Supplement to
THE
ENCYCLOPEDIA
★ ★ ★ ★ ★ of the ★ ★ ★ ★ ★
REPUBLICAN
PARTY

Supplement to

THE ENCYCLOPEDIA

★ ★ ★ ★ ★ *of the* ★ ★ ★ ★ ★

REPUBLICAN PARTY

Edited by

George Thomas Kurian

SHARPE REFERENCE

an imprint of M.E. Sharpe, Inc.

SHARPE REFERENCE

Sharpe Reference is an imprint of M.E. Sharpe INC.

M.E. Sharpe INC.
80 Business Park Drive
Armonk, NY 10504

© 2002 by *M.E. Sharpe* INC.

Library of Congress Cataloging-in-Publication Data

Kurian, George Thomas.
Supplement to the Encyclopedia of the Republican Party and the Encyclopedia of the
Democratic Party / George Thomas Kurian.
p. cm.
Includes bibliographical references and index.
ISBN 0-7656-8031-9 (set : alk. paper)
1. Republican Party (U.S.: 1854–)--Encyclopedias. 2. Democratic Party
(U.S.)—Encyclopedias. I. Encyclopedia of the Republican Party. II. Encyclopedia of the
Democratic Party. III. Title.

JK2352.K87 2002
324.2734′03--dc21

99-059982

Printed and bound in the United States of America

The paper used in this publication meets the minimum requirements of
American National Standard for Information Sciences—Permanence of
Paper for Printed Library Materials,
ANSI Z 39.48.1984.

BM (c) 10 9 8 7 6 5 4 3 2 1

CONTENTS

Contributors vii
Introduction ix

**Part I: Elections and Politics in the
    Twenty-first Century**

Campaign 2000 and the Florida Recount 3
The Bush Presidency: The First Hundred Days 16
The 2000 Census and the New Congress,
    2002–2012 26
The Electoral College 27

Part II: National Issues and Ideology

Affirmative Action 35
Budget and Fiscal Policy 36
Campaign Finance Reform 38
Civil Rights 40
Congressional Elections 42
Congressional Party Leadership 44
Drugs 46
Education 47
Foreign Policy 50
Gun Control 53
Healthcare 54
Immigration 56
Military 58
Party Organization 59
Social Security 61
Voting Behavior 63

Part III: National Leaders

William Bennett 69
George W. Bush 70
Dick Cheney 72
Tom DeLay 73
Elizabeth Dole 74
Newt Gingrich 75
Dennis Hastert 76
Henry Hyde 78
Trent Lott 79

John McCain 80
Mitch McConnell 81
George Pataki 82
Colin Powell 83
J.C. Watts 84

Part IV: Members of Congress

Representatives 89
Senators 163

Part V: Governors 191

Part VI: State Portraits: History and Politics 217

**Part VII: State Portraits: Elections
    and Statistics** 293

Part VIII: National Political Statistics

Presidential Election Results by State,
    1996 398
Presidential Election Results by State,
    2000 400
House of Representatives Election Results,
    1998 402
Senate Election Results, 1998 417
House of Representatives Election Results,
    2000 418
Senate Election Results, 2000 433
Party Composition in Congress,
    1788–2000 434
Party Victories in House of Representatives,
    1860–2000 437
Seats That Changed Party in Congress,
    1954–2000 439
Presidential Victories by State,
    1980–2000 441
Voter Registration and Partisan Enrollment,
    1998 443
Voter Registration and Partisan Enrollment,
    2000 445

Part IX: National Campaigns and Platforms

The Presidential Election of 1996 449
The Congressional Elections of 1998 450
Republican Party Platform, 1996 453
Republican Party Platform, 2000 501

Part X: Impeachment of President Clinton 555

General Index 565
Biographical Index 579
Geographical Index 583

Editor
George Thomas Kurian

Contributors

Jay Barth
Hendrix College

William C. Binning
Youngstown University

Steve D. Boilard
*Fiscal and Policy Analyst,
California Legislature*

Robert E. Dewhirst
*Northwest Missouri State
University*

Ethan Fenn

Richard A. Glenn
Youngstown University

Lisa Hacken

Alan S. Hammock
West Virginia University

Samuel Hoff
Delaware State University

Lisa Langenbach
*Middle Tennessee State
University*

Tom Lansford
New England College

Penny Miller
University of Kentucky

Gina Misiroglu

Tim Morris

William E. Pederson
Louisiana State University

Charles Prysby
*University of North Carolina,
Greensboro*

Steve Rowe

Frauke Schnell
West Chester University

Larry Schwab
John Carroll University

Steven Shaffer
Mississippi State University

Jeffrey D. Schultz
Colorado College

Carl Skutsch
School of Visual Arts

INTRODUCTION

The *Supplement to the Encyclopedia of the Republican Party* reviews the developments in the Republican Party between 1996, when the first edition of the encyclopedia was published, and 2001. This five-year period was an epochal one for Republicans in which they managed to preserve and consolidate their gains and to convert the party, for a short time, into the majority party at all levels of the United States government. During the opening months of the administration of George W. Bush, Republicans controlled the White House and both houses of Congress for the first time in almost half a century. (The Republican Party lost control of the Senate in June 2001 after one of its members, Senator James Jeffords of Vermont, left the party.) Republicans owe much of their good fortune to Bill Clinton, without whom they could not have achieved what they did. Despite his personal popularity, President Clinton gave Republicans a series of openings by his moral and ethical lapses. In 1994, Republicans managed to break the "curse" of the New Deal, under which they had been exiled into the political wilderness for many years. The New Deal—the popular government programs instituted by President Franklin D. Roosevelt and the Democrats in the 1930s—was to the Republicans what the Civil War had been to the Democrats in the 1860s—a disaster from which it was once thought they would never recover. Just as Democrats had been shut out of the presidency from 1861 to 1885, Republicans were shut out of it from 1933 to 1953. Power is to political parties what oxygen is to plants and humans, and exclusion from power for any long period stunts the growth of the party, as it did the Republicans in the mid-twentieth century.

Economic problems and foreign affairs debacles in the 1970s helped fuel the Republican resurgence in the 1980s, led by conservative president Ronald Reagan. Clinton, who defeated George H. W. Bush in 1992, gave Republicans more ammunition. His early failures, especially his healthcare reform plan, provided the setting for the return of the Republican Party to power in the Senate and the House. If Clinton was the "comeback kid," then the Republican Party, by the same token, became the comeback party. Clinton also provided the setting for the Republican Party to strengthen its ideological moorings and to develop core constituencies that it did not have before.

The Republican Party was born in the 1850s as a one-issue party dedicated to stopping the spread of slavery. Once slavery was abolished after the Civil War, the Republican Party found itself ideologically homeless. Controlling the White House for fifty-six of the seventy-two years from 1861 to 1933, the party began a long patron-client relationship with big business and other establishment institutions, which has continued ever since. But well into the mid-twentieth century, Republicans were neither inherently conservative nor tied to religious groups. They were simply defenders of the status quo, whatever that status quo was. Many were moderate and even liberal. During the Cold War they became staunch anticommunists. They also became increasingly identified with lower taxes and a smaller national government, two positions that launched the conservative takeover of the party by Ronald Reagan in the 1980s, followed by Representative Newt Gingrich (R-GA) in the 1990s. The newly invigorated party learned to sharpen its knives in assaults against liberals, Clinton, and the weakened Democratic Party. The occasion for one of these assaults, the impeachment hearings and trial in 1998 and 1999, was again provided by President Clinton.

The success of the Republicans in the 1980s and 1990s came in part from support from the religious right, which made the party more conservative on many social issues, such as abortion, school prayer, and gay rights. At long last, the Republican Party had found a strong ideological home. But the split between the moderate and liberal Republicans, on the one hand, and the hard core of the new Republican Party, on the other, persists. The split is now between the so-called social conservatives, who favor regulation of moral issues, and the fiscal conservatives, who are more libertarian. This split often makes it difficult for party leaders to act decisively on key issues and forces them to make compromises for the sake of bipartisanship, be it intraparty or interparty. By invoking his cry for "compassionate conservatism," President George W. Bush is attempting to bridge this chasm, although the resignation of Senator Jeffords from the party indicates that this chasm remains deep.

By 2001, the Republican Party has finally been able to bring an end to the era of the New Deal and escape the long shadow of Franklin Roosevelt. It has started off the twenty-first century, just as it did the twentieth, with a Republican president in the White House. Republicans control the House of Representatives, Republican-appointed justices form a majority on the Supreme Court, they hold two-thirds of all governorships, and they have the majority in over two-thirds of the state legislatures. The entire South is now solidly Republican. Democrats are on the defensive on many national issues, and with Clinton out of the White House, they have no single issue or individual to coalesce around. Whether Republicans can maintain this dominance will be the political question of the coming years.

The *Supplement to the Encyclopedia of the Republican Party* has benefited from the dedicated support of Andrew Gyory, executive editor at M. E. Sharpe, himself an astute student of American politics; Wendy Muto, project editor, who expertly managed this enterprise from start to finish; and Cathleen Prisco, editorial assistant, who gathered and compiled vital information and oversaw many of the details involved in this volume. As in all my works, I wish to thank my beloved wife and faithful companion, Annie Kurian, for her unfailing support and encouragement.

George Thomas Kurian

PART I

ELECTIONS AND POLITICS IN THE TWENTY-FIRST CENTURY

CAMPAIGN 2000 AND THE FLORIDA RECOUNT

INTRODUCTION

The 2000 campaign for the Republican Party's nomination seemed to end before it even began. George W. Bush, the two-term governor of Texas, was the first choice of Republican Party leaders, who clearly expected him to coast to the Republican nomination and then defeat Democratic Vice President Al Gore. But Bush's path was not quite that easy. He faced a strong challenge in the Republican primaries, and a tough race emerged between him and Gore. Even election day did not give Bush his victory, as an electoral crisis in Florida kept the nation in limbo for thirty-six days.

In the end, Bush did win the presidency, but only after a long and hard-fought campaign, which became much more interesting than anyone, including probably Bush himself, had expected or wanted.

GEORGE W. BUSH

In 1998, more than two years before the election took place, the Republicans already had a front-runner in the person of George W. Bush, son of former president George H. W. Bush. Bush was relatively inexperienced—he gained his only political experience as governor of Texas—but he had his father's name, a charming and unpretentious personal style, and early on most of the Republican establishment had gathered around him to offer their support. They desperately wanted someone who could beat Al Gore, the likely Democratic candidate, and end eight years of Democratic occupation of the White House.

Bush was born in New Haven, Connecticut, on July 6, 1946. He spent most of his youth in Texas before earning a B.A. at Yale University and an M.B.A. at Harvard Business School. Bush did not excel academically and his easy-going Texas style did not fit in with the East Coast Ivy League atmosphere, but he made lasting friends who later helped him in his political career. He served

George W. Bush (*left*) with his parents, former president George H. W. Bush and former first lady Barbara Bush, in Houston, Texas. (*Republican National Committee*)

in the Texas Air National Guard (1968–73) before entering the business world. His business endeavors were not particularly successful until 1989 when he became the head of a consortium that bought the Texas Rangers baseball team (his share of which he sold in 1994 for a substantial profit). Bush's only first-hand political experience during these years came when he ran for Congress in 1978—and lost. He also served as an aide and adviser during his father's presidential campaign (1988) and term as president (1989–93).

In 1994, Bush's second run for office was successful. Running for governor of Texas, he defeated the very popular incumbent, Ann Richards. This victory gave him national attention, and some Republicans started to mention his name as a possible presidential contender. Although the Texas constitution does not give its governor extensive powers (in some ways, the lieutenant governor has more real power), Bush served competently and was popular in a state Republicans had to win if they hoped to win the 2000 presidential election. He got along well with both Democrats and Republicans in the Texas State Legislature—although this was less difficult than it might seem, because in Texas, most Democrats are fairly conservative and politically not too far from their Republican opponents. Still, Bush was able to use his history of bipartisan cooperation to buttress his later promise that he would try to lessen the partisan rancor that had been increasing in Washington and the United States since the 1970s. By the time he was reelected governor in 1998, he had become the front-runner for the 2000 Republican nomination.

Bush's primary appeal for the Republican party was his name and his personal charm. Name recognition is a vital part of a presidential campaign, and despite losing his bid for a second term to Bill Clinton, Bush's father had been a popular president. Even better—in the eyes of Republican leaders—Bush had a relaxed and personable manner that reminded them of former president Ronald Reagan. In person, Bush was adept at making friends and had an easygoing public persona.

Almost as important as his name and charm was Bush's ability to satisfy the special-interest groups that had often sabotaged likely Republi-can candidates in the past. He told the National Rifle Association that he would oppose gun controls, assured abortion opponents that he would remain a staunch foe of abortion, and promised anti–big government Republicans that he would lower taxes.

From 1998 to 1999, Republicans from around the country came to visit Bush at his ranch in Texas to determine whether he was the right candidate for the 2000 campaign. Many of them liked what they saw. Those who were not completely sure were sometimes convinced by the pilgrimages themselves. The many visits took on a momentum of their own, and by early 1999 Bush seemed to be the inevitable choice of his party. He announced his candidacy in June 1999, and most observers believed he would win the Republican nomination easily.

Bush's weaknesses included his lack of political experience and occasional inarticulateness. Bush certainly was not a policy expert in the style of Bill Clinton. Early in his campaign he made a number of verbal blunders, such as referring to the inhabitants of Kosovo as Kosovonians (rather than Kosovars) and to Greeks as Grecians, and such mistakes continued, albeit less frequently, throughout the campaign. However, Bush was also careful to surround himself with established and knowledgeable political figures, such as Colin Powell and Dick Cheney, who balanced his lack of foreign policy expertise with their own extensive experience. While this deflected the criticism that he was unprepared for the presidency, it also gave the impression of a young neophyte in need of the guidance of his elders.

There were also stories, which Bush tacitly acknowledged, that he had been somewhat wild in his younger days. Bush, who later in life became a born-again Christian, insisted that those days were long gone and therefore irrelevant, but the stories lurked around the edges of the Bush bandwagon throughout the campaign. One antidote to these stories was the clearly solid relationship Bush had with his wife Laura, who seemed to personify traditional family values.

Bush described his political ideology as "compassionate conservatism," a phrase he often repeated. Its exact meaning was unclear, but it seemed to convey the idea that Bush would not hew to the hard-right positions of some Republican extremists. In this same vein, he emphasized his bipartisan approach to government and his willingness to cooperate with congressional Democrats. How these moderate words could coexist with Bush's promises to the right remained unclear, but his supporters, moderate and conservative, seemed satisfied.

Beyond his slogans of inclusion—"Nobody gets left behind" and "compassionate conservatism"—the issues that seemed to matter the most to Bush revolved around cutting taxes. He was a strong opponent of the estate tax—which, like many Republicans, he called the "death tax"—and he wished to cut income taxes across the board. Beyond tax cuts, the other issues he emphasized were improved education; national educational standards; school vouchers; and putting some Social Security funds into private accounts.

JOHN McCAIN

Although it was not immediately clear from the beginning of the campaign, Bush's chief rival for the Republican nomination was John McCain. An influential senator from Arizona, McCain was a war hero who had fought in Vietnam, and had spent five years in North Vietnam as a prisoner of war. He earned the Silver Star, the Bronze Star, the Legion of Merit, the Purple Heart, and the Distinguished Flying Cross before retiring from the military in 1981. He served in the House of Representatives for Arizona from 1983 to 1987 and as a U.S. senator from 1987 to the present.

Although he held several important positions in the Senate, McCain was not especially popular among his fellow Republicans. He was considered a maverick and a troublemaker and uncooperative with the party leadership. He tended to inspire strong emotions: either adoration or disdain. Politically he was quite conservative, but took independent positions. For example, he opposed abortion but thought that the best way to fight it was to encourage adoption; three of his own four children were adopted.

McCain's assets included his extensive legis-

lative experience and maverick image. He was also likable and particularly popular among reporters, an advantage for any presidential candidate.

While McCain was willing to take positions on numerous issues, the one he always returned to was campaign finance reform. Along with Democratic Senator Russell Feingold of Wisconsin, McCain had sponsored legislation that would have greatly decreased the ability of candidates to raise money, particularly so-called soft money, during their campaigns. The legislation was stalled in the Senate, but McCain did not give up on campaign finance reform. He called current campaign financing methods "an incumbent protection racket" and argued that it led to a perception of corruption and an increase in political apathy among America's younger voters. He saw his presidential bid as part of a crusade against the corrupt effects of money on the American political system.

OTHER CANDIDATES

Unlike the Democratic campaign, which was a simple contest between Gore and former New Jersey senator Bill Bradley, the Republicans had an abundance of candidates. Including Bush and McCain, there were twelve Republicans running for president in 1999, with most of them coming from the conservative wing of the party. The conservatives were Gary Bauer, Pat Buchanan, Steve Forbes, John R. Kasich, Alan Keyes, Dan Quayle, and Robert Smith. The small moderate contingent consisted of Lamar Alexander, Elizabeth Dole, and Orrin Hatch.

Most of these candidates faded before the election campaign had really begun. In July 1999, Representative Kasich of Ohio withdrew from the race without ever contesting any primary or caucus. Unable to raise the money necessary for a viable candidacy, Kasich, who had served eighteen years in Congress, threw his support to Bush. Senator Robert Smith of New Hampshire also dropped out of the Republican race in July. Unlike Kasich, however, Smith attacked his party as too willing to chase votes without integrity and vowed to lead an independent run for the presidency. "We need to clean out the pollsters and the consultants and the spin doctors and the bloated staffs who tell us what to say, how to say it, when to say it, and how long to say it." Smith's independent bid failed, and he faded from the public eye.

Lamar Alexander, a former Tennessee governor, withdrew in August 1999 after running an unsuccessful grass-roots campaign. Former vice president Dan Quayle retired from the field in September, having attracted even less attention than Alexander.

Elizabeth Dole, wife of former senator Bob Dole—the Republican presidential nominee in 1996—left the race in October 1999. The former president of the American Red Cross, Dole had attracted a number of moderate Republicans, especially women, but she failed to overcome a stiff speaking style and brittle manner. (Embarrassingly, even before she had retired from the race, her own husband suggested he might support McCain.)

Surviving into 2000 were Bush, McCain, Utah senator Orrin Hatch, Christian conservative Gary Bauer, magazine publisher Steve Forbes, and political commentator Alan Keyes.

BUCHANAN'S REFORM PARTY BID

Pat Buchanan, like Elizabeth Dole, had left the Republican race in October 1999, but Buchanan left only the Republican campaign, not the presidential campaign. Disgusted by his poor showing among traditional Republicans, Buchanan decided to transfer his populist movement to a different political party, namely the Reform Party founded by Ross Perot in 1992. Buchanan did not fit easily into any political category. He was a social conservative who opposed abortion and gay rights, but he also attacked rich Republicans who ignored the needs of working Americans. He had been accused of being a racist because of anti-immigrant statements he had made in the past. He had no practical political experience, being best known in his role as a pundit on the television show "Crossfire."

Buchanan's fight for the Reform Party nomination attracted some media attention and much intra-party squabbling. Many Reform Party leaders, most notably Minnesota governor Jesse Ventura, opposed Buchanan's nomination because they felt he was too interested in social issues and insufficiently sympathetic to the libertarian message of the Reform Party.

Despite Ventura's efforts (he even tried to get businessman Donald Trump to seek the nomination), Buchanan's supporters were able to gain the nomination for their candidate. The nomination gave Buchanan millions of dollars in matching funds that the Reform Party had earned because of its showing in the 1996 presidential race. In the end, even this money did not significantly affect the race, but it did give Buchanan enough cash for television advertisements pushing his pet issues (one much-criticized commercial suggested that English was in danger of being replaced as America's national language). Few Americans took Buchanan's candidacy seriously.

THE MONEY

The main reason for the early winnowing of the Republican field was the same for all the candidates: not enough money. Bush, the premier Republican fund-raiser, had acquired a campaign chest of $36 million by July 1999, and it continued to grow, making his opponents' contests increasingly difficult. By February 2000, he had raised more than $70 million. This enormous war chest served two purposes: First, it gave Bush the ability to outspend his rivals in advertising, critical in modern media-driven campaigns; and second, it helped to maintain his aura of inevitability. (At the center of the Bush fund-raising effort were his "pioneers," Republican party supporters who had each promised to raise at least $100,000 for the campaign.) It also made it difficult for his rivals to raise the funds they needed. Republican stalwarts were reluctant to give money to candidates who seemed to have little chance of beating Bush. All the early candidates cited money as one of the main reasons for their withdrawal from the campaign.

Bush's remaining opponents were not immune to money woes, but managed to overcome or ignore them, at least for a while. After Bush, McCain had been the most successful at raising funds, although he was a distant second compared with Bush; he compensated by maintaining a lean campaign team that operated on a shoestring budget. The other candidates had done even less well at raising money. Bauer survived with the grassroots support of religious groups; Forbes depended on his own vast fortune; and Keyes and Hatch got by largely on persistence. (Indeed, Keyes never officially conceded the Republican nomination.)

Still, surviving was not winning. Reporters and political operatives all assumed that Bush's money lead would spell victory. Money meant airtime, and airtime gained name recognition and votes. There were some Republicans who had never heard of Gary Bauer; everyone had heard of George Bush.

One of the reasons Bush had been able to raise so much money is that he had, controversially, decided not to accept federal matching funds. Candidates can receive federal matching funds only if they adhere to spending limits during the campaign. Bush had clearly decided that he would gain more from unlimited fund-raising than he would from any federal campaign assistance. Bush's opponents accused him of buying the election, but Bush simply argued that they envied his popularity in the party.

Accompanied by his wife, Laura Bush, George W. Bush campaigns in Dubuque, Iowa. *(Republican National Committee)*

IOWA AND NEW HAMPSHIRE

After money problems had already eliminated half the field, Bush faced his first electoral contests: the Iowa caucuses and the New Hampshire primary. Leading in the polls, Bush avoided risks. He resisted debating his opponents, believing that a debate could only help them: if he did well in a debate, nothing would change, while a bad performance might harm his chances. When an October 1999 Republican debate was scheduled in New Hampshire, therefore, Bush declined to appear. After much criticism, and some slippage in the polls, Bush appeared at other debates.

It became increasingly clear that Bush had only two real rivals: Forbes, who was focusing

his personal fortune on winning in Iowa, and McCain, who was waging a hard-driving campaign to win in New Hampshire. Of the two of them, McCain was slowly emerging as a dark horse who might be able to challenge Bush. As he crisscrossed the state in his bus, he drew larger and larger crowds. He went from 10 percent in polls taken during the summer of 1999 to 30 percent by the end of the year.

The other candidates were less impressive. Keyes made speeches attacking the United Nations and the federal income tax, while Hatch struggled to explain the details of Senate bills he had helped to pass. Both men, along with Gary Bauer, remained at the bottom of the polls.

Voting in the Iowa caucuses took place on January 24, 2000. As expected, Bush won, but his victory was not overwhelming. He got 41 percent of the vote, followed by Forbes with 30 percent, Keyes with 14 percent, Bauer with 9 percent, McCain (who had decided not to contest Iowa) with 5 percent, and Hatch with 1 percent. Two days later Hatch withdrew from the race.

Forbes's strong showing seemed to suggest he had a chance at the nomination, but New Hampshire was clearly the key state in the contest. By election eve, the dark horse McCain had moved ahead of Bush in the polls. One interesting element in the New Hampshire race was that independent voters were allowed to vote in either the Republican or Democratic primary. This meant that McCain and Democratic senator Bill Bradley, both of whom were popular among independents, were essentially competing against each other in addition to competing with their rivals in their own parties.

A close race was expected, but in a major upset McCain won a landslide victory in the February 1 contest. McCain gained 49 percent of the vote to Bush's 31 percent. Forbes received only 13 percent, Keyes 6 percent, and Bauer got less than 1 percent. As expected, McCain did well among independents, beating Bush by 41 percent, but he also beat Bush by a full 10 percent among Republicans, which was surprising, even given New Hampshire's notoriously independent Republican voters. Bush's nomination had ceased to seem inevitable.

McCain's role now became that of chief rival, and two more Republicans—Forbes and Bauer—dropped out of the race. Alan Keyes remained throughout the entire campaign, delivering fiery speeches to small crowds. He did not give up until the Republican convention, but he gained few votes and remained a marginal figure.

PRESS ISSUES

The two Republican front-runners approached the press quite differently. Bush avoided extended conversations with reporters and answered few unscripted questions. The Bush campaign advisers dealt with the media carefully. With Bush leading in the polls, he and his campaign had no wish to risk any embarrassing gaffes that might hurt his standing. They wanted their man to stay ahead in the race. This attitude was heightened by some reporters' questions, which sometimes seemed to have been designed to simply trip up Bush on foreign policy issues or mistakes made in his youth.

McCain, on the other hand, brought the press into his campaign and made them a central part of his strategy. In the campaign bus, which traveled through New Hampshire and beyond, McCain would gather with reporters and spend extended informal time with them. McCain's

charm was not as polished as Bush's, but he was more open than Bush and traded jokes with reporters. McCain was also remarkably open with reporters on political issues, admitting to mistakes and putting forward opinions that he knew would not be universally popular. The campaign bus came to be known as the "Straight Talk Express." Reporters gave McCain extensive and generally favorable coverage.

McCain's popularity with the press went against the usual Republican feeling that the press had a liberal bias (surveys regularly show that most reporters vote for Democrats). McCain was certainly no liberal—his Senate voting record showed that he was as conservative as Bush—but as an experienced campaigner, he recognized that as the underdog he had to take risks.

The result was favorable press coverage. McCain's straight-talking gamble seemed successful.

THE BUSH-McCAIN CONTEST

Despite McCain's New Hampshire victory, the contest remained an uphill one for the McCain camp. Bush had more money, the backing of the Republican establishment, and the advantage of advance preparation in every Republican state. McCain had focused on New Hampshire and now had to leverage his victory into national success.

McCain's chances were made more difficult by the recent tendency of both parties to "frontload" their primaries—that is, hold them early in the year rather than spread them out over the whole campaign season. Primary elections had been moved forward until more than 42 percent of Republican delegates would be chosen by March 7. Frontloading gave established candidates like Bush a huge advantage over upset candidates. They already had the money, infrastructure, and national name recognition. Given this tight schedule, McCain had little time to organize and capitalize on his early success.

McCain had the support of independents and some Democrats, but it was Republicans who voted in most primaries, and among them Bush had an edge in most states. But McCain's strong showing among Democrats and Independents did tempt some pragmatic Republicans who wanted a candidate who could win against Gore in November. If most conservatives were firmly in Bush's camp (barring the few who voted for Keyes), the moderates were wavering. And the McCain supporters—some calling themselves "McCainiacs"—tended to be more passionate than their Bush counterparts.

The next major contest, South Carolina's February 19 primary, became a bitter fight. Both men felt they had to do well. Bush had won Iowa and Delaware (although McCain gained 25 percent of the vote, despite having never set foot in the state) while McCain had the New Hampshire upset under his belt. Bush wanted to defeat the upstart, while McCain had to prove that New Hampshire was not just a fluke.

The next contest, for South Carolina's thirty-seven delegates, was fairly ugly, as both candidates released television attack advertisements accusing the other of hypocrisy. Particularly galling to McCain were suggestions by Bush supporters that he had not supported veterans' issues. Bush also criticized McCain's reform plans as empty and characterized himself as "a reformer with results." McCain's legislative record was necessarily more extensive than Bush's, but the phrase stuck in people's heads and seemed to gain Bush support and votes. Bush won the February 19 contest with 53 percent of the vote to McCain's 42 percent. It was a respectable showing given Bush's better preparation in the state, but not the upset the McCain camp had been hoping for.

Three days later McCain won the primaries in Arizona and Michigan, the latter a major upset. The Bush camp made a rebound on February 29 by winning in Virginia, North Dakota, and Washington. McCain had probably damaged his chances in Virginia by an election eve speech in which he attacked the religious right for being too extreme.

The Republican race ended with the "Super Tuesday" contests of March 7, when the candidates competed for delegates in California, New York, Ohio, Missouri, Georgia, Maine, Maryland, Massachusetts, Connecticut, Rhode Island, and

Vermont. McCain made respectable showings across the board but was able to win only in the small states of Connecticut, Vermont, Massachusetts, and Rhode Island, while Bush won the rest, including the giant prizes of New York and California.

McCain conceded on March 9 (the same day that Bill Bradley conceded to Al Gore), but stopped short of endorsing Bush. (He later did, however, and campaigned with him in the fall.) The campaign, particularly in South Carolina, had left a bitter taste in the senator's mouth. But with McCain out of the race, Bush was the Republican candidate.

BUSH V. GORE

During the remainder of the primary season, as Bush coasted to an easy victory in uncontested Republican primaries, he began to focus his energies and efforts on defeating Gore. His first priority was to pick a vice presidential running mate. On April 25, Bush named Dick Cheney to head his search for a vice president. Cheney was a respected conservative politician who had served many years in Congress and had also been President Gerald Ford's chief of staff and President George Bush's secretary of defense. Three months later, on July 25, Bush announced that he had chosen Cheney himself to be his vice president. Politically the move was unusual—it gave Bush no obvious electoral edge because Cheney's home state of Wyoming was already locked up for the Republicans. Many Americans saw Bush as relatively young and inexperienced; Dick Cheney, while only slightly older than Bush, had a great deal more political and governing experience. The impression was that Bush had chosen someone who could help guide him through the rough spots of his presidency.

Bush spent much of the spring focusing on his policy proposals, particularly his tax cut plans, while repeating that he planned to bring "integrity" back to the White House—a clear reference to scandals of Clinton's presidency. Gore, on the other hand, saw his poll numbers steadily slip against those of Bush. Bush's solid lead allowed

The newly nominated Republican ticket of George W. Bush and Dick Cheney, accompanied by their respective wives, Laura Bush (*left*) and Lynne Cheney (*right*), wave to the crowd at the Republican National Convention in Philadelphia. *(Republican National Committee)*

him to focus on Democratic stronghold states such as West Virginia, Tennessee, and California. Some of these efforts proved in the end to be a waste of time—Bush never came close to winning California—but others distracted Gore and forced him to shore up areas that he had thought were solidly in his camp. And in one critical case—Tennessee, Al Gore's home state—Bush's efforts resulted in a surprise Republican victory.

During the spring and summer, the contrast between the two men became clearer to the American people. Gore was clearly better versed in the issues. He was known as a policy "wonk," who stayed up late studying position papers. Bush, on the other hand, left policy study to his aides, seeing himself as a coordinator and driver rather than a details person. Gore believed that his knowledge of the minutiae of government would impress the American people and lead to a sure victory, but most Americans saw Gore as stiff and reserved. Bush, on the other hand, came across as relaxed and human. Bush even joked about his reputed thick-headedness. At one dinner, attended by the well-known conservative and fellow Yale graduate William F. Buckley,

Bush said, "William F. Buckley wrote a book at Yale. I read one."

The truth was that while Bush was probably more appealing on a personal level to most Americans, neither candidate was particularly inspiring to their party faithful. If Bush was doing better, it was more because of Gore's lack of popularity than because of Bush's massive appeal.

The Republican National Convention in Philadelphia, which was held from July 31 to August 3, boosted Bush's popularity further. It was orchestrated to highlight Bush's portrayal of himself as a "uniter, not a divider," and was largely successful. Bush's speech was clearly delivered and well received. He again emphasized values over specific policy points: "Our generation has a chance to reclaim some essential values—to show we have grown up before we grow old."

Bush was also aided by the third-party candidacy of Green Party nominee Ralph Nader. Nader, who announced his candidacy on February 21, 2000, and was chosen by the Green Party on June 25, was a consumer activist who had run on the Green Party ticket in 1996, but with little pas-

George W. Bush campaigned in many traditionally Democratic strongholds, such as Chicago, Illinois.
(Republican National Committee)

sion. This time he took his nomination more seriously and caused Gore genuine difficulties. Most third-party presidential campaigns have little success, but Nader had a large collection of dedicated and youthful followers who filled stadiums around the country. While Nader denounced both Bush and Gore, his strongest attacks were directed against Gore, and his followers were largely drawn from the left wing of the Democratic Party. Nader would probably be taking votes from Gore, not Bush. (Pat Buchanan, on the other hand, would probably cost Bush some votes, but he was not as popular as Nader.) Indirectly emphasizing the harm done to the Gore campaign by Nader, the Bush camp used clips from Nader's speeches in its own anti-Gore commercials.

Although Bush had a strong lead in the polls, in the late summer he saw it slip and his campaign went through a bad spell. The Democratic National Convention, which was held from August 14 to August 17, gave Gore a bump in the polls, as conventions always do, but the bump stayed and narrowed Bush's lead. An open-microphone gaffe in early September made Bush look mean-spirited. Seeing a *New York Times* reporter whom he disliked, Bush muttered an offensive, disparaging remark, which Cheney seconded. Both men's comments were picked up by the microphone, heard by journalists, including their target, and reported.

Bush was next damaged by his hesitancy to debate. The Bush team was clearly nervous about exposing their man to Gore, who was a more experienced debater, and tried to stall and avoid many direct confrontations. After much delay and backpedaling, Bush finally agreed to three presidential debates and one vice presidential debate. Bush's actions had made him seem afraid, and when the controversy was over, Gore had pulled slightly ahead in the polls.

Against all expectations, Bush did quite well in the debates and his poll numbers began to recover from the bad days of September. In the first debate, held on October 3, Gore was seen by viewers as overly aggressive. He interrupted Bush, sighed during his statements, and mugged off camera. His policy points were ignored—he criticized Bush's tax plan as a gift to the rich—and he came across as forced, impolite, and fussy. Bush, on the other hand, came across as calm and friendly. In the second debate, held on October 11, Gore was more passive and Bush was able to make his points with little contradiction. It was only in the last debate, October 17, that Gore scored well, but Bush was able to coast on the success of the first two debates.

Cheney also did well in the vice presidential debate, held on October 5. Senator Joseph Lieberman of Connecticut, Gore's vice presidential running mate, was generally expected to win the debate but Cheney held his own and thereby greatly exceeded expectations. The two men exchanged a few jokes and remained calm and civil. Some observers suggested that they were both more presidential in manner than their senior partners. Cheney had also been portrayed by Democrats as very conservative, but he projected a fairly moderate image during the debate.

The Bush-Cheney team were again up in the polls at the end of the debates and with barely two weeks to go in the campaign Bush's advisers began to leak to the press that their ticket had the election all locked up.

In the last days before the election, however, things began to shift. In the week before the election information emerged that in 1976 Bush had been arrested for driving under the influence of alcohol, had paid a $150 fine, and been released. The information did not seem to bother most Americans, but it may have shifted a few voters' minds at a critical juncture.

As Bush relaxed, looking forward to victory, Gore went into overdrive, moving from state to state, making speeches, and cheering on his supporters. In the last weekend before the election, with Bush taking it relatively easy, the poll numbers began to shift in Gore's favor and the Gore camp began to think they might be able to pull a miracle out of what had seemed like a lost election.

ELECTION NIGHT

Election night, November 7, was more tense than anyone would have predicted a year, or even a week, earlier. The Bush team knew that they had won most of the West and the South, while Gore had clinched the Northeast and Pacific Coast states. A few states were close calls but Republican hopes were focused on three big states that were tossups: Michigan (18 electoral votes), Pennsylvania (23 electoral votes), and Florida (25 electoral votes). Both sides believed that Gore probably had to win all three to have a chance of winning the election. Thinking they needed only one of these states to win, the Bush team went into the evening feeling fairly confident. However, as the evening wore on, it became clear that the election was going to be much closer than originally expected. Gore's last-minute whirlwind of cross-country trips and a strong Democratic get-out-the-vote effort seemed to be paying off for Gore.

After the polls began to close, television network forecasters, using data taken from exit polls, started calling the key states for Gore. First Florida and Michigan, and then Pennsylvania, were declared Gore victories by the network anchors covering the election. A Gore presidential victory seemed on the verge of occurring. But then as more returns came in, Florida again appeared too close to call. The networks were forced to take back their earlier predictions and put the state back into the undecided column. Shortly after 2:00 A.M. eastern standard time the networks began to call Florida again, but this time for Bush. At that point, with Florida in his pocket, Bush would have achieved a slim victory in the electoral college. Informed by his advisers that it was all over, Gore called Bush and offered his concession. He then got into his limousine to drive to where his supporters were gathered to offer a public concession.

As he left the limousine, however, and began his walk to the podium an assistant rushed after him with further news: still arriving returns suggested that Florida was again too close to call. Gore called Bush again and after a tense conversation told him that he was retracting his initial concession; Florida was a tossup and whoever won Florida would be the nation's next president. If Bush won the state, he would have 271 electoral votes to Gore's 267 and win a close victory; if Gore was victorious, he would have 292 electoral votes to Bush's 246. The winner in Florida, however, was to be determined only after thirty-six more days of legal maneuverings and heated verbal exchanges that would leave the country fascinated and the nation's next government in limbo.

THE FLORIDA RECOUNT CRISIS

Both the Gore and Bush teams woke up on November 8 believing that their man had probably won the election.

The Gore team knew that polling numbers in Florida favored Gore and they assumed that it was a simple counting glitch that had made it appear that Bush was winning. Moreover, it was clear that Gore had won a majority of the popular vote nationwide: 50,992,335 to Bush's 50,455,156. Legally this did not matter—the candidate with the most electoral votes would win the election—but the half million vote margin for Gore made him seem and feel like the country's next president.

The Bush team, however, was equally sure that the election was theirs. The returns left them with a 1,784 vote margin of victory in Florida. This was a tiny margin considering that almost 6 million Floridians had voted, but the Bush camp could also rely on the absentee ballots from soldiers stationed abroad, and most of these would probably go to Bush.

Florida law required that in an election this close a machine recount must automatically occur, and so Florida secretary of state Katherine Harris ordered the recount. Both campaigns then rushed teams down to Florida to push for a result favorable to their candidate. They hired legal help, appointed spokespersons, and began to delve into the intricacies of Florida election law, looking for an advantage for their man.

THE ISSUES

The course of the Florida recount crisis followed a number of parallel paths. First, some believed that confusing "butterfly" ballots in Palm Beach County had quite possibly led a few thousand voters to accidentally vote for Buchanan instead of Gore. The ballots placed the two candidates' names side by side in a way that might easily confuse elderly voters, and Palm Beach had many retirees. Certainly Buchanan's remarkably high showing in Palm Beach, the highest in Florida, was surprising given the county's large Jewish population and Buchanan's reputation for being hostile to Israel. (Buchanan himself, perhaps partly to annoy Bush, said he thought his high vote total was probably incorrect.) Many Buchanan votes might have been intended for Gore, but there was no way of determining that, and so the votes stood.

Second, there were reports that African-American voters had been disenfranchised in a number of counties. In some places, names of African-American voters were not on polling site lists of registered voters, in others, African Americans were disqualified after being misidentified as felons (it is illegal for felons to vote in Florida). There were also less well substantiated reports of police harassment of African Americans on their way to vote. In the end, none of these charges was considered strong enough to allow for a recount, but many African Americans, remembering the racism of the Old South that had kept them oppressed and disenfranchised for a hundred years after the Civil War, felt great resentment.

Third, there was the issue of inaccurate machine counts of ballots, and this in the end would be the most important element in the Florida recount. In many Florida counties, voting was conducted by punching holes in ballot cards, which were then counted by a machine. The machines were not perfectly constructed, and voters often did not punch all the way through a ballot card (leaving a little piece of paper called a "chad" hanging from the ballot card), so voting was never exactly accurate. Usually, however, the official count was close enough to the actual tally for the margin of error not to matter. With a margin of less than 2,000, this was, of course, no longer the case. Soon all of America would learn about ballot-counting machines, manual recounts, and chads.

While the debates over the recount went on in courtrooms, both parties used the press to argue that the other side was acting unfairly and trying to steal the election. The Republicans accused the Democrats of wanting to keep counting until their candidate won. The Democrats countered with the demand that "every vote" be counted. Both sides accused the other of using political maneuvers to interfere with the election.

If politics was going to matter, the Bush team had a clear advantage. The governor of Florida was Jeb Bush, George Bush's brother, Secretary of State Katherine Harris had been an early Bush supporter, and the Florida legislature was controlled by the Republican Party. The Democrats had only the state attorney general and the judges on the State Supreme Court, although the latters' decisions would be particularly important.

THE STRUGGLE

The first phase in the crisis came while the automatic machine recount was under way. The Democrats, arguing that machine recounts were less than perfectly accurate, requested hand recounts in Palm Beach, Broward, Volusia, and Miami-Dade counties—all Gore strongholds where unclear ballots would be statistically more likely to help Gore than Bush. On November 9, Palm Beach and Volusia agreed to do manual recounts. Both candidates kept a low profile while communicating with key aides. Bush was much more hands off than Gore, letting his legal and campaign staff handle the Florida crisis with little interference.

By November 10, tallies showed that the machine recounts were reducing Bush's lead by hundreds of votes; clearly through repeated handling, chads were falling off of ballot cards and transforming ballots that machines could not

count into ballots that could be counted, and many of these were Gore ballots. By the end of the machine recount Bush had only a 327 vote edge over Gore. It seemed likely that hand recounts would benefit Gore even further. On November 11, the Bush team filed a request in U.S. District Court to stop the hand recounts, claiming that manual recounts were inherently inaccurate (although Texas law allowed for hand recounts in close elections). The request was denied and Volusia and Palm Beach counties began the long process of a hand recount. Secretary of State Harris, however, said she would not extend the official deadline for submitting recount figures. Since this deadline was November 14, her ruling essentially precluded hand recounts. At the official deadline, 5 P.M. on November 14, Harris announced that Bush led by 300 votes. Republicans declared the race over, but Democrats did not concede.

On November 16, the Florida State Supreme Court ruled that the manual recounts could proceed. After further court battles, the State Supreme Court ruled that hand-recounted votes could be accepted until November 26. Miami-Dade county, claiming that the deadline was too tight, stopped their hand recount. Palm Beach continued to count, but took a Thanksgiving break. Broward County began a review of disputed ballots. Palm Beach, after taking a day off, missed the November 26 deadline. Harris declared Bush the winner of Florida's twenty-five electoral votes. The Democrats continued to make court appeals designed to restart the recount process and Gore made a speech on November 27 to the country asking for patience. Meanwhile, the Florida legislature began to discuss the possibility that, in case court rulings went against Bush, they would choose pro-Bush electors themselves, short-circuiting the Democrats maneuvers. If this legislative decision were to go through it would risk a disputed election, with both Republicans and Democrats sending delegations to the Electoral College and the "real" delegation being determined by Congress.

On December 8 the Democrats were handed a major victory when the Florida Supreme Court, in a four to three vote, called for a statewide manual recount. New recounts were begun, but on December 9 the United States Supreme Court, in a five to four decision, voted to temporarily stop the recount. On December 12 the United States Supreme Court, again in a five to four decision, voted to overturn the Florida Supreme Court's decision to allow a manual recount. The majority supporting the decision, consisting of William Rehnquist, Sandra Day O'Connor, Antonin Scalia, Anthony Kennedy, and Clarence Thomas—all Republican appointees—argued that there was no consistent standard for a recount and therefore it was a violation of the equal protection clause of the Constitution. The Court seemed to be at least in part motivated by a desire to have the election certified by midnight on December 12 in order to guarantee a smooth official Electoral College vote for president on the constitutionally scheduled date of December 18. The four disagreeing justices signed a dissent, written by Justice Stephen Breyer, that argued that the decision was bad for the country and risked "undermining the public's confidence in the court itself." The decision, nevertheless, stood.

At 9 P.M. eastern standard time on December 13, in what was generally agreed to be his best speech of the campaign, Gore conceded the election. "I know that many of my supporters are disappointed. I am, too. But our disappointment must be overcome by our love of country." An hour later Bush made his victory speech. "Whether you voted for me or not, I will do my best to serve your interests, and I will work to earn your respect."

PRESIDENT GEORGE W. BUSH

In the end the election had been closer than anyone had expected. Bush had won with a minority of the popular vote, with only 271 out of 538 electoral votes, and in Florida with an official margin of only 537 votes out of almost six million votes cast in that state. George W. Bush was now president-elect of the United States.

The Nader factor had also helped Bush. Although Nader received only received 2.7 percent of the national vote—substantially less than the 5 percent he and his supporters were hoping for—in two states, Florida and New Hampshire, the total of Nader voters was more than Bush's victory margin; in Florida it was far more. While it can not be known how these voters would have cast their ballots had Nader not been in the race, it is not unreasonable to assume that more of them would have voted for Gore than Bush. Democrats certainly spent the next few weeks attacking Nader for "losing" the election and giving a victory to Bush. Throughout these attacks, Nader remained unrepentant, and blamed Gore for losing his own election.

Buchanan, on the other hand, had a minimal effect on the election. Even though his Reform Party nomination gave him access to millions more dollars than Nader, he received less than 0.5 percent of the vote.

Finally, Bush had been helped by a friendly administration in Florida and a Supreme Court that favored the arguments of his lawyers over those of the Gore team.

Did Gore "really" win? Did Bush? In the months after the election, newspapers around the nation used Florida's liberal freedom of information laws to do their own, completely unofficial, ballot recounts. The results satisfied no one. Depending on which ballots were counted, and how they were judged, either Bush or Gore could be assigned the most ballots. It is unlikely that a historical consensus will ever emerge. Except, of course, that George W. Bush did become the nation's forty-third president.

The legacy of this bitterly contested campaign remains unclear. Certainly many Americans, almost all of them Democrats, believe that the Supreme Court overstepped its powers and handed the presidency to George W. Bush. Most Republicans, however, believe that the Supreme Court prevented an illegal attempt by the Gore camp to undo a fair election. That the difference of opinion in national surveys was split largely along party lines suggests that the country will never entirely agree on what happened or should have happened in November and December 2000.

Carl Skutsch

SEE ALSO: The Bush Presidency: The First Hundred Days; The Electoral College; Campaign Finance Reform; Voting Behavior; George W. Bush; Dick Cheney; John McCain; Elizabeth Dole; The Presidential Election of 1996.

BIBLIOGRAPHY

"Bush Outlines His Goals." *New York Times,* August 4, 2000.

"Bush Remark Off-Color, on Tape." *USA Today,* September 5, 2000.

"A Flawed Call Adds to High Drama." *New York Times,* November 8, 2000.

"Hedgehog and the Fox." *Sunday Times* (London), 5 November 2000.

Milbank, Dana. *Smashmouth: Two Years in the Gutter with Al Gore and George W. Bush.* New York: Basic Books, 2001.

New York Times Staff. *36 Days: The Complete Chronicle of the 2000 Presidential Election Crisis.* New York: Times Books, 2001.

"Sen. Smith Follows His Beliefs, Leaves GOP." *Boston Globe,* July 14, 1999.

Simon, Roger. *Divided We Stand: How Al Gore Beat George Bush and Lost the Presidency.* New York: Times Books, 2001.

THE BUSH PRESIDENCY: THE FIRST HUNDRED DAYS

INTRODUCTION

On November 7, 2000, more than 105 million Americans went to the polls to choose whether George W. Bush or Al Gore would be the next president of the United States. Although Gore won the popular vote by a very slim margin, Bush seemed to have won the Electoral College by an equally slim margin. "Seemed," because even after the polls had closed, there remained some doubt over the results in Florida, and whoever won Florida would have enough electoral votes to be the next president. Both candidates claimed victory. After thirty-six days of legal action, recounts, and a decision by the U.S. Supreme Court, Gore conceded that Bush had won

On January 20, 2001, George W. Bush takes the oath of office as the nation's forty-third president. *(Wally McNamee, White House)*

Florida's twenty-five electoral votes and therefore the election. On December 13, Bush became president-elect, and on January 20, 2001, he took the oath of office to become the nation's forty-third president.

BEGINNING IN CRISIS

George W. Bush's presidency began with the handicap of a very late start caused by the political crisis in Florida. For five weeks following the November 7 election, the Bush camp did not know for sure that their man would be the next president. This made the difficult process of planning for a new administration even more difficult. Media observers and critics wondered whether Bush and his advisers would be able to make up this lost time.

The Florida crisis was also the cause of a potentially even more severe handicap: A substantial portion of the electorate (more than 40 percent) thought that Bush had achieved his victory unfairly. The first hundred days in office—technically from January 20 to April 30, but a period generally lasting well into the spring—is often considered the honeymoon period of a new presidency. Bush's first hundred days would demonstrate whether he had overcome the heavy burdens caused by the Florida crisis as well as his failure to capture more popular votes than his opponent.

Surprising media Cassandras, Bush and his team were able to begin functioning in a coherent fashion and quickly put forward a legislative agenda that surprised both opponents and allies. Part of this success was owed to careful preinaugural planning—even during the weeks when the election remained in doubt—and part was probably due to Bush's administrative style, which emphasized delegating authority to trusted aids and advisers and maintaining a tight schedule. In pointed contrast to the haphazard, frenzied style of the Clinton presidency, Bush's administration projected an image of adult efficiency and competence.

The honeymoon for the Bush administration ended fairly quickly, however, and he was faced with a series of problems—from budget disagreements to a diplomatic conflict with China—that were handled with a mixed amount of success.

PICKING A CABINET

If a president's choice of cabinet sets the tone for his administration, Bush's choices were suggestive. During the 2000 campaign, Bush had promised to give America "compassionate conservatism," but in his cabinet choices the emphasis was on "conservatism." Before the January 20 inauguration, conservatives had expressed concerns that Bush might be more like his father: practicing lip-service conservatism but steering a more moderate course. In picking his cabinet, however, Bush was able to reassure them of his conservative bona fides. Liberal politicians were unlikely to be pleased with any Bush cabinet, but even moderate Republicans expressed some concerns about its conservative tone during the early weeks of the Bush administration.

The key person in Bush's cabinet was elected, not appointed: Vice President Dick Cheney. From the campaign trail to the White House, Cheney served a more prominent role on the Bush team than any previous vice president. A longtime politician—he had been President Gerald R. Ford's chief of staff in the 1970s and had served five terms in the House of Representatives in the late 1970s and 1980s—he provided Bush with a reservoir of experience, important for a president whose only previous governmental service was as governor of Texas. He also had impeccable conservative credentials: as a congressman, he had opposed both abortion and the Equal Rights Amendment. During the first months of the Bush administration, Cheney served as front man for Bush: the president would rule on policy, but it was often Cheney who was in charge of seeing that policies were carried out. He also served as the White House's chief contact person with Congress.

Cheney was given offices in both the Senate and the House and worked to maintain good relations with both Republican and Democratic members of Congress, a role that was widely appreciated: "You talk to Dick Cheney and things happen," said then Senate Republican leader Trent Lott. (Despite his conservative political views, Cheney's amiable personality allowed him to get along with politicians from all across the political spectrum.) Cheney's central role in the Bush presidency led some satirists to claim that it was really a Cheney administration, with Bush merely providing his name while the vice president did all the real work (a point of view that Cheney vigorously denied). One concern expressed during both the campaign and Bush's first hundred days was that Cheney's vital role might be threatened by his poor health—Cheney had a heart condition and had had four heart attacks—but his doctors assured the press and public that the vice president was healthy enough to continue his very active role.

CABINET CONTROVERSIES

Bush's first political hurdles came with the Senate confirmation hearings for his cabinet choices.

All cabinet-level offices must be confirmed by the Senate. The Democrats, many of them bitter after the Florida conflict, were eager to give Bush's nominees some political bruises. It does not seem that the framers of the Constitution foresaw the nature of these battles. As originally conceived, Senate approval of a cabinet was designed to prevent the instatement of someone egregiously incompetent. Despite their origins, however, confirmation hearings have become increasingly partisan over the years as senators and presidents have struggled for political dominance. During the Clinton presidency, the Republicans in Congress had used their powers to interfere with his agenda; now that a Republican was president, the Democrats were ready to reciprocate.

Bush's first cabinet appointment was uncontroversial: Colin Powell as secretary of state. Powell was a popular choice with both conservatives and moderates. A well-known and popular figure because of his role as chair of the Joint Chiefs of Staff during the 1991 Gulf War with Iraq, he was also a symbol of the possibility of African-American success in the United States. No other black man had ever been put in a position of such power, a position that places Powell in the line of presidential succession. Unlike many Republicans, Powell was supportive of some programs popular among liberals, including affirmative action. For many conservatives, however, foreign policy was not a central issue and Bush could afford to pick a moderate secretary of state, especially one with Powell's popularity. Powell and other uncontroversial picks were quickly confirmed by a voice vote in the Senate.

Some of Bush's other appointments suggested a more conservative direction for his presidency. His selection of then-senator John Ashcroft for the job of attorney general was most controversial. Ashcroft was a conservative Christian who opposed abortion and gay rights, and some critics worried that he would not be willing to firmly enforce laws protecting women seeking abortions or gays seeking to avoid discrimination. Ashcroft was also a hard-liner on law-and-order issues, supporting the death penalty (as do most Americans) and opposing gun control legislation (unlike most Americans). The appointment caused a storm of criticism and five weeks of debate. Ashcroft's many years in the Senate, however, made even some of his Democratic colleagues reluctant to oppose the appointment, a fact that the Bush administration had intelligently foreseen, and the Senate approved his nomination on February 1 with a fifty-eight to forty-two majority.

The choice of Gale Norton as secretary of the interior angered environmentalists. Norton had a reputation for favoring oil and timber companies over environmental groups, and these groups feared that her tenure in office would lead to a loosening of the environmental protections that had been put into place by previous administrations. Norton had been a protégé of James Watt—President Ronald Reagan's unpopular interior secretary who had favored opening up wilderness areas to oil and timber companies—and her friendliness to oil and chemical companies led some of her harshest critics to call her "James Watt in a skirt." The Senate approved her nomination on January 30 by a vote of seventy-five to twenty-four.

A later and closer confirmation struggle came with the appointment of Theodore B. Olson as solicitor general in May. Olson had angered many Democrats because he had served as one of Bush's key attorneys during the Florida recount struggle, representing Bush before the Supreme Court. Olson was also accused of being an extremist who had lied about his years as an anti-Clinton opponent. He had worked at the *American Spectator* magazine while it carried out the "Arkansas Project," a venture in which $2.4 million was used to search for Clinton indiscretions. Olson denied any direct involvement in the project, but many Democrats doubted his word. Olson's nomination passed on May 24 with a remarkably close vote of fifty-one to forty-seven.

Bush balanced these conservative cabinet selections with a number of moderates, including New Jersey governor Christine Todd Whitman as secretary of the Environmental Protection Agency (EPA) and Wisconsin governor Tommy Thompson as Secretary of Health and Human Services. But these moderates, like Powell, were not positioned to threaten conservative positions. Whitman, for example, had gained her reputation as a moderate in part because of her pro-choice position on abortion, but as EPA secretary, she would have no effect on the Bush administration's abortion policies.

Bush's cabinet also had a fairly broad ethnic makeup, with two African Americans serving in prominent jobs (Powell as secretary of state and Condoleezza Rice as national security adviser), alongside Hispanic Americans and one Asian American. This was a shift from the days of Ronald Reagan and George H. W. Bush—whose cabinets were a sea of white faces—as was the more prominent role given to women in the new cabinet.

Beyond its political complexion, Bush's cabinet was characterized by its extensive political experience. Unlike the Clinton presidency, which introduced many new faces to Washington, Bush was calling on individuals who had served in previous administrations, particularly those who had worked with his father and Reagan. Defense secretary Donald Rumsfeld's roots were even older: He had served as President Ford's secretary of defense. One of the few young faces was that of Condoleezza Rice.

THE BUSH STYLE

All presidents quickly imprint their style on the presidency, and Bush was no exception. The key work for the Bush administration seemed to be delegation and separation of responsibilities. Once Bush assigned a task to a member of his administration, he tended to leave him or her alone to accomplish it, and he discouraged interference from other branches and officials. Bush officials often used the metaphor of a business: Bush was a chief executive officer who handed down jobs to his senior management and let them handle the work as they saw fit, interfering only if they were having problems. Here again, Bush was obviously attempting to highlight the contrast between his own methods and President Clinton's more haphazard style. Critics, however, suggested that Bush's emphasis on delegation had created a hands-off president who was out of touch with the day-to-day business of his administration.

Bush's personal approach was amiable and joking. As was his habit from college days, he quickly handed out nicknames to cabinet officials, aides, members of Congress, and newspaper reporters. The *Hotline*, a political newsletter, listed 100 nicknames applied to those around Bush. Among them were "Balloonfoot," for Secretary of State Colin Powell; "Big George," for Democratic representative George Miller, "the Cobra," applied to *New York Times* columnist and prominent Bush critic Maureen Dowd; and "Ostrich Legs," given to Russian president Vladimir Putin. While some found the nicknames amusing, others were offended and felt they trivialized the presidency.

Bush was also less accessible to the media than some previous presidents. He generally avoided formal news conferences, preferring to take quick questions from reporters during public appearances. Even at those, Bush answered fewer questions than his predecessors did during photo opportunities (traditionally a time to pepper a president with topical questions). Reporters complained that taking questions in these impromptu contexts made it too easy for Bush to avoid questions that he did not wish to answer. In his public appearances, Bush was generally relaxed if sometimes awkward in the face of unexpected questions.

In his political relationships, Bush made efforts to cross partisan lines. He gave House minority leader Richard Gephardt a birthday cake, invited the Kennedy family to watch a screening of the movie *Thirteen Days*, and listened to members of the Congressional Black Caucus offer up their grievances. While Democrats acknowledged the importance of these gestures, many quickly became impatient with what they felt was Bush's lack of commitment to true bipartisanship. "Big George" Miller praised Bush's reaching out but argued that it had been too superficial. "President Bush is very friendly," he observed. "Many of his policies have been less so."

His work habits were steady and consistent, compared with those of his predecessor. Clinton's official schedule was always treated with amusement by the press corps and ignored by his staff; the Bush team kept tightly to its schedule. If a meeting was due to end at 3:00 P.M., it ended. On the other hand, Bush did not work as long hours as Clinton, who was notorious for keeping late hours, often working until midnight. Bush usually finished his workday by 6:00 P.M. and spent his evening hours relaxing.

THE FIRST DAYS

The early days of Bush's presidency probably benefited to some degree by the contrast with the Clinton presidency. Many people had been unhappy with Clinton's loose style, while his affair with intern Monica Lewinsky gave a tawdry tone to his last years in office. By comparison, Bush and his team seemed clean-cut and wholesome, a point repeatedly mentioned by reporters, pundits, and Bush staffers.

The contrast was made even more stark by the minor controversies that were swirling around after Clinton's last days in office. Clinton had made a number of last-minute pardons during his final days—something most presidents have done—and the shady pasts of some of those he had pardoned aroused Republican ire and media attention. There were also reports that the Clintons had taken more than they should have from the White House. These minor incidents helped to distract from the stumbles the Bush administration, like all incoming administrations, made.

Another minor yet distracting note was sounded in the first days of the Bush administration in reports that departing Clinton staffers had maliciously vandalized White House offices. Bush staffers leaked to the media reports claiming that telephone lines had been cut, filing cabinets glued shut, desks overturned, and lewd graffiti scribbled on office walls. There were also reports that the letter *W* had been removed from computer keyboards (a prank directed at President George W. Bush, whose middle initial was often used as a short-hand identifier by both critics and friends). Finally, there were stories that china and silverware with the presidential seal had been stolen off Air Force One. Ari Fleischer, Bush's press secretary, downplayed the incidents but used the moment to emphasize the change in tone planned by the Bush team: "It's a differ-

ent way of governing; it's a different way of leading."

Clinton staffers denied that there had been any major vandalism. But despite the denials, the impression left was of a disgruntled and vindictive Clinton staff being replaced by a more serious and mature Bush team, a tone that had been emphasized by Bush and his administration since Inauguration Day.

However, four months later it turned out that the Clinton denials probably were largely true. The General Services Administration, an agency responsible for maintaining government property, investigated the allegations and found no evidence of widespread vandalism. In its May report, the agency stated that "the condition of the real property was consistent with what we would expect to encounter when tenants vacate office space after an extended occupancy." (On February 13, Bush himself had already refuted the Air Force One story.)

TAXES FIRST

President Bush's first priority as president was cutting taxes. During his campaign, he had promised to lower income taxes and to eliminate the estate tax, and he clearly intended to make his campaign pledges good. Much of the energy of his first months in office, therefore, was spent trying to achieve these goals. In the process, he alienated a number of Democrats, but his determination, greatly helped by Republican control of both the House and the Senate, enabled him to achieve most of the tax cuts he sought.

Bush's tax-cutting plans were made possible by the prosperity the country had enjoyed during the Clinton years (and for which both parties claimed responsibility). A growing economy had led to larger-than-expected tax revenues and as a result had also created a substantial budget surplus, with larger surpluses predicted for the future. Both Democrats and Republicans agreed that a tax cut should be passed, but the Democrats wanted relatively modest cuts, thereby allowing for more spending on a number of federal programs. Bush disagreed and put forward a bold tax-cutting plan that surprised Congress with its audacity.

On February 8, Bush sent his tax plan to Congress. Arguing that it was time to give the American people back some of their money, he also suggested that the tax cut might help boost what seemed to be a sagging economy. The size of the proposed tax cut surprised many: $1.6 trillion over ten years.

The next few months saw acrimonious debate over the tax cut, with Democrats arguing that the cut benefited primarily the rich (which in raw monetary terms was true), while Republicans argued that in the long run it would benefit all Americans by fueling economic growth and rewarding entrepreneurship and innovation. Throughout the debate, Bush stuck to his theme that the money belonged to the American people and should be given back to them.

Final victory came on May 26, when Congress voted for a final $1.35 trillion tax cut package. While not as large as Bush had initially wished, it was the biggest tax cut since the Reagan cuts of the early 1980s. A number of Democrats in the House and the Senate joined their Republican colleagues to pass the tax plan with substantial majorities: 240 to 154 in the House, and 58 to 33 in the Senate. The tax plan would gradually phase in cuts for all income tax brackets, reaching its completion in 2010. That would be the year in which the estate tax would be repealed. The estate tax, often referred to as the "death tax" by its Republican opponents, had long been on the conservative agenda for elimination.

Bush was clearly proud of his achievement. "Tax relief was the right thing to do, and is the responsible thing to do, for the American people, and for the economy," he stated. "This is significant—and this is only the beginning."

DOMESTIC ISSUES

With his background as a state governor, it was hardly surprising that Bush's strongest emphasis in his early days in office was on domestic policy. Symbolically, he made this clear by his active schedule of domestic travel: in his first eight weeks in office, he visited eighteen states. By his hundredth day, he had visited twenty-six states. But his domestic policy initiatives went beyond simply traveling.

After taxes, Bush's budget was the next most important item on the domestic agenda. On February 27, before a joint session of Congress, he outlined a $1.9 trillion budget plan for fiscal year 2002. He called it "a new vision for governing the nation for a new generation."

On April 9, Bush delivered a more detailed budget. This $1.96 trillion budget allowed for a modest increase in federal spending. Social Security, education, and the military were some of the biggest beneficiaries of budget increases. The biggest losers were the Department of the Interior and the Environmental Protection Agency, both of which oversee programs designed to preserve wilderness areas and protect the environment. After some debate, the budget passed the House (May 9) and the Senate (May 10), with voting being mostly along party lines. Bush also pushed forward other domestic policies, although none with the impact of his tax cut.

As governor, Bush had made education a priority (albeit with little effect on Texas's very serious education problems). Even critics acknowledge his sincere desire to improve Americans' educational opportunities. As part of his education agenda, President Bush offered a program that would cut federal funding to schools that did not live up to national standards. He also supported the use of school vouchers and more standardized testing for students. These initiatives were criticized by some liberal opponents, but in this case, their importance was necessarily limited because the vast majority of funding for public schools comes from local governments, not the federal government. In his first proposed budget, Bush also offered an 11.5 percent spending increase for the Department of Education, the largest increase planned for any federal agency.

Critics and admirers alike agreed that Bush's presidency was very friendly to business interests in America. Bush worked to weaken federal regulations that he and his advisers felt restricted the competitiveness of American businesses.

Among those areas most under attack by Bush were job safety rules, which he felt were unfairly burdensome. Bush eliminated a number of safety rules that Clinton had put into effect by presidential decree, arguing that the rules were unnecessary and needlessly interfered with American business's ability to operate competitively in a world market.

Bush also had to deal with a growing energy crisis in California, which saw rolling blackouts across that state. Bush delegated the task of dealing with the crisis to Cheney, who headed a task force on national energy strategy. Cheney's team recommended increased efforts to find energy resources and an expansion of the use of coal and nuclear power. Both suggestions were strongly criticized by environmentalists.

That environmentalists were angry with Bush was hardly surprising. Bush's pro-business bias and pro-production (rather than conservation) stance on energy made him politically deaf to the interests of environmental lobbyists and advocates. His biggest domestic missteps were in the area of environmental policy. He began handicapped by his choice of Gale Norton as interior secretary. Norton was seen as too close to business interests to be properly protective of the environment. In his spending plans, Bush also made clear that he considered environmental issues to be secondary. While spending for oil and gas exploration went up, the budget for energy conservation and renewable energy sources was cut in half.

Bush also rescinded a number of regulations that Clinton had put into place to protect the environment. Bush, for example, refused to support regulations that would strictly limit the amount of arsenic allowable in drinking water, arguing that the standards were too rigid. He also backtracked on a campaign promise to cut carbon dioxide emissions, the main cause of global warning. In a letter to Senator Chuck Hagel (R-NE) explaining his reversal, the president cited a recent Department of Energy report that concluded it would be too costly to regulate carbon dioxide. When he called for allowing drilling for oil in the Arctic National Wildlife Refuge of Alaska, Wilderness Society president William H. Meadows claimed that Bush had "declared war on the environment." Finally, the Bush administration announced that it would not support the provisions of the Kyoto Protocol on global warming, a move that particularly angered environmentalists in the European Union.

RELIGION CENTER STAGE

During his campaign, Bush gained the support of evangelical and conservative Christians by promising that he would be more supportive of issues important to them than President Clinton had been. For the most part, his early days as president proved that he was as good as his word. The *Economist*—a moderately conservative magazine that endorsed Bush during the campaign—put it well in its May 19, 2001, issue: "We don't know whether George Bush will succeed in creating a more right-wing administration than Ronald Reagan's, although he is clearly trying his hardest. But he is certainly creating a more religious one. Mr. Reagan, an easy-going divorcee [sic], supported the church like a buttress, from the outside. Mr. Bush, a born-again Methodist, is more a pillar in the nave."

The Christian emphasis of the Bush administration was also apparent in small ways. The candidate himself claimed Jesus Christ as his favorite philosopher, while Attorney General Ashcroft held daily Bible study classes in his office.

One religious initiative that attracted much criticism was Bush's call for "faith-based organizations" to lead the fight against poverty and other social problems. Backing up this call, on January 29 Bush created the White House Office of Faith-Based and Community Initiatives, headed by Princeton scholar John J. DiIulio Jr. With DiIulio's office leading the fight, Bush wanted to distribute federal funds to religious groups that helped the poor and needy.

Critics on the left disliked the plan because they saw it as a threat to the traditional wall between church and state; they were afraid that many religious groups would use state-sponsored programs to attempt to convert those seeking help. More surprisingly, some conservative Christians also voiced some doubts about the program. Rev. Jerry Falwell expressed "deep concerns" that government money might also come with government requirements and restrictions that would prevent church organizations from carrying out some of their most important functions. In April 2001, 850 members of the clergy released a petition calling for Bush's plan to be rejected. "These provisions would entangle religion and government in an unprecedented and perilous way. The flow of government dollars and the accountability for how those funds are used will inevitably undermine the independence and integrity of houses of worship."

There were also doubts expressed about the method of choosing religious organizations. Bush said that the initiative would support Christian, Jewish, and Muslim groups but left unclear how eligibility would be determined. In the early days of the initiative, some of the groups expressing interest included the Unification Church of the Reverend Sun Myung Moon and the Scientologists, two groups often scorned by traditional Christian groups.

The Bush administration was taken aback by some of the possible applicants for its faith-based initiatives, but it clearly made a sincere attempt to broaden its religious base. Bush invited ministers, priests, rabbis, and a Muslim imam to the launching of his faith-based initiative. This was quite different from earlier conservative Christian initiatives, which focused on Protestant Christians, paying at best token lip service to the inclusion of Catholics and Jews. Bush, with his strong support among some categories of Catholic and Jewish voters, was clearly moving beyond this base.

Bush also followed through on his religiously centered message by his policy decisions opposing abortion. During the campaign, although he did not play it up, Bush made no secret of his opposition to abortion. He promised to take a pro-life position, in contrast to that of Clinton, who was pro-choice. On his first business day in office, January 21, Bush reinstated an abortion "gag order" on overseas organizations. The rule, initiated during the Reagan presidency, maintained by the first Bush administration, but rescinded by Clinton, forbade overseas organizations that received U.S. government funds from giving out any information on abortion. The ruling pleased Bush's supporters on the right but outraged pro-choice advocates. The rule cut funding not just from abortion providers but also from family-planning clinics that offered information on abortion.

FOREIGN POLICY

If Bush was generally viewed as stronger on domestic issues, foreign policy was clearly a weak point. Bush's previous experience had given him no real foreign policy background (unlike his father, who had had extensive international contacts when he became president). This was not necessarily a fatal handicap—President Clinton also had only his experience as governor behind him but still managed to maintain a strong grasp of foreign policy issues—but it was an area zeroed in on by many critics. More than Clinton, Bush also had a reputation for being uninterested in foreign policy issues. Bush had made some gaffes during the campaign—not being able to name the leaders of Pakistan or India, for example—that helped to contribute to this image.

The international community also doubted his abilities. An English tabloid printed a map with a big arrow pointing at England to help Bush find the country, and French papers were openly contemptuous of his intellectual abilities. Only in the Americas, particularly in Mexico, was Bush's victory viewed with approval. (Bush's fluency in Spanish helped gain him Hispanic voters during the campaign and Latin American support in the international community.) Europeans were also disturbed by statements that suggested Bush would be less involved in solving international problems. Condoleezza Rice, Bush's national security adviser, called for "a new division of labor" in European security arrangements, implying that the United States planned to reduce its European commitments. Bush's rejection of the Kyoto environmental accord also made Europeans unhappy.

During the first months of his term, Bush's travel plans did not do a great deal to dispel the perception that foreign policy was not his favorite topic. While he met with President Vicente

Fox of Mexico and other Latin American leaders, as well as Tony Blair, Britain's prime minister, his foreign travel was limited, and he did not meet with such major leaders as President Vladimir Putin of Russia or President Jiang Zemin of China.

CHINA CONFLICT

Bush's lack of focus on China was brought to an end by his first major foreign policy crisis. On April 1, a Chinese jet fighter and a U.S. Navy EP-3E reconnaissance plane crashed into each other over the South China Sea. The Chinese plane fell into the ocean, and its pilot was pronounced dead. The American plane, although damaged, was able to make an emergency landing in China, where the crew was immediately interned by Chinese military authorities.

For the next eleven days, China and the United States faced each other in a tense diplomatic confrontation. The Chinese expressed annoyance at being watched by American surveillance craft with electronic eavesdropping devices. They insisted that the American plane was responsible for the accident and demanded a full apology. Bush and Secretary of State Powell demanded the return of the Navy crew. For both nations, national pride was at stake.

The confrontation ended with Bush issuing a statement "regretting" that the incident had occurred, followed by the Chinese release of the twenty-four U.S. crew members (the plane was released three months later). While some criticized Bush's method of dealing with the crisis—hard-liners thought he was too easy on China—he probably did as well as possible given the difficult nature of the situation. Most Americans supported his handling of the crisis.

Late in April, Bush also raised Chinese hackles by a statement on a morning television show that he would "do whatever it took to help Taiwan defend herself." This suggestion that the United States might go to war on behalf of Taiwan, an island still claimed by mainland China, angered China. It also went against a long-standing American tradition of maintaining vagueness on the issue (the assumption being that if Chinese leaders did not know whether America would help Taiwan, they would not risk aggressive military action).

RUSSIA AND THE MISSILE SHIELD

Bush also had brushes with Russia, which led the London *Guardian* to refer to "fears of a new cold war." First, in February, the FBI revealed that one of its own agents, Robert Hanssen, had been spying for the Soviets on the United States for fifteen years. Hanssen was arrested, but Bush also ordered that more than fifty Russian diplomats involved with espionage be expelled from the United States. "I was presented with the facts," he said. "I made the decision. It was the right thing to do." Russia responded by ordering some American diplomats expelled from Moscow.

Tensions were further exacerbated by the Bush administration's plans to build a defensive missile shield to protect the United States against nuclear attacks. The idea of a missile shield had long been supported by Bush's secretary of defense Rumsfeld, and Bush argued that it was necessary for the nation's defense. Although the Bush administration insisted that the targets of the shield were "rogue" nations such as North Korea and Iraq, Russia was particularly disturbed by the plans. The Anti-Ballistic Missile Treaty, which the Soviet Union and the United States had concluded in 1972, restricted antimissile systems. Russia saw the new American position as destabilizing and a threat to the balance of power between the United States and Russia. Many European leaders agreed and put quiet pressure on the Bush administration to change its position, although without any success.

Domestic critics expressed doubts that any antimissile shield was even possible. They argued that spending money on a missile shield would be a waste that would benefit only military contractors.

SENATE SWITCH

The successes of Bush's early months were made possible by the Republican Party's control of both houses of Congress. Bush was the first Republican president since Dwight Eisenhower in the 1950s to have the Senate and the House under his party's control. Both his tax bill and his budget were made possible by the Republican-dominated Congress. But in late May, that changed.

On May 24, Vermont senator James Jeffords announced that he was leaving the Republican Party to become an Independent. Normally, one senator changing party affiliation would not be big news, but the United States Senate had been divided evenly between fifty Republicans and fifty Democrats, with Vice President Cheney using his tiebreaking vote to give his party majority control. Jeffords's departure from the party gave control of the Senate to the Democrats.

Bush's conservative politics—which had pleased the right wing of his party—may have been responsible for this damaging turn of events. Jeffords, a longtime moderate, had been angered by what he saw as Bush's extremist politics. There were also personal slights. Jeffords's moderate voting record had resulted in his receiving some political snubs from the Bush administration, such as not being invited to a White House ceremony honoring a Vermont teacher. There were also hints from Bush officials that they would not support subsidies for Vermont's dairy farmers. In retrospect, these hardball tactics may have been a mistake by the Bush White House. With the Democrats in control of the Senate, it became more difficult for Bush to carry out the rest of his agenda.

CONCLUSION

To most observers, Bush's first hundred days were a modest success. They do not bear comparison, of course, to the famous first hundred days of Franklin D. Roosevelt in 1933, but neither do they resemble Clinton's in 1993, which were marked by disorganization and policy reversals.

Bush's primary objective, a substantial tax cut, was well on the way to being achieved. The possibility of a serious recession also seemed to diminish. And although Bush had not scored many points among foreign allies and foes, he had managed to prevail in his first foreign policy crisis in the confrontation with China.

Bush also claimed to have created a new way of governing in Washington, with less partisanship. Commenting on his first hundred days, he said: "We're making progress toward changing the tone in Washington. There's less name-calling and finger-pointing. We're sharing credit. We are learning we can make our points without making enemies."

The public consensus on Bush was generally favorable. His approval rating at the end of April 2001 was about 62 percent, better than the 55 percent achieved by President Clinton after his first hundred days, although not as good as Ronald Reagan's 68 percent or even Jimmy Carter's 63 percent. (Vice President Cheney's approval rating was 64 percent.) More important, the country had moved past the election crisis and largely accepted Bush as its legitimate president.

Bush was not as popular with Congress as he was with the American people. To celebrate his first hundred days in office, Bush held a luncheon on April 30 and invited all the members of Congress. Many Republicans showed up; few Democrats did (missing were such key leaders as Representative Dick Gephardt and Senator Tom Daschle). And the May defection of Senator Jeffords guaranteed that in the future, Congress would be even less friendly to President Bush.

Carl Skutsch

SEE ALSO: Campaign 2000 and the Florida Recount; Budget and Fiscal Policy; Campaign Finance Reform; Congressional Elections; Education; Dennis Hastert; Trent Lott.

BIBLIOGRAPHY

"Back to the Bad Old Days?" *Guardian* (London), 23 March 2001.

"Bush Aides Mum on Reports of White House Vandalism." *Boston Globe*, January 26, 2001.

"Bush Backs Expulsion of 50 Russians." *Washington Post*, March 23, 2001.

"Bush Calls His 100-Day Accomplishments 'Only a Start.'" *Washington Times*, April 29, 2001.

"Bush Calls His Tax Cut Cautious with a 'Vision.'" *Washington Times*, March 1, 2001.

"Bush Drops Pledge to Curb Emissions." *Los Angeles Times*, March 14, 2001.

"Cheney Ever More Powerful as Crucial Link to Congress." *New York Times*, May 13, 2001.

"Clerics Attack Faith Initiative." *Washington Times*, May 1, 2001.

"Congress Passes Tax Cut, With Rebates This Summer." *New York Times*, May 27, 2001.

Economist, January to May 2001.

Financial Times, January to May 2001.

"God and Man in Washington." *Economist* (London), 19 May 2001.

"GSA Says There's No Truth to White House Vandal Scandal." *Seattle Times*, May 18, 2001.

"In Early Battles, Bush Learns Need for Compromises." *New York Times*, April 29, 2001.

New York Times, January to May 2001.

"Nicknames: The First 100 Names!" *The Hotline*, 27 April 2001.

"President Pledges Defense of Taiwan." *Washington Post*, April 26, 2001.

"US Turns Its Back on Climate Treaty." *Times* (London), 29 March 2001.

Washington Post, January to May 2001.

THE 2000 CENSUS AND THE NEW CONGRESS, 2002–2012

The Constitution requires that a census be taken every ten years to survey the American population for the purposes of determining the makeup of the House of Representatives. The number of representatives for each state is based on its total population in proportion to the whole country's population. Because the size of the House of Representatives is fixed at 435 members, when one state gains representatives because its population has increased, another state must lose representatives. For this reason, taking the census is both politically significant and a politicized process. It is carried out by the United States Census Bureau, an agency of the Department of Commerce.

The 2000 census began in controversy. For many years demographers had argued that the process of counting every single person was impractical and inaccurate. They believed that it missed people, particularly the poor, who are often difficult to reach or have no fixed residence.

According to an internal Census Bureau report, the 1990 census left out 8 million people—mostly minorities and city dwellers—while double-counting 4 million people—mostly white suburban home owners. Government demographers in the Census Bureau suggested that the 2000 census should use statistical sampling techniques to fill in the gaps in traditional counting methods. This proposal was opposed by Republicans in Congress, who argued that sampling was illegal and subject to political manipulation. It was also apparent that those most likely to be missed in a census count—ethnic minorities and the poor—were also those most likely to vote for Democrats. In *Department of Commerce v. United States House of Representatives*, the Supreme Court ruled statistical sampling techniques illegal in 1999. The 2000 census, therefore, was conducted by means of the same methods used for its predecessors.

The official result of the 2000 census put the total population of the United States at 281,421,906. With 435 members in the House, this means there are approximately 647,000 people for each representative.

Since 1990, the U.S. population had grown by more than 30 million—a 13 percent increase—but that population gain was not evenly distributed across the country. Regionally, the big winners were the West and South, which both saw large-scale migration from other parts of the country as well as foreign immigration. This population gain for the South and West translated into a gain of twelve congressional seats. In the West, Arizona gained two seats, while California, Colorado, and Nevada each gained one seat. In the South, Florida, Georgia, and Texas each gained two seats, while North Carolina gained one seat. The losers were mostly in the Northeast and Midwest. Connecticut, Illinois, Indiana, Michigan, Ohio, Oklahoma, and Wisconsin all lost one seat, while New York and Pennsylvania each lost two seats. Mississippi was the only southern state to lose a seat.

The results of the 2000 census were not accepted by all states without a struggle. Arguing that its 14,000 Mormon missionaries living abroad should have been counted in its census totals, Utah sued the Census Bureau. According to law, "residence" is where a person actually lives when the census is taken; the only exceptions are for military and diplomatic personnel. Utah was about 800 short of qualifying for an additional representative in Congress and so was eager to have its missionaries counted. The lawsuit failed. (If Utah had won, North Carolina would have lost its extra seat.)

Generally, the new census favored Republicans. The states won by George W. Bush in the 2000 election gained seven seats, and those won by Al Gore lost seven seats, so that if the election had been held using figures from the 2000 census, Bush's electoral margin would have been wider. The census results will also almost certainly help the Republicans in Congress. (The census figures will first affect the 108th Congress, which will be elected in 2002 and take office in 2003.) The areas that gained population, the West and the South, have tended to vote Republican; and if their voting trends continue, the Republicans are likely to widen the narrow gap held by the 107th Congress, elected in 2000.

In Arizona, for example, the 107th Congress has five Republicans and only one Democrat; extrapolating from those figures, there is a very good chance that in the 108th Congress, Arizona's two new seats will go to Republicans. In New York, nineteen of thirty-one seats went to Democrats; New York's loss of two seats could easily translate into a loss of two Democratic representatives. There are no guarantees, of course, and a great deal depends on who controls the state legislature in each state. Although laws vary, state legislatures are usually in charge of the process of redrawing the lines of congressional districts. Careful and creative redistricting can favor one party's representatives disproportionately. This fact gives Democrats an advantage in Georgia and allows Republicans to control the process in Florida. Overall, however, Republican- and Democratic-controlled legislatures supervise approximately the same number of congressional districts, and thus the consequences of partisanship tend to cancel each other out.

All other factors being equal, therefore, the census will probably give Republicans approximately ten extra seats in Congress. "All other fac-

tors," however, are never equal—a strong Bush presidency, for example, would boost Republican chances, a weak showing would do the opposite—and so the census, while important, will only be one among many factors determining the political balance for 2003 and the decade beyond.

Carl Skutsch

SEE ALSO: The Electoral College; Voting Behavior.

BIBLIOGRAPHY

Federal Election Commission Web site: www.fec. gov *and* fecweb1.fec.gov/pubrec/2000 presgeresults.htm

United States Census Bureau Web site: www. census.gov *and* www.census.gov/population/ www/censusdata/apportionment.html

THE ELECTORAL COLLEGE

The Electoral College is the political body that chooses the president and the vice president of the United States. Unlike other federal elective officials (such as representatives and senators), these two officials are not chosen directly by popular vote but rather by the votes of the 538 individuals who are selected to make up the Electoral College. Although the College has been an integral part of the process of choosing a president for more than 200 years, many Americans were unaware, before the November 2000 election, of what the College was or how it operated. That election, in which Al Gore won a majority of the popular vote but George W. Bush won a majority of the electoral vote and thus became president, made the institution of the Electoral College a major issue for the first time in many years.

HOW IT WORKS

The perception of many voters is that when they vote in a presidential election they are voting directly for a particular presidential candidate. This, however, is not true. A voter steps into a voting booth, but does not actually vote for a candidate but, rather, for a slate of electors. In most presidential elections, the difference is unimportant: The candidate with the most votes on election night is usually also the person who will become president the following January. However, there have been a number of elections—including the November 2000 election—in which the Electoral College's critical role in choosing the president raised public awareness of the institution.

The role of the Electoral College in choosing a president is unusual but not particularly complicated. Before a presidential election, each political party chooses a group of electoral candidates to represent it in every state. Although in almost every state voters simply pull a lever and make a mark next to the name of the presidential candidate, they are actually voting for the slate of electoral candidates, chosen by a presidential candidate's party. These electoral candidates are almost always party loyalists who have promised to vote for their party's chosen candidate. The victorious electoral candidates become the official electors for that state—members of the Electoral College—with the right to vote for the president. (Most states use a winner-take-all system in which the victorious presidential candidate wins all the electors; Maine and Nebraska are the only exceptions.)

For example, for the November 7, 2000, presidential election, the Republican and Democratic parties in New York State each chose thirty-three people to be possible electors. When the New York votes were tallied, Al Gore's electoral candidates had won the most votes in New York and therefore became official electors. George W. Bush's electoral candidates for New York played no further role in the election, even though they had received more than 2 million votes.

Once chosen, each state's victorious electors are required to meet in their respective state capitals on the first Monday after the second Wednesday in December. In 2000, this date fell on December 18. At these meetings, the electors cast their votes for president; these electoral votes are then sent on to Washington where members of the Senate and the House of Representatives count them. The candidate who receives a majority of the electoral votes becomes president. If no candidate receives a majority of

electoral votes, the House of Representatives is given the job of choosing a president from among the three candidates with the greatest number of electoral votes. Voting in this case goes by state, with each state's delegation in the House of Representatives getting only one vote (this unusual situation has happened only twice—after the elections of 1800 and 1824).

WHY IT CAME TO EXIST

When the United States Constitution was drafted in 1787, the men who wrote it—the "founding fathers"—were suspicious of unrestricted democracy. They were almost all men of property and distinction, and they worried about turning over the country to the less wealthy and less well-educated general population. The founding fathers felt that the vast majority of Americans were ill equipped to judge important issues such as the choice of a president. In the early drafts of the Constitution, the founding fathers had left the choice of president to Congress, bypassing the people entirely. Later, fearing that this method of choosing a president put too much power in the hands of Congress, they decided to allow the president to be elected through a separate process. To make sure, however, that the president would not be picked by a population swayed by sudden or transient passions, they designed a system that put a shield between the president and the population: That shield was the Electoral College. (The term "Electoral College" does not appear in the Constitution, but was coined later.)

Article 2, Section 1 of the United States Constitution explains how the Electoral College works: "Each State shall appoint, in such Manner as the Legislature thereof may direct, a Number of Electors, equal to the whole Number of Senators and Representatives to which the State may be entitled in the Congress." After voters in each state have chosen their party's electors in the general election, the electors meet—each state's delegation in its own state capital—and vote for president and vice president. Those votes are then sent to Congress, which tallies the vote and officially declares the winner of the election.

The number of electors is determined by the combined congressional representation of all the states. Each state is allocated one elector for each of its representatives in the House and two electors for its two senators. (The number of members each state has in the House of Representatives is based on its population, which is determined by the census every ten years. The number of representatives, 435, is based on the results of the 1910 census.) Thus, California, the largest state, receives 54 electors for its 52 representatives and 2 senators, while Vermont gets 3 electors for its 1 representative and 2 senators. The District of Columbia was granted 3 electors by the Twenty-Third Amendment to the Constitution, ratified in 1961. (Before that time, citizens of Washington, D.C., did not vote for president.)

During the drafting of the United States Constitution, deciding the size of the Electoral College required careful negotiation. The idea that the size of the Electoral College should be based on the size of each state's voting population was opposed by two groups. Delegates from small states, such as New Hampshire and Delaware, objected that big states would be able to dominate presidential elections; and delegates from southern states objected to a system that did not take into account their non-voting slave populations. Basing the Electoral College on congressional representation satisfied both of these groups of states. Small states received extra electoral votes because of the two senators that all states received, while slave states were credited with 60 percent of their slave populations when determining electoral representation because of the "three-fifths compromise," which allowed states to count each slave as three-fifths of a person for the purposes of determining representation in the House of Representatives.

The Electoral College, therefore, was not intended to be democratic. Because it was based on congressional representation, it favored small states and slave states. Large free states, like New York, suffered from this favoritism, and partly because of this, the debate over whether or not to adopt the Constitution was especially rancorous in New York. Moreover, the members of the Electoral College were not originally meant to be chosen by the people but instead by state legislatures. Despite these flaws, the Constitution, and the Electoral College along with it, was ratified by all thirteen of the original states. It was not a perfect document, but it may have been the best that could be achieved given the political realities of the day.

IN PRACTICE

As originally conceived there was to be no direct connection between the democratic will of the people and choice of president. State legislatures chose the electors, and the electors voted for president. The founding fathers believed that these electors, presumably men of education and stature in the community, would make a better choice than would the general population. In the 1796 elections, for example, almost half of presidential electors were chosen by state legislatures, rather than through popular elections. Moreover, most states limited the right to vote to white men with some wealth or property, further limiting the democratic nature of presidential elections.

Despite their undemocratic beginnings, presidential elections gradually became increasingly based on the will of the people. In the 1830s, the last property qualifications for voting were eliminated, and in most states, voters, not state legislatures, were given the responsibility for choosing each state's electors (South Carolina, the one exception, did not allow popular elections of electors until after the Civil War).

Nevertheless, whether chosen by state legislatures or by popular vote, the Electoral College was at the center of a number of presidential election controversies.

The first came in the election of 1800. Originally, the Constitution stated that each elector could vote for two people and the candidate with the most votes became president, while the runner up became vice president. In 1800, after a bitterly contested election between Federalist John Adams and Democrat-Republican Thomas Jefferson, Jefferson received 73 electoral votes, giving him a victory over Adams. However, Jefferson's vice presidential choice, Aaron Burr, also received 73 votes. Since neither Jefferson or Burr had won a majority, the election was thrown into the House of Representatives where Federalists, disliking Jefferson, did their best to throw the election to Burr. It was only in February 1801 that Federalists gave up this attempt and agreed to pick Jefferson. The Twelfth Amendment to the Constitution, ratified in 1804, prevented such a situation from happening again by requiring separate votes for president and vice president.

There have been several elections where the victorious presidential candidate failed to win a majority of the popular vote. In most of these elections, however, the victor had received more votes than any other candidate. In 1860, for example, Abraham Lincoln became president with 40 percent of the popular vote in a four-way race, but he had more votes than any other candidate and won a majority of electoral votes. More recently, Bill Clinton won 49.25 percent of the popular vote in 1996 and Bob Dole won 40.7 percent, with the remainder split among other candidates. Clinton easily won a majority of electoral votes, 379 to 159.

There have only been four elections, however, in which the candidate with the most popular votes lost in the Electoral College and therefore failed to be elected president. The elections occurred in 1824, 1876, 1888, and 2000.

In 1824, a four-way election gave no candidate a majority of popular or electoral votes, and the election was thrown into the House of Representatives. Andrew Jackson had won the largest number of both popular votes (155,872) and electoral votes (99), but the House voted for John Quincy Adams, who had received only 105,321 popular votes and 84 electoral votes. Adams became president. Jackson supporters cried foul and claimed that the election had been stolen.

In 1876, Democrat Samuel Tilden won a majority of the popular vote. He also won more electoral votes than his opponent, Republican Rutherford B. Hayes, but disputed vote counts in four states (Florida, Louisiana, South Carolina, and Oregon) prevented Tilden from winning a majority. The decision was thus left to Congress, which chose to award the election to Hayes. President Hayes was accused by critics of having gained the support of southern congressmen by

promising to end federal support of African-American voting rights.

In 1888, Republican Benjamin Harrison lost the popular vote by a small margin but won a clear electoral majority over Democrat Grover Cleveland. Cleveland accepted defeat and did not contest or dispute the election.

For the next twenty-seven presidential elections, the candidate who won the popular vote also won the electoral vote. Then came the 2000 election. Not counting the contested state of Florida, Gore's popular vote total was 50,996,039, more than a half million more than Bush's 50,456,141. But for weeks the Electoral College result was unclear. Gore was victorious in twenty states and Washington, D.C., giving him a probable total of 267 electoral votes; Bush won in twenty-nine states, but only had 246 electoral votes. The key state was Florida, whose 25 electoral votes were in dispute and where Bush held a razor-thin lead. After many recounts and court controversies, a December 12, 2000, United States Supreme Court decision effectively ended the possibility of continuing a Florida recount and therefore allowed Bush to maintain a 537-vote margin in Florida (of 6 million votes cast). Winning Florida's electoral votes guaranteed him the election. Gore conceded on the following evening. The final electoral vote tally was 271 to 266; one Washington, D.C., elector abstained instead of voting for Gore.

IS IT FAIR?

There is a long history of criticizing the Electoral College, a history as old as the College itself. From its beginnings, critics have argued that it is not a democratic institution. First, it puts the choice of president in the hands of presidential electors rather than the American people. Second, because its size is based on congressional representation rather than directly on population it gives some states disproportionate influence over presidential elections. Finally, because in most cases electors are chosen according to winner-take-all state laws, it is possible for the candidate with less popular support to win the election.

The first criticism has only limited validity. Potential electors are chosen because of their party loyalty and they rarely vote against the candidate they have pledged to support. Some states even have laws penalizing "faithless electors"—electors who do not vote as they have promised—although many constitutional scholars question the legality of those laws. In any case, there have been very few faithless electors, and they have never affected the outcome of a presidential contest. (In 1988, for example, Margarette Leach, an elector for Democratic presidential candidate Michael Dukakis, voted instead for Democratic vice presidential candidate Lloyd Bentsen in order to draw attention to the flaws in the Electoral College; her vote had no effect on the election.) When Americans vote for a president, the weight of tradition almost guarantees that the elector, if chosen, will carry out their wishes.

That the Electoral College favors some states over others is a stronger criticism. The Electoral College rewards sparsely populated states over heavily populated states. While the number of electors each state receives *approximately* matches its share of the United States population—because the size each state delegation is based in part on the number of representatives it has in the House of Representatives, which is in turn based upon population—smaller states receive a disproportionate number of electors because all states, no matter how sparsely populated, receive two senators. California's 33,871,648 people give it 54 electors, or 1 elector for every 615,848 people; Vermont's 608,837 people give it 3 electors, or 1 elector for every 202,945 people. This means that a voter in Vermont has three times more influence over a presidential contest than a voter in California.

The winner-take-all nature of electoral contests is perhaps the most flawed part of the system. Because most states (the exceptions are Maine and Nebraska) reward all electoral votes to whichever candidate gets a plurality of votes in that state, it makes it very possible for a candidate to win the popular vote but lose in the Electoral College, as has happened four times in the past. The problem stems from the fact that "extra" votes in a state do not help a candidate win

an election. Winning 4.1 million popular votes in New York (60 percent of the vote) gained Al Gore the state's 33 electoral votes; but if he had won only 3.5 million, he still would have had 51 percent of the popular vote and still gained New York's 33 electoral votes. In other words, 600,000 Gore supporters in New York could have stayed home and Gore still would have won all the state's electoral votes.

This is why Gore won the popular vote but lost the election. Gore's support was concentrated in several large states, such as New York and California, where his "extra" votes did nothing to help him. Bush, in contrast, won a couple of key large states, such as Ohio and Florida, by very narrow margins. Bush also had overwhelming support in several western states, such as Montana and Utah, whose small populations gave them disproportionate weight in the Electoral College.

Defenders of the Electoral College argue that it makes sure that small states will not be ignored because it forces candidates to spend time in every state, not just in those with the largest populations. Ignoring the undemocratic nature of this argument, it is also untrue. In the 2000 election campaigns as in past campaigns, presidential candidates focused their time and money on medium and large states where polling suggested there was a close contest. Small states and states where one candidate had overwhelming support were ignored by both campaigns. For example, Gore and Bush spent little time campaigning in New York, California, and Texas, because both campaigns knew that Gore was almost certain to win the first two states, while Bush had locked up Texas. Likewise, they both ignored small western states because these were all in Bush's column. The 2000 campaign concentrated on states such as Florida, Ohio, Pennsylvania, and Wisconsin, where the race was both close and electorally significant.

A stronger defense argues that in a very close election, the Electoral College shields the country from traumatic national recount. Recounts, when they occur, need to happen only in those states where the contest was close. This argument, however, remains hypothetical. In the past 100 years, the statistically closest popular vote in a presidential election came in 1960 when John F. Kennedy defeated Richard M. Nixon by fewer than 120,000 votes of almost 69 million cast. While this is close, it is unlikely to have been close enough to have made a national recount a possibility.

THE FUTURE

A number of reforms have been proposed by critics of the Electoral College, particularly after the controversial November 2000 election.

Some political scientists have suggested simply scrapping the College entirely and choosing the president by popular vote, a choice favored by most Americans questioned in opinion polls. These critics argue that the current system is not only undemocratic but also too confusing to the general public: it makes people think that their votes do not count. Eliminating the Electoral College would require a constitutional amendment.

Others have argued that the states should eliminate winner-take-all contests and instead adopt a system like that currently in use in Maine and Nebraska, wherein electors are chosen by legislative district. This would prevent extra votes in a state from being wasted votes (and if used in Florida would probably have resulted in a Gore presidential victory). This change has the advantage of not requiring a constitutional amendment: each state has the legal right to regulate the election process in any way it wishes.

None of these suggestions, however, seems likely to be put into effect. A constitutional amendment would require the agreement of three-fourths of the states and it is unlikely that the small states of the West and Northeast would vote to give up the advantages accruing to them under the current system. There is also the reality of political inertia. The Electoral College has worked, more or less, for more than two hundred years; there is no strong interest among politicians or the general population to change it; and there are strong constituencies who oppose any changes.

Carl Skutsch

SEE ALSO: Campaign 2000 and the Florida Recount; The 2000 Census and the New Congress, 2002–2012.

BIBLIOGRAPHY

Hardaway, Robert M. *The Electoral College and the Constitution: The Case for Preserving Federalism.* Westport, CT: Praeger, 1994.

Longley, Lawrence D., and Neal R. Pierce. *The Electoral College Primer 2000.* New Haven: Yale University Press, 1999.

Office of the Federal Register. "A Procedural Guide to the Electoral College." www.nara.gov/fedreg/elctcoll/proced.html

Witcover, Jules. *No Way to Pick a President.* New York: Farrar Straus & Giroux, 1999.

PART II

NATIONAL ISSUES AND IDEOLOGY

AFFIRMATIVE ACTION

Since the passage of the 1964 Civil Rights Act, affirmative action has been a program whose intent is to ensure fair hiring standards and access to education, housing, and government resources, such as government contracts, for all people regardless of their race, nationality, or gender. In the late 1990s and early twenty-first century, the policies that support the current state of affirmative action have been called into question. Some critics have charged that the policy of affirmative action has contributed to quotas—hiring a certain number of people of a particular race, ethnicity, or sex. Establishing quotas for one group of people, they argue, necessarily discriminates against another group of people. While the pursuit of equal opportunity and treatment for all Americans is the goal behind affirmative action, such groups as the Republican Party have clamored for reform of this policy.

The Republican Party has traditionally been seen as "not friendly" toward the spirit and law of affirmative action. At the Republican National Convention in Philadelphia in July 2000, General Colin Powell, a strong supporter of the policy, chided the Republicans for their often voiced opposition to affirmative action. Powell, one of the most prominent African Americans in the nation, challenged presidential candidate and Texas governor George W. Bush and the Republicans to continue supporting and innovating programs that would provide poorer Americans greater access to jobs, homes, education, and government resources designed for entrepreneurial ventures. Bush responded with a program that he hopes will initiate a period of "affirmative access" rather than affirmative action.

Inaugurated as president in 2001, George W. Bush has designed a plan to provide fair access to jobs, schooling, homes, and governmental resources. Bush does not want the image that the Republican Party does not care for the most impoverished in society to continue, but his plans do diverge from the traditional means of affirmative action. The president believes that equality can be more quickly achieved through ending the "soft bigotry of low expectations" in education. By strengthening schools and giving all American students a sound education, America will have given future leaders a strong start toward individual freedom. The hope is that a more educated populace will find better ways for individual success, rather than rely on government programs for survival. Along with strengthening education, Bush wants to eliminate quotas for jobs, education, and resources, a practice, he claims, that pits race against race and group against group. He argues that such programs as his Texas 10 Percent Plan and college savings accounts are the innovations needed to eliminate quotas but still provide full access to resources to all Americans. The 10 Percent Plan allows any student, regardless of race, religion, or nationality, who places in the top 10 percent of his or her high school class guaranteed admission to a Texas state university. The program is meant to bolster confidence that the government is opening doors for success that students will make use of.

Finally, Bush aims to base receipt of government resources and contracts on merit rather than quotas, but he also proposes changes in contract regulations and negotiations that would make it easier for minority-owned businesses (which are often smaller and have less experience) to win government contracts. For example, he would ease such regulations as high licensing fees and break up large contracts so that smaller businesses would be able to bid for them. He would also allow small businesses to team up with more established businesses to fulfill contracts. Further, he supports stronger state efforts to search out minority-owned businesses to bid for contracts. Those wanting government money for business start-up and contracts will have to prove their merit for receiving the money or contract rather than handing out these items to groups because a quota must be met. Bush and the Republicans argue that this will strengthen people by challenging them to prove their worth and abilities.

Bush and the Republicans also want to push "affirmative access" through cutting taxes, enhancing welfare reform, helping at-risk children, and enabling low-income Americans to purchase their own home instead of renting. With current welfare reforms that have helped families leave the welfare rolls and establish work independence, Bush advocates cutting taxes greatly so these families can keep more of what they earn. Because homeownership has traditionally been seen as one of the hallmarks of the American Dream, Bush and the Republicans are looking to implement the "American Dream Down Payment," a program designed to allow the half a million families drawing federal rent assistance to apply one year of their assistance money toward a down payment on their own home. Finally, Bush and the Republicans advocate strengthening faith-based and community-driven assistance groups to help all Americans, particularly at-risk children. The Republicans believe that these groups are often better equipped than government institutions to help people in need.

President Bush and the Republican Party want resources given on the basis of quotas to stop. Rather, they feel that giving Americans access to better education, tax breaks, government resources, and homeownership will better strengthen citizens and society.

President Bush selected John Ashcroft, a Republican senator from Missouri, as his attorney general. Ashcroft has stated his opposition to all forms of affirmative action. His appointment was criticized by civil rights leaders because he had campaigned against the nomination of African-American Missouri judge Ronnie White for a federal judgeship. On the other hand, Bush has appointed a very diverse group of top government officials, including General Colin Powell as secretary of state and Condoleezza Rice as national security adviser. The White House acknowledges that it has considered racial, ethnic, and gender diversity in suggesting appointments, but it has not relied on quotas or trade-offs. While maintaining his opposition to affirmative action requiring quotas, Bush has continued to stress affirmative access in his presidency.

Steve Rowe

SEE ALSO: Civil Rights; Immigration.

BIBLIOGRAPHY

Altschiller, Donald, ed. *Affirmative Action*. New York: H. W. Wilson, 1991.

Bacchi, Carol Lee. *The Politics of Affirmative Action: "Women," Equality and Category Politics*. Thousand Oaks, CA: Sage, 1996.

Belz, Hernan. *Equality Transformed: A Quarter-Century of Affirmative Action*. New Brunswick, NJ: Transaction, 1991.

Blanchard, Fletcher A., and Faye J. Crosby, eds. *Affirmative Action in Perspective*. New York: Springer-Verlag, 1989.

Cahn, Steven M., ed. *The Affirmative Action Debate*. New York: Routledge, 1995.

Carter, Stephen L. *Reflections of an Affirmative Action Baby*. New York: Basic Books, 1991.

Chin, Gabriel J., ed. *Affirmative Action and the Constitution*. New York: Garland, 1998.

Rosenfeld, Michael. *Affirmative Action and Justice: A Philosophical and Constitutional Inquiry*. New Haven: Yale University Press, 1991.

Wyzan, Michael L., ed. *The Political Economy of Ethnic Discrimination and Affirmative Action: A Comparative Perspective*. New York: Praeger, 1990.

BUDGET AND FISCAL POLICY

The issue of how to manage the budget of the United States government was often the one that starkly contrasted the Republicans and the Democrats. Republicans largely sought to reign in the government's spending in the hopes that current revenues would then alleviate any deficit. Whether or not a Republican was a budget-hawk was a sure test of fiscal conservatism. Republicans went so far as to propose a constitutional amendment that would have required a balanced federal budget. In the 1990s, this proposal was the battleground for contentious debate between the Republican members of Congress and the Clinton White House. However, huge economic growth during the decade enabled the federal government to balance the budget in 1998—for the first time in almost thirty years—and begin running a surplus. These developments largely ended Republican calls for a balanced budget amendment. The debate now focuses on what fiscal restraints should be implemented to maintain a balanced budget in the future and on what to do with the budget surplus. In 2000, the budget surplus was estimated to be more than $1.9 trillion over the next ten years.

While the country no longer faces large budget shortfalls, it does still have a national debt of more than $5 trillion. A budget deficit occurs when the government spends more money than it receives in taxes and must therefore borrow money to pay its debts. A surplus occurs when the government spends less money than it receives in taxes and therefore has extra, or surplus, funds left over. For much of the 1970s, 1980s, and 1990s, the federal government spent more than it collected and floated bonds to cover the deficit. The accumulation of these bonds and the promise to repay them with interest is what constitutes the national debt. The debate that currently separates Republicans from Democrats in the arena of budget and fiscal policy is where to spend the budget surplus and how much of it should be refunded in the form of tax relief.

Both parties recognize that the large budget surpluses are an opportunity to accomplish goals that otherwise might be too difficult to achieve. The Republicans believe that the booming economy and resulting surpluses are due in part to the efforts of the Republican-led Congress in the late 1990s to cut tax burdens while reining in spending. Republicans believe that this formula will continue to produce increased surpluses and will grow the economy out of its deficit.

To accomplish this, in 2001 President George W. Bush suggested a tax cut of $1.6 trillion over ten years. This major cut in taxes, according to Republicans, would produce a fairer tax structure and one that generates more revenue because the money not taken by the government would be invested or spent to help fuel the economy. The guiding principle behind this type of tax cut is that the surplus belongs to the people—the taxpayers—and should, if possible, be returned to them to spend or invest as they see fit.

The bulk of the tax cut would come from an across-the-board cut in marginal income tax rates. Marginal tax rates are the amount people pay on each taxable dollar earned after taking deductions. Decreasing the marginal tax rates would decrease the amount of taxes everyone pays, but in general, those who pay more in taxes—the wealthiest citizens—would receive the biggest cuts. President Bush also wants to phase out the estate tax, which is the tax paid by the heirs of large estates and some family businesses. He believes in eliminating the so-called marriage penalty tax by making the income ceiling for married couples twice that of single people, instead of its current level of 1.7 times the amount of a single person's income. Most Republicans and some moderate Democrats support the president's tax proposals, and in May 2001, Congress approved a $1.35 trillion tax cut, giving the president most but not all of what he sought.

Another element of the current debate over fiscal policy is the solvency of the Social Security Trust Fund. While the trust fund is an off-budget item, which means that it is not reported on the budget, the government does report its surpluses or deficits on a Unified Budget, which pulls together the general ledger and the trust fund. The result is that much of the early budget surpluses, in 1998 for example, was the result of large surpluses in the trust fund masking shortfalls in the budget itself. However, future revenue projections show that the budget itself will produce large surpluses and the trust fund will begin to run deficits as the baby boom generation—those born in the years after World War II—begins to retire. Republicans hope to solve that problem by partially privatizing Social Security so that the returns on the money invested by workers exceed the low sums currently earned on invested dollars. Republicans also contend that a plan that allows private individuals to invest a portion of their Social Security funds would further spur the economy and result in increased tax and Social Security revenues. In addition, they believe that part of the budget surplus ought to be set aside to shore up the trust fund. The Republicans' proposed 2002 budget saves the entire Social Security surplus and states the government's commitment to reforming the program, but it does not propose any modifications to Social Security or money to support the trust fund for the time being.

Republicans also believe that a portion of the budget surplus should be targeted at national debt reduction. However, this goal should not be sought at the detriment of the fundamental belief that tax relief and controlled spending are more effective ways of dealing with the national debt in the long run. Key to this viewpoint is that the national debt—while overwhelming in sheer numbers—is not a critical factor to the nation's economic health because it represents such a low number as a ratio to gross national product (GNP). In fact, the United States has the lowest ratio of debt to GNP of any major postindustrial nation. Over the course of the last few years, as annual deficits have subsided and the economy has grown, the debt has become less of a factor in the economy and the investment market. Republicans believe that the nation can grow itself out of the debt.

Finally, Republicans would take the opportunity to spend some of the surplus on programs in certain areas. Most of the ones favored by Republican lawmakers involve increased spending on the military, which according to them had been cut too severely during the Clinton administration. President George W. Bush has also made education spending among his top priorities, although Democrats believe he has not increased the Education Department's budget enough. Bush has proposed increased spending on healthcare, particularly for Medicare prescription drug benefits, as well as for farmers aid, veterans benefits, and biomedical research.

While calls for a balanced budget amendment have faded away over the last several years, the heart of Republican budget and fiscal policy has remained largely unchanged since the presidency of Ronald Reagan. Dubbed "Reaganomics" in the 1980s, the policy involves the cutting of taxes to spur investment on the part of individuals and the control of the growth of government spending. Republicans believe that it is largely this combination which has helped to create the current budget surpluses and which will continue to produce a growing economy and steady increases in federal revenues to cover future costs.

Jeffrey D. Schultz

SEE ALSO: Campaign Finance Reform; Foreign Policy; Military; Social Security.

BIBLIOGRAPHY

Gosling, James J. *Budgetary Politics in American Governments*. New York: Longman, 1992.

Hyde, Albert C., ed. *Government Budgeting: Theory, Process, and Politics*. 2d ed. Pacific Grove, CA: Brooks/Cole, 1992.

Koven, Steven G. *Public Budgeting in the United States: The Cultural and Ideological Setting*. Washington, DC: Georgetown University Press, 1999.

Minarik, Joseph J. *Making America's Budget Policy: From the 1980s to the 1990s*. Armonk, NY: M. E. Sharpe, 1990.

Ott, David J., and Attiat F. Ott. *Federal Budget Policy*. Washington, DC: Brookings Institution, 1977.

Schick, Allen. *The Federal Budget: Politics, Policy, Process*. Washington, DC: Brookings Institution, 1995.

CAMPAIGN FINANCE REFORM

It is difficult to define a single Republican position on campaign finance reform. Many individual Republicans support campaign reform, and many oppose it. Those who support it often tend to be more liberal on other issues, but not always. (While there may be no firm Republican position on campaign reform, Democrats almost universally espouse it, so it could be considered the liberal position on that basis.) The 2000 Republican Party platform reflected this confusion, containing a mix of expansions and contractions of the current campaign finance system. Exacerbating the difficulty of discerning a Republican stance is the fact that "poison pills" (amendments or alternative bills offered not on their merits but to take votes away from another proposal) are an unusually common tactic in the arena of campaign finance legislation. The bills a legislator introduces may thus be a poor indication of his or her actual position on campaign finance.

The major legislative vehicle for attempted

campaign finance reform in recent years has been the McCain-Feingold Bill, which was first introduced in 1996 by Senators John McCain (R-AZ) and Russ Feingold (D-WI). In its original form, it would have banned "soft money" contributions to political parties, banned political action committee (PAC) contributions to candidates, and set up a system of public financing, conditioned on voluntary spending limits, for congressional elections. The bill drew a number of Republican supporters: Representatives Christopher Shays (R-CT) and Linda Smith (R-WA) cosponsored the House version with Martin Meehan (D-MA), which became known as the Shays-Meehan Bill. It also drew Republican opponents, including Senator Mitch McConnell (R-KY) and Representative John Doolittle (R-CA), and ultimately failed to become law. Doubting the wisdom of McCain-Feingold, Representative Bill Thomas (R-CA) devised a more moderate counterproposal that would have required a majority of contributions to come from within a candidate's district, banned "bundling" of contributions to avoid individual contribution limits, and allowed political parties to contribute more to their candidates when opponents spent large amounts of money on their own campaigns. Thomas's proposal also went nowhere.

McCain-Feingold had another go-around in 1998, with momentum from hearings on campaign finance abuses chaired by Senator Fred Thompson (R-TN). Again, there was a moderate Republican counterproposal, this time from Senators James Jeffords (R-VT) and Olympia Snowe (R-ME). This proposal would have imposed disclosure requirements on independent issue campaigns, rather than banning them entirely. McCain and Feingold responded by watering down many provisions of their bill, but again, both McCain-Feingold and the alternative went down to defeat.

The bill was still on the table in 1999 and this time drew a spate of counterproposals. Representatives' positions that year pointed out starkly that campaign finance reform is not necessarily a moderate versus conservative issue in the Republican Party. Again, Christopher Shays cosponsored the House version of McCain-Feingold, but this time a group of twenty-nine Republicans led by Representative Zach Wamp (R-TN) and Marge Roukema (R-NJ) formed to pressure Speaker Dennis Hastert (R-IL) to bring the bill to a floor vote. Many staunch conservatives backed Shays-Meehan (or at least a vote on it), including Representatives Wamp, Bill Barrett (R-NE), Jack Metcalf (R-WA), and Mark Sanford (R-SC). In response to McCain-Feingold and Shays-Meehan came bills from Representative Doolittle to scrap all the current federal election law and replace it with a system of no limits and full disclosure of donor identities; from Representative Thomas to streamline the Federal Election Commission (FEC); and from Representative Asa Hutchinson (R-AR) to ban soft money donations but raise the limits on hard money contributions (that is, those which go directly to candidates). These competing proposals highlight the need to look beyond a bill's text for its author's true position. The presence of multiple alternatives allowed representatives to claim they voted for "campaign finance reform" while knowing that no individual proposal would garner a majority. Thomas's bill, in particular, was cited as giving the cover of a "yes" vote yet offering only piecemeal reform.

In 2000, McCain-Feingold was back on the agenda, this time propelled in part by McCain's bid for the Republican presidential nomination. Campaign finance reform was a major piece of his agenda, and he went so far as to hold a joint appearance on the issue with former senator Bill Bradley (D-NJ), who was campaigning for the Democratic nomination at the same time and had a similar emphasis on campaign finance. Again, there was a counterproposal to McCain-Feingold, this time from Senator Chuck Hagel (R-NE). Hagel's bill would have imposed looser restrictions on soft money than McCain's and was popular enough to yield at least lukewarm responses both from Democrats and from Senator McConnell, historically one of the Senate's most committed opponents of campaign finance reform. The 2000 session even saw Congress pass a bill on campaign finance reform, albeit a small area of it. Section 527 groups, named after a section of the Internal Revenue Code that gave them tax-exempt status, finally came under FEC disclosure rules, which they had not before.

The emphasis on campaign finance reform carried over to the Republican Party platform, which called for barring corporations and labor unions from making soft money donations and for preventing incumbents from rolling over campaign funds into a race for a different office. Reflecting the schizophrenia in the party, however, the platform would also adjust individual contribution limits for inflation and allow individuals to continue to make soft money contributions. Other campaign finance provisions in the platform would require full disclosure of contributions on the Internet and bar unions from spending dues money on politics without members' consent. The platform echoed the concern in the 1976 Supreme Court decision *Buckley v. Valeo* for freedom of speech but (in another nod to the party's split personality) did not explicitly call for unlimited spending.

In early April 2001, the McCain-Feingold Bill passed the Senate. As passed, the bill banned soft money contributions, required more stringent and efficient disclosure of donations, and doubled the amount individuals may directly contribute to candidates from $1,000 to $2,000. It also barred independent groups from airing "issue ads" that address a specific candidate sixty days before a general election and thirty days before a primary. However, Republicans in the House were reluctant to bring the bill to a vote there and delayed its consideration for as long as possible. Although the House had twice previously approved nearly identical bills, representatives no longer have the assurance that the bill will be killed in the Senate and are therefore much more hesitant about passing it.

Despite Senator McCain's staunch commitment to the bill, most members of the Republican Party were ambivalent at best about it. Most Republicans opposed it, and President George W. Bush would not consider promising his signature on any campaign finance reform bill until it went through both houses and he could view it in its final form.

Ethan Fenn

SEE ALSO: Budget and Fiscal Policy; Congressional Elections; Congressional Party Leadership; Party Organization; John McCain.

BIBLIOGRAPHY

"Campaign Dollar Rerun; Congress Seems Unlikely to Pass Campaign Finance Reform, and the Best Possibility for Reform May Lie with the Individual States." *The Nation*, March 9, 1998, 3.

Carney, Eliza Newlin. "Defending PACs." *National Journal* 28:28 (1996): 1518.

———. "Poison Pills for Campaign Reform." *National Journal* 31:34–35 (1999): 2430.

———. "The Speaker or the Cause?" *National Journal* 31:20 (1999): 1332.

———. "Staking the Wrong Reform." *National Journal* 30:15 (1998): 822.

Thomas, Bill. "Q: Was the GOP Proposal to Reform Campaign Finance a Good Idea? Yes: Require All Candidates to Raise Most of Their Funds from Within Their Electoral Districts." *Insight on the News*, August 19, 1996, 24.

CIVIL RIGHTS

The modern civil rights movement has far surpassed the very limited origins it had more than forty years ago. At that time, the concept of civil rights was largely limited to the political, legal, and social situation of African Americans and other minority racial groups and what remedies ought to be made to correct past injustice. Today, however, the issues that comprise the modern civil rights movement include women's rights, gay and lesbian rights, the rights of those who are disabled, and others. A key premise behind civil rights is that members of these groups need specific programs or affirmative action to overcome either historical inequalities or current discriminatory practices.

Among the three major civil rights issues for women are the securing of equal pay for equal work, breaking through the "glass ceiling," and effective prosecution and protection in cases of domestic violence. For African Americans and other minority groups, major issues include the continuation of affirmative action, the end to racial profiling by police and businesses (especially banking), and the continuation and extension of bilingual education. For Americans who are disabled, gaining access to work and educational opportunities has always been a challenge that they believe requires a proactive federal government. Gays and lesbians have sought to move into the mainstream of American life by demanding full legal rights protecting them from discrimination and hate crimes, as well as all the rights associated with a traditional family structure, including the right to have a marriage recognized by the government, the right to adopt children, and the ability to serve openly in the nation's armed forces.

Generally, the Republican Party has rejected attempts to level the playing field through the imposition of or creation of laws that attempt to redress the problems of groups of people who share a certain racial, ethnic, or gender identity or who otherwise face disadvantages or discrimination. The party has sought instead to promote equality of opportunity and equality before the law rather than to create new laws.

Despite this general predisposition against legislation, however, President George H. W. Bush and the Republican-controlled Congress of the Clinton administration sought to address some of these issues through the creation of new laws. For example, the first Bush administration (1989–93) was a leading advocate of the Americans with Disabilities Act of 1989. This law required that buildings and companies make reasonable accommodations for employees and patrons who are disabled. Therefore, it would be a mistake to claim categorically that Republicans do not support measures that address groups with a certain disadvantage. It is safe to say that in most cases Republicans believe either that the government should not be involved in any remedy or that the use of laws to assist certain groups of people is suspect.

Inaugurated in 2001, President George W. Bush has generally opposed legislative initiatives aimed at rectifying perceived inequalities based on membership in a specific group. He and the party reject affirmative action because it does not solve the underlying problems that make such policies necessary. Instead, Bush and the party see the reform of education, including the issuance of vouchers, as a way to break the cycle of poverty that has often trapped minorities. Bush has also supported what he calls "English-plus"

legislation that would permit education, signs, and other items to be in both English and another language.

Racial profiling—a law enforcement practice of using race to decide which individuals to stop and examine—and police brutality have consistently been volatile issues during Bush's campaign and presidency. In his campaign, Bush talked of wanting local governments to oversee such matters and expressed concerns about using the federal government to enforce control. Although his comments on the topic have been limited, in his first speech to Congress as president he pledged to end the practice. He came under fire for not addressing riots in Cincinnati in April 2001, which flared in response to the shooting of an unarmed black man by police, the fourth black man killed by Cincinnati police in six months and the fifteenth in six years. However, such leading Republicans as former New Jersey governor Christine Todd Whitman, now director of the Environmental Protection Agency, have publicly spoken out against the practice and have indicated that its use will be investigated.

On the issue of gay rights, the party's position is markedly more steadfast. While Republicans support the continuation of "Don't ask, don't tell" in the military, they are adamantly opposed to open homosexuals serving in the military. Additionally, they do not support gay adoption or gay marriage. The Republican-controlled Congress led the charge to prevent the nationalization of gay marriages through legislation that defined what constitutes a marriage. This was done to prevent several states and municipalities from giving legal status to ceremonies between members of the same sex. As governor, Bush also spoke out against gays in the Boy Scouts and stated that hate crime legislation should not extend to homosexuals.

As president, Bush chose Senator John Ashcroft as attorney general. Civil rights advocates were critical of Bush's selection because Ashcroft had led a campaign to block the nomination of a black judge to a federal judgeship in his home state of Missouri and generally has been viewed as hostile to civil rights legislation. Civil rights leaders also had reservations about Bush's nomination of Ralph Boyd, an African-American lawyer from Boston, as the assistant attorney general for civil rights, because he was mostly untested in the realm of civil rights litigation.

Generally speaking, then, the Republican Party does not support the notion that societal problems should be addressed through legislative manners when it comes to rectifying real or perceived inequities in a class-based system. Instead, the party believes that civil rights are those rights which belong to all American citizens based on the fact that they are citizens. From this viewpoint, preferential treatment such as affirmative action, extension of class status to homosexuals, and unique laws that protect behavior or require special treatment from other individuals violate the classical understanding of civil rights.

Jeffrey D. Schultz

SEE ALSO: Affirmative Action; Immigration.

BIBLIOGRAPHY

Adam, Barry D. *The Rise of a Gay and Lesbian Movement*. New York: Twayne Publishers, 1995.

Freeman, Jo, and Victoria Johnson, eds. *Waves of Protest: Social Movements Since the Sixties*. Lanham, MD: Rowman & Littlefield Publishers, 1999.

Martin, Waldo E., Jr., and Patricia Sullivan. *Civil Rights in the United States*. New York: Macmillan Reference USA, 2000.

Simpson, Andrea Y. *The Tie That Binds: Identity and Political Attitudes in the Post–Civil Rights Generation*. New York: New York University Press, 1998.

Steinberg, Stephen, ed. *Race and Ethnicity in the United States: Issues and Debates*. Malden, MA: Blackwell Publishers, 2000.

CONGRESSIONAL ELECTIONS

In 1994, the Republicans won control of both the House and Senate for the first time in forty years. In the 1996 election, the Republicans had the opportunity to win consecutive congressional elections for the first time since the 1920s.

The campaign battle between the parties in 1996 was shaped by the developments in Congress during the 104th Congress (1995–96). During much of 1995, the Republicans, especially in the House, were successful in passing key parts of their legislative agenda. Then, toward the end of 1995, the House and Senate Republicans began to have less success as President Bill Clinton and the congressional Democrats became more effective in challenging the Republicans' initiatives.

The turning point came in late 1995 and early 1996 when parts of the federal government were shut down over the budget fight between the Clinton administration and the Republican leadership in Congress. Polls indicated that a much higher proportion of the public supported the president and the Democrats than the Republicans in the budget conflict. And polls during the next several months showed that the public's support for the congressional Republicans, especially Speaker Newt Gingrich (R-GA), declined significantly. The momentum in the policy battle had shifted to the Democrats.

The 1996 presidential race was another problem for the congressional Republicans. President Clinton had a huge lead in the polls over Robert Dole, the Republican presidential candidate. Many party leaders feared that the weakness of Dole's support would make it more difficult for the Republicans to win in the House and Senate.

Consequently, the Republicans were on the defensive going into the election campaign. While most election analysts thought that the Republicans had a good chance of maintaining their majority in the Senate, many believed it was possible for the Republicans to lose control of the House. Several polls indicated that the House Democrats had a big lead over the House Republicans.

In the campaign, congressional Democrats went on the attack and criticized their Republican opponents for making devastating cuts in Medicare, education, and other popular items. Republicans responded by defending their record and claiming that the Democrats' attacks were unfair and untrue.

Toward the end of the campaign, many Republicans began running commercials warning the public about the dangers of electing both a Democratic president and a Democratic Congress. The Dole camp strongly protested this strategy since it showed that many Republican candidates had concluded that Bill Clinton was going to win the presidential election.

About two weeks before the 1996 presidential election, polls began indicating a shift in opinion toward the Republicans. This shift seemed to have saved the Republican majority in the House. In the election, the Republicans gained two seats in the Senate and lost eight seats in the House. The Senate Republicans' majority increased to 55, while the House Republicans' total dropped to 227.

In the following congressional election in 1998, the Republican prospects looked very good. The election was a midterm election in the sixth year of an administration. In almost all previous congressional elections, the party of the president had lost seats in midterm elections. And the losses in midterm elections during an administration's sixth year were especially large. In addition, the election campaign occurred during impeachment proceedings against President Clinton.

Surprisingly, however, most polls did not forecast a landslide Republican victory. Whereas Americans were disgusted with President Clinton's behavior, his job approval ratings remained high. With peace and a strong economy, polls indicated that the majority of the public supported the president and congressional incumbents from both parties. So instead of the Republicans winning a big victory, as it seemed they would, at best they made only small gains as a high percentage of Republican and Democratic incumbents won reelection and the parties split the open seats.

Additionally, the majority of citizens, according to the polls, were unhappy with many aspects of the Republicans' investigation of the president. They thought that the Republicans were spending too much time on impeachment and not enough time on the important social and economic issues. So in a strange twist, a scandal involving a Democratic president in some ways ended up hurting the election prospects of Republican candidates.

In the campaign, Republicans touted their record in Congress and claimed credit for the strong economy and the budget surplus. Some Republican candidates, particularly those in heavily Republican districts, emphasized the scandal, whereas others did not make it a key part of their campaigns. Close to the election, House Republican leaders decided to air campaign ads focusing on the scandal.

In the election, the Republicans maintained their majorities in both chambers but suffered a historic loss in the House. While they kept their fifty-five to forty-five advantage in the Senate, they lost five seats in the House. The Republican loss was one of the only times in American history that the opposition party of the president ever lost seats in a midterm election. And, to make it even more amazing, the loss occurred in the midst of a huge scandal involving the Democrats.

The Republican loss of House seats in the 1998 election produced a great deal of debate and finger-pointing among Republicans. Speaker Gingrich received most of the blame. His critics charged that his unpopularity and poor campaign strategy strongly contributed to the loss. Some Republicans demanded that Gingrich resign his position as Speaker. Gingrich at first said that he would stay and fight for his office but later changed his mind and resigned from the House.

Going into the 2000 race, most election analysts concluded that the Republicans had a good chance of keeping their Senate majority but had about a fifty-fifty chance of maintaining their House majority. In the Senate, the Republicans entered the campaign with only a few open seats to defend and only a few vulnerable incumbents. It seemed possible for the Democrats to gain two or three sets, but it appeared unlikely that they could win the five or six seats (depending on the outcome of the presidential election) they needed for a majority. As it turned out, they gained four seats, tying the Senate 50–50 for the first time since 1881. However, because newly elected vice president, Dick Cheney, presided over the Senate and cast the deciding vote in the case of a tie, the Senate remained in Republican control. This control ended in June 2001, though, after Republican senator James Jeffords of Vermont left the party and became an Independent, thereby giving Democrats a fifty to forty-nine edge in the Senate. In the House, the Democrats had fewer retirements and needed to pick up only 6 seats out of a total of 435 to regain a majority. Many analysts felt the Democrats' chances for a takeover rested on winning seats in close California elections. Democrats gained only two seats, however, leaving the Republicans with a slim 221 to 212 edge. Both parties acknowledge that such a closely divided Congress, on top of the incredibly close election of George W. Bush, requires an unprecedented level of bipartisanship to pass any meaningful legislation.

Larry Schwab

SEE ALSO: Campaign Finance Reform; Congressional Party Leadership; Party Organization.

BIBLIOGRAPHY

Abramson, Paul R., John H. Aldrich, and David W. Rohde. *Change and Continuity in the 1996 and 1998 Elections.* Washington, DC: Congressional Quarterly Press, 1999.

Crotty, William, and Jerome M. Mileur, eds. *America's Choice: The Election of 1996.* Guilford, CT: Dushkin/McGraw-Hill, 1997.

Duncan, Philip D., and Brian Nutting, eds. *Politics in America: The 106th Congress.* Washington, DC: Congressional Quarterly Press, 1999.

Nelson, Michael, ed. *The Elections of 1996.* Washington, DC: Congressional Quarterly Press, 1997.

Pomper, Gerald M., et al., eds. *The Election of 1996: Reports and Interpretations.* Chatham, NJ: Chatham House, 1997.

CONGRESSIONAL PARTY LEADERSHIP

For most of the latter half of the twentieth century, the Republican Party has been the minority party in Congress. During the lengthy periods when the Republicans were in the minority, two distinct styles of leadership emerged. One, exemplified by Minority Leader Robert Michel, emphasized accommodation with the Democrats. The other, typified by Newt Gingrich, took a confrontational approach in an attempt to undermine the Democrats. Gingrich used his position to draw media attention to problems in the Democratic Party and to highlight the Republican agenda. Gingrich also was instrumental in leading the Republican takeover of the House of Representatives in 1994 and was subsequently elected Speaker of the House for the 104th and 105th Congresses.

Since becoming the majority party, however, Republicans in the House have had a difficult time capitalizing on their legislative majority. In the House, the party lost seats in subsequent elections and failed to expand their majority significantly in the Senate. By the 106th Congress, the Republican majority in the House was only six seats. Gingrich's confrontational style, which had been so effective in the minority, alienated the White House and Democrats in Congress and led to legislative gridlock on a number of major issues. Gingrich also led a Republican shutdown of the government over budget disputes with the Clinton administration. This shutdown created a backlash against the GOP and reinforced the negative perceptions of the party. Gingrich's leadership was undermined by ethics charges that two partisan interest groups had illegally helped his 1990 reelection campaign. He was cleared of most charges, but in 1997, Gingrich was fined $300,000 for using a tax-exempt foundation for political purposes. In the midst of these investigations, Gingrich faced a Republican uprising over his bid to be reelected Speaker. Democrats accused the Speaker of pressuring GOP members of the Ethics Committee. Although he was reelected, his leadership had been undermined, and following Republican losses in the House in the 1998 elections, Gingrich announced he would resign both as Speaker and as a member of the House at the end of the year.

Republicans tapped Robert Livingston of Louisiana as Gingrich's successor. Livingston was a self-described "legislative mechanic" with a far less flamboyant leadership style than his predecessor. The presumptive Speaker's main priorities were to remove Social Security funds from the general budget and to reduce the overall size of the federal government. However, in an effort to expose what publisher Larry Flynt called the hypocrisy of the Clinton impeachment, *Hustler* magazine threatened to publish details of Livingston's personal life. Livingston resigned on March 1, 1999, before he could be formally elected Speaker.

Republicans chose Illinois representative Dennis Hastert as Gingrich's formal replacement in an election on January 6, 1999. Hastert pledged to improve relations with the Democrats and to try to develop bipartisan legislation. The slim Republican majority in the House at the time of his election (222 seats to 212) necessitated a more conciliatory relationship between the parties. Hastert pledged to heal the wounds left by the Clinton impeachment and to work with the Democrats to shore up the Social Security system and eliminate government waste. He was also able to gain approval for the reappointment of those who had been House managers during the impeachment trial by a vote of 223 to 198, with all Republicans and five Democrats voting in favor of reappointment. As Speaker, Hastert maintained much closer relations with the rank-and-file members of the House and was not as aloof as either Gingrich or Livingston.

There was widespread dissatisfaction with the leadership, and several ranking members faced significant challenges in their reelection efforts. Republican House majority leader Dick Armey of Texas defeated three challengers in his bid to be reelected. J. C. Watts of Oklahoma replaced John Boehner of Ohio as the conference chair, and became the highest ranking African American in the Republican congressional leadership. Finally, Tom Davis of Virginia replaced John Linder of Georgia as chair of the National Republican Campaign Committee. Several women legislators ran for Republican leadership positions in the House, but all were defeated. The majority whip, Tom DeLay, who had earned a reputation as a staunch disciplinarian and an effective manager, was unopposed in his reelection bid. Chris Cox became chair of the House Policy Committee. These House Republican leaders kept their leadership positions in the 107th Congress.

Unlike the troubled Republican leadership of the House, the Republicans in the Senate maintained their leadership team through the 104th, 105th, 106th, and 107th Congresses. Strom Thurmond of South Carolina became president pro tempore. After Republican majority leader Robert Dole resigned from the Senate in 1996 to concentrate on his campaign for president, Trent Lott of Mississippi was elected majority leader and then consistently reelected. Although a staunch conservative, Lott was less confrontational than Gingrich. During his tenure, Republicans maintained and even expanded their control of the Senate. In the 106th Congress, in addition to Lott, Don Nickles of Oklahoma ran unopposed as majority whip, and Larry Craig of Indiana was unopposed in his bid to return as chair of the Republican Policy Committee. Senator Connie Mack of Florida was reelected Republican Conference chair without opposition.

The major issue faced by the Senate leadership was the impeachment of President Clinton. During the proceedings, Lott was able to maintain a level of civility and decorum that had not been present in the House. He also maintained the discipline of the Senate Republicans through the votes in the trial. Thanks to Lott's leadership, by the end of the impeachment process, Republican senators faced much less of a public backlash than did members of the House.

Senator Mitch McConnell of Kentucky was challenged by Chuck Hagel of Nebraska in his reelection bid to be chair of the National Republican Senatorial Committee. McConnell, who opposed campaign finance reform, was criticized for his handling of the senatorial races in 1998, and the revolt against him was an expression of the dissatisfaction of a number of conservative senators over the party's strategy in the general elections. In the end, his extensive fund-raising experience and political connections prevailed, and he was reelected on a vote of thirty-nine to thirteen. However, in 2001, McConnell was replaced by Tennessee senator Bill Frist, who plans to increase Republican senators' involvement in the committee so that they work as a team to support one another's campaigns.

Otherwise, Senate Republican leadership changed very little in the early months of the 107th Congress. Connie Mack retired, and Rick Santorum of Pennsylvania replaced him as conference chair after beating Christopher "Kit" Bond of Missouri in a close race for the position. Because the Senate was divided evenly between Democrats and Republicans, with Vice President Dick Cheney as the scale-tipper toward the Republicans, Democrats challenged the existing leadership structure of the Senate. They proposed equal representation and cochairs of committees. They eventually struck an unprecedented power-sharing deal, with Senate Republicans granting them equal representation but maintaining GOP leadership in all committees. Republican leadership supported the compromise as the only realistic way to keep legislation from being blocked by Democratic opposition. The deal also included a clause that bills receiving a tie vote in committee, which would normally kill a bill, would be brought to the entire Senate floor for further consideration.

The deal held for several months until Republicans lost control of the Senate in June 2001 following Senator James Jeffords's resignation from the party to become an Independent. This gave Democrats a fifty to forty-nine edge and threw Republicans into the minority. As a result, Lott became Senate minority leader, Thurmond lost his position as president pro tempore, and Republicans lost their leadership positions on Senate committees.

Tom Lansford

SEE ALSO: Congressional Elections; Party Organization; Voting Behavior; Dennis Hastert; Trent Lott.

BIBLIOGRAPHY
Ceaser, James W., and Andrew E. Busch. *Losing to Win: The 1996 Elections and American Politics.* Lanham, MD: Rowman & Littlefield, 1997.

Drew, Elizabeth. *Showdown: The Struggle Between the Gingrich Congress and the Clinton White House.* New York: Simon & Schuster, 1996.

Jillson, Cal. *American Government: Political Change and Institutional Development.* Fort Worth, TX: Harcourt Brace College, 1999.

Jones, Charles O. *Clinton and Congress, 1993–1996: Risk, Restoration, and Reelection.* Norman: University of Oklahoma Press, 1999.

Light, Paul. *A Delicate Balance: An Essential Introduction to American Government.* New York: St. Martin's Press, 1997.

Sinclair, Barbara. *Legislators, Leaders, and Lawmaking: The U.S. House of Representatives in the Postreform Era.* Baltimore: Johns Hopkins University Press, 1995.

DRUGS

The issue of drug abuse in the United States is one that every political party takes seriously. Battling the importation, sale, and usage of illicit drugs is an ongoing war that consumes many resources. Each political party has its ideas as to how many resources and what plans are needed to fight the drug scourge, but in the end, all political parties push to stop the dependence and decay that drugs produce.

President George W. Bush presented his drug policy initiatives just over one hundred days into his presidency. His plan focused on eliminating domestic demand for drugs, dealing out harsh punishment for drug offenses, and targeting families, churches, schools, and community groups as the places for children to learn antidrug messages. He allocated a $1.1 billion increase for federal drug programs, making the total budget over $19 billion. He nominated John P. Walters, known largely as a "law-and-order conservative" who strongly supports tough sentences for low-level drug dealers, as his drug policy director. He ordered Tommy Thompson, the secretary of health and human services, to survey the states for their treatment needs and capacity in order to close the gap between addicts requiring treatment and facilities for them. In addition, he required Attorney General John Ashcroft to devise a plan for eradicating drugs from federal prisons. He also suggested that the White House department in charge of opening federal programs to religiously affiliated social services consider ways to form federal partnerships with local groups involved in antidrug efforts.

To encourage parents and schools to educate children on the dangers of drug use, some of Bush's proposed budget will go to strengthen educational programs. For example, he would continue to fund the Safe and Drug-Free Schools and Communities Act, which mandates penalties for students who take weapons or drugs to school. By reaching them earlier and more often with antidrug education, Bush and the Republicans hope that children will abstain from drug use. Also, Bush looks to parents to educate children at home on the ills of drug use and the problems drugs can create. He dedicated $25 million over five years to the creation of a "Parent Drug Corps" to provide parents with education and training in effective drug prevention.

Bush also advocates tougher laws and punishments in the United States, as well as toughening the fight against drugs in foreign lands. Bush advocates enforcing stronger penalties on first-time possession infractions. For instance, as the governor of Texas, Bush supported sending first-time offenders for cocaine possession to automatic jail terms rather than the typical probation-only punishment. Also, as governor of Texas, which shares a boundary with Mexico, Bush has dealt with drug-fighting border patrols. He has noted that many of the counties along the border are already tightly stretched on drug-fighting resources and wants the federal government to help out with funding to fight drug importation. Finally, Bush strongly supports assisting drug-growing nations in preventing the growing and exportation of drugs. The South American nation of Colombia is the source of many illegal drugs, and Bush favors providing resources to the Colombian military to help it fight the drug traders in the country. By stopping the drug trade at the source, Bush believes that the U.S. drug problem could significantly be reduced.

Vice President Dick Cheney has a strong legislative history of fighting drugs. As a member of Congress in the 1980s, Cheney supported many antidrug measures, cosponsoring House Bills 1946 (1986), 4446 (1988), and 4842 (1988), which aimed to combat the creation and sale of drugs, as well as to establish mandatory penalties for certain drug offenses. In 1988, Cheney also cosponsored H.R. 4470, which offered monetary awards to persons turning in drug offenders and providing monetary awards arising from drug forfeitures to the states where the drugs were eliminated. Cheney also has supported legislative measures that try to help foreign countries fight drug crops and sales of drugs that could end up in the United States. Finally, Cheney has supported measures that requested media participation in the fight against drugs.

Cheney's hope was for the entertainment industry to step up and come out against the use of drugs.

Generally, President Bush's and Vice President Cheney's views on drug policy are representative of those of the Republican Party. The party frowns on former president Bill Clinton's drug policy, often noting that drug abuse by high school students fell during the Republican leadership of President Ronald Reagan and President George H. W. Bush, but increased under President Clinton. The 2000 party platform reiterated the Republicans' commitment to drug-free schools, effective antidrug programs, and harsh punishments for all levels of drug dealers.

Steve Rowe

SEE ALSO: Foreign Policy; Healthcare; Military.

BIBLIOGRAPHY

Long, Robert Emmet, ed. *Drugs in America*. New York: H. W. Wilson, 1993.

Sharp, Elaine B. *The Dilemma of Drug Policy in the United States*. New York: HarperCollins College, 1994.

Stimmel, Barry. *Drug Abuse and Social Policy in America: The War That Must Be Won*. New York: Haworth Medical Press, 1996.

EDUCATION

Education issues have become some of the most important political issues over the last decade. With the economy in good shape and the end of the Cold War, politicians at all levels of government have turned their attention to the improvement of the educational experience of young Americans. Both parties agree that the future of the nation is tied to the quality of education today. However, each party approaches the problems with a different set of solutions, which reflect their underlying political philosophies.

Republicans have generally come to the conclusion that the public school system has failed because of a variety of factors including social promotion (the practice of passing poorly performing students so that they stay with students of the same age), bureaucratic administrative systems that are not responsive to the needs of the students, and a stranglehold on education reform because of the unwillingness of teachers unions (as distinct from individual teachers) to accept ongoing testing and other reforms. In addition to these factors, Republicans are discouraged by the system because it bars the use of prayer and religious teachings.

To combat these perceived failings, Republicans have advocated the use of market forces to spur competition to improve overall educational performance and to broaden the types of schools that children can attend. To accomplish these two goals in a practical manner, Republicans have promoted two ideas that are generally referred to as "school choice"—the creation of charter schools and the distribution of vouchers. By offering parents and students choice in the type of educational environment, Republicans believe that the overall quality of education in America will increase as poorly performing schools will cease to have students attending and as students choose better alternative schools. Charter schools are publicly funded and publicly controlled schools that are run privately, usually by an incorporated parents group, nonprofit educational organization, community group, or other such agencies. The advantage to charter schools is that they must follow fewer rules. They can also circumvent teachers unions by hiring nonunion staffing.

The other method of creating a market force in the educational realm is the distribution of vouchers. Under a plan supported by Republicans, parents are given a voucher by the school district that has a fixed value (usually less than the cost of educating a student for a year). Most plans call for vouchers in the range of $2,000 to $4,000, while the national average for one year of public education is $5,200. These vouchers are then used to help pay for the tuition at a private school or for any interdistrict charges that a student faces. The value of the voucher is usually much less than the actual cost of tuition at most private schools, which averages $8,500 a year. The goal of creating a system in which at least a portion of the money moves with the student is that schools that do not raise standards will be driven out of business by the competition. Such

competition, Republicans argue, will make public schools more accountable and force them to improve education.

Republicans cite the success of American higher education as an example of how a more market-driven educational system provides for superior education and educational opportunities at all levels. Yet the creation of school choice is not the only change that Republicans seek in the educational system or the only means of distinguishing between Republicans and Democrats. Similar to its positions on other social problems, the Republican Party sees education as largely a state and local issue that should not be constrained by numerous regulations promulgated in Washington. When Republicans took over Congress in 1995, House Speaker Newt Gingrich went so far as to advocate the abolition of the Department of Education, because he opposed national regulations on education. Republicans never followed through on Gingrich's idea, however, and recently the party has had a turnaround in its stance toward the department, including proposing a $44.5 billion budget in 2001. Republicans favor using the vast monetary resources of the Department of Education not for the development of national tests or other national programs but to provide block grants that districts may use wherever their school needs the money most.

George W. Bush's campaign and early education proposals indicate how vital education has become to political discussions. While campaigning, Bush promised to make education one of his priorities as president and repeatedly assured voters that his education proposals would "leave no child behind." In his acceptance speech to the Republican National Convention in August 2000, he mentioned several aspects of education reform, including ending the "soft bigotry of low expectations" that has "too many American children segregated into schools without standards, shuffled from grade to grade because of their age, regardless of their knowledge." He called for greater control of education at the local level, recognizing that "one size does not fit all when it comes to educating our children, so local people should control local schools." Parents should be able to "make a different choice" for their child when schools fail, and for Bush that means "parents should get the money" to spend at another school.

In May 2001, Congress considered President Bush's proposal for education reform. Bush and fellow conservative Republicans were forced to concede on the issue of private school vouchers. Due to the lack of support for the program in sectors of both parties, Bush decided to remove vouchers from the 2001 education bills on the floors of Congress in order to gain passage of other reforms. However, he still encouraged compromise legislation that would make it easier for low-income parents with children in failing schools to choose a different public school and to receive vouchers to pay for private tutoring if their local public school failed to improve after four years. In addition, he successfully lobbied for parents' right to choose among public schools in certain circumstances.

In addition to having to abandon vouchers in the bill, Bush discovered that he was also at odds with many Republicans on the issue of educational assessment and local control of federal education funds. Although like most Republicans Bush favors more local control over educational guidelines and spending, his proposal sought to increase significantly school accountability through much stricter testing regulations. He believes schools should have greater flexibility to determine how they will spend federal dollars in exchange for being held more accountable for student performance. To accomplish this, his policy mandated that all students in the third through the eighth grades be tested in reading and math every year. Because he wants school achievement to be comparable across school districts and for improvement to be measurable over time, Bush would like the tests to be uniform across each grade within each state, with the same test being given year after year. Furthermore, tests must meet national standards so that schools do not simply give easy tests. Thus, failing schools can be targeted and given aid (or eventually punished if they fail to improve), and parents can better assess how their local school compares to other schools.

Republican governors, however, balked at the idea of increased uniformity in testing and opposed federal education sanctions on states or districts with schools that fail to improve over the course of ten years. They insisted that any attempt by Bush to mandate such strict testing regulations would violate states' rights. Bush supported compromise legislation that would allow school districts more discretion in the allocation of funds and states more flexibility in meeting national testing standards. Most Democrats are opposed to such a plan and have argued that Bush's budget does not provide enough money to repair school buildings or hire new teachers. In late May 2001, however, in a show of bipartisanship, the House approved the education bill requiring annual testing of students in reading and math.

Still, the debate over education and school choice is one that puts the two parties on distinctly different paths. Republicans favor a market-driven system that will encourage competition (similar in some respects to American higher education). They also seek to return control of education to parents through the use of vouchers, charter schools, local standards testing, and the limiting of federal regulations on schools.

Jeffrey D. Schultz

SEE ALSO: Affirmative Action; Budget and Fiscal Policy; Drugs; Immigration.

BIBLIOGRAPHY

Bok, Derek. *The State of the Nation: Government and the Quest for a Better Society, 1960–1995.* Cambridge: Harvard University Press, 1996.

Chubb, John E., and Terry M. Moe. *Politics, Markets, and America's Schools.* Washington, DC: Brookings Institution, 1990.

Coleman, James S., et al. *Redesigning American Education.* Boulder, CO: Westview Press, 1997.

Finn, Chester E., Jr., and Theodor Rebarber, eds. *Education Reforms in the 90s.* New York: Macmillan, 1992.

Ravitch, Diane, ed. *Debating the Future of American Education: Do We Need National Standards and Assessments?* Washington, DC: Brookings Institution, 1995.

FOREIGN POLICY

Even after they gained majorities in both houses of Congress in 1994, the Republicans were unable to articulate a clear foreign policy vision during the Clinton administration. As a result, the party often appeared split or divided over major issues. The party's hawks were transformed into doves and often resisted the use of military force by the administration. Republicans opposed the use of U.S. forces in peacekeeping roles in various ethnic conflicts, including that in Bosnia. They argued that U.S. resources should be used only to protect national economic or strategic concerns. Contemporary Republican policy remains rooted in the promotion of U.S. interests and opposed to broad idealistic goals.

In general, the Clinton administration received support for most of its foreign policy goals, and in his second term, President Bill Clinton initially made a strong effort to build a bipartisan consensus. He nominated Republicans to key posts, including William S. Cohen as secretary of defense. He also nominated Madeleine Albright, generally regarded as a hawk who advocated a much more assertive foreign policy, as secretary of state. In 1997, the Senate easily confirmed the administration's new foreign and security policy team, although questions over Anthony Lake led the president to withdraw his nomination as the Central Intelligence Agency director and replace him with George Tenet. Foreign policy did not play a major part in the 1996 presidential campaign, as neither party advocated significant differences in diplomatic or security policy.

In Bill Clinton's second term, Republicans supported U.S. military actions in several strategic locations. In 1996, the GOP endorsed the deployment of U.S. military forces to Taiwan in response to Chinese maneuvers in the region. Congress also backed the administration's use of air strikes against Saddam Hussein's forces in Iraq after Hussein sent troops into the northern Kurdish areas of Iraq and ended compliance with United Nations (UN) weapons inspection resolutions. In 1999, the Republican leadership backed U.S. participation in the military intervention in Kosovo led by the North Atlantic

Treaty Organization (NATO), but many in the party questioned both the necessity and the scope of the effort. More than any other ethnic conflict at the time, that in Kosovo seemed to reignite the isolationist debate within the party. Prominent Republicans were also critical of the administration's handling of the intervention after the slow pace of air strikes allowed the Serbs to drive millions of ethnic Albanians from their homes.

On free trade issues, the Republicans in Congress worked with the Clinton administration to forge a tenuous bipartisan consensus. This consensus was reflected early on by Republican support for the North American Free Trade Agreement (NAFTA) in 1993, and later in support for maintaining most-favored-nation trade status for China (although within the party, relations with China remain a divisive issue as religious conservatives oppose closer ties with the regime in Beijing because of religious suppression). Key Republicans also supported China's entry in the World Trade Organization. The "free trade" wing of the party was countered by an equally substantial group of Republicans who opposed Chinese entry for national security concerns in light of Chinese espionage and for continuing human rights violations. Clinton was able to gain GOP approval for increased U.S. aid for such international organizations as the International Monetary Fund during the Asian economic crisis in 1997. A majority of Republicans also supported the failed effort to continue "fast-track" authority for the president to negotiate trade deals without subjecting them to congressional amendments.

With some notable exceptions, the Republican Senate supported the administration's European policies. The Senate ratified the second Strategic Arms Reduction Talks Treaty (START II Treaty) in 1996 and endorsed the administration's support for Russian president Boris Yeltsin in that year's presidential elections. The Senate also ratified the Chemical Weapons Convention in 1997. After considerable debate within the party over the scope and cost of enlargement, Republicans backed Clinton's plans for expansion of NATO to include three states from the former Warsaw Pact: the Czech Republic, Hungary, and Poland.

These new partners joined the military alliance in 1999.

Concurrently, Republicans occasionally utilized foreign policy to gain partisan victories over the Clinton White House. During the Clinton impeachment, Republicans roundly criticized the president's military strikes in Sudan and Afghanistan in the wake of the terrorist attacks in Kenya and Tanzania. Republicans were also at odds with the White House over military budgets, seeking much higher levels of spending for national defense. Congress added $30 billion to the defense budgets from 1996 through 1999. In one of the most contentious debates between the Republican leadership in Congress and the White House, Congress attempted to gain the president's support for a ballistic missile defense system. Such a system was opposed by Democrats, who asserted that it might lead to a renewed arms race and that it would destroy the Anti-Ballistic Missile Treaty of 1972. In 1999, in an embarrassing defeat for the administration, the Senate rejected the Comprehensive Test-Ban Treaty, which Clinton had signed in 1996. Republicans tied the rejection to the president's refusal to take meaningful steps toward a ballistic missile defense system, and the failure to ratify the measure cast shadows on the nation's ability to lead the nuclear nonproliferation movement.

Although there was a bipartisan effort to prevent the reelection of Boutros Boutros-Ghali as secretary-general of the UN and instead replace him with the more reform-minded Kofi Annan, partisan politics prevented consensus over U.S.-UN relations. Conservative senator Jesse Helms (R-NC) used his position as chair of the Senate Foreign Relations Committee to block U.S. payments to the UN. In addition, Republicans initially made efforts to block the appointment of Richard Holbrooke as UN ambassador following the appointment of Bill Richardson as secretary of energy.

With the end of both the Cold War and bipartisan consensus on foreign policy, Republican leaders have had to contend with opposing factions within the party. Advocates of free trade and global engagement have been opposed by the resurgent isolationist wing of the party, led by Pat Buchanan (who left the GOP for the Re-

form Party in late 1999). In addition, Republicans have utilized foreign policy as a means to win legislative victories over the White House. The presidential election in 2000 also made the Republican-led Congress less willing to grant the administration any dramatic foreign policy successes. This combination of factionalism within the party and opportunism has prevented the emergence of a new, coherent foreign policy agenda for the GOP.

During the 2000 campaign, in an attempt to appeal to the isolationist wing of the party while not alienating others, George W. Bush indicated that he did not support the use of American soldiers in peacekeeping missions but favored intervention only when issues related directly to U.S. strategic interests and goals. He stated the United States should not police the world or instruct other nations on how to do things.

President Bush's early administration reflected many of the ongoing splits within the Republican Party on issues of foreign affairs. His advisers were largely divided into two camps: Secretary of Defense Donald H. Rumsfeld and the Pentagon, who are mostly seen as conservative, hard-line hawks, less flexible in working with allies, and Secretary of State Colin Powell and the State Department, who are described as more moderate, focusing their efforts on sanctions and negotiations. Rumsfeld supported continuing American aid to the Iraqi National Congress, an opposition group fighting Iraqi president Saddam Hussein, in an attempt to oust Hussein from the inside. Powell, however, preferred to enforce stricter sanctions against the government while finding more ways to aid the Iraqi people. Overall, Bush's foreign policy team has been perceived as setting an early, hard-line approach to its affairs with the rest of the world. With regard to the Middle East peace process, Bush's national security adviser, Condoleezza Rice, announced that the Israelis and Palestinians should themselves assume responsibility for future negotiations. The Bush administration declared it would break with the Clinton administration's proposals and hands-on involvement in the region. When violence again broke out and reached alarming levels in the Middle East in May 2001, however, Bush and his foreign policy team began to signal a more active role in helping to quell the ongoing conflict and bloodshed.

Bush's two major foreign policy initiatives in his early presidency surrounded free trade and the creation of a missile defense program. He pushed a plan called the Free Trade Area of the Americas; he favored permanent, normal trading status with China (which was approved by Congress); and he supported opening trade with developing nations. Regaining fast-track authority, now called "trade promotion authority," is central to Bush's free trade proposal. In addition, he is against imposing stricter labor and environmental standards on trade agreements. Instead, he has argued that freer trade creates the social and economic conditions necessary for developing countries to improve their labor and environmental standards without the United States forcing its standards on others. Bush is also very much in favor of creating a missile defense shield, calling the 1972 Anti-Ballistic Missile Treaty a relic of the Cold War that can now be abandoned. However, many U.S. allies and other nations oppose the program, forcing Bush to wage a worldwide campaign to convince foreign leaders to accept it.

In appealing to other leaders on the proposed missile defense shield, Bush held a summit meeting in March 2001 with the president of South Korea in which he declared his unwillingness to resume Clinton administration negotiations to curtail North Korea's missile plans and expressed skepticism about dealing with the communist country's president. Yet others, including South Korea's president, urged the Bush administration to ease its tough stance on North Korea. China, North Korea's main ally, remained silent during this period. Early in his term, Bush encountered several challenging situations regarding relations with China. Opinions have long differed on whether to engage China, so that it would be forced into the world economy and therefore more dependent on the international community, or to contain it to stop its growing economic and political power. Clinton strongly favored engaging China, but Bush has been much tougher in his dealings. Much of the U.S.-China tension revolves around America's interactions with Taiwan, which split from China in

a 1949 civil war and which China still threatens to recover with force if necessary. When an American spy plane collided with a Chinese fighter plane off the coast of China in early April 2001, the Bush administration spent nearly two weeks working to broker a deal with China to release the American plane's crew, and the entire incident was fraught with tension on both sides and demands to compromise. Further, shortly after the incident, Bush offered the biggest arms sale to Taiwan made in nine years. Bush has also suggested the United States would come to Taiwan's aid if China attacked, a position only ambiguously hinted at by past Republican leaders.

In 2001, the United States was voted off of the United Nations Human Rights Commission, on which it had sat since its inception in 1947. The House of Representatives voted to withhold millions of dollars of back dues next year if the United States is not voted back onto the commission. President Bush does not support the measure, however, and it is unlikely to be considered in the Senate.

Tom Lansford

SEE ALSO: Immigration; Military.

BIBLIOGRAPHY

Gedmin, Jeffrey, ed. *European Integration and American Interests: What the New Europe Really Means for the United States.* Washington, DC: AEI Press, 1997.

Kennan, George F. *At a Century's Ending: Reflections, 1982–1995.* New York: W. W. Norton, 1996.

Lipset, Seymour Martin. *American Exceptionalism: A Double-Edged Sword.* New York: W. W. Norton, 1996.

Rosati, Jerel A., comp. *Readings in the Politics of U.S. Foreign Policy.* Fort Worth, TX: Harcourt Brace College, 1998.

Spanier, John, and Steven W. Hook. *American Foreign Policy Since World War II.* 14th ed. Washington, DC: Congressional Quarterly Press, 1998.

Wittkopf, Eugene R., and Christopher M. Jones, eds. *The Future of American Foreign Policy.* 3d ed. New York: Worth, 1999.

GUN CONTROL

The question of gun control has become an emotional and serious issue for many Americans. With the recent incidents of gun violence among youth and in society in general, many people have been clamoring for tougher restrictions on access to guns through the creation of more laws such as the federal Brady Bill, passed in 1993, which requires background checks on gun buyers at gun stores (but not gun shows). Some seek the elimination of guns altogether; others seek to eliminate major assault weapons and the ammunition for these weapons. Some groups, such as the National Rifle Association, are steadfastly fighting to keep any gun legislation to a bare minimum, arguing that the Second Amendment to the Constitution guarantees Americans the right to keep and bear arms.

The Republican Party defends the constitutional right to keep and bear arms. In keeping this right, the Republican Party asserts that individuals owning guns must responsibly use and store the firearms. This means that guns should be used only for sport or self-defense, and they should have the necessary safety mechanisms and storage to keep them from children or inexperienced users. Because the Republican Party feels that using guns for self-defense is a basic right, the party promotes training for the safe usage of guns. The Republicans support the enforcement of gun laws already enacted. They also back enforcing gun laws by prosecuting dangerous offenders identified as felons in instant background checks. The Republicans endorse programs, such as Project Exile, that hold criminals accountable for their actions when they use guns in violent or drug-related crimes. Operating in several states and local communities and supported by the National Rifle Association, Project Exile allows states and localities to apply federal gun possession laws—which often are much tougher than state and local laws—to prosecute felons and drug traffickers who use guns in their crimes. Even though the Republicans support background checks to ensure that guns do not get into the hands of the wrong people, they do oppose federal licensing and registration of guns.

This licensing and registration is viewed as a violation of the Second Amendment and an invasion of privacy.

During the 2000 presidential campaign, Republican candidate George W. Bush supported the right to own guns for protection and hunting. President Bush believes that some types of guns and ammunition need to be restricted, such as automatic weapons and high-capacity ammunition. Along with banning these items, Bush advocates raising the age limit for gun purchase to twenty-one years old. Bush has also indicated that he would sign, but not push for, certain gun restrictions, such as closing the loophole that allows people to buy guns at gun shows without the required background checks. Bush endorsed government funding of trigger locks for guns as a safety measure and banning guns in school zones.

Bush has argued that the best means of gun control is severe punishment of those convicted of committing violent crimes with guns. Republicans criticize former president Clinton for the 46 percent drop in gun law prosecutions during his administration. In 2001, President Bush proposed $550 million to start Project Safe Neighborhoods, which is inspired by Project Exile and would provide funds to hire new federal and state prosecutors to focus on gun violence and increase punishment of gun offenders. He also pledged money to improve federal record keeping so that it would be more difficult for convicts to obtain guns legally, to increase ballistic testing so that illegal weapons could be better traced, and to begin a youth gun interdiction program headed by the Bureau of Alcohol, Tobacco and Firearms. Further, the 2002 budget proposed by Bush also devoted federal matching funds to ChildSafe, which provides law enforcement agencies with programs and supplies that promote safe gun storage and the use of trigger locks.

Steve Rowe

SEE ALSO: Education; Military.

BIBLIOGRAPHY
Bijlefeld, Marjolijn, ed. *The Gun Control Debate: A Documentary History*. Westport, CT: Greenwood Press, 1997.

Carter, Gregg Lee. *The Gun Control Movement.* New York: Twayne, 1997.

Cottrol, Robert J. *Gun Control and the Constitution: Sources and Explorations on the Second Amendment.* New York: Garland, 1993.

Dizard, Jan E., Robert Merrill Muth, and Stephen P. Andrews, eds. *Guns in America: A Reader.* New York: New York University Press, 1999.

Kleck, Gary. *Point Blank: Guns and Violence in America.* New York: A. de Gruyter, 1991.

Spitzer, Robert J. *The Politics of Gun Control.* 2d ed. New York: Chatham House, 1998.

Utter, Glenn H. *Encyclopedia of Gun Control and Gun Rights.* Phoenix, AZ: Oryx Press, 2000.

HEALTHCARE

Healthcare in the United States is arguably the finest the world has ever known. Advances in research, treatment, and medicine have reached heights only imaginable in the mid-twentieth century. As medical science continues to advance, many in the United States are being squeezed out of receiving this treatment due to skyrocketing costs and inadequate medical insurance coverage. The presidential election of 2000 saw the issue of healthcare move to the forefront. With Medicare reform, prescription drug relief, and health insurance issues of vital importance to Americans, candidates from both major parties heavily emphasized their plan to address healthcare problems.

The American Medicare system is over thirty years old. This system, which many seniors and Americans who are disabled rely on for medical coverage, has seen coverage cutbacks and little advancement with current medical technology. The Republican Party strongly advocates bringing the Medicare system into the twenty-first century with enhancements to coverage and offering coverage choice to its recipients. The Republicans would like to see Medicare provide the same health coverage and policy choices that members of Congress receive in their healthcare programs. For example, since Medicare was created in the 1960s, there have been significant advances in treatments and screenings that are still not covered under Medicare. Medicare does not cover items that are considered routine, preventive tests, such as cholesterol screenings. It is due to such factors that Republicans want to see a cut in the 130,000-plus pages of Medicare regulations, reform the list of covered items, and offer recipients multiple programs that will best meet the needs of each policyholder. In the words of the 2000 Republican Party platform, the Republicans feel there is no longer room for a "one size fits all" medical coverage system that is antiquated and inefficient.

For those not eligible for the Medicare program, the Republicans look to enhance the access many impoverished Americans have to medical insurance. According to Republican National Committee research, there are nearly 44 million Americans with no medical insurance. The Republicans seek to provide affordable, quality health insurance to all Americans, via several options. First, the Republicans feel the greatest avenue for gaining health insurance is via employment. Through job creation, Americans become employed and can receive the benefit of health insurance through their jobs. This comes with a caveat though. The Republicans do realize that in many cases employers cannot offer health benefits to workers and remain profitable as a business, especially those in small businesses. Thus the Republicans propose to offer small business owners the opportunity to band together in associations that can derive the numbers needed to achieve group coverage for employee health insurance. The Republicans also advocate a tax credit that will help 27 million Americans buy private health insurance and a fully deductible health insurance tax credit to self-employed Americans. Finally, the Republican Party supports the creation of flexible savings accounts and medical savings accounts as means to save money for unforeseen medical expenses. These accounts should allow unused money to roll over from year to year, be tax deductible, and have both employer and employee contributions. With these accounts, employees will have a medical reserve that can be used in any way they need.

The Republican Party also looks to enhance the relationships patients have with their doctors and financial providers through the enactment of patients' rights laws. Early in his term, President George W. Bush outlined to Congress certain requirements he had for any patients' rights legislation. Many of his requests fall directly in line with the thinking of other Republicans. Most important, he would like to discourage lawsuits and court litigation to resolve disputes with health maintenance organizations (HMOs) and instead supports appeals through independent intermediary boards. These boards will hear cases concerning denials of treatment from a health provider organization. If a treatment is not given due to a provider's coverage decision, these quick appeal processes, supported by the Republicans, would allow a patient to appeal a decision in an attempt to gain the needed treatment without lengthy court trials. Doctors and any employers involved in this process should not be held accountable via lawsuits if a health provider neglects treatment. However, if an HMO does not follow the decision of an intermediary board to provide treatment, patients could hold the HMO liable in court and receive limited compensation.

During the 2000 campaign, Republican candidate George W. Bush called for strengthening Medicare, providing a prescription drug benefit for seniors, providing catastrophic Medicare coverage to keep seniors from having to pay more than $6,000 in costs a year during a lengthy illness, providing a patient's bill of rights for quality care, providing health insurance for the uninsured or underinsured, and supporting tax credits for those giving long-term care to an ill or aging person.

Bush promised that if he were elected he would implement immediate relief for seniors through the creation of a prescription drug plan and then would focus on overhauling Medicare later in his term. Soon after beginning his term, however, he began to encourage Congress to restructure the program, in addition to creating a prescription drug benefit, by the end of 2001. He backed a bill proposed by Senators John Breaux (D-LA) and Bill Frist (R-TN) that would save the program money by allowing seniors to choose among preapproved private health plans. Because Medicare would provide a standard portion of the premium, people who chose more

expensive plans would pay more of their own money for healthcare (although advocates of the bill claim that competition among the plans would bring down the costs). A government-run option similar to Medicare would still exist, but it would be subject to the same standard premiums as private providers. Bush has left the difficult details of changing the program to Congress. He has also expressed support for combining his Medicare visions with a plan he has dubbed the "Immediate Helping Hand." This is an approximated $48 billion program that will offer single Americans with an annual income less than $11,300 fully paid prescription drugs and married couples making $15,200 annually the same coverage. Single seniors with an annual income below $14,600 and married seniors with an annual income of $19,700 will be eligible for a partial prescription coverage plan.

Along with advocating a family tax credit for underinsured or uninsured Americans and the right for small businesses to band into "trade associations" for the benefit of group health coverage insurance, Bush wishes to set aside $3.6 billion for 1,200 new community health centers. These centers will be created in particular for areas with many underprivileged citizens. Also, these health centers will provide vaccines, screenings, counseling, and a host of other necessary services at little to no cost due to public funding and administration.

To round out these healthcare proposals, President Bush strongly advocates the creation of medical savings accounts (MSAs) and tax credits for those handling the long-term care of ill or elderly Americans. To help Americans set aside income for potential health-related needs, Bush feels that MSAs should become more mainstream and have some current restrictions lifted. For instance, the president believes that the $750,000 cap needs to be lifted. Medical savings accounts should also be made permanent and possibly even offered as an employment benefit where employees and employers can make matching contributions, much like some current 401(k) programs. Along with enhancing MSA programs, Bush feels that if the need arises for long-term care, Americans should receive some tax breaks to pay for or provide these services.

Money from an MSA will play a large role in paying for long-term care, but this may not provide enough. Bush would like to offer Americans $7.4 billion in tax breaks for nursing home coverage. Bush also strongly supports offering an additional tax exemption for older loved ones being cared for in someone else's home. With MSAs and long-term care tax reductions, Bush intends to help Americans prepare for any medical needs.

In summary, the Republican Party and its leaders have recognized the need for reforms and enhancements to America's current healthcare coverage system. With costs for treatment and coverage rising steadily, many Americans need help in planning and ultimately paying for healthcare. Revamping the current Medicare system to offer greater coverage and more policy options is a high priority. Along with this, the Republicans look to offer a prescription drug plan to help seniors pay for necessary medications. The Republicans also strongly advocate tax credits that will help poorer families obtain adequate health coverage and enable all American families to create medical savings accounts to offset any medical costs. The Republicans also advocate patients' rights to ensure that all individuals receive quality care and have all options and treatments fully available when required medically. The main goal the Republican Party endorses with these programs is to open the doors more fully to America's groundbreaking medical advances for all Americans.

Steve Rowe

SEE ALSO: Budget and Fiscal Policy; Education; Immigration; Social Security.

BIBLIOGRAPHY

Aaron, Henry J. *The Problem That Won't Go Away: Reforming U.S. Health Care Financing.* Washington, DC: Brookings Institution, 1996.

Andersen, Ronald M., Thomas H. Rice, and Gerald F. Kominski, eds. *Changing the U.S. Health Care System: Key Issues in Health Services, Policy, and Management.* San Francisco: Jossey-Bass, 1996.

Birenbaum, Arnold. *Putting Health Care on the National Agenda.* Westport, CT: Praeger, 1995.

DiIulio, John J., Jr., and Richard R. Nathan, eds. *Making Health Reform Work: The View from the States.* Washington, DC: Brookings Institution, 1994.

Fisk, Milton. *Toward a Healthy Society: The Morality and Politics of American Health Care Reform.* Lawrence: University Press of Kansas, 2000.

Marmor, Theodore R. *Understanding Health Care Reform.* New Haven: Yale University Press, 1994.

IMMIGRATION

The issue of immigration has always been a complex one in the United States. Although the country was settled by wave after wave of immigrants, Americans have debated whether or not the country can keep expanding to accommodate all peoples of the world in a single society. More practical than this philosophical question has been a simple economic one of the role immigrants play in the workforce. Currently, the United States admits more than 650,000 immigrants each year.

To some degree, both parties have wanted to limit immigration to the United States. For many Republicans, they often wanted to limit the number of new immigrants because of issues of Americanization. "Americanization" is the cultural process by which an immigrant sheds his or her former cultural identity and adopts one that is more American in content. Such a cultural identity would include the embracing of American political principles, including freedom, equality, self-reliance, and so on. It would also include such things as the adoption of English as the language of social interaction. Other Republicans have been concerned about immigration because of the impact that it might have on the labor market and the opinion that immigrants might be taking job opportunities away from citizens. This viewpoint is often held by the more isolationist wing of the party, which is a small but vocal segment.

In the mid-1990s, anti-immigration sentiment was a powerful force among Republicans. Although much of their ire was directed at illegal immigrants, the party also hoped to limit the numbers and rights of legal immigrants. The

1996 party platform suggested that "legal immigrants should depend for assistance on their sponsors, who are legally responsible for their financial well-being, not the American taxpayers. Just as we require 'deadbeat dads' to provide for the children they bring into the world, we should require 'deadbeat sponsors' to provide for the immigrants they bring into the country." In Congress, Republican legislators proposed that legal immigrants be limited to twelve months of welfare benefits and risk deportation if they exceeded that limit. The party platform supported legislation to prevent children born to immigrants who were in the country illegally or not long-term from being granted automatic citizenship. Further, it called for more crimes to be worthy of deportation if committed by an immigrant.

Illegal immigrants were particularly targeted by Republicans in the past decade and continue to be a point of focus today, even as the party softens its stance on legal immigrants. An estimated 275,000 illegal immigrants enter the nation each year, adding to the more than 5 million illegal aliens currently in the United States. This influx is not only a concern from a border control standpoint but also has a serious impact at the state level. Most of the illegal immigrants are centered in certain areas of the country such as California, New York, and Texas. Because these immigrants are often poor and poorly educated, they can heavily tax social services. In 1994, California passed Proposition 187, which specifically denied health and education benefits to illegal aliens on these grounds. Led by Governor Pete Wilson, Republicans strongly supported the measure, going so far as to applaud it in their 1996 party platform and base much of their proposed immigration legislation on it. The proposition was ultimately ruled unconstitutional.

The general stance of the Republican Party in the late 1990s was that legal immigration provides a vital infusion of workers in times of economic prosperity. Because of real shortages in both the high-end technological arena and the low-level physical labor area, many Republicans have argued for the expansion of work visas to allow companies to increase their recruiting efforts overseas. With the economy growing at a strong clip in these years, many jobs went unfilled because of lack of applicants. This situation was equally true in the service industry and high-tech industry. To this end, Republicans supported the increase in H-1B and H-2A worker visas. H-1B visas allow foreign professionals with a bachelor's degree to stay in the United States for six years. In particular, the American high-tech industry relies on these visas to fill highly skilled technical positions that the American labor pool is unable to fill, and high-tech industry has been credited with applying political pressure to raise limits on these visas. H-2A visas are for temporary agricultural workers. Plans to expand these visas have often included "streamlining" mechanisms that would give workers with these visas fewer labor and wage protections, making the visas more appealing to the agriculture industry, since the use of these visas is often undercut by illegal immigrant laborers.

In recent years, Republicans have generally been friendly to immigration because it is often the counterpart to increased free trade. Republicans support free trade agreements such as the North American Free Trade Agreement of 1994 (NAFTA), which established a free trade zone between the United States, Canada, and Mexico, thereby allowing goods to cross borders into or out of those countries without any tariffs or taxes. With the expansion of similar trade agreements across the Western Hemisphere, which President George W. Bush promotes, the flow of workers as well as of goods will become increasingly fluid. More movement of people will accompany fewer national trading barriers. Republicans have also urged reforming and streamlining the Immigration and Naturalization Service (INS) to better serve the needs of immigrants. Various proposals have been floated calling for the trimming of application time and procedures.

Bush has portrayed himself as being more compassionate toward immigrants and has given the Republican Party a kinder face on the issue. He supports INS reform, which would divide the agency into two parts to make it more immigrant-friendly. One part would focus on border and interior enforcement; the other would provide services for legitimate immigrants and process applications. Bush is pushing for increased border patrols, stating that it is more humane to turn people away at the border rather than to deport them once they have established a life in the United States. In addition, as described in the 2000 Republican Party platform, Bush wants to focus immigration admission on reuniting families, giving preference to spouses and children.

Bush also favored extending an immigration loophole that allowed some illegal immigrants to apply for a green card without the risks and expense of leaving the United States as is normally required. He has applauded the contributions of immigrants to the country and has especially welcomed Latinos. As governor of Texas, he promoted an "English-plus" program, which demanded that children become competent in the English language but also recognized the importance of Spanish to Texas culture and history. Finally, he has worked with Mexican president Vicente Fox to arrange a guest-worker program with Mexico, which would grant some legality to Mexican migrant workers who currently often enter the country illegally.

Tom Lansford

SEE ALSO: Affirmative Action; Civil Rights; Education; Foreign Policy; Healthcare.

BIBLIOGRAPHY

Cohen, Robin, and Zig Layton-Henry, eds. *The Politics of Migration*. Northampton, MA: E. Elgar, 1997.

DeLaet, Debra L. *U.S. Immigration Policy in an Age of Rights*. Westport, CT: Praeger, 2000.

Gorman, Robert F. *Mitigating Misery: An Inquiry into the Political and Humanitarian Aspects of U.S. and Global Refugee Policy*. Lanham, MD: University Press of America, 1993.

Lowell, Lindsay, and Demetrios G. Papademetriou, eds. *Immigration and U.S. Integration Policy Reforms*. Urbana, IL: Policy Studies Organization, 1992.

Mills, Nicolaus, ed. *Arguing Immigration: The Debate over the Changing Face of America*. New York: Simon & Schuster, 1994.

Schwartz, Warren F., ed. *Justice in Immigration*. New York: Cambridge University Press, 1995.

MILITARY

During the 2000 campaign, Republican presidential candidate George W. Bush focused heavily on national defense and military issues. He and other Republicans accused the Clinton administration of cutting back on the military, resulting both in equipment shortages and in degradation of service members' quality of life. Bush pledged to rebuild the military and boost morale.

In many ways, the Republican position on defense echoes the one taken by President Ronald Reagan in 1980. In that campaign, Reagan used the military as an effective campaign tool with such core groups as conservatives, men, and veterans. In 2001, Bush proposed a $1 billion hike in pay for service men and women. He also targeted $45 billion to be spent on modernizing facilities and equipment. Bush supports spending an additional $20 billion on research and development for post–Cold War weapons systems.

Defense has always been a top issue for Republicans, and it was among President George W. Bush's primary commitments. In pushing this issue during the campaign, Republicans advocated redefining the mission of the armed forces. Along with protecting the nation, the armed forces should have well-defined objectives when deployed, rather than more general peacekeeping goals. Republicans accused the Clinton administration of sending the military on vague, aimless, and seemingly endless assignments. In addition to shifting the military's focus, Bush has stated that he wants to revitalize the military by devoting more money to the pay and quality of life of military personnel. Republicans have expressed the need for modernizing the military to fight battles relating to technology and the information age. In keeping with this view, Bush has also called for the creation of a new military that meets the challenges of a new century.

In addition to these major initiatives, the Republicans have questioned the usefulness of the Anti-Ballistic Missile Treaty signed by the United States and the Soviet Union in 1972. Some Republicans even favor the abrogation of the 1972 accord because it would prevent the deployment of any strategic defense initiative. Moreover, while Russia and three other post–Soviet Union nuclear states have agreed to abide by the accord, Republicans argue that the potential nuclear proliferation caused by the breakup of the Soviet Union increases the need for such a defensive weapon.

President George W. Bush has been ardently in favor of abandoning the 1972 agreement altogether in order to develop a missile defense shield to deter attacks from "rogue" nations such as Iraq, Iran, and North Korea. In late April 2001, he announced the details of plans to move forward to create such a defense system. Many allies and other nations oppose the plan despite the group of diplomats Bush deployed to consult with and convince world leaders. Even though Bush has suggested that the shield would allow the United States to greatly shrink its nuclear arsenal, Germany, France, and Russia disapprove of the plan because they fear it would make the United States invulnerable enough to dominate world affairs completely and to intimidate other nations, leading to increased tensions.

China, the plan's greatest detractor, believes that the project would effectively neutralize its small arsenal of nuclear weapons and thereby compromise Chinese national security, particularly in relation to Taiwan, which the United States has suggested it would defend if China attacked. Bush also angered China by offering Taiwan a very large arms package. Although the ones offered for sale were not the most cutting-edge weapons available because they are supposedly to be used only defensively, the transaction was an affront to China and threatened to ignite an arms race between China and Taiwan. Bush and administration officials agreed that talks with allies and other nations about the plan would be ongoing.

Tom Lansford

SEE ALSO: Drugs; Foreign Policy; Gun Control.

BIBLIOGRAPHY

Asmus, Ronald D. *The New U.S. Strategic Debate.* Santa Monica, CA: Rand, 1993.

Binkin, Martin. *Who Will Fight the Next War?: The Changing Face of the American Military.* Washington, DC: Brookings Institution, 1993.

Blechman, Barry M. *The American Military in the Twenty-First Century.* New York: St. Martin's Press, 1993.

Evans, Ernest. *Wars Without Splendor: The U.S. Military and Low-Level Conflicts.* Westport, CT: Greenwood Press, 1987.

Hays, Peter L., Brenda J. Vallance, and Alan R. Van Tassel, eds. *American Defense Policy.* 7th ed. Baltimore: Johns Hopkins University Press, 1997.

PARTY ORGANIZATION

The Republican Party organization in Congress has four parts: leadership positions, conference, whip system, and party committees. House and Senate Republicans operate with a similar structure, but with some differences between the organizations in the two chambers. Differences also exist in the structure and operation of party organization in Congress depending on whether the party is in the majority or minority. In 1994, the Republicans won majority party control in both the House and the Senate for the first time in forty years. They remained in the majority in both chambers during the 105th Congress (1997–98), the 106th Congress (1999–2000), and the opening months of the 107th Congress, which convened in 2001. Their majority in the Senate in early 2001, however, was by the narrowest of margins. Split evenly at fifty apiece, Republicans held the majority due to Vice President Dick Cheney's tiebreaking vote. When Vermont senator James Jeffords resigned from the party and became an Independent, Republicans lost control of the Senate in June 2001.

Newt Gingrich (R-GA) led the House Republicans to victory in the 1994 election. Then, in 1995, he became the first Republican Speaker of the House since the mid-1950s. An articulate spokesman and chief policymaker, Gingrich became one of the most powerful Speakers of the century. He was able to shift some of the power on setting the agenda and formulating policy in bills from the standing committees to the majority party leaders. In early 1995, under his leadership, the House Republicans passed several key parts of their legislative agenda. However, by late 1995 and early 1996, Gingrich's influence had begun to decline as public opinion turned against the Republicans over the budget battle with President Bill Clinton and the shutdown of parts of the federal government. By 1997, power was moving back to the standing committees. In the summer of 1997, Gingrich faced a revolt against his leadership from a group of House Republicans and had to battle to retain his office. After the 1998 election, Gingrich's influence had decreased to such an extent that he decided to resign as Speaker and leave the House.

After Gingrich's resignation, the House Republicans elected Robert Livingston of Louisiana as their leader and candidate for Speaker. Livingston, however, resigned from the House a month later over revelations about extramarital affairs. These news stories were especially damaging because the House Republicans were considering whether to impeach President Clinton on activities related to a sex scandal.

With Livingston's resignation, the House Republicans chose Dennis Hastert of Illinois as their leader, and later, on the House floor, they elected him Speaker. Hastert's selection was a surprise because he was relatively unknown and did not hold a powerful position in the House. Hastert's leadership style is much different from Gingrich's. He does not concentrate as much power in the party leadership and focuses more on negotiating behind the scenes rather than playing a big public role.

The second highest position in the majority party of the House is the majority leader. Dick Armey of Texas became the majority leader in 1995. In November 1998, he survived a challenge from Steve Largent of Oklahoma and Jennifer Dunn of Washington for his position. His primary job is to aid the Speaker in the leadership functions. Armey is involved in the day-to-day activities associated with leading the majority party, especially scheduling the floor sessions and building majorities on floor votes.

In 1995, Tom DeLay of Texas was selected to the position of majority whip, the third highest office in the House majority party. He coordinates the whip system, a communication network between the leadership and the rank-and-file members. DeLay, who has become one of the most powerful members of Congress, has signif-

icant influence on the House Republicans' political and policy strategies. For example, he played an influential role in the decisions by House Republicans to vote for the impeachment of President Clinton and to select Dennis Hastert as Speaker.

The House Republican Conference selects the leaders and provides a forum for discussing policy issues and party matters. The House Republican Party committees are the Steering Committee (standing committee assignments), the Policy Committee (policy proposals), and the National Republican Congressional Committee (NRCC; campaign funds). The chairs of these committees in the 106th and 107th Congresses were Speaker Hastert (Steering), Christopher Cox of California (Policy), and Thomas Davis of Virginia (NRCC).

In the Senate, the Republican leader is the majority leader when the Republicans are in the majority and the minority leader when they are in the minority. After several years as the minority leader, Robert Dole of Kansas became the majority leader in 1995. In 1996, Senate Republicans elected Trent Lott of Mississippi to replace Dole after he decided to retire from the Senate to concentrate on his presidential campaign. As majority leader, Lott was the leader of both the Senate and the Senate Republicans. He negotiated the bills from the standing committees to the floor, scheduled the bills on the floor, and worked on building majority support for bills. While Lott's policy leadership was heavily influenced by his conservative ideology, he was willing, at times, to be a pragmatic deal maker in his relationship with Senate Democrats and the Clinton administration. For instance, he compromised with the Democrats in the 1996 session on several important bills (e.g., increasing the minimum wage and protecting drinking-water systems) to add to the congressional Republicans' record going into the election. He remained Senate majority leader until June 2001, when—following Jeffords's defection from the party and the resulting Republican loss of the Senate—he became Senate minority leader.

Don Nickles of Oklahoma, long the majority whip (or assistant majority leader), works with Lott to lead the Senate Republicans. While they usually agree on most policy areas, they have differed on a few major bills. Following the Republicans' loss of the Senate in June 2001, Nickles became minority whip.

Senate Republicans meet in their conference to select the leaders and discuss policy. And they operate with three party committees: the Committee on Committees (standing committee assignments), the Policy Committee (policy proposals), and the National Republican Senatorial Committee (campaign funds). In the 107th Congress, Idaho Republican Larry Craig was head of the Policy Committee, and Tennessee senator Bill Frist chaired the National Republican Senatorial Committee.

Because the 107th Senate was initially divided evenly between Democrats and Republicans, Democrats challenged the existing committee representation structure by proposing equal representation and sharing leadership of committees. After initial resistance, Republicans eventually agreed to a power-sharing deal whereby Democrats received equal representation, but the GOP kept leadership positions in all committees. This deal held until June 2001, when Democrats regained control of the Senate and Republicans lost their leadership positions.

Larry Schwab

SEE ALSO: Congressional Elections; Congressional Party Leadership; Voting Behavior.

BIBLIOGRAPHY

Bader, John B. *Taking the Initiative: Leadership Agendas in Congress and the "Contract with America."* Washington, DC: Georgetown University Press, 1996.

Congressional Quarterly. *How Congress Works*. 3d ed. Washington, DC: Congressional Quarterly Press, 1998.

Duncan, Philip D., and Brian Nutting, eds. *Politics in America: The 106th Congress.* Washington, DC: Congressional Quarterly Press, 1999.

Peters, Ronald M., Jr. *The American Speakership: The Office in Historical Perspective.* 2d ed. Baltimore: Johns Hopkins University Press, 1997.

Sinclair, Barbara. *Unorthodox Lawmaking: New Legislative Processes in the U.S. Congress.* Washington, DC: Congressional Quarterly Press, 1997.

SOCIAL SECURITY

The Social Security program was an initiative of the Democratic Party. It has turned into one of the most popular and successful social welfare programs ever instituted in the United States. Republicans have overcome their initial opposition to the system and have concentrated on maintaining the original mandate of the program and its fiscal solvency.

The growing number of retirees and the aging population's increasing size in the United States will put increased pressures on Social Security. In the 1950s, there were five workers for every retiree. In the twenty-first century, however, that ratio will drop to two workers for every retiree. Because Social Security is a pay-as-you-go system, the Social Security taxes of current workers are paid to current retirees. Hence, as there are proportionally fewer workers, the tax burden will have to increase dramatically to maintain the present system. Analysts predict that the system will be bankrupt by 2035. In an effort to save the system and in light of the success of private retirement plans such as 401(k)s and individual retirement accounts (IRAs), Republicans have called for the privatization of Social Security. However, Democrats have fervently resisted such efforts.

By the 1980s, Social Security had begun to run a surplus, but instead of allowing those moneys to remain in the trust fund, the federal government used the surplus for general expenditures. Although opposed in principle to the concept, Republicans have accepted this means to shore up the federal budget. This practice continued until 1999, when for the first time in thirty years, the government did not use excess Social Security funds as part of the general federal budget. Still, many believe that even if all future funds go directly into the program, by 2016 tax income will not be large enough to cover outlays, the government will have to begin liquidating its securities to pay benefits, and the fund will be completely exhausted in 2038.

Some reforms have been implemented with bipartisan support. In 2000, Congress approved Republican legislation, sponsored by Speaker of the House Dennis Hastert, that ended the long-standing penalty on seniors who work and receive Social Security payments. Democrats had opposed the measure for fear that it would further undercut the financial solvency of the system by depriving the trust fund of some $22 billion over a ten-year period. However, the popularity of the measure among seniors and the possibility that increased payroll taxes would offset the losses led the administration of Bill Clinton and congressional Democrats to shift their support in favor of the legislation. Republicans also sponsored so-called lock-box legislation, which would permanently place Social Security funds outside of the federal budget. Democrats initially resisted the legislation, but following an unexpected policy shift by the White House, they came to support the lock-box concept with one exception: Democrats wanted 15 percent of incoming Social Security funds to be used to shore up the Medicare program, an idea opposed by Republicans.

In 1994, the Clinton administration formed the bipartisan Advisory Council on Social Security to devise methods to save or prolong the life of Social Security. On January 6, 1997, the council presented its findings, which included such measures as the rejection of means testing so that wealthier Americans would continue to receive benefits and mandatory participation would be maintained in any future program. They could not agree on a single, broad, long-term solution, however, and provided three different plans. The first plan was known as the maintenance of benefits and called for increased taxes and a minimal decrease in some benefits. In addition, the government would invest as much as 40 percent of the trust fund in equity indexes (with the government assuming the risks if there were losses). In the second plan, the individual accounts proposal, a two-tier system would be created so that middle- and upper-income Americans would have reduced benefits. Meanwhile, those in the second tier would have an additional 1.6 percent of their income invested in plans of their choosing, similar to existing 401(k) plans. In this second plan, individuals would bear the risks of investments. The third and most sweeping plan, the personal savings account, would also create a two-tier system whereby all individuals would receive a monthly benefit equivalent to half the current payment. In addition, 5 percent of the employee's pay would go into individual investment accounts. In this plan also, individuals would be responsible for the risks, and there would be an additional 1.52 percent payroll tax on employers and employees to fund the transition period.

In his last State of the Union Address, delivered in 2000, Clinton proposed a variety of measures to shore up the program, most which were components of the advisory board's first plan. The president suggested transferring some 62 percent of the federal budget surplus over the next fifteen years to the program and an additional 15 percent to Medicare. Clinton also endorsed the proposal to transfer some percentage of the fund into private investments to maximize returns. Under these proposals, the life of Social Security could be extended until 2055. Clinton advocated the creation of universal savings accounts by which Americans could supplement Social Security by investing their own funds. The government would match these funds up to a certain percentage. To pay for the program, 11 percent of any future budget surpluses would be used.

Most Republicans opposed the Clinton plan. Instead, they favor some variation of the advisory board's third plan, based on the creation of individual investment accounts. Republicans favor such a system because a portion of each individual's Social Security taxes would go into his or her personal account. This would transform Social Security from an unfunded retirement plan to a fully funded system. Because individuals would provide for their own retirement, the plan would offer a permanent solution to the potential for insolvency in the program. Individuals would also be better able to plan for retirement because they would have control over investment options and a better sense of total assets. Since individuals would continue to receive some monthly benefit, albeit a sharply reduced payment, Republicans contend that this system could compensate for economic downturns in the stock or bond market and still provide a much more generous retirement for American workers.

President George W. Bush has insisted that to

avoid cutting benefits or raising taxes, Social Security must be reformed to increase the return on money going into the system. In the 2000 presidential election, he asserted his strong belief that individual private accounts are the only way to accomplish this goal. Throughout his campaign and in the early months of his presidency, however, he has been vague about how he would enact this reform. He has not detailed how he would provide the money for the transition to a system of individual accounts, which is predicted to cost around $1 trillion over ten years and is still likely to require politically painful benefit cuts. Taking steps to advance a new system, Bush planned to create a bipartisan commission, whose members would all be in favor of private accounts, to study the specifics of restructuring.

Tom Lansford

SEE ALSO: Budget and Fiscal Policy; Healthcare.

BIBLIOGRAPHY

Drew, Elizabeth. *Showdown: The Struggle Between the Gingrich Congress and the Clinton White House.* New York: Simon and Schuster, 1996.

Jones, Charles O. *Clinton and Congress, 1993–1996: Risk, Restoration, and Reelection.* Norman: University of Oklahoma Press, 1999.

Kurian, George Thomas, ed. *A Historical Guide to the U.S. Government.* New York: Oxford University Press, 1998.

Social Security Administration. *Social Security, Facts and Figures.* Washington, DC: Social Security Administration, 1999.

Social Security Advisory Council. *Report of the 1994–1996 Advisory Council on Social Security.* Washington, DC: GPO, 1997.

Steuerle, C. Eugene, and Jon M. Bakija. *Retooling Social Security for the 21st Century: Right and Wrong Approaches to Reform.* Washington, DC: Urban Institute Press, 1994.

VOTING BEHAVIOR

Republicans have made few proposals to reform the electoral system to raise voter turnout. In part, this may be because, as a conservative party, they are simply less likely to feel the need for political changes. Conservatives also tend to be more skeptical of expansive democracy. Finally, there is a maxim of campaign strategy that low turnout tends to benefit Republicans. The logic is that they have a larger core of committed voters who will show up no matter what. Whether or not this is true, the low turnout in recent years has benefited Republicans because the voters staying home have tended to be poorer and less educated, and these groups tend to vote Democratic.

Not surprisingly then, Republicans' reactions to others' reform proposals have largely been negative. The list of such proposals includes the National Voter Registration Act (the so-called Motor-Voter law), the political use of the Internet, early voting by mail, moving Election Day to a weekend or making it a holiday, voting by proportional representation, and permitting felons to vote. While generally negative, Republicans' reactions to these have been varied in strength, somewhat mixed in direction, and not always consonant with the party's best electoral strategy.

The Motor-Voter law required states to allow voter registration when applying for a driver's license or government benefits. Congress first passed a version of the law in 1992 when George H. W. Bush was president, but he vetoed it. Congress was unable to override the president's veto. When the bill came up in 1993, early in President Bill Clinton's term, opposition from Republican governors and members of Congress was just as strong. However, the Democratic-majority Congress easily passed it, and Clinton immediately signed it. After the Republicans won majorities in Congress in 1994, several members of Congress led unsuccessful repeal efforts: Representatives Bob Stump (R-AZ), John Linder (R-GA), Donald Manzullo (R-IL), and Bob Livingston (R-LA), and Senators Mitch McConnell (R-KY) and Paul Coverdell (R-GA). At the same time, a number of Republican governors challenged the law in various ways. Governor Pete Wilson of California refused to implement the law. Governor John Engler of Michigan exercised a line-item veto on the funding for the registration forms. Wilson, Governor George Allen of Virginia, and several other Republican governors launched unsuccessful court challenges. Fraud was one of the opposition's concerns, but the bill was also targeted at marginal voters with lower incomes and education levels—a traditional Democratic base. It turned out, however, that all this opposition may have been misplaced. Studies of the initial effects of Motor-Voter indicated that while more voters registered, not many more actually voted. Furthermore, any additional votes went as much to Republicans as to Democrats.

The Internet is one tool that Republicans could be expected to use to build turnout. After all, Internet users should tend to be wealthier and more educated, two demographics that lean Republican. At least early on, though, Republicans did not press this advantage: more Democrats than Republicans initially utilized the Web, and the Democrats conducted the first official Internet voting in an Arizona primary. Some of the more entrepreneurial members of the party have caught on to the Web, however. In 1999, Steve Forbes, for instance, launched his presidential campaign on the Internet and organized campaign precincts electronically. The Republican Party platform now reflects this position as well, positing that the Internet encourages individualism and freedom from excessive government.

Early voting by mail is another proposal to raise voter interest. Conservative Norman Ornstein has been one of the leading critics, on the grounds that the civic value of voting is diminished without a physical trip to the polling place. However, the practice does not appear to confer a political advantage on either party.

Some commentators posit that making Election Day a holiday or moving it to a weekend would raise turnout by giving people more free time to vote. No politician of either party seems to support this option. In the Republicans' case, the idea is consistent with their traditionalist bent, but it may be inconsistent with their short-run political interests. The employed, who would benefit from the day off, would seem to be more likely Republicans than would the unemployed.

Another plan that has not drawn Republican support is proportional representation. This plan would have all a state's representatives elected at large and in proportion to the party's state-wide vote, rather than (as is done now) in a discrete set of districts voting by plurality rule. Proponents hope that voters would be more ea-

ger if they could help their party gain seats even in a lopsided race. The plan would favor minority voters because they could elect a few representatives even with less than half the vote (and without gerrymandering majorities in a few districts while leaving the opposition stronger in the remaining ones). A few Democrats have therefore picked up the idea, but it is marginal enough that no Republican has indicated interest.

An idea that has shown more chance of success—and has consequently drawn more of a Republican response—is allowing felons the right to vote. Although most Republicans, such as former Massachusetts governor Paul Cellucci, have opposed granting former criminals voting rights, others have supported it. These include Florida governor Jeb Bush and Charles Colson, a former convict himself because of his involvement in the Watergate scandal in the 1970s but now a leader of the Prison Fellowship Ministries program.

On a more fundamental level, many contend that voter indifference is caused either by political cynicism or by the diminished role of government. If either of these arguments holds, then Republicans' mixed positions on campaign finance reform (a supposed cure for cynicism) and their calls for smaller government would work against added turnout.

Republicans were forced to take electoral reform more seriously after the 2000 elections, which were mired in controversy. The 2000 presidential election was extremely close, making every vote matter to the outcome. The focus on counting every vote revealed just how inaccurate vote tallying could be. Furthermore, the close election made it more difficult to predict the outcome on election night television coverage, yet the networks continued to make predictions before the polls closed and possibly affected voting behavior by discouraging people from going to the polls. The election disputes were blamed on outdated voting machines, confusing ballot designs, inaccurate voter rolls, and a lack of standard rules for reading unclear votes. Ultimately, the Republicans won the presidential race, and Republican members of Congress have moved more slowly on reform than Democrats who felt that sloppy voting procedures and outright discrimination against poor, minority, and elderly voters cost them the election.

Because the election brought issues of election reform to the forefront of American political consciousness, Republicans have made gestures toward reform. A few weeks into his presidency, George W. Bush asked Congress to consider four election issues: improving voting machines, making sure military personnel who are abroad have their votes counted, preventing felons from voting, and exploring whether network projections of election outcomes prior to the polls closing affect voters' behavior. Republican senator John McCain has urged reform before the 2002 interim elections. In addition, several Republican senators, particularly Mitch McConnell and Sam Brownback, have worked with Democrats to propose election reform legislation that is likely to be considered by Congress. Their bill includes grants to local governments to buy new voting equipment meeting government specifications, required compliance with the Voting Rights Act and civil rights laws, and mandatory provisional ballots (to allow people whose registration is in doubt to vote so their votes could be counted later if they were found eligible).

Frauke Schnell

SEE ALSO: Congressional Elections; Congressional Party Leadership; Party Organization.

BIBLIOGRAPHY

Broder, David S. "Keeping Voters Voting." *Washington Post*, October 11, 1998.

Carney, Eliza Newlin. "Opting Out of Politics." *National Journal*, January 17, 1998, 106.

Cloward, Richard A., and Frances Fox Piven. "Motor Voter Motives." *American Prospect*, November/December 1996, 18.

Dreier, Peter. "Detouring the Motor-Voter Law: Fear of Franchise; Republican Governor Pete Wilson of California Will Not Implement the National Voter Registration Act of 1993." *The Nation*, October 31, 1994, 490.

Gearey, Robyn. "Motor Voter's Breakdown Lane." *American Prospect*, September/October 1996, 48.

Grossman, Lawrence K. *The Electronic Republic: Reshaping Democracy in the Information Age.* New York: Viking, 1995.

"Is Online Voting Democratic?" *New Media Age*, March 16, 2000.

Keisling, Phil. "What If We Held an Election and Nobody Came? Voter Turnout Is Plummeting. How Vote-by-Mail Reverses the Trend; Oregon Used Vote-by-Mail in January 1996 to Fill Former Senator Bob Packwood's Seat." *Washington Monthly*, March 1, 1996, 40.

Leiter, Lisa. "Drive to Register Voters Pads Republican Rosters." *Insight on the News*, May 8, 1995, 44–47.

———. "Goodbye BBQ and Buttons: Hello Web and Home Page." *Insight on the News*, September 25, 1995, 23–25.

Lind, Michael. "Alice Doesn't Vote Here Anymore: Proportional Voting Versus Current Plurality System for Congress." *Mother Jones*, March 13, 1998, 52.

Malchow, Hal. "The Targeting Revolution in Political Direct Contact: Why Old Techniques Won't Win Elections of the Future." *Campaigns & Elections*, June 1997, 36.

Miller, John J. "Public Policy: Votes for Felons." *National Review*, April 3, 2000, 26–29.

Republican National Committee. "Republican Platform 2000: Renewing America's Purpose Together." Washington, DC: Republican National Committee, 2000.

Stein, Robert M. "Early Voting." *Public Opinion Quarterly*, March 22, 1998, 57.

Swanson, K. C. "Rules Eased, Voter Rolls Are Swelling." *National Journal*, October 19, 1996, 2231.

Wattenberg, Martin P. "Politics: Should Election Day Be a Holiday?" *Atlantic Monthly*, October 1, 1998.

West, Woody. "Good Folks Asleep? Let the Felons Vote." *Insight on the News*, March 29, 1999, 48.

"Why Citizens Shun the Polling Booth: An Interview with Curtis B. Gans." *American Perspective* 8:2 (1997): 42.

Part III

National Leaders

WILLIAM BENNETT

William J. Bennett was born on July 3, 1943, in New York City. After growing up in Brooklyn, he attended Williams College in Williamstown, Massachusetts, and earned a bachelor of arts degree in philosophy. Bennett continued his studies at the University of Texas, where he earned a Ph.D. in political philosophy. He also earned a law degree from Harvard University Law School.

While never holding elective office, Bennett has become one of the most influential members of the Republican Party. He began his public service at the national level when he became President Ronald Reagan's first chair of the National Endowment for the Humanities in 1981. From 1985 until 1988, Bennett served as the secretary of education in the Reagan administration, and in 1989, President George H. W. Bush appointed him the first director of the National Drug Control Policy, a position often referred to as "drug czar." In both roles, Bennett used his position as a bully pulpit by which to cajole, convince, and contradict.

After leaving government in 1990, Bennett achieved an even greater impact on the national political debate. A John M. Olin Distinguished Fellow at the Heritage Foundation, he cofounded Empower America with Jack Kemp. Bennett has

William Bennett (*Empower America*)

written for America's leading newspapers and magazines and has made frequent appearances on leading political talk shows. He has also written and edited eleven books—including *The Children's Book of Heroes* (1997), *Our Sacred Honor* (1997), and *The Death of Outrage: Bill Clinton and the Assault on American Ideals* (1998). Two of his books rank among the most successful of the 1990s: *The Book of Virtues* (1993) and *The Children's Book of Virtues* (1995). *The Book of Virtues* has been made into an animated series aired on PBS. Bennett has also become a leading critic of America's popular culture and waged campaigns against certain kinds of "gangsta rap" music and "trash television" talk shows. In addition, he supported the impeachment of Bill Clinton.

Although he is a well-known Republican, Bennett has consistently reached across party lines to pursue important common goals. He has worked closely with Democratic senator and vice presidential nominee Joseph Lieberman on the issues of popular culture and worldwide religious persecution. During the 2000 campaign, however, Bennett criticized Lieberman because he felt Lieberman had turned his back on their long history of work against Hollywood violence in order to gain the entertainment industry's financial support for the Democratic presidential ticket. He is cochair with former Democratic senator Sam Nunn of the National Commission on Civic Renewal. Bennett and former Democratic governor Mario Cuomo were named cochairs of the Partnership for a Drug-Free America.

Bennett was an unofficial adviser to several Republican presidential candidates during the 2000 primaries. In particular, he was very involved in developing George W. Bush's education policy, and he has continued to back the president's education proposals. In addition to his work as a writer and political analyst, in 2001 Bennett founded K12, an online private school for elementary through high school students. After paying various levels of enrollment fees, the school's curriculum will be available on the Internet for use by home-schooled students, children in after-school programs or charter schools, or adult education. Although he was once critical of Internet learning, Bennett hopes the school will make quality educational materials available to children across the country and eventually all over the world.

Jeffrey D. Schultz

SEE ALSO: Education.

BIBLIOGRAPHY

Bennett, William J., ed. *Our Sacred Honor: Words of Advice from the Founders in Stories, Letters, Poems, and Speeches.* Nashville, TN: Broadman and Holman, 1997.

Regier, Gerald P., ed. *Values & Public Policy.* Washington, DC: Family Research Council of America, 1988.

GEORGE W. BUSH

George Walker Bush was born on July 6, 1946, in New Haven, Connecticut, and was raised in Midland and Houston, Texas. He is the son of former president George H. W. Bush and Barbara Bush. Like his father, George W. Bush attended Phillips Academy in Andover, a New England prep school. In 1964, he once again followed in his father's footsteps and went to Yale University. An average student, he graduated from Yale in 1968 and was a fighter pilot in the Texas Air National Guard from 1969 to 1973. He received an M.B.A. from Harvard in 1975. He married a local Texas librarian, Laura Welch, in 1977, and they are the parents of two daughters.

In 1978, Bush ran as a Republican for Congress in Texas. He captured the Republican nomination by winning a Republican primary runoff by 1,400 votes. He lost the general election by a margin of 53 percent to 47 percent. He again tried to follow in his father's footsteps as a Texas oilman, but he was not particularly successful. His company was saddled with debt and he got out of that business. He and others who knew him well say his life changed in 1986, when he gave up alcohol and claimed to have found religion. Soon after, Bush enjoyed success as an adviser to his father's 1988 presidential campaign, and in 1989, he became a managing partner of the Texas Rangers baseball franchise. He later sold his share of that successful franchise at a handsome profit.

In 1994, Bush challenged incumbent Texas

George W. Bush *(Eric Draper)*

governor Ann Richards and won with 53.5 percent to Richards's 46 percent. In his 1998 reelection campaign, while the Republicans were doing quite poorly among Hispanic voters nationwide, Bush garnered 49 percent of the Texas Hispanic vote as part of his impressive 68.6 percent of the general vote. As governor, he was credited with increasing funding for schools, improving student performance, and cutting taxes. He was also considered more pragmatic than ideological, characterized by his charm and good political instincts.

When Bush launched his presidential campaign for the 2000 election, he emerged as the early frontrunner, stunning his opponents and political observers by raising over $50 million by the end of the summer of 1999. During the campaign, Bush characterized himself as a "compassionate conservative" to distinguish himself from the far right wing of the Republican Party. He played down explosive and divisive issues such as abortion, which many Republican leaders strongly oppose. Nevertheless, he enjoyed the support of most of the elected Republican leaders in the nation and beat back a challenge from Arizona senator John McCain to win the Republican nomination. His main challenger was Democratic candidate Al Gore, and the two remained neck and neck in the polls throughout much of the campaign. In the televised presidential debates in the fall, Bush's easy, unpretentious manner contrasted with Gore's articulateness. Bush's charm along the campaign trail quickly earned him the reputation of being a friendly, folksy Texan, and he prides himself on being honest and straightforward.

To make clear his "compassionate conservative" approach to leading the nation, Bush said he would care for those Americans who have been underserved in society and pledged to unify and empower all Americans. He stated he does not believe that government is the enemy of the people, but he also does not believe it is the answer to America's problems. Bush promoted the strengthening of faith-based organizations with federal money because he believes religious organizations should play a role in helping the poor and in providing solutions to drug and crime problems. In addition to these concerns, Bush focused squarely throughout his campaign on the issues of education, Social Security, Medicare, and taxes. He declared that his educational agenda would "leave no child behind," no matter the child's economic or cultural background, and pushed his school choice plan, which would offer federal vouchers to assist students wanting to get out of failing schools. In addition, Bush believes strongly in local rather than state control of schools and in holding schools accountable for their performance. Expressing concern over the future solvency of Social Security and Medicare, Bush promised overhauls of both systems and emphasized his politically controversial idea to privatize and introduce individual investment into Social Security. He also vowed to offer prescription drug benefits to senior citizens. And as he did while governor of Texas, Bush said he would cut taxes. He assured Americans of tax relief and an extensive tax cut that would jump-start a slowing

economy. Finally, Bush repeatedly campaigned on a promise to change the tone of Washington by reaching out to Democrats and leading a government based on bipartisanship rather than division.

This pledge of unity became particularly poignant following the extremely close election between Bush and Gore and the bitterly contested results in Florida, where the two candidates were locked in a race for the state's electoral votes. In December 2000, the Supreme Court, in a vote of five to four, effectively declared Bush the winner of the election by ruling to stop recounting disputed ballots. Leading up to his inauguration on January 20, 2001, political analysts as well as Bush's advisers worried that Bush would not have a clear mandate as president after such a controversial election. Bush assumed the presidency not having won the popular vote. Further, the Senate was split fifty-fifty, barely giving the Republicans a majority and underscoring the challenge Bush would face and the need to encourage compromise and bipartisanship on Capitol Hill.

Within days of taking office, media reports concluded that Bush had a 60 percent job approval rating. Some critics claimed Bush exhibited terrible unease and inexperience, having to rely heavily on his more experienced vice president, Dick Cheney, and other advisers. However, pundits were also stating that White House staff and officials, as well as Republican and Democratic members of Congress, were generally pleased with the style in which Bush was leading. Whereas President Bill Clinton liked to hold meetings with his staff into the late-night hours, Bush quickly became known as a no-nonsense president who rose early in the morning, was punctual, brief, and to the point in meetings, and was in bed by 10 P.M. In his first 100 days in office, Bush pushed his education proposal, budget and tax plan, and plans for a national missile defense shield to the forefront of his administration's business. While Bush's desire to improve the quality of life for military personnel by increasing their pay attracted no arguments from congressional leaders, most Democrats and many U.S. allies expressed skepticism over his missile defense plans. Bush was forced to enlist diplomats and foreign policy advisers to negotiate with world leaders and ease their fears about the defense system. In other matters of foreign policy, Bush attracted criticism for his tough, brusque dealings with problematic countries such as China, North Korea, and Russia. However, his administration's handling of a potentially explosive situation with China, in which a U.S. spy plane collided with a Chinese jet fighter, won him increased approval ratings.

Many of Bush's policies immediately drew opposition from Democratic lawmakers, forcing him to compromise on a number of his signature plans, including settling for a $1.35 trillion tax cut rather than the proposed $1.6 trillion and removing school vouchers from his education proposal. On these and other domestic issues, including the nation's energy policy and Bush's reversal of many Clinton administration programs to protect the environment, Democrats fiercely attacked Bush for what they perceived to be his increasing conservatism. Many charged that Bush's policies undercut efforts to help America's poorer citizens and threatened the nation's quality of life. Nevertheless, in the early months of his presidency, some of Bush's most important programs and policies received clear bipartisan support.

William C. Binning

SEE ALSO: Campaign 2000 and the Florida Recount; The Bush Presidency: The First Hundred Days.

BIBLIOGRAPHY

Bush, George W. *A Charge to Keep.* New York: Morrow, 1999.

Hatfield, J. H. *Fortunate Son: George W. Bush and the Making of an American President.* New York: Soft Skull Press, 2000.

Ivins, Molly, and Lou Dubose. *Shrub: The Short but Happy Political Life of George W. Bush.* New York: Random House, 2000.

Minutaglio, Bill. *First Son: George W. Bush and the Bush Family Dynasty.* New York: Times Books, 1999.

DICK CHENEY

Richard Bruce ("Dick") Cheney was born on January 30, 1941, in Lincoln, Nebraska, and grew up

Dick Cheney *(Government Printing Office)*

in Casper, Wyoming. He won a scholarship to Yale University but left after his first year. Returning home to Wyoming, he attended the University of Wyoming, earning his bachelor's degree in 1965 and his master's degree in political science in 1966. He started a doctoral program at the University of Wisconsin but left in 1968. He entered political life in 1969 when he became special assistant to Donald H. Rumsfeld, director of the Office of Economic Opportunity in the Richard Nixon administration. In 1970, he was appointed White House staff assistant and in 1971 assistant director of the Cost of Living Council. In 1973, Cheney left government service but returned a year later as deputy assistant to President Gerald R. Ford. He was quickly promoted to deputy White House chief of staff (Rumsfeld was chief of staff), and when Rumsfeld was appointed secretary of defense in 1975, Cheney, just thirty-four years old, became the youngest man to be appointed White House chief of staff.

After the defeat of President Ford in 1976,

Cheney returned to private life in Wyoming. In 1978, he ran a successful campaign for Congress and became the state's at-large representative. Reelected in each subsequent election, Cheney served ten years in the House of Representatives. During that time, he compiled a record as a committed conservative on both fiscal and social issues. He was one of President Ronald Reagan's leading supporters in the House. His commitment and abilities led to his election as minority whip despite being from a small electoral state. In 1989, President George H. W. Bush appointed him secretary of defense. A strong leader, Cheney directed the trimming back of defense budgets and strengthened the president's role in foreign affairs vis-à-vis the Congress. He also played a major role in overseeing the military activities in the Gulf War in 1991.

After the defeat of President Bush in 1992, Cheney, who is married to Lynne Cheney, former chair of the National Endowment for the Humanities, returned to private life in the gas and oil business in Texas. When Texas governor George W. Bush, son of the former president, launched his campaign for the presidency, Cheney became a key adviser, and when Bush emerged victorious in the primaries in early 2000, he appointed Cheney to head his vice presidential search committee. In the end, Bush selected Cheney to be his running mate. While Cheney did not bring a large electoral state to the Bush camp, he did bring solid conservative credentials and plenty of practical Washington experience.

Despite a history of heart problems, including a mild heart attack after the 2000 election and the implantation of a pacemaker five months into his term, Vice President Dick Cheney has been seen as a central force in the Bush administration. Political pundits and Democrats and Republicans alike have viewed Cheney as a linchpin in the workings of the Bush presidency. Entrusted to a visibly powerful position early in the administration, Cheney managed the presidential transition team and helped assemble Bush's cabinet. From there, he quickly built up a packed schedule that involves him in everything from discussions on missile defense to energy plans. He became a key figure in creating Bush's budget plan and in working with Democratic leaders to reach a compromise on the president's education bill. Furthermore, because of his years of experience in Congress and as a former White House chief of staff and secretary of defense, Cheney has been one of Bush's most trusted advisers on foreign policy. In May 2001, Cheney headed up a task force to work out Bush's energy policy. As vice president, Cheney had a vital role in the evenly divided Senate by giving Republicans a majority—and hence control of the chamber—and providing the tiebreaking vote. After Republicans lost control of the Senate in June 2001, however, Cheney's role in the Senate became less crucial.

Jeffrey D. Schultz

SEE ALSO: Campaign 2000 and the Florida Recount; The Bush Presidency: The First Hundred Days.

TOM DeLAY

Thomas Dale DeLay was born in Laredo, Texas, on April 8, 1947. He spent much of his youth in

Tom DeLay (*Government Printing Office*)

Venezuela, where his father was an oil drilling contractor. He attended Baylor University from 1965 to 1967, but graduated from the University of Houston in 1970. He opened a pest control business and also became active in local politics. In 1978, he was elected to the Texas House of Representatives, becoming the first Republican from Fort Bend County ever elected to the state house. Six years later, DeLay was elected to the United States House of Representatives from the 22nd District, which includes Brazoira, Fort Bend, and Harris Counties. In the House, DeLay has been a committed fiscal and social conservative.

During his tenure in the House, DeLay has held a number of leadership positions including Republican conference secretary, deputy whip, and chair of the Republican Study Committee. In 1992, he was elected House minority whip, the third highest leadership post in the House Republican Conference. He became responsible for pushing the Republican legislative agenda and worked closely with minority leader Newt Gingrich developing the "Contract with America" in 1994. A list of legislative goals, the Contract with America helped the Republican Party gain control of the House of Representatives for the first time in a generation.

DeLay became majority whip in 1995 and worked effectively with Gingrich, who became Speaker of the House. After Gingrich's resignation following the 1998 elections, DeLay played a key role in elevating J. Dennis Hastert to the Speaker's position.

An avowed and vocal Republican partisan, DeLay remains a controversial and extremely powerful representative. Known as "The Hammer" for his ability to maintain the party loyalty and discipline necessary to garner votes on key legislation, DeLay does not favor bipartisan politics. He fought bitterly with President Bill Clinton, precipitating a major budget standoff with him in 2000. Political analysts predicted DeLay would conflict with President George W. Bush's style of "compassionate conservatism" and balk at necessary compromises with Democrats in a Congress with such a small Republican majority, but DeLay has quieted his tactics to appease the Bush administration. In 2001, he fought for a larger tax cut than that requested by President Bush, but he has otherwise acquiesced to the more subtle political dealings of the Bush White House.

DeLay is well known as an avid and very skilled fund-raiser. His aggressive tactics to gain money from lobbyists and corporations have drawn criticism from both the left and the right, but his ability to cultivate the party's power and influence by getting money from and giving money to all the right causes and candidates is unquestioned. He is strongly opposed to campaign finance reform, preferring private rather than public money for financing campaigns. As a fundamentalist Christian, DeLay believes his mission as a representative is to inject conservative, Christian leadership and values into American culture and law. He is a dedicated advocate for child welfare, and particularly supports causes to eliminate child neglect and abuse. In addition to his role as majority whip, DeLay also serves on the Appropriations Committee, which produces all spending legislation in the House.

Jeffrey D. Schultz

SEE ALSO: The Bush Presidency: The First Hundred Days; Dennis Hastert.

ELIZABETH DOLE

Elizabeth Hanford Dole was born in Salisbury, North Carolina, on July 29, 1936. She earned a bachelor's degree from Duke University in 1958 and a master's degree in education and government from Harvard University in 1960. In 1965, she received a law degree from Harvard. Dole's public career began in 1966 when she became a staff assistant for the U.S. Department of Health, Education and Welfare. From 1968 to 1971, she served as executive director of the President's Commission for Consumer Interests under President Richard Nixon. From 1973 to 1979, Dole was a member of the Federal Trade Commission. She worked for the election of Ronald Reagan in 1980 and served as the president's assistant for public safety from 1981 to 1983.

In 1983, Reagan appointed her secretary of transportation, where she oversaw the privati-

Elizabeth Dole (*Office of Elizabeth Dole*)

zation of Conrail, the government-owned freight rail. She was the first woman to hold the position and the first woman in Reagan's cabinet. In 1989, President George H. W. Bush appointed her secretary of labor; as such, she strove to improve worker-management relations and was instrumental in settling the bitter Pittston coal strike.

Dole later became president of the American Red Cross. She held this position as an unpaid volunteer for her first year. She ultimately led the Red Cross for eight years and oversaw numerous reforms that made the organization one of the most efficient charitable institutions in the world.

Elizabeth Dole is half of one of the most prominent couples in the Republican Party. She married former Kansas senator and 1996 presidential candidate Robert Dole in 1975. After serving no less than six presidents and assisting her husband in his three bids for the presidency, Elizabeth Dole launched her own bid for the presidency in the 2000 election. Dole was the first woman of a major party to mount a serious presidential campaign, and she attracted many new voters, particularly young and professional

women, to the Republican Party. Dole campaigned on promises to improve education, eradicate guns from schools, promote a drug-free America, and strengthen America's defense and foreign policy. Despite her experience with campaigns and doing well in early poll contests in the summer of 1999, Dole was eventually forced to withdraw from the campaign because of lack of funds. In April 2001, Dole was selected to be the spokeswoman for a faith-based relief group working to build inexpensive housing for poor people around the world.

Tom Lansford

SEE ALSO: Campaign 2000 and the Florida Recount; The Presidential Election of 1996.

NEWT GINGRICH

Newton Gingrich was born on June 17, 1943, in Harrisburg, Pennsylvania, to Kathleen McPherson. His mother's second husband, Robert Gingrich, who was a career military officer, adopted him. The military family moved frequently. Gingrich graduated from Emory University in Atlanta in 1965 with a degree in history and received a Ph.D. in history from Tulane University in 1971.

A year before receiving his Ph.D., Gingrich received a faculty appointment at West Georgia College in Carrollton, Georgia. In 1974, Gingrich began his quest for a seat in the House of Representatives in Georgia's 6th Congressional District. He ran against the Democratic incumbent Jack Flynt in 1974 and 1976, losing both times. In 1978, Flynt did not run, and Gingrich finally was elected to the House of Representatives.

Gingrich brought a new style to the Republican minority in the House. Combative and aggressive, he worked to position the Republicans to capture the majority. He led the charge against Speaker of the House Jim Wright's ethical abuses, which led Wright to resign in June 1989.

Gingrich worked tirelessly to recruit and elect Republicans to Congress. In 1994, he engineered the Contract with America, a ten-point agenda of the House Republican campaign. The Republicans surprised the nation by winning the House

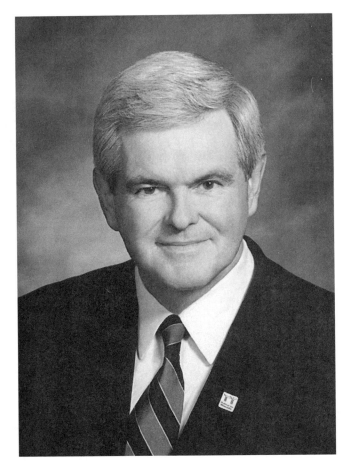

Newt Gingrich (*The Gingrich Group*)

and elected Gingrich as the first Republican Speaker of the House in forty years.

Gingrich took tight control of the majority and challenged President Bill Clinton's leadership at every turn. Assertive, ambitious, and telegenic, Gingrich pushed through numerous laws and was one of the most powerful Republicans in the country in the mid-1990s. He was also a lightning rod for controversy, and when Democrats charged him with ethical lapses stemming from a book deal and fund-raising abuses, he became a liability. His decision effectively to close down the government in late 1995 when he and Clinton could not agree on a budget further damaged his stature. The GOP majority slipped in the 1996 election and slipped further in 1998. Blamed for the losses, Gingrich resigned as Speaker and as a member of Congress in November 1998.

Since his resignation, Gingrich has kept a rel-

atively low profile. He became CEO of his own management consulting firm, The Gingrich Group, which is based in Atlanta. In addition, he is a political commentator for the Fox News Network, a senior fellow at the American Enterprise Institute, and a distinguished visiting fellow at the Hoover Institution at Stanford University.

William C. Binning

SEE ALSO: Tom DeLay; Dennis Hastert; The Congressional Election of 1998.

BIBLIOGRAPHY

Drew, Elizabeth. *Showdown: The Struggle Between the Gingrich Congress and the Clinton White House.* New York: Simon and Schuster, 1996.

Gingrich, Newt. *Lessons Learned the Hard Way: A Personal Report.* New York: HarperCollins, 1998.

DENNIS HASTERT

J. Dennis Hastert was born on January 2, 1942, in Aurora and grew up on a farm in Oswego, Illinois. In high school, he wrestled and played football. After graduating from Wheaton College in 1964, Hastert received his master's degree in 1967 from Northern Illinois University. From 1964 to 1980, he taught government and history and was the wrestling coach at Yorkville High School in Northern, Illinois. His team won a state championship, and he was named Illinois Coach of the Year in 1976.

His transition from government teacher to practitioner was sparked by a trip to Washington, D.C., in the late 1970s. On his return home, he served an internship in the state legislature with a local senator. In 1980, when he ran for a seat in the Illinois General Assembly, he finished third in the primary. Soon afterward, the incumbent became ill and Hastert was selected to replace him, a circumstance twice repeated that advanced his political career.

In March 1986, Hastert became the Republican replacement candidate for the 14th Congressional District after the incumbent—the former state senator for whom Hastert had interned and who was later elected to Congress—became fatally ill. Hastert won with 52 percent of the vote

Dennis Hastert (*Office of Rep. Hastert*)

and has steadily increased his margin of victory since then. From the outset of his congressional career, Hastert built a good working relationship with moderate Republican Illinois representative Robert H. Michel, then House minority leader. In early 1989, he worked with Representative Tom DeLay (R-TX) for a candidate narrowly defeated by a relative unknown, Newt Gingrich, for the position of whip. Following the Republican sweep of the House in the 1994 elections, Hastert was the chief organizer of Tom DeLay's successful campaign for majority whip, the only Republican leadership post won by a non-Gingrich candidate. In return, DeLay rewarded Hastert with the chief deputy whip post.

Fate intervened yet a third time in Hastert's political career in 1999. After Gingrich resigned as House Speaker and Representative Robert L. Livingston abruptly resigned as designate in 1998, Hastert was tapped to become Speaker of the House by Majority Whip DeLay and Representative Bill Paxton, once heir-designate to and friend of Gingrich who the previous summer had

plotted—unsuccessfully—with DeLay and Representative Richard Armey to replace Gingrich as Speaker.

As a result of these efforts, Hastert became Speaker of the House of Representatives on January 6, 1999. His low-key, workhorse leadership style sharply contrasts with the showhorse style of Gingrich. Hastert's style also contrasts with that of the ideologically inclined occupants of the two other highest leadership positions: Armey, the House majority leader, and DeLay, the House majority whip. Described often as "decent," "fair," and "easygoing," Hastert—the "accidental Speaker"—has tended to take a minimalist, team approach to leadership. Initially many criticized him as a captive of the House majority whip, but Hastert has been successful both in working with Republican Party factions and in working toward bipartisanship with Democrats. His relationship with House Minority Leader Richard A. Gephardt (D-MO) is strained, but he works well with House Minority Whip David E. Bonior (D-MI) and other Democrats.

Hastert was reelected Speaker of the House in the 107th Congress, and one Democrat, Representative James A. Traficant Jr. of Ohio, broke ranks with his party to vote for Hastert. When the 107th Congress came into session on January 3, 2001, Hastert called on Democratic members of the House to come together and cooperate with him and the Republicans on Bush's agenda to improve education, upgrade Medicare, strengthen Social Security, build a missile defense system, and cut taxes. Despite all the talk of party unity, however, Hastert again clashed with House Minority Leader Gephardt when the two failed to agree on a bipartisan approach to election reform. In March 2001, Hastert went to Lithuania to receive the Medal of Order of Grand Duke Gediminas, First Class, which is given to individuals for distinguished service to Lithuania. Hastert emphasized his district's connections to Lithuania and accepted the award on behalf of the Lithuanian community of Illinois.

William E. Pederson

SEE ALSO: The Bush Presidency: The First Hundred Days; Tom DeLay; Newt Gingrich.

BIBLIOGRAPHY

Cohen, Richard E., and David Baumann. "Speaking Up for Hastert." *National Journal* (1999): 3298–303.

Eilperin, Juliet, and Michael Grunwald. " 'Coach' Rallies a Fictitious Team." *Washington Post*, July 23, 1999.

HENRY HYDE

Henry John Hyde was born in Chicago, Illinois, on April 18, 1924. During World War II, Hyde enlisted in the U.S. Navy. After attending training at Duke University and the University of Notre Dame in 1943–44, he was commissioned an ensign. He saw active duty in the South Pacific in New Guinea and the Philippines. He left active duty and entered the reserves in 1946. He retired from the reserves in 1968. Returning to civilian life, Hyde attended Georgetown University, where he received a bachelor of science degree in 1947. In 1949, he earned his law degree

Henry Hyde *(Government Printing Office)*

from the Loyola University School of Law in Chicago.

Admitted to the bar in 1950, Hyde entered private practice, specializing in litigation. In 1967, Hyde decided to enter the political arena and was elected to the Illinois House of Representatives. He served in the state legislature until 1974, including serving as majority leader from 1971 to 1972. In 1974, Hyde ran for a seat in the House of Representatives. He was victorious in that election and has served in the House ever since, developing a reputation as a skilled parliamentarian as well as a conservative legislator.

A staunch supporter of the pro-life position, Hyde sponsored the so-called Hyde Amendment that bars the use of federal funds for abortions. He also chaired the Republican Platform Committee in 1996 and prevented the party's pro-life plank from being watered down. In addition to his social conservatism, Hyde has been a fiscal watchdog, seeking to curb wasteful government expenditures.

During his tenure in Congress, Hyde has served on a number of investigative committees. In 1987, he was the ranking Republican member of the Iran-Contra Hearings. As chair of the House Judiciary Committee from 1995 to 2001, he oversaw the impeachment of President Bill Clinton in 1998 and led the prosecution of President Clinton before the Senate the following year.

After winning reelection in 2000, Hyde was forced to step down as chair of the Judiciary Committee because of a 1994 Republican rule limiting committee chairs to a term of six years. At first he considered appealing the rule in order to continue chairing the committee, but instead he was appointed to chair the International Relations Committee in 2001. As chair of International Relations, he criticized China's handling of a collision between an American surveillance plane and a Chinese fighter plane. When the United States was voted off the United Nations Human Rights Commission in 2001, Hyde cosponsored a bill that would withhold back dues owed the United Nations unless the United States was voted back onto the commission in 2002. The bill passed the House.

Jeffrey D. Schultz

SEE ALSO: Impeachment of President Clinton.

TRENT LOTT

Trent Lott was born on October 9, 1941, in Grenada County, Mississippi. His father was a sharecropper who worked his way through school to eventually become a teacher. Lott earned his bachelor of science degree in public administration in 1963 and his Juris Doctor in 1967 from the University of Mississippi. He began his political career in 1968 when he became the administrative assistant to Representative William Colmer (D-MS).

In 1972, Lott decided to enter the political fray directly by running for the House of Representatives as a Republican. He was elected to the House that year and subsequently reelected

Trent Lott (*Government Printing Office*)

through the 1986 election. In 1979 while in the House, Lott was elected chair of the House Republican Research Committee—the fifth highest post in the House leadership. The following year he was elected Republican whip, the number two post in the Republican leadership. Lott took pride in the fact that he was the first southerner ever to hold that position, to which he was reelected three times.

In 1988, Lott ran for the United States Senate. Winning that election, he served in the Senate Republican leadership as secretary of the Senate Republican Conference. Reelected in 1994, he was selected as Senate majority whip in 1995. With that election, Lott became the first legislator to be elected whip in both the House and the Senate. When Senate majority leader Robert Dole decided to leave the Senate to focus on his presidential campaign, Lott was elevated to majority leader on June 12, 1996. During the difficult period in the Senate of President Bill Clinton's impeachment trial, Lott tried to balance the demands of competing forces in an effort to bring the matter to a quick and just conclusion. Sometimes controversial—as with his negative comments on homosexuality and speaking before a white supremacist group—Lott is generally well liked by both Democrats and Republicans for his ability to manage the business of the Senate effectively.

Before the 2000 elections, Lott, along with conservative leaders in the House, led a standoff with President Clinton over budget issues and fueled intense bickering in the Senate along party lines. He was elected for a third term in 2000. Because the 107th Senate was divided evenly between Democrats and Republicans, Lott's job as majority leader was more difficult than it had been in past years. Because every vote was so critical, he had to keep his party in line and behind President George W. Bush's proposals, in addition to negotiating with the Democrats. To prevent all legislation from getting backed up in committees, he brokered a power-sharing deal with Democratic minority leader Tom Daschle, which gave each party equal representation on committees while maintaining Republican leadership.

Following Vermont senator James Jeffords's

switch from Republican to Independent in May 2001, Democrats gained control of the Senate, and Lott became minority leader. He also serves on the Commerce, Science and Transportation Committee, the Finance Committee, and the Rules Committee. As is his style, Lott has evoked some controversy in the 107th Congress. He dismissed the Senate parliamentarian because he did not like some of his rulings. He also came under fire for trying to kill the McCain-Feingold campaign finance reform through procedural delays. On the other hand, he has been a staunch supporter of President Bush, supporting most of his proposals. In particular, he was very involved in affirming the appointment of his friend and former colleague John Ashcroft as attorney general. He also defends Bush's campaign promise to allow oil exploration in the Arctic National Wildlife Refuge. He came under heavy criticism for failing to prevent Jeffords from leaving the party, and some Republicans talked of removing Lott from his leadership position.

Jeffrey D. Schultz

SEE ALSO: The Bush Presidency: The First Hundred Days; Dennis Hastert.

JOHN McCAIN

John Sidney McCain III was born in a naval hospital on August 29, 1936, in the Panama Canal Zone. Both McCain's father and grandfather were Annapolis-educated navy admirals, and McCain entered the U.S. Naval Academy after graduating from Episcopal High School in Alexandria, Virginia. At the academy, McCain continued the family tradition of doing poorly and graduated fifth from the bottom of the class. Also like his father and grandfather, however, McCain served his country well. After graduating in 1958, he was commissioned an ensign and became an aircraft carrier pilot. A lieutenant commander by the time the Vietnam War began, McCain was shot down on October 25, 1967, after completing his twenty-third bombing mission. He was captured and spent the next five years— two in solitary confinement—as a prisoner of war in the infamous "Hanoi Hilton." McCain re-

John McCain (*Government Printing Office*)

fused to be used as a propaganda tool by the North Vietnamese, who beat him severely as a result. In 1973, McCain was released and returned home after the longest incarceration of an American POW in U.S. history.

McCain remained in the navy for several more years and had his last tour of duty as navy liaison to the U.S. Senate. Moving to Arizona, McCain decided to run for the United States House of Representatives in 1982. In a crowded Republican primary, McCain won the party's nomination and the election in the fall. Reelected in 1984, McCain served only two terms in the House. In 1986, McCain decided to seek the seat of retiring senator Barry Goldwater. McCain won that election and was handily reelected in 1992 and 1998. In the 1998 election, McCain won nearly 70 percent of the vote.

A rising star in the party, McCain served as national security adviser for Robert Dole in 1996 and delivered the speech nominating him for president at the Republican National Convention. In the Senate, he has chaired the Commerce,

Science, and Transportation Committee and served on the Armed Services and Indian Affairs Committees. He has also maintained his early reputation as a maverick. Never quite satisfied following rules, he has won many admirers for his work in the Senate, but at the cost of wielding power within the legislative chamber's inner circle. He has often championed such populist causes as campaign finance reform, even though many in his own party do not agree with his solution. He is also a longtime supporter of electoral reform and a line-item veto to combat pork-barrel spending.

In 1999, McCain decided to take that same independence that he has shown throughout his life and seek the Republican Party presidential nomination. After an early victory in the New Hampshire primary in January 2000, McCain emerged as the main challenger to the better-funded frontrunner, Texas governor George W. Bush. During the lively campaign, McCain gained wide support among independent voters and crossover Democrats. Bush ultimately prevailed, and McCain endorsed and campaigned for him. McCain remains both a Republican maverick and an influential senator.

In 2001, McCain cosponsored a number of bills with Democrats and continued to irk his party's leadership. His greatest success was the Senate's passage of the McCain-Feingold Bill on campaign finance reform, the cause he was most closely associated with in his campaign for the presidential nomination. Most of the Republican Party leadership opposes the bill and has tried to block its passage. McCain has also cosponsored legislation to close the gun show background check loophole, ensure patients' rights, ban betting on college sports, improve airline accountability to passengers, and open the prescription drug business to more generic drug manufacturers.

Jeffrey D. Schultz

SEE ALSO: Campaign 2000 and the Florida Recount; The Bush Presidency: The First Hundred Days; Campaign Finance Reform.

BIBLIOGRAPHY
McCain, John. *Faith of My Fathers: A Family Memoir*. New York: HarperPerennial, 2000.

MITCH McCONNELL

Mitchell McConnell was born on February 20, 1942, in Sheffield, Alabama, and raised in South Louisville, Kentucky. A political animal by nature, McConnell served as his student body president in high school and at the University of Louisville, where he earned a bachelor's degree in 1964. He attended the University of Kentucky's College of Law where he was president of the student bar association, earning his J.D. in 1967. McConnell began his career in public service soon after he finished his formal education and served as chief legislative assistant to Senator Marlow Cook. During the administration of Gerald R. Ford, McConnell was deputy assistant attorney general from 1974 to 1975. From 1978 until his election to the Senate in 1984, he served as a county judge-executive in Jefferson County.

Reelected in 1990 and 1996, McConnell is one of the Senate's most influential and powerful members. He served two terms as chair of the

Mitch McConnell (*Government Printing Office*)

National Republican Senatorial Committee, a post in which he is responsible for developing and supporting the campaigns of Republican Senate candidates. Until Republicans lost control of the Senate in June 2001, he was chair of both the Senate Rules Committee, which has jurisdiction over federal election law and the administration of the Senate, and the Foreign Operations Appropriations Subcommittee. He is also a senior member of the Agriculture and Appropriations Committees and a member of the Judiciary Committee. His party honored him by naming him chair of the Joint Congressional Committee on Inaugural Ceremonies, which was in charge of George W. Bush's inauguration ceremony. McConnell was the emcee of the 2001 ceremony and escorted the president to various festivities throughout Inauguration Day.

McConnell has been the leading opponent of campaign finance reform. Long outspoken on the issue, during the Senate debate of the McCain-Feingold Bill on campaign finance reform in 2001, he reiterated his belief that the proposed reforms would kill the political parties and that they violated the First Amendment. In 2001, he cosponsored legislation for electoral reform that would give localities money to buy modern voting equipment and enforce stricter standards for fairness and accuracy in tallying votes. McConnell will be up for reelection in 2002. He is married to Secretary of Labor Elaine L. Chao.

Jeffrey D. Schultz

SEE ALSO: Campaign Finance Reform.

GEORGE PATAKI

George E. Pataki was born on June 24, 1945, in Peekskill, New York, on his family's farm, which he still runs with his family. A strong student, Pataki graduated from Yale University in 1967, where he attended on an academic scholarship. He earned another scholarship to attend Columbia University Law School, graduating in 1970. Pataki held a number of private and public sector jobs in the 1970s and 1980s. He served ten years in the New York State legislature and as mayor of Peekskill.

George Pataki (*Government Printing Office*)

In 1994, Pataki ran for governor of New York against three-term incumbent Mario Cuomo. Although relatively unknown, Pataki had powerful backers, including Senator Alphonse D'Amato, and won the election. A moderate to conservative politician, Pataki used his first term to enact many of his campaign promises, including restoration of the death penalty, reduction of personal income taxes, and the requirement that many welfare recipients work for their benefits. Throughout his first term, the reduction of taxes in the hopes of stimulating New York's economy was a recurring theme as Pataki worked to cut energy taxes, sales taxes, property taxes, and add-on estate taxes (which were eliminated); he also spearheaded the largest corporate tax cut in history. The result was a strong growth economy. Yet taxes were not the only issues he tackled. He also sought to toughen sentences on violent criminals and signed Jenna's Law, which ended parole for first-time violent felons. He also led the legislative movement for education reform that included charter schools.

On November 3, 1998, Pataki was reelected by a margin of more than 1 million votes—the largest landslide for a Republican governor in New York history. Since his reelection, Pataki has continued to pursue the policies that made his first term successful, including additional tax cuts and education reform. The state has enjoyed explosive job growth and has seen its welfare lists decline by 38 percent. Pataki has taken his conservative approach directly to state government by cutting the number of state employees and using some of the state's surplus to erase the $5 billion deficit in the "Rainy Day" fund for revenue shortfalls. He has also pursued legislation that would be tougher on violent crimes, such as the elimination of parole for all violent offenders. Further, in 2000, he passed the strictest gun control legislation in the country.

Pataki was very involved in the 2000 elections. He strongly supported George W. Bush in the presidential election and expended much effort campaigning on his behalf. He handpicked New York's Republican senatorial candidate, Rick Lazio, who ran and lost against Hillary Rodham Clinton. Pataki will likely run for a third term as New York governor in 2002. Given the state's strong Democratic showing in the 2000 elections, particularly among minority voters, he began appealing to black and Hispanic voters early in 2001. He proposed reforms of the state's strict mandatory drug sentencing laws to shorten the sentences for nonviolent drug offenders. He also visited Vieques, Puerto Rico, and spoke out against the United States Navy's use of the island for practice bombing missions.

Jeffrey D. Schultz

COLIN POWELL

Colin Luther Powell was born on April 5, 1937, in Harlem, New York. His parents were immigrants from Jamaica who had moved to the United States before his birth. Raised in the South Bronx, he attended public schools and graduated from Morris High School in 1954. He attended the City College of New York, where he earned a bachelor of science degree in geology in 1958. While at City College, Powell began his military career when he joined the Reserve Officers' Training Corps (ROTC). He excelled in his training, becoming the company commander of the Pershing Rifles and eventually the commander of the entire Army ROTC program at City College. Commissioned a second lieutenant, he went to Fort Benning, Georgia, for his basic training.

Shortly after his marriage in 1962, Powell was sent to South Vietnam as a military adviser. This would be the first of two tours of duty in Vietnam. In 1968, he returned as a battalion executive officer and was awarded the Purple Heart. Returning home, Powell graduated from George Washington University with an MBA in 1971. A year later, he earned a post as a White House Fellow. This brought the midcareer military officer in contact with the more political aspect of defense.

For much of the next fifteen years, Powell held a series of positions both inside and outside the military, including positions as executive assistant to the secretary of energy and military assistant to the secretary of defense during the

Colin Powell (*Department of State*)

administration of President Jimmy Carter. In 1981, he was selected by the administration of Ronald Reagan to serve as senior military assistant to Secretary of Defense Caspar Weinberger. In 1987, Powell was appointed National Security Adviser by President Reagan. In this position, he was responsible for advising the president on the national security aspects of policies including those on the environment, trade, defense, budget, and education.

In 1989, President George H. W. Bush appointed Powell chairman of the Joint Chiefs of Staff, the highest military post in the nation. In this position, he was a key adviser during the Persian Gulf War, and his leadership in this conflict thrust him into the national spotlight. Powell retired from the military in 1993. He remained active in politics, declaring he was a Republican in the tradition of former New York governor Nelson Rockefeller. He became the CEO of an organization seeking to create volunteer solutions to social problems. In his 1995 autobiography, *My American Journey*, Powell described himself as "a fiscal conservative with a social conscience." In 1996, many Republicans sought to draft Powell as the party's presidential candidate. He declined to run for office and did so again in 2000.

He endorsed Texas governor George W. Bush for president and was appointed secretary of state in 2001. The first African American to hold this position, Powell remains one of the most influential and more moderate members of the Bush administration.

At the 2000 Republican National Convention, Powell gave a speech on opening night that stressed candidate George W. Bush's theme of "compassionate conservatism" with assurances that a Bush presidency would be caring, moderate, and strong. Already an exceedingly popular figure in national polls, Powell attracted great attention with the speech, which covered education, race relations, and the growth of social and economic opportunity, particularly for minorities and underserved Americans. As secretary of state, Powell immediately focused efforts on increasing funds to build up the infrastructure of the State Department. A significant force in defining Bush's foreign policy,

Powell has been committed to maintaining a strong national defense and has supported Bush's plans for a national missile defense shield. In addition to playing a central role in several key foreign policy issues in 2001 regarding relations with China, Russia, and the Middle East, Powell made a weeklong trip to Africa in May, where he focused on the issues of fighting AIDS around the continent and bringing peace to the civil war–torn Sudan.

Richard A. Glenn

SEE ALSO: Campaign 2000 and the Florida Recount; Foreign Policy; Military.

BIBLIOGRAPHY

Berenson, Lawrence. *The Colin Powell Story*. New York: Random House, 1996.

Powell, Colin L., with Joseph E. Persico. *My American Journey*. New York: Random House, 1995.

Soble, Ronald L. *Colin Powell*. New York: New American Library, 1995.

J. C. WATTS

Julius Caesar Watts Jr. was born on November 18, 1957, the fifth of six children, to Buddy and Helen Watts. Raised in Eufaula, Oklahoma, Watts was a standout athlete at Eufaula High School and attended the University of Oklahoma, where he played quarterback for the Sooners. While earning his bachelor of arts degree in journalism, he led his team to back-to-back Big Eight Championships and Orange Bowl victories. After being selected as the most valuable player in the 1980 and 1981 Orange Bowls, Watts became a star quarterback in the Canadian Football League (CFL) and played until 1986. In his rookie season he was named the most valuable Player of the Grey Cup, the CFL's Super Bowl.

Watts determined that a career in professional football was not his calling. Returning to Oklahoma, he served as a youth minister at Sunnylane Baptist Church in Del City, Oklahoma, from January 1987 until December 1994, when he became associate pastor. He began his political career in 1990 when he was elected to the Oklahoma State Corporation Commission. In

J. C. Watts (*Government Printing Office*)

1994, he ran for the House of Representatives in Oklahoma's 4th Congressional District.

Watts won the election and rose to national attention with a passionate speech at the Republican National Convention. In this speech, Watts, an African American and social conservative, argued that the Republican Party was better equipped to handle the issues that faced minorities. Easily winning reelection, Watts was selected to give the Republican response to President Clinton's 1997 State of the Union Address, and has become a national spokesperson for the Republican Party on such critical issues as the need to balance the budget, tax relief, and education reform. Watts has also been an active and faithful proponent of cultural renewal and

stronger families. He introduced the Community Renewal Project, which attempts to reinvigorate and strengthen communities by encouraging investment and savings, offering school choice, and allowing citizens the option to use faith-based programs. The project was passed into law in 2000.

His leadership has been recognized by his colleagues, who selected him to serve in the House leadership as House Republican Conference chair, the fourth highest post. In addition, Watts serves on the Armed Services Committee and is a member of both the Military Readiness Subcommittee and the Procurement Subcommittee. He is a member as well of the Special Oversight Panel on Terrorism. Watts was recognized by the Junior Chamber of Commerce as one of Ten Outstanding Young Americans in 1996. He has also been commended by the Christian Coalition, which awarded him its Friend of the Family Award, and has served as a spokesperson for the Fellowship of Christian Athletes. He is on the Board of Representatives of the Fellowship of Christian Athletes in Oklahoma and a leader of the Orphan Foundation of America.

Watts has been at the forefront of President George W. Bush's proposal to open more federal grant money to religious organizations that provide social services. In 2001, he sponsored "charitable choice" legislation, which would allow federally funded faith-based organizations to hire only workers who adhere to their religious views and practices. He disagreed with Bush's tax cut proposal and sought a larger cut. Watts has also sponsored legislation to honor slaves who helped build the Capitol building and White House, and he has gained considerable support for establishing a National Museum of African American History and Culture on the National Mall.

Jeffrey D. Schultz

SEE ALSO: Tom DeLay; Dennis Hastert.

PART IV

MEMBERS OF CONGRESS

REPRESENTATIVES

ROBERT B. ADERHOLT, Representative, Fourth District, Alabama

Born: Haleyville, AL, July 22, 1965

Resides: Haleyville, AL

Education: Graduated, Birmingham Southern University; J.D., Cumberland School of Law, Samford University

Career: Attorney; assistant legal adviser to Governor Fob James, 1995–96

Civic Activities and Awards: George Bush delegate, Republican National Convention, 1992

State and Local Office: Haleyville municipal judge, 1992–96

Elected to Congress: Elected to the 105th Congress in November 1996; reelected in 1998, 2000

W. TODD AKIN, Representative, Second District, Missouri

Born: New York, NY, July 5, 1947

Resides: Town and Country, MO

Education: B.S., Worchester Polytechnic Institute, 1971; M.Div., Covenant Seminary, St. Louis, 1984

Military Service: U.S. Army Corps of Engineers

Career: IBM, Laclede Steel

Civic Activities and Awards: Bicentennial Commission of the U.S. Constitution, 1987; Boy Scouts of America; former board member, Missouri Right to Life; board member, The Mission Gate Prison Ministry

State and Local Office: Missouri State House of Representatives, 1988–2001

Elected to Congress: Elected to the 107th Congress in November 2000

BILL ARCHER, former Representative, Seventh District, Texas

Born: Houston, TX, March 22, 1928

Resides: Houston, TX

Education: St. Thomas High School, salutatorian, 1945; attended Rice University, 1945–46; University of Texas, B.B.A., LL.B. (with honors), 1946–51

Military Service: U.S. Air Force, 1951–53; captain, U.S. Air Force Reserve

Career: Attorney and businessman; president, Uncle Johnny Mills, Inc., 1953–61

Civic Activities and Awards: Member of St. Anne's Catholic Church; member, Sigma Alpha Epsilon fraternity; chosen Houston Sigma Alpha Epsilon Man of the Year; St. Thomas High School Alumnus Award; Houston B'nai B'rith Good Heart Award; member, Phi Delta Phi legal fraternity; life member, Houston Livestock Show and Rodeo; Guardian of Small Business Award, National Federation of Independent Business Watchdog of the Treasury Award; National Alliance of Senior Citizens Golden Age Hall of Fame Award; president, Texas State Society of Washington, DC, 1974–75; Spring Branch–Memorial Chamber of Commerce Most Representative Citizen Award; Brotherhood Award, National Conference of Christians and Jews; University of

Rep. Bill Archer (*Government Printing Office*)

89

Texas 1981 Distinguished Alumnus Award; member, White House Commission on Regulatory Reform, 1975–76; chair, National Republican Study Committee Task Force on Regulatory Reform, 1975–76; member, National Commission on Social Security Reform, 1982–83; member, Republican Leadership's Task Force on Health, 1992–93; chair, Leader's Economic Task Force, 1993; Free Congress Foundation's Sound Dollar Award, 1994; Golden Bulldog Award, Watchdog of the Treasury; Jefferson Award, Citizens for a Sound Economy, 1994; National Association of Private Enterprise Entrepreneurs Perfect Partner Award, 1993; American Society of Association Executives, Beacon Award, 1992; American Business Council of the Gulf Counties, Open Door to the Middle East Award, 1993

State and Local Office: Councilman and mayor pro tempore, city of Hunters Creek Village, 1955–62; elected to Texas House of Representatives, 1966; reelected, 1968

Elected to Congress: Elected to the 92nd Congress in November 1970; reelected to each succeeding Congress through 2001; was not a candidate for reelection in 2000

DICK ARMEY, Representative, Twenty-Sixth District, Texas

Born: Cando, ND, July 7, 1940

Resides: Cooper Canyon, TX

Education: Cando High School, 1958; B.A., Jamestown College, ND, 1963; M.A., University of North Dakota, Grand Forks, 1964; Ph.D., University of Oklahoma, Norman, 1969

Career: Faculty, economics, University of Montana, 1964–65; assistant professor, West Texas State University, 1967–68; assistant professor, Austin College, 1968–72; associate professor, North Texas State University, 1972–77; chair, Department of Economics, North Texas State University, 1977–83; economics consultant and adviser; Distinguished Fellow of the Fisher Institute, Dallas, TX

Civic Activities and Awards: Omicron Delta Epsilon, economics honor society; Southwestern Social Sciences Association; Missouri Valley

Rep. Dick Armey *(Government Printing Office)*

Economics Association; former deacon, Presbyterian Church

Elected to Congress: Elected to the 99th Congress in November 1984; reelected to each succeeding Congress

SPENCER BACHUS, Representative, Sixth District, Alabama

Born: Birmingham, AL, December 28, 1947

Resides: Birmingham, AL

Education: B.A., Auburn University, 1969; J.D., University of Alabama, 1972

Career: Law firm, Bachus, Dempsey, Carson, and Steed, senior partner; practicing attorney, 1972–92

Civic Activities and Awards: Hunter Street Baptist Church; Republican Party chair, 1991–92; Guardian of Small Business Award; Watchdog of the Treasury Award; U.S. Chamber of Commerce, Spirit of Free Enterprise Award

State and Local Office: Alabama state representative, senator; school board

Elected to Congress: Elected to the 103rd Congress in November 1992; reelected to each succeeding Congress

RICHARD H. BAKER, Representative, Sixth District, Louisiana

Born: New Orleans, LA, May 22, 1948

Resides: Baton Rouge, LA

Education: University High School; B.A., Louisiana State University, Baton Rouge, 1971

Career: Real estate broker

Civic Activities and Awards: Member, Southern Legislative Conference, ALEC, Central Area Homebuilders, East Baton Rouge Airport Commission, Baton Rouge Masonic Lodge no. 372, Central Region Planning Commission; member, Blackwater Methodist Church

State and Local Office: Louisiana House of Representatives, 1972–86; chair, Committee on Transportation, Highways, and Public Works, 1980–86

Elected to Congress: Elected to the 100th Congress in November 1986; reelected to each succeeding Congress

CASS BALLENGER, Representative, Tenth District, North Carolina

Born: Hickory, NC, December 6, 1926

Resides: Hickory, NC

Education: Episcopal High School, 1944; attended University of North Carolina, Chapel Hill, 1944–45; B.A., Amherst College, 1948

Military Service: U.S. Naval Air Corps, aviation cadet, 1944–45

Career: Founder and president, Plastic Packaging, Inc., Hickory, NC, 1957–present

Civic Activities and Awards: Advisory Budget Commission, White House Advisory Committee, Community Ridge Day Care Center, Hickory Rotary Club, Hickory United Fund, Lenoir-Rhyne College Board of Development, Salvation Army Board of Directors, Florence Crittenton Home Board of Directors, Greater Hickory Chamber of Commerce (past director); sustaining member, North Carolina School of the Arts; patron, North

Carolina Symphony, North Carolina Arts Society

State and Local Office: North Carolina House of Representatives, 1974–76; North Carolina Senate, 1976–86; member, Catawba County Board of Commissioners (1966–74; chair, 1970–74)

Elected to Congress: Elected to the 99th Congress in November 1986, to complete the unexpired term of James Broyhill; deputy whip, 105th Congress; reelected to each succeeding Congress

BOB BARR, Representative, Seventh District, Georgia

Born: Iowa City, IA, November 5, 1948

Resides: Smyrna, GA

Education: Community High School (Teheran, Iran), 1966; B.A., University of Southern California, 1970; M.A., international affairs, George Washington University, 1972; J.D., Georgetown University, 1977

Career: Member of the Georgia and Florida bars; director, Southeastern Legal Foundation, 1990–92; private practice, 1978–86 and 1991–94; appointed U.S. attorney for the Northern District of Georgia, 1986–90; Central Intelligence Agency, 1971–78

Civic Activities and Awards: Member, Kiwanis, National Rifle Association, National Federation of Independent Business, Chamber of Commerce; attends Wesleyan Fellowship Church

Elected to Congress: Elected to the 104th Congress in November 1994; reelected to each succeeding Congress

WILLIAM E. (BILL) BARRETT, former Representative, Third District, Nebraska

Born: Lexington, NE, February 9, 1929

Resides: Lexington, NE

Education: Lexington High School; B.A., Hastings College, 1951; classes at universities of Connecticut, Nebraska, and Colorado

Military Service: U.S. Navy, 1951–52

Career: In real estate and insurance since 1956; president, Barrett-Housel and Associates, 1970–90

Civic Activities and Awards: Named Legislator of the Year by the National Republican Legislature

Association, 1990; named one of the five most influential state legislators by the *Lincoln Star*, 1988; Lexington School Board, 1962–68; Lexington Planning Commission; Lexington Airport Authority; Greater Lexington Development Corporation; Nebraska Association of Insurance Agents; National Association of Insurance Agents; past president, Dawson County Board of Realtors; past treasurer, Nebraska Realtors Association; Realtors National Marketing Institute; American Institute of Real Estate Appraisers; National Association of Realtors; National Association of Realtors' honorary fraternity, Omega Tau Rho; certified instructor, Nebraska Real Estate Commission; member: Nebraska Jaycees (past president); Lexington Rotary Club (past president); American Legion; elder, Presbyterian Church; trustee, Hastings College; served on the Republican State Executive Committee, 1964–66, 1973–79; chair, Nebraska Republican Party, 1973–75; Nebraska chair, president, Ford Committee, 1975–76; Republican National Committee, 1973–75

State and Local Office: Appointed to Nebraska legislature in 1979; elected to Nebraska legislature in 1980, 1984, 1988; elected speaker of the Nebraska legislature, 1987–90

Elected to Congress: Elected to the 102nd Congress in November 1990; reelected to each succeeding Congress through 2001; was not a candidate for reelection in 2000

ROSCOE G. BARTLETT, Representative, Sixth District, Maryland

Born: Moreland, KY, June 3, 1926

Resides: Frederick, MD

Education: B.A., Columbia Union College, 1947; University of Maryland, Ph.D., 1952

Career: Retired professor; engineer

Civic Activities and Awards: 1999 Jeffries Aerospace Medicine and Life Sciences Research Award from the American Institute of Aeronautics and Astronautics

Elected to Congress: Elected to the 103rd Congress in November 1992; reelected to each succeeding Congress

JOE L. BARTON, Representative, Sixth District, Texas

Born: Waco, TX, September 15, 1949

Resides: Ennis, TX

Education: Waco High School, 1968; B.S., industrial engineering, Texas A&M University, 1972; M.S., industrial administration, Purdue University, 1973

Career: Plant manager, assistant to the vice president, Ennis Business Forms, 1973–81; awarded White House Fellowship, 1981–82; served as aide to James B. Edwards, secretary, Department of Energy; member, Natural Gas Decontrol Task Force in the Office of Planning, Policy and Analysis; worked with the Department of Energy task force in support of the President's Private Sector Survey on Cost Control; natural gas decontrol and project cost control consultant, Atlantic Richfield Company

Civic Activities and Awards: Cofounder, Houston County Volunteer Ambulance Service, 1976; vice president, Houston County Industrial Development Authority, 1980; chair, Crockett Parks and Recreation Board, 1979–80; vice president, Houston County Chamber of Commerce, 1977–80; member, Dallas Energy Forum; Methodist

Elected to Congress: Elected to the 99th Congress in November 1984; reelected to each succeeding Congress

CHARLES BASS, Representative, Second District, New Hampshire

Born: Boston, MA, January 8, 1952

Resides: Peterborough, NH

Education: Holderness School, 1970; B.A., Dartmouth College, 1974

Career: Chief of Staff, Representative David Emery (Maine), 1976–79; vice president, High Standard, 1980–94; chair, Columbia Architectural Products, 1984–94

Civic Activities and Awards: Member, Monadnock Rotary Club (president, 1992–93), Anoskeag Veterans, Altemont Lodge, FA&M; trustee, New Hampshire Higher Education Assistance Foundation, Monadnock Conservancy, New Hampshire Humanities Council

State and Local Office: New Hampshire state representative, 1982–88; vice chair, Judiciary Committee; New Hampshire State Senate, 1988–92; chair, Public Affairs and Ethics committees, cochair, Economic Development Committee

Elected to Congress: Elected to the 104th Congress in November 1994; reelected to each succeeding Congress

HERBERT H. BATEMAN, former Representative, First District, Virginia

Born: Elizabeth City, NC, August 7, 1928

Education: College of William and Mary, B.A., 1949; Georgetown University Law Center, J.D., 1956

Military Service: U.S. Air Force, discharged as first lieutenant, 1953

Career: Attorney; teacher at Hampton High School, 1949–51; law clerk for Judge Walter M. Bastian, U.S. Court of Appeals, District of Columbia Circuit, 1956–57; general legal counsel, U.S. Jaycees, 1964–65

Civic Activities and Awards: Member, Joint Legislative Audit and Review Commission; member, Coal and Energy Study Commission, 1979–82; chair, Consumer Credit Study Committee, 1970–74; member, Study of Virginia Milk Commission, 1972–74; board of commissioners, Peninsula Ports Authority of Virginia, 1968–73; chair, Peninsula Arena-Auditorium Authority; board of directors, Peninsula Economic Development Council; member, past president, Virginia Jaycees; board of directors, Newport News Chapter, American Red Cross; president and campaign chair, Peninsula United Fund; Braxton-Perkins Post, American Legion; Omicron Delta Kappa; Phi Delta Phi; Pi Kappa Alpha; American Judicature Society

State and Local Office: Elected to the Virginia State Senate in 1967, reelected 1971, 1975, and 1979; committee assignments in finance, courts of justice, transportation, and rehabilitation and social services; former member and chair, agriculture, conservation and natural resources committees

Elected to Congress: Elected to the 98th Congress in November 1982; reelected to each succeeding Congress and served until his death on September 11, 2000

DOUG BEREUTER, Representative, First District, Nebraska

Born: York, NE, October 6, 1939

Resides: Cedar Bluffs, NE

Education: Utica High School, 1957; B.A., University of Nebraska, Lincoln, 1961; Sigma Alpha Epsilon; M.C.P., Harvard University, 1966; M.P.A., Harvard University, 1973

Military Service: Counterintelligence officer, First Infantry Division, U.S. Army, 1963–65

Career: Urban development consultant in states surrounding Nebraska; associate professor at University of Nebraska and Kansas State University; visiting lecturer, Harvard University; division director, Nebraska Department of Economic Development, 1967–68; director, State Office of Planning and Programming, 1968–70; appointee, Federal-State Relations Coordinator for Nebraska State Government, 1967–70

Civic Activities and Awards: Legislative Conservationist of the Year Award by the Nebraska and National Wildlife Federation in 1980; member: State Crime Commission, 1969–71; Phi Beta Kappa; Sigma Xi; board of trustees, Nebraska Wesleyan University

State and Local Office: State senator, Nebraska legislature, 1974–78; vice chair, Appropriations Committee and Committee on Administrative Rules and Regulations, 1977–78; chair, the Urban Development Committee of the National Conference of State Legislatures, 1977–78; member, Select Committee on Post-Secondary Education Coordination, 1977–78

Elected to Congress: Elected to the 96th Congress in November 1978; reelected to each succeeding Congress

JUDY BIGGERT, Representative, Thirteenth District, Illinois

Born: Chicago, IL, August 15, 1937

Resides: Hinsdale, IL

Education: New Trier High School, 1955; B.A., Stanford University, 1959; J.D., Northwestern University School of Law, 1963

Career: Attorney, 1975–98

State and Local Office: Illinois House of Representatives, 81st District, 1992–98; Assistant House Republican Leader, 1995–98

Elected to Congress: Elected to the 106th Congress in November 1998; reelected in 2000

BRIAN BILBRAY, former Representative, Forty-Ninth District, California

Born: Coronado, CA, January 28, 1951

Resides: Imperial Beach, CA

Education: Mar Vista High School; attended South Western College, 1972

Career: Tax consultant; city council, Imperial Beach, CA, 1976–78

Civic Activities and Awards: Member, Fleet Reserve Association

State and Local Office: Mayor, Imperial Beach, 1978–85; San Diego County Board of Supervisors, 1985–95

Elected to Congress: Elected to the 104th Congress in November 1994; reelected to each succeeding Congress through 2000; was an unsuccessful candidate for reelection in 2000

MICHAEL BILIRAKIS, Representative, Ninth District, Florida

Born: Tarpon Springs, FL, July 16, 1930

Resides: Palm Harbor, FL

Education: B.S. in engineering, University of Pittsburgh, 1955–59; accounting, George Washington University, Washington, DC, 1959–60; J.D., University of Florida, 1961–63

Military Service: U.S. Air Force, 1951–55

Career: Attorney and small businessman, petroleum engineer, aerospace contract administrator, geophysical engineer (offshore oil exploration), steelworker, and judge of various courts for eight years

Civic Activities and Awards: Phi Alpha Delta Annual Award for Outstanding Law Graduate; president of the student body of School of Engineering and Mines; Citizen of the Year Award for Greater Tarpon Springs, 1972–73; founder and charter president of Tarpon Springs Volunteer Ambulance Service; past president and four-year director of Greater Tarpon Springs Chamber of Commerce; past president, Rotary Club of Tarpon Springs; board of governors, Pinellas Suncoast Chamber of Commerce; board of development, Anclote Manor Psychiatric Hospital, AHEPA; elected commander, Post 173 American Legion, Holiday, FL (1977–79, two terms); 33rd degree Mason and Shriner; member, West Pasco Bar Association, American Judicature Society, Florida and American Bar Associations, University of Florida Law Center Association, Gator Boosters, American Legion, Veterans of Foreign Wars; member, Juvenile Diabetes Association, Elks, Eastern Star and White Shrine of Jerusalem, Royaler of Jesters of Egypt Temple Shrine District, Air Force Association; former member, Clearwater Bar Association, National Contract Management Association, American Society of Mining, Metallurgical and Petroleum Engineers, and Creative Education Foundation

Elected to Congress: Elected to the 98th Congress in November 1982; reelected to each succeeding Congress

TOM J. BLILEY, former Representative, Seventh District, Virginia

Born: Chesterfield County, January 28, 1932

Resides: Richmond, VA

Education: Benedictine High School, 1948; B.A., history, Georgetown University, 1952

Military Service: U.S. Navy, 1952–65, left active duty with the rank of lieutenant

Career: President, Joseph W. Bliley Funeral Homes, 1955–80

Civic Activities and Awards: Former board member, National League of Cities; past president, Virginia Municipal League; former board member, Metropolitan Richmond Chamber of Commerce; board member, Central Richmond Association; Virginia Home for Boys, board of governors; former board member, Cripples Children's Hospital; former member, board of visitors, Virginia Commonwealth University; former board member, Southern Bank and Trust Company; Richmond Rotary Club

State and Local Office: Elected to Richmond City Council, 1968; appointed vice mayor, 1968; reelected to council and appointed mayor, 1970–77

Elected to Congress: Elected to the 97th Congress in November 1980; reelected to each succeeding Congress through 2000; was not a candidate for reelection in 2000

ROY D. BLUNT, Representative, Seventh District, Missouri

Born: Niangua, MO, January 10, 1950

Resides: Strafford, MO

Education: B.A., 1970, Southwest Baptist University; M.A., 1972, Southwest Missouri State University

Career: Missouri secretary of state, 1984–93; president, Southwest Baptist University, 1993–96; author

Civic Activities and Awards: Past chair, Missouri Housing Development Commission and Governor's Council on Literacy; past cochair, Missouri Opportunity 2000 Commission; past member, Project Democracy Commission for Voter Participation in the United States; past board member, American Council of Young Political Leaders; served as first chair of the Missouri Prison Fellowship; named one of the Ten Outstanding Young Americans, 1986

Elected to Congress: Elected to the 105th Congress in November 1996

SHERWOOD L. BOEHLERT, Representative, Twenty-Third District, New York

Born: Utica, NY, September 28, 1936

Resides: New Hartford, NY

Education: Whitesboro Central High School; B.A., Utica College, 1961

Military Service: U.S. Army, 1956–58

Career: Wyandotte Chemicals Corporation, 1961–64; 1964–72, chief of staff for Congressman Alexander Pirnie; 1964–72, chief of staff for Congressman Donald J. Mitchell, 1973–79

Civic Activities and Awards: Past president, Administrative Assistants Association, U.S. House of Representatives; board of directors, Utica College Foundation; St. John the Evangelist Church, New Hartford; Distinguished Service Award, New York Air Force Association; honorary doctoral degree, Utica College of Syracuse University; Federal 100, Readers' Choice Award, *Federal Computer Week* magazine; Environmental Leadership Award, League of Conservation Voters of America; Sierra Club's Edgar Wayburn Award

State and Local Office: Oneida County executive, 1978–82

Elected to Congress: Elected to the 98th Congress in November 1982; reelected to each succeeding Congress

JOHN A. BOEHNER, Representative, Eighth District, Ohio

Born: Cincinnati, OH, November 17, 1949

Resides: West Chester, OH

Education: Moeller High School, 1968; B.S., Xavier University, 1977

Career: President, Nucite Sales, 1976–90

Civic Activities and Awards: Member, St. John Catholic Church, Ohio Farm Bureau, Lakota Hills Homeowners Association, Knights of Columbus; Union Chamber of Commerce, American Heart Association Board, Butler County Mental Health Association, YMCA Capital Campaign (cochair), Union Elementary School PTA, Middletown Chamber of Commerce, American Legion Post 218 of Middletown, Butler County Trustees and Clerks Association

State and Local Office: Ohio House of Representatives, 1984–90; ranking Republican member, Commerce and Labor Committee; Energy and Environment Committee; Judiciary and Criminal Justice Committee; elected, Union Township trustee, 1981; president, Union Township Board of Trustees, 1984

Elected to Congress: Elected to the 102nd Congress in November 1990; reelected to each succeeding Congress

HENRY BONILLA, Representative, Twenty-Third District, Texas

Born: San Antonio, TX, January 2, 1954

Resides: San Antonio, TX

Education: South San Antonio High School, 1972; B.J., University of Texas, Austin, 1976

Career: Executive news producer, KENS-TV, 1986–89; executive producer for public affairs, KENS-TV, San Antonio, 1989–92

Civic Activities and Awards: U.S. Chamber of Commerce's Spirit of Enterprise Award, 1996–99; National Federation of Independent Business, Guardian of Small Business Award, 1994, 1996; League of Private Property Owners, Champion of Private Property Rights Award, 1994; Watchdogs of the Treasury, Golden Bulldog Award, 1995–98; U.S. Hispanic Chamber of Commerce, President's Award, 1994; American Heart Association of Texas, Legislator of the Year, 1994; Vocational Home Economics Teachers Association of Texas, Golden Flame Award, 1994; Hispanic Heritage Conference Eagle Award, 1993; University of Texas Ex-Students Association, Outstanding Young Texas Executives Award, 1993; San Antonio Hispanic Chamber of Commerce, Corporate Community Service Award, 1990; San Antonio Hispanic Chamber of Commerce, Leadership Award, 1989

Elected to Congress: Elected to the 103rd Congress in November 1992; reelected to each succeeding Congress

MARY BONO, Representative, Forty-Fourth District, California

Born: Cleveland, OH, October 24, 1961

Resides: Palm Springs, CA

Education: Bachelor of Fine Arts, art history, University of Southern California, 1984

Civic Activities and Awards: San Gorgonio Chapter of the Girl Scouts of America, Woman of the Year 1993; board member: Palm Springs International Film Festival; first lady of Palm Springs and active in a wide range of community charities and service organizations; leadership role in support of the D.A.R.E. program, Olive Crest Home for Abused Children, Tiempos de Los Ninos

Elected to Congress: Elected to the 105th Congress on April 7, 1998, to fill the vacancy caused by the death of her husband, Sonny Bono; reelected in 1998, 2000

KEVIN BRADY, Representative, Eighth District, Texas

Born: Vermillion, SD, April 11, 1955

Resides: The Woodlands, TX

Education: B.S., business, University of South Dakota, 1990

Career: Executive, Woodlands Chamber of Commerce, 1978–96

Civic Activities and Awards: Achievement Award, Texas Conservative Coalition; Outstanding Young Texan (one of five), Texas Jaycees; Ten Best Legislators for Families and Children, State Bar of Texas; Legislative Standout, *Dallas Morning News*; Scholars Achievement Award for Excellence in Public Service, North Harris Montgomery Community College District; Victims Rights Equalizer Award, Texans for Equal Justice Center; Support for Family Issues Award, Texas Extension Homemakers Association; chair, Council of Chambers of Greater Houston; president, East Texas Chamber Executive Association; president, South Montgomery County Woodlands Chamber of Commerce, 1985–present; director, Texas Chamber of Commerce Executives; Rotarian; attends St. Simon and Jude Catholic Church

State and Local Office: Served in Texas House of Representatives, 1991–96

Elected to Congress: Elected to the 105th Congress in November 1996, reelected 1998, 2000

HENRY E. BROWN JR., Representative, First District, South Carolina

Born: Bishopville, SC, December 20, 1935

Resides: Hanahan, SC

Education: Attended Baptist College (The Citadel)

Military Service: South Carolina National Guard

Career: Vice president, Piggly Wiggly Carolina Co.

Civic Activities and Awards: The South Carolina Chamber Servant of the Year Award, 1995; Independent Colleges of South Carolina and the South Carolina College Legislators Legislator of the Year Award, 1995; Director Award, South Carolina Department of Revenue; South Carolina Taxpayers Watchdog, South Carolina Treasurer's Office; Guardian of Small Business Award, South Carolina Chapter, NFIB, 1996; South Carolina School Board Association's Outstanding Legislator Award, 1997; the South Carolina Association of Realtors' South Carolina Legislator of the Year Award, 1997; honorary degree of Doctor of Business Administration, The Citadel, 1998; the South Carolina Association of School Librarians Legislator of the Year Award, 1998–99; Legislator of the Year Award, National Republican Legislators Association, 1999; Legislator of the Year Award, South Carolina Vocational Directors Association, 1999; Order of the Palmetto, 2000; member, Cooper River Baptist Church; member, Hammerton Lodge no. 332 A.F.M.; member, North Charleston Rotary Club; past director, Crime Stoppers; past director, Berkeley Chamber of Commerce.

State and Local Office: Hanahan City Council, 1981–85; Hanahan Planning Commission; South Carolina House of Representatives, 1985–2000

Elected to Congress: Elected to the 107th Congress in November 2000

EDWARD BRYANT, Representative, Seventh District, Tennessee

Born: Jackson, TN, September 7, 1948

Resides: Henderson, TN

Education: Jackson High School; B.A., 1970, and J.D., 1972, University of Mississippi

Military Service: Army officer, ROTC in the Military Intelligence Branch, 1970; captain, Judge Advocate Generals Corps

Career: Teacher, U.S. Military Academy, West Point, NY, 1977–78; practicing attorney, 1978–90; U.S. attorney for the Western District of Tennessee, 1991–93; led an office of 29 attorneys who prosecuted Tennessee's largest mass murder case; ranked among the top nationally in the prosecution of violent criminals; one of the first to establish a task force to investigate abuse and fraud in the healthcare system

Civic Activities and Awards: Vice president, Sigma Nu; member, military honorary society and leadership society; president, Madison County Bar Association; board member of Rotary, Little League, Fellowship of Christian Athletes; member, Tennessee Farm Bureau

Elected to Congress: Elected to the 104th Congress in November 1994; reelected to each succeeding Congress

RICHARD BURR, Representative, Fifth District, North Carolina

Born: Charlottesville, VA, November 30, 1955

Resides: Winston-Salem, NC

Education: Reynolds High School, 1974; B.A., communications, Wake Forest University, 1978

Career: National sales manager, Carswell Distributing, 1978–94

Civic Activities and Awards: Member, Reynolds Rotary Club; cochair, North Carolina Taxpayers United, National Policy Forum Council on Economic Growth and Workplace Opportunity; cochair, Partnership for a Drug-Free North Carolina

Elected to Congress: Elected to the 104th Congress in November 1994; reelected to each succeeding Congress

DAN BURTON, Representative, Sixth District, Indiana

Born: Indianapolis, IN, June 21, 1938

Resides: Indianapolis, IN

Education: Shortridge High School, 1956; Indiana University, 1958–59; Cincinnati Bible Seminary, 1959–60

Military Service: U.S. Army, 1957–58; U.S. Army Reserves, 1958–62

Career: Insurance and real estate firm owner since 1968

Civic Activities and Awards: President, Volunteers of America, Indiana Christian Benevolent Association, Committee for Constitutional Government, Family Support Center; member, Jaycees; 33rd degree Mason, Scottish rite division; eleven Golden Bulldog awards from the Watchdogs of the Treasury; ten Taxpayers' Friend awards from the National Taxpayers Union; six Guardian of

Small Business awards from the National Federation of Independent Business; thirteen Spirit of Enterprise awards from the U.S. Chamber of Commerce

State and Local Office: Indiana House of Representatives, 1967–68, 1977–80; Indiana State Senate, 1969–70, 1981–82

Elected to Congress: Elected to the 98th Congress in November 1982; reelected to each succeeding Congress

STEVE BUYER, Representative, Fifth District, Indiana

Born: Rensselaer, IN, November 26, 1958

Resides: Monticello, IN

Education: North White High School, 1976; B.S., business administration, The Citadel, 1980; J.D., Valparaiso University School of Law, 1984

Military Service: U.S. Army Reserve, 1980–present; U.S. Army Judge Advocate General's Corps, 1984–87; major; legal counsel for the 22nd Theater Army in Operations Desert Shield and Desert Storm

Career: Deputy attorney general of Indiana, 1987–88; White County Republican Party, 1988–90; admitted to the Virginia and Indiana bars; family law practice, 1988–92

Elected to Congress: Elected to the 103rd Congress in November 1992; reelected to each succeeding Congress

SONNY CALLAHAN, Representative, First District, Alabama

Born: Mobile, AL, September 11, 1932

Resides: Mobile, AL

Education: McGill Institute (high school), 1950; University of Alabama, Mobile (night school), 1959–60

Military Service: U.S. Navy, seaman, 1952–54

Career: Businessman, Finch Companies, 1955–85; president, 1964–85

Civic Activities and Awards: Member, Mobile Area Chamber of Commerce

State and Local Office: Alabama House of Representatives, 1970–78; Alabama State Senate, 1978–82

Elected to Congress: Elected to the 99th Congress in November 1984; reelected to each succeeding Congress

KEN CALVERT, Representative, Forty-Third District, California

Born: Corona, CA, June 8, 1953

Resides: Corona, CA

Education: Chaffey College, A.A., 1973; San Diego State University, B.A. in economics, 1975

Career: Congressional aide to Rep. Victor V. Veysey, CA; general manager, Jolly Fox Restaurant, 1975–79; Marcus W. Meairs Co., 1979–81; president and general manager, Ken Calvert Real Properties, 1981–92; Riverside County Republican Party, 1984–88

Civic Activities and Awards: County youth chairman, Rep. Veysey's district, 1970, then 43rd District, 1972; Corona/Norco Youth Chairman for Nixon, 1968 and 1972; Reagan-Bush campaign worker, 1980; cochair, Wilson for Senate Campaign, 1982; Riverside Republican Party, chair, 1984–88; cochair, George Deukmejian election, 1978, 1982 and 1986; cochair, George Bush election, 1988; cochair, Pete Wilson Senate elections, 1982 and 1988; cochair, Pete Wilson for Governor election, 1990; Riverside County Republican Winners Circle, charter member; Corona/Norco Republican Assembly, former vice president; Lincoln Club of Riverside County, chair and charter member, 1986–90; Corona Rotary Club, president, 1991; Corona Elks; Navy League of Corona/Norco; Corona Chamber of Commerce, president, 1990; Norco Chamber of Commerce; County of Riverside Asset Leasing, chair; Corona/Norco Board of Realtors; Monday Morning Group; Corona Group, past chair; Economic Development Partnership, executive board; Corona Community Hospital Corporate 200 Club; Silver Eagles (March AFB Support Group), charter member; Corona Airport Advisory Commission

Elected to Congress: Elected to the 103rd Congress in November 1992; reelected to each succeeding Congress

DAVE CAMP, Representative, Fourth District, Michigan

Born: Midland, MI, July 9, 1953

Resides: Midland, MI

Education: Midland Dow High School, 1971; B.A., Albion College, 1975, magna cum laude; J.D., University of California at San Diego, 1978

Career: Attorney, member of state bar of Michigan, state bar of California, District of Columbia bar, U.S. Supreme Court bar; U.S. District Court bar (Eastern District of Michigan and Southern District of California), Midland County Bar Association; law practice, Midland, 1978–90; special assistant attorney general, 1980–84; administrative assistant to Congressman Bill Schuette, Michigan's 10th Congressional District, 1984–87

Civic Activities and Awards: Former president of Young Business People's Group; former member, Michigan's 10th Congressional District Republican Executive Committee; member, Midland County Republican Executive Committee

State and Local Office: State representative, Michigan's 102nd District, 1989–90

Elected to Congress: Elected to the 102nd Congress in November 1990; reelected to each succeeding Congress

TOM CAMPBELL, former Representative, Fifteenth District, California

Born: Chicago, IL, August 14, 1952

Resides: Campbell, CA

Education: B.A., M.A. (awarded simultaneously), economics, University of Chicago, 1973; J.D., magna cum laude, Harvard Law School, 1976, and editor of *Harvard Law Review;* Ph.D., economics, University of Chicago, 1980 (Lilly Fellowship)

Career: Admitted to the Illinois and District of Columbia bars in 1976; U.S. Supreme Court clerk, Justice Byron White, 1977–78; attorney in private practice, 1978–80; law professor, Stanford University (tenured, 1987); executive assistant to deputy U.S. attorney general, 1981; director, Bureau of Competition, Federal Trade Commission, 1981–83

Civic Activities and Awards: White House Fellow, 1980–81; member, White House Task Force on Women, 1981; term member, Council on Foreign Relations, 1981–86; member, San Francisco

Council on Foreign Relations, 1983–88; Chicago Council on Foreign Relations, 1978–80; council member, American Bar Association, 1983–88; rated single most fiscally responsible member of Congress by the National Taxpayers Union, 1992

State and Local Office: California State Senate, 1993–95

Elected to Congress: Elected to the 101st Congress in November 1988; reelected in 1990; was not a candidate for reelection in 1992, but was an unsuccessful candidate for election to the U.S. Senate; elected to the 104th Congress on December 12, 1995, by special election, to fill the vacancy caused by the resignation of Norman Mineta; reelected in 1996, 1998; was not a candidate for reelection in 2000, but was an unsuccessful candidate for election to the U.S. Senate

CHARLES T. CANADY, former Representative, Twelfth District, Florida

Born: Lakeland, FL, June 22, 1954

Resides: Lakeland, FL

Education: Lakeland High School; B.A., Haverford College, 1976; J.D., Yale Law School, 1979

Career: Practicing attorney, Lakeland, 1979–92

Civic Activities and Awards: Recipient, President's Award, Florida Public Library Association, 1988; Crime Fighters Award, Florida Department of Law Enforcement, 1989; board member, Volunteers in Service to the Elderly, Carenet, HUG (home for unwed mothers), Community Council on Substance Abuse, United Cerebral Palsy; member, Boy Scout Advisory Council

State and Local Office: Member, Florida House of Representatives, 1984–90

Elected to Congress: Elected to the 103rd Congress in November 1992; reelected to each succeeding Congress through 2001; was not a candidate for reelection in 2000

CHRISTOPHER B. CANNON, Representative, Third District, Utah

Born: Salt Lake City, UT, October 20, 1950

Resides: Mapleton, UT

Education: B.S., university studies, Brigham Young University, 1974; graduate work at Harvard School of Business, 1974–75; J.D., Brigham Young University, 1980

Career: Admitted to the Utah bar in 1980 and began practice in Provo, UT; attorney, Robinson, Seiler and Glazier; associate solicitor (1984–86) and deputy associate solicitor (1983–84), Department of the Interior; cofounder, Geneva Steel, Provo, 1987–90; founder, Cannon Industries, Salt Lake City; president and subsequently chair of Cannon Industries, Salt Lake City

Civic Activities and Awards: Member, Utah Republican Party Elephant Club and Finance Committee; Utah chair, Lamar Alexander for President; Utah finance chairman, Bush-Quayle '92

Elected to Congress: Elected to the 105th Congress in November 1996; reelected in 1998, 2000

ERIC CANTOR, Representative, Seventh District, Virginia

Born: Henrico County, VA, June 6, 1963

Resides: Henrico County, VA

Education: Bachelor's degree, George Washington University, 1985; J.D., College of William and Mary, 1988; M.S., Columbia University, 1989

Career: Attorney, Cantor and Cantor, Richmond

Civic Activities and Awards: Member, Western Henrico Rotary; member, Fraternal Lodge no. 53 AF and AM; member, Henrico County Republican Committee; former member, Board of Directors for the Jewish Community Center, Richmond; former member, Leadership Development Council for Greater Richmond Chapter of the American Red Cross; Board of Trustees, Elk Hill Farm; Board of Trustees, Virginia Holocaust Museum; former cochair, Virginia-Israel Partnership; president, Virginia-Israel Foundation; former chair, Joint Study Commission of Capital Access and Business Financing; former chair, Legislative Task Force on Truants and Runaways; former member, Virginia Commission on Youth

State and Local Office: Virginia House of Delegates, 1991–2001

Elected to Congress: Elected to the 107th Congress in November 2000

SHELLEY MOORE CAPITO, Representative, Second District, West Virginia

Born: Glendale, WV, November 26, 1953

Resides: Charleston, WV

Education: B.S., Duke University, 1975; M.Ed., University of Virginia, 1976

Career: Career counselor, West Virginia State College; director, Educational Information Center, West Virginia Board of Regents

Civic Activities and Awards: Past president and board member, YWCA; member, Community Council of the Kanawha Valley; member, West Virginia Interagency Council for Early Intervention; volunteer, Read Aloud; volunteer, Habitat for Humanity; member, First Presbyterian Church

State and Local Office: West Virginia House of Delegates, 1996–2001

Elected to Congress: Elected to the 107th Congress in November 2000

MICHAEL N. CASTLE, Representative at Large, Delaware

Born: Wilmington, DE, July 2, 1939

Resides: Wilmington, DE

Education: Tower Hill School, 1957; B.A., economics, Hamilton College, 1961; LL.B., Georgetown University Law School, 1964

Career: Attorney; admitted to the District of Columbia and Delaware bars, 1964; commenced practice in Wilmington; Delaware deputy attorney general, 1965–66

Civic Activities and Awards: Awarded honorary degrees, Wesley College (1986), Widener College (1986), Delaware State University (1986), Hamilton College (1991), Jefferson Medical College, Philadelphia, PA (1992), active in the National Governors' Association, serving three years as chair of the Human Resources Committee; co-vice chair for National Governors' Association Task Force on Health Care, with President Clinton; past president of the Council of State Governments; past chair of the Southern Governors'

Association; chaired the Republican Governors Association, 1988; American Diabetes Association's C. Everett Koop Award for Health Promotion and Awareness, 1992; member, Delaware Bar Association, American Bar Association; former member, National Governors' Association, Republican Governors Association, National Assessment Governing Board, Council of State Governors, Southern Governors' Association; honorary board of directors, Delaware Greenways

State and Local Office: Delaware House of Representatives, 1966–68; Delaware State Senate, 1968–76; lieutenant governor of Delaware, 1981–85; governor, 1985–92

Elected to Congress: Elected to the 103rd Congress in November 1992; reelected to each succeeding Congress

STEVE CHABOT, Representative, First District, Ohio

Born: Cincinnati, OH, January 22, 1953

Resides: Cincinnati, OH

Education: LaSalle High School; B.A., College of William and Mary, 1975; J.D., Salmon P. Chase College of Law, 1978

Career: Former schoolteacher; private practice lawyer, 1978–94

State and Local Office: Member, Cincinnati City Council, 1985–90; Hamilton County commissioner, 1990–94; chair, County Council's Urban Development and Law and Public Safety committees

Elected to Congress: Elected to the 104th Congress in November 1994; reelected to each succeeding Congress

SAXBY CHAMBLISS, Representative, Eighth District, Georgia

Born: Warrenton, NC, November 10, 1943

Resides: Macon, GA

Education: C.E. Byrd High School, 1962; B.A., University of Georgia, 1966; J.D., University of Tennessee College of Law, 1968

Civic Activities and Awards: Served on the Georgia state bar's Disciplinary Review Panel, 1969; member, Moultrie-Colquitt County Economic Development Authority, Colquitt County Economic Development Corporation

Elected to Congress: Elected to the 104th Congress in November 1994; reelected to each succeeding Congress

HELEN P. CHENOWETH-HAGE, former Representative, First District, Idaho

Born: Topeka, KS, January 27, 1938

Resides: Boise, ID

Education: Grants Pass High School; B.A., Whitworth College, 1962

Career: Self-employed medical and legal management consultant, 1964–75; guest instructor, University of Idaho School of Law; recruited physicians to towns and clinics in Northwest from medical schools nationwide; state executive director of Idaho Republican Party, 1975–77; chief of staff to then-Representative Steve Symms, 1977–78; co-owner, Consulting Associates, 1978–84

Civic Activities and Awards: Nationally recognized spokesperson for private property rights; U.S. Chamber of Commerce, Spirit of Enterprise Award, 1996–98; Idaho Chapter Safari Club International, Hunter's Appreciation Award; Food Distributors International, Thomas Jefferson Award; Idaho Army and Air National Guard, medal; National Taxpayer's Union, Taxpayer's Friend Award; Americans for Tax Reform, Friend of the Taxpayer Award, 1996–98; Christian Coalition Friend of the Family Award; National Rifle Association of America, NRA Legion of Honor Award; League of Private Property Voters, Property Rights Champion Award, 1997, 1998; Concerned Women for America, Statesman of the Year Award; Citizens Committee for the Right to Keep and Bear Arms, Gun Rights Defender of the Year; International Bible Reading Association, 1998 Bible Reader Marathon participant

Elected to Congress: Elected to the 104th Congress in November 1994; reelected in 1996, 1998; was not a candidate for reelection in 2000

JON CHRISTENSEN, former Representative, Second District, Nebraska

Born: St. Paul, NE, February 20, 1963

Resides: Omaha, NE

Education: St. Paul High School; B.A., Midland Lutheran College, 1985; J.D., South Texas College of Law, 1989

Career: Admitted to the Nebraska bar, 1992; vice president, COMREP, Inc.; marketing director, Connecticut Mutual Insurance Co.; insurance executive; formed Aguila Group, Inc.

Civic Activities and Awards: Elected freshman class president; member of the student senate; cofounded Midland's Fellowship of Christian Athletes; served as president of Law Week; member, Nebraska Farm Bureau, Nebraska Cattlemen's Association, National Federation of Independent Business, Northwest Rotary Club; member, American, Nebraska, and Omaha Bar Associations; member, Probate and Trust Division, National and Omaha Association of Life Underwriters; cochair, American Diabetes Association's Celebrity Breakfast

Elected to Congress: Elected to the 104th Congress in November 1994; reelected in 1996; was not a candidate for reelection in 1998; was an unsuccessful candidate for nomination as governor of Nebraska, 1998

HOWARD COBLE, Representative, Sixth District, North Carolina

Born: Greensboro, NC, March 18, 1931

Resides: Greensboro, NC

Education: Attended Appalachian State University, 1949–50; A.B., history, Guilford College, 1958; J.D., University of North Carolina School of Law, 1962

Military Service: Enlisted in U.S. Coast Guard as a seaman recruit, 1952; active duty, 1952–56 and 1977–78; reserve duty, 1960–81; presently holds rank of captain; last reserve duty assignment, commanding officer, U.S. Coast Guard Reserve Unit, Wilmington, NC

Career: Attorney; admitted to North Carolina bar, 1966; field claim representative and superintendent, auto insurance, 1961–67; assistant U.S. attorney, Middle District of North Carolina, 1969–73; commissioner (secretary), North Carolina

Department of Revenue, 1973–77; practiced law with law firm of Turner, Enochs and Sparrow, Greensboro, NC, 1979–83

Civic Activities and Awards: Member, Alamance Presbyterian Church, American Legion, Veterans of Foreign Wars of the United States, Lions Club, Greensboro Bar Association, North Carolina Bar Association; North Carolina state cochair, American Legislative Exchange Council, 1983–84

State and Local Office: North Carolina House of Representatives, 1969, 1979–84

Elected to Congress: Elected to the 99th Congress in November 1984; reelected to each succeeding Congress

THOMAS A. COBURN, former Representative, Second District, Oklahoma

Born: Casper, WY, March 14, 1948

Resides: Muskogee, OK

Education: Central High School, 1966; B.S., Oklahoma State University, 1970; Oklahoma University Medical School, 1983

Career: Manufacturing manager, Coburn Ophthalmic Division, Coburn Optical Industries, 1970–78; family physician, 1983–present

Civic Activities and Awards: Founder and cochair, Congressional Family Caucus; member, American Medical Association, Oklahoma State Medical Association, East Central County Medical Society, American Academy of Family Practice; member, First Baptist Church, ordained deacon; teacher, adult classes, First Baptist Church; Promise Keepers; medical mission trip to Iraq and Haiti

Elected to Congress: Elected to the 104th Congress in November 1994; reelected in 1996, 1998; was not a candidate for reelection in 2000

MAC COLLINS, Representative, Third District, Georgia

Born: Jackson, GA, October 14, 1944

Resides: Hampton, GA

Education: Jackson High School, 1962

Career: Owner, Collins Trucking Company, 1962–82

Civic Activities and Awards: Chair, Butts County Republican Party, 1981–82; director, Georgia Forestry Association; 32nd degree Mason; member, American Legislative Exchange Council and National Conference of State Legislatures

State and Local Office: Georgia State Senate, 1989–92; chair, Butts County Commission, 1977–80

Elected to Congress: Elected to the 103rd Congress in November 1992; reelected to each succeeding Congress; deputy whip

LARRY COMBEST, Representative, Nineteenth District, Texas

Born: Memphis, TX, March 20, 1945

Resides: Lubbock, TX

Education: Panhandle High School, 1963; B.B.A., West Texas State University, 1969

Career: Farmer; teacher; Agriculture Stabilization and Conservation Service of U.S. Department of Agriculture, 1971; legislative assistant to U.S. Senator John Tower of Texas, 1971–78; owner, Combest Distributing Company, 1978–85

Civic Activities and Awards: State treasurer for Senator Tower's reelection, 1978; member, St. John's Methodist Church, Lubbock Historical Society; "Who's Who in American Politics," 1971; "Personalities of the South," 1972

Elected to Congress: Elected to the 99th Congress in November 1984; reelected to each succeeding Congress

MERRILL COOK, former Representative, Second District, Utah

Born: Philadelphia, PA, May 6, 1946

Resides: Salt Lake City, UT

Education: East High School; B.A., University of Utah, 1969; M.B.A., Harvard University, 1971

Career: Business management consultant, Arthur D. Little, Inc., 1971–73; founder and president, Cook Slurry Company, Salt Lake City, 1973–96; KALL talk show host, *Merrill Cook Show*, 1995

Civic Activities and Awards: Reagan delegate to Republican National Convention, 1976; member, Central Committee of the Utah Republican Party, 1980s

Elected to Congress: Elected to the 105th Congress in November 1996; reelected in 1998; was an unsuccessful candidate for reelection in 2000

JOHN COOKSEY, Representative, Fifth District, Louisiana

Born: Alexandria, LA, August 20, 1941

Resides: Monroe, LA

Education: LaSalle High School; B.S., Louisiana State University, 1962; M.D., Louisiana State University Medical School, 1966; M.B.A., Louisiana State University, 1994

Military Service: U.S. Air Force, 1967–69, served in northern Thailand during Vietnam War; Air National Guard, 1969–72

Career: Physician-ophthalmologist; Ochsner Medical Foundation, New Orleans; private medical practice in Monroe, LA, 1972–96

Civic Activities and Awards: Made five medical mission trips to Maua Methodist Hospital in Maua, Kenya, to perform eye surgery; in 1986 raised enough money through private donations to build a modern eye clinic at Maua Hospital to be used by local and visiting ophthalmologists; received Downtown Rotary Club Paul Harris Fellow Award in 1989 for humanitarian work in Africa; member, Louisiana State Medical Society, Louisiana Association of Business and Industry, Monroe Chamber of Commerce, National Federation of Independent Business, St. Paul United Methodist Church (laity leader); president, Ouachita Parish Medical Society; president, Ophthalmology Association; Board of Trustees of the Billy Pomeroy Caney Conference Center (chair), Board of Trustees of the Louisiana Association of Business and Industry, Board of Trustees of the Public Affairs Research Council

Elected to Congress: Elected to the 105th Congress in November 1996; reelected in 1998, 2000

CHRISTOPHER COX, Representative, Forty-Seventh District, California

Born: St. Paul, MN, October 16, 1952

Resides: Newport Beach, CA

Education: St. Thomas Academy, 1970; B.A., University of Southern California, 1973; J.D., Harvard Law School, 1977; M.B.A., Harvard Business School, 1977

Career: Attorney; admitted to the California bar in 1978 and commenced practice in Los Angeles; law clerk, U.S. Court of Appeals, San Francisco, CA, and Honolulu, HI, 1977–78; associate, Latham and Watkins, Newport Beach, CA, 1978–84; lecturer, Harvard Business School, 1982–83; cofounder, Context Corporation, St. Paul, MN, 1984–86; partner, Latham and Watkins, Newport Beach, CA, 1984–86; senior associate counsel to the president, the White House, 1986–88

Civic Activities and Awards: Member, Republican Associates, California Republican Assembly, Rotary Club of Orange County

Elected to Congress: Elected to the 101st Congress in November 1988; reelected to each succeeding Congress

PHILIP M. CRANE, Representative, Eighth District, Illinois

Born: Chicago, IL, November 3, 1930

Resides: Wauconda, IL

Education: DePauw University, Hillsdale College, University of Michigan, and University of Vienna; B.A., 1952, M.A., 1961, and Ph.D., 1963, Indiana University

Military Service: U.S. Army, active duty, 1954–56

Career: Teacher, Indiana University, 1960–63; employed by the Republican Party as a public relations expert, 1962; teacher, United States and Latin American history, Bradley University, 1963–1967; director of schools, Westminster Academy, Northbrook, IL, 1967–68; author of three books and editor of numerous others; advertising manager, Hopkins Syndicate

Civic Activities and Awards: Honorary doctor of laws, Grove City College, 1973; honorary doctor of political science, Francisco Marroquin University (Guatemala), 1979; in 1964, served as director of research for the Illinois Goldwater Organization; at the request of Richard Nixon, served as one of his advisers and researchers on political and national issues, 1964–68; in 1976 served as chair of Illinois Citizens for Reagan Committee; trustee of Hillsdale College; chair, American

Conservative Union, 1977–79; director of the Intercollegiate Studies Institute; serves with more than 60 U.S. senators and representatives on the National Advisory Board of Young Americans for Freedom; chair of Republican Study Committee, 1983; appointed by President Reagan to the Commission on the Bicentennial of the United States Constitution

Elected to Congress: Elected to the 91st Congress on November 25, 1969, by special election, to fill the vacancy caused by the resignation of Donald Rumsfeld; reelected to each succeeding Congress

ANDER CRENSHAW, Representative, Fourth District, Florida

Born: Jacksonville, FL, September 1, 1944

Resides: Jacksonville, FL

Education: Robert E. Lee High School, Jacksonville; bachelor's degree, the University of Georgia; J.D., University of Florida

Career: Investment banker; senior vice president, William R. Hough & Co.

Civic Activities and Awards: Member, Florida Ethics Commission, 1983–85; member, Florida Constitution Revision Commission, 1997–98; member, Grace Episcopal Church

State and Local Office: Florida House of Representatives, 1973–76; Florida State Senate, 1986–94

Elected to Congress: Elected to the 107th Congress in November 2000

BARBARA CUBIN, Representative at Large, Wyoming

Born: Salinas, CA, November 30, 1946

Resides: Casper, WY

Education: Natrona County High School; B.S., Creighton University, 1969

Career: Manager, substitute teacher, social worker, chemist

Civic Activities and Awards: Member of St. Stephen's Episcopal Church; founding member of the Casper Suicide Prevention League, Casper Service League; president, Southridge Elementary School Parent/Teacher Organization; Mercer House, president and executive member; Casper Self-Help Center, board member; Seton House, board member; Central Wyoming Rescue Mission, volunteer cook and server; Wyoming State Choir and Casper Civic Chorale; Cub Scout leader; Sunday school teacher at St. Stephen's Episcopal Church; executive committee of the Energy Council; chair, Center for Legislators Energy and Environment Research (CLEER); National Council of State Legislature; vice chair, Energy Committee; 1994 Edison Electric Institutes' Wyoming Legislator of the Year; Toll Fellowship from the Council of State Governments, 1990; Republican precinct committee member, 1988–94; legislative liaison and member, Natrona County Republican Women; 1992 Wyoming state Republican convention parliamentarian; delegate, Wyoming State Republican Convention, 1990, 1992, and 1994; State Legislative Candidate Recruitment Committee for the Wyoming Republican Party in 1988, 1990, and 1992

State and Local Office: Wyoming House of Representatives, Minerals, Business and Economic Development, Revenue, Transportation committees, 1987–92; chair, Joint Interim Economic Development Subcommittee; Wyoming State Senate, Travel, Recreation, Wildlife, Cultural Resources, Revenue committees, 1992–94; chair, Wyoming Senate Republican Conference, 1992–94

Elected to Congress: Elected to the 104th Congress in November 1994; reelected to each succeeding Congress

JOHN ABNEY CULBERSON, Representative, Seventh District, Texas

Born: Houston, TX, August 24, 1956

Resides: Houston, TX

Education: Bachelor's degree, Southern Methodist University, 1981; J.D., South Texas College of Law, 1988

Career: Defense attorney

Civic Activities and Awards: Member, Memorial Drive United Methodist Church

State and Local Office: Texas House of Representatives, 1986–2001

Elected to Congress: Elected to the 107th Congress in November 2000

RANDY (DUKE) CUNNINGHAM, Representative, Fifty-First District, California

Born: Los Angeles, CA, December 8, 1941

Resides: San Diego, CA

Education: Shelbina High School; University of Missouri, B.A., education, 1964, and M.S. in education, 1965; M.B.A., National University, 1985

Military Service: Joined the U.S. Navy at the age of 25 and became one of the most highly decorated fighter pilots in the Vietnam War; retired in 1987 with the rank of commander

Career: Dean, School of Aviation and Flight Training, and businessman; coached swim teams at Hinsdale College and at the University of Missouri, training 36 All-Americans, 2 Olympic gold and silver medalists; author of *Fox Two*, on his experiences as a naval aviator, and produced *Top Gun—The Story Behind the Story*, video about his career as a fighter pilot instructor at Miramar NAS

Civic Activities and Awards: Member, Naval Aviation Hall of Fame, Golden Eagles, Miramar Aviation Hall of Fame, American Fighter Aces Association

Elected to Congress: Elected to the 102nd Congress in November 1990; reelected to each succeeding Congress

JO ANN DAVIS, Representative, First District, Virginia

Born: Rowan County, NC, June 29, 1950

Resides: Yorktown, VA

Education: Kecoughtan High School, 1968; attended Hampton Roads Business College, VA

Career: Real estate broker; owner, Davis Management Company, 1988; owner, Jo Ann Davis Realty, 1990; cofounder, International Military Relocation Center

Civic Activities and Awards: Member, Grievance Committee, Virginia Peninsula Association of Realtors; member, Professional Standards Committee, Virginia Peninsula Association of Realtors

State and Local Office: Virginia General Assembly, 1997–2001

Elected to Congress: Elected to the 107th Congress in November 2000

THOMAS M. DAVIS, Representative, Eleventh District, Virginia

Born: Minot, ND, January 5, 1949

Resides: Falls Church, VA

Education: U.S. Capitol Page School; B.A., 1971, Amherst College with honors in political science; J.D., 1975, University of Virginia; attended officer candidate school

Military Service: U.S. Army, 1971–72; Army Reserves, 1972–79

Career: Member, Fairfax County Board of Supervisors, 1980–94 (chair, 1992–94); vice president and general counsel of PRC, Inc., McLean, VA, 1977–84

Civic Activities and Awards: Past president, Washington Metropolitan Council of Governments; founding member and past president, Bailey's Crossroads Rotary Club

Elected to Congress: Elected to the 104th Congress in November 1994; reelected to each succeeding Congress

NATHAN DEAL, Representative, Ninth District, Georgia

Born: Millen, GA, August 25, 1942

Resides: Lula, GA

Education: Washington County High School, 1960; B.A., Mercer University, 1964; J.D., Mercer University, Walter F. George School of Law, 1966

Military Service: Captain, U.S. Army, 1966–68

Career: Admitted to the Georgia bar, 1966; Hall County attorney, 1966–70; assistant district attorney, Northeastern Judicial Circuit of Georgia, 1970–71; practicing attorney, 1971–92

Civic Activities and Awards: Member and ordained deacon, Gainesville First Baptist Church; Board of Trustees, Mercer University; Advisory Board of Honors programs, North Georgia College and State University; past president and lifetime member, Gainesville Rotary Club

State and Local Office: Hall County Juvenile Court

Judge, 1971–72; Georgia State Senate, 1981–92; president pro tempore, 1989–90, 1991–92

Elected to Congress: Elected to the 103rd Congress in November 1992; reelected to each succeeding Congress

TOM DeLAY, Representative, Twenty-Second District, Texas

Born: Laredo, TX, April 8, 1947

Resides: Sugar Land, TX

Education: Calallan High School, 1965; attended Baylor University, 1967; B.S., University of Houston, 1970

Career: Businessman; owner, Albo Pest Control, 1973–84

Civic Activities and Awards: Member, Oyster Creek Rotary, Ft. Bend 100 Club, Chamber of Commerce; board member, Youth Opportunities Unlimited

State and Local Office: Texas House of Representatives, 1979–84

Elected to Congress: Elected to the 99th Congress in November 1984; reelected to each succeeding Congress; elected by colleagues to post of majority whip, 104th Congress

JIM DeMINT, Representative, Fourth District, South Carolina

Born: Greenville, SC, September 2, 1951

Resides: Greenville, SC

Education: West Hampton High School, Greenville, SC, 1969; B.S., University of Tennessee, 1973; M.B.A., Clemson University, 1981

Career: Certified management consultant and certified quality trainer; advertising and marketing businessman; started his own company, DeMint Marketing, 1983

Civic Activities and Awards: Active in Greenville, SC, business and educational organizations

Elected to Congress: Elected to the 106th Congress in November 1998; reelected in 2000

LINCOLN DIAZ-BALART, Representative, Twenty-First District, Florida

Born: Havana, Cuba, August 13, 1954

Resides: Miami, FL

Education: American School of Madrid, Spain, 1972; B.A., New College of the University of South Florida, 1977; J.D., Case Western Reserve University Law School, 1979

Career: Attorney; admitted to the Florida bar, 1979; partner, Fowler, White, Burnett, Hurley, Banick and Strickroot, P.A., Miami

Civic Activities and Awards: Founding member, Miami-Westchester Lions Club; member, Organization for Retarded Citizens

State and Local Office: Florida House of Representatives, 1986–89; Florida State Senate, 1989–92

Elected to Congress: Elected to the 103rd Congress in November 1992; reelected to each succeeding Congress

JAY W. DICKEY JR., former Representative, Fourth District, Arkansas

Born: Pine Bluff, AR, December 14, 1939

Resides: Pine Bluff, AR

Education: Pine Bluff High School; University of Arkansas (B.A., 1961, J.D., 1963)

Career: Owned two Taco Bell restaurants; practicing attorney, 1963–92; Pine Bluff city attorney, 1968–70

Civic Activities and Awards: Former state chair, Christian Legal Society; past president, Pine Bluff Jaycees; recipient, Jaycees Distinguished Service Award; former board member, Bank of Bearden, Guaranty Savings and Loan Association, Pine Bluff Chamber of Commerce; life member, National Rifle Association; member, Ducks Unlimited, Pillars Club of the United Way, Century Club of the Boy Scouts

Elected to Congress: Elected to the 103rd Congress in November 1992; reelected to each succeeding Congress through 2001; was an unsuccessful candidate for reelection in 2000

JOHN T. DOOLITTLE, Representative, Fourth District, California

Born: Glendale, CA, October 30, 1950

Resides: Rocklin, CA

Education: Cupertino High School, 1968; University of California at Santa Cruz, B.A., 1972; University of the Pacific, McGeorge School of Law, J.D., 1978

Career: Practicing attorney, 1978–80; member, California bar

State and Local Office: Elected to the California State Senate, 1980, reelected 1984 and 1988; served as chair of the Senate Republican Caucus, May 1987–April 1990

Elected to Congress: Elected to the 102nd Congress in November 1990; elected in 1992 to newly drawn 4th Congressional District; reelected to each succeeding Congress

DAVID DREIER, Representative, Twenty-Eighth District, California

Born: Kansas City, MO, July 5, 1952

Resides: San Dimas, CA

Education: Claremont McKenna College, B.A. (cum laude), political science, 1975; Claremont Graduate School, M.A., American government, 1976

Career: Director, corporate relations, Claremont McKenna College, 1975–78; director, marketing and government affairs, Industrial Hydrocarbons, 1979–80; vice president, Dreier Development, 1985–present

Civic Activities and Awards: Winston S. Churchill Fellow; Phi Sigma Alpha; board of governors, James Madison Society; member, Republican State Central Committee of California, Los Angeles Town Hall; named Outstanding Young Man of America and Outstanding Young Californian, 1976 and 1978

Elected to Congress: Elected to the 97th Congress in November 1980; reelected to each succeeding Congress

JOHN J. DUNCAN JR., Representative, Second District, Tennessee

Born: Lebanon, TN, July 21, 1947

Resides: Knoxville, TN

Education: University of Tennessee, B.S. degree in journalism, 1969; National Law Center, George Washington University, J.D. degree, 1973

Military Service: Served in both the Army National Guard and the U.S. Army Reserve, 1970–87, retired with the rank of captain

Career: Practicing attorney, private law practice in Knoxville, 1973–81

Civic Activities and Awards: Member, American Legion Posts 40 and 8, Elks, Sertoma Club, Masons (Scottish rite), and Shrine; present or past board member, Red Cross, Girls' Club, YWCA, Sunshine Center for the Mentally Retarded, Beck Black Heritage Center, Knoxville Union Rescue Mission, Senior Citizens Home Aid Service; active elder at Eastminster Presbyterian Church

State and Local Office: Appointed state trial judge by Governor Lamar Alexander in 1981 and elected to a full eight-year term in 1982

Elected to Congress: Elected to both the 100th Congress (special election) and the 101st Congress in separate elections held in November 1988; reelected to each succeeding Congress

JENNIFER DUNN, Representative, Eighth District, Washington

Born: Seattle, WA, July 29, 1941

Resides: Bellevue, WA

Education: B.A., Stanford University, 1963

Career: Systems engineer, IBM, 1964–69; public relations, King County Assessors Office, 1978–80

Civic Activities and Awards: Chair, Washington State Republican Party, 1981–92; member, Republican National Committee (vice chair, Western Region); U.S. delegate to the United Nations Commission on the Status of Women, 1984, 1990; member, Preparatory Commission for the 1985 World Conference on the Status of Women; appointee, President's Advisory Council on Voluntary Services, President's Advisory Council on Historic Preservation, Executive Committee of the Small Business Administration Advisory Council; received Shavano Summit Award for Excellence in National Leadership, Hillsdale College, 1984; member, Seattle Junior League, board of Epiphany School, advisory board for KUOW-FM (National Public Radio), Metropolitan Opera National Council, Henry M. Jackson Foundation,

Rep. Jennifer Dunn (*Government Printing Office*)

International Women's Forum, and International Republican Institute

Elected to Congress: Elected to the 103rd Congress in November 1992; reelected to each succeeding Congress

VERNON J. EHLERS, former Representative, Third District, Michigan

Born: Pipestone, MN, February 6, 1934

Resides: Grand Rapids, MI

Education: Educated at home by his parents; attended Calvin College, 1952–55; Ph.D. in nuclear physics from University of California at Berkeley, 1960; NATO postdoctoral research fellow; University of Heidelberg, Germany, 1961–62

Career: Research physicist at Lawrence Berkeley Laboratory and lecturer in physics at the University of California; coauthored two books on the environment, *Earthkeeping in the '90s: Stewardship of Creation* and *Earthkeeping: Christian*

Stewardship of Natural Resources; coauthored two books on world hunger; professor, Calvin College, 1966–82

Civic Activities and Awards: Named an Outstanding Educator of the Year, 1970–73; appointed to INTERSET, a science advisory committee; chair, National Conference of State Legislatures Environment Committee; science adviser to then-Congressman Gerald Ford; member and former elder of Eastern Avenue Christian Reformed Church, Grand Rapids

State and Local Office: Elected to the Kent County Commission, 1975–82; elected to the state House of Representatives, 1982–86; Michigan Senate, 1986–93; president pro tempore, 1990–93

Elected to Congress: Elected to the 103rd Congress in December 1993, by special election, to fill the vacancy caused by the death of Paul B. Henry; reelected to each succeeding Congress through 2001; was not a candidate for reelection in 2000

ROBERT L. EHRLICH JR., Representative, Second District, Maryland

Born: Arbutus, MD, November 25, 1957

Resides: Timonium, MD

Education: B.A., Princeton University, 1979; J.D., Wake Forest University, 1982

Career: Admitted to Maryland bar, 1983; associate, Ober, Kaler, Grimes, and Shriver, 1982–92; of counsel, Ober, Kaler, Grimes, and Shriver, 1992–94

Civic Activities and Awards: Spirit of Enterprise Award from the U.S. Chamber of Commerce; Guardian of Small Business from the National Federation of Independent Business; National Association of Manufacturers' Legislative Excellence Award; Federal Official of the Year from the National Industries for the Blind; Cystic Fibrosis Foundation of Maryland; BPO Elks (Towson chapter); Community Assistance Network; Regional Manufacturing Institute; Izaak Walton League; Chesapeake Bay Foundation

State and Local Office: Maryland House of Delegates, 1986–94

Elected to Congress: Elected to the 104th Congress in November 1994; reelected to each succeeding Congress

JO ANN EMERSON, Representative, Eighth District, Missouri

Born: Washington, DC, September 16, 1950

Resides: Cape Girardeau, MO

Education: B.A., political science, Ohio Wesleyan University, 1972

Career: Deputy communications director, National Republican Congressional Committee, 1984–91; director, state relations and grassroots programs, National Restaurant Association, 1991–94; senior vice president of public affairs, American Insurance Association, 1994–96

Civic Activities and Awards: Member, PEO Women's Service Group, Cape Girardeau, MO; member, Copper Dome Society, Southeast Missouri State University; advisory committee, Children's Inn; National Institutes of Health; advisory board, Arneson Institute for Practical Politics and Public Affairs, Ohio Wesleyan University

Elected to Congress: Elected to the 104th Congress in November 1996, to serve the remainder of her late husband Bill Emerson's term; reelected to each succeeding Congress

PHIL S. ENGLISH, Representative, Twenty-First District, Pennsylvania

Born: Erie, PA, June 20, 1956

Resides: Erie, PA

Education: B.A., University of Pennsylvania, political science, 1978

Career: Staff aide, Pennsylvania Senate, 1980–84; chief of staff, State Senator Melissa Hart, 1990–92; executive director, State Senate Finance Committee, 1990–94

State and Local Office: Erie city controller, 1985–89

Elected to Congress: Elected to the 104th Congress in November 1994; reelected to each succeeding Congress

JOHN ENSIGN, former Representative, First District, Nevada

Born: Roseville, CA, March 25, 1958

Resides: Las Vegas, NV

Education: E. W. Clark High School, 1976; University of Las Vegas, 1976–79; B.S., Oregon State University, 1981; D.V.M., Colorado State University, 1985

Career: Veterinarian; general manager of a casino

Civic Activities and Awards: Member, Las Vegas Southwest Rotary, Las Vegas Chamber of Commerce, Sigma Chi fraternity, Prison Fellowship, Meadows Christian Fellowship

Elected to Congress: Elected to the 104th Congress in November 1994; reelected in 1996; was not a candidate for reelection in 1998, but was an unsuccessful candidate for election to the U.S. Senate

TERRY EVERETT, Representative, Second District, Alabama

Born: Dothan, AL, February 15, 1937

Resides: Enterprise, AL

Education: Attended Enterprise State Junior College

Military Service: U.S. Air Force, 1955–59

Career: Newspaper publisher; president, Premium Home Builders, Everett Land Development Company; president and chair of the board, *Union Springs Herald*, 1988–present; owner and operator, Hickory Ridge Farms

Civic Activities and Awards: Past chair, board of directors, Dothan Federal Savings Bank; Alabama Press Association

Elected to Congress: Elected to the 103rd Congress in November 1992; reelected to each succeeding Congress

THOMAS W. EWING, former Representative, Fifteenth District, Illinois

Born: Atlanta, IL, September 19, 1935

Resides: Pontiac, IL

Education: B.S., Milikin University, 1957; J.D., John Marshall Law School, 1968

Military Service: U.S. Army, 1957–59; Army Reserves, 1959–63

Career: Farm owner and businessman; executive director, Pontiac and Harvey Chambers of Com-

merce, 1963–68; assistant state attorney, Livingston County, 1968–73; practicing attorney, 1968–91

Civic Activities and Awards: Delegate, Republican National Convention, 1980, 1984, and 1988; secretary, Illinois delegation; delegation floor whip, 1984; named National Legislator of the Year by National Republican Legislators Association, 1988

State and Local Office: Illinois House of Representatives, 1974–91; assistant Republican minority leader, 1982–90; minority leader, 1990

Elected to Congress: Elected to the 102nd Congress on July 2, 1991, by special election, to fill the vacancy caused by the resignation of Edward Madigan; reelected to each succeeding Congress through 2001; was not a candidate for reelection in 2000

HARRIS W. FAWELL, former Representative, Thirteenth District, Illinois

Born: West Chicago, IL, March 25, 1929

Resides: Naperville, IL

Education: West Chicago Community High School; undergraduate, North Central College, 1947–49; LL.B., Chicago-Kent College of Law, 1952

Career: Engaged in private practice of law, Fawell, James and Brooks, Naperville, 1954–84; general counsel, Illinois Association of Park Districts, 1977–84; former assistant state's attorney, DuPage County, IL

Civic Activities and Awards: Member, DuPage County, IL, and American Bar Associations; U.S. District Court Trial Bar; Illinois and American Trial Lawyer Associations; American Judicature Society; highest legal ability rating, A, of Martindale-Hubbell law directory; member, Illinois Commission on Children, 1967–77; former chair, School Law Section Council, Illinois State Bar Association; active in many civic associations; elected fellow of the Chicago-Kent College of Law Honor Council "for contribution to the College of Law and high standards of legal profession," 1981; Illinois congressional representative to the Full Committee of the National Republican Congressional Committee; Speaker's Group on Health Care Reform; member, Wesley Methodist Church, Naperville, IL

State and Local Office: Illinois State Senate, 1963–77

Elected to Congress: Elected to the 99th Congress in November 1984; reelected to each succeeding Congress through 1999; was not a candidate for reelection in 1998

MICHAEL FERGUSON, Representative, Seventh District, New Jersey

Born: Ridgeway, NJ, June 22, 1970

Resides: Warren Township, NJ

Education: B.A., University of Notre Dame; M.A., Georgetown University

Career: Educator; small businessperson; high school teacher, Mount St. Michael Academy, Bronx, NY; founder and president, Strategic Education Initiatives Inc., an educational consulting firm; adjunct instructor of political science, Brookdale Community College, Lincroft, NJ; past executive director, Better Schools Foundation; former executive director, Catholic Campaign for America; past director, Save Our Schools

Civic Activities and Awards: National Federation of Independent Business; the New Jersey Chamber of Commerce; Knights of Columbus; Epilepsy Foundation of New Jersey; Delbarton School; the Friendly Sons of St. Patrick; National Italian-American Foundation, Warren Professional and Business Association; Sierra Club

Elected to Congress: Elected to the 107th Congress in November 2000

JEFF FLAKE, Representative, First District, Arizona

Born: Snow Flake, AZ, December 31, 1962

Resides: Mesa, AZ

Education: Bachelor's degree, Brigham Young University, 1986; M.A., Brigham Young University, 1987

Career: Former executive director, Foundation for Democracy; former executive director, Goldwater Institute

Elected to Congress: Elected to the 107th Congress in November 2000

ERNEST LEE FLETCHER, Representative, Sixth District, Kentucky

Born: Mount Sterling, KY, November 12, 1952

Resides: Lexington, KY

Education: LaFayette High School, 1970; B.S., University of Kentucky, 1974; USAF, 1974–80; University of Kentucky College of Medicine, 1984

Career: Physician, family medical practice; CEO, St. Joseph Medical Foundation, 1997–99

State and Local Office: Kentucky House of Representatives, 1994–96

Elected to Congress: Elected to the 106th Congress in November 1998; reelected in 2000

MARK A. FOLEY, Representative, Sixteenth District, Florida

Born: Newton, MA, September 8, 1954

Resides: West Palm Beach, FL

Education: Lake Worth High School; attended Palm Beach Community College

Career: President, Foley Smith and Associates, real estate company

State and Local Office: Lake Worth city commissioner, 1977–83; Lake Worth vice mayor, 1983–84; Florida House of Representatives, 1990–92; Florida Senate (Agriculture Committee chair), 1992–94

Elected to Congress: Elected to the 104th Congress in November 1994; reelected to each succeeding Congress

MICHAEL P. FORBES, former Representative, First District, New York

Born: Riverhead, NY, July 16, 1952

Resides: Quogue, NY

Education: Westhampton Beach High, 1971; State University of New York at Albany, 1983, B.A.

Career: Regional administrator, Small Business Administration, 1983–93; owned a public relations and marketing business, Forbes & Co., 1987–89; regional director, U.S. Chamber of Commerce, 1993–94; staff assistant, U.S. Senator

Alfonse D'Amato, 1980–83; staff assistant, U.S. Representative Sam Stratton, 1983–84; assistant aide, U.S. Representative Connie Mack, 1984–87

Civic Activities and Awards: Principal liaison for Chamber of Commerce of the United States; Knights of Columbus; Southampton Elks; Irish-American Society of the Hamptons

Elected to Congress: Elected to the 104th Congress in November 1994; reelected in 1996, 1998; changed party affiliation to Democrat in 1999; was an unsuccessful candidate for reelection in 2000

VITO FOSSELLA, Representative, Thirteenth District, New York

Born: Staten Island, NY, March 9, 1965

Resides: Staten Island, NY

Education: B.S., Wharton School, University of Pennsylvania, 1987; J.D., Fordham University School of Law, 1993

Career: Attorney; admitted to New York bar, 1994; practicing attorney, 1994

State and Local Office: New York City Council, 1994–97

Elected to Congress: Elected to the 105th Congress on November 4, 1997, in a special election, to fill the vacancy caused by the resignation of Susan Molinari; reelected in 1998, 2000

TILLIE K. FOWLER, Representative, Fourth District, Florida

Born: Milledgeville, GA, December 23, 1942

Resides: Jacksonville, FL

Education: B.A. and J.D., Emory University, 1964, 1967

Career: Attorney, admitted to Georgia bar, 1967; legislative assistant, Congressman Robert G. Stevens Jr., 1967–70; general counsel, deputy counsel, associate director of legislative affairs, White House Office of Consumer Affairs, 1970–71

Civic Activities and Awards: Member, Emory University Alumni Board of Governors; Civil Justice Reform Act Advisory Group for the United States District Court, Middle District of Florida; American Red Cross, Northeast Florida chapter; honorary member, St. Vincent's Health Care Sys-

tem Advisory Board; the National Security Caucus' National Security Leadership Award; the Watchdogs of the Treasury Golden Bulldog Award; 60 Plus Guardian of Seniors' Rights Award; U.S. Chamber of Commerce's Spirit of Enterprise Award; National Federation of Independent Business' Guardian of Small Business Award; Association of Emory University Alumni Emory Medal for distinguished achievement, 1996; National Guard Association of the United States Charles Dick Medal of Merit, 1997

State and Local Office: Member, Jacksonville City Council, 1985–92; president, Jacksonville City Council, 1989–90

Elected to Congress: Elected to the 103rd Congress in November 1992; reelected to each succeeding Congress through 2001; was not a candidate for reelection in 2000

JON D. FOX, former Representative, Thirteenth District, Pennsylvania

Born: Abington, PA, April 22, 1947

Resides: Elkins Park, PA

Education: Cheltenham High School, 1965; B.A., Pennsylvania State University, 1969; J.D., Delaware Law School (now Widener University School of Law), 1975

Military Service: U.S. Air Force Reserve, technical sergeant, 1969–75

Career: Admitted to the Pennsylvania state bar, 1976; U.S. General Services Administration, Washington, DC; assistant district attorney in Montgomery County, 1976–84

Civic Activities and Awards: Awarded the Lindsay Law Prize for excellence in legal research; guest lecturer for the Presidential Classroom for Young Americans; founder/chair, Legislative Coalition Against Drug and Alcohol Abuse; member, Legislative Coalition for Libraries, Pennsylvania Firefighters Legislative Caucus; served on the boards of Montgomery County Legal Aid, Eastern Montgomery County Red Cross, Jewish Community Relations Council (neighborhood division), Aldersgate Youth Service Bureau, Montgomery County Spinal Cord Association, American Cancer Society, Manor Junior College, Willow Grove Senior Citizens Center, the Citizen's Committee for Environmental Control, F&AM Friendship Lodge 400 (Jenkintown), Friends of the Abington Free Library, Glenside Kiwanis, Optimist Club of Lower Montgomery County, North Penn Elks, North Penn Veterans of Foreign Wars, Lansdale American Legion, Abington Senior Citizens Support Council, Advisory Council to the Montgomery County Office on Aging and Adult Services; cofounded, Montgomery County AIDS Task Force, 1987, which resulted in the creation of the Montgomery County Department of Health, 1989

State and Local Office: Vice chair, Board of Commissioners; Abington Township commissioner, 1980–84; Pennsylvania House of Representatives, 1984–90; Montgomery city commissioner, 1991–94; member, House Appropriations and Education committees; member, House Select committees on Services for the Handicapped and Long-Term Care; Republican chair, House Special Education Subcommittee; chair, Mental Health Task Force of the Children's Legislative Caucus

Elected to Congress: Elected to the 104th Congress in November 1994; reelected in 1996; unsuccessful candidate for reelection in 1998

BOB FRANKS, former Representative, Seventh District, New Jersey

Born: Hackensack, NJ, September 21, 1951

Resides: New Providence, NJ

Education: B.A., DePauw University, 1973; J.D., Southern Methodist University, 1976

Career: Political consultant, 1976–79; Med Data Inc., 1979–81; co-owner, *County News*, 1982–84; New Jersey Republican state chairman, 1988–89; 1990–92

Civic Activities and Awards: Member, Long-Term Planning Committee, Overlook Hospital Association, 1982–present; member, Children's Specialized Board of Managers, 1982–present

State and Local Office: Elected to New Jersey General Assembly, 1979–92; assembly majority conference leader, 1986–89; assembly policy chairman, 1992

Elected to Congress: Elected to the 103rd Congress in November 1992; reelected to each succeeding

Congress through 2001; was not a candidate for reelection in 2000, but was an unsuccessful candidate for election to the U.S. Senate

RODNEY P. FRELINGHUYSEN, Representative, Eleventh District, New Jersey

Born: New York, NY, April 29, 1946

Resides: Morristown, NJ

Education: Graduated, Hobart College, 1969; attended graduate school in Connecticut

Military Service: U.S. Army, 93rd Engineer Battalion, honorably discharged, 1971

Career: Morris County state and federal aid coordinator and administrative assistant, 1972–74

Civic Activities and Awards: Named Legislator of the Year by the Veterans of Foreign Wars, the New Jersey Association of Mental Health agencies, and the New Jersey Association of Retarded Citizens; honored by numerous organizations; served on welfare and mental health boards, human services and private industry councils; member, American Legion and Veterans of Foreign Wars; Watchdog of the Treasury Award; Tax Fighter Award; the Friends of Housing for the Disabled Award; the Guardian of Seniors' Rights Award; the Spirit of Small Business Award; Rutgers University Award and the University of Medicine and Dentistry's University Medal for outstanding support of higher education, 1998

State and Local Office: Served in the New Jersey General Assembly, 1983–94; chair, Assembly Appropriations Committee, 1988–89 and 1992–94; member, Morris County Board of Chosen Freeholders, 1974–83, director, 1980

Elected to Congress: Elected to the 104th Congress in November 1994; reelected to each succeeding Congress

ELTON GALLEGLY, Representative, Twenty-Third District, California

Born: Huntington Park, CA, March 7, 1944

Resides: Simi Valley, CA

Education: Huntington Park High School, 1962; attended Los Angeles State College, 1962–63

Career: Businessman; owner, real estate firm

Civic Activities and Awards: Former vice chair and chair, Ventura County Association of Governments; former member, board of directors, Moorpark College Foundation; delegate to 1988 Republican National Convention

State and Local Office: Member, Simi Valley City Council, 1979–80; mayor, city of Simi Valley, 1980–86

Elected to Congress: Elected to the 100th Congress in November 1986; reelected to each succeeding Congress

GREG GANSKE, Representative, Fourth District, Iowa

Born: New Hampton, IA, March 31, 1949

Resides: Des Moines, IA

Education: B.S., University of Iowa, 1972; M.D., University of Iowa School of Medicine, 1976; general surgery training at Oregon Health Science Center; reconstructive surgery training under Nobel laureate Joe Murray at Harvard, completed his reconstructive surgery residence in 1984

Military Service: U.S. Army Reserve, 1986–present, lieutenant colonel

Career: Plastic and reconstructive surgeon, practiced in Des Moines; active manager of 160 acres of farmland

Elected to Congress: Elected to the 104th Congress in November 1994; reelected to each succeeding Congress

GEORGE GEKAS, Representative, Seventeenth District, Pennsylvania

Born: Harrisburg, PA, April 14, 1930

Resides: Harrisburg, PA

Education: William Penn High School, 1948; B.A., Dickinson College, 1952; LL.B. and J.D., Dickinson School of Law, 1958

Military Service: Corporal in U.S. Army, 1953–55

Career: Attorney, admitted to the Pennsylvania bar in 1959, and commenced practice in Harrisburg; served as assistant district attorney, Dauphin County, PA, 1960–66

Civic Activities and Awards: Member, American

Judicature Society; Harrisburg Historical Society; board of trustees, Orthodox Church of Greater Harrisburg; Police Athletic League; March of Dimes Campaign; Cancer Crusade; member, Greek Orthodox Holy Trinity Cathedral

State and Local Office: Pennsylvania House of Representatives, 1966–74; Pennsylvania Senate, 1976–82

Elected to Congress: Elected to the 98th Congress in November 1982; reelected to each succeeding Congress

JAMES A. GIBBONS, Representative, Second District, Nevada

Born: Sparks, NV, December 16, 1944

Resides: Reno, NV

Education: B.S., geology, 1967 and M.S., mining geology, 1973, University of Nevada at Reno; J.D., Southwestern University, 1979

Military Service: Colonel, U.S. Air Force, 1967–71; vice commander of the Nevada Air Guard, 1975–95

Career: Pilot, Delta Airlines, 1987–96; mining geologist; admitted to the Nevada bar in 1982 and began practice in Reno; mining and water rights attorney

Civic Activities and Awards: Advisory board, Committee to Aid Abused Women; member, Nevada Landman's Association, American Association of Petroleum Landsmen, Nevada Bar Association, National Conference Board, University of Nevada Alumni Association, Reno Board of Realtors, Nevada Development Authority; board of directors, Nevada Council on Economic Education

State and Local Office: Nevada state assemblyman, 1988–94

Elected to Congress: Elected to the 105th Congress in November 1996; reelected in 1998, 2000

WAYNE T. GILCHREST, Representative, First District, Maryland

Born: Rahway, NJ, April 15, 1946

Resides: Kennedyville, MD

Education: Rahway High School, 1964; attended Wesley College, Dover, DE; B.A. in history, Delaware State College, Dover, 1973; graduate studies, Loyola University, Baltimore, MD, 1984

Military Service: U.S. Marine Corps, 1964–68; awarded the Purple Heart, Bronze Star, Navy Commendation Medal, Navy Unit Citation, and others

Career: Government and history teacher, Kent County High School, 1973–86; National Forest Service Worker, Bitterroot National Forest, 1986

Civic Activities and Awards: Member, Kent County Teachers Association, American Legion, Veterans of Foreign Wars, Order of the Purple Heart, Kennedyville Methodist Church

Elected to Congress: Elected to the 102nd Congress in November 1990; reelected to each succeeding Congress

PAUL E. GILLMOR, Representative, Fifth District, Ohio

Born: Tiffin, OH, February 1, 1939

Resides: Old Fort, OH

Education: Old Fort High School, 1957; B.A., Ohio Wesleyan University, 1961; J.D., University of Michigan Law School, 1964

Military Service: U.S. Air Force, captain, 1965–66

Career: Attorney; admitted to the Ohio bar, 1965; commenced practice in Tiffin, OH

State and Local Office: Ohio State Senate, 1967–88; minority leader and president, Ohio State Senate

Elected to Congress: Elected to the 101st Congress in November 1988; reelected to each succeeding Congress

BENJAMIN A. GILMAN, Representative, Twentieth District, New York

Born: Poughkeepsie, NY, December 6, 1922

Resides: Middletown, NY

Education: Middletown High School, 1941; B.S., Wharton School of Business and Finance, University of Pennsylvania, 1946; LL.B., New York Law School, 1950

Military Service: Veteran of World War II, 20th Air Force, 19th Bomb Group; awarded Distinguished Flying Cross and Air Medal for 35 missions over Japan; New York State Guard, 1981–present

Career: Appointed assistant attorney general, New York State Department of Law, 1953–55; founded the law firm of Gilman and Gilman, 1955, in Middletown, NY; attorney for New York State's temporary committee on the Courts

Civic Activities and Awards: Member, Southeastern Water Commission; member, Middletown, Orange County, New York State and American Bar Associations; member, the Association of the Bar of the City of New York, New York and American Trial Lawyers Associations; member of Orange County Republican Committee, American Legion, V.F.W., Masonic War Veterans Beth El Post no. 29, JWV (national legislative chairman), 33rd degree Mason in Hoffman Lodge; member, BPO Elks; International Narcotic Enforcement Officers Association, Zeta Beta Tau fraternity, Otisville Grange, Hudson-Delaware Boy Scout Council, Lamont-Doherty Geological Observatory Advisory Council, advisory committee of New York State Division of Youth's Start Center; past president of Capitol Hill Shrine Club; former board chairman of Middletown Little League; vice president of Orange County Mental Health Association and Orange County Heart Association; lieutenant colonel, Civil Air Patrol, congressional branch; member, Le Société des 40 Hommes et 8 Chevaux; colonel, New York Guard; United States Military Academy Board of Visitors, 1973–83; Presidential Commission Against World Hunger; Task Force on the Handicapped; Foundation for Better Health; Good Samaritan Hospital, Suffern, NY; board of directors, World Hunger Year

State and Local Office: Served for three terms in the New York State Assembly from the 95th District, 1967–72

Elected to Congress: Elected to the 93rd Congress in November 1972; reelected to each succeeding Congress

ROBERT W. (BOB) GOODLATTE, Representative, Sixth District, Virginia

Born: Holyoke, MA, September 22, 1952

Resides: Roanoke, VA

Education: B.A., Bates College, 1974; J.D., Washington and Lee University, 1977

Career: Admitted to the Massachusetts and Virginia bars; began practice in Roanoke, VA, 1979; district director for Congressman M. Caldwell Butler, 1977–79; attorney, sole practitioner, 1979–81; partner, 1981–92

Civic Activities and Awards: Chair, 6th District, Virginia Republican Committee, 1983–88; member, Civitan Club of Roanoke (president, 1989–90); former member, Building Better Boards Advisory Council; member, Parent-Teacher Association, Fishburn Park Elementary School

Elected to Congress: Elected to the 103rd Congress in November 1992; reelected to each succeeding Congress

WILLIAM F. GOODLING, former Representative, Nineteenth District, Pennsylvania

Born: Loganville, PA, December 5, 1927

Resides: Jacobus, PA

Education: William Penn Senior High School; B.S., University of Maryland, 1953; M.Ed., Western Maryland College, 1957; doctoral studies, Pennsylvania State University

Military Service: U.S. Army, 1946–48

Career: Various teaching positions including principal, West York Area High School, 1952–74; supervisor of student teachers for Pennsylvania State University; superintendent, Spring Grove area schools

Civic Activities and Awards: Member, Lions, various health associations, and Loganville United Methodist Church

State and Local Office: President, Dallastown area school board, 1966–67

Elected to Congress: Elected to the 94th Congress in November 1974; reelected to each succeeding Congress until 2000; was not a candidate for reelection in 2000

PORTER J. GOSS, Representative, Fourteenth District, Florida

Born: Waterbury, CT, November 26, 1938

Resides: Sanibel, FL

Education: B.A., Yale University, 1960

Military Service: U.S. Army, second lieutenant, 1960–62

Career: Clandestine services officer, CIA, 1960–71; newspaper publisher, small business owner, 1973–78; director, National Audubon Society

Civic Activities and Awards: Chair, State Advisory Committee on Coastal Management; vice chair, West Coast Inland Navigational District; past chairman, Metropolitan Planning Organization; port commissioner, Southwest Florida Regional Airport; member, Southwest Florida Mental Health District Board, Canterbury School, Lee County Mental Health Center, Sanibel-Captiva Conservation Foundation, Westminster Presbyterian Church

State and Local Office: Council member, city of Sanibel, 1974–82; Sanibel mayor, 1974–77; commissioner, Lee County, District 1, 1983–88; chair, Lee County Commission, 1985–86

Elected to Congress: Elected to the 101st Congress in November 1988; reelected to each succeeding Congress

LINDSEY GRAHAM, Representative, Third District, South Carolina

Born: Seneca, SC, July 9, 1955

Resides: Seneca, SC

Education: Daniel High School; B.A., University of South Carolina, 1977; M.A. in public administration, 1978; awarded J.D., 1981

Military Service: Joined the U.S. Air Force, 1982; served as the base legal and as area defense counsel; assigned to Rhein Main Air Force Base, Germany, 1984; chief prosecutor for U.S. Air Force; Meritorious Service Medal for active duty tour in Europe; presently major in the South Carolina Air National Guard, serving as base staff judge advocate at McEntyre Air National Guard Base, Eastover, SC

Career: Practicing attorney, 1988–92; assistant county attorney for Oconee County, 1988–92; city attorney for Central, SC, 1990–94

Civic Activities and Awards: Home Health Care Legislator of the Year, 1992; member, Seneca Sertoma, Walhalla Rotary, Anderson Chamber of Commerce, American Legion Post 120, Retired

Officers Association; served as fund-raising chairman, Oconee County chapter of the American Cancer Society; board member, Rosa Clark Free Medical Clinic in Seneca, SC; appointed to Judicial Arbitration Commission by the chief justice of the Supreme Court; member, Corinth Baptist Church

State and Local Office: South Carolina House of Representatives, 1992–94

Elected to Congress: Elected to the 104th Congress in November 1994; reelected to each succeeding Congress

KAY GRANGER, Representative, Twelfth District, Texas

Born: Greenville, TX, January 18, 1943

Resides: Ft. Worth, TX

Education: B.S., magna cum laude, Texas Wesleyan University, 1965

Career: Public school teacher, 1965–78; owner, Kay Granger Insurance Agency, 1985–present

Civic Activities and Awards: Honorary doctorate of humane letters, 1992, Texas Wesleyan University; past chair, Ft. Worth Zoning Commission; past board member, Dallas–Ft. Worth International Airport, North Texas Commission, Ft. Worth Convention and Visitors Bureau, U.S. Conference of Mayors' Advisory Board; Business and Professional Women's Woman of the Year, 1989

State and Local Office: Mayor of Ft. Worth, 1991–95; Ft. Worth city council member, 1989–91

Elected to Congress: Elected to the 105th Congress in November 1996; reelected in 1998, 2000

SAMUEL GRAVES, Representative, Sixth District, Missouri

Born: Tarkio, MO, November 7, 1963

Resides: Tarkio, MO

Education: Tarkio High School, 1982; B.A., University of Missouri-Columbia School of Agriculture

Career: Small businessman; farmer

Civic Activities and Awards: National Outstanding Young Farmer Award, Missouri Farm Bureau, 1990; Atchison County president and state chair-

man; Young Farmer and Rancher Committee; Missouri Spirit of Enterprise Award, Missouri Chamber of Commerce; Voice of Missouri Business Award, Associated Industries of Missouri; Tom Henderson Small Business Award, Small Business Development Corporation

State and Local Office: Missouri State House of Representatives, 1992–1994; Missouri State Senate, 1994–2001

Elected to Congress: Elected to the 107th Congress in November 2000

MARK GREEN, Representative, Eighth District, Wisconsin

Born: Boston, MA, June 1, 1960

Resides: Green Bay, WI

Education: B.A., University of Wisconsin-Eau Claire, 1983; J.D., University of Wisconsin Law School-Madison, 1987

Career: Attorney

State and Local Office: Wisconsin State Assembly, 4th District, 1992–98

Elected to Congress: Elected to the 106th Congress in November 1998; reelected in 2000

JAMES C. GREENWOOD, Representative, Eighth District, Pennsylvania

Born: Philadelphia, PA, May 4, 1951

Resides: Erwinna, PA

Education: Council Rock High School; B.A., Dickinson College, 1973

Career: Legislative assistant, Pennsylvania state representative John S. Renninger, 1972–76; campaign coordinator, Renninger for Congress Committee, 1976; caseworker, Bucks County Children and Youth Social Service Agency, 1977–80

Civic Activities and Awards: Head house parent, The Woods Schools, 1974–76; board of directors, Pennsylvania Trauma Systems Foundation, Pennsylvania Energy Development Authority, Pennsylvania Higher Education Assistance Agency; member, Governor's Commission for Children and Families, Children's Trust Fund Board, Joint Legislative Air and Water Pollution Control and Conservation Committee, Permanency Planning Task Force of the Committee on the Environment of the Eastern Regional Conference of the Council of State Governments; board of directors, Bucks County Council on Alcoholism, Parents Anonymous, Today, The Woods Schools; Public Citizen of the Year, 1990; Pennsylvania Chapter of the National Federation of Independent Business, Guardian of Small Business Award, 1990, 1994; Pennsylvania Association of Retarded Citizens, Outstanding Legislator, 1989; Progressive Education for Rubella Children Award, 1987; Pennsylvania Association of Rehabilitation Facilities, Distinguished Service Award, 1987; National Head Injury Foundation, Award of Appreciation, 1986; Humane Society of the United States Award, 1983

State and Local Office: Pennsylvania state representative, 1980–86; Pennsylvania state senator, 1986–93; chair, Joint State Government Commission Task Force on Services to Youth and Children, Pennsylvania Legislative Children's Caucus; member, Joint State Government Commission Task Force on Commonwealth Efficiency Study; vice chair, Assembly on the Legislature of the National Conference of State Legislatures

Elected to Congress: Elected to the 103rd Congress in November 1992; reelected to each succeeding Congress

FELIX J. GRUCCI JR., Representative, First District, New York

Born: Brookhaven, NY, November 25, 1951

Resides: Brookhaven, NY

Career: President, Fireworks by Grucci

Civic Activities and Awards: Past board member, American Pyrotechnics Association

State and Local Office: Suffolk County Planning Commission, 1988–91; Brookhaven councilman, 1993–95; Brookhaven town supervisor, 1995–2000

Elected to Congress: Elected to the 107th Congress in November 2000

GILBERT W. GUTKNECHT, Representative, First District, Minnesota

Born: Cedar Falls, IA, March 20, 1951

Resides: Rochester, MN

Education: Cedar Falls High School; B.A., University of Northern Iowa, 1973

Career: Real estate broker and auctioneer, 1979–94

Civic Activities and Awards: Member, Knights of Columbus, Chamber of Commerce

State and Local Office: State representative, 1982–94

Elected to Congress: Elected to the 104th Congress in November 1994; reelected to each succeeding Congress

JAMES V. HANSEN, Representative, First District, Utah

Born: Salt Lake City, UT, August 14, 1932

Resides: Farmington, UT

Education: B.S., University of Utah, 1960

Military Service: U.S. Navy, 1951–55

Career: President, James V. Hansen Insurance Agency; president, Woodland Springs Development Company

Civic Activities and Awards: Recipient, Legislator of the Year Award, 1980; member, Rotary Club; recipient, Citizen of the Year Award; member, Church of Jesus Christ of Latter-day Saints (Mormon)

State and Local Office: Member, Utah House of Representatives, 1973–80; speaker of the house, 1978–80

Elected to Congress: Elected to the 97th Congress in November 1980; reelected to each succeeding Congress

MELISSA A. HART, Representative, Fourth District, Pennsylvania

Born: Pittsburgh, PA, April 4, 1962

Resides: Bradford Woods, PA

Education: Bachelor's degree, Washington and Jefferson College, Pennsylvania, 1984; J.D., University of Pittsburgh, 1987

Career: Counsel, Doepken Keevican & Weiss, Pittsburgh

Civic Activities and Awards: Board member, Community College of Allegheny County; board member, Pennsylvania Partnership for Economic

Education; board member, Vietnam Veterans Leadership Program; board member, University of Pittsburgh Board of Trustees; board member, Children's Cancer Foundation; board member, Pittsburgh Film Office; board member, Pittsburgh Ballet Theatre

State and Local Office: Pennsylvania State Senate, 1990–2001

Elected to Congress: Elected to the 107th Congress in November 2000

J. DENNIS HASTERT, Representative, Fourteenth District, Illinois

Born: Aurora, IL, January 2, 1942

Resides: Yorkville, IL

Education: Oswego High School, 1960; B.A., Wheaton College, 1964; M.S., Northern Illinois University, 1967

Career: Teacher/coach, Yorkville High School; partner, family restaurant business

Civic Activities and Awards: Named one of Illinois' 20 top legislators in 1985 by *Chicago Sun-Times*; member, Yorkville Lions Club; board of directors, Aurora Family Support Center

State and Local Office: Member, Illinois General Assembly House of Representatives, 1980–86; Republican spokesman for the Appropriations II Committee; chair, Joint Committee on Public Utility Regulation; member, Legislative Audit Commission

Elected to Congress: Elected to the 100th Congress in November 1986; reelected to each succeeding Congress; elected Speaker of the House, 1998

DOC HASTINGS, Representative, Fourth District, Washington

Born: Spokane, WA, February 7, 1941

Resides: Pasco, WA

Education: Pasco High School, 1959; attended Columbia Basin College, 1959–61, and Central Washington State University, 1963–64

Military Service: U.S. Army Reserve, 1964–69

Career: President, Columbia Basin Paper and Supply, 1967–94

Civic Activities and Awards: Board of directors, Yakima Federal Savings and Loan; assistant majority leader, National Platform Committee, 1984; president, Pasco Chamber of Commerce, Pasco Downtown Development Association; Pasco Jaycees; chair, Franklin County Republican Central Committee, 1974–78; delegate, Republican National Convention, 1976–84

State and Local Office: Member, Washington State House of Representatives, 1979–87; assistant majority leader; Republican Caucus chairman; Republican nominee for U.S. House of Representatives, 1992

Elected to Congress: Elected to the 104th Congress in November 1994; reelected to each succeeding Congress

ROBERT (ROBIN) C. HAYES, Representative, Eighth District, North Carolina

Born: Concord, NC, August 14, 1945

Resides: Concord, NC

Education: B.A., history, Duke University, 1967

Career: Owner and operator, Mt. Pleasant Hosiery Mill, 1988–present

State and Local Office: North Carolina House of Representatives, 1992–96

Elected to Congress: Elected to the 106th Congress in November 1998; reelected in 2000

JOHN D. HAYWORTH, Representative, Sixth District, Arizona

Born: High Point, NC, July 12, 1958

Resides: Scottsdale, AZ

Education: High Point Central High School, 1976; B.A., speech communications and political science, cum laude, North Carolina State University, 1980

Career: Broadcaster, public relations consultant, insurance agent

Civic Activities and Awards: Member, Rotary Club of Phoenix (Paul Harris Fellow), Boy Scouts of America (Eagle Scout); speaker for D.A.R.E.

Elected to Congress: Elected to the 104th Congress in November 1994; reelected to each succeeding Congress

JOEL HEFLEY, Representative, Fifth District, Colorado

Born: Ardmore, OK, April 18, 1935

Resides: Colorado Springs, CO

Education: Classen High School, 1953; B.A., Oklahoma Baptist University, 1957; M.A., Oklahoma State University, 1962; Gates Fellow, Harvard University, 1984

Career: Management consultant; executive director, Community Planning and Research Council, 1966–86

State and Local Office: Colorado State House of Representatives, 1977–78; Colorado State Senate, 1979–86

Elected to Congress: Elected to the 100th Congress in November 1986; reelected to each succeeding Congress

WALLY HERGER, Representative, Second District, California

Born: Yuba City, CA, May 20, 1945

Resides: Marysville, CA

Education: East Nicolaus High School; attended California State University, Sacramento, 1968–69

Career: Cattle rancher; small businessman

Civic Activities and Awards: Member, East Nicolaus High School Board of Trustees, 1977–80; member, National Federation of Independent Business, Sutter County Taxpayers Association, Yuba-Sutter Farm Bureau, California Cattlemen's Association, California Chamber of Commerce, Big Brothers/Big Sisters board of directors, South Yuba Rotary Club

State and Local Office: California state assemblyman, 1980–86

Elected to Congress: Elected to the 100th Congress in November 1986; reelected to each succeeding Congress

RICK HILL, former Representative at Large, Montana

Born: Grand Rapids, MN, December 30, 1946

Resides: Helena, MT

Education: B.S., economics and political science, St. Cloud State University, 1968

Career: Businessman; president, Insurewest Inc., 1984–96; managing partner, Hill Properties, 1988–present

Civic Activities and Awards: Served as Republican precinct committee member and state committee member from Lewis and Clark County; served on board of directors, Montana Science and Technology Alliance; chair, State Worker's Compensation Board, 1993–96; past chair, Helena Chamber of Commerce, State Republican Party Government Affairs Committee; past president, Professional Insurance Agents, Green Meadow Country Club; member, Montana Ambassadors, Montana Contractors Association, National Surety Bond Association, National Rifle Association, National Ski Patrol; listed in *Who's Who in American Finance and Industry;* chair, Montana Republican Party, 1991–92

Elected to Congress: Elected to the 105th Congress in November 1996; reelected in 1998; was not a candidate for reelection in 2000

VAN HILLEARY, Representative, Fourth District, Tennessee

Born: Dayton, TN, June 20, 1959

Resides: Spring City, TN

Education: Rhea County High School; B.S., University of Tennessee, 1981; J.D., Cumberland School of Law, Samford University, 1990

Military Service: Major, U.S. Air Force Reserve, 1982–present; served two volunteer tours in Persian Gulf during Operations Desert Shield and Desert Storm, flying 24 missions on a C-130 aircraft; U.S. Air Medals, Aerial Achievement Medal, National Service Medal, Kuwait Liberation Medal, Southwest Asia Campaign Medal, Outstanding Unit Ribbon

Career: Director, planning and business development at SSM Industries, Spring City, TN, 1984–86, 1992–94; admitted to the Tennessee bar, 1991

Civic Activities and Awards: Member, Presbyterian Church, American Legion, Veterans of Foreign Wars, Kiwanis International

Elected to Congress: Elected to the 104th Congress in November 1994; reelected to each succeeding Congress

DAVID L. HOBSON, Representative, Seventh District, Ohio

Born: Cincinnati, OH, October 17, 1936

Resides: Springfield, OH

Education: Withrow High School, 1954; B.A., Ohio Wesleyan University, Delaware, OH, 1958; J.D., Ohio State College of Law, Columbus, 1963

Military Service: Ohio Air National Guard, 1958–63

Career: Admitted to the Kentucky bar, 1965; businessman

Civic Activities and Awards: Member, VFW Post no. 1031, Springfield Rotary, Shrine Club no. 5121, Moose no. 536, Elks no. 51; member, board of Ohio Wesleyan University

State and Local Office: Ohio State Senate, 1982–90; majority whip, 1986–88; president pro tempore, 1988–90

Elected to Congress: Elected to the 102nd Congress in November 1990; reelected to each succeeding Congress

PETER HOEKSTRA, Representative, Second District, Michigan

Born: Groningen, the Netherlands, October 30, 1953

Resides: Holland, MI

Education: Holland Christian High School; B.A., Hope College (Holland) 1975; M.B.A., University of Michigan, 1977

Career: Vice president for product management, Herman Miller, Inc., 1977–92

Elected to Congress: Elected to the 103rd Congress in November 1992; reelected to each succeeding Congress

STEPHEN HORN, Representative, Thirty-Eighth District, California

Born: San Juan Bautista, CA, May 31, 1931

Resides: Long Beach, CA

Education: San Benito County High School, 1949; A.B., with great distinction, political science, Stanford University, 1953; M.P.A., Harvard University, 1955; Ph.D., political science, Stanford University, 1958

Military Service: Strategic Intelligence Reserve, SP-7, U.S. Army, 1954–62

Career: Congressional fellow, American Political Science Association, 1958–59; administrative assistant to Secretary of Labor James P. Mitchell, 1959–60; legislative assistant to U.S. Senator Thomas H. Kuchel (R-CA), 1960–66; senior fellow in governmental studies, Brookings Institution, 1966–69; dean of graduate studies and research, American University, 1969–70; president, California State University, Long Beach, 1970–88; trustee professor of political science, California State University, Long Beach, 1988–92; author, *The Cabinet and Congress* (1960), *Unused Power: The Work of the Senate Committee on Appropriations* (1970); coauthor, *Congressional Ethics: The View from the House* (1975)

Civic Activities and Awards: Vice chair and member, U.S. Commission on Civil Rights, 1969–82; member, National Institute of Corrections, 1970–88 (chair, 1985–87); lecturer on human rights, education, and American government in 15 countries for the U.S. Information Agency, 1975–79; fellow, National Academy of Public Administration, 1986–present; chair, American Association of State Colleges and Universities, 1985–86; named one of the 100 most effective university presidents in the United States, 1986

Elected to Congress: Elected to the 103rd Congress on November 1992; reelected to each succeeding Congress

JOHN NATHAN HOSTETTLER, Representative, Eighth District, Indiana

Born: Evansville, IN, July 19, 1961

Resides: Wadesville, IN

Education: Graduated, North Posey High School, 1979; B.S., Rose-Hulman Polytechnic University, 1983

Career: Performance engineer, Southern Indiana Gas and Electric, 1983–94

Civic Activities and Awards: Member, Baptist Church

Elected to Congress: Elected to the 104th Congress in November 1994; reelected to each succeeding Congress

AMO HOUGHTON, Representative, Thirty-First District, New York

Born: Corning, NY, August 7, 1926; grandson of former congressman Alanson B. Houghton of New York

Resides: Corning, NY

Education: St. Paul's School; B.A., Harvard University, 1950; M.B.A., Harvard Business School, 1952

Military Service: U.S. Marine Corps, 1945–46 (World War II)

Career: Executive officer, Corning Glass Works, Corning, NY, 1951–86, chairman and CEO, 1964–86

Civic Activities and Awards: Honorary doctoral degrees, Alfred University (1963), Albion College (1964), Centre College (1966), Clarkson College of Technology (1968), Elmira College (1982), Hartwick College (1983); Houghton College (1983), St. Bonaventure University (1987), Hobart and William Smith College (1991); member, Grace Commission, Business Council of New York State, Business Advisory Commission for Governor of New York, Labor-Industry Coalition for International Trade, Corning Chamber of Commerce, Corning Rotary Club, Corning Elks Club; trustee, Brookings Institution

Elected to Congress: Elected to the 100th Congress in November 1986; reelected to each succeeding Congress

KENNY HULSHOF, Representative, Ninth District, Missouri

Born: Sikeston, MO, May 22, 1958

Resides: Columbia, MO

Education: Thomas W. Kelly High School; B.S., University of Missouri School of Agriculture, 1980; J.D., University of Mississippi Law School, 1983

Career: Attorney, admitted to Missouri and Mississippi bars in 1983; assistant public defender, 32nd Judicial Circuit, 1983–86; assistant prosecuting attorney, Cape Girardeau, MO, 1986–89; special prosecutor, attorney general, State of Missouri, 1989–96

Civic Activities and Awards: Member, Newman Center Catholic Church, Boone County Farm Bureau, Farm House Foundation, Ducks Unlimited

Elected to Congress: Elected to the 105th Congress in November 1996; reelected in 1998

DUNCAN HUNTER, Representative, Fifty-Second District, California

Born: Riverside, CA, May 31, 1948

Resides: Alpine, CA

Education: Rubidoux High School, 1966; J.D. and B.S.L., Western State University, 1976

Military Service: First lieutenant, U.S. Army Airborne, 1969–71

Career: Trial lawyer; admitted to the California bar, 1976; practicing attorney, 1976–80

Civic Activities and Awards: Member, Baptist Church, Navy League

Elected to Congress: Elected to the 97th Congress in November 1980; reelected to each succeeding Congress

ASA HUTCHINSON, Representative, Third District, Arkansas

Born: Gravette, AR, December 3, 1950

Resides: Fort Smith, AR

Education: B.S., accounting, Bob Jones University, 1972; J.D., University of Arkansas Law School, 1974

Career: Admitted to the Arkansas bar in 1975 and began practice in Bentonville; Bentonville city attorney, 1976; United States attorney, 1982–85; chair, Arkansas State Republican Committee, 1990–95

Elected to Congress: Elected to the 105th Congress in 1996; reelected in 1998

HENRY J. HYDE, Representative, Sixth District, Illinois

Born: Chicago, IL, April 18, 1924

Resides: Wood Dale, IL

Education: St. George High School, 1942; B.S., Georgetown University, 1947; J.D., Loyola University School of Law, 1949

Military Service: Ensign, U.S. Navy, 1944–46; commander, U.S. Naval Reserve (retired)

Career: Admitted to the Illinois bar, January 9, 1950; practicing attorney, 1950–75

State and Local Office: State representative in Illinois General Assembly, 1967–74; majority leader, Illinois House of Representatives, 1971–72

Elected to Congress: Elected to the 94th Congress in November 1974; reelected to each succeeding Congress

BOB INGLIS, former Representative, Fourth District, South Carolina

Born: Savannah, GA, October 11, 1959

Resides: Greenville, SC

Education: May River Academy, 1977; A.B., Duke University, 1981; J.D., University of Virginia Law School, 1984

Career: Attorney; admitted to the South Carolina bar, 1984; formerly shareholder, Leatherwood, Walker, Todd and Mann, P.C.

Civic Activities and Awards: Fourth District Chair, South Carolinians to Limit Congressional Terms; Leadership Greenville; United Way Loaned Executive; Second Presbyterian Church

Elected to Congress: Elected to the 103rd Congress in November 1992; reelected in 1994, 1996; was not a candidate for reelection in 1998, but was an unsuccessful candidate for election to the U.S. Senate

JOHNNY ISAKSON, Representative, Sixth District, Georgia

Born: Atlanta, GA, December 28, 1944

Resides: Marietta, GA

Education: B.B.A., University of Georgia, 1966

Career: Real estate executive; Northside Realty, 1967–99, president, 1979–99

Civic Activities and Awards: Republican National Committee, Best Legislator in America, 1989; chairman of the board, Georgian Club; trustee, Kennesaw State University; board of directors, Metro Atlanta and Georgia Chambers of Commerce; past president, Cobb Chamber of Commerce; executive committee, National Association of Realtors; president, Realty Alliance; advisory board, Federal National Mortgage Association

State and Local Office: Georgia State House of Representatives, 1976–1990; Georgia State Senate, 1992–1996; chair, Georgia Board of Education, 1996

Elected to Congress: Elected to the 106th Congress on February 23, 1999, by special election, to fill the vacancy created when Newt Gingrich did not take his seat; reelected in 2000

DARRELL E. ISSA, Representative, Forty-Eighth District, California

Born: Cleveland, OH, January 1, 1954

Resides: Vista, CA

Education: Bachelor's degree, Siena Heights University, Michigan, 1976

Military Service: United States Army, active duty, 1970–1972; U.S. Army Reserves, 1972–76; active duty, 1976–80; Army Reserves, 1980–90

Career: CEO, Directed Electronics, 1982–2001

Civic Activities and Awards: Past chair, Consumer Electronics Association; former governor, Electronic Industries Alliance; past director, Business-Industry Political Action Committee; past director, San Diego Economic Development Association; past director, Great San Diego County Chamber of Commerce; *Inc.* magazine's Entrepreneur of the Year Award, 1994; past president, American Task Force for Lebanon; Ellis Island Medal of Honor; board of trustees, Siena Heights University

Elected to Congress: Elected to the 107th Congress in November 2000

ERNEST J. ISTOOK JR., Representative, Fifth District, Oklahoma

Born: Ft. Worth, TX, February 11, 1950

Resides: Warr Acres, OK

Education: Castleberry High School, 1967; B.A., Baylor University, 1971; J.D., Oklahoma City University, 1976

Career: Attorney; admitted to the Oklahoma bar, 1977; reporter, 1972–77

Civic Activities and Awards: Library board chairman, Oklahoma City, 1985–86; director, Warr Acres Chamber of Commerce, 1986–92

State and Local Office: City councilman, Warr Acres, 1982–86; Oklahoma State House of Representatives, 1986–92

Elected to Congress: Elected to the 103rd Congress in November 1992; reelected to each succeeding Congress

WILLIAM LEWIS JENKINS, Representative, First District, Tennessee

Born: Detroit, MI, November 29, 1936

Resides: Rogersville, TN

Education: Rogersville High School, 1954; B.B.A. from Tennessee Tech, 1957; J.D., University of Tennessee College of Law, 1961

Military Service: U.S. Army, 1960–62

Career: Farmer, 1961–present; admitted to the Rogersville bar, 1962; attorney; commissioner of conservation, 1971–72; ; energy adviser to Governor Lamar Alexander; director, Tennessee Valley Authority, 1971–78; Tennessee circuit court judge, 1990–96

Civic Activities and Awards: TVA board member; delegate to the Republican National Convention, 1988; member, American Legion, Masonic Lodge, Tennessee Bar Association, Tennessee Farm Bureau

State and Local Office: Tennessee General Assembly, 1962–71; Speaker of the Tennessee House, 1969–71

Elected to Congress: Elected to the 105th Congress in November 1996; reelected in 1998

NANCY L. JOHNSON, Representative, Sixth District, Connecticut

Born: Chicago, IL, January 5, 1935

Resides: New Britain, CT

Education: University of Chicago Laboratory School, 1951; University of Chicago, 1953; B.A., Radcliffe College, cum laude, 1957; attended University of London (English Speaking Union Scholarship), 1957–58

Career: Adjunct professor (political science), Central Connecticut State College, 1968–71

Civic Activities and Awards: Member, board of directors, United Way of New Britain; president,

Sheldon Community Guidance Clinic; Unitarian Universalists Society of New Britain; founding president, Friends of New Britain Public Library; member, board of directors, New Britain Bank and Trust; New Britain Museum of American Art

State and Local Office: Connecticut State Senate, 1977–82

Elected to Congress: Elected to the 98th Congress in November 1982; reelected to each succeeding Congress

SAM JOHNSON, Representative, Third District, Texas

Born: San Antonio, TX, October 11, 1930

Resides: Dallas, TX

Education: B.S., business administration, Southern Methodist University, 1951; M.A., international affairs, George Washington University, 1974

Military Service: U.S. Air Force, 1950–79; Korea and Vietnam (POW in Vietnam, 6 years, 10 months); director, Air Force Fighter Weapons School; flew with Air Force Thunderbirds Precision Flying Demonstration Team; graduate of Armed Services Staff College and National War College; 2 Silver Stars, 2 Legions of Merit, Distinguished Flying Cross, Bronze Star with Valor, 2 Purple Hearts, 4 Air Medals, and 3 Outstanding Unit awards; ended career with rank of colonel and Air Division commander

Career: Opened home-building company, 1979

Civic Activities and Awards: Smithsonian Board of Regents; U.S./Russian Joint Commission on POW/MIA; executive board of Dedman College, Southern Methodist University; Associated Texans Against Crime; Texas State Society

State and Local Office: Texas House of Representatives, 1984–91

Elected to Congress: Elected to the 102nd Congress on May 18, 1991, by special election, to fill the vacancy caused by the resignation of Steve Bartlett; reelected to each succeeding Congress

TIMOTHY V. JOHNSON, Representative, Fifteenth District, Illinois

Born: Urbana, IL, July 23, 1946

Resides: Sidney, IL

Education: Urbana High School; U.S. Military Academy at West Point; graduated Phi Beta Kappa, University of Illinois, 1969; J.D., University of Illinois, 1972

Career: Attorney

State and Local Office: Urbana City Council, 1971–75; Illinois State House of Representatives, 1976–2000

Elected to Congress: Elected to the 107th Congress in November 2000

WALTER B. JONES, Representative, Third District, North Carolina

Born: Farmville, NC, February 10, 1943

Resides: Farmville, NC

Education: Hargrave Military Academy, 1961; B.A., Atlantic Christian College, 1966

Military Service: North Carolina National Guard, 1967–71

Career: Salesman, Dunn Associates, 1973–82; president, Benefit Reserves Inc., 1989–94; president, Judson Company, 1990–94

State and Local Office: Member, North Carolina General Assembly House of Representatives, 1983–92

Elected to Congress: Elected to the 104th Congress in November 1994; reelected to each succeeding Congress

JOHN R. KASICH, former Representative, Twelfth District, Ohio

Born: McKees Rocks, PA, May 13, 1952

Resides: Westerville, OH

Education: Sto-Rox High School, 1970; B.A., political science, Ohio State University, 1974

Career: Administrative assistant to State Senator Donald Lukens, 1975–77

Civic Activities and Awards: Member, board of trustees, Concord Counseling Service, Westerville, OH; Outstanding Young Men in America Award, 1976; Watchdog of the Treasury Award, 1979; Watchdog of the Treasury's Golden Bulldog Award, 1983–92; Northland Community Council

Rep. John R. Kasich *(Government Printing Office)*

President's Award, 1981–82; American Security Council's Leadership Award, Guardian of Small Business Award, 1983–92; Spirit of Enterprise Award, 1988–93; Taxpayer's Friend Award, 1989–91; Ohio Health Care Association's Buckeye Award; National Wholesale Grocers Association's Thomas Jefferson Award, 1992, 1994; Champion of the Merit Shop, 1985–92, Associated Builders and Contractors; National Association of Wholesaler-Distributors; Congressional Leadership Award, 1994

State and Local Office: Ohio Senate, 1979–82; chair, Health and Human Services Committee

Elected to Congress: Elected to the 98th Congress in November 1982; reelected to each succeeding Congress through 2001; was not a candidate for reelection in 2000

RICHARD (RIC) KELLER, Representative, Eighth District, Florida

Born: Johnson City, TN, September 5, 1964

Resides: Orlando, FL

Education: B.S., East Tennessee State University, 1986; J.D., Vanderbilt University, 1992

Career: Attorney; joke writer to Jeb Bush in his first, unsuccessful campaign for governor of Florida, 1994; partner, Rumberger, Kirk & Caldwell

Civic Activities and Awards: Past chair, Board of Directors, Orlando/Orange County COMPACT program

Elected to Congress: Elected to the 107th Congress in November 2000

SUE W. KELLY, Representative, Nineteenth District, New York

Born: Lima, OH, September 26, 1936

Resides: Katonah, NY

Education: Lima Central High School; B.A., Denison University, 1958; M.A., Sarah Lawrence College, 1985

Career: Educator, small business owner, patient advocate, rape crisis counselor; professor, Sarah Lawrence College, 1988–91

Civic Activities and Awards: Member, League of Women Voters, American Association of University Women, PTA, Bedford Recreation Committee; member, Bedford Presbyterian Church

Elected to Congress: Elected to the 104th Congress in November 1994; reelected to each succeeding Congress

MARK R. KENNEDY, Representative, Second District, Minnesota

Born: Benson, Swift County, MN, April 11, 1957

Resides: Watertown, MN

Education: B.A., St. John's University, 1978; M.B.A., University of Michigan, Ann Arbor, 1973

Career: Business executive; certified public accountant

Elected to Congress: Elected to the 107th Congress in November 2000

BRIAN D. KERNS, Representative, Seventh District, Indiana

Born: Terre Haute, IN, May 22, 1957

Resides: Prairieton, IN

Education: Bachelor's degree, Indiana State University, 1991; M.P.A., Indiana State University, 1992

Career: Reporter and photographer, WTWO Television, Terre Haute; public information specialist, State of Indiana Department of Natural Resources; director of publications and public relations, St. Joseph's College, Rensselaer

Civic Activities and Awards: United Press International's "Best Feature Story of the Year" Award; Zorah Shine Children's Advocate Award; member, St. Stephen's Episcopal Church; member, Masonic Lodge; member, Elks Lodge; member, Eagles Lodge

Elected to Congress: Elected to the 107th Congress in November 2000

JAY KIM, former Representative, Forty-First District, California

Born: Seoul, Korea, March 27, 1939

Resides: Diamond Bar, CA

Education: B.S., civil engineering, University of Southern California, 1967; M.S., civil engineering, University of Southern California, 1973; M.P.A., California State University, 1980

Military Service: Republic of Korea Army, 1959–61

Career: Civil engineer; founder, JAYKIM Engineers, a transportation design firm

Civic Activities and Awards: Member, American Society of Civil Engineers, American Public Works Association

State and Local Office: Member, city council, Diamond Bar, CA, 1990–91; mayor, Diamond Bar, 1991–92

Elected to Congress: Elected to the 103rd Congress in November 1992; reelected in 1994, 1996; unsuccessful candidate for reelection in 1998

PETER T. KING, Representative, Third District, New York

Born: New York, NY, April 5, 1944

Resides: Seaford, NY

Education: B.A., St. Francis College, 1965; J.D., University of Notre Dame Law School, 1968

Military Service: U.S. Army Reserve National Guard, 1968–73

Career: Admitted to New York bar, 1968; attorney; deputy Nassau County attorney, 1972–74; executive assistant to the Nassau County executive, 1974–76; general counsel, Nassau Off-Track Betting Corporation, 1977

Civic Activities and Awards: Member, Ancient Order of Hibernians, Long Island Committee for Soviet Jewry, Sons of Italy, Knights of Columbus, 69th Infantry Veterans Corps, American Legion

State and Local Office: Hempstead town councilman, 1978–81; Nassau County comptroller, 1981–92

Elected to Congress: Elected to the 103rd Congress in November 1992; reelected to each succeeding Congress

JACK KINGSTON, Representative, First District, Georgia

Born: Bryan, TX, April 24, 1955

Resides: Savannah, GA

Education: Michigan State University, 1973–74; B.S., University of Georgia, 1978

Career: Insurance salesman; vice president, Palmer and Cay/Carswell

Civic Activities and Awards: Member, Savannah Health Mission, Isle of Hope Community Association, Christ Church; each congressional term, has been named a Taxpayer Hero by Citizens Against Government Waste and was awarded the Watchdog of the Treasury Golden Bulldog Award; annually, received the U.S. Chamber of Commerce's Spirit of Enterprise Award; 91 percent rating (average is 46 percent) on the Deficit Reduction Scorecard, the Concord Coalition; Friend of the Farmer, Georgia Farm Bureau; Senior Friendly, 60 Plus Association; Guardian of Small Business, National Federation of Independent Business; first representative to receive the National Rural Water Association's Green Key Award for his commitment to protecting public health, quality of life, and the environment, 1997;

Georgia Peanut Commission's highest honor, the Distinguished Service Award, 1998

State and Local Office: Georgia House of Representatives, 1984–92

Elected to Congress: Elected to the 103rd Congress in November 1992; reelected to each succeeding Congress

MARK STEVEN KIRK, Representative, Tenth District, Illinois

Born: Champaign, IL, September 15, 1959

Resides: Wilmette, IL

Education: B.A., with honors, Cornell University, 1981; M.Sc., London School of Economics, London, 1982; J.D., Georgetown University Law Center, 1992; studied at the Universidad Nacional Autonoma de Mexico, Mexico City

Military Service: U.S. Naval Reserves

Career: Attorney; aide, Congressman John Porter, 1984, and chief of staff, 1987–90; officer, World Bank's International Finance Corporation, 1990; special assistant to the assistant secretary for Inter-American Affairs, U.S. State Department, 1992–93; lawyer, Baker & MacKenzie, 1993–95; counsel, U.S. House International Relations Committee, 1995

Elected to Congress: Elected to the 107th Congress in November 2000

SCOTT KLUG, former Representative, Second District, Wisconsin

Born: Milwaukee, WI, January 16, 1953

Resides: Madison, WI

Education: Marquette University High School, 1971; B.A., history, Lawrence University, 1975; M.S.J., Northwestern University, 1976; M.B.A., University of Wisconsin, Madison, 1990

Career: News reporter and news anchor for WKOW-TV; investigative reporter for WJLA-TV; vice president, business development, Blunt, Ellis, and Loem

Elected to Congress: Elected to the 102nd Congress in November 1990; reelected to each succeeding Congress through 1998; not a candidate for reelection in 1998

JOE KNOLLENBERG, Representative, Eleventh District, Michigan

Born: Mattoon, IL, November 28, 1933

Resides: Bloomfield Hills, MI

Education: Eastern Illinois University, B.S., 1995

Military Service: U.S. Army, 1955–57

Career: Operated family insurance agency, 1958–92

Civic Activities and Awards: Troy Chamber of Commerce, past vice chair; Birmingham Cable TV Community Advisory Board, past member; St. Bede's Parish Council, past president and board member; Evergreen School PTA, past president; Bloomfield Glens Homeowners Association, past president; Cranbrook Homeowners Association, past president; Southfield Ad Hoc Park and Recreational Development Committee, past coordinator; Southfield Mayor's Wage and Salary Committee, past member

Elected to Congress: Elected to the 103rd Congress in November 1992; reelected to each succeeding Congress

JIM KOLBE, Representative, Fifth District, Arizona

Born: Evanston, IL, June 28, 1942

Resides: Tucson, AZ

Education: U.S. Capitol Page School, 1960; B.A., political science, Northwestern University, 1965; M.B.A., Stanford University, 1967; study abroad program, International School of America, 1962–63

Military Service: U.S. Navy, 1968–69; lieutenant commander, U.S. Naval Reserves, 1970–77

Career: Vice president, Wood Canyon Corporation, Sonoita, AZ; consultant, real estate development and political affairs; special assistant to Governor Ogilvie of Illinois, 1972–73

Civic Activities and Awards: Board of directors, Arizona Foundation for Children; board of directors, Tucson Community Food Bank; presidential appointment, Commission on Presidential Scholars; director of operations, Vietnam Orphans Airlift, San Francisco, 1975

State and Local Office: Arizona state senator, 1977–

82; served on Appropriations, Education, and Agriculture committees, chair of Judiciary Committee

Elected to Congress: Elected to the 99th Congress in November 1984; reelected to each succeeding Congress

STEVEN T. KUYKENDALL, former Representative, Thirty-Sixth District, California

Born: Oklahoma City, OK, January 27, 1947

Resides: Rancho Palos Verdes, CA

Education: B.S., economics, Oklahoma City University, 1968; M.B.A., San Diego State University, 1974

Military Service: Second lieutenant, U.S. Marine Corps, 1968, retired as captain, 1973

Career: Former banker

State and Local Office: Mayor, Rancho Palos Verdes, CA, 1994; California State Assembly, 1994–98

Elected to Congress: Elected to the 106th Congress in November 1998; unsuccessful candidate for re-election in 2000

RAY LaHOOD, Representative, Eighteenth District, Illinois

Born: Peoria, IL, December 6, 1945

Resides: Peoria, IL

Education: Spalding High School; Canton Junior College; B.S., education and sociology, Bradley University, 1971

Career: Junior high school teacher, 1971–77; director of Rock Island County Youth Services Bureau, 1972–74; chief planner for Bi-State Metropolitan Planning Commission, 1974–76; administrative assistant to Congressman Tom Railsback, 1977–82; chief of staff, Representative Bob Michel, 1990–94

Civic Activities and Awards: Academy of Our Lady/Spalding Board of Education (past president); Notre Dame High School Board (past president); Peoria Area Retarded Citizens Board of Directors (past member); Bradley University National Alumni Board (past president); Peoria Area Chamber of Commerce board (past member); Peoria Economic Development Council board of directors; Heartland Water Resources Council; Children's Hospital of Illinois advisory board; Peoria Rotary Club; Junior League Community advisory committee; Pillars Society of the United Way; Holy Family Church; Ellis Island Medal of Honor; Chamber of Commerce, Spirit of Enterprise Award; Farm Bureau, Friend of Agriculture Award; National Pork Producers Council, Bronze Symbol of Service Award; National Federation of Independent Business, Guardian of Small Business Award; Food Distributors International, Thomas Jefferson Award; United Seniors Association, Guardian of Medicare Award; National Tax-Limitation Committee, Tax Fighter Award; Peoria Notre Dame High School, 1999 Distinguished Alumnus

State and Local Office: Member, Illinois House of Representatives, 1982

Elected to Congress: Elected to the 104th Congress in November 1994; reelected to each succeeding Congress

STEVE LARGENT, Representative, First District, Oklahoma

Born: Tulsa, OK, September 28, 1954

Resides: Tulsa, OK

Education: Putnam City High School; B.S., University of Tulsa, 1976

Career: Professional athlete, National Football League, Seattle Seahawks, 1976–89; proprietor, advertising and marketing consulting firm, 1989-present

Civic Activities and Awards: Inducted into the Pro Football Hall of Fame, 1995; advisory board, Tulsa Area Salvation Army; board of trustees, University of Tulsa; Fellowship of Christian Athletes; Focus on the Family; Fellowship Bible Church, Tulsa

Elected to Congress: Elected to the 104th Congress in November 1994; reelected to each succeeding Congress

TOM LATHAM, Representative, Fifth District, Iowa

Born: Hampton, IA, July 14, 1948

Resides: Alexandria, IA

Education: Alexander Community School; graduated, Cal (Latimer) Community College, 1966; attended Wartburg College, 1966–67; Iowa State University, 1976–70; agricultural business major

Career: Marketing representative, independent insurance agent, bank teller, bookkeeper; co-owner, Latham Seed Co., 1976–present

Civic Activities and Awards: Member and past president, Nazareth Lutheran Church; past chair, Franklin County Extension Council; secretary, Republican Party of Iowa; 5th District Representative, Republican State Central Committee; co-chair, Franklin County Republican Central Committee; Iowa delegation whip, 1992 Republican National Convention; member, Iowa Farm Bureau Federation, Iowa Soybean Association, American Seed Trade Association, Iowa Corn Growers Association, Iowa Seed Association, Agribusiness Association of Iowa, I.S.U. Extension Citizens Advisory Council

Elected to Congress: Elected to the 104th Congress in November 1994; reelected to each succeeding Congress

STEVEN C. LaTOURETTE, Representative, Nineteenth District, Ohio

Born: Cleveland, OH, July 22, 1954

Resides: Madison Village, OH

Education: Cleveland Heights High School, 1972; B.A., University of Michigan, 1976; J.D., Cleveland State University, 1979

Career: Assistant public defender, Public Defender's Office, Lake County, OH, 1980–83; associated with Painesville firm of Cannon, Stern, Aveni and Krivok, 1983–86; associated with firm of Baker, Hackenberg and Collins, 1986–88; prosecuting attorney, Lake County, OH, 1988–94

Civic Activities and Awards: Served on the Lake County Budget Commission; executive board of the Lake County Narcotics Agency; chair, County Task Force on Domestic Violence; trustee, Cleveland Policy Historical Society; director, regional forensic laboratory; member, Lake County Association of Police Chiefs, Ohio Prosecuting Attorneys Association, National District Attorneys Association; appointed to serve as a fellow of the American College of Prosecuting Attorneys

Elected to Congress: Elected to the 104th Congress in November 1994; reelected to each succeeding Congress

RICK A. LAZIO, former Representative, Second District, New York

Born: West Islip, NY, March 13, 1958

Resides: Brightwaters, NY

Education: B.A., Vassar College, 1980; J.D., American University, Washington College of Law, 1983

Career: Assistant district attorney, Suffolk County, 1983–88; admitted to the New York bar, 1984; practicing attorney, 1989–92

State and Local Office: Suffolk County Legislature, 1989–92

Elected to Congress: Elected to the 103rd Congress in November 1992; reelected to each succeeding Congress through 2000; was not a candidate for reelection in 2000, but was an unsuccessful candidate for election to the U.S. Senate

JAMES A. LEACH, Representative, First District, Iowa

Born: Davenport, IA, October 15, 1942

Resides: Davenport, IA

Education: Davenport High School, 1960; B.A., Princeton University, 1964; M.A., School of Advanced International Studies, Johns Hopkins University, 1966; further graduate studies at the London School of Economics, 1966–68

Career: Staff member for U.S. Representative Donald Rumsfeld, 1965–66; foreign service officer assigned to the Department of State, 1968–69; administrative assistant to the director of the Office of Economic Opportunity, 1969–70; foreign service officer assigned to the Arms Control and Disarmament Agency, 1971–72; president, Flamegas Companies, 1973–76

Civic Activities and Awards: Member, U.S. delegation to the Geneva Disarmament Conference (1971–72), U.S. delegation to the United Nations General Assembly (1972); U.S. delegation to the United Nations Conference on Natural Resources (1975), U.S. Advisory Commission on Interna-

tional Educational and Cultural Affairs (1975–76), Federal Home Loan Bank Board of Des Moines (1975–76); member, Bettendorf Chamber of Commerce, National Federation of Independent Business, Elks, Moose, Rotary, Episcopal Church

Elected to Congress: Elected to the 95th Congress in November 1976; reelected to each succeeding Congress

JERRY LEWIS, Representative, Fortieth District, California

Born: Seattle, WA, October 21, 1934

Resides: Redlands, CA

Education: San Bernardino High School, 1952; B.A., University of California at Los Angeles, 1956

Career: Graduate intern in public affairs, Coro Foundation; insurance executive, 1959–78

State and Local Office: Former member, San Bernardino school board; served in California State Assembly, 1968–78

Elected to Congress: Elected to the 96th Congress in November 1978; reelected to each succeeding Congress

RON LEWIS, Representative, Second District, Kentucky

Born: McKell, KY, September 14, 1946

Resides: Cecilia, KY

Education: McKell High School, 1964; B.A., University of Kentucky, 1969; U.S. Navy Officer Candidate School, 1972; M.A., higher education, Morehead State University, 1981

Career: Laborer, Morehead State, Armco Steel Corporation, Kentucky Highway Department, Eastern State Hospital; sales, Ashland Oil; teacher, Watterson College, 1980; Baptist minister, 1980–present

Civic Activities and Awards: Member, Elizabethtown Chamber of Commerce; past president, Hardin and Larue County jail ministry; member, Serverus Valley Ministerial Association; honored for his voting record by U.S. Term Limits, League of Private Property Rights, Council for Citizens Against Government Waste, National Federation of Independent Business; named a Guardian of Seniors' Rights by Tax Fairness for Seniors

Elected to Congress: Elected to the 104th Congress in May 1994; reelected to each succeeding Congress

JOHN LINDER, Representative, Eleventh District, Georgia

Born: Deer River, MN, September 9, 1942

Resides: Tucker, GA

Education: Deer River High School, 1957; B.S., 1963, and D.D.S., 1967, University of Minnesota

Military Service: Captain, U.S. Air Force, 1967–69

Career: Practicing dentist, 1969–82; president, Linder Financial Corporation, 1977–92

Civic Activities and Awards: Member, Georgia Republican Party, Rotary Club, American Legion

State and Local Office: Georgia state representative, 1975–80, 1983–90

Elected to Congress: Elected to the 103rd Congress in November 1992; reelected to each succeeding Congress

FRANK A. LoBIONDO, Representative, Second District, New Jersey

Born: Bridgeton, NJ, May 12, 1946

Resides: Vineland, NJ

Education: Georgetown Preparatory School, 1964; St. Joseph's University, 1968

Career: Operations manager, LoBiondo Brothers Motor Express, 1968–94

Civic Activities and Awards: Board of directors, Literacy Volunteers of America, Cape May County chapter; Vineland Rotary, 1987–95 (honorary as of January 1, 1995); board of directors, Young Men's Christian Association; honorary chair, Cumberland County Hospice annual fundraising drive, 1992; chair, American Heart Association, Cumberland County chapter, 1989–90; founder, Cumberland County Environmental Task Force; president, Cumberland County Guidance Center, 1982–84; director, Young Men's Christian Association, 1978–84; member, Cape May County Chamber of Commerce (honorary as of January 1, 1995)

State and Local Office: Cumberland County Board of Freeholders, 1985–88; New Jersey state assemblyman, 1988–94; chair, General Assembly Economic and Community Development, Agriculture and Tourism Committee, 1988–94

Elected to Congress: Elected to the 104th Congress in November 1994; reelected to each succeeding Congress

FRANK D. LUCAS, Representative, Sixth District, Oklahoma

Born: Cheyenne, OK, January 6, 1960

Resides: Cheyenne, OK

Education: Oklahoma State University, Agricultural Economics, 1982

Career: Rancher and farmer

Civic Activities and Awards: Member, Oklahoma Farm Bureau, Oklahoma Cattleman's Association, Oklahoma Shorthorn Association

State and Local Office: Served in Oklahoma State House of Representatives, 1989–94; secretary, House Republican Caucus, 1991–94

Elected to Congress: Elected to the 103rd Congress in May 1994, by special election, to fill the vacancy caused by the resignation of Glenn English; reelected to each succeeding Congress

DONALD MANZULLO, Representative, Sixteenth District, Illinois

Born: Rockford, IL, March 24, 1944

Resides: Egan, IL

Education: B.A., American University, 1967; J.D., Marquette University Law School, 1970

Career: Admitted to the Illinois bar, 1970; practicing attorney, 1970–72

Civic Activities and Awards: President, Ogle County Bar Association, 1971, 1973; adviser, Oregon Ambulance Corporation; founder, Oregon Youth; member, State of Illinois and City of Oregon Chambers of Commerce, Friends of Severson Dells, Natural Land Institute, Ogle County Historic Society, Northern Illinois Alliance for the Arts, Aircraft Owners and Pilots Association, Ogle County Pilots Association, Kiwanis International, Illinois Farm Bureau, Ogle County Farm Bureau, National Federation of

Independent Business; Citizens Against Government Waste, Taxpayer's Hero; National Taxpayers Union, Taxpayer's Friend; Illinois Agriculture Association, Friend of Agriculture; 60 Plus Association, Senior Friendly; National Federation of Independent Business, Guardian of Small Business Award; several endorsements from the U.S. Chamber of Commerce

Elected to Congress: Elected to the 103rd Congress in November 1992; reelected to each succeeding Congress

BILL McCOLLUM, former Representative, Eighth District, Florida

Born: Brooksville, FL, July 12, 1944

Resides: Altamonte Springs, FL

Education: Hernando High School, 1962; B.A., 1965, and J.D., 1968, University of Florida

Military Service: U.S. Navy, 1969–72; Naval Reserves, 1972–92

Career: Lawyer, admitted to the Florida bar in 1968 and commenced practice in Orlando, 1973; former partner, Pitts, Eubanks and Ross

Civic Activities and Awards: Member, Florida Bar Association; Florida Blue Key, Phi Delta Phi, and Omicron Delta Kappa; Kiwanis; Sertoma Club of Apopka; American Legion; *Who's Who in America;* Reserve Officers Association; Naval Reserve Officers Association; Military Order of World Wars; former chair, Seminole County Republican Executive Committee

Elected to Congress: Elected to the 97th Congress in November 1980; reelected to each succeeding Congress through 2001; was not a candidate for reelection in 2000, but was an unsuccessful candidate for election to the U.S. Senate

JIM McCRERY, Representative, Fourth District, Louisiana

Born: Shreveport, LA, September 18, 1949

Resides: Shreveport, LA

Education: Leesville High, 1967; B.A., Louisiana Tech University, 1971; J.D., Louisiana State University, 1975

Career: Attorney; admitted to the Louisiana bar in 1975 and commenced practice in Leesville, LA; Jackson, Smith, and Ford (Leesville), 1975–78; assistant city attorney, Shreveport, 1979–80; district manager, U.S. Representative Buddy Roemer, 1981–82; legislative director, U.S. Representative Buddy Roemer, 1982–84; regional manager for government affairs, Georgia-Pacific Corporation, 1984–88

Civic Activities and Awards: Board of directors, Louisiana Association of Business and Industry, 1986–87; chair, Regulatory Affairs Committee, Louisiana Forestry Association, 1987; National Federation of Independent Business, Guardian of Small Business Award; U.S. Chamber of Commerce, Spirit of Enterprise Award; 60 Plus Association, Guardian of Seniors' Rights Award

Elected to Congress: Elected to the 100th Congress on April 16, 1988, by special election, to fill the vacancy caused by the resignation of Charles E. (Buddy) Roemer; reelected to each succeeding Congress

JOSEPH M. McDADE, former Representative, Tenth District, Pennsylvania

Born: Scranton, PA, September 29, 1931

Resides: Clarks Summit, PA

Education: Attended St. Paul's School and Scranton Preparatory School; B.A. with honors, political science, University of Notre Dame, 1953; LL.B., University of Pennsylvania, 1956

Career: Clerkship in office of Federal Chief Judge John W. Murphy, Middle District of Pennsylvania; engaged in general practice of law in 1957; served as Scranton city solicitor, 1962

Civic Activities and Awards: Honorary degrees, St. Thomas Aquinas College, University of Scranton; Marywood College Presidential Medal; L.H.D., Misericordia College, 1981; H.H.D., Kings College, 1981; LL.D., Mansfield State College, 1982; member, James Wilson Law Club, Knights of Columbus, Elks Club, Scranton Chamber of Commerce; American, Pennsylvania, and Lackawanna County Bar Associations

Elected to Congress: Elected to the 88th Congress in November 1962; reelected to each succeeding Congress through 1998; was not a candidate for reelection in 1998

JOHN M. McHUGH, Representative, Twenty-Fourth District, New York

Born: Watertown, NY, September 29, 1948

Resides: Pierrepont Manor, NY

Education: Watertown High School, 1966; B.A., Utica College of Syracuse University, 1970; M.P.A., Nelson A. Rockefeller Graduate School of Public Affairs; State University of New York at Albany, 1977

Career: Assistant to the city manager, Watertown, 1971–76; liaison with local governments for New York state senator H. Douglas Barclay, 1976–84

Civic Activities and Awards: American Society of Young Political Leaders; Jefferson County Farm Bureau; BPOE of Watertown; National Conference of State Legislatures; Council of State Governments, Eastern Regional Conference Committee on Fiscal Affairs; U.S. Trade Representative's Intergovernmental Policy Advisory Committee on Trade

State and Local Office: Elected to the New York State Senate, 1984–92

Elected to Congress: Elected to the 103rd Congress in November 1992; reelected to each succeeding Congress

SCOTT McINNIS, Representative, Third District, Colorado

Born: Glenwood Springs, CO, May 9, 1953

Resides: Grand Junction, CO

Education: Glenwood Springs High School; attended Mesa College; B.A. in business administration from Ft. Lewis College, 1975; J.D., St. Mary's University, 1980

Career: Worked as police officer in Glenwood Springs, 1976; director of the Valley View Hospital; director of personnel at Holy Cross Electric Association; practicing attorney, 1980–92

Civic Activities and Awards: Received the Florence Sabin Award for contributions to rural health care; received several awards from the United Veterans Commission of Colorado; member, Colorado Tourism Board; Colorado Ski Country's Legislator of the Year and Legislative Achievement of the Decade; received the Lee Atwater Leadership Award for outstanding contributions and extraordinary achievements in public service; twice received the National Federation of Independent Business Guardian of Small Business Award; Watchdogs of the Treasury, Golden Bulldog Award; American Security Council, National Security Leadership Award; Korean Veterans Association, Man of the Year; Free Congress Foundation, Sound Dollar Award; U.S. Chamber of Commerce, Thomas Jefferson Award, Spirit of Free Enterprise Award; Colorado Association of Homebuilders Award for Government Service; Rocky Mountain chapter of Associated Builders and Contractor's Public Servant of the Year

State and Local Office: Colorado House of Representatives, 1983–92; chaired the Committee on Agriculture, Livestock, and Natural Resources; served on the Judiciary, Local Government, and Appropriations committees for 10 years; state house majority leader, 1990–92

Elected to Congress: Elected to the 103rd Congress in November 1992; reelected to each succeeding Congress

DAVID M. McINTOSH, former Representative, Second District, Indiana

Born: Oakland, CA, June 8, 1958

Resides: Muncie, IN

Education: East Noble High School; B.A., Yale University, 1980; J.D., University of Chicago, 1983

Career: Member of the Indiana state bar and the U.S. Supreme Court bar; special assistant to President Reagan for domestic affairs, special assistant to Attorney General Meese in the Reagan administration, 1986–87; liaison to President's Commission on Privatization; specialized in constitutional legal policy at the Justice Department; special assistant to Vice President Quayle, 1989–91; executive director of the President's Council on Competitiveness, 1989–92; legal counsel to Vice President Quayle; fellow, Hudson Institute Competitiveness Center, 1993–94; senior fellow, Citizens for a Sound Economy

Civic Activities and Awards: Founded the Federalist Society for Law and Public Policy (currently national cochair)

Elected to Congress: Elected to the 104th Congress in November 1994; reelected to each succeeding Congress through 2001; was not a candidate for reelection in 2000, but was an unsuccessful candidate for governor

HOWARD P. "BUCK" McKEON, Representative, Twenty-Fifth District, California

Born: Los Angeles, CA, September 9, 1939

Resides: Santa Clarita, CA

Education: Verdugo Hills High School; B.S., Brigham Young University, 1985

Career: Owner, Howard and Phil's Western Wear, 1973–present; chairman, Valencia National Bank, 1987–88

Civic Activities and Awards: Board of directors, Canyon Country Chamber of Commerce; California Republican State Central Committee; advisory council, Boy Scouts of America; president and trustee, William S. Hart School District, 1979–87; chair and director, Henry Mayo Newhall Memorial Hospital, 1983–87; honorary chair, Red Cross Community Support Campaign, 1992; honorary chair, Leukemia Society Celebrity Program, 1990 and 1994

State and Local Office: Santa Clarita mayor, 1987–88; Santa Clarita City Council, 1988–92

Elected to Congress: Elected to the 103rd Congress in November 1992; president, Republican Freshman Class of the 103rd Congress; reelected to each succeeding Congress

JACK METCALF, former Representative, Second District, Washington

Born: Marysville, WA, November 30, 1927

Resides: Marysville, WA

Education: B.A., Pacific Lutheran University, 1951; M.A., University of Washington, 1966

Military Service: U.S. Army, 1946–47

Career: U.S. Fish and Wildlife Service patrol boat skipper with U.S. Marshal Authority, 1947–48; teacher, Everett High School, 1951–81; owner of the Log Castle Bed and Breakfast, Langley, 1978–present

Civic Activities and Awards: Member, Concord Coalition, South Whidby (Washington) Historical Society, South Whidby (Washington) Kiwanis, Wildcat Steelhead Club, Back Country Horsemen—Skagit County chapter

State and Local Office: Washington State House of Representatives, 1960–64; Washington State Senate, 1966–74, 1980–92; chair, Washington State Senate Environment and Natural Resources Committee

Elected to Congress: Elected to the 104th Congress in November 1994; reelected in 1996, 1998; was not a candidate for reelection in 2000

JOHN L. MICA, Representative, Seventh District, Florida

Born: Binghamton, NY, January 27, 1943; brother of former congressman Daniel A. Mica

Resides: Winter Park, FL

Education: Miami-Edison High School; B.A., University of Florida, 1967

Career: Executive director, local government study commissions, Palm Beach County, 1970–72; executive director, Orange County local government study commission, 1972–74; president, MK Development, 1975–92; administrative assistant, U.S. Senator Paula Hawkins, 1981–85; managing general partner, Cellular Communications; partner, Mica, Dudinsky and Associates, 1985–92

Civic Activities and Awards: Florida State Good Government Award, 1973; one of five Florida Jaycees Outstanding Young Men of America, 1978; member, Kiwanis, Crime Line Board, Tiger Bay Club, Beth Johnson Mental Health Board, PTA Board, Chamber of Commerce, Florida Blue Key; U.S. Chamber of Commerce, Spirit of Enterprise Award, 1999; Taxpayers' Hero Award and Watchdog of the Treasury Award

State and Local Office: Florida State House of Representatives, 1976–80

Elected to Congress: Elected to the 103rd Congress in November 1992; reelected to each succeeding Congress

DAN MILLER, Representative, Thirteenth District, Florida

Born: Highland Park, MI, May 30, 1942

Resides: Bradenton, FL

Education: Manatee High School, 1960; B.S., B.A., University of Florida, 1964; M.B.A., Emory University, 1965; Ph.D., Louisiana State University, 1970

Career: Businessman; partner, Miller Enterprises, 1973–present

Elected to Congress: Elected to the 103rd Congress in November 1992; reelected to each succeeding Congress

GARY G. MILLER, Representative, Forty-First District, California

Born: Huntsville, AR, October 16, 1948

Resides: Diamond Bar, CA

Education: California High School, Whittier, CA; Lowell High School, LaHabra, CA; Mount San Antonio College, Walnut, CA, 1971, 1988–89

Military Service: Private, U.S. Army, 1967

Career: Developer, owner, G. Miller Development Company, 1971–98

State and Local Office: Diamond Bar City Council, 1989–95; mayor, Diamond Bar, 1992; California State Assembly, 1995–98

Elected to Congress: Elected to the 106th Congress in November 1998; reelected in 2000

SUSAN MOLINARI, former Representative, Thirteenth District, New York

Born: Staten Island, NY, March 27, 1958

Education: St. Joseph Hill Academy, 1976; B.A., 1980, M.A., 1982, State University of New York at Albany

Career: Research analyst; finance assistant, National Republican Governors Association; ethnic community liaison; Republican National Committee, 1983–84

State and Local Office: New York City Council, 1986–90

Elected to Congress: Elected to the 101st Congress on March 20, 1990, by special election, to fill the vacancy caused by the resignation of her father, Guy V. Molinari; reelected to each succeeding Congress and served until her resignation on August 2, 1997

JERRY MORAN, Representative, First District, Kansas

Born: Great Bend, KS, May 29, 1954

Resides: Hays, KS

Education: B.S., University of Kansas, 1976, J.D., University of Kansas, 1981

Career: Operations instructor, Consolidated State Bank, 1975–77; manager, Farmers State Bank and Trust Co., 1977–78; practicing attorney, 1981–96; instructor, Ft. Hays State University, 1986

Civic Activities and Awards: Rotary Club; Lions International; board of trustees, Ft. Hays State University Endowment Association

State and Local Office: Elected to the Kansas Senate, 1988–96; majority leader 1995–97

Elected to Congress: Elected to the 105th Congress in November 1996; reelected in 1998, 2000

CONSTANCE A. MORELLA, Representative, Eighth District, Maryland

Born: Somerville, MA, February 12, 1931

Resides: Bethesda, MD

Education: Somerville High School, 1948; A.B., Boston University, 1954; M.A., American University, 1967

Career: Professor, Montgomery College, 1970–86

Civic Activities and Awards: Honorary doctoral degrees from American University, Norwich University, Dickinson College, Mount Vernon College, and University of Maryland; trustee, Capitol College; charter member of Global Legislators for a Balanced Environment (GLOBE)

State and Local Office: Delegate, Maryland General Assembly, 1979–86

Elected to Congress: Elected to the 100th Congress in November 1986; reelected to each succeeding Congress

SUE MYRICK, Representative, Ninth District, North Carolina

Born: Tiffin, OH, August 1, 1941

Resides: Charlotte, NC

Education: Port Clinton High School; attended Heidelberg College, 1959–60

Career: President and CEO, Myrick Advertising and Myrick Enterprises, 1985–94

Civic Activities and Awards: Active with the National League of Cities and the U.S. Conference of Mayors; served on former president Bush's Affordable Housing Commission; member, Charlotte Chamber of Commerce, Muscular Dystrophy Association, March of Dimes, Elks Auxiliary, PTA, United Methodist Church; Cub Scout den mother; founder, Charitable Outreach Society; member, Republican Conference's Communications Working Group

State and Local Office: Charlotte City Council, 1983–85; mayor of Charlotte, NC, 1987–91

Elected to Congress: Elected to the 104th Congress in November 1994; reelected to each succeeding Congress

GEORGE R. NETHERCUTT JR., Representative, Fifth District, Washington

Born: Spokane, WA, October 7, 1944

Resides: Spokane, WA

Education: North Central High School; B.A., Washington State University, 1967; J.D., Gonzaga University School of Law, 1971

Career: Law clerk, federal Judge Ralph Plummer, U.S. District Court, Anchorage, AK, 1971–72; staff counsel and chief of staff, U.S. Senator Ted Stevens (R-AK), 1972–76; practicing attorney, 1976–94; town attorney for eastern Washington communities of Reardan, Creston, and Almira

Civic Activities and Awards: Cofounder, Vanessa Behan Crisis Nursery; past president, Spokane County Juvenile Diabetes Foundation; past chair, Spokane County Republican Party; member, Spokane Central Lions, Sigma Nu fraternity, Spokane Masonic Lodge no. 34 (Scottish rite), El Katif Shrine, Masonic Temple Foundation Trustees, Spokane School Levy Adviser Foundation

Elected to Congress: Elected to the 104th Congress in November 1994; reelected to each succeeding Congress

MARK W. NEUMANN, former Representative, First District, Wisconsin

Born: East Troy, WI, February 27, 1954

Resides: Janesville, WI

Education: East Troy High School, 1972; B.S., University of Wisconsin, Whitewater, 1975; M.S., University of Wisconsin, River Falls, 1977

Career: Home builder

Civic Activities and Awards: Member of St. Matthew's Evangelical Lutheran Church of Janesville; past president of the Milton Chamber of Commerce; member, Optimist Club, Forward Janesville, South Central Wisconsin Builders Association, National Federation of Independent Business, Janesville Board of Realtors, Board of Regents of Wisconsin Lutheran College; director of the Boys and Girls Club of Janesville; recipient of the Entrepreneur of the Year Award from the University of Wisconsin–Whitewater Entrepreneurship Program

Elected to Congress: Elected to the 104th Congress in November 1994; reelected in 1996; was not a candidate for reelection in 1998, but was an unsuccessful candidate for election to the U.S. Senate

ROBERT NEY, Representative, Eighteenth District, Ohio

Born: Wheeling, WV, July 5, 1954

Resides: St. Clairsville, OH

Education: St. John's High School; B.S., Ohio State University, 1976

Career: Teacher, Iran, 1978; program manager, Ohio Office of Appalacia, 1979; Bellaire Safety Director, 1980

Civic Activities and Awards: Member, Elks, Lions, Kiwanis, National Rifle Association

State and Local Office: Ohio House of Representatives, 1980–82; Ohio Senate, 1984–94

Elected to Congress: Elected to the 104th Congress in November 1994; reelected to each succeeding Congress

ANNE MEAGHER NORTHUP, Representative, Third District, Kentucky

Born: Louisville, KY, January 22, 1948

Resides: Louisville, KY

Education: Sacred Heart Academy, 1966; B.A., St. Mary's College, 1970

Civic Activities and Awards: Board member, Greater Louisville Public Radio, Community Advisory Board for the Junior League of Louisville, Hospice of Louisville, Kentucky Cancer Consortium, Partnership for Kentucky School Reform; member, Institute for Republican Women; Association of Equipment Distributors, Legislator of the Year, 1999; U.S. Chamber of Commerce, Spirit of Enterprise Award, 1999; Susan B. Anthony Congressional Award, 1999; Southern Economic Development Council, Inc., Honor Roll of Legislative Achievement in Economic Development, 1999; Watchdogs of the Treasury, Bulldog Award, 1999; Citizens for a Sound Economy, Jefferson Award, 1998; NFIB, Guardian of Small Business Award, 1997–98; the Environmental Industry Association, Legislator of the Year, 1997; National Industries for the Blind, Outstanding Freshman Member of Congress, 1997; U.S. Chamber of Commerce, Spirit of Enterprise Award, 1997; National Association of Manufacturers, Award for Manufacturing Legislative Excellence; Sacred Heat Academy Alumna Award, 1994; Catholic Schools Distinguished Alumni Award, 1991; University of Notre Dame Award of the Year, 1991

State and Local Office: Kentucky House of Representatives, 1987–96

Elected to Congress: Elected to the 105th Congress in November 1996; reelected in 1998, 2000

CHARLES W. NORWOOD JR., Representative, Tenth District, Georgia

Born: Valdosta, GA, July 27, 1941

Resides: Evans, GA

Education: Baylor Military High School, 1959; B.S., Georgia Southern University, 1964; D.D.S., Georgetown University Dental School, 1967

Military Service: Served as captain, U.S. Army, 1967–69, including tour of duty in Vietnam with the 173rd Airborne Brigade; awarded the Combat Medic Badge and two Bronze Stars

Career: Began dentistry practice, Augusta, GA, 1969; started several small businesses over the years, including Northwood Tree Nursery in

Evans, GA, and Park Avenue Fabrics in Augusta, GA

Civic Activities and Awards: Elected president of the Georgia Dental Association, 1983; member, Trinity-on-the-Hill United Methodist Church, Augusta, GA

Elected to Congress: Elected to the 104th Congress in November 1994; reelected to each succeeding Congress

JIM NUSSLE, Representative, Second District, Iowa

Born: Des Moines, IA, June 27, 1960

Resides: Manchester, IA

Education: Carl Sandburg High School, 1978; attended Ronshoved Hojskole (Denmark), 1978–79; Luther College, B.A., 1983; Drake University Law School, J.D., 1985

Career: Admitted to the bar, January 1986; Delaware County attorney, 1986–90; practicing attorney, 1985–86

Elected to Congress: Elected to the 102nd Congress in November 1990; reelected to each succeeding Congress

THOMAS OSBORNE, Representative, Third District, Nebraska

Born: Hastings, NE, February 23, 1937

Resides: LeMoyne, NE

Education: B.A., Hastings College, 1959; M.A., University of Nebraska, 1963; Ph.D., University of Nebraska-Lincoln, 1965

Career: Professional football player, National Football League, 1959–60; head football coach, University of Nebraska Cornhuskers, 1972–97; creator, Teammates Program, 1991; author, *More Than Willing*

Elected to Congress: Elected to the 107th Congress in November 2000

DOUGLAS A. OSE, Representative, Third District, California

Born: Sacramento, CA, June 27, 1955

Resides: Sacramento, CA

Education: Rio Americano High School; B.S., business administration, University of California at Berkeley, 1977

Civic Activities and Awards: Citrus Heights Incorporation Project Board of Directors; California State Automobile Association Board of Directors; Citrus Heights Chamber of Commerce; Sacramento Housing and Redevelopment Commission; Sacramento Rotary Club

Elected to Congress: Elected to the 106th Congress in November 1998; reelected in 2000

C. L. "BUTCH" OTTER, Representative, First District, Idaho

Born: Caldwell, ID, May 3, 1942

Resides: Star, ID

Education: Bachelor's degree, College of Idaho, 1967; attended Armored Intelligence and Reconnaissance School, Fort Knox, Kentucky, 1968

Military Service: U.S. National Guard, 1968–73

Career: Director, Food Products Division, J. R. Simplot; president, Simplot Livestock; president, Simplot International.

Civic Activities and Awards: Honorary doctorate, Mindanao State University, Philippines; member, Board of Directors, J. R. Simplot Company; member, Board of Directors, Kyn-Ten Oil Drilling Company; Republican Party Central Committee; past chair, Canyon County Republican Party; past member, President Ronald Reagan's Task Force on International Private Enterprise; past member, the World Bank's Agricultural Advisory Committee; past member, the Center for International Private Enterprise; past member, Idaho Association of Commerce and Industry; past member, the Idaho Young President's Organization, past member, the Pacific Northwest Waterways Association; past member, Northwest Food Producers; past member, Board of the National Cowboy Hall of Fame; member, Regional Advisory Board for the Museum of the Rockies; member, the Idaho International Trade Council; member, Elks Club, 1967–present; member, National Rifle Association; member, Maple Grove State Grange, 1958–present; member, the Idaho Cowboys Association; member, the American Legion; member, Idaho 4-H Million Dollar Club;

member, Grand Slam Member of Ducks Unlimited; member, Roman Catholic Church

State and Local Office: Idaho State House of Representatives, 1972–76; Idaho lieutenant governor, 1987–2001

Elected to Congress: Elected to the 107th Congress in November 2000

MICHAEL G. OXLEY, Representative, Fourth District, Ohio

Born: Findlay, OH, February 11, 1944

Resides: Findlay, OH

Education: Findlay Senior High School, 1962; B.A., government, Miami University, 1966; J.D., Ohio State University College of Law, 1969

Career: Admitted to Ohio bar, 1969; FBI special agent, Washington, DC, Boston, and New York City, 1969–72; attorney, Oxley, Malone, Fitzgerald, Hollister, 1972–81

Civic Activities and Awards: Member, Trinity Lutheran Church, Findlay, OH; American, Ohio, and Findlay Bar Associations; Sigma Chi fraternity; Omicron Delta Kappa men's honorary fraternity; Society of Former Special Agents of the FBI; Rotary International; Ohio Farm Bureau; Findlay Area Chamber of Commerce

State and Local Office: Ohio House of Representatives, 1972–81; member, financial institutions committee and state government committee; ranking minority member, judiciary and criminal justice committee

Elected to Congress: Elected to the 97th Congress on June 25, 1981, in a special election, to fill the vacancy caused by the death of Tennyson Guyer; reelected to each succeeding Congress

RON PACKARD, former Representative, Forty-Eighth District, California

Born: Meridian, ID, January 19, 1931

Resides: Oceanside, CA

Education: Meridian High School, 1948; attended Brigham Young University, 1948–50; Portland State University, 1952–53; D.M.D., University of Oregon Dental School, 1957

Military Service: Lieutenant, U.S. Navy Dental Corps, 1957–59

Career: Dentist

Civic Activities and Awards: Director, Carlsbad Chamber of Commerce, 1972–76; Carlsbad Planning Commission, 1974–76; Carlsbad chair of the Boy Scouts of America, 1977–79; member, North County Armed Services YMCA, North County Transit District, San Diego Association for Government, Coastal Policy Committee and Transportation Policy Committee, California League of Cities; president, San Diego Division of the California League of Cities; Mormon Church

State and Local Office: Carlsbad School District Board, 1960–72; Carlsbad City Council, 1976–78; mayor of Carlsbad, 1978–82

Elected to Congress: Elected to the 98th Congress in November 1982; reelected to each succeeding Congress through 2001; was not a candidate for reelection in 2000

MICHAEL (MIKE) PAPPAS, former Representative, Twelfth District, New Jersey

Born: New Brunswick, NJ, December 29, 1960

Resides: Rocky Hill, NJ

Education: Alma Preparatory School; attended Seton Hall University

Career: Insurance executive and partner, Pappas Insurance Agency

Civic Activities and Awards: Chair, Human Services and Education Steering Committee, National Association of Counties; member, National Policy Forum, Republican National Committee; president, New Jersey Association of Counties, 1994; past chair, New Jersey Judicial Unification Transition Committee; spearheaded Somerset County Youth Council; board of trustees, Somerset Medical Center; past member, Somerset County 4-H Association, Franklin Township Lions Club, Order of AHEPA, Central Jersey Club of the Deaf; Franklin Township Lions Club Citizen of the Year Award, 1988; Somerville Area Jaycees Distinguished Service Award, 1992

State and Local Office: Somerset County freeholder, 1984–86, serving as director, deputy director, and board of social services chair; Franklin township councilman, 1982–87; mayor of Franklin, 1983–84

Elected to Congress: Elected to the 105th Congress in November 1996; was an unsuccessful candidate for reelection in 1998

MIKE PARKER, former Representative, Fourth District, Mississippi

Born: Laurel, MS, October 31, 1949

Resides: Brookhaven, MS

Education: Franklin High School, 1967; B.A., William Carey College, 1970

Career: Small businessman

Civic Activities and Awards: Member, Faith Presbyterian Church

Elected to Congress: Elected to the 101st Congress in November 1988; reelected to each succeeding Congress through 1998; was not a candidate for reelection in 1998

RON E. PAUL, Representative, Fourteenth District, Texas

Born: Pittsburgh, PA, August 20, 1935

Resides: Surfside Beach, TX

Education: B.A., Gettysburg College, 1957; M.D., Duke College of Medicine, 1961

Military Service: Captain, U.S. Air Force, 1963–68

Career: Practicing obstetrician and gynecologist, 1968–96

State and Local Office: Represented Texas's 22nd District in the U.S. House of Representatives, 1978–84

Elected to Congress: Elected to the 105th Congress in November 1996; reelected in 1998, 2000

EDWARD A. PEASE, former Representative, Seventh District, Indiana

Born: Terre Haute, IN, May 22, 1951

Resides: Seelyville, IN

Education: B.A. with distinction, 1973, and J.D., cum laude, 1977, Indiana University; postgraduate study in English, Indiana State University, 1978–84

Career: Admitted to the Indiana bar in 1977 and began practice in Brazil, IN; vice president for university advancement, Indiana State University; city attorney, Brazil, IN, 1980; department attorney, Clay County Department of Public Welfare, 1978–79; partner, Thomas, Thomas, and Pease, Attorneys at Law, 1977–84; general counsel, Indiana State University, 1984–93

Civic Activities and Awards: Member, former chapter adviser, and former national president, Pi Kappa Alpha fraternity; member, Phi Beta Kappa and Phi Eta Sigma scholastic fraternities; member of the advisory council and chair of the National Order of the Arrow Committee, National Council of Boy Scouts of America; member, executive committee, Wabash Valley Council, Boy Scouts of America; board of directors, National Interfraternity Conference; lay leader, First United Methodist Church of Brazil

State and Local Office: Indiana State Senate, 1980–92

Elected to Congress: Elected to the 105th Congress in November 1996; reelected in 1998; was not a candidate for reelection in 2000

MIKE PENCE, Representative, Second District, Indiana

Born: Columbus, IN, June 7, 1959

Resides: Edinburgh, IN

Education: Bachelor's degree, Hanover College, Indiana, 1981; J.D., Indiana University, 1986

Career: Broadcast consultant; former radio talk show host

Elected to Congress: Unsuccessful candidate for election 1988 and 1990; elected to the 107th Congress in November 2000

JOHN E. PETERSON, Representative, Fifth District, Pennsylvania

Born: Titusville, PA, December 25, 1938

Resides: Pleasantville, PA

Education: Attended Pennsylvania State University, 1974–76

Military Service: U.S. Army, 1958–64

Career: Owner, Peterson's Golden Dawn Food Market, 1958–84

Civic Activities and Awards: Past president, Pleasantville Lions Club, Titusville Chamber of Commerce, Pleasantville PTA, and Pleasantville

Borough Council; formerly served on boards of directors of Titusville Hospital and University of Pittsburgh's Titusville and Bradford campuses, advisory board of Pennsylvania State University School of Forest Resources, and advisory committee of the University of Pittsburgh Graduate School of Public Health

State and Local Office: Pleasantville borough councilman, 1968–77; Pennsylvania State House of Representatives, 1977–84; Pennsylvania State Senate, 1985–96

Elected to Congress: Elected to the 105th Congress in November 1996; reelected in 1998, 2000

THOMAS E. PETRI, Representative, Sixth District, Wisconsin

Born: Marinette, WI, May 28, 1940

Resides: Fond du Lac, WI

Education: Lowell P. Goodrich High School, 1958; B.A., Harvard University, 1962; J.D., Harvard Law School, 1965

Career: Lawyer; admitted to the Wisconsin state and Fond du Lac county bar associations, 1965; law clerk to federal Judge James Doyle, 1965–66; White House aide, 1969; commenced practice in Fond du Lac in 1970–79

Civic Activities and Awards: Peace Corps volunteer, 1966–67

State and Local Office: Wisconsin State Senate, 1972–79

Elected to Congress: Elected to the 96th Congress on April 3, 1979, by special election, to fill the vacancy caused by the death of William A. Steiger; reelected to each succeeding Congress

CHARLES W. "CHIP" PICKERING JR., Representative, Third District, Mississippi

Born: Laurel, MS, August 10, 1963

Resides: Laurel, MS

Education: B.A., business administration, University of Mississippi, 1986; M.B.A., Baylor University, 1988

Career: Farmer; legislative aide to Senate majority leader Trent Lott, 1990–94; Bush administration appointee, U.S. Department of Agriculture, 1989–91

Civic Activities and Awards: Southern Baptist missionary to Budapest, Hungary, 1986–87; U.S. Chamber of Commerce, Spirit of Enterprise Award, 1998; Americans for Tax Reform, Friend of the Taxpayer Award

Elected to Congress: Elected to the 105th Congress in November 1996; reelected in 1998, 2000

JOSEPH R. PITTS, Representative, Sixteenth District, Pennsylvania

Born: Lexington, KY, October 10, 1939

Resides: Kennett Square, PA

Education: B.A., philosophy and religion, Asbury College, 1961; M.Ed., West Chester University, 1972

Military Service: U.S. Air Force, 1963–69, rising from second lieutenant to captain

Career: Math and science teacher, Great Valley High School, Malvern, PA, 1969–72; nursery business owner and operator, 1974–90; teacher, Mortonsville Elementary School, Versailles, KY

State and Local Office: Member, Pennsylvania House of Representatives, 1972–96, serving as chair of Appropriations Committee, 1989–96, and of Labor Relations Committee, 1981–88

Elected to Congress: Elected to the 105th Congress in November 1996; reelected in 1998, 2000

TODD RUSSELL PLATTS, Representative, Nineteenth District, Pennsylvania

Born: York, PA, March 5, 1962

Resides: Springettsbury Township, PA

Education: York Suburban High School, 1980; B.S., summa cum laude, Shippensburg University of Pennsylvania, 1984; J.D., cum laude, Pepperdine University School of Law, 1991

Career: Attorney; associate, Barley, Snyder, Senft & Cohen Law Firm, 1992–93

Civic Activities and Awards: Co-chair, York County Transportation Coalition; legislative chair, York Metropolitan Planning Organization; Statewide Children's Health Insurance Advisory Committee; Central Pennsylvania Hugh O'Brian Youth Leadership Seminar; Junior Achievement of South Central Pennsylvania

State and Local Office: Pennsylvania State House of Representatives, 1993–2000

Elected to Congress: Elected to the 107th Congress in November 2000

RICHARD W. POMBO, Representative, Eleventh District, California

Born: Tracy, CA, January 8, 1961

Resides: Tracy, CA

Education: Attended California Polytechnic Institute, 1979–82

Career: Rancher

Civic Activities and Awards: Cofounder, San Joaquin County Citizens Land Alliance; member, Tracy Rotary Club

State and Local Office: Tracy city council member, 1990–92

Elected to Congress: Elected to the 103rd Congress in November 1992; reelected to each succeeding Congress

JOHN EDWARD PORTER, former Representative, Tenth District, Illinois

Born: Evanston, IL, June 1, 1935

Resides: Wilmette, IL

Education: Evanston Township High School, 1953; attended Massachusetts Institute of Technology, 1953–54; B.S.B.A., Northwestern University School of Business, Evanston, IL, 1957; J.D. with distinction, University of Michigan Law School, 1961 (law review)

Military Service: U.S. Army Signal Corps (Reserve), 1958–64

Career: Engaged in the practice of law in Evanston, IL; admitted to practice before the Supreme Court of the United States, U.S. Court of Claims, and the Illinois state bar; attorney, U.S. Department of Justice, Washington, DC, 1961–63

Civic Activities and Awards: Member or officer of many civic and philanthropic organizations; repeatedly recognized by the National Taxpayers Union, Watchdogs of the Treasury, Inc., and many other groups as one of the Congress's most fiscally conservative members; in 1992, one of six (out of 435) House members named a Taxpayer

Superhero by the Grace Commission's Citizens Against Government Waste; in 1994, one of 35 House members to be cited by the Grace Commission for his votes against higher spending and taxes; in 1997, received the best score of any House member in the bipartisan Concord Coalition's analysis of spending votes, earning him a place on the Coalition's Honor Roll of members with the strongest commitment to eliminating deficits and balancing the budget; placed on the Concord Coalition's Honor Roll, 1998, for his voting record; member, U.S. Congressional Delegation to the United Nations Conference on Environment and Development (UNCED), better known as the Earth Summit, 1992; vice chair, Global Legislators Organization for a Balanced Environment (GLOBEUSA), 1993–present

State and Local Office: Illinois House of Representatives, 1973–79

Elected to Congress: Elected to the 96th Congress on January 22, 1980, by special election to fill the vacancy caused by the resignation of Abner J. Mikva; reelected to each succeeding Congress through 2001; was not a candidate for reelection in 2000

ROB PORTMAN, Representative, Second District, Ohio

Born: Cincinnati, OH, December 19, 1955

Resides: Terrace Park, OH

Education: Cincinnati Country Day School; B.A., Dartmouth College, 1979; J.D., University of Michigan Law School, 1984

Career: Admitted to the Ohio and Washington, DC, bars, 1984; practicing attorney, 1984–88; associate counsel to former president Bush, 1989; deputy assistant to the president and director, White House Office of Legislative Affairs, 1990–91; alternative U.S. Representative to the U.N. Human Rights Commission, 1992

Elected to Congress: Elected to the 103rd Congress on May 4, 1993, by special election, to fill the vacancy caused by the resignation of William Gradison; reelected to each succeeding Congress

DEBORAH PRYCE, Representative, Fifteenth District, Ohio

Born: Warren, OH, July 29, 1951

Resides: Columbus, OH

Education: B.A., cum laude, Ohio State University, 1973; J.D., Capital University Law School, 1976

Career: Attorney; admitted to the Ohio bar in 1976; administrative law judge, Ohio Department of Insurance, 1976–78; first assistant city prosecutor, senior assistant city attorney, and assistant city attorney, Columbus City Attorney's Office, 1978–85; presiding judge for two terms, Franklin County Municipal Court; attorney, Hamilton, Kramer, Myers & Cheek, 1992

Civic Activities and Awards: Ohio Supreme Court Victims of Crime Award, 1986–92; YWCA Woman of the Year Award, 1995; member, Ohio Supreme Court Committee on Dispute Resolution; chair, Municipal Court Subcommittee; member, Jail Capacity Management Board, Domestic Violence Task Force, Corrections Planning Board, Alliance for Cooperative Justice Policy Board, Columbus Inns of Court and Action for Children; member, Franklin County Alcohol, Drug Addiction and Mental Health Services (ADAMH) Advisory Committee; American Council of Young Political Leaders, delegate to Australia, 1986; session member, former deacon, and stewardship chair, Indianola Presbyterian Church

Elected to Congress: Elected to the 103rd Congress in November 1992; reelected to each succeeding Congress

ADAM H. PUTNAM, Representative, Twelfth District, Florida

Born: Bartow, FL, July 31, 1974

Resides: Bartow, FL

Education: Bartow High School; B.S., University of Florida, 1995

Career: Family citrus and cattle business

Civic Activities and Awards: Past president, Florida 4-H Foundation; member, Polk County Farm Bureau; member, Florida Sheriff's Youth Villa Board of Associates; member, Polk County Cattleman's Association; member, Polk County Historical Association; Outstanding Male Graduate, University of Florida, 1995

State and Local Office: Florida State House of Representatives, 1996–2000

Elected to Congress: Elected to the 107th Congress in November 2000

JACK QUINN, Representative, Thirtieth District, New York

Born: Buffalo, NY, April 13, 1951

Resides: Hamburg, NY

Education: B.A., Siena College, 1973; M.A., State University of New York, Buffalo, 1978

Career: Teacher and coach, Orchard Park Central School, 1973–83

Civic Activities and Awards: Founder, DARE, 1984; U.S. Chamber of Commerce, Spirit of Enterprise Award; National Coalition of Homeless Veterans, Legislative Leadership Award; Amherst Gaelic League, Irishman of the Year; *Congressional Quarterly*, one of the Top 50 Most Effective Lawmakers in Washington; National Trails Award for recognizing the significance of the Seaway Trail and making transportation improvements to Lake Shore Road in Hamburg; Greater Buffalo Chapter of the American Red Cross, Ruth C. Roberts Award; Buffalo AFL-CIO Council, Government Service Award for work on behalf of the working men and women; TR Fund, Teddy Roosevelt Award for outstanding environmental efforts; Citizens Against Government Waste, Sound Dollar Award; Medaille College, honorary doctoral degree; inducted into the distinguished Bishop Timon-St. Jude John Timon Society; Hilbert College, Mother Colette Hilbert Award for service to others

State and Local Office: Council member, Hamburg, 1982–84; town supervisor, Hamburg, 1983–92

Elected to Congress: Elected to the 103rd Congress in November 1992; reelected to each succeeding Congress

GEORGE RADANOVICH, Representative, Nineteenth District, California

Born: Mariposa, CA, June 20, 1955

Resides: Mariposa, CA

Education: Mariposa County High School; B.S., California State Polytechnic University, 1978

Career: Assistant manager, Yosemite Bank, 1980–83; farmer; opened Mariposa County's first winery, Radanovich Winery, 1986–present

Civic Activities and Awards: Charter member and president of the Mariposa Wine Grape Growers Association; treasurer, Mariposa Historical Society, 1982–83; Mariposa County Planning Commission, 1982–86; founder, Mariposa Creek Parkway, 1985; chair, Mariposa County Board of Supervisors, 1989–92; member, Wine Institute, California Farm Bureau, California Association of Wine Grape Growers, Chambers of Commerce; California Ag Leadership, class 21; executive director, California State Mining and Mineral Museum Association

Elected to Congress: Elected to the 104th Congress in November 1994; reelected to each succeeding Congress

JIM RAMSTAD, Representative, Third District, Minnesota

Born: Jamestown, ND, May 6, 1946

Resides: Minnetonka, MN

Education: University of Minnesota, B.A., Phi Beta Kappa, 1968; George Washington University, J.D. with honors, 1973

Military Service: First lieutenant, U.S. Army Reserve, 1968–74

Career: Practicing attorney, 1973–80; adjunct professor, American University, 1975–78

Civic Activities and Awards: Board member, Minnesota DARE; Lake Country Food Bank; Violence Against Women Coalition

State and Local Office: Minnesota State Senate, 1980–90; assistant minority leader

Elected to Congress: Elected to the 102nd Congress in November 1990; reelected to each succeeding Congress

BILL REDMOND, former Representative, Third District, New Mexico

Born: Chicago, IL, January 28, 1955

Resides: Santa Fe, NM

Education: B.A., ministry and administration, Lincoln Christian College, 1979; master's, philosophy, science, counseling, history, and administration, Lincoln Christian Seminary, 1988; attended Murray State University

Military Service: U.S. Army Reserve, Army Chaplain Candidate Program

Career: Special education instructor, 1980–83; author; teacher at University of New Mexico

Civic Activities and Awards: Albuquerque Lodge of B'nai Brith, Albuquerque Humane Association

Elected to Congress: Elected to the 105th Congress on May 13, 1997, to fill the vacancy caused by the resignation of Bill Richardson; unsuccessful candidate for reelection in 1998

RALPH REGULA, Representative, Sixteenth District, Ohio

Born: Beach City, OH, December 3, 1924

Resides: Navarre, OH

Education: B.A., Mount Union College, 1948; LL.B., William McKinley School of Law, 1952

Military Service: U.S. Navy, 1944–46 (World War II)

Career: Attorney at law; admitted to Ohio bar and began practice in Navarre, OH, 1952–73

Civic Activities and Awards: Member, Ohio State Board of Education, 1960–64; St. Timothy Episcopal Church, Massillon, OH; board of trustees, Mount Union College; honorary member, board of advisers, Walsh College; Kiwanis; Grange; trustee, Starl County Historical Society

State and Local Office: Ohio State House of Representatives, 1965–66, Ohio State Senate, 1967–72

Elected to Congress: Elected to the 93rd Congress in November 1972; reelected to each succeeding Congress

DENNIS R. REHBERG, Representative at Large, Montana

Born: Billings, MT, October 5, 1955

Resides: Billings, MT

Education: B.A., Washington State University, 1977

Career: Rancher

State and Local Office: Montana State Senate, 1977–79; Montana State House of Representatives, 1984–91; Montana lieutenant governor, 1991–96

Elected to Congress: Unsuccessful candidate for the U.S. Senate in 1996; elected to the 107th Congress in November 2000

THOMAS M. REYNOLDS, Representative, Twenty-Seventh District, New York

Born: Belafonte, PA, September 3, 1950

Resides: Springville, NY

Education: Attended Kent State University

Civic Activities and Awards: Former director, Better Business Bureau, cooperative extension and central referral service

State and Local Office: Erie County legislator, 1982–88; New York State Assembly, 1988–98

Elected to Congress: Elected to the 106th Congress in November 1998; reelected in 2000

BILL RICHARDSON, former Representative, Third District, New Mexico

Born: Pasadena, CA, November 15, 1947

Education: B.A., Tufts University, 1970; M.A., Fletcher School of Law and Diplomacy, 1971

Career: Congressional and federal employee, 1971–78; executive director, New Mexico State Democratic Party and Bernalillo County Democratic Party, 1978; international business consultant, 1978–82; secretary of energy, 1998–2000

Elected to Congress: Unsuccessful candidate for election to the 97th Congress in 1980; elected to the 98th Congress in November 1982; reelected to each succeeding Congress and served until his resignation on February 2, 1997, to become U.S. ambassador to the United Nations

FRANK DUNCAN RIGGS, former Representative, First District, California

Born: Louisville, KY, September 5, 1950

Resides: Windsor, CA

Education: San Rafael High School; St. Mary's Golden Gate University, 1980, B.A. in administration of justice, summa cum laude

Military Service: U.S. Army, military police investigator, 1972–75

Career: Real estate developer and vice president

of an educational software company; former police officer and deputy sheriff

Civic Activities and Awards: Member, California State Job Training Coordinating Council, Governor's Committee for Employment of Disabled Persons

State and Local Office: Member, Windsor School Board, 1984–88; two-term board president

Elected to Congress: Elected to the 102nd Congress in November 1990; was an unsuccessful candidate for reelection in 1992; elected to the 104th Congress in November 1994; reelected in 1996; was not a candidate for reelection in 1998

ROBERT RILEY, Representative, Third District, Alabama

Born: Ashland, AL, October 3, 1944

Resides: Ashland, AL

Education: Clay County High School, 1962; B.A. in business administration, University of Alabama, 1965

Career: Businessman; owner of Midway Ford, Chrysler, Plymouth, Dodge and Jeep Eagle; owner, Midway Transit Trucking Company, 1965–present; involved in commercial and residential real estate; cattleman

Civic Activities and Awards: Member, First Baptist Church of Ashland, Ashland Jaycees, Alabama Cattleman's Association, APEA; Shriner; Mason

State and Local Office: Ashland City Council, 1972–76

Elected to Congress: Elected to the 105th Congress in November 1996; reelected in 1998, 2000

CHARLES E. "BUDDY" ROEMER, former Representative, Fourth District, Louisiana

Born: Shreveport, LA, October 4, 1943

Resides: Bossier City, LA

Education: B.S., 1964, M.A., 1967, Harvard University

Career: Businessman, farmer, banker

State and Local Office: Louisiana Constitutional Convention, 1972; delegate, Democratic National Convention, 1972; Louisiana governor, 1987–92

Elected to Congress: Elected to the 97th Congress in 1980; reelected to each succeeding Congress and served until his resignation on March 14, 1988

JAMES E. ROGAN, former Representative, Twenty-Seventh District, California

Born: San Francisco, CA, August 21, 1957

Resides: Glendale, CA

Education: B.A., University of California, Berkeley, 1979; J.D., University of California at Los Angeles, Law School, 1983

Career: Admitted to the California bar in 1984 and began practice in Los Angeles; Los Angeles County deputy district attorney, 1985–90; attorney; Glendale Municipal Court judge, 1990–94

State and Local Office: California State Assembly, 1994–96, serving as assembly majority leader in 1996

Elected to Congress: Elected to the 105th Congress in November 1996; reelected in 1998; was an unsuccessful candidate for reelection in 2000

HAROLD ROGERS, Representative, Eighth District, Kentucky

Born: Barrier, KY, December 31, 1937

Resides: Somerset, KY

Education: Wayne County High School, 1955; attended Western Kentucky University, 1956–57; B.A., University of Kentucky, 1962; J.D., University of Kentucky Law School, 1964

Military Service: Member, North Carolina and Kentucky National Guards, 1957–64

Career: Lawyer, admitted to the Kentucky state bar, 1964; commenced practice in Somerset; associate, Smith and Blackburn, 1964–67; private practice, 1967–69; commonwealth attorney, Pulaski and Rockcastle Counties, KY, 1969–80

Civic Activities and Awards: Delegate, Republican National Convention, 1972, 1976, 1984, and 1988; past president, Kentucky Commonwealth Attorneys Association; member and past president, Somerset-Pulaski County Chamber of Commerce and Pulaski County Industrial Foundation; founder, Southern Kentucky Economic Development Council, 1986; member, Chowder and Marching Society, 1981–present

Elected to Congress: Elected to the 97th Congress in November 1980; reelected to each succeeding Congress

MIKE ROGERS, Representative, Eighth District, Michigan

Born: Livingston County, MI, June 2, 1963

Resides: Brighton, MI

Education: Bachelor's degree, Adrian College, Michigan; University of Michigan ROTC; FBI Academy

Military Service: United States Army, 1985–88

Career: Special agent, Federal Bureau of Investigation; cofounder, E.B.I. Builders, Inc.

Civic Activities and Awards: Member, Society of Former Special Agents for the Federal Bureau of Investigation; honorary member, Brighton Rotary Club; member, Cleary College Board of Trustees.

State and Local Office: Michigan State Senate, 1994–2000

Elected to Congress: Elected to the 107th Congress in November 2000

DANA ROHRABACHER, Representative, Forty-Fifth District, California

Born: Coronado, CA, June 21, 1947

Resides: Huntington Beach, CA

Education: Palos Verdes High School, CA, 1965; attended Los Angeles Harbor College, 1965–67; B.A., Long Beach State College, 1969; M.A., University of Southern California, 1975

Career: Writer/journalist, 1970–80; reporter, City News Service/Radio News West, and editorial writer, *Orange County Register*, 1972–80; assistant press secretary, Reagan/Bush Committee, 1980; speechwriter and special assistant to President Ronald Reagan, 1981–88

Elected to Congress: Elected to the 101st Congress in November 1988; reelected to each succeeding Congress

ILEANA ROS-LEHTINEN, Representative, Eighteenth District, Florida

Born: Havana, Cuba, July 15, 1952

Resides: Miami, FL

Education: B.S., Florida International University, 1975; M.S., educational leadership, Florida International University, 1986; doctoral candidate in education, University of Miami

Career: Certified Florida schoolteacher; founder and former owner, Eastern Academy Elementary School, 1978–85

Civic Activities and Awards: Former president, Bilingual Private School Association; regular contributor to leading Spanish-language newspaper

State and Local Office: Florida House of Representatives, 1982–86; Florida State Senate, 1986–89

Elected to Congress: Elected to the 101st Congress on August 29, 1989, in a special election, to fill the vacancy caused by the death of Claude Pepper; reelected to each succeeding Congress

MARGE ROUKEMA, Representative, Fifth District, New Jersey

Born: West Orange, NJ, September 19, 1929

Resides: Ridgewood, NJ

Education: B.A., Montclair State College in New Jersey, political science and English; studies in urban and regional planning at Rutgers University

Career: Teacher, history and English, Livingston and Ridgewood, NJ, 1951–55

Civic Activities and Awards: Chair, Ridgewood Better Government Committee; member, Mayor's Advisory Charter Study Commission, New Jersey Business and Professional Women, College Club of Ridgewood, Distributive Education Clubs of America Congressional Advisory Board; active member, board of directors of public service organizations including Ridgewood Family Counseling Service, Leukemia Society of Northern New Jersey, Ridgewood Senior Citizens Housing Corporation (cofounder), Spring House residential center for the treatment of alcoholism, Spectrum for Living; National PTA Children's Advocacy Award, Concord Coalition's House Honor Roll, U.S. Chamber of Commerce Spirit of Enterprise Award; National Federation of Independent Businesses, Guardian of Small Business Award

State and Local Office: Trustee and vice president, Ridgewood Board of Education, 1970–73

Elected to Congress: Elected to the 97th Congress in November 1980; reelected to each succeeding Congress

ED ROYCE, Representative, Thirty-Ninth District, California

Born: Los Angeles, CA, October 12, 1951

Resides: Fullerton, CA

Education: B.A., California State University, Fullerton, 1977

Career: Small business owner; controller; corporate tax manager

Civic Activities and Awards: Member, Fullerton Chamber of Commerce; board member, Literacy Volunteers of America; California Interscholastic Athletic Foundation board of advisers

State and Local Office: California State Senate, 1982–92

Elected to Congress: Elected to the 103rd Congress in November 1992; reelected to each succeeding Congress

PAUL RYAN, Representative, First District, Wisconsin

Born: Janesville, WI, January 29, 1970

Resides: Janesville, WI

Education: Joseph A. Craig High School; B.A., Miami University of Ohio, 1992

Career: Professional marketing consultant, Ryan Inc., Central, 1997–98; aide to former U.S. Senator Bob Kasten (R-WI), 1992; adviser to former vice presidential candidate Jack Kemp, and U.S. drug czar Bill Bennett; legislative director, U.S. Senator Sam Brownback, 1995–97

Civic Activities and Awards: Janesville YMCA; Janesville Bowmen, Inc.; Ducks Unlimited

Elected to Congress: Elected to the 106th Congress in November 1998; reelected in 2000

JIM RYUN, Representative, Second District, Kansas

Born: Wichita, KS, May 29, 1947

Resides: Topeka, KS

Education: Wichita East High School, 1965; B.A., photojournalism, University of Kansas, 1970

Career: Product development consultant, president of Jim Ryun Sports; professional photographer and author of two books; U.S. Olympian, track and field, represented the United States in three consecutive Olympics (1964, 1968, 1972): silver medal in the 1,500-meter race, 1968, and world record holder in the 880-yard, mile, and 1,500-meter races

Civic Activities and Awards: Sports Illustrated Sportsman of the Year, 1966; AAU Sullivan Award; Jaycees of America Top Ten Young Men of the United States, 1968

Elected to Congress: Elected to the 105th Congress in November 1996; reelected in 1998

MATT SALMON, former Representative, First District, Arizona

Born: Salt Lake City, UT, January 21, 1958

Resides: Mesa, AZ

Education: Mesa High School, 1976; B.A., Arizona State University, 1981; M.A., Brigham Young University, 1986

Career: Telecommunications executive; community affairs manager, U.S. West Communications, Phoenix, AZ, 1981–94

Civic Activities and Awards: Member, East Valley Child Crisis Center; Council on Families, Youth and Children; Mesa United Way; Arizona Science and Technology Museum

State and Local Office: Arizona State Senate, 1991–94; assistant majority leader, 1993–94; chairman, Rules Committee, 1993–94; Appropriations and Finance committees and Appropriations Subcommittee on Education

Elected to Congress: Elected to the 104th Congress in November 1994; reelected to each succeeding Congress through 2001; was not a candidate for reelection in 2000

MARSHALL (MARK) CLEMENT SANFORD JR., former Representative, First District, South Carolina

Born: Ft. Lauderdale, FL, May 28, 1960

Resides: Charleston, SC

Education: Attended high school in Beaufort, SC; B.A., Furman University, 1983; M.B.A., University of Virginia, Darden School of Business, 1988

Career: Owner, real estate investment firm, 1992–present

Civic Activities and Awards: Member, Preservation Society of Charleston, National Trust; attends St. Stephen's Episcopal Church

Elected to Congress: Elected to the 104th Congress in November 1994; reelected in 1996, 1998; was not a candidate for reelection in 2000

JIM SAXTON, Representative, Third District, New Jersey

Born: Nicholson, PA, January 22, 1943

Resides: Mount Holly, NJ

Education: Lackawanna Trail High School, 1961; B.A., education, East Stroudsburg State College, 1965; graduate courses in elementary education, Temple University, Philadelphia, PA, 1968

Career: Public school teacher, 1965–68; realtor, owner of Jim Saxton Realty Company, 1968–84

Civic Activities and Awards: Chair, State Republican Platform Committee, 1983; former member, Chamber of Commerce, Association of the U.S. Air Force, Leadership Foundation of New Jersey, Boy Scouts of America, Rotary International; former chair, American Cancer Committee

State and Local Office: New Jersey General Assembly, 1976–82; New Jersey State Senate, 1982–84

Elected to Congress: Elected to the 98th Congress on November 6, 1984, by special election, to fill the vacancy caused by the death of Edwin B. Forsythe; reelected to each succeeding Congress

JOE SCARBOROUGH, Representative, First District, Florida

Born: Atlanta, GA, April 9, 1963

Resides: Pensacola, FL

Education: Catholic High School; B.A. in history, University of Alabama, 1985; J.D., University of Florida, 1990

Career: Admitted to the Florida bar, 1991; teacher, 1985–87; practicing attorney, 1990–94

Civic Activities and Awards: Served on the executive board of the Escambia–Santa Rosa Bar Association; board of directors for the Navy League of the Pensacola area; Emerald Coast Pediatric Primary Care; member, Gulf Coast Economics Club, Chamber of Commerce, Inns of Court, Challenger Committee, Rotary Club, Young Lawyers Association, Fellowship of Christian Athletes; attends First Baptist Church of Pensacola

Elected to Congress: Elected to the 104th Congress in November 1994; reelected to each succeeding Congress

DAN SCHAEFER, former Representative, Sixth District, Colorado

Born: Guttenberg, IA, January 25, 1936

Resides: Lakewood, CO

Education: B.A., Niagara University, 1961

Military Service: U.S. Marine Corps, sergeant, 1955–57

Career: Public relations consultant, 1967–83

Civic Activities and Awards: Member, West Chamber of Commerce, South Metro Chamber of Commerce, Golden Chamber of Commerce, Englewood Chamber of Commerce, Evergreen Chamber of Commerce, Conifer Chamber of Commerce, Century Club, Chatfield YMCA, Chatfield Jaycees; honorary doctor of laws (1986), Niagara University

State and Local Office: Colorado General Assembly, 1977–78; Colorado State Senate, 1979–83

Elected to Congress: Elected to the 103rd Congress on March 29, 1983, by special election, to fill the vacancy caused by the death of John L. Swigert; reelected to each succeeding Congress through 1998; was not a candidate for reelection in 1998

BOB SCHAFFER, Representative, Fourth District, Colorado

Born: Cincinnati, OH, July 24, 1962

Resides: Ft. Collins, CO

Education: B.S., political science, University of Dayton, 1984

Career: Legislative assistant; former press secretary for Republican senators; Colorado General Assembly, 1985–87; owner, Northern Front Range Marketing Company, 1989–94

Civic Activities and Awards: Named National Legislator of the Year, 1995, by National Republican Legislators Association; named Business Legislator of the Year by Colorado Association of Commerce and Industry; named Guardian of Small Business by the National Federation of Independent Business; named Taxpayer Champion by the Colorado Union of Taxpayers

State and Local Office: Colorado state senator, 1987–96

Elected to Congress: Elected to the 105th Congress in November 1996; reelected in 1998, 2000

STEVEN SCHIFF, former Representative, First District, New Mexico

Born: Chicago, IL, March 18, 1947

Education: B.A., University of Illinois, Chicago, political science, 1968; J.D., University of New Mexico Law School, 1972

Military Service: New Mexico Air National Guard, 1969–88

Career: Assistant district attorney of Bernalillo County, NM, 1972–77; trial attorney, 1977–79; assistant city attorney and counsel for Albuquerque Police Department, 1979–81; district attorney, Bernalillo County, 1980–88

Civic Activities and Awards: Member, Civitan International, New Mexico and national district attorneys associations, Albuquerque Lodge of B'nai B'rith, Albuquerque Humane Association

Elected to Congress: Elected to the 101st Congress in November 1988; reelected to each succeeding Congress and served until his death in Albuquerque, NM, on March 25, 1998

EDWARD L. SCHROCK, Representative, Second District, Virginia

Born: Middletown, OH, April 6, 1941

Resides: Virginia Beach, VA

Education: Bachelor's degree, Alderson-Broaddus College, West Virginia, 1964; M.A., American University, 1975

Military Service: United States Navy, attaining the rank of captain, 1964–88

Career: Investment broker

Civic Activities and Awards: Harborfest, the International Azalea Festival and Tradefest; member, board of Directors, Lee's Friends, a cancer victim support organization; past member, Library Board of Virginia; member, Library of Virginia Foundation Board; past president, Friends of the Virginia Beach Public Library; past president, Parent/Faculty Association, Cape Henry Collegiate School

State and Local Office: Virginia State Senate, 1995–2001

Elected to Congress: Elected to the 107th Congress in November 2000

F. JAMES SENSENBRENNER JR., Representative, Ninth District, Wisconsin

Born: Chicago, IL, June 14, 1943

Resides: Menomonee Falls, WI

Education: Milwaukee Country Day School, 1961; A.B., Stanford University, 1965; J.D., University of Wisconsin Law School, 1968

Career: Staff member of former U.S. congressman J. Arthur Younger of California, 1965; admitted to the Wisconsin bar, 1968; commenced practice in Cedarburg, WI; admitted to practice before the U.S. Supreme Court in 1972

Civic Activities and Awards: Member, Waukesha County Republican Party, Wisconsin Bar Association, Riveredge Nature Center, American Philatelic Society

State and Local Office: Wisconsin Assembly, 1968–74; Wisconsin State Senate, 1974–78; assistant minority leader, 1976

Elected to Congress: Elected to the 96th Congress in November 1978; reelected to each succeeding Congress

PETE SESSIONS, Representative, Fifth District, Texas

Born: Waco, TX, March 22, 1955

Resides: Dallas, TX

Education: B.A., Southwestern University, 1978

Career: Worked for Southwestern Bell and Bell Communications Research (formerly Bell Labs), 1978–93, rising to the position of district manager; past vice president for public policy, National Center for Policy Analysis, 1994–95

Civic Activities and Awards: Board member, East Dallas YMCA; team leader, Adopt-a-Shoreline; past chair, East Dallas Chamber of Commerce; past district chair, White Rock Council of the Boy Scouts of America; member, East Dallas Rotary Club

Elected to Congress: Elected to the 105th Congress in November 1996; reelected in 1998, 2000

JOHN B. SHADEGG, Representative, Fourth District, Arizona

Born: Phoenix, AZ, October 22, 1949

Resides: Phoenix, AZ

Education: Camelback High School; B.A., University of Arizona, Tucson, 1972; J.D., University of Arizona, 1975

Military Service: Air National Guard, 1969–75

Career: Admitted to the Arizona bar, 1976; private practice; special assistant attorney general, 1983–90; special counsel, Arizona House Republican Caucus, 1991–92

Civic Activities and Awards: Adviser, U.S. Sentencing Commission; founding director and executive committee member, Goldwater Institute for Public Policy; member and former president, Crime Victim Foundation; chair, Arizona Juvenile Justice Advisory Council; advisory board, Salvation Army; vestry, Christ Church of the Ascension Episcopal, 1989–91; member, Law Society, ASU College of Law; chair, Arizona Republican Caucus, 1985–87; chair, Proposition 108—Two-Thirds Tax Limitation Initiative, 1992; member, Fiscal Accountability and Reform Efforts (FARE) Committee, 1991–92; counsel, Arizonans for Wildlife Conservation (No on Proposition 200), 1992; Victims Bill of Rights Task Force, 1989–90

Elected to Congress: Elected to the 104th Congress in November 1994; reelected to each succeeding Congress

E. CLAY SHAW JR., Representative, Twenty-Second District, Florida

Born: Miami, FL, April 19, 1939

Resides: Ft. Lauderdale, FL

Education: Miami Edison Senior High School, 1957; B.A., Stetson University, 1961; M.B.A., University of Alabama, 1963; J.D., Stetson University College of Law, 1966

Career: Former certified public accountant; lawyer; admitted to the Florida state bar in 1966 and commenced practice in Ft. Lauderdale; admitted to practice before the federal court in the Southern District of Florida and the U.S. Supreme Court; assistant city attorney, Ft. Lauderdale, 1968; chief city prosecutor, 1968–69; assistant municipal judge, 1969–71; U.S. special ambassador, Papua New Guinea (under President Ford)

Civic Activities and Awards: Executive committee, U.S. Conference of Mayors; executive committee, Republican National Committee; president, National Conference of Republican Mayors; director, Ft. Lauderdale Chamber of Commerce; vice chair, Sun Belt Mayor's Task Force; Broward County Charter Commission; national vice chair, Mayors for Reagan, 1980; member, St. Anthony's Church

State and Local Office: Ft. Lauderdale city commissioner, 1971–73; vice mayor, 1973–75; mayor, 1975–80

Elected to Congress: Elected to the 97th Congress in November 1980; reelected to each succeeding Congress

CHRISTOPHER SHAYS, Representative, Fourth District, Connecticut

Born: Stamford, CT, October 18, 1945

Resides: Stamford, CT

Education: Darien High School, 1964; B.A., Principia College, 1968; M.B.A., New York University Graduate School of Business, 1974; M.P.A., New York University Graduate School of Public Administration, 1978

Career: Peace Corps, Fiji Islands, 1968–70; business consultant; college instructor; realtor; executive aide, Trumbull first selectman, 1971–72

State and Local Office: Connecticut State House of Representatives, 1974–87

Elected to Congress: Elected to the 100th Congress on August 18, 1987, by special election, to fill the vacancy caused by the death of Stewart B. Mc-Kinney; reelected to each succeeding Congress

DON SHERWOOD, Representative, Tenth District, Pennsylvania

Born: Nicholson, PA, March 5, 1941

Resides: Tunkhannock, PA

Education: Lackawanna Trail High School; Wyoming Seminary Preparatory School; B.A., Dartmouth College, 1963

Military Service: U.S. Army, 1964–66, first lieutenant

Career: Small businessman; founder and owner, Sherwood Chevrolet and Horiacher-Sherwood Forestry Equipment

Civic Activities and Awards: Tunkhannock Area School Board, 1975–98

Elected to Congress: Elected to the 106th Congress in November 1998; reelected in 2000

JOHN M. SHIMKUS, Representative, Twentieth District, Illinois

Born: Collinsville, IL, February 21, 1958

Resides: Collinsville, IL

Education: Collinsville High School; B.S., United States Military Academy, West Point, NY, 1980; teaching certificate, Christ College, 1990; M.B.A., Southern Illinois University, 1997

Military Service: U.S. Army, 1980–85; Army Reserves, 1985–present

Career: Government and history teacher, Collinsville High School

State and Local Office: Collinsville township trustee, 1989–93; Madison county treasurer, 1990–96

Elected to Congress: Elected to the 105th Congress in November 1996; reelected in 1998, 2000

BUD SHUSTER, former Representative, Ninth District, Pennsylvania

Born: Glassport, PA, January 23, 1932

Resides: Everett, PA

Education: B.S., University of Pittsburgh, 1954; M.B.A., Duquesne University, 1960; Ph.D., American University, 1967

Military Service: U.S. Army, 1954–56

Career: Former vice president of RCA's computer division, 1965–68; founder and chair of a computer software company, 1968–72; authored award-winning book, *Believing in America*

Civic Activities and Awards: Member, Phi Beta Kappa, Sigma Chi (Significant Sig Award), Chowder and Marching Society; delegate, Republican National Convention (1976, 1980, 1984, 1988, 1992, 1996); member, Authors Guild

Elected to Congress: Elected to the 93rd Congress in November 1972; reelected to each succeeding Congress and served until his resignation on February 3, 2001

ROBERT SIMMONS, Representative, Second District, Connecticut

Born: New York, NY, February 11, 1943

Resides: Stonington, CT

Education: Bachelor's degree, Haverford College, 1965; M.P.A., Harvard University's Kennedy School of Government, 1979; Ph.D., University of Connecticut, 1992

Military Service: United States Army, 1965–67; two Bronze Star medals for his service in Vietnam; colonel, U.S. Army Reserves

Career: Operations officer, Central Intelligence Agency, 1969–79; staff member, Senator John H. Chafee, 1979; staff director, Permanent Select Committee on Intelligence, 1981–85

Civic Activities and Awards: CIA Seal Medallion; visiting lecturer, Political Science Department, Yale University, 1985–95; past president, Stonington Community Center, 1986–88; chair, Stonington Police Commission, 1987–88; chair, Stonington Republican Town Committee, 1988–92; teaching assistant, University of Connecticut, 1988–91, Reserve Officer Association's Outstanding USAR Small Unit Award, 1996; Knowlton Award, 1998; adjutant, American Legion Post no. 58; lector, Calvary Episcopal Church; member, Asylum Lodge no. 57 (AF&AM), Stonington; associate fellow, Berkeley College, Yale

State and Local Office: Connecticut General Assembly, 1991–2001

Elected to Congress: Elected to the 107th Congress in November 2000

MICHAEL K. SIMPSON, Representative, Second District, Idaho

Born: Burley, ID, September 8, 1950

Resides: Blackfoot, ID

Education: Blackfoot High School, 1968; Utah State University, 1972; Washington University School of Dental Medicine, 1977

Career: Dentist, private practice

State and Local Office: Blackfoot City Council, 1982–86; Idaho State House of Representatives, 1984–98; Idaho speaker of the house 1993–98

Elected to Congress: Elected to the 106th Congress in November 1998; reelected in 2000

JOE R. SKEEN, Representative, Second District, New Mexico

Born: Roswell, NM, June 30, 1927

Resides: Picacho, NM

Education: B.S., engineering, Texas A&M University, 1950

Military Service: U.S. Navy, 1945–46; U.S. Air Force Reserve, 1949–52

Career: Soil and water engineer, Zuni and Ramah Navajo Indian Council, 1951; ran family sheep ranching operation in Lincoln County, NM; operated a flying service, Ruidoso, NM

Civic Activities and Awards: Served three years as state Republican chair; member, New Mexico Woolgrowers Association, New Mexico Cattle Growers Association, New Mexico Farm and Livestock Bureau, Conquistadores Council, Boy Scouts of America, Elks, Eagles; Catholic

State and Local Office: New Mexico State Senate, 1960–70; minority leader, 1965–70

Elected to Congress: Elected to the 97th Congress in 1980 as a write-in candidate, after the incumbent died in office and the Republican Party was denied a place on the ballot by the courts; reelected to each succeeding Congress

CHRISTOPHER H. SMITH, Representative, Fourth District, New Jersey

Born: Rahway, NJ, March 4, 1953

Resides: Washington Township, NJ

Education: B.S., Trenton State College, 1975; attended Worcester College (England), 1974

Career: Businessman

Civic Activities and Awards: Executive director, New Jersey Right to Life Committee, 1976–78; Catholic

Elected to Congress: Elected to the 97th Congress in November 1980; reelected to each succeeding Congress

ROBERT F. (BOB) SMITH, former Representative, Second District, Oregon

Born: Portland, OR, June 16, 1931

Resides: Medford, OR

Education: B.A., business administration and economics, Willamette University, 1953

Career: Rancher and businessman

Civic Activities and Awards: Board of trustees, Willamette University

State and Local Office: Oregon House of Representatives, 1960–72; house majority leader and speaker pro tempore of Oregon legislature, 1964–66; speaker of the house, 1968–72; state senator, 1972–82, and senate Republican leader, 1978–82

Elected to Congress: Elected to the 98th Congress in November 1982; reelected to each succeeding Congress through 1994; was not a candidate for reelection in 1994; elected to the 105th Congress in November 1996; was not a candidate for reelection in 1998

LAMAR S. SMITH, Representative, Twenty-First District, Texas

Born: San Antonio, TX, November 19, 1947

Resides: San Antonio, TX

Education: Texas Military Institute, 1965; B.A., Yale University, 1969; J.D., Southern Methodist University School of Law, 1975

Career: Management intern, Small Business Administration, Washington, DC, 1969–70; business and financial writer, *Christian Science Monitor*, 1970–72; admitted to the state bar of Texas, 1975, and commenced practice in San Antonio with the firm of Maebius and Duncan; partner, Lamar Seeligson Ranch, Jim Wells County, TX

Civic Activities and Awards: Chair of the Republican Party of Bexar County, TX

State and Local Office: Texas House of Representatives, 1981–82; Bexar County commissioner, 1982–85

Elected to Congress: Elected to the 100th Congress in November 1986; reelected to each succeeding Congress

LINDA A. SMITH, former Representative, Third District, Washington

Born: LaJunta, CO, July 16, 1950

Resides: Vancouver, WA

Education: Ft. Vancouver High School, 1968

Career: Manager of seven tax preparation offices for nine years

Civic Activities and Awards: Attends Glad Tidings Church, Vancouver

State and Local Office: Washington state representative, 1983–86; Washington state senator, 1987–94; chair, Children and Family Services Committee; vice chair, Republican Caucus

Elected to Congress: Elected to the 104th Congress in November 1994; reelected in 1996; was not a candidate for reelection in 1998; was an unsuccessful candidate for election to the U.S. Senate in 1998

NICK SMITH, Representative, Seventh District, Michigan

Born: Addison, MI, November 5, 1934

Resides: Addison, MI

Education: Attended Addison community schools; B.A., Michigan State University, 1957; M.S., University of Delaware, 1959

Military Service: Captain, military intelligence, U.S. Air Force, 1959–61

Career: State chair, Agriculture Stabilization and Conservation Service, 1969–72; director, Michigan Farm Bureau; national director of energy for the U.S. Department of Agriculture, 1972–74

Civic Activities and Awards: Member, Addison Community Hospital Board; member, National Delegation on U.S.-Soviet Cooperation and Trade; Kellogg Foundation Fellow; Outstanding Young Men of America Award

State and Local Office: Elected Addison Township trustee, 1962–68, supervisor, 1966–68, county board member, 1966–68; Michigan House of Representatives, 1978–82; Michigan State Senate, 1982–92; president pro tempore, 1983–90

Elected to Congress: Elected to the 103rd Congress in November 1992; reelected to each succeeding Congress

VINCENT K. SNOWBARGER, former Representative, Third District, Kansas

Born: Kankakee, IL, September 16, 1949

Resides: Olathe, KS

Education: Shawnee Mission South High School, 1967; B.A., history, Southern Nazarene University, 1971; M.A., political science, University of Illinois, 1974; J.D., University of Kansas, 1977

Career: Attorney, admitted to Kansas bar in 1977; assistant public defender, 32nd Judicial Circuit, 1983–86; Olathe City Planning Commission, 1982–84

Civic Activities and Awards: Member, Rotary International, Olathe Area Chamber of Commerce, Mid-America Nazarene College Foundation, National Federation of Independent Business

State and Local Office: Kansas House of Representatives, 1985–96; majority leader, 1993–96

Elected to Congress: Elected to the 105th Congress in November 1996; was an unsuccessful candidate for reelection in 1998

GERALD B. H. SOLOMON, former Representative, Twenty-Second District, New York

Born: Okeechobee, FL, August 14, 1930

Resides: Glens Falls, NY

Education: Bethlehem Central High School; attended Siena College, 1949–50, and St. Lawrence University, 1953–54

Military Service: U.S. Marine Corps, 1951–52

Career: Founding partner of insurance and investment firm, 1963

Civic Activities and Awards: President, Chamber of Commerce; member, First Presbyterian Church,

Masons, Kiwanis, Grange, Farm Bureau, Jaycees, Queensbury Fire Department, Elks Lodge, Boy Scouts, Oriental Shrine, Amvets, Marine Corps League, American Legion, Disabled American Veterans

State and Local Office: Member, New York State Assembly, 1973–78; Queensbury town supervisor and Warren County legislator, 1968–72

Elected to Congress: Elected to the 96th Congress in November 1978; reelected to each succeeding Congress through 1998; was not a candidate for reelection in 1998

MARK E. SOUDER, Representative, Fourth District, Indiana

Born: Grabill, IN, July 18, 1950

Resides: Ft. Wayne, IN

Education: Leo High School, 1968; B.S., Indiana University-Purdue University, Ft. Wayne, 1972; M.B.A., University of Notre Dame Graduate School of Business, 1974

Career: Partner, Historic Souder's of Grabill; majority owner of Souder's General Store; vice president, Our County Home, fixture manufacturing business; served as economic development liaison for then-Representative Dan Coats (IN, 4th District); appointed Republican staff director for the House Select Committee on Children, Youth and Families, 1984–89; legislative director and deputy chief of staff for Congressman Coats, 1989–93

Civic Activities and Awards: Attends Emmanuel Community Church; member, Grabill Chamber of Commerce; former head of Congressional Action Committee of Ft. Wayne Chamber of Commerce

Elected to Congress: Elected to the 104th Congress in November 1994; reelected to each succeeding Congress

FLOYD SPENCE, Representative, Second District, South Carolina

Born: Columbia, SC, April 9, 1928

Resides: Lexington, SC

Education: Lexington High School; B.A., English, University of South Carolina, 1952; U.S. Navy ROTC; LL.B., University of South Carolina Law School, 1956

Military Service: U.S. Navy, retired as captain; captain, U.S. Naval Reserves

Career: Author and lecturer; lawyer; former partner in law firm of Callison and Spence, West Columbia, SC

Civic Activities and Awards: Former Sunday school teacher and council member, Sons of Confederate Veterans, commander of Wade Hampton Camp; advisory board of Civil Air Patrol; executive board member of the Indian Waters Council of the Boy Scouts of America; member of Farm Bureau, Chamber of Commerce, American Legion, Veterans of Foreign Wars, Lexington Voiture, Reserve Officers Association, Naval Reserve Association, U.S. Supreme Court bar, Lexington County Bar Association, South Carolina Bar Association, and American Bar Association, Legislator of the Year, 1998; Senior Army Reserve Commanders Association, Distinguished Service Award; United States Air Force Auxiliary Civil Air Patrol, Distinguished Recognition Award, 1998; Americans for Tax Reform, Friend of the Taxpayer Award; the Military Order of the World Wars, Gold Patrick Henry Medallion for Patriotic Achievement; Congressional Medal of Honor Society of the United States, National Patriot's Award; Veterans of Foreign Wars of the United States, VFW Congressional Award for 1996; United States Chamber of Commerce, Spirit of Enterprise Award

State and Local Office: South Carolina House of Representatives, 1956–62; South Carolina State Senate, 1966–1970; minority leader of South Carolina State Senate, 1966–70; chairman of Joint Senate–House Internal Security Committee in South Carolina, 1967–70

Elected to Congress: Elected to the 92nd Congress in November 1970; reelected to each succeeding Congress

CLIFF B. STEARNS, Representative, Sixth District, Florida

Born: Washington, DC, April 16, 1941

Resides: Ocala, FL

Education: Woodrow Wilson High, 1959; B.S., electrical engineering, George Washington University, 1963; Air Force ROTC; graduate work, University of California, Los Angeles, 1965

Military Service: U.S. Air Force (captain), 1963–67

Career: Businessman

Civic Activities and Awards: Past president, Silver Springs Kiwanis; member, Marion County/Ocala Energy Task Force, Tourist Development Council, Ocala Board of Realtors, American Hotel/Motel Association in Florida, American Hotel/Motel Association of the United States, Grace Presbyterian Church; board of directors, Boys Club of Ocala; trustee, Munroe Regional Hospital

Elected to Congress: Elected to the 101st Congress in November 1988; reelected to each succeeding Congress

BOB STUMP, Representative, Third District, Arizona

Born: Phoenix, AZ, April 4, 1927

Resides: Tolleson, AZ

Education: Tolleson High School, 1947; B.S., Arizona State University, 1951

Military Service: U.S. Navy, 1943–46 (World War II)

Career: Cotton farmer

Civic Activities and Awards: Barry M. Goldwater Scholarship and Excellence in Education Foundation; NFIB, Guardian of Small Business Award; 1998 VFW Congressional Award; NCOA 1994 L. Mendel Rivers Award for Legislative Action; U.S. Chamber of Commerce, Spirit of Enterprise Award; American Ex-Prisoners of War, 1995 Barbed Wire Award; AMVETS, 1994 Silver Helmet Congressional Award; Watchdogs of the Treasury, Golden Bulldog Award; American Farm Bureau, Golden Plow Award; National Taxpayers' Union, Taxpayer's Friend Award (15 times); 1995 FFA Arizona Agriculturist of the Year; 1996 Vietnam Veterans Association, Legislator of the Year Award; 60 Plus Association, Guardian of Senior Rights Award, 1998

State and Local Office: Arizona House of Representatives, 1959–67; Arizona State Senate, 1967–76; president, Arizona State Senate, 1975–76

Elected to Congress: Elected to the 95th Congress in November 1976; reelected to each succeeding Congress

JOHN E. SUNUNU, Representative, First District, New Hampshire

Born: Boston, MA, September 10, 1964; son of Governor John H. Sununu

Resides: Bedford, NH

Education: Salem High School, 1982; B.S. in mechanical engineering, Massachusetts Institute of Technology, 1986; M.S., mechanical engineering, Massachusetts Institute of Technology, 1987; M.B.A., Harvard University Business School, 1991

Career: Design engineer, Remec Inc., 1987–89; manager and operations specialist, Pittiglio, Rabin, Todd & McGrath, 1990–92; chief financial officer and director of operations, Teletrol Systems, 1993–95; consultant, JHS Associates, 1995–96

Elected to Congress: Elected to the 105th Congress in November 1996; reelected in 1998, 2000

JOHN E. SWEENEY, Representative, Twenty-Second District, New York

Born: Troy, NY, August 9, 1955

Resides: Clifton Park, NY

Education: B.A., Russell Sage College, Troy, NY, 1981; J.D., Western New England School of Law, 1990

Career: Attorney

State and Local Office: New York State commissioner of labor, 1995–97; deputy secretary to Governor George Pataki, 1997–98

Elected to Congress: Elected to the 106th Congress in November 1998; reelected in 2000

JAMES M. TALENT, former Representative, Second District, Missouri

Born: Des Peres, MO, October 18, 1956; related to Congressman Richard A. Gephardt

Resides: Chesterfield, MO

Education: Kirkwood High School, 1973; B.S., Washington University, 1978; J.D., University of Chicago Law School, 1981

Career: Admitted to the Missouri bar, 1981; clerk for Judge Richard Posner, U.S. Court of Appeals, 7th Circuit, 1982–83; associate of Moller, Talent, Kuelthau, and Welch; of counsel, Lashly and Baer

Civic Activities and Awards: Member, West County Chamber of Commerce, Chesterfield Chamber of Commerce, Twin Oaks Presbyterian Church

State and Local Office: Missouri State House of Representatives, 1985–92, elected minority leader, 1989–92

Elected to Congress: Elected to the 103rd Congress in November 1992; reelected to each succeeding Congress through 2001; was not a candidate for reelection in 2000, but was an unsuccessful candidate for governor

THOMAS G. TANCREDO, Representative, Sixth District, Colorado

Born: North Denver, CO, December 20, 1945

Resides: Littleton, CO

Education: Holy Family High School, 1964; B.A., University of North Colorado, 1968

Career: President, Independence Institute, a public policy research organization in Golden, CO, 1993–98

State and Local Office: Colorado State House of Representatives 1976–81; secretary of education's regional representative, 1981–93

Elected to Congress: Elected to the 106th Congress in November 1998; reelected in 2000

W. J. (BILLY) TAUZIN, Representative, Third District, Louisiana

Born: Chackbay, LA, June 14, 1943

Resides: Chackbay, LA

Education: Thibodaux High School, 1961; B.A., history, prelaw, Nicholls State University, 1964; J.D., Louisiana State University, 1967

Career: Legislative aide in Louisiana State Senate; admitted to the Louisiana bar in 1968; commenced practice in Houma, LA; law partner, Marcel, Marcel, Fanguy and Tauzin, 1968–72; private practice, 1972; partner, Sonnier and Tauzin, 1976

Civic Activities and Awards: American Electronics Association, High-Tech Hall of Fame Award; Brain Injury Association, Silvio O. Conte Award for Public Awareness and Education; National Association of Manufacturers, Award for Legislative Excellence; National Association of Businessmen, Watchdogs of the Treasury Award

State and Local Office: Louisiana House of Representatives, 1971–79

Elected to Congress: Elected to the 96th Congress on May 22, 1980, by special election, to fill the vacancy caused by the resignation of David C. Treen; reelected to each succeeding Congress

CHARLES H. TAYLOR, Representative, Eleventh District, North Carolina

Born: Brevard, NC, January 23, 1941

Resides: Brevard, NC

Education: Brevard High School; B.A., Wake Forest University, 1963; J.D., Wake Forest University, 1966

Career: Tree farmer

Civic Activities and Awards: Member, North Carolina Board of Transportation, North Carolina Energy Policy Council; vice chair, Western North Carolina Environmental Council; chair, North Carolina Parks and Recreation Council; member, Board of Visitors to the Military Academy

State and Local Office: Member, North Carolina State House, 1966–72; minority leader, 1968–72; North Carolina state senator and minority leader, 1972–74

Elected to Congress: Elected to the 102nd Congress in November 1990; reelected to each succeeding Congress

LEE TERRY, Representative, Second District, Nebraska

Born: Omaha, NE, January 29, 1962

Resides: Omaha, NE

Education: B.A., University of Nebraska, 1984; J.D., Creighton Law School, 1987

Career: Attorney

State and Local Office: Omaha City Council, 1990–98; served as vice president and president

Elected to Congress: Elected to the 106th Congress in November 1998; reelected in 2000

BILL THOMAS, Representative, Twenty-First District, California

Born: Wallace, ID, December 6, 1941

Resides: Bakersfield, CA

Education: Garden Grove High School, 1959; A.A., Santa Ana Community College, 1961; B.A., San Francisco State University, 1963; M.A., San Francisco State University, 1965

Career: Professor, Bakersfield Community College, 1965–74

Civic Activities and Awards: Selected by the American Council of Young Political Leaders as a delegate to the Soviet Union, 1977; National Federation of Independent Business, Guardian of Small Business Award; U.S. Chamber of Commerce, Spirit of Enterprise Award

State and Local Office: California State Assembly,

Rep. Bill Thomas (*Government Printing Office*)

1974–78; Agriculture, Revenue and Taxation, and Rules committees

Elected to Congress: Elected to the 96th Congress in November 1978; reelected to each succeeding Congress

WILLIAM M. (MAC) THORNBERRY, Representative, Thirteenth District, Texas

Born: Clarendon, TX, July 15, 1958

Resides: Clarendon, TX

Education: Clarendon High School; B.A., Texas Tech University, 1980; J.D., University of Texas Law School, 1983

Career: Rancher; chief of staff, U.S. Representative Larry Combest, 1985–88; deputy assistant secretary of state for legislative affairs, 1988–89; practicing attorney, 1989–94

Civic Activities and Awards: Member, Texas and Southwestern Cattle Raisers; member, First Presbyterian Church of Amarillo; Congressional Rural Caucus; Board of Visitors for the Department of Defense; Centers for Regional Security Studies; Board of Visitors, Joint Forces Command; Congressional Internet Caucus; Congressional Oil and Gas Caucus; Tax Reform Working Group; Rural Health Care Coalition; Republican Mainstream Alliance; Boot Caucus

Elected to Congress: Elected to the 104th Congress in November 1994; reelected to each succeeding Congress

JOHN R. THUNE, Representative at Large, South Dakota

Born: Pierre, SD, January 7, 1961

Resides: Pierre, SD

Education: Jones County High School, 1979; B.A., business administration, Biola University, 1973; M.B.A., University of South Dakota, 1984

Career: State railroad director, 1991–93; former congressional legislative assistant and deputy staff director

Civic Activities and Awards: Executive director, South Dakota Municipal League; board of directors, National League of Cities; executive director, South Dakota Republican Party, 1989–91

Elected to Congress: Elected to the 105th Congress in November 1996; reelected in 1998

TODD TIAHRT, Representative, Fourth District, Kansas

Born: Vermillion, SD, June 15, 1951

Resides: Goddard, KS

Education: Attended South Dakota School of Mines and Technology; B.A., Evangel College, 1975; M.B.A., Southwest Missouri State, 1989

Career: Proposal manager, Boeing Company, 1985–94

Elected to Congress: Elected to the 104th Congress in November 1994; reelected to each succeeding Congress

PATRICK (PAT) J. TIBERI, Representative, Twelfth District, Ohio

Born: Columbus, OH, October 21, 1962

Resides: Columbus, OH

Education: Northland High School; B.A., Ohio State University, 1985

Career: Assistant to Congressman John Kasich; realtor, ReMax Achievers

Civic Activities and Awards: Past president, Forest Park Civic Association, Columbus; member, American Red Cross Columbus Chapter Advisory Board; member, Court Appointed Special Advocates (CASA) board, Franklin County; co-founder, Windsor Terrace Learning Center; co-founder, Columbus Young Leaders Group; member, Sons of Italy; chair, Columbus Italian Festival, 1999; more than a dozen statewide "Legislator of the Year" awards from groups ranging from the Buckeye State Sheriffs Association to the National Federation of Independent Business, Ohio; Watchdog of the Treasury Award; member, St. John the Baptist Catholic Church

State and Local Office: Ohio State House of Representatives, 1993–2000; assistant majority floor leader, 1996; majority floor leader, 1998

Elected to Congress: Elected to the 107th Congress in November 2000

PATRICK J. TOOMEY, Representative, Fifteenth District, Pennsylvania

Born: Providence, RI, November 17, 1961

Resides: Allentown, PA

Education: B.A., Harvard University, 1984

Career: Investment banker; international financial consultant; restaurateur

State and Local Office: Allentown, PA, Government Study Commission, 1994

Elected to Congress: Elected to the 106th Congress in November 1998; reelected in 2000

FRED UPTON, Representative, Sixth District, Michigan

Born: St. Joseph, MI, April 23, 1953

Resides: St. Joseph, MI

Education: Shattuck School, 1971; B.A., journalism, University of Michigan, 1975

Career: Field manager, Dave Stockman campaign, 1976; staff member, Congressman Dave Stockman, 1976–80; legislative assistant, Office of Management and Budget, 1981–83; deputy director of legislative affairs, 1983–84; director of legislative affairs, 1984–85

Civic Activities and Awards: Member, First Congregational Church, Emil Verbin Society

Elected to Congress: Elected to the 100th Congress in November 1986; reelected to each succeeding Congress

DAVID VITTER, Representative, First District, Louisiana

Born: May 3, 1961

Resides: Metairie, LA

Education: A.B., Harvard University, 1983; B.A., Oxford University, Rhodes Scholar, 1985; J.D., Tulane University School of Law, 1988

Career: Lawyer (business attorney); adjunct law professor, Tulane and Loyola universities

Civic Activities and Awards: Alliance for Good Government, Legislator of the Year; Victims and Citizens Against Crime, Outstanding Legislator and Lifetime Achievement Award

State and Local Office: Louisiana House of Representatives, 1991–99

Elected to Congress: Elected to the 106th Congress on May 29, 1999, by special election, to fill the vacancy caused by the resignation of Robert Livingston; reelected in 2000

GREGORY PAUL WALDEN, Representative, Second District, Oregon

Born: The Dalles, OR, January 10, 1957

Resides: Hood River, OR

Education: B.S., University of Oregon, 1981

Career: Owner, Columbia Gorge Broadcasters, Inc., 1986–present

Civic Activities and Awards: National Republican Legislators Association Legislator of the Year, 1993; Oregon Jaycees Outstanding Young Oregonian, 1991; member, Associated Oregon Industries; Oregon Health Sciences Foundation; Hood River Rotary Club; Hood River Elk's Club; National Federation of Independent Business; Hood River Chamber of Commerce; Hood River Memorial Hospital; Columbia Bancorp

State and Local Office: Oregon State House of Representatives, 1988–94, majority leader, 1991–93; Oregon State Senate, 1994–96, assistant majority leader

Elected to Congress: Elected to the 106th Congress in November 1998; reelected in 2000

JAMES T. WALSH, Representative, Twenty-Fifth District, New York

Born: Syracuse, NY, June 19, 1947; son of U.S. Representative William F. Walsh

Resides: Syracuse, NY

Education: B.A., St. Bonaventure University, 1970

Career: Marketing executive, NYNEX, 1974–88

Civic Activities and Awards: President, Syracuse Common Council; member, Syracuse Board of Estimates, board of trustees of Erie Canal Museum, Vera House, and Everson Museum, advisory council of the Catholic Schools Drug-Free Schools and Communities Consortium, Valley Men's Club, South Side Businessmen's Club, Nine Mile Republican Club, Onondaga Anglers Association, Oneida Lake Association, Otisco Lake Association

Elected to Congress: Elected to the 101st Congress in November 1988; reelected to each succeeding Congress

ZACHARY P. (ZACH) WAMP, Representative, Third District, Tennessee

Born: Ft. Benning, GA, October 28, 1957

Resides: Chattanooga, TN

Education: McCallie School, 1976; attended University of North Carolina at Chapel Hill and University of Tennessee

Career: Commercial and industrial real estate broker

Civic Activities and Awards: Member, Red Bank Baptist Church; named Chattanooga Business Leader of the Year; chair, Hamilton County Republican Party; YMCA youth basketball coach; regional director, Tennessee Republican Party; received Tennessee Jaycees' Outstanding Young Tennessean Award, 1996; U.S. Chamber of Commerce Spirit of Enterprise Award; Citizens Against Government Waste A rating; National Taxpayers Union Friend of the Taxpayer Award; recognized by the Citizens Taxpayers Association of Hamilton County, the National Federation of Independent Business and the Concord Coalition for casting tough votes to reduce spending

Elected to Congress: Elected to the 104th Congress in November 1994; reelected to each succeeding Congress

WES WATKINS, Representative, Third District, Oklahoma

Born: DeQueen, AR, December 15, 1938

Resides: Stillwater, OK

Education: B.S., 1960, M.S., 1961, Oklahoma State University

Military: Oklahoma National Guard, 1960–67

Career: President, World Export Services, an oil, real estate, and telecommunications investment company, 1990–96

Civic Activities and Awards: Founding member, Congressional Trade Caucus; past president,

House Rural Caucus and U.S. Congress Prayer Breakfast Group

State and Local Office: Oklahoma State Senate, 1974–76

Elected to Congress: Elected to the 95th Congress (as a Democrat) in November 1976; reelected to each succeeding Congress until 1991; was not a candidate for reelection in 1990, but was an unsuccessful candidate for election as governor of Oklahoma; changed party affiliation to Republican; elected to the 105th Congress in November 1996; reelected in 1998, 2000

JULIUS C. WATTS JR., Representative, Fourth District, Oklahoma

Born: Eufaula, OK, November 18, 1957

Resides: Norman, OK

Education: Eufaula High School, 1976; B.A., journalism, University of Oklahoma, 1981

Career: Quarterback, Canadian Football League, 1981–86; ordained minister, 1993; youth minister, 1987–95

Civic Activities and Awards: Oklahoma Corporate Commission, 1991–95 (commission chair, 1992–95); served on the National Drinking Water Advisory Council, Electricity Committee of the National Association of Regulatory Utility Commissioners; member, Fellowship of Christian Athletes, Oklahoma Special Olympics; national speaking tour, anti-drug campaign; honorary chair, Susan G. Komen Breast Cancer Foundation; leader, Orphan Foundation of America

Elected to Congress: Elected to the 104th Congress in November 1994; reelected to each succeeding Congress

CURT WELDON, Representative, Seventh District, Pennsylvania

Born: Marcus Hook, PA, July 22, 1947

Resides: Aston, PA

Education: B.A., West Chester State College, 1969; graduate work, Cabrini College, Temple University, St. Joseph's University

Career: Administrator and teacher

Civic Activities and Awards: Concord Coalition's Deficit Hawk Award; United Seniors Association, Guardian of Medicare Award; U.S. Chamber of Commerce, Spirit of Enterprise Award; Rotary International, Paul Harris Fellow; 60 Plus Association, Senior Friendly Award; Consortium for Oceanographic Research and Education, CORE Award for efforts to promote oceanographic research and protection of the seas; American Diabetes Association and Junior Diabetes Association, Diabetes Award for ongoing efforts to battle diabetes; Food Distributors International, Thomas Jefferson Award; Delaware County Library System, Outstanding Public Official for Libraries Award; National Council for Adoption, Friend of Adoption Award; National Federation of Independent Business, Guardian of Small Business Award; Nature Conservancy, Nature Conservancy Award; Delaware County Chamber of Commerce, Free Enterprise Award; Community Action Association, Outstanding Public Official of the Year Award; Valley Forge Council of the Boy Scouts of America, Good Scout Award; Watchdogs of the Treasury, Inc., Golden Bulldog Award; Community Action Association of Delaware County, Legislator Award for efforts in Congress to increase funding for the Community Service Block Grant and continued support of Community Action Agencies

State and Local Office: Mayor of Marcus Hook Borough, 1977–82; member, Delaware County Council, 1981–86; chairman, 1985–86

Elected to Congress: Elected to the 100th Congress in November 1986; reelected to each succeeding Congress

DAVE WELDON, Representative, Fifteenth District, Florida

Born: Amityville, NY, August 31, 1953

Resides: Palm Bay, FL

Education: Farmingdale High School, 1971; B.S., biochemistry, State University of New York, Stony Brook, 1978; M.D., State University of New York, Buffalo, 1981

Military Service U.S. Medical Corps, 1981–87; Army Reserves, 1987–92

Career: Practicing physician, internal medicine, 1987–94

Civic Activities and Awards: Member, Florida

Medical Association, Brevard County Medical Society, Brevard Veterans Council, Vietnam Veterans of Brevard, American Legion; volunteer, Veterans Outpatient Clinic, Viera, Florida

Elected to Congress: Elected to the 104th Congress in November 1994; reelected to each succeeding Congress

JERRY WELLER, Representative, Eleventh District, Illinois

Born: Streator, IL, July 7, 1957

Resides: Morris, IL

Education: Dwight High School, 1975; B.S., agriculture, University of Illinois, 1979

Career: Aide to Congressman Tom Corcoran, 1980–81; aide to John R. Block (U.S. secretary of agriculture), 1981–85

Civic Activities and Awards: National Republican Legislative Association Legislator of the Year

State and Local Office: Illinois House of Representatives, 1988–94

Elected to Congress: Elected to the 104th Congress in November 1994; reelected to each succeeding Congress

RICHARD (RICK) WHITE, former Representative, First District, Washington

Born: Bloomington, IN, November 6, 1953

Resides: Bainbridge Island, WA

Education: B.A., Dartmouth College, 1975; attended Pantheon-Sorbonne in Paris; J.D., Georgetown University, 1980

Career: Partner, Perkins Cole law firm; private-sector jobs ranging from dock foreman to assembly-line worker to grill cook

Civic Activities and Awards: Founder and director, Books for Kids (a literacy program); YMCA's Indian Guides program; Law Explorers adviser for Boy Scouts; elder, Rolling Bay Presbyterian Church; member of Leadership Tomorrow; leader, Republican Party Farm Team (encouraging young professionals to get involved in the party); served on Queen Anne Community Council, 1986–88; delegate to various districts

Elected to Congress: Elected to the 104th Congress

in November 1994; reelected in 1996; was an unsuccessful candidate for reelection in 1998

EDWARD WHITFIELD, Representative, First District, Kentucky

Born: Hopkinsville, KY, May 25, 1943

Resides: Hopkinsville, KY

Education: Madisonville High School; B.S., University of Kentucky, 1965; J.D., University of Kentucky, 1969; attended American University's Wesley Theological Seminary

Military Service: First lieutenant, U.S. Army Reserve, 1967–73

Career: Admitted to Kentucky bar, 1970, and Florida bar, 1993; attorney, private practice, 1970–79; vice president, CSX Corporation, 1983–91; counsel, Interstate Commerce Commission, 1991–93

Civic Activities and Awards: Watchdog of the Treasury Award; League of Private Property Voters, Champion of Private Property Rights; U.S. Chamber of Commerce, Spirit of Enterprise Award; National Federation of Independent Business, Guardian of Small Business Award

State and Local Office: Kentucky State House of Representatives, 1973–75

Elected to Congress: Elected to the 104th Congress in November 1994; reelected to each succeeding Congress

ROGER F. WICKER, Representative, First District, Mississippi

Born: Pontotoc, MS, July 5, 1951

Resides: Tupelo, MS

Education: Pontotoc High School; B.A. and J.D., University of Mississippi, 1973 and 1975 (law review); Air Force ROTC

Military Service: U.S. Air Force, 1976–80; lieutenant colonel, U.S. Air Force Reserve, 1980–present

Career: Attorney at law; U.S. House Rules Committee staff for Representative Trent Lott, 1980–82; private law practice, 1982–94; Lee County public defender, 1984–87; Tupelo City judge pro tempore, 1986–87

Civic Activities and Awards: Member, Lions Club, Promise Keepers; Ole Miss Hall of Fame; Sigma

Nu fraternity; Omicron Delta Kappa; Phi Delta Phi; president of Tupelo Community Theater; president, Lee County Young Lawyers; North Mississippi Medical Center Development Council; member, Community Development Foundation Education Roundtable, CDF Skills and Technology Task Force; deacon, Sunday school teacher, adult choir of First Baptist Church, Tupelo, MS

State and Local Office: Member, Mississippi State Senate, 1988–94; chair, Electric Committee, 1992, Public Health and Welfare Committee, 1993; Education, Judiciary, Finance, Elections, and Constitution committees; Senate Rules Committee, 1993

Elected to Congress: Elected to the 104th Congress in November 1994; reelected to each succeeding Congress

HEATHER ANN WILSON, Representative, First District, New Mexico

Born: Keene, NH, December 30, 1960

Resides: Albuquerque, NM

Education: Keene High School, NH; B.S., United States Air Force Academy, 1982; Oxford University, Rhodes Scholar; master's degree (1984), doctoral degrees in philosophy (international relations), 1985

Military Service: United States Air Force, 1982–89; captain

Career: President, Keystone International, Inc., 1991–95

State and Local Office: New Mexico Secretary of Children, Youth, and Families, 1995–98

Elected to Congress: Elected to the 105th Congress on June 23, 1998, by special election, to fill the vacancy caused by the death of Steven Schiff; reelected in November 1998, 2000

FRANK R. WOLF, Representative, Tenth District, Virginia

Born: Philadelphia, PA, January 30, 1939

Resides: Vienna, VA

Education: B.A., Pennsylvania State University, 1961; LL.B., Georgetown University Law School, 1965

Military Service: U.S. Army, 1962–63; Army Reserves, 1963–67

Career: Legislative assistant for former U.S. congressman Edward G. Biester Jr., 1968–71; assistant to Secretary of the Interior Rogers C. B. Morton, 1971–74; deputy assistant secretary for congressional and legislative affairs, Department of the Interior, 1974–75; practicing attorney, 1975–80

Civic Activities and Awards: Member, Vienna Presbyterian Church

Elected to Congress: Elected to the 97th Congress in November 1980; reelected to each succeeding Congress

C. W. (BILL) YOUNG, Representative, Tenth District, Florida

Born: Harmarville, PA, December 16, 1930

Resides: Indian Rocks Beach, FL

Military: Army National Guard, 1948–57

Career: Aide, U.S. Representative William Cramer, 1957–60

Civic Activities and Awards: National committee member, Florida Young Republicans, 1957–59; state chair, Florida Young Republicans, 1959–61; member, Florida Constitution Revision Commission, 1965–67; founder, C.W. Bill Young Marrow Donor Recruitment and Research Program

State and Local Office: Florida State Senate, 1960–70, minority leader, 1966–70

Elected to Congress: Elected to the 92nd Congress in November 1970; reelected to each succeeding Congress

DONALD E. YOUNG, Representative at Large, Alaska

Born: Meridian, CA, June 9, 1933

Resides: Ft. Yukon, AK

Education: A.A., Yuba Junior College, 1952; B.A., Chico State College, 1958

Military Service: U.S. Army, 41st Tank Battalion, 1955–57

Career: Educator for nine years; riverboat captain

Civic Activities and Awards: Honorary doctorate of laws, University of Alaska, Fairbanks; member, National Education Association, Elks, Lions, Jaycees

State and Local Office: Ft. Yukon City Council, 1960–64; Fort Yukon Mayor, 1964–68; Alaska State House of Representatives, 1966–70; Alaska State Senate, 1970–73

Elected to Congress: Elected to the 93rd Congress on March 6, 1973, in a special election, to fill the vacancy created by the death of Congressman Nick Begich; reelected to each succeeding Congress

SENATORS

SPENCER ABRAHAM, former Senator, Michigan

Born: East Lansing, MI, June 12, 1952

Resides: Auburn Hills, MI

Education: East Lansing High School; B.A., Michigan State University, 1974; J.D., Harvard Law School, 1979

Career: Practicing attorney; admitted to District of Columbia and State of Michigan bars; office counsel, Miller Canfield, Paddock, and Stone, 1992–94; deputy chief of staff to Vice President Dan Quayle, 1990

Civic Activities and Awards: Chair, Michigan Republican Party, 1983–89; cochair, National Republican Campaign Committees, 1990–92; founder and board member, Federalist Society; founder and president, *Harvard Journal of Law and Public Policy*

Elected to Congress: Elected to the U.S. Senate in November 1994; was an unsuccessful candidate for reelection in 2000

WAYNE ALLARD, Senator, Colorado

Born: Ft. Collins, CO, December 2, 1943

Resides: Loveland, CO

Education: Ft. Collins High School, 1963; preveterinary studies, Colorado State University, 1964; D.V.M., Colorado State University, 1968

Sen. Wayne Allard *(Government Printing Office)*

Career: Received veterinarian license in Colorado; chief health officer, Loveland, CO, 1970–78; Larimer County Board of Health, 1978–82; owner, Allard Animal Hospital, 1970–90

Civic Activities and Awards: Member, American Veterinary Medical Association, Chamber of Commerce

State and Local Office: Colorado State Senate, 1982–90; chair, majority caucus

Elected to Congress: U.S. Representative, 1991–96; elected to the U.S. Senate in November 1996

GEORGE ALLEN, Senator, Virginia

Born: Whittier, CA, March 8, 1952

Resides: Chesterfield, VA

Education: B.A., University of Virginia, 1974; J.D., University of Virginia, 1977

Career: Attorney; partner, McGuire Woods Battle & Boothe, 1998–2001

Civic Activities and Awards: Chair, Youth for Reagan, 1976; fellow, the Heritage Foundation, 1998–

Sen. Robert F. Bennett *(Office of Sen. Bennett)*

99; fellow, the National Center for Policy Analysis, 1998–99; Jeffersonian scholar, American Legislative Exchange Council, 1998–2000

State and Local Office: Virginia House of Delegates, 1983–91; governor of Virginia, 1994–98

Elected to Congress: Elected to the U.S. House of Representatives by special election in November 1991, to fill the vacancy caused by the resignation of D. French Slaughter Jr., served from 1991–93; elected to the U.S. Senate in November 2000

JOHN ASHCROFT, former Senator, Missouri

Born: Chicago, IL, May 9, 1942

Resides: Springfield, MO

Education: Hillcrest High School; A.B. cum laude, Yale University, 1964; J.D., University of Chicago School of Law, 1967

Career: Admitted to the Springfield bar, 1967; practicing attorney

State and Local Office: Governor of Missouri, 1985–93; attorney general of Missouri, 1976–85; state auditor of Missouri, 1973–75

Elected to Congress: Elected to the U.S. Senate in November 1994; was an unsuccessful candidate for reelection in 2000; appointed U.S. attorney general in 2001

ROBERT F. BENNETT, Senator, Utah

Born: Salt Lake City, UT, September 18, 1933

Resides: Salt Lake City, UT

Education: B.S., University of Utah, 1957

Career: Chief executive officer of Franklin Quest, Salt Lake City, 1984–91; chief congressional liaison, U.S. Department of Transportation; chair of Utah Education Strategic Planning Commission, 1988; author, *Gaining Control*

Civic Activities and Awards: Entrepreneur of the Year, *Inc.* magazine, 1989; Light of Learning Award, 1989

Elected to Congress: Elected to the U.S. Senate in November 1992; reelected in 1998

CHRISTOPHER S. (KIT) BOND, Senator, Missouri

Born: St. Louis, MO, March 6, 1939

Resides: Mexico, MO

Education: B.A., cum laude, Woodrow Wilson School of Public and International Affairs, Princeton University, 1960; J.D., valedictorian, University of Virginia, 1963

Career: Held a clerkship with the U.S. Court of Appeals for the Fifth Circuit until 1964; practiced law in Washington, DC, and returned to Missouri, 1967; practicing attorney

State and Local Office: Assistant attorney general of Missouri, 1969–70; state auditor, 1970–72; governor of Missouri, 1973–77, 1981–85

Elected to Congress: Elected to the Senate in November 1986; reelected in 1992, 1998

SAMUEL DALE BROWNBACK, Senator, Kansas

Born: Garrett, KS, September 12, 1956

Resides: Topeka, KS

Education: Prairie View High School, 1974; B.S.

Sen. Kit Bond (*Office of Sen. Bond*)

Sen. Sam Brownback (*Office of Sen. Brownback*)

with honors, Kansas State University, 1978; J.D., University of Kansas, 1982

Career: Admitted to the Kansas bar; attorney, broadcaster, teacher; White House Fellow, Office of the U.S. Trade Representative, 1990–91

Civic Activities and Awards: Member, Topeka Fellowship Council, Kansas Bar Association, Kansas State University and Kansas University alumni associations

State and Local Office: State secretary of agriculture, 1986–93

Elected to Congress: U.S. House of Representatives, 1994–96; elected to the U.S. Senate in November 1996, to fill the remainder of the vacancy caused by the resignation of former senator Bob Dole; reelected in 1998

JIM BUNNING, Senator, Kentucky

Born: Campbell County, KY, October 23, 1931

Resides: Southgate, KY

Education: St. Xavier High School, Cincinnati,

OH, 1949; B.S., Xavier University, Cincinnati, OH, 1953

Career: Professional baseball player, hall of fame; investment broker and agent; president, Jim Bunning Agency, Inc.; appointed member, Ohio, Kentucky, and Indiana Regional Council of Governments, Cincinnati, OH; National Committeeman, Republican National Committee, 1983–92; appointed member, President's National Advisory Board on International Education Programs, 1984–88

Civic Activities and Awards: Board of directors, Kentucky special Olympics; Ft. Thomas (KY) Lions Club, Brighton Street Center Community Action Group

State and Local Office: Kentucky State Senate, minority floor leader, 1979–83; member, Ft. Thomas City Council, 1977–79

Elected to Congress: U.S. House of Representatives, 1986–98; elected to the U.S. Senate in November 1998

Sen. Jim Bunning (*Office of Sen. Bunning*)

Sen. Conrad Burns (*Government Printing Office*)

CONRAD R. BURNS, Senator, Montana

Born: Gallatin, MO, January 25, 1935

Resides: Billings, MT

Education: Gallatin High School, 1952; attended University of Missouri, Columbia, 1953–54

Military Service: U.S. Marine Corps, corporal, 1955–57

Career: Farm broadcaster and auctioneer

Civic Activities and Awards: Member, Rotary, American Legion, National Association of Farm Broadcasters, American Association of Farm Broadcasters, Atonement Lutheran Church

State and Local Office: County commissioner, Yellowstone County, 1986

Elected to Congress: Elected to the U.S. Senate in November 1988; reelected in 1994, 2000

BEN NIGHTHORSE CAMPBELL, Senator, Colorado

Born: Auburn, CA, April 13, 1933

Resides: Ignacio, CO

Education: Attended Placer High School, 1951; quit high school to join Air Force (earned his GED while in Air Force); attended graduation exercises and received a diploma in 1991; B.A., San Jose State University, 1957; attended Meiji University (Tokyo) as special research student, 1960–64

Military Service: U.S. Air Force in Korea, airman second class, 1951–53

Career: Jewelry designer who has won more than 200 first-place and best-of-show awards; rancher who raised, trained, and showed horses; All-American in judo, captain of the U.S. Olympic Judo Team in 1964, gold medal in the Pan-American Games of 1963

Civic Activities and Awards: Appointed adviser to the Colorado Commission on International Trade and Colorado Commission on the Arts and Humanities; voted by colleagues one of Ten Best Legislators in the *Denver Post*—News Center 4 survey, 1984; 1984 Outstanding Legislator Award

Sen. Ben Nighthorse Campbell (*Government Printing Office*)

from Colorado Bankers Association; inducted into the Council of 44 Chiefs, Northern Cheyenne Indian Tribe; member, Durango Chamber of Commerce, American Quarter Horse Association, American Paint Horse Association, American Brangus Association, Aircraft Owners and Pilot Association; senior technical adviser, U.S. Judo Association

State and Local Office: Elected Colorado state legislator in 1982, serving 1983–86 on the Agriculture and Natural Affairs and Business and Labor committees

Elected to Congress: U.S. Representative, 1987–92; elected to the U.S. Senate in November 1992; reelected in 1998

JOHN H. CHAFEE, former Senator, Rhode Island

Born: Providence, RI, October 22, 1922

Education: Deerfield Academy, 1940; B.A., Yale University, 1947; LL.B., Harvard Law School, 1950

Military Service: U.S. Marine Corps; served in original landing on Guadalcanal, August 1942; commissioned second lieutenant, participated in fighting in Okinawa; recalled to active duty in Marines in Korean conflict, 1951; served in Korea as rifle company commander; discharged with rank of captain, 1952

Career: Admitted to the bar in Rhode Island, 1950; practiced law in Providence, 1952–63; secretary of the navy, January 1969 to May 1972

Civic Activities and Awards: Chair, Republican Governors Association, 1968; Chubb fellow, Yale University, 1966; board of visitors, John F. Kennedy School of Government, Harvard University, 1969–72; Yale University, board of trustees, 1972–78; honorary degrees, Brown University, Providence College, University of Rhode Island, Rhode Island College, Roger Williams College, Salve Regina College, Suffolk University, Jacksonville University, Bryant College; Legislator of the Year Award, National League of Women Voters, 1992; Environmental Law Institute Award, 1991; 1992 Audubon Medal; 1992 Excellence in Health Care Award

State and Local Office: Member, Rhode Island House of Representatives, 1957–63; minority leader, 1959–63; governor of Rhode Island, 1963–69

Elected to Congress: Elected to the U.S. Senate in November 1976; reelected to each succeeding Congress and served until his death on October 24, 1999

LINCOLN CHAFEE, Senator, Rhode Island

Born: Providence, RI, March 26, 1953

Resides: Warwick, RI

Education: B.A., classics, Brown University, 1975 (received Francis M. Driscoll Award for leadership, scholarships and athletics); LL.B., Harvard University, 1950

Military Service: Marine Corps, 1942–45, 1951–53

Career: Farrier, manufacturing management; planner, General Dynamics facility at Quonset

Point; executive director of the Northeast Corridor Initiative

State and Local Office: Delegate, Rhode Island Constitutional Convention, 1985; Warwick City Council, 1986–92; mayor, City of Warwick, 1992–1999

Elected to Congress: Appointed to the 106th Congress on November 2, 1999, to fill the vacancy caused by the death of his father, John H. Chafee; reelected in 2000

DAN COATS, former Senator, Indiana

Born: Jackson, MI, May 16, 1943

Resides: Ft. Wayne, IN

Education: Jackson High School, 1961; B.A., Wheaton College, 1965; J.D., Indiana University School of Law, cum laude, 1971 (associate editor, law review)

Military Service: Staff sergeant, U.S. Army, 1966–68

Career: Attorney, admitted to the Indiana state bar in 1972 and commenced practice in Ft. Wayne; Mutual Security Life Insurance Company, Ft. Wayne, assistant vice president and counsel for mortgage loan and real estate investments; district director, U.S. Representative Dan Quayle, 1976–80

Civic Activities and Awards: Board member, board of visitors of Wheaton College, Big Brothers/Big Sisters of America, International Republican Institute, Military Academy Board of Advisers at West Point, Center for Effective Compassion; numerous honorary board memberships; member, McLean Presbyterian Church, Quest Club; Emil Verbin Society; Indiana University School of Law, Distinguished Alumni Award, 1995; L. Mendel Rivers Award, 1993; numerous National Federation of Independent Business, Guardian of Small Business awards; Region 5 Head Start Man of the Year, 1991; numerous Watchdog of the Treasury awards; 1986 Leadership Award, Coalition for Peace Through Strength; Spirit of Enterprise Award; Sagamore of the Wabash, 1985; 1988 Congressional Baseball Game, MVP; honorary degrees, Huntington College, Wheaton College, Olivet College

Elected to Congress: U.S. Representative, 1980–88; appointed by Indiana governor Robert Orr in 1988 to the U.S. Senate seat vacated by Vice President–elect Dan Quayle; elected November 6, 1990, to complete the term ending January 3, 1993; reelected in 1992; was not a candidate for reelection in 1998

THAD COCHRAN, Senator, Mississippi

Born: Pontotoc, MS, December 7, 1937

Resides: Jackson, MS

Education: Bryam High School, 1955; B.A., University of Mississippi, 1959; J.D., University of Mississippi Law School, 1965; studied international law and jurisprudence at Trinity College, University of Dublin, Ireland, 1963–64

Military Service: U.S. Navy, 1959–61

Career: Admitted to Mississippi bar in 1965; partner, Watkins & Eager law firm, Jackson

Civic Activities and Awards: Rotary Foundation Fellowship; board of directors, Jackson Rotary Club, 1970–71; Outstanding Young Man of the

Sen. Thad Cochran *(Government Printing Office)*

Year Award, Junior Chamber of Commerce in Mississippi, 1971; president, young lawyers division of Mississippi state bar, 1972–73

Elected to Congress: U.S. Representative, 1972–78; elected to the U.S. Senate in November 1978; subsequently appointed by the governor on December 27, 1978, to fill the vacancy caused by the resignation of Senator James O. Eastland; reelected to each succeeding term

SUSAN COLLINS, Senator, Maine

Born: Caribou, ME, December 7, 1952

Resides: Bangor, ME

Education: Caribou High School, 1971; B.A., magna cum laude, Phi Beta Kappa, St. Lawrence University, 1975

Career: Staff director, Senate Subcommittee on the Oversight of Government Management, 1981–87; for 12 years, principal adviser on business issues to former senator William S. Cohen; commissioner of professional and financial regulation for Maine governor John R. McKernan Jr., 1987; New England administrator, Small Business Administration, 1992–93; appointed deputy treasurer of Massachusetts, 1993; founding executive director, Husson College Center for Family Business, 1994–96

Civic Activities and Awards: Outstanding Alumni Award, St. Lawrence University, 1992

Elected to Congress: Elected to the U.S. Senate in November 1996

PAUL D. COVERDELL, former Senator, Georgia

Born: Des Moines, IA, January 20, 1939

Education: Lee's Summit High School, 1957; B.A., journalism, University of Missouri, 1961

Military Service: Officer, U.S. Army, in Okinawa, Taiwan, and Korea, 1962–64

Career: Founder and president, Coverdell & Company, 1964–89; chair, Georgia Republican Party, 1985–87; director, U.S. Peace Corps, 1989–91

Civic Activities and Awards: Good Government Award, Atlanta Jaycees, 1976; Ten Leading State Legislators, *Atlanta Journal Constitution*, 1980; National Republican Legislator's Association Legislator of the Year, 1982; Liberty Bell Award, Atlanta Bar Association, 1982; Honorable William E. Brock Award, 1984; Hermione Weil Alexander Fund Award of Appreciation, 1984, for the battle against drunk driving; Atlanta Fulton County League of Women Voters, second Sidney Marcus Public Service Award, 1985; Leadership Atlanta, Leadership Georgia; Georgia Institute of Technology Distinguished Service Award, 1989; Appreciation Award from the Atlanta Association for Retarded Citizens, 1981

State and Local Office: Georgia State Senate, 1970–89

Elected to Congress: Elected to the U.S. Senate in November 1992, in a special runoff election; reelected in 1998, and served until his death on July 18, 2000

LARRY E. CRAIG, Senator, Idaho

Born: Midvale, ID, July 20, 1945

Resides: Payette, ID

Sen. Larry E. Craig (*Office of Sen. Craig*)

Education: Attended Midvale public schools; B.A., 1969, University of Idaho; graduate work in economics and the politics of developing nations, George Washington University, 1970

Military Service: Army National Guard, 1970–74

Career: Farmer-rancher, Midvale area, for ten years

Civic Activities and Awards: Idaho state president and national vice president, Future Farmers of America, 1966–67; member, National Foundation for Defense Analysis; Idaho State Republican Executive Committee, 1976–78; president, Young Republican League of Idaho, 1976–77; chair, Republican Central Committee, Washington County, 1971–72; board of directors, National Rifle Association; policy chair, Republican Study Committee, 1990; delegate, Idaho State Republican Conventions, 1976–78

State and Local Office: Idaho State Senate, 1974–80; chair, Senate Commerce and Labor Committee

Elected to Congress: U.S. Representative, 1981–91; elected to the U.S. Senate in November 1990, reelected in 1996

Sen. Mike Crapo *(Office of Sen. Crapo)*

MIKE CRAPO, Senator, Idaho

Born: Idaho Falls, ID, May 20, 1951

Resides: Idaho Falls, ID

Education: Idaho Falls High School, 1969; B.A., Brigham Young University, 1973; J.D., Harvard University Law School, 1977

Career: Attorney; admitted to the California bar, 1977; admitted to the Idaho bar, 1979; law clerk, Hon. James M. Carter, judge of the U.S. Court of Appeals for the Ninth Circuit, San Diego, CA, 1977–78; associate attorney, Gibson, Dunn, and Crutcher, San Diego, 1978–79; attorney, Holden, Kidwell, Hahn, and Crapo, 1979–92; partner, 1983–92

Civic Activities and Awards: Member, American Bar Association, Boy Scouts of America, Idaho Falls Rotary Club, 1984–88

State and Local Office: Idaho State Senate, 1984–92, assistant majority leader, 1987–89, president pro tempore, 1988–92

Elected to Congress: U.S. Representative, 1992–98; elected to the U.S. Senate in November 1998

MIKE DeWINE, Senator, Ohio

Born: Springfield, OH, January 5, 1947

Resides: Cedarville, OH

Education: Yellow Springs High School; B.S., Miami University, 1969; J.D., Ohio Northern University, 1972

Career: Attorney, admitted to the Ohio state bar, 1972; Greene County assistant prosecuting attorney, 1973–75

State and Local Office: Ohio state senator, 1980–82; lieutenant governor of Ohio, 1990–94

Elected to Congress: U.S. Representative, 1983–91; elected to the U.S. Senate in November 1994; reelected in 2000

PETE V. DOMENICI, Senator, New Mexico

Born: Albuquerque, NM, May 7, 1932

Resides: Albuquerque, NM

Education: St. Mary's High School, 1950; University of New Mexico, B.S., 1954; Denver University, LL.D., 1958

Sen. Mike DeWine *(Government Printing Office)*

Sen. Pete V. Domenici *(Government Printing Office)*

Career: Admitted to New Mexico bar, 1958; entered private practice, 1958

State and Local Office: Elected to Albuquerque City Commission, 1966; chair (ex officio mayor), 1967

Elected to Congress: Elected to the U.S. Senate in November 1972; reelected to each succeeding term

JOHN ENSIGN, Senator, Nevada

Born: Roseville, CA, March 25, 1958

Resides: Las Vegas, NV

Education: E. W. Clark High School, Las Vegas, 1976; attended University of Nevada, 1979; B.S., Oregon State University, Corvallis, 1981; D.V.M., Colorado State University, Fort Collins, 1985

Career: Owner, West Flamingo Animal Hospital, Las Vegas, 1987–94; owner, South Shores Animal Hospital, Las Vegas, 1994–present

Elected to Congress: U.S. House of Representatives, 1995–99; was not a candidate in 1998 for reelection to the U.S. House of Representatives but was an unsuccessful candidate for election to the U.S. Senate; elected to the U.S. Senate in November 2000

MICHAEL B. ENZI, Senator, Wyoming

Born: Bremerton, WA, February 1, 1944

Resides: Gillette, WY

Education: Sheridan High School, 1962; B.S., accounting, George Washington University, 1966; M.B.A., Denver University, 1968

Military Service: Served in Wyoming Air National Guard, 1967–73

Career: Accounting manager and computer programmer, Dunbar Well Service, 1985–97; director, Black Hills Corporation, 1992–96; chairman, founding board of directors, First Wyoming Bank of Gillette, 1978–88; owner, with wife, of NZ Shoes, 1969–95

Civic Activities and Awards: Commissioner, Western Interstate Commission for Higher Education, 1995–96; served on the Education Commission of the States, 1989–93; president, Wyoming Association of Municipalities, 1980–82; president, Wyoming Jaycees, 1973–74; member, Lions Club; elder, Presbyterian Church; Eagle Scout

Sen. Michael B. Enzi (*Government Printing Office*)

Sen. Peter G. Fitzgerald (*Government Printing Office*)

Sen. Bill Frist (*Government Printing Office*)

State and Local Office: Served in Wyoming State House of Representatives, 1987–91, and in Wyoming State Senate, 1991–96; mayor of Gillette, 1975–82

Elected to Congress: Elected to the U.S. Senate in November 1996

PETER G. FITZGERALD, Senator, Illinois

Born: Elgin, IL, October 20, 1960

Resides: Iverness, IL

Education: Portsmouth Abbey, 1978; B.A., Dartmouth College, 1982; J.D., University of Michigan School of Law, 1986

Career: Corporate attorney

State and Local Office: Illinois General Assembly, 1992–98

Elected to Congress: Elected to the U.S. Senate in November 1998

WILLIAM (BILL) H. FRIST, Senator, Tennessee

Born: Nashville, TN, February 22, 1952

Resides: Nashville, TN

Education: Montgomery Bell Academy, 1970; A.B., Princeton University, Woodrow Wilson School of Public and International Affairs, 1974; M.D., Harvard Medical School, 1978, with honors; residency in general surgery (1978–84) and thoracic surgery (1983–84), Massachusetts General Hospital; cardiovascular and transplant fellowship, Stanford University Medical Center, 1985–86

Career: Heart and lung transplant surgeon; founding director, Vanderbilt Transplant Center; teaching faculty, Vanderbilt University Medical Center, 1986–93; staff surgeon, Nashville Veterans' Administration Hospital; board certified in both general surgery and cardiothoracic surgery; commercial pilot, author of 100 scientific articles, chapters and abstracts (subjects: fibroblast growth factor, thoracic surgery, artificial heart, transplantation, immunosuppression); author of *Transplant* (1989); coeditor, *Grand Rounds in Transplantation* (1995)

Civic Activities and Awards: Medical Center Ethics Committee, 1991–93; chair, Tennessee Medicaid Task Force, 1992–93; Distinguished Service Award, Tennessee Medical Association; president, Middle Tennessee Heart Association; member, Smithsonian Institution Board of Regents, Princeton University Board of Trustees, American College of Surgeons, Society of Thoracic Surgeons, Southern Thoracic Surgical Association, American College of Chest Physicians, American Medical Association, Tennessee Medical Association, American Society of Transplant Surgeons, Association of Academic Surgery, International Society for Heart and Lung Transplantation, Tennessee Transplant Society, Alpha Omega Alpha, Rotary Club, United Way, de Tocqueville Society; board member, YMCA Foundation of Metropolitan Nashville, Sergeant York Historical Association

Elected to Congress: Elected to the U.S. Senate in November 1994; reelected in 2000

SLADE GORTON, former Senator, Washington

Born: Chicago, IL, January 8, 1928

Resides: Bellevue, WA

Education: Graduated from high school in Evanston, IL, 1945; A.B., international relations, Dartmouth College, 1950; LL.B., with honors, Columbia University Law School, 1953

Military Service: U.S. Army, 1945–46; U.S. Air Force, 1953–56; retired colonel, Air Force Reserves, 1956–80

Career: Admitted to bar, Washington state, 1953

Civic Activities and Awards: Member, National Association of Attorneys General, 1969–80, president 1976–77; Washington State Law and Justice Commission, 1969–80, chair 1969–76; State Criminal Justice Training Commission, 1969–80, chair 1969–76; member, President's Consumer Advisory Council, 1975–77; Wyman Award winner, 1980

State and Local Office: Elected to Washington State House of Representatives, 46th District, Seattle, 1958; reelected 1960, 1962, 1964, 1966, majority leader 1967–68; elected Washington state attorney general, 1968; reelected 1972, 1976

Elected to Congress: Elected to the U.S. Senate in November 1980; unsuccessful candidate for reelection, 1986; elected to the U.S. Senate in November 1988; reelected in 1994; was an unsuccessful candidate for reelection in 2000

PHIL GRAMM, Senator, Texas

Born: Ft. Benning, GA, July 8, 1942

Resides: College Station, TX

Education: B.A., 1964, Ph.D., 1967, economics, University of Georgia

Career: Professor of economics, Texas A&M University, 1967–78; author of several books, including *The Evolution of Modern Demand Theory* and *The Economics of Mineral Extraction*

Civic Activities and Awards: Episcopalian

Elected to Congress: U.S. Representative, 1978–82; resigned from the House on Jan. 5, 1983, upon being denied a seat on the House Budget Committee; reelected to the House in a special election on February 12, 1983; elected to the U.S. Senate in November 1984; reelected in 1990, 1996

Sen. Phil Gramm (*Government Printing Office*)

ROD GRAMS, former Senator, Minnesota

Born: Princeton, MN, February 4, 1948

Resides: Ramsey, MN

Education: St. Francis High School; attended Anoka-Ramsey Junior College, Brown Institute, Carroll College

Career: Producer and anchor, 1982–91, at KMSP-TV (Minneapolis/St. Paul, MN), KFBB-TV (Great Falls, MT), WSAU-TV (Wausau, WI), and WIFR-TV (Rockford, IL); home builder; land developer; president and CEO, Sun Ridge Builders, 1985; congressional delegate to the UN General Assembly, 1996, 1998

Elected to Congress: U.S. Representative, 1992–1994; Republican whip for the 103rd Congress; elected to the U.S. Senate in November 1994; was an unsuccessful candidate for reelection in 2000

CHARLES (CHUCK) GRASSLEY, Senator, Iowa

Born: New Hartford, IA, September 17, 1933

Resides: New Hartford, IA

Education: New Hartford Community High School, 1951; B.A., University of Northern Iowa, 1955; M.A., University of Northern Iowa, 1956; doctoral studies, University of Iowa, 1957–58

Career: Farmer

Civic Activities and Awards: Farm Bureau, State and County Historical Society, Masons, Baptist Church, International Association of Machinists

State and Local Office: Member, Iowa House of Representatives, 1958–74

Elected to Congress: U.S. Representative, 1974–80; elected to the U.S. Senate in November 1980; reelected to each succeeding term

JUDD GREGG, Senator, New Hampshire

Born: Nashua, NH, February 14, 1947

Resides: Rye, NH

Education: Phillips Exeter Academy, 1965; A.B., Columbia University, 1969; J.D., 1972, and LL.M., 1975, Boston University

Sen. Charles Grassley (*Government Printing Office*)

Sen. Judd Gregg *(Office of Sen. Gregg)*

Education: St. Bonaventure High School, 1964; Brown Institute for Radio and Television; University of Nebraska

Military Service: U.S. Army, Vietnam, 1968; received two Purple Hearts, other decorations

Career: President, McCarthy and Company, Omaha, NE; president and CEO, Private Sector Council (PSC), Washington, DC; deputy director and CEO, Economic Summit of Industrialized Nations (G-7 Summit), 1990; president and CEO, World USO; cofounder, director, and executive vice president, VANGUARD Cellular Systems, Inc.; cofounder and chair of VANGUARD subsidiary, Communications Corporation International: president, Collins, Hagel and Clarke; former deputy administrator, Veterans' Administration; former administrative assistant to Congressman John Y. McCollister; former newscaster and talk show host, Omaha radio stations KBON and KLNG

Civic Activities and Awards: Member, American Legion, Veterans of Foreign Wars, Disabled

Career: Attorney, admitted to the New Hampshire bar, 1972; commenced practice in Nashua; practiced law, 1976–80

Civic Activities and Awards: Member, Governor's Executive Council, 1978–80; president, Crotched Mountain Rehabilitation Foundation; awards from the National Taxpayers Union, Citizens Against Government Waste, the National Federation of Independent Businesses, the Concord Coalition, the Watchdogs of the Treasury, Inc., Citizens for a Sound Economy

State and Local Office: Governor of New Hampshire, 1988–92

Elected to Congress: U.S. Representative, 1981–89; elected to the U.S. Senate in November 1992; reelected in 1998

CHARLES (CHUCK) HAGEL, Senator, Nebraska

Born: North Platte, NE, October 4, 1946

Resides: Omaha, NE

Sen. Chuck Hagel *(Government Printing Office)*

American Veterans, Military Order of the Purple Heart, board of directors, Omaha Chamber of Commerce; board of trustees, Bellevue University, Hastings College, Heartland Chapter of the American Red Cross; campaign chair, Great Plains Chapter of Paralyzed Veterans of America; board of directors and national advisory committee, Friends of the Vietnam Veterans' Memorial; board of directors, Arlington National Cemetery Historical Society; chair of the board, No Greater Love; first-ever World USO Leadership Award; Distinguished Alumni Award, University of Nebraska, Omaha, 1988; Freedom Foundation (Omaha Chapter) 1993 Recognition Award

Elected to Congress: Elected to the U.S. Senate in November 1996

ORRIN G. HATCH, Senator, Utah

Born: Pittsburgh, PA, March 22, 1934

Resides: Salt Lake City, UT

Education: B.S., Brigham Young University, 1959; J.D., University of Pittsburgh, 1962

Career: Worked at the metal lathing building trade; practiced law in Salt Lake City, UT, and Pittsburgh, PA; senior partner, Hatch and Plumb law firm, Salt Lake City; author, "The Equal Rights Amendment Extension: A Critical Analysis," *Harvard Journal of Law and Public Policy;* "Should the Capital Vote in Congress? A Critical Analysis of the D.C. Representation Amendment," *Fordham Urban Law Journal;* "Alternative Dispute Resolution in the Federal Government: A View from Congress," *Touro Law Review;* "The First Amendment and Our National Heritage," *Oklahoma City University Law Review;* "Avoidance of Constitutional Conflicts," *University of Pittsburgh Law Review;* "The Role of Congress in Sentencing: The United State Sentencing Commission, Mandatory Minimum Sentences, and the Search for a Certain and Effective Sentencing System," *Wake Forest Law Review*

Civic Activities and Awards: Member, AFL-CIO; holds Av rating in Martindale-Hubbell Law Directory; member, Salt Lake County Bar Association, Utah Bar Association, American Bar Association, Pennsylvania Bar Association, Alle-

Sen. Orrin G. Hatch (*Government Printing Office*)

gheny County Bar Association, numerous other professional and fraternal organizations; member, Church of Jesus Christ of Latter-day Saints; honorary degrees, University of Maryland, Pepperdine University, Southern Utah State University; honorary National Ski Patrol member; Help Eliminate Litter and Pollution (HELP) Association

Elected to Congress: Elected to the U.S. Senate in November 1976; reelected to each succeeding term

JESSE HELMS, Senator, North Carolina

Born: Monroe, NC, October 18, 1921

Resides: Raleigh, NC

Education: Attended Wingate Junior College and Wake Forest College

Military Service: U.S. Navy, 1942–45

Career: Former city editor, *Raleigh Times;* administrative assistant to U.S. Senator Willis Smith, 1951–53, and to U.S. Senator Alton Lennon, 1953;

Sen. Jesse Helms *(Government Printing Office)*

Elected to Congress: Elected to the U.S. Senate in November 1972; reelected to each succeeding term

TIM HUTCHINSON, Senator, Arkansas

Born: Gravette, AR, August 11, 1949

Resides: Bentonville, AR

Education: Springdale High School, 1967; B.A., Bob Jones University, 1979; M.A., University of Arkansas, 1990

Career: College instructor, John Brown University; co-owner, KBCV radio station, 1982–89

Civic Activities and Awards: Member, Kiwanis, Chamber of Commerce, Our Farm Board, Northwest Community College Foundation, Emmanuel Baptist Church

State and Local Office: Arkansas state legislature, 1985–92

Elected to Congress: U.S. Representative, 1992–96; elected to the U.S. Senate in November 1996

executive director, North Carolina Bankers Association, 1953–60; executive vice president, Capitol Broadcasting Company; wrote editorials for WRAL-TV and Tobacco Radio Network, 1960–72

Civic Activities and Awards: Deacon and Sunday school teacher, Hayes Barton Baptist Church, Raleigh; recipient of two Freedom Foundation awards for radio and television editorials; recipient of annual citizenship awards from North Carolina American Legion, North Carolina Veterans of Foreign Wars; president, Raleigh Rotary Club, 1969–70; 33rd degree Mason; Grand Orator, Grand Lodge of Masons of North Carolina, 1964–65, 1982, 1991; member, board of directors, North Carolina Cerebral Palsy Hospital; member, board of directors of Camp Willow Run, a youth camp for Christ at Littleton, NC

State and Local Office: Member, Raleigh City Council, chair of Law and Finance Committee, 1957–61

Sen. Tim Hutchinson *(Government Printing Office)*

Sen. Kay Bailey Hutchison (*Government Printing Office*)

KAY BAILEY HUTCHISON, Senator, Texas

Born: Galveston, TX, July 22, 1943

Resides: Dallas, TX

Education: Graduate of the University of Texas at Austin and University of Texas School of Law

Career: Political and legal correspondent for KPRC-TV, Houston, 1967–70; appointed vice chair of the National Transportation Safety Board, 1976–78; senior vice president and general counsel, RepublicBank Corporation, 1978–82; co-founded Fidelity National Bank of Dallas; owner, McCraw Candies, 1984–88

Civic Activities and Awards: Episcopalian; member, development boards of Southern Methodist University and Texas A&M schools of business; trustee of the University of Texas Law School Foundation

State and Local Office: Texas State House of Representatives, 1972–76; Texas state treasurer, 1990–93

Elected to Congress: Elected to the U.S. Senate on June 5, 1993, by special election, to fill the vacancy caused by the resignation of Lloyd Bentsen; reelected in 1994, 2000

JAMES M. INHOFE, Senator, Oklahoma

Born: Des Moines, IA, November 17, 1934

Resides: Tulsa, OK

Education: Central High School, 1953; B.A., University of Tulsa, 1973

Military Service: U.S. Army, private first class, 1957–58

Career: Businessman; active pilot; president, Quaker Life Insurance Company

Civic Activities and Awards: Member, First Presbyterian Church of Tulsa

State and Local Office: Oklahoma State House of Representatives, 1967–69; Oklahoma State Senate, 1969–77; mayor of Tulsa, 1978–84

Elected to Congress: U.S. Representative, 1986–94; elected to the U.S. Senate in November 1994 to

Sen. James M. Inhofe (*Government Printing Office*)

complete the unexpired term of Senator David Boren upon his resignation; reelected in 2000

JAMES M. JEFFORDS, Senator, Vermont

Born: Rutland, VT, May 11, 1934

Resides: Shrewsbury, VT

Education: Attended public schools in Rutland; received B.S., Yale University, 1956; L.D., LL.B., Harvard University, 1962

Military Service: U.S. Navy, 1956–59, lieutenant (jg); captain, U.S. Naval Reserve, 1959–90

Career: Admitted to the Vermont bar, 1962; practicing attorney, 1963–69

State and Local Office: State senator, 1967–68; attorney general, State of Vermont, 1969–73

Elected to Congress: U.S. Representative, 1974–88; elected to the U.S. Senate in November 1988; reelected 1994, 2000; resigned from the Republican Party and became an Independent in May 2001

DIRK KEMPTHORNE, former Senator, Idaho

Born: San Diego, CA, October 29, 1951

Resides: Boise, ID

Education: B.A., University of Idaho, 1976

Career: Executive assistant to the director, Idaho Department of Lands, 1976–78; executive vice president, Idaho Home Builders Association, 1978–81; Idaho public affairs manager, FMC Corporation, 1983–86

Civic Activities and Awards: U.S. Conference of Mayors Advisory Board, 1991–93; chair, U.S. Conference of Mayors; first vice president, Association of Idaho Cities, 1991–93; board of directors, Parents and Youth Against Drug and Alcohol Abuse (PAYADA); honorary chair, Working Partners

State and Local Office: Mayor, city of Boise, 1985–92

Elected to Congress: Elected to the U.S. Senate in November 1992; was not a candidate for reelection in 1998

JON KYL, Senator, Arizona

Born: Oakland, NE, April 25, 1942

Resides: Phoenix, AZ

Sen. Jon Kyl (*Government Printing Office*)

Education: Bloomfield High School, 1960; B.A., University of Arizona, 1964 (Phi Beta Kappa, Phi Kappa Phi); LL.B., University of Arizona, 1966 (editor in chief, *Arizona Law Review*)

Career: Attorney, admitted to the Arizona state bar, 1966; former partner in Phoenix law firm of Jennings, Strouss and Salmon, 1966–86

Civic Activities and Awards: Chair, Phoenix Chamber of Commerce (1984–85)

Elected to Congress: U.S. Representative, 1986–94; elected to the U.S. Senate in November 1994; reelected in 2000

TRENT LOTT, Senator, Mississippi

Born: Grenada, MS, October 9, 1941

Resides: Pascagoula, MS

Education: University of Mississippi, B.A., 1963, J.D., 1967

Career: Served as field representative for the University of Mississippi, 1963–65; acting law alumni secretary of the Ole Miss Alumni Association, 1966–67; practiced law in Pascagoula in 1967 with Bryan and Gordon law firm; administrative assistant to Congressman William M. Colmer, 1968–72

Civic Activities and Awards: Member, Sigma Nu social fraternity, Phi Alpha Delta legal fraternity, Jackson County Bar Association, American Bar Association, Masons, First Baptist Church of Pascagoula

Elected to Congress: U.S. Representative, 1972–88; elected to the U.S. Senate in November 1988; reelected in 1994, 2000

RICHARD G. LUGAR, Senator, Indiana

Born: Indianapolis, IN, April 4, 1932

Resides: Indianapolis, IN

Education: Shortridge High School, 1950; B.A., Denison University, 1954; M.A., Pembroke College (Oxford University, Rhodes Scholar), 1956

Military Service: U.S. Navy, 1957–60

Sen. Richard G. Lugar *(Government Printing Office)*

Career: Businessman; treasurer, Lugar Stock Farms, a livestock and grain operation; vice president and treasurer, 1960–67, Thomas L. Green and Co., manufacturers of food production machinery; visiting professor of political science, director of public affairs, Indiana Central University; professor, University of Indianapolis, 1976; member, Rotary Club; Indiana Farm Bureau; Kiwanis; Youth for Understanding

Civic Activities and Awards: Member, advisory board, U.S. Conference of Mayors, 1969–75; National League of Cities, advisory council, 1972–75, president, 1971; Advisory Commission on Intergovernmental Relations, 1969–75, vice chair, 1971–75; board of trustees, Denison University; advisory board, Indiana University–Purdue University at Indianapolis; 34 honorary doctorates from 11 states; recipient of Fiorello La Guardia Award, 1975; Republican National Convention keynote speaker, 1972; Senate Foreign Relations Committee chair, 1985–86; National Republican Senatorial Committee chair, 1983–84; member, St. Luke's Methodist Church

State and Local Office: Indianapolis Board of School Commissioners, 1964–67; mayor of Indianapolis, 1968–75

Elected to Congress: Elected to the U.S. Senate in November 1976; reelected to each succeeding term

CONNIE MACK, former Senator, Florida

Born: Philadelphia, PA, October 29, 1940

Resides: Cape Coral, FL

Education: Ft. Myers High School, 1959; B.A., marketing, University of Florida, Gainesville, 1966

Career: Banker, 1966–82

Civic Activities and Awards: Ft. Myers Chamber of Commerce; Kiwanis Club; board of directors, Palmer Drug Abuse Center; Ft. Myers Rotary; appointed to Federal Reserve Board (Miami branch)

Elected to Congress: U.S. Representative, 1982–88; elected to the U.S. Senate in November 1988; reelected in 1994; was not a candidate for reelection in 2000

JOHN McCAIN, Senator, Arizona

Born: Panama Canal Zone, August 29, 1936

Resides: Phoenix, AZ

Education: Episcopal High School, 1954; graduated, U.S. Naval Academy, 1958; National War College, 1973–74

Military Service: Retired captain (pilot), U.S. Navy, 1958–81; Silver Star, Bronze Star, Legion of Merit, Purple Heart, Distinguished Flying Cross

Civic Activities and Awards: Chair, International Republican Institute, 1993–present; named to *Time* magazine's "Top 25 Most Influential People in America," 1997

Elected to Congress: U.S. Representative, 1982–86; elected to the U.S. Senate in November 1986; reelected in 1992, 1998; was an unsuccessful candidate for presidential nomination in 2000

MITCH McCONNELL, Senator, Kentucky

Born: Sheffield, AL, February 20, 1942

Resides: Louisville, KY

Education: Manual High School, 1960; B.A. with honors, University of Louisville, 1964; J.D., University of Kentucky Law School, 1967

Career: Attorney, admitted to the Kentucky bar, 1967; chief legislative assistant to U.S. Senator Marlow Cook, 1968–70; deputy assistant U.S. attorney general, 1974–75

Civic Activities and Awards: President, Kentucky Association of County Judge/Executives, 1982; named Outstanding Young Man in Jefferson County, 1974; named Outstanding Young Man in Kentucky, 1977; named Conservationist of the Year by the League of Kentucky Sportsmen, 1983; founder and chair, Kentucky Task Force on Exploited and Missing Children, 1982; cochair, National Child Tragedies Coalition, 1981; advisory board member, National Institute of Justice, 1982–84; appointed chair of the Council of Elected Officials by Republican National Committee Chair Haley Barbour; member, Crescent Hill Baptist Church, Louisville, KY

State and Local Office: Judge/executive of Jefferson County, KY, 1978–84

Elected to Congress: Elected to the U.S. Senate in November 1984; reelected 1990, 1996

FRANK H. MURKOWSKI, Senator, Alaska

Born: Seattle, WA, March 28, 1933

Resides: Fairbanks, AK

Education: Ketchikan High School, 1951; attended University of Santa Clara, 1951–53; B.A., economics, Seattle University, 1955

Military Service: U.S. Coast Guard, active duty, 1955–56

Career: Banker; Alaska Commissioner of Economic Development, 1966–70; president, Alaska National Bank, Fairbanks, 1971–80

Civic Activities and Awards: President, Alaska Bankers Association, 1972; president, Alaska Chamber of Commerce, 1977; member, Elks, Lions, Pioneers of Alaska, Young Presidents Organization, American Legion

Elected to Congress: Elected to the U.S. Senate in November 1980; reelected to each succeeding term

Sen. Frank H. Murkowski (*Government Printing Office*)

Sen. Don Nickles (*Government Printing Office*)

PAT ROBERTS, Senator, Kansas

Born: Topeka, KS, April 20, 1936

Resides: Dodge City, KS

Education: Holton High School, 1954; B.A., journalism, Kansas State University, 1958

Military Service: Captain, U.S. Marine Corps, 1958–62

Career: Editor and reporter, Arizona newspapers, 1962–67; aide to Senator Frank Carlson, 1967–68; aide to Representative Keith Sebelius, 1969–80

Civic Activities and Awards: Honorary American farmer, Future Farmers of America; 1993 Wheat Man of the Year, Kansas Association of Wheat Growers; Golden Carrot Award, Public Voice; Golden Bulldog Award, Watchdogs of the Treasury; numerous Guardian of Small Business awards, National Federation of Independent Business; 1995 Dwight D. Eisenhower Medal, Eisenhower Exchange Fellowship

Elected to Congress: U.S. Representative, 1980–96; elected to the U.S. Senate in November 1996

DON NICKLES, Senator, Oklahoma

Born: Ponca City, OK, December 6, 1948

Resides: Ponca City, OK

Education: Ponca City High School, 1967; B.A., business administration, Oklahoma State University, 1971

Military Service: National Guard, 1970–76

Career: Vice president and general manager, Nickles Machine Corporation, 1976–80

Civic Activities and Awards: Cofounder and member, Oklahoma Coalition for Peace Through Strength; served on the boards of Ponca City United Way, St Mary's Catholic Church Parish Council, Chamber of Commerce, Kay County Council for Retarded Children; Rotary Club; Fellowship of Christian Athletes

State and Local Office: Served in Oklahoma State Senate, 1979–80

Elected to Congress: Elected to the U.S. Senate in November 1980; reelected to each succeeding term

Sen. Pat Roberts (*Office of Sen. Roberts*)

WILLIAM V. ROTH JR., former Senator, Delaware

Born: Great Falls, MT, July 22, 1921

Resides: Wilmington, DE

Education: B.A., University of Oregon, 1944; M.B.A., Harvard Business School; LL.B., Harvard Law School, 1947

Military Service: Enlisted as private in U.S. Army, 1943; served in Pacific; Bronze Star; discharged in 1946 as captain

Career: Member, Delaware and California bars, admitted to practice before U.S. Supreme Court; author of *The Power to Destroy*

Civic Activities and Awards: Episcopalian; chair of Delaware Republican State Committee, 1961–64; Republican National Committee, 1961–64

Elected to Congress: U.S. Representative, 1966–70; elected to the U.S. Senate in November 1970; re-elected to each succeeding term through 2001; was an unsuccessful candidate for reelection in 2000

RICHARD (RICK) JOHN SANTORUM, Senator, Pennsylvania

Born: Winchester, VA, May 10, 1958

Resides: Penn Hills, PA

Education: Carmel High School 1976; B.A., Pennsylvania State University, 1980; M.B.A., University of Pittsburgh, 1981; J.D., Dickinson School of Law, 1986

Career: Admitted to the Pennsylvania bar; administrative assistant to State Senator J. Doyle Corman (R-Centre), 1981–86; director of the Senate Local Government Committee, 1981–84; director of the Pennsylvania Senate Transportation Committee, 1984–86; associate attorney, Kirkpatrick and Lockhart, Pittsburgh, PA, 1986–90

Civic Activities and Awards: Rotary, Bethel Park USC; Italian Sons and Daughters Association; Knights of Columbus; Big Brothers and Sisters of Greater Pittsburgh Advisory Board; Tyrolean Society, Western Pennsylvania; Sons of Italy

Elected to Congress: U.S. Representative, 1991–93; elected to the U.S. Senate in November 1994; re-elected in 2000

Sen. Rick Santorum *(Government Printing Office)*

JEFFERSON (JEFF) BEAUREGARD SESSIONS III, Senator, Alabama

Born: Hybard, AL, December 24, 1946

Resides: Mobile, AL

Education: Wilcox County High School; B.A., Huntingdon College, 1969; J.D., University of Alabama, 1973

Military Service: U.S. Army Reserves, captain, 1973–86

Career: Attorney; admitted to the Alabama bar in 1973 and commenced practice for Guin, Bouldin and Porch in Russellville, 1973–75; assistant U.S. attorney, South District of Alabama, 1975–77; attorney for Stockman and Bedsole, 1977–81; U.S. attorney, South District of Alabama, 1981–93; attorney for Stockman, Bedsole and Sessions, 1993–94; attorney general, State of Alabama, 1995–97

Civic Activities and Awards: Huntingdon College Board of Trustees; delegate, General Conference, United Methodist Church; Mobile Lions Club; Mobile United Methodist Inner City Mission;

Sen. Jeff Sessions *(Office of Sen. Sessions)*

Sen. Richard C. Shelby *(Office of Sen. Shelby)*

American Bar Association; Ashland Place United Methodist Church; Recipient of the Teddy Roosevelt Environmental Award, the Watchdog of the Treasury Award, the Alabama Farmers Federation's Service to Agriculture Award

Elected to Congress: Elected to the U.S. Senate in November 1996

RICHARD C. SHELBY, Senator, Alabama

Born: Birmingham, AL, May 6, 1934

Resides: Tuscaloosa, AL

Education: Attended the public schools; B.A., University of Alabama, 1957; LL.B., University of Alabama School of Law, 1963

Career: Admitted to the Alabama bar in 1961 and commenced practice in Tuscaloosa; attorney, 1963–78; law clerk, Supreme Court of Alabama, 1961–62; city prosecutor, Tuscaloosa, 1963–71; U.S. magistrate, Northern District of Alabama, 1966–70; special assistant attorney general, State of Alabama, 1969–71

Civic Activities and Awards: Former president, Tuscaloosa County Mental Health Association; Alabama Code Revision Committee, 1971–75; Phi Alpha Delta legal fraternity, Tuscaloosa County; Alabama and American Bar Associations; First Presbyterian Church of Tuscaloosa; Exchange Club; American Judicature Society; Alabama Law Institute

State and Local Office: Alabama State Senate, 1970–78; chair, legislative council of Alabama state legislature, 1977–78

Elected to Congress: U.S. Representative, 1979–87; elected to the U.S. Senate in November 1986; reelected in 1992, 1998

GORDON HAROLD SMITH, Senator, Oregon

Born: Pendleton, OR, May 25, 1952

Resides: Pendleton, OR

Education: B.A., 1976, Brigham Young University; LL.B., 1979, Southwestern University

Career: Served as law clerk to Justice H. Vernon

Payne of the New Mexico Supreme Court and practiced law in Arizona; president/owner of Smith Frozen Foods since 1981

State and Local Office: Member, Oregon State Senate, 1992–97; elected Oregon senate president, 1995–97

Elected to Congress: Elected to the U.S. Senate in November 1996

ROBERT C. SMITH, Senator, New Hampshire

Born: Trenton, NJ, March 30, 1941

Resides: Tuftonboro, NH

Education: B.S., government and history, Lafayette College, Easton, PA, 1965; graduate work at Long Beach State College

Military Service: U.S. Navy, 1965–76; one year of duty in Vietnam, five years in U.S. Naval Reserve

Career: Teacher, realtor

Elected to Congress: U.S. Representative, 1985–90; elected to the U.S. Senate in November 1990; re-elected in 1996

OLYMPIA J. SNOWE, Senator, Maine

Born: Augusta, ME, February 21, 1947

Resides: Auburn, ME

Education: Edward Little High School, 1965; B.A., University of Maine, 1969

Career: Director, Superior Concrete Company, 1969–78; Auburn Board of Voter Registration, 1971–73

Civic Activities and Awards: Member, Holy Trinity Greek Orthodox Church of Lewiston-Auburn; active member of civic and community organizations

State and Local Office: Elected to the Maine State House of Representatives, 1973, to the seat vacated by the death of her first husband, the late Peter Snowe; reelected for a full two-year term in 1974; elected to the Maine State Senate, 1976; chaired the Joint Standing Committee on Health and Institutional Services

Elected to Congress: U.S. Representative, 1978–94; elected to the U.S. Senate in November 1994; re-elected in 2000

Sen. Olympia J. Snowe *(Government Printing Office)*

ARLEN SPECTER, Senator, Pennsylvania

Born: Wichita, KS, February 12, 1930

Resides: Philadelphia, PA

Education: Russell High School, 1947; University of Pennsylvania, 1951, B.A., international relations, Phi Beta Kappa; Yale Law School, LL.B., 1956 (law review)

Military Service: U.S. Air Force, 1951–53, attaining rank of first lieutenant

Career: Member, served as assistant counsel to the Warren Commission, 1964; Pennsylvania assistant attorney general, 1964–65; law firm of Dechert, Price and Rhoads before and after two terms as district attorney of Philadelphia, 1965–73

Civic Activities and Awards: Served on Pennsylvania's State Planning Board, the White House Conference on Youth, the National Commission on Criminal Justice, and the Peace Corps National Advisory Council

Elected to Congress: Elected to the U.S. Senate in

Sen. Arlen Specter *(Government Printing Office)*   **Sen. Ted Stevens** *(Government Printing Office)*

November 1980; reelected to each succeeding term

TED STEVENS, Senator, Alaska

Born: Indianapolis, IN, November 18, 1923

Resides: Girdwood, AK

Education: B.A., University of California at Los Angeles, 1947; LL.B., Harvard Law School, 1950

Military Service: First lieutenant (pilot), 1943–46; 14th Air Force in China, 1944–45

Career: Practiced law in Washington, DC, and Fairbanks, AK, 1950–53; U.S. attorney, Fairbanks, 1953–56; legislative counsel, U.S. Department of the Interior, 1956–58; assistant to Secretary of the Interior Fred Seaton, 1958–60; appointed solicitor of the Department of the Interior by President Eisenhower, 1960; opened law office, Anchorage, AK, 1961

Civic Activities and Awards: Member, American, Federal, California, Alaska, and District of Columbia Bar Associations; member, Rotary, Amer-

ican Legion, Veterans of Foreign Wars, Igloo no. 4 Pioneers of Alaska

State and Local Office: Alaska House of Representatives, 1964–68

Elected to Congress: Appointed to the U.S. Senate in December 1968, following the death of Alaska's senator E. L. Bob Bartlett; subsequently elected for a full term in 1972; reelected to each succeeding term

CRAIG THOMAS, Senator, Wyoming

Born: Cody, WY, February 17, 1933

Resides: Casper, WY

Education: Cody High School; B.S., University of Wyoming, 1954; LL.B., LaSalle University, 1968

Military Service: U.S. Marine Corps, captain, 1955–59

Career: Small businessman; vice president, Wyoming Farm Bureau, 1959–66; American Farm Bureau, 1966–75; general manager, Wyoming Rural Electric Association, 1975–89

Sen. Craig Thomas *(Government Printing Office)*

State and Local Office: Member, Wyoming House of Representatives, 1984–89

Elected to Congress: U.S. Representative, 1989–94; elected to the U.S. Senate in November 1994; reelected in 2000

FRED THOMPSON, Senator, Tennessee

Born: Sheffield, AL, August 19, 1942

Resides: Nashville, TN

Education: Lawrence County High School, 1960; B.S., Memphis State University, 1964; J.D., Vanderbilt University, 1967

Career: Admitted to the Tennessee bar, 1967; assistant U.S. attorney, 1969–72; minority counsel, Senate Select Committee on Presidential Campaign Activities (Watergate Committee), 1973–74; special counsel to Governor Lamar Alexander (Tennessee) during the first three months of his administration in 1980; special counsel, Senate Foreign Relations Committee (Haig confirmation), 1980–81; special counsel, Senate Intelli-

gence Committee, 1982; film actor, 18 motion pictures

Civic Activities and Awards: Member, Nashville, Tennessee, and American Bar Associations; member, Appellate Court Nominating Commission for the State of Tennessee, 1985–87; author of the Watergate memoir *At That Point in Time*

Elected to Congress: Elected to the U.S. Senate in 1994; reelected in 2000

STROM THURMOND, Senator, South Carolina

Born: Edgefield, SC, December 5, 1902

Resides: Aiken, SC

Education: 1923, B.S., Clemson University; studied law at night with his father; holds twenty-seven honorary degrees

Military Service: Reserve officer, 1923–59; while serving as judge, volunteered for active duty in World War II the day war was declared against Germany; served with Headquarters First Army (1942–46), American, European, and Pacific the-

Sen. Fred Thompson *(Government Printing Office)*

Sen. Strom Thurmond (*Office of Sen. Thurmond*)

aters; participated in Normandy invasion with 82nd Airborne Division and landed on D Day; awarded 5 battle stars and 18 decorations, medals, and awards, including the Legion of Merit with Oak Leaf Cluster, Bronze Star Medal with V, Purple Heart, Belgian Order of the Crown, and French Croix de Guerre; major general, U.S. Army Reserves

Career: Admitted to South Carolina bar, 1930, and admitted to practice in all federal courts, including the U.S. Supreme Court; attorney and educator; teacher and athletic coach (1923–29); county superintendent of education (1929–33); city attorney and county attorney (1930–38); state senator (1933–38); circuit judge (1938–46); practiced law in Edgefield, SC (1930–38) and in Aiken, SC (1951–55); adjunct professor of political science at Clemson University and distinguished lecturer at the Strom Thurmond Institute, State's Rights candidate for U.S. president, 1948

Civic Activities and Awards: Chair of Southern Governors Conference (1950); member, Presi-

dent's Commission on Organized Crime and Commission on the Bicentennial of the Constitution; past national president of Reserve Officers Association (ROA) of the United States (1954–55); Clemson University Alumni Association Distinguished Service Award (1961), Clemson Medallion (1981) and Clemson University Athletic Hall of Fame (1988); Disabled American Veterans Outstanding and Unselfish Service awards (1964 and 1981); Military Order of World Wars Distinguished Service Award (1964); Order of AHEPA Dedicated Public Service Award (1968); WIS radio-TV (Columbia, SC) South Carolinian of the Year (1968); 33rd degree Mason (1969); first president of ROA to receive Minuteman of the Year Award (1971); Noncommissioned Officers Association, L. Mendel Rivers Award for Legislative Action (1971); Congressional Medal of Honor Society, National Patriots Award (1974); Retired Officers Association Distinguished Service Award (1974); Association of U.S. Army, Distinguished Service Citation (1974); American Legion Distinguished Public Service Award (1975); Medal of the Knesset, Israel (1982); Distinguished Service Medal (1984); Military Order of the Purple Heart Congressional Award (1976); Amvets Silver Helmet Congressional Award (1977); Veterans of Foreign Wars Dwight D. Eisenhower Service Award (1977) and Congressional Award (1985), Touchdown Club of Washington, DC, "Mr. Sam" Award for contributions to sports (1978); South Carolina Trial Lawyers Association Service Award (1980); Navy League of U.S. Meritorious Service Citation (1980); American Judges Association Distinguished Service Citation (1981); South Carolina Hall of Fame (1982); Audie Murphy Patriotism Award (1982); National Guard Association of United States, Harry S. Truman Distinguished Services Award (1982); New York Board of Trade Textile Man of the Year (1984); Napoleon Hill Gold Medal Humanitarian Achievement Award (1985); Order of the Palmetto Award; Presidential Citizens Medal by President Ronald Reagan; Award for Life Service to Veterans (1989); Noncommissioned Officers Association Lifetime Legislative Achievement Award, (1990); Adjutants General Association of the United States, George Washington Freedom Award (1991); U.S. Marshals Service, America's Star Award, (1991); Presidential Medal of Freedom (1992); over 20 honorary degrees; numerous Watchdog of the Treasury awards and Guardian of Small Business awards; Order of Distinguished Diplomatic Service Merit Medal, South Korea (1974); Order of Kim Khanh Award, Republic of Vietnam (1975); Grand Cross in the Order of Orange-Nassau, the Netherlands (1982); numerous other international distinctions; U.S. Army Ranger Hall of Fame Medal (1994); Senior Army Reserve Commanders Association Hall of Fame Medal (1995); Baptist; Shriner; South Carolina and American bar associations; numerous defense, veteran, civic, fraternal, and farm organizations; delegate to six Democratic national conventions (chair of South Carolina delegation and national committeeperson, 1948); switched from Democratic to Republican Party, September 16, 1964; delegate to eight Republican national conventions (chair of South Carolina delegation, 1984)

State and Local Office: Governor of South Carolina, 1947–51

Elected to Congress: Elected to the U.S. Senate on November 2, 1954, as a write-in candidate (first person in U.S. history elected to a major office in this manner); resigned as U.S. senator on April 4, 1956, to place the office in a primary, pursuant to a promise made to the people during the 1954 campaign; renominated and reelected to the U.S. Senate in 1956, resuming duties on November 7, 1956; reelected to each succeeding term

GEORGE V. VOINOVICH, Senator, Ohio

Born: Cleveland, OH, July 15, 1936

Resides: Columbus, OH

Education: B.A., Ohio University, 1958; J.D., College of Law, Ohio State University, 1961; honorary doctorate of law, Ohio University, 1981; honorary doctorate of public administration, Findlay University, 1993

Civic Activities and Awards: President, National League of Cities, 1985; chair, National Governor's Association, 1997–98

State and Local Office: Assistant attorney general, Ohio, 1963–64; Ohio House of Representatives,

Sen. George V. Voinovich (*Government Printing Office*)

1966–71; Cuyahoga County auditor, 1971–76; Cuyahoga County commissioner, 1977–78; lieutenant governor, Ohio, 1978–79; mayor, Cleveland, OH, 1979–89; 65th governor of Ohio, 1990–98

Elected to Congress: Elected to the U.S. Senate in November 1998

JOHN W. WARNER, Senator, Virginia

Born: Washington, DC, February 18, 1927

Resides: Middleburg, VA

Education: Washington and Lee University (engineering), 1949; entered University of Virginia Law School, 1949; received LL.B. from University of Virginia, 1953

Military Service: U.S. Navy, 1945–46, third-class electronics technician; U.S. Marine Corps, served in Korea as first lieutenant, communications officer, 1st Marine Air Wing, September 1950–May 1952

Sen. John W. Warner *(Government Printing Office)*

Career: Former owner and operator of Atoka, a cattle and crops farm, 1961–94; law clerk to E. Barrett Prettyman, late chief judge for the U.S. Court of Appeals for D.C. Circuit, 1953–54; private law practice, 1954–56; assistant U.S. attorney, 1956–60; private law practice, 1960–69; undersecretary, U.S. Navy, February 1969–April 1972; secretary, U.S. Navy, May 1972–April 1974; Department of Defense delegate to Law of the Sea conferences, 1969–72, head of U.S. delegation for Incidents at Sea Conference, treaty signed in Moscow, May 1972; administrator, American Revolution Bicentennial Administration, April 1974–October 1976

Civic Activities and Awards: Trustee, Protestant Episcopal Cathedral of Mount St. Albans, 1967–72; member, board of trustees, Washington and Lee University, 1968–79

Elected to Congress: Elected to the U.S. Senate in November 1978; reelected to each succeeding term

PART V

GOVERNORS

GOVERNORS

GEORGE ALLEN, former governor of Virginia, was born on March 8, 1952, in Whittier, California. He received his B.A. degree from the University of Virginia in 1974, before pursuing a J.D. degree from the university, which he was awarded in 1977. Allen served in the Virginia House of Delegates from 1983 to 1991. He was elected to the U.S. House of Representatives by special election on November 5, 1991, to fill the vacancy caused by the resignation of D. French Slaughter Jr., and served in the House until January 1993. He was elected governor of Virginia that year and served one term (Virginia governors can serve only one four-year term). After his governorship, Allen went to work for the Richmond-based law firm McGuire Woods Battle & Boothe. Allen was elected to the U.S. Senate in November 2000. Elected 1993. Term expired 1998.

LINCOLN ALMOND, governor of Rhode Island, was born June 16, 1936, in Pawtucket, Rhode Island. He was a member of the U.S. Naval Reserve Submarine Service from 1953 to 1961. He received a bachelor's degree from the University of Rhode Island in 1958 and a law degree from Boston University Law School in 1961. He was appointed Lincoln town administrator in 1963, a position he held until 1969. He was U.S. attorney from 1969 to 1978 and from 1981 to 1993. In 1992, he was inducted into the Historic Central Falls Hall of Fame. He was president of the Blackstone Valley Development Foundation, Inc., a private, nonprofit land development organization, until his election as governor in November 1994. One of his first acts was to privatize the Rhode Island Department of Economic Development, establishing the quasi-public Economic Development Corporation, charged with providing state employers the tools needed to remain competitive and with encouraging job growth. Governor Almond also created the Economic Policy Council in response to the need for an unbiased organization that could conduct research, provide analysis, recommend policies, and assist state leaders in setting an economic vision for the state. During Governor Al-

Gov. Lincoln Almond (*Government Printing Office*)

mond's first term in office, the unemployment rate was reduced significantly, the state's budget went from a deficit to a historic surplus, and the state made its greatest investment in public higher education in any four-year period. Governor Almond has also worked to downsize state government, eliminating several cabinet departments and reducing the state workforce. He has enacted sweeping welfare reform and restructured the state's utility law. Elected 1994, 1998. Term expires 2003.

PHILIP E. BATT, former governor of Idaho, was born on March 4, 1927, in Wilder, Idaho. Batt served in the U.S. Army in 1945–46, prior to attending and graduating from the University of Idaho in 1948. He spent most of his early career as an Idaho onion farmer. After serving in the Idaho House of Representatives and State Senate, Batt was elected to the position of lieutenant governor in 1978, a post he held until 1982. Although he ran for governor that year, he lost to John Evans as part of a long Democratic streak in the governor's mansion. After his success as Republican state chair in 1992, in 1994 he ran for governor on a platform of lowering taxes. As governor, he established a property tax cut of $40 million in 1995 and reduced the number of state employees by 300. Elected 1994. Term expired 1999.

DAVID BEASLEY, former governor of South Carolina, was born on February 26, 1957, in Lamar, South Carolina. Educated in South Carolina public schools, Beasley graduated from Lamar High School and was a student-athlete at Clemson University, majoring in microbiology. As a twenty-year-old junior at Clemson, Beasley ran for the South Carolina House of Representatives. Upon election, he transferred to the University of South Carolina (USC), where he received his J.D. degree from the USC School of Law in 1983. As a member of the South Carolina House of Representatives from 1979 to 1992, Beasley rose quickly in the party leadership, becoming both the youngest majority whip and youngest house speaker pro tempore in the United States. During his thirteen years in the legislature, Beasley served as chair of the Education and Public Works Committee, chair of the Joint Legislative Study Committee on Education, and vice-chair of the Joint Legislative Committee on Children. Beasley was elected governor in 1994. During his first legislative session as governor, Beasley was able to pass his agenda in its entirety: tax reduction, comprehensive welfare reform, anticrime measures, and economic development incentives. Beasley's priority during his second legislative session as governor was education, in which he focused on the implementation of a statewide educational technology plan, as well as his campaign theme of "Putting Families First," which challenged state agencies to make every service family-friendly. Beasley has been awarded honorary Doctor of Law degrees from the University of South Carolina, the Citadel, Re-

gent University, and Charleston Southern University. Elected 1994. Term expired 1999.

TERRY EDWARD BRANSTAD, former governor of Iowa, was born November 17, 1946, in Leland, Iowa. Branstad graduated from the University of Iowa with a B.A. degree in 1969 and from Drake University with a J.D. degree in 1974. He also served in the U.S. Army from 1969 to 1971. Branstad was elected to the Iowa House of Representatives in 1972, just before turning twenty-six, and served for three terms. He was also a farmer and senior partner in the law firm of Branstad-Schwarm in Lake Mills, Iowa. Branstad was elected lieutenant governor in 1978; in 1982, he was elected governor. Despite his administration's antitax and antigambling stance, he increased the sales tax by one cent in 1983 and approved a lottery in 1985. Throughout the 1980s and 1990s, Branstad supported active government programs, including Community Economic Betterment Account business subsidies (1985), a groundwater protection act (1987), and the Iowa Communications Network, which connected all schools to fiber-optic cables (1989). Elected 1982, 1986, 1990, 1994. Term expired 1999.

GEORGE W. BUSH, former governor of Texas and son of President George H. W. Bush, was born July 6, 1946, in New Haven, Connecticut, moved to Texas with his parents as a toddler, and grew up in Midland and Houston. He was an F-102 fighter pilot in the Texas Air National Guard from 1968 to 1973. He received a bachelor's degree from Yale University in 1968 and earned a master's degree in business administration from Harvard University in 1975. He began his career in the oil and gas business in Midland in 1975 and worked in the energy industry into the mid- to late-1980s. He moved to Washington to serve as a senior adviser for his father's presidential campaign in 1988. He assembled the group of partners that purchased the Texas Rangers baseball franchise in 1989 and later built the Rangers's new home, the Ballpark in Arlington. He served as managing general partner of the Texas Rangers until he was elected governor on November 8, 1994. In a historic reelection victory, he became the first Texas governor to be elected to consecutive four-year terms, winning 68.6 percent of the vote. In his second term, Governor Bush called himself a "compassionate conservative" and shaped policy based on the principles of limited government, personal responsibility, strong families, and local control. During two Texas legislative sessions, Bush worked in a spirit of bipartisan cooperation with the lieutenant governor, speaker of the house, and members of the Texas legislature to enact historic reforms to improve public schools, put welfare recipients to work, curb frivolous lawsuits, and strengthen criminal justice laws. Elected 1994, 1998. Served until December 21, 2000, when he became president-elect of the United States.

JEB BUSH, governor of Florida, son of former President George H. W. Bush and brother of President George W. Bush, was born February

Gov. Jeb Bush (*Government Printing Office*)

11, 1953, in Midland, Texas. In 1981, he helped start a real estate development company, the Codina Group, now the largest full-service commercial real estate company in southern Florida. He was its president and chief operating officer until December 1994. He served as Florida's secretary of commerce from 1987 to 1988 and was the unsuccessful Republican nominee for governor in 1994. He has volunteered his time to assist the Miami Children's Hospital, the United Negro College Fund of South Florida, the United Way of Dade County, and the Dade County Homeless Trust. He established the Foundation for Florida's Future, a nonprofit organization that seeks to affect public policy at the grassroots level. As chair of the foundation, Bush cofounded the Liberty City Charter School with the Urban League of Greater Miami. This independent public school, one of the state's first, now serves more than 180 underprivileged kindergartners and first, second, third, and fourth graders from the poorest sections of Miami. Bush also successfully led an effort to cut unemployment compensation taxes for Florida businesses while expanding benefits for the unemployed. His foundation trained law enforcement officers to respond better to cases of elder abuse and neglect, and in 1995, he authored a book profiling fourteen of Florida's civic heroes. Elected 1998. Term expires 2003.

ARNE CARLSON, former governor of Minnesota, was born on September 24, 1934, in New York City. He received his bachelor's degree from Williams College in 1957 and engaged in postgraduate studies at the University of Minnesota from 1957 to 1958. Carlson had a strong public service history prior to being elected governor: He served on the Minneapolis City Council from 1965 to 1967; as floor whip in the Minnesota House of Representatives, where he served eight years; and as Minnesota state auditor from 1978 to 1990. Carlson was first elected Minnesota's governor in 1990 and reelected in 1994 by the largest margin in the state's history. The highlights of his second administration included workers' compensation reform; a welfare reform package that emphasized return to the workforce and child care; putting computers in schools; and an education tax credit for tutoring, summer school, and alternative learning. Carlson received awards from the National Audubon Society, the National Women's Political Caucus, and the Minnesota Children's Defense Fund. In 1993, he was named "Republican of the Year" by the National Ripon Society. Elected 1990, 1994. Term expired 1999.

ARGEO PAUL CELLUCCI, former governor of Massachusetts, was born April 24, 1948, in Marlborough, Massachusetts. In 1970, he graduated from the Boston College School of Management, where he served in the Reserve Officers' Training Corps (ROTC). He received his law degree from Boston College Law School in 1973. Cellucci served in the U.S. Army Reserves from 1970 until 1978, when he was honorably discharged with the rank of captain. His private sector experience

Former Gov. Argeo Paul Cellucci *(State Department)*

includes almost thirty years of work at his family's automobile dealership and seventeen years in the private practice of law, eventually as partner in a Hudson law firm. His career in government began in 1970, when he was elected to the Hudson Charter Commission. One year later, he won a seat on the Hudson Board of Selectmen, and he served on that panel until 1977. In 1976, he was elected to the first of four terms in the Massachusetts House of Representatives. Cellucci was elected to the Massachusetts State Senate in 1984; during his third senate term, he became the assistant Republican leader. He was elected lieutenant governor of Massachusetts in 1990 and was reelected in 1994 by a historic margin of 71 percent. On July 29, 1997, he was sworn in as governor to complete the remainder of the term of William F. Weld. He was reelected in November 1998. A strong advocate for smaller government and lower taxes, Cellucci offered a major cut in the Massachusetts income tax on his first day in office. He was a leader in education reform, access to healthcare, and the fight against domestic violence. Elected 1998. On February 13, 2001, President George W. Bush nominated Cellucci as U.S. ambassador to Canada. The Senate confirmed his appointment on April 5, 2001, and he vacated the office on April 10, 2001.

LAWTON MAINOR CHILES JR., former governor of Florida, was born on April 3, 1930, in Lakeland, Florida. After graduating from the University of Florida in 1952, Chiles served as a U.S. Army artillery officer during the Korean War. He went on to earn his law degree from the University of Florida in 1955 and began practicing law in Lakeland until he ran for public office three years later. First elected to the Florida House of Representatives in 1958 and then to the Florida Senate in 1966, in 1970 Chiles began a most unusual campaign for the U.S. Senate: He walked over 1,000 miles from Pensacola to Dade County. Known thereafter as "Walkin' Lawton," voters elected him three times to the U.S. Senate, where he spent the next eighteen years, from 1971 to 1989. After his retirement from the Senate, Chiles reentered state politics and won the governorship in 1990. During his first term in office, Chiles proposed major healthcare and tax reforms, continuing those policies into his second term. His second term emphasized programs and legislation for Florida children and saw the completion of efforts to sue tobacco companies to pay for healthcare costs that resulted from smoking. Elected 1990, 1994. Died on December 12, 1998, three weeks before the end of his second term of office. Term expired 1999.

DONALD T. DiFRANCESCO, acting governor of New Jersey, was born on November 20, 1944, in Scotch Plains, New Jersey. DiFrancesco is a graduate of Penn State University and Seton Hall School of Law. After graduating, DiFrancesco pursued a law career, eventually becoming a partner in a New Jersey law firm. DiFrancesco began his legislative career in the General Assembly in 1976 and was first elected to the New Jersey Senate in 1979. A lifelong New Jersey resident, he represents the 22d District, which includes parts of Middlesex, Morris, Somerset, and Union Counties. DiFrancesco became acting governor of New Jersey on January 31, 2001, when Governor Christine Todd Whitman resigned to become administrator of the U.S. Environmental Protection Agency. DiFrancesco retains his duties as senate president, a post to which his senate colleagues have elected him for an unprecedented five two-year terms. Acting Governor DiFrancesco has laid out an agenda that includes providing property tax relief, helping needy children, improving public schools and workplace basic skills, reforming healthcare, protecting drinking water, promoting "smart" growth, and eliminating racial profiling. Term expires 2002.

JAMES (JIM) EDGAR, former governor of Illinois, was born on July 22, 1946, in Vinita, Oklahoma. After graduating from Eastern Illinois University in 1968, Edgar entered politics as an aide to leaders in Illinois's General Assembly. From there, he went on to serve two terms as state representative, from 1976 to 1979; became director of legislative affairs for then-governor James R. Thompson; and in 1981 was appointed secretary of state, an office he held until he took over the reins of state government in 1990. Edgar's administration is remembered for bringing the state through a severe fiscal crisis in the early 1990s without a tax increase, the reform of Chicago's schools, government payroll caps, and increased funding for the state's poorer school districts. His "Earnfare" program encouraged welfare mothers to work and required mothers aged eighteen and under to stay in high school to be eligible for welfare payments. By early 1997, his budget was in surplus, and the state's unemployment rate was well below the national average. Since leaving office in 1999, Edgar has served as a distinguished fellow at the University of Illinois Institute of Government and Public Affairs. Elected 1990, 1994. Term expired 1999.

JOHN ENGLER, governor of Michigan, was born October 12, 1948, in Mt. Pleasant, Michigan, and grew up in Beal City, a small farming community. He earned a bachelor's degree in agricultural economics from Michigan State University in 1971 and a law degree from Thomas M. Cooley Law School in 1981. Prior to his first term as governor, he served for twenty years in the state legislature, including seven years as senate majority leader. Improving education has been the top priority of his administration, and a new focus on high standards, more accountability, and strengthened local control has helped student test scores climb to record highs. More than 173 charter schools are in operation, and funding for elementary and secondary schools has increased more than 50 percent. Governor Engler led the fight to enact Proposal A, a landmark 1994 ballot initiative that cut school property taxes and created a portable foundation grant for each student that dramatically reduced the disparity in funding among school districts. His welfare strategy to require work and remove the barriers to employment has helped more than 250,000 families leave welfare rolls for private payrolls and independence. During the 1990s, tax cuts saved families and businesses more than $15 billion and helped create more than 825,000 jobs. Engler has transformed a $1.8 billion budget deficit into a $1.2 billion surplus by cutting spending, reducing bureaucracy, reorganizing state government, and setting new priorities. Excluding public safety personnel, state government is 23 percent smaller. Engler is past chair of the National Education Goals Panel, the Council of Great Lakes Governors, and the Republican Governors' Association. He is a member of the National Governors' Association Executive Committee. Elected 1990, 1994, 1998. Term expires 2003.

KIRK FORDICE, former governor of Mississippi, was born February 10, 1934, in Memphis, Tennessee. He earned a bachelor's degree in civil engineering in 1956 and a master's degree in industrial management in 1957 from Purdue University. Following graduate school, he served two years' active duty as an engineer officer in the First Division of the U.S. Army and became airborne-qualified. He served eighteen more years in the Army Reserves, from which he retired in 1977 with the rank of colonel. Before his election as governor, he was a professional engineer and CEO of Fordice Construction Com-

Former Gov. Kirk Fordice *(Hawkins Photography)*

pany. He is a past president of the Associated General Contractors of America. During his tenure as governor, he returned Mississippi to fiscal integrity and maximized its economic development potential; emphasized accountability in education; cut taxes; accomplished civil justice (tort) reform; secured more than 171,000 new jobs for Mississippians; built additional prison space; ensured truth-in-sentencing; cut excessive inmate "perks"; and reduced the welfare caseload by 60 percent. Fordice is past chair of the Southern Governors' Association, the Southern Growth Policies Board, the Tennessee-Tombigbee Waterway Development Authority, the Southern States Energy Board, and the Southern Technology Council. Fordice is honorary chair of the Initiative and Referendum Institute and Mississippi Citizens for Legislative Term Limits. He is a member of the National Board of Advisors of the Washington Legal Foundation. In 1991, he became the first Republican to be elected governor of Mississippi in 118 years; his reelection in 1995 made him the only Mississippi governor elected to serve two consecutive four-year terms in this century. Elected 1991, 1995. Term expired 2000.

M. J. "MIKE" FOSTER, governor of Louisiana, was born July 11, 1930, in Shreveport, Louisiana. He graduated from Louisiana State University with a bachelor of science degree in chemistry in 1952. He served in the U.S. Air Force in Korea from 1952 to 1955 and then served as a captain in the U.S. Air Force Reserve. Beginning in 1987, he was elected to two terms in the state senate, where he chaired the Commerce Committee and was a member of the Transportation, Highways and Public Works, and Judiciary Committees. He has served as president of the St. Mary's Parish Farm Bureau, chair of the Sugar Growers' Committee of the Louisiana Farm Bureau, and vice president of the Franklin Jaycees. He was president of Sterling Sugars, Inc., managing partner of Maryland Corporation, and president of Bayou Sale Contractors, Inc., until his inauguration as governor in January 1996. Elected November 1995, 1999. Term expires 2004.

JIM GERINGER, governor of Wyoming, was born April 24, 1944, in Wheatland, Wyoming,

Gov. Mike Foster *(Government Printing Office)*

Gov. Jim Geringer *(Government Printing Office)*

and raised on the family farm. He received a bachelor's degree in mechanical engineering from Kansas State University in 1967 and was an active member of the U.S. Air Force from 1967 to 1977, working on a variety of aerospace programs for both the Air Force and NASA, including launches of reconnaissance satellites, the NASA Viking Mars lander, an interim upper-stage booster for the space shuttle, and the beginning of the global positioning satellite system. During this time, he also served as chief of computer programming at a ground receiving station for early warning satellites. In 1979, he went into farming and cattle feeding full time in rural Wyoming. He was elected to the Wyoming House of Representatives in 1982 and had served for six years when he was elected to the Wyoming State Senate. During this period, the Geringers continued to operate their farm, and he participated in the Air Force Reserve. He was first elected governor in 1994. Geringer has focused on local com-

munities as central to each government service or action, with the state providing resources and support for locally driven programs. Education has been a continuing priority, and he has pushed for higher standards, proper assessment of achievement, and effective use of technology for basic and distance learning. Geringer has advocated economic growth through the newly created Wyoming Business Council, with the underpinning of the state's economy as a combination of traditional business and diversification through new business. He is immediate past chair of the Interstate Oil and Gas Compact Commission and has served as chair of the Great Plains Partnership. He chairs the Western Governors' Association and is chair-elect of the Education Commission of the States. Elected 1994, 1998. Term expires 2003.

JAMES S. GILMORE III, governor of Virginia, was born October 6, 1949, in Richmond, Virginia.

Gov. James S. Gilmore *(Government Printing Office)*

Standards of Learning. The cut in the car tax will result in $435 million in tax relief over two years. By 2002, more than 90 percent of Virginians will not pay the car tax, and $1.5 billion per year will be returned to the taxpayers. Gilmore currently is chair-elect of the Southern States Energy Board. Elected 1997. Term expires 2002.

BILL GRAVES, governor of Kansas, was born January 9, 1953, in Salina, Kansas. He grew up learning every aspect of the family trucking company, from working on the loading docks to working in management. He received a bachelor's degree from Kansas Wesleyan College in 1975, and he studied business administration at the University of Kansas from 1976 to 1979. He was appointed assistant secretary of state of Kansas in 1985, elected secretary of state in 1986, and reelected in 1990. In 1991, the International Association of Corporation Administrators recognized the office of secretary of state, under his

He received an undergraduate degree from the University of Virginia in 1971. After graduating, he volunteered for the U.S. Army and was assigned to U.S. Army counterintelligence in West Germany. During his military service, he earned the Joint Service Commendation medal for service to the North Atlantic Treaty Organization (NATO). He returned to Virginia and entered the University of Virginia law school, graduating in 1977. After working for a decade in community service and as an attorney and small businessman, he was elected the commonwealth's attorney for Henrico County in 1987 and was reelected in 1991. In 1993, he was elected Virginia's attorney general, establishing a record of accomplishments in education, public safety, and the environment. Governor Gilmore has worked to cut taxes and provide children with quality education. One year into his term, he helped pass the largest tax cut in Virginia history and worked to implement Virginia's nationally acclaimed

Gov. Bill Graves *(Government Printing Office)*

leadership, for its outstanding service to the businesses it served. Since his election as governor in 1994, Graves has focused on a commonsense approach to state government issues. He is working hard to reduce taxes and government spending. The state government budget approved by the Kansas legislature in 1996 was the first in a generation to spend less than in the prior year. Since taking office, Graves has pushed through tax relief for Kansas residents totaling more than $3.7 billion. Involved in civic and community activities, Graves has served on the executive committee of the Jayhawk Area Council of the Boy Scouts of America and is a member of the boards of trustees for Kansas Wesleyan University and the Sunflower State Games. He is a member of the Kansas Chamber of Commerce and Industry and the Kansas Cavalry and is an alumnus of the 1985 class of Leadership Kansas. Elected 1994, 1998. Term expires 2003.

KENNY C. GUINN, governor of Nevada, was born August 24, 1936, in Garland, Arkansas, and grew up in Exeter, California. He earned undergraduate and graduate degrees in physical education from Fresno State University in 1957 and 1958, respectively, and a doctorate in education from Utah State University in Logan in 1970. In 1964, Guinn went to work for the Clark County School District as a planning specialist. Within five years, he was named superintendent of schools in Clark County and served with distinction in that position until 1978, when he was named administrative vice president for Nevada Savings and Loan in Las Vegas, which later became PriMerit Bank. At PriMerit, he quickly advanced through management ranks and in 1987 was appointed chair of the board of directors. Soon thereafter, Guinn was recruited to the energy business as president of Southwest Gas Corporation, eventually becoming chair of the board of directors of that utility in 1993. In 1994, Guinn was recruited by the University of Nevada Board of Regents to serve as interim president of the University of Nevada at Las Vegas (UNLV). During that year, he restored credibility to the university's basketball program and instituted administrative and policy initiatives that enabled the school to expand successfully. Guinn has

Gov. Kenny Guinn (*Government Printing Office*)

served on the Clark County Community College Advisory Committee, the UNLV Foundation Board of Trustees, the White House Conference on Children and Youth, the Las Vegas Citizens' Advisory Committee on Downtown Development, the Governor's Commission on Government Reorganization (which he chaired in 1991–92), the Metropolitan Police Fiscal Affairs Committee, the Nevada Educational Development Council, and the Advisory Group for Civil Justice Reform. Elected 1998. Term expires 2003.

JOHN HOEVEN, governor of North Dakota, was born on March 13, 1957, in Bismarck, North Dakota. He earned a bachelor's degree from Dartmouth College in 1979 and a master's degree in business administration from the J. L. Kellogg Graduate School of Management at Northwestern University in 1981. He served as executive vice president for First Western Bank in Minot from 1986 to 1993. From 1993 to 2000, he was president and CEO of Bank of North Dakota, overseeing the bank's growth from $900 million in assets to $1.6 billion. He received statewide and regional honors from the U.S. Small Business Administration for his economic development leadership, served as an economic adviser for North Dakota's universities, and served as a trustee at Bismarck State College and as a regent at Minot State University. In addition, Hoeven was a member of the board of directors for First Western Bank and Trust, North Dakota Bankers Broadcasting, North Dakota Economic Developers Association, Bismarck YMCA, and the Harold Schafer Leadership Center. For two years, he served as chair of the Minot Area Development Corporation. Elected 2000. Term expires 2005.

MIKE HUCKABEE, governor of Arkansas, was born August 24, 1955, in Hope, Arkansas. In 1972, he was elected Arkansas Boys State gov-

Gov. Mike Huckabee (*Office of Gov. Huckabee*)

ernor. In 1975, he graduated magna cum laude from Ouachita Baptist University after two and a half years of study. He pastored churches in Arkadelphia, Pine Bluff, and Texarkana, Arkansas, and served two terms as president of the Arkansas Baptist State Convention, from 1989 to 1991. In 1993, he was elected lieutenant governor, and he was reelected in 1994 to a four-year term. On July 15, 1996, he was sworn in as governor to complete the remainder of the term of Jim Guy Tucker. In his legislative session, Governor Huckabee signed legislation creating ARKids First, a program that provides health insurance to children of working parents who make too much money to qualify for Medicaid but not enough to afford private coverage. He signed the first major, broad-based tax cut in state history and simplified the procedure for renewing car tags. Under his leadership, Arkansas's welfare rolls were reduced by 41.5 percent in sixteen months. He has written two books: *Character Is the Issue*, which chronicles his political career, and *Kids Who Kill*, which addresses juvenile violence. He was named the 1997 American Sportsfishing Association Man of the Year. Governor Huckabee was the first vice-chair of the Southern Governors' Association and became chair in 1999–2000; he was vice-chair of the National Governors' Association Committee on Human Resources. Huckabee became governor on July 15, 1996, when the previous governor resigned. Elected 1998. Term expires 2003.

JANE DEE HULL, governor of Arizona, was born August 8, 1935, in Kansas City, Missouri. She received a bachelor's degree in elementary education from the University of Kansas at Lawrence in 1957 and did postgraduate work in political science and economics at Arizona State University from 1974 to 1978. She is a graduate of Josephson Ethics Institute and has served on the boards of numerous community and service organizations. She began her involvement in politics as a precinct committeeperson and deputy registrar in 1965 and subsequently worked on several campaigns. In 1978, she was elected to the Arizona House of Representatives. In 1989, she was chosen by her fellow representatives to

Gov. Jane Dee Hull (*Office of Gov. Hull*)

serve as speaker of the house, the first woman to hold that position in Arizona. She served as speaker from 1989 to 1992. In 1993, she ran a successful campaign for secretary of state, becoming the second woman to hold that office and the first Republican since 1931. On September 5, 1997, she was sworn in as governor to complete the remainder of the term of Fife Symington, and in November 1998, she was overwhelmingly elected to her first full term. As governor, she has made education, children, the economy, and preserving the state's natural beauty her top priorities. Her Students FIRST school facilities funding program received broad bipartisan support. Governor Hull's KidsCare program provides health insurance to the working poor, and her Growing Smarter plan offers practical steps to control area growth. She helped pass tax cuts for a record nine consecutive years, and with the property tax cuts resulting from the Students FIRST legisla-

tion, she has given state taxpayers the largest tax cut in Arizona history. Elected 1998. Term expires 2003.

FORREST HOOD "FOB" JAMES, former governor of Alabama, was born on September 15, 1934, in Lanett, Alabama. He earned a B.S. degree in civil engineering at Auburn Polytechnic Institute (now Auburn University), where he was an All-American halfback on the Auburn football team. In 1956, James played professional football with the Montreal Alouettes before entering the U.S. Army, serving two years as a lieutenant in the U.S. Corps of Engineers. In 1962, James founded Diversified Products, Inc., an athletic equipment company. From 1972 to 1974, he was president of the Alabama Citizens for Transportation, a statewide committee that developed a twenty-year highway program subsequently adopted by the Alabama Legislature. In 1978, James was elected governor of Alabama as a Democrat and served a four-year term, from 1979 to 1983. During his administration, James was reasonably successful in attaining his education reform package, improving the state's mental health system, remedying prison overcrowding, and reestablishing the once financially challenged Medicaid system. Additionally, James consolidated various state agencies to reduce state spending and improved the state's highways as a result of earmarking a substantial reparation budget from the state's oil windfall funds. James switched to the Republican Party in April 1994 and was reelected governor in November 1994—making him the only Alabamian who was first elected governor as a Democrat and then reelected as a Republican. Elected 1994. Term expired 1999.

WILLIAM J. JANKLOW, governor of South Dakota, was born September 13, 1939, in Chicago, Illinois. After serving in the U.S. Marine Corps from 1956 to 1959, he received a bachelor's degree from the University of South Dakota in 1964 and a law degree from the University of South Dakota Law School in 1966. He served as chief legal officer for the South Dakota Legal Services System on the Rosebud Reservation from 1966 to

1973, when he left to begin a private law practice. He was state attorney general from 1975 to 1979 and served two terms as governor, from 1979 to 1987. He then returned to private practice until his reelection as governor in November 1994. In 1995, Janklow won legislative approval for his 20 percent statewide reduction in property taxes for agricultural land and owner-occupied homes. Under his policies, prison crews build affordable housing for the elderly and equip schools with fiber-optic lines for technology and advanced telecommunications. His emphasis on doing more for children includes an expanded immunization program, more adoptions of children who would otherwise be placed in long-term foster care, and more technology in education. Governor Janklow was reelected in November 1998, becoming the first South Dakota governor to be elected four times. Elected 1978, 1982, 1994, 1998. Term expires 2003.

MIKE JOHANNS, governor of Nebraska, was born June 18, 1950, in Osage, Iowa. He received a bachelor's degree from St. Mary's College in 1971 and a doctor of jurisprudence degree from Creighton University in 1974. After graduating, he clerked for a year before joining the law firm of Cronin and Hannon for two years. He then moved to Lincoln, Nebraska, and became a partner at Nelson, Johanns, Morris, Holdeman, and Titus. In 1982, he was elected to the Lancaster County Board of Commissioners. While on the county board, he served on the City/County Common and the City/County Joint Budget Committees. In 1989, he was elected to the Lincoln City Council as an at-large member. He was elected mayor of Lincoln, Nebraska, in 1991, and reelected in 1995 with no opposition. In March 1992, he launched the Lincoln Community Development Partnership, a coalition of thirteen local agencies, to facilitate low-income housing projects. As mayor, he headed the expansion of a summer youth employment program targeted to Lincoln's at-risk and minority youth. For this expansion, he received a 1993 Job Training Partnership Act Presidential Award in the outstanding civic leader category. He served on the executive committee of the U.S. Conference of Mayors and was named president of the League

Gov. Mike Johanns (*Office of Gov. Johanns*)

of Nebraska Municipalities in 1996. In his first year as governor, Johanns was selected to lead the Western governors' efforts to ensure Congress is addressing the needs of the region's agricultural interests when it takes up legislation to reauthorize the Farm Bill before it expires in 2002. Johanns has also served as vice-chair of the Governors' Ethanol Coalition and become chair in 2001. The goals of the coalition are to increase ethanol's use, decrease the nation's dependence on imported energy resources, improve the environment, and stimulate the national economy. Elected 1998. Term expires 2003.

GARY E. JOHNSON, governor of New Mexico, was born January 1, 1953, in Minot, North Dakota. He received a bachelor's degree in political science from the University of New Mexico in 1975. In 1974, he began seeking construction and remodeling jobs; in 1976, that led him to found a construction company, which has been placed

Gov. Gary E. Johnson *(Government Printing Office)*

"For the Children's Sake" plan. He is a nationally ranked triathlete and the first governor to compete in Hawaii's Ironman Triathlon. Elected 1994, 1998. Term expires 2003.

FRANK KEATING, governor of Oklahoma, was born February 10, 1944, in St. Louis, Missouri, and grew up in Tulsa, Oklahoma. He received a bachelor's degree in history from Georgetown University in 1966 and a law degree from the University of Oklahoma College of Law in 1969. He worked for the Federal Bureau of Investigation before being elected to the Oklahoma legislature, where he served in the house and senate. In 1981, he was named U.S. attorney for the northern district of Oklahoma. He later served in the Reagan and Bush administrations as assistant secretary of the treasury, associate attorney general and general counsel, and acting deputy secretary at the U.S. Department of Housing and Urban Development. In 1994, Governor Keating

in a blind trust while he is in office. He served on the board of directors of the Greater Albuquerque Chamber of Commerce and on the board of advisors at the University of New Mexico's Center for Entrepreneurship and Economic Development at the Anderson School of Management. In his first term, Governor Johnson cut taxes and reduced the number of state employees by 6 percent. He signed a $1.2 billion highway improvement package to upgrade 500 miles of state roads and convert them to four lanes. Governor Johnson has also overseen the successful implementation of Salud!, his managed care program for Medicaid recipients. He has held growth of state government to around 4 percent. Under the governor's leadership, two new privatized prisons have been built. Johnson's top priority is to improve education. In addition to signing legislation to invest more than $300 million in additional funds in education programs, he has initiated education reform through his

Gov. Frank Keating *(Office of Gov. Keating)*

was elected to his first term. His reelection in 1998 makes him the state's first Republican governor to serve consecutive terms. Keating and his wife were named recipients of the William Booth Award by the Salvation Army for their leadership during the 1995 federal building bombing crisis in Oklahoma City. Keating succeeded in setting a reform and growth agenda for Oklahoma during his first term with the creation of 128,000 new jobs. He also has been a major advocate of education reform, environmental protection, road building, and tougher law enforcement. Keating serves on the National Governors' Association Executive Committee. Elected 1994, 1998. Term expires 2003.

DIRK KEMPTHORNE, governor of Idaho, was born October 29, 1951, in San Diego, California. He attended the University of Idaho, earning a bachelor's degree in political science in 1975. Kempthorne was elected mayor of Boise, Idaho,

Gov. Dirk Kempthorne (*Office of Gov. Kempthorne*)

in 1986 and served for seven years. He was elected to the U.S. Senate in November 1992. His first bill, legislation to end unfunded federal mandates on state and local governments, became Senate Bill 1 in the 104th Congress. It became law on March 22, 1995, at a Rose Garden signing ceremony. Kempthorne authored the new Safe Drinking Water Act in 1996, which provided clean, safe, and affordable drinking water without federal restrictions. He was a member of the Environment and Public Works Committee that recently produced a highway bill dramatically increasing the amount of federal funds coming to the states for road, bridge, and infrastructure repair. He chaired the Drinking Water, Fisheries, and Wildlife Subcommittee and served on the Armed Services Committee, chairing the Military Personnel Subcommittee, and on the Small Business Committee. The Idaho Jaycees selected him as Outstanding Young Idahoan in 1988, and he has earned the Distinguished Service Medal, the top civilian honor from the Idaho National Guard. Governor Kempthorne serves on the National Governors' Association Executive Committee. Elected 1998. Term expires 2003.

MICHAEL O. LEAVITT, governor of Utah, was born February 11, 1951, and raised in Cedar City, Utah. He earned a bachelor's degree in business and economics from Southern Utah University in 1976. He is past president and chief executive officer of a large regional insurance firm and served as an outside director of several major corporations. He has been a member of the Utah State Board of Regents, which oversees Utah's nine colleges and universities. During his tenure as governor, Leavitt enhanced education, reformed welfare, expanded healthcare, protected open space, renovated highways, cut taxes, and led the state in an era of unprecedented prosperity. He negotiated the largest land exchange since the United States acquired Alaska, to dramatically expand funding for the schoolchildren of Utah. He created a new distance-learning partnership by cofounding Western Governors' University. During his term, Utah has received national and international recognition, including being named the site for the 2002 Winter Olympics. Utah also has been named the best-managed and most livable state in America by *Financial World* magazine. Governor Leavitt was the driving force behind the creation of the first western presidential primary, held in March 2000. He coauthored Enlibra, a new shared doctrine for environmental management that provides commonsense tools for protecting the environment and its natural resources. He has held regional and national leadership roles, serving as past chair of the Republican Governors' Association and the Western Governors' Association. He received the American Legislative Exchange Council's Thomas Jefferson Award, which recognized him for his long-standing leadership in returning power from the federal government to the states. Leavitt served as vice-chair of the National Governors' Association and became chair in August 1999, a position he held until July 2000. Elected 1992, 1996, 2000. Term expires 2005.

JAMES SCOTT McCALLUM, governor of Wisconsin, was born on May 2, 1950, in Fond du Lac, Wisconsin. After graduating from Macalester College in St. Paul, Minnesota, in 1972 with a B.A. degree in both economics and political science, McCallum earned a master's degree in international economics from Johns Hopkins University in 1974. He then went to work in Washington, D.C., as an aide to the late representative William Steiger. He later returned to Fond du Lac, where he founded and managed a property development firm and served as a YMCA Program Director. In 1976, at the age of twenty-six, McCallum ran for and was elected to the state senate seat representing his hometown of Fond du Lac. In the state senate, McCallum earned a reputation for strong, aggressive action, pushing for action on a variety of important state issues. McCallum chaired the State Senate Campaign Committee from 1976 to 1980, a period during which state senate seats held by Republicans increased by almost 50 percent. In 1982, McCallum won the Republican U.S. Senate primary with 72 percent of the vote. In 1986, he announced his candidacy for lieutenant governor and ran on a platform of restoring confidence in state government, revitalizing the state's economy, and rebuilding confidence in the state's

ability to confront any issue. After serving for fourteen years as Wisconsin's lieutenant governor, McCallum was sworn in on February 1, 2001, as Wisconsin's forty-third governor, after Governor Tommy G. Thompson resigned to accept an appointment as secretary of health and human services in President Bush's cabinet. McCallum has been an active volunteer coach for youth sports teams, has served on the board of directors for Wisconsin Special Olympics, and has served as state chair of the YMCA Youth in Government. Term expires 2003.

JUDY MARTZ, governor of Montana, was born on July 28, 1943, in Big Timber, Montana. Since 1973, Martz has co-owned and operated Martz Disposal Service, a commercial solid waste firm in Butte. In the early 1990s, she served as president of the Butte Chamber of Commerce and on the board of the St. James Community Hospital from 1992 to 1998. She was field representative for Senator Conrad Burns, a position she held until she was elected lieutenant governor in 1996. As lieutenant governor, she chaired the Drought Advisory Council, overseeing preparations for threatening weather conditions that could affect Montana's agricultural families and economy. As cochair of the Montana-Alberta Boundary Advisory Commission, she led programs to facilitate constructive relations with Canada in the areas of transportation, agriculture, trade, education, and the arts. Martz also served as chair of Montana's Y2K Readiness Council; chair of the Montana Census Council; chair of the Governor's Council on Organ and Tissue Donor Awareness; and Chair of the Governor's Summit on Youth/ Montana's Promise. During the wildfire season of 2000, she was a creator of the "I Care a Ton Program" to help agricultural producers in need of donated hay for their livestock. Elected 2000. Term expires 2005.

BILL OWENS, governor of Colorado, was born October 22, 1950, in Fort Worth, Texas. He attended Austin State University, graduating in 1973 with a bachelor's degree in political science. He was awarded a two-year fellowship to the Lyndon B. Johnson School of Public Affairs at the University of Texas, where he received a master's

Gov. Bill Owens (*Government Printing Office*)

degree in public administration in 1975. After graduating, Owens joined the accounting firm of Touche Ross and Company in Washington, D.C., as a management consultant. He moved to Colorado in 1977 to work with the management team at the Gates Corporation in Denver. He was named executive director of a statewide trade association in 1982. Owens chaired the Aurora Planning Commission from 1979 to 1981 and served in the state legislature from 1982 to 1994. He was elected state treasurer in 1994. Owens sponsored legislation that created charter schools, toughened prison sentences, modernized state child abuse statutes, and helped reform Colorado's tort system. Elected 1998. Term expires 2003.

GEORGE E. PATAKI, governor of New York, was born June 24, 1945, in Peekskill, New York. He received a bachelor's degree from Yale University in 1967 and a law degree from Columbia

University Law School in 1970. He worked for a New York law firm and served as counsel to two state senate committees. He served two terms as mayor of Peekskill, from 1982 to 1984, and was a member of the New York State Assembly from 1985 to 1992. In 1992, he was elected to the New York State Senate, a position he held until he was inaugurated governor in January 1995. In 1996, the Cato Institute, a libertarian, Washington, D.C.-based organization that studies fiscal policy, rated Governor Pataki the nation's most effective governor at cutting taxes and controlling state spending. Cato awarded him high marks again in 1998. Since Pataki took office, he has reduced state spending for the first time since 1943, and New York has cut taxes more than any other state. Since January 1995, 419,300 private sector jobs have been created. Pataki's welfare-to-workfare policies have reduced welfare rolls by more than 632,000, to the lowest number in more than thirty years. He has restored the death penalty, imposed longer sentences on violent felons, and eliminated parole for all violent offenders. New York leads major states in reducing violent crime, which is at its lowest level since 1970. In 1998, he won approval of a strong charter school law. For his work in reforming child support laws to ensure that deadbeat parents meet their obligations, Pataki was honored in 1997 with the national Golden Heart Award from the Association for Children for Enforcement of Support. Pataki chairs the National Governors' Association Committee on Economic Development and Commerce. Elected 1994, 1998. Term expires 2003.

JAMES RICHARD (RICK) PERRY, governor of Texas, was born on March 4, 1950, in Paint Creek, Texas, where he was raised on his family's farm. Perry is a 1972 graduate of Texas A&M University, where he was a member of the Corps of Cadets. Between 1972 and 1977, Governor Perry served in the U.S. Air Force, flying C-130 tactical airlift aircraft in the United States, Europe, and the Middle East. From 1978 to 1986, Perry served as a member of the State Board of Education. Perry began his public career in 1984, when he was elected to the Texas House of Representatives, serving a rural West Texas district from

1985 to 1991. Texans chose Rick Perry to be the first agribusinessman in forty years to serve as Commissioner of Agriculture, and he was overwhelmingly reelected in 1994 with 63 percent of the vote. He was elected lieutenant governor of Texas in 1998 and in that capacity worked with legislators of both parties to pass a balanced state budget that included record tax cuts, record teacher pay raises, and a historic school funding increase. He was sworn in as the state's forty-seventh governor on December 21, 2000, after Governor George W. Bush resigned the office following his election as president of the United States. As governor, Perry is committed to continued reform in the Texas public school system, advancing higher education; addressing traffic congestion; expanding healthcare, infrastructure, and educational opportunity; and ensuring Texas is at the forefront of the digital revolution. Term expires 2002.

MARC RACICOT, former governor of Montana, was born July 24, 1948, in Thompson Falls, Montana, and spent most of his childhood in Libby. He received a bachelor of arts degree in 1970 from Carroll College in Helena, where he served as student body president and set still-standing basketball records. He earned a law degree in 1973 from the University of Montana School of Law. Following graduation, he joined the U.S. Army and was stationed in West Germany, where he was a prosecutor in the Judge Advocate General's Corps. As a captain, he became the chief prosecutor for the largest U.S. military jurisdiction in Europe. He returned to the United States in 1976, when he took a position as deputy county attorney for Missoula County. In 1977, he became assistant attorney general and Montana's first special prosecutor. He was elected attorney general in 1988 and governor in 1992. In 1996, Governor Racicot was reelected with 80 percent of the vote, the largest margin in state history. Some of the successes under Racicot's leadership include reforming a troubled state workers' compensation system, enacting significant healthcare reform, and initiating sweeping welfare reform, with a 30 percent caseload reduction. After working with the legislature to eliminate a $200 million deficit in 1993, the Racicot administration helped

produce a $22.4 million budget surplus in 1995, which was returned to Montana taxpayers at the governor's insistence. The governor and the 1997 legislature also created tax relief totaling almost $70 million. In December 1997, he became chair of the board of directors of Jobs for America's Graduates, a program that successfully targets at-risk youth. Elected 1992, 1996. Term expired 2001.

TOM RIDGE, former governor of Pennsylvania, was born August 26, 1945, in Munhall, Pennsylvania. Raised in a working-class family, he won a scholarship to Harvard, graduating with a bachelor's degree in government studies in 1967, then attended Dickinson School of Law. His studies were interrupted when he was drafted in 1968. He served as an infantry staff sergeant in Vietnam until 1970, where he won the Bronze Star for Valor, the Vietnamese Cross of Gallantry, and the Combat Infantry Badge. He returned to law school, graduating in 1972, and served as an

Former Gov. Tom Ridge (*Government Printing Office*)

assistant district attorney in Erie County before his election to the U.S. House of Representatives in 1982. The first enlisted Vietnam veteran in the House, he served six consecutive terms before his election as governor in November 1994. In his first term, he cut taxes, reformed education and welfare, and fought crime. Governor Ridge's tax cuts, workers' compensation reform, and fostering of electric industry competition helped Pennsylvania create nearly 250,000 new jobs. Ridge won legislation to create charter schools and to overhaul the state's teacher sabbatical law, while increasing education funding by more than $300 million. He championed other education reforms such as school choice, tougher academic standards for students, and tougher preparatory standards for teachers. He fulfilled a campaign pledge with a special session on crime that produced forty new crime-fighting measures. He imposed tough new work requirements on childless welfare recipients, then invested much of the savings in child care and job readiness training. Ridge's land recycling law has become a national model. On November 3, 1998, he was reelected by the largest victory margin accorded to a Republican governor in state history. Elected 1994, 1998. Ridge resigned in October 2001 to become Director of the Office of Homeland Security.

JOHN G. ROWLAND, governor of Connecticut, was born May 24, 1957, in Waterbury, Connecticut. He received a bachelor's degree from Villanova University in 1979. His public service career includes two terms in the Connecticut state legislature, from 1981 to 1984, and three terms in the U.S. House of Representatives, from 1985 to 1990. While in the U.S. House of Representatives, he served on the Armed Services Committee, the Intelligence Committee, the Veterans' Affairs Committee, the House Select Committee on Narcotics Abuse and Control, and the House Republican Anti-drug Task Force. He received the Watchdog of the Treasury Award for his efforts against unnecessary government spending. In 1992, he served as the Connecticut campaign chair for President George Bush. He was elected governor in 1994, the youngest person ever elected to this office in Connecticut. He was reelected in 1998 by an overwhelming margin. A

Gov. John G. Rowland (*Government Printing Office*)

major focus of Rowland's administration has been to improve the quality of life for Connecticut's citizens and to make the state more attractive to businesses. Income tax rates and taxes on businesses have been cut, and Rowland has called for and signed reforms in the state welfare system. Elected 1994, 1998. Term expires 2003.

GEORGE H. RYAN, governor of Illinois, was born February 24, 1934, in Maquoketa, Iowa. He earned a bachelor's degree in pharmacy from Ferris State College in 1961 and at one time owned a chain of family-run pharmacies. Ryan served as chair of the Kankakee County Board and was elected five times to the Illinois House of Representatives, serving as speaker during the 1981–82 session. Ryan served two terms as lieutenant governor before being elected secretary of state in 1990. During his tenure in public office, he has promoted organ and tissue donor awareness, adult literacy programs, and the application

Gov. George H. Ryan (*Office of Gov. Ryan*)

of new information technologies. He is a strong advocate for the prevention of drunk driving, and he successfully pushed for Illinois to lower the blood alcohol level limit to .08 percent, the lowest in the Midwest. Elected 1998. Term expires 2003.

EDWARD T. SCHAFER, former governor of North Dakota, was born August 8, 1946, and raised in Bismarck, North Dakota. He graduated from the University of North Dakota with a degree in business administration in 1969, then earned a master's degree in business administration from Denver University. He was elected president of the Gold Seal Company in 1978. He was elected governor in 1992 and was reelected to a second term in 1996. With an aggressive agenda for economic development, Schafer fostered a growing economy that generated millions of new dollars for education, health, and safety programs, without income tax increases. Under Schafer's leadership, North Dakota achieved record low unemployment rates and a 10 percent increase in jobs. He lowered unemployment insurance tax rates and reduced workers' compensation rates to make millions of dollars available to employers. Schafer significantly increased funding for education and directed more than $70 million to help care for the state's older adults. He supported significant investments in technology and water development projects to improve the delivery of services to people in remote areas and to provide solid infrastructure for continued economic growth. He reduced the number of state government employees and the cost of the state government as a percentage of personal income. During his tenure as governor, North Dakota's population stabilized after a decade-long trend of outmigration. Governor Schafer is a past chair of the Midwestern Governors' Association, the Interstate Oil and Gas Compact, and the Western Governors' Association. Elected 1992, 1996. Term expired 2001.

DON SUNDQUIST, governor of Tennessee, was born March 5, 1936, in Moline, Illinois. He received a bachelor's degree from Augustana College in 1957 and served in the U.S. Navy until 1959. He has an extensive business background, including management and corporate positions at Josten's, a company that makes college rings. He also started his own printing and advertising firm and was a cofounder of the first Red, Hot, and Blue Barbecue restaurant. His first elected position was in the U.S. House of Representatives, where he served six terms and earned a reputation for being a fiscal conservative. He was elected governor of Tennessee in 1994 and was reelected in 1998 by a record margin. His Families First welfare reform program has reduced the number of employable adults on welfare by 60 percent. During his tenure, Tennessee became the first state in the nation to offer universal health insurance, covering every child through age eighteen who cannot otherwise get coverage. Through the ConnecTen project, Tennessee also became the first state to connect all its public schools and libraries to the Internet. Under Sundquist's leadership, Tennessee has attracted a rec-

Gov. Don Sundquist *(Office of Gov. Sundquist)*

ord $5.4 billion in new capital investment. Elected 1994, 1998. Term expires 2003.

JANE SWIFT, governor of Massachusetts, was born on February 24, 1965, in North Adams, Massachusetts. Swift received her bachelor's degree from Trinity College in 1987. Swift's career as an elected official began in 1991, when she was the youngest woman ever elected to the Massachusetts State Senate. She quickly became the youngest woman in state senate history to hold a leadership position, rising to the rank of assistant minority leader in 1993. Swift served as director of regional airport development at the Massachusetts Port Authority in 1997. That year, Governor William F. Weld appointed her as director of the Office of Consumer Affairs and Business Regulation. Elected lieutenant governor of Massachusetts in 1998, she worked as "co-governor" with Governor Paul Cellucci to stimulate economic growth, impose fiscal discipline,

improve public education, and enhance the quality of life for working families. Swift became the first woman governor of Massachusetts on April 10, 2001, when Governor Cellucci resigned to become the U.S. ambassador to Canada. Swift is also the youngest governor in the country and the first governor to give birth (to twin girls on May 15, 2001) while in office. As governor, Swift signed the "no-new-taxes pledge" and filed legislation to expand the state's Earned Income Tax Credit to assist low-income families. Swift has also championed solutions that protect consumer privacy, provide a guaranteed college education for foster children, and enable state employees to better balance the demands of work and family. Term expires 2003.

JOHN FIFE SYMINGTON III, former governor of Arizona, was born on August 12, 1945, in New York City. He graduated from Harvard University in 1968. Symington served with the U.S. Air Force, receiving the Bronze Star for service in Vietnam and attaining the rank of captain. He was a partner with Lincoln Property Company from 1972 to 1976 and was the founder of the Symington Company, with which he was involved from 1976 to 1989. Elected governor in a runoff election held February 26, 1991, Symington took office on March 6, 1991. Governor Symington served as chair of the Western Governors' Conference from 1992 to 1993. Symington enjoyed some policy successes in his second administration, including a fourth consecutive tax decrease in 1995, reducing income tax liability by a total of 21 percent, or $1.5 billion; tougher juvenile justice laws; and his 700,000-acre Arizona Preserve Initiative in 1996. Symington resigned from office on September 5, 1997, after being convicted in a federal court of fraud on September 3. Elected 1991, 1995.

BOB TAFT, governor of Ohio, was born on January 8, 1942. His father and grandfather were U.S. senators, and his great-grandfather was William Howard Taft, the twenty-seventh president of the United States and a chief justice of the U.S. Supreme Court. Taft earned his bachelor's degree at Yale University in 1963, his master's degree in government from Princeton University in 1967,

Gov. Bob Taft *(Government Printing Office)*

and his doctor of jurisprudence degree from the University of Cincinnati Law School in 1976. From 1963 to 1965, he worked as a teacher for the Peace Corps in Tanzania, East Africa. He served the U.S. State Department in Vietnam from 1967 to 1969. From 1969 to 1973, he was budget officer and assistant director of Illinois's Bureau of the Budget. Taft was elected to the Ohio House of Representatives in 1976. In 1981, he was elected Hamilton County commissioner and served in that post for ten years. In 1991, he was elected secretary of state for Ohio. Elected 1998. Term expires 2003.

TOMMY G. THOMPSON, former governor of Wisconsin, was born November 19, 1941, in Elroy, Wisconsin. He received his bachelor's degree in political science in 1963 and his law degree in 1966 from the University of Wisconsin. He is a former army captain and a former member of the U.S. Army Reserve. Thompson was first elected

to the Wisconsin Assembly in 1966 and was elected assistant minority leader in 1973. In 1981, he was elected Republican floor leader. He is a member of the Wisconsin Bar Association, the Juneau County Bar Association, the Juneau County Republican Party, and St. Patrick's Catholic Church. Thompson is the recipient of the American Legislative Exchange Council's 1991 Thomas Jefferson Award, *City and State* magazine's Most Valuable Public Official Award, the Free Congress Foundation's Government Award, *Governing* magazine's 1997 Public Official of the Year Award, the American Legion's 1998 National Award for Americanism, and the 1998 Horatio Alger Award. Thompson is the current chair of the Council of State Governments and the Amtrak Reform Board. He is also a member of the Export/Import Bank Chairman's Advisory Board, the Inter-American Dialogue, the National Education Goals Panel, and ACHIEVE, a resource center for governors and business leaders on academic standards, assessment, accountability, and technology. He is a past chair of the National Governors' Association, the Education Commission of the States, the Republican Governors' Association, the Council of Great Lakes Governors, the Midwest Governors' Conference, the Intergovernmental Policy Advisory Committee, and ACHIEVE. Thompson resigned as governor on January 31, 2001, to become secretary of health and human services. Elected 1986, 1990, 1994, 1998.

CECIL H. UNDERWOOD, former governor of West Virginia, was born November 5, 1922, in Josephs Mills, West Virginia. He earned his bachelor's degree from Salem College in West Virginia in 1943 and his master's degree from West Virginia University in 1952. He served six terms in the West Virginia House of Delegates, from 1945 to 1956, the last four terms as minority leader. He was elected governor in 1956, at age thirty-four, and was the youngest governor in the state's history. From 1972 to 1975, he was president of Bethany College. He has served as chair of Morgantown Industrial/Research Park, president of the National Association of State Councils on Vocational Education, and president of the West Virginia State Council. He taught at both the high school and college levels and was adjunct professor in political science at Marshall University before he became governor again in January 1997. Governor Underwood is an emeritus member of the board of directors and former chair of Appalachian Regional Health Care. He also served on the board of directors of the American Cancer Society at both the state and national levels and is the former lay leader of Johnson Memorial Methodist Church in Huntington. He was the director of the United Methodist Charities of West Virginia and was elected as a delegate to the general and jurisdictional conferences of the United Methodist Church in 1988, 1992, and 1996. In 1992, Underwood was named West Virginian of the Year by the Public Relations Society of America. Since returning to public office, Underwood has accepted leadership positions in several regional and national organizations, including the Southern Technology Council, Southern Growth Policies Board, Southern States Energy Board, National Education Goals Panel, Southern Regional Education Board, and Jobs for America's Graduates. Elected 1956, 1996. Term expired 2001.

GEORGE VOINOVICH, former governor of Ohio, was born on July 15, 1936, in Cleveland, Ohio. He received his B.A. degree in government from Ohio University in 1958, and his J.D. degree from Ohio State University College of Law in 1961. Voinovich's career in public service dates back to 1963 when he was appointed assistant attorney general for the state of Ohio. He later served as a state representative from 1967 to 1971, Cuyahoga County auditor from 1971 to 1976, Cuyahoga County commissioner from 1977 to 1978, and lieutenant governor of the state of Ohio in 1979. In 1979, he was elected mayor of Cleveland, a post he held for ten years. Voinovich was elected governor in November 1990 and reelected in 1994, garnering 72 percent of the vote—a twentieth-century Ohio record and the largest margin of victory in the United States in 1994 by a candidate for governor. As governor, Voinovich is the only person to have served as chair of the National Governors' Association and president of the National League of Cities. Voi-

novich played a major role in shaping legislative achievements, including welfare reform, the Unfunded Mandate Reform Act, the Safe Drinking Water Act Amendments, and expanded healthcare. Under Voinovich, Ohio's unemployment rate fell to a twenty-five-year low, more than 500,000 new jobs were created, and Ohio was ranked first in the nation by *Site Selection* magazine for new and expanded business facilities. Voinovich held Ohio's budget to its lowest growth rate in thirty years, while dramatically increasing state support for programs that help children, families, and older adults. At the same time, he reduced welfare rolls by more than 362,000 persons—a 55 percent drop during his two terms as governor—by eliminating general assistance and by providing training to move people off welfare. Voinovich was elected to the U.S. Senate in November 1998. Elected 1990, 1994. Term expired 1999.

CHRISTINE T. WHITMAN, former governor of New Jersey, was born September 26, 1946, in New York City and was raised in Oldwick in Hunterdon County, New Jersey. She earned a bachelor's degree in government in 1968 from Wheaton College in Norton, Massachusetts. She is a former director of the Somerset County Board of Freeholders and a former president of the New Jersey Board of Utilities. She was elected governor in 1993, becoming the first woman to hold that office in New Jersey. During her term in office, Whitman enacted thirty-eight tax cuts, including a 30 percent income tax cut. She rolled back or eliminated several business taxes and enacted meaningful tort reform. She enacted legislation reducing auto insurance rates for good drivers by 15 percent. Four of nineteen departments of state government were eliminated or merged. Prison medical services and state-run motor vehicle offices were privatized. Governor Whitman enacted a new method of state funding for public schools, tied to rigorous academic standards. Voters approved Whitman's proposal to provide state funds to reach her goal of permanently preserving 1 million acres of open space and farmland by 2010. She signed several tough anticrime bills, including the so-called Megan's Law and Three Strikes and You're

In. Her crime-fighting initiatives helped New Jersey post its lowest crime rate in twenty-six years. Whitman implemented a far-reaching welfare reform plan that establishes a lifetime limit of five years on welfare benefits and enforces tougher job requirements while increasing funding for child care and job placement. Welfare caseloads were reduced by 50 percent during her term in office. Elected 1993, 1997. Whitman resigned on January 31, 2001, to become administrator of the U.S. Environmental Protection Agency.

PETER BARTON WILSON, former governor of California, was born on August 23, 1933, in Lake Forest, Illinois. He attended Yale University on an ROTC scholarship and graduated in 1956. He served three years as a Marine Corps infantry officer before continuing on to earn a law degree from the University of California School of Law at Berkeley in 1962. Wilson was admitted to the California bar in 1963 and commenced practice in San Diego, California, before beginning nearly three decades of public service: as a member of the California legislature from 1966 to 1971, as mayor of San Diego from 1971 to 1983, and as a two-term U.S. senator who served from 1983 to 1991, when he resigned following his election as governor of California. As governor, amid a tight state budget, Wilson enacted his program of "preventative government" to benefit children. He maintained per-pupil spending in California classrooms, protected public safety by increasing funding for corrections, and saved several key California military bases from closure. He also began a major overhaul of government in an effort to make the state government a partner in creating jobs for California businesses. Elected 1990, 1994. Term expired 1999.

PART VI

STATE PORTRAITS: HISTORY AND POLITICS

STATES

ALABAMA

For almost a century, from the end of the Civil War to the 1950s, Alabama was a solidly one-party Democratic state. Blacks were effectively barred from voting and if there was any electoral competition, it was only within the Democratic Party. The first major break in the Democratic phalanx came in 1928 with the nomination of Al Smith, a Catholic, as presidential candidate. The rumblings continued under Franklin D. Roosevelt, as white supremacists and states' righters held their ground against a growing liberal wing more sympathetic to civil rights. Republicans made their first inroads in the presidential election of 1952 when Dwight Eisenhower won 35 percent of the vote, a level of support unheard of before World War II. This support grew to 39 percent in 1956 and 41 percent in 1960. A major breakthrough came in 1964 when Barry Goldwater won 69.5 percent of the vote, and on his coattails more than ninety Republicans were elected to office, including five to the U.S. Congress. Although 1964 marked a disaster for Republicans nationwide, in Alabama, it marked the dawn of growing Republican influence in the state.

The popularity of Democratic governor George Wallace, who dominated Alabama politics in the 1960s and 1970s, prevented Republicans from making more headway in the state. Nevertheless, Republicans carried Alabama in five of the seven presidential elections held between 1968 and 1992 and also held two of the seven U.S. house seats. In 1980 Alabama Republicans won their first ever U.S. Senate seat with the election of Jeremiah Denton and followed that success by capturing the governor's office with Guy Hunt in 1986. Republicans made significant gains in the 1990s, but both houses of the state legislature remained in the hands of Democrats in 2000, who held roughly two-thirds of the seats.

One reason for Republican renewal in Alabama is the large-scale defection of white Democrats, a phenomenon common in the South in the 1980s and early 1990s. Democratic stalwarts like Senator Richard Shelby and Governor "Fob" James Jr. switched to the Republican Party and inspired many Democrats to follow them. Such defections proved costly to the Democratic hopes of keeping their historic majority in elections to state and national offices.

As the Republican tide continued to mount, Republican organizations became more professional and better funded. Republicans, however, are active primarily in urban areas, and there are large rural areas in Alabama where there is no Republican presence of any kind. This explains the continued strength of the Democratic Party in elections to the state legislature. Republicans find it harder to recruit good candidates for many of the seats and have to depend on defections for this purpose.

The three levels of Republican Party organization are the county, the congressional district, and the state. However, there are several counties and congressional districts without any Republican committee. The state committee, working through its executive committee, is all powerful. It directs, manages, and supervises party business, prescribes rules for conventions and primaries, settles controversies, and builds and promotes Republican interests.

Republican Presidential Victories, 1860–2000
Total: 10 (1868, 1872, 1964, 1972, 1980, 1984, 1988, 1992, 1996, 2000)

Republican Governors of Alabama, 1860–2000
William Hugh Smith, 1868–1870; David P. Lewis, 1872–1874; Harold Guy Hunt, 1987–1993; Forest Hood "Fob" James Jr., 1995–1999.

ADDRESS: Republican Party of Alabama, P. O. Box 361784, Birmingham, AL 35232

Tel.: (205) 978-2500
www.algop.org

BIBLIOGRAPHY

Cosman, Bernard, and Robert J. Huckshorn, eds. *Republican Politics: The 1964 Campaign and Its Aftermath for the Party.* New York: Praeger, 1968.

Havard, William C., ed. *The Changing Politics of the South.* Baton Rouge: Louisiana University Press, 1972.

Alabama Congressional Delegation, Voting Record as Assessed by Key Groups, 1998

	ADA	ACLU	AFS	LCV	CON	NTU	NFIB	COC	ACU	NTLC	CHC
Senators											
R. C. Shelby	5	14	11	0	2	64	89	78	92	85	100
J. Sessions	0	14	0	0	71	74	100	89	100	100	100
Representatives											
S. Callahan	0	7	0	8	8	50	92	100	96	100	100
B. Riley	5	6	11	0	13	49	100	89	100	100	100
T. Everett	5	7	11	0	33	51	100	89	100	97	100
R. Aderholt	10	6	33	0	13	46	93	83	96	97	100
S. Bachus	5	0	11	8	50	59	93	89	84	92	100

ADA: Americans for Democratic Action; ACLU: American Civil Liberties Union; AFS: American Federation of State, County, and Municipal Employees; LCV: League of Conservation Voters; CON: Concord Coalition; NTU: National Taxpayers Union; COC: Chamber of Commerce of the United States; NFIB: National Federation of Independent Business; ACU: American Conservative Union; NTLC: National Tax-Limitation Committee; CHC: Christian Coalition.

ALASKA

Political parties have played a muted role in Alaskan politics where "partisanship" is a word of opprobrium rather than commendation. Alaskan political culture developed late, primarily after statehood in 1959. Even then, the state's small population, large area, and relative isolation tended to make political ideology less divisive than it is in other states. The state electoral laws also militate against party-driven elections. For many years, Alaska had a blanket primary in which voters received a ballot with a list of all candidates for all offices to choose from. This system was declared illegal by the U.S. District Court in 1992, but was reinstated by the Supreme Court in 1996.

Although Republicans appear to have a weaker organization than Democrats, they currently hold more national and state offices. Both U.S. senators are Republican, as is the sole U.S. House member. Republicans also control both houses of the state legislature. In 1994, Democrat Tony Knowles was elected governor. Reelected in 1998, he holds the only major office in the state in Democratic hands.

Although the Republican Party leads in number of voters identifying themselves as members, it has lost its lead in funding because of factional infighting among three groups. The first consists of the old guard, who are mostly moderates, and the other two belong to the Christian Right. One faction of the Christian Right is known as the Prevo Conservatives, and they hold moderate positions on all issues except abortion rights. The other faction is more extreme and militant and eschews any toleration of moderate positions. Both Christian groups have broken with the more liberal old guard on the abortion issue.

Unlike the Democratic Party, the GOP's strength is exclusively in urban Alaska. The party flourishes in the Southcentral region, which includes Anchorage, with over one-half of the state population. However, Republicans tend to ignore the rural areas where most of the Alaskan Indians live. Republican prospects are also clouded by the presence of the Alaska Independence Party, a strong third party, which has attracted many Alaskans, including Walter J. Hickel, who served as Republican governor in the 1960s. He was reelected governor in 1990 on the Alaska Independence Party.

Republican Presidential Victories, 1960–2000
Total: 10 (1960, 1968, 1972, 1976, 1980, 1984, 1988, 1992, 1996, 2000)

Republican Governors of Alaska, 1960–2000
Walter J. Hickel, 1966–1969; Keith Harvey Miller, 1969–1970; Jay Sterner Hammond, 1974–1982.

ADDRESS: Republican Party of Alaska, 1001 West Fireweed Lane, Anchorage, AK 99503

Tel.: (907) 276-4467

www.alaskarepublicans.com

BIBLIOGRAPHY
McBeath, Gerald A., and Thomas A. Morehouse. *Alaska Politics & Government.* Lincoln: University of Nebraska Press, 1994.
Sorauf, Frank. *Party Politics in America.* 5th ed. Boston: Little, Brown, 1984.

Alaska Congressional Delegation, Voting Record as Assessed by Key Groups, 1998*

	ADA	ACLU	AFS	LCV	CON	NTU	NFIB	COC	ACU	NTLC	CHC
Senators											
T. Stevens	20	43	11	0	67	54	89	94	56	71	73
F. Murkowski	5	29	11	0	55	68	100	100	78	82	90
Representative											
D. Young	20	20	44	0	2	48	85	78	84	83	100

*For abbreviations, see p. 220.

ARIZONA

Even before Arizona became a state in 1912, Democrats dominated Arizona politics. They won eleven of the fifteen contests for seats in the territorial legislature and had a comfortable majority in the state legislature, from 1880 to 1912. Their position did not change after the advent of statehood, and the Democratic era lasted well into the 1960s. During these years, the registered Democrats outnumbered registered Republicans by two to one, and during the Great Depression of the 1930s, Republicans reached their nadir with only 12 percent of registered voters. For much of this period Republicans all but disappeared from the state's political scene.

In the 1960s, Republican fortunes took a turn for the better for the first time. As liberals began to dominate the Democratic Party, many conservatives and moderates sought a new home within the Republican Party. Between 1950 and 1970 the number of voters registered as Republicans rose from 25 to 45 percent. Initially, the GOP captured the high-visibility offices such as governor and U.S. Senator, thus sending signals to the Democratic establishment that the days of their unchallenged supremacy were over. In 1966, a court-ordered reapportionment plan increased the Republican representation of Phoenix and other Republican areas and helped Republicans gain control of both houses of the legislature. Since then, the GOP has dominated the state house and senate. Major state and national offices, however, have routinely alternated between the two parties.

The person most responsible for the growth of the Republican Party in Arizona was longtime senator Barry Goldwater, who ran for president in 1964. Goldwater helped to unify the state party, attract national exposure, and streamline party activities. The party was built from the grassroots up, with volunteers registering voters and getting the party faithful out to vote on election day. The GOP in Arizona now provides more services to candidates and holds regular fund-raising events under a full-time executive director. After Goldwater left active politics in 1987, increased factionalism and threats from the right threatened Republican unity. The ascendancy of Evan Mecham, supported by the ultra-conservatives, were bleak years for the party.

Republican lawmakers passed a resolution declaring America to be a Christian nation and scuttled making Martin Luther King's birthday a state holiday. Mecham was later impeached and removed from office for his involvement in a scandal.

The organizational pyramid begins with the 1,846 precinct committees—the total count in 1994. Above the precinct level are the county committees, whose heads are automatically members of the state committee. The state committee meets in the state capital every year in January to elect a chair, a secretary, and a treasurer from among its members. Actual day-to-day party administration is in the hands of the executive committee in which the counties as well as the congressional districts are represented. Fund-raising is institutionalized through membership programs. The GOP appears to have survived the worst of the factionalism of the 1980s and to have adopted more of the big-tent approach, avoiding any approach to issues that might alienate large segments of the electorate. The short-lived Senator McCain insurgency on the national scene during the 2000 Republican presidential primary illustrates the continuing influence of Barry Goldwater. McCain is the logical successor to Goldwater with his strong conservative beliefs on military affairs and his affinity to libertarianism.

Republican Presidential Victories, 1912–2000
Total: 15 (1920, 1924, 1928, 1952, 1956, 1960, 1964, 1968, 1972, 1976, 1980, 1984, 1988, 1992, 2000)

Republican Governors of Arizona, 1912–2000
Thomas Edward Campbell 1917, 1919–1923; John C. Phillips, 1929–1931; John Howard Pyle, 1951–1955; Paul Jones Fannin, 1959–1965; John Richard Williams, 1967–1975; Evan Mecham, 1987–1988; Fife Symington, 1991–1999; Jane Dee Hull, 1999– .

ADDRESS: Arizona Republican Party, 3501 North 24th Street, Phoenix, AZ 85016

Tel.: (602) 957-7770
www.azgop.org

BIBLIOGRAPHY
Berman, David R. *Arizona Politics & Government: The Quest for Autonomy, Democracy, and Development.* Lincoln: University of Nebraska Press, 1998.
Smith, Zachary A., ed. *Politics and Public Policy in Arizona.* 2d ed. Westport, CT: Praeger, 1996.

Arizona Congressional Delegation, Voting Record as Assessed by Key Groups, 1998*

	ADA	ACLU	AFS	LCV	CON	NTU	NFIB	COC	ACU	NTLC	CHC
Senators											
J. McCain	20	14	33	0	93	73	100	76	68	96	73
J. Kyle	0	14	0	0	95	88	88	76	96	100	100
Representatives											
M. Salmon	5	6	0	8	92	82	93	83	96	95	100
B. Stump	0	13	0	0	60	79	100	78	96	100	100
J. Shadegg	0	20	0	0	70	76	76	93	89	100	100
J. Kolbe	15	14	11	23	65	63	100	89	72	82	58
J. D. Hayworth	0	6	0	15	70	72	100	89	100	97	100

*For abbreviations, see p. 220.

ARKANSAS

Arkansas had a strong tradition as a Democratic state from the time of the Reconstruction. The Democratic era lasted for well over 100 years into the 1990s. During this period the voters elected Democrats consistently and exclusively to state and national offices. The state first voted for a Republican president in 1972, after most of the other Southern states. It elected its first Republican senator, Tim Hutchinson, only in 1996. From statehood in 1836 to 1995, with the exception of the Reconstruction period, only four Republicans represented Arkansas in the U.S. House of Representatives and, until Mike Huckabee became governor in 1996, only two Republicans—Winthrop Rockefeller and Frank White—had held that office. As late as 1994, Republicans were a minority of nineteen in the 135-member state legislature and only in the Ozarks did any of them serve in local offices. In the 107th Congress (2001–2002), one U.S. senator (Hutchison) from Arkansas is Republican and one of four U.S. House seats is held by a Republican.

The first cracks in Democratic dominance appeared in the 1960s under the aegis of Governor Winthrop Rockefeller, who spent millions of dollars, primarily on his own elections (1964, 1966, 1968, 1970) but also on building up the party. After his death, however, the party went into further decline, although during the same period, Republicans garnered more votes in presidential elections. Republicans received another boost when Frank White upset Governor Bill Clinton in 1980.

In the early 1990s Republicans began to capitalize on the growing pro-Republican sentiments in the South by adopting a proactive policy, known as Optimal Republican Voting Strength, in which the GOP plays a hands-on role in recruiting candidates, encouraging Democrats to switch parties, and targeting certain localities for extensive campaigning. In this they were helped by the presidency of Bill Clinton, who had served as Arkansas governor from 1979 to 1981 and 1983 to 1992. From the beginning of Clinton's presidency in 1993, the Democratic Party in Arkansas was on the defensive, trying to put out the fires of scandals that Clinton seemed to generate periodically. At the same time, the Republican National Committee (RNC) allocated more funds to Arkansas in hope of discrediting the Democrats in Clinton's home state. The Whitewater investigation in the mid-1990s proved a bonanza for Republicans as it exposed corruption among leading Arkansans Democrats. In 1993 Huckabee was elected lieutenant governor

and he became governor when Jim Guy Tucker, Clinton's successor, was forced to resign after being convicted of fraud and other charges.

Republicans also gained a significant legal victory in 1995 when the Eighth U.S. Circuit Court of Appeals declared unconstitutional the state law that required parties to conduct and pay for their own primary elections. The law was thereupon revised to require the state to pay for primaries, thus ensuring that voters will be able to vote in either party primary in all precincts. Democrats still control the state senate and the house by a wide margin, but Republicans are becoming more assertive and confident. In the 2000 presidential election Al Gore lost Arkansas by a wide margin.

The Arkansas Republican Party maintains its state headquarters in Little Rock. The state committee consists of 350 members and the state executive committee, between forty-five and fifty members. The state convention meets in the fall of even-numbered election years to elect the state party chair and members of the state committee and the executive committee. The executive committee meets up to twelve times a year. The party chair has a guiding influence on the party, even when the governor is a Republican. The chair is the chief spokesperson for the party, and also serves as a lobbyist and watchdog. There are four full-time paid staff members including the executive director and a finance director. Republicans have fewer auxiliary organizations than the Democrats, but the Arkansas Federation of Republican Women has been consistently one of the most active in the state. The state party relies very much on the RNC for advice, guidance, and funding. The state GOP is visited a number of times each year by RNC representatives to coordinate fund-raising efforts and political strategies. The county Republican organizations are fairly autonomous, although county party officials serve on the state committees. Local organizations are very strong in the northwestern part of the state, where Republicans have managed to displace Democrats in county legislative bodies. State Republican officeholders, such as the governor, also maintain their personal organizations with only loose ties to the state parties.

Republican Presidential Victories, 1860–2000
Total: 5 (1868, 1980, 1984, 1988, 2000)

Republican Governors of Arkansas, 1860–2000
Powell Clayton, 1868–1871; Ozra A. Hadley, 1871–1873; Elisha Baxter, 1873–1874; Frank D. White, 1981–1983; Mike Huckabee 1996– .

ADDRESS: Arkansas Republican Party, 1201 West Sixth Street, Little Rock, AR 72201

Tel.: (501) 372-7301

www.arkgop.com

BIBLIOGRAPHY
Blair, Diane D. "Arkansas." In *The 1984 Presidential Election in the South: Patterns of Southern Party Politics*, ed. Robert P. Steed, Laurence W. Moreland, and Tod A. Baker, 14–17. New York: Praeger, 1985.

———. "Arkansas: Ground Zero in the Presidential Race." In *The 1992 Presidential Election in the South: Current Patterns of Southern Party and Electoral Politics*, ed. Robert P. Steed, Laurence W. Moreland, and Tod A. Baker, 112–19. Westport, CT: Praeger, 1994.

———. *Arkansas Politics & Government: Do the People Rule?* Lincoln: University of Nebraska Press, 1988.

Urwin, Cathy Kunzinger. *Agenda for Reform: Winthrop Rockefeller as Governor of Arkansas, 1967–71.* Fayetteville: University of Arkansas Press, 1991.

Arkansas Congressional Delegation, Voting Record as Assessed by Key Groups, 1998*

	ADA	ACLU	AFS	LCV	CON	NTU	NFIB	COC	ACU	NTLC	CHC
Senator											
T. Hutchinson	5	14	0	0	65	70	100	89	100	100	100
Representatives											
A. Hutchinson	5	19	0	23	33	50	93	94	92	89	83
J. W. Dickey	5	13	11	8	26	51	100	94	96	97	100

*For abbreviations, see p. 220.

CALIFORNIA

After California achieved statehood in 1850, Republicans and Democrats contested most elections, with such offices as the governorship frequently changing hands. By the end of the century, however, Republicans clearly became the dominant party. In one forty-year period, from 1899 to 1938, every governor was a Republican. The party, however, was often divided between its conservative and more moderate, progressive wings. Early on, the reformers and the progressives gained the upper hand, and they consolidated their gains by changing the electoral laws; for example, they introduced a uniform ballot in 1872, and followed with the introduction of an Australian ballot (printed by the government rather than by the parties). A 1906 political scandal involving San Francisco political boss Abraham Reuf and the Southern Pacific Railroad precipitated the founding of the Lincoln-Roosevelt League, led by progressive Republican Hiram Johnson, who was elected governor in 1910. Johnson introduced the system of candidate cross-filing, non-partisan judicial and local elections, and the procedure of citizen initiative and recall. These reforms strengthened the power of Republican moderates by preempting extremists. Johnson bolted the party in 1912 to run for vice president on the Progressive Party ticket headed by Teddy Roosevelt. After losing, he returned to the Republican Party and served in the U.S. Senate from 1917 to 1945. The Republican moderates remained in power through the Great Depression and into the postwar era.

The greatest Republican moderate was Earl Warren. After winning the gubernatorial election in 1942, he won reelection with both Republican and Democratic support in 1946, the only time in California history when a candidate won 92 percent of the vote. Warren ran unsuccessfully for vice president in 1948 but was later appointed chief justice of the United States. After World War II, conservative Republicans in California mounted strong challenges to the moderate wing of the party. Senator William Knowland, elected in 1945, and Richard Nixon, elected representative in 1946, senator in 1950, and vice president in 1952, helped move the party to the right. In 1958, Republicans lost both the governor's mansion and the state legislature. The election of Ronald Reagan as governor in 1966 continued the conservative direction of the California Republican Party, a direction reinforced by governors George Deukmejian in the 1980s and Pete Wilson in the 1990s.

The November 1998 elections were devastating to California's Republican Party. After sixteen years of Republican governors, voters elected Democrat Gray Davis to the governorship with 58 percent of the vote. Republicans fared poorly in most other statewide contests as well. The only statewide offices held by Republicans after the election were those of secretary of state (Bill Jones) and insurance commissioner (Chuck Quackenbush). A major financial scandal at the Insurance Commission in 2000 raised the specter of impeachment for Quackenbush, who subsequently resigned.

Neither did Republicans fare well in the 1998 legislative races. Republicans could not add to the fifteen seats (out of forty) they held in the state senate. In the lower house (the assembly), the party dropped from thirty-seven to thirty-two seats (out of eighty). As a result of the Republicans' poor showing at that election, the Republican assembly leadership underwent a prolonged shakeup, ultimately resulting in Scott Baugh's assuming the post of minority leader. In the senate, the more moderate Jim Brulte retained his post. The party lost seats in the 2000 election, and as of 2001 there are fourteen Republicans in the state senate and thirty in the assembly. California Republicans also lost ground in the U.S. House of Representatives in 2000, winning only nineteen of fifty-two seats and failing to gain a U.S. Senate seat.

Many analysts have cited Governor Pete Wilson's endorsement of several controversial initiatives as a critical reason for the Republicans' political losses in 1998. Those initiatives include one that denied certain welfare benefits to illegal immigrants and one that virtually eliminated bilingual education. Latino voters were said to be offended by the supposed attack on their ethnic group. However, many Latinos in fact supported those initiatives, particularly the ban on bilingual education. Furthermore, despite striking increases in their political mobilization, Latinos still constituted a relatively small portion of the total number of voters in that election. More likely, the Republicans' demise was prompted by the combination of a weak economy during much of Deukmejian's and Wilson's terms and a perceived rightward drift of the party—particularly with regard to social issues such as abortion. In addition, California's new "blanket primary" system, which allows voters to choose candidates regardless of party affiliation, may also have affected the electoral outcomes.

The Republicans were poised for future hard times after the reapportionment based on the 2000 census. Lacking both a majority in the legislature and a base in the governor's office, the Republicans could neither control the redistricting bill nor veto it. It was almost inevitable that the Republicans would challenge the Democrat-created redistricting in court. If that challenge was not successful, the party could expect to spend the first decade of the twenty-first century as a minority legislative party.

Like its national counterpart, the California Republican Party emphasizes the importance of personal liberty and limited government. Upon these bedrock beliefs is built a generally cohesive party platform addressing a variety of more tangible issues.

The party platform asserts that one of the primary functions of government is to maintain law and order "so that individuals can be free to pursue the fruits of life and liberty." In general, the party links the promotion of law and order to putting more police on the street, limiting opportunities to appeal court decisions, and imposing harsh sentences. The party embraces "three-strikes" laws (which impose a mandatory life sentence on persons convicted of three felonies) as an especially effective weapon against crime. The party also supports the death penalty as both a deterrent to crime and a just punishment for certain crimes.

The party tends to distinguish its position on crime from that of the state's Democrats by emphasizing the rights of victims over the rights of the accused and the incarcerated. The state's Republicans also oppose "judicial activism." Several Republican members of the legislature, including state senator Richard Rainey and assemblyman George House, are former police officers.

Notably, the party's platform on crime does not include support for stricter gun control. Instead, the party advocates amending the state constitution to affirm explicitly the right of citizens to own and use firearms. The party opposes gun registration laws and similar gun-control provisions.

The Republicans' faith in the market as an efficient and just mechanism for creating and allocating wealth drives their calls for less regulation of business and less taxation of income and profits. For the party, this translates into certain policy prescriptions tailored to the particular circumstances of California.

For example, California experiences an ongoing tension between the desire to protect the state's natural resources (such as its coastline, forests, and vast agricultural areas) and the need to accommodate a burgeoning population (which in the 1990s rose 10 percent, from 30 million to 33 million). The party emphasizes the protection of private property rights, rather than government regulation, as the best way to ensure the protection of those resources. It also takes a strong position against illegal immigration which, according to the party, harms the state's economy and exacerbates its population pressures.

In the late 1990s and into the new millennium the party has emphasized its opposition to taxes and other financial restrictions on automobiles. Assemblyman Tom McClintock in particular led the party in an attack on the vehicle license fee, or "car tax," levied each year on automobiles. The party has also attacked gasoline taxes and has pushed for shifting more state funding from rail and bus projects to highways and roads. The state Republican Party has continually de-

fended the property tax limit passed in 1978 by a voter initiative known as Proposition 13. The party also advocates shifting property tax revenues currently controlled by the state government to local governments.

Like the national Republican Party, California Republicans experience considerable internal conflict over the issue of abortion. For the more conservative wing of the party, which views abortion in all but the most exceptional circumstances to be tantamount to murder, this is a litmus test issue of the party's support for religious values and morality. More moderate party members consider the legal and practical questions surrounding the abortion issue to be too complex and nuanced to be answered with a simple policy statement.

The party's platform declares the Republicans to be "the Party of Life" and expresses the party's opposition to taxpayer funding for abortion of any kind. The platform calls for a reversal of *Roe v. Wade*, although it does not specify which provisions of that landmark compromise should be reversed. The party also opposes partial-birth abortion, which in the late 1990s became a dramatic and graphic rallying point for abortion opponents.

Republican Presidential Victories, 1860–2000
Total: 23 (1860, 1864, 1868, 1872, 1876, 1884, 1888, 1896, 1900, 1904, 1908, 1920, 1924, 1928, 1952, 1956, 1960, 1968, 1972, 1976, 1980, 1984, 1988)

Republican Governors of California, 1860–2000
Leland Stanford, 1862–1863; Frederick Ferdinand Low, 1863–1867; Newton Booth, 1871–1875; Romualdo Pacheco, 1875; George Clement Perkins, 1880–1883; Robert Whitney Waterman, 1887–1891; Henry Harrison Markham, 1891–1895; Henry Tifft Gage, 1899–1903; George Cooper Pardee, 1903–1907; James Norris Gillett, 1907–1911; Hiram Warren Johnson, 1911–1917; William Dennison Stephens, 1917–1923; Friend William Richardson, 1923–1927; Clement Calhoun Young, 1927–1931; James "Sunny Jim" Rolph Jr., 1931–1934; Frank Finley Merriam, 1934–1939; Earl Warren, 1943–1953; Goodwin Jess Knight, 1953–1959; Ronald Wilson Reagan, 1967–1975; George Deukmejian, 1983–1991; Peter Barton Wilson, 1991–1999.

ADDRESS: California Republican Party, 1903 West Magnolia, Burbank, CA 91506

Tel.: (818) 841-5210

www.cagop.org

BIBLIOGRAPHY

Bell, Charles G., and Charles M. Price. *California Government Today: Politics of Reform.* 4th ed. Pacific Grove, CA: Brooks/Cole, 1992.

Cresap, Dean Russell. *Party Politics in the Golden State.* Los Angeles: Haynes Foundation, 1954.

Jewell, Malcolm E., and David M. Olson. *Political Parties and Elections in American States.* 3d ed. Chicago: Dorsey Press, 1988.

Owens, John R., Edmond Constantini, and Louis F. Wechsler. *California Politics and Parties.* New York: Macmillan, 1970.

Sorauf, Frank J. *Party Politics in America.* 5th ed. Boston: Little, Brown, 1984.

California Congressional Delegation, Voting Record as Assessed by Key Groups, 1998*

	ADA	ACLU	AFS	LCV	CON	NTU	NFIB	COC	ACU	NTLC	CHC
Representatives											
W. Herger	0	6	0	0	45	73	100	88	100	95	100
J. Doolittle	5	6	11	0	13	55	100	89	100	95	100
R. Pombo	10	6	11	0	13	56	86	89	96	95	100
T. Campbell	35	56	44	46	96	68	71	72	52	55	42
G. Radonovich	0	7	0	0	42	65	86	94	100	95	100
B. Thomas	0	25	11	8	2	52	93	100	92	92	67
E. Gallegly	15	13	22	8	13	48	100	83	76	87	100
H. P. McKeon	5	6	0	8	19	51	100	100	96	95	100
J. E. Rogan	0	6	0	15	60	59	85	100	100	95	100
D. Dreier	0	13	11	8	33	54	85	100	92	97	100
S. Horn	20	50	33	54	26	42	79	83	56	53	33
E. Royce	5	6	14	15	84	83	100	71	100	94	100
J. Lewis	10	31	22	15	13	44	100	100	75	73	73
K. Calvert	0	13	0	8	13	49	100	100	92	100	100
D. Rohrabacher	5	13	22	15	96	81	93	67	100	97	100
C. Cox	0	13	11	15	79	75	93	83	100	97	100
R. C. Packard	5	7	0	8	13	50	100	100	96	95	100
B. P. Bilbray	20	20	33	85	74	52	79	61	64	63	75
R. Cunningham	0	8	0	8	21	54	100	100	100	91	100
D. Hunter	5	6	13	8	42	66	86	71	100	97	100

*For abbreviations, see p. 220.

COLORADO

Historically, Colorado has been a strong Republican state, but since the 1960s Democrats have had flash successes at the congressional and gubernatorial levels. The state legislature has been under Republican control since 1960, except for four years between 1964 and 1968. From 1975 to 1999, however, two Democratic veterans, Richard

Lamm and Roy Romer, served as governor. The Democratic run ended when Bill Owens defeated his Democratic opponent by a narrow margin in 1998. In 2001 both U.S. senators from Colorado are Republicans and so are four of the six House members. Republican strength in the state is concentrated in Colorado Springs, a center of Christian evangelistic organizations; Fort Collins; and Greeley, north of Denver. The GOP also does well in rural areas, especially in Grand Junction. The swing votes are found in Jefferson County, to the west of Denver, and Arapahoe County, to the south, which generally vote Republican except when the Democrats have a strong candidate. Republicans fare worst in Denver, where many African Americans live; Pueblo, a major union stronghold; and Boulder, where the state university is located.

Rank-and-file members play a greater role in the nominating process in Colorado. Party conventions are held by law prior to the party primaries, and candidates for elective offices must win at least 30 percent of the vote at a county or state convention to win a place on the primary ballot.

The organizational pyramid consists of three levels: precinct, county, and state. The state central committee oversees all operations under the direction of the chair and executive director. One of the major responsibilities of the committee is to raise soft money, but it also provides candidates with in-kind support services such as demographic research, polling, and press releases. Republican headquarters is in downtown Denver on South Jackson Street. Republicans are stronger than Democrats in fund-raising and in providing in-kind services. These services include telephone banks and bulk mailing. Colorado Republicans were the first in the nation to introduce a state party computer bulletin board, which in-

cludes talking points on major issues, a review of GOP bills in the legislature, and candidate biographies. The state party tracks all elections, tries to identify seats that will be closely contested in the next general election, and generates data that could be used to devise appropriate strategy.

Republican Presidential Victories, 1876–2000
Total: 21 (1876, 1880, 1884, 1888, 1904, 1920, 1924, 1928, 1940, 1944, 1952, 1956, 1960, 1968, 1972, 1976, 1980, 1984, 1988, 1996, 2000)

Republican Governors of Colorado, 1876–2000
John Long Routt, 1876–1879, 1891–1893; Frederick Walker Pitkin, 1879–1883; Benjamin Harrison Eaton, 1885–1887; Job Adams Cooper, 1889–1891; Albert Willis McIntire, 1895–1897; James Hamilton Peabody, 1903–1905; 1905; Jesse Fuller McDonald, 1905–1907; Henry Augustus Buchtel, 1907–1909; George Alfred Carlson, 1915–1917; Oliver Henry Nelson Shoup, 1919–1923; Clarence J. Morley, 1925–1927; Ralph L. Carr, 1939–1943; John Charles Vivian, 1943–1947; Daniel Isaac Thornton, 1951–1955; John A. Love, 1963–1973; John David Vanderhoof, 1973–1975; Bill Owens, 1999– .

ADDRESS: Republican Party of Colorado, 1776 South Jackson Street, Suite 210, Denver, CO 80210

Tel.: (303) 758-3333
www.cologop.org

BIBLIOGRAPHY

Cronin, Thomas E., and Robert D. Loevy. *Colorado Politics and Government: Governing the Centennial State.* Lincoln: University of Nebraska Press, 1993.

Martin, Curtis W., and Rudolph Gomez. *Colorado Government and Politics.* Boulder, CO: Pruett Press, 1972.

Colorado Congressional Delegation, Voting Record as Assessed by Key Groups, 1998*

	ADA	ACLU	AFS	LCV	CON	NTU	NFIB	COC	ACU	NTLC	CHC
Senators											
B. N. Campbell	25	29	33	0	0	54	89	83	76	71	82
W. Allard	5	14	0	0	81	74	89	83	100	96	100

	ADA	ACLU	AFS	LCV	CON	NTU	NFIB	COC	ACU	NTLC	CHC
Representatives											
S. McInnis	5	6	0	15	26	53	100	100	96	94	92
B. Schaffer	5	19	0	8	60	82	100	78	100	97	100
L. Hefly	0	6	11	15	66	72	100	75	100	100	100

*For abbreviations, see p. 220.

CONNECTICUT

From 1896 through the New Deal, Republicans considered Connecticut their own bailiwick. During that time they carried the state in eight of the nine presidential elections (all except 1912), and won fifteen of the eighteen gubernatorial elections (all except 1910, 1912, and 1930). The New Deal dealt a blow to GOP dominance and put it on the defensive for the next half century. Between 1931 and 1999 there were seven Republican governors and eight Democratic governors. But the U.S. senators from Connecticut have been overwhelmingly Democratic, and both U.S. senators in 2001 are Democratic. Of the six U.S. House members from Connecticut, three are Republican. Democrats control both houses of the state legislature, but Republican governor John Rowland remains popular. It may, therefore, be correct to describe Connecticut as a strong two-party state with a Democratic edge.

According to the electoral rolls, far more Democrats are registered in Connecticut than Republicans, but the GOP has managed to cut the Democrats' margin. In the early 1980s Democrats led the Republicans in party identification by 36 percent to 21 percent, but this lead had been cut to 32 percent and 24 percent, respectively, by the early 1990s, with 39 percent of the voters claiming to be independent.

Connecticut operates on a nominating system called the challenge primary, according to which candidates may be nominated by a convention or caucus; but any candidate who receives a minimum of 15 percent of the convention or caucus vote may challenge the party's choice in a primary. Nevertheless the "boss" tradition is still strong, and most voters acquiesce in party deci-

sions and support the party nominee. The years from 1960 to 1994 were the wilderness years for Republicans, as they saw their majorities whittled down in the legislature and the party itself torn by ideological divisions. The maverick Lowell Weicker actually depressed the party fortunes by siphoning off moderate Republicans and forming a short-lived Connecticut Party to bolster his gubernatorial ambitions. The election of John Rowland in 1996 provided the party with a major boost, as it acquired a focus of power in the struggle against the Democratic legislature. The Republicans contest virtually every available seat in the state. The chair of the Republican state committee has considerable leeway in making operational and political decisions but must obtain the approval of the state central committee on budgetary and policy issues. The party is very unified under Rowland, helped by the departure of Lowell Weicker and the absence of a strong prolife or Christian Right faction. The GOP is particularly well organized in small towns.

Republican Presidential Victories, 1860–2000
Total: 22 (1860, 1864, 1868, 1872, 1880, 1896, 1900, 1904, 1908, 1916, 1920, 1924, 1928, 1932, 1948, 1952, 1956, 1972, 1976, 1980, 1984, 1988)

Republican Governors of Connecticut, 1860–2000
William Alfred Buckingham, 1858–1866; Joseph Roswell Hawley, 1866–1867; Marshall Jewell, 1869–1870, 1871–1873; Charles Bartlett Andrews 1879–1881; Hobart B. Bigelow, 1881–1883; Henry Baldwin Harrison, 1885–1887; Phineas Chapman Lounsbury, 1887–1889; Morgan Gardner Bulkeley, 1889–1893; Owen Vincent Coffin, 1895–1897; Lorrin Alamson Cooke, 1897–1889; George Edward Lounsbury, 1899–1901; George Payne McLean, 1901–1903; Abiram Chamberlain, 1903–1905; Henry Roberts, 1905–1907; Rollins

Simmons Woodruff, 1907–1909; George Leavens Lilley, 1903–1908; Frank Bentley Weeks, 1909–1911; Marcus Hensye Holcomb, 1915–1921; Everett John Lake, 1921–1923; Charles Augustus Templeton, 1923–1925; Hiram Bingham, 1925; John Harper Trumbull, 1925–1931; Raymond Earl Baldwin, 1939–1941, 1943–1946; James Lukens McConaughy, 1947–1948; James Coughlin Shannon, 1948–1949; John Davis Lodge, 1951–1955; Thomas Joseph Meskill, 1971–1975; John G. Rowland, 1995– .

ADDRESS: Connecticut Republican Party, 97 Elm Street, Hartford, CT 06106

Tel.: (860) 547-0589

www.ctgop.org

BIBLIOGRAPHY

Lockard, Duane. *New England State Politics.* Princeton: Princeton University Press, 1959.

Rose, Gary L. *Connecticut Politics at the Crossroads.* Lanham, MD: University Press of America, 1992.

Connecticut Congressional Delegation, Voting Record as Assessed by Key Groups, 1998*

	ADA	ACLU	AFS	LCV	CON	NTU	NFIB	COC	ACU	NTLC	CHC
Representatives											
C. Shays	45	63	33	100	92	67	57	56	40	42	58
N. L. Johnson	55	63	67	77	62	28	71	83	16	34	17

*For abbreviations, see p. 220.

DELAWARE

Delaware's Republican Party was established in 1860, the year Abraham Lincoln was elected president (although he did not win Delaware). Republicans made few inroads in the state in the nineteenth century, winning just one of nine gubernatorial elections between 1866 and 1896 and one of eight presidential contests from 1864 through 1892.

The national party realignment of 1896 reversed the trend, with state Republicans gaining the upper hand. From 1900 through 1932, Republicans won all nine gubernatorial elections. From 1898 to 1932, Republicans held a majority in both state legislative chambers for two-thirds of this period and controlled both chambers simultaneously for eighteen years. In U.S. House elections held between 1898 and 1932, Delaware Republicans were victorious in thirteen of eighteen contests. Starting with the popular election of U.S. senators in 1916, Republicans captured four of six seats through 1934. Delaware backed Republican presidential candidates in every election except one from 1896 to 1932.

After the New Deal realignment of the 1930s, Delaware Republicans had as strong an impact on the direction of state and national politics as state Democrats. Although they tied with state Democrats in endorsing eight of sixteen presidential candidates between 1936 and 1996, Republicans won nine of fifteen gubernatorial contests, sixteen of twenty-nine U.S. House races, and twelve of eighteen U.S. Senate elections.

In 2001, Republican state officials included the attorney general and the state auditor. The state legislature has witnessed split party control of the two chambers for several successive sessions, with Republicans retaining a majority of the state house. The only U.S. House member from Delaware is Michael Castle, a five-term incumbent who served two terms as governor from 1985 to 1993. Both of Delaware's U.S. senators are Democrats.

The rules of the Delaware Republican Party were last revised in 1993. Organizationally, the party is divided into seven convention districts: Wilmington, Brandywine, Christiana-Mill Creek, Colonial, Newark, Kent, and Sussex. Like the Democratic state headquarters, the Republican home base is in Wilmington. The officers of the state Republican Party, elected for two-year terms, include a chair, a vice chair, a secretary, and a treasurer.

State conventions within the Republican Party encompass three types: organizational, held in odd-numbered years; general, held in even-numbered years; and special organizational. Whereas the organizational convention chooses state party officers and receives annual reports, the general convention endorses candidates for national and statewide posts. The state party committee is composed of party officers and representatives from each convention district and affiliated organizations. The Republican state committee has two standing committees: Rules and Finance.

After Delaware's party and legislative leaders agreed, a law was passed in 1995 that scheduled the state's first-ever presidential primary four days after the New Hampshire primary. When New Hampshire and national party personnel pressured Delaware to change the date of the election, state officials refused. As a result, only Steve Forbes visited the state in 1996. Not coincidentally, Forbes won the Delaware primary that year, besting Bob Dole by 33 to 27 percent. When the same dispute with New Hampshire recurred in 2000, Delaware Republicans abandoned the state-sponsored primary, scheduling a party-financed and -run event on February 8. The election furnished George W. Bush with his first primary victory of the 2000 presidential nomination period. Thirty-six percent of registered voters in Delaware identify themselves as Republican.

Republican Presidential Victories, 1860–2000
Total: 18 (1872, 1896, 1900, 1904, 1908, 1916, 1920, 1924, 1928, 1932, 1948, 1952, 1956, 1968, 1972, 1980, 1984, 1988)

Republican Governors of Delaware, 1860–2000
Joshua Hopkins Marvil, 1895; John Hunn, 1901–1905; Preston Lea, 1905–1909; Simeon Selby Pennewell, 1909–1913; Charles Miller, 1913–1917, John Gillis Townsend Jr., 1917–1921; William Du Hamel Denney, 1921–1925; Robert P. Robinson, 1925–1929; Clayton Douglass Buck Sr., 1929–1937; Walter W. Bacon, 1941–1949; James Caleb Boggs, 1953–1960; David Penrose Buckson, 1960–1961; Russell Wilbur Peterson, 1969–1973; Pierre Samuel du Pont IV, 1977–1985; Michael Newbold Castle, 1985–1992; Dale Edward Wolf, 1992–1993.

ADDRESS: Delaware Republican Party, 2 Mill Road, Suite 108, Wilmington, DE 19806

Tel.: (302) 651-0260
www.delawaregop.com

BIBLIOGRAPHY
Christensen, Gardell Dano, and Eugenia Burney. *Colonial Delaware.* Nashville, TN: T. Nelson, 1974.

Gosnell, Harold F., and Richard G. Smolka. *American Parties and Elections.* Columbus, OH: Merrill, 1976.

Hancock, Harold B. *Delaware During the Civil War, A Political History.* Wilmington, DE: Historical Society of Delaware, 1961.

———. *Delaware Two Hundred Years Ago, 1780–1800.* Wilmington, DE: Middle Atlantic Press, 1987.

———. *Liberty and Independence: The Delaware State During the American Revolution.* Wilmington, DE: Delaware American Revolution Bicentennial Commission, 1976.

Hoff, Samuel B. "Delaware." In *State Party Profiles, A 50-State Guide to Development, Organization, and Resources,* ed. Andrew M. Appleton and Daniel S. Ward, 52–27. Washington, DC: Congressional Quarterly, 1997.

Hoffecker, Carol E. *Delaware, The First State.* Wilmington, DE: Middle Atlantic Press, 1988.

Jewell, Malcolm E., and David M. Olson. *Political Parties and Elections in American States.* 3d ed. Chicago: Dorsey Press, 1988.

Martin, Roger A. *A History of Delaware Through Its Governors, 1776–1984.* Wilmington, DE: McClafferty Print, 1984.

Munroe, John A. *Delaware Becomes a State.* Newark: University of Delaware Press, 1953.

———. *History of Delaware.* Newark: University of Delaware Press, 1979.

Spruance, John S. *Delaware Stays in the Union; The Civil War Period, 1860–1865.* Newark: University of Delaware Press, 1955.

Delaware Congressional Delegation, Voting Record as Assessed by Key Groups, 1998*

	ADA	ACLU	AFS	LCV	CON	NTU	NFIB	COC	ACU	NTLC	CHC
Senator											
W. Roth	15	33	11	38	39	59	78	78	65	67	55
Representative											
M. N. Castle	30	44	26	69	99	54	79	67	42	55	42

*For abbreviations, see p. 220.

FLORIDA

The Civil War virtually shut out the Republican Party in the South, and Florida was no exception. From 1877 to the 1950s, the GOP did not matter in the least in Florida politics. It was not politics but demographics that helped the GOP to gain a foothold in Florida. The new immigrants into Florida after World War II did not share the racial or political profile of the earlier generations, neither did they have the historic loyalty of southerners to the Democratic Party and to the Confederacy. Many were wealthy retirees with conservative patterns of thinking on social and fiscal issues. Next came large numbers of Cuban exiles fleeing Fidel Castro's ascension to power in 1959. Their conservative background and hatred of socialism clearly marked them as potential Republicans. In fact, Cubans formed the nucleus of the Republican Party in Dade County. The fallout from this demographic change was first felt in the 1960s. The first Republican governor was elected in 1966 and the first Republican U.S. senator, in 1968. In 1990, the GOP also gained a majority of the state congressional delegation. In 1999, Republicans controlled the governor's office, both houses of legislature, fifteen of twenty-three U.S. House seats, and one U.S. Senate seat.

In terms of registered Republicans, the shift in power is even more remarkable. In 1964 about 70 percent of registered voters identified themselves as Democrats. By 1994, only 32 percent identified themselves as Democrats, whereas 33 percent identified themselves as Republicans. Most of the GOP increase came from the white and Cuban population. Demographic changes also affected the organizational structure of the Republican Party. Party membership was concentrated in only four urban counties, which had two votes each on the state executive committee. On the other hand, ten northern rural counties with only a few registered Republicans controlled twenty votes. This inequity was corrected in a party re-organization in the late 1960s. Court-ordered re-apportionment of electoral districts also helped Republicans, as the more Democratic rural districts lost votes to the more populous urban centers that were more Republican.

The Republican Party is organized in each of the state's sixty-seven counties and twenty-three congressional districts. The county executive committees elect members to the state executive committees which, in turn, elect members of the district committees and the national party committee. At each level, conventions are held. Highly urbanized counties have year-round headquarters with full-time executive directors. The Florida GOP gets support from the Republican National Committee in organizational and electoral matters. Modernization has transformed the party into a full-service organization providing campaign support, direct mail, research, and other services for candidates. State and local levels of the party work together in get-the-vote-out drives, mailing lists, and voter registration drives. The state party also maintains close relations with the legislative caucus. With a Republican governor and a Republican legislature, the GOP is in a strong position to initiate a conservative legislative agenda without interference from the Democrats.

Republican Presidential Victories, 1860–2000
Total: 14 (1868, 1872, 1876, 1928, 1952, 1956, 1960, 1968, 1972, 1980, 1984, 1988, 1992, 2000)

Republican Governors of Florida, 1860–2000

Harrison Reed, 1868–1873; Ossian Bingley Hart, 1873–1874; Marcellus Lovejoy Stearns, 1874–1877; Claude Roy Kirk Jr., 1967–1971; Robert Martinez, 1987–1991; John Ellis "Jeb" Bush, 1999– .

ADDRESS: Republican Party of Florida, 420 East Jefferson Street, Tallahassee, FL 32301

Tel.: (850) 222-7920

www.rpof.org

BIBLIOGRAPHY

Dauer, Manning J., ed. *Florida's Politics and Government.* Gainesville: University Presses of Florida, 1980.

Huckshorn, Robert J., ed. *Government and Politics in Florida.* Gainesville: University of Florida Press, 1991.

Klingman, Peter D. *Neither Dies nor Surrenders: A History of the Republican Party in Florida, 1867–1970.* Gainesville: University Presses of Florida, 1984.

Florida Congressional Delegation, Voting Record as Assessed by Key Groups, 1998*

	ADA	ACLU	AFS	LCV	CON	NTU	NFIB	COC	ACU	NTLC	CHC
Senator											
C. Mack	0	29	0	0	67	64	100	89	80	89	82
Representatives											
J. Scarborough	10	6	11	31	87	77	79	78	96	92	100
T. K. Fowler	5	25	14	15	28	46	100	94	88	86	67
C. Stearns	5	6	11	8	77	66	100	83	96	92	100
J. L. Mica	10	6	11	15	65	54	100	89	92	95	100
B. McCollum	5	13	11	15	30	61	79	94	84	84	92
M. Bilirakis	5	6	11	46	2	53	100	89	92	89	100
C. W. Young	0	8	0	15	2	63	92	93	90	86	83
C. Canady	5	6	11	15	21	53	93	89	88	89	92
D. Miller	10	40	11	31	92	78	100	76	88	95	83
P. J. Goss	5	19	14	31	46	72	100	86	91	89	100
D. Weldon	0	13	0	15	42	54	93	89	92	92	100
M. Foley	20	31	22	38	4	60	93	100	80	92	67
I. Ros-Lehtinen	15	27	57	46	28	50	92	67	80	69	92
L. Daiz-Balart	25	27	56	38	13	44	79	72	68	66	92
E. C. Shaw Jr.	10	38	11	31	33	36	86	100	72	76	75

*For abbreviations, see p. 220.

GEORGIA

Georgia is a typical Southern state over which Democrats exercised unchallenged control from the end of Reconstruction to the 1960s. Georgia politics consisted mainly of struggles within the Democratic Party between conservatives and the progressives. Georgia Republicans did not even nominate a candidate for governor between 1876 and 1962. The Georgia delegation to Congress did not contain a single Republican until 1977–1978, and there was only a solitary one before 1992. The 1994 elections marked a watershed in the state's political history. When the elections were over, the Georgia delegation to the U.S. Congress consisted of eight Republican representatives out of eleven and one U.S. Senator. Democrats still control the state legislature and the governor's office, but their hold on these offices is tenuous.

The single most important reason for the Republican gains was the identification of the Democratic Party with the Civil Rights movement. Many Georgians increasingly perceived Democrats as the party of black power, welfare, abortion, and big government. The court-directed reapportionment of electoral districts worked against the Democrats. With most African Americans concentrated in a few districts, the white majority districts fell easily to the Republicans.

But the Republicans had to make a lot of leeway in order to achieve a level playing field. The lack of an opposition had made the Democratic Party flabby, cumbrous, and faction-ridden, but it also reduced the Republican Party to a no-show in most electoral districts. For most of the twentieth century few candidates wanted to stand on the Republican ticket and few GOP voters existed to organize. The election of Republican Mack Mattingly to the Senate and Newt Gingrich to the U.S. House of Representatives in 1978 signaled that the GOP had arrived. By the mid-1980s, the party had managed to establish a sizable presence in the electoral field, with experienced candidates, strong budgets, and improved campaign technology.

During the Reagan and Bush years, the GOP was saddled with deep ideological divisions between conservatives—mainly the Christian Right—and moderates. Although these disputes tended to become somewhat ugly at times, Republican leaders like "Bo" Callaway, managed to smooth things over before they erupted in public forums. Since the rise of Newt Gingrich in 1994, factional disputes have been contained, although, as in other state Republican parties, internal tensions remain a constant feature of GOP politics. Newt Gingrich was never a force in Georgia politics as he was on the national scene, and his downfall has not hurt the state party's fortunes.

Republicans are currently organized in 150 of the state's 159 counties. Republican organizational style of top–down flow of authority has apparently worked in Georgia, where fundraising is a function of the state party. One of the main handicaps for the party is the lack of eligible candidates with broad appeal. The Republican state convention meets in odd-numbered years, and the state chairs serve two-year terms. The state convention is the principal venue where the battles for the control of the state party take place.

Republican Presidential Victories, 1860–2000
Total: 6 (1964, 1972, 1984, 1988, 1996, 2000)

Republican Governors of Georgia, 1860–2000
Rufus Brown Bullock, 1868–1871; Benjamin Conley, 1871–1872.

ADDRESS: Georgia Republican Party, 5600 Roswell Road, Northeast, East Building, Suite 200, Atlanta, GA 30342

Tel.: (404) 257-5559
www.gagop.org

BIBLIOGRAPHY

Fleischmann, Arnold, and Carol Pierannunzi. *Politics in Georgia*. Atlanta: University of Georgia Press, 1997.

Grantham, Dewey W. *The Life & Death of the Solid South: A Political History*. Lexington: University Press of Kentucky, 1988.

Georgia Congressional Delegation, Voting Record as Assessed by Key Groups, 1998*

	ADA	ACLU	AFS	LCV	CON	NTU	NFIB	COC	ACU	NTLC	CHC
Senator											
P. Coverdell	0	14	11	0	2	66	100	89	92	93	82

	ADA	ACLU	AFS	LCV	CON	NTU	NFIB	COC	ACU	NTLC	CHC
Representatives											
J. Kingston	0	6	0	8	66	69	100	82	100	100	100
M. Collins	0	6	0	0	50	61	100	83	100	95	91
B. Barr	5	7	13	0	87	76	100	72	100	100	100
S. Chambliss	0	6	0	8	2	49	100	94	96	92	91
N. Deal	10	0	11	8	81	73	100	67	88	97	100
C. Norwood	5	6	11	8	21	50	100	83	100	97	100
J. Linder	0	6	0	8	26	53	100	100	100	97	100

*For abbreviations, see p. 220.

HAWAII

Hawaii's political history is a cautionary story for the GOP. Once a Republican bastion where the Democrats barely survived, it has so completely reversed the standing of the two parties that Republicans have barely a foothold in the islands. Virtually all national and state offices are occupied by Democrats. In the state senate Republicans have only three seats of twenty-five, and in the state house, they hold less than one-third of the total. Only one Republican governor, William Quinn, the state's first, who served from 1959 to 1962, has ever been elected to office. What doomed the Republicans were the changing demographics after World War II. Japanese Americans and other ethnic groups who now form the majority on the islands have by and large found a permanent home in the Democratic Party. The old white establishment, known in Hawaiian as *haole*, has been relegated to the position of an embattled minority, a status it shares now with its old defender, the Republican Party. For all practical purposes, Hawaii is a one-party state, and on this score, it ranks at the top of all fifty states.

In contrast to the Democrats, Republicans have such difficulty recruiting candidates that in many cases a number of Democrats run unopposed. To compound the problem, Republicans did not have the kind of strong leadership that the Democrats had under Governor John Burns.

The Democrats have 40 percent more registered party members than do the Republicans. Over the years, the Democrats, using all the media techniques at their command, have managed to create a negative image of the Republicans as the *haole* party.

The Republican county committees are quite weak, for the party does not have any following in the rural areas and is limited to urban pockets. Party decisions are made almost entirely by the state committee. But given its minority status for over forty years, the state committee itself is quite anemic. There are no patronage positions to hand out, and the party's central coffers are almost always empty. Party meetings are held both annually and biennially. Precinct committees and the state committee meet annually, but the county conventions and district committees meet in odd-numbered years The state platform convention takes place in even-numbered years in Honolulu. The state organizational convention takes place in odd-numbered years.

Republican Presidential Victories, 1960–2000
Total: 2 (1972, 1984)

Republican Governors of Hawaii, 1959–2000
William Francis Quinn, 1959–1962.

ADDRESS: Republican Party of Hawaii, 725 Kapiolani Boulevard, Suite C-105, Honolulu, HI 96813

Tel.: (808) 593-8180
www.gophawaii.com

BIBLIOGRAPHY

Coffman, Tom. *Catch a Wave: A Case Study of Hawaii's New Politics.* Honolulu: University Press of Hawaii, 1973.

Wang, James C. F. *Hawaii State and Local Politics.* Hilo, HI: J.C.F. Wang, 1982.

IDAHO

Many of Idaho's early settlers after the Civil War were Confederates and Mormons who allied with the Democratic Party. Settlers opposed to the Mormons tended to be Republicans. Some lived in southeast Idaho, and others, who wanted to unite with Washington State, lived in the north. Their control of the legislature enabled them to disenfranchise Mormons from 1884 to 1896, and when Idaho achieved statehood in 1890, the first three governors were Republican. The turn of the century was a period of fluid change in political party power as Populists, Democrats, Silver Republicans, and a number of third parties vied for control of the statehouse. Populist and Progressive candidates dominated the interwar years.

However, after World War II, when Idaho became more Republican, Mormons were welcomed into the party. The rise of many ultraconservative groups in Idaho, like the John Birch Society, was evidence of a trend toward the right that was accentuated through the Cold War years. The state Republican committee was controlled for a long time by a small group of conservatives but the moderate wing of the party managed to stave off total domination. As a result, Barry Goldwater lost Idaho in 1964 by 1 percent. In 2001, Republicans hold the governor's office and have a commanding lead in the state legislatures; both U.S. senators and the state's two representatives are Republican.

The GOP is better organized than the Democratic Party. Republicans have healthy local organizations in all fifty-four Idaho counties, while there are several counties without a Democratic presence. However, the right–moderate rift periodically resurfaces within the GOP, and the fight over abortion rights particularly becomes bitter and divisive. Regionalism also plays a part in this factional divide. The right wing of the party comes from southeastern Idaho, while moderates are largely from the urban southwest.

Republican Presidential Victories, 1892–2000

Total: 17 (1904, 1908, 1920, 1924, 1928, 1952, 1956, 1960, 1968, 1972, 1976, 1980, 1984, 1988, 1992, 1996, 2000)

Republican Governors of Idaho, 1890–2000

George Laird Shoup, 1890; Norman Bushnell Willey, 1890–1893; William John McConnell, 1893–1897; John Tracy Morrison, 1903–1905; Frank Robert Gooding, 1905–1909; James Henry Brady, 1909–1911; John Michiner Haines, 1913–1915; David William Davis, 1919–1923; Charles Calvin Moore, 1923–1927; H. Clarence Baldridge, 1927–1931; Clarence Alfred Bottolfson, 1939–1941, 1943–1945; Charles Armington Robins, 1947–1951; Leonard Beck Jordan, 1951–1955; Robert Eben Smylie, 1955–1967; Don William Samuelson, 1967–1971; Philip E. Batt, 1995–1999; Dick Kempthorne, 1999– .

ADDRESS: Idaho Republican Party, P.O. Box 2267, Boise, ID 83701

Tel.: (208) 343-6405

www.idgop.org

BIBLIOGRAPHY

Blank, Robert H. *Individualism in Idaho: The Territorial Foundations.* Pullman: Washington State University Press, 1988.

Stapilus, Randy. *Paradox Politics: People and Power in Idaho.* Boise, ID: Ridenbaugh Press, 1988.

Idaho Congressional Delegation, Voting Record as Assessed by Key Groups, 1998*

	ADA	ACLU	AFS	LCV	CON	NTU	NFIB	COC	ACU	NTLC	CHC
Senators											
L. Craig	5	14	0	0	14	65	100	100	84	86	91
M. Crapo	10	13	25	15	21	51	92	94	83	73	100

	ADA	ACLU	AFS	LCV	CON	NTU	NFIB	COC	ACU	NTLC	CHC
Representative											
H. Chenoweth	20	6	33	8	33	60	86	67	92	84	100

*For abbreviations, see p. 220.

ILLINOIS

Illinois has a special place in Republican Party history as the home state of Abraham Lincoln and the scene of some of its greatest triumphs. It was in Chicago in 1860 that Lincoln was nominated for president and became the first Republican to capture the White House. The momentum helped the GOP to maintain itself in power for the next half century. During this period the Democrats led a precarious existence in their power base in southern Illinois, especially in Williamson County where there had been an effort to secede from the Union during the Civil War. Except for those in the immigrant neighborhoods of Chicago, Democrats were largely shut out of state power in the late nineteenth century.

By the early 1900s, Chicago was becoming so populous that its numbers determined elections. Chicago interests took over the party, and rural GOP representatives were simply stampeded into following the lead of the city bosses. Of these, the most prominent during the interwar years was William Hale "Big Bill" Thompson, elected mayor in 1915 and reelected in 1919 and 1927. Republicans continued to do well in national races, but they had to yield to Democrats in many local off-year elections. Finally, in 1932, as Franklin D. Roosevelt triumphed throughout the nation, Lincoln's home state abandoned the Republican Party and joined the Democratic bandwagon until the 1970s. The Democratic Chicago political machine was among the strongest in the nation. Created by Mayor Anton Cermak in 1931, it became a virtual steamroller under Mayor Richard J. Daley. Although Daley's reach was limited to Chicago and Cook County, he had the power to change outside elections, and he provided the victory margin for John F. Kennedy in 1960. But the 1960s elections also proved that the Republicans had bottomed out. Cook County

politics became an odious feature of Democratic politics, and Republicans—whose strength lay in the suburbs, particularly the so-called collar counties of DuPage, Kane, Lake, McHenry, and Will—began to look squeaky clean beside the Daley machine. Thus, the voting patterns in Illinois were reset as not merely Democrat versus Republican, but the city of Chicago versus the rest of the state.

Republicans also were helped by a number of other factors. One was the Supreme Court decision of 1990 banning the hiring, promotion, or transfer of public employees based on their party affiliation, a practice that had sustained the Daley organization for many years. In 1972, the Supreme Court had voided the so-called twenty-three-month rule prohibiting a voter from voting in one party's primary within twenty-three-months of having voted in another party's primary. By opening up party primaries to all voters, the Court's decision marked the end of machine politics. Also, there was internal unrest in the Democratic Party against Daley's autocratic rule. The death of Daley in 1976 and the subsequent rise of black influence in the Democratic Party meant that a Democratic era had ended and the field was reopened for intense two-party competition. Since 1977 Republicans have occupied the governor's mansion continuously.

The GOP maintains offices in both Chicago and Springfield. Central committee members are elected for four-year terms from each of the twenty congressional districts during the off-year primary. Each district elects one central committee member and a nonvoting deputy who is not of the same gender as the member. The GOP does not endorse any candidate in the primaries, a practice that has now been adopted by the Democrats.

Republican Presidential Victories, 1860–2000
Total: 24 (1860, 1864, 1868, 1872, 1876, 1880, 1884,

1888, 1896, 1900, 1904, 1908, 1916, 1920, 1924, 1928, 1952, 1956, 1968, 1972, 1976, 1980, 1984, 1988)

Republican Governors of Illinois, 1860–2000

John Wood, 1860–1861; Richard Yates, 1861–1865; Richard James Oglesby, 1865–1869, 1873; 1885–1889; John McAuley Palmer, 1869–1873; John Lourie Beveridge, 1873–1877; Shelby Moore Cullom, 1877–1883; John Marshall Hamilton, 1883–1885; Joseph Wilson Fifer, 1889–1893; John Riley Tanner, 1897–1901; Richard Yates, 1901–1905; Charles Samuel Deneen, 1905–1913; Frank Orren Lowden, 1917–1921; Lennington Small, 1921–1929; Louis Lincoln Emmerson, 1929–1933; Dwight Herbert Green, 1941–1949; William Grant Stratton, 1953–1961; Richard Buell Ogilvie, 1969–

1973; James Robert Thompson, 1977–1991; James Edgar, 1991–1999; George H. Ryan, 1999– .

ADDRESS: Illinois Republican Party, P.O. Box 78, Springfield, IL 62705

Tel.: (217) 525-0011

www.ilgop.org

BIBLIOGRAPHY

Crane, Edgar G., Jr., ed. with the assistance of Robin M. Crane. *Illinois, Political Processes and Governmental Performance.* Dubuque, IA: Kendall/Hunt, 1980.

Kenney, David, and Barbara L. Brown. *Basic Illinois Government: A Systematic Explanation.* 3d ed. Carbondale: Southern Illinois University Press, 1993.

Illinois Congressional Delegation, Voting Record as Assessed by Key Groups, 1998*

	ADA	ACLU	AFS	LCV	CON	NTU	NFIB	COC	ACU	NTLC	CHC
Representatives											
H. Hyde	0	6	0	8	40	61	79	88	92	89	92
P. M. Crane	0	7	0	0	87	83	92	81	96	100	100
J. E. Porter	15	38	11	69	78	51	86	83	46	45	50
G. C. Weller	15	13	44	31	13	47	86	88	92	76	100
J. D. Hastert	0	6	0	23	26	51	100	100	100	97	100
T. Ewing	0	7	0	23	26	50	100	100	91	84	92
D. Manzullo	0	6	0	23	63	63	100	94	92	89	100
R. LaHood	20	13	44	31	76	45	64	83	60	68	83
J. M. Shimkus	10	6	33	8	13	50	86	94	88	89	100

*For abbreviations, see p. 220.

INDIANA

Indiana is perceived as a Republican bastion, yet the Hoosier State has a strong two-party tradition. For over a hundred years, Republicans have had the edge on all counts: the number of registered voters, the percentage of votes, and control of the legislature. However, they have remained vulnerable to upsets by Democrats and have never enjoyed a veto-proof majority.

Party influence and strength have been shaped by both external and internal events that have forced changes in the way the GOP mobilizes its resources and the way its constituencies respond. Court-ordered reapportionment and redistricting of the state legislature and congressional districts have required changes in the party's strategy for winning seats. The replacement of convention nominations by primaries has required changes in the recruitment and nomination of candidates. As personal candidacies have become common, county chairs have lost their former role as brokers and deal makers. To boost the office of county chair, the Indiana General Assembly passed legislation that made it almost impossible for county chairs to be deposed. However, most candidates for statewide offices tend to ignore the county chairs during fund-raising and campaigning and to deal more often with the state committee. Developments in campaign techniques and technologies have given the party more mileage for its campaign dollars and enabled it to reach wider audiences more economically. Because the courts have stripped both parties of patronage rights and perquisites, the parties have had to search for alternative sources of funds. Republicans are more active in volunteer and candidate recruitment. They have benefited from the presence of a number of think tanks in the state, notably, the Hudson Institute and the Public Policy Institute.

The Republican state committee has amassed more power and influence as a result of the decline of the county-level organization. The state committee is involved in all the key activities: fund-raising, development of resources, and campaign coordination.

The factional divide within the Republican Party is somewhat muted. The religious right has not been able to take over the party, which is more or less in the hands of the pro-business and socially moderate conservatives.

Republican Presidential Victories, 1860–2000
Total: 29 (1860, 1864, 1868, 1872, 1880, 1888, 1896, 1900, 1904, 1908, 1916, 1920, 1924, 1928, 1940, 1944, 1948, 1952, 1956, 1960, 1968, 1972, 1976, 1980, 1984, 1988, 1992, 1996, 2000)

Republican Governors of Indiana, 1860–2000
Henry Smith Lane, 1861; Oliver Perry Morton, 1861–1867; Conrad Baker, 1867–1873; Albert Gallatin Porter, 1881–1885; Alvin Peterson Hovey, 1899–1891; Ira Joy Chase, 1891–1893; James Atwell Mount, 1897–1901; Winfield Taylor Durbin, 1901–1905; James Franklin Hanly, 1905–1909, James Putnam Goodrich, 1917–1921; Warren Terry McCray, 1921–1924; Emmett Forest Branch, 1924–1925; Edward L. Jackson, 1925–1929; Harry Guyer Leslie, 1929–1933; Ralph Fesler Gates, 1945–1949; George North Craig, 1953–1957; Harold Willis Handley, 1957–1961; Edgar Doud Whitcomb, 1969–1973; Otis Ray Bowen, 1973–1981; Robert D. Orr, 1981–1989.

ADDRESS: Indiana Republican Party, 200 South Meridian, Suite 400, Indianapolis, IN 46225

Tel.: (317) 635-7561

www.indgop.org

BIBLIOGRAPHY

Harmon, Robert B. *Government and Politics in Indiana: An Information Source Survey*. Monticello, IL: Vance Bibliographies, 1978.

Peirce, Neal R., and John Keefe. *The Great Lakes States of America: People, Politics and Power in the Five Great Lakes States*. New York: Norton, 1980.

Indiana Congressional Delegation, Voting Record as Assessed by Key Groups, 1998*

	ADA	ACLU	AFS	LCV	CON	NTU	NFIB	COC	ACU	NTLC	CHC
Senator											
R. G. Luger	0	29	0	13	91	63	100	94	68	68	82
Representatives											
D. McIntosh	0	7	0	8	45	66	92	94	100	91	100
M. Souder	15	13	25	8	66	63	100	76	83	89	100
S. Buyer	15	14	22	8	13	45	100	94	88	95	91
D. Burton	5	7	0	0	5	51	100	93	96	95	100
E. Pease	0	6	11	31	13	51	86	100	100	89	100
J. Hostettler	10	19	11	0	65	58	93	78	92	89	92

*For abbreviations, see p. 220.

IOWA

Republicans enjoyed unchallenged supremacy in Iowa politics until the 1950s. Republican influence declined as a result of urbanization and industrialization in the 1950s and 1960s when the state lost its rustic character. The Democratic challenge was orchestrated by Governor Harold Hughes, who served from 1963 to 1969. However, the organizational resurgence of the Democrats has not been strong enough to displace the Republicans, who have continued to win elective offices regularly. Currently, Democrats occupy the governor's office. Republicans control both houses of the state legislature and hold one U.S. Senate seat (Chuck Grassley) and four of five House seats.

Iowa is noted as a grassroots state where the people shape party institutions and policies in a more direct way than in other states. Iowa's first-in-the-nation caucus, devised for the presidential nomination process, has become the mechanism that fuels party growth. The caucus also provides an opportunity for the state party to organize fund-raisers and receive contributions from candidates in return for goodwill as well as votes.

The state party committee is headquartered in Des Moines. It is composed of three members from each of Iowa's five congressional districts and two national committeepersons, one man and one woman. The Christian right has been active in Iowa since 1992 when they gained a majority on the state committee. Tempering their zeal is Terry Branstad, the moderate conservative who served as governor from 1983 to 1999. Another strong faction within the GOP comprises farmers. The Farm Bureau is informally aligned with the Republican Party, and they fight their battles together.

Republican Presidential Victories, 1860–2000
Total: 27 (1860, 1864, 1868, 1872, 1876, 1880, 1884, 1888, 1892, 1896, 1900, 1904, 1908, 1916, 1920, 1924, 1928, 1940, 1944, 1952, 1956, 1960, 1968, 1972, 1976, 1980, 1984)

Republican Governors of Iowa, 1860–2000
Samuel Jordan Kirkwood, 1860–1864, 1876–1877; William Milo Stone, 1864–1868; Samuel Merrill, 1868–1872; Cyrus Clay Carpenter, 1872–1876; Josha G. Newbold, 1877–1878; John Henry Gear, 1878–1882; Buren Robinson Sherman, 1882–1886; William Larrabee, 1886–1890; Frank Darr Jackson, 1894–1896; Francis Marion Drake, 1896–1898; Leslie Mortimer Shaw, 1898–1902; Albert Baird Cummins, 1902–1908; Warren Garst, 1908–1909; Beryl Franklin Carroll, 1909–1913; George W. Clarke, 1913–1917; William Lloyd Harding, 1917–1921; Nathan Edward Kendall, 1921–1925; John Hammill, 1925–1931; Daniel Webster Turner, 1931–1933; George Allison Wilson, 1939–1943; Bourke Blakemore Hickenlooper, 1943–1945; Robert Donald Blue, 1945–1949; William S. Beardsley, 1949–1954; Leo Elthon, 1954–1955; Leo Arthur Hoegh, 1955–1957; Norman Arthur Erbe, 1961–1963; Robert D. Ray, 1969–1983; Terry Branstad, 1983–1999.

ADDRESS: Republican Party of Iowa, 521 East Locust Street, Des Moines, IA 50309

Tel.: (515) 282-8105
www.iowagop.org

BIBLIOGRAPHY
Gannaway, John W. *The Development of Party Organization in Iowa.* Iowa City: State Historical Society of Iowa, 1903.
Jewell, Malcolm E., and David M. Olson. *Political Parties and Elections in American States.* Chicago: Dorsey Press, 1988.

Iowa Congressional Delegation, Voting Record as Assessed by Key Groups, 1998*

	ADA	ACLU	AFS	LCV	CON	NTU	NFIB	COC	ACU	NTLS	CHC
Senator											
C. Grassley	5	14	22	0	92	56	89	83	80	75	91

	ADA	ACLU	AFS	LCV	CON	NTU	NFIB	COC	ACU	NTLS	CHC
Representatives											
J. Leach	45	56	50	85	30	42	71	89	32	50	33
J. Nussle	10	13	11	31	42	49	100	100	84	92	100
G. Ganske	5	20	33	46	38	36	67	81	64	63	83
T. Latham	0	6	0	15	13	48	100	100	92	95	100

*For abbreviations, see p. 220.

KANSAS

Kansas is a bastion of classic Republicanism. In the last century, it has produced a number of influential leaders such as Charles Curtis, Alfred Landon, Dwight Eisenhower, Robert Dole, and Nancy Landon Kassebaum. Its dominance is also reflected in the numbers of elections won and the offices held. Since statehood in 1861, Kansas has elected just nine Democratic governors and only five since 1960. In the U.S. Senate and House elections, Republicans usually win hands down with over 60 percent of the vote. Since 1960, control of the state senate and house has never slipped from Republican hands. Currently, Republicans hold both U.S. Senate seats, three of four U.S. House seats, and the governor's mansion.

Republican support is based in two geographic areas: the western half of the state and Johnson County, a wealthy suburb in the east. Both areas are predominantly white.

Republicans have so dominated the state that Democrats have not won a U.S. Senate seat since the Great Depression. On the other hand, the GOP plans and campaigns hard for state legislative contests by targeting its resources toward specific races in which the Democratic candidate is vulnerable. The GOP depends on direct mail and telemarketing for fund-raising. To reduce full-time staff, it depends on professional consultants, especially those who worked on Robert Dole's presidential campaign in 1996.

Since the election of Bill Graves as governor in 1994, the Christian right has controlled three of the four state party congressional district delegations and has secured a majority of the Republican state central committee. In 1995 the socially conservative David Miller was elected as Kansas Democratic Party state chair. The factional divide between social conservatives and moderates has, however, had little effect on electoral outcomes.

Republican Presidential Victories, 1864–2000
Total: 28 (1864, 1868, 1872, 1876, 1880, 1884, 1888, 1900, 1904, 1908, 1920, 1924, 1928, 1940, 1944, 1948, 1952, 1956, 1960, 1968, 1972, 1976, 1980, 1984, 1988, 1992, 1996, 2000)

Republican Governors of Kansas, 1861–2000
Charles Lawrence Robinson, 1861–1863; Thomas Carney, 1863–1865; Samuel Johnson Crawford, 1865–1868; Nehemiah Green, 1868–1869; James Madison Harvey, 1869–1873; Thomas Andrew Osborn, 1873–1877; George Tobey Anthony, 1877–1879; John Pierce St. John, 1879–1883; John Alexander Martin, 1885–1889; Lyman Underwood Humphrey, 1889–1893; Edmund Needham Morrill, 1895–1897; William Eugene Stanley, 1899–1903; Willis Joshua Bailey, 1903–1905; Edward Wallis Hoch, 1905–1909; Walter Roscoe Stubbs, 1909–1913; Arthur Capper, 1915–1919; Henry Justin Allen, 1919–1923; Benjamin Sanford Paulen, 1925–1929; Clyde Martin Reed, 1929–1931; Alfred Mossman Landon, 1933–1937; Payne Harry Ratner, 1939–1943; Andrew Frank Schoeppel, 1943–1947; Frank Carlson, 1947–1950; Frank Leslie Hagaman, 1950–1951; Edward Ferdinand Arn, 1951–1955; Frederick Lee Hall, 1955–1957; John Berridge McCuish, 1957; John Anderson Jr., 1961–1965; William Henry Avery, 1965–1967; Robert Frederick Bennett, 1975–1979; John Michael "Mike" Hayden, 1987–1991; Bill Graves, 1995– .

ADDRESS: Republican Party of Kansas, 2025 Southwest Gage, Topeka, KS 66604

Tel.: (785) 234-3456
www.ksgop.org

BIBLIOGRAPHY

Harder, Marvin, and Carolyn Rampey. *The Kansas Legislature: Procedures, Personalities, and Prob-* *lems.* Lawrence: University Press of Kansas, 1972.

Sundquist, James L. *Dynamics of the Party System: Alignment and Realignment of Political Parties in the United States.* Washington, DC: Brookings Institution, 1983.

Kansas Congressional Delegation, Voting Record as Assessed by Key Groups, 1998*

	ADA	ACLU	AFS	LCV	CON	NTU	NFIB	COC	ACU	NTLC	CHC
Senators											
S. Brownback	0	14	0	0	52	68	100	94	92	100	100
P. Roberts	0	14	0	0	4	56	88	100	84	79	91
Representatives											
J. Moran	10	19	11	15	13	55	100	100	92	87	92
J. Ryun	0	6	0	0	13	54	100	100	100	100	100
T. Tiahrt	0	6	0	0	2	57	100	94	100	97	100

*For abbreviations, see p. 220.

KENTUCKY

In Kentucky Democratic dominance, which had persisted after the Civil War, ended in 1896 when many conservative Democrats switched parties. Kentucky remained a strong two-party state until the New Deal restored Democrats to office. Unlike other states in the South, the Republican Party retained much of its appeal in Kentucky. With a base of support in the southeastern mountains and the larger cities, the party received at least 40 percent of the vote in national and statewide elections until the Eisenhower era. From 1931 to 1967, the Republicans elected only one governor. Although they have done well in national and statewide elections, they have been unable to elect a governor since 1971 or make any inroads into entrenched Democratic power in local governments. The Republican Party has not controlled either house of the state legislature since 1920 and in recent years has held less than one-third membership.

Republicans have a mixed and spotty track record in nominating strong candidates, especially for gubernatorial races. But with U.S. Senator Mitch McConnell, a leading voice in the national Republican Party and in charge of the Republican campaigns, Kentucky has received a fair share of campaign funds and RNC support in the 1990s. Republicans have a large and elaborate organization at precinct, county, congressional district and state levels with the state convention at the apex. The 350 to 500 members of the state central committee are chosen by the state convention. The state central committee is largely symbolic; actual day-to-day party affairs are handled by the executive committee. The party headquarters is located at Frankfort. It is responsible for targeting races, providing support services to candidates, fund-raising, polling, recruitment, voter registration drives, and furnishing information. Despite such organizational flair, the GOP is not always able to field candidates for all local and legislative seats. It generally plays safe by concentrating on districts where it tends to do well, such as the large metropolitan areas of Lexington, Louisville, Covington, and Newport. Although pressed on the right by Christian conservatives, the Republican Party remains true to the big-tent concept. On the other hand, Democrats have been in some disarray, especially in the First and Second Congressional districts in western Kentucky. At present, the Republicans have both U.S. Senate seats and five of six U.S. House seats. But at home, the Democrats have the governorship and both houses of the legislature.

Republican Presidential Victories, 1860–2000
Total: 11 (1896, 1924, 1928, 1956, 1960, 1968, 1972, 1980, 1984, 1988, 2000)

Republican Governors of Kentucky, 1860–2000
William O'Connell Bradley, 1895–1899; William Sylvester Taylor, 1899–1900; Augustus Everett Willson, 1907–1911; Edwin Porch Morrow, 1919–1923; Flemon Davis Sampson, 1927–1931; Simeon

Slavens Willis, 1943–1947; Louis Brady Nunn, 1967–1971.

ADDRESS: Republican Party of Kentucky, P.O. Box 1068, Frankfort, KY 40602

Tel.: (502) 875-5130

www.rpk.org

BIBLIOGRAPHY
Jewell, Malcolm E., and Everett W. Cunningham. *Kentucky Politics.* Lexington: University of Kentucky Press, 1968.

Miller, Penny M., and Malcolm E. Jewell. *Political Parties and Primaries in Kentucky.* Lexington: University Press of Kentucky, 1990.

Kentucky Congressional Delegation, Voting Record as Assessed by Key Groups, 1998*

	ADA	ACLU	AFS	LCV	CON	NTU	NFIB	COC	ACU	NTLC	CHC
Senators											
M. McConnell	0	14	0	0	14	63	100	94	92	93	91
J. Bunning	0	7	0	8	2	46	100	94	92	92	10
Representatives											
E. Whitfield	5	13	22	23	32	47	100	88	96	92	100
R. Lewis	0	6	0	0	2	51	100	100	100	100	100
A. Northrup	0	13	11	8	13	47	100	100	88	87	100
H. Rogers	5	6	13	15	13	46	100	88	92	95	100

*For abbreviations, see p. 220.

LOUISIANA

The story of Louisiana politics is the recent transformation of a one-party state in the Deep South into a strong two-party state with Republicans emerging as a viable alternative to the Democratic Party. In the 1980s Louisiana had its first Republican governor in the twentieth century and five of seven seats in the U.S. House of Representatives. It was a big step forward for a party that had been in the political wilderness for over a hundred years. It is all the more remarkable because registered Democrats outnumber registered Republicans by two to one. Republicans have now set their sights on gaining control of the state legislature and on ousting the two Democratic U.S. senators.

In Congress, the Democratic Party–sponsored Civil Rights Bill of 1957 set in motion the train of events that empowered the Republican Party to challenge the Democratic Party, initially in national elections and then in statewide elections. In 1956, Dwight Eisenhower won Louisiana against Adlai Stevenson, and this Republican win was repeated in 1964 when Barry Goldwater carried the state despite Lyndon Johnson's landslide national victory. In the 1970s the Republican social agenda began attracting many conservative pro-life Catholics and Protestants, and the Republican economic agenda wooed the middle classes. In 1975 Democrats retaliated by discarding the closed party primary for an open one that forced Republicans to face the same intense competition in the primary that Democrats had faced for years. If no candidate received a majority in the open primary, the two top candidates, regardless of party affiliation, met in a runoff. Even with this disadvantage, Republicans won the office of the governor in 1979 for the first time in the twentieth century.

Before the 1960s, the Republican Party existed only in name in Louisiana. After Eisenhower's surprising win in 1956, three businessmen—Charles Lyons, George Despot, and Tom Stagg, all anti–civil rights conservatives—began recruiting candidates to run for state-level offices, and in doing so, they founded, in 1965, the Republican state central committee. The anti–civil rights stance of the party proved immensely popular and may have helped the party to elect David Treen as governor in 1979. Continued efforts to build grass-roots support on social, fiscal, and racial issues paid off handsomely in the Reagan and Bush years. A caucus was organized in the legislature as the number of Republican legislators grew.

Because of the difference in size between the Democratic and Republican parties, they are subject to different state laws with regard to membership, elections, and committees. Unlike other states, Louisiana is divided into parishes, rather than counties, and Republicans have parish executive committees at the local level and a state central committee at the state level. They also have a state council, which is the central committee's political arm overseeing elections and party building. Some of the districts have district chairs. Other members of the state committee are all statewide and federal Republican elected officials, Republican state legislators, and representatives of para organizations, such as Young Republicans, Black Republicans, College Republicans, Hispanic Republicans, and Women Republicans. The social conservatives and fiscal conservatives form the two main wings of the party, but factional loyalties are not as yet disruptive of party unity.

Republican Presidential Victories, 1860–2000
Total: 8 (1876, 1956, 1964, 1972, 1980, 1984, 1988, 2000)

Republican Governors of Louisiana, 1860–2000
Henry Clay Warmoth, 1868–1872; Pinckney Benton Stewart Pinchback, 1872–1873; John McEnery, 1873; William Pitt Kellogg, 1873–1877; David Conner Treen, 1980–1984; Charles Elson "Buddy" Roemer III, 1988–1992; Murphy J. "Mike" Foster, 1996– .

ADDRESS: Louisiana Republican Party, 7916 Wrenwood Blvd., Suite E, Baton Rouge, LA 70809

Tel.: (225) 928-2998
www.lagop.com

BIBLIOGRAPHY
Lamis, Alexander P. *The Two-Party South.* New York: Oxford University Press, 1990.
Theodoulou, Stella Z. *The Louisiana Republican Party, 1948–1984: The Building of a State Political Party.* Tulane Studies in Political Science, vol. 18. New Orleans: Tulane University Department of Political Science, 1985.

Louisiana Congressional Delegation, Voting Record as Assessed by Key Groups, 1998*

	ADA	ACLU	AFS	LCV	CON	NTU	NFIB	COC	ACU	NTLC	CHC
Representatives											
W. J. Tauzin	5	7	0	8	13	47	100	100	88	89	92
J. McCrery	5	21	11	8	6	60	100	100	96	86	83
J. Cooksey	0	14	17	8	13	48	100	100	96	89	91
R. H. Baker	0	6	0	8	21	51	100	100	95	95	100

*For abbreviations, see p. 220.

MAINE

Maine, which was once a part of Massachusetts, was a solid Republican state between 1854 and 1954. It had only five Democratic governors in its history. However, since 1954 the two parties have alternated in power at both the gubernatorial and legislative levels. At the presidential level, the turnaround was significant. Between 1860 and 1960, Maine voted Democratic in only one presidential election, but has voted Democratic in five of ten presidential elections since 1964, when it helped Lyndon Johnson trounce Barry Goldwater. Changing demographics pushed Democrats to the fore in electoral politics in the 1950s. The Republican Party also began to feel the effects of ideological strife between moderates and the new social and religious conservatives. It was this tension that led to the election of Edmund Muskie as governor in 1954.

As the parties became even in their electoral strengths, they also became parallel in their organizational modes. The thirty years from 1960 to 1990 were the worst in Maine's Republican Party history, as the party periodically lost control of the legislature, the governor's office, and even its majority in the U.S. congressional delegation. Maine tends to be a moderate state, and historically Maine Republicans have been more interested in competent administration than in ideology. As conservatives gained influence within the party, however, internal disagreements precluded efforts by state leaders to focus on party organization at the local levels. Moderates regained control of the party in the 1980s, and since then party fortunes have improved somewhat. The party went so far as to endorse the Equal Rights Amendment in 1984 and a pro-choice plank on abortion in 1988.

The basic unit of party organization is the town or municipal committee elected biannually by the town caucus. At the next level is the county committee, of which there are fourteen. The Republican state committee at the apex of the organizational pyramid has fifty-nine members—two to five members from each county in addition to representatives of the legislative caucus, Republican members of Congress from the state, two members of the RNC, and representatives of para groups such as Maine Young Republicans. The state executive committee sets the agenda for the party and determines party policies and programs. The annual conventions set forth the party platform and provide a forum for campaigning by prospective candidates.

The major trend in party organization is toward centralization. The state committee has reasserted its rights to direct and monitor more closely the activities of the town and county committees. The state organization has also developed the technology to handle fund-raising for candidates and, as a result, has gained power relative to the legislative caucus.

Republican Presidential Victories, 1860–2000
Total: 30 (1860, 1864, 1868, 1872, 1876, 1880, 1884, 1888, 1892, 1896, 1900, 1904, 1908, 1916, 1920, 1924, 1928, 1932, 1936, 1940, 1944, 1948, 1952, 1956, 1960, 1972, 1976, 1980, 1984, 1988)

Republican Governors of Maine, 1860–2000
Lot Myrick Morrill, 1858–1861; Israel Washburn Jr., 1861–1863; Abner Coburn, 1863–1864; Samuel Cony, 1864–1867; Joshua Lawrence Chamberlain, 1867–1871; Sidney Perham, 1871–1874; Nelson Dingley Jr., 1874–1876; Seldon Connor, 1876–1879; Daniel Franklin Davis, 1880–1881; Frederick Robie, 1883–1887; Joseph Robinson Bodwell, 1887; Sebastian Streeter Marble, 1887–1889; Edwin Chick Burleigh, 1889–1893; Henry B. Cleaves, 1893–1897; Llewellyn Powers, 1897–1901; John Fremont Hill, 1901–1905; William Titcomb Cobb, 1905–1909; Bert Manfred Fernald, 1909–1911; William Thomas Haines, 1913–1915; Carl Elias Milliken, 1917–1921; Frederick Hale Parkhurst, 1921; Percival Proctor Baxter, 1921–1925; Ralph Owen Brewster, 1925–1929; William Turdor Gardiner, 1929–1933; Lewis Orin Barrows, 1937–1941; Sumner Sewall, 1941–1945; Horace Augustus Hildreth, 1945–1949; Frederick George Payne, 1949–1952; Burton Melvin Cross, 1952–1955; Nathaniel M. Haskell, 1953; Robert Nelson Haskell, 1959; John Hathaway Reed, 1959–1967; John Rettie McKernan, 1987–1995.

ADDRESS: Maine Republican Party, 100 Water Street, Hallowell, ME 04347

Tel.: (207) 622-6247
www.mainegop.com

BIBLIOGRAPHY
Hayes, Kenneth P. "Maine Political Parties." In *New England Political Parties*, ed. Josephine F. Milburn, and William Doyle. Cambridge, MA: Schenkman, 1983.

Palmer, Kenneth T., G. Thomas Taylor, and Marcus A. LiBrizzi. *Maine Politics & Government*. Lincoln: University of Nebraska Press, 1992.

Maine Congressional Delegation, Voting Record as Assessed by Key Groups, 1998*

	ADA	ACLU	AFS	LCV	CON	NTU	NFIB	COC	ACU	NTLC	CHC
Senators											
O. Snowe	35	57	56	50	59	49	89	78	40	36	36
S. Collins	35	57	44	50	59	53	100	78	36	50	36

*For abbreviations, see p. 220.

MARYLAND

Maryland is a state where Democrats have held an overwhelming superiority in numbers and organization since the Civil War. Unlike states in the Deep South, the Democratic majority in Maryland was not rolled back during the civil rights struggle of the 1950s and 1960s, and Republicans have been unable to gain sufficient traction to displace their rivals in major national and statewide elections, much less in local ones. The last time the GOP controlled the state legislature was in 1918. There have been only five Republican governors in the state's history.

Republicans had their best chance to make inroads in the state after the election of Spiro Agnew as governor in 1966 and his selection as Nixon's vice presidential candidate in 1968. Agnew's conviction for bribery and the resignation of the vice presidency in 1973, however, proved a major setback. Party leaders tried to recover by initiating a number of organizational reforms, including the establishment of a permanent headquarters in Annapolis, the selection of Artis T. Allen as the party's first African American chair, and the introduction of computerized information and fund-raising networks. These efforts, however, failed to produce the desired results, and Democrats continued to win elections. Tensions between conservatives and moderates also took a heavy toll on party unity. The 1994 Republican tide helped to lift the Maryland Republicans. In the 107th Congress, the brightest feature for Republicans is the four of eight seats they hold in the U.S. House. In all other offices, they trail Democrats badly. However, in the state legislature, they have made some progress from the days when there were so few Republican legislators that the Republican minority leader regularly attended Democratic leadership meetings until 1991. Since 1994 Republicans tend to be more united on substantive issues than the Democrats, especially during election years. The Republican state central committee is more involved in recruiting candidates, but does not distribute cash contributions.

Republican Presidential Victories, 1860–2000
Total: 12 (1864, 1896, 1900, 1920, 1924, 1928, 1948, 1952, 1956, 1972, 1984, 1988)

Republican Governors of Maryland, 1860–2000
Lloyd Lowndes Jr., 1896–1900; Phillips Lee Goldsborough, 1912–1916; Harry Whinna Nice, 1935–1939; Theodore Roosevelt McKeldin, 1951–1959; Spiro Theodore Agnew, 1967–1969.

ADDRESS: Maryland Republican Party, 15 West Street, Annapolis, MD 21401

Tel.: (410) 269-0113
www.mdgop.org

BIBLIOGRAPHY
Callcott, George H. *Maryland Political Behavior: Four Centuries of Political Culture*. Baltimore: Maryland Historical Society, 1986.

Kent, Frank Richardson. *The Story of Maryland Politics*. Hatboro, PA: Tradition Press, 1968.

Maryland Congressional Delegation, Voting Record as Assessed by Key Groups, 1998*

	ADA	ACLU	AFS	LCV	CON	NTU	NFIB	COC	ACU	NTLS	CHC
Representatives											
W. T. Gilchrest	35	44	22	62	13	42	77	89	44	66	64
R. L. Ehrlich Jr.	5	25	11	15	42	55	93	94	92	95	75
R. G. Bartlett	5	6	11	0	77	66	100	78	100	97	100
C. A. Morella	65	81	78	92	85	40	36	56	20	34	17

*For abbreviations, see p. 220.

MASSACHUSETTS

The Republican Party has not fared well in Massachusetts in the twentieth century. In other states, GOP fortunes have followed a rhythm of their own, in tune with periodic realignments and changing demographics. However, there has been no significant resurgence of even moderate conservatism in the Bay State since the end of World War II. This contrasts with the dominance of Federalist–Whig–Republican rule for a whole century from the Revolution when the old-stock Yankee elites controlled all the levers of power in politics as well as in commerce, religion, and industry. In the ninety-three state elections from 1797 to 1890 (Massachusetts had annual elections until 1920) Republicans won all but ten and controlled both houses of legislature.

The decline in GOP power began in the 1920s with the great Irish immigration adding boatloads every day to the Democratic party rolls. In 1948 Republicans lost control of the state government for the first time. They recovered briefly in 1952, but not for too long. With the arrival of the Kennedy clan in 1952 (the year John F. Kennedy was elected senator), the Republican Party was in full retreat. The Kennedy presidency was the shining moment for Massachusetts Democrats. The party swept into all the important constitutional offices, and Tip O'Neill began his long, illustrious career as the first Democratic Speaker. In the course of the next twenty years the whole state became a Democratic fiefdom, and for every Republican in the state legislature there were four Democrats. Very soon the GOP did not have candidates to run for more than half the legislative seats. The only visible office that they succeeded in retaining periodically was that of the governor. From 1962 to 2000, Republicans have occupied the governor's office for twenty years as against eighteen for the Democrats. A succession of Republican leaders, including John Volpe, Francis Sargent, and William Weld, were responsible for this bright spot on an otherwise bleak picture for the GOP. It is significant that all these Republican leaders were moderates.

One hopeful feature for the GOP is that the unusual ethnicity-driven political culture of the state is seen as subsiding after many decades. The great cultural antagonism between the English, Protestant Republicans and the Irish, Catholic, and working-class Democrats has lost much of its relevance. A new middle class of socially moderate and economically affluent voters is less guided by ethnic loyalties at the voting booth and is capable of splitting votes in races where issues predominate.

As in all one-party states, party organization is weak in Massachusetts: in the case of the Democrats, because they would win elections anyway with or without a disciplined party to support them; in the case of the Republicans, because even the best organization could not help them overcome their handicaps. The lack of a strong opposition has produced weak political parties. Unlike the faction-ridden Democratic Party, the Republicans are well disciplined and united on most issues, and they are also free of sniping from the religious right or from hard-core conservatives.

Under state law, Republicans are organized on two levels: local town and ward committees and the state committee. One man and one woman are elected for four-year terms to the party's central committee from each of the state's forty Senate districts. The state committee includes state as well as U. S. legislative leaders, but they do not have a vote. Executive functions are assigned to an executive committee and legislative functions to the state committee. Only elected officials make policy and manage the party while state committee and party convention regulars merely ratify the decisions of party leaders. Delegates to the state convention are chosen at town and ward committee meetings.

Republican Presidential Victories, 1860–2000

Total: 20 (1860, 1864, 1868. 1872, 1876, 1880, 1884, 1888, 1892, 1896, 1900, 1904, 1908, 1916, 1920, 1924, 1952, 1956, 1980, 1984)

Republican Governors of Massachusetts, 1860–2000

Nathaniel Prentice Banks, 1858–1861; John Albion Andrew, 1861–1866; Alexander Hamilton Bullock, 1866–1869; William Claflin, 1869–1872; William Barrett Washburn, 1872–1874; Thomas Talbot, 1874–1875, 1879–1880; Alexander Hamilton Rice, 1876–1879; John Davis Long, 1880–1883; George Dexter Robinson, 1884–1887; Oliver Ames, 1887–1890; John Quincy Adams Brackett, 1890–1891; Frederick Thomas Greenhalge, 1894–1896; Roger Wolcott, 1896–1900; Winthrop Murray Crane, 1900–1903; John Lewis Bates, 1903–1905; Curtis Guild Jr., 1906–1909; Eben Sumner Draper, 1909–1911; Samuel Walker McCall, 1916–1919; Calvin Coolidge, 1919–1921; Channing Harris Cox, 1921–1925; Alvan Tufts Fuller, 1925–1929; Frank G. Allen, 1929–1931; Leverett Saltonstall, 1939–1945; Robert Fiske Bradford, 1947–1949; Christian Archibald Herter, 1953–1957; John Anthony Volpe, 1961–1963, 1965–1969; Francis William Sargent, 1969–1975; William Weld, 1991–1997; Paul Cellucci, 1997–2001; Jane Swift, 2001– .

ADDRESS: Massachusetts Republican Party, 21 Milk Street, Fourth Floor, Boston, MA 02109

Tel.: (617) 357-1998

www.massgop.com

BIBLIOGRAPHY

Barbrook, Alec. *God Save the Commonwealth: An Electoral History of Massachusetts*. Amherst: University of Massachusetts Press, 1973.

Frier, Ted, and Larry Overlan. *Time for a Change: The Return of the Republican Party in Massachusetts*. Boston: Lafayette Graphics/Davis Press, 1992.

MICHIGAN

Michigan has a special place in the history of the Republican Party, for it was in Jackson, Michigan, that the GOP officially took its name, adopted a platform, and nominated its first candidates. The association stuck for over 100 years. There was only one Democratic governor between 1894 and 1932. No Democrats were elected to the legislature for many sessions, and only a few before 1946. This long honeymoon lasted until after World War II when the influx of African Americans into Michigan, and particularly Detroit, swelled the Democratic Party rolls. The watershed was Democratic G. Mennen Williams's governorship beginning in 1949. Since then, seats in the governor's office and the legislature have alternated between the two parties. In the 107th Congress, Democrats have both U. S. Senate seats and nine of the sixteen U. S. House seats.

Republicans have managed partially to stem the Democratic tide with the help of strong leaders such as George Romney, William Milliken, and the current governor, John Engler. Democrats, on the other hand, have had only two governors between 1961 and 2000. In 1961 a Republican plan of action to maintain party strength set forth new directions in six key areas: research, education, press relations, advertisement and promotion, special events, and field organization. The party organization was geared to a full-time operation, and it adopted business marketing methods to sell the conservative ideology as a product. The revitalized Republican agenda was a sensational triumph for the party. At this time, ticket splitting became common at the ballot box, encouraged by the George Romney wing of the party, which refused to endorse Barry Goldwater for president in 1964. By 1970 Republicans were gaining support in urban areas as a result of a Democratic debacle over busing. It also benefited from a white backlash against the growing power of unions and African Americans in the Democratic Party and imbroglios over party primaries.

The Republican Party is ranked as organizationally strong both at the state and local levels. Both the state and local party organizations are dominated by John Engler, who is active in party affairs. He sets the political agenda, suggests party chairs, raises millions in party funds, and monitors recruitment of candidates. He has also been successful in fending off takeover efforts by the religious right and the prolife wing.

Republican Presidential Victories, 1860–2000
Total: 26 (1860, 1864, 1868, 1872, 1876, 1880, 1884, 1888, 1892, 1896, 1900, 1904, 1908, 1916, 1920, 1924, 1928, 1940, 1948, 1952, 1956, 1972, 1976, 1980, 1984, 1988)

Republican Governors of Michigan, 1860–2000
Moses Wisner, 1859–1861; Austin Blair, 1861–1865; Henry Howland Crapo, 1865–1869; Henry Porter Baldwin, 1869–1873; John Judson Bagley, 1873–1877; Charles Miller Crosswell, 1877–1881; David Howell Jerome, 1881–1883; Russell Alexander Alger, 1885–1887; Cyrus Gray Luce, 1887–1891; John Tyler Rich, 1893–1897; Hazen Stuart Pingree, 1897–1901; Aaron Thomas Bliss, 1901–1905; Fred Maltby Warner, 1905–1911; Chase Salmon Osborn, 1911–1913; Albert Edson Sleeper, 1917–1921; Alexander Joseph Groesbeck, 1921–1927; Fred Warren Green, 1927–1931; Wilber Marion Bruckner, 1931–1933; Frank Dwight Fitzgerald, 1935–1937; 1939; Luren Dudley Dickinson, 1939–1941; Harry Francis Kelly, 1943–1947; Kim Sigler, 1947–1949; George Wilken Romney, 1963–1969; William Grawn Milliken, 1969–1983; John Engler, 1991– .

ADDRESS: Michigan Republican Party, 2121 East Grand River, Lansing, MI 48912

Tel.: (517) 487-5413

www.migop.org

BIBLIOGRAPHY
Browne, William P., and Kenneth VerBurg. *Michigan Politics and Government: Facing Change in a Complex State*. Lincoln: University of Nebraska Press, 1995.

Stieber, Carolyn. *The Politics of Change in Michigan*. East Lansing: Michigan State University Press, 1970.

Michigan Congressional Delegation, Voting Record as Assessed by Key Groups, 1998*

	ADA	ACLU	AFS	LCV	CON	NTU	NFIB	COC	ACU	NTLC	CHC
Senator											
S. Abraham	5	14	22	13	67	65	100	83	76	89	91
Representatives											
P. Hoekstra	5	13	11	15	74	83	100	82	100	97	100
V. J. Ehlers	25	31	33	69	50	51	100	89	56	58	92
D. Camp	10	13	0	23	13	50	100	100	96	87	92
F. Upton	15	19	22	46	50	51	93	89	56	71	75
N. Smith	20	14	23	31	60	62	100	83	76	89	100
J. Knollenberg	0	13	11	8	13	50	100	100	96	95	100

*For abbreviations, see p. 220.

MINNESOTA

From the year Minnesota joined the union in 1858, Republicans dominated the state. Up to 1898 Republicans won every gubernatorial and presidential election. They also had the overwhelming majority in U.S. Senate and House elections. When former president Teddy Roosevelt, who had bolted the Republican Party and run as a Progressive, carried Minnesota in 1912, it marked the first time a Republican presidential candidate did not win the state. Twenty years later, Franklin D. Roosevelt became the first Democratic presidential candidate to win Minnesota, a feat he repeated in 1936 and 1940. In the early 1900s, Democrats, Independents, and later the Farmer-Labor Party (organized in 1944) began whittling away at the Republicans by winning local and statewide offices. Nevertheless, Republicans managed to hold the governor's office for thirty-six of the fifty-two years from 1901 to 1953. During this time, Republicans represented the state 72 percent of the time in the U.S. Senate. In the House, Republicans served 82 percent of the time, Farmer-Laborites 12 percent, and Democrats 6 percent. The Republicans took a big blow in 1948 when Hubert Humphrey became the first popularly elected Democratic U.S. Senator from Minnesota. In 1954, DFL candidate Orville Freeman won the governorship, the first time a Democrat had won that office in forty years. In 1958 Eugene McCarthy won a U.S. Senate seat, and when Humphrey became vice president in 1965, Walter Mondale was appointed to the U.S. Senate to fill his seat. These names dominated Minnesota politics for more than a third of a century, often shutting out the Republicans. The GOP has not controlled the state legislature since the 1970s. In 2001, they hold only three of eight U.S. House seats and no U.S. Senate seats.

In 1975, Minnesota Republicans tried to energize the party by calling themselves the Independent-Republican Party. They achieved some major successes by winning both U.S. Senate seats and the governorship in 1978. However, as undiluted Republicanism returned to national prominence in 1994, the name Independent was dropped the following year.

In a close three-way race in 1998, former wrestler and Reform Party candidate Jesse Ventura was elected governor, becoming the party's highest ranking elected official in the nation. However, Ventura left the party in 2000 and joined the Independence Party. The Republican Party is one of the three parties that meet the definition of a "major political party" under Minnesota law, the other two being the DFL and the Reform Party. The bottom level of the political pyramid is the precinct, but in the GOP hierarchy, the county, or state legislative district, is the basic unit. This level endorses candidates for offices within its region and selects delegates to the state committee. The state committee has 325 members, and the membership of the state executive committee is a more manageable number, typically about one-tenth the size of the state central committee. The key officers of the central committee are the chair and the executive director. Technically, the state convention is the ultimate arbiter of political platforms, policies, and programs. The conventions also choose presidential delegates in appropriate years.

Republican Presidential Victories, 1860–2000
Total: 20 (1860, 1864, 1868, 1872, 1876, 1880, 1884, 1888, 1892, 1896, 1900, 1904, 1908, 1916, 1920, 1924, 1928, 1952, 1956, 1972)

Republican Governors of Minnesota, 1860–2000
Alexander Ramsey, 1860–1863; Henry Adoniram Swift, 1863–1864; Stephen Miller, 1864–1866; William Rogerson Marshall, 1866–1870; Horace Austin, 1870–1874; Cushman Kellogg Davis, 1874–1876; John Sargent Pillsbury, 1876–1882; Lucius Frederick Hubbard, 1882–1887; Andrew Ryan McGill, 1887–1889; William Rush Merriam, 1889–1893; Knute Nelson, 1893–1895; David Marston Clough, 1895–1899; Samuel Rinnah Van Sant, 1901–1905; Adolph Olson Eberhart, 1909–1915; Joseph Alfred Arner Burnquist, 1915–1921; Jacob Aall Ottesen Preus, 1921–1925; Theodore Christianson, 1925–1931; Harold Edward Stassen, 1939–1943; Edward John Thye, 1943–1947; Luther Wallace Youngdahl, 1947–1951; Clyde Elmer Anderson, 1951–1955; Elmer Lee Anderson, 1961–1963; Harold LeVander, 1967–1971; Albert Harold Quie, 1979–1983; Arne Carlson, 1991–1999.

ADDRESS: Republican Party of Minnesota, 480 Cedar Street, Suite 560, St. Paul, MN 55101

Tel.: (651) 222-0022
www.gopmn.org

BIBLIOGRAPHY
Gieske, Millard L., and Edward R. Brandt, eds. *Perspectives on Minnesota Government and Politics.* Dubuque, IA: Kendall/Hunt, 1977.
Mitau, G. Theodore. *Politics in Minnesota.* 2d ed. Minneapolis: University of Minnesota Press, 1970.

Minnesota Congressional Delegation, Voting Record as Assessed by Key Groups, 1998*

	ADA	ACLU	AFS	LCV	CON	NTU	NFIB	COC	ACU	NTLC	CHC
Senator											
R. Grams	0	14	0	0	95	73	89	94	88	96	100
Representatives											
G. Gutknecht	5	6	11	8	31	48	93	94	92	92	100
J. Ramstad	20	13	0	85	33	48	93	94	60	50	42

*For abbreviations, see p. 220.

*For abbreviations, see p. 220.

MISSISSIPPI

After the Civil War, the Republican Party emerged in Mississippi in the 1860s as a progressive, biracial party, but quickly split into all-white and nearly all-black factions. Historically the minority party in the state, it became more electorally competitive in the 1960s and 1970s as the national Democratic Party nominated more liberal presidential candidates, and today the Republican Party is nearly as strong as the Democratic Party.

As members of a national party opposing the extension of slavery into western territories, Republican presidential candidates received no votes in Mississippi until 1868. Ulysses S. Grant became the first and only Republican presidential candidate to win Mississippi until Barry Goldwater ran in 1964. During Reconstruction in the 1860s and 1870s, the enfranchisement of African Americans and disenfranchisement of some Confederate whites led to Republican political control, as the party elected four successive white governors, two African-American secretaries of state, and one white and one black lieutenant governor. In addition to blacks, the party included some businessmen, northern migrants, and those who before the war were pro-union and upper-class Whigs.

By 1882 the state party had racially split into the Lily White (all white) and Black and Tans (biracial) factions. Republicans were unable to win any state or federal offices after Reconstruction, and factional conflicts within the party became a battle for national party recognition and for distribution of federal patronage during Re-

publican presidencies. After alternations in factional control of the party, whites in a special meeting in 1915 elected M.J. Muldihill as state party chair, who, despite a challenge from black attorney Perry Howard and black dentist S.D. Redmond, was recognized by the national committee. After the Mississippi party sent separate delegations to the 1920 national convention, the 1924 convention seated the Black and Tans and recognized them as the official state party. The Lily Whites were repeatedly unsuccessful in unseating these regular Republicans, and in most presidential elections they offered a rival slate of electors to state voters. In 1954, after registering first under a state party registration law and pursuing a court challenge, the Lily Whites gained state recognition as the official Republican Party. Despite a compromise that seated both factions at the 1956 national convention, the Dwight Eisenhower administration began channeling patronage to the Lily Whites in an effort to gain white votes. In 1960 Howard declined to challenge Lily White recognition by the national party, and the state party began to desegregate.

As the state party attracted more young, urban professionals in the 1950s, it opened a permanent state headquarters in Jackson in 1959. Under party chairman Wirt Yerger Jr., organizational activity increased, campaign workshops were held for party workers, nationally known Republicans such as Barry Goldwater spoke to the party faithful, and platform resolutions reflected the conservative nature of the party. The first two Republicans to win office in the twentieth century were a candidate for a county attorney position in 1961 and a candidate for the state legislature in 1962. The spirited but unsuccessful gubernatorial campaigns of party-switching public service commissioner Rubel Phillips in 1963 and 1967 and of progressive businessman Gil Carmichael in 1975 and 1979 helped build the party, though Phillips's second defeat cost the party the three state legislative seats it had gained in his previous bid.

The state party has benefited from a succession of aggressive state party chairs. By 1968, under Clarke Reed, the party was organized in all counties, some African-American professionals were recruited as party workers, and Teen Age Republican clubs were started. State party campaign assistance to Thad Cochran and Trent Lott helped elect both of them to the U.S. House in 1972. In 1978, Cochran was elected to the U.S. Senate. Ebbie Spivey and Evelyn McPhail led the growing party in the 1980s and early 1990s when the party elected Lott as its second GOP senator and Kirk Fordice as the state's first Republican governor since Reconstruction.

Organizationally, the state executive committee consists of fifty members with ten elected for each of the five congressional districts. County committees vary in size, averaging about twelve members, and are most active in urban areas. Affiliated groups are the Mississippi Federation of Republican Women, the Mississippi Republican Elected Officials Association, the Teen Age Republicans with thirty chapters across the state, and the Mississippi College Republican Federation, which unites the College Republican groups established at most schools.

The party operates a modern headquarters in the state capital with a staff including the chair, executive director, directors of finance, politics, communications, and information systems, and two assistants. Its quarterly newsletter is entitled *Party Lines*. Its impressive fund-raising operation includes the United Republican Fund for small donors who contribute monthly, and the Capital Foundation for larger donors. National Republican officeholders typically keynote annual fund-raising dinners, and the state party financially supports its candidates. The party also honors the party faithful and has sought to combat voter

fraud by requiring that voters show an identification card.

Some problems facing the party include difficulty in fully staffing the county executive committees, though committee members are more active during campaigns than their Democratic counterparts. Few African Americans hold party or elected positions. As late as 1999 the party failed to contest all elected offices including half of the seats in a state legislature that was two-thirds Democratic and failed to contest over two-thirds of county supervisory offices. Yet Republicans have closed the partisan identification gap with Democrats among average citizens, as many conservative whites became Republican during the Fordice administration. In the 107th Congress (2001–2002), both Mississippi senators are Republican as are two of five members in the U.S. House of Representatives.

Republican Presidential Victories, 1860–2000
Total: 9 (1872, 1964, 1972, 1980, 1984, 1988, 1992, 1996, 2000)

Republican Governors of Mississippi, 1860–2000
Adelbert Ames, 1868–1870, 1874–1876; James Lusk Alcorn, 1870–1871; Ridgely Ceylon Powers, 1871–1874; Kirk Fordice, 1992–2000.

ADDRESS: Republican Party of Mississippi, 415 Yazoo Street, Jackson, MS 39201

Tel.: (601) 948-5191

www.msgop.org

BIBLIOGRAPHY

Breaux, David, Stephen D. Shaffer, and Thomas Wilson. "Mississippi." In *State Party Profiles: A 50-State Guide to Development, Organization, and Resources*, ed. Andrew M. Appleton and Daniel S. Ward, 79–80. Washington, DC: Congressional Quarterly, 1997.

Ginzl, David J. "Lily-Whites Versus Black-and-Tans: Mississippi Republicans During the Hoover Administration." *The Journal of Mississippi History* 42 (1980): 194–211.

Hathorn, Billy Burton. "Challenging the Status Quo: Rubel Lex Phillips and the Mississippi

Republican Party, 1963–1967." *The Journal of Mississippi History* 47 (1985): 240–64.

Hy, Ronn, and Richard T. Saeger. "The Nature and Role of Political Parties." In *Mississippi Government and Politics in Transition*, ed. David M. Landry and Joseph B. Parker, 204–17. Dubuque, IA: Kendall/Hunt, 1976.

Krane, Dale, and Stephen D. Shaffer. *Mississippi Government and Politics: Modernizers Versus Traditionalists*. Lincoln: University of Nebraska Press, 1992.

Land, Guy Paul. "Mississippi Republicanism and the 1960 Presidential Election." *The Journal of Mississippi History* 40 (1991): 33–48.

Loewen, James W., and Charles Sallis, eds. *Mississippi: Conflict & Change*. New York: Pantheon Books, 1974.

Parker, Joseph B., ed. *Politics in Mississippi*. Salem, WI: Sheffield, 1993.

Shaffer, Stephen D., and David A. Breaux. "Mississippi: The 'True Believers' Challenge the Party of Everyone." In *Southern State Party Organizations and Activists*, ed. Charles D. Hadley and Lewis Bowman, 65–74. Westport, CT: Praeger, 1995.

Walton, Hanes. *Black Republicans: The Politics of the Black and Tans*. Metuchen, NJ: Scarecrow Press, 1975.

Mississippi Congressional Delegation, Voting Record as Assessed by Key Groups, 1998*

	ADA	ACLU	AFS	LCV	CON	NTU	NFIB	COC	ACU	NTLC	CHC
Senators											
T. Cochran	0	29	0	0	67	57	89	100	81	63	73
T. Lott	0	14	0	0	14	61	100	94	92	82	100
Representatives											
R. Wicker	0	6	0	8	4	53	100	100	96	97	100
C. Pickering	0	7	0	8	13	52	100	94	100	100	100

*For abbreviations, see p. 220.

MISSOURI

Missouri's Republican Party, long playing catch-up in state politics, rallied in the last three decades of the twentieth century to attain a competitive stance against the Democrats. In the nineteenth century the party won the struggle to remain in the union during the Civil War and then dominated politics briefly during the postwar era of disenfranchised former Confederates. The party spent the rest of the century winning only occasional victories, primarily when factional disputes divided the Democrats. Electoral victories became more frequent in the first few decades of the new century, but become rare again with the ascendancy of the Democrats' nationwide New Deal coalition of voters in the 1930s and 1940s.

Missouri Republicans' struggles continued until 1968, when John Danforth upset the incumbent attorney general to win the first statewide post for the party since the end of World War II. Danforth's victory energized the Republican faithful and inspired subsequent fund-raising efforts. Momentum from this victory helped another young candidate, Christopher "Kit" Bond, capture the state auditor's office in 1971. Bond then ran for governor in 1972. Based largely upon candidate organizational and fund-raising momentum, coupled with Richard Nixon's landslide victory for the presidency at the top of the ticket, Missouri's Republicans, led by Bond, won races for the governor, lieutenant governor, and state auditor. Bond became the first Republican governor since 1945. Clearly, the party had arrived.

The party's successes in the 1970s and 1980s

were anchored in the success of their three political stars at winning an array of statewide offices: John Danforth, Christopher Bond, and John Ashcroft. The trio dominated Missouri's three biggest political prizes—the governorship and both United States Senate seats—for most of those two decades. Only Bond's loss of the governorship in 1976 (which he recaptured four years later) marred their collective winning streak. Danforth, Bond, and Ashcroft won consistently. Their aggressive fund-raising efforts financed extensive and efficient personal organizations coupled with professional media campaigns produced by experts outside the state.

Meanwhile, other party nominees began winning top offices. Republicans captured the offices of lieutenant governor, secretary of state, and state auditor regularly during the 1970s and 1980s. During this time, the party's congressional delegation grew steadily, if less spectacularly, until four of the state's nine representatives were Republicans and held what became widely viewed as electorally "safe" seats. By 2001, five of the state's nine representatives were Republican.

In addition, the party maintained a state headquarters in Jefferson City staffed by an executive director and a cadre of full-time field organizers. Overall, the party maintained its ability to raise more funds than the Democrats.

On the other hand, Republican stalwarts continued to be frustrated in attempts to capture either chamber of the state's General Assembly. However, the size of the party's minority delegation continued to increase throughout this period as the number of Republicans came to rival that of the majority Democrats. Republicans increased their policy-making clout in these years by frequently forming coalitions with conservative Democrats to win important legislative victories.

Moreover, although party faithful hail 1968 as a breakthrough year marked by Danforth's victory, they bemoan 1992. That year the party's scandal-plagued gubernatorial nominee, state Attorney General William Webster, led the Republican's entire statewide ticket to a bitter defeat.

Among the voters, the statewide base of power for Missouri Republicans traditionally has been anchored within two areas—primarily the rural counties of the Ozark region in the southwestern part of the state and in the wealthy suburbs of west and southwest St. Louis County. In addition, the party traditionally dominated a few isolated counties along the northern border with Iowa. However, as the century drew to a close, Republicans increasingly gained strength in the state's southeastern counties, popularly known as the Missouri "bootheel" region. In addition, party candidates have been increasingly successful in several areas of northern Missouri, winning selected General Assembly and the U.S. House of Representatives Ninth District seats.

On the other hand, the party's base in populous St. Louis County has been significantly threatened by an influx of Democrats moving north, northwest, and southward from the city of St. Louis. Republican electoral strength likewise has been evolving outward as party voters also migrated to neighboring, traditionally bedroom, communities in nearby counties to the north, west, and southwest.

Across the state the party's evolution generally has been slower in the Kansas City, Missouri, metropolitan area. Instead of going to nearby suburbs in Missouri, Republicans migrating from that city tended to move westward across the state line into the wealthier suburbs of Johnson County, Kansas. This further weakened the position of the party faithful remaining in one of Missouri's traditionally Democratic strongholds. Likewise, wealthier Republicans moving into the Kansas City metropolitan area from around the nation increasingly were settling in the plush Kansas suburbs instead of choosing to live in the established comfortable neighborhoods of the city.

Thus, successful Republican statewide candidates have won with a strategy of carrying vote-rich St. Louis County by a comfortably large margin coupled with attaining even bigger margins among Missouri's rural counties, particularly those in the Ozarks.

Although occasional infighting has attracted news coverage, the party has more recently escaped the factional strife between economic conservatives and social conservatives that at times has plagued Republicans nationwide. In general, social conservatives appear to have gained the upper hand politically among the party statewide. Party fund-raising in Missouri has tended to attract donations from organizations traditionally associated with Republicans nationwide—major corporations, including those prominent in the state's economy as well as outsiders with interests in the outcome of Missouri elections.

State laws extensively regulate the organization and operation of political parties in Missouri. Parties are mandated to establish committees at six levels: county, legislative district, senatorial district, circuit judicial district, congressional district, and statewide. State committees are composed of sixty-eight members—one man and one woman representing each of the thirty-four state senatorial district committees. Regulations direct state committees when to hold annual meetings, nominate candidates, and write platforms. Although not required, major political parties have chosen to locate state headquarters near the capitol in Jefferson City.

In sum, Missouri's Republicans have made the state generally competitive politically. They have won many statewide contests in the last three decades of the twentieth century and, at the beginning of the twenty-first century, are challenging Democrats for control of the Missouri General Assembly. A key to their continued competitiveness remains their superior fund-raising ability. Nurturing and even increasing this important advantage is probably essential to continued electoral success.

Republican Presidential Victories, 1860–2000
Total: 14 (1864, 1868, 1904, 1908, 1920, 1924, 1928, 1952, 1968, 1972, 1980, 1984, 1988, 2000)

Republican Governors of Missouri, 1860–2000
Thomas Clement Fletcher, 1865–1869; Joseph Washington McClurg, 1869–1871; Herbert Spencer Hadley, 1909–1913; Arthur Mastick Hyde, 1921–1925; Samuel Aaron Baker, 1925–1929; Henry Stewart Caulfield, 1929–1933; Forrest Donnell, 1941–1945; Christopher S. "Kit" Bond, 1973–1977, 1981–1985; John Ashcroft, 1985–1993.

ADDRESS: Missouri Republican Party, P.O. Box 73, Jefferson City, MO 65102

Tel.: (573) 636-3146

www.mogop.org

BIBLIOGRAPHY

Burnett, R. E., and Cordell E. Smith. "Missourians and the Political Parties." In *Missouri Government and Politics*, ed. Richard J. Hardy, Richard R. Dohm, and David A. Leuthold, 56–69. Columbia: University of Missouri Press, 1995.

Dewhirst, Robert E. *The Almanac of Missouri Politics 2000*. Elmhurst, IL: Star Point Press, 2000.

Hardy, Richard J., and Richard R. Dohm, eds. *Missouri Government and Politics*. Columbia: University of Missouri Press, 1985.

Karsch, Robert F. *The Government of Missouri*. Columbia, MO: Lucas Bros., 1978.

Paddock, Joel. "Political Parties." In *Reinventing Missouri Government: A Case Study in State Experiments at Work*, ed. Denny E. Pilant, 24–36. Fort Worth, TX: Harcourt Brace, 1994.

———. "Missouri." In *State Party Profiles: A 50-State Guide to Development, Organization, and Resources*, ed. Andrew Appleton and Daniel Ward, 177–84. Washington, DC: Congressional Quarterly Press, 1997.

Missouri Congressional Delegation, Voting Record as Assessed by Key Groups, 1998*

	ADA	ACLU	AFS	LCV	CON	NTU	NFIB	COC	ACU	NTLC	CHC
Senators											
C. S. Bond	15	29	11	0	25	53	100	89	72	68	72
J. Ashcroft	5	14	0	0	89	80	89	78	100	100	100

(continued)

Missouri Congressional Delegation, Voting Record as Assessed by Key Groups, 1998* *(continued)*

	ADA	ACLU	AFS	LCV	CON	NTU	NFIB	COC	ACU	NTLC	CHC
Representatives											
J. M. Talent	5	6	0	15	2	51	100	100	96	95	100
R. Blunt	0	6	0	8	4	54	100	82	100	95	92
J. A. Emerson	5	6	11	8	33	51	93	83	92	89	100
K. Hulshof	15	6	0	38	21	48	100	100	88	84	92

*For abbreviations, see p. 220.

MONTANA

The chief distinguishing feature of Montana politics is the high level of partisanship and electoral competition. Between 1972 (when the present state constitution was adopted) and 1996, the governor and the majority in each house of the state legislature were of the same party for only six years. For another six years, both parties were equally matched in the state legislature. Usually, state legislative seats are won with less than 55 percent of the popular vote. Also, since 1984, state senate seats have tended to change party control regularly.

This state of affairs came to an end in the early 1990s, when the Republicans trounced the Democrats at the polls, and the Democrats spent the rest of the decade regrouping. In 1994 Republicans won their largest majority in the state Senate and House: 62 and 68 percent, respectively. Currently, the only major office held by a Democrat is that of one U. S. Senator.

Party organizations are relatively weak in Montana for several reasons. Initiative and referendum provide Montanans a means of bypassing political parties. Because of the low population base, parties are unable to generate funds for their candidates in a meaningful way and thus have no means of influencing their success. The use of the direct primary to nominate all elective candidates and the use of the nonpartisan ballot to elect judges and city and school board officials also removes political parties from two common avenues of political participation. Political parties also tend to be highly regulated. The state-mandated political organization has

three levels: precinct, county, and state. The state central committee has delegates from the state's fifty-six counties.

The Republicans are more generally a rural and small-town party with its strongest geographic base in the rural "coyote" counties in eastern and central Montana. They do well in the middle-class suburbs of Billings and Great Falls. Republicans also do well among conservatives, prolifers, anti–gun control advocates, and a marginal group consisting of those who oppose taxation and disgruntled former union workers in industries hard hit by environmental laws. New immigrants from California, who tend to be wealthy and older, have settled in the western part of the state and have added to the Republican rolls. Montana has an open primary, which discourages party identification as do the nonpartisan primaries for local elections to the judicial or school boards. Open primaries encourage raiding, a practice in which members of one party pose as members of the other in order to boost the weakest candidate and prevent strong candidates from emerging for the rival party. However, the Republican presidential primary is nonbinding. National convention delegates picked by the state delegate convention may choose any candidate that they favor.

Republican Presidential Victories, 1892–2000
Total: 17 (1892, 1904, 1908, 1920, 1924, 1928, 1952, 1956, 1960, 1968, 1972, 1976, 1980 1984, 1988, 1996, 2000)

Republican Governors of Montana, 1889–2000
John Ezra Rickards, 1893–1897; Joseph Moore Dixon, 1921–1925; Samuel Clarence Ford, 1941–1949; John Hugo Aronson, 1953–1961; Donald

Grant Nutter, 1961–1962; Tim M. Babcock, 1962–1969; Stan Stephens, 1989–1993; Marc Francis Racicot, 1993–2001; Judy Martz, 2001– .

ADDRESS: Montana Republican Party, 1419-B Helena Avenue, Helena, MT 59601

Tel.: (406) 442-6469

www.mtgop.org

BIBLIOGRAPHY

Lopach, James J., ed. *We the People of Montana: The Workings of a Popular Government.* Missoula, MT: Mountain Press, 1983.

Waldron, Ellis, and Paul B. Wilson. *Atlas of Montana Elections, 1889–1976.* Missoula: University of Montana, 1978.

Montana Congressional Delegation, Voting Record as Assessed by Key Groups, 1998*

	ADA	ACLU	AFS	LCV	CON	NTU	NFIB	COC	ACU	NTLC	CHC
Senator											
C. Burns	0	29	11	0	14	64	100	100	84	81	91
Representative											
R. Hill	10	7	24	8	89	46	79	83	79	78	92

*For abbreviations, see p. 220.

NEBRASKA

Republicans dominated Nebraska politics from statehood in 1867, to the 1890s, when hard economic times offered Democrats and independents a number of electoral opportunities of which they took immediate advantage. Democrats adopted a strategy by which they would back fusion candidates representing any of a number of opposition groups. However, Republicans crept back into power after the courts declared fusion candidates illegal. In 1934, just after the New Deal, Republicans gained when an amendment to the state constitution created a unicameral legislature elected on a nonpartisan basis. This change in the electoral landscape helped Republican incumbents and shielded them from the national swing to the Democrats in the 1930s and 1940s. Another shift occurred in the 1950s when the Republicans tended to lose out to better Democratic candidates, mostly in state legislative elections. It was not until 1994 that Republicans turned back the tide. In 2001, Republicans hold the governor's office, one U.S. Senate seat, and all three U.S. House seats.

Nebraska political culture is unusual in that it is generally muted and devoid of the stridency common in other states. Factionalism is rare, but conservatives generally have their way in state conventions and draft the party conventions to include much of their agenda. Republicans hold an edge over Democrats in organizational depth and in funding. Party leaders tend to stay on the sidelines during the nonpartisan legislative elections, and they also contribute only a small portion of their candidates' campaign chest during crucial races. Party leaders also do not take sides during primary elections.

Republican Presidential Victories, 1868–2000
Total: 27 (1868, 1872, 1876, 1880, 1884, 1888, 1892, 1900, 1904, 1920, 1924, 1928, 1940, 1944, 1948, 1952, 1956, 1960, 1968, 1972, 1976, 1980, 1984, 1988, 1992, 1996, 2000)

Republican Governors of Nebraska, 1868–2000
David C. Butler, 1867–1871; William Hartford James, 1871–1873; Robert Wilkinson Furnas, 1873–1875; Silas Garber, 1875–1879; Albinus Nance, 1879–1883; James William Dawes, 1883–1887; John Milton Thayer, 1887–1891, 1891–1892; Lorenzo Crounse, 1893–1895; Charles Henry Dietrich, 1901; Ezra Perin Savage, 1901–1903; John Hopgood Mickey, 1903–1907; George Lawson Sheldon, 1907–1909; Chester Hardy Aldrich, 1911–1913; Samuel Roy McKelvie, 1919–1923; Adam McMullen, 1925–1929; Arthur J. Weaver,

1929–1931; Dwight Palmer Griswold, 1941–1947; Frederick Val demar Erastus Peterson, 1947–1953; Robert Berkey Crosby, 1953–1955; Victor Emmanuel Anderson, 1955–1959; Dwight Willard Burney, 1960–1961; Norbert Theodore Tiemann, 1967–1971; Charles Thone 1979–1983; Kay A. Orr, 1987–1991; Mike Johanns, 1999– .

ADDRESS: Republican Party of Nebraska, 421 South 9th Street, Suite 233, Lincoln, NE 68508

Tel.: (402) 475-2122

www.negop.org

BIBLIOGRAPHY

League of Women Voters in Nebraska. *Nebraska State Government*. 3d ed. Lincoln: League of Women Voters in Nebraska, 1972.

Miewald, Robert D., ed. *Nebraska Government & Politics*. Lincoln, NE: University of Nebraska Press, 1984.

Nebraska Congressional Delegation, Voting Record as Assessed by Key Groups, 1998*

	ADA	ACLU	AFS	LCV	CON	NTU	NFIB	COC	ACU	NTLC	CHC
Senator											
C. Hagel	0	29	0	0	78	66	89	94	72	86	100
Representatives											
D. K. Bereuter	5	6	0	15	26	33	79	100	64	67	83
B. Barrett	15	6	22	8	60	61	100	89	76	82	83

*For abbreviations, see p. 220.

NEVADA

Nevada's early history from 1864 to 1890 was dominated by Republicans, but the half century that followed saw third parties—especially the Silver Party, Populists, and Democrats—displacing the Republicans in local and national elections.

The years from 1906 through 1932 were somewhat better for Republicans, who fared better in high-profile national and statewide elections. But their fortunes sank again during the New Deal years of the 1930s when Republicans nearly vanished from the state legislature. In the 1960s, the number of registered Democrats was double that of Republicans. The wilderness period for the Republicans ended in the 1970s, when some parity between the two parties returned to the state legislature as well as in voter registration figures. This was a hopeful augury for the Republicans, who had been the underdogs for a long time. In 2001 Republicans occupy the governor's office and have a majority in the state senate; but Democrats hold one U.S. Senate seat and one of two U.S. House seats.

The turnaround in Republican Party prospects that began in the early 1970s was fueled by three developments. One was that the state's moderately conservative population was alienated by the drift of the Democratic Party to the left. Second, most new immigrants to the state are the relatively wealthy older people from traditionally Republican districts in southern California. Third, the Republican Party was adept at taking advantage of modern computer techniques for fund-raising and voter-registration drives and had more funds to devote to these programs. Republicans also have improved their grass-roots activity and candidate recruitment. The Democrats no longer have the advantage of having the best candidates in every election.

The Nevada Republican Party has the three-tier system common to most states—precinct, county, and state—each level electing delegates to the next higher one. The county committee chairs wield considerable influence within the party and are themselves members of the state committee. The Republican Party has a paid full-time executive director who manages day-to-day affairs and communicates with county and precinct-level committees. Unlike Democrats, who have retained their caucus, Republicans hold a primary to nominate their presidential candidate. Candidates for state offices are selected by closed primaries. Nevada Republicans have managed to stave off attempts by the religious right to take over the party and now follow a big-tent approach to problems and policies.

Republican Presidential Victories, 1864–2000
Total: 19 (1864, 1868, 1872, 1876, 1884, 1888, 1904, 1920, 1924, 1928, 1952, 1956, 1968, 1972, 1976, 1980, 1984, 1988, 2000)

Republican Governors of Nevada, 1864–2000
Henry Goode Blasdel, 1864–1871; John Henry Kinkead, 1879–1883; Charles Clark Stevenson, 1887–1890; Francis Jardine Bell, 1890–1891; Roswell Keyes Colcord, 1891–1895; Tasker Lowndes Oddie, 1911–1915; Frederick Bennett Balzar, 1927–1934; Morley Isaac Griswold, 1934–1935; Charles Hinton Russell, 1951–1959; Paul Dominique Laxalt, 1967–1971; Robert Frank List, 1979–1983; Kenny Guinn, 1999– .

ADDRESS: Nevada Republican Party, 8625 West Sahara Avenue, Las Vegas, NV 89117

Tel.: (702) 258-9182

www.nevadagop.org

BIBLIOGRAPHY

Elliot, Russell R. *History of Nevada.* Lincoln: University of Nebraska Press, 1987.

Hulse, James W. *Forty Years in the Wilderness: Impressions of Nevada, 1940–1980.* Reno: University of Nevada Press, 1986.

Nevada Congressional Delegation, Voting Record as Assessed by Key Groups, 1998*

	ADA	ACLU	AFS	LCV	CON	NTU	NFIB	COC	ACU	NTLC	CHC
Representative											
J. Gibbons	20	19	22	8	2	52	100	89	92	92	82

*For abbreviations, see p. 220.

NEW HAMPSHIRE

The Granite State occupies a special place in Republican history as one of its oldest bastions. In 1853 Amos Tuck called a meeting at his home in Exeter, New Hampshire, where the party was christened. Republicans elected their first state governor in 1857 and since then there have been only six Democratic governors and forty-seven Republican governors.

New Hampshire politics has three unusual features. The first is the state's first-in-the-nation primary, which makes New Hampshire a harbinger of presidential elections. The second is the influence of its leading conservative newspaper, the *Manchester Union Leader,* which acts as the voice of the Republican Party. Although its impact has declined in recent years, it is still widely respected as the conservative conscience of the state and as its kingmaker. The third is the very large size of its legislature, which has a membership of 424 (400 for the house and 24 for the sen-ate). Such a large number poses difficulties in the recruitment of proper candidates and in ensuring the ideological sympathies of those candidates. In any case, the distinction between Democrats and Republicans is not ideological in the strict sense, because both parties have liberals and conservatives; liberal Republicans have more in common with liberal Democrats than with their conservative fellow Republicans. The GOP has come to be a loose and convenient coalition of no particular ideological persuasion or loyalties, and some Democrats masquerade as Republicans in districts inhospitable to the Democratic Party. Since there is little formal recruitment or screening of candidates and since candidates do not spend much time preparing for elections, there is little party intervention and only modest services to candidates. Power within the party is dispersed and decentralized and flows in many directions. Because the state is a light regulator of political parties, the GOP is not required to set minimum standards for the composition and functions of its committees. Local party structure is not defined in the Republican Party bylaws. The state convention, the state committee, and the state executive committee are the most active party organs. State conventions adopt party platforms and nominate presidential electors. The state committee is the hub of the party, and its core is the collective membership of the county committees. Between meetings of the state committee, the executive committee, which includes all Republican county chairs and the mayors of the state's four largest cities, conducts all business.

The New Hampshire primary is a unique political institution of which the people of the state are proud, but it creates tensions within the party and between the national and state parties, because state leaders openly espouse the cause of one candidate over others.

Republican Presidential Victories, 1860–2000
Total: 28 (1860, 1864, 1868, 1872, 1876, 1880, 1884, 1888, 1892, 1896, 1900, 1904, 1908, 1920, 1924, 1928, 1932, 1948, 1952, 1956, 1960, 1968, 1972, 1976, 1980, 1984, 1988, 2000)

Republican Governors of New Hampshire, 1860–2000
Ichabod Goodwin, 1859–1861; Nathaniel Springer Berry, 1861–1863; Joseph Albree Gilmore, 1863–1865; Walter Harriman, 1867–1869; Onslow Stearns, 1869–1871; Ezekiel Albert Straw, 1872–1874; Person Colby Cheney, 1875–1877; Benjamin Franklin Prescott, 1877–1879; Nathaniel Head, 1879–1881; Charles Henry Bell, 1881–1883; Samuel Whitney Hale, 1883–1885; Moody Currier, 1885–1887; Charles Henry Sawyer, 1887–1889; David Harvey Goodell, 1889–1891; Hiram Americus Tuttle, 1891–1893; John Butler Smith, 1893–1895; Charles Albert Busiell, 1895–1897; George Allen Ramsdell, 1897–1899; Frank West Rollins, 1899–1901; Chester Bradley Jordan, 1901–1903; Nahum Josiah Batchelder, 1903–1905; John McLane, 1905–1907; Charles Miller Floyd, 1907–1909; Henry Brewer Quinby, 1909–1911; Robert Perkins Bass, 1911–1913; Rolland Harty Spaulding, 1915–1917; Henry Wilder Keyes, 1917–1919; John Henry Bartlett, 1919–1921; Albert Oscar Brown, 1921–1923; John Gilbert Winant, 1925–1927, 1931–1935; Huntley Nowel Spaulding, 1927–1929; Charles William Tobey, 1929–1931; Henry Styles Bridges, 1935–1937; Francis Parnell Murphy, 1937–1941; Robert Oscar Blood, 1941–1945; Charles Milby Dale, 1945–1949; Sherman Adams, 1949–1953; Hugh Gregg, 1953–1955; Lane Dwinell, 1955–1959; Wesley Powell, 1959–1963; Walter Rutherford Peterson, 1969–1973; Meldrim Thomson Jr., 1973–1979; Vesta M. Roy, 1982–1983; John Henry Sununu, 1983–1989; Judd Alan Gregg, 1989–1993; Stephen "Steve" Merrill, 1993–1997.

ADDRESS: New Hampshire Republican Party, 134 North Main Street, Concord, NH 03301

Tel.: (603) 225-9341

www.nhgop.org

BIBLIOGRAPHY
Milburn, Josephine F., and William Doyle. *New England Political Parties.* Cambridge, MA: Schenkman, 1983.

Peirce, Neal R. *The New England States: People, Politics, and Power in the Six New England States.* New York: Norton, 1976.

New Hampshire Congressional Delegation, Voting Record as Assessed by Key Groups, 1998*

	ADA	ACLU	AFS	LCV	CON	NTU	NFIB	COC	ACU	NTLC	CHC
Senators											
B. Smith	5	14	0	0	81	81	89	78	100	100	100
J. Gregg	5	29	11	50	52	63	100	89	78	86	91
Representatives											
J. E. Sununu	0	6	0	31	74	56	100	94	92	89	100
C. Bass	10	25	11	54	26	47	100	94	63	68	75

*For abbreviations, see p. 220.

NEW JERSEY

Situated between New York and Pennsylvania, New Jersey shares the political traditions of its neighbors. The strong urban character of the states' population and the large proportion of immigrants tend to strengthen the Democratic hold; but arrayed against these Democratic constituencies are the affluent, suburban rural areas where the GOP has long been entrenched. Like New York, New Jersey had strong political bosses in both the Republican and Democratic Parties. In Atlantic County, the legendary Enoch "Nucky" Johnson and Frank S. "Hap" Farley were kingmakers until the 1970s, when they were indicted for criminal fraud. New Jersey also suffers from its proximity to the great media centers of New York City and Philadelphia. New Jersey has no major city and, despite a large number of local newspapers, has no major media outlets. As a result, New Jersey politics and issues often get less coverage than those of neighboring states.

However, New Jersey may be characterized as a typical two-party state where no party has a built-in advantage. New Jersey has voted Republican more often than Democratic in presidential and gubernatorial elections, and the Republicans have also kept a close grip on the state legislature. The latter was an important leverage, for many of the Democratic governors were hobbled by a contrary legislature. Their strength was derived from the malapportionment of the legislature. The forty assembly districts are apportioned by population, but there are more rural districts than urban districts. The house has two members per district and the senate, one. Thus, a few Republican legislators representing the small districts could hold up or defeat any legislation that is not in their interests. While Republicans control the governor's house and both houses of the legislature in 2001, they have only six of the thirteen U.S. House seats and neither of the two U.S. Senate seats. New Jersey Republicans also tend to be more moderate than fellow Republicans in the Midwest and the South.

There are three levels of GOP organization—municipal, county, and state—but they are parallel organizations with few up-down links, and more hierarchical ones. Under Governor Christine Todd Whitman the GOP transformed itself into a full-service party, which provides all kinds of assistance to candidates. Because Republicans are dominant in the legislature, the party works closely with the legislative caucus. There is a legislative steering committee, which includes the state party chair. The steering committee has two divisions: the senate Republican majority (SRM) and the assembly Republican majority (ARM).

Republican Presidential Victories, 1860–2000

Total: 19 (1860, 1872, 1896, 1900, 1904, 1908, 1916, 1920, 1924, 1928 1948, 1952, 1956, 1968, 1972, 1976, 1980, 1984, 1988)

Republican Governors of New Jersey, 1860–2000

Charles Smith Olden, 1860–1863; Marcus Lawrence Ward, 1866–1869; John William Griggs, 1896–1898; Foster McGowan Voorhees, 1898, 1899–1902; David Ogden Watkins, 1898–1899; Franklin Murphy, 1902–1905; Edward Casper Stokes, 1905–1908; John Franklin Fort, 1908–1911; Walter Evans Edge, 1917–1919; William Nelson Runyon, 1919–1920; Clarence Edwards Case, 1920; Morgan Foster Larson, 1929–1932; Clifford R. Powell, 1935; Horace Griggs Prall, 1935; Harold Giles Hoffman, 1935–1938; Watter E. Edge, 1944–1947; Alfred Eastlack Driscoll, 1947–1954; William Thomas Cahill, 1970–1974; Thomas H. Kean, 1982–1990; Christine Todd Whitman, 1994–2001; Donald DiFrancesco (acting), 2001.

ADDRESS: New Jersey Republican Party, 28 West State Street, Suite 305, Trenton, NJ 08608

Tel.: (609) 989-7300

www.njgop.org

BIBLIOGRAPHY

Pomper, Gerald M., ed. *The Political State of New Jersey*. New Brunswick, NJ: Rutgers University Press, 1986.

Rosenthal, Alan, and John Blydenburgh, eds. *Politics in New Jersey*. New Brunswick, NJ: Rutgers University, 1975.

New Jersey Congressional Delegation, Voting Record as Assessed by Key Groups, 1998*

	ADA	ACLU	AFS	LCV	CON	NTU	NFIB	COC	ACU	NTLC	CHC
Representatives											
F. A. LoBiondo	30	13	44	69	26	46	86	78	68	47	67
J. Saxton	25	25	43	69	28	46	85	81	63	58	83
C. H. Smith	25	6	33	85	30	48	79	61	72	53	92
M. Roukema	20	19	22	69	30	52	71	78	60	50	42
B. Franks	25	31	33	77	33	50	86	83	52	45	50
R. Frelinghuysen	10	38	11	54	42	57	86	83	52	50	50

*For abbreviations, see p. 220.

NEW MEXICO

New Mexico, which became a state in 1912, has a short political history. Between 1912 and the New Deal, the Republicans were in the ascendant, although they suffered some electoral defeats until 1924. The Republicans were strongly entrenched in the northern counties, while the Democrats were equally strong in the southeastern region known as Little Texas. The New Deal changed the political landscape as the Republicans were forced to retreat. The influence of both parties on electoral outcomes was reduced by the state's adoption of direct primaries in 1939.

The Hispanic vote determines success in New Mexico politics. Hispanics hold the balance of power in the ten northern counties. The other key regions are Little Texas and Bernalillo County, where Albuquerque is located. Hispanic loyalties in the northern counties, once solidly Republican, have been won over by the Democrats. On the other hand, Little Texas, once Democratic, has shifted to the GOP. But no region is more vote-rich than Bernalillo, which has more often than not come down on the GOP side in major elections. In 2001, Republicans hold one U.S. Senate seat, two of three U.S. House seats, and the governor's office. Democrats control both houses of the legislature, as they have done since 1933, with two brief exceptions. At the county level, the Republicans have made some gains, but are outnumbered by Democrats.

Republicans have more financial resources than Democrats and typically outspend their rivals. In an effort to streamline their fund-raising and candidate recruitment and support services, they have adopted several programs, including financial clubs such as the Solomon Luna Club for those donating $1,000, the Candidate Financial Assistance and Priority Committee to deal with fund disbursements to candidates; and the Campaign Committee for New Mexico to address campaign finance reforms.

The Republican Party is organized at the precinct, ward, county, and state levels. The strongest Republican county committees are in Bernalillo and in the Anglo rural counties outside Little Texas, such as Ontero, San Juan, and Los Alamos. Although there are moderate and conservative wings within the party, outbreaks of factional infighting have been rare. When such internal struggles take place, they can be very costly in terms of voter support, as was proved during the 2000 Republican primary. Governor Johnson is an outspoken libertarian who has run often into problems with the RNC.

Republican Presidential Victories, 1912–2000
Total: 11 (1920, 1924, 1928, 1952, 1956, 1968, 1972, 1976, 1980, 1984, 1988)

Republican Governors of New Mexico, 1912–2000
Washington Ellsworth Lindsey, 1917–1919; Octaviano Amrosio Larrazolo, 1919–1921; Merritt Cramer Mechem, 1921–1923; Richard Charles Dillon, 1927–1931; Edwin Leard Mechem, 1951–1955, 1957–1959, 1961–1962; Thomas Felix Bolack, 1962–1963; David Francis Cargo, 1967–1971;

Garrey Edward Carruthers, 1987–1991; Gary E. Johnson, 1995– .

ADDRESS: Republican Party of New Mexico, 2901 Juan Tabo Street NE, Suite 116, Albuquerque, NM 87112

Tel.: (505) 998-5254

www.gopnm.org

BIBLIOGRAPHY

Holmes, Jack E. *Politics in New Mexico.* Albuquerque: University of New Mexico Press, 1967.

Vigil, Maurilio E., Michael Olsen, and Roy Lujan. *New Mexico Government and Politics.* Lanham, MD: University Press of America, 1990.

New Mexico Congressional Delegation, Voting Record as Assessed by Key Groups, 1998*

	ADA	ACLU	AFS	LCV	CON	NTU	NFIB	COC	ACU	NTLC	CHC
Senator											
P. V. Domenici	5	43	13	0	45	58	100	100	70	71	82
Representative											
J. Skeen	10	13	11	15	13	44	100	100	84	92	83

*For abbreviations, see p. 220.

NEW YORK

The political fault lines in New York were clearly defined by the Revolution. When the Republican Party came into existence in the 1850s, it assumed the mantle of the earlier Whig Party. Whereas the Democratic Party was identified with immigrants—mostly Irish—and the poor, the Republicans were associated with the wealthier and the native-born. There was also a dichotomy between New York City, where Democrats have tended to dominate, and the rest of the state, where Republicans are stronger. This dichotomy continued to play a part in New York politics throughout the nineteenth and twentieth centuries.

The New York GOP has produced some of the party's great national leaders, including Theodore Roosevelt and Charles Evans Hughes, both of whom served as governors. Nelson Rockefeller, who served as governor from 1959 to 1973, refashioned the modern state party and made it more liberal than the national party. But with the departure of Rockefeller in 1973 and the Supreme Court's legislative reapportionment decision in 1973, the GOP fell into the doldrums for more than twenty years. The earlier apportionment of legislative districts was overturned by the Su-

preme Court, which established a new one person–one vote rule. The result was that rural districts in which Republicans were strong had fewer votes than the more populous urban districts. Alfonse D'Amato, elected senator in 1980, dominated the party for the next two decades and engineered the nomination of George Pataki, who was elected governor in 1994. Former prosecutor Rudolph Giuliani, was elected mayor of New York City in 1993. Giuliani, more moderate on social issues, opposed Pataki's election in 1994, and the two, jockeying for control of the Republican Party, have long had tense relations.

The Republican state committee consists of 300 members, two from each of the state's 150 assembly districts. Like the Democrats, Republicans also have gender parity in all their elective offices. The committee employs an executive director with a main office in Albany and a satellite office in New York City.

Republican Presidential Victories, 1860–2000
Total: 19 (1860, 1864, 1872, 1880, 1888, 1896, 1900, 1904, 1908, 1916, 1920, 1924, 1928, 1948, 1952, 1956, 1972, 1980, 1984)

Republican Governors of New York, 1860–2000
Edwin Denison Morgan, 1859–1863; Reuben Eaton Fenton, 1865–1869; John Adams Dix, 1873–1875; Alonzo B. Cornell, 1880–1883; Levi Parsons

Morton, 1895–1897; Frank Swett Black, 1897–1899; Theodore Roosevelt, 1899–1901; Benjamin Baker Odell Jr., 1901–1905; Frank Wayland Higgins, 1905–1907; Charles Evans Hughes, 1907–1910; Horace White, 1910–1911; Charles Seymour Whitman, 1915–1919; Nathan Lewis Miller, 1921–1923; Thomas Edmund Dewey, 1943–1955; Nelson Aldrich Rockefeller, 1959–1973; Malcolm Wilson, 1973–1975; George Pataki, 1995– .

ADDRESS: Republican Party of New York, 315 State Street, Albany, NY 12210

Tel.: (518) 462-2601

www.nygop.org

BIBLIOGRAPHY

Colby, Peter W., and John K. White. *New York State Today: Politics, Government, Public Policy.* 2d ed. Albany: State University of New York Press, 1989.

Zimmerman, Joseph F. *The Government and Politics of New York State.* New York: New York University Press, 1981.

New York Congressional Delegation, Voting Record as Assessed by Key Groups, 1998*

	ADA	ACLU	AFS	LCV	CON	NTU	NFIB	COC	ACU	NTLC	CHC
Representatives											
R. A. Lazio	40	25	44	77	13	43	79	89	52	50	73
P. T. King	10	13	33	15	31	52	79	82	76	71	100
V. Fossella	0	8	0	31	26	50	100	100	96	90	100
S. W. Kelly	45	38	56	85	6	43	71	83	48	49	58
B. A. Gilman	45	56	63	77	2	42	69	71	38	47	50
S. L. Boehlert	60	69	78	92	33	28	50	61	24	39	25
J. M. McHugh	25	13	44	31	13	42	86	89	68	74	80
J. T. Walsh	30	13	33	69	26	30	79	89	44	53	83
J. Quinn	30	6	56	62	23	41	86	76	48	57	75
A. Houghton	30	56	50	15	26	29	82	100	29	40	27

*For abbreviations, see p. 220.

NORTH CAROLINA

During Reconstruction, the Republican Party made significant inroads in North Carolina, holding the governor's office from 1868 to 1876. It also held several seats in Congress. The party declined in the late nineteenth century, however, and languished for half a century. Not until 1972 did Republicans elect their first governor of the twentieth century, James Holshouser, and first senator, Jesse Helms. The Republican Party grew rapidly, and in 1994 Republicans won a majority of the state assembly seats and a near majority in the state senate. The overall pattern since the 1990s has been one of growth for the Republicans, but the state remains highly competitive.

Divided outcomes are still common, and neither party has been able to win more than 55 percent of the vote in a national election. As of 2001, Republicans in North Carolina hold one U.S. Senate seat and seven of twelve seats in the U.S. House of Representatives.

The Republican resurgence in North Carolina in the late twentieth century was helped by a stronger state party organization. This organization consists of a chairperson and other officers, a central committee, and an executive committee. The chair is the executive head, although the party may also appoint an executive director to assist in administrative tasks. The executive committee is a body of over 500 individuals, including party officers, elected officials, other ex officio members, and close to 200 members from the congressional districts. This large body meets at least twice per year. The central committee, which meets at least bimonthly, is a smaller body of thirty voting members, including state party officers, congressional district chairs, leaders of certain auxiliary organizations, and selected legislative leaders.

Below the state level, the counties and congressional districts are the most important organizational units, although judicial and state legislative district organizations exist as well. The county party organization consists of a chairman and an executive committee, which is a body of ten or more individuals including the county chair, other county officers, and five or more members elected by the county convention. County executive committees meet at least twice per year, but some meet more frequently, even monthly.

The congressional district also is an important organizational unit. Each district has an executive committee, which meets quarterly; it is composed of district officers, the chairs and vice-chairs of the counties within the district, and the elected district members of the state executive committee. Over 40 percent of the state executive committee consists of these elected district members and the district officers, who are ex officio members.

The lowest party organizational unit is the precinct. The precinct committee consists of three officers—a chair, a vice-chair, and a secretary—and as many members-at-large as the precinct meeting chooses to elect. Precinct meetings are open to all registered Republicans living in the precinct.

Conventions are held at the county, congressional district, and state levels in odd-numbered years and in presidential election years. Precinct meetings are held on the same schedule. The conventions elect officers and conduct other business, but they have little to do with the nomination of candidates. By law, party candidates for local, state, and congressional offices are chosen in primary elections. Unlike the situation in some other states, party conventions play no role in nominations, and organizational endorsements of primary candidates are not permitted. The state convention does play a role in the presidential nomination process, even though the state has a presidential primary, as the state convention selects some of the delegates to the national party convention, the others being selected at the congressional district level. However, the delegation's first ballot at the national convention must be cast in accordance with the primary outcome.

In the early 1970s, the Republican state party headquarters was a small operation located in rented office space in Raleigh, with a full-time staff of three individuals. Even this modest headquarters was more than the party had in the early 1960s. By the early 1980s, the state party owned its own headquarters and had doubled its staff to six. In 1988, the party had a staff of nine individuals and a budget of roughly $1.6 million; and there was an affiliated campaign organization, "Victory '88," with a sizable staff and budget for coordinated campaign activities. Increased party organization and activity have continued into the 1990s, as the two major parties continue to contest elections closely.

The state party headquarters in 1999, a year in which no state or congressional elections were held, had six full-time staff members and an operating budget of approximately $1 million. In 1998 there were seven full-time staff members and a budget of about $1.8 million. Presidential election years, which also are when the governor and other major statewide offices are elected, bring the highest level of activity. In 1996, for example, there were ten full-time staff members and a budget of $2 million, plus another $3 million in the coordinated "Victory '96" campaign directed by the state party.

The state party funds its operating and campaign budgets primarily from contributions from individuals and from party transfer funds. Some contributions are designated for campaign activities and are subject to the contribution limits established by federal or state law. Other contributions, such as those to support the operating budget or party-building activities, are not so restricted and are sometimes termed "soft money." Another significant source of state party funds is the state income tax check-off system. These disbursements to the state parties are the greatest in presidential election years.

Although campaigning is largely conducted by individual candidates and their campaign organizations, the state party provides campaign assistance to candidates. Voter registration drives and get-out-the-vote activities, which benefit the entire ticket, have been emphasized in recent election years, particularly by phoning and sending mail to targeted registered voters. In 1998, about 700,000 pieces of mail were sent and about one million phone calls were made in this effort. Candidates in key competitive races may receive financial and other support. Also, the state party routinely runs training seminars, which are useful for candidates who lack experience in campaigning.

County party activity varies across the state. Almost every county party holds a convention. About 75 percent have an executive committee that meets regularly, and nearly that many hold an annual fund-raising event. Only around 20 percent have a permanent county headquarters, but about another 50 percent establish a county headquarters during the fall of election years. Of course, counties range from large urban ones to small rural ones, and the extent of party organization and activity is related to differences in size. Republican precinct organization also varies. At least one-third of the precincts have an active committee, one that meets on schedule and engages in some activity. Probably at least two-thirds of the precincts have a chair.

In sum, the Republican Party organization has developed considerably at all levels, from the precinct to the state, over the past thirty years.

Republican Presidential Victories, 1860–2000
Total: 11 (1868, 1872, 1928, 1968, 1972, 1980, 1984, 1988, 1992, 1996, 2000)

Republican Governors of North Carolina, 1860–2000
William Woods Holden, 1865, 1868–1870; Ted Robinson Caldwell, 1870–1874; Curtis Hooks Brogden, 1874–1877; James Eubert Holshouser Jr., 1973–1977; James Grubbs Martin, 1985–1993.

ADDRESS: Republican Party of North Carolina, P.O. Box 12905, 1410 Hillsborough, Raleigh, NC 27605

Tel.: (919) 828-6423
www.ncgop.org

BIBLIOGRAPHY
Fleer, Jack D. *North Carolina Government and Politics.* Lincoln: University of Nebraska Press, 1994

Luebke, Paul. *Tarheel Politics: Myths and Realities.* Chapel Hill: University of North Carolina Press, 1990.

———. *Tarheel Politics 2000.* Chapel Hill: University of North Carolina Press, 1998.

Prysby, Charles. "North Carolina: Emerging Two-Party Politics." In *Southern State Party Organizations and Activists,* ed. Charles D. Hadley and Lewis Bowman, 37–53. Westport, CT: Praeger, 1995.

———. "North Carolina." In *State Party Profiles, A 50-State Guide to Development, Organization, and Resources,* ed. Andrew M. Appleton and Daniel S. Ward, 234–43. Washington, DC: Congressional Quarterly, 1997.

North Carolina Congressional Delegation, Voting Record as Assessed by Key Groups, 1998*

	ADA	ACLU	AFS	LCV	CON	NTU	NFIB	COC	ACU	NTLC	CHC
Senator											
J. Helms	0	20	0	0	34	71	88	88	100	93	100
Representatives											
W. B. Jones	5	6	11	8	81	77	100	72	100	100	100
R. Burr	5	13	11	8	86	75	100	82	92	92	92
H. Coble	10	6	13	0	65	62	86	89	96	97	100
S. Myrick	5	13	11	8	70	73	100	83	83	95	100

	ADA	ACLU	AFS	LCV	CON	NTU	NFIB	COC	ACU	NTLC	CHC
C. Ballenger	5	6	0	8	86	69	100	82	91	95	100
C. H. Taylor	5	6	22	0	4	62	100	88	96	97	100

*For abbreviations, see p. 220.

NORTH DAKOTA

When North Dakota entered the union in 1889, Republicans were the clear favorites among the voters. However, their popularity was not due to any particular allegiance to Republican ideology, and therefore GOP dominance was very shallow and easily challenged. Republican supremacy lasted until World War I, when an economic slump promoted dissident parties with populist appeal. Foremost among these parties was the Non Partisan League (NPL) which swept the 1916 and 1918 elections. Eventually, in 1956, NPL merged with the Democratic Party. Republicans were able to recapture their control of the legislature under Dwight Eisenhower and have held on to it tenaciously. In 2001, the Republicans control the state legislature and the governor's office, but the Democrats claim the sole U.S. House seat and both U.S. Senate seats.

North Dakota political culture has been distinguished by two characteristics: egalitarianism and nonpartisanship, and both militate against the development of strong political parties. Characteristically, the districts, rather than the precincts, are the active units of electoral activity. The district committees or executive committees meet regularly. Recruitment of candidates, as well as retaining sitting legislators, is difficult because legislators are poorly paid and heavily overworked, and the rewards are minimal. Because there are fewer candidates than seats, primary contests are rare. The state party assumes greater responsibility for conducting the campaigns of these candidates once they are persuaded to run. Congressional seats are more sought after because of the greater rewards and prestige and because the RNC bears a significant portion of campaign financing.

The Republican Party does not involve itself in county-level elections. Under state law, the state committee consists of legislative-district chairpersons, two national committeepersons, and any additional members, including state party officers, state finance chair, Republican congressional office holders (none in 1999), floor leaders of the state senate and house, elected state officeholders, past chairperson, president of the Federation of Republican Women, chair of the Young Republicans, and the chair of the College Republicans. Districts meet part of the expenses of the state committee. Besides the full-time staff at headquarters, the party relies on volunteers between elections.

In keeping with the state's nonpartisan tradition, the GOP provides electoral services, but no ideological discipline, to its activists. As a result, religious conservatives have made little headway in the state. Even the party platform is more of a statement of ideals than a rigorous mandate.

Republican Presidential Victories, 1896–2000
Total: 22 (1896, 1900, 1904, 1908, 1920, 1924, 1928, 1940, 1944, 1948, 1952, 1956, 1960, 1968, 1972, 1976, 1980, 1984, 1988, 1992, 1996, 2000)

Republican Governors of North Dakota, 1889–2000
John Miller, 1889–1891; Andrew Horace Burke, 1891–1893; Roger Allin, 1895–1897; Frank Arlington Briggs, 1897–1898; John McMurray Devine, 1898–1899; Frederick Bartlett Fancher, 1899–1901; Frank White, 1901–1905; Elmore Y. Sarles, 1905–1907; Louis Benjamin Hanna, 1913–1917; Lynn Joseph Frazier, 1917–1921; Regnvold Anderson Nestos, 1921–1925; Arthur Gustav Sorlie, 1925–1928; Walter Jeremiah Maddock, 1928–1929; George F. Shafer, 1929–1933; William Langer, 1933–1934; 1937–1939; Ole H. Olson, 1934–1935; Walter Welford, 1935–1937; Fred George Aandahl, 1945–1951; Clarence Norman Brunsdale, 1951–1957; John Edward Davis, 1957–1961; Allen Ingvar Oslon, 1981–1984; Edward Thomas Schafer, 1992–2000; John Hoeven, 2000– .

ADDRESS: Republican Party of North Dakota, P.O. Box 1917, 101 East Broadway Avenue, Bismarck, ND 58501

Tel.: (701) 255-0030

www.ndgop.com

BIBLIOGRAPHY

Howard, Thomas Wilson, and Charles Nelson Howard. *North Dakota Political Tradition.* Ames: Iowa State University Press, 1981.

Wilkins, Robert P., and Wynona Huchette Wilkins. *North Dakota: A Bicentennial History.* New York: Norton, 1977.

OHIO

The Republican Party gained power in Ohio during the Civil War and has maintained it by drawing on its natural constituency—farmers and owners of small and large businesses—which enabled it to offset Democratic strength among labor, teachers, and ethnic groups. Because Republicans and Democrats were equal in number from the Civil War to World War I and Ohio was an essential state for Republicans in presidential elections, more Ohioan Republicans have been nominated for the White House than those of any other state. After World War II, Republicans had the advantage of a strong leader in Ray C. Bliss, chair of the Republican Party, who was able to keep the party coalition from fracturing under the pressure of postwar demographic and economic changes. Bliss rebuilt the county machines and secured support among business groups and candidate organizations. The momentum was carried through under Governor James Rhodes, governor for sixteen years (1963–1971 and 1975–1983). Another period of renewal followed under James Tilling, secretary of the Ohio senate (1984–1994), and under state chair Robert Bennett. In 2001, Republicans hold both U.S. Senate seats, eleven of nineteen House seats, and the governor's office. They also control the state legislature.

Political parties in Ohio are heavily regulated under state law. The structure of the GOP organization therefore hews closely to the state law. Primary voters in each congressional district elect one man and one woman to the state central committee for four-year terms. The state convention, which is held in even-numbered years, drafts the party platform and nominates presidential electors. Delegates to the state convention are chosen by the county executive committees. Each county committee is represented on the county board of elections, and likewise the state committee is represented on the Ohio Elections Commission. There are also numerous party auxiliaries such as the senate and house legislative campaign committees as well as organizations representing Republican women, students, business, and youth. Because Ohio is a swing state, the RNC keeps a close watch on the health of the state party and commits funds and personnel to bolster Republican prospects.

Under law, the GOP may endorse candidates during primary elections and also fill legislative, county, and municipal offices when vacancies occur between elections.

Republican Presidential Victories, 1860–2000

Total: 26 (1860, 1864, 1868, 1872, 1876, 1880, 1884, 1888, 1892, 1896, 1900, 1904, 1908, 1920, 1924, 1928, 1944, 1952, 1956, 1960, 1968, 1972, 1980, 1984, 1988, 2000)

Republican Governors of Ohio, 1860–2000

William Dennison Jr., 1860–1862; Jacob Dolson Cox, 1866–1868; Rutherford Birchard Hayes, 1868–1872, 1876–1877; Edward Follansbee Noyes, 1872–1874; Thomas Lowry Young, 1877–1878; Charles Foster, 1880–1884; Joseph Benson Foraker, 1886–1890; William McKinley, 1892–1896; Asa Smith Bushnell, 1896–1900; George Kilborn Nash, 1900–1904; Myron Timothy Herrick, 1904–1906; Andrew Lintner Harris, 1906–1909; Frank Bartlett Willis, 1915–1917; Harry Lyman Davis, 1921–1923; Myers Young Cooper, 1929–1931; John William Bricker, 1939–1945; Thomas James Herbert, 1947–1949; John William Brown, 1957; C. William O'Neill, 1957–1959; James Allen Rhodes, 1963–1971, 1975–1983; George Victor Voinovich, 1991–1998; Nancy P. Hollister, Dec. 31, 1998–Jan. 10, 1999; Robert A. Taft II, 1999– .

ADDRESS: Ohio Republican Party, 211 South Fifth Street, Columbus, OH 43215

Tel.: (614) 228-2481

www.ohiogop.org

BIBLIOGRAPHY

Lamis, Alexander P., and Mary Ann Sharkey, eds. *Ohio Politics*. Kent, OH: Kent State University Press, 1994.

Lieberman, Carl, ed. *Government and Politics in Ohio*. Lanham, MD: University Press of America, 1984.

Ohio Congressional Delegation, Voting Record as Assessed by Key Groups, 1998*

	ADA	ACLU	AFS	LCV	CON	NTU	NFIB	COC	ACU	NTLC	CHC
Senator											
M. De Wine	10	14	1	0	75	49	100	89	64	68	91
Representatives											
S. Chabot	0	13	0	38	92	82	100	83	96	92	100
R. Portman	5	6	0	31	94	73	100	78	88	84	100
M. G. Oxley	5	20	11	8	13	48	100	100	96	95	92
P. E. Gillmor	5	0	0	15	45	42	93	100	68	81	92
D. Hobson	5	31	22	23	70	65	100	82	88	89	83
J. A. Boehner	0	7	0	8	50	66	100	89	96	100	100
J. R. Kasich	0	6	0	23	70	69	100	82	96	92	100
D. Pryce	5	31	29	15	46	54	100	100	83	84	73
R. Regula	20	13	44	23	2	42	100	89	64	66	67
R. Ney	15	13	33	8	31	47	100	83	80	68	75
S. C. Latourette	40	27	67	46	33	42	86	78	52	58	83

*For abbreviations, see p. 220.

OKLAHOMA

Oklahoma began as a Democratic state and ended up in the Republican camp. Except for a brief time in 1920, the pre–World War II legislature was entirely in non-Republican hands. After barely surviving the New Deal years, the Republican presence in the legislature was reduced to a handful of members in the 1950s because nearly half the seats went uncontested by the GOP for lack of candidates. Not a single Republican served as governor during the half-century following statehood in 1907; in 1958 the Republican gubernatorial candidate received only 19 percent of the popular vote and lost all seventy-seven counties. For the first two-thirds of the twentieth century, political analysts considered Oklahoma a one-party Democratic state.

The first break in this bleak Republican picture came when Dwight Eisenhower carried the state in 1952 and 1956. Since then, Republican presidential candidates have swept the state in all elections except in 1964. In 1962 Henry Bellmon was elected the first Republican governor, followed by Dewey Bartlett and Frank Keating. Bellmon and Bartlett later captured U.S. Senate seats for the GOP. Congressional seats fell next. In 2001, Republicans hold both U.S. Senate seats, five of six House seats, and the governor's office. The state house and senate are still under Democratic control, but the GOP is well on its way to taking over the legislature.

The Republican strength is based in the northern half of the state and in the two largest cities, Oklahoma City and Tulsa. Strong party leaders such as Bellmon and recent party chairs Tom Cole (1991–1993) and Clinton Key (1993–1995), have managed to keep the party united at election times despite the bickering among the party's factional wings, particularly small farmers and owners of small businesses, Christian conservatives, and traditional elites. Intraparty factionalism is muted, and there are few personality-driven conflicts.

The transformation of the Oklahoma GOP from a loose coterie of wealthy urban individuals into a strong grassroots-driven organization was the work of Bellmon, Cole, and Key. Bellmon's Operation Countdown emphasized finance, candidate recruitment, and registration of Republican voters. Bellmon created county organizations where they did not exist before. Bellmon, Cole, and Key went outside safe Republican seats to target the more vulnerable Democratic seats. These efforts have paid off handsomely since 1994.

Organizationally, the Republican Party is heavily concentrated in Tulsa and Oklahoma City, which accounted for 43 percent of all delegates to the 1995 state party convention. The state party committee includes the budget committee and the executive committee. The executive committee consists of thirty-two members including district party chairs and vice chairs, Republican legislative leaders, and state officials. The state committee includes executive committee members, four officers from each of the counties, and other elected officials. The GOP is no longer the elitist organization it used to be and is beginning to think and act like a majority party. The result of this new focus is that the GOP is finding more candidates seeking to run on the Republican ticket than ever before. The party is also becoming more diverse, going outside its traditional turf to enlist African-American and Hispanic voters.

Republican Presidential Victories, 1908–2000
Total: 14 (1920, 1928, 1952, 1956, 1960, 1968, 1972, 1976, 1980, 1984, 1988, 1992, 1996, 2000)

Republican Governors of Oklahoma, 1907–2000
Henry Louis Bellmon, 1963–1967, 1987–1991; Dewey Follett Bartlett, 1967–1971; Frank Keating, 1995– .

ADDRESS: Oklahoma Republican Party, 4031 North Lincoln Boulevard, Oklahoma City, OK 73105

Tel.: (405) 528-3501
www.okgop.com

BIBLIOGRAPHY
Jones, Stephen. *Oklahoma Politics in State and Nation.* Enid, OK: Haymaker Press, 1974.
Scales, James R., and Danney Goble. *Oklahoma Politics: A History.* Norman: University of Oklahoma Press, 1982.

Oklahama Congressional Delegation, Voting Record as Assessed by Key Groups, 1998*

	ADA	ACLU	AFS	LCV	CON	NTU	NFIB	COC	ACU	NTLC	CHC
Senators											
D. Nickles	0	14	0	0	81	80	100	83	96	96	100
J. M. Inhofe	5	14	0	0	71	74	89	76	100	100	100
Representatives											
S. Largent	10	13	11	15	87	79	93	82	92	97	100
T. Coburn	5	6	25	0	93	78	92	71	100	97	100
W. Watkins	5	13	11	8	21	54	100	100	92	91	100
J. C. Watts	10	13	11	0	21	50	100	94	84	97	100
E. J. Istook Jr.	0	0	0	8	59	6	93	94	95	97	100
F. Lucas	0	6	0	0	21	55	100	100	100	97	100

*For abbreviations, see p. 220.

OREGON

The Republican regime in Oregon lasted from 1880 to 1950, one of the longest stretches of one-party rule among the states. Republicans won every presidential election from 1860 to 1932, except two. Between 1882 and 1910, Republicans held all statewide offices except for one governor, one secretary of state, and one attorney general. During this period, Republicans won every U.S. Senate election. But increased challenge from the Democratic Party became a common feature of Oregon politics after 1950, as demographics, especially the influx of younger voters, favored the Democrats. The Republican lead in voter registration narrowed sharply between 1932 and 1954. The percentage of registered voters was seventy-one to twenty-six in favor of the Republicans in 1932, but it shrank to forty-nine to forty-nine in 1954. The percentage of registered Republicans continued to decrease during the next forty years until it reached 36 percent as compared to Democrats at 43 percent. In 1954 Richard Neuberger became the first elected Democratic U.S. Senator from Oregon in over forty years. The 1956 election proved a decisive turning point when Democrats took control of both houses of the state legislature for the first time since 1878. They also captured the governorship, both U.S. Senate seats, and three of four U.S. House seats.

Since 1956, Oregon has emerged as a competitive two-party state with party fortunes constantly shifting. Although Democrats continued to dominate the state legislature, they lost both U.S. Senate seats in 1968 to moderate Republicans Mark Hatfield and Robert Packwood. Depending on the state of the economy, there were wild swings in electoral outcomes. After electing conservative Republican Victor Atiyeh as governor in 1978 and 1982, Oregon voters elected a liberal Democrat to succeed him. After backing Republican presidents from 1968 to 1984, they chose Michael Dukakis in 1988 and Bill Clinton in 1992 and 1996. Fluidity of political loyalties was also demonstrated by the 24.2 percent of the popular vote received by Ross Perot in 1992. Democrats have fared slightly better in Oregon in the 1990s than in other comparable states. They won the governorship in 1990, 1994, and 1998, although they lost both houses of the state legislature. They also regained the seat vacated by Senator Packwood. Democrats lead Republicans by 7 percent in voter registration, but nearly 21 percent of the voters are not registered with either party.

Although Packwood lost power in the Oregon Republican Party, he was instrumental in strengthening the moderate wing of the Republican Party in the state, a group that favored reproductive rights, women's rights, and other socially liberal issues. One of Packwood's legacies was the so-called Dorchester Conference, a sounding board for liberal policy ideas. The liberal wing is actively opposed by Christian conservatives, but the conservatives' numbers have not been large enough to allow them to take over the party. The struggle between moderates and conservatives continues to divide Oregon Republicans in the twenty-first century. Occasionally, the moderates have threatened to leave the party whenever the conservatives have made significant gains in imposing their agenda on the party.

Republican Presidential Victories, 1860–2000
Total: 25 (1860, 1864, 1872, 1876, 1880, 1884, 1888, 1892, 1896, 1900, 1904, 1908, 1916, 1920, 1924, 1928, 1948, 1952, 1956, 1960, 1968, 1972, 1976, 1980, 1984)

Republican Governors of Oregon, 1860–2000
Addison Crandall Gibbs, 1862–1866; George L. Woods, 1866–1870; Zenas Ferry Moody, 1882–1887; William Paine Lord, 1895–1899; Theodore Thurston Geer, 1899–1903; Frank Williamson Benson, 1909–1910; Jay Bowerman, 1910–1911; James Withycombe, 1915–1919; Ben Wilson Olcott, 1919–1923; Isaac Lee Patterson, 1927–1929; Albin Walter Norblad, 1929–1931; Charles Arthur Sprague, 1939–1943; Earl Wilcox Snell, 1943–1947; John Hubert Hall, 1947–1949; Douglas James McKay, 1949–1952; Paul Linton Patterson, 1952–1956; Elmo Everett Smith, 1956–1957; Mark Odom Hatfield, 1959–1967; Thomas Lawson McCall, 1967–1975; Victor George Atiyeh, 1979–1987.

ADDRESS: Republican Party of Oregon, 570 Liberty Street SE, Suite 200, Salem, OR 97301

Tel.: (503) 587-9233
www.orgop.org

BIBLIOGRAPHY
The Almanac of Oregon Politics. Corvallis: Almanac of Oregon Politics, 1998.

Jewell, Malcolm E., and David M. Olson. *Political Parties and Elections in American States*. 3d ed. Chicago: Dorsey Press, 1988.

Oregon Congressional Delegation, Voting Record as Assessed by Key Groups, 1998*

	ADA	ACLU	AFS	LCV	CON	NTU	NFIB	COC	ACU	NTLC	CHC
Senator											
G. H. Smith	5	29	22	13	38	54	100	94	72	68	82

*For abbreviations, see p. 220.

PENNSYLVANIA

From the Civil War to the 1930s, Pennsylvania was known as a rock-solid Republican state where GOP influence was largely unchallenged. From 1900 to 1934, Republicans won every race for governor and U.S. senator and controlled both houses of the state legislature. So regular was the electoral defeat of Democratic candidates that many Republicans went unopposed. Republican dominance during the seventy years was buttressed by a well-oiled machine that milked the patronage system through a practice known as "macing" or forcing public employees to contribute to party funds. Municipal and state contractors were also asked to pay quite openly. Three bosses ran this machine from 1865 to 1921: Simon Cameron (1865–1887), Matthew S. Quay (1887–1904), and Boise Penrose (1904–1921).

The New Deal dealt a death blow to this state of affairs. The watershed was Franklin D. Roosevelt's second term when George H. Earle was elected Pennsylvania's first Democratic governor in the twentieth century and Joseph F. Guffey was elected U.S. senator. The Democrats also captured both houses of the legislature. Catholics, African Americans, Jews, and East Europeans joined FDR's coalition, while the rural and suburban middle classes, Protestants, and upper-income families formed the Republican phalanx. With labor unions staunchly behind FDR's New Deal as well as Governor Earle's "Little New Deal," the Democratic voter base continued to expand from the 1950s to the 1960s. Philadelphia became a dependable Democratic city under Mayor Joseph S. Clark (1951–1956) and later, Mayor Richardson Dilworth (1956–1962). In the statewide elections that followed in the 1960s and 1970s, Philadelphia provided the vote margins that tilted the balance against Republicans.

By the 1960s Pennsylvania had become a strongly competitive state with the two parties alternating in office at all levels. On only a few occasions did either party win consecutive elections to any office. Although the number of registered Democrats exceeded the number of registered Republicans, both parties were even in their control of the vital institutions. The legislature was split most of the time between the GOP and the Democrats. The growing decline of party identification among Pennsylvania voters contributed to the growing volatility of the political system. Ticket splitting also became very common. The loss of patronage after the governorship of Democrat George Leader also reduced one of the most powerful means by which both parties perpetuated themselves in power. Incumbency became a deciding factor in many elections. Both parties had enough safe seats to maintain their strength but not enough to challenge the status quo. In 2001, Republicans hold the office of the governor, both U.S. Senate seats, and eleven of twenty-one U. S. House seats. They control both houses of the legislature.

Because of the large number of undecided voters in the state, Republican political leaders tend to be pragmatic and moderate, and they are careful not to alienate any significant segment of the population. Pennsylvania has produced a large number of moderate Republicans: William Scranton, Raymond Shafer, Dick Thornburgh, Tom Ridge, James Duff, Hugh Scott, Richard Schweiker, Henry John Heinz, and Arlen Specter. Conservative senator Rick Santorum, elected in 1994, is the only exception to this trend.

Pennsylvania has sixty-seven counties, each of which has a Republican committee and a chair who serve two-year terms. The Republican state committee consists of 300 members. Until the New Deal era, Republicans were associated with big-money interests. Since then, however, Republicans have opted for the "big tent" approach in which small business and rural areas and small towns are well represented. The Christian Coalition has had some success and may hold about 25 to 30 percent of state committee seats. Because Republicans controlled both the legislature and the governor's office, they were in a much stronger position at the end of the twentieth century than they were in the middle, and the state party, the legislative caucus, and the governor work together to ensure that the party's interests are advanced through appropriate policies and programs. Because of its tactical strength the GOP is also able to generate more funds and attract more candidates to run for office.

Republican Presidential Victories, 1860–2000
Total: 25 (1860, 1864, 1868, 1872, 1876, 1880, 1884, 1888, 1892, 1896, 1900, 1904, 1908, 1916, 1920, 1924, 1928, 1932, 1948, 1952, 1956, 1972, 1980, 1984, 1988)

Republican Governors of Pennsylvania, 1860–2001
Andrew Gregg Curtin, 1861–1867; John White Geary, 1867–1873; John Frederick Hartranft, 1873–1879; Henry Martyn Hoyt, 1879–1883; James Addams Beaver, 1887–1891; Daniel Hartman Hastings, 1895–1899; William Alexis Stone, 1899–1903; Samuel Whitaker Pennypacker, 1903–1907; Edwin Sydney Stuart, 1907–1911; John Kinley Tener, 1911–1915; Martin Grove Brumbaugh, 1915–1919; William Cameron Sproul, 1919–1923; Gifford Pinchot, 1923–1927, 1931–1935; John Stuchell Fisher, 1927–1931; Arthur Horace James, 1939–1943; Edward Martin, 1943–1947; John Cromwell Bell Jr., 1947; James Henderson Duff, 1947–1951; John Sidney Fine, 1951–1955; William Warren Scranton, 1963–1967; Raymond Philip Shafer, 1967–1971; Richard Lewis "Dick" Thornburgh, 1979–1987; Tom Ridge, 1995–2001; Mark Schweiker 2001– .

ADDRESS: Republican Party of Pennsylvania, 112 State Street, Harrisburg, PA 17101

Tel.: (717) 234-4901

www.pagop.org

BIBLIOGRAPHY
Beers, Paul B. *Pennsylvania Politics: Today and Yesterday: The Tolerable Accommodation.* University Park: Pennsylvania State University Press, 1980.

Klein, Philip S., and Ari Hoogenboom. *A History of Pennsylvania.* 2d ed. University Park: Pennsylvania State University Press, 1980.

Pennsylvania Congressional Delegation, Voting Record as Assessed by Key Groups, 1998*

	ADA	ACLU	AFS	LCV	CON	NTU	NFIB	COC	ACU	NTLC	CHC
Senators											
A. Specter	45	50	80	50	58	44	63	60	33	48	20
R. Santorum	0	14	0	0	71	69	100	89	84	89	91
Representatives											
J. E. Peterson	0	6	0	0	13	51	100	100	96	97	100
C. Weldon	25	0	44	69	35	51	93	78	60	66	92
J. Greenwood	25	53	22	69	26	47	100	94	48	58	50
B. Shuster	10	7	13	8	26	52	92	94	96	97	92
J. R. Pitts	0	6	0	15	13	54	100	100	96	92	100
G. W. Gekas	10	13	0	8	13	46	100	100	84	92	92
W. Goodling	5	7	13	15	13	52	100	88	92	92	100
P. English	35	33	44	31	6	46	93	89	68	58	92

*For abbreviations, see p. 220.

RHODE ISLAND

Rhode Island, a quintessentially Yankee state, was Republican for seventy-four years from 1856 to 1930. During this period, Republican governors were in power for sixty-three years, and the state voted for Republican presidential candidates in seventeen of eighteen elections. The break came with the New Deal, which shattered the Republican majority. Since then, Republican governors have held power for only twenty years, and the state has voted for Republican presidential candidates in only four elections. Like Massachusetts, it has become a Democratic bastion where even the successful Republicans, like former governor and senator John Chafee, tend to be moderate and fairly liberal. It took only one election in 1932 to achieve this remarkable turnaround. The heavily Roman Catholic state had voted for the Catholic Al Smith in 1928, but in the 1932 elections, voted for Franklin D. Roosevelt; Rhode Islanders also elected Theodore Green, a Democrat, as governor and bestowed a majority in the state legislature on the Democrats. But in Rhode Island as in all other states, the 1960s also witnessed the beginning of a shift in party loyalties. Republican John Chafee won three successive terms as governor in the 1960s, followed by Edward DiPrete in the 1980s. Chafee also served as senator from 1977 to 1999. So while the Democrats are the favorites in most elections, they are not dominant and the voters are becoming more bipartisan. In 2001, Republicans hold one seat in the U.S. Senate and control the governorship. Democrats hold both U. S. House seats and an overwhelming majority in the state legislature.

Because the Republicans are concentrating on the visible national and statewide offices, they have tended to ignore the legislative elections. The Democratic lopsided majority in the legislature is the result of this Republican strategy. The Republicans are stronger in the suburbs than in the cities, but since Rhode Island is more urban than suburban, the urban Democrats usually carry the day.

Rhode Island has no precincts as such, only voting districts. Therefore there is no party activity at the precinct level. There are no county or regional units either. There are only two levels of party organization: the town or city committees and the state committee. In addition, there are 100 representative- and 50 senatorial-district committees. Representative-district committees have three to five members each and the senatorial-district committees, five to seven members each. The members of these committees are chosen at the party primaries. Republican state-committee membership is based on a complex system. Each of the thirty-nine cities and towns sends three delegates each except for Cranston and Warwick, which send eight delegates; Providence, which sends ten, and another eight of the larger towns, which send three or four delegates. The state committee also includes twenty-three at-large members. State law also mandates that the Republican Party hold its annual convention prior to the general election. The convention adopts the party platform, a routine exercise. Because Republicans are a small minority in the legislature, the party caucus plays a lesser role in relation to the state party committee than is the case with Democrats. Given the small size of the state, Republicans maintain only one office in the state in Providence.

Republican Presidential Victories, 1860–2000
Total: 20 (1860, 1864, 1868, 1872, 1876, 1880, 1884, 1888, 1892, 1896, 1900, 1904, 1908, 1916, 1920, 1924, 1952, 1956, 1972, 1984)

Republican Governors of Rhode Island, 1860–2000
Ambrose Everett Burnside, 1866–1869; Seth Padelford, 1869–1873; Henry Howard, 1873–1875; Henry Lippitt, 1875–1877; Charles Collins Van Zandt, 1877–1880; Alfred Henry Littlefield, 1880–1883; Augustus Osborn Bourn, 1883–1885; George Peabody Wetmore, 1885–1887; Royal Chapin Taft, 1888–1889; Herbert Warren Ladd, 1889–1890, 1891–1892; Daniel Russell Brown, 1892–1895; Charles Warren Lippitt, 1895–1897; Elisha Dyer III, 1897–1900; William Gregory, 1900–1901; Charles Dean Kimball, 1901–1903; George Herbert Utter, 1905–1907; Aram J. Pothier, 1909–1915, 1925–1928; Robert Livingston Beeckman, 1915–1921; Emery John San Souci, 1921–1923; Norman Stanley Case, 1928–1933; William Henry Vanderbilt, 1939–1941; Christo-

pher Del Sesto, 1959–1961; John Hubbard Chafee, 1963–1969; Edward Daniel DiPrete, 1985–1991; Lincoln C. Almond, 1995– .

ADDRESS: Republican Party of Rhode Island, 551 South Main Street, Providence, RI 02903

Tel.: (401) 453-4100

BIBLIOGRAPHY

Lockard, Duane. *New England State Politics.* Princeton, NJ: Princeton University Press, 1959.

McLoughlin, William G. *Rhode Island: A Bicentennial History.* New York: Norton, 1978.

Rhode Island Congressional Delegation, Voting Record as Assessed by Key Groups, 1998*

	ADA	ACLU	AFS	LCV	CON	NTU	NFIB	CPC	ACU	NTLC	CHC
Senator											
J. H. Chafee**	45	86	56	50	75	36	89	89	32	46	20

*For abbreviations, see p. 220.
**Senator Chafee died in 1999.

SOUTH CAROLINA

South Carolina was a Democratic fiefdom until the 1960s. Ironically, the first Republican presidential candidate it voted for was Barry Goldwater in 1964, when the Republicans lost almost all other states. Democrats had long monopolized the state, often winning with more than 90 percent of the popular vote. In the races for the U. S. Senate, state legislature, U. S. House of Representatives, and the governor's office, when the Democrats ran unopposed most of the time, the disspirited Republicans did not even bother to put up a token candidate.

What ended the Democratic stranglehold was the same racial tension that had brought South Carolina into the Democratic camp in the Civil War era. As the white supremacy and the Jim Crow system came under increasing attack in the 1950s and 1960s, white South Carolinians began to flee the Democratic Party, which nationally had become identified with the civil rights movement. Strom Thurmond, the popular governor of South Carolina, was the first to take up the standard against the Democratic Party by running as a States' Rights presidential candidate in 1948. In 1964 he switched to the Republican Party and helped Barry Goldwater to carry the state. In 1965, Republicans gained their first U.S. House seat in the twentieth century when Democrat Albert Watson switched parties and was elected to Congress as a Republican, and in 1966 Re-

publicans became bold enough to nominate Joseph Rogers as their gubernatorial candidate. Although Rogers lost, he received 42 percent of the vote, an unheard-of percentage for Republicans. Republicans also won sixteen seats in the state house. The Republican Party had arrived in South Carolina.

Since the mid-1960s Republicans have chalked up a string of successes. They have won every presidential election since then with the exception of 1976, when southerner Jimmy Carter headed the Democratic ticket. In 2001 Republicans hold the majority in the state house, one U. S. Senate seat, and four of six U.S. House seats. Thurmond has served in the Senate since 1954, making him the longest serving senator in American history.

Before 1964 Republicans did not need a formal organization in the state because the party existed mainly on paper. But success brought with it the need to create a multilevel organization. Much of the funding in the early days came from Roger Milliken, president of the multibillion-dollar Milliken–Deering textile corporation. By the 1970s the party had not only a well-staffed state headquarters but also county organizations in every county and precinct-level organizations in some areas. Republicans' improved morale is evident in the data on party membership, campaign effectiveness, increased ability to raise funds, candidate recruitment, and more effective use of polling and computer technology. The goal of the GOP now is to keep up the momentum of their growth and to capitalize on the failed social policies of the Democratic Party.

Republican Presidential Victories, 1860–2000
Total: 12 (1868, 1872, 1876, 1964, 1968, 1972, 1980, 1984, 1988, 1992, 1996, 2000)

Republican Governors of South Carolina, 1860–2000
James Lawrence Orr, 1865–1868; Robert Kingston Scott, 1868–1872; Franklin J. Moses Jr., 1872–1874; Daniel Henry Chamberlain, 1874–1877; James Burrows Edwards, 1975–1979; Carroll Ashmore Campbell Jr., 1987–1995; David Beasley, 1995–1999.

ADDRESS: Republican Party of South Carolina, 1508 Lady Street, Columbia, SC 29201

Tel.: (803) 988-8440

www.scgop.com

BIBLIOGRAPHY
Carter, Luther F., and David S. Mann, eds. *Government in the Palmetto State.* Columbia: University of South Carolina, 1983.

Hadley, Charles D., and Lewis Bowman, eds. *Southern State Party Organizations and Activists.* Westport, CT: Praeger, 1995.

South Carolina Congressional Delegation, Voting Record as Assessed by Key Groups, 1998*

	ADA	ACLU	AFS	LCV	CON	NTU	NTIB	COC	ACU	NTLC	CHC
Senator											
S. Thurmond	0	29	0	0	14	62	100	94	76	93	82
Representatives											
M. Sanford	20	19	22	38	100	90	86	71	72	76	100
F. Spence	5	6	11	8	13	53	100	78	100	97	100
L. Graham	15	0	11	8	86	72	100	76	88	97	100

*For abbreviations, see p. 220.

SOUTH DAKOTA

South Dakota, like its sister state to the north, was Republican turf from statehood in 1889 to the 1960s. From 1889 to 1994, the Republican Party won 78 percent of the elections for president, U.S. Senate, U.S. House, and governor. It also voted for Republican presidential candidates in all elections since statehood except on four occasions. Its Republican credentials are evidenced by the fact that it chose Richard Nixon over its own native son, Senator George McGovern, in 1972. South Dakotan Republican leaders lean to the right just as much as South Dakotan Democratic leaders such as Tom Daschle and George McGovern, lean to the left. But Republican moderates, such as Larry Pressner and James Abdnor, tend to get elected more often than conservatives. Although factional cleavages exist within the Republican Party, they rarely erupt into the open.

South Dakota has relatively weak parties whose weakness is rooted in history. First, South Dakotans are very egalitarian and have less prominent class divisions than other regions and no elite ruling classes. Party nominations are made in the primaries, thus leaving political parties without any relevant function. Furthermore, state law is very restrictive regarding campaign finances. Political parties in themselves have neither the expertise nor the money to advance the electoral interests of their candidates.

The political pyramid has at its base the precinct. Each precinct has a committeeman and a commiteewoman to represent the registered party members in the county central committee and in the state convention. Often these positions remain unfilled for a long time. At the next level is the county, where most of the partisan activity takes place. The 200-member Republican state central committee is composed of three persons from each county. The executive committee has a much smaller membership, and it is charged with the actual management of party affairs when the state committee is not in session. Another powerful body is the state convention, which drafts the party platform, nominates any state candidate not voted on in the primary, elects the state party chair, and chooses presidential electors. The Republican state headquarters is in Pierre.

Republican Presidential Victories, 1892–2000
Total: 23 (1892, 1900, 1904, 1908, 1916, 1920, 1924, 1928, 1940, 1944, 1948, 1952, 1956, 1960, 1968, 1972, 1976, 1980, 1984, 1988, 1992, 1996, 2000)

Republican Governors of South Dakota, 1889–2000
Arthur Calvin Mellette, 1889–1893; Charles Henry Sheldon, 1893–1897; Charles Nelson Herreid, 1901–1905; Samuel Harrison Elrod, 1905–1907; Coe Isaac Crawford, 1907–1909; Robert Scaddon Vessey, 1909–1913; Frank Michael Byrne, 1913–1917; Peter Norbeck, 1917–1921; William Henry McMaster, 1921–1925; Carl Gunderson, 1925–1927; Warren Everett Green, 1931–1933; Leslie Jensen, 1937–1939; Harlan John Bushfield, 1939–1943; Merrill Quentin Sharpe, 1943–1947; George Theodore Mickelson, 1947–1951; Sigurd Anderson, 1951–1955; Joseph Jacob Foss, 1955–1959; Archie M. Gubbrud, 1961–1965; Nils Andreas Boe, 1965–1969; Frank Leroy Farrar, 1969–1971; William John Janklow, 1979–1987; George Speaker Mickelson, 1987–1993; Walter Dale Miller, 1993–1995; William John Janklow, 1995– .

ADDRESS: Republican Party of South Dakota, P.O. Box 1099, Pierre, SD 57501

Tel.: (605) 224-7347

BIBLIOGRAPHY
Clem, Alan L. *Prairie State Politics: Popular Democracy in South Dakota*. Washington, DC: Public Affairs Press, 1967.
Schell, Herbert S. *History of South Dakota*. Lincoln: University of Nebraska Press, 1961.

South Dakota Congressional Delegation, Voting Record as Assessed by Key Groups, 1998*

	ADA	ACLU	AFS	LCV	CON	NTU	NFIB	COC	ACU	NTLC	CHC
Representative											
John Thune	5	6	0	23	13	48	100	100	92	89	92

*For abbreviations, see p. 220.

TENNESSEE

Tennessee was the most divided non-border state in the South during the Civil War. Its Democratic governor, Andrew Johnson, ran for vice president at the urging of President Abraham Lincoln in 1864, and Republicans managed to retain a toehold in the state into the next century, electing two governors in the early 1900s. It is not surprising, therefore, that Tennessee was the first southern state to experience the Republican resurgence. By the 1950s, Tennessee was voting for Republican presidential candidates, and by 1970, Republicans had elbowed out prominent Democrats from their U.S. Senate and House seats, elected a governor, and gained control of the state legislature. Within the space of two decades, the century-old Democratic power machine was in shambles.

However, Democrats quickly recovered. In 1976, Democrat Jim Sasser upset incumbent William Brock for the U.S. Senate seat, and in 1984, Al Gore captured the U.S. Senate seat left vacant by the retirement of Howard Baker Jr. By 1992, Tennesseans had reverted to the Democratic column in the presidential election of Bill Clinton and awarded both U.S. Senate seats and six of the nine U.S. House seats to Democrats. Democrats captured the governorship in 1986 and 1990 and reduced the Republican percentage of the state house and senate seats.

In 1994, Republicans rebounded by capturing both U.S. Senate seats and the majority of the

U.S. House seats, and winning the governorship. In 2001, they continue to hold both U.S. Senate seats, five of nine U.S. House seats, and the governor's office. Democrats are in control of the state legislature.

The Republicans had always been strong in east Tennessee and the six Highland Rim counties of west Tennessee, which had voted to remain in the Union before the Civil War. Outside these areas, the GOP established its presence only after Barry Goldwater's candidacy provided momentum in 1964. However, even by the 1980s, the party had no presence in more than three-fourths of the counties. In 1993, the party was also deeply in debt and disspirited. However, the 1994 election was a shot in the arm.

State law regulates both party structure and operations. It weakens the party role in elections by mandating primaries to select party nominees for governor, the legislature, and U.S. Senate and House members. The absence of party registration and straight-ticket voting debilitates party identification. State law also regulates the composition of the state party committees, procedures for their election, and their meeting dates and venues. Members of the state party committee are elected at the August primary in gubernatorial election years. At the local level, Republicans generally employ a multistage process to select county executive-committee members, differentiating between counties with fewer than 100,000 inhabitants and those with more than 100,000 inhabitants. The electoral fortunes of party candidates across the state influence the

relationship between state and local parties. Generally, the state party provides technical assistance to local parties and receive, in turn, limited financial assistance. In terms of their organization, Republicans have gained a marked edge over the Democrats, because, coming from the outside as challengers, they work harder to build and maintain their grass-roots base.

Republican Presidential Victories, 1860–2000

Total: 12 (1868, 1920, 1928, 1952, 1956, 1960, 1968, 1972, 1980, 1984, 1988, 2000)

Republican Governors of Tennessee, 1860–2000

William Gannaway Brownlow, 1865–1869; DeWitt Clinton Senter, 1869–1871; Alvin Hawkins, 1881–1883; Ben W. Hooper, 1911–1915; Alfred Alexander Taylor, 1921–1923; Bryant Winfield Culberson Dunn, 1971–1975; (Andrew) Lamar Alexander, 1979–1987; Don Sundquist, 1995– .

ADDRESS: Republican Party of Tennessee, 1922 West End Avenue, Nashville, TN 37203

Tel.: (615) 329-9595

www.tngop.org

BIBLIOGRAPHY

Bass, Jack, and Walter De Vries. *The Transformation of Southern Politics: Social Change and Political Consequence Since 1945.* New York: Basic Books, 1976.

Lamis, Alexander P. *The Two-Party South.* New York: Oxford University Press, 1990.

Swansborough, Robert H. *Political Change in Tennessee, 1948–1978: Party Politics Trickles Down.* Knoxville: University of Tennessee, 1980.

Tennessee Congressional Delegation, Voting Record as Assessed by Key Groups, 1998*

	ADA	ACLU	AFS	LCV	CON	NTU	NFIB	COC	ACU	NTLC	CHC
Senators											
F. D. Thompson	10	0	11	0	52	70	89	89	84	89	82
W. Frist	5	14	11	13	14	59	100	94	80	81	82
Representatives											
B. Jenkins	5	6	11	0	13	50	93	89	100	92	92
J. J. Duncan Jr.	15	0	11	8	65	65	100	78	84	92	92

	ADA	ACLU	AFS	LCV	CON	NTU	NFIB	COC	ACU	NTLC	CHC
Representatives											
Z. Wamp	15	0	11	8	66	71	93	76	84	92	100
V. Hilleary	5	6	11	8	21	61	93	83	96	95	100
E. Bryant	0	6	0	8	13	50	93	100	100	100	100

*For abbreviations, see p. 220.

TEXAS

As the Democratic Party embraced civil rights and liberalism nationwide in the 1960s, many whites fled the party in Texas and joined the Republicans. The Republican Party in Texas also gained adherents among newer immigrants who were more conservative than native Texans. These factors coupled with the ideological rift between liberals and conservatives within the Democratic Party gave Republicans their first chance to gain statewide office since the end of Reconstruction. The first sign that this was happening was the election of Republican John Tower to the Senate seat vacated by Lyndon B. Johnson when he became vice president of the United States in 1961. Competitiveness at lower statewide levels came only slowly and fitfully. As late as 1950, Republican gubernatorial candidates averaged only 11 percent of the vote. But with every succeeding election, Republicans increased their percentage until 1978 when, with Bill Clements running, they won the governorship for the first time in the twentieth century. They won it again with George W. Bush in 1994 and 1998. Bush has proved extremely popular, manifesting a broad appeal to conservatives and moderate Democrats as well as Hispanics, while advocating an approach he terms "compassionate conservatism." The track record was the same in other races. In 1970, the GOP fielded candidates for fewer than one-third of the races for the state house, but this percentage rose to 60 percent in 1990. In 1990 they also won 50 percent of the vote in the legislative elections.

Following John Tower's victory in 1961, the GOP received an organizational facelift. Republicans consolidated their success by streamlining and professionalizing their operations. The party headquarters was moved from Houston to Austin. The party received a further boost in 1973 when Governor John Connally changed his affiliation from Democrat to Republican and Clements won the governorship in 1978. During this period, Republicans were fortunate in having the leadership of two innovative chairs: Ray Bliss and Bill Brock, who helped to launch mail order blitzes by using sophisticated direct-mail technologies.

Although there are ideological rifts within the party, the GOP is relatively homogeneous, in general agreement on fiscal issues and quarreling only on social issues. The conservative wing consistently controls the state party platform, which has always included a pro-life plank. But party platforms rarely constrain the legislative caucus. Republicans also have benefited from a spate of defections from the Democratic Party. As a result, Republicans may well control both the state legislature and the governor's mansion within a few years. Governor George W. Bush, son of former president George H. W. Bush, was elected president in 2000 and his lieutenant governor, Rick Perry, became governor in December 2000.

Republican Presidential Victories, 1860–2000
Total: 10 (1928, 1952, 1956, 1972, 1980, 1984, 1988, 1992, 1996, 2000)

Republican Governors of Texas, 1860–2000
Edmund Jackson Davis, 1870–1874; William Perry Clements Jr., 1979–1983, 1987–1991; George W. Bush, 1995–2000; James Richard Perry, 2000– .

ADDRESS: Republican Party of Texas, 211 East 7th Street, Suite 620, Austin, TX 78701

Tel.: (512) 477-9821
www.texasgop.org

BIBLIOGRAPHY
Casdorph, Paul D. *A History of the Republican Party in Texas, 1865–1965.* Austin, TX: Pemberton Press, 1965.

Havard, William C., ed. *The Changing Politics of the South.* Baton Rouge: Louisiana State University Press, 1972.

Texas Congressional Delegation, Voting Record as Assessed by Key Groups, 1998*

	ADA	ACLU	AFS	LCV	CON	NTU	NFIB	COC	ACU	NTLC	CHC
Senators											
P. Gramm	0	14	0	0	90	73	89	94	96	96	100
K. B. Hutchinson	0	17	11	0	14	64	100	100	88	93	91
Representatives											
S. Johnson	0	6	0	0	43	78	100	88	100	100	100
P. Sessions	0	6	0	0	60	70	100	89	100	97	100
J. Barton	5	6	0	8	81	75	93	78	100	100	100
W. Archer	0	7	0	15	31	65	100	100	92	95	100
K. Brady	0	6	0	0	45	60	100	94	96	95	100
K. Granger	5	19	11	8	13	49	100	100	84	89	100
M. Thornberry	5	6	0	0	60	69	100	89	100	100	92
R. Paul	20	40	38	23	97	88	79	65	88	71	91
L. Combest	0	6	0	0	33	52	100	94	100	97	100
L. S. Smith	0	7	0	8	13	50	100	100	92	97	100
T. DeLay	0	6	0	0	26	57	100	100	96	95	100
H. Bonilla	10	25	13	0	35	66	100	88	92	94	100
R. Armey	0	6	0	8	28	55	100	100	100	97	100

*For abbreviations, see p. 220.

UTAH

In 1887, the People's Party, which had until then controlled every seat in the Utah territorial legislature, chose the Democratic Party as its successor. In 1890 the Democratic Party was formally established, followed by the Republican Party a year later. After Utah achieved statehood in 1896, Republican presidential candidates won four elections in a row from 1900 to 1912. Things changed with the 1916 election, however, when Woodrow Wilson, a Democrat, carried the state. Franklin D. Roosevelt's New Deal brought Utah firmly into the Democratic camp in the 1930s, and some of the most prominent New Dealers were Utah Mormons. In 1940 FDR carried Utah by 62 percent.

Utah made an ideological U-turn in the 1960s, forsaking Democrats with a vengeance. In every presidential election since 1972 Utah has given Republican presidential candidates the highest percentage of their votes. In 1992, Bill Clinton received only 25 percent of the state's popular vote. Since 1976, both U.S. Senate seats from Utah have been held by Republicans, and since 1985, the governor's office has also been in Republican hands. Two of three U.S. House seats are held by Republicans. In the state legislature, Democrats form a tiny minority. There was a time in the

1980s when the highest Democratic office holder in the state was the sheriff of Salt Lake County. In short, Republicans have made a clean sweep of Utah.

Part of the reason for Republican dominance is the GOP's ability to raise funds using sophisticated direct-mail techniques, such as the Elephant Club: Contributors who give large donations become members of the club and gain greater access to party leaders. The party is also engaged in electoral mobilization of its constituents. Because of the open-primary system in Utah, voter identification and mobilization are top priorities for the party. An aggressive absentee-ballot program is an element of this program. The GOP's status as a majority party helps it to recruit the best possible candidates, and it often has a surplus of able candidates for any particular office.

The strongest influence on party policies and programs is wielded by the governor, the two U.S. senators, and the state committee chair. In the 1994 convention, the state-committee chair was given even greater authority than before in the conduct of party affairs. The twenty-member executive committee is the de facto governing authority.

Utah's current position as the strongest Republican state in the union has facilitated a good working relationship with the RNC, which provides symbolic and material help to the state Republican committee. The GOP is a relatively homogeneous party with a well-defined constituency. Groups committed to the conservative ideology, like the College Republicans, the Women's Federation, and the Hispanic Republican Assembly, are well represented in the state committee. Both the Christian right and pro-lifers work within the party and exercise considerable influence beyond their actual numbers.

Republican Presidential Victories, 1896–2000
Total: 19 (1900, 1904, 1908, 1912, 1920, 1924, 1928, 1952, 1956, 1960, 1968, 1972, 1976, 1980, 1984, 1988, 1992, 1996, 2000)

Republican Governors of Utah, 1896–2000
Heber Manning Wells, 1896–1905; John Christopher Cutler, 1905–1909; William Spry, 1909–1917; Charles Rendell Mabey, 1921–1925; Joseph Bracken Lee, 1949–1957; George Dewey Clyde, 1957–1965; Norman Howard Bangerter, 1985–1993; Michael Okerlund Leavitt, 1993– .

ADDRESS: Republican Party of Utah, 117 East South Temple, Salt Lake City, UT 84111

Tel.: (801) 533-9777

www.utgop.org

BIBLIOGRAPHY

Gladerisi, Peter F., et al., eds. *The Politics of Realignment: Party Change in the Mountain West.* Boulder, CO: Westview Press, 1987.

Jonas, Frank H., ed. *Politics in the American West.* Salt Lake City: University of Utah Press, 1969.

Utah Congressional Delegation, Voting Record as Assessed by Key Groups, 1998*

	ADA	ACLU	AFS	LCV	CON	NTU	NFIB	COC	ACU	NTLC	CHC
Senators											
O. G. Hatch	5	14	11	13	14	57	100	94	80	75	62
R. Bennett	10	33	22	13	2	50	100	89	64	74	82
Representatives											
J. V. Hansen	5	7	0	0	23	56	93	100	100	94	100
M. Cook	15	6	11	8	13	48	100	89	84	84	92
C. Cannon	5	13	0	8	7	62	100	100	95	91	91

*For abbreviations, see p. 220.

VERMONT

Vermont is a textbook case of a state whose Republican affiliation seemed for over a hundred years to have been carved in granite; yet, since 1962, some of its highest state offices have fallen into the hands of the Democrats and Independents. In 1974 Patrick Leahy became the state's first Democratic U.S. senator and has remained so ever since. In 1990, Bernard Sanders, a socialist born in New York City, won the state's lone U.S. House seat as an Independent. There have been four Democratic governors since 1962. Yet, this is the same state that voted for GOP presidential candidates in every presidential election from 1856 to 1960—the longest such record in political history. Not only did Vermont choose GOP presidential candidates, it voted for them with resounding majorities. For a whole century from 1854 through 1958, Republicans held every major statewide office as well as U.S. Senate and House seats without a break. Although such one-party rule was common in the South, it was unusual for a northern state.

The state's transformation from a one-party Republican state was slow and engineered by demographics. Throughout the 1960s, non-Vermonters poured into the state, many of them young professionals with Democratic credentials. Soon, the Republican Vermonters were outnumbered. In 1964 Barry Goldwater became the first Republican to lose the state, revealing the transition in the state's political loyalties. The trend has continued ever since. Even when Vermont voted for Republican presidential candidates after 1964, it was tepid in its support. This support stopped entirely in 1992 and 1996 when Vermont moved to the Democratic column and helped to elect Bill Clinton. In 2001, Vermont is represented in the U.S. Congress by the Independent Bernard Sanders, the liberal Democrat Patrick Leahy, and the Independent Senator James Jeffords, who collectively compose one of the most liberal contingents from any state. Jeffords, elected as a Republican senator in 1988 and reelected in 1994 and 2000, left the party in 2001 to become an Independent. Jeffords's switch had national repercussions, as it gave the Democratic Party control of the U.S. Senate.

Electoral volatility, unknown in Vermont until the 1960s, has become a common feature of all contests. State offices are now divided between the GOP and the Democrats as state voters select candidates from opposite parties for key office. This trend was promoted by the office-bloc ballot form, in use since 1978, under which candidates are grouped together by office, so ticket-splitting is easier. Vermont also witnessed another rare phenomenon when incumbents, who were formerly assured of reelection, began to lose with increasing frequency. This, however, did not apply to U.S. senators from Vermont. In the twenty-one reelections since 1914, Vermont's elected U.S. senators have always won reelections.

The Republican Party is strongest along the Massachusetts border and the Upper Connecticut Valley. It is weakest in Burlington, Winooski, Barre, and other towns. In the era of Republican dominance, when Vermonters elected twenty-eight one-term Republican governors in a row, the party was organizationally strong throughout the state. Because GOP control was complete, the offices belonged to the party and not to the incumbent. Party discipline was prized over personality. However, by the 1940s liberal factions had appeared in the party, helped by the crossover of Democrats masquerading as Republicans. To contain factionalism, the party tried to modernize its operations under the direction of Richard Snelling, a business executive and later governor. Despite modernization, the GOP has become a minority party in Vermont, outnumbered in both houses of legislature and out of the governor's office.

Republican Presidential Victories, 1860–2000
Total: 32 (1860, 1864, 1868, 1872, 1876, 1880, 1884, 1888, 1892, 1896, 1900, 1904, 1908, 1912, 1916, 1920, 1924, 1928, 1932, 1936, 1940, 1944, 1948, 1952, 1956, 1960, 1968, 1972, 1976, 1980, 1984, 1988)

Republican Governors of Vermont, 1860–2000
Erastus Fairbanks, 1860–1861; Frederick Holbrook, 1861–1863; John Gregory Smith, 1863–1865; Paul Dillingham Jr., 1865–1867; John Boardman Page, 1867–1869; Peter Thacher Washburn, 1869–1870; George Whitman Hendee, 1870; John Wolcott Stewart, 1870–1872; Julius

Converse, 1872–1874; Asahel Peck, 1874–1876; Horace Fairbanks, 1876–1878; Redfield Proctor Jr., 1878–1880; Roswell Farnham, 1880–1882; John Lester Barstow, 1882–1884; Samuel Everett Pingree, 1884–1886; Ebenezer Jolls Ormsbee, 1886–1888; William Paul Dillingham, 1888–1890; Carroll Smalley Page, 1890–1892; Levi Knight Fuller, 1892–1894; Urban Andrain Woodbury, 1894–1896; Josiah Grout, 1896–1898; Edward Curtis Smith, 1898–1900; William Wallace Stickney, 1900–1902; John Griffith McCullough, 1902–1904; Charles James Bell, 1904–1906; Fletcher Dutton Proctor, 1906–1908; George Herbert Prouty, 1908–1910; John Abner Mead, 1910–1912; Allen Miller Fletcher, 1912–1915; Charles Winslow Gates, 1915–1917; Horace French Graham, 1917–1919; Percival Wood Clement, 1919–1921; James Hartness, 1921–1923; Redfield Proctor Jr., 1923–1925; Franklin Swift Billings, 1925–1927; John Eliakim Weeks, 1927–1931; Stanley Calef Wilson, 1931–1935; Charles Manley Smith, 1935–1937; George David Aiken, 1937–1941; William Henry Wills, 1941–1945; Mortimer Robinson Proctor, 1945–1947; Ernest William Gibson Jr., 1947–1950; Harold John Arthur, 1950–1951; Lee Earl Emerson, 1951–1955; John Blaine Johnson, 1955–1959; Robert Theodore Stafford, 1959–1961; Frank Ray Keyser Jr., 1961–1963; Deane Chandler Davis, 1969–1973; Richard A. Snelling, 1977–1985, 1991.

ADDRESS: Republican Party of Vermont, 100 State Street, Suite 2, Montpelier, VT 05601

Tel.: (802) 223-3411

www.vermontgop.org

BIBLIOGRAPHY

Doyle, William. *The Vermont Political Tradition, and Those Who Helped to Make It.* Montpelier, VT: W. Doyle, 1984.

Sherman, Michael, ed. *Vermont State Government Since 1965.* Burlington: University of Vermont, 1999.

Vermont Congressional Delegation, Voting Record as Assessed by Key Groups, 1998*

	ADA	ACLU	AFS	LCV	CON	NTU	NFIB	COC	ACU	NTLC	CHC
Senator											
J. M. Jeffords	55	57	44	50	36	32	89	89	24	32	9

*For abbreviations, see p. 220.

VIRGINIA

For much of its history, the Republican Party in Virginia seemed consigned to permanent minority status. The politics of the Old Dominion were dominated by powerful Democratic machines that controlled politics to such an extent that the Republicans did not even present a significant opposition party. However, the gradual shift in voting patterns in the South and the movement of new residents to the state has dramatically increased the influence of the party and created a rough parity in the state legislature.

The dominance of the Democratic Party in Virginia was initially broken by the Civil War and Reconstruction. In the late 1870s, a new third party arose known as the Readjusters, who called for a recalculation of the state debt. Led by William Mahone, the Readjusters were composed mainly of Republicans, and from 1877 to 1883 they controlled the state legislature and elected several members to Congress. Mahone established a powerful political machine, but corruption among public officials became so rampant that Democrats were able to erode the machine's power and regain control of state politics.

An election law passed in 1884 gave the Democrats vast control over the election machinery and by the 1890s, the Republicans had been virtually eliminated from state politics. At the 1902 constitutional convention, eighty-eight of the 100 delegates were Democrats. The resultant constitution established a large poll tax and discriminatory voter registration rules that ultimately disenfranchised African Americans and poor whites who supported the Republicans. In 1905, direct primaries became required for all state office elections and this further constrained the ability of the GOP to capture positions.

Though its roots were in the nineteenth century, the Democratic Party machine in the Old Dominion reached its peak in the early twentieth century. After the death of Senator Thomas S. Martin in 1919, Harry Flood Byrd gained control of the party machinery. The conservative Byrd developed a unique and highly powerful political machine whose influence lasted well into later years of the twentieth century. The distinctiveness of the Byrd machine was that it was not based on the usual enticements of patronage and material rewards, but on a set of conservative principles that included fiscal responsibility. Since Virginia Democrats were often more conservative than their Republican counterparts, it made it especially difficult for the Republicans to make inroads in the electorate.

When Byrd began his term as governor in 1926, he initiated a series of political reforms that concentrated most political power in the hands of the governor (governors in the Old Dominion are limited to one term). The Byrd machine handpicked the Democratic candidate for governor, and Republican challengers made little headway as the Democrats controlled the governor's mansion until 1969.

Ironically, the conservative nature of the Byrd machine ultimately set the stage for the growth of the Republican Party in the state. Since national Democratic candidates were usually more liberal than Virginia's Democrats, the electorate often gave a majority of votes to the Republicans in presidential elections, but a majority of votes to the Democrats in state elections. In order to prevent Republican gains, Byrd split the state and national elections so that elections for the Old Dominion's legislature and governorship are held in odd, and thereby, non-presidential election years. This only reinforced the Republican trend as Virginia became one of the first southern states consistently to vote Republican in presidential elections. The Democratic Party was also weakened by election laws that do not require citizens to register by party.

Demographic trends also aided the rise in Republican strength in the state. The Byrd machine's main base consisted of rural, white,

conservative Democrats. The growth of Virginia's cities increased the number of Republicans as many of the new residents disagreed with the Byrd "pay-as-you-go" policy, which prevented the use of bonds to fund road and school construction. The implementation of the Voting Rights Act of 1965 brought African Americans into the Democratic Party, and they worked for a much more liberal agenda. Conservatives in the Democratic Party balked at the growing liberalism of the party and many became Republicans. After Byrd's death in 1966, his son, Harry F. Byrd Jr., took over control of the machine, but its influence had begun to fade. In 1969, Linwood Holton was elected the first Republican governor of Virginia in the twentieth century. He was followed by two other Republicans, including Miles Godwin, who had previously been elected governor as a Byrd Democrat in 1965.

Throughout the 1970s, the Republicans steadily gained strength in Virginia, and by the 1980s, the state had a viable two-party system. In the 1970s and 1980s, the Republicans controlled a majority of the state's representation in the U.S. House. Nonetheless, while the GOP was able to capture the governorship and U.S. Senate and House seats, it seemed unable to gain a majority in the state legislature.

After Republican control of the governor's mansion through the 1970s, the Democrats captured the governorship for twelve straight years as the Democrats fielded candidates who were socially liberal but fiscally conservative. However, the Republicans subsequently won two gubernatorial races. The popularity of Republican governors George Allen (1994–1998) and James Gilmore (1998–2001) helped boost the party's fortunes. Allen's campaign centered on a "get tough" approach to crime, and Gilmore campaigned to repeal an unpopular tax. In the state senate, Republicans have increased their number from four in 1960 to a twenty-two to eighteen majority in 2001. In the state house of delegates, Republicans hold the majority. Statewide polls now indicate that Virginia's population is almost evenly split between Republicans and Democrats.

While the party continues to gain in the state, factionalism has become a problem. The Old Dominion is home to the main leaders and institutions of the Christian Right, and the GOP now faces divisions between conservatives and moderates. Supporters of the Christian Coalition constitute a working majority within the party, but not within the electorate. These differences manifested themselves in the 1994 senatorial election between Oliver North and Democrat Charles Robb, and in several statewide races. North narrowly lost to Robb but in 2000, former governor Allen easily defeated Robb.

Republican Presidential Victories, 1860–2000
Total: 14 (1872, 1928, 1952, 1956, 1960, 1968, 1972, 1976, 1980, 1984, 1988, 1992, 1996, 2000)

Republican Governors of Virginia, 1860–2000
Abner Linwood Holton, 1970–1974; Mills Edwin Godwin Jr., 1974–1978; John Nichols Dalton, 1978–1982; George Felix Allen, 1994–1998; James S. Gilmore III, 1998– .

ADDRESS: Republican Party of Virginia, 115 East Grace Street, Richmond, VA 23219

Tel.: (804) 780-0111
www.rpv.org

BIBLIOGRAPHY
Barone, Michael, William Lilley III, and Laurence J. DeFranco. *State Legislative Elections: Voting Patterns and Demographics.* Washington, DC: Congressional Quarterly, 1998.

Hadley, Charles D., and Lewis Bowman, eds. *Southern State Party Organizations and Activists.* Westport, CT: Praeger, 1995.

Havard, William C., ed. *The Changing Politics of the South.* Baton Rouge: Louisiana State University Press, 1972.

Kidd, Quentin, ed. *Government and Politics in Virginia: The Old Dominion at the 21st Century.* Needham Heights, MA: Simon & Schuster Custom, 1999.

Lowe, Richard. *Republicans and Reconstruction in Virginia, 1856–70.* Charlottesville: University Press of Virginia, 1991.

Moakley, Maureen, ed. *Party Realignment and State Politics.* Columbus: Ohio State University Press, 1992.

Moger, Allen W. *Virginia: Bourbonism to Byrd, 1870–1925.* Charlottesville: University Press of Virginia, 1968.

Roback, Thomas H. *Recruitment and Incentive Patterns Among Grassroots Republican Officials: Continuity and Change in Two States.* Beverly Hills, CA: Sage, 1974.

Rozell, Mark J., and Clyde Wilcox. *Second Coming: The New Christian Right in Virginia Politics.* Baltimore, MD: Johns Hopkins University Press, 1996.

Sabato, Larry. *The Democratic Party Primary in Virginia: Tantamount to Election No Longer.* Charlottesville: University Press of Virginia, 1977.

Steed, Robert P., Laurence W. Moreland, and Todd A. Baker, eds. *Southern Parties and Elections: Studies in Regional Political Change.* Tuscaloosa: University of Alabama Press, 1997.

Virginia Congressional Delegation, Voting Record as Assessed by Key Groups, 1998*

	ADA	ACLU	AFS	LCV	CON	NTU	NFIB	COC	ACU	NTLC	CHC
Senator											
J. W. Warner	20	29	11	13	38	63	100	100	79	86	80
Representatives											
H. H. Bateman	5	15	25	15	5	43	83	100	86	84	83
B. Goodlatte	0	6	0	8	21	61	93	100	100	95	92
T. Bliley	0	13	13	8	13	50	93	100	100	95	100
F. R. Wolf	10	13	22	15	81	66	93	72	80	89	100
T. Davis	15	69	33	38	42	41	86	100	64	67	75

*For abbreviations, see p. 220.

WASHINGTON

From statehood in 1889 to the New Deal in the 1930s, Republicans dominated Washington. The GOP was so powerful from 1900 to 1932 that Democrats could not muster candidates for many statewide elections. However, the tables were turned after the New Deal when the minority Democrats found themselves in the majority and Republicans found themselves swept out of office for almost a whole decade. Some semblance of a two-party competitive system was restored after World War II when divided government became the norm. Republicans were more successful in electing members of the U.S. Congress, and Democrats in maintaining their control of the legislature. However, with the introduction in the 1950s of the blanket primary, which outlawed preprimary endorsements, parties lost their leverage in nominating candidates. At the same time, conservative Democrats began either to defect to the Republicans or to sabotage Democratic legislative programs.

Hit by the blanket primary, the Republican Party began efforts to recoup its influence through centralization of its operations at the state level; professionalization of its staff; and concentrating on postprimary activities including political communication, campaign management, and fund-raising. The state committee became a service-vendor institution devoted to demographic studies, data processing, polling, and voter registration. The state committee created a central pool of service-oriented programs that all Republican candidates could draw on. Voter registration information is one of the crucial information packages that the party delivers to candidates for a small fee. This transformation has made the Washington State Republican Party one of the strongest among the nation's state parties.

There are three hierarchical levels of party organization: precinct, county, and state. Because of the large number of precincts—5,860 statewide—precinct workers are in short supply. The thirty-nine counties are the units where partisan-ship begins actively to exert its influence. In counties that contain multiple legislative districts, a single committee may be set up for each district. The state committee has seventy-eight members, one man and one woman from each county. In practice, the state executive committee handles most of the routine day-to-day affairs. County and state conventions are held in alternate years.

Conservatives are very vocal and active in the Republican Party and captured many important party posts in the early 1990s. Pushing the Contract with America and other conservative programs they attracted many socially conservative Democrats east of the Cascade Mountains. The result was the historic defeat of House Speaker Thomas Foley and many of his fellow Democrats in 1994.

Republican Presidential Victories, 1892–2000
Total: 14 (1892, 1900, 1904, 1908 1920, 1924, 1928, 1952, 1956, 1960, 1972, 1976, 1980, 1984)

Republican Governors of Washington, 1889–2000
Elisha Peyre Ferry, 1889–1893; John Harte McGraw, 1893–1897; Henry McBride, 1901–1905; Albert Edward Mead, 1905–1909; Samuel Goodlove Cosgrove, 1909; Marion E. Hay, 1909–1913; Louis Folwell Hart, 1919–1925; Roland Hill Hartley, 1925–1933; Arthur Bernard Langlie, 1941–1945, 1949–1957; Daniel Jackson Evans, 1965–1977; John D. Spellman, 1981–1985.

ADDRESS: Republican Party of Washington, 16400 Southcenter Parkway, Suite 200, Seattle, WA 98188

Tel.: (206) 575-2900
www.wsrp.org

BIBLIOGRAPHY

Mullen, W. Frank, and John Pierce, eds. *The Government and Politics of Washington State.* Pullman: Washington State University Press, 1978.

Nice, David C., John C. Pierce, and Charles H. Sheldon, eds. *Government and Politics in the Evergreen State.* Pullman: Washington State University Press, 1992.

Washington Congressional Delegation, Voting Record as Assessed by Key Groups, 1998*

	ADA	ACLU	AFS	LCV	CON	NTU	NFIB	COC	ACU	NTLC	CHC
Senator											
S. Gorton	0	14	0	0	45	56	100	89	72	64	82
Representatives											
J. Metcalf	20	0	33	23	2	49	86	83	80	71	100
D. Hastings	0	7	0	8	21	59	100	94	100	100	100
G. Nethercutt	0	13	0	8	60	64	100	89	96	95	92
J. Dunn	0	13	0	8	13	51	100	100	96	100	83

*For abbreviations, see p. 220.

WEST VIRGINIA

The Republican Party has long been in the minority in West Virginia, one of the most solidly Democratic states in the country. Just how much of a minority party is revealed in the number of statewide races Republicans have won since 1932—exactly eight (out of 127 total). These include the election of two Republican governors, Arch Moore, who served three terms (two consecutive), and Cecil Underwood, who served two terms. Locally, the party has enjoyed some success, notably in small, mostly rural counties that have been Republican since Civil War days (a relatively small band of counties stretching from the Ohio River across the middle of the state), but politics in most counties in West Virginia, too, is dominated by Democrats.

The Republican Party's minority status is, in part, a function of party registration in the state. Democrats outnumber Republicans two to one in party registration. It takes an extraordinary Republican candidate or a bitter split within the Democratic Party to enable Republicans to win statewide elections. One such Republican candidate was Arch Moore, the three-term governor. After a defeat in a bid for an unprecedented fourth term, however, Moore was convicted of violating federal campaign finance statutes and sent to prison. This was obviously yet another blow to the Republican Party.

The last Republican governor, Cecil Underwood, has the distinction of having served the state as both the youngest and the oldest governor, having first been elected in 1956 and then again in 1996. His election in 1996, however, came only after the Democratic Party split badly, and the Democratic nominee, Charlotte Pritt, could not expand beyond her original electoral base of political liberals, union members, teachers, and environmentalists.

Although the core of Republican Party support in West Virginia is a relatively small ribbon of rural counties running largely through the center and northern parts of the state (Morgan, Grant, Preston, Upshur, Doddridge, Tyler, Ritchie, Jackson, and Roane Counties), it enjoys a measure of support in five urban counties that allows it to be somewhat competitive in statewide races and more than competitive with regard to legislative seats. Kanawha County, for example, has approximately 63,000 registered Democrats and 33,000 Republicans, but because it is home to the state capital—Charleston—where many white-collar, upper-income persons reside and work, the race between Republican and Democratic candidates is often quite close. Likewise, Wood County, a relatively urban county along the Ohio River containing the city of Parkersburg and containing approximately twenty-one thousand Democrats and nineteen thousand Republicans, is always a very competitive county for the two parties. The same is true of Berkeley County, in the eastern panhandle of the state, near Washington, D.C., where there are about fourteen thousand Democrats and twelve thousand Republicans and where the competition between the parties is always high as well.

The ideological base of the Republican Party is the business community, but a minority segment of the party supports a heavy social agenda. Republicans are at the forefront of sponsoring antiabortion and antipornography laws in the state legislature. They have also been the principal sponsors of a bill to reinstate the death penalty. As the minority party, however, they have not been successful in these endeavors. Still, joining with conservative Democrats from time to time, they have been on the winning side of many issues such as giving tax breaks to business, limiting the effect of environmental regulations, and advancing the interests of selected special interests such as the timber industry, the coal industry, the oil and gas industries, and the public utilities. In a sense, therefore, despite its minority status, the Republican Party in West Virginia has been successful in advancing the core of its business-oriented agenda with or without winning elections. This Republican Party scored a major victory in 2000 when George W. Bush carried the state. Without West Virginia's electoral votes, Bush would have lost the election.

Republican Presidential Victories, 1864–2000
Total: 15 (1864, 1868, 1872, 1896, 1900, 1904, 1908, 1916, 1920, 1924, 1928, 1956, 1972, 1984, 2000)

Republican Governors of West Virginia, 1860–2000
Arthur Ingram Boreman, 1863–1869; Daniel Duane Tompkins Farnsworth, 1869; William Erskine Stevenson, 1869–1871; George Wesley Atkinson, 1897–1901; Albert Blakeslee White, 1901–1905; William Mercer Owens Dawson, 1905–1909; William Ellsworth Glasscock, 1909–1913; Henry Drury Hatfield, 1913–1917; Ephraim Franklin Morgan, 1921–1925; Howard Mason Gore, 1925–1929; William Gustavus Conley, 1929–1933; Cecil H. Underwood, 1957–1961, 1997–2001; Arch Alfred Moore Jr., 1969–1977, 1985–1989.

ADDRESS: Republican Party of West Virginia, 1620 Kanawha Boulevard East, Suite 4B, Charleston, WV 25311

Tel.: (304) 344-3446
www.wvgop.com

BIBLIOGRAPHY

Brisbin, Richard A., Jr., et al., eds. *West Virginia Government and Politics.* Lincoln: University of Nebraska Press, 1996.

Hammock, Allan S. "West Virginia." In *State Party Profiles: A 50-State Guide to Development, Organization, and Resources,* ed. Andrew M. Appleton and Daniel S. Ward, 349–58. Washington, DC: Congressional Quarterly Press, 1997.

WISCONSIN

When Wisconsin became a state in 1848, the Democratic Party was at the acme of its power and the Republican Party was not yet born. It was in a small schoolhouse in Ripon, Wisconsin, that Whigs, Free-Soilers, and antislavery Democrats gathered to form the Republican Party. Republicans quickly became the majority party, a status they retained for most of the next century. The party faced a major challenge when the popular Robert M. La Follette, governor (1901–1906) and later U.S. Senator (1906–1925), bolted the Republicans and ran for the White House in 1924 on the Progressive Party platform. La Follette lost, however, and with his departure, the conservative Stalwarts took over the party. The Stalwart leader, William Campbell, is considered the father of modern Republicanism in the state. Meanwhile, the Progressives dominated Wisconsin politics for over a decade until they became extinct by 1946. The downfall and death of Senator Joseph McCarthy in 1957 provided an opening for Democrats, who soon began to have an impact on state politics. From then on, Republicans have lost the governor's office in three stretches: 1958 to 1964, 1970 to 1978, and 1982 to 1986. Democrats also controlled the state assembly from 1970 to 1974 and the state senate from 1974 to 1993. But the pendulum swung back when Tommy Thompson became governor in 1987. The GOP momentum held throughout the 1990s. Whereas 42 percent of Wisconsin residents identified themselves as Democrats in 1980 and 26 percent as Republicans, the relative numbers had changed by 1995 to 37 percent in favor of Republicans and 30 percent for Democrats.

The Christian right and Right to Life groups are very active in Wisconsin, but they have not yet threatened party unity. However, Wisconsin is an issue-oriented state and philosophical divisions can cause problems for party leaders. The open primary and the lack of partisan registration have prompted the GOP state committee to depend on telemarketing to identify its supporters.

With the exception of Milwaukee County, the county organization is the basic unit. (In Milwaukee, the basic unit is the club). The next level is the congressional district. Each congressional district elects two representatives to the state convention committee. At the state level are the state committee, the executive committee, and the state convention. The state officers consist of a chair, five vice chairs, a state finance chair, a secretary, a treasurer, and a national committeeman and a national committeewoman. Three of the vice chairs represent auxiliary organizations. The executive committee consists of all state officers plus the chair and vice chair of each congressional district; the state chairs of the Wisconsin College Republicans, the Wisconsin Black Republican Council, and the Wisconsin Republic Heritage Groups; the immediate past state chair; and representatives of the state senate caucus, the assembly caucus, and the Republican delegation to the U.S. Congress. The state convention is held annually. In even-numbered years, the convention adopts a party platform. The Republican Party's lead reflected the popularity of Governor Tommy Thompson, who was elected to a record fourth term as governor in 1998 and enjoyed a 70 percent approval rating in public opinion polls. Thompson has played an active role in building the Republican Party in the state. After Thompson resigned to become secretary of health and human services in 2001, the Republican Lieutenant Governor Scott McCallum became governor.

Republican Presidential Victories, 1860–2000
Total: 23 (1860, 1864, 1868, 1872, 1876, 1880, 1884, 1888, 1896, 1900, 1904, 1908, 1916, 1920, 1928, 1944, 1952, 1956, 1960, 1968, 1972, 1980, 1984)

Republican Governors of Wisconsin, 1860–2001
Alexander Williams Randall, 1858–1862; Louis Powell Harvey, 1862; Edward P. Salomon, 1862–1864; James Taylor Lewis, 1864–1866; Lucius Fairchild, 1866–1872; Cadwallader Colden Washburn, 1872–1874; Harrison Ludington, 1876–1878; William E. Smith, 1878–1882; Jeremiah McLain Rusk, 1882–1889; William Dempster Hoard, 1889–1891; William Henry Upham, 1895–1897; Edward Scofield, 1897–1901; Robert Marion La Follette, 1901–1906; James Ole Davidson, 1906–1911; Francis Edward McGovern, 1911–1915; Emanuel Lorenz Philipp, 1915–1921; John James Blaine, 1921–1927; Fred R. Zimmerman, 1927–1929; Walter Jodok Kohler Sr., 1929–1931; Philip F. La Follette, 1931–1933; Julius Peter Heil, 1939–1943; Walter Samuel Goodland, 1943–1947; Oscar Rennebohm, 1947–1951; Walter Jodok Kohler Jr., 1951–1957; Vernon Wallace Thomson, 1957–1959; Warren Perley Knowles, 1965–1971; Lee Sherman Dreyfus, 1979–1983; Tommy George Thompson, 1987–2001; Scott McCallum, 2001– .

ADDRESS: Republican Party of Wisconsin, P.O. Box 31, Madison WI, 53701

Tel: (608) 257-4765
www.wisgop.org

BIBLIOGRAPHY
Crane, Wilder, and A. Clarke Hagensick. *Wisconsin Government and Politics*. Milwaukee: University of Wisconsin, 1976.

Epstein, Leon D. *Politics in Wisconsin*. Madison: University of Wisconsin Press, 1958.

Haney, Richard Carlton, ed. *A Concise History of the Modern Republican Party of Wisconsin, 1925–1975*. Madison: Republican Party of Wisconsin, 1976.

Wisconsin Congressional Delegation, Voting Record as Assessed by Key Groups, 1998*

	ADA	ACLU	AFS	LCV	CON	NTU	NFIB	COC	ACU	NTLC	CHC
Representatives											
T. E. Petri	15	13	11	46	65	70	100	94	88	84	100
J. Sensenbrenner	5	6	0	38	77	87	100	78	92	92	100

*For abbreviations, see p. 220.

WYOMING

Republican dominance in Wyoming has not changed in the last 110 years. After statehood in 1890 Republicans swept all the state offices and won a majority in both houses of the state legislature. In 1994 they won in an identical fashion all the five state government offices and a majority of both houses of the legislature and retained both U. S. Senate seats and the lone House seat. The legislature, particularly, has been a Republican bailiwick, with the GOP in power 96 percent of the time in the senate and 85 percent of the time in the house. With the exception of the governor's office, where Democrats have enjoyed some success, Republicans have dominated all state offices. More than 60 percent of the registered voters identify themselves as Republican and 33 percent as Democrats. The percentage of registered Democrats has been falling for some time, so that the party does not have much of a future in Wyoming.

The Republican political machine was crafted by the first governor of Wyoming, Francis E. Warren, who later served as U.S. senator for thirty-seven years until 1929. He made the Republican Party the favorite of the cattle ranchers, the most powerful political group in the state. Also popular in the state was Alan Simpson, who served in the U. S. Senate from 1979 to 1997. Ronald Reagan also helped to advance the GOP image in the state.

The basic unit of GOP organization is the precinct, each of which elects a commiteeman and a commiteewoman to the county central committee. The state central committee is composed of county party chairs plus a state committeeman and a state committeewoman elected from each county. State conventions are held in even-numbered years. All county and statewide candidates are elected in primary elections. Because Democrats do not pose a threat to Republican hegemony, winners in Republican primaries are a shoo-in. Democrats generally win only when there are bitter intraparty GOP postprimary fights.

Republican Presidential Victories, 1890–2000
Total: 20 (1892, 1900, 1904, 1908, 1920, 1924, 1928, 1944, 1952, 1956, 1960, 1968, 1972, 1976, 1980, 1984, 1988, 1992, 1996, 2000)

Republican Governors of Wyoming, 1890–2000
Francis Emroy Warren, 1890; Amos Walker Barber, 1890–1893; William Alford Richards, 1895–1899; DeForest Richards, 1899–1903; Fenimore Chatterton, 1903–1905; Bryant Butler Brooks, 1905–1911; Joseph Maull Carey, 1911–1915; Robert Davis Carey, 1919–1923; Franklin Earl Lucas, 1924–1925; Frank Collins Emerson, 1927–1931; Alonzo Monroe Clark, 1931–1933; Nels Hanson Smith, 1939–1943; Arthur Griswold Crane, 1949–1951; Frank Aloysius Barrett, 1951–1953; Clifford Joy "Doc" Rogers, 1953–1955; Milward Lee Simpson, 1955–1959; Clifford Peter Hansen, 1963–1967; Stanley Knapp Hathaway, 1967–1975; Jim Geringer, 1995–1999.

ADDRESS: Republican Party of Wyoming, 400 East First Street, Suite 314, Casper, WY 82601

Tel.: (307) 234-9166

www.wygop.org

BIBLIOGRAPHY

Cawley, Gregg, et al. *The Equality State: Governmental Politics in Wyoming.* Dubuque, IA: Eddie Bowers, 1991.

Larson, T.A. *History of Wyoming.* Lincoln: University of Nebraska Press, 1965.

Wyoming Congressional Delegation, Voting Record as Assessed by Key Groups, 1998*

	ADA	ACLU	AFS	LCV	CON	NTU	NFIB	COC	ACU	NTLC	CHC
Senators											
C. Thomas	5	29	0	0	71	72	89	89	84	86	91
M. Enzi	0	14	0	0	84	70	89	94	92	93	100
Representative											
B. Cubin	5	13	0	0	42	63	93	94	100	97	100

*For abbreviations, see p. 220.

PART VII

STATE PORTRAITS: ELECTIONS AND STATISTICS

ALABAMA

2000 Electoral Votes: 9

Election Results, U.S. President, 1972–2000

Year	Democrat	Republican	Win[a]	Total Vote	Dem Vote	Rep Vote	Other Vote	Dem %	Rep %	Other %	R Margin	R Mar %
00	Gore	G. W. Bush	R	1,666,272	692,611	941,173	32,488	41.6	56.5	1.9	248,562	14.9
96	Clinton	Dole	R	1,533,226	662,165	769,044	102,017	43.2	50.2	6.7	106,879	7.0
92	Clinton	G. Bush	r	1,677,472	690,080	804,283	183,109	41.1	48.0	10.9	114,203	6.8
88	Dukakis	G. Bush	R	1,377,970	549,506	815,576	12,888	39.9	59.2	0.9	266,070	19.3
84	Mondale	Reagan	R	1,424,748	551,899	872,849	0	38.7	61.3	0.0	320,950	22.5
80	Carter	Reagan	R	1,307,403	636,730	654,192	16,481	48.7	50.0	1.3	17,462	1.3
76	Carter	Ford	D	1,163,240	659,170	504,070	0	56.7	43.3	0.0	−155,100	−13.3
72	McGovern	Nixon	R	1,006,111	256,923	728,701	20,487	25.5	72.4	2.0	471,778	46.9

Election Results, U.S. Senate, 1980–1998

Year	Democrat	Republican	Win[a]	Total Vote	Dem Vote	Rep Vote	Other Vote	Dem %	Rep %	Other %	R Margin	R Mar %
98	Suddith	Shelby	R	1,292,541	474,568	817,973	0	36.7	63.3	0.0	343,405	26.6
96	Bedford	Sessions	R	1,498,760	681,651	786,436	30,673	45.5	52.5	2.1	104,785	7.0
92	Shelby	Sellers	D	1,544,713	1,022,698	522,015	0	66.2	33.8	0.0	−500,683	−32.4
90	Heflin	Cabaniss	D	1,185,004	717,814	467,190	0	60.6	39.4	0.0	−250,624	−21.1
86	Shelby	Denton	D	1,211,897	609,360	602,537	0	50.3	49.7	0.0	−6,823	−0.6
84	Heflin	Smith, Jr.	D	1,371,234	860,535	498,508	12,191	62.8	36.4	0.9	−362,027	−26.4
80	Folsom	Denton	R	1,296,757	610,175	650,362	36,220	47.1	50.2	2.8	40,187	3.1

Election Results, Governor, 1982–1998

Year	Democrat	Republican	Win[a]	Total Vote	Dem Vote	Rep Vote	Other Vote	Dem %	Rep %	Other %	R Margin	R Mar %
98	Siegelman	James	D	1,314,901	760,155	554,746	0	57.8	42.2	0.0	−205,409	−15.6
94	Folsom	James	R	1,199,095	594,169	604,926	0	49.6	50.5	0.0	10,757	0.9
90	Hubbert	Hunt	R	1,215,626	582,106	633,520	0	47.9	52.1	0.0	51,414	4.2
86	Baxley	Hunt	R	1,233,366	537,163	696,203	0	43.6	56.5	0.0	159,040	12.9
82	Wallace	Folmar	D	1,128,595	650,538	440,815	37,242	57.6	39.1	3.3	−209,723	−18.6

(continued)

ALABAMA (continued)

Population, Registration, and Turnout, 1980–2000

Year	Population	Vot Age Pop	Registration	Dem %	Rep %	Other %	Unregistered	Turnout	TAPV[b]	Rank	TAPR[c]	Rank
00	4,447,100	3,333,000	2,528,963	n/a	n/a	n/a	1,918,137	1,666,272	50.0	36	65.9	25
98	4,351,999	3,267,864	2,316,598	n/a	n/a	n/a	951,266	1,314,901	40.2	24	56.8	8
96	4,273,084	3,172,837	2,470,766	n/a	n/a	n/a	702,071	1,533,226	48.3	38	62.1	38
94	4,218,792	3,138,000	2,283,484	n/a	n/a	n/a	854,516	1,199,095	38.2	38	52.5	36
92	4,136,000	3,058,000	2,367,972	n/a	n/a	n/a	690,028	1,677,472	54.9	31	70.8	43
90	4,040,587	2,981,799	2,381,992	n/a	n/a	n/a	599,807	1,215,626	40.8	22	51.0	37
88	3,990,200	3,010,000	2,451,494	n/a	n/a	n/a	558,506	1,377,970	45.8	40	56.2	48
86	4,052,300	2,949,000	2,362,361	n/a	n/a	n/a	586,639	1,233,366	41.8	19	52.2	37
84	3,990,200	2,893,000	2,343,448	n/a	n/a	n/a	549,552	1,441,713	49.8	41	61.5	48
82	3,945,709	2,823,000	2,135,722	n/a	n/a	n/a	687,278	1,128,595	40.0	36	52.8	42
80	3,893,888	2,730,753	2,132,139	n/a	n/a	n/a	598,614	1,341,929	49.1	41	62.9	46

[a] Upper case indicates victory with a majority of votes cast; lower case, victory with a plurality of votes cast.
[b] TAPV = turnout as a % of voting age population. Rankings are among all states.
[c] TAPR = turnout as a % of registration. Rankings are among all states.

Sources: Alabama Democratic Party, Alabama Republican Party, Federal Election Commission, U.S. Census Bureau.

ALASKA

2000 Electoral Votes: 3

Election Results, U.S. President, 1972–2000

Year	Democrat	Republican	Win[a]	Total Vote	Dem Vote	Rep Vote	Other Vote	Dem %	Rep %	Other %	R Margin	R Mar %
00	Gore	G. W. Bush	R	285,560	79,004	167,398	39,158	27.7	58.6	13.7	88,394	14.9
96	Clinton	Dole	R	240,986	80,380	122,746	37,860	33.4	50.9	15.7	42,366	17.6
92	Clinton	G. Bush	r	253,775	78,294	102,000	73,481	30.9	40.2	29.0	23,706	9.3
88	Dukakis	G. Bush	R	199,159	72,584	119,251	7,324	36.5	59.9	3.7	46,667	23.4
84	Mondale	Reagan	R	200,384	62,007	138,377	0	30.9	69.1	0.0	76,370	38.1
80	Carter	Reagan	R	139,109	41,842	86,112	11,155	30.1	61.9	8.0	44,270	31.8
76	Carter	Ford	R	115,613	44,058	71,555	0	38.1	61.9	0.0	27,497	23.8
72	McGovern	Nixon	R	95,219	32,967	55,349	6,903	34.6	58.1	7.3	22,382	23.5

Election Results, U.S. Senate, 1980–1998

Year	Democrat	Republican	Win[a]	Total Vote	Dem Vote	Rep Vote	Other Vote	Dem %	Rep %	Other %	R Margin	R Mar %
98	Sonneman	Murkowski	R	221,142	43,743	165,227	12,172	19.8	74.7	5.5	121,484	54.9
96	Obermeyer	Stevens	R	230,907	23,977	177,893	29,037	10.4	77.0	12.6	148,856	64.5
92	Smith	Murkowski	R	239,247	92,065	127,163	20,019	38.5	53.2	8.4	35,098	14.7
90	Beasley	Stevens	R	186,958	61,152	125,806	0	32.7	67.3	0.0	64,654	34.6
86	Olds	Murkowski	R	180,562	79,727	97,674	3,161	44.2	54.1	1.8	17,947	9.9
84	Havelock	Stevens	R	205,723	58,804	146,919	0	28.6	71.4	0.0	88,115	42.8
80	Gruening	Murkowski	R	156,762	72,007	84,159	596	45.9	53.7	0.4	12,152	7.8

Election Results, Governor, 1982–1998

Year	Democrat	Republican	Win[a]	Total Vote	Dem Vote	Rep Vote	Other Vote	Dem %	Rep %	Other %	R Margin	R Mar %
98	Knowles	Lindauer	D	176,606	112,879	39,331	24,396	63.9	22.3	13.8	−73,548	−41.6
94	Knowles	Campbell	d	213,127	87,701	87,118	38,308	41.2	40.9	18.0	−583	−0.3
90	Knowles	Sturgulewski	o	186,913	60,201	50,991	75,721	32.2	27.3	40.5	−9,210	−4.9
86	Cowper	Sturgulewski	d	172,521	84,943	76,515	11,063	49.2	44.4	6.4	−8,428	−4.9
82	Sheffield	Fink	d	194,511	89,918	72,291	32,302	46.2	37.2	16.6	−17,627	−9.1

(continued)

ALASKA *(continued)*

Population, Registration, and Turnout, 1980–2000

Year	Population	Vot Age Pop	Registration*	Dem %	Rep %	Other %	Unregistered*	Turnout	TAPV[b]	Rank	TAPR[c]	Rank
00	626,932	430,000	473,648	16.2	24.7	59.1	153,284	285,560	66.4	3	60.3	41
98	614,010	421,749	459,903	16.7	24.8	58.5	−38,154	222,831	52.8	2	48.5	23
96	607,007	414,364	414,815	16.9	24.5	58.7	−451	240,986	58.2	13	58.1	46
94	606,276	414,000	342,107	17.5	23.0	59.5	71,893	213,127	51.5	8	62.3	17
92	587,000	401,000	315,058	18.9	21.9	59.2	85,942	253,775	63.3	16	80.5	14
90	550,043	377,699	300,467	19.3	21.0	59.7	77,232	186,958	49.5	10	62.2	15
88	524,000	385,000	280,904	21.0	20.8	58.3	104,096	199,159	51.7	26	70.9	30
86	534,000	373,000	290,808	22.4	21.1	56.5	82,192	180,562	48.4	9	62.1	12
84	505,000	348,000	305,262	23.7	19.9	56.5	42,738	206,788	59.4	14	67.7	43
82	438,000	310,000	266,224	26.4	16.6	57.0	43,776	194,511	62.7	1	73.1	4
80	401,851	271,051	258,742	26.6	16.5	57.0	12,309	157,588	58.1	21	60.9	47

*Registration figures include out-of-state and out-of-country voters who are not officially included in the voting age population.

[a]Upper case indicates victory with a majority of votes cast; lower case, victory with a plurality of votes cast.

[b]TAPV = turnout as a % of voting age population. Rankings are among all states.

[c]TAPR = turnout as a % of registration. Rankings are among all states.

Sources: Alaska Democratic Party, Alaska Republican Party, Federal Election Commission, U.S. Census Bureau, Alaska Division of Elections Web site <www.gov.state.ak.us/ltgov/elections>

ARIZONA

2000 Electoral Votes: 8

Election Results, U.S. President, 1972–2000

Year	Democrat	Republican	Win[a]	Total Vote	Dem Vote	Rep Vote	Other Vote	Dem %	Rep %	Other %	R Margin	R Mar %
00	Gore	G. W. Bush	R	1,532,016	685,341	781,652	65,023	44.7	51.0	4.2	96,311	6.3
96	Clinton	Dole	d	1,401,791	653,288	622,073	126,430	46.6	44.4	9.0	−31,215	−2.2
92	Clinton	G. Bush	r	1,468,877	543,050	572,086	353,741	37.0	39.0	24.1	29,036	2.0
88	Dukakis	G. Bush	R	1,171,873	454,029	702,541	15,303	38.7	60.0	1.3	248,512	21.2
84	Mondale	Reagan	R	1,015,270	333,854	681,416	0	32.9	67.1	0.0	347,562	34.2
80	Carter	Reagan	R	853,483	246,843	529,688	76,952	28.9	62.1	9.0	282,845	33.1
76	Carter	Ford	R	733,473	295,602	418,642	19,229	40.3	57.1	2.6	123,040	16.8
72	McGovern	Nixon	R	622,926	198,540	402,812	21,574	31.9	64.7	3.5	204,272	32.8

Election Results, U.S. Senate, 1980–2000

Year	Democrat	Republican	Win[a]	Total Vote	Dem Vote	Rep Vote	Other Vote	Dem %	Rep %	Other %	R Margin	R Mar %
00	unopposed	Kyl	R	1,397,076	–	1,108,196	288,880	–	79.3	20.7	1,108,196	79.3
98	Ranger	McCain	R	1,013,093	275,224	696,577	41,292	27.2	68.8	4.1	421,353	41.6
94	Coppersmith	Kyl	R	1,119,002	442,510	600,999	75,493	39.6	53.7	6.8	158,489	14.2
92	Sargent	McCain	R	1,353,077	436,321	771,395	145,361	32.3	57.0	10.7	335,074	24.8
88	DeConcini	DeGreen	D	1,159,312	660,403	478,060	20,849	57.0	41.2	1.8	−182,343	−15.7
86	Kimball	McCain	R	862,815	340,965	521,850	0	39.5	60.5	0.0	180,885	21.0
82	DeConcini	Dunn	D	723,885	411,970	291,749	20,166	56.9	40.3	2.8	−120,221	−16.6
80	Schulz	Goldwater	r	874,238	422,972	432,371	18,895	48.4	49.5	2.2	9,399	1.1

Election Results, Governor, 1982–1998

Year	Democrat	Republican	Win[a]	Total Vote	Dem Vote	Rep Vote	Other Vote	Dem %	Rep %	Other %	R Margin	R Mar %
98	Johnson	Hull	R	1,017,261	361,552	620,188	35,521	35.5	61.0	3.5	258,636	25.4
94	Basha	Symington	R	1,129,416	500,702	593,492	35,222	44.3	52.6	3.1	92,790	8.2
90	Goddard	Symington	r	1,055,277	519,691	523,984	11,602	49.3	49.7	1.1	4,293	0.4
86	Warner	Mecham	r	866,984	298,986	343,913	224,085	34.5	39.7	25.9	44,927	5.2
82	Babbitt	Corbet	D	726,321	453,795	235,877	36,649	62.5	32.5	5.1	−217,918	−30.0

(continued)

ARIZONA *(continued)*

Population, Registration, and Turnout, 1980–2000

Year	Population	Vot Age Pop	Registration	Dem %	Rep %	Other %	Unregistered	Turnout	TAPV[b]	Rank	TAPR[c]	Rank
00	5,130,632	3,625,000	2,173,122	38.2	43.4	18.4	2,957,510	1,532,016	42.3	50	70.5	11
98	4,668,631	3,405,227	2,592,676	40.0	44.4	15.6	812,551	1,017,261	29.9	46	39.2	42
96	4,428,068	3,024,670	2,244,672	40.7	45.2	14.1	779,998	1,401,791	46.3	43	62.4	37
94	4,075,052	2,936,000	2,075,322	42.1	45.0	12.9	860,678	1,129,416	38.5	32	54.4	34
92	3,832,000	2,785,000	1,965,094	42.5	45.3	12.2	819,906	1,468,877	52.7	37	74.7	33
90	3,665,228	2,684,109	1,859,956	41.9	46.9	11.2	824,153	1,055,277	39.3	26	56.7	27
88	3,052,900	2,605,000	1,797,716	42.8	45.8	11.4	807,284	1,171,873	45.0	43	65.2	41
86	3,279,700	2,399,000	1,597,934	43.1	45.5	11.4	801,066	866,984	36.1	36	54.3	29
84	3,052,900	2,257,000	1,462,818	45.4	44.3	10.3	794,182	1,025,897	45.5	46	70.1	37
82	2,878,036	2,091,000	1,140,849	46.9	44.5	8.6	950,151	726,321	34.7	43	63.7	24
80	2,718,215	1,926,705	1,121,169	47.5	43.8	8.8	805,536	874,238	45.4	45	78.0	14

[a]Upper case indicates victory with a majority of votes cast; lower case, victory with a plurality of votes cast.

[b]TAPV = turnout as a % of voting age population. Rankings are among all states.

[c]TAPR = turnout as a % of registration. Rankings are among all states.

Sources: Arizona Democratic Party, Arizona Republican Party, Federal Election Commission, U.S. Census Bureau, Arizona Secretary of State Web site <www.sosaz.com>

ARKANSAS

2000 Electoral Votes: 6

Election Results, U.S. President, 1972–2000

Year	Democrat	Republican	Win[a]	Total Vote	Dem Vote	Rep Vote	Other Vote	Dem %	Rep %	Other %	R Margin	R Mar %
00	Gore	G. W. Bush	R	921,781	422,768	472,940	26,073	45.9	51.3	2.8	50,172	5.4
96	Clinton	Dole	D	884,262	475,171	325,416	83,675	53.7	36.8	9.5	−149,755	−16.9
92	Clinton	G. Bush	D	942,279	505,823	337,324	99,132	53.7	35.8	10.5	−168,499	−17.9
88	Dukakis	G. Bush	R	827,738	349,237	466,578	11,923	42.2	56.4	1.4	117,341	14.2
84	Mondale	Reagan	R	873,420	338,646	534,774	0	38.8	61.2	0.0	196,128	22.5
80	Carter	Reagan	r	823,673	398,041	403,164	22,468	48.3	49.0	2.7	5,123	0.6
76	Carter	Ford	D	767,146	498,604	267,903	639	65.0	34.9	0.1	−230,701	−30.1
72	McGovern	Nixon	R	651,320	199,892	448,541	2,887	30.7	68.9	0.4	248,649	38.2

Election Results, U.S. Senate, 1980–1998

Year	Democrat	Republican	Win[a]	Total Vote	Dem Vote	Rep Vote	Other Vote	Dem %	Rep %	Other %	R Margin	R Mar %
98	Lambert-Lincoln	Boozeman	D	700,644	385,878	292,906	21,860	55.1	41.8	3.1	−92,972	−13.3
96	Bryant	Hutchinson	R	846,183	400,241	445,942	0	47.3	52.7	0.0	45,701	5.4
92	Bumpers	Huckabee	D	920,008	553,635	366,373	0	60.2	39.8	0.0	−187,262	−20.4
90	Pryor	unopposed	D	493,910	493,910	–	0	100.0	–	0.0	−493,910	−100.0
86	Bumpers	Hutchinson	D	695,435	433,122	262,313	0	62.3	37.7	0.0	−170,809	−24.6
84	Pryor	Bethune	D	875,956	502,341	373,615	0	57.4	42.7	0.0	−128,726	−14.7
80	Bumpers	Clark	D	808,481	477,905	330,576	0	59.1	40.9	0.0	−147,329	−18.2

Election Results, Governor, 1980–1998

Year	Democrat	Republican	Win[a]	Total Vote	Dem Vote	Rep Vote	Other Vote	Dem %	Rep %	Other %	R Margin	R Mar %
98	Bristow	Huckabee	R	706,011	272,923	421,989	11,099	38.7	59.8	1.6	149,066	21.1
94	Tucker	Nelson	D	716,840	428,936	287,904	0	59.8	40.2	0.0	−141,032	−19.7
90	Clinton	Nelson	D	696,311	400,386	295,925	0	57.5	42.5	0.0	−104,461	−15.0
86	Clinton	White	D	688,266	439,851	248,415	0	63.9	36.1	0.0	−191,436	−27.8
84	Clinton	Freeman	D	886,548	554,561	331,987	0	62.6	37.5	0.0	−222,574	−25.1
82	Clinton	White	D	789,351	431,855	357,496	0	54.7	45.3	0.0	−74,359	−9.4
80	Clinton	White	R	838,925	403,241	435,684	0	48.1	51.9	0.0	32,443	3.9

(continued)

ARKANSAS *(continued)*

Population, Registration, and Turnout, 1980–2000

Year	Population	Vot Age Pop	Registration	Dem %	Rep %	Other %	Unregistered	Turnout	TAPV[b]	Rank	TAPR[c]	Rank
00	2,673,400	1,929,000	1,555,809	n/a	n/a	n/a	1,117,591	921,781	47.8	42	59.2	42
98	2,538,303	1,884,582	1,471,413	n/a	n/a	n/a	413,169	706,011	37.5	29	48.0	27
96	2,509,793	1,834,248	1,369,459	n/a	n/a	n/a	464,789	884,262	48.2	37	64.6	32
94	2,452,671	1,812,000	1,274,885	n/a	n/a	n/a	537,115	716,840	39.6	29	56.2	29
92	2,399,000	1,770,000	1,317,944	n/a	n/a	n/a	452,056	942,279	53.2	36	71.5	41
90	2,350,725	1,729,594	1,218,525	n/a	n/a	n/a	511,069	696,311	40.3	25	57.1	26
88	2,349,200	1,761,000	1,203,016	n/a	n/a	n/a	557,984	827,738	47.0	39	68.8	34
86	2,372,200	1,729,000	1,197,841	n/a	n/a	n/a	531,159	695,435	40.2	25	58.1	22
84	2,349,200	1,705,000	1,159,588	n/a	n/a	n/a	545,412	886,548	52.0	35	76.5	14
82	2,303,857	1,661,000	1,116,082	n/a	n/a	n/a	544,918	789,351	47.5	13	70.7	7
80	2,286,435	1,615,232	1,185,902	n/a	n/a	n/a	429,330	838,925	51.9	35	70.7	36

[a] Upper case indicates victory with a majority of votes cast; lower case, victory with a plurality of votes cast.
[b] TAPV= turnout as a % of voting age population. Rankings are among all states.
[c] TAPR= turnout as a % of registration. Rankings are among all states.

Sources: Arkansas Democratic Party, Arkansas Republican Party, Federal Election Commission, U.S. Census Bureau.

CALIFORNIA

2000 Electoral Votes: 54

Election Results, U.S. President, 1972–2000

Year	Democrat	Republican	Win[a]	Total Vote	Dem Vote	Rep Vote	Other Vote	Dem %	Rep %	Other %	R Margin	R Mar %
00	Gore	G. W. Bush	D	10,965,856	5,861,203	4,567,429	537,224	53.4	41.7	4.9	−1,293,774	−11.8
96	Clinton	Dole	D	10,018,615	5,119,835	3,828,380	1,070,400	51.1	38.2	10.7	−1,291,455	−12.9
92	Clinton	G. Bush	d	11,047,906	5,121,325	3,630,575	2,296,006	46.4	32.9	20.8	−1,490,750	−13.5
88	Dukakis	G. Bush	R	9,886,254	4,702,233	5,054,917	129,104	47.6	51.1	1.3	352,684	3.6
84	Mondale	Reagan	R	9,389,528	3,922,519	5,467,009	0	41.8	58.2	0.0	1,544,490	16.4
80	Carter	Reagan	R	8,348,352	3,083,661	4,524,858	739,833	36.9	54.2	8.9	1,441,197	17.3
76	Carter	Ford	R	7,682,940	3,742,284	3,882,244	58,412	48.7	50.5	0.8	139,960	1.8
72	McGovern	Nixon	R	8,367,862	3,475,847	4,602,096	289,919	41.5	55.0	3.5	1,126,249	13.5

Election Results, U.S. Senate, 1980–2000

Year	Democrat	Republican	Win[a]	Total Vote	Dem Vote	Rep Vote	Other Vote	Dem %	Rep %	Other %	R Margin	R Mar %
00	Feinstein	Campbell	D	10,623,614	5,932,522	3,886,853	804,239	55.8	36.6	7.6	−2,045,669	−19.3
98	Boxer	Fong	D	8,311,905	4,410,056	3,575,078	326,771	53.1	43.0	3.9	−834,978	−10.0
94	Feinstein	Huffington	d	8,502,891	3,977,063	3,811,501	714,327	46.8	44.8	8.4	−165,562	−1.9
92	Boxer	Herschensohn	d	10,563,178	5,173,443	4,644,139	745,596	49.0	44.0	7.1	−529,304	−5.0
92	Feinstein	Seymour	D	9,947,109	5,853,621	4,093,488	0	58.9	41.2	0.0	−1,760,133	−17.7
88	McCarthy	Wilson	R	9,743,547	4,287,253	5,143,409	312,885	44.0	52.8	3.2	856,156	8.8
86	Cranston	Zschau	d	7,398,462	3,646,672	3,541,804	209,986	49.3	47.9	2.8	−104,868	−1.4
82	Brown, Jr.	Wilson	R	7,805,450	3,494,968	4,022,565	287,917	44.8	51.5	3.7	527,597	6.8
80	Cranston	Gann	D	8,327,308	4,705,399	3,093,426	528,483	56.5	37.2	6.4	−1,611,973	−19.4

Election Results, Governor, 1982–1998

Year	Democrat	Republican	Win[a]	Total Vote	Dem Vote	Rep Vote	Other Vote	Dem %	Rep %	Other %	R Margin	R Mar %
98	Davis	Lungren	D	8,381,850	4,858,817	3,216,749	306,284	58.0	38.4	3.7	−1,642,068	−19.6
94	Brown	Wilson	R	8,658,662	3,517,777	4,777,674	363,211	40.6	55.2	4.2	1,259,897	14.6
90	Feinstein	Wilson	r	7,699,185	3,525,197	3,791,904	382,084	45.8	49.3	5.0	266,707	3.5
86	Bradley	Deukmejian	R	7,443,485	2,781,714	4,506,601	155,170	37.4	60.5	2.1	1,724,887	23.2
82	Bradley	Deukmejian	r	7,876,335	3,787,669	3,881,014	207,652	48.1	49.3	2.6	93,345	1.2

(continued)

CALIFORNIA *(continued)*

Population, Registration, and Turnout, 1980–2000

Year	Population	Vot Age Pop	Registration	Dem %	Rep %	Other %	Unregistered	Turnout	TAPV[b]	Rank	TAPR[c]	Rank
00	33,871,648	24,873,000	15,707,307	45.4	34.9	19.7	18,164,341	10,965,822	44.1	46	69.8	12
98	32,666,550	23,755,178	14,969,185	46.7	35.5	17.8	8,785,993	8,381,850	35.3	38	56.0	9
96	31,878,234	22,795,537	15,662,075	47.2	36.4	16.4	7,133,462	10,018,615	43.9	46	64.0	35
94	31,430,697	22,753,000	14,723,784	49.0	37.2	13.8	8,029,216	8,658,662	38.1	37	58.8	25
92	30,867,000	22,445,000	15,101,473	49.1	37.0	13.9	7,343,527	11,047,906	49.2	47	73.2	37
90	29,760,022	22,009,296	13,478,027	49.5	39.3	11.3	8,531,269	7,699,185	35.0	37	57.1	25
88	28,314,000	20,875,000	14,004,873	50.4	38.6	11.0	6,870,127	9,886,254	47.4	38	70.6	29
86	26,981,000	19,811,000	12,833,920	50.8	38.3	10.9	6,977,080	7,443,485	37.6	30	58.0	21
84	25,795,000	19,094,000	13,073,630	52.1	36.5	11.5	6,020,370	9,559,423	50.1	40	73.1	27
82	24,628,000	18,357,000	11,557,335	53.2	34.9	11.9	6,799,665	7,876,335	42.9	29	68.2	13
80	23,667,902	17,284,322	11,361,623	53.2	34.7	12.1	5,922,699	8,585,821	49.7	39	75.6	22

[a]Upper case indicates victory with a majority of votes cast; lower case, victory with a plurality of votes cast.
[b]TAPV= turnout as a % of voting age population. Rankings are among all states.
[c]TAPR= turnout as a % of registration. Rankings are among all states.

Sources: California Democratic Party, California Republican Party, Federal Election Commission, U.S. Census Bureau, California Secretary of State Web site <www.ss.ca.gov>

COLORADO

2000 Electoral Votes: 8

Election Results, U.S. President, 1972–2000

Year	Democrat	Republican	Win[a]	Total Vote	Dem Vote	Rep Vote	Other Vote	Dem %	Rep %	Other %	R Margin	R Mar %
00	Gore	G. W. Bush	R	1,741,368	738,227	883,748	119,393	42.4	50.8	6.9	145,521	8.4
96	Clinton	Dole	r	1,510,704	671,152	691,848	147,704	44.4	45.8	9.8	20,696	1.4
92	Clinton	G. Bush	d	1,558,541	629,681	562,850	366,010	40.4	36.1	23.5	−66,831	−4.3
88	Dukakis	G. Bush	R	1,372,395	621,453	728,177	22,765	45.3	53.1	1.7	106,724	7.8
84	Mondale	Reagan	R	1,276,792	454,975	821,817	0	35.6	64.4	0.0	366,842	28.7
80	Carter	Reagan	R	1,150,870	367,973	652,264	130,633	32.0	56.7	11.4	284,291	24.7
76	Carter	Ford	R	1,070,827	460,353	584,367	26,107	43.0	54.6	2.4	124,014	11.6
72	McGovern	Nixon	R	953,884	329,980	597,189	26,715	34.6	62.6	2.8	267,209	28.0

Election Results, U.S. Senate, 1980–1998

Year	Democrat	Republican	Win[a]	Total Vote	Dem Vote	Rep Vote	Other Vote	Dem %	Rep %	Other %	R Margin	R Mar %
98	Lamm	Campbell	R	1,327,235	464,754	829,370	33,111	35.0	62.5	2.5	364,616	27.5
96	Strickland	Allard	R	1,469,545	677,600	750,325	41,620	46.1	51.1	2.8	72,725	4.9
92	Campbell	Considine	D	1,466,618	803,725	662,893	0	54.8	45.2	0.0	−140,832	−9.6
90	Heath	Brown	R	994,794	425,746	569,048	0	42.8	57.2	0.0	143,302	14.4
86	Wirth	Kramer	d	1,060,765	529,449	512,994	18,322	49.9	48.4	1.7	−16,455	−1.6
84	Dick	Armstrong	R	1,297,809	449,327	833,821	14,661	34.6	64.3	1.1	384,494	29.6
80	Hart	Buchanan	D	1,173,142	590,501	571,295	11,346	50.3	48.7	1.0	−19,206	−1.6

Election Results, Governor, 1982–1998

Year	Democrat	Republican	Win[a]	Total Vote	Dem Vote	Rep Vote	Other Vote	Dem %	Rep %	Other %	R Margin	R Mar %
98	Schoettler	Owens	r	1,321,307	639,905	648,202	33,200	48.4	49.1	2.5	8,297	0.6
94	Romer	Benson	D	1,116,184	619,205	432,042	64,937	55.5	38.7	5.8	−187,163	−16.8
90	Romer	Andrews	D	984,435	626,032	358,403	0	63.6	36.4	0.0	−267,629	−27.2
86	Romer	Strickland	D	1,058,928	616,325	434,420	8,183	58.2	41.0	0.8	−181,905	−17.2
82	Lamm	Fuhr	D	956,021	627,960	302,740	25,321	65.7	31.7	2.7	−325,220	−34.0

(continued)

306

COLORADO *(continued)*

Population, Registration, and Turnout, 1980–2000

Year	Population	Vot Age Pop	Registration	Dem %	Rep %	Other %	Unregistered	Turnout	TAPV[b]	Rank	TAPR[c]	Rank
00	4,301,261	3,067,000	2,274,152	30.0	35.4	34.6	2,027,109	1,741,368	56.8	18	76.6	4
98	3,970,971	2,930,391	2,563,441	30.6	35.7	33.8	366,950	1,327,235	45.3	14	51.8	16
96	3,822,676	2,765,385	2,285,503	31.5	36.1	32.5	479,882	1,510,704	54.6	23	66.1	28
94	3,655,647	2,685,000	2,034,338	32.9	34.2	32.9	650,662	1,116,184	41.6	26	54.9	33
92	3,470,000	2,561,000	2,003,375	34.0	33.4	32.7	557,625	1,558,541	60.9	20	77.8	23
90	3,294,394	2,433,128	1,932,725	31.1	34.0	34.9	500,403	994,794	40.9	21	51.5	34
88	3,301,000	2,489,000	2,029,518	30.5	32.9	36.5	459,482	1,372,395	55.1	19	67.6	36
86	3,267,000	2,432,000	1,817,370	31.0	33.1	36.0	614,630	1,060,765	43.6	13	58.4	20
84	3,190,000	2,347,000	1,621,306	31.9	31.8	36.3	725,694	1,297,809	55.3	27	80.0	7
82	3,045,000	2,256,000	1,455,734	31.8	31.6	36.6	800,266	956,021	42.4	30	65.7	17
80	2,889,964	2,079,958	1,434,257	31.8	30.7	37.6	645,701	1,184,415	56.9	24	82.6	2

[a]Upper case indicates victory with a majority of votes cast; lower case, victory with a plurality of votes cast.

[b]TAPV = turnout as a % of voting age population. Rankings are among all states.

[c]TAPR = turnout as a % of registration. Rankings are among all states.

Sources: Colorado Democratic Party, Colorado Republican Party, Federal Election Commission, U.S. Census Bureau, Colorado Secretary of State.

CONNECTICUT

2000 Electoral Votes: 8

Election Results, U.S. President, 1972–2000

Year	Democrat	Republican	Win[a]	Total Vote	Dem Vote	Rep Vote	Other Vote	Dem %	Rep %	Other %	R Margin	R Mar %
00	Gore	G. W. Bush	D	1,459,525	816,015	561,094	82,416	55.9	38.4	5.6	−254,921	−17.5
96	Clinton	Dole	D	1,392,609	735,740	483,109	173,760	52.8	34.7	12.5	−252,631	−18.1
92	Clinton	G. Bush	d	1,609,402	682,318	578,313	348,771	42.4	35.9	21.7	−104,005	−6.5
88	Dukakis	G. Bush	R	1,443,387	676,584	750,241	16,562	46.9	52.0	1.2	73,657	5.1
84	Mondale	Reagan	R	1,460,474	569,597	890,877	0	39.0	61.0	0.0	321,280	22.0
80	Carter	Reagan	r	1,390,749	541,732	677,210	171,807	39.0	48.7	12.4	135,478	9.7
76	Carter	Ford	R	1,367,156	647,895	719,261	0	47.4	52.6	0.0	71,366	5.2
72	McGovern	Nixon	R	1,384,277	555,498	810,763	18,016	40.1	58.6	1.3	255,265	18.4

Election Results, U.S. Senate, 1980–2000

Year	Democrat	Republican	Win[a]	Total Vote	Dem Vote	Rep Vote	Other Vote	Dem %	Rep %	Other %	R Margin	R Mar %
00	Lieberman	Giordana	D	1,311,261	828,902	448,077	34,282	63.2	34.2	2.6	−380,825	−29.0
98	Dodd	Franks	D	964,457	628,306	312,177	23,974	65.2	32.4	2.5	−316,129	−32.8
94	Lieberman	Labriola	D	1,079,664	723,842	334,833	20,989	67.0	31.0	1.9	−389,009	−36.0
92	Dodd	Johnson	D	1,454,605	882,569	572,036	0	60.7	39.3	0.0	−310,533	−21.3
88	Lieberman	Weicker	d	1,383,516	688,499	678,454	16,563	49.8	49.0	1.2	−10,045	−0.7
86	Dodd	Eddy	D	976,933	632,695	340,438	3,800	64.8	34.9	0.4	−292,257	−29.9
82	Moffett	Weicker	R	1,083,508	499,146	545,987	38,375	46.1	50.4	3.5	46,841	4.3
80	Dodd	Buckley	D	1,355,961	763,969	581,884	10,108	56.3	42.9	0.8	−182,085	−13.4

Election Results, Governor, 1982–1998

Year	Democrat	Republican	Win[a]	Total Vote	Dem Vote	Rep Vote	Other Vote	Dem %	Rep %	Other %	R Margin	R Mar %
98	Kennelly	Rowland	R	999,535	354,187	628,707	16,641	35.4	62.9	1.7	274,520	27.5
94	Curry	Rowland	r	1,147,054	375,133	415,201	356,720	32.7	36.2	31.1	40,068	3.5
90	Morrison	Rowland	o	1,125,057	236,641	427,840	460,576	21.0	38.0	40.9	191,199	17.0
86	O'Neill	Belaga	D	993,692	575,638	408,489	9,565	57.9	41.1	1.0	−167,149	−16.8
82	O'Neill	Rome	D	1,083,876	578,264	497,773	7,839	53.4	45.9	0.7	−80,491	−7.4

(continued)

CONNECTICUT (continued)

Population, Registration, and Turnout, 1980–2000

Year	Population	Vot Age Pop	Registration	Dem %	Rep %	Other %	Unregistered	Turnout	TAPV[b]	Rank	TAPR[c]	Rank
00	3,405,565	2,499,000	1,874,245	34.4	24.2	41.5	1,531,320	1,459,526	58.4	12	77.9	3
98	3,274,069	2,483,354	1,964,763	35.6	24.3	40.1	518,591	999,535	40.2	23	50.9	19
96	3,274,238	2,476,929	1,881,323	35.7	25.2	39.1	595,606	1,392,609	56.2	18	74.0	4
94	3,275,251	2,487,000	1,795,895	37.6	25.9	36.5	691,105	1,147,054	46.1	16	63.9	12
92	3,281,000	2,508,000	1,961,643	37.7	25.9	36.4	546,357	1,609,402	64.2	13	82.0	8
90	3,287,116	2,537,535	1,703,049	39.2	27.1	33.7	834,486	1,125,057	44.3	16	66.1	8
88	3,233,000	2,492,000	1,795,419	39.2	27.1	33.8	696,581	1,443,387	57.9	13	80.4	5
86	3,189,000	2,445,000	1,670,798	40.1	26.6	33.3	774,202	993,692	40.6	21	59.5	17
84	3,155,000	2,408,000	1,809,017	39.8	26.5	33.8	598,983	1,466,900	60.9	10	81.1	4
82	3,153,000	2,359,000	1,647,514	40.2	26.5	33.4	711,486	1,083,879	45.9	19	65.8	16
80	3,107,576	2,283,820	1,719,108	39.2	26.4	34.4	564,712	1,405,449	61.5	11	81.8	4

[a] Upper case indicates victory with a majority of votes cast; lower case, victory with a plurality of votes cast.

[b] TAPV = turnout as a % of voting age population. Rankings are among all states.

[c] TAPR = turnout as a % of registration. Rankings are among all states.

Sources: Connecticut Democratic Party, Connecticut Republican Party, Federal Election Commission, U.S. Census Bureau, Connecticut Secretary of State.

DELAWARE

2000 Electoral Votes: 3

Election Results, U.S. President, 1972–2000

Year	Democrat	Republican	Win[a]	Total Vote	Dem Vote	Rep Vote	Other Vote	Dem %	Rep %	Other %	R Margin	R Mar %
00	Gore	G. W. Bush	D	327,529	180,068	137,288	10,173	55.0	41.9	3.1	−42,780	−13.1
96	Clinton	Dole	D	270,810	140,355	99,062	31,393	51.8	36.6	11.6	−41,293	−15.2
92	Clinton	G. Bush	d	287,580	126,054	102,313	59,213	43.8	35.6	20.6	−23,741	−8.3
88	Dukakis	G. Bush	R	248,286	108,647	139,639	0	43.8	56.2	0.0	30,992	12.5
84	Mondale	Reagan	R	253,846	101,656	152,190	0	40.1	60.0	0.0	50,534	19.9
80	Carter	Reagan	r	233,294	105,754	111,252	16,288	45.3	47.7	7.0	5,498	2.4
76	Carter	Ford	D	234,864	122,596	109,831	2,437	52.2	46.8	1.0	−12,765	−5.4
72	McGovern	Nixon	R	235,516	92,283	140,357	2,876	39.2	59.6	1.2	48,074	20.4

Election Results, U.S. Senate, 1982–2000

Year	Democrat	Republican	Win[a]	Total Vote	Dem Vote	Rep Vote	Other Vote	Dem %	Rep %	Other %	R Margin	R Mar %
00	Carper	Roth	D	327,017	181,566	142,891	2,560	55.5	43.7	0.8	−38,675	−11.8
96	Biden	Clatworthy	D	275,591	165,465	105,088	5,038	60.0	38.1	1.8	−60,377	−21.9
94	Oberly	Roth	R	199,029	84,554	111,088	3,387	42.5	55.8	1.7	26,534	13.3
90	Biden	Brady	D	180,152	112,918	64,554	2,680	62.7	35.8	1.5	−48,364	−26.8
88	Woo	Roth	R	243,493	92,378	151,115	0	37.9	62.1	0.0	58,737	24.1
84	Biden, Jr.	Burris	D	245,932	147,831	98,101	0	60.1	39.9	0.0	−49,730	−20.2
82	Levinson	Roth	R	190,960	84,413	105,357	1,190	44.2	55.2	0.6	20,944	11.0

Election Results, Governor, 1980–2000

Year	Democrat	Republican	Win[a]	Total Vote	Dem Vote	Rep Vote	Other Vote	Dem %	Rep %	Other %	R Margin	R Mar %
00	Miner	Burris	D	323,569	191,695	128,603	3,271	59.2	39.7	1.0	−63,092	−19.5
96	Carper	Rzewnicki	D	270,954	188,300	82,654	0	69.5	30.5	0.0	−105,646	−39.0
92	Carper	Scott	D	270,090	179,365	90,725	0	66.4	33.6	0.0	−88,640	−32.8
88	Kreshtool	Castle	R	239,969	70,236	169,733	0	29.3	70.7	0.0	99,497	41.5
84	Quillen	Castle	R	243,565	108,315	135,250	0	44.5	55.5	0.0	26,935	11.1
80	Gordy	Du Pont IV	R	225,036	64,217	159,004	1,815	28.5	70.7	0.8	94,787	42.1

(continued)

DELAWARE *(continued)*

Population, Registration, and Turnout, 1980–2000

Year	Population	Vot Age Pop	Registration	Dem %	Rep %	Other %	Unregistered	Turnout	TAPV[b]	Rank	TAPR[c]	Rank
00	783,600	582,000	503,360	42.6	34.0	23.4	280,240	327,529	56.3	20	64.8	27
98	743,603	564,532	469,159	42.0	34.5	23.5	95,373	180,463	32.0	43	38.5	41
96	724,842	538,371	419,695	42.4	35.5	22.2	118,676	275,591	51.2	27	65.7	27
94	706,351	530,000	348,122	43.3	36.4	20.4	181,878	199,029	37.6	36	57.2	27
92	689,000	518,000	342,088	43.4	36.8	19.8	175,912	287,580	55.5	29	84.1	3
90	666,168	502,827	299,150	42.6	37.7	19.7	203,677	180,152	35.8	33	60.2	19
88	660,000	490,000	318,362	43.6	36.1	20.3	171,638	248,286	50.7	29	78.0	8
86	633,000	469,000	296,436	44.5	34.6	20.9	172,564	160,757	34.3	39	54.2	28
84	614,000	458,000	314,034	44.7	33.6	21.7	143,966	254,908	55.7	24	81.2	3
82	602,000	445,000	285,736	44.6	32.9	22.6	159,264	190,960	42.9	28	66.8	14
80	594,338	427,849	300,600	43.9	32.7	23.4	127,249	235,668	55.1	28	78.4	13

[a] Upper case indicates victory with a majority of votes cast; lower case, victory with a plurality of votes cast.

[b] TAPV = turnout as a % of voting age population. Rankings are among all states.

[c] TAPR = turnout as a % of registration. Rankings are among all states.

Sources: Delaware Democratic Party, Delaware Republican Party, Federal Election Commission, U.S. Census Bureau, Delaware Commissioner of Elections.

DISTRICT OF COLUMBIA

2000 Electoral Votes: 3

Election Results, U.S. President, 1972–2000

Year	Democrat	Republican	Win[a]	Total Vote	Dem Vote	Rep Vote	Other Vote	Dem %	Rep %	Other %	R Margin	R Mar %
00	Gore	G. W. Bush	D	201,894	171,923	18,073	11,898	85.2	9.0	5.9	−153,850	−76.2
96	Clinton	Dole	D	185,078	158,220	17,339	9,519	85.5	9.4	5.1	−140,881	−76.1
92	Clinton	Bush	D	222,998	192,619	20,698	9,681	86.4	9.3	4.3	−171,921	−77.1
88	Dukakis	Bush	D	191,182	159,407	27,590	4,185	83.4	14.4	2.2	−131,817	−68.9
84	Mondale	Reagan	D	209,417	180,408	29,009	0	86.2	13.9	0.0	−151,399	−72.3
80	Carter	Reagan	D	169,675	130,231	23,313	16,131	76.8	13.7	9.5	−106,918	−63.0
76	Carter	Ford	D	165,691	137,818	27,873	0	83.2	16.8	0.0	−109,945	−66.4
72	McGovern	Nixon	D	163,421	127,627	35,226	568	78.1	21.6	0.4	−92,401	−56.5

Population, Registration, and Turnout, 1980–2000

Year	Population	Vot Age Pop	Registration	Dem %	Rep %	Other %	Unregistered	Turnout	TAPV[b]	Rank	TAPR[c]	Rank
00	572,059	411,000	354,410	76.6	7.5	16.0	217,649	201,894	49.1	38	57.0	46
98	523,124	420,165	356,381	77.7	7.2	15.1	63,784	136,359	32.5	41	38.3	43
96	543,213	439,604	361,419	78.2	7.1	14.8	78,185	185,078	42.1	49	51.2	49
94	570,175	452,000	361,890	79.1	7.1	13.8	90,110	183,649	40.6	27	50.7	38
92	589,000	471,000	340,953	n/a	n/a	n/a	130,047	222,998	47.3	49	65.4	47
90	606,900	489,808	308,105	n/a	n/a	n/a	181,703	n/a	n/a	n/a	n/a	n/a
88	617,000	489,000	299,757	n/a	n/a	n/a	189,243	191,182	39.1	51	63.8	44
86	626,000	483,000	280,175	n/a	n/a	n/a	202,825	n/a	n/a	n/a	n/a	n/a
84	625,000	488,000	282,169	n/a	n/a	n/a	205,831	209,417	42.9	48	74.2	24
82	631,000	489,000	360,648	n/a	n/a	n/a	128,352	110,664	22.6	50	30.7	48
80	638,333	494,978	288,837	n/a	n/a	n/a	206,141	173,199	35.0	51	60.0	49

[a]Upper case indicates victory with a majority of votes cast; lower case, victory with a plurality of votes cast.
[b]TAPV = turnout as a % of voting age population. Rankings are among all states.
[c]TAPR = turnout as a % of registration. Rankings are among all states.
Sources: District of Columbia Democratic Party, District of Columbia Republican Party, Federal Election Commission, U.S. Census Bureau, District of Columbia Board of Elections and Ethics Web site <www.dcboee.org>

FLORIDA

2000 Electoral Votes: 25

Election Results, U.S. President, 1972–2000

Year	Democrat	Republican	Win[a]	Total Vote	Dem Vote	Rep Vote	Other Vote	Dem %	Rep %	Other %	R Margin	R Mar %
00	Gore	G. W. Bush	r	5,963,110	2,912,253	2,912,790	138,067	48.8	48.8	2.3	537	0.0
96	Clinton	Dole	d	5,297,019	2,545,968	2,243,324	507,727	48.1	42.4	9.6	−302,644	−5.7
92	Clinton	G. Bush	r	5,295,913	2,071,651	2,171,781	1,052,481	39.1	41.0	19.9	100,130	1.9
88	Dukakis	G. Bush	R	4,299,122	1,655,851	2,616,597	26,674	38.5	60.9	0.6	960,746	22.3
84	Mondale	Reagan	R	4,179,166	1,448,816	2,730,350	0	34.7	65.3	0.0	1,281,534	30.7
80	Carter	Reagan	R	3,656,118	1,419,475	2,046,951	189,692	38.8	56.0	5.2	627,476	17.2
76	Carter	Ford	D	3,129,174	1,636,000	1,469,531	23,643	52.3	47.0	0.8	−166,469	−5.3
72	McGovern	Nixon	R	2,583,283	718,117	1,857,759	7,407	27.8	71.9	0.3	1,139,642	44.1

Election Results, U.S. Senate, 1980–2000

Year	Democrat	Republican	Win[a]	Total Vote	Dem Vote	Rep Vote	Other Vote	Dem %	Rep %	Other %	R Margin	R Mar %
00	Nelson	McCollum	D	5,856,731	2,989,487	2,705,348	161,896	51.0	46.2	2.8	−284,139	−4.9
98	Graham	Crist	D	3,900,162	2,436,407	1,463,755	0	62.5	37.5	0.0	−972,652	−24.9
94	Rodham	Mack	R	4,105,138	1,210,412	2,894,726	0	29.5	70.5	0.0	1,684,314	41.0
92	Graham	Grant	D	4,959,455	3,244,299	1,715,156	0	65.4	34.6	0.0	−1,529,143	−30.8
88	McKay	Mack	R	4,065,431	2,015,717	2,049,329	385	49.6	50.4	0.0	33,612	0.8
86	Graham	Hawkins	D	3,429,919	1,877,543	1,552,376	0	54.7	45.3	0.0	−325,167	−9.5
82	Chiles	Poole	D	2,651,829	1,636,857	1,014,551	421	61.7	38.3	0.0	−622,306	−23.5
80	Gunter	Hawkins	R	3,528,028	1,705,409	1,822,460	159	48.3	51.7	0.0	117,051	3.3

Election Results, Governor, 1982–1998

Year	Democrat	Republican	Win[a]	Total Vote	Dem Vote	Rep Vote	Other Vote	Dem %	Rep %	Other %	R Margin	R Mar %
98	Mackay	Bush	R	3,965,159	1,773,054	2,192,105	0	44.7	55.3	0.0	419,051	10.6
94	Chiles	Bush	D	4,206,076	2,135,008	2,071,068	0	50.8	49.2	0.0	−63,940	−1.5
90	Chiles	Martinez	D	3,530,274	1,995,206	1,535,068	0	56.5	43.5	0.0	−460,138	−13.0
86	Pajcic	Martinez	R	3,386,145	1,538,620	1,847,525	0	45.4	54.6	0.0	308,905	9.1
82	Graham	Bafalis	D	2,688,576	1,739,553	949,023	0	64.7	35.3	0.0	−790,530	−29.4

Population, Registration, and Turnout, 1980–2000

Year	Population	Vot Age Pop	Registration	Dem %	Rep %	Other %	Unregistered	Turnout	TAPV[b]	Rank	TAPR[c]	Rank
00	15,982,378	11,774,000	8,752,717	43.5	39.2	17.4	7,229,661	5,963,110	50.6	33	68.1	17
98	14,915,980	11,376,048	8,220,266	44.9	40.1	15.0	3,155,782	3,965,159	34.9	37	48.2	26
96	14,399,985	10,794,242	8,077,877	46.2	41.0	12.9	2,716,365	5,297,019	49.1	32	65.6	26
94	13,952,714	10,690,000	6,559,598	49.5	41.9	8.6	4,130,402	4,206,076	39.3	31	64.1	11
92	13,488,000	10,381,000	6,541,825	50.7	40.9	8.4	3,839,175	5,295,913	51.0	41	81.0	13
90	12,937,926	10,071,689	6,031,161	52.2	40.6	7.2	4,040,528	3,530,274	35.1	36	58.5	23
88	12,335,000	9,614,000	6,047,347	54.0	39.0	7.0	3,566,653	4,299,122	44.7	42	71.1	28
86	11,675,000	9,111,000	5,631,188	57.1	36.2	6.7	3,479,812	3,429,919	37.6	29	60.9	14
84	11,050,000	8,631,000	5,574,472	59.4	34.0	6.6	3,056,528	4,180,051	48.4	44	75.0	22
82	10,416,000	8,090,000	4,865,636	63.0	30.8	6.2	3,224,364	2,688,576	33.2	44	55.3	39
80	9,746,324	7,385,363	4,809,721	64.2	29.7	6.1	2,575,642	3,686,177	49.9	38	76.6	17

[a] Upper case indicates victory with a majority of votes cast; lower case, victory with a plurality of votes cast.

[b] TAPV = turnout as a % of voting age population. Rankings are among all states.

[c] TAPR = turnout as a % of registration. Rankings are among all states.

Sources: Florida Democratic Party, Florida Republican Party, Federal Election Commission, U.S. Census Bureau, Florida Department of State Division of Elections Web site <www.dos.state.fl.us>

GEORGIA

2000 Electoral Votes: 13

Election Results, U.S. President, 1972–2000

Year	Democrat	Republican	Win[a]	Total Vote	Dem Vote	Rep Vote	Other Vote	Dem %	Rep %	Other %	R Margin	R Mar %
00	Dole	G. W. Bush	R	2,596,645	1,116,230	1,419,720	60,695	43.0	54.7	2.3	303,490	11.7
96	Clinton	Dole	r	2,298,899	1,053,849	1,080,843	164,207	45.8	47.0	7.1	26,994	1.2
92	Clinton	G. Bush	d	2,313,875	1,008,966	995,252	309,657	43.6	43.0	13.4	–13,714	–0.6
88	Dukakis	G. Bush	R	1,809,657	714,792	1,081,331	13,534	39.5	59.8	0.8	366,539	20.3
84	Mondale	Reagan	R	1,775,350	706,628	1,068,722	0	39.8	60.2	0.0	362,094	20.4
80	Carter	Reagan	D	1,580,956	890,733	654,168	36,055	56.3	41.4	2.3	–236,565	–15.0
76	Carter	Ford	D	1,463,152	979,409	483,743	0	66.9	33.1	0.0	–495,666	–33.9
72	McGovern	Nixon	R	1,174,772	289,529	881,496	3,747	24.7	75.0	0.3	591,967	50.4

Election Results, U.S. Senate, 1980–2000

Year	Democrat	Republican	Win[a]	Total Vote	Dem Vote	Rep Vote	Other Vote	Dem %	Rep %	Other %	R Margin	R Mar %
00	Miller	Mattingly	D	2,428,513	1,413,224	920,478	94,811	58.2	37.9	3.9	–492,746	–20.3
98	Coles	Coverdell	R	1,753,911	791,904	918,540	43,467	45.2	52.4	2.5	126,636	7.2
96	Cleland	Millner	d	2,259,224	1,103,993	1,073,969	81,262	48.9	47.5	3.6	–30,024	–1.3
92	Fowler, Jr.	Coverdell	d	2,251,576	1,108,416	1,073,282	69,878	49.2	47.7	3.1	–35,134	–1.6
92	Fowler, Jr.	Coverdell	R	1,253,991	618,877	635,114	—	49.4	50.7	0.0	16,237	1.3
90	Nunn	unopposed	D	1,033,439	1,033,439	—	0	100.0	—	0.0	1,033,439	–100.0
86	Fowler, Jr.	Mattingly	D	1,224,948	623,707	601,241	0	50.9	49.1	0.0	–22,466	–1.8
84	Nunn	Hicks	D	1,681,300	1,344,104	337,196	0	79.9	20.1	0.0	–1,006,908	–59.9
80	Talmadge	Mattingly	R	1,579,829	776,143	803,686	0	49.1	50.9	0.0	27,543	1.7

Election Results, Governor, 1982–1998

Year	Democrat	Republican	Win[a]	Total Vote	Dem Vote	Rep Vote	Other Vote	Dem %	Rep %	Other %	R Margin	R Mar %
98	Barnes	Millner	D	1,792,808	941,076	790,201	61,531	52.5	44.1	3.4	–150,875	–8.4
94	Miller	Millner	D	1,545,297	788,926	756,371	0	51.1	49.0	0.0	–32,555	–2.1
90	Miller	Isakson	D	1,412,287	766,662	645,625	0	54.3	45.7	0.0	–121,037	–8.6
86	Harris	Davis	D	1,174,977	828,465	346,512	0	70.5	29.5	0.0	–481,953	–41.0
82	Harris	Bell	D	1,168,586	734,090	434,496	0	62.8	37.2	0.0	–299,594	–25.6

Population, Registration, and Turnout, 1980–2000

Year	Population	Vot Age Pop	Registration	Dem %	Rep %	Other %	Unregistered	Turnout	TAPVᵇ	Rank	TAPRᶜ	Rank
00	8,186,453	5,893,000	3,859,960	n/a	n/a	n/a	4,326,493	2,583,208	43.8	47	66.9	21
98	7,642,207	5,619,856	3,910,740	n/a	n/a	n/a	1,709,116	1,792,808	31.9	42	45.8	28
96	7,353,225	5,277,288	3,811,384	n/a	n/a	n/a	1,465,904	2,298,899	43.6	45	60.3	42
94	7,055,336	5,164,000	3,003,527	n/a	n/a	n/a	2,160,473	1,545,297	29.9	49	51.4	42
92	6,751,000	4,949,000	3,177,061	n/a	n/a	n/a	1,771,939	2,313,875	46.8	48	72.8	36
90	6,478,216	4,750,913	2,772,816	n/a	n/a	n/a	1,978,097	1,412,287	29.7	46	50.9	36
88	6,342,000	4,665,000	2,941,339	n/a	n/a	n/a	1,723,661	1,809,657	38.8	50	61.5	46
86	6,104,000	4,402,000	2,575,819	n/a	n/a	n/a	1,826,181	1,224,948	27.8	47	47.6	39
84	5,842,000	4,228,000	2,732,332	n/a	n/a	n/a	1,495,668	1,776,120	42.0	50	65.0	47
82	5,639,000	4,049,000	2,316,718	n/a	n/a	n/a	1,732,282	1,168,604	28.9	48	50.4	44
80	5,463,105	3,813,692	2,466,786	n/a	n/a	n/a	1,346,906	1,596,583	41.9	49	64.7	45

[a]Upper case indicates victory with a majority of votes cast; lower case, victory with a plurality of votes cast.
[b]TAPV = turnout as a % of voting age population. Rankings are among all states.
[c]TAPR = turnout as a % of registration. Rankings are among all states.

Sources: Georgia Democratic Party, Georgia Republican Party, Federal Election Commission, U.S. Census Bureau.

HAWAII

2000 Electoral Votes: 4

Election Results, U.S. President, 1972–2000

Year	Democrat	Republican	Win[a]	Total Vote	Dem Vote	Rep Vote	Other Vote	Dem %	Rep %	Other %	R Margin	R Mar %
00	Gore	G. W. Bush	D	367,951	205,286	137,845	24,820	55.8	37.5	6.7	−67,441	−18.3
96	Clinton	Dole	D	360,120	205,012	113,943	41,165	56.9	31.6	11.4	−91,069	−25.3
92	Clinton	G. Bush	d	369,135	179,310	136,822	53,003	48.6	37.1	14.4	−42,488	−11.5
88	Dukakis	G. Bush	D	354,461	192,364	158,625	3,472	54.3	44.8	1.0	−33,739	−9.5
84	Mondale	Reagan	R	332,204	147,154	185,050	0	44.3	55.7	0.0	37,896	11.4
80	Carter	Reagan	d	298,012	135,879	130,112	32,021	45.6	43.7	10.8	−5,767	−1.9
76	Carter	Ford	D	287,378	147,375	140,003	0	51.3	48.7	0.0	−7,372	−2.6
72	McGovern	Nixon	R	270,366	101,433	168,933	0	37.5	62.5	0.0	67,500	25.0

Election Results, U.S. Senate, 1980–2000

Year	Democrat	Republican	Win[a]	Total Vote	Dem Vote	Rep Vote	Other Vote	Dem %	Rep %	Other %	R Margin	R Mar %
00	Akaka	Carroll	D	345,623	251,215	84,701	9,707	72.7	24.5	2.8	−166,514	−48.2
98	Inouye	Young	D	398,124	315,252	70,964	11,908	79.2	17.8	3.0	−244,288	−61.4
94	Akaka	Hustace	D	356,902	256,189	86,320	14,393	71.8	24.2	4.0	−169,869	−47.6
92	Inouye	Reed	D	356,115	208,266	97,928	49,921	58.5	27.5	14.0	−110,338	−31.0
90	Akaka	Saiki	D	344,879	188,901	155,978	0	54.8	45.2	0.0	−32,923	−9.5
88	Matsunaga	Hustace	D	323,876	247,941	66,987	8,948	76.6	20.7	2.8	−180,954	−55.9
86	Inouye	Hutchinson	D	328,797	241,887	86,910	0	73.6	26.4	0.0	−154,977	−47.1
82	Matsunaga	Brown	D	306,410	245,386	52,071	8,953	80.1	17.0	2.9	−193,315	−63.1
80	Inouye	Brown	D	288,006	224,485	53,068	10,453	78.0	18.4	3.6	−171,417	−59.5

Election Results, Governor, 1982–1998

Year	Democrat	Republican	Win[a]	Total Vote	Dem Vote	Rep Vote	Other Vote	Dem %	Rep %	Other %	R Margin	R Mar %
98	Cayetano	Lingle	D	407,556	204,206	198,952	4,398	50.1	48.8	1.1	−5,254	−1.3
94	Cayetano	Saiki	d	369,013	134,978	107,908	126,127	36.6	29.2	34.2	−27,070	−7.3
90	Waihee	Hemmings	D	334,801	203,491	131,310	0	60.8	39.2	0.0	−72,181	−21.6
86	Waihee	Anderson	D	334,115	173,655	160,460	0	52.0	48.0	0.0	−13,195	−3.9
82	Ariyoshi	Anderson	d	311,853	141,043	81,507	89,303	45.2	26.1	28.6	−59,536	−19.1

Population, Registration, and Turnout, 1980–2000

Year	Population	Vot Age Pop	Registration	Dem %	Rep %	Other %	Unregistered	Turnout	TAPV[b]	Rank	TAPR[c]	Rank
00	1,211,537	909,000	637,349	n/a	n/a	n/a	574,188	367,951	40.5	51	57.7	44
98	1,193,001	894,674	601,404	n/a	n/a	n/a	293,270	407,556	45.6	8	67.8	3
96	1,183,723	877,553	544,916	n/a	n/a	n/a	332,637	360,120	41.0	51	66.1	25
94	1,178,564	874,000	488,889	n/a	n/a	n/a	385,111	369,013	42.2	25	75.5	2
92	1,160,000	867,000	464,495	n/a	n/a	n/a	402,505	369,135	42.6	51	79.5	17
90	1,108,229	828,103	453,389	n/a	n/a	n/a	374,714	344,879	41.6	19	76.1	1
88	1,098,000	824,000	443,742	n/a	n/a	n/a	380,258	354,461	43.0	47	79.9	4
86	1,062,000	782,000	419,794	n/a	n/a	n/a	362,206	334,115	42.7	18	79.6	1
84	1,037,000	758,000	418,904	n/a	n/a	n/a	339,096	335,846	44.3	47	80.2	6
82	994,000	725,000	405,005	n/a	n/a	n/a	319,995	311,853	43.0	27	77.0	1
80	964,691	689,540	402,795	n/a	n/a	n/a	286,745	303,287	44.0	47	75.3	27

[a]Upper case indicates victory with a majority of votes cast; lower case, victory with a plurality of votes cast.

[b]TAPV = turnout as a % of voting age population. Rankings are among all states.

[c]TAPR = turnout as a % of registration. Rankings are among all states.

Sources: Hawaii Democratic Party, Hawaii Republican Party, Federal Election Commission, U.S. Census Bureau.

IDAHO

2000 Electoral Votes: 4

Election Results, U.S. President, 1972–2000

Year	Democrat	Republican	Win[a]	Total Vote	Dem Vote	Rep Vote	Other Vote	Dem %	Rep %	Other %	R Margin	R Mar %
00	Gore	G. W. Bush	R	501,615	138,637	336,937	26,041	27.6	67.2	5.2	198,300	39.5
96	Clinton	Dole	R	491,711	165,443	256,595	69,673	33.7	52.2	14.2	91,152	18.5
92	Clinton	G. Bush	r	470,053	137,013	202,645	130,395	29.2	43.1	27.7	65,632	14.0
88	Dukakis	G. Bush	R	408,968	147,272	253,881	7,815	36.0	62.1	1.9	106,609	26.1
84	Mondale	Reagan	R	406,033	108,510	297,523	0	26.7	73.3	0.0	189,013	46.6
80	Carter	Reagan	R	427,949	110,192	290,699	27,058	25.8	67.9	6.3	180,507	42.2
76	Carter	Ford	R	330,700	126,549	204,151	0	38.3	61.7	0.0	77,602	23.5
72	McGovern	Nixon	R	310,379	80,826	199,384	30,169	26.0	64.2	9.7	118,558	38.2

Election Results, U.S. Senate, 1980–1998

Year	Democrat	Republican	Win[a]	Total Vote	Dem Vote	Rep Vote	Other Vote	Dem %	Rep %	Other %	R Margin	R Mar %
98	Mauk	Crapo	R	378,174	107,375	262,966	7,833	28.4	69.5	2.1	155,591	41.1
96	Minnick	Craig	R	497,233	198,422	283,532	15,279	39.9	57.0	3.1	85,110	17.1
92	Stallings	Kempthorne	R	478,504	208,036	270,468	0	43.5	56.5	0.0	62,432	13.0
90	Twilegar	Craig	R	315,936	122,295	193,641	0	38.7	61.3	0.0	71,346	22.6
86	Evans	Symms	R	382,024	185,066	196,958	0	48.4	51.6	0.0	11,892	3.1
84	Busch	McClure	R	406,168	105,591	293,193	7,384	26.0	72.2	1.8	187,602	46.2
80	Church	Symms	r	439,647	214,439	218,701	6,507	48.8	49.8	1.5	4,262	1.0

Election Results, Governor, 1982–1998

Year	Democrat	Republican	Win[a]	Total Vote	Dem Vote	Rep Vote	Other Vote	Dem %	Rep %	Other %	R Margin	R Mar %
98	Huntley	Kempthorne	R	381,248	110,815	258,095	12,338	29.1	67.7	3.2	147,280	38.6
94	EchoHawk	Batt	R	413,279	181,363	216,123	15,793	43.9	52.3	3.8	34,760	8.4
90	Andrus	Fairchild	D	320,610	218,673	101,937	0	68.2	31.8	0.0	−116,736	−36.4
86	Andrus	Leroy	d	387,426	193,429	189,794	4,203	49.9	49.0	1.1	−3,635	−0.9
82	Evans	Batt	D	326,522	165,365	161,157	0	50.6	49.4	0.0	−4,208	−1.3

Population, Registration, and Turnout, 1980–2000

Year	Population	Vot Age Pop	Registration	Dem %	Rep %	Other %	Unregistered	Turnout	TAPV[b]	Rank	TAPR[c]	Rank
00	1,293,953	921,000	728,085	n/a	n/a	n/a	565,868	501,615	54.5	22	68.9	13
98	1,228,684	877,526	661,433	n/a	n/a	n/a	216,093	381,248	43.4	16	57.6	6
96	1,189,251	815,337	700,430	n/a	n/a	n/a	114,907	497,233	61.0	6	71.0	11
94	1,133,034	794,000	625,803	n/a	n/a	n/a	168,197	413,279	52.1	7	66.0	9
92	1,067,000	743,000	611,121	n/a	n/a	n/a	131,879	478,504	64.4	12	78.3	22
90	1,006,749	698,344	540,247	n/a	n/a	n/a	158,097	320,610	45.9	15	59.3	22
88	1,003,000	701,000	572,430	n/a	n/a	n/a	128,570	408,968	58.3	12	71.4	27
86	1,003,000	705,000	549,934	n/a	n/a	n/a	155,066	387,426	55.0	3	70.4	7
84	999,000	689,000	582,196	n/a	n/a	n/a	106,804	411,144	59.7	12	70.6	35
82	975,000	665,000	541,164	n/a	n/a	n/a	123,836	326,522	49.1	10	60.3	33
80	943,935	636,858	581,006	n/a	n/a	n/a	55,852	439,647	69.0	2	75.7	21

[a]Upper case indicates victory with a majority of votes cast; lower case, victory with a plurality of votes cast.
[b]TAPV = turnout as a % of voting age population. Rankings are among all states.
[c]TAPR = turnout as a % of registration. Rankings are among all states.
Sources: Idaho Democratic Party, Idaho Republican Party, Federal Election Commission, U.S. Census Bureau.

ILLINOIS

Election Results, U.S. President, 1972–2000

2000 Electoral Votes: 22

Year	Democrat	Republican	Win[a]	Total Vote	Dem Vote	Rep Vote	Other Vote	Dem %	Rep %	Other %	R Margin	R Mar %
00	Gore	G. W. Bush	D	4,742,108	2,589,026	2,019,421	133,661	54.6	42.6	2.8	−569,605	−12.0
96	Clinton	Dole	D	4,309,933	2,341,744	1,587,021	381,168	54.3	36.8	8.8	−754,723	−17.5
92	Clinton	G. Bush	d	5,027,961	2,453,350	1,734,096	840,515	48.8	34.5	16.7	−719,254	−14.3
88	Dukakis	G. Bush	R	4,559,120	2,215,940	2,310,939	32,241	48.6	50.7	0.7	94,999	2.1
84	Mondale	Reagan	R	4,793,602	2,086,499	2,707,103	0	43.5	56.5	0.0	620,604	12.9
80	Carter	Reagan	R	4,686,216	1,981,413	2,358,049	346,754	42.3	50.3	7.4	376,636	8.0
76	Carter	Ford	R	4,691,503	2,271,295	2,364,269	55,939	48.4	50.4	1.2	92,974	2.0
72	McGovern	Nixon	R	4,723,236	1,913,472	2,788,179	21,585	40.5	59.0	0.5	874,707	18.5

Election Results, U.S. Senate, 1980–1998

Year	Democrat	Republican	Win[a]	Total Vote	Dem Vote	Rep Vote	Other Vote	Dem %	Rep %	Other %	R Margin	R Mar %
98	Moseley-Braun	Fitzgerald	R	3,394,241	1,610,496	1,709,041	74,704	47.5	50.4	2.2	98,545	2.9
96	Durbin	Salvi	D	4,246,494	2,384,028	1,728,824	133,642	56.1	40.7	3.2	−655,204	−15.4
92	Braun	Williamson	D	4,758,062	2,631,229	2,126,833	0	55.3	44.7	0.0	−504,396	−10.6
90	Simon	Martin	D	3,251,005	2,115,377	1,135,628	0	65.1	34.9	0.0	−979,749	−30.1
86	Dixon	Koehler	D	3,122,883	2,033,783	1,053,734	35,366	65.1	33.7	1.1	−980,049	−31.4
84	Simon	Percy	D	4,787,200	2,397,303	2,308,039	81,858	50.1	48.2	1.7	−89,264	−1.9
80	Dixon	O'Neal	D	4,579,933	2,565,302	1,946,296	68,335	56.0	42.5	1.5	−619,006	−13.5

Election Results, Governor, 1982–1998

Year	Democrat	Republican	Win[a]	Total Vote	Dem Vote	Rep Vote	Other Vote	Dem %	Rep %	Other %	R Margin	R Mar %
98	Poshard	Ryan	R	3,358,657	1,594,191	1,714,094	50,372	47.5	51.0	1.5	119,903	3.6
94	Netsch	Edgar	R	3,106,556	1,069,850	1,984,318	52,388	34.4	63.9	1.7	914,468	29.4
90	Hartigan	Edgar	R	3,222,343	1,569,217	1,653,126	0	48.7	51.3	0.0	83,909	2.6
86	unopposed	Thompson	R	3,143,978	–	1,655,849	1,488,129	–	52.7	47.3	1,655,849	52.7
82	Stevenson	Thompson	r	3,673,546	1,811,027	1,816,101	46,418	49.3	49.4	1.3	5,074	0.1

Population, Registration, and Turnout, 1980–2000

Year	Population	Vot Age Pop	Registration	Dem %	Rep %	Other %	Unregistered	Turnout	TAPV[b]	Rank	TAPR[c]	Rank
00	12,419,293	8,983,000	7,129,026	n/a	n/a	n/a	5,290,267	4,742,115	52.8	28	66.5	22
98	12,045,326	8,857,994	6,754,998	n/a	n/a	n/a	2,102,996	3,394,241	38.3	28	50.2	20
96	11,846,544	8,704,046	6,663,301	n/a	n/a	n/a	2,040,745	4,309,933	49.5	29	64.7	31
94	11,751,774	8,668,000	6,119,001	n/a	n/a	n/a	2,548,999	3,106,556	35.8	41	50.8	41
92	11,631,000	8,603,000	6,600,358	n/a	n/a	n/a	2,002,642	5,027,961	58.4	27	76.2	28
90	11,430,602	8,484,236	6,031,858	n/a	n/a	n/a	2,452,378	3,251,005	38.3	29	53.9	32
88	11,614,000	8,550,000	6,356,940	n/a	n/a	n/a	2,193,060	4,559,120	53.3	24	71.7	24
86	11,553,000	8,490,000	6,003,811	n/a	n/a	n/a	2,486,189	3,143,794	37.0	33	52.4	36
84	11,522,000	8,436,000	6,470,438	n/a	n/a	n/a	1,965,562	4,819,088	57.1	20	74.5	21
82	11,448,000	8,344,000	5,965,514	n/a	n/a	n/a	2,378,486	3,690,616	44.2	22	61.9	28
80	11,426,518	8,179,101	6,230,332	n/a	n/a	n/a	1,948,769	4,749,117	58.1	20	76.2	20

[a]Upper case indicates victory with a majority of votes cast; lower case, victory with a plurality of votes cast.

[b]TAPV = turnout as a % of voting age population. Rankings are among all states.

[c]TAPR = turnout as a % of registration. Rankings are among all states.

Sources: Illinois Democratic Party, Illinois Republican Party, Federal Election Commission, U.S. Census Bureau, Illinois State Board of Elections.

INDIANA

2000 Electoral Votes: 12

Election Results, U.S. President, 1972–2000

Year	Democrat	Republican	Win[a]	Total Vote	Dem Vote	Rep Vote	Other Vote	Dem %	Rep %	Other %	R Margin	R Mar %
00	Gore	G. W. Bush	R	2,199,302	901,980	1,245,836	51,486	41.0	56.6	2.3	343,856	15.6
96	Clinton	Dole	r	2,134,048	887,424	1,006,693	239,931	41.6	47.2	11.2	119,269	5.6
92	Clinton	G. Bush	r	2,293,729	848,420	989,375	455,934	37.0	43.1	19.9	140,955	6.1
88	Dukakis	G. Bush	R	2,168,621	860,643	1,297,763	10,215	39.7	59.8	0.5	437,120	20.2
84	Mondale	Reagan	R	2,218,711	841,481	1,377,230	0	37.9	62.1	0.0	535,749	24.1
80	Carter	Reagan	R	2,211,492	844,197	1,255,656	111,639	38.2	56.8	5.1	411,459	18.6
76	Carter	Ford	R	2,198,672	1,014,714	1,183,958	0	46.2	53.9	0.0	169,244	7.7
72	McGovern	Nixon	R	2,125,529	708,568	1,405,154	11,807	33.3	66.1	0.6	696,586	32.8

Election Results, U.S. Senate, 1980–2000

Year	Democrat	Republican	Win[a]	Total Vote	Dem Vote	Rep Vote	Other Vote	Dem %	Rep %	Other %	R Margin	R Mar %
00	Johnson	Lugar	R	2,145,209	683,273	1,427,944	33,992	31.9	66.6	1.6	744,671	34.7
98	Bayh	Helmke	D	1,588,617	1,012,244	552,732	23,641	63.7	34.8	1.5	−459,512	−28.9
94	Jontz	Lugar	R	1,543,568	470,799	1,039,625	33,144	30.5	67.4	2.2	568,826	36.9
92	Hogsett	Coats	R	2,168,120	900,148	1,267,972	0	41.5	58.5	0.0	367,824	17.0
90	Hill	Coats	R	1,502,687	696,639	806,048	0	46.4	53.6	0.0	109,409	7.3
88	Wickes	Lugar	R	2,099,303	668,778	1,430,525	0	31.9	68.1	0.0	761,747	36.3
86	Long	Quayle	R	1,545,563	595,192	936,143	14,228	38.5	60.6	0.9	340,951	22.1
82	Fithian	Lugar	R	1,817,287	828,400	978,301	10,586	45.6	53.8	0.6	149,901	8.2
80	Bayh	Quayle	R	2,198,376	1,015,962	1,182,414	0	46.2	53.8	0.0	166,452	7.6

Election Results, Governor, 1980–2000

Year	Democrat	Republican	Win[a]	Total Vote	Dem Vote	Rep Vote	Other Vote	Dem %	Rep %	Other %	R Margin	R Mar %
00	O'Bannon	McIntosh	D	2,179,268	1,232,525	908,285	38,458	56.6	41.7	1.8	−324,240	−14.9
96	O'Bannon	Goldsmith	D	2,109,915	1,087,128	986,982	35,805	51.5	46.8	1.7	−100,146	−4.7
92	Bayh	Pearson	D	2,204,684	1,382,151	822,533	0	62.7	37.3	0.0	−559,618	−25.4
88	Bayh	Mutz	D	2,140,781	1,138,574	1,002,207	0	53.2	46.8	0.0	−136,367	−6.4
84	Townsend	Orr	R	2,197,988	1,036,922	1,146,497	14,569	47.2	52.2	0.7	109,575	5.0
80	Hillenbrand	Orr	R	2,178,403	913,116	1,257,383	7,904	41.9	57.7	0.4	344,267	15.8

Population, Registration, and Turnout, 1980–2000

Year	Population	Vot Age Pop	Registration	Dem %	Rep %	Other %	Unregistered	Turnout	TAPV[b]	Rank	TAPR[c]	Rank
00	6,080,485	4,448,000	4,000,809	n/a	n/a	n/a	2,079,676	2,180,305	49.0	39	54.5	49
98	5,899,195	4,381,829	3,693,982	n/a	n/a	n/a	687,847	1,588,617	36.3	33	43.0	38
96	5,840,528	4,316,112	3,488,088	n/a	n/a	n/a	828,024	2,134,048	49.4	31	61.2	40
94	5,752,073	4,280,000	2,976,255	n/a	n/a	n/a	1,303,745	1,543,568	36.1	40	51.9	37
92	5,662,000	4,200,000	3,180,167	n/a	n/a	n/a	1,019,833	2,293,729	54.6	30	72.1	40
90	5,544,159	4,088,195	2,764,768	n/a	n/a	n/a	1,323,427	1,502,687	36.8	31	54.4	31
88	5,556,000	4,068,000	2,865,852	n/a	n/a	n/a	1,202,148	2,168,621	53.3	23	75.7	13
86	5,503,000	4,033,000	2,878,498	n/a	n/a	n/a	1,154,502	1,555,507	38.6	26	54.0	27
84	5,492,000	3,998,000	3,049,590	n/a	n/a	n/a	948,410	2,233,069	55.9	23	73.2	26
82	5,471,000	3,942,000	2,936,978	n/a	n/a	n/a	1,005,022	1,817,287	46.1	18	61.9	27
80	5,490,224	3,871,249	2,944,311	n/a	n/a	n/a	926,938	2,242,033	57.9	19	76.1	19

[a]Upper case indicates victory with a majority of votes cast; lower case, victory with a plurality of votes cast.

[b]TAPV = turnout as a % of voting age population. Rankings are among all states.

[c]TAPR = turnout as a % of registration. Rankings are among all states.

Sources: Indiana Democratic Party, Indiana Republican Party, Federal Election Commission, U.S. Census Bureau, Indiana Secretary of State Web site <www.state.in.us/sos.index.html>

324

IOWA

2000 Electoral Votes: 7

Election Results, U.S. President, 1972–2000

Year	Democrat	Republican	Win[a]	Total Vote	Dem Vote	Rep Vote	Other Vote	Dem %	Rep %	Other %	R Margin	R Mar %
00	Gore	G. W. Bush	d	1,315,563	638,517	634,373	42,673	48.5	48.2	3.2	−4,144	−0.3
96	Clinton	Dole	D	1,232,835	620,258	492,644	119,933	50.3	40.0	9.7	−127,614	−10.4
92	Clinton	G. Bush	d	1,344,712	586,353	504,891	253,468	43.6	37.6	18.9	−81,462	−6.1
88	Dukakis	G. Bush	D	1,224,000	670,557	545,355	8,088	54.8	44.6	0.7	−125,202	−10.2
84	Mondale	Reagan	R	1,308,708	605,620	703,088	0	46.3	53.7	0.0	97,468	7.4
80	Carter	Reagan	R	1,300,331	508,672	676,026	115,633	39.1	52.0	8.9	167,354	12.9
76	Carter	Ford	r	1,272,845	619,931	632,863	20,051	48.7	49.7	1.6	12,932	1.0
72	McGovern	Nixon	R	1,225,944	496,206	706,207	23,531	40.5	57.6	1.9	210,001	17.1

Election Results, U.S. Senate, 1980–1998

Year	Democrat	Republican	Win[a]	Total Vote	Dem Vote	Rep Vote	Other Vote	Dem %	Rep %	Other %	R Margin	R Mar %
98	Osterberg	Grassley	R	947,632	289,049	648,480	10,103	30.5	68.4	1.1	359,431	37.9
96	Harkin	Lightfoot	D	1,223,774	634,166	571,807	17,801	51.8	46.7	1.5	−62,359	−5.1
92	Lloyd-Jones	Grassley	R	1,251,322	351,561	899,761	0	28.1	71.9	0.0	548,200	43.8
90	Harkin	Tauke	D	982,844	535,975	446,869	0	54.5	45.5	0.0	−89,106	−9.1
86	Roehrick	Grassley	R	888,286	299,406	588,880	0	33.7	66.3	0.0	289,474	32.6
84	Harkin	Jepsen	D	1,292,278	716,883	564,381	11,014	55.5	43.7	0.9	−152,502	−11.8
80	Culver	Grassley	R	1,276,986	581,545	683,014	12,427	45.5	53.5	1.0	101,469	7.9

Election Results, Governor, 1982–1998

Year	Democrat	Republican	Win[a]	Total Vote	Dem Vote	Rep Vote	Other Vote	Dem %	Rep %	Other %	R Margin	R Mar %
98	Vilsack	Lightfoot	D	955,774	500,231	444,787	10,756	52.3	46.5	1.1	−55,444	−5.8
94	Campbell	Branstad	R	993,632	414,453	566,395	12,784	41.7	57.0	1.3	151,942	15.3
90	Avenson	Branstad	R	971,224	379,372	591,852	0	39.1	60.9	0.0	212,480	21.9
86	Junkins	Branstad	R	909,699	436,987	472,712	0	48.0	52.0	0.0	35,725	3.9
82	Conlin	Branstad	R	1,037,678	483,291	548,313	6,074	46.6	52.8	0.6	65,022	6.3

Population, Registration, and Turnout, 1980–2000

Year	Population	Vot Age Pop	Registration	Dem %	Rep %	Other %	Unregistered	Turnout	TAPV[b]	Rank	TAPR[c]	Rank
00	2,926,324	2,165,000	1,841,346	30.2	31.6	38.2	1,084,978	1,314,395	60.7	8	71.4	10
98	2,862,447	2,140,308	1,865,520	32.0	33.0	35.0	274,788	955,774	44.7	13	51.2	18
96	2,851,792	2,117,253	1,741,958	33.0	34.6	32.3	375,295	1,232,835	58.2	12	70.8	10
94	2,829,252	2,101,000	1,631,126	35.6	36.0	28.4	469,874	993,632	47.3	14	60.9	20
92	2,812,000	2,079,000	1,703,532	37.4	31.2	31.4	375,468	1,344,712	64.7	10	78.9	18
90	2,776,755	2,057,875	1,580,160	38.0	31.4	30.7	477,715	982,844	47.8	12	62.2	14
88	2,834,000	2,068,000	1,690,093	36.1	31.1	32.8	377,907	1,224,000	59.2	9	72.4	23
86	2,851,000	2,115,000	1,621,538	35.3	31.2	33.5	493,462	909,699	43.0	17	56.1	25
84	2,903,000	2,121,000	1,762,841	34.7	31.1	34.2	358,159	1,319,805	62.2	9	74.9	20
82	2,905,000	2,113,000	1,586,345	34.6	32.0	33.5	526,655	1,037,678	49.1	9	65.4	21
80	2,913,808	2,086,367	1,746,725	32.4	31.6	36.0	339,642	1,317,142	63.1	9	75.4	26

[a]Upper case indicates victory with a majority of votes cast; lower case, victory with a plurality of votes cast.
[b]TAPV = turnout as a % of voting age population. Rankings are among all states.
[c]TAPR = turnout as a % of registration. Rankings are among all states.
Sources: Iowa Democratic Party, Iowa Republican Party, Federal Election Commission, U.S. Census Bureau, Iowa Secretary of State.

KANSAS

2000 Electoral Votes: 6

Election Results, U.S. President, 1972–2000

Year	Democrat	Republican	Win[a]	Total Vote	Dem Vote	Rep Vote	Other Vote	Dem %	Rep %	Other %	R Margin	R Mar %
00	Gore	G. W. Bush	R	1,072,216	399,276	622,332	50,608	37.2	58.0	4.7	223,056	20.8
96	Clinton	Dole	R	1,073,274	387,659	583,245	102,370	36.1	54.3	9.5	195,586	18.2
92	Clinton	G. Bush	r	1,152,743	390,434	449,951	312,358	33.9	39.0	27.1	59,517	5.2
88	Dukakis	G. Bush	R	993,024	422,636	554,049	16,339	42.6	55.8	1.7	131,413	13.2
84	Mondale	Reagan	R	1,010,445	333,149	677,296	0	33.0	67.0	0.0	344,147	34.1
80	Carter	Reagan	R	961,193	326,150	566,812	68,231	33.9	59.0	7.1	240,662	25.0
76	Carter	Ford	R	946,358	430,421	502,752	13,185	45.5	53.1	1.4	72,331	7.6
72	McGovern	Nixon	R	916,095	270,287	619,812	25,996	29.5	67.7	2.8	349,525	38.2

Election Results, U.S. Senate, 1980–1998

Year	Democrat	Republican	Win[a]	Total Vote	Dem Vote	Rep Vote	Other Vote	Dem %	Rep %	Other %	R Margin	R Mar %
98	Feleciano	Brownback	R	727,236	229,718	474,639	22,879	31.6	65.3	3.2	244,921	33.7
96	Thompson	Roberts	R	1,052,120	362,200	652,677	37,243	34.4	62.0	3.5	290,477	27.6
96	Docking	Brownback	R	1,064,716	461,344	574,021	29,351	43.3	53.9	2.8	112,677	10.6
92	O'Dell	Dole	R	1,101,194	349,525	706,246	45,423	31.7	64.1	4.1	356,721	32.4
90	Williams	Kassebaum	R	786,096	207,491	578,605	0	26.4	73.6	0.0	371,114	47.2
86	MacDonald	Dole	R	823,566	246,664	576,902	0	30.0	70.1	0.0	330,238	40.1
84	Maher	Kassebaum	R	996,729	211,664	757,402	27,663	21.2	76.0	2.8	545,738	54.8
80	Simpson	Dole	R	938,957	340,271	598,686	0	36.2	63.8	0.0	258,415	27.5

Election Results, Governor, 1982–1998

Year	Democrat	Republican	Win[a]	Total Vote	Dem Vote	Rep Vote	Other Vote	Dem %	Rep %	Other %	R Margin	R Mar %
98	Sawyer	Graves	R	742,665	168,243	544,882	29,540	22.7	73.4	4.0	376,639	50.7
94	Slattery	Graves	R	820,846	294,733	526,113	0	35.9	64.1	0.0	231,380	28.2
90	Finney	Hayden	d	783,325	380,609	333,589	69,127	48.6	42.6	8.8	−47,020	−6.0
86	Docking	Hayden	R	840,605	404,338	436,267	0	48.1	51.9	0.0	31,929	3.8
82	Carlin	Hardage	D	763,263	405,772	339,356	18,135	53.2	44.5	2.4	−66,416	−8.7

Population, Registration, and Turnout, 1980–2000

Year	Population	Vot Age Pop	Registration	Dem %	Rep %	Other %	Unregistered	Turnout	TAPV[b]	Rank	TAPR[c]	Rank
00	2,688,418	1,983,000	1,623,623	27.7	45.3	27.0	1,064,795	1,072,216	54.1	25	66.0	24
98	2,629,067	1,931,615	1,513,685	28.7	45.3	26.1	417,930	742,665	38.4	27	49.1	22
96	2,572,150	1,872,567	1,439,999	29.5	45.3	25.2	432,568	1,073,274	57.3	16	74.5	2
94	2,554,047	1,863,000	1,314,213	30.8	44.3	24.9	548,787	820,846	44.1	18	62.5	14
92	2,523,000	1,843,000	1,365,849	31.1	43.0	25.9	477,151	1,152,743	62.5	15	84.4	2
90	2,477,574	1,815,960	1,204,574	29.8	44.1	26.2	611,386	786,096	43.3	18	65.3	9
88	2,495,000	1,829,000	1,265,958	28.5	41.3	30.2	563,042	993,024	54.3	21	78.4	7
86	2,461,000	1,809,000	1,184,497	29.2	41.3	29.6	624,503	840,605	46.5	10	71.0	4
84	2,440,000	1,791,000	1,113,379	28.8	38.4	32.8	677,621	1,021,991	57.1	19	91.8	1
82	2,408,000	1,768,000	1,186,513	29.4	38.5	32.1	581,487	763,263	43.2	26	64.3	23
80	2,363,679	1,714,282	1,159,071	28.9	37.5	33.6	555,211	979,795	57.2	23	84.5	1

[a] Upper case indicates victory with a majority of votes cast; lower case, victory with a plurality of votes cast.

[b] TAPV = turnout as a % of voting age population. Rankings are among all states.

[c] TAPR = turnout as a % of registration. Rankings are among all states.

Sources: Kansas Democratic Party, Kansas Republican Party, Federal Election Commission, U.S. Census Bureau, Kansas Secretary of State Web site <www.kssos.org>

KENTUCKY

2000 Electoral Votes: 8

Election Results, U.S. President, 1972–2000

Year	Democrat	Republican	Win[a]	Total Vote	Dem Vote	Rep Vote	Other Vote	Dem %	Rep %	Other %	R Margin	R Mar %
00	Gore	G. W. Bush	R	1,544,187	638,898	872,492	32,797	41.4	56.5	2.1	233,594	15.1
96	Clinton	Dole	d	1,387,999	636,614	623,283	128,102	45.9	44.9	9.2	-13,331	-1.0
92	Clinton	G. Bush	d	1,486,226	665,104	617,178	203,944	44.8	41.5	13.7	-47,926	-3.2
88	Dukakis	G. Bush	R	1,322,517	580,368	734,281	7,868	43.9	55.5	0.6	153,913	11.6
84	Mondale	Reagan	R	1,362,371	539,589	822,782	0	39.6	60.4	0.0	283,193	20.8
80	Carter	Reagan	r	1,283,818	617,417	635,274	31,127	48.1	49.5	2.4	17,857	1.4
76	Carter	Ford	D	1,154,406	615,717	531,852	6,837	53.3	46.1	0.6	-83,865	-7.3
72	McGovern	Nixon	R	1,067,499	371,159	676,446	19,894	34.8	63.4	1.9	305,287	28.6

Election Results, U.S. Senate, 1980–1998

Year	Democrat	Republican	Win[a]	Total Vote	Dem Vote	Rep Vote	Other Vote	Dem %	Rep %	Other %	R Margin	R Mar %
98	Baesler	Bunning	r	1,145,414	563,051	569,817	12,546	49.2	49.8	1.1	6,766	0.6
96	Beshear	McConnell	R	1,307,029	560,012	724,794	22,223	42.9	55.5	1.7	164,782	12.6
92	Ford	Williams	D	1,313,492	836,888	476,604	0	63.7	36.3	0.0	-360,284	-27.4
90	Sloane	McConnell	R	916,010	437,976	478,034	0	47.8	52.2	0.0	40,058	4.4
86	Ford	Andrews	D	677,105	503,775	173,330	0	74.4	25.6	0.0	-330,445	-48.8
84	Huddleston	McConnell	r	1,292,407	639,721	644,990	7,696	49.5	49.9	0.6	5,269	0.4
80	Ford	Foust	D	1,106,890	720,861	386,029	0	65.1	34.9	0.0	-334,832	-30.2

Election Results, Governor, 1983–1999

Year	Democrat	Republican	Win[a]	Total Vote	Dem Vote	Rep Vote	Other Vote	Dem %	Rep %	Other %	R Margin	R Mar %
99	Patton	Martin	D	580,074	325,099	128,788	126,187	56.0	22.2	21.8	-196,311	-33.8
95	Patton	Forgy	D	980,014	500,787	479,227	0	51.1	48.9	0.0	-21,560	-2.2
91	Jones	Hopkins	D	834,920	540,468	294,452	0	64.7	35.3	0.0	-246,016	-29.5
87	Wilkinson	Harper	D	777,815	504,674	273,141	0	64.9	35.1	0.0	-231,533	-29.8
83	Collins	Bunning	D	1,030,671	561,674	454,650	14,347	54.5	44.1	1.4	-107,024	-10.4

Population, Registration, and Turnout, 1980–2000

Year	Population	Vot Age Pop	Registration	Dem %	Rep %	Other %	Unregistered	Turnout	TAPV[b]	Rank	TAPR[c]	Rank
00	4,041,769	2,993,000	2,556,815	60.2	33.1	6.7	1,484,954	1,544,026	51.6	30	60.4	40
98	3,936,499	2,948,206	2,590,338	60.6	32.3	7.1	357,868	1,145,414	38.9	26	44.2	33
96	3,883,723	2,887,511	2,396,086	61.6	31.1	7.3	491,425	1,387,999	48.1	36	57.9	45
94	3,826,794	2,857,000	2,132,152	65.6	30.2	4.2	724,848	784,268	27.5	50	36.8	48
92	3,755,000	2,792,000	2,076,263	66.2	29.7	4.2	715,737	1,486,226	53.2	35	71.6	39
90	3,685,296	2,731,202	1,854,315	67.4	29.6	3.1	876,887	916,010	33.5	40	49.4	40
88	3,727,000	2,746,000	2,026,307	67.2	29.4	3.4	719,693	1,322,517	48.2	35	65.3	40
86	3,728,000	2,728,000	1,998,899	68.1	28.7	3.2	729,101	677,105	24.8	49	33.9	47
84	3,720,000	2,696,000	2,022,995	67.7	28.6	3.7	673,005	1,369,345	50.8	39	67.7	42
82	3,667,000	2,654,000	1,826,590	68.2	28.6	3.3	827,410	700,292	26.4	49	38.3	47
80	3,660,777	2,576,584	1,821,417	67.9	28.6	3.6	755,167	1,295,627	50.3	37	71.1	35

[a]Upper case indicates victory with a majority of votes cast; lower case, victory with a plurality of votes cast.
[b]TAPV = turnout as a % of voting age population. Rankings are among all states.
[c]TAPR = turnout as a % of registration. Rankings are among all states.

Sources: Kentucky Democratic Party, Kentucky Republican Party, Federal Election Commission, U.S. Census Bureau, Kentucky Secretary of State Web site <www.sos.state.ky.us>

LOUISIANA

2000 Electoral Votes: 9

Election Results, U.S. President, 1972–2000

Year	Democrat	Republican	Win[a]	Total Vote	Dem Vote	Rep Vote	Other Vote	Dem %	Rep %	Other %	R Margin	R Mar %
00	Gore	G. W. Bush	R	1,765,656	792,344	927,871	45,441	44.9	52.6	2.6	135,527	7.7
96	Clinton	Dole	D	1,783,959	927,837	712,586	143,536	52.0	39.9	8.1	−215,251	−12.1
92	Clinton	G. Bush	d	1,760,835	815,971	733,386	211,478	46.3	41.7	12.0	−82,585	−4.7
88	Dukakis	G. Bush	R	1,628,202	717,460	883,702	27,040	44.1	54.3	1.7	166,242	10.2
84	Mondale	Reagan	R	1,688,885	651,586	1,037,299	0	38.6	61.4	0.0	385,713	22.8
80	Carter	Reagan	R	1,527,651	708,453	792,853	26,345	46.4	51.9	1.7	84,400	5.5
76	Carter	Ford	D	1,255,399	661,365	587,446	6,588	52.7	46.8	0.5	−73,919	−5.9
72	McGovern	Nixon	R	1,051,491	298,142	686,852	66,497	28.4	65.3	6.3	388,710	37.0

Election Results, U.S. Senate, 1980–1998

Year	Democrat	Republican	Win[a]	Total Vote	Dem Vote	Rep Vote	Other Vote	Dem %	Rep %	Other %	R Margin	R Mar %
98	Breaux	Donelon	D	969,165	620,502	306,616	42,047	64.0	31.6	4.3	−313,886	−32.4
96	Landrieu	Jenkins	D	1,700,102	852,945	847,157	0	50.2	49.8	0.0	−5,788	−0.3
90	Johnston	Duke	D	1,360,293	752,902	607,391	0	55.4	44.7	0.0	−145,511	−10.7
86	Breaux	Moore	D	1,369,897	723,586	646,311	0	52.8	47.2	0.0	−77,275	−5.6
84	Johnston	unopposed*	–	–	–	–	–	–	–	–	–	–
80	Long	unopposed*	–	–	–	–	–	–	–	–	–	–

Election Results, Governor, 1983–1999

Year	Democrat	Republican	Win[a]	Total Vote	Dem Vote	Rep Vote	Other Vote	Dem %	Rep %	Other %	R Margin	R Mar %
99	Jefferson	Foster	R	1,295,205	382,445	805,203	107,557	29.5	62.2	8.3	422,758	32.6
95	Fields	Foster	R	1,550,360	565,861	984,499	0	36.5	63.5	0.0	418,638	27.0
91	Edwards	Duke	D	1,728,040	1,057,031	671,009	0	61.2	38.8	0.0	−386,022	−22.3
87	Roemer	Livingston	o	1,558,730	516,078	287,780	754,872	33.1	18.5	48.4	−228,298	−14.6
83	Edwards	Treen	D	1,615,905	1,006,561	588,508	20,836	62.3	36.4	1.3	−418,053	−25.9

Population, Registration, and Turnout, 1980–2000

Year	Population	Vot Age Pop	Registration	Dem %	Rep %	Other %	Unregistered	Turnout	TAPV[b]	Rank	TAPR[c]	Rank
00	4,468,976	3,255,000	2,730,380	59.9	22.1	18.1	1,738,596	1,765,656	54.2	24	64.7	28
98	4,368,967	3,177,555	2,686,561	62.5	21.5	16.1	490,994	969,165	30.5	44	36.1	44
96	4,350,579	3,103,120	2,559,352	65.1	21.1	13.8	543,768	1,783,959	57.5	11	69.7	14
94	4,315,085	3,080,000	2,212,927	70.7	19.3	10.0	867,073	824,324	26.8	51	37.3	47
92	4,287,000	3,049,000	2,292,129	71.3	19.1	9.6	756,871	1,760,835	57.8	26	76.8	27
90	4,219,973	2,992,704	2,169,099	74.0	17.8	8.2	823,605	1,360,293	45.5	14	62.7	11
88	4,408,000	3,175,000	2,190,634	75.2	16.4	8.4	984,366	1,628,202	51.3	28	74.3	20
86	4,501,000	3,186,000	2,179,317	78.2	13.5	8.3	1,006,683	1,369,897	43.0	16	62.9	10
84	4,461,000	3,124,000	2,244,469	81.6	10.5	7.9	879,531	1,706,822	54.6	26	76.0	17
82	4,362,000	3,050,000	1,958,676	85.2	8.3	6.5	1,091,324	n/a	n/a	n/a	n/a	n/a
80	4,205,900	2,873,896	2,015,402	86.6	7.4	6.0	858,494	1,548,591	53.9	29	76.8	16

*Under Louisiana law, a candidate who wins a majority of the votes in the primary election is elected. When no candidate wins a majority, the two top vote-getters—regardless of party—face each other in a runoff election. A candidate who runs unopposed in the primary is declared elected and is not listed on the ballot in either the primary or general election.

[a] Upper case indicates victory with a majority of votes cast; lower case, victory with a plurality of votes cast.

[b] TAPV = turnout as a % of voting age population. Rankings are among all states.

[c] TAPR = turnout as a % of registration. Rankings are among all states.

Sources: Louisiana Democratic Party, Louisiana Republican Party, Federal Election Commission, U.S. Census Bureau, Louisiana Department of Elections and Registration Web site <www.laelections.org>

MAINE

2000 Electoral Votes: 4

Election Results, U.S. President, 1972–2000

Year	Democrat	Republican	Win[a]	Total Vote	Dem Vote	Rep Vote	Other Vote	Dem %	Rep %	Other %	R Margin	R Mar %
00	Gore	G. W. Bush	d	651,817	319,951	286,616	45,250	49.1	44.0	6.9	−33,335	−5.1
96	Clinton	Dole	D	605,753	312,788	186,378	106,587	51.6	30.8	17.6	−126,410	−20.9
92	Clinton	G. Bush	d	676,744	263,420	206,504	206,820	38.9	30.5	30.6	−56,916	−8.4
88	Dukakis	G. Bush	R	554,805	243,569	307,131	4,105	43.9	55.4	0.7	63,562	11.5
84	Mondale	Reagan	R	551,015	214,515	336,500	0	38.9	61.1	0.0	121,985	22.1
84	Carter	Reagan	r	512,823	220,974	238,522	53,327	43.1	46.5	10.4	17,548	3.4
80	Carter	Ford	r	479,478	232,279	236,320	10,879	48.4	49.3	2.3	4,041	0.8
72	McGovern	Nixon	R	417,042	160,584	256,458	0	38.5	61.5	0.0	95,874	23.0

Election Results, U.S. Senate, 1982–2000

Year	Democrat	Republican	Win[a]	Total Vote	Dem Vote	Rep Vote	Other Vote	Dem %	Rep %	Other %	R Margin	R Mar %
00	Lawrence	Snowe	R	634,872	197,183	437,689	0	31.1	68.9	0.0	240,506	37.9
96	Brennan	Collins	r	606,707	266,226	298,422	42,059	43.9	49.2	6.9	32,196	5.3
94	Andrews	Snowe	R	511,491	186,042	308,244	17,205	36.4	60.3	3.4	122,202	23.9
90	Rolde	Cohen	R	520,220	201,053	319,167	0	38.7	61.4	0.0	118,114	22.7
88	Mitchell	Wyman	D	556,695	452,590	104,105	0	81.3	18.7	0.0	−348,485	−62.6
84	Mitchell	Cohen	R	551,378	142,626	404,414	4,338	25.9	73.4	0.8	261,788	47.5
82	Mitchell	Emery	D	459,715	279,819	179,882	14	60.9	39.1	0.0	−99,937	−21.7

Election Results, Governor, 1982–1998

Year	Democrat	Republican	Win[a]	Total Vote	Dem Vote	Rep Vote	Other Vote	Dem %	Rep %	Other %	R Margin	R Mar %
98	Connolly	Longley	O	421,009	50,506	79,716	290,787	12.0	18.9	69.1	−167,056	−39.7
94	Brennan	Collins	o	511,041	172,951	117,990	220,100	33.8	23.1	43.1	−102,110	−20.0
90	Brennan	McKernan	r	522,181	230,038	243,766	48,377	44.1	46.7	9.3	13,728	2.6
86	Tierney	McKernan	r	426,847	128,744	170,312	127,791	30.2	39.9	29.9	41,568	9.7
82	Brennan	Cragin	D	460,292	281,066	172,949	6,277	61.1	37.6	1.4	−108,117	−23.5

Population, Registration, and Turnout, 1980–2000

Year	Population	Vot Age Pop	Registration*	Dem %	Rep %	Other %	Unregistered*	Turnout	TAPVᵇ	Rank	TAPRᶜ	Rank
00	1,274,923	968,000	882,337	31.8	30.1	38.0	392,586	651,817	67.3	2	73.9	9
98	1,244,250	952,665	933,753	31.8	28.7	39.5	18,912	421,009	44.2	15	45.1	29
96	1,243,316	936,487	1,001,292	31.8	28.8	39.5	−64,805	606,707	64.8	2	60.6	39
94	1,240,209	934,000	938,240	33.1	29.2	37.7	−4,240	511,491	54.8	4	54.5	32
92	1,235,000	931,000	974,605	33.0	29.3	37.7	−43,605	676,744	72.7	1	69.4	45
90	1,227,928	918,926	871,697	32.9	29.9	37.2	47,229	520,220	56.6	1	59.7	18
88	1,205,000	893,000	854,764	33.6	30.2	36.2	38,236	556,695	62.3	6	65.1	39
86	1,174,000	874,000	790,083	34.0	30.4	35.6	83,917	426,847	48.8	7	54.0	26
84	1,156,000	856,000	810,661	33.9	29.5	36.7	45,339	553,144	64.6	3	68.2	41
82	1,133,000	830,000	766,285	33.7	30.6	35.7	63,715	460,292	55.5	5	60.1	32
80	1,124,660	802,498	759,978	35.4	31.9	32.7	42,520	522,927	65.2	8	68.8	40

*Registration figures include out-of-state and out-of-country voters who are not officially included in the voting age population.

ᵃUpper case indicates victory with a majority of votes cast; lower case, victory with a plurality of votes cast.

ᵇTAPV = turnout as a % of voting age population. Rankings are among all states.

ᶜTAPR = turnout as a % of registration. Rankings are among all states.

Sources: Maine Democratic Party, Maine Republican Party, Federal Election Commission, U.S. Census Bureau, Maine Secretary of State Web site <www.state.me.us/sos>

MARYLAND

2000 Electoral Votes: 10

Election Results, U.S. President, 1972–2000

Year	Democrat	Republican	Win[a]	Total Vote	Dem Vote	Rep Vote	Other Vote	Dem %	Rep %	Other %	R Margin	R Mar %
00	Gore	G. W. Bush	D	2,023,735	1,144,008	813,827	65,900	56.5	40.2	3.3	−330,181	−16.3
96	Clinton	Dole	D	1,778,233	966,207	681,530	130,496	54.3	38.3	7.3	−284,677	−16.0
92	Clinton	G. Bush	D	1,977,079	988,571	707,094	281,414	50.0	35.8	14.2	−281,477	−14.2
88	Dukakis	G. Bush	R	1,714,358	826,304	876,167	11,887	48.2	51.1	0.7	49,863	2.9
84	Mondale	Reagan	R	1,667,853	787,935	879,918	0	47.2	52.8	0.0	91,983	5.5
80	Carter	Reagan	d	1,526,304	726,161	680,606	119,537	47.6	44.6	7.8	−45,555	−3.0
76	Carter	Ford	D	1,432,273	759,612	672,661	0	53.0	47.0	0.0	−86,951	−6.1
72	McGovern	Nixon	R	1,353,812	505,781	829,305	18,726	37.4	61.3	1.4	323,534	23.9

Election Results, U.S. Senate, 1980–2000

Year	Democrat	Republican	Win[a]	Total Vote	Dem Vote	Rep Vote	Other Vote	Dem %	Rep %	Other %	R Margin	R Mar %
00	Sarbanes	Rappaport	D	1,946,898	1,230,013	715,178	1,707	63.2	36.7	0.1	−514,835	−26.4
98	Mikulski	Pierpont	D	1,507,447	1,062,810	444,637	0	70.5	29.5	0.0	−618,173	−41.0
94	Sarbanes	Brock	D	1,369,033	809,125	559,908	0	59.1	40.9	0.0	−249,217	−18.2
92	Mikulski	Keyes	D	1,841,298	1,307,610	533,688	0	71.0	29.0	0.0	−773,922	−42.0
88	Sarbanes	Keyes	D	1,616,703	999,166	617,537	0	61.8	38.2	0.0	−381,629	−23.6
86	Mikulski	Chavez	D	1,112,636	675,225	437,411	0	60.7	39.3	0.0	−237,814	−21.4
82	Sarbanes	Hogan	D	1,114,690	707,356	407,334	0	63.5	36.5	0.0	−300,022	−26.9
80	Conroy	Mathias	R	1,286,088	435,118	850,970	0	33.8	66.2	0.0	415,852	32.3

Election Results, Governor, 1982–1998

Year	Democrat	Republican	Win[a]	Total Vote	Dem Vote	Rep Vote	Other Vote	Dem %	Rep %	Other %	R Margin	R Mar %
98	Glendening	Sauerbrey	D	1,535,329	846,972	688,357	0	55.2	44.8	0.0	−158,615	−10.3
94	Glendening	Sauerbrey	D	1,410,195	708,094	702,101	0	50.2	49.8	0.0	−5,993	−0.4
90	Schaefer	Shepard	D	1,110,995	664,015	446,980	0	59.8	40.2	0.0	−217,035	−19.5
86	Schaefer	Mooney	D	1,101,476	907,291	194,185	0	82.4	17.6	0.0	−713,106	−64.7
82	Hughes	Pascal	D	1,139,149	705,910	432,826	413	62.0	38.0	0.0	−273,084	−24.0

Population, Registration, and Turnout, 1980–2000

Year	Population	Vot Age Pop	Registration	Dem %	Rep %	Other %	Unregistered	Turnout	TAPV[b]	Rank	TAPR[c]	Rank
00	5,296,486	3,925,000	2,715,366	57.0	29.7	13.3	2,581,120	2,023,735	51.6	31	74.5	7
98	5,134,808	3,847,618	2,577,698	57.6	30.3	12.2	1,269,920	1,535,329	39.9	22	59.6	5
96	5,071,604	3,770,472	2,587,977	58.7	30.0	11.4	1,182,495	1,778,233	47.2	40	68.7	16
94	5,006,265	3,742,000	2,367,166	61.0	29.4	9.7	1,374,834	1,410,195	37.7	35	59.6	22
92	4,908,000	3,683,000	2,463,010	61.2	29.2	9.7	1,219,990	1,977,079	53.7	33	80.3	16
90	4,781,468	3,619,227	2,134,732	63.1	28.9	8.0	1,484,495	1,110,995	30.7	43	52.0	33
88	4,622,000	3,491,000	2,310,133	64.2	27.7	8.1	1,180,867	1,714,358	49.1	33	74.2	19
86	4,463,000	3,333,000	2,139,690	67.5	25.1	7.5	1,193,310	1,112,636	33.4	41	52.0	35
84	4,349,000	3,259,000	2,253,150	67.9	24.3	7.9	1,005,850	1,675,873	51.4	38	74.4	23
82	4,265,000	3,176,000	1,968,498	69.1	23.6	7.3	1,207,502	1,139,149	35.9	41	57.9	34
80	4,216,975	3,049,869	2,064,883	68.8	23.4	7.8	984,986	1,540,496	50.5	36	74.6	25

[a] Upper case indicates victory with a majority of votes cast; lower case, victory with a plurality of votes cast.

[b] TAPV = turnout as a % of voting age population. Rankings are among all states.

[c] TAPR = turnout as a % of registration. Rankings are among all states.

Sources: Maryland Democratic Party, Maryland Republican Party, Federal Election Commission, U.S. Census Bureau, Maryland State Board of Elections Web site <www.elections.state.md.us>

MASSACHUSETTS

2000 Electoral Votes: 12

Election Results, U.S. President, 1972–2000

Year	Democrat	Republican	Win[a]	Total Vote	Dem Vote	Rep Vote	Other Vote	Dem %	Rep %	Other %	R Margin	R Mar %
00	Gore	G. W. Bush	D	2,702,984	1,616,487	878,502	207,995	59.8	32.5	7.7	−737,985	−27.3
96	Clinton	Dole	D	2,545,656	1,571,509	718,058	256,089	61.7	28.2	10.1	−853,451	−33.5
92	Clinton	G. Bush	d	2,754,442	1,318,662	805,049	630,731	47.9	29.2	22.9	−513,613	−18.6
88	Dukakis	G. Bush	D	2,629,891	1,401,415	1,194,635	33,841	53.3	45.4	1.3	−206,780	−7.9
84	Mondale	Reagan	R	2,550,542	1,239,606	1,310,936	0	48.6	51.4	0.0	71,330	2.8
80	Carter	Reagan	r	2,493,972	1,053,802	1,057,631	382,539	42.3	42.4	15.3	3,829	0.2
76	Carter	Ford	D	2,525,388	1,429,475	1,030,276	65,637	56.6	40.8	2.6	−399,199	−15.8
72	McGovern	Nixon	D	2,458,756	1,332,540	1,112,078	14,138	54.2	45.2	0.6	−220,462	−9.0

Election Results, U.S. Senate, 1982–2000

Year	Democrat	Republican	Win[a]	Total Vote	Dem Vote	Rep Vote	Other Vote	Dem %	Rep %	Other %	R Margin	R Mar %
00	Kennedy	Robinson III	D	2,599,420	1,889,494	334,341	375,585	72.7	12.9	14.4	−1,555,153	−59.8
96	Kerry	Weld	D	2,554,431	1,334,135	1,143,120	77,176	52.2	44.8	3.0	−191,015	−7.5
94	Kennedy	Romney	D	2,179,257	1,265,997	894,000	19,260	58.1	41.0	0.9	−371,997	−17.1
90	Kerry	Rappaport	D	2,314,629	1,321,712	992,917	0	57.1	42.9	0.0	−328,795	−14.2
88	Kennedy	Malone	D	2,606,018	1,693,344	884,267	28,407	65.0	33.9	1.1	−809,077	−31.0
84	Kerry	Shamie	D	2,519,871	1,384,395	1,135,476	0	54.9	45.1	0.0	−248,919	−9.9
82	Kennedy	Shamie	D	2,050,751	1,247,084	784,602	19,065	60.8	38.3	0.9	−462,482	−22.6

Election Results, Governor, 1982–1998

Year	Democrat	Republican	Win[a]	Total Vote	Dem Vote	Rep Vote	Other Vote	Dem %	Rep %	Other %	R Margin	R Mar %
98	Harshbarger	Cellucci	R	1,903,336	901,843	967,160	34,333	47.4	50.8	1.8	65,317	3.4
94	Roosevelt	Weld	R	2,163,626	611,641	1,533,380	18,605	28.3	70.9	0.9	921,739	42.6
90	Silber	Weld	R	2,275,695	1,099,878	1,175,817	0	48.3	51.7	0.0	75,939	3.3
86	Dukakis	Kariotis	D	1,683,150	1,157,786	525,364	0	68.8	31.2	0.0	−632,422	−37.6
82	Dukakis	Sears	D	2,050,254	1,219,109	749,679	81,466	59.5	36.6	4.0	−469,430	−22.9

Population, Registration, and Turnout, 1980–2000

Year	Population	Vot Age Pop	Registration	Dem %	Rep %	Other %	Unregistered	Turnout	TAPV[b]	Rank	TAPR[c]	Rank
00	6,349,097	4,749,000	4,008,796	36.4	13.6	49.9	2,340,301	2,734,006	57.6	14	68.2	16
98	6,147,132	4,689,429	3,706,404	37.5	13.1	49.4	983,025	1,903,336	40.6	21	51.4	17
96	6,092,352	4,641,696	3,459,193	38.2	13.8	48.1	1,182,503	2,554,431	55.0	22	73.8	3
94	6,041,123	4,617,000	3,153,378	40.2	13.3	46.6	1,463,622	2,179,257	47.2	13	69.1	5
92	5,998,000	4,614,000	3,351,918	40.2	13.4	46.5	1,262,082	2,754,442	59.7	23	82.2	7
90	6,016,425	4,663,350	3,213,763	41.8	13.8	44.5	1,449,587	2,314,629	49.6	9	72.0	4
88	5,889,000	4,535,000	3,274,777	46.4	13.5	40.1	1,260,223	2,629,891	58.0	11	80.3	3
86	5,832,000	4,525,000	3,005,729	46.6	13.3	40.1	1,519,271	1,683,150	37.2	32	56.0	24
84	5,798,000	4,459,000	3,253,775	48.5	12.7	38.7	1,205,225	2,559,383	57.4	18	78.7	10
82	5,781,000	4,358,000	3,026,868	45.3	14.0	40.7	1,331,132	2,050,751	47.1	16	67.8	12
80	5,737,037	4,244,947	3,156,672	46.2	15.3	38.5	1,088,275	2,519,745	59.4	15	79.8	7

[a] Upper case indicates victory with a majority of votes cast; lower case, victory with a plurality of votes cast.

[b] TAPV = turnout as a % of voting age population. Rankings are among all states.

[c] TAPR = turnout as a % of registration. Rankings are among all states.

Sources: Massachusetts Democratic Party, Massachusetts Republican Party, Federal Election Commission, U.S. Census Bureau, Secretary of the Commonwealth of Massachusetts Web site <www.state.ma.us/sec>

MICHIGAN

2000 Electoral Votes: 18

Election Results, U.S. President, 1972–2000

Year	Democrat	Republican	Win[a]	Total Vote	Dem Vote	Rep Vote	Other Vote	Dem %	Rep %	Other %	R Margin	R Mar %
00	Gore	G. W. Bush	D	4,232,501	2,170,418	1,953,139	108,944	51.3	46.1	2.6	−217,279	−5.1
96	Clinton	Dole	D	3,844,166	1,989,653	1,481,212	373,301	51.8	38.5	9.7	−508,441	−13.2
92	Clinton	G. Bush	d	4,250,935	1,871,182	1,554,940	824,813	44.0	36.6	19.4	−316,242	−7.4
88	Dukakis	G. Bush	R	3,668,261	1,675,783	1,965,486	26,992	45.7	53.6	0.7	289,703	7.9
84	Mondale	Reagan	R	3,781,209	1,529,638	2,251,571	0	40.5	59.6	0.0	721,933	19.1
80	Carter	Reagan	r	3,851,980	1,661,532	1,915,225	275,223	43.1	49.7	7.2	253,693	6.6
76	Carter	Ford	R	3,638,361	1,696,714	1,893,742	47,905	46.6	52.1	1.3	197,028	5.4
72	McGovern	Nixon	R	3,489,727	1,459,435	1,961,721	68,571	41.8	56.2	2.0	502,286	14.4

Election Results, U.S. Senate, 1982–2000

Year	Democrat	Republican	Win[a]	Total Vote	Dem Vote	Rep Vote	Other Vote	Dem %	Rep %	Other %	R Margin	R Mar %
00	Stabenow	Abraham	d	4,167,685	2,061,952	1,994,693	111,040	49.5	47.9	2.7	−67,259	−1.6
96	Levin	Romney	D	3,762,721	2,195,738	1,500,106	66,427	58.4	39.9	1.8	−695,632	−18.5
94	Carr	Abraham	R	3,042,879	1,300,960	1,578,770	163,149	42.8	51.9	5.4	277,810	9.1
90	Levin	Schuette	D	2,527,448	1,471,753	1,055,695	0	58.2	41.8	0.0	−416,058	−16.5
88	Riegle	Dunn	D	3,505,929	2,116,865	1,348,219	40,845	60.4	38.5	1.2	−768,646	−21.9
84	Levin	Lousma	D	3,700,915	1,915,831	1,745,302	39,782	51.8	47.2	1.1	−170,529	−4.6
82	Riegle	Ruppe	D	2,994,292	1,728,793	1,223,288	42,211	57.7	40.9	1.4	−505,505	−16.9

Election Results, Governor, 1982–1998

Year	Democrat	Republican	Win[a]	Total Vote	Dem Vote	Rep Vote	Other Vote	Dem %	Rep %	Other %	R Margin	R Mar %
98	Fieger	Engler	R	3,026,579	1,143,574	1,883,005	0	37.8	62.2	0.0	739,431	24.4
94	Wolpe	Engler	R	3,087,539	1,188,438	1,899,101	0	38.5	61.5	0.0	710,663	23.0
90	Blanchard	Engler	R	2,534,673	1,258,539	1,276,134	0	49.7	50.4	0.0	17,595	0.7
86	Blanchard	Lucas	D	2,395,262	1,632,138	753,647	9,477	68.1	31.5	0.4	−878,491	−36.7
82	Blanchard	Headlee	D	3,039,782	1,561,291	1,369,582	108,909	51.4	45.1	3.6	−191,709	−6.3

Population, Registration, and Turnout, 1980–2000

Year	Population	Vot Age Pop	Registration	Dem %	Rep %	Other %	Unregistered	Turnout	TAPV[b]	Rank	TAPR[c]	Rank
00	9,938,444	7,358,000	6,861,342	n/a	n/a	n/a	3,077,102	4,232,501	57.5	15	61.7	36
98	9,817,242	7,265,627	6,915,613	n/a	n/a	n/a	350,014	3,036,886	41.8	17	43.9	32
96	9,594,350	7,029,898	6,677,079	n/a	n/a	n/a	352,819	3,844,166	54.7	21	57.6	44
94	9,496,147	6,971,000	6,207,662	n/a	n/a	n/a	763,338	3,087,539	44.3	17	49.7	43
92	9,437,000	6,928,000	6,147,083	n/a	n/a	n/a	780,917	4,250,935	61.4	19	69.2	44
90	9,295,297	6,836,532	5,892,001	n/a	n/a	n/a	944,531	2,534,673	37.1	30	43.0	45
88	9,240,000	6,791,000	5,952,513	n/a	n/a	n/a	838,487	3,668,261	54.0	20	61.6	45
86	9,145,000	6,633,000	5,790,753	n/a	n/a	n/a	842,247	2,395,262	36.1	35	41.4	45
84	9,058,000	6,591,000	5,888,808	n/a	n/a	n/a	702,192	3,801,658	57.7	16	64.6	46
82	9,109,000	6,543,000	5,624,573	n/a	n/a	n/a	918,427	3,039,782	46.5	15	54.0	41
80	9,262,078	6,509,710	5,725,713	n/a	n/a	n/a	783,997	3,908,769	60.0	12	68.3	43

[a] Upper case indicates victory with a majority of votes cast; lower case, victory with a plurality of votes cast.
[b] TAPV = turnout as a % of voting age population. Rankings are among all states.
[c] TAPR = turnout as a % of registration. Rankings are among all states.
Sources: Michigan Democratic Party, Michigan Republican Party, Federal Election Commission, U.S. Census Bureau.

MINNESOTA

2000 Electoral Votes: 10

Election Results, U.S. President, 1972–2000

Year	Democrat	Republican	Win[a]	Total Vote	Dem Vote	Rep Vote	Other Vote	Dem %	Rep %	Other %	R Margin	R Mar %
00	Gore	G. W. Bush	d	2,438,685	1,168,266	1,109,659	160,760	47.9	45.5	6.6	–58,607	–2.4
96	Clinton	Dole	D	2,189,737	1,120,438	766,476	302,823	51.2	35.0	13.8	–353,962	–16.2
92	Clinton	G. Bush	d	2,331,344	1,020,997	747,841	562,506	43.8	32.1	24.1	–273,156	–11.7
88	Dukakis	G. Bush	D	2,093,176	1,109,471	962,337	21,368	53.0	46.0	1.0	–147,134	–7.0
84	Mondale	Reagan	D	2,068,967	1,036,364	1,032,603	0	50.1	49.9	0.0	–3,761	–0.2
80	Carter	Reagan	d	2,002,432	954,174	873,268	174,990	47.7	43.6	8.7	–80,906	–4.0
76	Carter	Ford	D	1,925,325	1,070,440	819,395	35,490	55.6	42.6	1.8	–251,045	–13.0
72	McGovern	Nixon	R	1,741,652	802,346	898,269	41,037	46.1	51.6	2.4	95,923	5.5

Election Results, U.S. Senate, 1982–2000

Year	Democrat	Republican	Win[a]	Total Vote	Dem Vote	Rep Vote	Other Vote	Dem %	Rep %	Other %	R Margin	R Mar %
00	Dayton	Grams	d	2,419,520	1,181,553	1,047,474	190,493	48.8	43.3	7.9	–134,079	–5.5
96	Wellstone	Boschwitz	D	2,181,932	1,098,493	901,282	182,157	50.3	41.3	8.4	–197,211	–9.0
94	Wynia	Grams	r	1,770,315	781,860	869,653	118,802	44.2	49.1	6.7	87,793	5.0
90	Wellstone	Boschwitz	D	1,806,194	911,999	864,375	29,820	50.5	47.9	1.7	–47,624	–2.6
88	Humphrey	Durenberger	R	2,093,538	856,694	1,176,210	60,634	40.9	56.2	2.9	319,516	15.3
84	Growe	Boschwitz	R	2,065,903	852,844	1,199,926	13,133	41.3	58.1	0.6	347,082	16.8
82	Dayton	Durenberger	R	1,804,675	840,401	949,207	15,067	46.6	52.6	0.8	108,806	6.0

Election Results, Governor, 1982–1998

Year	Democrat	Republican	Win[a]	Total Vote	Dem Vote	Rep Vote	Other Vote	Dem %	Rep %	Other %	R Margin	R Mar %
98	Humphrey	Coleman	o	2,090,990	587,528	717,350	786,112	28.1	34.3	37.6	–56,363	–2.7
94	Marty	Carlson	R	1,727,394	589,344	1,094,165	43,885	34.1	63.3	2.5	504,821	29.2
90	Perpich	Carlson	R	1,788,158	836,218	895,988	55,952	46.8	50.1	3.1	59,770	3.3
86	Perpich	Ludeman	D	1,396,893	790,138	606,755	0	56.6	43.4	0.0	–183,383	–13.1
82	Perpich	Whitney	D	1,785,539	1,049,104	711,796	24,639	58.8	39.9	1.4	–337,308	–18.9

Population, Registration, and Turnout, 1980–2000

Year	Population	Vot Age Pop	Registration	Dem %	Rep %	Other %	Unregistered	Turnout	TAPV[b]	Rank	TAPR[c]	Rank
00	4,919,479	3,547,000	3,265,324	n/a	n/a	n/a	1,654,155	2,438,685	68.8	1	74.7	5
98	4,725,419	3,465,972	3,000,412	n/a	n/a	n/a	465,560	2,090,990	60.3	1	69.7	2
96	4,657,758	3,364,056	3,067,802	n/a	n/a	n/a	296,254	2,189,737	65.1	1	71.4	9
94	4,567,267	3,327,000	2,857,463	n/a	n/a	n/a	469,537	1,770,315	53.2	6	62.0	16
92	4,480,000	3,273,000	3,138,901	n/a	n/a	n/a	134,099	2,331,344	71.2	2	74.3	34
90	4,375,099	3,208,316	2,830,649	n/a	n/a	n/a	377,667	1,806,194	56.3	2	63.8	10
88	4,307,000	3,161,000	2,916,957	n/a	n/a	n/a	244,043	2,093,538	66.2	1	71.8	22
86	4,214,000	3,098,000	2,615,137	n/a	n/a	n/a	482,863	1,396,893	45.1	12	53.4	32
84	4,163,000	3,048,000	2,893,049	n/a	n/a	n/a	154,951	2,084,449	68.4	1	72.1	34
82	4,133,000	3,001,000	2,667,522	n/a	n/a	n/a	333,478	1,804,675	60.1	2	67.7	11
80	4,075,970	2,901,768	2,787,277	n/a	n/a	n/a	114,491	2,045,560	70.5	1	73.4	31

[a] Upper case indicates victory with a majority of votes cast; lower case, victory with a plurality of votes cast.

[b] TAPV = turnout as a % of voting age population. Rankings are among all states.

[c] TAPR = turnout as a % of registration. Rankings are among all states.

Sources: Minnesota Democratic Party, Minnesota Republican Party, Federal Election Commission, U.S. Census Bureau.

MISSISSIPPI

2000 Electoral Votes: 7

Election Results, U.S. President, 1972–2000

Year	Democrat	Republican	Win[a]	Total Vote	Dem Vote	Rep Vote	Other Vote	Dem %	Rep %	Other %	R Margin	R Mar %
00	Gore	G. W. Bush	R	994,184	404,614	572,844	16,726	40.7	57.6	1.7	168,230	16.9
96	Clinton	Dole	r	893,857	394,022	439,838	59,997	44.1	49.2	6.7	45,816	5.1
92	Clinton	G. Bush	R	973,677	400,258	487,793	85,626	41.1	50.1	8.8	87,535	9.0
88	Dukakis	G. Bush	R	931,527	363,921	557,890	9,716	39.1	59.9	1.0	193,969	20.8
84	Mondale	Reagan	R	934,569	352,192	582,377	0	37.7	62.3	0.0	230,185	24.6
80	Carter	Reagan	r	882,406	429,281	441,089	12,036	48.7	50.0	1.4	11,808	1.3
76	Carter	Ford	D	752,229	381,309	366,846	4,074	50.7	48.8	0.5	-14,463	-1.9
72	McGovern	Nixon	R	645,963	126,782	505,125	14,056	19.6	78.2	2.2	378,343	58.6

Election Results, U.S. Senate, 1982–2000

Year	Democrat	Republican	Win[a]	Total Vote	Dem Vote	Rep Vote	Other Vote	Dem %	Rep %	Other %	R Margin	R Mar %
00	Brown	Lott	R	994,144	314,090	654,941	25,113	31.6	65.9	2.5	340,851	34.3
96	Hunt	Cochran	R	878,662	240,647	624,154	13,861	27.4	71.0	1.6	383,507	43.6
94	Harper	Lott	R	608,085	189,752	418,333	0	31.2	68.8	0.0	228,581	37.6
90	unopposed	Cochran	R	274,244	–	274,244	0	–	100.0	0.0	274,244	100.0
88	Dowdy	Lott	R	946,719	436,339	510,380	0	46.1	53.9	0.0	74,041	7.8
84	Winter	Cochran	R	952,240	371,926	580,314	0	39.1	60.9	0.0	208,388	21.9
82	Stennis	Barbour	D	645,026	414,099	230,927	0	64.2	35.8	0.0	-183,172	-28.4

Election Results, Governor, 1983–1999

Year	Democrat	Republican	Win[a]	Total Vote	Dem Vote	Rep Vote	Other Vote	Dem %	Rep %	Other %	R Margin	R Mar %
99	Musgrove	Parker	d	763,938	379,034	370,691	14,213	49.6	48.5	1.9	-8,343	-1.1
95	Molpus	Fordice	R	819,471	364,210	455,261	0	44.4	55.6	0.0	91,051	11.1
91	Mabus	Fordice	R	699,935	338,435	361,500	0	48.4	51.7	0.0	23,065	3.3
87	Mabus	Reed	D	721,695	385,689	336,006	0	53.4	46.6	0.0	-49,683	-6.9
83	Allain	Bramlett	D	737,842	407,676	286,920	43,246	55.3	38.9	5.9	-120,756	-16.4

Population, Registration, and Turnout, 1980–2000

Year	Population	Vot Age Pop	Registration	Dem %	Rep %	Other %	Unregistered	Turnout	TAPV[b]	Rank	TAPR[c]	Rank
00	2,844,658	2,047,000	1,739,858	n/a	n/a	n/a	1,104,800	994,184	48.6	41	57.1	45
98	2,752,092	1,995,217	1,806,868	n/a	n/a	n/a	188,349	550,917	27.6	47	30.5	49
96	2,716,115	1,935,334	1,715,913	n/a	n/a	n/a	219,421	893,857	46.2	42	52.1	48
94	2,669,111	1,914,000	1,658,445	n/a	n/a	n/a	255,555	608,085	31.8	46	36.7	49
92	2,614,000	1,867,000	1,640,150	n/a	n/a	n/a	226,850	973,677	52.2	39	59.4	49
90	2,573,216	1,826,455	1,592,992	n/a	n/a	n/a	233,463	274,244	15.0	50	17.2	48
88	2,620,000	1,867,000	1,595,826	n/a	n/a	n/a	271,174	946,719	50.7	27	59.3	47
86	2,625,000	1,833,000	1,643,191	n/a	n/a	n/a	189,809	523,563	28.6	45	31.9	48
84	2,598,000	1,804,000	1,669,539	n/a	n/a	n/a	134,461	952,240	52.8	31	57.0	49
82	2,551,000	1,772,000	1,507,669	n/a	n/a	n/a	264,331	645,026	36.4	40	42.8	46
80	2,520,638	1,703,822	1,485,539	n/a	n/a	n/a	218,283	892,620	52.4	34	60.1	48

[a]Upper case indicates victory with a majority of votes cast; lower case, victory with a plurality of votes cast.
[b]TAPV = turnout as a % of voting age population. Rankings are among all states.
[c]TAPR = turnout as a % of registration. Rankings are among all states.

Sources: Mississippi Democratic Party, Mississippi Republican Party, Federal Election Commission, U.S. Census Bureau.

MONTANA

2000 Electoral Votes: 3

Election Results, U.S. President, 1972–2000

Year	Democrat	Republican	Win[a]	Total Vote	Dem Vote	Rep Vote	Other Vote	Dem %	Rep %	Other %	R Margin	R Mar %
00	Gore	G. W. Bush	R	410,997	137,126	240,178	33,693	33.4	58.4	8.2	103,052	25.1
96	Clinton	Dole	r	407,083	167,922	179,652	59,509	41.3	44.1	14.6	11,730	2.9
92	Clinton	G. Bush	d	405,939	154,507	144,207	107,225	38.1	35.5	26.4	−10,300	−2.5
88	Dukakis	G. Bush	R	365,674	168,936	190,412	6,326	46.2	52.1	1.7	21,476	5.9
84	Mondale	Reagan	R	379,192	146,742	232,450	0	38.7	61.3	0.0	85,708	22.6
80	Carter	Reagan	R	354,127	118,032	206,814	29,281	33.3	58.4	8.3	88,782	25.1
76	Carter	Ford	R	322,962	149,259	173,703	0	46.2	53.8	0.0	24,444	7.6
72	McGovern	Nixon	R	317,603	120,197	183,976	13,430	37.9	57.9	4.2	63,779	20.1

Election Results, U.S. Senate, 1982–2000

Year	Democrat	Republican	Win[a]	Total Vote	Dem Vote	Rep Vote	Other Vote	Dem %	Rep %	Other %	R Margin	R Mar %
00	Schweitzer	Burns	R	411,601	194,430	208,082	9,089	47.2	50.6	2.2	13,652	3.3
96	Baucus	Rehberg	d	407,490	201,935	182,111	23,444	49.6	44.7	5.8	−19,824	−4.9
94	Mudd	Burns	R	350,387	131,845	218,542	0	37.6	62.4	0.0	86,697	24.7
90	Baucus	Kolstad	D	311,399	217,563	93,836	0	69.9	30.1	0.0	−123,727	−39.7
88	Melcher	Burns	R	365,254	175,809	189,445	0	48.1	51.9	0.0	13,636	3.7
84	Baucus	Cozzens	D	379,155	215,704	154,308	9,143	56.9	40.7	2.4	−61,396	−16.2
82	Melcher	Williams	D	321,062	174,861	133,789	12,412	54.5	41.7	3.9	−41,072	−12.8

Election Results, Governor, 1980–2000

Year	Democrat	Republican	Win[a]	Total Vote	Dem Vote	Rep Vote	Other Vote	Dem %	Rep %	Other %	R Margin	R Mar %
00	O'Keefe	Martz	R	410,192	193,131	209,135	7,926	47.1	51.0	1.9	16,004	3.9
96	Jacobson	Racicot	R	405,175	76,471	320,768	7,936	18.9	79.2	2.0	244,297	60.3
92	Bradley	Racicot	R	407,822	198,421	209,401	0	48.7	51.4	0.0	10,980	2.7
88	Judge	Stephens	R	367,021	169,313	190,604	7,104	46.1	51.9	1.9	21,291	5.8
84	Schwinden	Goodover	D	378,970	266,578	100,070	12,322	70.3	26.4	3.3	−166,508	−43.9
80	Schwinden	Ramirez	D	360,466	199,574	160,892	0	55.4	44.6	0.0	−38,682	−10.7

Population, Registration, and Turnout, 1980–2000

Year	Population	Vot Age Pop	Registration	Dem %	Rep %	Other %	Unregistered	Turnout	TAPV[b]	Rank	TAPR[c]	Rank
00	902,195	668,000	698,260	n/a	n/a	n/a	203,935	410,986	61.5	7	58.9	43
98	880,453	656,050	639,241	n/a	n/a	n/a	16,809	331,551	50.5	3	51.9	15
96	879,372	634,147	590,751	n/a	n/a	n/a	43,396	407,490	64.3	3	69.0	15
94	856,047	619,000	514,051	n/a	n/a	n/a	104,949	352,133	56.9	3	68.5	4
92	824,000	598,000	529,822	n/a	n/a	n/a	68,178	407,822	68.2	5	77.0	26
90	799,065	576,961	435,900	n/a	n/a	n/a	141,061	311,399	54.0	3	71.4	5
88	805,000	586,000	505,541	n/a	n/a	n/a	80,459	367,071	62.6	2	72.6	21
86	819,000	595,000	443,935	n/a	n/a	n/a	151,065	317,862	53.4	4	71.6	2
84	823,000	588,000	526,841	n/a	n/a	n/a	61,159	384,377	65.4	2	73.0	25
82	804,000	576,000	445,888	n/a	n/a	n/a	130,112	321,062	55.7	4	72.0	5
80	786,690	554,887	496,402	n/a	n/a	n/a	58,485	363,952	65.6	7	73.3	30

[a]Upper case indicates victory with a majority of votes cast; lower case, victory with a plurality of votes cast.

[b]TAPV = turnout as a % of voting age population. Rankings are among all states.

[c]TAPR = turnout as a % of registration. Rankings are among all states.

Sources: Montana Democratic Party, Montana Republican Party, Federal Election Commission, U.S. Census Bureau, Montana Secretary of State Web site <www.sos.state.mt.us>

MISSOURI

2000 Electoral Votes: 11

Election Results, U.S. President, 1972–2000

Year	Democrat	Republican	Win[a]	Total Vote	Dem Vote	Rep Vote	Other Vote	Dem %	Rep %	Other %	R Margin	R Mar %
00	Gore	G. W. Bush	R	2,359,892	1,111,138	1,189,924	58,830	47.1	50.4	2.5	78,786	3.3
96	Clinton	Dole	d	2,157,469	1,025,935	890,016	241,518	47.6	41.3	11.2	−135,919	−6.3
92	Clinton	G. Bush	d	2,383,773	1,053,873	811,159	518,741	44.2	34.0	21.8	−242,714	−10.2
88	Dukakis	G. Bush	R	2,093,228	1,001,619	1,084,953	6,656	47.9	51.8	0.3	83,334	4.0
84	Mondale	Reagan	R	2,122,771	848,583	1,274,188	0	40.0	60.0	0.0	425,605	20.0
80	Carter	Reagan	R	2,083,283	931,182	1,074,181	77,920	44.7	51.6	3.7	142,999	6.9
76	Carter	Ford	D	1,952,300	999,163	928,808	24,329	51.2	47.6	1.3	−70,355	−3.6
72	McGovern	Nixon	R	1,857,393	698,531	1,154,058	4,804	37.6	62.1	0.3	455,527	24.5

Election Results, U.S. Senate, 1980–2000

Year	Democrat	Republican	Win[a]	Total Vote	Dem Vote	Rep Vote	Other Vote	Dem %	Rep %	Other %	R Margin	R Mar %
00	Carnahan*	Ashcroft	D	2,361,586	1,191,812	1,142,852	26,922	50.5	48.4	1.1	−48,960	−2.1
98	Nixon	Bond	R	1,576,857	690,208	830,625	56,024	43.8	52.7	3.6	140,417	8.9
94	Wheat	Ashcroft	R	1,775,110	633,697	1,060,149	81,264	35.7	59.7	4.6	426,452	24.0
92	Rothman-Serot	Bond	R	2,354,916	1,057,967	1,221,901	75,048	44.9	51.9	3.2	163,934	7.0
88	Nixon	Danforth	R	2,078,871	660,045	1,407,416	11,410	31.8	67.7	0.6	747,371	36.0
86	Woods	Bond	R	1,477,327	699,624	777,612	91	47.4	52.6	0.0	77,988	5.3
82	Woods	Danforth	R	1,543,505	758,629	784,876	0	49.2	50.9	0.0	26,247	1.7
80	Eagleton	McNary	D	2,066,965	1,074,859	985,399	6,707	52.0	47.7	0.3	−89,460	−4.3

Election Results, Governor, 1980–2000

Year	Democrat	Republican	Win[a]	Total Vote	Dem Vote	Rep Vote	Other Vote	Dem %	Rep %	Other %	R Margin	R Mar %
00	Holden	Talent	d	2,346,830	1,152,752	1,131,307	62,771	49.1	48.2	2.7	−21,445	−0.9
96	Carnahan	Kelly	D	2,142,501	1,224,801	866,268	51,432	57.2	40.4	2.4	−358,533	−16.7
92	Carnahan	Webster	D	2,343,999	1,375,425	968,574	0	58.7	41.3	0.0	−406,851	−17.4
88	Hearnes	Ashcroft	R	2,085,917	724,919	1,339,531	21,467	34.8	64.2	1.0	614,612	29.5
84	Rothman	Ashcroft	R	2,108,206	913,700	1,194,506	0	43.3	56.7	0.0	280,806	13.3
80	Teasdale	Bond	R	2,088,027	981,884	1,098,950	7,193	47.0	52.6	0.3	117,066	5.6

Population, Registration, and Turnout, 1980–2000

Year	Population	Vot Age Pop	Registration	Dem %	Rep %	Other %	Unregistered	Turnout	TAPVᵇ	Rank	TAPRᶜ	Rank
00	5,595,211	4,105,000	3,860,672	n/a	n/a	n/a	1,734,539	2,359,892	57.5	16	61.1	38
98	5,438,559	4,031,943	3,635,991	n/a	n/a	n/a	395,952	1,576,857	39.1	25	43.4	37
96	5,358,692	3,941,971	3,342,849	n/a	n/a	n/a	599,122	2,157,469	54.7	20	64.5	30
94	5,277,640	3,899,000	2,952,642	n/a	n/a	n/a	946,358	1,775,110	45.5	15	60.1	21
92	5,193,000	3,844,000	3,057,413	n/a	n/a	n/a	786,587	2,383,773	62.0	17	78.0	21
90	5,117,073	3,802,247	2,747,693	n/a	n/a	n/a	1,054,554	1,324,184	34.8	35	48.2	41
88	5,141,000	3,821,000	2,943,025	n/a	n/a	n/a	877,975	2,093,538	54.8	18	71.1	26
86	5,066,000	3,744,000	2,769,184	n/a	n/a	n/a	974,816	1,477,327	39.5	24	53.3	31
84	5,001,000	3,697,000	2,969,300	n/a	n/a	n/a	727,700	2,122,783	57.4	17	71.5	33
82	4,949,000	3,636,000	2,748,726	n/a	n/a	n/a	887,274	1,543,505	42.5	25	56.2	35
80	4,916,686	3,552,402	2,845,023	n/a	n/a	n/a	707,379	2,099,220	59.1	14	73.8	28

*Carnahan died before the election; his widow, Lynn Carnahan, was appointed to fill the vacancy.

[a]Upper case indicates victory with a majority of votes cast; lower case, victory with a plurality of votes cast.

[b]TAPV = turnout as a % of voting age population. Rankings are among all states.

[c]TAPR = turnout as a % of registration. Rankings are among all states.

Sources: Missouri Democratic Party, Missouri Republican Party, Federal Election Commission, U.S. Census Bureau, Missouri Secretary of State Web site <http://mosl.sos.state.mo.us>

NEBRASKA

2000 Electoral Votes: 5

Election Results, U.S. President, 1972–2000

Year	Democrat	Republican	Win[a]	Total Vote	Dem Vote	Rep Vote	Other Vote	Dem %	Rep %	Other %	R Margin	R Mar %
00	Gore	G. W. Bush	R	697,019	231,780	433,862	31,377	33.3	62.2	4.5	202,082	29.0
96	Clinton	Dole	R	677,415	236,761	363,467	77,187	35.0	53.7	11.4	126,706	18.7
92	Clinton	G. Bush	r	734,646	216,864	343,678	174,104	29.5	46.8	23.7	126,814	17.3
88	Dukakis	G. Bush	R	661,465	259,235	397,956	4,274	39.2	60.2	0.7	138,721	21.0
84	Mondale	Reagan	R	646,610	187,475	459,135	0	29.0	71.0	0.0	271,660	42.0
80	Carter	Reagan	R	630,492	166,424	419,214	44,854	26.4	66.5	7.1	252,790	40.1
76	Carter	Ford	R	601,895	233,293	359,219	9,383	38.8	59.7	1.6	125,926	20.9
72	McGovern	Nixon	R	576,289	169,991	406,298	0	29.5	70.5	0.0	236,307	41.0

Election Results, U.S. Senate, 1982–2000

Year	Democrat	Republican	Win[a]	Total Vote	Dem Vote	Rep Vote	Other Vote	Dem %	Rep %	Other %	R Margin	R Mar %
00	Nelson	Stenberg	D	692,350	353,093	337,977	1,280	51.0	48.8	0.2	−15,116	−2.2
96	Nelson	Hagel	R	676,126	281,904	379,933	14,289	41.7	56.2	2.1	98,029	14.5
94	Kerrey	Stoney	D	577,965	317,297	260,668	0	54.9	45.1	0.0	−56,629	−9.8
90	Exon	Daub	D	592,792	349,779	243,013	0	59.0	41.0	0.0	−106,766	−18.0
88	Kerrey	Karnes	D	667,339	378,717	278,250	10,372	56.8	41.7	1.6	−100,467	−15.1
84	Exon	Hoch	D	639,364	332,217	307,147	0	52.0	48.0	0.0	−25,070	−3.9
82	Zorinsky	Keck	D	545,553	363,350	155,760	26,443	66.6	28.6	4.9	−207,590	−38.1

Election Results, Governor, 1982–1998

Year	Democrat	Republican	Win[a]	Total Vote	Dem Vote	Rep Vote	Other Vote	Dem %	Rep %	Other %	R Margin	R Mar %
98	Hoppner	Johanns	R	544,588	250,678	293,910	0	46.0	54.0	0.0	43,232	7.9
94	Nelson	Spence	D	571,500	423,270	148,230	0	74.1	25.9	0.0	−275,040	−48.1
90	Nelson	Orr	D	581,512	292,771	288,741	0	50.4	49.7	0.0	−4,030	−0.7
86	Boosalis	Orr	R	563,481	265,156	298,325	0	47.1	52.9	0.0	33,169	5.9
82	Kerrey	Thone	D	547,639	277,436	270,203	0	50.7	49.3	0.0	−7,233	−1.3

Population, Registration, and Turnout, 1980–2000

Year	Population	Vot Age Pop	Registration	Dem %	Rep %	Other %	Unregistered	Turnout	TAPV[b]	Rank	TAPR[c]	Rank
00	1,711,263	1,234,000	1,085,217	36.2	49.5	14.3	626,046	697,019	56.5	19	64.2	30
98	1,662,719	1,217,077	1,056,351	37.0	49.3	13.7	160,726	544,588	44.7	12	51.6	14
96	1,652,093	1,193,815	1,015,056	37.9	49.5	12.7	178,759	677,415	56.7	15	66.7	19
94	1,622,858	1,182,000	919,321	39.8	49.7	10.6	262,679	577,965	48.9	11	62.9	13
92	1,606,000	1,165,000	951,395	40.9	48.9	10.2	213,605	734,646	63.1	14	77.2	25
90	1,578,385	1,149,373	890,579	42.0	50.5	7.6	258,794	592,792	51.6	6	66.6	7
88	1,602,000	1,167,000	898,959	42.1	50.7	7.2	268,041	667,339	57.2	14	74.2	18
86	1,598,000	1,177,000	849,762	42.3	51.2	6.5	327,238	563,481	47.9	8	66.3	9
84	1,605,000	1,169,000	902,626	42.8	50.4	6.8	266,374	652,090	55.8	22	72.2	32
82	1,586,000	1,151,000	832,121	43.5	50.1	6.4	318,879	547,639	47.6	12	65.8	15
80	1,569,825	1,122,364	856,186	44.0	49.6	6.4	266,178	639,533	57.0	22	74.7	24

[a]Upper case indicates victory with a majority of votes cast; lower case, victory with a plurality of votes cast.

[b]TAPV = turnout as a % of voting age population. Rankings are among all states.

[c]TAPR = turnout as a % of registration. Rankings are among all states.

Sources: Nebraska Democratic Party, Nebraska Republican Party, Federal Election Commission, U.S. Census Bureau, Nebraska Secretary of State Web site <www.nol.org/home/SOS>

NEVADA

2000 Electoral Votes: 4

Election Results, U.S. President, 1972–2000

Year	Democrat	Republican	Win[a]	Total Vote	Dem Vote	Rep Vote	Other Vote	Dem %	Rep %	Other %	R Margin	R Mar %
00	Gore	G. W. Bush	r	608,970	279,978	301,575	27,417	46.0	49.5	4.5	21,597	3.5
96	Clinton	Dole	d	464,279	203,974	199,244	61,061	43.9	42.9	13.2	−4,730	−1.0
92	Clinton	G. Bush	d	497,556	189,148	175,828	132,580	38.0	35.3	26.7	−13,320	−2.7
88	Dukakis	G. Bush	R	343,133	132,738	206,040	4,355	38.7	60.1	1.3	73,302	21.4
84	Mondale	Reagan	R	280,425	91,655	188,770	0	32.7	67.3	0.0	97,115	34.6
80	Carter	Reagan	R	239,334	66,666	155,017	17,651	27.9	64.8	7.4	88,351	36.9
76	Carter	Ford	R	193,752	92,479	101,273	0	47.7	52.3	0.0	8,794	4.5
72	McGovern	Nixon	R	181,766	66,016	115,750	0	36.3	63.7	0.0	49,734	27.4

Election Results, U.S. Senate, 1980–2000

Year	Democrat	Republican	Win[a]	Total Vote	Dem Vote	Rep Vote	Other Vote	Dem %	Rep %	Other %	R Margin	R Mar %
00	Bernstein	Ensign	R	600,250	238,260	330,687	31,303	39.7	55.1	5.2	92,427	15.4
98	Reid	Ensign	d	435,790	208,650	208,222	18,918	47.9	47.8	4.3	−428	−0.1
94	Bryan	Furman	D	380,530	193,804	156,020	30,706	50.9	41.0	8.1	−37,784	−9.9
92	Reid	Dahl	D	452,563	253,150	199,413	0	55.9	44.1	0.0	−53,737	−11.9
88	Bryan	Hecht	D	342,407	175,548	161,336	5,523	51.3	47.1	1.6	−14,212	−4.2
86	Reid	Santini	d	261,932	130,955	116,606	14,371	50.0	44.5	5.5	−14,349	−5.5
82	Cannon	Hecht	R	240,394	114,720	120,377	5,297	47.7	50.1	2.2	5,657	2.4
80	Gojack	Laxalt	R	243,273	92,129	144,224	6,920	37.9	59.3	2.8	52,095	21.4

Election Results, Governor, 1982–1998

Year	Democrat	Republican	Win[a]	Total Vote	Dem Vote	Rep Vote	Other Vote	Dem %	Rep %	Other %	R Margin	R Mar %
98	Jones	Guinn	R	420,989	182,281	223,892	14,816	43.3	53.2	3.5	41,611	9.9
94	Miller	Gibbons	D	379,676	200,026	156,875	22,775	52.7	41.3	6.0	−43,151	−11.4
90	Miller	Gallaway	D	303,667	207,878	95,789	0	68.5	31.5	0.0	−112,089	−36.9
86	Bryan	Cafferata	D	260,375	187,268	65,081	8,026	71.9	25.0	3.1	−122,187	−46.9
82	Bryan	List	D	239,751	128,132	100,104	11,515	53.4	41.8	4.8	−28,028	−11.7

Population, Registration, and Turnout, 1980–2000

Year	Population	Vot Age Pop	Registration	Dem %	Rep %	Other %	Unregistered	Turnout	TAPV[b]	Rank	TAPR[c]	Rank
00	1,998,257	1,390,000	898,347	41.5	41.7	16.8	1,099,910	608,970	43.8	48	67.8	18
98	1,746,898	1,279,791	898,055	41.5	41.8	16.7	381,736	435,790	34.1	39	48.5	21
96	1,603,163	1,131,522	778,134	41.8	42.4	15.8	353,388	464,279	41.0	50	59.7	41
94	1,457,028	1,082,000	626,224	43.2	41.4	15.4	455,776	380,530	35.2	42	60.8	19
92	1,327,000	989,000	649,931	45.4	39.4	15.2	339,069	497,556	50.3	45	76.6	24
90	1,201,833	904,885	516,423	45.0	42.9	12.2	388,462	303,667	33.6	39	58.8	21
88	1,054,000	780,000	444,933	47.1	42.5	10.5	335,067	344,173	44.1	46	77.4	11
86	963,000	724,000	367,596	50.1	42.9	7.1	356,404	261,932	36.2	34	71.3	3
84	917,000	686,000	356,405	51.7	41.1	7.2	329,595	286,667	41.8	49	80.4	5
82	877,000	652,000	322,290	54.1	38.5	7.4	329,710	240,394	36.9	39	74.6	2
80	800,493	584,912	297,318	53.4	38.7	7.9	287,594	243,692	41.7	48	82.0	3

[a] Upper case indicates victory with a majority of votes cast; lower case, victory with a plurality of votes cast.
[b] TAPV = turnout as a % of voting age population. Rankings are among all states.
[c] TAPR = turnout as a % of registration. Rankings are among all states.

Sources: Nevada Democratic Party, Nevada Republican Party, Federal Election Commission, U.S. Census Bureau, Nevada Secretary of State Web site <www.sos.state.nv.us>

NEW HAMPSHIRE

2000 Electoral Votes: 4

Election Results, U.S. President, 1972–2000

Year	Democrat	Republican	Win[a]	Total Vote	Dem Vote	Rep Vote	Other Vote	Dem %	Rep %	Other %	R Margin	R Mar %
00	Gore	G. W. Bush	r	569,071	266,348	273,559	29,164	46.8	48.1	5.1	7,211	1.3
96	Clinton	Dole	d	496,597	246,166	196,486	53,945	49.6	39.6	10.9	−49,680	−10.0
92	Clinton	G. Bush	d	532,861	209,040	202,484	121,337	39.2	38.0	22.8	−6,556	−1.2
88	Dukakis	G. Bush	R	450,525	163,696	281,537	5,292	36.3	62.5	1.2	117,841	26.2
84	Mondale	Reagan	R	387,397	120,347	267,050	0	31.1	68.9	0.0	146,703	37.9
80	Carter	Reagan	R	380,262	108,864	221,705	49,693	28.6	58.3	13.1	112,841	29.7
76	Carter	Ford	R	337,665	147,635	185,935	4,095	43.7	55.1	1.2	38,300	11.3
72	McGovern	Nixon	R	334,055	116,435	213,724	3,896	34.9	64.0	1.2	97,289	29.1

Election Results, U.S. Senate, 1980–1998

Year	Democrat	Republican	Win[a]	Total Vote	Dem Vote	Rep Vote	Other Vote	Dem %	Rep %	Other %	R Margin	R Mar %
98	Condodemetrak	Gregg	R	314,696	88,883	213,477	12,336	28.2	67.8	3.9	124,594	39.6
96	Swett	Smith	r	491,873	227,355	242,257	22,261	46.2	49.3	4.5	14,902	3.0
92	Rauh	Gregg	r	502,787	234,982	249,591	18,214	46.7	49.6	3.6	14,609	2.9
90	Durkin	Smith	R	280,892	91,262	189,630	0	32.5	67.5	0.0	98,368	35.0
86	Peabody	Rudman	R	244,735	79,222	154,090	11,423	32.4	63.0	4.7	74,868	30.6
84	D'Amours	Humphrey	R	384,369	157,447	225,828	1,094	41.0	58.8	0.3	68,381	17.8
80	Durkin	Rudman	R	375,018	179,455	195,563	0	47.9	52.2	0.0	16,108	4.3

Election Results, Governor, 1988–2000

Year	Democrat	Republican	Win[a]	Total Vote	Dem Vote	Rep Vote	Other Vote	Dem %	Rep %	Other %	R Margin	R Mar %
00	Shaheen	Humphrey	d	564,340	275,038	246,952	42,350	48.7	43.8	7.5	−28,086	−5.0
98	Shaheen	Lucas	D	317,897	210,769	98,473	8,655	66.3	31.0	2.7	−112,296	−35.3
96	Shaheen	Lamontagne	D	496,669	284,131	196,278	16,260	57.2	39.5	3.3	−87,853	−17.7
94	King	Merrill	R	311,529	79,686	218,134	13,709	25.6	70.0	4.4	138,448	44.4
92	Arnesen	Merrill	R	516,065	206,232	289,170	20,663	40.0	56.0	4.0	82,938	16.1
90	Grandmaison	Gregg	R	293,845	101,886	177,611	14,348	34.7	60.4	4.9	75,725	25.8
88	McEachern	Gregg	R	441,823	172,543	267,064	2,216	39.1	60.5	0.5	94,521	21.4

Population, Registration, and Turnout, 1980–2000

Year	Population	Vot Age Pop	Registration	Dem %	Rep %	Other %	Unregistered	Turnout	TAPV[b]	Rank	TAPR[c]	Rank
00	1,235,786	911,000	856,519	26.2	35.3	38.4	379,267	569,081	62.5	6	66.4	23
98	1,185,048	886,438	747,397	27.2	36.4	36.4	139,041	317,897	35.9	32	42.5	36
96	1,162,481	853,284	713,236	28.9	38.7	32.4	140,048	496,669	58.2	10	69.6	13
94	1,136,820	846,000	665,021	31.7	37.9	30.4	180,979	311,529	36.8	39	46.8	45
92	1,111,000	831,000	660,985	33.3	38.9	27.8	170,015	532,861	64.1	11	80.6	12
90	1,109,252	830,497	658,716	29.2	38.6	32.3	171,781	293,845	35.4	34	44.6	44
88	1,085,000	823,000	649,780	30.4	38.9	30.7	173,220	450,524	54.7	17	69.3	33
86	1,027,000	765,000	551,257	30.4	36.7	33.0	213,743	250,966	32.8	40	45.5	41
84	978,000	734,000	543,790	31.2	37.1	31.6	190,210	388,904	53.0	30	71.5	31
82	951,000	699,000	462,457	29.6	40.8	29.7	236,543	284,943	40.8	32	61.6	26
80	920,610	661,936	551,432	32.5	40.3	27.2	110,504	383,932	58.0	18	69.6	38

[a] Upper case indicates victory with a majority of votes cast; lower case, victory with a plurality of votes cast.

[b] TAPV = turnout as a % of voting age population. Rankings are among all states.

[c] TAPR = turnout as a % of registration. Rankings are among all states.

Sources: New Hampshire Democratic Party, New Hampshire Republican Party, Federal Election Commission, U.S. Census Bureau, New Hampshire Department of State.

NEW JERSEY

2000 Electoral Votes: 15

Election Results, U.S. President, 1972–2000

Year	Democrat	Republican	Win[a]	Total Vote	Dem Vote	Rep Vote	Other Vote	Dem %	Rep %	Other %	R Margin	R Mar %
00	Gore	G. W. Bush	D	3,187,226	1,788,850	1,284,173	114,203	56.1	40.3	3.6	−504,677	−15.8
96	Clinton	Dole	D	3,075,860	1,652,361	1,103,099	320,400	53.7	35.9	10.4	−549,262	−17.9
92	Clinton	G. Bush	d	3,314,900	1,436,206	1,356,865	521,829	43.3	40.9	15.7	−79,341	−2.4
88	Dukakis	G. Bush	R	3,099,553	1,320,352	1,743,192	36,009	42.6	56.2	1.2	422,840	13.6
84	Mondale	Reagan	R	3,194,953	1,261,323	1,933,630	0	39.5	60.5	0.0	672,307	21.0
80	Carter	Reagan	R	2,928,553	1,147,364	1,546,557	234,632	39.2	52.8	8.0	399,193	13.6
76	Carter	Ford	R	2,987,058	1,444,653	1,509,688	32,717	48.4	50.5	1.1	65,035	2.2
72	McGovern	Nixon	R	2,997,229	1,102,211	1,845,502	49,516	36.8	61.6	1.7	743,291	24.8

Election Results, U.S. Senate, 1982–2000

Year	Democrat	Republican	Win[a]	Total Vote	Dem Vote	Rep Vote	Other Vote	Dem %	Rep %	Other %	R Margin	R Mar %
00	Corzine	Franks	D	3,015,662	1,511,237	1,420,267	84,158	50.1	47.1	2.8	−90,970	−3.0
96	Torricelli	Zimmer	D	2,883,466	1,519,154	1,227,351	136,961	52.7	42.6	4.8	−291,803	−10.1
94	Lautenberg	Haytaian	D	2,054,887	1,033,487	966,244	55,156	50.3	47.0	2.7	−67,243	−3.3
90	Bradley	Whitman	D	1,896,684	977,810	918,874	0	51.6	48.5	0.0	−58,936	−3.1
88	Lautenberg	Dawkins	D	2,987,634	1,599,905	1,349,937	37,792	53.6	45.2	1.3	−249,968	−8.4
84	Bradley	Mochary	D	3,096,456	1,986,644	1,080,100	29,712	64.2	34.9	1.0	−906,544	−29.3
82	Lautenberg	Fenwick	D	2,193,945	1,117,549	1,047,626	28,770	50.9	47.8	1.3	−69,923	−3.2

Election Results, Governor, 1981–1997

Year	Democrat	Republican	Win[a]	Total Vote	Dem Vote	Rep Vote	Other Vote	Dem %	Rep %	Other %	R Margin	R Mar %
97	McGreevey	Whitman	r	2,416,104	1,107,968	1,133,394	174,742	45.9	46.9	7.2	25,426	1.1
93	Florio	Whitman	R	2,446,155	1,210,031	1,236,124	0	49.5	50.5	0.0	26,093	1.1
89	Florio	Courter	D	2,256,654	1,379,937	838,553	38,164	61.2	37.2	1.7	−541,384	−24.0
85	Shapiro	Kean	R	1,910,038	573,005	1,337,033	0	30.0	70.0	0.0	764,028	40.0
81	Florio	Kean	r	2,316,291	1,143,788	1,145,465	27,038	49.4	49.5	1.2	1,677	0.1

Population, Registration, and Turnout, 1980–2000

Year	Population	Vot Age Pop	Registration	Dem %	Rep %	Other %	Unregistered	Turnout	TAPV[b]	Rank	TAPR[c]	Rank
00	8,414,350	6,245,000	4,710,768	25.0	18.6	56.4	3,703,582	3,187,226	51.0	32	67.7	19
98	8,115,011	6,124,572	4,538,944	25.2	19.2	55.6	1,585,628	1,815,489	29.6	45	40.0	40
96	7,987,933	5,981,775	4,320,866	25.5	20.1	54.5	1,660,909	3,075,860	51.4	26	71.2	8
94	7,903,925	5,974,000	3,859,245	28.8	22.1	49.1	2,114,755	2,054,887	34.4	45	53.2	35
92	7,789,000	5,925,000	4,063,541	28.9	20.1	50.9	1,861,459	3,314,900	55.9	28	81.6	6
90	7,730,188	5,930,726	3,718,598	32.3	21.2	46.6	2,212,128	1,896,684	32.0	41	51.0	35
88	7,721,000	5,943,000	4,010,790	31.6	20.1	48.4	1,932,210	2,987,634	50.3	31	74.5	15
86	7,620,000	5,815,000	3,777,278	34.3	20.4	45.3	2,037,722	1,553,545	26.7	48	41.1	44
84	7,517,000	5,709,000	4,072,639	33.5	21.3	45.2	1,636,361	3,217,862	56.4	21	79.0	9
82	7,438,000	5,551,000	3,681,211	33.9	21.6	44.5	1,869,789	2,193,945	39.5	35	59.6	31
80	7,364,823	5,372,524	3,761,428	32.8	20.8	46.4	1,611,096	2,975,684	55.4	27	79.1	10

[a] Upper case indicates victory with a majority of votes cast; lower case, victory with a plurality of votes cast.

[b] TAPV = turnout as a % of voting age population. Rankings are among all states.

[c] TAPR = turnout as a % of registration. Rankings are among all states.

Sources: New Jersey Democratic Party, New Jersey Republican Party, Federal Election Commission, U.S. Census Bureau, New Jersey Department of Law & Public Safety, Division of Elections Web site <www.state.nj.us/lps/elections/electionshome.htm>

NEW MEXICO

2000 Electoral Votes: 5

Election Results, U.S. President, 1972–2000

Year	Democrat	Republican	Win[a]	Total Vote	Dem Vote	Rep Vote	Other Vote	Dem %	Rep %	Other %	R Margin	R Mar %
00	Gore	G. W. Bush	d	598,605	286,783	286,417	25,405	47.9	47.8	4.2	−366	−0.1
96	Clinton	Dole	d	556,074	273,495	232,751	49,828	49.2	41.9	9.0	−40,744	−7.3
92	Clinton	G. Bush	d	566,336	261,617	212,824	91,895	46.2	37.6	16.2	−48,793	−8.6
88	Dukakis	G. Bush	R	521,194	244,497	270,341	6,356	46.9	51.9	1.2	25,844	5.0
84	Mondale	Reagan	R	508,870	201,769	307,101	0	39.7	60.4	0.0	105,332	20.7
80	Carter	Reagan	R	448,064	167,826	250,779	29,459	37.5	56.0	6.6	82,953	18.5
76	Carter	Ford	R	412,567	201,148	211,419	0	48.8	51.3	0.0	10,271	2.5
72	McGovern	Nixon	R	386,241	141,084	235,606	9,551	36.5	61.0	2.5	94,522	24.5

Election Results, U.S. Senate, 1982–2000

Year	Democrat	Republican	Win[a]	Total Vote	Dem Vote	Rep Vote	Other Vote	Dem %	Rep %	Other %	R Margin	R Mar %
00	Bingaman	Redmond	D	589,526	363,744	225,517	265	61.7	38.3	0.0	−138,227	−23.4
96	Trujillo	Domenici	R	551,821	164,356	357,171	30,294	29.8	64.7	5.5	192,815	34.9
94	Bingaman	McMillan	D	463,014	249,989	213,025	0	54.0	46.0	0.0	−36,964	−8.0
90	Benavides	Domenici	R	406,745	110,033	296,712	0	27.1	73.0	0.0	186,679	45.9
88	Bingaman	Valentine	D	508,562	321,983	186,579	0	63.3	36.7	0.0	−135,404	−26.6
84	Pratt	Domenici	R	502,624	141,253	361,371	0	28.1	71.9	0.0	220,118	43.8
82	Bingaman	Schmitt	D	404,810	217,682	187,128	0	53.8	46.2	0.0	−30,554	−7.5

Election Results, Governor, 1982–1998

Year	Democrat	Republican	Win[a]	Total Vote	Dem Vote	Rep Vote	Other Vote	Dem %	Rep %	Other %	R Margin	R Mar %
98	Chavez	Johnson	R	498,703	226,755	271,948	0	45.5	54.5	0.0	45,193	9.1
94	King	Johnson	r	467,621	186,686	232,945	47,990	39.9	49.8	10.3	46,259	9.9
90	King	Bond	D	410,256	224,564	185,692	0	54.7	45.3	0.0	−38,872	−9.5
86	Powell	Carruthers	R	394,833	185,378	209,455	0	47.0	53.1	0.0	24,077	6.1
82	Anaya	Irick	D	407,466	215,840	191,626	0	53.0	47.0	0.0	−24,214	−5.9

Population, Registration, and Turnout, 1980–2000

Year	Population	Vot Age Pop	Registration	Dem %	Rep %	Other %	Unregistered	Turnout	TAPV[b]	Rank	TAPR[c]	Rank
00	1,819,046	1,263,000	972,895	52.2	32.7	15.1	846,151	598,605	47.4	43	61.5	37
98	1,736,931	1,232,721	912,964	53.8	32.9	13.3	319,757	498,703	40.5	20	54.6	10
96	1,713,407	1,185,302	837,794	54.6	33.7	11.7	347,508	556,074	46.9	39	66.4	24
94	1,653,521	1,156,000	713,645	57.7	34.1	8.3	442,355	467,621	40.5	28	65.5	8
92	1,581,000	1,114,000	707,012	58.2	33.9	8.0	406,988	566,336	50.8	40	80.1	15
90	1,515,069	1,068,328	658,374	58.9	35.5	5.7	409,954	410,256	38.4	28	62.3	13
88	1,507,000	1,101,000	674,826	58.5	35.4	6.1	426,174	521,194	47.3	37	77.2	10
86	1,479,000	1,035,000	632,787	60.1	34.0	5.9	402,213	394,833	38.1	28	62.4	11
84	1,426,000	995,000	650,929	61.5	32.0	6.5	344,071	514,370	51.7	34	79.0	8
82	1,367,000	951,000	582,646	63.0	30.3	6.7	368,354	407,466	42.8	24	69.9	8
80	1,302,894	885,156	652,687	62.7	29.8	7.6	232,469	456,237	51.5	33	69.9	37

[a]Upper case indicates victory with a majority of votes cast; lower case, victory with a plurality of votes cast.
[b]TAPV = turnout as a % of voting age population. Rankings are among all states.
[c]TAPR = turnout as a % of registration. Rankings are among all states.

Sources: New Mexico Democratic Party, New Mexico Republican Party, Federal Election Commission, U.S. Census Bureau, New Mexico Secretary of State Web site <www.sos.state.nm.us>

NEW YORK

2000 Electoral Votes: 33

Election Results, U.S. President, 1972–2000

Year	Democrat	Republican	Win[a]	Total Vote	Dem Vote	Rep Vote	Other Vote	Dem %	Rep %	Other %	R Margin	R Mar %
00	Gore	G. W. Bush	D	6,821,999	4,107,697	2,403,374	310,928	60.2	35.2	4.6	−1,704,323	−25.0
96	Clinton	Dole	D	6,316,129	3,756,177	1,933,492	626,460	59.5	30.6	9.9	−1,822,685	−28.9
92	Clinton	G. Bush	D	6,881,820	3,444,450	2,346,649	1,090,721	50.1	34.1	15.9	−1,097,801	−16.0
88	Dukakis	G. Bush	D	6,485,683	3,347,882	3,081,871	55,930	51.6	47.5	0.9	−266,011	−4.1
84	Mondale	Reagan	R	6,784,372	3,119,609	3,664,763	0	46.0	54.0	0.0	545,154	8.0
80	Carter	Reagan	r	6,090,004	2,728,372	2,893,831	467,801	44.8	47.5	7.7	165,459	2.7
76	Carter	Ford	D	6,490,349	3,389,558	3,100,791	0	52.2	47.8	0.0	−288,767	−4.4
72	McGovern	Nixon	R	7,165,919	2,951,084	4,192,778	22,057	41.2	58.5	0.3	1,241,694	17.3

Election Results, U.S. Senate, 1980–2000

Year	Democrat	Republican	Win[a]	Total Vote	Dem Vote	Rep Vote	Other Vote	Dem %	Rep %	Other %	R Margin	R Mar %
00	Clinton	Lazio	D	6,779,839	3,747,310	2,915,730	116,799	55.3	43.0	1.7	−831,580	−12.3
98	Schumer	D'Amato	D	4,670,805	2,551,065	2,058,988	60,752	54.6	44.1	1.3	−492,077	−10.5
94	Moynihan	Castro	D	4,790,336	2,646,541	1,988,308	155,487	55.3	41.5	3.3	−658,233	−13.7
92	Abrams	D'Amato	R	6,253,194	3,086,200	3,166,994	0	49.4	50.7	0.0	80,794	1.3
88	Moynihan	McMillan	D	6,040,924	4,048,649	1,875,784	116,491	67.0	31.1	1.9	−2,172,865	−36.0
86	Green	D'Amato	R	4,179,447	1,723,216	2,378,197	78,034	41.2	56.9	1.9	654,981	15.7
82	Moynihan	Sullivan	D	4,967,497	3,232,146	1,696,766	38,585	65.1	34.2	0.8	−1,535,380	−30.9
80	Holtzman	D'Amato	r	5,982,857	2,618,661	2,699,652	664,544	43.8	45.1	11.1	80,991	1.4

Election Results, Governor, 1982–1998

Year	Democrat	Republican	Win[a]	Total Vote	Dem Vote	Rep Vote	Other Vote	Dem %	Rep %	Other %	R Margin	R Mar %
98	Vallone	Pataki	R	4,737,775	1,570,317	2,571,991	595,467	33.1	54.3	12.6	1,001,674	21.1
94	Cuomo	Pataki	r	5,203,762	2,364,904	2,538,702	300,156	45.5	48.8	5.8	173,798	3.3
90	Cuomo	Rinfret	D	4,056,896	2,157,087	865,948	1,033,861	53.2	21.4	25.5	−1,291,139	−31.8
86	Cuomo	O'Rourke	D	4,293,971	2,775,229	1,363,810	154,932	64.6	31.8	3.6	−1,411,419	−32.9
82	Cuomo	Lehrman	D	5,222,396	2,675,213	2,494,827	52,356	51.2	47.8	1.0	−180,386	−3.5

Population, Registration, and Turnout, 1980–2000

Year	Population	Vot Age Pop	Registration	Dem %	Rep %	Other %	Unregistered	Turnout	TAPV[b]	Rank	TAPR[c]	Rank
00	18,976,457	13,805,000	11,262,816	46.6	28.2	25.3	7,713,641	6,960,215	50.4	34	61.8	35
98	18,175,301	13,672,690	10,740,788	46.5	29.0	24.5	2,931,902	4,737,775	34.7	36	44.1	31
96	18,184,774	13,599,219	10,162,156	46.6	29.5	23.9	3,437,063	6,316,129	46.4	41	62.2	36
94	18,169,051	13,658,000	8,818,691	47.0	30.7	22.3	4,839,309	5,203,762	38.1	34	59.0	24
92	18,119,000	13,697,000	9,193,391	47.0	32.3	20.7	4,503,609	6,881,820	50.2	44	74.9	32
90	17,990,456	13,730,906	8,201,532	58.0	39.1	2.9	5,529,374	4,056,896	29.5	45	49.5	38
88	17,909,000	13,480,000	8,581,276	47.5	34.5	18.0	4,898,724	5,499,006	40.8	48	64.1	43
86	17,772,000	13,472,000	8,071,004	48.1	33.6	18.4	5,400,996	4,293,971	31.9	42	53.2	30
84	17,746,000	13,362,000	9,044,208	48.2	34.2	17.6	4,317,792	6,806,810	50.9	37	75.3	19
82	17,659,000	13,142,000	7,634,992	47.2	35.4	17.4	5,507,008	5,222,396	39.7	34	68.4	10
80	17,558,072	12,869,227	7,897,555	48.9	36.8	14.3	4,971,672	6,200,715	48.2	43	78.5	9

[a] Upper case indicates victory with a majority of votes cast; lower case, victory with a plurality of votes cast.
[b] TAPV = turnout as a % of voting age population. Rankings are among all states.
[c] TAPR = turnout as a % of registration. Rankings are among all states.

Sources: New York Democratic Party, New York Republican Party, Federal Election Commission, U.S. Census Bureau, New York State Board of Elections Web site <www.elections.state.ny.us>

NORTH CAROLINA

2000 Electoral Votes: 14

Election Results, U.S. President, 1972–2000

Year	Democrat	Republican	Win[a]	Total Vote	Dem Vote	Rep Vote	Other Vote	Dem %	Rep %	Other %	R Margin	R Mar %
00	Gore	G. W. Bush	R	2,914,990	1,257,692	1,631,163	26,135	43.1	56.0	0.9	373,471	12.8
96	Clinton	Dole	r	2,513,357	1,107,849	1,225,938	179,570	44.1	48.8	7.1	118,089	4.7
92	Clinton	G. Bush	r	2,606,567	1,114,042	1,134,661	357,864	42.7	43.5	13.7	20,619	0.8
88	Dukakis	G. Bush	R	2,134,370	890,167	1,237,258	6,945	41.7	58.0	0.3	347,091	16.3
84	Mondale	Reagan	R	2,170,768	824,287	1,346,481	0	38.0	62.0	0.0	522,194	24.1
80	Carter	Reagan	r	1,843,453	875,635	915,018	52,800	47.5	49.6	2.9	39,383	2.1
76	Carter	Ford	D	1,669,325	927,365	741,960	0	55.6	44.5	0.0	−185,405	−11.1
72	McGovern	Nixon	R	1,518,612	438,705	1,054,889	25,018	28.9	69.5	1.7	616,184	40.6

Election Results, U.S. Senate, 1980–1998

Year	Democrat	Republican	Win[a]	Total Vote	Dem Vote	Rep Vote	Other Vote	Dem %	Rep %	Other %	R Margin	R Mar %
98	Edwards	Faircloth	D	2,012,143	1,029,237	945,943	36,963	51.2	47.0	1.8	−83,294	−4.1
96	Gantt	Helms	R	2,556,313	1,173,875	1,345,833	36,605	45.9	52.7	1.4	171,958	6.7
92	Sanford	Faircloth	R	2,577,855	1,194,015	1,297,892	85,948	46.3	50.4	3.3	103,877	4.0
90	Gantt	Helms	R	2,069,904	981,573	1,088,331	0	47.4	52.6	0.0	106,758	5.2
86	Sanford	Broyhill	D	1,591,330	823,662	767,668	0	51.8	48.2	0.0	−55,994	−3.5
84	Hunt	Helms	R	2,239,051	1,070,488	1,156,768	11,795	47.8	51.7	0.5	86,280	3.9
80	Morgan	East	r	1,797,665	887,653	898,064	11,948	49.4	50.0	0.7	10,411	0.6

Election Results, Governor, 1980–2000

Year	Democrat	Republican	Win[a]	Total Vote	Dem Vote	Rep Vote	Other Vote	Dem %	Rep %	Other %	R Margin	R Mar %
00	Easley	Vinroot	D	2,942,062	1,530,324	1,360,960	50,778	52.0	46.3	1.7	−169,364	−5.8
96	Hunt	Hayes	D	2,566,042	1,436,638	1,097,053	32,351	56.0	42.8	1.3	−339,585	−13.2
92	Hunt	Gardner	D	2,595,184	1,368,246	1,121,955	104,983	52.7	43.2	4.1	−246,291	−9.5
88	Jordan	Martin	R	2,180,025	957,687	1,222,338	0	43.9	56.1	0.0	264,651	12.1
84	Edmisten	Martin	R	2,226,727	1,011,209	1,208,167	7,351	45.4	54.3	0.3	196,958	8.8
80	Hunt	Lake	D	1,847,432	1,143,145	691,449	12,838	61.9	37.4	0.7	−451,696	−24.4

Population, Registration, and Turnout, 1980–2000

Year	Population	Vot Age Pop	Registration	Dem %	Rep %	Other %	Unregistered	Turnout	TAPV[b]	Rank	TAPR[c]	Rank
00	8,049,313	5,797,000	5,122,123	49.9	34.0	16.1	2,927,190	2,914,990	50.3	35	56.9	47
98	7,546,493	5,626,719	4,708,421	52.1	33.8	14.1	918,298	2,012,143	35.8	31	42.7	35
96	7,322,870	5,396,019	4,317,543	54.4	33.7	11.9	1,078,476	2,566,042	47.6	35	59.4	43
94	7,069,836	5,315,000	3,635,875	58.6	32.8	8.7	1,679,125	1,588,157	29.9	47	43.7	46
92	6,843,000	5,180,000	3,817,380	60.6	31.9	7.5	1,362,620	2,606,567	50.3	43	68.3	46
90	6,628,637	5,022,488	3,347,635	63.7	30.8	5.5	1,674,853	2,069,904	41.2	20	61.8	12
88	6,489,000	4,913,000	3,432,042	65.5	29.6	4.9	1,480,958	2,180,025	44.4	45	63.5	42
86	6,331,000	4,748,000	3,080,990	68.6	27.2	4.2	1,667,010	1,591,330	33.5	38	51.7	34
84	6,166,000	4,600,000	3,270,933	70.0	25.6	4.4	1,329,067	2,239,051	48.7	43	68.5	39
82	6,019,000	4,429,000	2,674,787	72.0	24.0	4.1	1,754,213	1,321,080	29.8	45	49.4	45
80	5,881,766	4,222,405	2,774,844	71.2	24.4	4.4	1,447,561	1,855,833	44.0	46	66.9	44

[a]Upper case indicates victory with a majority of votes cast; lower case, victory with a plurality of votes cast.

[b]TAPV = turnout as a % of voting age population. Rankings are among all states.

[c]TAPR = turnout as a % of registration. Rankings are among all states.

Sources: North Carolina Democratic Party, North Carolina Republican Party, Federal Election Commission, U.S. Census Bureau, North Carolina State Board of Elections Web site <www.sboe.state.nc.us>

NORTH DAKOTA

2000 Electoral Votes: 3

Election Results, U.S. President, 1972–2000

Year	Democrat	Republican	Win[a]	Total Vote	Dem Vote	Rep Vote	Other Vote	Dem %	Rep %	Other %	R Margin	R Mar %
00	Gore	G. W. Bush	R	288,256	95,284	174,852	18,120	33.1	60.7	6.3	79,568	27.6
96	Clinton	Dole	r	266,411	106,905	125,050	34,456	40.1	46.9	12.9	18,145	6.8
92	Clinton	G. Bush	r	306,496	99,168	136,244	71,084	32.4	44.5	23.2	37,076	12.1
88	Dukakis	G. Bush	R	297,261	127,739	166,559	2,963	43.0	56.0	1.0	38,820	13.1
84	Mondale	Reagan	R	304,765	104,429	200,336	0	34.3	65.7	0.0	95,907	31.5
80	Carter	Reagan	R	296,524	79,189	193,695	23,640	26.7	65.3	8.0	114,506	38.6
76	Carter	Ford	R	292,500	136,078	153,470	2,952	46.5	52.5	1.0	17,392	5.9
72	McGovern	Nixon	R	280,514	100,384	174,109	6,021	35.8	62.1	2.2	73,725	26.3

Election Results, U.S. Senate, 1980–2000

Year	Democrat	Republican	Win[a]	Total Vote	Dem Vote	Rep Vote	Other Vote	Dem %	Rep %	Other %	R Margin	R Mar %
00	Conrad	Sand	D	287,539	176,470	111,069	0	61.4	38.6	0.0	−65,401	−22.7
98	Dorgan	Nalewaja	D	213,358	134,747	75,013	3,598	63.2	35.2	1.7	−59,734	−28.0
94	Conrad	Clayburgh	D	236,547	137,157	99,390	0	58.0	42.0	0.0	−37,767	−16.0
92	Dorgan	Sydness	D	297,509	179,347	118,162	0	60.3	39.7	0.0	−61,185	−20.6
92	Conrad	Dalrymple	D	158,440	103,246	55,194	0	65.2	34.8	0.0	−48,052	−30.3
88	Burdick	Strinden	D	289,170	171,899	112,937	4,334	59.5	39.1	1.5	−58,962	−20.4
86	Conrad	Andrews	d	289,013	143,932	141,812	3,269	49.8	49.1	1.1	−2,120	−0.7
82	Burdick	Knorr	D	262,465	164,873	89,304	8,288	62.8	34.0	3.2	−75,569	−28.8
80	Johanneson	Andrews	R	299,272	86,658	210,347	2,267	29.0	70.3	0.8	123,689	41.3

Election Results, Governor, 1980–2000

Year	Democrat	Republican	Win[a]	Total Vote	Dem Vote	Rep Vote	Other Vote	Dem %	Rep %	Other %	R Margin	R Mar %
00	Keitkamp	Hoeven	R	289,412	130,144	159,255	13	45.0	55.0	0.0	29,111	10.1
96	Kaldor	Schafer	R	264,286	89,349	174,937	0	33.8	66.2	0.0	85,588	32.4
92	Spaeth	Schafer	R	300,243	123,845	176,398	0	41.3	58.8	0.0	52,553	17.5
88	Sinner	Mallberg	D	299,080	179,094	119,986	0	59.9	40.1	0.0	−59,108	−19.8
84	Sinner	Olson	D	314,382	173,922	140,460	0	55.3	44.7	0.0	−33,462	−10.6
80	Link	Olson	R	302,621	140,391	162,230	0	46.4	53.6	0.0	21,839	7.2

Population, Registration, and Turnout, 1980–2000

Year	Population	Vot Age Pop	Registration*	Dem %	Rep %	Other %	Unregistered*	Turnout	TAPV[b]	Rank	TAPR[c]	Rank
00	642,200	477,000	n/a	n/a	n/a	n/a	n/a	288,256	60.4	10	n/a	n/a
98	638,244	475,633	n/a	n/a	n/a	n/a	n/a	213,358	44.9	11	n/a	n/a
96	643,539	470,922	n/a	n/a	n/a	n/a	n/a	266,411	56.6	14	n/a	n/a
94	637,988	467,000	n/a	n/a	n/a	n/a	n/a	236,547	50.7	9	n/a	n/a
92	636,000	465,000	n/a	n/a	n/a	n/a	n/a	306,496	65.9	8	n/a	n/a
90	638,800	463,415	n/a	n/a	n/a	n/a	n/a	221,890	47.9	11	n/a	n/a
88	667,000	483,000	n/a	n/a	n/a	n/a	n/a	299,080	61.9	5	n/a	n/a
86	679,000	495,000	n/a	n/a	n/a	n/a	n/a	289,013	58.4	2	n/a	n/a
84	687,000	491,000	n/a	n/a	n/a	n/a	n/a	314,382	64.0	5	n/a	n/a
82	670,000	480,000	n/a	n/a	n/a	n/a	n/a	262,465	54.7	6	n/a	n/a
80	652,717	461,053	n/a	n/a	n/a	n/a	n/a	302,621	65.6	6	n/a	n/a

*North Dakota does not register voters.

[a]Upper case indicates victory with a majority of votes cast; lower case, victory with a plurality of votes cast.

[b]TAPV = turnout as a % of voting age population. Rankings are among all states.

[c]TAPR = turnout as a % of registration. Rankings are among all states.

Sources: North Dakota Democratic Party, North Dakota Republican Party, Federal Election Commission, U.S. Census Bureau, North Dakota Secretary of State Web site <www.state.nd.us/sec>

364

OHIO

2000 Electoral Votes: 21

Election Results, U.S. President, 1972–2000

Year	Democrat	Republican	Win[a]	Total Vote	Dem Vote	Rep Vote	Other Vote	Dem %	Rep %	Other %	R Margin	R Mar %
00	Gore	G. W. Bush	r	4,701,998	2,183,628	2,350,363	168,007	46.4	50.0	3.6	166,735	3.5
96	Clinton	Dole	d	4,531,457	2,148,222	1,859,883	523,352	47.4	41.0	11.6	−288,339	−6.4
92	Clinton	G. Bush	d	4,915,678	1,984,942	1,894,310	1,036,426	40.4	38.5	21.1	−90,632	−1.8
88	Dukakis	G. Bush	R	4,393,235	1,939,629	2,416,549	37,057	44.2	55.0	0.8	476,920	10.9
84	Mondale	Reagan	R	4,504,000	1,825,440	2,678,560	0	40.5	59.5	0.0	853,120	18.9
80	Carter	Reagan	R	4,213,431	1,752,414	2,206,545	254,472	41.6	52.4	6.0	454,131	10.8
76	Carter	Ford	d	4,068,852	2,009,959	2,000,626	58,267	49.4	49.2	1.4	−9,333	−0.2
72	McGovern	Nixon	R	4,094,787	1,558,889	2,441,827	94,071	38.1	59.6	2.3	882,938	21.6

Election Results, U.S. Senate, 1980–2000

Year	Democrat	Republican	Win[a]	Total Vote	Dem Vote	Rep Vote	Other Vote	Dem %	Rep %	Other %	R Margin	R Mar %
00	Celeste	DeWine	R	4,448,801	1,595,066	2,665,512	188,223	35.9	59.9	4.2	1,070,446	24.1
98	Boyle	Voinovich	R	3,404,351	1,482,054	1,922,087	210	43.5	56.5	0.0	440,033	12.9
94	Hyatt	DeWine	R	3,436,800	1,348,213	1,836,556	252,031	39.2	53.4	7.3	488,343	14.2
92	Glenn	DeWine	D	4,793,953	2,444,419	2,028,300	321,234	51.0	42.3	6.7	−416,119	−8.7
88	Metzenbaum	Voinovich	D	4,352,754	2,480,038	1,872,716	0	57.0	43.0	0.0	−607,322	−14.0
86	Glenn	Kindness	D	3,121,189	1,949,208	1,171,893	88	62.5	37.6	0.0	−777,315	−24.9
82	Metzenbaum	Pfeifer	D	3,395,463	1,923,767	1,396,790	74,906	56.7	41.1	2.2	−526,977	−15.5
80	Glenn	Betts	D	4,027,303	2,770,786	1,137,695	118,822	68.8	28.3	3.0	−1,633,091	−40.6

Election Results, Governor, 1982–1998

Year	Democrat	Republican	Win[a]	Total Vote	Dem Vote	Rep Vote	Other Vote	Dem %	Rep %	Other %	R Margin	R Mar %
98	Fisher	Taft	R	3,354,213	1,498,956	1,678,721	176,536	44.7	50.1	5.3	179,765	5.4
94	Burch	Voinovich	R	3,346,166	835,849	2,401,572	108,745	25.0	71.8	3.3	1,565,723	46.8
90	Celebrezze	Voinovich	R	3,477,582	1,539,479	1,938,103	0	44.3	55.7	0.0	398,624	11.5
86	Celeste	Rhodes	D	3,066,611	1,858,372	1,207,264	975	60.6	39.4	0.0	−651,108	−21.2
82	Celeste	Brown	D	3,356,721	1,981,882	1,303,962	70,877	59.0	38.9	2.1	−677,920	−20.2

Population, Registration, and Turnout, 1980–2000

Year	Population	Vot Age Pop	Registration	Dem %	Rep %	Other %	Unregistered	Turnout	TAPV[b]	Rank	TAPR[c]	Rank
00	11,353,140	8,433,000	7,537,822	13.5	18.9	67.6	3,815,318	4,701,998	55.8	21	62.4	32
98	11,209,493	8,365,488	7,127,879	17.4	17.5	65.1	1,237,609	3,404,351	40.7	19	47.8	25
96	11,172,782	8,290,658	6,879,687	19.3	19.5	61.3	1,410,971	4,531,457	54.7	19	65.9	23
94	11,102,198	8,248,000	6,253,321	25.0	20.4	54.6	1,994,679	3,436,800	41.7	24	55.0	31
92	11,016,000	8,197,000	6,544,098	23.5	18.8	57.7	1,652,902	4,915,678	60.0	22	75.1	31
90	10,847,115	8,047,371	5,928,008	31.4	21.1	47.5	2,119,363	3,477,582	43.2	17	58.7	20
88	10,855,000	7,970,000	5,945,616	32.1	21.0	46.9	2,024,384	4,393,235	55.1	16	73.9	17
86	10,752,000	7,891,000	5,954,800	31.7	19.4	48.9	1,936,200	3,121,189	39.6	23	52.4	33
84	10,740,000	7,857,000	6,358,558	30.1	18.8	51.1	1,498,442	4,563,235	58.1	15	71.8	30
82	10,791,000	7,818,000	5,674,128	31.0	21.2	47.9	2,143,872	3,395,463	43.4	23	59.8	30
80	10,797,630	7,703,789	5,926,864	26.1	17.9	56.0	1,776,925	4,283,603	55.6	25	72.3	34

[a]Upper case indicates victory with a majority of votes cast; lower case, victory with a plurality of votes cast.
[b]TAPV = turnout as a % of voting age population. Rankings are among all states.
[c]TAPR = turnout as a % of registration. Rankings are among all states.

Sources: Ohio Democratic Party, Ohio Republican Party, Federal Election Commission, U.S. Census Bureau, Ohio Secretary of State Web site <www.state.oh.us/sos>

OKLAHOMA

2000 Electoral Votes: 8

Election Results, U.S. President, 1972–2000

Year	Democrat	Republican	Win[a]	Total Vote	Dem Vote	Rep Vote	Other Vote	Dem %	Rep %	Other %	R Margin	R Mar %
00	Gore	G. W. Bush	R	1,234,229	474,276	744,337	15,616	38.4	60.3	1.3	270,061	21.9
96	Clinton	Dole	r	1,206,713	488,105	582,315	136,293	40.5	48.3	11.3	94,210	7.8
92	Clinton	G. Bush	r	1,385,873	473,066	592,929	319,878	34.1	42.8	23.1	119,863	8.6
88	Dukakis	G. Bush	R	1,171,036	483,423	678,367	9,246	41.3	57.9	0.8	194,944	16.6
84	Mondale	Reagan	R	1,246,610	385,080	861,530	0	30.9	69.1	0.0	476,450	38.2
80	Carter	Reagan	R	1,135,880	402,026	695,570	38,284	35.4	61.2	3.4	293,544	25.8
76	Carter	Ford	r	1,092,251	532,442	545,708	14,101	48.8	50.0	1.3	13,266	1.2
72	McGovern	Nixon	R	1,029,900	247,147	759,025	23,728	24.0	73.7	2.3	511,878	49.7

Election Results, U.S. Senate, 1980–1998

Year	Democrat	Republican	Win[a]	Total Vote	Dem Vote	Rep Vote	Other Vote	Dem %	Rep %	Other %	R Margin	R Mar %
98	Carroll	Nickles	R	859,713	268,898	570,682	20,133	31.3	66.4	2.3	301,784	35.1
96	Boren	Inhofe	R	1,183,150	474,162	670,610	38,378	40.1	56.7	3.2	196,448	16.6
94	McCurdy	Inhofe	R	982,430	392,488	542,390	47,552	40.0	55.2	4.8	149,902	15.3
92	Lewis	Nickles	R	1,252,226	494,350	757,876	0	39.5	60.5	0.0	263,526	21.0
90	Boren	Jones	D	884,498	735,684	148,814	0	83.2	16.8	0.0	−586,870	−66.4
86	Jones	Nickles	R	893,666	400,230	493,436	0	44.8	55.2	0.0	93,206	10.4
84	Boren	Crozier	D	1,197,937	906,131	280,638	11,168	75.6	23.4	0.9	−625,493	−52.2
80	Coats	Nickles	R	1,098,294	478,283	587,252	32,759	43.6	53.5	3.0	108,969	9.9

Election Results, Governor, 1982–1998

Year	Democrat	Republican	Win[a]	Total Vote	Dem Vote	Rep Vote	Other Vote	Dem %	Rep %	Other %	R Margin	R Mar %
98	Boyd	Keating	R	873,585	357,552	505,498	10,535	40.9	57.9	1.2	147,946	16.9
94	Mildren	Keating	r	995,012	294,936	466,740	233,336	29.6	46.9	23.5	171,804	17.3
90	Walters	Price	D	911,314	523,196	297,584	90,534	57.4	32.7	9.9	−225,612	−24.8
86	Walters	Bellmon	r	909,925	405,295	431,762	72,868	44.5	47.5	8.0	26,467	2.9
82	Nigh	Daxon	D	883,130	548,159	332,207	2,764	62.1	37.6	0.3	−215,952	−24.5

Population, Registration, and Turnout, 1980–2000

Year	Population	Vot Age Pop	Registration	Dem %	Rep %	Other %	Unregistered	Turnout	TAPV[b]	Rank	TAPR[c]	Rank
00	3,450,654	2,531,000	2,233,602	55.3	35.7	9.0	1,217,052	1,234,229	48.8	40	55.3	48
98	3,346,713	2,467,346	2,034,793	58.0	35.1	6.9	432,553	873,585	35.4	35	42.9	34
96	3,300,902	2,399,648	1,823,748	61.0	34.2	4.8	575,900	1,206,713	50.3	28	66.2	22
94	3,258,069	2,378,000	1,966,144	63.6	33.4	3.0	411,856	995,012	41.8	23	50.6	40
92	3,212,000	2,354,000	2,302,279	63.1	33.7	3.2	51,721	1,385,873	58.9	24	60.2	48
90	3,145,585	2,308,578	2,010,684	64.9	32.7	2.4	297,894	911,314	39.5	24	45.3	43
88	3,242,000	2,404,000	2,199,014	65.3	32.1	2.6	204,986	1,171,036	48.7	32	53.3	49
86	3,305,000	2,445,000	2,018,401	67.1	30.3	2.6	426,599	909,925	37.2	31	45.1	42
84	3,310,000	2,401,000	1,928,638	67.6	29.8	2.6	472,362	1,255,676	52.3	33	65.1	45
82	3,212,000	2,345,000	1,613,827	71.0	26.7	2.3	731,173	883,130	37.7	37	54.7	38
80	3,025,290	2,169,693	1,469,320	71.8	26.0	2.2	700,373	1,149,708	53.0	31	78.2	12

[a]Upper case indicates victory with a majority of votes cast; lower case, victory with a plurality of votes cast.
[b]TAPV = turnout as a % of voting age population. Rankings are among all states.
[c]TAPR = turnout as a % of registration. Rankings are among all states.

Sources: Oklahoma Democratic Party, Oklahoma Republican Party, Federal Election Commission, U.S. Census Bureau, Oklahoma State Election Board Web site <www.state.ok.us/~elections>

OREGON

2000 Electoral Votes: 7

Election Results, U.S. President, 1972–2000

Year	Democrat	Republican	Win[a]	Total Vote	Dem Vote	Rep Vote	Other Vote	Dem %	Rep %	Other %	R Margin	R Mar %
00	Gore	G. W. Bush	d	1,533,968	720,342	713,577	100,049	47.0	46.5	6.5	−6,765	−0.4
96	Clinton	Dole	d	1,375,431	649,641	538,152	187,638	47.2	39.1	13.6	−111,489	−8.1
92	Clinton	Bush	d	1,451,162	621,314	475,757	354,091	42.8	32.8	24.4	−145,557	−10.0
88	Dukakis	Bush	D	1,176,332	616,206	560,126	0	52.4	47.6	0.0	−56,080	−4.8
84	Mondale	Reagan	R	1,222,179	536,479	685,700	0	43.9	56.1	0.0	149,221	12.2
80	Carter	Reagan	R	1,140,323	456,890	571,044	112,389	40.1	50.1	9.9	114,154	10.0
76	Carter	Ford	r	1,022,734	490,407	492,120	40,207	48.0	48.1	3.9	1,713	0.2
72	McGovern	Nixon	R	927,946	392,760	486,686	48,500	42.3	52.5	5.2	93,926	10.1

Election Results, U.S. Senate, 1980–1998

Year	Democrat	Republican	Win[a]	Total Vote	Dem Vote	Rep Vote	Other Vote	Dem %	Rep %	Other %	R Margin	R Mar %
98	Wyden	Lim	D	1,107,962	682,425	377,739	47,798	61.6	34.1	4.3	−304,686	−27.5
96*	Bruggere	Smith	r	1,358,828	624,370	677,336	57,122	46.0	49.9	4.2	52,966	3.9
96*	Wyden	Smith	d	1,181,650	571,739	553,519	56,392	48.4	46.8	4.8	−18,220	−1.5
92	AuCoin	Packwood	R	1,357,306	639,851	717,455	0	47.1	52.9	0.0	77,604	5.7
90	Lonsdale	Hatfield	R	1,097,838	507,743	590,095	0	46.3	53.8	0.0	82,352	7.5
86	Bauman	Packwood	R	1,032,052	375,735	656,317	0	36.4	63.6	0.0	280,582	27.2
84	Hendriksen	Hatfield	R	1,214,274	406,122	808,152	0	33.5	66.6	0.0	402,030	33.1
80	Kulongoski	Packwood	R	1,139,939	501,963	594,290	43,686	44.0	52.1	3.8	92,327	8.1

Election Results, Governor, 1982–1998

Year	Democrat	Republican	Win[a]	Total Vote	Dem Vote	Rep Vote	Other Vote	Dem %	Rep %	Other %	R Margin	R Mar %
98	Kitzhaber	Sizemore	D	1,110,844	717,061	334,001	59,782	64.6	30.1	5.4	−383,060	−34.5
94	Kitzhaber	Smith	D	1,218,589	622,083	517,874	78,632	51.1	42.5	6.5	−104,209	−8.6
90	Roberts	Frohnmayer	d	1,097,457	508,749	444,646	144,062	46.4	40.5	13.1	−64,103	−5.8
86	Goldschmidt	Paulus	D	1,056,442	549,456	506,986	0	52.0	48.0	0.0	−42,470	−4.0
82	Kulongoski	Atiyeh	R	1,042,003	374,316	639,841	27,846	35.9	61.4	2.7	265,525	25.5

Population, Registration, and Turnout, 1980–2000

Year	Population	Vot Age Pop	Registration	Dem %	Rep %	Other %	Unregistered	Turnout	TAPV[b]	Rank	TAPR[c]	Rank
00	3,421,399	2,530,000	1,943,699	39.4	35.8	24.8	1,477,700	1,533,968	60.6	9	78.9	2
98	3,281,974	2,456,804	1,965,981	40.3	35.8	23.9	490,823	1,110,844	45.2	10	56.5	7
96	3,203,735	2,343,545	1,962,155	41.0	36.4	22.5	381,390	1,375,431	58.7	8	70.1	12
94	3,086,188	2,303,000	1,837,125	42.8	36.3	20.8	465,875	1,218,589	52.9	5	66.3	7
92	2,977,000	2,210,000	1,786,086	44.6	36.1	19.3	423,914	1,451,162	65.7	7	81.2	11
90	2,842,321	2,118,191	1,476,500	46.9	38.7	14.5	641,691	1,097,838	51.8	5	74.4	2
88	2,767,000	2,051,000	1,524,446	48.3	38.7	13.1	526,554	1,197,720	58.4	10	78.6	6
86	2,698,000	2,016,000	1,502,244	48.5	39.1	12.4	513,756	1,056,442	52.4	5	70.3	6
84	2,676,000	1,990,000	1,608,693	49.3	37.0	13.8	381,307	1,226,527	61.6	8	76.2	16
82	2,673,000	1,953,000	1,516,589	49.5	36.4	14.1	436,411	1,042,003	53.4	8	68.7	9
80	2,633,105	1,909,296	1,569,296	50.0	36.0	14.0	340,000	1,179,803	61.8	10	75.2	23

*Following the resignation of Senator Packwood, a special election was held in January 1996 to fill the unexpired portion of his term. In this election, Ronald Wyden defeated Gordon Smith. Ten months later, in the regular election for Oregon's other Senate seat, Smith defeated Tom Bruggere.

[a]Upper case indicates victory with a majority of votes cast; lower case, victory with a plurality of votes cast.

[b]TAPV = turnout as a % of voting age population. Rankings are among all states.

[c]TAPR = turnout as a % of registration. Rankings are among all states.

Sources: Oregon Democratic Party, Oregon Republican Party, Federal Election Commission, U.S. Census Bureau, Oregon Secretary of State Web site <www.sos.state.or.us>

PENNSYLVANIA

2000 Electoral Votes: 23

Election Results, U.S. President, 1972–2000

Year	Democrat	Republican	Win[a]	Total Vote	Dem Vote	Rep Vote	Other Vote	Dem %	Rep %	Other %	R Margin	R Mar %
00	Gore	G. W. Bush	D	4,913,119	2,485,967	2,281,127	146,025	50.6	46.4	3.0	−204,840	−4.2
96	Clinton	Dole	d	4,501,307	2,215,819	1,801,169	484,319	49.2	40.0	10.8	−414,650	−9.2
92	Clinton	G. Bush	d	4,937,672	2,239,164	1,791,841	906,667	45.4	36.3	18.4	−447,323	−9.1
88	Dukakis	G. Bush	R	4,536,251	2,194,944	2,300,087	41,220	48.4	50.7	0.9	105,143	2.3
84	Mondale	Reagan	R	4,812,454	2,228,131	2,584,323	0	46.3	53.7	0.0	356,192	7.4
80	Carter	Reagan	R	4,492,333	1,937,540	2,261,872	292,921	43.1	50.4	6.5	324,332	7.2
76	Carter	Ford	D	4,584,865	2,328,677	2,205,604	50,584	50.8	48.1	1.1	−123,073	−2.7
72	McGovern	Nixon	R	4,592,106	1,796,951	2,714,521	80,634	39.1	59.1	1.8	917,570	20.0

Election Results, U.S. Senate, 1980–2000

Year	Democrat	Republican	Win[a]	Total Vote	Dem Vote	Rep Vote	Other Vote	Dem %	Rep %	Other %	R Margin	R Mar %
00	Klink	Santorum	R	4,735,504	2,154,908	2,481,962	98,634	45.5	52.4	2.1	327,054	6.9
98	Lloyd	Specter	R	2,957,499	1,028,839	1,814,180	114,480	34.8	61.3	3.9	785,341	26.6
94	Wofford	Santorum	r	3,513,112	1,648,481	1,735,691	128,940	46.9	49.4	3.7	87,210	2.5
92	Yeakel	Specter	r	4,802,410	2,224,966	2,358,125	219,319	46.3	49.1	4.6	133,159	2.8
91	Wofford	Thornburgh	D	3,382,746	1,860,760	1,521,986	0	55.0	45.0	0.0	−338,774	−10.0
88	Vignola	Heinz	R	4,366,598	1,416,764	2,901,715	48,119	32.5	66.5	1.1	1,484,951	34.0
86	Edgar	Specter	R	3,378,226	1,448,219	1,906,537	23,470	42.9	56.4	0.7	458,318	13.6
82	Wecht	Heinz	R	3,604,108	1,412,965	2,136,418	54,725	39.2	59.3	1.5	723,453	20.1
80	Flaherty	Specter	R	4,418,042	2,122,391	2,230,404	65,247	50.5	52.0	1.5	108,013	2.4

Election Results, Governor, 1982–1998

Year	Democrat	Republican	Win[a]	Total Vote	Dem Vote	Rep Vote	Other Vote	Dem %	Rep %	Other %	R Margin	R Mar %
98	Itkin	Ridge	R	3,024,941	938,745	1,736,844	349,352	31.0	57.4	11.6	798,099	26.4
94	Singel	Ridge	r	3,585,181	1,430,099	1,627,976	527,106	39.9	45.4	14.7	197,877	5.5
90	Casey	Hafer	D	3,052,760	2,065,244	987,516	0	67.7	32.4	0.0	−1,077,728	−35.3
86	Casey	Scranton III	D	3,388,275	1,717,484	1,638,268	32,523	50.7	48.4	1.0	−79,216	−2.3
82	Ertel	Thornburgh	R	3,683,985	1,772,353	1,872,784	38,848	48.1	50.8	1.1	100,431	2.7

Population, Registration, and Turnout, 1980–2000

Year	Population	Vot Age Pop	Registration	Dem %	Rep %	Other %	Unregistered	Turnout	TAPV[b]	Rank	TAPR[c]	Rank
00	12,281,054	9,155,000	7,781,997	48.0	41.8	10.2	4,499,057	4,912,185	53.7	26	63.1	31
98	12,001,451	9,141,623	7,258,822	48.4	42.3	9.3	1,882,801	3,024,941	33.1	40	41.7	39
96	12,056,112	9,162,540	6,805,612	49.0	42.8	8.2	2,356,928	4,501,307	49.1	30	66.1	21
94	12,052,367	9,155,000	5,879,093	50.3	43.1	6.6	3,275,907	3,585,181	39.2	30	61.0	18
92	12,009,000	9,164,000	5,993,002	50.8	42.8	6.4	3,170,998	4,937,672	53.9	32	82.4	5
90	11,881,643	9,086,833	5,659,189	51.4	43.8	4.9	3,427,644	3,052,760	33.6	38	53.9	30
88	12,001,000	9,060,000	5,875,943	52.2	42.9	4.9	3,184,057	4,536,251	50.1	30	77.2	9
86	11,889,000	9,023,000	5,846,975	53.5	41.4	5.1	3,176,025	3,388,275	37.6	27	57.9	19
84	11,887,000	8,996,000	6,193,702	54.6	40.2	5.3	2,802,298	4,844,903	53.9	28	78.2	12
82	11,865,000	8,909,000	5,702,557	53.2	41.3	5.4	3,206,443	3,683,985	41.4	31	64.6	20
80	11,863,895	8,738,361	5,754,287	53.4	41.3	5.3	2,984,074	4,561,501	52.2	32	79.3	8

[a] Upper case indicates victory with a majority of votes cast; lower case, victory with a plurality of votes cast.

[b] TAPV = turnout as a % of voting age population. Rankings are among all states.

[c] TAPR = turnout as a % of registration. Rankings are among all states.

Sources: Pennsylvania Democratic Party, Pennsylvania Republican Party, Federal Election Commission, U.S. Census Bureau, Pennsylvania Department of State Web site <www.dos.state.pa.us>

RHODE ISLAND

2000 Electoral Votes: 4

Election Results, U.S. President, 1972–2000

Year	Democrat	Republican	Win[a]	Total Vote	Dem Vote	Rep Vote	Other Vote	Dem %	Rep %	Other %	R Margin	R Mar %
00	Gore	G. W. Bush	D	408,783	249,508	130,555	28,720	61.0	31.9	7.0	-118,953	-29.1
96	Clinton	Dole	D	390,247	233,050	104,683	52,514	59.7	26.8	13.5	-128,367	-32.9
92	Clinton	G. Bush	d	449,945	213,299	131,601	105,045	47.4	29.3	23.4	-81,698	-18.2
88	Dukakis	G. Bush	D	404,569	225,123	177,761	1,685	55.7	43.9	0.4	-47,362	-11.7
84	Mondale	Reagan	R	409,186	197,106	212,080	0	48.2	51.8	0.0	14,974	3.7
80	Carter	Reagan	d	412,954	198,342	154,793	59,819	48.0	37.5	14.5	-43,549	-10.5
76	Carter	Ford	D	408,885	227,636	181,249	0	55.7	44.3	0.0	-46,387	-11.3
72	McGovern	Nixon	R	415,808	194,645	220,383	780	46.8	53.0	0.2	25,738	6.2

Election Results, U.S. Senate, 1982–2000

Year	Democrat	Republican	Win[a]	Total Vote	Dem Vote	Rep Vote	Other Vote	Dem %	Rep %	Other %	R Margin	R Mar %
00	Weygand	Chafee	R	391,537	161,023	222,588	7,926	41.1	56.8	2.0	61,565	15.7
96	Reed	Meyer	D	363,371	230,676	127,368	5,327	63.5	35.1	1.5	-103,308	-28.4
94	Kushner	Chafee	R	345,388	122,532	222,856	0	35.5	64.5	0.0	100,324	29.0
90	Pell	Schneider	D	364,052	225,105	138,947	0	61.8	38.2	0.0	-86,158	-23.7
88	Licht	Chafee	R	397,990	180,717	217,273	0	45.4	54.6	0.0	36,556	9.2
84	Pell	Leonard	D	395,272	286,780	108,492	0	72.6	27.5	0.0	-178,288	-45.1
82	Michaelson	Chafee	R	342,778	167,283	175,495	0	48.8	51.2	0.0	8,212	2.4

Election Results, Governor, 1980–1998

Year	Democrat	Republican	Win[a]	Total Vote	Dem Vote	Rep Vote	Other Vote	Dem %	Rep %	Other %	R Margin	R Mar %
98	York	Almond	R	306,383	129,105	156,180	21,098	42.1	51.0	6.9	27,075	8.8
94	York	Almond	r	361,377	157,361	171,194	32,822	43.5	47.4	9.1	13,833	3.8
92	Sundlun	Leonard	D	421,585	261,484	145,590	14,511	62.0	34.5	3.4	-115,894	-27.5
90	Sundlin	DiPrete	D	356,588	264,411	92,177	0	74.2	25.9	0.0	-172,234	-48.3
88	Sundlun	DiPrete	R	400,486	196,936	203,550	0	49.2	50.8	0.0	6,614	1.7
86	Sundlun	DiPrete	R	316,810	104,508	208,822	3,480	33.0	65.9	1.1	104,314	32.9
84	Solomon	DiPrete	R	408,370	163,311	245,059	0	40.0	60.0	0.0	81,748	20.0
82	Garrahy	Marzullo	D	336,661	246,566	79,602	10,493	73.2	23.7	3.1	-166,964	-49.6
80	Garrahy	Cianci	D	405,903	299,174	106,729	0	73.7	26.3	0.0	-192,445	-47.4

373

Population, Registration, and Turnout, 1980–2000

Year	Population	Vote Age Pop	Registration	Dem %	Rep %	Other %	Unregistered	Turnout	TAPV[b]	Rank	TAPR[c]	Rank
00	1,048,319	753,000	655,107	n/a	n/a	n/a	393,212	408,783	54.3	23	62.4	33
98	988,480	750,563	632,955	n/a	n/a	n/a	117,608	306,383	40.8	18	48.4	24
96	990,225	752,183	602,692	n/a	n/a	n/a	149,491	390,247	51.9	25	64.8	29
94	996,757	757,000	552,638	n/a	n/a	n/a	204,362	361,377	47.7	12	65.4	10
92	1,005,000	771,000	554,664	n/a	n/a	n/a	216,336	449,945	58.4	25	81.1	10
90	1,003,464	777,774	536,773	n/a	n/a	n/a	241,001	364,052	46.8	13	67.8	6
88	993,000	764,000	548,758	n/a	n/a	n/a	215,242	404,569	53.0	22	73.7	16
86	975,000	750,000	524,664	n/a	n/a	n/a	225,336	322,085	42.9	15	61.4	13
84	962,000	738,000	542,216	n/a	n/a	n/a	195,784	409,186	55.4	25	75.5	15
82	958,000	723,000	533,853	n/a	n/a	n/a	189,147	342,778	47.4	14	64.2	22
80	947,154	703,984	547,472	n/a	n/a	n/a	156,512	415,967	59.1	13	76.0	18

[a]Upper case indicates victory with a majority of votes cast; lower case, victory with a plurality of votes cast.
[b]TAPV = turnout as a % of voting age population. Rankings are among all states.
[c]TAPR = turnout as a % of registration. Rankings are among all states.

Sources: Rhode Island Democratic Party, Rhode Island Republican Party, Federal Election Commission, U.S. Census Bureau.

SOUTH CAROLINA

2000 Electoral Votes: 8

Election Results, U.S. President, 1972–2000

Year	Democrat	Republican	Win[a]	Total Vote	Dem Vote	Rep Vote	Other Vote	Dem %	Rep %	Other %	R Margin	R Mar %
00	Gore	G. W. Bush	R	1,384,253	566,039	786,892	31,322	40.9	56.8	2.3	220,853	16.0
96	Clinton	Dole	r	1,151,689	506,283	573,458	71,948	44.0	49.8	6.3	67,175	5.8
92	Clinton	G. Bush	r	1,195,893	479,514	577,507	138,872	40.1	48.3	11.6	97,993	8.2
88	Dukakis	G. Bush	R	986,009	370,554	606,443	9,012	37.6	61.5	0.9	235,889	23.9
84	Mondale	Reagan	R	959,998	344,459	615,539	0	35.9	64.1	0.0	271,080	28.2
80	Carter	Reagan	r	882,917	427,560	441,207	14,150	48.4	50.0	1.6	13,647	1.5
76	Carter	Ford	D	796,965	450,825	346,140	0	56.6	43.4	0.0	−104,685	−13.1
72	McGovern	Nixon	R	673,960	186,824	477,044	10,092	27.7	70.8	1.5	290,220	43.1

Election Results, U.S. Senate, 1980–1998

Year	Democrat	Republican	Win[a]	Total Vote	Dem Vote	Rep Vote	Other Vote	Dem %	Rep %	Other %	R Margin	R Mar %
98	Hollings	Inglis	D	1,067,910	562,791	488,132	16,987	52.7	45.7	1.6	−74,659	−7.0
96	Close	Thurmond	R	1,161,231	510,951	619,859	30,421	44.0	53.4	2.6	108,908	9.4
92	Hollings	Hartnett	D	1,145,205	591,030	554,175	0	51.6	48.4	0.0	−36,855	−3.2
90	Cunningham	Thurmond	R	726,144	244,112	482,032	0	33.6	66.4	0.0	237,920	32.8
86	Hollings	McMaster	D	737,763	465,500	262,886	9,377	63.1	35.6	1.3	−202,614	−27.5
84	Pervis	Thurmond	R	965,130	306,982	644,815	13,333	31.8	66.8	1.4	337,833	35.0
80	Hollings	Mays	D	870,502	612,556	257,946	0	70.4	29.6	0.0	−354,610	−40.7

Election Results, Governor, 1982–1998

Year	Democrat	Republican	Win[a]	Total Vote	Dem Vote	Rep Vote	Other Vote	Dem %	Rep %	Other %	R Margin	R Mar %
98	Hodges	Beasley	D	1,070,443	570,070	484,088	16,285	53.3	45.2	1.5	−85,982	−8.0
94	Theodore	Beasley	R	932,672	447,002	470,756	14,914	47.9	50.5	1.6	23,754	2.5
90	Mitchell	Campbell, Jr.	R	740,865	212,034	528,831	0	28.6	71.4	0.0	316,797	42.8
86	Daniel	Campbell, Jr.	R	753,410	361,325	384,565	7,520	48.0	51.0	1.0	23,240	3.1
82	Riley	Workman, Jr.	D	671,625	468,819	202,806	0	69.8	30.2	0.0	−266,013	−39.6

Population, Registration, and Turnout, 1980–2000

Year	Population	Vot Age Pop	Registration	Dem %	Rep %	Other %	Unregistered	Turnout	TAPV[b]	Rank	TAPR[c]	Rank
00	4,012,012	2,977,000	2,157,006	n/a	n/a	n/a	1,855,006	1,386,331	46.6	44	64.3	29
98	3,835,962	2,876,666	2,021,766	n/a	n/a	n/a	854,900	1,070,443	37.2	30	52.9	13
96	3,698,746	2,728,903	1,814,777	n/a	n/a	n/a	914,126	1,161,231	42.6	47	64.0	34
94	3,663,984	2,712,000	1,499,589	n/a	n/a	n/a	1,212,411	932,672	34.4	44	62.2	15
92	3,603,000	2,658,000	1,537,140	n/a	n/a	n/a	1,120,860	1,195,893	45.0	50	77.8	20
90	3,486,703	2,566,496	1,354,807	n/a	n/a	n/a	1,211,689	749,681	29.2	47	55.3	29
88	3,470,000	2,534,000	1,447,151	n/a	n/a	n/a	1,086,849	991,372	39.1	49	68.5	32
86	3,376,000	2,467,000	1,298,857	n/a	n/a	n/a	1,168,143	753,410	30.5	43	58.0	18
84	3,302,000	2,389,000	1,395,714	n/a	n/a	n/a	993,286	968,529	40.5	51	69.4	38
82	3,203,000	2,309,000	1,229,319	n/a	n/a	n/a	1,079,681	671,625	29.1	47	54.6	37
80	3,121,820	2,178,526	1,235,521	n/a	n/a	n/a	943,005	889,707	40.8	50	72.0	33

[a]Upper case indicates victory with a majority of votes cast; lower case, victory with a plurality of votes cast.

[b]TAPV = turnout as a % of voting age population. Rankings are among all states.

[c]TAPR = turnout as a % of registration. Rankings are among all states.

Sources: South Carolina Democratic Party, South Carolina Republican Party, Federal Election Commission, U.S. Census Bureau.

SOUTH DAKOTA

2000 Electoral Votes: 3

Election Results, U.S. President, 1972–2000

Year	Democrat	Republican	Win[a]	Total Vote	Dem Vote	Rep Vote	Other Vote	Dem %	Rep %	Other %	R Margin	R Mar %
00	Gore	G. W. Bush	R	316,269	118,804	190,700	6,765	37.6	60.3	2.1	71,896	22.7
96	Clinton	Dole	r	323,826	139,333	150,543	33,950	43.0	46.5	10.5	11,210	3.5
92	Clinton	G. Bush	r	334,901	124,888	136,718	73,295	37.3	40.8	21.9	11,830	3.5
88	Dukakis	G. Bush	R	312,991	145,560	165,415	2,016	46.5	52.9	0.6	19,855	6.3
84	Mondale	Reagan	R	316,380	116,113	200,267	0	36.7	63.3	0.0	84,154	26.6
80	Carter	Reagan	R	323,629	103,855	198,343	21,431	32.1	61.3	6.6	94,488	29.2
76	Carter	Ford	R	298,573	147,068	151,505	0	49.3	50.7	0.0	4,437	1.5
72	McGovern	Nixon	R	307,415	139,945	166,476	994	45.5	54.2	0.3	26,531	8.6

Election Results, U.S. Senate, 1980–1998

Year	Democrat	Republican	Win[a]	Total Vote	Dem Vote	Rep Vote	Other Vote	Dem %	Rep %	Other %	R Margin	R Mar %
98	Daschle	Schmidt	D	262,111	162,884	95,431	3,796	62.1	36.4	1.5	−67,453	−25.7
96	Johnson	Pressler	D	324,487	166,533	157,954	0	51.3	48.7	0.0	−8,579	−2.
92	Daschle	Haar	D	325,828	217,095	108,733	0	66.6	33.4	0.0	−108,362	−33.3
90	Muenster	Pressler	R	252,409	116,727	135,682	0	46.3	53.8	0.0	18,955	7.5
86	Daschle	Abdnor	D	295,830	152,657	143,173	0	51.6	48.4	0.0	−9,484	−3.2
84	Cunningham	Pressler	R	315,713	80,537	235,176	0	25.5	74.5	0.0	154,639	49.0
80	McGovern	Abdnor	R	327,478	129,018	190,594	7,866	39.4	58.2	2.4	61,576	18.8

Election Results, Governor, 1982–1998

Year	Democrat	Republican	Win[a]	Total Vote	Dem Vote	Rep Vote	Other Vote	Dem %	Rep %	Other %	R Margin	R Mar %
98	Hunhoff	Janklow	R	260,187	85,473	166,621	8,093	32.9	64.0	3.1	81,148	31.2
94	Beddow	Janklow	R	311,613	126,273	172,515	12,825	40.5	55.4	4.1	46,242	14.8
90	Samuelson	Mickelson	R	256,723	105,525	151,198	0	41.1	58.9	0.0	45,673	17.8
86	Herseth	Mickelson	R	294,441	141,898	152,543	0	48.2	51.8	0.0	10,645	3.6
82	O'Connor	Janklow	R	278,562	81,136	197,426	0	29.1	70.9	0.0	116,290	41.7

Population, Registration, and Turnout, 1980–2000

Year	Population	Vot Age Pop	Registration	Dem %	Rep %	Other %	Unregistered	Turnout	TAPV[b]	Rank	TAPR[c]	Rank
00	754,844	543,000	471,152	38.4	48.2	13.4	283,692	316,269	58.2	13	67.1	20
98	738,171	537,234	496,718	36.1	44.2	19.7	40,516	262,111	48.8	5	52.8	12
96	732,405	522,598	459,971	40.1	48.7	11.3	62,627	324,487	62.1	5	70.5	7
94	721,164	512,000	431,873	41.0	49.2	9.8	80,127	311,613	60.9	1	72.2	3
92	711,000	508,000	448,292	42.4	48.0	9.6	59,708	334,901	65.9	6	74.7	30
90	696,004	497,542	420,351	42.9	49.3	7.9	77,191	256,723	51.6	4	61.1	16
88	713,000	509,000	440,301	42.8	49.2	8.0	68,699	312,991	61.5	4	71.1	25
86	708,000	509,000	428,097	43.2	48.8	8.1	80,903	295,830	58.1	1	69.1	8
84	705,000	504,000	442,790	43.4	47.7	8.9	61,210	317,867	63.1	6	71.8	29
82	697,000	494,000	426,511	44.5	47.0	8.5	67,489	278,562	56.4	3	65.3	19
80	690,768	484,234	447,508	45.2	46.1	8.7	36,726	327,703	67.7	4	73.2	29

[a] Upper case indicates victory with a majority of votes cast; lower case, victory with a plurality of votes cast.
[b] TAPV = turnout as a % of voting age population. Rankings are among all states.
[c] TAPR = turnout as a % of registration. Rankings are among all states.

Sources: South Dakota Democratic Party, South Dakota Republican Party, Federal Election Commission, U.S. Census Bureau, South Dakota Secretary of State Web site <www.state.sd.us/sos>

TENNESSEE

2000 Electoral Votes: 11

Election Results, U.S. President, 1972–2000

Year	Democrat	Republican	Win[a]	Total Vote	Dem Vote	Rep Vote	Other Vote	Dem %	Rep %	Other %	R Margin	R Mar %
00	Gore	G. W. Bush	R	2,076,181	981,720	1,061,949	32,512	47.3	51.1	1.6	80,229	3.9
96	Clinton	Dole	d	1,893,915	909,146	863,530	121,239	48.0	45.6	6.4	−45,616	−2.4
92	Clinton	G. Bush	d	1,974,789	933,521	841,300	199,968	47.3	42.6	10.1	−92,221	−4.7
88	Dukakis	G. Bush	R	1,627,027	679,794	947,233	0	41.8	58.2	0.0	267,439	16.4
84	Mondale	Reagan	R	1,701,926	711,714	990,212	0	41.8	58.2	0.0	278,498	16.4
80	Carter	Reagan	r	1,606,803	783,051	787,761	35,991	48.7	49.0	2.2	4,710	0.3
76	Carter	Ford	D	1,464,852	825,879	633,969	5,004	56.4	43.3	0.3	−191,910	−13.1
72	McGovern	Nixon	R	1,201,182	357,293	813,147	30,742	29.8	67.7	2.6	455,854	38.0

Election Results, U.S. Senate, 1982–2000

Year	Democrat	Republican	Win[a]	Total Vote	Dem Vote	Rep Vote	Other Vote	Dem %	Rep %	Other %	R Margin	R Mar %
00	Clark	Frist	R	1,928,613	621,152	1,255,444	52,017	32.2	65.1	2.7	634,292	32.9
96	Gordon	Thompson	R	1,778,603	654,937	1,091,554	32,112	36.8	61.4	1.8	436,617	24.5
94	Sasser	Frist	R	1,480,352	623,164	834,226	22,962	42.1	56.4	1.6	211,062	14.3
94	Cooper	Thompson	R	1,465,835	565,930	885,998	13,907	38.6	60.4	1.0	320,068	21.8
90	Gore	Hawkins	D	764,601	530,898	233,703	0	69.4	30.6	0.0	−297,195	−38.9
88	Sasser	Andersen	D	1,567,136	1,020,061	541,033	6,042	65.1	34.5	0.4	−479,028	−30.6
84	Gore	Ashe	D	1,648,036	1,000,607	557,016	90,413	60.7	33.8	5.5	−443,591	−26.9
82	Sasser	Beard	D	1,259,755	780,113	479,642	0	61.9	38.1	0.0	−300,471	−23.9

Election Results, Governor, 1982–1998

Year	Democrat	Republican	Win[a]	Total Vote	Dem Vote	Rep Vote	Other Vote	Dem %	Rep %	Other %	R Margin	R Mar %
98	Hooker	Sundquist	R	975,688	287,750	669,973	17,965	29.5	68.7	1.8	382,223	39.2
94	Bredesen	Sundquist	R	1,487,049	664,252	807,104	15,693	44.7	54.3	1.1	142,852	9.6
90	McWherter	Henry	D	770,233	480,885	289,348	0	62.4	37.6	0.0	−191,537	−24.9
86	McWherter	Dunn	D	1,210,051	656,602	553,449	0	54.3	45.7	0.0	−103,153	−8.5
82	Tyree	Alexander	R	1,238,900	500,937	737,963	0	40.4	59.6	0.0	237,026	19.1

Population, Registration, and Turnout, 1980–2000

Year	Population	Vot Age Pop	Registration	Dem %	Rep %	Other %	Unregistered	Turnout	TAPV[b]	Rank	TAPR[c]	Rank
00	5,689,283	4,221,000	3,181,108	n/a	n/a	n/a	2,508,175	2,076,181	49.2	37	65.3	26
98	5,430,621	4,099,219	3,154,487	n/a	n/a	n/a	944,732	975,688	23.8	50	30.9	48
96	5,319,654	3,945,754	2,849,910	n/a	n/a	n/a	1,095,844	1,893,915	48.0	34	66.5	18
94	5,175,240	3,878,000	2,693,003	n/a	n/a	n/a	1,184,997	1,487,049	38.3	33	55.2	30
92	5,024,000	3,778,000	2,726,449	n/a	n/a	n/a	1,051,551	1,974,789	52.3	38	72.4	38
90	4,877,185	3,660,581	2,491,098	n/a	n/a	n/a	1,169,483	770,233	21.0	49	30.9	47
88	4,895,000	3,661,000	2,417,033	n/a	n/a	n/a	1,243,967	1,653,965	45.2	41	68.4	35
86	4,803,000	3,563,000	2,445,803	n/a	n/a	n/a	1,117,197	1,210,051	34.0	37	49.5	38
84	4,726,000	3,490,000	2,579,504	n/a	n/a	n/a	910,496	1,711,993	49.1	42	66.4	44
82	4,651,000	3,408,000	2,272,782	n/a	n/a	n/a	1,135,218	1,259,755	37.0	38	55.4	36
80	4,591,120	3,290,972	2,359,002	n/a	n/a	n/a	931,970	1,617,464	49.1	40	68.6	39

[a]Upper case indicates victory with a majority of votes cast; lower case, victory with a plurality of votes cast.
[b]TAPV = turnout as a % of voting age population. Rankings are among all states.
[c]TAPR = turnout as a % of registration. Rankings are among all states.
Sources: Tennessee Democratic Party, Tennessee Republican Party, Federal Election Commission, U.S. Census Bureau.

TEXAS

2000 Electoral Votes: 32

Election Results, U.S. President, 1972–2000

Year	Democrat	Republican	Win[a]	Total Vote	Dem Vote	Rep Vote	Other Vote	Dem %	Rep %	Other %	R Margin	R Mar %
00	Gore	G. W. Bush	R	6,407,637	2,433,746	3,799,639	174,252	38.0	59.3	2.7	1,365,893	21.3
96	Clinton	Dole	r	5,606,537	2,459,683	2,736,167	410,687	43.9	48.8	7.3	276,484	4.9
92	Clinton	G. Bush	r	6,132,667	2,281,815	2,496,071	1,354,781	37.2	40.7	22.1	214,256	3.5
88	Dukakis	G. Bush	R	5,427,140	2,352,748	3,036,829	37,563	43.4	56.0	0.7	684,081	12.6
84	Mondale	Reagan	R	5,382,704	1,949,276	3,433,428	0	36.2	63.8	0.0	1,484,152	27.6
80	Carter	Reagan	R	4,503,465	1,881,147	2,510,705	111,613	41.8	55.8	2.5	629,558	14.0
76	Carter	Ford	D	4,055,737	2,082,319	1,953,300	20,118	51.3	48.2	0.5	−129,019	−3.2
72	McGovern	Nixon	R	3,471,281	1,154,289	2,298,896	18,096	33.3	66.2	0.5	1,144,607	33.0

Election Results, U.S. Senate, 1982–2000

Year	Democrat	Republican	Win[a]	Total Vote	Dem Vote	Rep Vote	Other Vote	Dem %	Rep %	Other %	R Margin	R Mar %
00	Kelly	Hutchison	R	6,276,652	2,030,315	4,082,091	164,246	32.3	65.0	2.6	2,051,776	32.7
96	Morales	Gramm	R	5,527,441	2,428,776	3,027,680	70,985	43.9	54.8	1.3	598,904	10.8
94	Fisher	Hutchison	R	4,279,940	1,639,615	2,604,218	36,107	38.3	60.9	0.8	964,603	22.5
93	Krueger	Hutchison	R	1,765,254	576,538	1,188,716	0	32.7	67.3	0.0	612,178	34.7
90	Parmer	Gramm	R	3,732,343	1,429,986	2,302,357	0	38.3	61.7	0.0	872,371	23.4
88	Bentsen	Boulter	D	5,323,023	3,149,806	2,129,228	43,989	59.2	40.0	0.8	−1,020,578	−19.2
84	Doggett	Gramm	R	5,313,905	2,202,557	3,111,348	0	41.5	58.6	0.0	908,791	17.1
82	Bentsen	Collins	D	3,103,167	1,818,223	1,256,759	28,185	58.6	40.5	0.9	−561,464	−18.1

Election Results, Governor, 1982–1998

Year	Democrat	Republican	Win[a]	Total Vote	Dem Vote	Rep Vote	Other Vote	Dem %	Rep %	Other %	R Margin	R Mar %
98	Mauro	Bush	R	3,737,102	1,165,592	2,550,821	20,689	31.2	68.3	0.6	1,385,229	37.1
94	Richards	Bush	R	4,396,242	2,016,928	2,350,994	28,320	45.9	53.5	0.6	334,066	7.6
90	Richards	Williams	D	3,752,101	1,925,670	1,826,431	0	51.3	48.7	0.0	−99,239	−2.6
86	White	Clements, Jr.	R	3,440,790	1,584,515	1,813,779	42,496	46.1	52.7	1.2	229,264	6.7
82	White	Clements, Jr.	D	3,191,091	1,697,870	1,465,937	27,284	53.2	45.9	0.9	−231,933	−7.3

Population, Registration, and Turnout, 1980–2000

Year	Population	Vot Age Pop	Registration	Dem %	Rep %	Other %	Unregistered	Turnout	TAPV[b]	Rank	TAPR[c]	Rank
00	20,851,820	14,850,000	10,267,639	n/a	n/a	n/a	10,584,181	6,407,037	43.1	49	62.4	34
98	19,759,614	14,130,414	11,538,235	n/a	n/a	n/a	2,592,179	3,737,102	26.4	48	32.4	46
96	19,128,261	13,323,574	10,540,678	n/a	n/a	n/a	2,782,896	5,606,537	42.1	48	53.2	47
94	18,378,185	13,077,000	8,641,848	n/a	n/a	n/a	4,435,152	4,396,242	33.6	43	50.9	39
92	17,656,000	12,583,000	8,439,874	n/a	n/a	n/a	4,143,126	6,132,667	48.7	46	72.7	35
90	16,986,510	12,150,671	7,701,499	n/a	n/a	n/a	4,449,172	3,752,101	30.9	42	48.7	39
88	16,841,000	12,270,000	8,201,856	n/a	n/a	n/a	4,068,144	5,427,140	44.2	44	66.2	38
86	16,682,000	11,891,000	7,287,173	n/a	n/a	n/a	4,603,827	3,440,790	28.9	44	47.2	40
84	16,083,000	11,410,000	7,900,167	n/a	n/a	n/a	3,509,833	5,397,571	47.3	45	68.3	40
82	15,280,000	10,883,000	6,414,988	n/a	n/a	n/a	4,468,012	3,191,091	29.3	46	49.7	43
80	14,229,191	9,921,522	6,639,661	n/a	n/a	n/a	3,281,861	4,541,108	45.8	44	68.4	42

[a] Upper case indicates victory with a majority of votes cast; lower case, victory with a plurality of votes cast.

[b] TAPV = turnout as a % of voting age population. Rankings are among all states.

[c] TAPR = turnout as a % of registration. Rankings are among all states.

Sources: Texas Democratic Party, Texas Republican Party, Federal Election Commission, U.S. Census Bureau.

UTAH

2000 Electoral Votes: 5

Election Results, U.S. President, 1972–2000

Year	Democrat	Republican	Win[a]	Total Vote	Dem Vote	Rep Vote	Other Vote	Dem %	Rep %	Other %	R Margin	R Mar %
00	Gore	G. W. Bush	R	770,754	203,053	515,096	52,605	26.3	66.8	6.8	213,043	40.5
96	Clinton	Dole	R	665,470	221,633	361,911	81,926	33.3	54.4	12.3	140,278	21.1
92	Clinton	G. Bush	r	709,461	183,429	322,632	203,400	25.9	45.5	28.7	139,203	19.6
88	Dukakis	G. Bush	R	647,016	207,352	428,442	11,222	32.1	66.2	1.7	221,090	34.2
84	Mondale	Reagan	R	624,474	155,369	469,105	0	24.9	75.1	0.0	313,736	50.2
80	Carter	Reagan	R	594,237	124,266	439,687	30,284	20.9	74.0	5.1	315,421	53.1
76	Carter	Ford	R	520,018	182,110	337,908	0	35.0	65.0	0.0	155,798	30.0
72	McGovern	Nixon	R	478,476	126,284	323,643	28,549	26.4	67.6	6.0	197,359	41.2

Election Results, U.S. Senate, 1980–2000

Year	Democrat	Republican	Win[a]	Total Vote	Dem Vote	Rep Vote	Other Vote	Dem %	Rep %	Other %	R Margin	R Mar %
00	Howell	Hatch	R	769,704	242,569	504,803	22,332	31.5	65.6	2.9	262,234	34.1
98	Leckman	Bennett	R	494,897	163,172	316,652	15,073	33.0	64.0	3.1	153,480	31.0
94	Shea	Hatch	R	519,304	146,938	357,297	15,069	28.3	68.8	2.9	210,359	40.5
92	Owens	Bennett	R	721,297	301,228	420,069	0	41.8	58.2	0.0	118,841	16.5
88	Moss	Hatch	R	640,697	203,364	430,084	7,249	31.7	67.1	1.1	226,720	35.4
86	Oliver	Garn	R	435,017	115,523	314,608	4,886	26.6	72.3	1.1	199,085	45.8
82	Wilson	Hatch	R	530,802	219,482	309,332	1,988	41.4	58.3	0.4	89,850	16.9
80	Berman	Garn	R	594,298	151,454	437,675	5,169	25.5	73.7	0.9	286,221	48.2

Election Results, Governor, 1980–2000

Year	Democrat	Republican	Win[a]	Total Vote	Dem Vote	Rep Vote	Other Vote	Dem %	Rep %	Other %	R Margin	R Mar %
00	Orton	Leavitt	R	761,806	321,979	424,837	14,990	42.3	55.8	2.0	102,858	13.5
96	Bradley	Leavitt	R	671,864	156,616	503,693	11,555	23.3	75.0	1.7	347,077	51.7
92	Hanson	Leavitt	r	754,647	177,181	321,713	255,753	23.5	42.6	33.9	144,532	19.2
88	Wilson	Bangerter	r	649,114	249,321	260,462	139,331	38.4	40.1	21.5	11,141	1.7
84	Owens	Bangerter	R	629,619	275,669	351,792	2,158	43.8	55.9	0.3	76,123	12.1
80	Matheson	Wright	D	600,019	330,974	266,578	2,467	55.2	44.4	0.4	−64,396	−10.7

Population, Registration, and Turnout, 1980–2000

Year	Population	Vot Age Pop	Registration	Dem %	Rep %	Other %	Unregistered	Turnout	TAPV[b]	Rank	TAPR[c]	Rank
00	2,233,169	1,465,000	1,123,238	n/a	n/a	n/a	1,109,931	770,754	52.6	29	68.6	15
98	2,099,758	1,398,458	1,115,821	n/a	n/a	n/a	282,637	494,897	35.4	34	44.4	30
96	2,000,494	1,276,790	1,050,452	n/a	n/a	n/a	226,338	671,864	52.6	24	64.0	33
94	1,907,936	1,235,000	921,981	n/a	n/a	n/a	313,019	519,304	42.0	22	56.3	28
92	1,813,000	1,159,000	965,211	n/a	n/a	n/a	193,789	754,647	65.1	9	78.2	19
90	1,722,850	1,095,406	780,555	n/a	n/a	n/a	314,851	437,859	40.0	23	56.1	28
88	1,690,000	1,078,000	806,934	n/a	n/a	n/a	271,066	649,114	60.2	7	80.4	2
86	1,665,000	1,058,000	763,057	n/a	n/a	n/a	294,943	435,017	41.1	20	57.0	23
84	1,623,000	1,024,000	840,416	n/a	n/a	n/a	183,584	629,656	61.5	7	74.9	18
82	1,554,000	993,000	748,730	n/a	n/a	n/a	244,270	530,802	53.5	7	70.9	6
80	1,461,037	921,533	781,711	n/a	n/a	n/a	139,822	604,098	65.6	5	77.3	15

[a] Upper case indicates victory with a majority of votes cast; lower case, victory with a plurality of votes cast.
[b] TAPV = turnout as a % of voting age population. Rankings are among all states.
[c] TAPR = turnout as a % of registration. Rankings are among all states.

Sources: Utah Democratic Party, Utah Republican Party, Federal Election Commission, U.S. Census Bureau, Utah State Elections Office Web site <www.elections.utah.gov>

VERMONT

2000 Electoral Votes: 3

Election Results, U.S. President, 1972–2000

Year	Democrat	Republican	Win[a]	Total Vote	Dem Vote	Rep Vote	Other Vote	Dem %	Rep %	Other %	R Margin	R Mar %
00	Gore	G. W. Bush	D	294,308	149,022	119,775	25,511	50.6	40.7	8.7	−29,247	−9.9
96	Clinton	Dole	D	257,889	137,894	80,352	39,643	53.5	31.2	15.4	−57,542	−22.3
92	Clinton	G. Bush	d	287,705	133,592	88,122	65,991	46.4	30.6	22.9	−45,470	−15.8
88	Dukakis	G. Bush	R	242,194	115,775	124,331	2,088	47.8	51.3	0.9	8,556	3.5
84	Mondale	Reagan	R	231,595	95,730	135,865	0	41.3	58.7	0.0	40,135	17.3
80	Carter	Reagan	r	208,249	81,891	94,598	31,760	39.3	45.4	15.3	12,707	6.1
76	Carter	Ford	R	183,177	78,789	100,387	4,001	43.0	54.8	2.2	21,598	11.8
72	McGovern	Nixon	R	186,946	68,174	117,149	1,623	36.5	62.7	0.9	48,975	26.2

Election Results, U.S. Senate, 1980–2000

Year	Democrat	Republican	Win[a]	Total Vote	Dem Vote	Rep Vote	Other Vote	Dem %	Rep %	Other %	R Margin	R Mar %
00	Flanagan	Jeffords	R	288,500	73,352	189,133	26,015	25.4	65.6	9.0	115,781	40.1
98	Leahy	Tuttle	D	213,407	154,567	48,051	10,789	72.4	22.5	5.1	−106,516	−49.9
94	Backus	Jeffords	R	211,480	85,868	106,505	19,107	40.6	50.4	9.0	20,637	9.8
92	Leahy	Douglas	D	278,616	154,762	123,854	0	55.6	44.5	0.0	−30,908	−11.1
88	Gray	Jeffords	R	239,600	71,460	163,183	4,957	29.8	68.1	2.1	91,723	38.3
86	Leahy	Snelling	D	196,467	124,123	67,798	4,546	63.2	34.5	2.3	−56,325	−28.7
82	Guest	Stafford	R	168,003	79,340	84,450	4,213	47.2	50.3	2.5	5,110	3.0
80	Leahy	Ledbetter	d	209,188	104,089	101,647	3,452	49.8	48.6	1.7	−2,442	−1.2

Election Results, Governor, 1988–2000

Year	Democrat	Republican	Win[a]	Total Vote	Dem Vote	Rep Vote	Other Vote	Dem %	Rep %	Other %	R Margin	R Mar %
00	Dean	Dwyer	D	293,473	148,059	111,359	34,055	50.5	37.9	11.6	−36,700	−12.5
98	Dean	Dwyer	D	217,774	121,425	89,726	6,623	55.8	41.2	3.0	−31,699	−14.6
96	Dean	Gropper	D	253,987	179,544	57,161	17,282	70.7	22.5	6.8	−122,383	−48.2
94	Dean	Kelley	D	210,586	145,661	40,292	24,633	69.2	19.1	11.7	−105,369	−50.0
92	Dean	McClaughry	D	279,360	213,523	65,837	0	76.4	23.6	0.0	−147,686	−52.9
90	Welch	Snelling	R	211,027	97,321	109,540	4,166	46.1	51.9	2.0	12,219	5.8
88	Kunin	Bernhardt	D	242,548	134,438	105,191	2,919	55.4	43.4	1.2	−29,247	−12.1

Population, Registration, and Turnout, 1980–2000

Year	Population	Vot Age Pop	Registration	Dem %	Rep %	Other %	Unregistered	Turnout	TAPV[b]	Rank	TAPR[c]	Rank
00	608,827	460,000	427,354	n/a	n/a	n/a	181,473	294,308	64.0	5	68.9	14
98	590,883	449,536	402,603	n/a	n/a	n/a	46,933	217,774	48.4	6	54.1	11
96	588,654	438,011	385,328	n/a	n/a	n/a	52,683	257,889	58.9	7	66.9	17
94	580,209	434,000	373,442	n/a	n/a	n/a	60,558	211,480	48.7	10	56.6	26
92	570,000	425,000	383,371	n/a	n/a	n/a	41,629	287,705	67.7	4	75.0	29
90	562,758	419,675	350,349	n/a	n/a	n/a	69,326	211,027	50.3	8	60.2	17
88	557,000	412,000	348,312	n/a	n/a	n/a	63,688	242,548	58.9	8	69.6	31
86	541,000	401,000	328,466	n/a	n/a	n/a	72,534	196,633	49.0	6	59.9	16
84	530,000	392,000	333,778	n/a	n/a	n/a	58,222	234,561	59.8	11	70.3	36
82	516,000	381,000	315,767	n/a	n/a	n/a	65,233	169,251	44.4	21	53.6	40
80	511,456	365,451	311,919	n/a	n/a	n/a	53,532	212,795	58.2	17	68.2	41

[a]Upper case indicates victory with a majority of votes cast; lower case, victory with a plurality of votes cast.
[b]TAPV = turnout as a % of voting age population. Rankings are among all states.
[c]TAPR = turnout as a % of registration. Rankings are among all states.

Sources: Vermont Democratic Party, Vermont Republican Party, Federal Election Commission, U.S. Census Bureau, Vermont Secretary of State Web site <www.sec.state.vt.us>

VIRGINIA

2000 Electoral Votes: 13

Election Results, U.S. President, 1972–2000

Year	Democrat	Republican	Win[a]	Total Vote	Dem Vote	Rep Vote	Other Vote	Dem %	Rep %	Other %	R Margin	R Mar %
00	Gore	G. W. Bush	R	2,739,447	1,217,290	1,437,490	84,667	44.4	52.5	3.1	220,200	8.0
96	Clinton	Dole	r	2,416,642	1,091,060	1,138,350	187,232	45.2	47.1	7.8	47,290	2.0
92	Clinton	G. Bush	r	2,537,806	1,038,650	1,150,517	348,639	40.9	45.3	13.7	111,867	4.4
88	Dukakis	G. Bush	R	2,191,609	859,799	1,309,162	22,648	39.2	59.7	1.0	449,363	20.5
84	Mondale	Reagan	R	2,133,328	796,250	1,337,078	0	37.3	62.7	0.0	540,828	25.4
80	Carter	Reagan	R	1,837,201	752,174	989,609	95,418	40.9	53.9	5.2	237,435	12.9
76	Carter	Ford	R	1,650,450	813,896	836,554	0	49.3	50.7	0.0	22,658	1.4
72	McGovern	Nixon	R	1,457,019	438,887	988,493	29,639	30.1	67.8	2.0	549,606	37.7

Election Results, U.S. Senate, 1982–2000

Year	Democrat	Republican	Win[a]	Total Vote	Dem Vote	Rep Vote	Other Vote	Dem %	Rep %	Other %	R Margin	R Mar %
00	Robb	Allen	R	2,718,301	1,296,093	1,420,460	1,748	47.7	52.3	0.1	124,367	4.6
96	Warner	Warner	R	2,351,726	1,115,982	1,235,744	0	47.5	52.6	0.0	119,762	5.1
94	Robb	North	d	2,055,913	938,376	882,213	235,324	45.6	42.9	11.5	−56,163	−2.7
90	unopposed	Warner	R	1,073,537	—	876,782	196,755	—	81.7	18.3	680,027	63.3
88	Robb	Dawkins	D	2,067,738	1,474,086	593,652	0	71.3	28.7	0.0	−880,434	−42.6
84	Harrison	Warner	R	2,007,336	601,142	1,406,194	0	30.0	70.1	0.0	805,052	40.1
82	Davis	Trible	R	1,415,410	690,839	724,571	0	48.8	51.2	0.0	33,732	2.4

Election Results, Governor, 1981–1997

Year	Democrat	Republican	Win[a]	Total Vote	Dem Vote	Rep Vote	Other Vote	Dem %	Rep %	Other %	R Margin	R Mar %
97	Beyer	Gillmore	R	1,733,988	738,971	969,062	25,955	42.6	55.9	1.5	230,091	13.3
93	Terry	Allen	R	1,793,244	733,527	1,045,319	14,398	40.9	58.3	0.8	311,792	17.4
89	Wilder	Coleman	D	1,787,131	896,936	890,195	0	50.2	49.8	0.0	−6,741	−0.4
85	Baliles	Durrette	D	1,343,090	741,438	601,652	0	55.2	44.8	0.0	−139,786	−10.4
81	Robb	Coleman	D	1,420,611	760,357	659,398	856	53.5	46.4	0.1	−100,959	−7.1

Population, Registration, and Turnout, 1980–2000

Year	Population	Vot Age Pop	Registration	Dem %	Rep %	Other %	Unregistered	Turnout	TAPV[b]	Rank	TAPR[c]	Rank
00	7,078,515	5,263,000	3,770,273	n/a	n/a	n/a	3,308,242	2,789,808	53.0	27.0	74.0	8
98	6,791,345	5,146,667	3,725,921	n/a	n/a	n/a	1,420,746	1,137,437	22.1	51	30.5	47
96	6,675,451	5,005,831	3,322,135	n/a	n/a	n/a	1,683,696	2,416,642	48.3	33	72.7	6
94	6,551,522	4,948,000	3,004,169	n/a	n/a	n/a	1,943,831	2,055,913	41.6	21	68.4	6
92	6,377,000	4,814,000	3,054,662	n/a	n/a	n/a	1,759,338	2,537,806	52.7	34	83.1	4
90	6,187,358	4,682,620	2,738,029	n/a	n/a	n/a	1,944,591	1,073,537	22.9	48	39.2	46
88	6,015,000	4,544,000	2,878,718	n/a	n/a	n/a	1,665,282	2,191,609	48.2	34	76.1	12
86	5,787,000	4,377,000	2,612,060	n/a	n/a	n/a	1,764,940	1,041,416	23.8	50	39.9	46
84	5,636,000	4,241,000	2,543,763	n/a	n/a	n/a	1,697,237	2,146,635	50.6	36	84.4	2
82	5,491,000	4,075,000	2,234,011	n/a	n/a	n/a	1,840,989	1,415,410	34.7	42	63.4	25
80	5,346,818	3,872,859	2,302,405	n/a	n/a	n/a	1,570,454	1,866,032	48.2	42	81.0	6

[a]Upper case indicates victory with a majority of votes cast; lower case, victory with a plurality of votes cast.
[b]TAPV = turnout as a % of voting age population. Rankings are among all states.
[c]TAPR = turnout as a % of registration. Rankings are among all states.
Sources: Virginia Democratic Party, Virginia Republican Party, Federal Election Commission, U.S. Census Bureau.

WASHINGTON

2000 Electoral Votes: 11

Election Results, U.S. President, 1972–2000

Year	Democrat	Republican	Win[a]	Total Vote	Dem Vote	Rep Vote	Other Vote	Dem %	Rep %	Other %	R Margin	R Mar %
00	Gore	G. W. Bush	D	2,487,433	1,247,652	1,108,864	130,917	50.2	44.6	5.3	−138,788	−5.6
96	Clinton	Dole	d	2,253,837	1,123,323	840,712	289,802	49.8	37.3	12.9	−282,611	−12.5
92	Clinton	G. Bush	d	2,266,051	993,037	731,234	541,780	43.8	32.3	23.9	−261,803	−11.6
88	Dukakis	G. Bush	D	1,865,253	933,516	903,835	27,902	50.1	48.5	1.5	−29,681	−1.6
84	Mondale	Reagan	R	1,850,022	798,352	1,051,670	0	43.2	56.9	0.0	253,318	13.7
80	Carter	Reagan	R	1,700,510	650,193	865,244	185,073	38.2	50.9	10.9	215,051	12.6
76	Carter	Ford	R	1,532,041	717,323	777,732	36,986	46.8	50.8	2.4	60,409	3.9
72	McGovern	Nixon	R	1,470,847	568,334	837,135	65,378	38.6	56.9	4.4	268,801	18.3

Election Results, U.S. Senate, 1980–2000

Year	Democrat	Republican	Win[a]	Total Vote	Dem Vote	Rep Vote	Other Vote	Dem %	Rep %	Other %	R Margin	R Mar %
00	Cantwell	Gorton	d	2,461,379	1,199,437	1,197,208	64,734	48.7	48.6	2.6	−2,229	−0.1
98	Murray	Smith	D	1,888,561	1,103,184	785,377	0	58.4	41.6	0.0	−317,807	−16.8
94	Sims	Gorton	R	1,700,173	752,352	947,821	0	44.3	55.8	0.0	195,469	11.5
92	Murray	Chandler	D	2,218,802	1,197,973	1,020,829	0	54.0	46.0	0.0	−177,144	−8.0
88	Lowry	Gorton	R	1,848,542	904,183	944,359	0	48.9	51.1	0.0	40,176	2.2
86	Adams	Gorton	D	1,337,367	677,471	650,931	8,965	50.7	48.7	0.7	−26,540	−2.0
83	Lowry	Evans	R	1,213,307	540,981	672,326	0	44.6	55.4	0.0	131,345	10.8
82	Jackson	Jewett	D	1,368,476	943,655	332,273	92,548	69.0	24.3	6.8	−611,382	−44.7
80	Magnuson	Gorton	R	1,728,369	792,052	936,317	0	45.8	54.2	0.0	144,265	8.3

Election Results, Governor, 1980–2000

Year	Democrat	Republican	Win[a]	Total Vote	Dem Vote	Rep Vote	Other Vote	Dem %	Rep %	Other %	R Margin	R Mar %
00	Locke	Carlson	D	2,469,852	1,441,973	980,060	47,819	58.4	39.7	1.9	−461,913	−18.7
96	Locke	Craswell	D	2,237,030	1,296,492	940,538	0	58.0	42.0	0.0	−355,954	−15.9
92	Lowry	Eikenberry	D	2,270,531	1,184,315	1,086,216	0	52.2	47.8	0.0	−98,099	−4.3
88	Gardner	Williams	D	1,874,929	1,166,448	708,481	0	62.2	37.8	0.0	−457,967	−24.4
84	Gardner	Spellman	D	1,888,987	1,006,993	881,994	0	53.3	46.7	0.0	−124,999	−6.6
80	McDermott	Spellman	R	1,730,896	749,813	981,083	0	43.3	56.7	0.0	231,270	13.4

Population, Registration, and Turnout, 1980–2000

Year	Population	Vot Age Pop	Registration	Dem %	Rep %	Other %	Unregistered	Turnout	TAPV[b]	Rank	TAPR[c]	Rank
00	5,894,121	4,368,000	3,335,714	n/a	n/a	n/a	2,558,407	2,487,433	56.9	17	74.6	6
98	5,689,263	4,216,773	3,119,562	n/a	n/a	n/a	1,097,211	1,888,561	44.8	9	60.5	4
96	5,532,939	4,012,536	3,078,128	n/a	n/a	n/a	934,408	2,253,837	56.2	17	73.2	5
94	5,343,090	3,935,000	2,896,519	n/a	n/a	n/a	1,038,481	1,700,173	43.2	19	58.7	23
92	5,136,000	3,781,000	2,814,680	n/a	n/a	n/a	966,320	2,270,531	60.1	21	80.7	9
90	4,866,692	3,605,305	2,225,101	n/a	n/a	n/a	1,380,204	1,292,682	35.9	32	58.1	24
88	4,648,000	3,417,000	2,499,309	n/a	n/a	n/a	917,691	1,874,929	54.9	15	75.0	14
86	4,463,000	3,317,000	2,230,354	n/a	n/a	n/a	1,086,646	1,337,367	40.3	22	60.0	15
84	4,349,000	3,228,000	2,457,667	n/a	n/a	n/a	770,333	1,888,987	58.5	13	76.9	13
82	4,283,000	3,136,000	2,105,563	n/a	n/a	n/a	1,030,437	1,368,476	43.6	20	65.0	18
80	4,132,156	2,992,563	2,236,603	n/a	n/a	n/a	755,960	1,742,394	58.2	16	77.9	11

[a]Upper case indicates victory with a majority of votes cast; lower case, victory with a plurality of votes cast.
[b]TAPV = turnout as a % of voting age population. Rankings are among all states.
[c]TAPR = turnout as a % of registration. Rankings are among all states.

Sources: Washington Democratic Party, Washington Republican Party, Federal Election Commission, U.S. Census Bureau, Washington Secretary of State Web site <www.secstate.wa.gov>

WEST VIRGINIA

2000 Electoral Votes: 5

Election Results, U.S. President, 1972–2000

Year	Democrat	Republican	Win[a]	Total Vote	Dem Vote	Rep Vote	Other Vote	Dem %	Rep %	Other %	R Margin	R Mar %
00	Gore	G. W. Bush	R	648,124	295,497	336,475	16,152	45.6	51.9	2.5	40,978	6.3
96	Clinton	Dole	D	636,459	327,812	233,946	74,701	51.5	36.8	11.7	−93,866	−14.7
92	Clinton	G. Bush	d	681,804	331,001	241,974	108,829	48.6	35.5	16.0	−89,027	−13.1
88	Dukakis	G. Bush	D	653,311	341,016	310,065	2,230	52.2	47.5	0.3	−30,951	−4.7
84	Mondale	Reagan	R	733,640	328,157	405,483	0	44.7	55.3	0.0	77,326	10.5
80	Carter	Reagan	D	733,359	367,462	334,206	31,691	50.1	45.6	4.3	−33,256	−4.5
76	Carter	Ford	D	750,674	435,914	314,760	0	58.1	41.9	0.0	−121,154	−16.1
72	McGovern	Nixon	R	762,399	277,435	484,964	0	36.4	63.6	0.0	207,529	27.2

Election Results, U.S. Senate, 1982–2000

Year	Democrat	Republican	Win[a]	Total Vote	Dem Vote	Rep Vote	Other Vote	Dem %	Rep %	Other %	R Margin	R Mar %
00	Byrd	Gallaher	D	603,477	469,215	121,635	12,627	77.8	20.2	2.1	−347,580	−57.6
96	Rockefeller	Burks	D	595,614	456,526	139,088	0	76.7	23.4	0.0	−317,438	−53.3
94	Byrd	Klos	D	420,936	290,495	130,441	0	69.0	31.0	0.0	−160,054	−38.0
80	Rockefeller	Yoder	D	404,305	276,234	128,071	0	68.3	31.7	0.0	−148,163	−36.6
88	Byrd	Wolfe	D	634,547	410,983	223,564	0	64.8	35.2	0.0	−187,419	−29.5
84	Rockefeller	Raese	D	722,429	374,233	344,680	3,516	51.8	47.7	0.5	−29,553	−4.1
82	Byrd	Benedict	D	565,314	387,170	173,910	4,234	68.5	30.8	0.8	−213,260	−37.7

Election Results, Governor, 1980–2000

Year	Democrat	Republican	Win[a]	Total Vote	Dem Vote	Rep Vote	Other Vote	Dem %	Rep %	Other %	R Margin	R Mar %
00	Wise	Underwood	D	648,047	324,822	305,926	17,299	50.1	47.2	2.7	−18,896	−2.9
96	Pritt	Underwood	R	628,559	287,870	324,518	16,171	45.8	51.6	2.6	36,648	5.8
92	Caperton	Benedict	D	657,565	368,302	240,390	48,873	56.0	36.6	7.4	−127,912	−19.5
88	Caperton	Moore	D	649,593	382,421	267,172	0	58.9	41.1	0.0	−115,249	−17.7
84	See	Moore	R	741,502	346,565	394,937	0	46.7	53.3	0.0	48,372	6.5
80	Rockefeller IV	Moore	D	742,150	401,863	337,240	3,047	54.2	45.4	0.4	−64,623	−8.7

Population, Registration, and Turnout, 1980–2000

Year	Population	Vot Age Pop	Registration	Dem %	Rep %	Other %	Unregistered	Turnout	TAPV[b]	Rank	TAPR[c]	Rank
00	1,808,344	1,416,000	1,067,822	61.8	29.0	9.2	740,522	648,124	45.8	45	60.7	39
98	1,811,156	1,406,902	1,007,811	62.7	29.4	7.9	399,091	351,277	25.0	49	34.9	45
96	1,825,754	1,406,272	970,743	63.5	29.7	6.8	435,529	636,459	45.3	44	65.6	20
94	1,822,021	1,393,000	884,315	65.2	30.4	4.4	508,685	420,936	30.2	48	47.6	44
92	1,812,000	1,376,000	956,172	65.7	30.5	3.9	419,828	681,804	49.5	42	71.3	42
90	1,793,477	1,349,900	884,839	66.2	31.1	2.7	465,061	404,305	30.0	44	45.7	42
88	1,876,000	1,398,000	968,619	66.1	31.3	2.6	429,381	653,311	46.7	36	67.4	37
86	1,919,000	1,435,000	946,039	66.8	31.0	2.2	488,961	395,820	27.6	46	41.8	43
84	1,951,000	1,432,000	1,025,230	67.2	30.8	2.0	406,770	741,502	51.8	32	72.3	28
82	1,948,000	1,419,000	948,329	66.6	31.2	2.2	470,671	565,314	39.8	33	59.6	29
80	1,949,644	1,389,711	1,034,546	66.8	30.9	2.3	355,165	742,150	53.4	30	71.7	32

[a]Upper case indicates victory with a majority of votes cast; lower case, victory with a plurality of votes cast.
[b]TAPV = turnout as a % of voting age population. Rankings are among all states.
[c]TAPR = turnout as a % of registration. Rankings are among all states.

Sources: West Virginia Democratic Party, West Virginia Republican Party, Federal Election Commission, U.S. Census Bureau, West Virginia Secretary of State Web site <www.state.wv.us/sos>

WISCONSIN

2000 Electoral Votes: 11

Election Results, U.S. President, 1972–2000

Year	Democrat	Republican	Win[a]	Total Vote	Dem Vote	Rep Vote	Other Vote	Dem %	Rep %	Other %	R Margin	R Mar %
00	Gore	G. W. Bush	d	2,598,607	1,242,987	1,237,279	118,341	47.8	47.6	4.6	−5,708	−0.2
96	Clinton	Dole	d	2,193,845	1,071,971	845,029	276,845	48.9	38.5	12.6	−226,942	−10.3
92	Clinton	G. Bush	d	2,516,400	1,041,066	930,855	544,479	41.4	37.0	21.6	−110,211	−4.4
88	Dukakis	G. Bush	D	2,189,335	1,126,794	1,047,499	15,042	51.5	47.9	0.7	−79,295	−3.6
84	Mondale	Reagan	R	2,194,324	995,740	1,198,584	0	45.4	54.6	0.0	202,844	9.2
80	Carter	Reagan	r	2,231,086	981,584	1,088,845	160,657	44.0	48.8	7.2	107,261	4.8
76	Carter	Ford	D	2,080,162	1,040,232	1,004,987	34,943	50.0	48.3	1.7	−35,245	−1.7
72	McGovern	Nixon	R	1,852,890	810,174	989,430	53,286	43.7	53.4	2.9	179,256	9.7

Election Results, U.S. Senate, 1980–2000

Year	Democrat	Republican	Win[a]	Total Vote	Dem Vote	Rep Vote	Other Vote	Dem %	Rep %	Other %	R Margin	R Mar %
00	Kohl	Gillespie	D	2,540,083	1,563,238	940,744	36,101	61.5	37.0	1.4	−622,494	−24.5
98	Feingold	Neumann	D	1,760,129	890,068	852,272	17,789	50.6	48.4	1.0	−37,796	−2.1
94	Kohl	Welch	D	1,565,090	912,662	636,989	15,439	58.3	40.7	1.0	−275,673	−17.6
92	Feingold	Kasten	D	2,420,261	1,290,662	1,129,599	0	53.3	46.7	0.0	−161,063	−6.7
88	Kohl	Engeleiter	D	2,167,257	1,128,625	1,030,440	8,192	52.1	47.6	0.4	−98,185	−4.5
86	Garvey	Kasten	R	1,481,962	702,963	754,573	24,426	47.4	50.9	1.7	51,610	3.5
82	Proxmire	McCallum	D	1,544,981	983,311	527,355	34,315	63.7	34.1	2.2	−455,956	−29.5
80	Nelson	Kasten	R	2,204,135	1,065,487	1,106,311	32,337	48.3	50.2	1.5	40,824	1.9

Election Results, Governor, 1982–1998

Year	Democrat	Republican	Win[a]	Total Vote	Dem Vote	Rep Vote	Other Vote	Dem %	Rep %	Other %	R Margin	R Mar %
98	Garvey	Thompson	R	1,755,198	679,553	1,047,716	27,929	38.7	59.7	1.6	368,163	21.0
94	Chvala	Thompson	R	1,563,153	482,850	1,051,326	28,977	30.9	67.3	1.9	568,476	36.4
90	Loftus	Thompson	R	1,378,601	576,280	802,321	0	41.8	58.2	0.0	226,041	16.4
86	Earl	Thompson	R	1,526,572	705,578	805,090	15,904	46.2	52.7	1.0	99,512	6.5
82	Earl	Kohler	D	1,580,344	896,812	662,838	20,694	56.8	41.9	1.3	−233,974	−14.8

Population, Registration, and Turnout, 1980–2000

Year	Population	Vot Age Pop	Registration*	Dem %	Rep %	Other %	Unregistered	Turnout	TAPV[b]	Rank	TAPR[c]	Rank
00	5,363,675	3,930,000	2,598,607	n/a	n/a	n/a	1,331,393	2,598,607	66.1	4	n/a	n/a
98	5,223,500	3,872,456	1,760,129	n/a	n/a	n/a	2,112,327	1,760,129	45.5	7	n/a	n/a
96	5,159,795	3,769,666	2,193,845	n/a	n/a	n/a	1,575,821	2,193,845	58.2	9	n/a	n/a
94	5,081,658	3,735,000	1,565,090	n/a	n/a	n/a	2,169,910	1,565,090	41.9	20	n/a	n/a
92	5,007,000	3,677,000	2,516,400	n/a	n/a	n/a	1,160,600	2,516,400	68.4	3	n/a	n/a
90	4,891,769	3,602,787	1,378,601	n/a	n/a	n/a	2,224,186	1,378,601	38.3	27	n/a	n/a
88	4,855,000	3,536,000	2,189,335	n/a	n/a	n/a	1,346,665	2,189,335	61.9	3	n/a	n/a
86	4,785,000	3,515,000	1,526,572	n/a	n/a	n/a	1,988,428	1,526,572	43.4	14	n/a	n/a
84	4,762,000	3,479,000	2,211,789	n/a	n/a	n/a	1,267,211	2,211,789	63.6	4	n/a	n/a
82	4,765,000	3,446,000	1,580,344	n/a	n/a	n/a	1,865,656	1,580,344	45.9	17	n/a	n/a
80	4,705,767	3,346,330	2,271,884	n/a	n/a	n/a	1,074,446	2,271,884	67.9	3	n/a	n/a

*Wisconsin has election day registration at the polls.

[a] Upper case indicates victory with a majority of votes cast; lower case, victory with a plurality of votes cast.

[b] TAPV = turnout as a % of voting age population. Rankings are among all states.

[c] TAPR = turnout as a % of registration. Rankings are among all states.

Sources: Wisconsin Democratic Party, Wisconsin Republican Party, Federal Election Commission, U.S. Census Bureau.

WYOMING

2000 Electoral Votes: 3

Election Results, U.S. President, 1972–2000

Year	Democrat	Republican	Win[a]	Total Vote	Dem Vote	Rep Vote	Other Vote	Dem %	Rep %	Other %	R Margin	R Mar %
00	Gore	G. W. Bush	R	218,351	60,481	147,947	9,923	27.7	67.8	4.5	87,466	40.1
96	Clinton	Dole	r	211,571	77,934	105,388	28,249	36.8	49.8	13.4	27,454	13.0
92	Clinton	G. Bush	r	198,770	68,160	79,347	51,263	34.3	39.9	25.8	11,187	5.6
88	Dukakis	G. Bush	R	176,551	67,113	106,867	2,571	38.0	60.5	1.5	39,754	22.5
84	Mondale	Reagan	R	186,611	53,370	133,241	0	28.6	71.4	0.0	79,871	42.8
80	Carter	Reagan	R	172,199	49,427	110,700	12,072	28.7	64.3	7.0	61,273	35.6
76	Carter	Ford	R	155,580	62,239	92,717	624	40.0	59.6	0.4	30,478	19.6
72	McGovern	Nixon	R	145,570	44,358	100,464	748	30.5	69.0	0.5	56,106	38.5

Election Results, U.S. Senate, 1982–2000

Year	Democrat	Republican	Win[a]	Total Vote	Dem Vote	Rep Vote	Other Vote	Dem %	Rep %	Other %	R Margin	R Mar %
00	Logan	Thomas	R	213,659	47,087	157,622	8,950	22.0	73.8	4.2	110,535	51.7
96	Karpan	Enzi	R	211,077	89,103	114,116	7,858	42.2	54.1	3.7	25,013	11.9
94	Sullivan	Thomas	R	201,710	79,287	118,754	3,669	39.3	58.9	1.8	39,467	19.6
90	Helling	Simpson	R	157,632	56,848	100,784	0	36.1	63.9	0.0	43,936	27.9
88	Vinich	Wallop	R	180,964	89,821	91,143	0	49.6	50.4	0.0	1,322	0.7
84	Ryan	Simpson	R	186,898	40,525	146,373	0	21.7	78.3	0.0	105,848	56.6
82	McDaniel	Wallop	R	167,191	72,466	94,725	0	43.3	56.7	0.0	22,259	13.3

Election Results, Governor, 1982–1998

Year	Democrat	Republican	Win[a]	Total Vote	Dem Vote	Rep Vote	Other Vote	Dem %	Rep %	Other %	R Margin	R Mar %
98	Vinich	Geringer	R	174,888	70,754	97,235	6,899	40.5	55.6	3.9	26,481	15.1
94	Karpan	Geringer	R	200,990	80,747	118,016	2,227	40.2	58.7	1.1	37,269	18.5
90	Sullivan	Mead	D	160,109	104,638	55,471	0	65.4	34.7	0.0	−49,167	−30.7
86	Sullivan	Simpson	D	164,720	88,879	75,841	0	54.0	46.0	0.0	−13,038	−7.9
82	Herschler	Morton	D	168,555	106,427	62,128	0	63.1	36.9	0.0	−44,299	−26.3

Population, Registration, and Turnout, 1980–2000

Year	Population	Vot Age Pop	Registration	Dem %	Rep %	Other %	Unregistered	Turnout	TAPVᵇ	Rank	TAPRᶜ	Rank
00	493,782	358,000	220,012	29.1	60.9	10.0	273,770	213,726	59.7	11	97.1	1
98	480,907	351,501	239,539	29.6	59.5	10.9	111,962	174,888	49.8	4	73.0	1
96	481,400	343,916	240,711	31.0	58.3	10.6	103,205	211,571	61.5	4	87.9	1
94	475,981	339,000	237,836	33.4	56.9	9.8	101,164	201,710	59.5	2	84.8	1
92	466,000	328,000	234,260	35.5	53.5	11.0	93,740	198,770	60.6	18	84.9	1
90	453,588	318,063	222,331	34.7	56.6	8.7	95,732	160,109	50.3	7	72.0	3
88	479,000	351,000	226,189	35.8	54.9	9.3	124,811	180,964	51.6	25	80.0	1
86	507,000	360,000	235,292	32.8	57.6	9.6	124,708	164,720	45.8	11	70.0	5
84	513,000	354,000	239,974	36.7	51.4	11.9	114,026	187,904	53.1	29	78.3	11
82	508,000	353,000	230,074	36.9	51.1	12.0	122,926	168,555	47.7	11	73.3	3
80	469,557	323,576	219,423	37.0	49.4	13.6	104,153	176,713	54.6	26	80.5	5

[a]Upper case indicates victory with a majority of votes cast; lower case, victory with a plurality of votes cast. Rankings are among all states.

[b]TAPV = turnout as a % of voting age population. Rankings are among all states.

[c]TAPR = turnout as a % of registration. Rankings are among all states.

Sources: Wyoming Democratic Party, Wyoming Republican Party, Federal Election Commission, U.S. Census Bureau, Wyoming Secretary of State Web site <soswy.state.wy.us>

PART VIII

NATIONAL POLITICAL STATISTICS

Presidential Election Results by State, 1996

State	Clinton	Dole	Other	Total	Rep. Margin	Win[a]	Clinton %	Dole %	Other %
AL	662,165	769,044	102,017	1,533,226	106,879	R	43.2	50.2	6.7
AK	80,380	122,746	37,860	240,986	42,366	R	33.4	50.9	15.7
AZ	653,288	622,073	126,430	1,401,791	−31,215	d	46.6	44.4	9.0
AR	475,171	325,416	83,675	884,262	−149,755	D	53.7	36.8	9.5
CA	5,119,835	3,828,380	1,070,400	10,018,615	−1,291,455	D	51.1	38.2	10.7
CO	671,152	691,848	147,704	1,510,704	20,696	r	44.4	45.8	9.8
CT	735,740	483,109	173,760	1,392,609	−252,631	D	52.8	34.7	12.5
DE	140,355	99,062	31,393	270,810	−41,293	D	51.8	36.6	11.6
DC	158,220	17,339	9,519	185,078	−140,881	D	85.5	9.4	5.1
FL	2,545,968	2,243,324	507,727	5,297,019	−302,644	d	48.1	42.4	9.6
GA	1,053,849	1,080,843	164,207	2,298,899	26,994	r	45.8	47.0	7.1
HI	205,012	113,943	41,165	360,120	−91,069	D	56.9	31.6	11.4
ID	165,443	256,595	69,673	491,711	91,152	R	33.7	52.2	14.2
IL	2,341,744	1,587,021	381,168	4,309,933	−754,723	D	54.3	36.8	8.8
IN	887,424	1,006,693	239,931	2,134,048	119,269	r	41.6	47.2	11.2
IA	620,258	492,644	119,933	1,232,835	−127,614	D	50.3	40.0	9.7
KS	387,659	583,245	102,370	1,073,274	195,586	R	36.1	54.3	9.5
KY	636,614	623,283	128,102	1,387,999	−13,331	d	45.9	44.9	9.2
LA	927,837	712,586	143,536	1,783,959	−215,251	D	52.0	39.9	8.1
ME	312,788	186,378	106,587	605,753	−126,410	D	51.6	30.8	17.6
MD	966,207	681,530	130,496	1,778,233	−284,677	D	54.3	38.3	7.3
MA	1,571,509	718,058	256,089	2,545,656	−853,451	D	61.7	28.2	10.1
MI	1,989,653	1,481,212	373,301	3,844,166	−508,441	D	51.8	38.5	9.7
MN	1,120,438	766,476	302,823	2,189,737	−353,962	D	51.2	35.0	13.8
MS	394,022	439,838	59,997	893,857	45,816	r	44.1	49.2	6.7
MO	1,025,935	890,016	241,518	2,157,469	−135,919	d	47.6	41.3	11.2
MT	167,922	179,652	59,509	407,083	11,730	r	41.3	44.1	14.6
NE	236,761	363,467	77,187	677,415	126,706	R	35.0	53.7	11.4
NV	203,974	199,244	61,061	464,279	−4,730	d	43.9	42.9	13.2
NH	246,166	196,486	53,945	496,597	−49,680	d	49.6	39.6	10.9
NJ	1,652,361	1,103,099	320,400	3,075,860	−549,262	D	53.7	35.9	10.4
NM	273,495	232,751	49,828	556,074	−40,744	d	49.2	41.9	9.0
NY	3,756,177	1,933,492	626,460	6,316,129	−1,822,685	D	59.5	30.6	9.9
NC	1,107,849	1,225,938	179,570	2,513,357	118,089	r	44.1	48.8	7.1
ND	106,905	125,050	34,456	266,411	18,145	r	40.1	46.9	12.9
OH	2,148,222	1,859,883	523,352	4,531,457	−288,339	d	47.4	41.0	11.6
OK	488,105	582,315	136,293	1,206,713	94,210	r	40.5	48.3	11.3
OR	649,641	538,152	187,638	1,375,431	−111,489	d	47.2	39.1	13.6
PA	2,215,819	1,801,169	484,319	4,501,307	−414,650	d	49.2	40.0	10.8
RI	233,050	104,683	52,514	390,247	−128,367	D	59.7	26.8	13.5
SC	506,283	573,458	71,948	1,151,689	67,175	r	44.0	49.8	6.3
SD	139,333	150,543	33,950	323,826	11,210	r	43.0	46.5	10.5
TN	909,146	863,530	121,239	1,893,915	−45,616	d	48.0	45.6	6.4
TX	2,459,683	2,736,167	410,687	5,606,537	276,484	r	43.9	48.8	7.3
UT	221,633	361,911	81,926	665,470	140,278	R	33.3	54.4	12.3

State	Clinton	Dole	Other	Total	Rep. Margin	Win[a]	Clinton %	Dole %	Other %
VT	137,894	80,352	39,643	257,889	−57,542	D	53.5	31.2	15.4
VA	1,091,060	1,138,350	187,232	2,416,642	47,290	r	45.2	47.1	7.8
WA	1,123,323	840,712	289,802	2,253,837	−282,611	d	49.8	37.3	12.9
WV	327,812	233,946	74,701	636,459	−93,866	D	51.5	36.8	11.7
WI	1,071,971	845,029	276,845	2,193,845	−226,942	d	48.9	38.5	12.6
WY	77,934	105,388	28,249	211,571	27,454	r	36.8	49.8	13.4
US	47,401,185	39,197,469	9,614,135	96,212,789	−8,203,716	d	49.3	40.7	10.0

[a]Upper case indicates victory with a majority of votes cast; lower case, a plurality of votes cast.
Source: Federal Election Commission Web site: www.fec.gov

Presidential Election Results by State, 2000

State	G.W. Bush	Gore	Other	Total	Rep. Margin	Win[a]	Bush %	Gore %	Other %
AL	941,173	692,611	32,488	1,666,272	248,562	R	56.5	41.6	1.9
AK	167,398	79,004	39,158	285,560	88,394	R	58.6	27.7	13.7
AZ	781,652	685,341	65,023	1,532,016	96,311	R	51.0	44.7	4.2
AR	472,940	422,768	26,073	921,781	50,172	R	51.3	45.9	2.8
CA	4,567,429	5,861,203	537,224	10,965,856	−1,293,774	D	41.7	53.4	4.9
CO	883,748	738,227	119,393	1,741,368	145,521	R	50.8	42.4	6.9
CT	561,094	816,015	82,416	1,459,525	−254,921	D	38.4	55.9	5.6
DE	137,288	180,068	10,173	327,529	−42,780	D	41.9	55.0	3.1
DC	18,073	171,923	11,898	201,894	−153,850	D	9.0	85.2	5.9
FL	2,912,790	2,912,253	138,067	5,963,110	537	r	48.8	48.8	2.3
GA	1,419,720	1,116,230	60,695	2,596,645	303,490	R	54.7	43.0	2.3
HI	137,845	205,286	24,820	367,951	−67,441	D	37.5	55.8	6.7
ID	336,937	138,637	26,041	501,615	198,300	R	67.2	27.6	5.2
IL	2,019,421	2,589,026	133,661	4,742,108	−569,605	D	42.6	54.6	2.8
IN	1,245,836	901,980	51,486	2,199,302	343,856	R	56.6	41.0	2.3
IA	634,373	638,517	42,673	1,315,563	−4,144	d	48.2	48.5	3.2
KS	622,332	399,276	50,608	1,072,216	223,056	R	58.0	37.2	4.7
KY	872,492	638,898	32,797	1,544,187	233,594	R	56.5	41.4	2.1
LA	927,871	792,344	45,441	1,765,656	135,527	R	52.6	44.9	2.6
ME	286,616	319,951	45,250	651,817	−33,335	d	44.0	49.1	6.9
MD	813,827	1,144,008	65,900	2,023,735	−330,181	D	40.2	56.5	3.3
MA	878,502	1,616,487	207,995	2,702,984	−737,985	D	32.5	59.8	7.7
MI	1,953,139	2,170,418	108,944	4,232,501	−217,279	D	46.1	51.3	2.6
MN	1,109,659	1,168,266	160,760	2,438,685	−58,607	d	45.5	47.9	6.6
MS	572,844	404,614	16,726	994,184	168,230	R	57.6	40.7	1.7
MO	1,189,924	1,111,138	58,830	2,359,892	78,786	R	50.4	47.1	2.5
MT	240,178	137,126	33,693	410,997	103,052	R	58.4	33.4	8.2
NE	433,862	231,780	31,377	697,019	202,082	R	62.2	33.3	4.5
NV	301,575	279,978	27,417	608,970	21,597	r	49.5	46.0	4.5
NH	273,559	266,348	29,164	569,071	7,211	r	48.1	46.8	5.1
NJ	1,284,173	1,788,850	114,203	3,187,226	−504,677	D	40.3	56.1	3.6
NM	286,417	286,783	25,405	598,605	−366	d	47.8	47.9	4.2
NY	2,403,374	4,107,697	310,928	6,821,999	−1,704,323	D	35.2	60.2	4.6
NC	1,631,163	1,257,692	26,135	2,914,990	373,471	R	56.0	43.1	0.9
ND	174,852	95,284	18,120	288,256	79,568	R	60.7	33.1	6.3
OH	2,350,363	2,183,628	168,007	4,701,998	166,735	r	50.0	46.4	3.6
OK	744,337	474,276	15,616	1,234,229	270,061	R	60.3	38.4	1.3
OR	713,577	720,342	100,049	1,533,968	−6,765	d	46.5	47.0	6.5
PA	2,281,127	2,485,967	146,025	4,913,119	−204,840	D	46.4	50.6	3.0
RI	130,555	249,508	28,720	408,783	−118,953	D	31.9	61.0	7.0
SC	786,892	566,039	31,322	1,384,253	220,853	R	56.8	40.9	2.3
SD	190,700	118,804	6,765	316,269	71,896	R	60.3	37.6	2.1
TN	1,061,949	981,720	32,512	2,076,181	80,229	R	51.1	47.3	1.6
TX	3,799,639	2,433,746	174,252	6,407,637	1,365,893	R	59.3	38.0	2.7
UT	515,096	203,053	52,605	770,754	312,043	R	66.8	26.3	6.8

State	G.W. Bush	Gore	Other	Total	Rep. Margin	Win[a]	Bush %	Gore %	Other %
VT	119,775	149,022	25,511	294,308	−29,247	D	40.7	50.6	8.7
VA	1,437,490	1,217,290	84,667	2,739,447	220,200	R	52.5	44.4	3.1
WA	1,108,864	1,247,652	130,917	2,487,433	−138,788	D	44.6	50.2	5.3
WV	336,475	295,497	16,152	648,124	40,978	R	51.9	45.6	2.5
WI	1,237,279	1,242,987	118,341	2,598,607	−5,708	d	47.6	47.8	4.6
WY	147,947	60,481	9,923	218,351	87,466	R	67.8	27.7	4.5
US	50,456,141	50,996,039	3,952,366	105,404,546	−539,898	d	47.9	48.4	3.7

[a]Upper case indicates victory with a majority of votes cast; lower case, a plurality of votes cast.
Source: Federal Election Commission Web site: www.fec.gov

House of Representatives Election Results, 1998

State/District	Democrat	Republican	Total Vote	Dem Vote	Rep Vote	Other Vote	Dem %	Rep %	Other %
Alabama									
1	unopposed	**H. L. Callahan**	113,564	0	112,872	692	0.0	99.4	0.6
2	Joe Fondren	**Terry Everett**	189,669	58,136	131,428	105	30.7	69.3	0.1
3	Joe Turnham	**Bob Riley**	175,217	73,357	101,731	129	41.9	58.1	0.1
4	Don Bevill	**Robert Aderholt**	188,476	82,065	106,297	114	43.5	56.4	0.1
5	**Bud Cramer**	Gil Aust	193,490	134,819	58,536	135	69.7	30.3	0.1
6	D. W. Smalley	**Spencer Bachus**	215,582	60,657	154,761	164	28.1	71.8	0.1
7	**Earl Hilliard**	unopposed	139,181	136,431	–	2,750	98.0	–	2.0
Alaska									
	Jim Duncan	**Don Young**	223,300	77,232	139,676	6,392	34.6	62.6	2.9
Arizona									
1	David Mendoza	**Matt Salmon**	152,948	54,108	98,840	0	35.4	64.6	0.0
2	**Ed Pastor**	Ed Barron	84,363	57,178	23,628	3,557	67.8	28.0	4.2
3	Stuart Marc Starky	**Bob Stump**	204,623	66,979	137,618	26	32.7	67.3	0.0
4	Eric Ehst	**John Shadegg**	158,822	49,538	102,722	6,562	31.2	64.7	4.1
5	Tom Volgy	**Jim Kolbe**	201,473	91,030	103,952	6,491	45.2	51.6	3.2
6	Steve Owens	**J. D. Hayworth**	201,537	88,001	106,891	6,645	43.7	53.0	3.3
Arkansas									
1	**Marion Berry**	unopposed	–	–	–	–	–	–	–
2	**Vic Snyder**	Phil Wyrick	173,071	100,334	72,737	0	58.0	42.0	0.0
3	unopposed	**Asa Hutchinson**	191,697	–	154,780	36,917	–	80.7	19.3
4	Judy Smith	**Jay Dickey**	160,540	68,194	92,346	0	42.5	57.5	0.0
California									
1	**Mike Thompson**	Mark Luce	196,772	121,713	64,622	10,437	61.9	32.8	5.3
2	Rob Braden	**Wally Herger**	205,367	70,837	128,372	6,158	34.5	62.5	3.0
3	Sandie Dunn	**Doug Ose**	192,006	86,471	100,621	4,914	45.0	52.4	2.6
4	David Shapiro	**John Dolittle**	248,224	85,394	155,306	7,524	34.4	62.6	3.0
5	**Robert Matsui**	Robert Dinsmore	181,838	130,715	47,307	3,816	71.9	26.0	2.1
6	**Lynn Woolsey**	Ken McAuliffe	232,981	158,446	69,295	5,240	68.0	29.7	2.2
7	**George Miller**	Norman Reece	164,132	125,842	38,290	0	76.7	23.3	0.0
8	**Nancy Pelosi**	David Martz	172,462	148,027	20,781	3,654	85.8	12.0	2.1
9	**Barbara Lee**	Clay Sanders	169,895	140,722	22,431	6,742	82.8	13.2	4.0

No.	Winner	Challenger	Total	(D) votes	(R) votes	Other	(D) %	(R) %	Other %
10	**Ellen Tauscher**	Charles Ball	237,809	127,134	103,299	7,376	53.5	43.4	3.1
11	**Richard Pombo**	Robert Figueroa	155,449	56,345	95,496	3,608	36.2	61.4	2.3
12	**Tom Lantos**	Robert Evans Jr.	173,212	128,135	36,562	8,515	74.0	21.1	4.9
13	**Fortney Stark**	James R. Goetz	142,787	101,671	38,050	3,066	71.2	26.6	2.1
14	**Ann Eshoo**	John Haugen	188,910	129,663	53,719	5,528	68.6	28.4	2.9
15	**Tom Campbell**	Dick Lane	184,786	70,059	111,876	2,851	37.9	60.5	1.5
16	**Zoe Lofgren**	Horace Thayn	117,414	85,503	27,494	4,417	72.8	23.4	3.8
17	**Sam Farr**	Bill McCampbell	160,690	103,719	52,470	4,501	64.5	32.7	2.8
18	**Gary Condit**	unopposed	136,931	118,842	—	18,089	86.8	—	13.2
19	**George Radanovich**	unopposed	165,149	—	131,105	34,044	—	79.4	20.6
20	**Cal Dooley**	Cliff Unruh	99,782	60,599	39,183	—	60.7	39.3	—
21	**Bill Thomas**	unopposed	146,983	—	115,989	30,994	—	78.9	21.1
22	**Lois Capps**	Tom Bordonaro Jr.	202,190	111,388	86,921	3,881	55.1	43.0	1.9
23	**Elton Gallegly**	Daniel Gonzalez	160,430	64,068	96,362	0	39.9	60.1	0.0
24	**Brad Sherman**	Randy Hoffman	180,580	103,491	69,501	7,588	57.3	38.5	4.2
25	**Howard McKeon**	unopposed	152,682	—	114,013	38,669	—	74.7	25.3
26	**Howard Berman**	unopposed	83,662	69,000	—	14,662	82.5	—	17.5
27	**James Rogan**	Barry Gordon	159,066	73,875	80,702	4,489	46.4	50.7	2.8
28	**David Dreier**	Janice Nelson	157,200	61,721	90,607	4,872	39.3	57.6	3.1
29	**Henry Waxman**	Mike Gottlieb	178,094	131,561	40,282	6,251	73.9	22.6	3.5
30	**Xavier Becerra**	Patricia Parker	71,671	58,230	13,441	0	81.2	18.8	0.0
31	**Matthew Martinez**	Frank Moreno	87,360	61,173	19,786	6,401	70.0	22.6	7.3
32	**Julian Dixon**	Laurence Ardito	129,492	112,253	14,622	2,617	86.7	11.3	2.0
33	**Lucille Roybal-Allard**	Wayne Miller	49,674	43,310	6,364	0	87.2	12.8	0.0
34	**G. F. Napolitano**	Ed Perez	113,075	76,471	32,321	4,283	67.6	28.6	3.8
35	**Maxine Waters**	unopposed	88,145	78,732	—	9,413	89.3	—	10.7
36	**Steven Kuykendall**	Janice Hahn	181,706	84,624	88,843	8,239	46.6	48.9	4.5
37	**J. Millender-McDonald**	Saul Lankster	82,327	70,026	12,301	0	85.1	14.9	0.0
38	**Steve Horn**	Peter Mathews	134,875	59,767	71,386	3,722	44.3	52.9	2.8
39	**Ed Royce**	A. R. Groom	155,465	52,815	97,366	5,284	34.0	62.6	3.4
40	**Jerry Lewis**	Robert Conaway	150,125	47,897	97,406	4,822	31.9	64.9	3.2
41	**Gary Miller**	Eileen Ansari	128,414	52,264	68,310	7,840	40.7	53.2	6.1
42	**George Brown Jr.**	Elia Pirozzi	112,520	62,207	45,328	4,985	55.3	40.3	4.4
43	**Ken Calvert**	Mike Rayburn	149,071	56,373	83,012	9,686	37.8	55.7	6.5
44	**Mary Bono**	Ralph Waite	161,528	57,697	97,013	6,818	35.7	60.1	4.2
45	**Dana Rohrabacher**	Patricia Neal	160,770	60,022	94,296	6,452	37.3	58.7	4.0
46	**Loretta Sanchez**	R. K. Dornan	85,002	47,964	33,388	3,650	56.4	39.3	4.3

(continued)

House of Representatives Election Results, 1998 (continued)

State/District	Democrat	Republican	Total Vote	Dem Vote	Rep Vote	Other Vote	Dem %	Rep %	Other %
California (cont.)									
47	Christina Avalos	**Christopher Cox**	196,316	57,938	132,711	5,667	29.5	67.6	2.9
48	unopposed	**Ron Packard**	180,719	–	138,948	41,771	–	76.9	23.1
49	Christine Kehoe	**Brian Bilbray**	185,519	86,400	90,516	8,603	46.6	48.8	4.6
50	**Bob Filner**	unopposed	77,991	77,354	–	637	99.2	–	0.8
51	Dan Kripke	**Randy Cunningham**	206,878	71,706	126,229	8,943	34.7	61.0	4.3
52	unopposed	**Duncan Hunter**	153,568	–	116,251	37,317	–	75.7	24.3
Colorado									
1	**Diana DeGette**	Nancy McClanahan	174,305	116,628	52,452	5,225	66.9	30.1	3.0
2	**Mark Udall**	Bob Greenlee	228,442	113,946	108,385	6,111	49.9	47.4	2.7
3	Robert Kelley	**Scott McInnis**	236,653	74,479	156,501	5,673	31.5	66.1	2.4
4	Susan Kirkpatrick	**Bob Schaffer**	221,291	89,973	131,318	0	40.7	59.3	0.0
5	Ken Alford	**Joel Hefley**	214,270	55,609	155,790	2,871	26.0	72.7	1.3
6	Henry Strauss	**Tom Tancredo**	199,188	82,662	111,374	5,152	41.5	55.9	2.6
Connecticut									
1	**John Larson**	Kevin O'Connor	168,264	97,681	69,668	915	58.1	41.4	0.5
2	**Sam Gejdenson**	Gary Koval	163,202	99,567	57,860	5,775	61.0	35.5	3.5
3	**Rosa DeLauro**	Martin Reust	153,851	109,726	42,090	2,035	71.3	27.4	1.3
4	Jonathan Kantrowitz	**Christopher Shays**	137,204	40,988	94,767	1,449	29.9	69.1	1.1
5	**Jim Maloney**	Mark Nielsen	157,157	78,394	76,051	2,712	49.9	48.4	1.7
6	Charlotte Koskoff	Nancy Johnson	174,781	69,201	101,630	3,950	39.6	58.1	2.3
Delaware	Dennis Williams	**Michael Castle**	180,527	57,446	119,811	3,270	31.8	66.4	1.8
District of Columbia	**E. H. Norton**	E. H. Wolterbeek	136,359	122,228	8,610	5,521	89.6	6.3	4.0
Florida[a]									
1	unopposed	**Joe Scarborouch**	141,188	–	140,525	663	–	99.5	0.5
2	**Allen Boyd**	unopposed	145,420	138,440	–	6,980	95.2	–	4.8
3	**Corrine Brown**	Bill Randall	120,151	66,621	53,530	0	55.4	44.6	0.0
4	unopposed	**Tillie Fowler**	–	–	–	–	–	–	–
5	**Karen Thurman**	unopposed	199,152	132,005	–	67,147	66.3	–	33.7
6	unopposed	**Clifford Stearns**	–	–	–	–	–	–	–

	Candidate	Candidate	Total	Vote	Vote	Other	%	%	%
7	unopposed	**John Mica**	—	—	—	—	—	—	—
8	Al Krulick	**Bill McCollum**	158,575	54,245	104,298	32	34.2	65.8	0.0
9	unopposed	**Michael Bilirakis**	—	—	—	—	—	—	—
10	unopposed	**C. W. Bill Young**	—	—	—	—	—	—	—
11	**Jim Davis**	Joe Chillura	131,438	85,262	46,176	0	64.9	35.1	0.0
12	unopposed	**Charles Canady**	—	—	—	—	—	—	—
13	unopposed	**Dan Miller**	—	—	—	—	—	—	—
14	unopposed	**Porter Goss**	—	—	—	—	—	—	—
15	David Golding	**Dave Weldon**	204,932	75,654	129,278	0	36.9	63.1	0.0
16	unopposed	**Mark Foley**	—	—	—	—	—	—	—
17	**Carrie Meek**	unopposed	—	—	—	—	—	—	—
18	unopposed	**Ileana Ros-Lehtinen**	—	—	—	—	—	—	—
19	**Robert Wexler**	unopposed	—	—	—	—	—	—	—
20	**Peter Deutsch**	unopposed	—	—	—	—	—	—	—
21	Patrick Cusack	**L. Diaz-Balart**	112,396	28,378	84,018	0	25.2	74.8	0.0
22	unopposed	**Clay Shaw**	—	—	—	—	—	—	—
23	**Alcee Hastings**	unopposed	—	—	—	—	—	—	—
Georgia									
1	unopposed	**Jack Kingston**	92,229	—	92,229	0	—	10.0	0.0
2	**S. D. Bishop Jr.**	J. F. McCormick Jr.	137,258	77,953	59,305	0	56.8	43.2	0.0
3	unopposed	**Michael Collins**	123,064	—	123,064	0	—	10.0	0.0
4	**Cynthia McKinney**	Sunny Warren	164,768	100,622	64,146	0	61.1	38.9	0.0
5	**John Lewis**	John J. Lewis Sr.	139,054	109,177	29,877	0	78.5	21.5	0.0
6	Gary Pelphrey	**Newt Gingrich**	233,332	68,366	164,966	0	29.3	70.7	0.0
7	James Williams	**Bob Barr**	155,275	69,293	85,982	0	44.6	55.4	0.0
8	Ronald Cain	**Saxby Chambliss**	141,072	53,079	87,993	0	37.6	62.4	0.0
9	unopposed	**Nathan Deal**	122,713	—	122,713	0	—	10.0	0.0
10	M. D. Freeman	**Charlie Norwood**	148,531	60,004	88,527	0	40.4	59.6	0.0
11	Vincent Littman	**John Linder**	174,419	53,510	120,909	0	30.7	69.3	0.0
Hawaii									
1	**Neil Abercrombie**	Gene Ward	189,571	116,693	68,905	3,973	61.6	36.3	2.1
2	**Patsy Mink**	Carol Douglass	207,871	144,254	50,423	13,194	69.4	24.3	6.3
Idaho									
1	Dan Williams	**Helen Chenoweth**	204,884	91,653	113,231	0	44.7	55.3	0.0
2	Richard Stallings	**Mike Simpson**	173,945	77,736	91,337	4,872	44.7	52.5	2.8

(continued)

House of Representatives Election Results, 1998 *(continued)*

State/District	Democrat	Republican	Total Vote	Dem Vote	Rep Vote	Other Vote	Dem %	Rep %	Other %
Illinois									
1	**Bobby Rush**	Marlene Ahimaz	174,365	151,890	18,429	4,046	87.1	10.6	2.3
2	**Jesse Jackson Jr.**	Robert Gordon III	166,668	148,985	16,075	1,608	89.4	9.6	1.0
3	**William Lipinski**	Robert Marshall	159,899	115,887	44,012	0	72.5	27.5	0.0
4	**Luis Gutierrez**	John Birch	66,356	54,244	10,529	1,583	81.7	15.9	2.4
5	**Rod Blagojevich**	Alan Spitz	129,425	95,738	33,687	0	74.0	26.0	0.0
6	Thomas Cramer	**Henry Hyde**	165,708	49,906	111,603	4,199	30.1	67.3	2.5
7	**Danny Davis**	unopposed	140,968	130,984	–	9,984	92.9	–	7.1
8	Mike Rothman	**Philip Crane**	151,856	47,614	104,242	0	31.4	68.6	0.0
9	**Janice Schakowsky**	Herbert Sohn	144,610	107,878	33,448	3,284	74.6	23.1	2.3
10	unopposed	**John Porter**	138,429	–	138,429	0	–	100.0	0.0
11	Gary Mueller	Gerald Weller	171,055	70,458	100,597	0	41.2	58.8	0.0
12	**Jerry Costello**	William Price	165,014	99,605	65,409	0	60.4	39.6	0.0
13	Susan Hynes	**Judy Biggert**	199,767	77,878	121,889	0	39.0	61.0	0.0
14	Robert Cozzi Jr.	**Dennis Hastert**	168,148	50,844	117,304	0	30.2	69.8	0.0
15	Laurel Prussing	**Thomas Ewing**	169,309	65,054	104,255	0	38.4	61.6	0.0
16	unopposed	**Donald Manzullo**	143,686	–	143,686	0	–	100.0	0.0
17	**Lane Evans**	Mark Baker	194,200	100,128	94,072	0	51.6	48.4	0.0
18	unopposed	**Ray LaHood**	158,177	–	158,175	2	–	100.0	0.0
19	**David Phelps**	Brent Winters	210,044	122,430	87,614	0	58.3	41.7	0.0
20	Rick Verticchio	**John Shimkus**	197,578	76,475	121,103	0	38.7	61.3	0.0
Indiana									
1	**Peter Visclosky**	Michael Petyo	127,754	92,634	33,503	1,617	72.5	26.2	1.3
2	Sherman Boles	**David McIntosh**	164,296	62,452	99,608	2,236	38.0	60.6	1.4
3	**Tim Roemer**	Daniel Holtz	145,666	84,625	61,041	0	58.1	41.9	0.0
4	Mark Wehrle	**Mark Souder**	147,957	54,286	93,671	0	36.7	63.3	0.0
5	David Steele III	**Steve Buyer**	162,388	58,504	101,567	2,317	36.0	62.5	1.4
6	Bob Kern	**Dan Burton**	187,827	31,472	135,250	21,105	16.8	72.0	11.2
7	Samuel Hillenburg	**Edward Pease**	159,314	44,823	109,712	4,779	28.1	68.9	3.0
8	Gail Riecken	**John Hostettler**	178,057	81,871	92,785	3,401	46.0	52.1	1.9
9	**Baron Hill**	Jean Leising	183,176	92,973	87,797	2,406	50.8	47.9	1.3
10	**Julia Carson**	Gary Hofmeister	119,436	69,682	47,017	2,737	58.3	39.4	2.3

State / District	Democrat	Republican	Total vote	Dem. vote	Rep. vote	Other vote	Dem. %	Rep. %	Other %
Iowa									
1	Bob Rush	**Jim Leach**	188,208	79,529	106,419	2,260	42.3	56.5	1.2
2	Rob Tully	**Jim Nussle**	189,574	83,405	104,613	1,556	44.0	55.2	0.8
3	**Leonard Boswell**	Larry McKibben	189,752	107,947	78,063	3,742	56.9	41.1	2.0
4	Jon Dvorak	**Greg Ganske**	199,396	67,550	129,942	1,904	33.9	65.2	1.0
5	unopposed	**Tom Latham**	133,771	–	132,730	1,041	–	99.2	0.8
Kansas									
1	Jim Phillips	**Jerry Moran**	189,393	36,618	152,775	0	19.3	80.7	0.0
2	Jim Clark	**Jim Ryun**	178,048	69,521	108,527	0	39.0	61.0	0.0
3	**Dennis Moore**	Vince Snowbarger	197,314	103,376	93,938	0	52.4	47.6	0.0
4	Jim Lawing	**Todd Tiahrt**	162,693	62,737	94,785	5,171	38.6	58.3	3.2
Kentucky									
1	Tom Barlow	**Ed Whitfield**	172,710	77,402	95,308	0	44.8	55.2	0.0
2	Bob Evans	**Ron Lewis**	177,966	62,848	113,285	1,833	35.3	63.7	1.0
3	Chris Gorman	**Anne Northup**	195,436	92,865	100,690	1,881	47.5	51.5	1.0
4	**Ken Lucas**	Gex Williams	175,032	93,485	81,547	0	53.4	46.6	0.0
5	S. J. Bailey-Bamer	**Harold Rogers**	181,800	39,585	142,215	0	21.8	78.2	0.0
6	Ernesto Scorsone	**Ernie Fletcher**	195,918	90,033	104,046	1,839	46.0	53.1	0.9
Louisiana[b]									
1	unopposed	**Robert Livingston**	–	–	–	–	–	–	–
2	**William Jefferson**	unopposed	118,949	102,247	–	16,702	86.0	–	14.0
3	unopposed	**Billy Tauzin**	–	–	–	–	–	–	–
4	unopposed	**Jim McCrery**	–	–	–	–	–	–	–
5	unopposed	**John Cooksey**	–	–	–	–	–	–	–
6	Marjorie McKeithen	**Richard Baker**	191,245	94,201	97,044	0	49.3	50.7	0.0
7	**Chris John**	unopposed	–	–	–	–	–	–	–
Maine									
1	**Thomas Allen**	Ross Connelly	222,677	134,335	79,160	9,182	60.3	35.5	4.1
2	**John Baldacci**	Jonathan Reisman	191,876	146,202	45,674	0	76.2	23.8	0.0
Maryland									
1	Irving Pinder	**Wayne Gilchrest**	196,221	60,450	135,771	0	30.8	69.2	0.0
2	Kenneth Bosley	**Robert Ehrlich**	210,206	64,474	145,711	21	30.7	69.3	0.0
3	**Benjamin Cardin**	Colin Harby	177,168	137,501	39,667	0	77.6	22.4	0.0

(continued)

Header: House of Representatives Election Results, 1998 (continued)

State/District	Democrat	Republican	Total Vote	Dem Vote	Rep Vote	Other Vote	Dem %	Rep %	Other %
Maryland *(cont.)*									
4	**Albert Wynn**	John Kimble	150,657	129,139	21,518	0	85.7	14.3	0.0
5	**Steny Hoyer**	Robert Ostrom	193,968	126,792	67,176	0	65.4	34.6	0.0
6	Timothy McCown	**Roscoe Bartlett**	201,530	73,728	127,802	0	36.6	63.4	0.0
7	**Elijah Cummings**	Kenneth Kondner	131,447	112,699	18,742	6	85.7	14.3	0.0
8	Ralph Neas	**Constance Morella**	220,748	87,497	133,145	106	39.6	60.3	0.0
Massachusetts									
1	**John Olver**	Gregory Morgan	169,976	121,863	48,055	58	71.7	28.3	0.0
2	**Richard Neal**	unopposed	131,933	130,550	–	1,383	99.0	–	1.0
3	**James McGovern**	Matthew Amorello	190,878	108,613	79,174	3,091	56.9	41.5	1.6
4	**Barney Frank**	unopposed	150,720	148,340	–	2,380	98.4	–	1.6
5	**Martin Meehan**	David Coleman	180,230	127,418	52,725	87	70.7	29.3	0.0
6	**John Tierney**	Peter Torkildsen	214,706	117,132	90,986	6,588	54.6	42.4	3.1
7	**Edward Markey**	Patricia Long	194,305	137,178	56,977	150	70.6	29.3	0.1
8	**Michael Capuano**	Philip Hyde III	121,887	99,603	14,125	8,159	81.7	11.6	6.7
9	**John Moakley**	unopposed	151,555	150,667	–	888	99.4	–	0.6
10	**William Delahunt**	Eric Bleicken	235,563	164,917	70,466	180	70.0	29.9	0.1
Michigan									
1	**Bart Stupak**	Michelle McManus	221,796	130,129	87,630	4,037	58.7	39.5	1.8
2	Bob Schrauger	**Peter Hoekstra**	213,622	63,573	146,854	3,195	29.8	68.7	1.5
3	John Ferguson	**Vernon Ehlers**	200,251	49,489	146,364	4,398	24.7	73.1	2.2
4	unopposed	**Dave Camp**	170,109	–	155,343	14,766	–	91.3	8.7
5	**James Barcia**	Donald Brewster	189,971	135,254	51,442	3,275	71.2	27.1	1.7
6	Clarence Annen	**Fred Upton**	161,627	45,358	113,292	2,977	28.1	70.1	1.8
7	Jim Berryman	**Nick Smith**	182,127	72,998	104,656	4,473	40.1	57.5	2.5
8	**Debbie Stabenow**	Susan Munsell	218,040	125,169	84,254	8,617	57.4	38.6	4.0
9	**Dale Kildee**	Tom McMillin	188,525	105,457	79,062	4,006	55.9	41.9	2.1
10	**David Bonior**	Brian Palmer	207,524	108,770	94,027	4,727	52.4	45.3	2.3
11	Travis Reeds	**Joe Knollenberg**	225,804	76,107	144,264	5,433	33.7	63.9	2.4
12	**Sander Levin**	Leslie Touma	189,428	105,824	79,619	3,985	55.9	42.0	2.1
13	**Lynn Rivers**	Tom Hickey	171,887	99,935	68,328	3,624	58.1	39.8	2.1
14	**John Conyers Jr.**	Vendella Collins	145,305	126,321	16,140	2,844	86.9	11.1	2.0
15	**C. C. Kilpatrick**	C. D. Boyd-Fields	124,860	108,582	12,887	3,391	87.0	10.3	2.7
16	**John Dingell**	William Morse	174,357	116,145	54,121	4,091	66.6	31.0	2.3

State	District	Democrat	Republican	Total	Dem Votes	Rep Votes	Other Votes	Dem %	Rep %	Other %
Minnesota	1	Tracy Beckman	**Gil Gutknecht**	239,903	108,420	131,233	250	45.2	54.7	0.1
	2	**David Minge**	Craig Duehring	261,127	148,933	99,490	12,704	57.0	38.1	4.9
	3	Stan Leino	**Jim Ramstad**	283,309	66,505	203,731	13,073	23.5	71.9	4.6
	4	**Bruce Vento**	Dennis Newinski	239,746	128,726	95,388	15,632	53.7	39.8	6.5
	5	**Martin Sabo**	Frank Taylor	217,612	145,535	60,035	12,042	66.9	27.6	5.5
	6	**Bill Luther**	John Kline	297,701	148,728	136,866	12,107	50.0	46.0	4.1
	7	**Collin Peterson**	Aleta Edin	236,942	169,907	66,562	473	71.7	28.1	0.2
	8	**James Oberstar**	Jerry Shuster	263,263	173,734	69,667	19,862	66.0	26.5	7.5
Mississippi	1	Rex Weathers	**Roger Wicker**	99,333	30,438	66,738	2,157	30.6	67.2	2.2
	2	**Bennie Thompson**	unopposed	113,040	80,507	—	32,533	71.2	—	28.8
	3	unopposed	**Charles Pickering Jr.**	100,250	—	84,785	15,465	—	84.6	15.4
	4	**Ronnie Shows**	Delbert Hosemann	137,199	73,252	61,551	2,396	53.4	44.9	1.7
	5	**Gene Taylor**	Randy McDonnell	101,095	78,661	19,341	3,093	77.8	19.1	3.1
Missouri	1	**William Clay Sr.**	Richmond Soluade Sr.	125,051	90,840	30,635	3,576	72.6	24.5	2.9
	2	John Ross	**James Talent**	203,259	57,565	142,313	3,381	28.3	70.0	1.7
	3	**Richard Gephardt**	William Federer	176,099	98,287	74,005	3,807	55.8	42.0	2.2
	4	**Ike Skelton**	Cecilia Noland	187,616	133,173	51,005	3,438	71.0	27.2	1.8
	5	**Karen McCarthy**	Penny Bennett	153,685	101,313	47,582	4,790	65.9	31.0	3.1
	6	**Pat Danner**	Jeff Bailey	192,777	136,774	51,679	4,324	70.9	26.8	2.2
	7	Marc Perkel	**Roy Blunt**	178,801	43,416	129,746	5,639	24.3	72.6	3.2
	8	Tony Heckemeyer	**JoAnn Emerson**	166,524	59,426	104,271	2,827	35.7	62.6	1.7
	9	Linda Vogt	**Kenny Hulshof**	188,305	66,861	117,196	4,248	35.5	62.2	2.3
Montana		Dusty Deschamps	**Rick Hill**	331,551	147,073	175,748	8,730	44.4	53.0	2.6
Nebraska	1	Don Eret	**Doug Bereuter**	185,227	48,826	136,058	343	26.4	73.5	0.2
	2	Michael Scott	**Lee Terry**	163,003	55,722	106,782	499	34.2	65.5	0.3
	3	unopposed	**Bill Barrett**	177,729	—	149,896	27,833	—	84.3	15.7
Nevada	1	**Shelley Berkley**	Don Chairez	161,082	79,315	73,540	8,227	49.2	45.7	5.1
	2	unopposed	**Jim Gibbons**	248,763	—	201,623	47,140	—	81.1	18.9

(continued)

House of Representatives Election Results, 1998 *(continued)*

State/District	Democrat	Republican	Total Vote	Dem Vote	Rep Vote	Other Vote	Dem %	Rep %	Other %
New Hampshire									
1	Peter Flood	**John Sununu**	156,369	51,783	104,430	156	33.1	66.8	0.1
2	Mary Rauh	**Charles Bass**	161,376	72,217	85,740	3,419	44.8	53.1	2.1
New Jersey									
1	**Robert Andrews**	Ronald Richards	123,342	90,279	27,855	5,208	73.2	22.6	4.2
2	Derek Hunsberger	**Frank LoBiondo**	141,514	43,563	93,248	4,703	30.8	65.9	3.3
3	Steven Polansky	**Jim Saxton**	157,239	55,248	97,508	4,483	35.1	62.0	2.9
4	Larry Schneider	**Christopher Smith**	149,577	52,281	92,991	4,305	35.0	62.2	2.9
5	Mike Schneider	**Marge Roukema**	166,818	55,487	106,304	5,027	33.3	63.7	3.0
6	**Frank Pallone**	Michael Ferguson	137,012	78,102	55,180	3,730	57.0	40.3	2.7
7	Maryanne Connelly	**Bob Franks**	148,042	65,776	77,751	4,515	44.4	52.5	3.0
8	**Bill Pascrell**	Matthew Kirnan	130,588	81,068	46,289	3,231	62.1	35.4	2.5
9	**Steven Rothman**	Steve Lonegan	141,459	91,330	47,817	2,312	64.6	33.8	1.6
10	**Donald Payne**	W. S. Wnuck	98,494	82,244	10,678	5,572	83.5	10.8	5.7
11	John Scollo	**R. P. Frelinghuysen**	148,971	44,160	100,910	3,901	29.6	67.7	2.6
12	**Rush Holt**	Michael Pappas	184,610	92,528	87,221	4,861	50.1	47.2	2.6
13	**Robert Menendez**	Theresa deLeon	87,823	70,308	14,615	2,900	80.1	16.6	3.3
New Mexico									
1	Phillip Maloof	**Heather Wilson**	179,168	75,040	86,784	17,344	41.9	48.4	9.7
2	Shirley Baca	**Joe Skeen**	146,873	61,796	85,077	0	42.1	57.9	0.0
3	**Tom Udall**	Bill Redmond	171,649	91,248	74,266	6,135	53.2	43.3	3.6
New York									
1	William Holst	**Michael Forbes**	155,090	55,630	99,460	0	35.9	64.1	0.0
2	John Bace	**Rick Lazio**	128,438	37,949	85,089	5,400	29.5	66.2	4.2
3	Kevin Langberg	**Peter King**	182,383	63,628	117,258	1,497	34.9	64.3	0.8
4	**Carolyn McCarthy**	Gregory Becker	171,583	90,256	79,984	1,343	52.6	46.6	0.8
5	**Gary Ackerman**	David Pinzon	149,862	97,404	49,586	2,872	65.0	33.1	1.9
6	**Gregory Meeks**	unopposed	76,122	76,122	–	0	100.0	–	0.0
7	**Joseph Crowley**	James Dillon	73,780	50,924	18,896	3,960	69.0	25.6	5.4
8	**Jerrold Nadler**	Theodore Howard	131,331	112,948	18,383	0	86.0	14.0	0.0
9	**Anthony Weiner**	Louis Telano	104,522	69,439	24,486	10,597	66.4	23.4	10.1

District	Democratic candidate	Republican candidate	Total vote	Dem. vote	Rep. vote	Other vote	Dem. %	Rep. %	Other %
10	**Edolphus Towns**	Ernestine Brown	90,501	83,528	5,577	1,396	92.3	6.2	1.5
11	**Major Owens**	David Greene	84,201	75,773	7,284	1,144	90.0	8.7	1.4
12	**Nydia Velazquez**	Rosemarie Markgraf	63,706	53,269	7,405	3,032	83.6	11.6	4.8
13	Eugene Prisco	**Vito Fossella**	117,550	40,167	76,138	1,245	34.2	64.8	1.1
14	**Carolyn Maloney**	Stephanie Kupferman	143,530	111,072	32,458	0	77.4	22.6	0.0
15	**Charles Rangel**	David Cunningham	97,139	90,424	5,633	1,082	93.1	5.8	1.1
16	**Jose Serrano**	Thomas Bayley	70,580	67,367	2,457	756	95.4	3.5	1.1
17	**Eliot Engel**	Peter Fiumefreddo	91,984	80,947	11,037	0	88.0	12.0	0.0
18	**Nita Lowey**	unopposed	110,702	91,623	—	19,079	82.8	—	17.2
19	Dick Collins	**Sue Kelly**	167,832	56,378	104,467	6,987	33.6	62.2	4.2
20	Paul Feiner	**Benjamin Gilman**	168,904	65,589	98,546	4,769	38.8	58.3	2.8
21	**Michael McNulty**	Lauren Ayers	197,570	146,639	50,931	0	74.2	25.8	0.0
22	Jean Bordewich	**John Sweeney**	193,266	81,296	106,919	5,051	42.1	55.3	2.6
23	unopposed	**Sherwood Boehlert**	137,735	—	111,242	26,493	—	80.8	19.2
24	Neil Tallon	**John McHugh**	147,693	31,011	116,682	0	21.0	79.0	0.0
25	Yvonne Rothenberg	**James Walsh**	174,665	53,461	121,204	0	30.6	69.4	0.0
26	**Maurice Hinchey**	Wm. H. Bud Walker	175,140	108,204	54,776	12,160	61.8	31.3	6.9
27	Bill Cook	**Thomas Reynolds**	178,020	75,978	102,042	0	42.7	57.3	0.0
28	**Louise Slaughter**	Richard Kaplan	183,458	118,856	56,443	8,159	64.8	30.8	4.4
29	**John La Face**	Chris Collins	170,529	97,235	69,481	3,813	57.0	40.7	2.2
30	Crystal Peoples	**Jack Quinn**	171,292	55,199	116,093	0	32.2	67.8	0.0
31	Caleb Rossiter	**Amo Houghton**	158,252	40,091	107,615	10,546	25.3	68.0	6.7

North Carolina

District	Democratic candidate	Republican candidate	Total vote	Dem. vote	Rep. vote	Other vote	Dem. %	Rep. %	Other %
1	**Eva Clayton**	Ted Tyler	136,747	85,125	50,578	1,044	62.2	37.0	0.8
2	**Bob Etheridge**	Dan Page	175,194	100,550	72,997	1,647	57.4	41.7	0.9
3	Jon Williams	**Walter Jones**	134,912	50,041	83,529	1,342	37.1	61.9	1.0
4	**David Price**	Tom Roberg	224,910	129,157	93,469	2,284	57.4	41.6	1.0
5	Mike Robinson	**Richard Burr**	176,291	55,806	119,103	1,382	31.7	67.6	0.8
6	unopposed	**Howard Coble**	127,194	—	112,740	14,454	—	88.6	11.4
7	**Mike McIntyre**	unopposed	136,290	124,366	—	11,924	91.3	—	8.7
8	Mike Taylor	**Robert Hayes**	133,124	64,127	67,505	1,492	48.2	50.7	1.1
9	Rory Blake	**Sue Myrick**	174,082	51,345	120,570	2,167	29.5	69.3	1.2
10	unopposed	**T. Cass Ballenger**	138,511	—	118,541	19,970	—	85.6	14.4
11	David Young	**Charles Taylor**	199,423	84,256	112,908	2,259	42.2	56.6	1.1
12	**Mel Watt**	John Keadle	147,088	82,305	62,070	2,713	56.0	42.2	1.8

(continued)

House of Representatives Election Results, 1998 (continued)

State/District	Democrat	Republican	Total Vote	Dem Vote	Rep Vote	Other Vote	Dem %	Rep %	Other %
North Dakota	Earl Pomeroy	Kevin Cramer	212,888	119,668	87,511	5,709	56.2	41.1	2.7
Ohio									
1	Roxanne Qualls	Steve Chabot	174,424	82,003	92,421	0	47.0	53.0	0.0
2	Charles Sanders	Rob Portman	203,637	49,293	154,344	0	24.2	75.8	0.0
3	Tony Hall	John Shondel	164,742	114,198	50,544	0	69.3	30.7	0.0
4	Paul McClain	Michael Oxley	175,540	63,529	112,011	0	36.2	63.8	0.0
5	Susan Darrow	Paul Gillmor	185,905	61,926	123,979	0	33.3	66.7	0.0
6	Ted Strickland	Nancy Hollister	180,563	102,852	77,711	0	57.0	43.0	0.0
7	Donald Minor Jr.	Dave Hobson	179,697	49,780	120,765	9,152	27.7	67.2	5.1
8	John Griffin	John Boehner	180,891	52,912	127,979	0	29.3	70.7	0.0
9	Marcy Kaptur	Edward Emery	161,105	130,793	30,312	0	81.2	18.8	0.0
10	Dennis Kucinich	Joe Slovenec	165,567	110,552	55,015	0	66.8	33.2	0.0
11	Stephanie Jones	James Hereford	143,295	115,226	18,592	9,477	80.4	13.0	6.6
12	Edward Brown	John Kasich	184,891	60,694	124,197	0	32.8	67.2	0.0
13	Sherrod Brown	Grace Drake	188,975	116,309	72,666	0	61.5	38.5	0.0
14	Thomas Sawyer	Tom Watkins	169,073	106,046	63,027	0	62.7	37.3	0.0
15	Adam Clay Miller	Deborah Pryce	173,176	49,334	113,846	9,996	28.5	65.7	5.8
16	Peter Ferguson	Ralph Regula	183,473	66,047	117,426	0	36.0	64.0	0.0
17	James Traficant Jr.	Paul Alberty	181,421	123,718	57,703	0	68.2	31.8	0.0
18	Robert Burch	Bob Ney	187,690	74,571	113,119	0	39.7	60.3	0.0
19	Elizabeth Kelley	Steven LaTourette	190,876	64,090	126,786	0	33.6	66.4	0.0
Oklahoma									
1	Howard Plowman	Steve Largent	147,340	56,309	91,031	0	38.2	61.8	0.0
2	Kent Pharaoh	Tom Coburn	148,264	59,042	85,581	3,641	39.8	57.7	2.5
3	Walt Roberts	Wes Watkins	144,995	55,163	89,832	0	38.0	62.0	0.0
4	Ben Odom	J. C. Watts Jr.	135,379	52,107	83,272	0	38.5	61.5	0.0
5	M. C. Smothermon	Ernest Istook	151,399	48,182	103,217	0	31.8	68.2	0.0
6	Paul Barby	Frank Lucas	131,271	43,555	85,261	2,455	33.2	65.0	1.9
Oregon									
1	David Wu	Molly Bordonaro	239,496	119,993	112,827	6,676	50.1	47.1	2.8
2	Kevin Campbell	Greg Walden	215,216	74,924	132,316	7,976	34.8	61.5	3.7
3	Earl Blumenauer	unopposed	183,351	153,889	–	29,462	83.9	–	16.1

District	Candidate	Opponent							
4	**Peter DeFazio**	Steve Webb	224,637	157,524	64,143	2,970	70.1	28.6	1.3
5	**Darlene Hooley**	Marylin Shannon	227,657	124,916	92,215	10,526	54.9	40.5	4.6
Pennsylvania									
1	**Robert Brady**	William Harrison	95,848	77,788	15,898	2,162	81.2	16.6	2.3
2	**Chaka Fattah**	Anne Marie Mulligan	118,764	102,763	16,001	0	86.5	13.5	0.0
3	**Robert Borski**	Charles Dougherty	111,660	66,270	45,390	0	59.3	40.7	0.0
4	**Ron Klink**	Mike Turzai	161,685	103,183	58,485	17	63.8	36.2	0.0
5	**John Peterson**	unopposed	117,323	–	99,502	17,821	–	84.8	15.2
6	**Tim Holden**	John Meckley	139,953	85,374	54,579	0	61.0	39.0	0.0
7	**Curt Weldon**	Martin D'Urso	166,411	46,920	119,491	0	28.2	71.8	0.0
8	**Jim Greenwood**	Bill Tuthill	148,200	48,320	93,697	6,183	32.6	63.2	4.2
9	**Bud Shuster**	unopposed	126,027	–	125,409	618	–	99.5	0.5
10	**Don Sherwood**	Patrick Casey	173,056	83,760	84,275	5,021	48.4	48.7	2.9
11	**Paul Kanjorski**	Stephen Urban	133,065	88,933	44,123	9	66.8	33.2	0.0
12	**John Murtha**	Timothy Holloway	146,780	100,528	46,239	13	68.5	31.5	0.0
13	**Joseph Hoeffel**	Jon Fox	184,490	95,105	85,915	3,470	51.6	46.6	1.9
14	**William Coyne**	Bill Ravotti	137,736	83,355	52,745	1,636	60.5	38.3	1.2
15	**Pat Toomey**	Roy Afflerbach	148,706	66,930	81,755	21	45.0	55.0	0.0
16	**Joseph Pitts**	Robert Yorczyk	136,085	40,092	95,979	14	29.5	70.5	0.0
17	**George Gekas**	unopposed	115,107	–	114,931	176	–	99.8	0.2
18	**Mike Doyle**	Dick Walker	145,337	98,363	46,945	29	67.7	32.3	0.0
19	**Bill Goodling**	Linda Ropp	142,489	40,674	96,284	5,531	28.5	67.6	3.9
20	**Frank Mascara**	unopposed	98,075	97,885	–	190	99.8	–	0.2
21	**Phil English**	Larry Klemens	149,115	54,591	94,518	6	36.6	63.4	0.0
Rhode Island									
1	**Patrick Kennedy**	Ronald Santa	138,895	92,788	38,460	7,647	66.8	27.7	5.5
2	**Robert Weygand**	John Matson	154,053	110,917	38,170	4,966	72.0	24.8	3.2
South Carolina									
1	**Mark Sanford**	unopposed	130,071	–	118,414	11,657	–	91.0	9.0
2	**Floyd Spence**	Jane Frederick	206,763	84,864	119,583	2,316	41.0	57.8	1.1
3	**Lindsey Graham**	unopposed	129,449	–	129,047	402	–	99.7	0.3
4	**Jim DeMint**	Glenn Reese	182,550	73,314	105,264	3,972	40.2	57.7	2.2
5	**John Spratt**	Mike Burkhold	164,267	95,105	66,299	2,863	57.9	40.4	1.7
6	**James Clyburn**	Gary McLeod	160,576	116,507	41,421	2,648	72.6	25.8	1.6

(continued)

House of Representatives Election Results, 1998 (continued)

State/District	Democrat	Republican	Total Vote	Dem Vote	Rep Vote	Other Vote	Dem %	Rep %	Other %
South Dakota	Jeff Moser	John Thune	258,590	64,433	194,157	0	24.9	75.1	0.0
Tennessee									
1	Kay White	**William Jenkins**	99,689	30,710	68,904	75	30.8	69.1	0.1
2	unopposed	**John Duncan**	102,502	—	90,860	11,642	—	88.6	11.4
3	James Lewis Jr.	**Zack Wamp**	113,786	37,144	75,100	1,542	32.6	66.0	1.4
4	Jerry Cooper	**Van Hilleary**	105,479	42,627	62,829	23	40.4	59.6	0.0
5	**Bob Clement**	unopposed	90,102	74,611	—	15,491	82.8	—	17.2
6	**Bart Gordon**	Walt Massey	137,436	75,055	62,277	104	54.6	45.3	0.1
7	unopposed	**Ed Bryant**	91,980	—	91,503	477	—	99.5	0.5
8	**John Tanner**	unopposed	76,825	76,803	—	22	100.0	—	0.0
9	**Harold Ford Jr.**	Claude Burdikoff	95,782	75,428	18,078	2,276	78.7	18.9	2.4
Texas									
1	**Max Sandlin**	Dennis Boerner	135,979	80,788	55,191	0	59.4	40.6	0.0
2	**Jim Turner**	Brian Babin	139,589	81,556	56,891	1,142	58.4	40.8	0.8
3	unopposed	**Sam Johnson**	116,978	—	106,690	10,288	—	91.2	8.8
4	**Ralph Hall**	Jim Lohmeyer	144,080	82,989	58,954	2,137	57.6	40.9	1.5
5	Victor Morales	**Pete Sessions**	110,667	48,073	61,714	880	43.4	55.8	0.8
6	Ben Boothe	**Joe Barton**	154,886	40,112	112,957	1,817	25.9	72.9	1.2
7	unopposed	**Bill Archer**	118,946	—	111,010	7,936	—	93.3	6.7
8	unopposed	**Kevin Brady**	132,948	—	123,372	9,576	—	92.8	7.2
9	**Nick Lampson**	Tom Cottar	135,162	86,055	49,107	0	63.7	36.3	0.0
10	**Lloyd Doggett**	unopposed	136,282	116,127	—	20,155	85.2	—	14.8
11	**Chet Edwards**	unopposed	86,303	71,142	—	15,161	82.4	—	17.6
12	Tom Hall	**Kay Granger**	107,741	39,084	66,740	1,917	36.3	61.9	1.8
13	Mark Harmon	**Mac Thornberry**	119,466	37,027	81,141	1,298	31.0	67.9	1.1
14	Loy Sneary	**Ron Paul**	152,863	68,014	84,459	390	44.5	55.3	0.3
15	**Ruben Hinojosa**	Tom Haughey	82,178	47,957	34,221	0	58.4	41.6	0.0
16	**Silvestre Reyes**	unopposed	76,767	67,486	—	9,281	87.9	—	12.1
17	**Charlie Stenholm**	Rudy Izzard	140,685	75,367	63,700	1,618	53.6	45.3	1.2
18	**Sheila Jackson Lee**	unopposed	91,267	82,091	—	9,176	89.9	—	10.1
19	Sidney Blankenship	**Larry Combest**	129,428	21,162	108,266	0	16.4	83.6	0.0
20	**Charlie Gonzalez**	James Walker	79,713	50,356	28,347	1,010	63.2	35.6	1.3
21	unopposed	**Lamar Smith**	180,608	—	165,047	15,561	—	91.4	8.6

District	Candidate 1	Candidate 2	Total	Votes 1	Votes 2	Other	% 1	% 2	% Other
22	Hill Kemp	**Tom DeLay**	134,720	45,386	87,840	1,494	33.7	65.2	1.1
23	Charlie Jones	**Henry Bonilla**	114,720	40,281	73,177	1,262	35.1	63.8	1.1
24	**Martin Frost**	Shawn Terry	97,992	56,321	40,105	1,566	57.5	40.9	1.6
25	**Ken Bentsen**	John Sanchez	101,269	58,591	41,848	830	57.9	41.3	0.8
26	unopposed	**Dick Armey**	136,514	—	120,332	16,182	—	88.1	11.9
27	**Solomon Ortiz**	Erol Stone	97,398	61,638	34,284	1,476	63.3	35.2	1.5
28	**Ciro Rodriguez**	unopposed	79,353	71,849	—	7,504	90.5	—	9.5
29	**Gene Green**	unopposed	47,631	44,179	—	3,452	92.8	—	7.2
30	**Eddie Bernice Johnson**	Carrie Kelleher	79,752	57,603	21,338	811	72.2	26.8	1.0
Utah									
1	Steve Beierlein	**James Hansen**	162,085	49,307	109,708	3,070	30.4	67.7	1.9
2	Lily Eskelsen	**Merrill Cook**	177,641	77,198	93,718	6,725	43.5	52.8	3.8
3	unopposed	**Chris Cannon**	131,123	—	100,830	30,293	—	76.9	23.1
Vermont									
	unopposed	Mark Candon	215,133	—	70,740	144,393	—	32.9	67.1
Virginia									
1	unopposed	**Herbert Bateman**	100,057	—	76,474	23,583	—	76.4	23.6
2	**Owen Pickett**	unopposed	72,091	67,975	—	4,116	94.3	—	5.7
3	**Robert Scott**	unopposed	63,354	48,129	—	15,225	76.0	—	24.0
4	**Norman Sisisky**	unopposed	66,579	64,563	—	2,016	97.0	—	3.0
5	**Virgil Goode Jr.**	unopposed	73,882	73,097	—	785	98.9	—	1.1
6	David Bowers	**Robert Goodlatte**	128,730	39,487	89,177	66	30.7	69.3	0.1
7	unopposed	**Thomas Bliley Jr.**	97,889	—	77,044	20,845	—	78.7	21.3
8	**James Moran Jr.**	Demaris Miller	146,287	97,545	48,352	390	66.7	33.1	0.3
9	**Frederick Boucher**	J. A. Barta	143,126	87,163	55,918	45	60.9	39.1	0.0
10	Cornell Brooks	**Frank Wolf**	144,755	36,476	103,648	4,631	25.2	71.6	3.2
11	unopposed	**Thomas Davis III**	112,111	—	91,603	20,508	—	81.7	18.3
Washington									
1	**Jay Inslee**	Rick White	226,473	112,726	99,910	13,837	49.8	44.1	6.1
2	Grethe Cammermeyer	**Jack Metcalf**	224,901	100,776	124,125	0	44.8	55.2	0.0
3	**Brian Baird**	Don Benton	220,219	120,364	99,855	0	54.7	45.3	0.0
4	Gordon Pross	**Doc Hastings**	176,090	43,043	121,684	11,363	24.4	69.1	6.5
5	Brad Lyons	**George Nethercutt**	193,258	73,545	110,040	9,673	38.1	56.9	5.0
6	**Norm Dicks**	Bob Lawrence	209,599	143,308	66,291	0	68.4	31.6	0.0
7	**Jim McDermott**	unopposed	207,542	183,076	—	24,466	88.2	—	11.8

(continued)

House of Representatives Election Results, 1998 (continued)

State/District	Democrat	Republican	Total Vote	Dem Vote	Rep Vote	Other Vote	Dem %	Rep %	Other %
Washington (cont.)									
8	H. Behrens-Benedict	**Jennifer Dunn**	226,910	91,371	135,539	0	40.3	59.7	0.0
9	**Adam Smith**	Ron Taber	173,056	111,948	61,108	0	64.7	35.3	0.0
West Virginia									
1	**Alan Mollohan**	unopposed	124,114	105,101	–	19,013	84.7	–	15.3
2	**Bob Wise**	Sally Anne Kay	136,153	99,357	29,136	7,660	73.0	21.4	5.6
3	**Nick Joe Rahall II**	unopposed	91,010	78,814	–	12,196	86.6	–	13.4
Wisconsin									
1	Lydia Spottswood	**Paul Ryan**	189,946	81,164	108,475	307	42.7	57.1	0.2
2	**Tammy Baldwin**	Josephine Musser	221,693	116,377	103,528	1,788	52.5	46.7	0.8
3	**Ron Kind**	Troy Brechler	179,448	128,256	51,001	191	71.5	28.4	0.1
4	**Jerry Kleczka**	Tom Reynolds	182,701	105,841	76,666	194	57.9	42.0	0.1
5	**Tom Barrett**	Jack Melvin	154,861	121,129	33,506	226	78.2	21.6	0.1
6	unopposed	**Thomas Petri**	155,669	–	144,144	11,525	–	92.6	7.4
7	**David Obey**	Scott West	190,865	115,613	75,049	203	60.6	39.3	0.1
8	Jay Johnson	**Mark Green**	205,974	93,441	112,418	115	45.4	54.6	0.1
9	unopposed	**J. Sensenbrenner Jr.**	192,318	–	175,533	16,785	–	91.3	8.7
Wyoming	Scott Farris	**Barbara Cubin**	174,219	67,399	100,687	6,133	38.7	57.8	3.5

Names in boldface type denote the winner.

[a] Under Florida law, a candidate who runs unopposed in the general election is not listed on the ballot and is declared elected.

[b] Under Louisiana law, a candidate who wins a majority of the votes in the primary election is elected. When no candidate wins a majority, the two top vote-getters—regardless of party—face each other in a runoff election. A candidate who runs unopposed in the primary is declared elected and is not listed on the ballot in either the primary or general election.

Source: Federal Election Commission Web site: www.fec.gov/pubrec/fe98/alh.htm

Senate Election Results, 1998

State	Democrat	Republican	Total Vote	Dem Vote	Rep Vote	Other Vote	Dem %	Rep %	Other %
AL	Clayton Suddith	**Richard Shelby**	1,293,405	474,568	817,973	864	36.7	63.2	0.1
AK	Joseph A. Sonneman	**Frank H. Murkowski**	221,807	43,743	165,227	12,837	19.7	74.5	5.8
AZ	Ed Ranger	**John McCain**	1,013,280	275,224	696,577	41,479	27.2	68.7	4.1
AR	**Blanche Lincoln**	Fay Boozman	700,644	385,878	295,870	18,896	55.1	42.2	2.7
CA	**Barbara Boxer**	Matt Fong	8,314,953	4,411,705	3,576,351	326,897	53.1	43.0	3.9
CO	Dottie Lam	**B. N. Campbell**	1,327,235	464,754	829,370	33,111	35.0	62.5	2.5
CT	**Christopher J. Dodd**	Gary A. Franks	964,457	628,306	312,177	23,974	65.2	32.4	2.5
FL	**Bob Graham**	Charlie Crist	3,900,162	2,436,407	1,463,755	0	62.5	37.5	0.0
GA	Michael J. Coles	**P. D. Coverdell**	1,753,911	791,904	918,540	43,467	45.2	52.4	2.5
HI	**Daniel K. Inouye**	Crystal Young	398,124	315,252	70,964	11,908	79.2	17.8	3.0
ID	Bill Mauk	**Mike Crapo**	378,174	107,375	262,966	7,833	28.4	69.5	2.1
IL	Carol Moseley-Braun	**Peter G. Fitzgerald**	3,394,521	1,610,496	1,709,041	74,984	47.4	50.4	2.2
IN	**Evan Bayh**	Paul Helmke	1,588,617	1,012,244	552,732	23,641	63.7	34.8	1.5
IA	David Osterberg	**Chuck Grassley**	947,907	289,049	648,480	10,378	30.5	68.4	1.1
KS	Paul Feleciano Jr.	**Sam Brownback**	727,236	229,718	474,639	22,879	31.6	65.3	3.1
KY	Scotty Baesler	**Jim Bunning**	1,145,414	563,051	569,817	12,546	49.2	49.8	1.1
LA	**John B. Breaux**	Jim Donelon	969,165	620,502	306,616	42,047	64.0	31.6	4.3
MD	**Barbara Ann Mikulski**	Ross Z. Pierpont	1,507,447	1,062,810	444,637	0	70.5	29.5	0.0
MO	Jeremiah W. Nixon	**Christopher Bond**	1,576,857	690,208	830,625	56,024	43.8	52.7	3.6
NV	**Harry Reid**	John Ensign	435,790	208,650	208,222	18,918	47.9	47.8	4.3
NH	G. Condodemetraky	**Judd Gregg**	314,956	88,883	213,477	12,596	28.2	67.8	4.0
NY	**Charles E. Schumer**	Al D'Amato	4,670,805	2,551,065	2,058,988	60,752	54.6	44.1	1.3
NC	**John Edwards**	Lauch Faircloth	2,012,143	1,029,237	945,943	36,963	51.2	47.0	1.8
ND	**Byron L. Dorgan**	Donna Nalewaja	213,358	134,747	75,013	3,598	63.2	35.2	1.7
OH	Mary O. Boyle	**George V. Voinovich**	3,404,351	1,482,054	1,922,087	210	43.5	56.5	0.0
OK	Don E. Carroll	**Don Nickles**	859,713	268,898	570,682	20,133	31.3	66.4	2.3
OR	**Ron Wyden**	John Lim	1,117,747	682,425	377,739	57,583	61.1	33.8	5.2
PA	Bill Lloyd	**Arlen Specter**	2,957,772	1,028,839	1,814,180	114,753	34.8	61.3	3.9
SC	**Fritz Hollings**	Bob Inglis	1,068,367	562,791	488,132	17,444	52.7	45.7	1.6
SD	**Tom Daschle**	Ron Schmidt	262,111	162,884	95,431	3,796	62.1	36.4	1.5
UT	Scott Leckman	**Robert F. Bennett**	494,909	163,172	316,652	15,085	33.0	64.0	3.0
VT	**Patrick Leahy**	Fred H. Tuttle	214,036	154,567	48,051	11,418	72.2	22.5	5.3
WA	**Patty Murray**	Linda Smith	1,888,561	1,103,184	785,377	0	58.4	41.6	0.0
WI	**Russell Feingold**	Mark W. Neumann	1,760,836	890,059	852,272	18,505	50.6	48.4	1.1

Names in boldface type denote the winner.

Source: Federal Election Commission Web site: www.fec.gov/pubrec/fe98/98senate.htm

House of Representatives Election Results, 2000

State/District	Democrat	Republican	Total Vote	Dem Vote	Rep Vote	Other Vote	Dem %	Rep %	Other %
Alabama									
1	unopposed	**H. L. Callahan**	165,669	–	151,188	14,481	–	91.3	8.7
2	Charles Woods	**Terry Everett**	222,636	64,958	151,830	5,848	29.2	68.2	2.6
3	unopposed	**Bob Riley**	169,519	–	147,317	22,202	–	86.9	13.1
4	Marsha Folsom	**Robert Aderholt**	231,106	86,400	140,009	4,697	37.4	60.6	2.0
5	**Bud Cramer**	unopposed	209,514	186,059	–	23,455	88.8	–	11.2
6	unopposed	**Spencer Bachus**	241,917	–	212,751	29,166	–	87.9	12.1
7	**Earl Hilliard**	Ed Martin	198,633	148,243	46,134	4,256	74.6	23.2	2.1
Alaska									
	Clifford Mark Greene	**Don Young**	274,393	45,372	190,862	38,159	16.5	69.6	13.9
Arizona									
1	David Mendoza	**Jeff Flake**	229,971	97,455	123,289	9,227	42.4	53.6	4.0
2	**Ed Pastor**	Bill Barenholtz	122,605	84,034	32,990	5,581	68.5	26.9	4.6
3	Gene Scharer	**Bob Stump**	301,970	94,676	198,367	8,927	31.4	65.7	3.0
4	Ben Jankowski	**John Shadegg**	219,497	71,803	140,396	7,298	32.7	64.0	3.3
5	George Cunningham	**Jim Kolbe**	287,609	101,564	172,986	13,059	35.3	60.1	4.5
6	Larry Nelson	**J. D. Hayworth**	304,004	108,317	186,687	9,000	35.6	61.4	3.0
Arkansas									
1	**Marion Berry**	Susan Myshka	199,956	120,266	79,437	253	60.1	39.7	0.1
2	**Vic Snyder**	Bob Thomas	220,649	126,957	93,692	0	57.5	42.5	0.0
3	unopposed	**Asa Hutchinson**	–	–	–	–	–	–	–
4	**Mike Ross**	Jay Dickey	212,160	108,143	104,017	0	51.0	49.0	0.0
California									
1	**Mike Thompson**	Russel Chase	239,335	155,638	66,987	16,710	65.0	28.0	7.0
2	Stan Morgan	**Wally Herger**	255,856	72,075	168,172	15,609	28.2	65.7	6.1
3	Bob Kent	**Doug Ose**	230,182	93,067	129,254	7,861	40.4	56.2	3.4
4	Mark Norberg	**John Dolittle**	311,423	97,974	197,503	15,946	31.5	63.4	5.1
5	**Robert Matsui**	Ken Payne	214,059	147,025	55,945	11,089	68.7	26.1	5.2
6	**Lynn Woolsey**	Ken McAuliffe	283,118	182,116	80,169	20,833	64.3	28.3	7.4
7	**George Miller**	Christopher Hoffman	208,789	159,692	44,154	4,943	76.5	21.1	2.4
8	**Nancy Pelosi**	Adam Sparks	215,428	181,847	25,298	8,283	84.4	11.7	3.8
9	**Barbara Lee**	Arneze Washington	214,650	182,352	21,033	11,265	85.0	9.8	5.2

10	**Ellen Tauscher**	Claude Hutchison Jr.	304,819	160,429	134,863	9,527	52.6	44.2	3.1
11	Tom Santos	**Richard Pombo**	208,607	79,539	120,635	8,433	38.1	57.8	4.0
12	**Tom Lantos**	Mike Garza	212,556	158,404	44,162	9,990	74.5	20.8	4.7
13	**Fortney Pete Stark**	James Goetz	183,146	129,012	44,499	9,635	70.4	24.3	5.3
14	**Anna Eshoo**	Bill Quraishi	230,262	161,720	59,338	9,204	70.2	25.8	4.0
15	**Mike Honda**	Jim Cunneen	236,904	128,545	99,866	8,493	54.3	42.2	3.6
16	**Zoe Lofgren**	Horace Thayn	159,746	115,118	37,213	7,415	72.1	23.3	4.6
17	**Sam Farr**	Clint Engler	208,760	143,219	51,557	13,984	68.6	24.7	6.7
18	**Gary Condit**	Steve Wilson	180,328	121,003	56,465	2,860	67.1	31.3	1.6
19	Dan Rosenberg	**George Radanovich**	222,615	70,578	144,517	7,520	31.7	64.9	3.4
20	**Cal Dooley**	Rich Rodriguez	126,534	66,235	57,563	2,736	52.3	45.5	2.2
21	Pedro Martinez Jr.	**Bill Thomas**	199,100	49,318	142,539	7,243	24.8	71.6	3.6
22	**Lois Capps**	Mike Stoker	255,070	135,538	113,094	6,438	53.1	44.3	2.5
23	Michael Case	**Elton Gallegly**	221,034	89,918	119,479	11,637	40.7	54.1	5.3
24	**Brad Sherman**	Jerry Doyle	235,444	155,398	70,169	9,877	66.0	29.8	4.2
25	Sid Gold	**Howard McKeon**	222,778	73,921	138,628	10,229	33.2	62.2	4.6
26	**Howard Berman**	unopposed	114,786	96,500	–	18,286	84.1	–	15.9
27	**Adam Schiff**	James Rogan	215,774	113,708	94,518	7,548	52.7	43.8	3.5
28	Janice Nelson	**David Dreier**	205,199	81,804	116,557	6,838	39.9	56.8	3.3
29	**Henry Waxman**	Jim Scileppi	238,201	180,295	45,784	12,122	75.7	19.2	5.1
30	**Xavier Becerra**	Tony Goss	99,920	83,223	11,788	4,909	83.3	11.8	4.9
31	**Hilda Solis**	unopposed	112,914	89,600	–	23,314	79.4	–	20.6
32	**Julian Dixon**	Kathy Williamson	164,527	137,447	19,924	7,156	83.5	12.1	4.3
33	**Lucille Roybal-Allard**	Wayne Miller	71,571	60,510	8,260	2,801	84.5	11.5	3.9
34	**Grace Napolitano**	Robert Arthur Canales	148,723	105,980	33,445	9,298	71.3	22.5	6.3
35	**Maxine Waters**	Carl McGill	116,215	100,569	12,582	3,064	86.5	10.8	2.6
36	**Jane Harman**	Steven Kuykendall	239,131	115,651	111,199	12,281	48.4	46.5	5.1
37	**J. Millender-McDonald**	Vernon Van	113,275	93,269	12,762	7,244	82.3	11.3	6.4
38	Gerrie Schipske	**Steve Horn**	180,122	85,498	87,266	7,358	47.5	48.4	4.1
39	Gill Kanel	**Ed Royce**	206,104	64,938	129,294	11,872	31.5	62.7	5.8
40	unopposed	**Jerry Lewis**	189,022	–	151,069	37,953	–	79.9	20.1
41	Rodolfo Favila	Gary Miller	177,616	66,361	104,695	6,560	37.4	58.9	3.7
42	**Joe Baca**	Elia Pirozzi	151,577	90,585	53,239	7,753	59.8	35.1	5.1
43	unopposed	**Ken Calvert**	190,332	–	140,201	50,131	–	73.7	26.3
44	Ron Oden	**Mary Bono**	209,187	79,302	123,738	6,147	37.9	59.2	2.9
45	Ted Crisell	**Dana Rohrabacher**	219,385	71,066	136,275	12,044	32.4	62.1	5.5
46	**Loretta Sanchez**	Gloria Matta Tuchman	116,908	70,381	40,928	5,599	60.2	35.0	4.8

(continued)

House of Representatives Election Results, 2000 (continued)

State/District	Democrat	Republican	Total Vote	Dem Vote	Rep Vote	Other Vote	Dem %	Rep %	Other %
California (cont.)									
47	John Graham	**Christopher Cox**	276,401	83,186	181,365	11,850	30.1	65.6	4.3
48	Peter Kouvelis	**Darrell Issa**	261,478	74,073	160,627	26,778	28.3	61.4	10.2
49	**Susan Davis**	Brian Bilbray	228,489	113,400	105,515	9,574	49.6	46.2	4.2
50	**Bob Filner**	Bob Divine	139,472	95,191	38,526	5,755	68.3	27.6	4.1
51	George Barraza	**Randy Cunningham**	267,799	81,408	172,291	14,100	30.4	64.3	5.3
52	Craig Barkacs	**Duncan Hunter**	202,994	63,537	131,345	8,112	31.3	64.7	4.0
Colorado									
1	**Diana DeGette**	Jesse Thomas	206,434	141,831	56,291	8,312	68.7	27.3	4.0
2	**Mark Udall**	Carolyn Cox	283,116	155,725	109,338	18,053	55.0	38.6	6.4
3	Curtis Imrie	**Scott McInnis**	302,540	87,921	199,204	15,415	29.1	65.8	5.1
4	unopposed	**Bob Schaffer**	263,006	–	209,078	53,928	–	79.5	20.5
5	unopposed	**Joel Hefley**	306,309	–	253,330	52,979	–	82.7	17.3
6	Kenneth Toltz	**Tom Tancredo**	262,477	110,568	141,410	10,499	42.1	53.9	4.0
Connecticut									
1	**John Larson**	Bob Backlund	211,263	151,932	59,331	0	71.9	28.1	0.0
2	Sam Gejdenson	**Rob Simmons**	225,900	111,520	114,380	0	49.4	50.6	0.0
3	**Rosa DeLauro**	June Gold	218,205	156,910	60,037	1,258	71.9	27.5	0.6
4	Stephanie Sanchez	**Christopher Shays**	206,758	84,472	119,155	3,131	40.9	57.6	1.5
5	**Jim Maloney**	Mark Nielsen	221,821	118,932	98,229	4,660	53.6	44.3	2.1
6	Paul Valenti	**Nancy Johnson**	229,543	75,471	143,698	10,374	32.9	62.6	4.5
Delaware	Michael Miller	**Michael Castle**	313,171	96,488	211,797	4,886	30.8	67.6	1.6
District of Columbia	**E. H. Norton**	E. H. Wolterbeek	175,631	158,824	10,258	6,549	90.4	5.8	3.7
Florida									
1	unopposed	**Joe Scarborough**	227,539	–	226,473	1,066	–	99.5	0.5
2	**Allen Boyd**	Doug Dodd	257,403	185,579	71,754	70	72.1	27.9	0.0
3	**Corrine Brown**	Jennifer Carroll	177,372	102,143	75,228	1	57.6	42.4	0.0
4	Tom Sullivan	**Ander Crenshaw**	303,286	94,587	203,090	5,609	31.2	67.0	1.8
5	**Karen Thurman**	Pete Enwall	280,598	180,338	100,244	16	64.3	35.7	0.0
6	unopposed	**Clifford Stearns**	178,972	–	178,789	183	–	99.9	0.1
7	Dan Vaughen	**John Mica**	270,560	99,531	171,018	11	36.8	63.2	0.0

District	Candidate 1	Candidate 2	Total Vote	Cand. 1 Vote	Cand. 2 Vote	Other Vote	Cand. 1 %	Cand. 2 %	Other %
8	Linda Chapin	**Ric Keller**	246,593	121,295	125,253	45	49.2	50.8	0.0
9	unopposed	**Michael Bilirakis**	256,794	–	210,318	46,476	–	81.9	18.1
10	unopposed	**C. W. Bill Young**	194,003	–	146,799	47,204	–	75.7	24.3
11	**Jim Davis**	unopposed	176,683	149,465	–	27,218	84.6	–	15.4
12	Mike Stedem	**Adam Putnam**	219,625	94,395	125,224	6	43.0	57.0	0.0
13	Daniel Dunn	**Dan Miller**	275,587	99,568	175,918	101	36.1	63.8	0.0
14	unopposed	**Porter Goss**	284,615	–	242,614	42,001	–	85.2	14.8
15	Patsy Ann Kurth	**Dave Weldon**	299,445	117,511	176,189	5,745	39.2	58.8	1.9
16	Jean Elliott Brown	**Mark Foley**	292,500	108,782	176,153	7,565	37.2	60.2	2.6
17	**Carrie Meek**	unopposed	100,718	100,715	–	3	100.0	–	0.0
18	unopposed	**Ileana Ros-Lehtinen**	112,991	–	112,968	23	–	100.0	0.0
19	**Robert Wexler**	Morris Kent Thompson	238,869	171,080	67,789	0	71.6	28.4	0.0
20	**Peter Deutsch**	unopposed	156,952	156,765	–	187	99.9	–	0.1
21	unopposed	**Lincoln Diaz-Balart**	132,342	–	132,317	25	–	100.0	0.0
22	Elaine Bloom	**Clay Shaw**	211,112	105,256	105,855	1	49.9	50.1	0.0
23	**Alcee Hastings**	Bill Lambert	116,813	89,179	27,630	4	76.3	23.7	0.0
Georgia									
1	Joyce Marie Griggs	**Jack Kingston**	190,460	58,776	131,684	0	30.9	69.1	0.0
2	**Sanford Bishop**	Dylan Glenn	180,300	96,430	83,870	0	53.5	46.5	0.0
3	Gail Notti	**Mac Collins**	236,706	86,309	150,200	197	36.5	63.5	0.1
4	**Cynthia McKinney**	Sunny Warren	229,856	139,579	90,277	0	60.7	39.3	0.0
5	**John Lewis**	Hank Schwab	177,942	137,333	40,606	3	77.2	22.8	0.0
6	Brett DeHart	**Johnny Isakson**	343,261	86,666	256,595	0	25.2	74.8	0.0
7	Roger Kahn	**Bob Barr**	228,584	102,272	126,312	0	44.7	55.3	0.0
8	Jim Marshall	**Saxby Chambliss**	192,431	79,051	113,380	0	41.1	58.9	0.0
9	James Harrington	**Nathan Deal**	243,531	60,360	183,171	0	24.8	75.2	0.0
10	Denise Freeman	**Charlie Norwood**	193,899	71,309	122,590	0	36.8	63.2	0.0
11	unopposed	**John Linder**	199,652	–	199,652	0	–	100.0	0.0
Hawaii									
1	**Neil Abercrombie**	Phil Meyers	157,194	108,517	44,989	3,688	69.0	28.6	2.3
2	**Patsy Takemoto Mink**	Russ Francis	183,230	112,856	65,906	4,468	61.6	36.0	2.4
Idaho									
1	Linda Pall	**C. L. Otter**	268,116	84,080	173,743	10,293	31.4	64.8	3.8
2	Craig Williams	**Mike Simpson**	224,719	58,265	158,912	7,542	25.9	70.7	3.4

(continued)

House of Representatives Election Results, 2000 *(continued)*

State/District	Democrat	Republican	Total Vote	Dem Vote	Rep Vote	Other Vote	Dem %	Rep %	Other %
Illinois									
1	**Bobby Rush**	Raymond Wardingley	196,186	172,271	23,915	0	87.8	12.2	0.0
2	**Jesse Jackson Jr.**	Robert Gordon III	195,901	175,995	19,906	0	89.8	10.2	0.0
3	**William Lipinski**	Karl Groth	192,503	145,498	47,005	0	75.6	24.4	0.0
4	**Luis Gutierrez**	unopposed	100,963	89,487	–	11,476	88.6	–	11.4
5	**Rod Blagojevich**	unopposed	162,889	142,161	–	20,728	87.3	–	12.7
6	Brent Christensen	Henry Hyde	226,207	92,880	133,327	0	41.1	58.9	0.0
7	**Danny Davis**	Robert Dallas	191,027	164,155	26,872	0	85.9	14.1	0.0
8	Lance Pressl	Philip Crane	232,695	90,777	141,918	0	39.0	61.0	0.0
9	**Jan Schakowsky**	Dennis Driscoll	192,346	147,002	45,344	0	76.4	23.6	0.0
10	Lauren Beth Gash	Mark Steven Kirk	237,506	115,924	121,582	0	48.8	51.2	0.0
11	James Stevenson	Gerald Weller	234,869	102,485	132,384	0	43.6	56.4	0.0
12	**Jerry Costello**	unopposed	183,257	183,208	–	49	100.0	–	0.0
13	Thomas Mason	**Judy Biggert**	292,018	98,768	193,250	0	33.8	66.2	0.0
14	Vern Deljonson	**Dennis Hastert**	254,909	66,309	188,597	3	26.0	74.0	0.0
15	F. Michael Kelleher Jr.	**Tim Johnson**	236,622	110,679	125,943	0	46.8	53.2	0.0
16	Charles Hendrickson	**Donald Manzullo**	267,071	88,781	178,174	116	33.2	66.7	0.0
17	**Lane Evans**	Mark Baker	241,347	132,494	108,853	0	54.9	45.1	0.0
18	Joyce Harant	**Ray LaHood**	259,023	85,317	173,706	0	32.9	67.1	0.0
19	**David Phelps**	James Eatherly	240,238	155,101	85,137	0	64.6	35.4	0.0
20	Jeffrey Cooper	**John Shimkus**	255,775	94,382	161,393	0	36.9	63.1	0.0
Indiana									
1	**Peter Visclosky**	Jack Reynolds	207,790	148,683	56,200	2,907	71.6	27.0	1.4
2	Robert Rock	**Mike Pence**	208,407	80,885	106,023	21,499	38.8	50.9	10.3
3	**Tim Roemer**	Chris Chocola	208,315	107,438	98,822	2,055	51.6	47.4	1.0
4	Michael Dewayne Foster	**Mark Souder**	210,430	74,492	131,051	4,887	35.4	62.3	2.3
5	Greg Goodnight	**Steve Buyer**	216,985	81,427	132,051	3,507	37.5	60.9	1.6
6	Darin Patrick Griesey	Dan Burton	283,175	74,881	199,207	9,087	26.4	70.3	3.2
7	Michael Douglas Graf	Brian Kerns	209,665	66,764	135,869	7,032	31.8	64.8	3.4
8	Paul Perry	**John Hostettler**	221,992	100,488	116,879	4,625	45.3	52.7	2.1
9	**Baron Hill**	Michael Bailey	233,283	126,420	102,219	4,644	54.2	43.8	2.0
10	**Julia Carson**	Marvin Scott	156,702	91,689	62,233	2,780	58.5	39.7	1.8

State / District	Candidate	Candidate	Total	Votes	Votes	Other	%	%	%
Iowa									
1	Bob Simpson	**Jim Leach**	266,990	96,283	164,972	5,735	36.1	61.8	2.1
2	Donna Smith	**Jim Nussle**	252,567	110,327	139,906	2,334	43.7	55.4	0.9
3	**Leonard Boswell**	Jay Marcus	248,926	156,327	83,810	8,789	62.8	33.7	3.5
4	Michael Huston	**Greg Ganske**	275,645	101,112	169,267	5,266	36.7	61.4	1.9
5	Mike Palecek	**Tom Latham**	231,806	67,593	159,367	4,846	29.2	68.8	2.1
Kansas									
1	unopposed	**Jerry Moran**	242,327	–	216,484	25,843	–	89.3	10.7
2	Stanley Wiles	**Jim Ryun**	244,759	71,709	164,951	8,099	29.3	67.4	3.3
3	**Dennis Moore**	Phill Kline	308,710	154,505	144,672	9,533	50.0	46.9	3.1
4	Carlos Nolla	**Todd Tiahrt**	242,583	101,980	131,871	8,732	42.0	54.4	3.6
Kentucky									
1	Brian Roy	**Edward Whitfield**	227,921	95,806	132,115	0	42.0	58.0	0.0
2	Brian Pedigo	**Ron Lewis**	237,462	74,537	160,800	2,125	31.4	67.7	0.9
3	Eleanor Jordan	**Ann Northup**	268,785	118,875	142,106	7,804	44.2	52.9	2.9
4	**Ken Lucas**	Don Bell	231,963	125,872	100,943	5,148	54.3	43.5	2.2
5	Sindey Jane Bailey	**Harold Rogers**	198,475	52,495	145,980	0	26.4	73.6	0.0
6	Scotty Baesler	**Ernie Fletcher**	270,803	94,167	142,971	33,665	34.8	52.8	12.4
Louisiana[a]									
1	Michael Armato	**David Vitter**	237,810	29,935	191,379	16,496	12.6	80.5	6.9
2	**William Jefferson**	unopposed	–	–	–	–	–	–	–
3	unopposed	**W. J. Tauzin**	183,960	–	143,446	40,514	–	78.0	22.0
4	Phillip Green	**Jim McCrery**	173,967	43,600	122,678	7,689	25.1	70.5	4.4
5	Roger Beall	**John Cooksey**	179,473	42,977	123,975	12,521	23.9	69.1	7.0
6	Kathy Rogillio	**Richard Baker**	243,478	72,192	165,637	5,649	29.7	68.0	2.3
7	unopposed	**Chris John**	183,483	152,796	–	30,687	83.3	–	16.7
Maine									
1	**Thomas Allen**	Jane Amero	339,094	202,823	123,915	12,356	59.8	36.5	3.6
2	**John Baldacci**	Richard Campbell	299,305	219,783	79,522	0	73.4	26.6	0.0
Maryland									
1	Bennett Bozman	**Wayne Gilchrest**	256,682	91,022	165,293	367	35.5	64.4	0.1
2	Kenneth Bosley	**Robert Ehrlich Jr.**	260,432	81,591	178,556	285	31.3	68.6	0.1

(continued)

House of Representatives Election Results, 2000 (continued)

State/District	Democrat	Republican	Total Vote	Dem Vote	Rep Vote	Other Vote	Dem %	Rep %	Other %
Maryland (cont.)									
3	Benjamin Cardin	Colin Harby	223,818	169,347	53,827	644	75.7	24.0	0.3
4	Albert Wynn	John Kimble	197,969	172,624	24,973	372	87.2	12.6	0.2
5	Steny Hoyer	Thomas Hutchins	255,375	166,231	89,019	125	65.1	34.9	0.0
6	Donald DeArmon	Roscoe Bartlett	278,045	109,136	168,624	285	39.3	60.6	0.1
7	Elijah Cummings	Kenneth Kondner	153,974	134,066	19,773	135	87.1	12.8	0.1
8	Terry Lierman	Constance Morella	300,469	136,840	156,241	7,388	45.5	52.0	2.5
Massachusetts									
1	John Olver	Peter Abair	248,201	169,375	73,580	5,246	68.2	29.6	2.1
2	Richard Neal	unopposed	198,846	196,670	–	2,176	98.9	–	1.1
3	James McGovern	unopposed	215,561	213,065	–	2,496	98.8	–	1.2
4	Barney Frank	Martin Travis	267,880	200,638	56,553	10,689	74.9	21.1	4.0
5	Martin Meehan	unopposed	203,641	199,601	–	4,040	98.0	–	2.0
6	John Tierney	Paul McCarthy	289,043	205,324	83,501	218	71.0	28.9	0.1
7	Edward Markey	unopposed	213,811	211,543	–	2,268	98.9	–	1.1
8	Michael Capuano	unopposed	145,072	144,031	–	1,041	99.3	–	0.7
9	John Joseph Moakley	Janet Jeghelian	248,756	193,020	48,672	7,064	77.6	19.6	2.8
10	William Delahunt	Eric Bleicken	316,564	234,675	81,192	697	74.1	25.6	0.2
Michigan									
1	Bart Stupak	Chuck Yob	290,569	169,649	117,300	3,620	58.4	40.4	1.2
2	Bob Shrauger	Peter Hoekstra	289,925	96,370	186,762	6,793	33.2	64.4	2.3
3	Timothy Steele	Vernon Ehlers	276,263	91,309	179,539	5,415	33.1	65.0	2.0
4	Lawrence Hollenbeck	Dave Camp	267,819	78,019	182,128	7,672	29.1	68.0	2.9
5	James Barcia	Ronald Actis	247,737	184,048	59,274	4,415	74.3	23.9	1.8
6	James Bupp	Fred Upton	234,640	68,532	159,373	6,735	29.2	67.9	2.9
7	Jennie Crittendon	Nick Smith	241,010	86,080	147,369	7,561	35.7	61.1	3.1
8	Dianne Byrum	Mike Rogers	297,609	145,079	145,190	7,340	48.7	48.8	2.5
9	Dale Kildee	Grant Garrett	258,928	158,184	92,926	7,818	61.1	35.9	3.0
10	David Bonior	Tom Turner	282,269	181,818	93,713	6,738	64.4	33.2	2.4
11	Matthew Frumin	Joe Knollenberg	306,302	124,053	170,790	11,459	40.5	55.8	3.7
12	Sander Levin	Bart Baron	245,169	157,720	78,795	8,654	64.3	32.1	3.5
13	Lynn Nancy Rivers	Carl Berry	247,521	160,084	79,445	7,992	64.7	32.1	3.2
14	John Conyers Jr.	William Ashe	189,707	168,982	17,582	3,143	89.1	9.3	1.7

District	Candidate 1	Candidate 2	Total	Vote 1	Vote 2	Vote 3	% 1	% 2	% 3
15	**Carolyn Kilpatrick**	C. D. Boyd-Fields	158,751	140,609	14,336	3,806	88.6	9.0	2.4
16	**John Dingell**	William Morse	235,517	167,142	62,469	5,906	71.0	26.5	2.5
Minnesota									
1	Mary Rieder	**Gil Gutknecht**	283,221	117,946	159,835	5,440	41.6	56.4	1.9
2	David Minge	**Mark Kennedy**	288,900	138,802	138,957	11,141	48.0	48.1	3.9
3	Sue Shuff	**Jim Ramstad**	329,062	98,219	222,571	8,272	29.8	67.6	2.5
4	**Betty McCollum**	Linda Runbeck	271,439	130,403	83,852	57,184	48.0	30.9	21.1
5	**Martin Olav Sabo**	Frank Taylor	255,145	176,629	58,191	20,325	69.2	22.8	8.0
6	**Bill Luther**	John Kline	355,824	176,340	170,900	8,584	49.6	48.0	2.4
7	**Collin Peterson**	Glen Menze	270,496	185,771	79,175	5,550	68.7	29.3	2.1
8	**James Oberstar**	Bob Lemen	309,651	210,094	79,890	19,667	67.8	25.8	6.4
Mississippi									
1	Joe Grist Jr.	**Roger Wicker**	209,040	59,763	145,967	3,310	28.6	69.8	1.6
2	**Bennie Thompson**	Hardy Caraway	173,307	112,777	54,090	6,440	65.1	31.2	3.7
3	William Thrash	**Charles Pickering**	210,363	54,151	153,899	2,313	25.7	73.2	1.1
4	**Ronnie Shows**	Dunn Lampton	199,034	115,732	79,218	4,084	58.1	39.8	2.1
5	**Gene Taylor**	Randy McDonnell	194,395	153,264	35,309	5,822	78.8	18.2	3.0
Missouri									
1	**William Lacy Clay**	Z. Dwight Billingsly	198,347	149,173	42,730	6,444	75.2	21.5	3.2
2	Ted House	**Todd Akin**	298,062	126,441	164,926	6,695	42.4	55.3	2.2
3	**Richard Gephardt**	Bill Federer	254,539	147,222	100,967	6,350	57.8	39.7	2.5
4	**Ike Skelton**	Jim Noland	269,889	180,634	84,406	4,849	66.9	31.3	1.8
5	**Karen McCarthy**	Steve Gordon	232,137	159,826	66,439	5,872	68.8	28.6	2.5
6	Steve Danner	**Samuel Graves Jr.**	273,201	127,792	138,925	6,484	46.8	50.9	2.4
7	Charles Christrup	**Roy Blunt**	273,937	65,510	202,305	6,122	23.9	73.9	2.2
8	Bob Camp	**Jo Ann Emerson**	234,066	67,760	162,239	4,067	28.9	69.3	1.7
9	Steven Carroll	**Kenny Hulshof**	291,610	111,662	172,787	7,161	38.3	59.3	2.5
Montana									
	Nancy Keenan	**Dennis Rehberg**	410,523	189,971	211,418	9,134	46.3	51.5	2.2
Nebraska									
1	Alan Jacobsen	**Doug Bereuter**	234,698	72,859	155,485	6,354	31.0	66.2	2.7
2	Shelley Kiel	**Lee Terry**	226,280	70,268	148,911	7,101	31.1	65.8	3.1
3	Roland Reynolds	**Tom Osborne**	222,093	34,944	182,117	5,032	15.7	82.0	2.3

(continued)

House of Representatives Election Results, 2000 (continued)

State/District	Democrat	Republican	Total Vote	Dem Vote	Rep Vote	Other Vote	Dem %	Rep %	Other %
Nevada									
1	Shelley Berkley	Jon Porter	229,235	118,469	101,276	9,490	51.7	44.2	4.1
2	Tierney Cahill	Jim Gibbons	355,969	106,379	229,608	19,982	29.9	64.5	5.6
New Hampshire									
1	Martha Fuller Clark	John Sununu	284,862	128,387	150,609	5,866	45.1	52.9	2.1
2	Barney Brannen	Charles Bass	271,555	110,367	152,581	8,607	40.6	56.2	3.2
New Jersey									
1	Robert Andrews	Charlene Cathcart	219,612	167,327	46,455	5,830	76.2	21.2	2.7
2	Edward Janosik	Frank LoBiondo	233,859	74,632	155,187	4,040	31.9	66.4	1.7
3	Susan Bass Levin	Jim Saxton	274,083	112,848	157,053	4,182	41.2	57.3	1.5
4	Reed Gusciora	Christopher Smith	250,810	87,956	158,515	4,339	35.1	63.2	1.7
5	Linda Mercurio	Marge Roukema	268,524	81,715	175,546	11,263	30.4	65.4	4.2
6	Frank Pallone Jr.	Brian Kennedy	209,852	141,698	62,454	5,700	67.5	29.8	2.7
7	Maryanne Connelly	Mike Ferguson	248,999	113,479	128,434	7,086	45.6	51.6	2.8
8	Bill Pascrell Jr.	Anthony Fusco Jr.	200,132	134,074	60,606	5,452	67.0	30.3	2.7
9	Steven Rothman	Joseph Tedeschi	206,771	140,462	61,984	4,325	67.9	30.0	2.1
10	Donald Payne	Dirk Weber	152,045	133,073	18,436	536	87.5	12.1	0.4
11	John Scollo	Rodney Frelinghuysen	273,838	80,958	186,140	6,740	29.6	68.0	2.5
12	Rush Holt	Dick Zimmer	299,942	146,162	145,511	8,269	48.7	48.5	2.8
13	Robert Menendez	Theresa de Leon	149,766	117,856	27,849	4,061	78.7	18.6	2.7
New Mexico									
1	John Kelly	Heather Wilson	213,139	92,187	107,296	13,656	43.3	50.3	6.4
2	Michael Montoya	Joe Skeen	173,356	72,614	100,742	0	41.9	58.1	0.0
3	Tom Udall	Lisa Lutz	201,019	135,040	65,979	0	67.2	32.8	0.0
New York									
1	Regina Seltzer	Felix Grucci Jr.	239,604	97,299	133,020	9,285	40.6	55.5	3.9
2	Steve Isreal	Joan Johnson	188,632	90,438	65,880	32,314	47.9	34.9	17.1
3	Dal LaMagna	Peter King	240,428	95,787	143,126	1,515	39.8	59.5	0.6
4	Carolyn McCarthy	Gregory Becker	225,755	136,703	87,830	1,222	60.6	38.9	0.5
5	Gary Ackerman	Edward Elkowitz	202,614	137,684	61,084	3,846	68.0	30.1	1.9

District	Candidate (1)	Candidate (2)	Total Vote	Vote (1)	Vote (2)	Other Vote	% (1)	% (2)	Other %
6	**Gregory Meeks**	unopposed	120,818	120,818	—	0	100.0	—	0.0
7	**Joseph Crowley**	Rose Robles Birtley	109,101	78,207	24,592	6,302	71.7	22.5	5.8
8	**Jerrold Nadler**	Marian Henry	184,969	150,273	27,057	7,639	81.2	14.6	4.1
9	**Anthony Weiner**	Noach Dear	144,632	98,983	45,649	0	68.4	31.6	0.0
10	**Edolphus Towns**	Ernestine Brown	133,884	120,700	6,852	6,332	90.2	5.1	4.7
11	**Major Owens**	Susan Cleary	128,784	112,050	8,406	8,328	87.0	6.5	6.5
12	**Nydia Velazquez**	Rosemary Markgraf	99,080	86,288	10,052	2,740	87.1	10.1	2.8
13	Katina Johnstone	**Vito Fossella**	170,062	57,603	109,806	2,653	33.9	64.6	1.6
14	**Carolyn Maloney**	Adrienne Rhodes	200,348	148,080	45,453	6,815	73.9	22.7	3.4
15	**Charles Rangel**	Jose Augustin Suero	141,664	130,161	7,346	4,157	91.9	5.2	2.9
16	**Jose Serrano**	Aaron Justice	107,546	103,041	3,934	571	95.8	3.7	0.5
17	**Eliot Engel**	Patrick McManus	128,294	115,093	13,201	0	89.7	10.3	0.0
18	**Nita Lowey**	John Vonglis	188,647	126,878	58,022	3,747	67.3	30.8	2.0
19	Larry Otis Graham	**Sue Kelly**	239,151	85,871	145,532	7,748	35.9	60.9	3.2
20	Paul Feiner	**Benjamin Gilman**	236,033	94,646	136,016	5,371	40.1	57.6	2.3
21	**Michael McNulty**	Thomas Pillsworth	235,672	175,339	60,333	0	74.4	25.6	0.0
22	Kenneth McCallion	**John Sweeney**	246,479	79,111	167,368	0	32.1	67.9	0.0
23	Richard Englebrecht	**Sherwood Boehlert**	205,035	38,049	124,132	42,854	18.6	60.5	20.9
24	Neil Tallon	**John McHugh**	186,187	42,698	138,322	5,167	22.9	74.3	2.8
25	Francis Gavin	**James Walsh**	220,243	64,533	151,880	3,830	29.3	69.0	1.7
26	**Maurice Hinchey**	Bob Moppert	226,579	140,395	78,103	8,081	62.0	34.5	3.6
27	Thomas Pecoraro	**Thomas Reynolds**	227,564	69,870	157,694	0	30.7	69.3	0.0
28	**Louise Slaughter**	Mark Johns	230,856	151,688	75,348	3,820	65.7	32.6	1.7
29	**John LaFalce**	Brett Sommer	209,487	128,328	81,159	0	61.3	38.7	0.0
30	John Fee	**Jack Quinn**	206,271	67,819	138,452	0	32.9	67.1	0.0
31	Kisun Peters	**Amo Houghton**	199,431	45,193	154,238	0	22.7	77.3	0.0

North Carolina

District	Candidate (1)	Candidate (2)	Total Vote	Vote (1)	Vote (2)	Other Vote	% (1)	% (2)	Other %
1	**Eva Clayton**	Duane Kratzer Jr.	189,168	124,171	62,198	2,799	65.6	32.9	1.5
2	**Bob Etheridge**	Doug Haynes	251,838	146,733	103,011	2,094	58.3	40.9	0.8
3	Leigh Harvey McNairy	**Walter Jones**	198,455	74,058	121,940	2,457	37.3	61.4	1.2
4	**David Price**	Jess Ward	325,870	200,885	119,412	5,573	61.6	36.6	1.7
5	unopposed	**Richard Burr**	185,855	—	172,489	13,366	—	92.8	7.2
6	unopposed	**Howard Coble**	215,085	—	195,727	19,358	—	91.0	9.0
7	**Mike McIntyre**	James Adams	229,666	160,185	66,463	3,018	69.7	28.9	1.3
8	Mike Taylor	**Robert Hayes**	203,464	89,505	111,950	2,009	44.0	55.0	1.0
9	Ed McGuire	**Sue Myrick**	264,220	79,382	181,161	3,677	30.0	68.6	1.4

House of Representatives Election Results, 2000 *(continued)*

State/District	Democrat	Republican	Total Vote	Dem Vote	Rep Vote	Other Vote	Dem %	Rep %	Other %
North Carolina *(cont.)*									
10	Delmas Parker	**T. Cass Ballenger**	240,658	70,877	164,182	5,599	29.5	68.2	2.3
11	Sam Neill	**Charles Taylor**	266,377	112,234	146,677	7,466	42.1	55.1	2.8
12	**Mel Watt**	Chad Mitchell	209,144	135,570	69,596	3,978	64.8	33.3	1.9
North Dakota	**Earl Pomeroy**	John Dorso	285,658	151,173	127,251	7,234	52.9	44.5	2.5
Ohio									
1	John Cranley	**Steve Chabot**	220,428	98,328	116,768	5,332	44.6	53.0	2.4
2	Charles Sanders	**Rob Portman**	277,541	64,091	204,184	9,266	23.1	73.6	3.3
3	**Tony Hall**	unopposed	214,247	177,731	–	36,516	83.0	–	17.0
4	Daniel Dickman	**Michael Oxley**	232,118	67,330	156,510	8,278	29.0	67.4	3.6
5	Dannie Edmon	**Paul Gillmor**	243,340	62,138	169,857	11,345	25.5	69.8	4.7
6	**Ted Strickland**	Mike Azinger	240,574	138,849	96,966	4,759	57.7	40.3	2.0
7	**Donald Minor**	Dave Hobson	242,186	60,755	163,646	17,785	25.1	67.6	7.3
8	John Parks	**John Boehner**	253,303	66,293	179,756	7,254	26.2	71.0	2.9
9	**Marcy Kaptur**	Dwight Bryan	225,328	168,547	49,446	7,335	74.8	21.9	3.3
10	**Dennis Kucinich**	Bill Smith	222,755	167,063	48,930	6,762	75.0	22.0	3.0
11	**Stephanie Jones**	James Sykora	193,519	164,134	21,630	7,755	84.8	11.2	4.0
12	M. O'Shaughnessy	**Pat Tiberi**	263,386	115,432	139,242	8,712	43.8	52.9	3.3
13	**Sherrod Brown**	Rick Jeric	263,298	170,058	84,295	8,945	64.6	32.0	3.4
14	**Thomas Sawyer**	Rick Wood	230,088	149,184	71,432	9,472	64.8	31.0	4.1
15	Bill Buckel	**Deborah Pryce**	232,297	64,805	156,792	10,700	27.9	67.5	4.6
16	William Smith	**Ralph Regula**	234,400	62,709	162,294	9,397	26.8	69.2	4.0
17	**James Traficant**	Paul Alberty	240,877	120,333	54,751	65,793	50.0	22.7	27.3
18	Marc Guthrie	**Bob Ney**	236,505	79,232	152,325	4,948	33.5	64.4	2.1
19	Dale Blanchard	**Steven LaTourette**	251,648	70,429	174,262	6,957	28.0	69.2	2.8
Oklahoma									
1	Dan Lowe	**Steve Largent**	200,005	58,493	138,528	2,984	29.2	69.3	1.5
2	**Brad Carson**	Andy Ewing	195,412	107,273	81,672	6,467	54.9	41.8	3.3
3	unopposed	**Wes Watkins**	159,216	–	137,826	21,390	–	86.6	13.4
4	Larry Weatherford	**J. C. Watts Jr.**	175,684	54,808	114,000	6,876	31.2	64.9	3.9
5	Garland McWatters	**Ernest Istook**	196,022	53,275	134,159	8,588	27.2	68.4	4.4
6	Randy Beutler	**Frank Lucas**	161,176	63,106	95,635	2,435	39.2	59.3	1.5

Oregon

Dist.	Candidate		Total						
1	David Wu	Charles Starr	303,521	176,902	115,303	11,316	58.3	38.0	3.7
2	Greg Walden	Walter Ponsford	298,907	78,101	220,086	720	26.1	73.6	0.2
3	Earl Blumenauer	Jeffrey Pollock	271,161	181,049	64,128	25,984	66.8	23.6	9.6
4	Peter DeFazio	John Lindsey	291,065	197,998	88,950	4,117	68.0	30.6	1.4
5	Darlene Hooley	Brian Boquist	275,348	156,315	118,631	402	56.8	43.1	0.1

Pennsylvania

Dist.	Candidate		Total						
1	Robert Brady	Steven Kush	169,541	149,621	19,920	0	88.3	11.7	0.0
2	Chaka Fattah	unopposed	183,694	180,021	–	3,673	98.0	–	2.0
3	Robert Borski	Charles Dougherty	189,871	130,528	59,343	0	68.7	31.3	0.0
4	Melissa Hart	Terry Van Horne	246,467	100,995	145,390	82	41.0	59.0	0.0
5	John Peterson	unopposed	172,517	–	147,570	24,947	–	85.5	14.5
6	Tim Holden	Thomas Kopel	211,313	140,084	71,227	2	66.3	33.7	0.0
7	Curt Weldon	Peter Lennon	266,256	93,687	172,569	0	35.2	64.8	0.0
8	Jim Greenwood	Ronald Strouse	260,710	100,617	154,090	6,003	38.6	59.1	2.3
9	Bud Shuster	unopposed	185,466	–	184,401	1,065	–	99.4	0.6
10	Don Sherwood	Pat Casey	237,435	112,580	124,830	25	47.4	52.6	0.0
11	Paul Kanjorski	Stephen Urban	198,665	131,948	66,699	18	66.4	33.6	0.0
12	John Murtha	Bill Choby	205,448	145,538	56,575	3,335	70.8	27.5	1.6
13	Joseph Hoeffel	Stewart Greenleaf	276,751	146,026	126,501	4,224	52.8	45.7	1.5
14	William Coyne	unopposed	147,749	147,533	–	216	99.9	–	0.1
15	Pat Toomey	Ed O'Brien	222,184	103,864	118,307	13	46.7	53.2	0.0
16	Joseph Pitts	Bob Yorczyk	242,589	80,177	162,403	9	33.1	66.9	0.0
17	George Gekas	L. H. Herrmann	232,460	66,190	166,236	34	28.5	71.5	0.0
18	Mike Doyle	Craig Stephens	224,956	156,131	68,798	27	69.4	30.6	0.0
19	Todd Platts	Jeff Sanders	232,622	61,538	168,722	2,362	26.5	72.5	1.0
20	Frank Mascara	Ronald Davis	225,463	145,131	80,312	20	64.4	35.6	0.0
21	Phil English	Marc Flitter	222,190	87,018	135,164	8	39.2	60.8	0.0

Rhode Island

Dist.	Candidate		Total						
1	Patrick Kennedy	Stephen Cabral	185,163	123,442	61,522	199	66.7	33.2	0.1
2	James Langevin	Robert Tingle	198,964	123,805	27,932	47,227	62.2	14.0	23.7

South Carolina

Dist.	Candidate		Total						
1	Henry Brown	Andy Brack	231,446	82,622	139,597	9,227	35.7	60.3	4.0
2	Floyd Spence	Jane Frederick	270,976	110,672	154,338	5,966	40.8	57.0	2.2

(continued)

House of Representatives Election Results, 2000 (continued)

State/District	Democrat	Republican	Total Vote	Dem Vote	Rep Vote	Other Vote	Dem %	Rep %	Other %
South Carolina (cont.)									
3	George Brightharp	Lindsey Graham	221,621	67,174	150,176	4,271	30.3	67.8	1.9
4	unopposed	Jim DeMint	189,051	–	150,436	38,615	–	79.6	20.4
5	John Spratt	Carl Gullick	215,838	126,877	85,247	3,714	58.8	39.5	1.7
6	James Clyburn	Vince Ellison	192,380	138,053	50,005	4,322	71.8	26.0	2.2
South Dakota	Curt Hohn	John Thune	314,761	78,321	231,083	5,357	24.9	73.4	1.7
Tennessee									
1	unopposed	William Jenkins	157,848	–	157,828	20	–	100.0	0.0
2	unopposed	John Duncan Jr.	209,485	–	187,154	22,331	–	89.3	10.7
3	William Callaway	Zack Wamp	218,940	75,785	139,840	3,315	34.6	63.9	1.5
4	David Dunaway	Van Hilleary	203,210	67,165	133,622	2,423	33.1	65.8	1.2
5	Bob Clement	Stan Scott	205,933	149,277	50,386	6,270	72.5	24.5	3.0
6	Bart Gordon	David Charles	271,899	168,861	97,169	5,869	62.1	35.7	2.2
7	Richard Sims	Ed Bryant	245,649	71,587	171,056	3,006	29.1	69.6	1.2
8	John Tanner	Billy Yancy	198,080	143,127	54,929	24	72.3	27.7	0.0
9	Harold Ford Jr.	unopposed	143,334	143,298	–	36	100.0	–	0.0
Texas									
1	Max Sandlin	Noble Willingham	211,848	118,157	91,912	1,779	55.8	43.4	0.8
2	Jim Turner	unopposed	178,830	162,891	–	15,939	91.1	–	8.9
3	Billy Wayne Zachary	Sam Johnson	261,897	67,233	187,486	7,178	25.7	71.6	2.7
4	Ralph Hall	Jon Newton	241,878	145,887	91,574	4,417	60.3	37.9	1.8
5	R. M. Coggins	Pete Sessions	185,958	82,629	100,487	2,842	44.4	54.0	1.5
6	unopposed	Joe Barton	252,741	–	222,685	30,056	–	88.1	11.9
7	Jeff Sell	John Culberson	248,593	60,694	183,712	4,187	24.4	73.9	1.7
8	unopposed	Kevin Brady	255,216	–	233,848	21,368	–	91.6	8.4
9	Nick Lampson	Paul Williams	219,816	130,143	87,165	2,508	59.2	39.7	1.1
10	Lloyd Doggett	unopposed	240,831	203,628	–	37,203	84.6	–	15.4
11	Chet Edwards	Ramsey Farley	192,918	105,782	85,546	1,590	54.8	44.3	0.8
12	Mark Greene	Kay Granger	187,916	67,612	117,739	2,565	36.0	62.7	1.4
13	Curtis Clinesmith	Mac Thornberry	174,475	54,343	117,995	2,137	31.1	67.6	1.2
14	Loy Sneary	Ron Paul	230,059	92,689	137,370	0	40.3	59.7	0.0
15	Ruben Hinojosa	unopposed	120,448	106,570	–	13,878	88.5	–	11.5
16	Silvestre Reyes	Daniel Power	135,650	92,649	40,921	2,080	68.3	30.2	1.5

District	Candidate 1	Candidate 2	Total vote	Cand. 1 vote	Cand. 2 vote	Other vote	Cand. 1 %	Cand. 2 %	Other %
17	**Charlie Stenholm**	Darrell Clements	204,430	120,670	72,535	11,225	59.0	35.5	5.5
18	**Sheila Jackson Lee**	Bob Levy	172,378	131,857	38,191	2,330	76.5	22.2	1.4
19	unopposed	**Larry Combest**	185,898	—	170,319	15,579	—	91.6	8.4
20	**Charles Gonzalez**	unopposed	122,574	107,487	—	15,087	87.7	—	12.3
21	Jim Green	**Lamar Smith**	330,878	73,326	251,049	6,503	22.2	75.9	2.0
22	Jo Ann Matranga	**Tom DeLay**	256,267	92,645	154,662	8,960	36.2	60.4	3.5
23	Isidro Garza Jr.	**Henry Bonilla**	201,754	78,274	119,679	3,801	38.8	59.3	1.9
24	**Martin Frost**	James Wright	166,948	103,152	61,235	2,561	61.8	36.7	1.5
25	**Ken Bentsen**	Phil Sudan	176,522	106,112	68,010	2,400	60.1	38.5	1.4
26	Steve Love	**Dick Armey**	295,272	75,601	214,025	5,646	25.6	72.5	1.9
27	**Solomon Ortiz**	Pat Ahumada	161,072	102,088	54,660	4,324	63.4	33.9	2.7
28	**Ciro Rodriguez**	unopposed	138,260	123,104	—	15,156	89.0	—	11.0
29	**Gene Green**	Allen Goforth	115,475	84,665	29,606	1,204	73.3	25.6	1.0
30	**E. B. Johnson**	unopposed	118,961	109,163	—	9,798	91.8	—	8.2
Utah									
1	K. M. Collinwood	**James Hansen**	261,805	71,229	180,591	9,985	27.2	69.0	3.8
2	**Jim Matheson**	Derek Smith	259,601	145,021	107,114	7,466	55.9	41.3	2.9
3	Donald Dunn	**Chris Cannon**	237,348	88,547	138,943	9,858	37.3	58.5	4.2
Vermont[b]	Pete Diamondstone	Karen Ann Kerin	283,366	14,918	51,977	216,471	5.3	18.3	76.4
Virginia									
1	Lawrence Davies	**Jo Ann Davis**	263,014	97,399	151,344	14,271	37.0	57.5	5.4
2	Jody Wagner	**Edward Schrock**	188,329	90,328	97,856	145	48.0	52.0	0.1
3	**Robert Scott**	unopposed	140,753	137,527	—	3,226	97.7	—	2.3
4	**Norman Sisisky**	unopposed	191,895	189,787	—	2,108	98.9	—	1.1
5[c]	John Boyd Jr.		212,705	65,387	—	147,318	30.7	—	69.3
6	unopposed	**Robert Goodlatte**	154,483	—	153,338	1,145	—	99.3	0.7
7	Warren Stewart	**Eric Cantor**	287,891	94,935	192,652	304	33.0	66.9	0.1
8	**James Moran Jr.**	Demaris Miller	259,199	164,178	88,262	6,759	63.3	34.1	2.6
9	**Frederick Boucher**	Michael Osborne	196,855	137,488	59,335	32	69.8	30.1	0.0
10	unopposed	**Frank Wolf**	283,637	—	238,817	44,820	—	84.2	15.8
11	M. L. Corrigan	**Thomas Davis, III**	242,968	83,455	150,395	9,118	34.3	61.9	3.8
Washington									
1	**Jay Inslee**	Dan McDonald	285,636	155,820	121,823	7,993	54.6	42.6	2.8
2	**Rick Larsen**	John Koster	293,180	146,617	134,660	11,903	50.0	45.9	4.1

(continued)

House of Representatives Election Results, 2000 (continued)

State/District	Democrat	Republican	Total Vote	Dem Vote	Rep Vote	Other Vote	Dem %	Rep %	Other %
Washington (cont.)									
3	Brian Baird	Trent Matson	282,664	159,428	114,861	8,375	56.4	40.6	3.0
4	Jim Davis	Doc Hastings	235,104	87,585	143,259	4,260	37.3	60.9	1.8
5	Tom Keefe	George Nethercutt Jr.	251,214	97,703	144,038	9,473	38.9	57.3	3.8
6	Norm Dicks	Bob Lawrence	254,713	164,853	79,215	10,645	64.7	31.1	4.2
7	Jim McDermott	unopposed	265,809	193,470	–	72,339	72.8	–	27.2
8	H. Behrens-Benedict	Jennifer Dunn	294,468	104,944	183,255	6,269	35.6	62.2	2.1
9	Adam Smith	Chris Vance	219,623	135,452	76,766	7,405	61.7	35.0	3.4
West Virginia									
1	Alan Mollohan	unopposed	194,771	170,974	–	23,797	87.8	–	12.2
2	Jim Humphreys	Shelley Moore Capito	224,315	103,003	108,769	12,543	45.9	48.5	5.6
3	Nick Joe Rahall, II	unopposed	160,786	146,807	–	13,979	91.3	–	8.7
Wisconsin									
1	Jeffrey Thomas	Paul Ryan	266,791	88,885	177,612	294	33.3	66.6	0.1
2	Tammy Baldwin	John Sharpless	318,380	163,534	154,632	214	51.4	48.6	0.1
3	Ron Kind	Susan Tully	272,212	173,505	97,741	966	63.7	35.9	0.4
4	Jerry Kleczka	Tim Riener	269,265	163,622	101,811	3,832	60.8	37.8	1.4
5	Tom Barrett	Jonathan Smith	223,852	173,893	49,296	663	77.7	22.0	0.3
6	Dan Flaherty	Tom Petri	275,605	96,125	179,205	275	34.9	65.0	0.1
7	David Obey	Sean Cronin	273,460	173,007	100,264	189	63.3	36.7	0.1
8	Dean Reich	Mark Green	283,294	71,575	211,388	331	25.3	74.6	0.1
9	Mike Clawson	F. J. Sensenbrenner Jr.	323,455	83,720	239,498	237	25.9	74.0	0.1
Wyoming	Michael Allen Green	Barbara Cubin	212,312	60,638	141,848	9,826	28.6	66.8	4.6

Names in boldface type denote the winner.

a Under Louisiana law, a candidate who wins a majority of the votes in the primary election is elected. When no candidate wins a majority, the two top vote-getters—regardless of party—face each other in a runoff election. A candidate who runs unopposed in the primary is declared elected and is not listed on the ballot in either the primary or general election.

b The Independent candidate, Bernie Sanders, won the election with 196,118 votes.

c The Independent candidate, Virgil H. Goode Jr., won the election with 143,312 votes.

Source: Federal Election Commission. Federal Elections 2000. Washington, DC: Federal Election Commission, 2001.

Senate Election Results, 2000

State	Democrat	Republican	Total Vote	Dem Vote	Rep Vote	Other Vote	Dem %	Rep %	Other %
AZ	unopposed	**Jon Kyl**	1,397,076	0	1,108,196	288,880	0.0	79.3	20.7
CA	**Dianne Feinstein**	Tom Campbell	10,623,614	5,932,522	3,886,853	804,239	55.8	36.6	7.6
CT	**Joe Lieberman**	Phil Giordano	1,311,261	828,902	448,077	34,282	63.2	34.2	2.6
DE	**Thomas R. Carper**	William V. Roth Jr.	327,017	181,566	142,891	2,560	55.5	43.7	0.8
FL	**Bill Nelson**	Bill McCollum	5,856,731	2,989,487	2,705,348	161,896	51.0	46.2	2.8
GA	**Zell Miller**	Mack Mattingly	2,428,513	1,413,224	920,478	94,811	58.2	37.9	3.9
HI	**Daniel K. Akaka**	John Carroll	345,623	251,215	84,701	9,707	72.7	24.5	2.8
IN	David L. Johnson	**Richard G. Lugar**	2,145,209	683,273	1,427,944	33,992	31.9	66.6	1.6
ME	Mark W. Lawrence	**Olympia J. Snowe**	634,872	197,183	437,689	0	31.1	68.9	0.0
MD	**Paul S. Sarbanes**	Paul H. Rappaport	1,946,898	1,230,013	715,178	1,707	63.2	36.7	0.1
MA	**Edward M. Kennedy**	Jack E. Robinson III	2,599,420	1,889,494	334,341	375,585	72.7	12.9	14.4
MI	**Debbie Stabenow**	Spence Abraham	4,167,685	2,061,952	1,994,693	111,040	49.5	47.9	2.7
MN	**Mark Dayton**	Rod Grams	2,419,520	1,181,553	1,047,474	190,493	48.8	43.3	7.9
MS	Troy D. Brown Sr.	**Trent Lott**	994,144	314,090	654,941	25,113	31.6	65.9	2.5
MO	**Mel Carnahan***	John Ashcroft	2,361,586	1,191,812	1,142,852	26,922	50.5	48.4	1.1
MT	Brian Schweitzer	**Conrad Burns**	411,601	194,430	208,082	9,089	47.2	50.6	2.2
NE	**Ben Nelson**	Don Stenberg	692,350	353,093	337,977	1,280	51.0	48.8	0.2
NV	Ed Bernstein	**John Ensign**	600,250	238,260	330,687	31,303	39.7	55.1	5.2
NJ	**Jon S. Corzine**	Bob Franks	3,015,662	1,511,237	1,420,267	84,158	50.1	47.1	2.8
NM	**Jeff Bingaman**	Bill Redmond	589,526	363,744	225,517	265	61.7	38.3	0.0
NY	**Hillary Rodham Clinton**	Rick Lazio	6,779,839	3,747,310	2,915,730	116,799	55.3	43.0	1.7
ND	**Kent Conrad**	Duane Sand	287,539	176,470	111,069	0	61.4	38.6	0.0
OH	Ted Celeste	**Mike DeWine**	4,448,801	1,595,066	2,665,512	188,223	35.9	59.9	4.2
PA	Ron Klink	**Rick Santorum**	4,735,504	2,154,908	2,481,962	98,634	45.5	52.4	2.1
RI	Robert A. Weygand	**Lincoln D. Chafee**	391,537	161,023	222,588	7,926	41.1	56.8	2.0
TN	Jeff Clark	**Bill Frist**	1,928,613	621,152	1,255,444	52,017	32.2	65.1	2.7
TX	Gene Kelly	**Kay Bailey Hutchison**	6,276,652	2,030,315	4,082,091	164,246	32.3	65.0	2.6
UT	Scott N. Howell	**Orrin G. Hatch**	769,704	242,569	504,803	22,332	31.5	65.6	2.9
VT	Ed Flanagan	**Jim Jeffords**	288,500	73,352	189,133	26,015	25.4	65.6	9.0
VA	Charles S. Robb	**George F. Allen**	2,718,301	1,296,093	1,420,460	1,748	47.7	52.3	0.1
WA	**Maria Cantwell**	Slade Gorton	2,461,379	1,199,437	1,197,208	64,734	48.7	48.6	2.6
WV	**Robert C. Byrd**	David T. Gallaher	603,477	469,215	121,635	12,627	77.8	20.2	2.1
WI	**Herbert H. Kohl**	John Gillespie	2,540,083	1,563,238	940,744	36,101	61.5	37.0	1.4
WY	Mel Logan	**Craig Thomas**	213,659	47,087	157,622	8,950	22.0	73.8	4.2

Names in boldface type denote the winner.

*Carnahan died before the election. His widow, Lynn Carnahan, was appointed to fill the vacancy.

Source: Federal Election Commission. *Federal Elections 2000.* Washington, DC: Federal Election Commission, 2001.

Party Composition in Congress, 1788–2000

Year	Congress	House Dem.[a]	House Rep.[b]	House Other	House Gains/losses[c] Dem.	House Gains/losses[c] Rep.	Senate Dem.[a]	Senate Rep.[b]	Senate Other	Senate Gains/losses[c] Dem.	Senate Gains/losses[c] Rep.	President[d]
1788	1st	26	38				9	17				Washington (F)
1790	2d	33	37				13	16				
1792	3d	57	48				13	17				Washington (F)
1794	4th	52	54				13	19				
1796	5th	48	58				12	20				J. Adams (F)
1798	6th	42	64				13	19				
1800	7th	69	36				18	13				Jefferson (DR)
1802	8th	102	39				25	9				
1804	9th	116	25				27	7				Jefferson (DR)
1806	10th	118	24				28	6				
1808	11th	94	48				28	6				Madison (DR)
1810	12th	108	36				30	6				
1812	13th	112	68				27	9				Madison (DR)
1814	14th	117	65				25	11				
1816	15th	141	42				34	10				Monroe (DR)
1818	16th	156	27				35	7				
1820	17th	158	25				44	4				Monroe (DR)
1822	18th	187	26				44	4				
1824	19th	105	97				26	20				J. Q. Adams (DR)
1826	20th	94	119				20	28				
1828	21st	139	74				26	22				Jackson (D)
1830	22d	141	58				25	21				
1832	23d	147	53				20	20				Jackson (D)
1834	24th	145	98				27	25				
1836	25th	108	107	24			30	18	4			Van Buren (D)
1838	26th	124	118				28	22				
1840	27th	102	133	6			28	22				Harrison (W)
1842	28th	142	79	1			25	28				Tyler (W)
1844	29th	143	77	6			31	25				Polk (D)
1846	30th	108	115	4			36	21	1			
1848	31st	112	109	9			35	25	2			Taylor (W)
1850	32d	140	88	5			35	24	3			Fillmore (W)
1852	33d	159	71	4			38	22	2			Pierce (D)
1854	34th	83	108	43			42	15	5			
1856	35th	131	92	14	+48	−16	39	20	5	−3	+5	Buchanan (D)
1858	36th	101	113	23	−30	+21	38	26	2	−1	+6	
1860	37th	42	106	28	−59	−7	11	31	7	−27	+5	Lincoln (R)
1862	38th	80	103		+38	−3	12	39		+1	+8	
1864	39th	46	145		−34	+42	10	42		−2	+3	Lincoln (R)
1866	40th	49	143		+3	−2	11	42		+1	0	A. Johnson (R)
1868	41st	73	170		+24	+27	11	61		0	+19	Grant (R)

		House			Gains/ losses[c]		Senate			Gains/ losses[c]		
Year	Congress	Dem.[a]	Rep.[b]	Other	Dem.	Rep.	Dem.[a]	Rep.[b]	Other	Dem.	Rep.	President[d]
1870	42d	104	139		+31	−31	17	57		+6	−4	
1872	43d	88	203		−16	+64	19	54		+2	−3	Grant (R)
1874	44th	181	107	3	+93	−96	29	46		+10	−8	
1876	45th	156	137		−25	+30	36	39	1	+7	−7	Hayes (R)
1878	46th	150	128	14	−6	−9	43	33		+7	−6	
1880	47th	130	152	11	−20	+24	37	37	2	−6	+4	Garfield (R)
1882	48th	200	119	6	+70	−33	36	40		−1	+3	Arthur (R)
1884	49th	182	140	2	−18	+21	34	41		−2	+2	Cleveland (D)
1886	50th	170	151	4	−12	+11	37	39		+3	−2	
1888	51st	156	173	1	−14	+22	37	47		0	+8	Harrison (R)
1890	52d	231	88	14	+75	−85	39	47	2	+2	0	
1892	53d	220	126	8	−11	+38	44	38	3	+5	−9	Cleveland (D)
1894	54th	104	246	7	−116	+120	39	44	5	−5	+6	
1896	55th	134	206	16	+30	−40	34	46	10	−5	+2	McKinley (R)
1898	56th	163	185	9	+29	−21	26	53	11	−8	+7	
1900	57th	153	198	5	−10	+13	29	56	3	+3	+3	McKinley (R)
1902	58th	178	207		+25	+9	32	58		+3	+2	T. Roosevelt (R)
1904	59th	136	250		−42	+43	32	58		0	0	T. Roosevelt (R)
1906	60th	164	222		+28	−28	29	61		−3	−3	
1908	61st	172	219		+8	−3	32	59		+3	−2	Taft (R)
1910	62d	228	162	1	+56	−57	42	49		+10	−10	
1912	63d	290	127	18	+62	−35	51	44	1	+9	−5	Wilson (D)
1914	64th	231	193	8	−59	+66	56	39	1	+5	−5	
1916	65th	210	216	9	−21	+23	53	42	1	−3	+3	Wilson (D)
1918	66th	191	237	7	−19	+21	47	48	1	−6	+6	
1920	67th	132	300	1	−59	+63	37	59		−10	+11	Harding (R)
1922	68th	207	225	3	+75	−75	43	51	2	+6	−8	
1924	69th	183	247	5	−24	+22	40	54	1	−3	+3	Coolidge (R)
1926	70th	195	237	3	+12	−10	47	48	1	+7	−6	
1928	71st	163	267	1	−32	+30	39	56	1	−8	+8	Hoover (R)
1930	72d	216	218	1	+53	−49	47	48	1	+8	−8	
1932	73d	313	117	5	+97	−101	59	36	1	+12	−12	F. D. Roosevelt (D)
1934	74th	322	103	10	+9	−14	69	25	2	+10	−11	
1936	75th	333	89	13	+11	−14	75	17	4	+6	−8	F. D. Roosevelt (D)
1938	76th	262	169	4	−71	+80	69	23	4	−6	+6	
1940	77th	267	162	6	+5	−7	66	28	2	−3	+5	F. D. Roosevelt (D)
1942	78th	222	209	4	−45	+47	57	38	1	−9	+10	
1944	79th	243	190	2	+21	−19	57	38	1	0	0	F. D. Roosevelt (D)
1946	80th	188	246	1	−55	+56	45	51		−12	+13	Truman (D)
1948	81st	263	171	1	+75	−75	54	42		+9	−9	Truman (D)

(continued)

Party Composition in Congress, 1788–2000 *(continued)*

Year	Congress	House Dem.[a]	House Rep.[b]	House Other	House Gains/losses[c] Dem.	House Gains/losses[c] Rep.	Senate Dem.[a]	Senate Rep.[b]	Senate Other	Senate Gains/losses[c] Dem.	Senate Gains/losses[c] Rep.	President[d]
1950	82d	234	199	2	−29	+28	48	47	1	−6	+5	
1952	83d	213	221	1	−21	+22	47	48	1	−1	+1	Eisenhower (R)
1954	84th	232	203		+19	−18	48	47	1	+1	−1	
1956	85th	234	201		+2	−2	49	47		+1	0	Eisenhower (R)
1958	86th	283	154		+49	−47	64	34		+17	−13	
1960	87th	263	174		−20	+20	64	36		−2	+2	Kennedy (D)
1962	88th	258	176	1	−4	+2	67	33		+4	−4	
1964	89th	295	140		+38	−38	68	32		+2	−2	L. Johnson (D)
1966	90th	248	187		−47	+47	64	36		−3	+3	
1968	91st	243	192		−4	+4	58	42		−5	+5	Nixon (R)
1970	92d	255	180		+12	−12	55	45		−4	+2	
1972	93d	243	192		−12	+12	57	43		+2	−2	Nixon (R)
1974	94th	291	144		+43	−43	61	38		+3	−3	Ford (R)
1976	95th	292	143		+1	−1	62	38		0	0	Carter (D)
1978	96th	277	158		−11	+11	59	41		−3	+3	
1980	97th	243	192		−33	+33	47	53		−12	+12	Reagan (R)
1982	98th	269	166		+26	−26	46	54		0	0	
1984	99th	253	182		−14	+14	47	53		+2	−2	Reagan (R)
1986	100th	258	177		+5	−5	55	45		+8	−8	
1988	101st	260	175		+3	−3	55	45		+1	−1	G. Bush (R)
1990	102d	267	167	1	+9	−8	56	44		+1	−1	
1992	103d	258	176	1	−10	+10	57	43		0	0	Clinton (D)
1994	104th	203	231	1	−53	+53	48[e]	52[e]		+7[e]	−7[e]	
1996	105th	206	227	1		−4	45	55		−3	+3	Clinton (D)
1998	106th	211	223	1	+8	−8	45	55		−0	−0	Clinton (D)
2000	107th	210	222	3	−1	−1	50[f]	50[f]		+5	−5	G. W. Bush (R)

[a] "Democratic" column indicates "Opposition" in 1788, "Democratic Republicans" from 1790 to 1822, "Jacksonians" in 1824 and 1826, and Democratic partisans in 1828 and later.

[b] The "Republican" column indicates "Administration" in 1788, "Federalists" from 1790 to 1822, "Administration" in 1824 and 1826, "National Republicans" in 1828 and 1830, "Anti-Masons" in 1832, "Whigs" from 1834 to 1852, and Republican partisans, 1854 on.

[c] Because of changes in the overall number of seats in the Senate and House, in the number of seats won by third parties, and in the number of vacancies, a Republican loss is not always matched precisely by a Democratic gain, or vice versa. Gains/losses reflect preelection/postelection changes. Deaths, resignations, and special elections can cause further changes in party makeup. In the 1930 election, for example, Republicans won majority control, but when Congress organized, special elections held to fill fourteen vacancies resulted in a Democratic majority.

[d] President elected in the year indicated or, if a midterm election year, nonelected president in office at the time of the midterm election.

[e] In 1994 Alabama senator Richard Shelby switched from Democrat to Republican the day after the election. With his switch the partisan balance became 53–47 and the Republicans gained eight seats.

[f] In spring 2001, Vermont senator James Jeffords switched from the Republican Party to become an Independent, thereby giving Democrats a 50 to 49 advantage in the Senate.

Sources: 1788–1852: *Bureau of the Census, Historical Statistics of the United States, Colonial Times to 1970* (Washington, D.C.: U.S. Government Printing Office, 1975), 1083–1084; 1854: *Congressional Quarterly, Elections 84* (Washington, D.C.: Congressional Quarterly, 1984), 106; 1856–1984: *Congressional Quarterly's Guide to U.S. Elections,* 2d ed. (Washington, D.C.: Congressional Quarterly, 1985), 1124; 1986–1990: *Congressional Quarterly Weekly Report* (1986), 2811, 2843; (1988), 3249, 3264, 3269; (1990), 3796; (1992), 3557, 3570, 3719, 3821; (1994), 3232, 3240.

Party Victories in House of Representatives, 1860–2000

State	1860–1895 Dem.	Rep.	1896–1931 Dem.	Rep.	1932–1965 Dem.	Rep.	1966–1995 Dem.	Rep.	1996–1999 Dem.	Rep.	2000 Dem.	Rep.
Alabama	92	19	170	0	146	5	68	40	4	10	2	5
Alaska	—	—	—	—	4	0	2	14	0	2	0	1
Arizona	—	—	11	0	26	7	22	4	2	10	1	5
Arkansas	54	5	124	0	109	0	40	19	4	4	3	1
California[a]	29	46	30	133	234	212	383	281	58	46	32	20
Colorado	1	9	21	34	43	26	40	39	4	8	2	4
Connecticut	33	36	11	77	58	44	55	35	8	4	3	3
Delaware	15	3	5	14	9	8	5	10	0	2	0	1
Florida	18	8	57	4	111	8	155	97	15	31	8	15
Georgia	111	11	207	0	170	1	126	27	6	16	3	8
Hawaii	—	—	0	0	6	0	28	2	4	0	2	0
Idaho	0	4	5	42	20	14	6	24	0	4	0	2
Illinois	118	191	136	333	220	221	184	162	20	20	10	10
Indiana	104	105	97	139	85	108	80	69	8	12	4	6
Iowa	16	131	10	193	35	105	36	55	2	8	1	4
Kansas	0	62	30	114	16	90	19	54	0	8	1	3
Kentucky	133	20	151	54	122	25	63	41	2	10	1	5
Louisiana	69	20	136	0	139	0	88	32	4	10	2	5
Maine	3	76	4	71	8	41	12	18	4	0	2	0
Maryland	74	15	63	49	87	25	80	43	8	8	4	4
Massachusetts	31	165	60	211	103	136	138	34	20	0	10	0
Michigan	33	118	12	214	112	187	156	119	20	12	9	7
Minnesota	11	51	8	146	44	91	69	51	12	4	5	3
Mississippi	70	17	142	0	110	1	59	17	5	5	3	2
Missouri	143	43	202	88	157	49	106	37	10	8	4	5
Montana	1	3	13	14	23	12	17	12	0	2	0	1
Nebraska	3	28	36	63	21	50	5	40	0	6	0	3
Nevada	4	9	5	10	14	3	13	8	1	3	1	1
New Hampshire	11	33	3	33	3	31	7	23	0	4	0	2
New Jersey	53	58	66	137	84	158	130	87	13	13	7	6
New Mexico	—	—	7	5	29	0	14	23	1	5	1	2
New York	236	312	328	397	387	368	339	213	36	26	18	13
North Carolina	78	32	157	11	189	9	113	54	11	13	5	7
North Dakota	0	4	0	44	2	33	9	9	2	0	1	0
Ohio	146	186	123	264	163	238	134	197	17	21	8	11
Oklahoma	—	—	70	27	112	14	65	25	0	12	1	5
Oregon	7	13	2	44	22	41	46	21	8	2	4	1
Pennsylvania	158	300	83	522	255	291	197	168	22	20	10	11
Rhode Island	8	32	13	34	32	2	23	8	4	0	2	0
South Carolina	62	30	127	0	97	2	59	32	4	8	2	4
South Dakota	6	11	3	42	7	27	12	11	0	2	0	1
Tennessee	83	52	139	39	121	37	77	52	8	10	4	5
Texas	110	1	295	7	365	8	297	88	34	26	17	13

(continued)

Party Victories in House of Representatives, 1860–2000 *(continued)*

State	1860–1895		1896–1931		1932–1965		1966–1995		1996–1999		2000	
	Dem.	Rep.	Dem.	Rep.	Dem.	Rep.	Dem.	Rep.	Dem.	Rep.	Dem.	Rep.
Utah	—	—	7	23	23	11	14	23	0	6	1	2
Vermont	0	42	0	36	1	16	0	12	0	0	0	0
Virginia	81	23	167	15	147	15	75	74	12	10	3	7
Washington	0	6	8	61	54	55	80	35	8	10	6	3
West Virginia	37	15	23	75	84	16	58	3	6	0	2	1
Wisconsin	40	94	18	176	46	105	73	67	10	8	5	4
Wyoming	1	2	1	17	3	14	4	11	0	2	0	1

Note: "——" indicates that the state was not yet admitted to the Union. The 1966–1995 period does not include special elections; candidates endorsed by both major and minor parties are counted as major party candidates. [a]When it could be determined, candidates who ran as both Republican and Democrat were classified by their usual party affiliation.

Sources: Congressional Quarterly's Guide to U.S. Elections, 2d ed. (Washington, DC: Congressional Quarterly, 1985), 1118–1119; 1986–1994: *Congressional Quarterly Weekly Report* (1986), 2843, (1988), 3269, (1990), 3802, (1992), 3571, (1994), 3236.

Seats That Changed Party in Congress, 1954–2000

Chamber/year	Total changes	Incumbent Defeated		Open Seat	
		Democrat to Republican	Republican to Democrat	Democrat to Republican	Republican to Democrat
House					
1954	26	3	18	2	3
1956	20	7	7	2	4
1958	50	1	35	0	14
1960	37	23	2	6	6
1962	19	9	5	2	3
1964	57	5	39	5	8
1966	47	39	1	4	3
1968	11	5	0	2	4
1970	25	2	9	6	8
1972	23	6	3	9	5
1974	55	4	36	2	13
1976	22	7	5	3	7
1978	33	14	5	8	6
1980	41	27	3	10	1
1982	31	1	22	3	5
1984	22	13	3	5	1
1986	21	1	5	7	8
1988	9	2	4	1	2
1990	21	6	9	0	6
1992	43	16	8	11	8
1994	61	35	0	22	4
1996	62	2	13	33	29
1998	40	0	4	19	17
2000	39	3	4	9	23
Senate					
1954	8	2	4	1	1
1956	8	1	3	3	1
1958	13	0	11	0	2
1960	2	1	0	1	0
1962	8	2	3	0	3
1964	4	1	3	0	0
1966	3	1	0	2	0
1968	9	4	0	3	2
1970	6	3	2	1	0
1972	10	1	4	3	2
1974	6	0	2	1	3
1976	14	5	4	2	3
1978	13	5	2	3	3
1980	12	9	0	3	0
1982	4	1	1	1	1

(continued)

Seats That Changed Party in Congress, 1954–2000 *(continued)*

Chamber/year	Total changes	Incumbent Defeated		Open Seat	
		Democrat to Republican	Republican to Democrat	Democrat to Republican	Republican to Democrat
1984	4	1	2	0	1
1986	10	0	7	1	2
1988	7	1	3	2	1
1990	1	0	1	0	0
1992	4	2	2	0	0
1994	8	2	0	6	0
1996	16	1	1	9	5
1998	8	0	2	3	2
2000	10	1	4	0	5

Note: This table reflects shifts in party control from before to after the November elections. It does not include shifts from the creation of districts or the reduction of two districts to one.

Sources: 1954–1992: Norman J. Ornstein et al., eds., *Vital Statistics on Congress, 1993–1994* (Washington, DC: Congressional Quarterly, 1994), 54, 56; 1994: *Congressional Quarterly Weekly Report* (1994), 3232–3233, 3240.

Presidential Victories by State, 1980–2000

State Abbr.	State Name	Democrat Wins	Republican Wins
AL	Alabama		00R; 96R; 92r; 88R; 84R; 80R
AK	Alaska		00R; 96R; 92r; 88R; 84R; 80R
AZ	Arizona	96d	00R; 92r; 88R; 84R; 80R
AR	Arkansas	96D; 92D	00R; 88R; 84R; 80r
CA	California	00D; 96D; 92d	88R; 84R; 80R
CO	Colorado	92d	00R; 96r; 88R; 84R; 80R
CT	Connecticut	00D; 96D; 92d	88R; 84R; 80r
DE	Delaware	00D; 96D; 92d	88R; 84R; 80r
DC	District of Columbia	00D; 96D; 92d; 88D; 84D; 80d	
FL	Florida	96d	00r; 92r; 88R; 84R; 80R
GA	Georgia	92d; 80D	00R; 96r; 88R; 84R
HI	Hawaii	00D; 96D; 92d; 88D; 80d	84R
ID	Idaho		00R; 96R; 92r; 88R; 84R; 80R
IL	Illinois	00D; 96D; 92d	88R; 84R; 80R
IN	Indiana		00R; 96r; 92r; 88R; 84R; 80R
IA	Iowa	00d; 96D; 92d; 88D	84R; 80R
KS	Kansas		00R; 96R; 92r; 88R; 84R; 80R
KY	Kentucky	96d; 92d	00R; 88R; 84R; 80r
LA	Louisiana	96D; 92d	00R; 88R; 84R; 80R
ME	Maine	00d; 96D; 92d	88R; 84R; 80r
MD	Maryland	00D; 96D; 92D; 80d	88R; 84R
MA	Massachusetts	00D; 96D; 92d; 88D	84R; 80r
MI	Michigan	00D; 96D; 92d	88R; 84R; 80r
MN	Minnesota	00d; 96D; 92d; 88D; 84D; 80d	
MS	Mississippi		00R; 96r; 92R; 88R; 84R; 80r
MO	Missouri	96d; 92d	00R; 88R; 84R; 80R
MT	Montana	92d	00R; 96r; 88R; 84R; 80R
NE	Nebraska		00R; 96R; 92r; 88R; 84R; 80R
NV	Nevada	96d; 92d	00r; 88R; 84R; 80R
NH	New Hampshire	96d; 92d	00r; 88R; 84R; 80R
NJ	New Jersey	00D; 96D; 92d	88R; 84R; 80R
NM	New Mexico	00d; 96d; 92d	88R; 84R; 80R
NY	New York	00D; 96D; 92D; 88D	84R; 80r
NC	North Carolina		00R; 96r; 92r; 88R; 84R; 80r
ND	North Dakota		00R; 96r; 92r; 88R; 84R; 80R
OH	Ohio	96d; 92d	00r; 88R; 84R; 80R
OK	Oklahoma		00R; 96r; 92r; 88R; 84R; 80R
OR	Oregon	00d; 96d; 92d; 88D	84R; 80R
PA	Pennsylvania	00D; 96d; 92d	88R; 84R; 80R
RI	Rhode Island	00D; 96D; 92d; 88D; 80d	84R
SC	South Carolina		00R; 96r; 92r; 88R; 84R; 80r
SD	South Dakota		00R; 96r; 92r; 88R; 84R; 80R
TN	Tennessee	96d; 92d	00R; 88R; 84R; 80r
TX	Texas		00R; 96r; 92r; 88R; 84R; 80R

(continued)

Presidential Victories by State, 1980–2000 *(continued)*

State Abbr.	State Name	Democrat Wins	Republican Wins
UT	Utah		00R; 96R; 92r; 88R; 84R; 80R
VT	Vermont	00D; 96D; 92d	88R; 84R; 80r
VA	Virginia		00R; 96r; 92r; 88R; 84R; 80R
WA	Washington	00D; 96d; 92d; 88D	84R; 80R
WV	West Virginia	96D; 92d; 88D; 80D	00R; 84R
WI	Wisconsin	00d; 96d; 92d; 88D	84R; 80r
WY	Wyoming		00R; 96r; 92r; 88R; 84R; 80R

Note: R = Republican majority, r = Republican plurality, D = Democratic majority, d = Democratic plurality.
Source: Statistical Abstract.

Voter Registration and Partisan Enrollment, 1998

State	Total Registration	Democrat	Republican	Other	Maj.[a]	Dem %	Rep %	Other %
AL	2,316,598	n/a*	n/a*	n/a*		n/a	n/a	n/a
AK	459,903	77,001	113,993	268,909	O[c]	16.7	24.8	58.5
AZ	2,592,676	1,036,519	1,151,549	404,608	r	40.0	44.4	15.6
AR	1,471,413	n/a	n/a	n/a		n/a	n/a	n/a
CA	14,969,185	6,989,006	5,314,912	2,665,267	d	46.7	35.5	17.8
CO	2,563,441	783,044	914,486	865,911	r	30.5	35.7	33.8
CT	1,964,763	699,766	477,684	787,313	o	35.6	24.3	40.1
DE	469,159	196,860	161,989	110,310	d	42.0	34.5	23.5
DC	356,381	276,955	25,667	53,759	D	77.7	7.2	15.1
FL	8,220,266	3,691,742	3,292,589	1,235,935	d	44.9	40.1	15.0
GA	3,910,740	n/a	n/a	n/a		n/a	n/a	n/a
HI	601,404	n/a	n/a	n/a		n/a	n/a	n/a
ID	661,433	n/a	n/a	n/a		n/a	n/a	n/a
IL	6,754,998	n/a	n/a	n/a		n/a	n/a	n/a
IN	3,693,982	n/a	n/a	n/a		n/a	n/a	n/a
IA	1,865,520	597,146	614,655	653,719	o	32.0	32.9	35.0
KS	1,513,685	433,759	685,107	394,819	r	28.7	45.3	26.1
KY	2,590,338	1,570,461	835,465	184,412	D	60.6	32.3	7.1
LA	2,686,561	1,677,833	577,136	431,592	D	62.5	21.5	16.1
ME	933,753	296,970	268,276	368,507	o	31.8	28.7	39.5
MD	2,577,698	1,484,062	780,331	313,305	D	57.6	30.3	12.2
MA	3,706,404	1,387,987	485,825	1,832,592	o	37.4	13.1	49.4
MI	6,915,613	n/a	n/a	n/a		n/a	n/a	n/a
MN	3,000,412	n/a	n/a	n/a		n/a	n/a	n/a
MS	1,806,868	n/a	n/a	n/a		n/a	n/a	n/a
MO	3,635,991	n/a	n/a	n/a		n/a	n/a	n/a
MT	639,241	n/a	n/a	n/a		n/a	n/a	n/a
NE	1,056,351	390,776	521,137	144,438	r	37.0	49.3	13.7
NV	898,055	372,289	375,541	150,225	r	41.5	41.8	16.7
NH	747,397	203,567	272,115	271,715	r	27.2	36.4	36.4
NJ	4,538,944	1,141,593	872,349	2,525,002	O	25.2	19.2	55.6
NM	912,964	491,337	300,344	121,283	D	53.8	32.9	13.3
NY	10,740,788	4,997,773	3,114,832	2,628,183	d	46.5	29.0	24.5
NC	4,708,421	2,454,656	1,590,453	663,312	D	52.1	33.8	14.1
ND[b]	n/a	n/a	n/a	n/a		n/a	n/a	n/a
OH	7,127,879	1,239,742	1,249,913	4,638,224	O	17.4	17.5	65.1
OK	2,034,793	1,181,004	714,163	139,626	D	58.0	35.1	6.9
OR	1,965,981	791,970	704,593	469,418	d	40.3	35.8	23.9
PA	7,258,822	3,514,970	3,072,299	671,553	d	48.4	42.3	9.3
RI	632,955	n/a	n/a	n/a		n/a	n/a	n/a
SC	2,021,766	n/a	n/a	n/a		n/a	n/a	n/a
SD	496,718	179,195	209,624	107,899	r	36.1	42.2	21.7
TN	3,154,487	n/a	n/a	n/a		n/a	n/a	n/a
TX	11,538,235	n/a	n/a	n/a		n/a	n/a	n/a

(continued)

Voter Registration and Partisan Enrollment, 1998 *(continued)*

State	Total Registration	Democrat	Republican	Other	Maj.[a]	Dem %	Rep %	Other %
UT	1,115,821	n/a	n/a	n/a		n/a	n/a	n/a
VT	402,603	n/a	n/a	n/a		n/a	n/a	n/a
VA	3,725,921	n/a	n/a	n/a		n/a	n/a	n/a
WA	3,119,562	n/a	n/a	n/a		n/a	n/a	n/a
WV	1,007,811	632,288	295,825	79,698	D	62.7	29.4	7.9
WI	1,760,129	n/a	n/a	n/a		n/a	n/a	n/a
WY	239,539	70,926	142,447	26,166	R	29.6	59.5	10.9
Totals	154,084,368	38,861,197	29,135,299	23,207,700				

*n/a = 22 states do not register voters by party.

[a]Upper case indicates a majority; lower case a plurality.

[b]North Dakota does not register voters.

[c]O = other.

Sources: See individual state entries in Part VII.

Voter Registration and Partisan Enrollment, 2000

State	Total Registration	Democrat	Republican	Other	Maj.[a]	Dem %	Rep %	Other %
AL	2,528,963	n/a*	n/a*	n/a*		n/a	n/a	n/a
AK	473,648							
AZ	2,173,122	830,904	942,078	400,140	r	38.2	43.4	18.4
AR	1,555,809	n/a	n/a	n/a		n/a	n/a	n/a
CA	15,707,307	7,134,601	5,485,492	3,087,214	d	45.4	34.9	19.7
CO	2,274,152							
CT	1,874,245	643,822	452,654	777,769		34.4	24.2	41.5
DE	503,360							
DC	354,410	271,380	26,485	56,545	D	76.6	7.5	16.0
FL	8,752,717	3,803,081	3,430,238	1,519,398	d	43.5	39.2	17.4
GA	3,859,960	n/a	n/a	n/a		n/a	n/a	n/a
HI	637,349	n/a	n/a	n/a		n/a	n/a	n/a
ID	728,085	n/a	n/a	n/a		n/a	n/a	n/a
IL	7,129,026	n/a	n/a	n/a		n/a	n/a	n/a
IN	4,000,809	n/a	n/a	n/a		n/a	n/a	n/a
IA	1,841,346							
KS	1,623,623	449,445	735,435	438,743	r	27.7	45.3	27.0
KY	2,556,815	1,539,562	846,621	170,632	D	60.2	33.1	6.7
LA	2,730,380							
ME	882,337	280,987	265,889	335,461	o[c]	31.8	30.1	38.0
MD	2,715,366	1,547,117	805,894	362,355	D	57.0	29.7	13.3
MA	4,008,796	1,460,881	546,333	2,001,582	o	36.4	13.6	49.9
MI	6,861,342	n/a	n/a	n/a		n/a	n/a	n/a
MN	3,265,324	n/a	n/a	n/a		n/a	n/a	n/a
MS	1,739,858	n/a	n/a	n/a		n/a	n/a	n/a
MO	3,860,672	n/a	n/a	n/a		n/a	n/a	n/a
MT	698,260	n/a	n/a	n/a		n/a	n/a	n/a
NE	1,085,217	392,344	537,605	155,268	r	36.2	49.5	14.3
NV	898,347	372,889	374,196	151,262	r	41.5	41.7	16.8
NH	856,519							
NJ	4,710,768	1,179,577	876,386	2,654,805	O	25.0	18.6	56.4
NM	972,895							
NY	11,262,816	5,243,617	3,171,044	2,848,155	d	46.6	28.2	25.3
NC	5,122,123	2,555,577	1,742,720	823,826	d	49.9	34.0	16.1
ND[b]	n/a	n/a	n/a	n/a		n/a	n/a	n/a
OH	7,537,822	1,021,214	1,422,767	5,093,841	O	13.5	18.9	67.6
OK	2,233,602	1,234,297	798,149	201,156	D	55.3	35.7	9.0
OR	1,943,699	765,641	696,657	481,401	d	39.4	35.8	24.8
PA	7,781,997	3,736,304	3,250,764	794,929	d	48.0	41.8	10.2
RI	655,107	n/a	n/a	n/a		n/a	n/a	n/a
SC	2,157,006	n/a	n/a	n/a		n/a	n/a	n/a
SD	471,152	181,129	226,906	63,117	r	38.4	48.2	13.4
TN	3,181,108	n/a	n/a	n/a		n/a	n/a	n/a
TX	10,267,639	n/a	n/a	n/a		n/a	n/a	n/a

(continued)

Voter Registration and Partisan Enrollment, 2000 *(continued)*

State	Total Registration	Democrat	Republican	Other	Maj.[a]	Dem %	Rep %	Other %
UT	1,123,238	n/a	n/a	n/a		n/a	n/a	n/a
VT	427,354	n/a	n/a	n/a		n/a	n/a	n/a
VA	3,770,273	n/a	n/a	n/a		n/a	n/a	n/a
WA	3,335,714	n/a	n/a	n/a		n/a	n/a	n/a
WV	1,067,822	659,838	309,970	98,014	D	61.8	29.0	9.2
WI	2,598,607	n/a	n/a	n/a		n/a	n/a	n/a
WY	220,012	63,994	133,927	22,091	R	29.1	60.9	10.0
Totals	159,017,918	35,368,201	27,078,210	22,537,704				

*n/a = 22 states do not register voters by party.
[a]Upper case indicates a majority; lower case a plurality.
[b]North Dakota does not register voters.
[c]O = other.
Sources: See individual state entries in Part VII.

PART IX

NATIONAL CAMPAIGNS
AND
PLATFORMS

THE PRESIDENTIAL ELECTION OF 1996

REPUBLICAN CONVENTION

As Republicans met at their national convention in San Diego, California, in mid-August 1996, there was largely a feeling that the party's nominee, former Kansas senator Robert "Bob" Dole, had already been beaten by the incumbent Democratic standard-bearer, Bill Clinton. In fact, many seasoned Republican political operatives referred to the convention as more of a wake than a kickoff to a campaign season. Speculation ran high as to who would be chosen as the vice presidential candidate. The delegates hoped that whoever was chosen would be strong enough to give their party the lift it needed. Dole chose former New York congressman and Reagan administration Department of Housing and Urban Development secretary Jack Kemp as his running mate. The selection was widely hailed as the conservative Kemp, a former professional football player for the San Diego Chargers, was seen as an aggressive campaigner and younger star of the Republican Party.

In addition to the devastating lead that President Clinton had over Bob Dole in every national poll, Dole—who won the nomination as a reward for his many years of service to the party, including his 1976 run as vice president on the ticket of Gerald Ford—had to contend with a largely fractured party that remained from the 1992 convention when a "culture war" between the social conservatives and the more moderate wing had divided the party. To curtail a repeat, many alternative voices in the party—such as Patrick Buchanan—were not given prominent or any time slots to speak. Of the keynote speakers, retired general Colin Powell and Dole's wife, Elizabeth, were the two highlights of the convention. Former presidents Gerald Ford and George Bush also spoke, as did former first lady Nancy Reagan.

Powell, who many Republicans had wanted as the nominee or the vice presidential candidate, gave a strong speech that outlined his political views and why he was a Republican. His prime-time appearance was an obvious call to African Americans that the GOP was a viable home for them as well. Emphasizing a social agenda, Powell called on the party not to abandon its social responsibilities in its defining of the party's principles.

The highlight of the entire convention was the speech given by Elizabeth Dole. Having taken a leave of absence from her duties as president of the American Red Cross, Elizabeth Dole was a veteran of several Republican administrations from Nixon to Reagan, wherein she served as secretary of transportation. She surprised the convention by leaving the podium and strolling through the audience at the convention as she gave a loving portrayal of her husband. The speech was so effective that many speculated that Hillary Clinton would mimic it in the Democratic Convention. That speech helped lay the groundwork at a national level for Elizabeth Dole to run for the Republican presidential nomination in 2000.

When Bob Dole accepted the nomination on the convention's final night, there was a certain resignation among the delegates that they had little chance of winning in November. Dole gave a speech that built off of the convention theme, "Restoring the American Dream." In the speech, which lasted nearly an hour, Dole addressed the issue of his age and argued that he represented a more secure bridge to America's past. His opponent, President Clinton, would take that imagery of a bridge and use it against Dole, arguing that while Dole was a bridge to the past, Clinton and the Democrats represented the bridge to the twenty-first century.

ELECTION

The 1996 presidential election was an uphill battle for the Republicans. At no time in the campaign did they have a lead or even appear to be within striking distance. While the enthusiastic campaigning of Kemp and the hard push by Dole in the last ninety-six hours closed some of the margins of victory for Democratic incumbents President Bill Clinton and Vice President Al Gore, the vote was never close. Clinton received 47,401,185 popular votes (49.3 percent), Dole 39,197,469 (40.7 percent). Clinton easily won the electoral college, 379 to 159. (Ross Perot, running as an Independent, received 8,085,294 popular votes, or 8.4 percent.) It seemed from the very start that Dole's campaign was out of touch with the direction the country wanted to take. Choosing the theme "Renewing America," the campaign often spoke of the country's illustrious past and the sacrifices previous generations had made. This was sharply contrasted by Clinton's "bridge to the twenty-first century." At age seventy-three, Dole was also perceived as too old by many voters. Many in the party supported Dole out of a sense that he deserved a chance to run. Little of the man underneath the harsh exterior came through until after the election, especially when Dole appeared on *Late Night with David Letterman*. After seeing that show, many viewers commented that they wished they had seen that Bob Dole sooner.

Republican congressional leaders where hopeful that they would be able to maintain and perhaps extend the majorities that they had gained in the off-year 1994 elections. Clinton did not provide sweeping coattails for the Democrats, who were able to cut the Republican majority by only ten seats (228–206), still leaving Republican Newt Gingrich as Speaker of the House. The key to the Republicans holding the House was the reelection of most of the freshman representatives who first came to Washington in 1994. The Senate was never in serious danger of switching from the Republicans to the Democrats. In the Senate the balance remained in favor of the Republicans with a 55–45 split.

Jeffrey D. Schultz

BIBLIOGRAPHY

Abramson, Paul R., John H. Aldrich, and David W. Rohde. *Change and Continuity in the 1996 and 1998 Elections*. Washington, DC: Congressional Quarterly Press, 1999.

Nelson, Michael, ed. *The Elections of 1996*. Washington, DC: Congressional Quarterly Press, 1997.

Pomper, Gerald M., et al., eds. *The Elections of 1996: Reports and Interpretations*. Chatham, NJ: Chatham House, 1997.

THE CONGRESSIONAL ELECTIONS OF 1998

In the days leading up to the 1998 off-year elections, many Republicans had high hopes not only that they would win the elections but also that there would be substantial gains in the number of Republican seats in both the House of Representatives and the Senate. In fact, Republicans were looking for a gain of twenty-five to thirty seats in the House and a filibuster-proof pickup of five seats in the Senate for a total of sixty. Why were the Republicans so optimistic? Historically, the party out of power (i.e., the party not in control of the White House) gains in off-year elections. Additionally, Republicans believed that the Clinton-Lewinsky scandal and, to a lesser degree, the campaign finance scandal would drive people in large numbers to vote Republican.

By election night, however, it was clear that most Republican leaders and strategists had overplayed the Lewinsky card. Not only did Republicans not gain large majorities in the House of Representatives, but the margin of power was cut from 228–206 to a meager 223–211. The division in the Senate remained the same: 55–45. While Republicans held on to the Senate, they lost two key Senate seats. The first was incumbent Republican Al D'Amato of New York, who led the investigation into campaign finance charges against the Clinton-Gore camp. D'Amato was defeated by Representative Charles Schumer. In North Carolina, widespread support from African-American voters helped Democratic attorney John Edwards defeat conservative Republican senator Lauch Faircloth.

Even in state elections, Republicans lost the governor's mansion in California to Lieutenant Governor Gray Davis. Perhaps the only bright spots were the reelection of George W. Bush as governor of Texas and the election of his brother Jeb Bush as governor of Florida, both of whom are sons of former president George H. W. Bush.

On the whole, the 1998 elections were ones that most Republicans would sooner forget.

Jeffrey D. Schultz

BIBLIOGRAPHY

Abramson, Paul R., John H. Aldrich, and David W. Rohde. *Change and Continuity in the 1996 and 1998 Elections*. Washington, DC: Congressional Quarterly Press, 1999.

McWilliams, Wilson Carey. *Beyond the Politics of Disappointment?: American Elections, 1980–1998*. New York: Chatham House/Seven Bridges Press, 2000.

Thurber, James A., ed. *The Battle for Congress: Consultants, Candidates, and Voters*. Washington, DC: Brookings Institution Press, 2001.

Wilson, James Q., and John J. DiIulio Jr. *American Government: Institutions and Policies*. 7th ed. Boston: Houghton Mifflin, 1998.

REPUBLICAN PARTY PLATFORM, 1996

PREAMBLE

We meet to nominate a candidate and pass a platform at a moment of measureless national opportunity. A new century beckons, and Americans are more than equal to its challenges. But there is a problem. The Clinton administration has proven unequal to the heritage of our past, the promise of our times, and the character of the American people. They require more and demand better. With them, we raise our voices and raise our sights.

We are the heirs of world leadership that was earned by bravery and sacrifice on half a thousand battlefields. We will soon nominate for the presidency a man who knew battle and so loves peace, a man who lives bravely and so walks humbly with his God and his fellow citizens. We walk with him now as he joins one more battle, every bit as crucial for our country's future as was the crusade in which he served.

Just when America should be leading the world, we have an administration squandering the international respect it did not earn and does not value. Just when America should be demonstrating anew the dynamic power of economic freedom, we have an administration working against both history and public opinion to expand the reach and burden of government. Just when Americans are reasserting their deepest values, we have an administration locked into the counterculture battles of its youth.

Americans are right to say we are on the wrong track. Our prestige in the world is declining. Economic growth here at home is anemic. Our society grows more violent and less decent. The only way the Clinton administration can magnify its questionable accomplishments is to lower our expectations. Those who lead the Democratic Party call America to smaller tasks and downsized dreams.

That is not the calling of an American president.

Today's Democratic leaders do not understand leadership. They reduce principles to tactics. They talk endlessly and confront nothing. They offer, not convictions, but alibis. They are paralyzed by indecision, weakened by scandal, and guided only by the perpetuation of their own power.

We asked for change. We worked for reform. We offered cooperation and consensus. Now, the asking is over. The Clinton administration cannot be reinvented; it must be replaced.

Republicans do not duplicate or fabricate or counterfeit a vision for the land we love. With our fellow citizens, we assert the present power of timeless truths.

This is what we want for America: real prosperity that reaches beyond the stock market to every family, small business, and worker; an economy expanding as fast as American enterprise and creativity will carry it, free from unnecessary taxes, regulation, and litigation.

This is what we want for America: the restoration of self-government by breaking Washington's monopoly on power. The American people want their country back. We will help them to regain it.

This too we want for America: moral clarity in our culture and ethical leadership in the White House. We offer America, not a harsh moralism, but our sincere conviction that the values we hold in our hearts determine the success of our lives and the shape of our society. It matters greatly that our leaders reflect and communicate those values, not undermine or mock them.

The diversity of our nation is reflected in this platform. We ask for the support and participation of all who substantially share our agenda. In one way or another, every Republican is a dissenter. At the same time, we are not morally indifferent. In this, as in many things, Lincoln is our model. At a time of great crisis, he spoke both words of healing and words of conviction. We do likewise, not for the peace of a political party, but because we citizens are bound together in a great enterprise for our children's future.

The platform that follows marshals these principles and sends them into action. We aim at nothing less than an economy of dynamic growth; a renewal of community, self-government and citizenship; and a national reaffirmation of the enduring principles on which America's greatness depends. We will count our victories, not in elections won or in economic numbers on a chart, but in the everyday achievements of the American Dream: when a man or woman discovers the dignity and confidence of a job, when a child rejects drugs and embraces life, when an entrepreneur turns an idea into an industry, when a family once again feels the security of its savings and has control over the education of its children.

None of the extraordinary things about our country are gifts of government. They are the accomplishments of free people in a free society. They are achievements, not entitlements—and are sweeter for that fact. They result when men and women live in obedience to their conscience, not to the state. All our efforts as Republicans are guided by the fixed star of this single principle: that freedom always exceeds our highest expectations.

This is the greatest task before the Republican Party: to raise the bar of American expectations. Of the potential of our economy. Of the border and civility of our culture. Of what a president can be, and what the presidency must be again.

There is a continuing revolution in the yellowed parchment and faded ink of the American creed . . . a revolution that will long outlive us. It can carry the weight of all our hopes. It can reward every dreamer. It is the reason that America's finest hour is never a memory and always a goal.

With trust in God and in fidelity to generations past and generations to come, we respectfully submit this platform to the American people.

PRINCIPLES OF THE 1996 REPUBLICAN PLATFORM

Introduction

Because Americans are a diverse and tolerant people, they have differences of opinion on many issues. But as a people, we share a common dream and common goals:

- A strong America that protects its citizens and champions their democratic ideals throughout the world;
- An America with a vibrant and growing economy that improves the standard of living for all;
- An America with a smaller, more effective, and less intrusive government that trusts its people to decide what is best for them;
- An America whose people feel safe and secure in their homes, on their streets, and in their communities;
- An America where our children receive the best education in the world and learn the values like decency and responsibility that made this country great;
- And an America with the compassion to care for those who cannot care for themselves.

Principles

1. Because the American Dream fulfills the promise of liberty, we believe it should be attainable by all through more and secure

jobs, home ownership, personal security, and education that meets the challenges of the century ahead.

2. Because a dynamic and growing economy is the best way to create more and better-paying jobs, with greater security in the workplace, we believe in lower taxes within a simpler tax system, in tandem with fair and open trade and a balanced federal budget.

3. Because wasteful government spending and over-regulation, fueled by higher taxes, are the greatest obstacles to job creation and economic growth, we believe in a Balanced Budget Amendment to the Constitution and a common-sense approach to government rules and red tape.

4. Because we recognize our obligation to foster hope and opportunity for those unable to care for themselves, we believe in welfare reform that eliminates waste, fraud, and abuse; requires work from those who are capable; limits time on public assistance; discourages illegitimacy; and reduces the burden on the taxpayers.

5. Because all Americans have the right to be safe in their homes, on their streets, and in their communities, we believe in tough law enforcement, especially against juvenile crime and the drug traffic, with stiff penalties, no loopholes, and judges who respect the rights of law-abiding Americans.

6. Because institutions like the family are the backbone of a healthy society, we believe government must support the rights of the family; and recognizing within our own ranks different approaches toward our common goal, we reaffirm respect for the sanctity of human life.

7. Because our children need and are entitled to the best education in the world, we believe in parental involvement and family choice in schooling, teacher authority and accountability, more control to local school boards, and emphasis upon the basics of learning in safe classrooms.

8. Because older Americans have built our past and direct us, in wisdom and experience, toward the future, we believe we must meet our nation's commitments to them by pre-serving and protecting Medicare and Social Security.

9. Because a good society rests on an ethical foundation, we believe families, communities, and religious institutions can best teach the American values of honesty, responsibility, hard work, compassion, and mutual respect.

10. Because our country's greatest strength is its people, not its government, we believe today's government is too large and intrusive and does too many things the people could do better for themselves.

11. Because we trust our fellow Americans, rather than centralized government, we believe the people, acting through their State and local elected officials, should have control over programs like education and welfare—thereby pushing power away from official Washington and returning it to the people in their communities and states.

12. Because we view the careful development of our country's natural resources as stewardship of creation, we believe property rights must be honored in our efforts to restore, protect, and enhance the environment for the generations to come.

13. Because we are all one America, we oppose discrimination. We believe in the equality of all people before the law and that individuals should be judged by their ability rather than their race, creed, or disability.

14. Because this is a difficult and dangerous world, we believe that peace can be assured only through strength, that a strong national defense is necessary to protect America at home and secure its interests abroad, and that we must restore leadership and character to the presidency as the best way to restore America's leadership and credibility throughout the world.

BUILDING A BETTER AMERICA

This is no time for diminished expectations. This is no time to sell America's potential short. This is a time to let go of the 20th century and embrace

the 21st—to seize the promise of the new era by liberating the genius of the American people.
    —Bob Dole, September 5, 1995,
    in Chicago

Improving the Standard of Living

We are the party of America's earners, savers, and taxpayers—the people who work hard, take risks and build a better future for our families and our communities. Our party believes that we can best improve the standard of living in America by empowering the American people to act in their own behalf by:

- cutting the near-record tax burden on Americans;
- reducing government spending and its size, while balancing the budget;
- creating jobs;
- using the benefits of science, technology, and innovations to improve both our lives and our competitiveness in the global economy;
- dramatically increasing the number of families who can own their home; and
- unleashing the competitiveness and will to win of individual Americans on the world trade scene with free but fair trade.

That's not wishful thinking; it's what we, the American people, used to take for granted before the growth of big government began to shadow our days and smother our hopes. In the 1980s—when we cut taxes, restrained regulation, and reduced government spending as a share of the nation's economy—prosperity made a comeback. Jobs were created, incomes rose, and poverty fell for seven straight years. Then the Democrat-controlled Congress forced the tax hikes of 1990 and jammed through Bill Clinton's tax bill of 1993.

Since then, Clintonomics has produced an economy that is squeezing the middle class between high taxes and low growth. The astounding fact is that we were growing 50 percent faster in 1992, when Bill Clinton described the economy as the worst in five decades. We've managed to avoid a recession only because the Republican Congress put the brakes on Bill Clinton's rush to ruin by substantially reducing gov-

ernment spending over the last two years. But we cannot go on like this. For millions of families, the American Dream is fading. Our goal is to revive it, and extend it to all who reach for it.

Our formula for growth, opportunity, and a better family life is simple: Trust the people, cut their taxes, scale back the size and scope of government, foster job creation, and get out of the way. We've done it before; we can do it again.

Tax Relief for Economic Growth

American families are suffering from the twin burdens of stagnant incomes and near-record taxes. This is the key cause of middle-class anxiety. It is why people feel they are working harder, but falling further behind; why they fear the current generation will not be as successful as the last generation; why they believe their children will be worse off; and why they feel so anxious about their own economic future.

After averaging 1.7 percent growth annually during the expansion following the 1981 tax cut, family incomes have failed to grow at all under Bill Clinton. Since 1990, families have actually lost much of the ground they gained during the low-tax, high-growth 1980s.

Anemic economic growth under Bill Clinton is largely responsible for this lost ground. The current economic expansion has not only failed to compare to the growth seen in the decade preceding his administration, it is the slowest recovery in the last 100 years. Since 1992, the economy has grown by only 2.4 percent per year, compared to 3.2 percent in the previous 10 years, and 3.9 percent between 1983 and 1989.

Bill Clinton has demonstrated that he fails to understand the role excessive tax burdens play on the economy and family incomes. In the first year of his administration, he pushed through the largest tax increase in history, raising taxes on families, senior citizens, and small businesses. Confronted with Republican attempts to cut family and business taxes, he vetoed the 1995 Balanced Budget Act, which included the $500-per-child tax credit as well as incentives to increase savings, economic growth, and job creation.

The Clinton tax increase has produced the second-highest tax burden in American history.

Federal tax and local taxes take more than 38 cents out of every dollar the American family earns. The federal tax burden alone is now approaching a record 25 percent of family income.

American families deserve better. They should be allowed to keep more of their hard-earned money so they can spend on their priorities, as opposed to sending ever-increasing amounts to Washington to be spent on the priorities of federal bureaucrats.

In response to this unprecedented burden confronting America, we support an across-the-board, 15 percent tax cut to marginal tax rates. Fifteen percent represents the total increase in the federal tax burden since Bill Clinton took office, and we believe such a cut should be the first step toward reducing overall tax burdens while promoting the economic growth that will raise family incomes and our overall standard of living.

Another drag on family finances has been government's failure to maintain the personal and dependent exemption at historic levels. If the personal and dependent exemption that was $600 in 1950 had kept pace with inflation, it would be $3,800 rather than the current $2,500. That is why Republicans have made the $500-per-child family tax credit one of the primary features of our tax cut package.

Job creation and increasing family incomes depend on economic growth, and a precondition for economic growth is a healthy rate of saving and investment. Nevertheless, Bill Clinton vetoed Republican bills to provide these incentives, including expanded and more generous IRAs—and new spousal IRAs—which could be used for health care, education, and home-buying. As a result, today's personal savings rate is less than half what it was two decades ago. Republicans support expansion of IRAs and the establishment of spousal IRAs to encourage savings and investment.

Bill Clinton also vetoed provisions to reduce the capital gains tax rate. Excessive taxes on investment cripple the American economy and kill American jobs by increasing the cost of capital, locking in resources, and stifling small business growth and entrepreneurial activity. Largely because of these excessive taxes, American businesses face a competitive disadvantage with respect to our major trading partners, hurting their ability to export products abroad and create jobs. To remove impediments to job creation and economic growth, we support reducing the top tax rate on capital gains by 50 percent.

In 1993, Bill Clinton raised taxes on millions of middle-class retirees by dramatically increasing the income tax on Social Security benefits. This targeted attack on the economic security of our elderly was unfair and misguided. Republicans believe that this Clinton initiative must be repealed.

These proposals making the current tax code fairer and less burdensome should be viewed as an interim step towards comprehensive tax reform. The current tax code is ridiculously complex and unfair. It is also an unnecessary drag on the economy. At a time when business investment plans are greatly diminished and savings rates are unacceptably low, we must reform our tax system to remove existing artificial, government-induced bias against saving and investment.

To that end, we firmly commit to a tax code for the 21st century that will raise revenue sufficient for a smaller, more effective, and less wasteful government without increasing the national debt. That new tax system must be flatter, fairer, and simpler, with a minimum of exclusions from its coverage, and one set of rules applying to all. It must be simple enough to be understood by all and enforced by few, with a low cost of compliance which replaces the current stack of endless forms with a calculation which can be performed on the back of a postcard.

It must expand the economy and increase opportunity by rewarding initiative and hard work. It must foster job creation and end bias against saving. It must promote personal freedom and innovation. It must do all this in order to boost wages and raise living standards for all of America's working families.

A simple, fair tax system that is pro-growth and pro-family will not need today's burdensome IRS. That agency has become a nightmare for law-abiding taxpayers. It must be dramatically downsized—with resources going to more important efforts like drug enforcement—and made less intrusive.

To protect the American people from those who would undo their forthcoming victory over big government, we support legislation requiring a super-majority vote in both houses of Congress to raise taxes.

We also support a government that keeps its word. Retroactive taxation, like Bill Clinton's infamous 1993 tax hike, breaks that word. We pledge a legislative or constitutional remedy to prohibit its repetition. Because of their vital role in fostering charity and patriotism, we oppose taxing religious and fraternal benefit societies. We will not tolerate attempts to impose taxes by federal judges.

Balancing the Budget and Reducing Spending

We didn't dig ourselves into a $5 trillion debt because the American people are undertaxed. We got that $5 trillion debt because government overspends.

The budget deficit is a "stealth tax" that pushes up interest rates and costs the typical family $36,000 on an average home mortgage, $1,400 on an ordinary student loan, and $700 on a car loan.
                                                                   —Bob Dole

Raising tax rates is the wrong way to balance the budget. It enables the Clinton tax addicts to wastefully spend the public's money. Republicans support a Balanced Budget Amendment to the Constitution, phased in over a short period and with appropriate safeguards for national emergencies. We passed it in the House of Representatives, but Bill Clinton and his allies—especially the Senate's somersault six, who switched their long-standing position on the issue—blocked it by a single vote. As president, Bob Dole will lead the fight for that amendment, and in the states, Republicans will finish the fight for its speedy ratification.

Once and for all, we declare:

- the budget deficit and high taxes are two halves of the vise that is producing the Clinton middle-class squeeze;

- a balanced budget and lower taxes go hand in hand, not in separate directions;
- reducing the budget deficit by shrinking government produces a fiscal dividend in stronger growth and lower interest rates;
- ending that deficit will make possible a dramatic return of resources to the American people;
- tax relief is the only way to return the economy to the growth rates our country enjoyed from World War II to the coming of Bill Clinton; and
- we will not mortgage our children's future by incurring deficits.

A president should be Commander-in-Chief in the nation's budget battle as well as in military conflicts. Bill Clinton has been AWOL—Absent Without Leadership. Congressional Republicans had to fight his Senate allies for over a year just to give him a line-item veto for appropriation bills. Instead of helping us strengthen the presidency in this way, he set an historic precedent: vetoing whole appropriation bills because they spent too little money! His vetoes essentially shut down much of the government.

We make this promise: A Republican president will veto money bills that spend too much, not too little, and will use the line-item veto to lead the charge against wasteful spending. A Republican president will build on the achievements of our Republican Congress, which has cut spending in excess of $53 billion over the last two years.

The Clinton Administration's tactic of using irresponsible monetary policy to hide the effects of their bad fiscal policies leads to:

- higher inflation,
- lower growth,
- fewer jobs, and
- scarcity of capital to fund small businesses.

This is not only bad economics; it is a hidden tax against both income and savings. We pledge a non-political monetary policy to keep prices stable and maintain public confidence in the value of the dollar.

Creating Jobs for Americans

Our goal is to empower the American people by expanding employment and entrepreneurial opportunities. Fundamentally, jobs are created in the private sector.

Small businesses are the engines of growth and job creation. They generate 75 percent of new jobs and 55 percent of our gross domestic product. The Republican Party is committed to the survival, the revival, and the resurgence of small business. In addition to our overall program of lower taxes, regulatory reform, and less spending, we will:

- allow small businesses to deduct the costs of their health insurance;
- restore the fair home-office deduction so important to start-up businesses;
- assure that no one who inherits a small business or farm has to sell it to pay inheritance taxes;
- make the IRS stop its discrimination against independent contractors;
- enact both legal reform and product liability legislation to shield small businesses and protect jobs from the threat of unfair litigation; and
- transfer from the public sector services that can be provided by the private sector more efficiently and cost effectively.

Small business is a force for enormous progress, socially, politically, and economically. This is both an economic and a civil rights agenda. Small businesses owned by women now employ more people than all the Fortune 500 companies combined. Republican-created enterprise zones will offer dramatic opportunities to workers employed by small businesses, particularly minorities and the "Forgotten Workers." Republicans support the creation of jobs in all areas of the country, from the inner city to rural America.

We must create the workplace of the future so that it becomes a vehicle for personal liberation for those who seek a foothold on the opportunity ladder. We advocate increased access to capital for businesses to expand, export, and bring new products and technologies to market. We propose to consolidate federal training programs and to transfer their administration to the States and local governments.

Restraining the size and spending of government is only part of the job. We must transform official policies and attitudes toward productive Americans. Many of our labor laws and job training programs are out of date and out of touch with the needs of today's workers. Both the Davis-Bacon Act and the Service Contract Act, for example, have come to restrict opportunity, increase costs, and inhibit innovation.

Congressional Republicans have already launched a fight against the union bosses' ban on flex-time and comp-time in private industry. Those innovations are especially important to families with children. Government has no business forbidding America's workers to arrange their schedules to suit the needs of their own families.

In the same spirit, we will enact the TEAM Act to empower employers and employees to act as a team, rather than as adversaries, to advance their common interests. (It is opposed only by those who profit from labor conflict, for whom Bill Clinton has vetoed the bill.) Another way to replace conflict with concerted action is to transform OSHA from an adversarial agency into a pioneering advocate of safer productivity. We will mesh its activities with the work of councils formed under the TEAM Act to advance worker protection from the ground up.

In contrast, the Clinton Administration has produced no regulatory reform, no tax relief, no product liability reform, and no legal reform.

Our vision is that everyone who seeks a job will have a job. We will break the "job lock" and bring employment opportunities to all Americans.

Science, Technology, and Innovation in the 21st Century

Our goal is to empower the American people by using the benefits of advanced science to improve their quality of life without undue restraint from government. Our bottom line is more jobs, better jobs, and a higher standard of living for the families of America.

As we prepare for the dawn of a new century, it is essential that our public policies keep pace with an evolving economy. Increased productivity is essential to expand the economy and improve the standard of living of all Americans. A recent report by the Office of Technology Assessment attributes at least half of all economic growth in the United States to advances in technology.

America is expanding its leadership role as a country that fosters innovation and technological advances, the essential ingredients of increased productivity. Leading these efforts are the men and women—and high-technology businesses—that foster creative solutions to world problems. We must create policies that enable these thoughtful leaders to continue to invest in research and development. U.S. research and development (R&D) investment has increased significantly over the past two decades and currently accounts for about 2.6 percent of the nation's gross domestic product. The private sector has been the main engine behind this growth, contributing over 60 percent of the national R&D investment. Such investment has led to increased employment and high-quality jobs. Businesses that invest heavily in R&D tend to create more jobs and to employ high-skilled workers in those new jobs at above-average wage levels.

Research and development is our commitment to the future. It is our investment in the future. We must design tax and regulatory policies that encourage private-sector research and experimentation, while lowering the cost of such investments.

We believe the marketplace, not bureaucrats, can determine which technologies and entrepreneurs best meet the needs of the public. American companies must use the most advanced product technologies, telecommunications, and information management systems. Technological advance means economic growth, higher productivity, and more security. We therefore support private-sector funding of applied research, especially in emerging technologies, and improved education in science and engineering. American workers must have the knowledge and

training to effectively utilize the capabilities of those new systems.

Federal science programs must emphasize basic research. The tax code must foster research and development. These policies will increase the pace of technological developments by de-emphasizing the role of government and strengthening the role of the private sector. We will advance the innovative ideas and pioneering spirit that make possible the impossible.

New discoveries to bolster America's international competitiveness are essential. The fruits of federally funded research led to the creation of the biotechnology industry through the Bayh-Dole Act. This is an example of innovation and risk-taking, creating 2,000 biotechnology companies employing thousands of employees and selling billions of dollars of products to keep us first and foremost in the global marketplace.

The communications revolution empowers individuals, enhances health care, opens up opportunity for rural areas, and strengthens families and institutions. A Dole-led Congress passed the Telecommunications Act of 1996 to promote the full and open competition and freedom of choice in the telecommunications marketplace. In contrast, the Clinton-Gore Administration repeatedly defended big-government regulation. This micromanagement of the Information Age is an impediment to the development of America's information superhighway.

We support the broadest access to telecommunications networks and services, based upon marketplace capabilities. The Internet today is the most staggering example of how the Information Age can and will enhance the lives of Americans everywhere. To further this explosion of new-found freedoms and opportunities, privacy, through secured communications, has never been more important. Bob Dole and the Republican Party will promote policies that ensure that the U.S. remains the world leader in science, technology, and innovation.

Homeownership

Homeownership is central to the American Dream. It is a commitment to a safe and stable community. It is not something government gives to the people, but rather something they can attain for themselves in a non-inflationary, growing economy. For most Americans, our home is our primary asset. Mortgage interest should remain deductible from the income tax.

We applaud Republican congressional efforts to pursue federal budget policies that will result in lower interest rates. Lower interest rates will open up more housing opportunities for more Americans than any program Washington could devise.

Republicans support regulatory reform efforts that make buying a house easy, understandable, and affordable.

We affirm our commitment to open housing, without quotas or controls, and we condemn the Clinton Administration's abuse of fair housing laws to harass citizens exercising their First Amendment rights.

In addition, we support transforming public housing into private housing, converting low-income families into proud homeowners. Resident management of public housing is a first step toward that goal, which includes eliminating the Department of Housing and Urban Development (HUD). HUD's core functions will be turned over to the States. Its civil rights component will be administered by the appropriate federal agency while enforcement will remain with the Department of Justice.

With the housing sector representing such a significant segment of the nation's economy, housing policy is and should continue to be a priority. We believe in a federal role which supplements, not directs or competes with, States and localities. We believe in federal programs which augment, not displace, private-sector capital and resources.

The federal government should not impose prescriptive solutions on State and local governments. Republicans believe that States and localities should have maximum flexibility to design programs which meet the individual needs of their communities. Washington must abandon the "one size fits all" approach and concentrate on adding value to the efforts of States, localities, private and faith-based organizations and individuals. Republicans believe we can and will ac-

complish this without disrupting services to the elderly, disabled, and families with children.

Promoting Trade and International Prosperity

Republicans believe that the United States, as the sole superpower in the world today, has a responsibility to lead—economically, militarily, diplomatically, and morally—so that we have a peaceful and prosperous world.

Republicans support free and fair trade. In the American Century ahead, our country will lead in international trade. American workers will be the winners in any fair competition, and American technology will drive a prosperity revolution around the world. Exports already fuel our economy; their continuing expansion is essential for full employment and long-term prosperity. That is possible only within the context of expanding trade, and we can do it better without a Department of Commerce.

Our country's merchandise trade deficit exploded to $175 billion in 1995 and will likely set an all-time record in 1996, siphoning American wealth into the hands of foreigners. Trade deficits with all our major trading partners were worse in 1995 than in 1992. With China alone, the deficit more than doubled to $35 billion in the last three and a half years. With Japan, Bill Clinton announced a series of hollow agreements that have done little to improve market access. With Russia, he approved a $1 billion Export-Import Bank loan to foster competition with the American aircraft industry. With Canada, he tolerates discrimination against the United States beverage industry and focused on our lumber crisis too late to help closed logging mills. With Mexico, he ignored injury to American agriculture from massive surges in imports.

We should vigorously implement the North American Free Trade Agreement, while carefully monitoring its progress, to guarantee that its promised benefits and protections are realized by all American workers and consumers.

Republicans are for vigorous enforcement of the trade agreements we already have on the books, unlike the Clinton Administration that uses United States trade policy as a bargaining chip and as a vehicle for pursuing a host of other social agenda items. Republicans will enforce United States trade laws, including our anti-dumping laws, and will use the Super 301 investigations that give the president authority to challenge foreign barriers to our exports. And we will use the Export Enhancement Program to boost American farm exports. To advance economic freedom, we insist that United States foreign aid, whether bilateral or through the World Bank and International Monetary Fund, promote market reforms, limit regulation, and encourage free trade. Republicans will stop subsidizing socialism in the less-developed nations. Republicans will not allow the World Trade Organization to undermine United States sovereignty and will support a World Trade Organization oversight commission.

Free market capitalism is the right model for economic development throughout the world. The Soviet model of a state-controlled economy has been discredited, and neither stage of development nor geographic location can justify economic authoritarianism. Human nature and aspirations are the same everywhere, and everywhere the family is the building block of economic and social progress. We therefore will protect the rights of families in international programs and will not fund organizations involved in abortion. The cost of turning our back on the global marketplace is the loss of opportunity and millions of jobs for United States citizens.

CHANGING WASHINGTON FROM THE GROUND UP

On November 8, 1994, the American people sent a message to Washington. . . . Their message is my mandate: To rein in government and reconnect it to the values of the American people. That means making government a whole lot smaller, a lot less arrogant, and getting it out of matters best left to the states, cities, and families across America.
—Bob Dole, March 10, 1995,
in Washington, D.C.

We are the party of small, responsible, and efficient government, joining our neighbors in cities

and counties, rather than distant bureaucrats, to build a just society and caring communities. We therefore assert the power of the American people over government, rather than the other way around. Our agenda for change, profound and permanent change in the way government behaves, is based on the Tenth Amendment to the Constitution:

The powers not delegated to the United States by the Constitution, nor prohibited by it to the States, are reserved to the States respectively, or to the people.

For more than half a century, that solemn compact has been scorned by liberal Democrats and the judicial activism of the judges they have appointed. We will restore the force of the Tenth Amendment and, in the process, renew the trust and respect which hold together a free society. As its first initiative enacted into law, the new Republican majority on Capitol Hill launched that effort early in 1995 by forbidding the imposition of new unfunded mandates upon State and local taxpayers. From now on, if official Washington promises benefits, official Washington must pay for them. We will apply that same principle to the ill-conceived Motor-Voter Act, the Democrats' costly invitation to ballot fraud.

To permanently restore balance in the federal system, States must have the proper tools to act as a counterforce to the federal government. Our country's founders attempted to carefully balance power between the two levels. The Tenth Amendment, as well as the ability of State legislatures to initiate constitutional amendments, and other constitutional tools given to States to protect their role in the system have now been either eroded away, given away, or rendered impossible to use. Thus, States lack the tools necessary to do their job as a counterbalance to the national government.

We call upon Congress, governors, State legislators, and local leaders to adopt structural reforms that will permanently restore balance in our federal system. In this Information Era of uncertainty and rapid change, it is government close to home, controlled by neighborhood and community leaders, that can best respond to the needs and values of all citizens.

As a first step in reforming government, we

support elimination of the Departments of Commerce, Housing and Urban Development, Education, and Energy, and the elimination, defunding, or privatization of agencies which are obsolete, redundant, of limited value, or too regional in focus. Examples of agencies we seek to defund or to privatize are the National Endowment for the Arts, the National Endowment for the Humanities, the Corporation for Public Broadcasting, and the Legal Services Corporation.

In addition, we support Republican-sponsored legislation that would require the original sponsor of proposed federal legislation to cite specific constitutional authority for the measure.

A Citizens' Congress

Even with these structural changes, a system of government is only as good as the women and men who serve within it. When the voters of 1994 elected Republican majorities in both the House and Senate for the first time in forty years, Capitol Hill had been an institution steeped in corruption and contemptuous of reform. Congressional Republicans changed things, from the ground up. They:

- applied all laws to Congress, so that those who make the rules will have to live by them;
- slashed congressional spending and cut back the staff on Capitol Hill;
- ordered an unprecedented audit of the House of Representatives, with devastating exposure of the Democrats' four decades of mismanagement;
- streamlined legislative procedures by reducing the number of committees and subcommittees;
- imposed term limits for House committee chairs and leadership positions—something the Democrats still refuse to do;
- abolished proxy voting in House committees, ending the scandal of absentee Members casting phony votes;
- required any Representative charged [and] indicted of a felony offense to relinquish positions of authority within Congress until cleared of wrongdoing;
- ended the Democrats' secret sessions by opening to the press and the public all committee meetings;
- brought to a vote, in both the House and Senate, a constitutional amendment to impose term limits on members of Congress. It failed to secure the necessary two-thirds vote in the House, where 80 percent of Republicans voted for it and 80 percent of Democrats voted against it. Every Senate Republican voted to allow a vote on term limits, but the Democrats killed it by a filibuster. It will take expanded Republican majorities in the 105th Congress to send to the States a term limits constitutional amendment;
- and passed historic legislation banning gifts to members of Congress and their staff.

We will continue our fight against gerrymandered congressional districts designed to thwart majority rule. We will eliminate made-in-Washington schemes to rig the election process under the guise of campaign reform. True reform is indeed needed: ending taxpayer subsidies for campaigns; strengthening party structures to guard against rogue operations; requiring full and immediate disclosure of all contributions; and cracking down on the indirect support, or "soft money," by which special interest groups underwrite their favored candidates.

Cleaning Up Government

In 1992, Bill Clinton promised "the most ethical Administration in the history of the Republic." Instead, the Clinton Administration has been rife with scandal. An unprecedented four Independent Counsels have been appointed since the Clinton inauguration to investigate various allegations of wrongdoing by members of this administration. The Clinton White House has abused executive power in both the White House Travel Office firings situation and in the FBI files matter. The FBI director said there have been "egregious violations of privacy" in the gathering of FBI files of officials who worked in the White House under Republican administrations.

We believe that misuse of law enforcement authorities for partisan political ends is no trivial matter. Such abuses strike at the heart of the relationship between citizen and government and undermine the rule of law and confidence in our leaders.

Scandals in government are not limited to possible criminal violations. The public trust is violated when taxpayers' money is treated as a slush fund for special interest groups who oppose urgently needed reforms. For example, the Democrats have denied school vouchers for poor children in the nation's capital at the demand of special interest unions. They have blocked urgently needed legal reforms at the command of the trial lawyers, now the biggest source of revenue for the Democratic Party. They have rejected reforms to improve the workplace to please union bosses who committed $35 million to aid the Clinton reelection effort.

It is time to restore honor and integrity to government. We propose to:

- revoke pension rights of public officials who have been convicted of crimes;
- strengthen citizen privacy laws and reform the FBI to guard against the politicization of law enforcement that we have seen by the Clinton White House;
- refuse to allow special interest groups to block innovative solutions for the poor or to block workplace or legal reforms that would help all working Americans; and
- recruit for public service, at all levels, men and women of integrity and high ethical standards.

We will end welfare for lobbyists. Every year, the federal government gives away billions of dollars in grants. Much of that money goes to interest groups which engage in political activity and issue advocacy at the taxpayers' expense. This is an intolerable abuse of the public's money. A Republican Congress will enact legislation, currently blocked by Bill Clinton's congressional allies, to make groups choose between grants and lobbying.

We will establish Truth in Testimony, requiring organizations which receive government funds and testify before Congress to disclose those funds. Our "Let America Know" legislation will force public disclosure of all taxpayer subsidies and lobbying by groups seeking grants. We will permit "private attorney general" lawsuits against federal grantees to ensure better enforcement of anti-lobbying restrictions. A Republican administration will impose accountability on grantees, to reveal what the public is getting for its money, and will end the process of automatic grant renewal. We will halt the funding of frivolous and politicized research grants.

Streamlining Government

Republicans believe we can streamline government and make it more effective through competition and privatization. We applaud the Republican Congress and Republican officials across the country for initiatives to expand the use of competition and privatization in government. It is greater competition—not unchallenged government bureaucracies—that will cut the cost of government, improve delivery of services, and ensure wise investment in infrastructure. A Dole administration will make competition a centerpiece of government, eliminating duplication and increasing efficiency.

Honest Budgets and Real Numbers

We have a moral responsibility not to leave our children a legacy of monstrous debt. Spending $1.6 trillion a year should be more than an accounting exercise. Restraining government spending, discussed elsewhere in this platform, is part of the solution. Reforming the entire budget is the rest of it.

Our goal is clarity, simplicity, and accountability in the nation's budget. The keystone of that agenda is the enactment of a constitutional amendment to require a balanced budget, which a majority of congressional Democrats have vigorously opposed. We do not take that step lightly; but then, a $5 trillion debt is no laughing matter for tomorrow's taxpayers. We vow to offer that amendment again and again, until Congress sends it to the States for ratification.

In addition, we must eliminate all built-in biases toward spending. For example, the "current service baseline" builds in automatic budget increases for inflation and other factors and works like this: If the Democrats want a $1 billion program to grow to $2 billion, then they count an increase to $1.5 billion as a half-billion dollar cut—and the media dutifully report it as such. This is a deceptive and reprehensible shell game that must be stopped.

A Republican president will fight wasteful spending with the line-item veto, which was finally enacted by congressional Republicans this year over bitter Democrat opposition, 120 years after President Grant first proposed it.

Even more important, we will stop the runaway growth of entitlement spending—the programs which automatically grow without any action required by Congress or the president. This spending has jumped 11-fold since 1970 and consumes more than half the federal budget. We will take entitlements off automatic pilot and make Congress accountable for their funding. To end outdated and wasteful programs, we will make the Government Performance and Results Act an integral part of our budget process.

Regulatory Reform

Regulatory reform is needed more than ever. Bill Clinton promised to "reinvent government," but he returned to the old mindset of controls and red tape. To make matters worse, he vetoed a comprehensive regulatory reform bill crafted by Republicans in the House and Senate. That measure will become law when Bob Dole is president.

We commend House Speaker Newt Gingrich and congressional Republicans in their innovative efforts to rescind, overturn, and zero-out absurd bureaucratic red tape and rules through the process known as "Corrections Day."

A Republican administration will require periodic review of existing regulations to ensure they are effective and do away with obsolete and conflicting rules. We will encourage civil servants to find ways to reduce regulatory burdens on the public and will require federal agencies to disclose the costs of new regulations on individuals and small businesses. A new regulatory budget will reveal the total cost of regulations on the American people.

We will target resources on the most serious risks to health, safety, and the environment, rather than on politically inspired causes, and will require peer-reviewed risk assessments based on sound science. We will require agencies to conduct cost-benefit analyses of their regulations and pursue alternatives to the outdated Clinton command-and-control approach. These common-sense reforms will restore fairness and predictability to government rules and, even more important, will enable us to achieve equal or superior levels of protection for the public at lower cost.

Just as important, we recognize that all too often, in its ever-present zeal to expand into every aspect of our daily lives, the federal government intrudes into the private economy by establishing new services in direct competition with already existing private firms. We oppose the use of taxpayer funds to provide a competitive advantage for government agencies seeking to compete with private firms in the free market.

Restoring Justice to the Courts

When I am president, only conservative judges need apply.

—Bob Dole, May 28, 1996,
in Aurora, Colorado

The American people have lost faith in their courts, and for good reason. Some members of the federal judiciary threaten the safety, the values, and the freedom of law-abiding citizens. They make up laws and invent new rights as they go along, arrogating to themselves powers King George III never dared to exercise. They free vicious criminals, pamper felons in prison, frivolously overturn State laws enacted by citizen referenda, and abdicate the responsibility of providing meaningful review of administrative decisions.

The delicate balance of power between the respective branches of our national government and the governments of the 50 states has been eroded. The notion of judicial review has in some cases come to resemble judicial supremacy, affecting all segments of public and private endeavor. Make no mistake, the separation of powers doctrine, complete and unabridged, is the linchpin of a government of laws. A Republican Congress and president will restore true separation of powers and guarantee the American people a government of law.

The federal judiciary, including the U.S. Supreme Court, has overstepped its authority under the Constitution. It has usurped the right of citizen legislators and popularly elected executives to make law by declaring duly enacted laws to be "unconstitutional" through the misapplication of the principle of judicial review. Any other role for the judiciary, especially when personal preferences masquerade as interpreting the law, is fundamentally at odds with our system of government in which the people and their representatives decide issues great and small.

No systemic reform of the judiciary can substitute for the wise exercise of power of appointment vested in the president of the United States. A Republican president will ensure that a process is established to select for the federal judiciary nominees who understand that their task is first and foremost to be faithful to the Constitution and to the intent of those who framed it. In that process, the American Bar Association will no longer have the right to meddle in a way that distorts a nominee's credentials and advances the liberal agenda of litigious lawyers and their allies.

Justice is mocked by some of today's litigation practices, which hinder our country's competitiveness, and drain billions of dollars away from productive Americans. While we fully support the role of the judiciary in vindicating the constitutional and statutory rights of individuals and organizations, we believe the proliferation of litigation hits the consumer with higher prices and cripples the practice of medicine. Despite bipartisan congressional efforts to enact legal reforms, Bill Clinton vetoed such legislation at the behest of his financial friends: the trial lawyers. A Republican president will sign that bill, and more. We encourage State governments to adopt reforms similar to those we propose to restore fairness to the federal system:

- strengthen judicial sanctions for lawsuits that are substantially without merit, thereby hitting unethical lawyers in their pocketbooks;
- apply the Racketeer Influenced and Corrupt Organizations law (RICO) as originally intended, to criminal proceedings, not civil litigation;
- award punitive damages on a fair and reasonable basis after clear proof of wrongdoing, with limits that discourage opportunistic litigation. Since punitive damages are intended to punish egregious wrongdoing, a substantial portion of the amount awarded should go to a crime-victim compensation fund or similar program;
- restore limited liability to non-profit organizations—churches, civic and community groups, and the volunteers who sustain them—to provide protection against profit-seeking lawsuits and to encourage volunteerism;
- increase sanctions for abuses of the discovery process used to intimidate opponents and drive up the costs of litigation;
- reform medical malpractice to reduce health care costs and keep doctors practicing in critical areas like obstetrics;
- eliminate the use of "junk science" by opportunistic attorneys by requiring courts to verify that the science of those called as expert witnesses is reasonably acceptable within the scientific community, and forbid the practice of making their fees conditional upon a favorable verdict. This action will reduce the practice of so-called hired-gun "experts," who make up theories to fit the facts of the case in which they are testifying;
- eliminate joint and several liability in order to ensure that responsible parties pay their "fair share" in proportion to their degree of fault; and
- guard against non-meritorious lawsuits that are designed to have a chilling effect on First Amendment rights.

A federal products liability law goes hand in hand with legal reform. Its absence not only penalizes consumers with higher costs and keeps needed products off the market, but also gives foreign nations a competitive edge over American workers. Bill Clinton doesn't mind that. He vetoed Republican reforms that would have saved the public tens of billions of dollars.

Bill Clinton even vetoed the Securities Litigation Reform Act, a Republican initiative to protect shareholders against avaricious litigation. That obstructionism was too much for even the Democrats in Congress, many of whom joined in overriding his veto. A Republican president will work with Congress to restore justice to the nation's courts and fair play to the practice of law.

The Nation's Capital

The District of Columbia should be an example for the rest of the country. Instead, decades of domination by the Democratic Party has left the city bankrupt and dangerous. Its residents—and all Americans—deserve better than that.

We reaffirm the constitutional status of the District of Columbia as the seat of government of the United States and reject calls for statehood for the District.

We call for structural reform of the city's government and its education system. For both efficiency and public safety, we will transfer water and sewer management in the District to the Army Corps of Engineers or to a regional entity.

We endorse proposals by the congressional Republican Leadership for dramatic reductions in federal taxes—and the city's own outrageous marginal tax rate—within the District. Bill Clinton opposes that idea. A Republican president will make it part of a comprehensive agenda to transform the nation's capital into a renewal community, an enterprise zone leading the way for the rest of urban America to follow.

Americans in the Territories

We welcome greater participation in all aspects of the political process by Americans residing in Guam, the Virgin Islands, American Samoa, the Northern Marianas, and Puerto Rico. No single approach can meet the needs of those diverse communities. We therefore emphasize respect for their wishes regarding their relationship to the rest of the Union. We affirm their right to seek the full extension of the Constitution, with all the rights and responsibilities it entails.

We support the Native American Samoans' efforts to preserve their culture and land-tenure system, which fosters self-reliance and strong extended family values.

We recognize that the people of Guam have voted for a closer relationship with the United States of America, and we affirm our support of their right to mutually improve their political relationship through commonwealth.

We support the right of the United States citizens of Puerto Rico to be admitted to the Union as a fully sovereign state after they freely so determine.

We endorse initiatives of the congressional Republican leadership to provide for Puerto Rico's smooth transition to statehood if its citizens choose to alter their current status, or to set them on their own path to become an independent nation.

INDIVIDUAL RIGHTS AND PERSONAL SAFETY

We are discovering as a nation that many of our deepest social problems are problems of character and belief. We will never solve those problems until the hearts of parents are turned toward their children; until respect is restored for life and property; until a commitment is renewed to love and serve our neighbor. The common good requires that goodness be common.

—Bob Dole, May 23, 1996, in Philadelphia

Upholding the Rights of All

This section of our platform deals with rights and responsibilities. But it deals also with something larger: the common good, our shared sense of what makes a society decent and noble. That takes us beyond government policies and programs to what we are as a people, and what we want to be.

We are the party of the open door. As we approach the start of a new century, the Republican Party is more dedicated than ever to strengthening the social, cultural, and political ties that bind us together as a free people, the greatest force for good the world has ever seen. While our party remains steadfast in its commitment to advancing its historic principles and ideals, we also recognize that members of our party have deeply held and sometimes differing views. We view this diversity of views as a source of strength, not as a sign of weakness, and we welcome into our ranks all Americans who may hold differing positions. We are committed to resolving our differences in a spirit of civility, hope, and mutual respect.

Americans do not want to be afraid of those they pass on the street, suspicious of strangers, fearful for their children. They do not want to have to fight a constant battle against brutality and degradation in what passes for entertainment. We oppose sexual harassment in the workplace, and must ensure that no one in America is forced to choose between a job and submitting to unwelcome advances. We also oppose indoctrination in the classroom. Americans should not have to tolerate the decline of ethical standards and the collapse of behavioral norms. Most important, they should not have to doubt the truthfulness of their elected leaders.

Reversing those trends won't be easy, but our homes and our children are worth the effort. Government has a small, but vital, role. But most of the burden must be ours: as parents, as consumers, as citizens whose right of free speech empowers us to stand up for the weak and vulnerable—and speak out against the profiteers of violence and moral decay.

That needs to be done, both in our house and in the White House. Bill Clinton can't—or won't—do it. So we will do it without him, and with new national leadership of character and conscience.

We are the party of individual Americans, whose rights we protect and defend as the foundation for opportunity and security for all. Today, as at our founding in the day of Lincoln, we insist no one's rights are negotiable.

As we strive to forge a national consensus on the divisive issues of our time, we call on all Republicans and all Americans to reject the forces of hatred and bigotry. Accordingly, we denounce all who practice or promote racism, anti-Semitism, ethnic prejudice, and religious intolerance. We condemn attempts by the EEOC or any other arm of government to regulate or ban religious symbols from the workplace, and we assert the right of religious leaders to speak out on public issues. We condemn the desecration of

places of worship and are proud that congressional Republicans led the fight against church arsons. We believe religious institutions and schools should not be taxed. When government funds privately operated social, welfare, or educational programs, it must not discriminate against religious institutions, whose record in providing services to those in need far exceeds that of the public sector.

The sole source of equal opportunity for all is equality before the law. Therefore, we oppose discrimination based on sex, race, age, creed, or national origin and will vigorously enforce anti-discrimination statutes. We reject the distortion of those laws to cover sexual preference, and we endorse the Defense of Marriage Act to prevent states from being forced to recognize same-sex unions. Because we believe rights inhere in individuals, not in groups, we will attain our nation's goal of equal rights without quotas or other forms of preferential treatment. We scorn Bill Clinton's notion that any person should be denied a job, promotion, contract, or a chance at higher education because of their race or gender. Instead, we endorse the Dole-Canady Equal Opportunity Act to end discrimination by the federal government. We likewise endorse this year's Proposition 209, the California Civil Rights Initiative, to restore to law the original meaning of civil rights.

We renew our historic Republican commitment to equal opportunity for women. In the early days of the suffragist movement, we pioneered the women's right to vote. We take pride in this year's remarkable array of Republican women serving in and running for office and their role in leadership positions in our party, in Congress, and in the states. Two women serve in our House leadership—a record untouched by the Democrats during their 40 years in power. The full exercise of legal rights depends upon opportunity, and economic growth is the key to continuing progress for women in all fields of endeavor. Public policy must respect and accommodate women, whether they are full-time homemakers or pursue a career.

Under Senator Dole's sponsorship, the Americans with Disabilities Act was enacted to ensure full participation by disabled citizens in our country's life. Republicans emphasize community integration and inclusion of persons with disabilities, both by personal example and by practical enforcement of the Individuals with Disabilities Education Act, the Air Carriers Access Act, and other laws. We will safeguard the interests of disabled persons in Medicare and Medicaid, as well as in federal workforce programs. Under a Republican renewal, the abilities of all will be needed in an expanding economy, which alone can carry forward the assistive technology that offers personal progress for everyone. We support full access to the polls, and the entire political process, by disabled citizens. We oppose the non-consensual withholding of health care or treatment because of handicap, age, or infirmity, just as we oppose euthanasia and assisted suicide, which, especially for the poor and those on the margins of society, threaten the sanctity of human life.

The unborn child has a fundamental individual right to life which cannot be infringed. We support a human life amendment to the Constitution, and we endorse legislation to make clear that the Fourteenth Amendment's protections apply to unborn children. Our purpose is to have legislative and judicial protection of that right against those who perform abortions. We oppose using public revenues for abortion and will not fund organizations which advocate it. We support the appointment of judges who respect traditional family values and the sanctity of innocent human life.

Our goal is to ensure that women with problem pregnancies have the kind of support, material and otherwise, they need for themselves and for their babies, not to be punitive towards those for whose difficult situation we have only compassion. We oppose abortion, but our pro-life agenda does not include punitive action against women who have an abortion. We salute those who provide alternatives to abortion and offer adoption services. Republicans in Congress took the lead in expanding assistance both for the costs of adoption and for the continuing care of adoptive children with special needs. Bill Clinton vetoed our adoption tax credit the first time around—and opposed our efforts to remove racial barriers to adoption—before joining in this

long overdue measure of support for adoptive families.

Worse than that, he vetoed the ban on partial-birth abortions, a procedure denounced by a committee of the American Medical Association and rightly branded as four-fifths infanticide. We applaud Bob Dole's commitment to revoke the Clinton executive orders concerning abortion and to sign into law an end to partial-birth abortions.

We reaffirm the promise of the Fifth Amendment: "nor shall private property be taken for public use, without just compensation." This Takings Clause protects the homes and livelihood of Americans against the governmental greed and abuse of power that characterizes the Clinton Administration; we will strictly enforce it.

We defend the constitutional right to keep and bear arms. We will promote training in the safe usage of firearms, especially in programs for women and the elderly. We strongly support Bob Dole's National Instant Check Initiative, which will help keep all guns out of the hands of convicted felons. The point-of-purchase instant check has worked well in many states, and now it is time to extend this system all across America. We applaud Bob Dole's commitment to have the national instant check system operational by the end of 1997. In one of the strangest actions of his tenure, Bill Clinton abolished Operation Triggerlock, the Republican initiative to jail any felon caught with a gun. We will restore that effort and will set by law minimum mandatory penalties for the use of guns in committing a crime: 5 years for possession, 10 years for brandishing, and 20 for discharge.

We affirm the right of individuals to participate in labor organizations and to bargain collectively, consistent with State laws. Because that participation should always be voluntary, we support the right of States to enact right-to-work laws. We will restore the original scope of the Hobbs Act, barring union officials from extortion and violence. We will vigorously implement the Supreme Court's Beck decision to ensure that workers are not compelled to subsidize political activity, like the $35 million slush fund extorted this year from rank-and-file members by

Washington-based labor leaders. We will reverse Bill Clinton's unconscionable Executive Order that deprived workers of their right to know how their union dues are spent.

A Sensible Immigration Policy

As a nation of immigrants, we welcome those who follow our laws and come to our land to seek a better life. New Americans strengthen our economy, enrich our culture, and defend the nation in war and in peace. At the same time, we are determined to reform the system by which we welcome them to the American family. We must set immigration at manageable levels, balance the competing goals of uniting families of our citizens and admitting specially talented persons, and end asylum abuses through expedited exclusion of false claimants.

Bill Clinton's immigration record does not match his rhetoric. While talking tough on illegal immigration, he has proposed a reduction in the number of border patrol agents authorized by the Republicans in Congress, has opposed the most successful border control program in decades (Operation Hold the Line in Texas), has opposed Proposition 187 in California which 60 percent of Californians supported, and has opposed Republican efforts to ensure that noncitizens not take advantage of expensive welfare programs. Unlike Bill Clinton, we stand with the American people on immigration policy and will continue to reform and enforce our immigration laws to ensure that they reflect America's national interest.

We also support efforts to secure our borders from the threat of illegal immigration. Illegal immigration has reached crisis proportions, with more than four million illegal aliens now present in the United States. That number, growing by 300,000 each year, burdens taxpayers, strains public services, takes jobs, and increases crime. Republicans in both the House and Senate have passed bills that tighten border enforcement, speed up deportation of criminal aliens, toughen penalties for overstaying visas, and streamline the Immigration and Naturalization Service.

Illegal aliens should not receive public benefits other than emergency aid, and those who become parents while illegally in the United States should not be qualified to claim benefits for their offspring. Legal immigrants should depend for assistance on their sponsors, who are legally responsible for their financial well-being, not the American taxpayers. Just as we require "deadbeat dads" to provide for the children they bring into the world, we should require "deadbeat sponsors" to provide for the immigrants they bring into the country. We support a constitutional amendment or constitutionally valid legislation declaring that children born in the United States of parents who are not legally present in the United States or who are not long-term residents are not automatically citizens.

We endorse the Dole/Coverdell proposal to make crimes of domestic violence, stalking, child abuse, child neglect, and child abandonment committed by aliens residing in this country deportable offenses under our immigration laws.

We call for harsh penalties against exploiters who smuggle illegal aliens and for those who profit from the production of false documents. Republicans believe that by eliminating the magnet for illegal immigration, increasing border security, enforcing our immigration laws, and producing counterfeit-proof documents, we will finally put an end to the illegal immigration crisis. We oppose the creation of any national ID card.

From Many, One

America's ethnic diversity within a shared national culture is one of our country's greatest strengths. While we benefit from our differences, we must also strengthen the ties that bind us to one another. Foremost among those is the flag. Its deliberate desecration is not "free speech," but an assault against our history and our hopes. We support a constitutional amendment that will restore to the people, through their elected representatives, their right to safeguard Old Glory. We condemn Bill Clinton's refusal, once again, to protect and preserve the most precious symbol of our Republic.

English, our common language, provides a shared foundation which has allowed people from every corner of the world to come together to build the American nation. The use of English is indispensable to all who wish to participate fully in our society and realize the American Dream. As Bob Dole has said: "For more than two centuries now, English has been a force for unity, indispensable to the process of transforming untold millions of immigrants from all parts of the globe into citizens of the most open and free society the world has ever seen." For newcomers, learning the English language has always been the fastest route to the mainstream of American life. That should be the goal of bilingual education programs. We support the official recognition of English as the nation's common language. We advocate foreign language training in our schools and retention of heritage languages in homes and cultural institutions. Foreign language fluency is also an essential component of America's competitiveness in the world market.

We will strengthen Native Americans' self-determination by respecting tribal sovereignty, encouraging a pro-business and pro-development climate on reservations. We uphold the unique government-to-government relationship between the tribes and the United States, and we honor our nation's trust obligations to them. In fulfillment thereof, we will ensure that the resources, financial and otherwise, which the United States holds in trust are well managed, audited, and protected. We second Bob Dole's call for legislation authorizing tribal governments to reorganize the Bureau of Indian Affairs and the Indian Health Service. We endorse efforts to ensure equitable participation in federal programs by Native Americans, Native Alaskans, and Native Hawaiians and to preserve their culture and languages.

Getting Tough on Crime

Women in America know better than anyone about the randomness and ruthlessness of crime. It is a shameful, national disgrace that nightfall has become synonymous with fear for so many of America's women.

— Bob Dole, May 28, 1996, in Aurora, Colorado

During Bill Clinton's tenure, America has become a more fearful place, especially for the elderly and for women and children. Violent crime has turned our homes into prisons, our streets and schoolyards into battlegrounds. It devours half a trillion dollars every year. Unfortunately, far worse could be coming in the near future. While we acknowledge the extraordinary efforts of single parents, we recognize that a generation of fatherless boys raises the prospect of soaring juvenile crime.

This is, in part, the legacy of liberalism—in the old Democrat Congress, in the Clinton Department of Justice, and in the courts, where judges appointed by Democrat presidents continue their assault against the rights of law-abiding Americans. For too long government policy has been controlled by criminals and their defense lawyers. Democrat Congresses cared more about the rights of criminals than safety for Americans. Bill Clinton arbitrarily closed off Pennsylvania Avenue, the nation's Main Street, for his protection, while his policies left the public unprotected against vicious criminals. As a symbol of our determination to restore the rule of law—in the White House as well as in our streets—we will reopen Pennsylvania Avenue.

After the elections of 1994, the new Republican majorities in the House and Senate fought back with legislation that ends frivolous, costly, and unnecessarily lengthy death-row appeals, requires criminals to pay restitution to their victims, speeds the removal of criminal aliens, and steps up the fight against terrorism. Congressional Republicans put into law a truth-in-sentencing prison grant program to provide incentives to states which enact laws requiring violent felons to serve at least 85 percent of their sentences and replaced a myriad of Democrat "Washington knows best" prevention programs with bloc grants to cities and counties to use to fight crime as they see fit. They put an end to federal court early-release orders for prison overcrowding and made it much harder for prisoners to file frivolous lawsuits about prison conditions.

There's more to do, once Bill Clinton's veto threats no longer block the way. We will establish no-frills prisons where prisoners are required to work productively and make the threat of jail a real deterrent to crime. Prisons should not be places of rest and relaxation. We will reform the Supreme Court's fanciful exclusionary rule, which has allowed a generation of criminals to get off on technicalities.

Juvenile crime is one of the most difficult challenges facing our nation. The juvenile justice system is broken. It fails to punish the minor crimes that lead to larger offenses, and lacks early intervention to keep delinquency from turning into violent crime. Truancy laws are not enforced, positive role models are lacking, and parental responsibility is overlooked. We will stress accountability at every step in the system and require adult trials for juveniles who commit adult crimes.

In addition, not only is juvenile crime on the rise, but unsupervised juveniles (especially at night) are most often the victims of abuse in our society. Recognizing that local jurisdictions have a clear and concise understanding of their problems, we encourage them to develop and enact innovative programs to address juvenile crime. We also encourage them to consider juvenile nocturnal curfews as an effective law enforcement tool in helping reduce juvenile crime and juvenile victimization.

Juvenile criminal proceedings should be open to victims and the public. Juvenile conviction records should not be sealed but made available to law enforcement agencies, the courts, and those who hire for sensitive work in schools and day-care centers.

Because liberal jurists keep expanding the rights of the accused, Republicans propose a constitutional amendment to protect victims' rights: audio and visual testimony of victims kept on file for future hearings, full restitution, protection from intimidation or violence by the offender, notification of court proceedings, a chance to be heard in plea bargains, the right to remain in court during trials and hearings concerning the crimes committed against them, a voice in the sentencing proceedings, and notice of the release or escape of offenders. Bill Clinton hypocritically endorsed our Victim's Rights Amendment while naming judges who opposed capital punishment, turned felons loose, and even excused

murder as a form of social protest. Bob Dole, the next Republican president, will end that nonsense and make our courts once again an instrument of justice.

While the federal government's role is essential, most law enforcement must remain in the hands of local communities, directed by State and local officials who are closely answerable to the people whose lives are affected by crime. In that regard, we support community policing; nothing inhibits local crime like an officer in the neighborhood. Bill Clinton promised 100,000 more police officers on the beat but, according to his own attorney general, delivered no more than 17,000. He ignored local law enforcers by tying the program in knots of red tape and high costs. Now he is diverting millions of its dollars, appropriated by congressional Republicans to fight street crime, to state parks and environmental projects. It's time to return those anti-crime resources to communities and let them decide what works best to keep their homes, schools, and workplaces safe. This would result in far more new police officers than Bill Clinton's program and give communities additional crime-fighting resources they need.

We will work with local authorities to prevent prison inmates from receiving disability or other government entitlements while incarcerated. We support efforts to allow peace officers, including qualified retirees, to assist their colleagues and protect their communities even when they are out of their home jurisdictions to the extent this is consistent with applicable state and local law. We will amend the Fair Labor Standards Act so that corrections officers can volunteer to assist local law enforcement.

Crimes against women and children demand an emphatic response. Under Bob Dole and Dick Zimmer's leadership, Republicans in Congress pushed through Megan's Law—the requirement that local communities be notified when sex offenders and kidnappers are released—in response to the growing number of violent sexual assaults and murders like the brutal murder of a little girl in New Jersey. We call for special penalties against thugs who assault or batter pregnant women and harm them or their unborn children. We endorse Bob Dole's call to bring federal penalties for child pornography in line with far tougher State penalties: ten years for a first offense, fifteen for the second, and life for a third. We believe it is time to revisit the Supreme Court's arbitrary decision of 1977 that protects even the most vicious rapists from the death penalty. Bob Dole authored a tough federal statute which provides for the admissibility of prior similar criminal acts of defendants in sexual assault cases. This important law enforcement tool should serve as a model for the states. We continue our strong support of capital punishment for those who commit heinous federal crimes, including the kingpins of the narcotics trade.

We wish to express our support and sympathy for all victims of terrorism and their families. Acts of terrorism against Americans and American interests must be stopped, and those who commit them must be brought to justice. We recommend a presidentially appointed "blue ribbon" commission to study more effective methods of prosecuting terrorists.

Only Republican resolve can prepare our nation to deal with the four deadly threats facing us in the early years of the 21st century: violent crime, drugs, terrorism, and international organized crime. Those perils are interlocked—and all are escalating. This is no time for excuses. It's time for a change.

Solving the Drug Crisis

The verdict is in on Bill Clinton's moral leadership: After 11 years of steady decline, the use of marijuana among teens doubled in the two years after 1992. At the same time, the use of cocaine and methamphetamines dramatically increased.

That shocks but should not surprise. For in the war on drugs—an essential component of the fight against crime—today's Democratic Party has been a conscientious objector. Nowhere is the discrepancy between Bill Clinton's rhetoric and his actions more apparent. Mr. Clinton's personal record has been a betrayal of the nation's trust, sending the worst possible signal to the nation's youth. At the urging of the Secret Service, the White House had to institute a drug-testing pro-

gram for Clinton staffers who were known to be recent users of illegal narcotics. At the same time, he drastically cut funding for drug interdiction. The Office of National Drug Control Policy was cut by 80 percent, and federal drug prosecutions dropped 25 percent. His attorney general proposed to reduce mandatory minimum sentences for drug trafficking and related crimes, and his surgeon general advocated legalization of narcotics. Hundreds of suspected drug smugglers have been allowed to go free at the border. Simultaneously, the use of marijuana, cocaine, and heroin has increased, especially among young people. Now, narcotics are again fueling the acceleration of crime rates, putting the nation on a collision course with the future.

Bill Clinton's weakness in international affairs has worsened the situation here at home. One case in point: He certified that Mexico has cooperated with our drug interdiction effort when 70 percent of drugs smuggled into the U.S. come across our southern border—and when the Mexican government ignored 165 extradition orders for drug criminals. Discredited at home and abroad, he lacks both the stature and the credibility to lead us toward a drug-free America.

A war against drugs requires moral leadership now lacking in the White House. Throughout the 1980s, the Republican approach—no legalization, no tolerance, no excuses—turned the tide against drug abuse. We can do it again by emphasizing prevention, interdiction, a tough international approach, and a crack-down on users. That requires reversing one of Bill Clinton's most offensive actions: his shocking purge of every U.S. attorney in the country shortly after he took office. This unprecedented firing destroyed our first line of defense against drug trafficking and other career criminals. Our country's most experienced and dedicated prosecutors were replaced with Clintonite liberals, some of whom have refused to prosecute major drug dealers, foreign narcotics smugglers, and child pornographers.

In a Dole administration, U.S. attorneys will prosecute and jail those who prey upon the innocent. We support upgrading our interdiction effort by establishing a Deputy Commissioner for

Drug Enforcement within the Customs Service. We will intensify our intelligence efforts against international drug traffickers and use whatever means necessary to destroy their operations and seize their personal accounts.

We support strong penalties, including mandatory minimum sentences, for drug trafficking, distribution, and drug-related crimes. Drug use is closely related to crime and recidivism. Drug testing should be made a routine feature of the criminal justice process at every stage, including the juvenile justice system. Test results should be used in deciding pretrial release, sentencing, and probation revocation.

A safer America must include highways without drunk or drug-impaired drivers. We support the toughest possible State laws to deal with drivers impaired by substance abuse and advocate federal cooperation, not compulsion, toward that end.

The Bottom Line: From the Top Down

Making America safe again will be a tremendous undertaking, in its own way as heroic as was the liberation of Europe from a different kind of criminal half a century ago. At the grassroots, that crusade already has enlisted the men and women of local law enforcement. Now they need a leader worthy of their cause—someone whose life reflects respect for the law, not evasion of it. Bill Clinton need not apply.

Bob Dole will be a president committed to the protection and safety of all Americans. However, his strength is diminished without a court system supportive of the national fight against violent crime. That is the bottom line of this year's presidential election: Who should chart the course of law enforcement for the next generation by naming as many as an additional 30 percent of our federal judges and the next several justices to the U.S. Supreme Court? Bill Clinton, the master of excuse and evasion? Or Bob Dole, whose life has been an exercise in honor and duty?

FAMILIES AND SOCIETY

The alternative to cold bureaucracy is not indifference. It is the warmth of families and neigh- *borhoods, charities, churches, synagogues, and communities. These value-shaping institutions have the tools to reclaim lives—individual responsibility, tough love, and spiritual renewal. They do more than care for the body; they restore the spirit.*
—Bob Dole, May 23, 1996, in Philadelphia

Stronger Families

We are the party of the American family, educating children, caring for the sick, learning from the elderly, and helping the less fortunate. We believe that strengthening family life is the best way to improve the quality of life for everyone.

Families foster the virtues that make a free society strong. We rely on the home and its supportive institutions to instill honesty, self-discipline, mutual respect, and the other virtues that sustain democracy. Our goal is to promote those values by respecting the rights of families and by assisting, where appropriate, the institutions which mediate between government and the home. While recognizing a role for government in dealing with social ills, we look to mediating institutions—religious and community groups, private associations of all kinds—to take the lead in tackling the social ills that some government programs have only worsened.

This is the clearest distinction between Republicans and Clinton Democrats: We believe the family is the core institution of our society. Bill Clinton thinks government should hold that place. It's little wonder, then, that today's families feel under siege. They seem to work harder with less reward for their labor. They can no longer expect that life will be better for their children than it was for them.

Their problem starts in the White House. Bill Clinton has hit families with higher taxes, vetoed their tax relief, and given their money to special interest groups. He has meddled in their schools, fought family choice in education, and promoted lifestyles inimical to their values. He repeatedly vetoed pro-family welfare reforms before surrendering to the demands of the American people. He tried to impose a ruinous government takeover of health care; led a scare campaign against Republican efforts to preserve, protect, and strengthen Medicare; and appointed to major positions in his administration social theorists whose bizarre views are alien to those of most Americans.

Republicans want to get our society back on track—toward good schools with great teachers, welfare that really helps, and health care responsive to the needs of people, not government. We want to make sure our most important programs—like Social Security and Medicare—are there when people need them. In all those cases, we start with the family as the building block of a safe and caring society.

Our agenda for more secure families runs throughout this platform. Here we take special notice of the way congressional Republicans have advanced adoption assistance, promoted foster care reform, and fought the marriage penalty in the tax code. They have worked to let parents have flex-time and comp-time in private industry, and have safeguarded family choice in child care against the Democrats' attempts to control it. They passed the Defense of Marriage Act, which defines "marriage" for purposes of federal law as the legal union of one man and one woman and prevents federal judges and bureaucrats from forcing states to recognize other living arrangements as "marriages." Further, they have advanced the Family Rights and Privacy Act—a bill of rights against the intrusions of big government and its grantees.

In the House and Senate, Republicans have championed the economic rights of the family and made a $500-per-child tax credit the centerpiece of their reform agenda. But that overdue measure of relief for households with children was vetoed.

We salute parents working at the State level to ensure constitutional protection for the rights of the family. We urge State legislators to review divorce laws to foster the stability of the home and protect the economic rights of the innocent spouse and children.

Improving Education

At the center of all that afflicts our schools is a denial of free choice. Our public schools are in trouble because they are no longer run by the public. Instead, they're controlled by narrow special interest groups who regard public education not as a public trust, but as political territory to be guarded at all costs.

—Bob Dole, July 17, 1996, in Minneapolis

The American people know that something is terribly wrong with our education system. The evidence is everywhere: children who cannot read, graduates who cannot reason, danger in schoolyards, indoctrination in classrooms.

To this crisis in our schools, Bill Clinton responds with the same liberal dogmas that created the mess: more federal control and more spending on all the wrong things. He opposes family rights in education and opportunity scholarships for poor children. When it comes to saving our schools, he flunks.

Americans should have the best education in the world. We spend more per pupil than any other nation, and the great majority of our teachers are dedicated and skilled educators, whose interests are ignored by political union bosses. Our goal is nothing less than a renaissance in American education, begun by returning its control to parents, teachers, local school boards, and, through them, to communities and local taxpayers.

Our formula is as simple as it is sweeping: The federal government has no constitutional authority to be involved in school curricula or to control jobs in the workplace. That is why we will abolish the Department of Education, end federal meddling in our schools, and promote family choice at all levels of learning. We therefore call for prompt repeal of the Goals 2000 program and the School-to-Work Act of 1994, which put new federal controls, as well as unfunded mandates, on the States. We further urge that federal attempts to impose outcome- or performance-based education on local schools be ended.

We know what works in education, and it isn't the liberal fads of the last thirty years. It's discipline, parental involvement, emphasis on basics including computer technology, phonics instead of look-say reading, and dedicated teaching.

Abstinence education in the home will lead to less need for birth control services and fewer abortions. We support educational initiatives to promote chastity until marriage as the expected standard of behavior. This education initiative is the best preventive measure to avoid the emotional trauma of sexually transmitted diseases and teen pregnancies that are serious problems among our young people. While recognizing that something must be done to help children when parental consent or supervision is not possible, we oppose school-based clinics, which provide referrals, counseling, and related services for contraception and abortion.

We encourage a reform agenda on the local level and urge State legislators to ensure quality education for all through programs of parental choice among public, private, and religious schools. That includes the option of home schooling, and Republicans will defend the right of families to make that choice. We support and vigorously work for mechanisms, such as opportunity scholarships, block grants, school rebates, charter schools, and vouchers, to make parental choice in education a reality for all parents.

On the federal level, we endorse legislation—like the Watts-Talent Low-Income Educational Opportunity Act, which is part of the Community Renewal Act of 1996, and the Coats-Kasich Educational Choice and Equity Act—to set up model programs for empowering the families who need good schooling the most.

We will continue to work for the return of voluntary prayer to our schools and will strongly enforce the Republican legislation that guarantees equal access to school facilities by student religious groups. We encourage State legislatures to pass statutes which prohibit local school boards from adopting policies of denial regarding voluntary school prayer.

We endorse Bob Dole's pledge that all federal education policies will be guided by his Education Consumer's Warranty. The Education Consumer's Warranty says that all American children should expect to:

- attend a safe school;
- be free from educational malpractice at the hands of bad schools, incompetent teachers, timid principals, and intrusive bureaucrats;
- find out exactly how well they and their school

are doing (in terms of achievement) in relation to how well they ought to be doing;
- learn the three R's through proven methods;
- learn the nation's history and democratic values and study the classics of Western civilization;
- attend a school that is free to innovate and isn't tied down by federal red tape;
- be confident that their high school diploma signifies a solid education, suitable for college or a good job;
- choose the school that's right for them;
- know that their tax dollars are reaching the classroom, not being siphoned off into overhead and bureaucracy; and,
- count on being able to arrive at college prepared to do freshman-level work.

To reinforce our American heritage, we believe our nation's governors, State legislators, and local school boards should support requiring our public schools to dedicate one full day each year solely to studying the Declaration of Independence and the Constitution.

America's families find themselves on a college treadmill: The more they work to pay tuition, the faster it seems to increase. Tuition has escalated far in excess of inflation, in defiance of market factors, and shows no sign of slowing down. Billions of dollars are wasted on regulations, paperwork, and "political correctness," which impedes the ability of the faculty to teach. We call for a national reassessment of the economics of higher education, to stop the treadmill and restore fiscal accountability to higher education. Congressional Republicans budgeted a 50 percent increase in student loans while fighting Bill Clinton's intrusion of big government into their financing. Heeding the outcry from the nation's campuses, we will end the Clinton Administration's perverse direct lending program. We support proposals to assist families to prepare for the financial strains of higher education, like the American Dream Savings Account, passed by congressional Republicans but vetoed.

To protect the nation's colleges and universities against intolerance, we will work with independent educators to create alternatives to ideological accrediting bodies. We believe meeting the higher education needs of America will require new public and private institutions that are flexible, able to apply new technologies, willing to provide access to all those who need it, cost-effective, and that place no burden on the American taxpayer.

Improving America's Health Care

Our goal is to maintain the quality of America's health care—the best in the world, bar none—while making health care and health insurance more accessible and more affordable. That means allowing health care providers to respond to consumer demand through consumer choice.

That approach stands in stark contrast to Bill Clinton's health plan of 1993. "Clintoncare" would have been a poison pill for the nation's health care system. Congressional Republicans countered with the right prescription:

- make insurance portable from job to job;
- ensure that persons are not denied coverage because of preexisting health conditions when changing employment;
- crack down on Medicare and Medicaid fraud, while preserving the confidentiality of medical records from inappropriate scrutiny and without imposing criminal penalties for clerical errors and billing mistakes;
- reform malpractice laws, to reduce the costly practice of "defensive medicine" and to make it easier for doctors to specialize in fields like obstetrics. We also recognize the vital importance of maintaining the confidentiality of the national practitioners data base;
- let individuals set up tax-free Medical Savings Accounts (MSAs), so they can plan for their own medical needs instead of relying on government or insurance companies. Republicans believe that Medicare and Medicaid recipients should also have the option to utilize MSAs, which would result in huge savings for the American taxpayers;
- overhaul the Food and Drug Administration to get better products on the market faster and at less cost to consumers;
- change IRS rules that restrict coverage; let employer groups offer tax-exempt policies and make premiums 100 percent deductible for farmers, small businesses, and all the self-employed;
- promote a private market for long-term care insurance;
- reduce paperwork through electronic billing;
- change anti-trust laws to let health care providers cooperate in holding down charges;
- avoid mandatory coverages that make consumers pay for more insurance than they need;
- allow multi-employer purchasing groups and form "risk pools" in the States to make employee health insurance more affordable;
- remove regulatory barriers to the use of managed care for those who choose it. Traditionally, all Americans have had the freedom to choose their health care plans, as well as the providers who treat them. To ensure quality of care, it is imperative that patients continue to enjoy the freedoms to which they have been accustomed. Communications between providers and patients should be free and open, and allow for full discussion of the patient's medical care. Financial arrangements should not be a barrier to a patient's receiving quality medical care;
- permit families with incomes up to twice the poverty level to buy into Medicaid;
- promote rural health care through telecommunications and emergency air transport; and
- increase funding for Community and Migrant Health Centers.

Bill Clinton and most congressional Democrats opposed many of these reforms, especially Medical Savings Accounts and changes in malpractice laws. Congressional Republicans rallied the nation to win a long overdue victory for consumers and for common sense. Three months away from the November elections, Bill Clinton caved in and promised to sign into law the Republican solution to America's health care problems.

But the Clinton Democrats are still blocking Republican efforts to preserve, protect, and strengthen Medicare. Until Medicare is financially secure again, our job is not finished. More than 39 million people depend on Medicare, which is rushing toward bankruptcy even more quickly than predicted. Bill Clinton doesn't seem to mind. Despite repeated Republican efforts to work with his administration to save Medicare, his response has been a barrage of propaganda. We proposed Medisave; he indulged in Mediscare. We say this with solemn deliberation: Bill Clinton lied about the condition of Medicare and lied about our attempts to save it.

We reaffirm our determination to protect Medicare. We will ensure a significant annual expansion in Medicare. That isn't "cutting Medicare." It's a projected average annual rate of growth of 7.1 percent per year—more than twice the rate of inflation—to ensure coverage for those who need it now and those who will need it in the future. We propose to allow unprecedented patient choice in Medicare, so that older Americans can select health care arrangements that work best for them, including provider-sponsored organizations offering quality care with strong consumer protections.

Our commitment is to protect the most vulnerable of our people: children, the elderly, the disabled. That is why we are determined to restructure Medicaid, the federal-State program of health care for the poor. Rife with fraud, poorly administered, with no incentives for patient or provider savings, Medicaid has mushroomed into the nation's biggest welfare program. Its staggering rate of growth threatens to overwhelm State budgets, while thwarting congressional progress towards a federal balanced budget. Bill Clinton's response has been to ignore the problem—and attack Republicans for trying to solve it.

We must find better ways to ensure quality health care for the poor. Medicaid should be turned over to State management with leeway for restructuring and reform. Low-income persons should have access to managed care programs and Medical Savings Accounts, just as other persons do, and State officials should have authority to weed out substandard providers and to eliminate excess costs. We endorse Republican legislation extending federal tort claim coverage to health care professionals who provide free medical services to persons who cannot afford them.

Preventive care is key to both wellness and

lower medical bills, and strong families are the most powerful form of preventive care. Responsible families mean less child abuse, lower mortality, fewer unvaccinated youngsters, fewer teen pregnancies, and less involvement with drugs, alcohol, and tobacco. To help low-income families toward those goals, we will unify scattered federal resources into block grants.

We reaffirm our traditional support for generous funding of medical research, especially through the National Institutes of Health, and for continuing federal support for teaching hospitals and medical schools. We remain committed to, and place a high priority on, finding a cure for HIV disease. We support increased funding for research targeted at conditions that touch the families of most Americans, like Alzheimer's, breast cancer, prostate cancer, and diabetes. We call for an increased emphasis on prevention of diseases that threaten the lives of women. This requires dramatic expansion of outreach and education to expand public awareness. We call for fetal protection in biomedical research and will enforce the rights of human subjects in all federally funded studies.

The value of medical research and preventive care to wellness and lower health care spending can be highlighted by the example of diabetes. Approximately 16 million people in the U.S. have diabetes, and 50 percent of people above age 65 are at risk for developing some form of the disease. Diabetes is a leading cause of adult blindness, kidney disease, heart disease, stroke, and amputations, and reduces life expectancy by up to 30 percent. As much as 25 percent of Medicare expenditures are incurred in the treatment of diabetes-related complications. Scientific discoveries, made possible by federal funding of medical research, have led to new efforts to prevent diabetes, as well as new treatment strategies to forestall the development of its debilitating and life-threatening complications. Today, people stricken with diabetes can, in concert with their health care providers, delay or prevent the serious and deadly complications of the disease. In other words, we now have the opportunity to reduce the burden of diabetes.

Renewing Hope and Opportunity

Thirty years ago, the "Great Society" was liberalism's greatest hope, its greatest boast. Today, it stands as its greatest shame, a grand failure that has crushed the spirit, destroyed the families, and decimated the culture of those who have become enmeshed in its web.

—Bob Dole, May 21, 1996,
in Fond du Lac, Wisconsin

Within a few weeks, Bill Clinton will sign into law a Republican reform of welfare. With a straight face, after twice vetoing similar legislation, he will attempt to take credit for what we have accomplished.

So be it. Our cause is justice for both the taxpayers and for the poor. Our purpose in welfare reform is not to save money but to bring into the mainstream of American life those who now are on the margins of our society and our economy. We will, in the words of the Speaker of the House of Representatives Newt Gingrich, replace the welfare state with an opportunity [in] society for all. The Clinton administration's "Reinventing Government" program to reform the welfare state bureaucracy has failed. In fact, management reforms of the Reagan years were repealed and new labor-management councils that diluted efficient management were added as additional bureaucracy and red tape. We will revoke these Clinton administration policies and oppose the liberal philosophy that bureaucracy can reform welfare.

The current welfare system has spent $5 trillion in the last thirty years and has been a catastrophic failure. Despite this massive effort, conditions in our nation's poor communities have grown measurably worse. Poverty used to be an economic problem; now it is a social pathology.

The key to welfare reform is restoring personal responsibility and encouraging two-parent households. The path to that goal lies outside of official Washington. In the hands of State and local officials, and under the eye of local taxpayers, welfare can again become a hand up instead of a handout. All able-bodied adults must be required to work, either in private-sector jobs or in community work projects. Illegal aliens must be ineligible for all but emergency benefits. And a firm time limit for receipt of welfare must be enforced.

Because illegitimacy is the most serious cause of child poverty, we will encourage States to stop cash payments to unmarried teens and set a family cap on payments for additional children. When benefits of any kind are extended to teen mothers, they must be conditioned upon their attendance at school and their living at home with a parent, adult relative, or guardian. About half the children of today's teen welfare mothers were fathered in statutory rape. We echo Bob Dole's call to our nation's governors to toughen and enforce State laws in this regard, as well as those concerning enforcement of child support.

Restoring common sense to welfare programs is only one side of the Republican equation for hope and opportunity. The other side is giving low-income households the tools with which they can build their own future. We propose to do this along the lines of the American Community Renewal Act, a Republican congressional initiative that would establish throughout the nation up to 100 renewal communities where residents, businesses, and investors would have unprecedented economic freedom and incentives to create prosperity. School choice for low-income families is an integral part of that initiative.

We call for the removal of structural impediments which liberals throw in the path of poor people: over-regulation of start-up enterprises, excessive licensing requirements, needless restrictions on formation of schools and child care centers catering to poor families, restrictions on providing public services in fields like transport and sanitation, and rigged franchises that close the opportunity door to all but a favored few.

Not everyone can make it on their own. Government at various levels has a role—and some aid programs do work well—and so do private individuals and charitable and faith-based organizations, whose record of success far outshines that of any public welfare program. To promote personal involvement with anti-poverty efforts, we call for a Charity Tax Credit that will be consistent with the fundamental changes we propose in the nation's system of taxation. To ensure that religiously affiliated institutions can fulfill their helping mission, we endorse Republican legislation to stop discrimination against them in government programs.

Older Americans

Our commitment to older Americans runs throughout this platform. It strengthens our call for tax fairness, shows in our action agenda against violent crime, and motivates our crusade to preserve, protect, and strengthen Medicare.

The Republican Party has always opposed the earnings limitation for Social Security benefits, a confiscatory tax that discourages older Americans from active engagement in all walks of life. While Bill Clinton imposed his new tax on Social Security benefits, he also initially vetoed our legislation to reform the earnings limitation, just as he vetoed our estate tax reform.

The Social Security system remains the cornerstone of personal security for millions of the elderly. In 1983, a Republican president, working with the Republican Chairman of the Senate Finance Committee—Bob Dole—saved the Social Security system from fiscal disaster. We have a legal and moral responsibility to America's seniors and will continue to do everything in our power to ensure that government honors our commitment to Social Security beneficiaries, now and in the future. We will keep it financially sound and keep politics out of its administration. We will work to ensure the integrity and solvency of the Social Security trust funds.

Those who are not older Americans now will one day be so. Our common goal is a secure economic future. To that end, public policy should encourage cooperative efforts by businesses and employees alike to expand the availability of savings vehicles for all. We want to expand retirement options so that individual choice, not government fiat, steers the decision-making process. We must increase both the amount and the portability of personal savings, especially in today's rapidly changing and unpredictable economy. We salute congressional Republicans for their landmark legislation simplifying pension law, cutting away the red tape that prevented many businesses from offering pension plans, and establishing a new pension system designed to meet the needs of workers in small businesses.

We also salute congressional Republicans for making long-term care more affordable and more available to those who need it. Too many seniors live in fear that they one day will incur long-term care costs that will wipe out their life savings and burden their children. The Republican Congress has passed legislation giving long-term care insurance policies the same tax-preferred treatment that health insurance policies now receive. Over the years, this legislation will give millions of Americans peace of mind and the financial wherewithal to obtain nursing home care of the highest quality.

A CLEANER, SAFER, HEALTHIER AMERICA

Those of us who grew up with a common set of values, a code of living that stays with us all our lives. Love of God and country and family. Commitment to honesty, decency, and personal responsibility. Self-reliance tempered by a sense of community . . . Those values made us the greatest country on earth. And the secret to getting our country back on track is simply to return to them as a matter of national policy.
                                                        —Bob Dole, August 19, 1995, in Ames, Iowa

We are the party of America's farmers, ranchers, foresters, and all who hold the earth in stewardship with the Creator. Republican leadership established the Land Grant College System under Abraham Lincoln, the National Park System under Ulysses Grant, the National Wildlife Refuge System under Teddy Roosevelt, and today's legal protections for clean air and water in more recent decades. We reaffirm our commitment to agricultural progress, environmental improvement, and the prudent development of our natural resources.

Our goal is to continue the progress we have made to achieve a cleaner, safer, healthier environment for all Americans—and to pass on to our children and grandchildren a better environment than we have today. We must recognize the unique role our States, localities, and private sector have in improving our environment. The States and communities are the laboratories of environmental innovation. Inflexible requirements hurt the environment, add unnecessary costs, and reduce technology development. While we have made substantial environmental progress, we must reject failed approaches created by fearmongering and centralized control which will not serve our environment well in the century ahead.

The Superfund program to clean up abandoned toxic waste sites is a case in point. More than half of the $30 billion already spent on Superfund has gone for litigation and administration. In other words, trial lawyers have profited from the current flawed and unfair liability scheme, while toxic waste sites wait to be cleaned up. Without the opposition of Bill Clinton, we will fix the broken Superfund law. We will direct resources to clean up sites where there are real risks, and cooperate with citizens, States, and localities who want to help, rather than harassing them with unwarranted lawsuits.

The States have been leaders in returning contaminated sites to productive use under "brownfields" programs. These programs tailor clean-up standards appropriate for expected future use, thus enabling environmental clean-up and economic development. Accordingly, as an essential component of our comprehensive Superfund reform, we will remove disincentives in current federal law in order to allow States to expand their innovative "brownfields" programs.

Inconsistent federal policies have created a nightmare for our nation's ports at a critical time of growth and change in international trade. We must protect the environment while recognizing the unique situation of each port. There must be a coordination of State, local, and federal roles in encouraging our ports to expand to meet current and future needs.

Republicans trust Americans to honor their shared desire to live and raise their children in a clean and healthy environment. For all environmental problems, we propose a common-sense approach based on flexibility and consensus, that builds a better future on free enterprise, local control, sound science, and technology development. This is our positive and proactive agenda:

- assure that the air and water are clean and safe for our children and future generations;
- assure that everyone has access to public outdoor recreation areas, and that historic and environmentally significant wilderness and wetlands areas will be protected without compromising our commitment to the rights of property owners;
- set reasonable standards for environmental improvement that incorporate flexibility, acknowledge geographic differences, and create incentives for development of new technologies;
- base all government environmental decisions on the best peer-reviewed scientific evidence, while encouraging advancements in research;
- achieve progress, as much as possible, through incentives rather than compulsion, and improve compliance by letting States and localities play a greater role in setting and maintaining standards. Many States have enacted environmental education and "voluntary self-audit" laws to encourage people to find and correct pollution; the Congress should remove disincentives for States to achieve these goals; and
- assure private property owners of due process to protect their rights, and make environmental decisions in concert with those whose homes, businesses, and communities are directly affected.

Our commitment to an improved environment is best embodied in the recently enacted amendments to the Safe Drinking Water Act. This Republican initiative will guarantee all Americans a safe and clean source of drinking water and will grant local communities the flexibility to avoid unnecessary requirements.

The Clinton Democrats disagree with our principles. They have increased spending by creating new bureaucratic programs, creating new paperwork requirements, and funding pet projects of their special interest friends. However, the Clinton Administration has failed to reduce regulatory burdens on States, localities, and individuals. It has failed to create incentives for environmental improvements or use sound science and cooperation to achieve environmental goals. Today, they are planning to impose scientifically unsupported, massive new regulations on ozone and particulates. These rules will impose new requirements on cities, add unnecessary costs, and destroy jobs without adequate justification.

Republicans support the ongoing efforts of the States and communities to ensure reliable and safe water supplies. As the federal government moves away from its past role as a grant giver and direct lender in the development of water-related infrastructure, we will encourage the establishment of public-private partnerships to build and finance our nation's water infrastructure.

We recognize [that] the Great Lakes encompass one-fifth of the fresh water supply of the entire world, and we oppose any diversion of Great Lakes water.

Republicans have always advocated conserving our animal and plant resources, but we recognize the current Endangered Species Act is seriously flawed and, indeed, is often counterproductive because of its reliance on federal command-and-control measures. The adherence of Clinton Democrats to these discredited ESA provisions has devastated the environment they pretend to protect by virtually encouraging landowners to remove habitat for marginal species to avoid government seizure of their property. We will improve the ESA by implementing an incentive-based program in cooperation with State, local, and tribal governments and private individuals to recognize the critical relationship between a healthy environment and a healthy economy founded on private property rights and responsibilities.

Securing Property Rights

Republicans consider private property rights the cornerstone of environmental progress. That lesson has been confirmed in the tragic environmental record of Communist rule and of socialist regimes in the less developed world. By safeguarding those rights—by enforcing the Takings Clause of the Fifth Amendment and by provid-

ing compensation—we not only stand true to the Constitution but advance sound environmentalism as well. Republicans, led by Senator Dole, have spearheaded efforts in Congress to protect private property rights.

Improving Public Lands

The nation's public lands—half the territory in the West—must be administered both for today's multiple uses and for tomorrow's generations. We support multiple use conducted in an environmentally and economically sustainable manner. We will preserve priority wilderness and wetlands—real wetlands of environmental significance, not the damp grounds of a bureaucrat's imagination.

We support a thorough review of the lands owned by the federal government with a goal of transferring lands that can best be managed by State, county, or municipal governments. This review should ensure that the federal government retains ownership to unique property worthy of national oversight. Properties transferred from federal control must recognize existing property and mineral rights, including water, mining claims, grazing permits, rights of access, hunting, fishing, and contracts.

We recognize the historic use of public lands for livestock production in compliance with legal requirements. Our renewable rangeland should continue to be available under conditions that ensure both expanded production of livestock and protection of the rangeland environment. We condemn the Clinton Administration's range war against this pillar of the Western economy.

We recognize the need to keep our National Park System healthy and accessible to all. Our national parks have a backlog of more than $4 billion in maintenance and infrastructure repair projects. The nation's natural crown jewels are losing some of their luster, tarnished by neglect and indifference. Our park system needs to be rebuilt, restructured, and reinvigorated to ensure that all Americans can enjoy and be proud of their parks.

We stand for sustainable forestry to stabilize and provide continuity for our timber industry and to improve the health of the country's public forests. This requires active management practices, such as the responsible salvage harvesting of dead and diseased trees. The Democrats' hands-off approach has made our great forests vulnerable to ravaging fires, insects, and disease.

The Democrats' policies have devastated the economy of timber-dependent communities across the Pacific Northwest and in the Tongass National Forest, the nation's largest and most productive, to please elite special interests. We join families and communities in rural America who rely on public forests for their livelihood in calling for the federal government to carefully evaluate the socioeconomic impacts of its actions and to live up to its commitments to provide an adequate timber supply to dependent communities through sustainable forest management.

We reaffirm the traditional deference by the federal government to the States in the allocation and appropriation of water. We deplore the Clinton Administration's disregard for State primacy through attempts to preempt State law with respect to water usage and watershed protection. We also recognize the need to protect adequate supplies of water for agriculture without unreasonable government mandates.

We support the original intent of the Mining Law of 1872: to provide the certainty and land tenure necessary for miners to risk tremendous capital investment on federal lands, thus preserving jobs—indeed, whole industries—and bolstering our domestic economy. We support appropriate changes to the law to ensure the taxpayer will receive a reasonable return for the value of extracted minerals. We oppose extremist attempts to shut down American mining in favor of our international competitors.

Power for Progress

Our goal is an energy supply available to all—competitively priced, secure, and clean—produced by healthy industries operating in an environmentally responsible manner using domestically available resources to the greatest extent practicable.

No one should take that for granted. Today's energy boom was hard won by Republican reforms in the 1980s, ending more than three decades of ruinous federal meddling that drove up prices and drove down supplies. Now that progress is under attack from the same quarters that brought us energy crises, gas rationing, and dangerous dependence on unreliable supplies of foreign oil. That dependency is 50 percent today, and will be two-thirds in only a few short years.

It does not have to be this way. The Clinton Administration has learned nothing from the collapse of liberalism. It clings to outdated regulation that stifles production and drives up consumer prices. Clinton proposed a punishing BTU energy tax that would have penalized consumers and cost thousands of jobs. After Republicans derailed that bad idea, Bill Clinton championed—and congressional Democrats approved—a 4.7-cent per gallon gas tax hike, not to improve roads and bridges, but for general spending.

Now the Clinton Administration demands lighter cars and family trucks to meet its Corporate Average Fuel Economy (CAFE) goals, at the cost of thousands of lives lost every year in auto accidents—not to mention the cost in jobs lost to foreign auto makers.

Nowhere has the failure of presidential leadership been more apparent than in Clinton's position on finding a reasonable long-term solution to our nation's nuclear waste disposal problem. We support the federal government's obligation under contract to take possession of nuclear waste and remove it from temporary storage in over 30 states across the country. At the same time, we believe that the siting and licensing of both permanent and interim storage facilities should be based on sound science and not solely upon political expediency.

The Clinton approach hobbles the nation's progress. Our program of energy renewal, on the other hand, is an essential component of broader opportunity for all. We must finish the job of preparing America's energy capacity to meet the challenges of the 21st century.

Today, Republican governors and the States are leading the way to true and meaningful electric utility industry deregulation and competition and lower rates for all consumers. Restructuring the electric utility industry presents both great opportunities and challenges for our nation. We support greater competition as we move toward a market-based approach, with true and meaningful deregulation, after an appropriate and fair transition period that allows for competitive retail markets while ensuring reliability of service in a cost-effective manner for all consumers.

We support elimination of the Department of Energy to emphasize the need for greater privatization and to reduce the size of the federal government. The Department of Energy's defense concerns should be transferred to an independent agency under the Defense Department. Other necessary programs should be farmed out to other departments and offices.

We support environmentally responsible energy extraction from public and private lands. We will not tolerate poor reclamation or pollution from mining or drilling. We advocate environmentally sound oil production in the largest known onshore or offshore petroleum reserve in the nation—the small coastal plain portion of the 19-million-acre Arctic National Wildlife Refuge. Oil produced there, traveling through an existing pipeline, will bring billions of dollars in revenues to reduce the federal budget deficit. On the other hand, without ANWR coastal plain development, we will lose hundreds of thousands of potential jobs, and untold billions of American dollars will be paid to foreign governments for the oil not produced from our home reserves.

We continue to support and encourage the development of our domestic natural gas industry. Natural gas is a clean, abundant, and domestically available resource, which can be provided, transported, and consumed in an environmentally responsible manner.

We will delegate management and collection of federal oil and gas royalties to the States, thereby increasing receipts both to the States and to the federal Treasury. This action will reduce bureaucratic involvement and administrative costs to the federal government. We urge the federal government to expedite and streamline the exploration, leasing, and permitting process for the domestic oil and gas industry.

The coal industry now supplies more than half of all electric generation and is vital for our entire economy. We encourage research for cleaner coal combustion technologies and will require that objective, peer-reviewed science be the basis for environmental decisions that increase costs for electric rate payers.

Because no single source of energy can reliably supply the needs of the American people, we believe in fostering alternative and renewable energy sources to assist in reducing dependence on unreliable foreign oil supplies. We anticipate the continuing development of energy from coal, oil, natural gas, agricultural products such as ethanol and biodiesel, nuclear, and hydro sources and where economically competitive, from wind, solar, and geothermal power.

The United States should continue its commitment to addressing global climate change in a prudent and effective manner that does not punish the U.S. economy. Despite scientific uncertainty about the role of human activity in climate change, the Clinton Administration has leapfrogged over reasoned scientific inquiry and now favors misdirected measures, such as binding targets and timetables, imposed only on the United States and certain other developed countries, to further reduce greenhouse gas emissions. Republicans deplore the arbitrary and premature abandonment of the previous policy of voluntary reductions of greenhouse gas emissions. We further deplore ceding U.S. sovereignty on environmental issues to international bureaucrats and our foreign economic competitors.

Energy policy and transportation policy go hand in hand. To prepare the National Highway System and the National Aviation System for the 21st century, we will maintain the integrity of the federal transportation trust funds and respect the call by Republican governors to ensure those funds are returned to the States with a minimum of federal red tape. Trusting the people, congressional Republicans passed the National Highway System Designation Act of 1995, returning to the States decisions about highway safety. We support reasonable speed limits, reflecting local needs and geography, and prudent personal safety measures, but we oppose Washington's one-size-fits-all approach to the mobility of the American people.

Agriculture in the 21st Century

The moral strength abundant on America's farms and rural communities has been the foundation and source of strength for our nation since its earliest days. America's settlers built their farming communities on values like faith, hard work, dedication, and self-sacrifice.

Republicans see a very bright future for agriculture and rural America. Our program to strengthen rural America will benefit every sector of the economy and every part of the nation. First and foremost, we will reduce the tax burden—both the estate tax and the capital gains levy—on those who produce America's food and fiber. This is essential to preserve production agriculture. Just like urban businesses, rural producers need full deductibility of health insurance premiums and an overall tax structure that is simpler and fairer.

Deficit spending by government is death by strangulation for agriculture. Our farms are major users of capital, with over $150 billion in current borrowing. Interest payments are one of their heaviest burdens. The Republican balanced budget of last year, vetoed by Bill Clinton, would have saved farmers more than $15 billion in interest costs by the year 2002. We stand with the American farmer in demanding an end to the spending excesses in official Washington.

The elections of 1994 were a resounding victory for American agriculture. The first Republican majorities in both the House and Senate in 40 years won an historic breakthrough with the "Freedom to Farm" act. For the first time in six decades, federal policy will allow individual farmers to grow what makes sense on their own land, not what a bureaucrat wants grown there. "Freedom to Farm" will permit them to respond to world trade opportunities for value-added exports that bring new jobs and broader prosperity to rural America.

Moreover, the Republican "Freedom to Farm" act is the most pro-environment farm bill ever. By liberating high-tech, high-yield U.S. agriculture to pursue ever-greater levels of efficiency, it will enable growers to produce more from less land, saving wildlife habitat and fragile soils from the plow. The new law allows farmers to rotate crops, thereby reducing use of pesticides, herbicides, and fertilizer. It continues the Conservation and Wetland Reserve Programs and creates a new Environmental Quality Incentive Program to help farmers do what they do best— conserve the land and pass it on, enriched and enhanced, to future generations.

While promising to modernize farm programs, the Clinton Administration instead advanced failed "New Deal" policies. Throughout the ensuing debate, they fought every effort by Congress to get the hand of government out of agriculture. Finally, having agreed to "Freedom to Farm," Bill Clinton is threatening to repeal this historic legislation, undercutting long-term planning by farmers across the country.

In contrast, "Freedom to Farm" ends the command-and-control policies that have choked the entrepreneurial spirit of rural America. "Freedom to Farm" permits experimentation with new crops and new markets, just in time to meet an explosion in worldwide demand for food, fiber, fuels, and industrial products. We reaffirm our historical and continuing support for the expanded use of biodiesel and ethanol to improve the rural economy and reduce our dependence on imported oil.

Experts predict the need for U.S. producers to triple their output over the next 40 years. "Freedom to Farm" positions them to meet the challenge of feeding a hungry and troubled world.

While "Freedom to Farm" greatly reduced USDA paperwork imposed on farmers, much remains to be done to reduce the regulations that add about $6,000 per farm per year to the cost of farming. Our extensive program of regulatory reform is explained in this platform.

Republicans worked hard for and applaud the repeal of the Delaney Clause and the reform of food safety laws. These changes allow a responsible approach toward crop production and ensure the quality of the nation's food supply, with special protections for our children.

We reaffirm the Republican Party's historic commitment to agricultural progress through research and education, starting with the system of land grant colleges established in 1862. For the new century, as in the days of Lincoln, farming must look ahead to innovation and constant improvement, especially biotechnology and precision farming techniques.

RESTORING AMERICAN WORLD LEADERSHIP

It's time to restore American leadership throughout the world. Our future security depends on American leadership that is respected, American leadership that is trusted, and when necessary, American leadership that is feared.

—Bob Dole

We are the party of peace through strength. Republicans put the interests of our country over those of other nations—and of the United Nations. We believe the safety and prosperity of the American home and workplace depend upon ensuring our national security in a dangerous world. This principle was proven in our long struggle against communism, and—as recent events have tragically shown—it is still true today. The gains we made for democracy around the world under two Republican presidents are now imperiled by a rudderless foreign policy. We vigorously support restoring the promotion of democracy worldwide as a cornerstone of U.S. foreign policy. Democracy is the best guarantor of peace and will ensure greater respect for fundamental human rights and the rule of law.

The international situation—and our country's security against the purveyors of evil—has worsened over the last three and a half years. Today, Russia's democratic future is more uncertain than at any time since the hammer and sickle was torn from the Kremlin towers. With impunity, Fidel Castro has shot American citizens out of the skies over international waters. North Korea has won unprecedented concessions regarding its nuclear capability from the Clinton Administration. Much of Africa has dissolved in tragedy—Somalia, Rwanda, Burundi, Liberia. The Clinton Administration objected to lifting the arms embargo on Bosnia while it facilitated the flow of Iranian weapons to that country. Bill Clinton made tough campaign pledges on China

but subsequently failed in his attempt to bluff the Chinese government—diminishing American prestige while not addressing the serious issues of human rights, regional stability, and nuclear proliferation. Bill Clinton's weakness, indecision, and double-talk have undermined America's role as leader of the free world.

In 1996, the nation's choice is clear: Either we return responsible leadership to the White House, or Bill Clinton's lack of international purpose results in catastrophe. We must keep our country strong and sovereign, and assert the interests and values of the United States in the international arena.

The Atlantic Alliance and Europe

Let us begin by reaffirming that Europe's security is indispensable to the security of the United States, and that American leadership is absolutely indispensable to the security of Europe.

—Bob Dole, June 25, 1996

Our relations with the nations of Europe must continue to be based on the NATO alliance, which remains the world's strongest bulwark of freedom and international stability. Our policy will strive to consolidate our Cold War victory in Europe and to build a firm foundation for a new century of peace. In the same spirit that Ronald Reagan called for the integration of Spain into the NATO alliance, we call for the immediate expansion of the framework for peace to include those countries of Central Europe which demonstrate the strongest commitment to the democratic ideals NATO was created to protect.

With the people of Poland, the Czech Republic, and Hungary we have special bonds. These nations—and others—are rightfully part of the future of Europe. As Bob Dole said, "It is an outrage that the patriots who threw off the chains of Soviet bondage have been told by Bill Clinton that they must wait to join the NATO alliance." We strongly endorse Bob Dole's call for Poland, the Czech Republic, and Hungary to enter NATO by 1998.

Bosnia

We support America's men and women in uniform who are serving in Bosnia and Herzegovina. However, we did not support the ill-conceived and inconsistent policies that led to their deployment. In 1992, candidate Bill Clinton pledged to lift the arms embargo on Bosnia, but once in office he ignored his promises. For three years, Bill Clinton upheld the illegal and unjust arms embargo on Bosnia and allowed genocidal aggression to go virtually unchallenged, while Bob Dole successfully led the effort in the Congress to lift the U.S. arms embargo. Once again, Bill Clinton subordinated American national interests to the United Nations in vetoing bipartisan legislation that would have lifted the U.S. arms embargo and rendered the deployment of American forces unnecessary. At the same time Bill Clinton was opposing congressional efforts to lift the arms embargo, he made a secret decision to allow the terrorist Iranian regime to supply arms to Bosnia. This duplicitous policy has endangered U.S. and allied forces and given Iran a foothold in Europe.

We look forward to a timely withdrawal of U.S. forces from Bosnia and recognize that providing the Bosnian Federation with adequate weapons and training is the only realistic exit strategy. We support the democratic process in Bosnia and, when conditions exist, the conduct of free and fair elections. We support bringing indicted war criminals to justice. We encourage the peoples of the region—and in particular those of Croatia, Bosnia and Herzegovina, and Serbia and Montenegro—to play a constructive role in fostering peace and stability there. We note with concern that repression and human rights abuses are escalating in Kosovo and support the appointment of a U.S. special envoy to help resolve the situation there.

Russia

We salute the people of Russia in their quest for democracy and a free market economy. During this crucial period, the Clinton Administration has pursued an accommodationist and misguided policy toward Moscow. Bill Clinton's comparison of Russia's extreme brutality in Chechnya to the American Civil War is offensive. The Clinton Administration's passivity in the face of Russia's intimidation and economic blackmail against countries of the former Soviet Union

has encouraged the rise of extreme nationalist and undemocratic forces. Its willingness to accept Russian changes to already agreed-to arms control treaties has undermined security. Its complacency over Russia's sale of nuclear technology to Iran and Cuba has contributed to the threat of nuclear proliferation.

Our foreign policy toward Russia should put American interests first and consolidate our Cold War victory in Europe. We have a national interest in a security relationship with a democratic Russia. Specifically, we will encourage Russia to respect the sovereignty and independence of its neighbors; support a special security arrangement between Russia and NATO—but not Moscow's veto over NATO enlargement; support Russian entry to the G-7 after its reforms have been achieved; and link U.S. assistance to Russian adherence to international treaty obligations.

Newly Independent States

We reaffirm our party's historic commitment to the independence of all former Captive Nations still recovering from the long night of Soviet communism, especially Latvia, Lithuania, Estonia, Armenia, and Ukraine. We endorse Republican legislation to establish in Washington, D.C., funded by private contributions, an international memorial to the 100 million victims of communism.

Ireland

We support efforts to establish peace with justice in Northern Ireland through a peace process inclusive of all parties who reject violence. During this difficult period in Irish history, we encourage private U.S. investment in the North, fully consistent with the MacBride principles for fair employment, in order to address the systemic discriminatory practices that still exist, especially against Catholics, in the workplace and elsewhere. We call on all parties to renounce terrorism in the Northern Ireland conflict.

Cyprus

We encourage a peaceful settlement for Cyprus and respect by all parties for the wishes of the Cypriot people. Concerned about continuing tension in the Aegean Sea, we will maintain close ties to both Greece and Turkey and urge all parties to refrain from precipitous actions and assertions contrary to legally established territorial arrangements.

Defending America Against Missile Attack

We face two scandalous situations. First, most Americans do not realize our country has no defense against long-range missile attack. Second, the current occupant of the Oval Office refuses to tell them of that danger. So we will.

This is the frightening truth: The United States provided the technology to Israel to protect it from Iraqi missile attacks during the Persian Gulf War, but President Clinton refuses to provide the technology—technology that is readily available—to the American people to protect our country from the growing threat posed by long-range ballistic missiles. The Strategic Defense Initiative (SDI) of the last two Republican administrations has been dismantled by Bill Clinton, who—contrary to the national security interests of the United States—clings to the obsolete Cold War ABM Treaty. Clinton slashed the funding budgeted by past presidents for missile defense and even violates the law by slowing down critical-theater missile defenses. He has pursued negotiations to actually expand the outdated ABM Treaty, further tying America's hands, and hobbling our self-defense. He now seeks new limitations that will hinder the United States from developing and deploying even-theater ballistic missile defenses to protect our troops abroad.

In a peaceful world, such limitations would be imprudent. In today's world, they are immoral. The danger of a missile attack with nuclear, chemical, or biological weapons is the most serious threat to our national security. Communist China has mocked our vulnerability by threatening to attack Los Angeles if we stand by our historic commitment to the Republic of China on Taiwan. We are vulnerable to blackmail—nuclear or otherwise—from a host of terrorist states that are now trying to acquire the instruments of doom. In the face of those dangers, Bill Clinton has ignored his responsibilities. In the most egre-

gious instance, he directed that a National Intelligence Estimate focus only on the missile threat to the continental United States, deliberately ignoring the near-term menace posed to Alaska and Hawaii by long-range missiles now being developed or otherwise acquired by the Communists who rule North Korea.

America will be increasingly threatened by long-range ballistic missiles in the near future, but there also exists today a more immediate threat from the proliferation of shorter-range, or "theater" missiles. Bill Clinton says that theater missile defense (TMD) is a top priority of his administration, yet refuses to provide adequate funding for our most promising and effective TMD programs. For example, not only has he recently cut funding by 40 percent for the Theater High Altitude Area Defense (THAAD) program, but he has also failed to request sufficient funds to develop and deploy the Navy Upper Tier system. Republicans will fully fund and deploy these and other TMD systems to protect American troops and vital interests abroad.

The Republican Party is committed to the protection of all Americans—including our two million citizens in Alaska and Hawaii—against missile attack. We are determined to deploy land-based and sea-based theater missile defenses as soon as possible, and a national system thereafter. We will not permit the mistakes of past diplomacy, based on the immoral concept of Mutual Assured Destruction, to imperil the safety of our nation, our Armed Forces abroad, and our allies. Arms control will be a means to enhance American national security, not an end in itself. We therefore endorse the Defend America Act of 1996, introduced by Senator Bob Dole, which calls for a national missile defense system for all fifty States by the year 2003.

To cope with the threat of the proliferation of weapons of mass destruction, the United States will have to deter the threat or use of weapons of mass destruction by rogue states. This in turn will require the continuing maintenance and development of nuclear weapons and their periodic testing. The Clinton Administration's proposed Comprehensive Test Ban Treaty (CTBT) is inconsistent with American security interests.

Rebuilding America's Strength

Republicans are committed to ensuring the status of the United States as the world's preeminent military power. We must reverse the decline in what our nation spends for defense. In just three and a half years, an amateur approach to military matters and dramatic reductions in defense spending under the Clinton Administration have had a serious negative impact on the readiness and capabilities of our armed forces. In 1994, three of the Army's primary combat divisions reported unacceptably low levels of readiness, and all forward-deployed Army divisions reported below-par readiness ratings. Not since the "Hollow Army" days of Jimmy Carter have Army readiness levels been so low. Funding shortfalls and shortages of spare parts and munitions are limiting training opportunities and thus the combat readiness of our forces. At the same time, Bill Clinton's peacekeeping operations and other global ventures have increased the operational demands on the limited forces available, extended the duration of their deployments, and put immense strains on service members and their families—without any discernible benefit to U.S. national security.

Republicans faced a similar situation with a deteriorating military in 1981, but then two Republican presidents turned things around and restored America's world leadership. We must do it again, and quickly. The All-Volunteer force is composed of the finest military personnel in the world today. These outstanding men and women deserve a civilian leadership committed to providing them with the resources, technology, and equipment they need to safely and successfully perform their missions. They deserve nothing but the best from the people they protect.

We recognize that today's military research and development, as well as procurement, is tomorrow's readiness. We are committed to readiness not just today, but also tomorrow. Bill Clinton has decimated our research and development effort, and slashed procurement for our armed forces. Not since 1950 have we spent so little on new weapons for our military. Fortunately, the Republican Congress has restored some of the funding Bill Clinton sought to cut for research and development and for procurement. Only a Commander-in-Chief who fully understands and respects the military can rebuild America's defense capabilities.

The Clinton Administration's own inadequate defense "strategy" has been underfunded. The mismatch between strategy, forces, and resources poses an enormous potential risk to America's military personnel and vital interests. This mismatch must be resolved now, before regional crises erupt and find our nation unprepared. A Republican president will immediately conduct a thorough review that will require resources and programs to be redirected according to goals set by the president instead of by the bureaucracy.

Money alone is not the answer. It must be spent the right way, with long-term efficiencies in mind. We call for reductions in the overhead and infrastructure of the Defense Department and successful demonstrations of weapons and equipment prior to full-scale purchases. Budgetary decisions must be made with an eye to preserving the nation's defense industrial base, accelerating procurement of key military and dual-use technologies, incorporating emerging technologies into military operations, and maintaining an adequate, safe, and reliable capability in nuclear weapons.

Only a Republican president and a Republican Congress can fulfill these duties.

Protecting American Interests

We scorn the Clintonite view that soon "nationhood as we know it will be obsolete; all states will recognize a single global authority." This is nonsense, but it explains why the Democrat administration has lurched from one foreign policy fiasco to the next—and why Bill Clinton vetoed the first legislative restructuring of America's diplomatic institutions in a half-century. A Republican president will reform the Department of State to ensure that America's interests always come first.

Republicans will not subordinate United States sovereignty to any international authority. We oppose the commitment of American troops to

U.S. "peacekeeping" operations under foreign commanders and will never compel American servicemen to wear foreign uniforms or insignia. We will insist on an end to waste, mismanagement, and fraud at the United Nations. We will ensure American interests are pursued and defended at the United Nations; will not tolerate any international taxation by the organization; nor will we permit any international court to seize, try, or punish American citizens. Before his departure from the Senate, Bob Dole introduced legislation prohibiting U.S. payments to the United Nations and any of its agencies if they attempt to implement global taxes. We support the passage of the Prohibition on United Nations Taxation Act of 1996 to preserve America's sovereignty and the American taxpayer's right to taxation with representation.

A Republican president will withdraw from Senate consideration any pending international conventions or treaties that erode the constitutional foundations of our Republic and will neither negotiate nor submit such agreements in the future. We will ensure that our future relations with international organizations not infringe upon either the sovereignty of the United States or the earnings of the American taxpayer.

American citizens must retain ownership of their private property, and must maintain full control of our national and state parks, without international interference.

International Terrorism

Terrorist states have made a comeback during Bill Clinton's Administration. He has treated their rulers with undue respect and failed to curb their acquisition of weapons of mass destruction. Although congressional Republicans passed anti-terrorism legislation earlier this year, the Clinton Administration has not implemented many key provisions of the law. It has not been used to freeze terrorists' assets, deny terrorists' visas, cut off foreign aid to supporters of terrorist states, or halt terrorist fundraising in the United States. The Clinton Administration has not implemented the anti-terrorist research program established and funded by Congress in the 1990 Aviation Security Act.

A Republican president will forcefully lead the world community to isolate and punish state sponsors of terrorism. It is vital to our security that we actively work to reverse the threat posed by these regimes—through imposition and enforcement of sanctions, banning investment, and leading our allies in effective policies. The governments of North Korea, Iran, Syria, Iraq, Libya, Sudan, and Cuba must know that America's first line of defense is not our shoreline, but their own borders. We will be proactive, not reactive, to strike the hand of terrorism before it can be raised against Americans.

We denounce terrorist attacks made on American citizens at home or abroad. We must take all legitimate steps to swiftly apprehend and severely punish persons committing terrorist acts. However, we must also denounce any attempts to deprive law-abiding citizens of their God-given, constitutionally protected rights while fighting terrorism. To take away the liberty of the American people while fighting terrorism is repugnant to the history and character of our nation. We firmly oppose any legislation that would infringe upon the rights of American citizens to freedom of religion, speech, press, and assembly; the right to keep and bear arms; and the right to judicial due process.

Africa

We support those U.S. aid programs to Africa which have proven records of success, especially the Child Survival Program of vitamins, immunizations, sanitation, and oral rehydration. We hail the social and economic progress of those nations which have used the free market to liberate the talent and striving of their people. They deserve our attention, but our outreach must be on a case-by-case basis. Our hope for the future of South Africa, for example, stands in contrast with the military rule now imposed on Nigeria, the continent's most populous country.

The Republican Party's commitment to freedom and human rights in Africa is as old as the establishment of the Republic of Liberia. Today, the tragic fate of that small nation symbolizes the larger tragedy that has befallen much of the continent. The Clinton Administration's dismal performance in Somalia, resulting in needless American deaths, set the stage for international passivity in the face of genocide in Rwanda and Burundi. The Clinton Administration has even failed to rally the world against the slave trade sponsored by the government of the Sudan, whose persecution of Sudanese Christians and others is nothing short of genocide. A Republican president will not tolerate this unconscionable treatment of children and women.

Asia

Bill Clinton's foreign policy failures loom large in Asia. Four years ago, most of that continent was rushing toward democratic reform. Today it threatens to slip backwards into conflict and repression. A Republican administration will keep the mutual security treaties with Japan and with the Republic of Korea as the foundation of our role in the region. We will halt Bill Clinton's efforts to appease North Korea by rewarding treaty-breaking with American taxpayer-financed oil and nuclear reactors. We will make further improvement of relations with Vietnam and North Korea contingent upon their cooperation in achieving a full and complete according of our POW's and MIA's from those Asian conflicts.

China and Taiwan

We support the aspiration of the Chinese people for both economic and political liberty, which includes respect for the human rights of the people of Tibet. Our relationship with the Chinese government will be based on vigilance with regard to its military potential, proliferation activities, and its attitude toward human rights, especially in Hong Kong. The Taiwan Relations Act must remain the basis of our relations with the Republic of China on Taiwan. We reaffirm our commitment to Taiwan's security and will regard any threat to alter its status by force as a threat to our own security interests. We will make available to Taiwan the material it needs for self-defense, particularly theater missile defense and coastal patrol submarines. In recognition of its growing importance in the global economy, we

support a larger role for Taiwan in international organizations.

Philippines

We reaffirm our historic friendship with the Philippine people, which has endured through changing circumstances.

The Middle East

Peace through strength continues to be central in the Middle East. Saddam Hussein reminded us just five years ago of the potential for aggression by radical states in this region. Republicans understand the importance of maintaining a robust U.S. military capability in the Eastern Mediterranean and the Persian Gulf, cooperating with our allies to ensure regional stability. Republicans also understand the need to be willing to use force to deter aggression and, where deterrence fails, to defeat it. That is why Republicans were the bedrock of support for the congressional vote to authorize the use of force against Iraq's aggression in 1991, while most Democrats voted against Operation Desert Storm.

The Middle East remains a region vital to American security. Our enduring goals there are to promote freedom and stability, secure access to oil resources, and maintain the security of Israel, our one democratic ally in the region with whom we share moral bonds and common strategic interests. Most of the world's oil exports flow from the Middle East, and thus its strategic significance remains. But it is still the most volatile region in the world. Islamic radicalism, increasing terrorism, and rogue states like Iran, Iraq, Syria, and Libya threaten regional and international stability.

In this environment, Israel's demonstrated strategic importance to the U.S. as our most reliable and capable ally in this part of the world is more critical than ever. That is why Israel's security is central to U.S. interests in the region. That is why Republican administrations initiated efforts with Israel to pre-position military equipment, to conduct joint contingency planning and joint military exercises. That is why we advocate continuing cooperation on the Arrow Missile, boost phase intercept, and the Nautilus programs. That is why we look toward the greater integration of Israel into our regional defense planning and wish to explore ways to enhance our strategic cooperation. That is why we have continued to support full funding for aid to Israel despite cuts in the foreign assistance budget, and why we applaud the country's commitment toward economic self-sufficiency.

We reaffirm that Republican commitment to maintain Israel's qualitative military advantage over any adversary or group of adversaries. While we fully support Israel's efforts to find peace and security with its neighbors, we will judge the peace process by the security it generates both for Israel and for the United States. In that context, we support Israel's right to make its own decisions regarding security and boundaries. We strongly oppose the Clinton Administration's attempt to interfere in Israel's democratic process.

We applaud the Republican Congress for enacting legislation to recognize Jerusalem as the undivided capital of Israel. A Republican administration will ensure that the U.S. Embassy is moved to Jerusalem by May 1999.

We honor the memory of Israeli Prime Minister Yitzhak Rabin, and express our support for the new government of Prime Minister Benjamin Netanyahu. We applaud those leaders in the Arab world, President Mubarak and King Hussein, who have spoken courageously and acted boldly for the cause of peace. We endorse continued assistance and support for countries which have made peace with Israel—led by Egypt and later joined by Jordan. Republican leadership will support others who follow their example, while isolating terrorist states until they are fit to rejoin the community of nations.

Western Hemisphere

The U.S. commitment to democratic institutions and market economies in the Western Hemisphere has paralleled our enduring interest in the security of the region, as laid out in the Monroe Doctrine. The success of Republican national security policies in the 1980s halted Soviet imperialism and promoted the process of economic and political reform in Latin America—defeating totalitarianism of the right and of the left. During the last decade and a half, Latin American countries have made enormous progress developing democratic institutions. We applaud their progress and offer our assistance to further expand and deepen democratic conditions in the region.

Hemispheric progress toward free and democratic societies has stalled during the Clinton Administration. A government bought and paid for by drug traffickers holds power in Colombia. Mexico—with whom we share hundreds of miles of border—is increasingly tainted by narcotics-related corruption at all levels of society. Similarly, there are signs of backsliding on democracy in Latin America, most notably in Paraguay, where a coup was narrowly averted earlier this year.

We call for a new partnership among the democratic nations of the Western Hemisphere to protect our hard-won victories against dictatorial government. This new partnership must address the most recent and dangerous threat to the hemisphere—narcotics traffickers and their trade. The emergence of the Western Hemisphere as an area—apart from Cuba—which shares our ideals of economic and political liberty must also mean close cooperation with the United States on a range of security issues. The Clinton Administration's policy of denying most Latin American nations the opportunity to replace their obsolescent military equipment, raise the professional competence of their armed forces, and cooperate fully with the United States in joint military training and exercises will be reversed by a Republican administration.

We cherish our special relationship with the people of Mexico and Canada. In a spirit of mutual respect, we believe the forthright discussion of economic and social issues that may divide us is in the best interest of all three nations.

Bill Clinton's outreach to Castro has only delayed the emergence of "Cuba Libre," extending the duration of Communist tyranny. The Republican Party has not wavered and will not waver in its goal of a democratic Cuba. We affirm our policy of isolating the Castro regime, including full implementation of the Helms-Burton Act to penalize foreign firms which do business there.

Bill Clinton's awkward and misguided intervention in Haiti has cost American taxpayers some $3 billion and risked the lives of American military personnel for a less-than-vital interest. We reject Clinton Administration claims of "success" in its military intervention in Haiti. Human rights abuses by government forces go unpunished; promised economic reforms have not been made; and the democratic process is deeply flawed.

Security and Foreign Assistance

America is and must remain the leader of the world. We did not win the Cold War without allies and friends, and we hope to face future challenges with them. Our country should not bear world burdens alone. Providing friendly nations with access to U.S. defense equipment can protect American security interests abroad and reduce the likelihood that American forces will have to be directly engaged in military conflict. The Clinton Administration has been blind to that wisdom.

We have seen the result in Bosnia, where American ground forces have been deployed because the Clinton Administration denied Bosnia the opportunity to acquire defense equipment in the United States.

The Clinton Administration has diverted aid from our friends to support U.N. operations and social welfare spending in the Third World. Congressional Republicans have done all they could to resist this folly. Only a Republican president can put an end to it.

The Clinton Administration's failure to couple American interests abroad with foreign aid has produced wasteful spending and has presented an impediment to achieving a balanced budget. A Republican administration will ensure foreign aid is cost-effective and based on its important role in directly promoting American national interests.

Protecting America's Technological Edge

American scientific and industrial leadership is one of the critical factors sustaining American security. Our technological edge is at risk not only because of the Clinton Administration's refusal to sustain an adequate investment in defense modernization, but also its virtual abandonment of national security–related export controls. Acquisition of technology by aspiring proliferators of weapons of mass destruction has been irresponsibly facilitated. A Republican administration will protect the American technological edge. It will do so by expanding investment in defense modernization, ensuring that the Defense Department has a key role in approving exports of militarily critical technology, and restoring the effectiveness of export control regimes.

The Men and Women of Defense

As Commander-in-Chief, Bill Clinton has been out of touch with the needs of the troops under his command. Bob Dole has served in the military and will protect military families against inflation, restore appropriate funding levels for billets and family housing, and ensure an environment where promotions and awards are made on the basis of military merit. A Republican president who has been on active duty will not casually disrupt military family life by sending troops on non-military missions around the world.

We have a solemn obligation to those who fight for America. Our military personnel should not be denied a cost of living increase, as Bill Clinton proposed in his first year in office. A Republican president will ensure a high priority for the quality of life of our military personnel and their families.

We will maintain the All-Volunteer force and will resist attempts to bring back the draft, whether directly or through Democrat schemes for compulsory national service. We will maintain our Armed Forces as a meritocracy, a model for the rest of our society, without special preferences or double standards for any group.

We salute the men and women of the National Guard and Reserve, citizen soldiers who have been—and must continue to be—a tradition in America. They perform important military functions as an integral part of our warfighting capability, and provide a critical link between our national security efforts and every community in the country. Our National Guard and Reserve forces must not be treated as an afterthought.

We oppose Bill Clinton's assault on the culture and traditions of the Armed Forces, especially his attempt to lift the ban on homosexuals in the military. We affirm that homosexuality is incompatible with military service.

We support the advancement of women in the military. We reaffirm our support for the exemption of women from ground combat units and are concerned about the current policy of involuntarily assigning women to combat or near-combat units. A Republican president will continue to reevaluate and revise, as necessary, current policies in light of evidence with regard to the effect on military morale, discipline, and overall readiness. We will not tolerate sexual harassment or misconduct toward anyone in the uniform, but we oppose politically motivated witch hunts that smear the innocent and destroy honorable careers. To promote the dignity of all members of the Armed Forces and their families, we endorse the efforts of congressional Republicans to halt the sale, in military facilities, of pornographic materials.

We deplore Bill Clinton's shameless attempt to use protections afforded active-duty military personnel under the Soldiers' and Sailors' Civil Relief Act of 1940 to protect himself from a sexual harassment lawsuit. We will amend the Soldiers' and Sailors' Civil Relief Act of 1940 to make clear that its protection against civil suits while on active duty does not extend to the occupant of the Oval Office.

The Republican Party has always been the advocate of the nation's veterans and remains unequivocally committed to the faithful fulfillment of America's obligations to them. We have no greater duty than providing for the courageous men and women who have risked their lives in defense of our country, a major reason why we defeated Bill Clinton's plan to replace veterans' health care with socialized medicine. We will continue to meet the nation's promises to those who make the military their career. That is why Republicans proposed and created a separate Department of Veterans Affairs, support veterans' preference in federal employment education and retraining programs, and pledge sufficient fund-

ing for veterans' hospitals, medical care, and employment programs.

Intelligence

The intelligence community should be our first line of defense against terrorism, drug trafficking, nuclear proliferation, and foreign espionage. Bill Clinton's neglect of our country's intelligence service is one of his most serious sins of omission. He has underfunded, misutilized, and marginalized critical intelligence missions and capabilities. No wonder his first appointee as Director of Central Intelligence has endorsed Bob Dole. The nation's security—and the personal safety of our citizens—cannot be placed at risk.

Effective intelligence can be expensive. But what it costs is measured in dollars rather than lives—an important lesson of the Gulf War. A Republican Administration will reverse the decline in funding for intelligence personnel and operations while better managing the development of futuristic capabilities. We will not constrain U.S. intelligence personnel with "politically correct" standards that impede their ability to collect and act on intelligence information. We will conduct whatever intelligence operations are necessary to safeguard American lives against the terrorists who bomb our airplanes and buildings.

Space

The Republican Party led America into space and remains committed to its exploration and mastery. We consider space travel and space science a national priority with virtually unlimited benefits, in areas ranging from medicine to micromachinery, for those on earth. Development of space will give us a growing economic resource and a source of new scientific discoveries. We look toward our country's return to the moon and to completion of the International Space Station, not just as a unique orbiting laboratory but also a framework for world cooperation in pursuit of expanding human knowledge.

Those and other ventures require leadership now lacking at the White House. The Democratic Party approaches space issues with a confined vision and misplaced appropriations, encouraging inefficient investments and pork-barrel spending. Bill Clinton gives lip service to our space program but denies it crucial resources. A Republican president and a Republican Congress will work together to make space an American frontier again. We will develop the Reusable Launch Vehicle, promote markets for commercial space launch services, and push technology to its creative limits. Commercial space development holds the key to expanding our aerospace industry and strengthening our technology base, but it can be promoted only by removing unnecessary and artificial regulatory, legal, and tax barriers.

Space exploration and exploitation are a matter of national security. Our Armed Forces already rely on space assets to support their operations on earth, and space technology will rapidly become more critical to successful military operations. Space is the ocean of tomorrow, and we cannot allow its domination by another power. We must ensure that America can work and prosper there, securely and without outside influence. A new Republican team will secure the high frontier for peace on earth and for unlimited human opportunity.

The Goal Is Freedom

America stands on the brink of a new century. After victory in the "long twilight struggle" against Soviet Communism, Americans can feel justifiably proud of the role they played in defeating history's most corrupt and predatory empire. The end of the Cold War has not spelled the end of history, but it has instead unleashed forces contained for nearly fifty years of superpower confrontation. Today America faces new challenges and new threats to our vital interests which can only be protected by our continued engagement in the world. Our nation must resist the temptation to turn inward and neglect the exercise of American leadership and our proper role in the world. Will the 21st century confer new opportunities and new benefits on America, or will it prove to be an era of weakness and decline? This will depend on whether we have a strong, decisive leader like Bob Dole who will

protect Americans at home and abroad and vigorously pursue the nation's interests around the globe.

The U.S. Constitution, the finest document for human governance ever devised, establishes the mission of providing for the common defense as a chief purpose of the federal government, in order to secure the blessings of liberty for ourselves and our posterity. The president's primary constitutional duty and most sacred responsibility is the role of Commander-in-Chief. Above all else, he must be able to ensure that the American people and our interests are defended. That requires strong, combat-ready military forces and a sound foreign policy. If the president fails in this office, then America's freedom, independence, and prosperity will be jeopardized, and all other issues—domestic and economic—become moot.

The bravery, skill, and sacrifice of America's fighting forces; the dedication, industry, and ingenuity of the American people; the superiority of U.S. technology; and the abundance of America's wealth and resources are sufficient to overcome any foreign threat or challenge. But these gifts are cause for gratitude and humility, not complacency. And these national treasures can be used to safeguard the nation effectively in a time of volatile change only if genuine leadership, wisdom, discernment, courage, and honor are present in the Commander-in-Chief and in the officials he or she appoints to critical national security posts. With such a president at the helm, America will know a new birth of freedom, security, and prosperity. And this nation, and the benefits it has bestowed upon mankind throughout our history, shall not perish from the earth.

CONCLUSION

As we begin a new era and a new millennium, we deem it essential to reaffirm the truths of the Declaration of Independence:

- That all men are created equal;
- That they are endowed by their Creator with certain unalienable rights, among these are life, liberty, and the pursuit of happiness;

- That government derives its just powers only from the consent of the governed.

We close this platform with the wisdom of our forefathers who had the courage to set their names to the Declaration of Independence as they too began a new era. Like them, we appeal to the Supreme Judge of the world for the rectitude of our intentions. With a firm reliance on the protection of Divine Providence, we pledge to each other and to the American people an unfaltering commitment to restore to America a deep respect for the values of human freedom.

APPENDIX I

Minority Views:
Amendments Considered by the Full Committee on Resolutions

Individual Rights and Personal Safety
In this section, 33 amendments were agreed to, 6 were withdrawn, and 9 were not accepted, as follows:

Page 467, strike language in the second paragraph and insert:
"The Republican Party believes that Republicans are people of principle on each side of the abortion issue who firmly and intractably hold those beliefs; by establishing a party position, we recognize that a resolution will not change these beliefs, but will serve to divide the party on other issues; and urge all Republicans to firmly debate these beliefs and vote their consciences in the November referendum."

Page 468, remove reference to "indoctrination in the classroom."

Page 469, replace paragraph on abortion with the following:
"As Republicans, we share a reverence for life and a deep belief in the traditional nuclear family and in parents as the best provider to children of love, moral values, and the sense of duty and responsibility that all children need to become decent and responsible adults.

"We are committed as a party and as individuals to significantly reducing the number of abortions in America.

"We believe that the decline in abortions we seek will be far better achieved by persuasion of individuals to choose—as a matter of individual conscience—behavior that will not produce unwanted pregnancies, than by governmental mandate and invasion of privacy.

"We believe that parents—fathers and mothers who provide their children with the love, guidance, and direction they need—should be the major influence in shaping their child's character, values, and conduct through teaching that love, marriage, and pre-marital abstinence are the right, moral, and responsible choices.

"We believe that both men and women who do not practice abstinence, but are unwilling or unprepared to accept the heavy responsibility of parenthood, have the strongest moral obligation to take effective contraceptive measures to prevent pregnancy and thereby prevent circumstances that lead to abortions or alternatively, to the epidemic social pathology caused by tragic childhoods of abuse, neglect, and fatherlessness.

"We believe that the role of government is to reinforce the teachings of parents, not replace them. Government should encourage abstinence among youth and contraception among adults unprepared for the responsibility of parenthood. We should vigorously prosecute statutory rape, vigorously enforce payment of child support, reform welfare laws that reward irresponsible behavior, and otherwise create strong disincentives for irresponsible sexual behavior on the part of men and women.

"For children who lack the love and guidance of a responsible parent in their lives, government should better promote adoption or encourage the influence of some other adult mentor in a child's life.

"Upon all foregoing points we agree as Republicans, whether conscientiously pro-life or conscientiously pro-choice. As Republicans, we acknowledge and respect the honest convictions that divide us on the question of abortion. Unlike the Democratic Party, we will not censor members of our party who hold opposing views on this issue. We are a party confident enough in our beliefs to tolerate dissent.

"And while differing on this issue, both pro-life and pro-choice Republicans are totally united in our belief that Bob Dole will provide the integrity, courage, and leadership America needs to lead the free world into a 21st century that will offer our children unparalleled individual freedom and opportunity if they meet the challenge of exercising personal responsibility."

Page 468, toward the end of the second paragraph, after the words "who may hold differing positions" add "on issues such as abortion and capital punishment."

Page 473, strike "it is time to revisit the Supreme Court's arbitrary decision of 1977 that protects even the most vicious rapists from the death penalty."

Page 473, in the same sentence strike "arbitrary."

Page 473, at the bottom insert:
"Safety on college and university campuses was mandated by law, passed and signed by President Bush in 1990. Clinton's administration has refused to enforce the law, and crimes against students continue to increase at alarming rates. Without this enforcement, students will continue to suffer from unacceptably high rates of crime during their college careers. A Dole administration will assure maximum safety for our future leaders of this country by enforcing the 1990 Campus Security Act, and enacting the Open Police Campus Logs Act of 1995 so that crimes on campus can be detected and punished."

Page 473, add to the second paragraph the word "domestic."

Withdrawn:

Page 467, strike language in the second paragraph and insert:
"As we approach the beginning of a new century, the Republican Party is more dedicated than ever to strengthening the social, cultural, and political ties that bind us together as a free people, the greatest force for good the world has ever seen.

While the party remains steadfast in its commitment to advancing its historic principles and ideals, we also recognize that members of our party have deeply held and sometimes differing views on issues of personal conscience like abortion and capital punishment. We view this diversity of views as a source of strength, not as a sign of weakness, and we welcome into our ranks all Americans who may hold differing positions on these and other issues. Recognizing that tolerance is a virtue, we are committed to resolving our differences in a spirit of civility, hope, and mutual respect. As we struggle to forge a national consensus on the divisive issues of our time, we call on all Republicans and all Americans to reject the forces of hatred and bigotry."

Families and Society
In this section, 13 amendments were agreed to, 2 were withdrawn, 2 were not accepted, as follows:

Page 478, in the third paragraph after the words "We call for an increased emphasis on prevention of diseases that threaten the lives of women," insert "in particular of cervical cancer as the sexually transmitted disease with the greatest impact on women, and of induced abortion as the single most avoidable known risk factor for breast cancer."

Page 480, at the top insert:
"We support a small business renaissance in our inner cities. We call upon city governments to cut taxes and eliminate burdensome regulations to unleash the spirit of enterprise and entrepreneurship."

Restoring American World Leadership
In this section, 9 amendments were agreed to, 1 was not accepted, as follows:

Page 486, add the following new paragraph: "Because we believe in treating tyrannies differently than other governments, we favor denying most-favored-nation privileges to regimes that practice religious persecution or coercive abortion or that engage in slave labor."

A Cleaner, Safer, Healthier America
In this section, 8 amendments were agreed to, 1 was withdrawn.

Changing Washington from the Ground Up
In this section, 7 amendments were agreed to.

Building a Better America
In this section, 3 amendments were agreed to.

APPENDIX II

Remarks by Bob Dole
Republican Candidate for President of the United States
Satellite Broadcast to RNC Platform Committee
Washington, D.C.
Tuesday, August 6, 1996

It's good to visit with you today. I'm proud of our party, and proud to be the Republican nominee. And I'm absolutely confident of victory on November fifth.

Yesterday in Chicago I outlined my economic growth plan to repeal the current tax code, to end the IRS as we know it, and to get the American family's income moving up again.

Not surprisingly, the Clinton team denounced my growth plan even before they heard the details. Why? Because to them, specifics aren't important; they simply don't believe in cutting taxes. They believe in raising taxes. They don't want to control spending, they want to increase spending. The dividing line in this campaign is crystal clear: I believe Washington takes too much of your hard-earned money. Bill Clinton does not.

The Clinton team says my plan isn't realistic. But how can anyone in America believe Bill Clinton when it comes to taxes? After all, he ran for president promising middle-class tax relief, then as president hit the American people with the largest tax increase in history. Those are the facts. And as John Adams put it, "facts are stubborn things."

President Clinton suggested yesterday that my plan will cause the deficit to go up. I'm touched by his new-found concern for a balanced budget. But here again, the facts tell a different story. It was Bill Clinton, not Bob Dole, who pressured six Democrats to switch sides on the Balanced Budget Amendment, causing it to lose narrowly in the Senate. So here is my challenge to President Clinton: If you're truly worried about the deficit, sit down right now with two Democratic senators and persuade them to support the Balanced Budget Amendment. Then we can have another vote. Help us get the job done, Mr. President. Find two votes. Make the calls today. If you're so eager to balance the budget, then take this action. If you're not—if your concern is just a ploy—then the American people will know it quickly.

The issue of credibility in this campaign will come down to a contrast between words and actions—President Clinton's words, and my actions. He'll use the rhetoric of reform. I've spent my entire career fighting to balance the budget, create more opportunities for people, and prevent government from growing beyond the consent of the governed. These will be the first principles and the legacy of my presidency. My administration won't be satisfied with second, third, or fourth best. America will be Number One again.

We've had many debates in our party about which should come first—tax cuts, or a balanced budget. I say it's time to get to work on both. The fact is that the budget deficit and high taxes are two halves of the vise that is producing the Clinton middle-class squeeze. High taxes pick the American family's pocket directly. Incredibly, that family now spends more on taxes than on food, clothing, and shelter combined. And the budget deficit is a "stealth tax" that pushes up interest rates.

There is no magic in fixing this problem. With today's pro-growth Republican Congress, cutting taxes and balancing the budget are just a matter of presidential will. If you have it, you can do it. I have it. I will do it. I will support and work for the Balanced Budget Amendment. I will reduce the size of the federal government. I will balance the budget by the year 2002.

And my tax plan, in a nutshell, is this: I intend to lower the federal income tax bill of a family of four making $35,000 a year by 56 percent—cutting it by more than half. We'll have a 15 percent tax cut, across the board, that will repeal the Clinton tax hike on the middle class. In fact, it will return total taxes to where they were when

Ronald Reagan left office. That's a big, big step in the right direction.

We'll give every middle-income tax-paying family a $500-per-child tax credit. We'll cut the top rate of the capital gains tax in half—because the capital gains tax hits smaller and growing businesses hardest, and they're the ones who will create most of our new jobs in the decade ahead. I want those businesses to use their growing value to give people better jobs, better opportunities, and better incomes—not just to pay more taxes.

I will call for expansion of Individual Retirement Accounts so people can put more away for their old age. I'll also ask for a repeal of the 1993 Clinton tax hike on Social Security benefits. And I will call for a super-majority—a 60 percent vote of Congress—before income tax rates can ever be raised again on the American people.

We're also going to change the IRS, which has grown to twice the size of the CIA and five times the size of the FBI. It takes the equivalent of nearly three million people working full time—more people than serve in the U.S. Armed Forces—just to comply with our tax laws.

My plan will downsize the IRS and upsize the amount of money Americans get to keep. It will also end the Clinton Administration's exemption of the IRS from the Paperwork Reduction Act. We simply cannot put this economy back on the right track unless we change the bureaucratic culture of the IRS—and, for that matter, the rest of Washington. As president, I will insist that all regulations—both new and existing—be reviewed to determine what works, what doesn't, what's too expensive, and what's too oppressive.

We must also change the culture that has permitted a litigation explosion in this country. Our lawsuit system is out of control; it's a drag on growth; and it undermines our competitiveness. President Clinton vetoed lawsuit reform at the behest of his biggest campaign contributors— the trial lawyers. When I'm president, we'll do the right thing and fix the broken-down lawsuit system. We'll limit outrageous punitive awards. We'll promote early settlements. We'll revoke the trial lawyers' license to search for deep pockets,

and ensure that most of the award money in the contingency fee system goes to those who were injured, instead of to lawyers. My administration will do the people's business, instead of doing the bidding of the trial lawyers.

No plan to strengthen the economy would be complete without education reform to make children and workers ready for the jobs of the future. The Clinton Administration has placed our educational destiny in the hands of bureaucrats and the liberal ideologues of the national teachers' unions. I will do things differently. My program includes Opportunity Scholarships, to enable parents to choose the best school for their children. We'll allow low- and middle-income students and parents to deduct interest on student loans and set up tax-free "Education Investment Accounts." I will take education out of the hands of the unions and bureaucrats and put it back in the hands of parents—where it belongs.

As you can see, my plan is about much more than simply reducing taxes and balancing the budget. It's about a vision for a healthy, vigorous, growing economy where all Americans can participate, and where no one is left behind. It's about a whole range of policies that will help wage-earners, small business owners, entrepreneurs, and everyone else in America who dreams of a better life for themselves and for their children.

President Clinton is completely satisfied with the status quo. He inherited a fast-growing economy and turned it into a slow-growing economy. His own forecasters project growth through the end of this decade at an incredibly lackluster 2.3 percent. In their view, that's good enough. Well, I don't believe that. And I know you don't, either. There is so much more potential in this economy, if only we will turn loose the greatness of the American people.

So as of now, Bill Clinton and his party are the defenders of the status quo, and we are the party of change. We are the party of ideas; they are the party of excuses. And for the next three months, the debate will focus on our ideas, our growth plan, and our vision for America going into the next century.

This is the message of our campaign: We're going to lift up this country—lift up our economy, lift up our schools, lift up our families, lift up our values. We're going to make the American Dream a reality for every generation that follows us here, in the greatest nation on the face of the earth.

We have some exciting days and weeks ahead of us. Thanks for listening, and thanks for all your hard work to deliver a strong, clear, confident message to the American people. God bless you all.

REPUBLICAN PARTY PLATFORM, 2000

PREAMBLE

We meet at a remarkable time in the life of our country. Our powerful economy gives America a unique chance to confront persistent challenges. Our country, after an era of drift, must now set itself to important tasks and higher goals. The Republican Party has the vision and leadership to address these issues.

Our platform is uplifting and visionary. It reflects the views of countless Americans all across this country who believe in prosperity with a purpose—who believe in Renewing America's Purpose. Together.

This platform makes clear that we are the party of ideas. We are the party that follows its bold words with bold deeds.

Since the election of 1860, the Republican Party has had a special calling—to advance the founding principles of freedom and limited government and the dignity and worth of every individual.

These principles form the foundation of both an agenda for America in the year 2000 and this platform for our party. They point us toward reforms in government, a restoration of timeless values, and a renewal of our national purpose.

The twenty-fifth man to receive our party's nomination is equal to the challenges facing our country. After a period of bitter division in national politics, our nominee is a leader who brings people together. In a time of fierce partisanship, he calls all citizens to common goals.

To longstanding problems, he brings a fresh outlook and innovative ideas—and a record of results.

Under his leadership, the Republican Party commits itself to bold reforms in education—to make every school a place of learning and achievement for every child. We will preserve local control of public schools, while demanding high standards and accountability for results.

We commit ourselves to saving and strengthening Social Security. After years of neglect and delay, we will keep this fundamental commitment to the senior citizens of today and tomorrow.

We commit ourselves to rebuilding the American military and returning to a foreign policy of strength and purpose and a renewed commitment to our allies. We will deploy defenses against ballistic missiles and develop the weapons and strategies needed to win battles in this new technological era.

We commit ourselves to tax reforms that will sustain our nation's prosperity and reflect its decency. We will reduce the burden on all Americans, especially those who struggle most.

We commit ourselves to aiding and encouraging the work of charitable and faith-based organizations, which today are making great strides in overcoming poverty and other social problems, bringing new hope into millions of lives. For every American there must be a ladder of opportunity, and for those most in need, a safety net of care.

We recommit ourselves to the values that strengthen our culture and sustain our nation: family, faith, personal responsibility, and a belief in the dignity of every human life.

We offer not only a new agenda, but also a new approach—a vision of a welcoming society in which all have a place. To all Americans, particularly immigrants and minorities, we send a clear message: This is the party of freedom and progress, and it is your home.

The diversity of our nation is reflected in this platform. We ask for the support and participation of all who substantially share our agenda. In one way or another, every Republican is a dissenter. At the same time, we are not morally indifferent. In this, as in many things, Lincoln is our model. He spoke words of healing and words of conviction. We do likewise, for we are bound together in a great enterprise for our children's future.

We seek to be faithful to the best traditions of our party. We are the party that ended slavery, granted homesteads, built land grant colleges, and moved control of government out of Washington, back into the hands of the people. We believe in service to the common good—and that good is not common until it is shared.

We believe that from freedom comes opportunity; from opportunity comes growth; and from growth comes progress and prosperity.

Our vision is one of clear direction, new ideas, civility in public life, and leadership with honor and distinction.

This is an election with clear alternatives. The Republican Party offers America a chance to begin anew: To give purpose to our plenty. To apply enduring principles to new challenges. To extend to all citizens the full promise of American life.

With confidence in our fellow Americans and great hopes for the future of our country, we respectfully submit this platform to the people of the United States.

This platform is dedicated to the memory of Paul Douglas Coverdell (1939–2000), United States Senator from Georgia, practical visionary, principled unifier, proud American, and our friend.

THE AMERICAN DREAM: PROSPERITY WITH A PURPOSE

Old Truths for the New Economy

The highest hopes of the American people—a world at peace, scientific progress, a just and caring society—cannot be achieved by prosperity alone, but neither can they be fulfilled without it. Yet prosperity is not an end in itself. Rather, it is the means by which great things can be achieved for the common good. Our commitment to the nation's economic growth is an affirmation of the real riches of our country: the works of compassion that link home to home, community to community, and hand to helping hand. This is the foundation of America, and that foundation is sound. Even though our economy, and that of the world to which we are now so closely tied, has been utterly transformed over the last two decades, Americans remain true to the faith of our founding fathers.

Yesterday's wildest dreams are today's realities, and there is no limit on the promise of tomorrow. The headiness of technological progress has made our society more future-oriented than ever before. But the fascination with the future means that, more than ever, we need to preserve the foundation that has served us so well. We must not overlook the practical experience of the past. To successfully chart where we should go in the years ahead, we must first look back to see how we got where we are today.

Twenty years ago, the economy was in shambles. Unemployment was at 7.1 percent, inflation at 13.5 percent, and interest rates at 15.3 percent. The Democratic Party accepted the malaise as the price the nation had to pay for big government, and in so doing lost the confidence of the American people. Inspired by Presidents Reagan and Bush, Republicans hammered into place the framework for today's prosperity and surpluses. We cut tax rates, simplified the tax code, deregulated industries, and opened world markets to American enterprise. The result was the tremendous growth in the 1980s that created the venture capital to launch the technology revolution of the 1990s.

That's the origin of what is now called the New Economy: the longest economic boom in the twentieth century, 40 million new jobs, the lowest inflation and unemployment in memory. The stock market, once a preserve of the well-to-do, now drives forward with the modest investments of tens of millions of households as ownership in America's economy becomes the norm rather than the exception.

The Republican Congress

We could have lost it all after the Democratic Congress passed the largest tax hike in history in 1993 that threatened to bring back the tax-and-spend follies of the bad old days. But the voters wouldn't have it and, in the next election, for the first time in forty years, they put Republican majorities in charge of both houses of Congress. The difference that made can be put into numbers. In the four decades from 1954 to 1994, government spending increased at an average annual rate of 7.9 percent, and the public's debt increased from $224 billion to $3.4 trillion. Since 1994, with Republicans leading the House and Senate, spending has been held to an annual 3.1 percent rate of growth, and the nation's debt will be nearly $400 billion lower by the end of this year. The federal government has operated in the black for the last two years and is now projected to run a surplus of nearly $5 trillion over ten years.

That wasn't magic. It took honesty and guts from a Congress that manages the nation's purse strings. Over a five-year period, as surpluses continue to grow, we will return half a trillion dollars to the taxpayers who really own it, without touching the Social Security surplus. That's what we mean by our lock box: The Social Security surplus is off-limits, off-budget, and will not be touched. We will not stop there, for we are also determined to protect Medicare and to pay down the national debt. Reducing that debt is both a sound policy goal and a moral imperative. Our families and most states are required to balance their budgets; it is reasonable to assume the federal government should do the same. Therefore, we reaffirm our support for a constitutional amendment to require a balanced budget.

Taxes and Budget: Render to Caesar, but Let the People Keep Their Own

I believe our country must be prosperous, but prosperity must have a purpose: to make sure the American Dream touches every willing heart.

—George W. Bush

It takes both candor and courage to say, as George W. Bush has said, that even in times of large surpluses, the economy is far from perfect and we should not be satisfied with the status quo. Budget surpluses are the result of over-taxation of the American people. The weak link in the chain of prosperity is the tax system. It not only burdens the American people; it threatens to slow, and perhaps to reverse, the economic expansion:

- The federal tax code is dysfunctional. It penalizes hard work, marriage, thrift, and success—the very factors that are the foundations for lasting prosperity.
- Federal taxes are the highest they have ever been in peacetime.
- Taxes at all levels of government absorb 36 percent of the net national product.

When the average American family has to work more than four months out of every year to fund all levels of government, it's time to change the tax system, to make it simpler, flatter, and fairer for everyone. It's time for an economics of inclusion that will let people keep more of what they earn and accelerate movement up the opportunity ladder.

We therefore enthusiastically endorse the principles of Governor Bush's Tax Cut with a Purpose:

- Replace the five current tax brackets with four lower ones, ensuring all taxpayers significant tax relief while targeting it especially toward low-income workers.
- Help families by doubling the child tax credit to $1,000, making it available to more families, and eliminating the marriage penalty.
- Encourage entrepreneurship and growth by capping the top marginal rate, ending the

death tax, and making permanent the Research and Development credit.

- Promote charitable giving and education.
- Foster capital investment and savings to boost today's dangerously low personal savings rate.

This is more than just an economic program to promote growth and job creation. It is our blueprint for the kind of society we want for our children and grandchildren. It is a call to conscience, a reminder that, even in times of great prosperity, there are those who bear great burdens. That is why, with the tax cuts we propose, while every taxpayer benefits, six million families—one in five taxpaying families with children—will no longer pay any federal income tax.

It took a Republican Congress to stand up to the Internal Revenue Service by publicly exposing its abuses and enacting a Taxpayer's Bill of Rights. Within the simpler and fairer tax system proposed by Governor Bush, the IRS will be downsized and made less intrusive. IRS rules should be understandable by all, enforced by few, with low-cost compliance. We applaud the efforts of the Republican Congress to expand the use and availability of Individual Retirement Accounts.

In 1997 the Republican Congress cut the capital gains tax from 28 percent to 20 percent. As a result capital gains for Americans doubled and federal government tax receipts from capital gains jumped from $50 billion in 1996 to $75 billion in 1997. These tax cuts produce more economic growth and often more tax revenues. We cheer their lowering of the capital gains tax rate and look forward to further reductions that will stimulate property sales and development to bring jobs and renewal to our urban neighborhoods.

To guard against future tax hikes, we support legislation requiring a super-majority vote in both houses of Congress to raise taxes. We will prohibit retroactive taxation and will not tolerate attempts by federal judges to impose taxes. Because of the vital role of religious and fraternal benevolent societies in fostering charity and patriotism, they should not be subject to taxation.

Income taxes and payroll taxes are the most obvious parts of the public's tax burden but con-

sumers foot the bills in higher prices for most of the user fees that are nothing but under-radar taxes. Excise taxes of all kinds have snowballed, because they shift public resentment from government to the businesses that are forced to collect them. One example is the gas tax of 1993. Another is the phone tax imposed to finance the Spanish-American War—and still in place a century later. We call for the immediate repeal of the phone tax.

Homeownership

Homeownership is central to the American Dream, and Republicans want to make it more accessible for everyone. That starts with access to capital for entrepeneurs and access to credit for consumers. Our proposals for helping millions of low-income families move from renting to owning are detailed elsewhere in this platform as major elements in Governor Bush's program for a New Prosperity. For those families, and for all other potential homebuyers, low interest rates make mortgages affordable and open up more housing opportunities than any government program.

Affordable housing is in the national interest. That is why the mortgage interest deduction for primary residences was put into the federal tax code, and why tax reform of any kind should continue to encourage homeownership. At the same time, a balanced national housing policy must recognize that decent housing includes apartments, and addresses the needs of all citizens, including renters.

We will turn over to local communities foreclosed and abandoned HUD properties for urban homesteading, a citizen renovation effort that has been remarkably successful in revitalizing neighborhoods. We affirm our commitment to open housing, without quotas or controls, and we applaud the proactive efforts by the realty and housing industries to assure access for everyone.

In many areas, housing prices are higher than they need to be because of regulations that drive up building costs. Some regulation is of course necessary, and so is sensible zoning. But we urge states and localities to work with local builders and lenders to eliminate unnecessary burdens that price many families out of the market. We see no role for any federal regulation of home-building, but we do foresee a larger role for State and local governments in controlling the federally assisted housing that has been so poorly managed from Washington. We also encourage the modification of restrictions that inhibit the rehabilitation of existing distressed properties.

Small Business: Where Prosperity Starts

Small businesses are the underlying essence of our economy. Small businesses create most of the new jobs and keep this country a land of opportunity. They have been the primary engines of economic advance by American women, whose dynamic entry into small business in recent years has accounted for much of the nation's growth. Small businesses generate more than half the gross domestic product. Their willingness to give people a chance, and their ability to train individuals new to the workforce, made welfare reform the success that it is. They deserve far better treatment from government than they have received. We will provide it through many of the initiatives explained elsewhere in this platform: lower tax rates, ending the death tax, cutting through red tape, legal and product liability reform, and the aggressive expansion of overseas markets for their goods and services.

We will end the harassment of small businesses by federal agencies. In the case of OSHA, we will withdraw its proposed ergonomics standard, ban its bureaucracy from the homes of telecommuting workers, and change the agency from an adversary to a partner for safer productivity. We will halt the IRS discrimination against independent contractors and, in order to guard against unwise regulation, will include the agency in the current procedures of the Small Business Regulatory Enforcement Fairness Act.

Providing health insurance is a major challenge for small business owners. Almost 60 percent of uninsured workers are either employed by small business or are self-employed. That is a compelling reason to immediately allow 100 percent deductibility of health insurance premiums and to let small businesses band together, across State lines, to purchase insurance through association health plans.

Workplace of the Future

Individual Americans, on their own initiative, are already creating the workplace of the future. Employees and employers alike need to act as a team, not as adversaries, to be competitive in the world market. Republicans want to empower them to do all of that, because we believe they know what is best for their families, their earnings, and their advancement in an opportunity economy. To help them reach their goals, government must replace antiquated laws that restrict opportunity, increase costs, and inhibit innovation.

Trade: The Force of Economic Freedom

The fearful build walls; the confident demolish them. I am confident in American workers, farmers, and producers, and I am confident that America's best is the best in the world.

—George W. Bush

International trade has become the world's most powerful economic force. International trade is not the creation of the world's rulers, but of the world's peoples, who strive for a better future and break down any barriers governments may erect to it. The result is today's global economy of open markets in democratic nations. That system is poised to sweep away both the counterproductive vestiges of protectionism and the backwater remnants of Marxism. We launched this revolution during the Reagan and Bush Administrations. Now we will bring it to completion: U.S. leadership of a global economy without limits to growth.

For our country, that outcome will be critical. Exports account for almost one-third of U.S. economic growth, while average wages in export-related industries are significantly higher. As for agriculture, expanding exports is key to saving the family farm. We must secure America's competitive advantage in the New Economy by preventing other countries from erecting barriers to innovation. For American producers and consumers alike, the benefits of free trade are already enormous. In the near future, they will be incalculable.

But free trade must be fair trade, within an open, rules-based international trading system. That will depend on American leadership, which has been lacking for the last eight years. The administration's failure to renew fast-track (expedited legislative procedures to approve free trade legislation) has undermined its ability to open new markets abroad for American goods and services. As a result, America's trade deficit with the rest of the world has surged to record highs. We must be at the table when trade agreements are negotiated, make the interests of American workers and farmers paramount, and ensure that the drive to open new markets is successful.

The vitality of that agenda depends upon the vigorous enforcement of U.S. trade laws against unfair competition. We will not tolerate the foreign practices, rules, and subsidization that put our exports on an unequal footing. It is not enough to secure signatures on a piece of paper; our trading partners must follow through on the promises they make. First and foremost, we must restore the credibility of U.S. trade leadership. We therefore propose to:

- Launch a new and ambitious round of multi-lateral negotiations focused solely on opening markets.
- Revitalize the World Trade Organization negotiations on agriculture and services.
- Give the next president fast-track negotiating authority.
- Negotiate reductions in tariffs on U.S. industrial goods and the elimination of other trade barriers so that our autos, heavy machinery, textiles, and other products will no longer be shut out of foreign markets.
- Take action against any trading partner that uses pseudo-science to block importation of U.S. bioengineered crops.
- Advance a Free Trade Area of the Americas to take advantage of burgeoning new markets at our doorstep.
- Revise export controls to tighten control over

military technology and ease restrictions on technology already available commercially.

Technology and the New Economy: The Force for Change

Governments don't create wealth. Wealth is created by Americans—by creativity and enterprise and risk-taking. The great engine of wealth has become the human mind—creating value out of genius.

—George W. Bush

The innovation at the heart of our New Economy has become the greatest force for change all over the world. With information technology, people in bondage can taste freedom, and people in freedom can bond more securely with each other. People who used to work for others are now independent entrepreneurs. And citizens are drilling through layers of entrenched bureaucracy to directly access information and transact business.

Republicans have embraced this change, for it advances the central values of our party and our country: a reduced role for government, greater personal liberty, economic freedom, reliance on the market, and decentralized decision-making. This revolution also suits our national character—rewarding creativity, hard work, tenacity, and a willingness to take risks. It empowers. This is America's moment.

Republicans recognize that the role of government in the New Economy is to foster an environment where innovation can flourish. The Information Revolution is the product of the creative efforts and hard work of men and women in the private sector, and not of government bureaucrats. At the same time, we recognize the magnitude and pace of change require vigilance to make the most of its opportunities and to mitigate its possible difficulties. For what we have experienced thus far is surely only the beginning of almost unimaginable growth, change, and more change. Let others be timid in the face of it, but let this country seize the opportunity.

The Republican Congress deserves great credit

for what it has already done to fulfill its historic E-Contract with the American people:

- The Internet Tax Freedom Act put a three-year moratorium on new Internet taxes to ensure that electronic commerce would not be smothered in its infancy.
- An expanded visa program (H-1B) provided much of the highly skilled labor that makes rapid technological progress possible.
- The Securities Litigation Reform Act, enacted by overriding a veto, is preventing trial lawyers from preying on new cutting-edge companies. The threat of abusive lawsuits must not be allowed to cripple the capital formation that will drive the Information Revolution.
- A codified World Intellectual Property Organization (WIPO) agreement ensured that content providers are protected from foreign criminals.
- Our extended research and development tax credit allows companies to innovate, when innovation is the name of the high-tech game.
- Deregulation of telecommunications, still in its early stages, shattered monopolies and opened the door to worldwide communication.

The initiatives are grounded in a steadfast commitment to open markets, to minimal regulations, and to reducing taxes that snuff out innovation—principles at the heart of the New Economy and our party.

Our latest breakthrough, enacted only weeks ago, is a landmark commercial law granting electronic signatures used in the formation of contracts online the same legal validity as pen and ink signatures on paper. With this single stroke, business-to-business e-commerce will explode, paperwork costs will decline, convenience will increase, and consumers rack up another major victory.

The impact of the Internet on the daily workings of government to make it more responsive and citizen-centered is considered elsewhere in this platform. But Republicans welcome the Information Revolution to the political arena too. Democracy thrives on well-informed citizens, and now the public will have unprecedented access to the workings of government, including the voting records of their Members of Congress and the written opinions of judges, whose decisions will now be reviewable in the court of public opinion. Where do we go from here?

- First, commit to global markets and free trade. Internet curtains must not take the place of the Iron Curtain through tariffs, duties, or taxes on Internet access. We call for a permanent ban on access taxes and an extension of the current moratorium on new and discriminatory taxes, which shall not prohibit a state from collecting taxes that are currently authorized by law.
- Second, maintain a highly educated workforce so that continued progress need not depend on imported personnel. Like Governor Bush, we have made this a vital part of our education program that is detailed elsewhere in this platform. Instead of burdening schools with red tape and narrow government programs, we will give them maximum flexibility in using federal education technology dollars to meet their specific needs—whether it be for computers, teacher training, software development, or systems integration.
- Third, speed up the research and innovation that drive technological progress, along the lines of our proposed tax reforms, National Institutes of Health (NIH) funding, and a $20 billion increase in the research and development budget of the Defense Department.
- Fourth, protect the technology industry from modern-day pirates at home and abroad: both those who violate copyrights and those who loot by litigation.
- Restrain the hand of government so that it cannot smother or slow the growth of worldwide commerce and communication through the Internet.

In addition, we must encourage government at all levels to work with the private sector to ensure that the Internet must be a medium for everyone. The old liberal approach—using the threat of stifling regulations to redistribute wealth and opportunity—will work no better than it ever has, and perhaps much worse, in the New Economy. The Republican Party embraces a creative, incentive-based, public/private approach, and a Republican president will use the influence of his office to urge high-tech philanthropy, with such initiatives as Governor Bush's plan to create and strengthen more than 2,000 community technology centers every year—centers which provide such services as free Internet access and technology skills training. The prosperity of our New Economy provides unprecedented opportunities for philanthropic giving.

What holds true for the Internet applies as well to other areas of scientific advance, from biotechnology to chemistry. These fields require enormous infusions of capital, as well as regulatory flexibility by government. The federal government must refocus and reinvigorate its role in promoting cutting-edge, basic research, and the tax code must foster research and development. These policies will increase the pace of technological developments by de-emphasizing the direct role of government while strengthening private-public partnerships and the role of the private sector. In addition, the Republican Party will remain committed to America's leadership in space research and exploration. We will ensure that this nation can expand our knowledge of the universe, and with the support of the American people, continue the exploration of Mars and the rest of the solar system. We consider space travel and space science a national priority with virtually unlimited benefits, in areas ranging from medicine to micro-machinery, for those on earth. Development of space will give us a growing economic resource and a source of new scientific discoveries. The potential benefits of new science and technology to the American people, indeed to all humanity, are incalculable and can only be hastened by the international free market in ideas that the Information Revolution has created.

Privacy and Secure Technologies

Government also has a responsibility to protect personal privacy, which is the single greatest concern Americans now have about the Information Revolution. Citizens must have the confidence that their personal privacy will be respected in the use of technology by both business and government. That privacy is an essen-

tial part of our personal freedom and our family life, and it must not be sacrificed in the name of progress. At the same time, consumers should have the benefit of new products, services, and treatments that result from the legitimate use of data with appropriate safeguards. We applaud the leadership already demonstrated in this regard by many outstanding businesses, which are ensuring individuals' privacy in various ways and promoting public education about the consumer's right to privacy.

EDUCATION AND OPPORTUNITY: LEAVE NO AMERICAN BEHIND

A Responsibility Era

Sometimes it's important to state the obvious. This is one of those times. America is a great country. There are many reasons for this, foremost among them our long tradition of personal responsibility, the demand for high standards and clear values, and the central importance of family in social and economic progress.

In recent years, America seemed to move away from some of the qualities that make her great, but we are now relearning some important lessons. The key is to acknowledge the mistakes, fix them, learn from them, and move on.

We're coming to understand that a good and civil society cannot be packaged into government programs but must originate in our homes, in our neighborhoods, and in the private institutions that bring us together, in all our diversity, for the works of mercy and labors of love.

This section of our platform deals with some of America's most enduring, and seemingly intractable, challenges. We approach these challenges with compassionate conservatism, a concept that is as old as the pioneers heading west in wagon trains, in which everyone had responsibility to follow the rules, but no one would be left behind.

Real Education Reform: Strengthening Accountability and Empowering Parents

No child in America should be segregated by low expectations ... imprisoned by illiteracy, aban-

doned to frustration and the darkness of self-doubt.

—George W. Bush

The question is "Are our schools better off now than they were eight years ago?" At a time of remarkable economic growth, when a world of opportunity awaits students who are prepared for it, American colleges and universities are offering remedial courses and American businesses are unable to find enough qualified or trainable workers to meet the demand. Worst of all, so many of our children, America's most precious asset, are headed toward failure in school, and that will hold them back throughout their lives. Republicans desire a better result. We believe that every child in this land should have access to a high-quality, indeed, a world-class education, and we're determined to meet that goal.

It's long past time to debate what works in education. The verdict is in, and our Republican governors provided the key testimony: strong parental involvement, excellent teachers, safe and orderly classrooms, high academic standards, and a commitment to teaching the basics—from an early start in phonics to mastery of computer technology. Federal programs that fail to support these fundamental principles are sadly out of date and, under the next president, out of time. For dramatic and swift improvement, we endorse the principles of Governor Bush's education reforms, which will:

- Raise academic standards through increased local control and accountability to parents, shrinking a multitude of federal programs into five flexible grants in exchange for real, measured progress in student achievement.
- Assist states in closing the achievement gap and empower needy families to escape persistently failing schools by allowing federal dollars to follow their children to the school of their choice.
- Expand parental choice and encourage competition by providing parents with information on their child's school, increasing the number of charter schools, and expanding education savings accounts for use from kindergarten through college.

- Help states ensure school safety by letting children in dangerous schools transfer to schools that are safe for learning and by forcefully prosecuting youths who carry or use guns and the adults who provide them.
- Ensure that all children learn to read by reforming Head Start and by facilitating state reading initiatives that focus on scientifically based reading research, including phonics.

Nothing is more important than literacy, and yet many children have trouble reading. This problem must be addressed at all grade levels. And as is so often the case in education, the solution is parent and child working together with teachers to help break a cycle of illiteracy that may have extended from generation to generation. We want to replace that pattern with the rich legacy of reading.

We recognize that under the American constitutional system, education is a state, local, and family responsibility, not a federal obligation. Since over 90 percent of public school funding is state and local, not federal, it is obvious that state and local governments must assume most of the responsibility to improve the schools, and the role of the federal government must be progressively limited as we return control to parents, teachers, and local school boards. Programs beginning the process by congressional Republicans to return power to the people, such as "Straight A's" legislation and "Dollars to the Classroom" are a good step to reach this goal. The Republican Congress rightly opposed attempts by the Department of Education to establish federal testing that would set the stage for a national curriculum. We believe it's time to test the Department, and each of its programs, instead.

Over thirty years ago, the federal government assumed a special financial responsibility to advance the education of disadvantaged children through the Title 1 program. Today, $120 billion later, the achievement gap between those youngsters and their peers has only widened. The fiscal loss is not a good thing, but the human loss is tragic. We cannot allow another generation of kids to be written off. For dramatic and swift improvement, we endorse Governor Bush's principles of local control, with accountability, parental choice, and meaningful student achievement as essential to education reform.

Qualified teachers are the vanguard of education reform. With mastery of their subjects, a contagious enthusiasm for learning, and a heartfelt commitment to their students, they can make any school great. That is why we advocate merit pay for them and expanded opportunities for professional development. Today, however, many teachers face danger and disrespect in the classroom, and their efforts to maintain order are hampered by the threat of litigation. We propose special legal protection for teachers to shield them from meritless lawsuits. We advocate a zero-tolerance policy toward all students who disrupt the classroom and we reaffirm that school officials must have the right and responsibility to appropriately discipline all students, including students with disabilities, who are disruptive or violent. Toward the same end, we will encourage faith-based and community organizations to take leading roles in after-school programs that build character and improve behavior. We propose to improve teacher training and recruiting by expanding the Troops-to-Teachers program, which places retired military personnel in the classroom, and by rewarding states that enact a system for teacher accountability. We will expand teacher loan-forgiveness to encourage qualified candidates to serve in high-need schools. As a matter of fairness, we will establish a teacher tax deduction to help defray the out-of-pocket teaching expenses so many good home, private, and public school teachers make to benefit their students.

Local responsibility for neighborhood schools has been the key to successful education since the days of the little red schoolhouse. We salute congressional Republicans for their continuing efforts, through Ed-Flex and other initiatives, to shift decision-making away from the federal bureaucracy and back to localities. We strongly endorse Governor Bush's proposal to consolidate cumbersome categorical programs into flexible performance grants, targeting resources to the classroom and tying them directly to student achievement. That is real reform.

In the Individuals with Disabilities Education Act (IDEA), the Congress required that every community in the country provide a free and appropriate education for all students with special needs and fund their schooling at higher levels. In return, the federal government promised to pay 40 percent of the average per pupil expenditure to cover the excess costs. During all the years the Democrats controlled Congress that was not done. It was congressional Republicans who took the first real strides toward fulfillment of the IDEA promise. We applaud them for recognizing that federal mandates must include federal funding. We will strive to promote the early diagnosis of learning deficiencies. Preventive efforts in early childhood should reduce the demand for special education and help many youngsters move beyond the need for IDEA's protections.

In the final analysis, education remains a parental right and responsibility. We advocate choice in education, not as an abstract theory, but as the surest way for families, especially low-income families, to free their youngsters from failing or dangerous schools and put them onto the road to opportunity and success. By the same token, we defend the option for home schooling and call for vigilant enforcement of laws designed to protect family rights and privacy in education. Children should not be compelled to answer offensive or intrusive questionnaires. We will continue to work for the return of voluntary school prayer to our schools and will strongly enforce the Republican legislation that guarantees equal access to school facilities by student religious groups. We strongly support voluntary student-initiated prayer in school without governmental interference. We strongly disagree with the Supreme Court's recent ruling, backed by the current administration, against student-initiated prayer.

Higher Education: Increased Access for All

One of the most profound changes in American society in the last half-century was the opening of post-secondary education to virtually everyone. Competition among institutions has been the key to that success. What began with the GI Bill in the 1940s has now, through student loans and grants, become the best higher education system in the world. Ours is a system in which achievement can count for more than money or social status. Americans are rightly proud of that. Now the challenges we face in the technological revolution and in the global economy require us to continue to expand the extent and excellence of higher education.

That is why both Governor Bush and congressional Republicans have given priority to programs that increase access to higher education for qualified students. The centerpiece of this effort has been education savings accounts—the ideal combination of minimal red tape and maximum consumer choice. Along with that innovation, congressional Republicans passed legislation to allow tax-free distributions from state pre-paid tuition plans, enhance the tax deduction for student loans, and make it more practicable for employers to provide educational assistance to train workers. Unfortunately, that legislation was vetoed. Next year, a Republican president will sign it into law.

Meanwhile, under Republican fiscal discipline, interest rates on federally guaranteed student loans are lower than ever before so student aspirations can reach higher than ever before. Pell Grants, the doorway to learning for millions of low-income families, are greater than ever—and will become a dynamic force in math, science, and technology when a Republican Congress enacts Governor Bush's proposal to:

- Target increased benefits to students taking challenging courses in those fields.
- Form partnerships with colleges and universities to improve science and math education.
- Attract science, math, and engineering grads to low-income schools and areas with shortages of those teachers.

Overall college costs, however, continue to climb, usually far ahead of inflation. Whatever the reasons, these costs squeeze the budgets of the middle class. Many families feel they're on a treadmill, working harder to pay tuition bills that never stop rising. We call upon campus administrators to search for ways to hold down that price spiral; and, in fairness to them, we propose a presidentially directed study on the effect of government regulation and paperwork demands.

At many institutions of higher learning, the ideal of academic freedom is threatened by intolerance. Students should not be compelled to support, through mandatory student fees, anyone's political agenda. The Republican Party stands in solidarity with the dedicated faculty who are penalized for their conservatism and also with the courageous students who run independent campus newspapers to confront the powerful with the power of truth. To protect the nation's colleges and universities against intolerance, we will work with independent educators to maintain alternatives to ideological accrediting bodies. We also support a reasonable approach to Title IX that seeks to expand opportunities for women without adversely affecting men's teams.

A New Prosperity: Seats for All at the Welcome Table

America has been successful because it offers a realistic shot at a better life. America has been successful because poverty has been a stage, not a fate. America has been successful because anyone can ascend the ladder and transcend their birth.

—George W. Bush

We want to expand opportunity instead of government. Governor Bush calls this "the Duty of Hope." We see it as our duty to act. But whatever we name it, the goal is the same—to give hope and real upward mobility to those who have never known either. It's clear that the old left-liberal order of social policy has collapsed in failure; and its failure was the most egregious among whom it most professed to serve: the poor and those on the margins of society.

The time is here to act, to bring hope, to expand opportunity. Republican governors throughout the country sparked a revolution that brought about the greatest social policy change in nearly 60 years—welfare reform. Inspired by the innovative reforms of Republican governors that successfully moved families from welfare dependence to the independence of work, congressional Republicans passed landmark welfare reform legislation in 1996 that has helped millions of Americans break the cycle of welfare and gain independence for their families. Because of that legislation—turning welfare resources and decision-making back to the states, with the understanding that recipients must meet a work requirement and such assistance would be only temporary—about six million Americans are now gainfully employed, many for the first time. We salute them.

And now it's time to take more steps in the right direction by helping these families climb the opportunity ladder. It won't be easy, but welfare reform wasn't easy either, though the results were surely worth the fight. Here are our next steps:

- Reward work with tax reform that takes 6 million families off the tax rolls, cuts the rate for those who remain on the rolls, and doubles the child tax credit to $1,000.
- Implement the "American Dream Down Payment" program, which will allow a half million families who currently draw federal rental assistance to become homeowners, and allow families receiving federal rental payments to apply one year's worth of their existing assistance money toward the purchase of their own first home, thus becoming independent of any further government housing assistance. This approach builds upon our longstanding commitment to resident management of public housing and other initiatives.
- Increase the supply of affordable housing for low-income working families and rehabilitate abandoned housing that blights neighborhoods by establishing the Renewing the Dream tax credit. This investor-based tax credit will create or renovate more than 100,000 single-family housing units in distressed communities.
- Build savings and personal wealth through Individual Development Accounts, in partnership with banks, to accelerate the savings of low-income earners.

For many individuals, poverty signals more than the lack of money. It often represents obstacles that cannot be overcome with just a paycheck. These are the challenging cases, where

government aid is least effective. These, too, are the situations where neighborhood and faith-based intervention has its greatest power. For this reason, the Republican Congress mandated charitable choice in the welfare reform law of 1996, allowing states to contract with faith-based providers for welfare services on the same basis as any other providers. The current administration has done its utmost to block the implementation of that provision, insisting that all symbols of religion must be removed or covered over—precisely what the 1996 provisions set out to prevent. The result is that many of the most successful service programs are essentially blacklisted because they will neither conceal nor compromise the faith that makes them so effective in changing lives. While this is unfair to faith-based organizations, it is unjust to those whom they could help conquer abuse, addiction, and hopelessness.

Texas was the first state to implement charitable choice in welfare, and its governor intends to expand it to all federally funded human services programs. We support his plans to unbar the gates of the government ghetto, inviting into the American Dream those who are now in its shadows and using the dedication and expertise of faith communities to make it happen.

This is what we propose:

- Apply charitable choice to all federal social service programs.
- Encourage an outpouring of giving by extending the current federal charity tax deduction to the 70 percent of all tax filers who do not itemize their deductions and by allowing people to make donations tax-free from their IRAs.
- Promote corporate giving by raising the cap on their charitable deductions and assuring them liability protection for their in-kind donations.

The renewal of entire communities is an awesome task and involves one human face, one human heart at a time. But the American people have a long and seasoned history of working wonders. Government does have a role to play, but as a partner, not a rival, to the armies of compassion. These forces have roots in the areas they serve, and their leaders are people to whom the disadvantaged are not statistics, but neighbors, friends, and moral individuals created in the image of God. With these approaches government becomes a partner with community and faith-based providers in supporting families and children and helping them improve their opportunities for a better life.

Children at Risk

Republicans recognize the importance of having a father and a mother in the home. The two-parent family still provides the best environment of stability, discipline, responsibility, and character. Documentation shows that where the father has deserted his family, children are more likely to commit a crime, drop out of school, become violent, become teen parents, take illegal drugs, become mired in poverty, or have emotional or behavioral problems. We support the courageous efforts of single-parent families to have a stable home.

The participation of faith-based and community groups will be especially important in dealing with the twin problems of non-marital pregnancy and substance abuse. Reducing those behaviors is the surest way to end the cycle of child poverty. After-school programs should be fully open to the community and faith-based groups that know best how to reach out to our children and help them reach their true potential.

We renew our call for replacing "family planning" programs for teens with increased funding for abstinence education, which teaches abstinence until marriage as the responsible and expected standard of behavior. Abstinence from sexual activity is the only protection that is 100 percent effective against out-of-wedlock pregnancies and sexually transmitted diseases, including HIV/AIDS, when transmitted sexually. We oppose school-based clinics that provide referrals, counseling, and related services for contraception and abortion. We urge the states to enforce laws against statutory rape, which accounts for an enormous portion of teen pregnancy. We support the establishment of Second Chance Maternity Homes, like the ones Governor Bush has proposed, to give young unwed mothers the opportunity to develop parenting skills, finish school, and enter the workforce. Because many youngsters fall into poverty as a re-

sult of divorce, we also encourage states to review their divorce laws and to support projects that strengthen marriage, promote successful parenting, bolster the stability of the home, and protect the economic rights of the innocent spouse and children. Finally, because so many social ills plaguing America are fueled by the absence of fathers, we support initiatives that strengthen marriage rates and promote committed fatherhood.

The entire nation has suffered from the administration's virtual surrender in the war against drugs, but children in poor communities have paid the highest price in the threat of addiction and the daily reality of violence. Drug kingpins have turned entire neighborhoods into wastelands and ruined uncounted lives with their poison. The statistics are shocking. Since 1992, among 10th graders, overall drug use has increased 55 percent, marijuana and hashish use has risen 91 percent, heroin use has gone up 92 percent, and cocaine use has soared 133 percent. Not surprisingly, teen attitudes toward drug abuse have veered sharply away from disapproval. With abundant supplies in their deadly arsenal, drug traffickers are targeting younger children, as well as rural kids.

Still, there is no substitute for presidential leadership, whether internationally or here at home, where America's families cry out for safe, drug-free schools. A Republican president will hear those cries and work with parents to protect children. We will bring accountability to anti-drug programs, promote those that work, and cease funding for those that waste resources. Equally important, in a Republican administration the Department of Justice will require all federal prosecutors to aggressively pursue drug dealers, from the kingpins to the lackeys. We renew our support for capital punishment for drug traffickers who take innocent life.

Illegal drugs and alcohol abuse are closely related to the incidence of child abuse. Government at all levels spends about $20 billion annually on a confusing array of programs to help either the children or adults in abusive or neglectful families. While the largest federal effort is the open-ended entitlements aimed at foster care and adoption, very little is allotted to preventive and family support services. We must decrease abuse caseloads and increase accountability throughout the child protection system. We propose to restructure that system along the lines of our welfare reform success, by combining the separate and competing funding sources into a Child Protection Block Grant with guaranteed levels of funding. This will empower the states to respond more quickly, more flexibly, and with greater compassion to children in peril. We call for the stringent and effective enforcement of laws against the abuse of children.

For many of those children, adoption may be the only route to a stable and loving home. Government at all levels should work with the charitable and faith-based groups that provide adoption services to remove the obstacles they sometimes encounter in their efforts to unite children in need with families who need them.

We call for state and local efforts to help the more than two million children of prisoners through pre-schools, mentoring, and family rebuilding programs. These children are often the ignored victims of crime. Early intervention in their plight is essential to reduce the cycle of violence and to save a child. We should be tough on criminals but compassionate toward our children.

Renewing Family and Community

Individual rights—and the responsibilities that go with them—are the foundation of a free society. In protecting those rights, and in asserting those responsibilities, we affirm the common good, and common goals, that should unite all Americans.

We are the party of the open door, determined to strengthen the social, cultural, and political ties that bind us together and make our country the greatest force for good in the world. Steadfast in our commitment to our ideals, we recognize that members of our party can have deeply held and sometimes differing views. This diversity is a source of strength, not a sign of weakness, and so we welcome into our ranks all who may hold differing positions. We commit to resolve our differences with civility, trust, and mutual respect.

Family Matters

The family is society's central core of energy. That is why efforts to strengthen family life are the surest way to improve life for everyone. For this reason, congressional Republicans made adoption easier and enacted the child tax credit—and that is why Governor Bush wants to double that credit to $1,000 per child and increase the adoption credit. It's why we advocate a family-friendly tax code, why we promote comp-time and flex-time to accommodate family needs, and why we advocate choice in child care. We support the traditional definition of "marriage" as the legal union of one man and one woman, and we believe that federal judges and bureaucrats should not force states to recognize other living arrangements as marriages. We rely on the home, as did the founders of the American Republic, to instill the virtues that sustain democracy itself. That belief led Congress to enact the Defense of Marriage Act, which a Republican Department of Justice will energetically defend in the courts. For the same reason, we do not believe sexual preference should be given special legal protection or standing in law.

Just as environmental pollution affects our physical health, so too does the pollution of our culture affect the health of our communities. There is much to celebrate in contemporary culture, but also much to deplore: the glorification of violence, the glamorizing of drugs, the abuse of women and children—whether in music or videos, advertising, or tabloid journalism. Still, there are individuals and organizations using their power as citizens and consumers to advance a cultural renewal in all aspects of American life. We support and applaud them.

Their efforts will be critically important in the Information Age, which, with all its tremendous benefits, brings a major challenge to families. When the FBI reports that porn sites are the most frequently accessed on the Internet, it's time for parents at home—and communities through their public institutions—to take action. We endorse Republican legislation pending in the Congress to require schools and libraries to secure their computers against on-line porn and predators if they accept federal subsidies to connect to the Internet. This is not a question of free speech. Kids in a public library should not be victims of filth, and porn addicts should not use library facilities for their addiction. Therefore, public libraries and schools should secure their computers against on-line pornography.

Upholding the Rights of All

Equality of individuals before the law has always been a cornerstone of our party. We therefore oppose discrimination based on sex, race, age, religion, creed, disability, or national origin and will vigorously enforce anti-discrimination statutes. As we strive to forge a national consensus on the crucial issues of our time, we call on all Americans to reject the forces of hatred and bigotry. Accordingly, we denounce all who practice or promote racism, anti-Semitism, ethnic prejudice, and religious intolerance.

Our country was founded in faith and upon the truth that self-government is rooted in religious conviction. While the Constitution guards against the establishment of state-sponsored religion, it also honors the free exercise of religion. We believe the federal courts must respect this freedom and the original intent of the framers. We assert the right of religious leaders to speak out on public issues and will not allow the EEOC or any other arm of government to regulate or ban religious symbols from the workplace. We condemn the desecration of places of worship and objects of religious devotion, and call upon the media to reconsider their role in fostering bias through negative stereotyping of religious citizens. We support the First Amendment right of freedom of association and stand united with private organizations, such as the Boy Scouts of America, and support their positions.

Because we treasure freedom of conscience, we oppose attempts to compel individuals or institutions to violate their moral standards in providing health-related services. We believe religious institutions and schools should not be taxed. When government funds privately operated social, welfare, or educational programs, it must not discriminate against faith-based organizations, whose record in providing services to those in need far exceeds that of the public sector. Their participation should be actively encour-

aged, and never conditioned upon the covering or removing of religious objects or symbols.

We believe rights inhere in individuals, not in groups. We will attain our nation's goal of equal opportunity without quotas or other forms of preferential treatment. It is as simple as this: No one should be denied a job, promotion, contract, or chance at higher education because of their race or gender. Equal access, energetically offered, should guarantee every person a fair shot based on their potential and merit.

The Supreme Court's recent decision, prohibiting states from banning partial-birth abortions—a procedure denounced by a committee of the American Medical Association and rightly branded as four-fifths infanticide—shocks the conscience of the nation. As a country, we must keep our pledge to the first guarantee of the Declaration of Independence. That is why we say the unborn child has a fundamental individual right to life which cannot be infringed. We support a human life amendment to the Constitution, and we endorse legislation to make clear that the Fourteenth Amendment's protections apply to unborn children. Our purpose is to have legislative and judicial protection of that right against those who perform abortions. We oppose using public revenues for abortion and will not fund organizations which advocate it. We support the appointment of judges who respect traditional family values and the sanctity of innocent human life.

Our goal is to ensure that women with problem pregnancies have the kind of support, material and otherwise, they need for themselves and for their babies, not to be punitive towards those for whose difficult situation we have only compassion. We oppose abortion, but our pro-life agenda does not include punitive action against women who have an abortion. We salute those who provide alternatives to abortion and offer adoption services, and we commend congressional Republicans for expanding assistance to adopting families and for removing racial barriers to adoption. The impact of those measures and of our Adoption and Safe Families Act of 1997 has been spectacular. Adoptions out of foster care have jumped 40 percent and the incidence of child abuse and neglect has actually declined. We second Governor Bush's call to make permanent the adoption tax credit and expand it to $7,500.

An essential part of a culture that respects life is integration and inclusion of persons with disabilities. That is the goal of Governor Bush's New Freedom Initiative, a comprehensive agenda for the breakthrough research and practical assistance that can help individuals with disabilities live independently, hold jobs, and take part in the daily life of their communities. We applaud this proposal, and we salute congressional Republicans for the way they have protected access to health care for individuals with disabilities against the administration's attempts to ration it. We pledge continued vigilance in that regard, especially in Medicare and Medicaid.

We oppose the non-consensual withholding of care or treatment because of disability, age, or infirmity, just as we oppose euthanasia and assisted suicide, which endanger especially the poor and those on the margins of society. We applaud congressional Republicans for their leadership against those abuses and their pioneering legislation to focus research and treatment resources on the alleviation of pain and the care of terminally ill patients.

Seeking the counsel of those who would be most affected by it, the Republican Congress enacted the new Ticket-to-Work law, empowering persons with disabilities to choose their own support services by voucher. Equally important, and with the inspiration of initiatives by some Republican governors, we have made it possible for millions of individuals with disabilities to rejoin the workforce without losing their health benefits. We pledge full enforcement of these and prior enactments that have helped bring individuals with disabilities into the mainstream of a society that needs their skills and their industry. We support their full access to the polls and to the entire political process. The promise of assistive technology, so costly but offering hope to so many, makes it all the more crucial that we maintain the expanding economy that sustains the investment necessary to make miracles happen.

We defend the constitutional right to keep and bear arms, and we affirm the individual responsibility to safely use and store firearms. Because self-defense is a basic human right, we will promote training in their safe usage, especially in federal programs for women and the elderly. A Republican administration will vigorously enforce current gun laws, neglected by the Democrats, especially by prosecuting dangerous offenders identified as felons in instant background checks. Although we support background checks to ensure that guns do not fall into the hands of criminals, we oppose federal licensing of law-abiding gun owners and national gun registration as a violation of the Second Amendment and an invasion of privacy of honest citizens. Through programs like Project Exile, we will hold criminals individually accountable for their actions by strong enforcement of federal and state firearm laws, especially when guns are used in violent or drug-related crimes. With a special emphasis upon school safety, we propose the crackdown on youth violence explained elsewhere in this platform.

We affirm the right of individuals to voluntarily participate in labor organizations and to bargain collectively. We therefore support the right of states to enact Right-to-Work laws. No one should be forced to contribute to a campaign or a candidate, so we will vigorously implement the Supreme Court's *Beck* decision to stop the involuntary use of union dues for political purposes. We will revoke the illegal executive order excluding millions of workers from federal contracts, and safeguard the unemployment compensation system against the diversion of its funds for political purposes.

From Many, One

Our country's ethnic diversity within a shared national culture is unique in all the world. We benefit from our differences, but we must also strengthen the ties that bind us to one another. Foremost among those is the flag. Its deliberate desecration is not "free speech" but an assault against both our proud history and our greatest hopes. We therefore support a constitutional amendment that will restore to the people, through their elected representatives, their right to safeguard Old Glory.

Another sign of our unity is the role of English as our common language. It has enabled people from every corner of the world to come together to build this nation. For newcomers, it has always been the fastest route to the mainstream of American life. English empowers. That is why fluency in English must be the goal of bilingual education programs. We support the recognition of English as the nation's common language. At the same time, mastery of other languages is important for America's competitiveness in the world market. We advocate foreign language training in our schools and the fostering of respect for other languages and cultures throughout our society.

We have reaped enormous human capital in the genius and talent and industry of those who have escaped nations captive to totalitarianism. Our country still attracts the best and brightest to invent here, create wealth here, improve the quality of life here. As a nation of immigrants, we welcome all new Americans who have entered lawfully and are prepared to follow our laws and provide for themselves and their families. In their search for a better life, they strengthen our economy, enrich our culture, and defend the nation in war and in peace. To ensure fairness for those wishing to reside in this country, and to meet the manpower needs of our expanding economy, a total overhaul of the immigration system is sorely needed.

The administration's lax enforcement of our borders had led to tragic exploitation of smuggled immigrants, and untold suffering, at the hands of law-breakers. We call for harsh penalties against smugglers and those who provide fake documents. We oppose the creation of any national ID card.

Because free trade is the most powerful force for the kind of development that creates a middle class and offers opportunity at home, the long-term solution for illegal immigration is economic growth in Mexico, Central America, and the Caribbean. In the short run, however, decisive action is needed. We therefore endorse the recommendations of the U.S. Commission on Immigration Reform:

- Restore credibility to enforcement by devoting more resources both to border control and to internal operations.
- Reorganize family unification preferences to give priority to spouses and children, rather than extended family members.
- Emphasize needed skills in determining eligibility for admission.
- Overhaul the failed Labor Certification Program to end the huge delays in matching qualified workers with urgent work.
- Reform the Immigration and Naturalization Service by splitting its functions into two agencies, one focusing on enforcement and one exclusively devoted to service.

The education reforms we propose elsewhere in this platform will, over time, greatly increase the number of highly qualified workers in all sectors of the American economy. To meet immediate needs, however, we support increasing the number of H-1B visas to ensure high-tech workers in specialized positions, provided such workers do not pose a national security risk; and we will expand the H-2A program for the temporary agricultural workers so important to the nation's farms.

Justice and Safety

Most Americans over the age of fifty remember a time when streets and schoolyards were safe, doors unlocked, windows unbarred. The elderly did not live in fear and the young did not die in gunfire. That world is gone, swept away in the social upheaval provoked by the welfare, drug, and crime policies of the 1960s and later.

We cannot go back to that time of innocence, but we can go forward, step by difficult step, to recreate respect for law—and law that is worthy of respect. Most of that effort must come on the state and local levels, which have the primary responsibility for law enforcement. While we support community policing and other proven initiatives against crime, we strongly oppose any erosion of that responsibility by the federal government. Our Republican governors, legislators, and local leaders have taken a zero-tolerance approach to crime that has led to the lowest crime and murder rates in a generation.

At the same time, we recognize the crucial leadership role the president and the Congress should play in restoring public safety. The congressional half of that team, in cooperation with governors and local officials who are the front line against crime, has been hard at work. Within proper federal jurisdiction, the Republican Congress has enacted legislation for an effective deterrent death penalty, restitution to victims, removal of criminal aliens, and vigilance against terrorism. They stopped federal judges from releasing criminals because of prison overcrowding, made it harder to file lawsuits about prison conditions, and, with a truth-in-sentencing law, pushed states to make sure violent felons actually do time. They have also provided billions of dollars, in the form of block grants, for law enforcement agencies to hire police and acquire new equipment and technology.

The other part of the team—a president engaged in the fight against crime—has been ineffective for the last eight years. To the contrary, sixteen hard-core terrorists were granted clemency, sending the wrong signal to others who would use terror against the American people. The administration started out by slashing the nation's funding for drug interdiction and overseas operations against the narcotics cartel. It finishes by presiding over the near collapse of drug policy. The only bright spot has been the determination of the Republican Congress. Its Western Hemisphere Drug Elimination Act of 1998 has just begun to restore the nation's ability to strike at the source of illegal drugs. Now the Congress is taking the lead to assist Colombia against the narco-insurgents who control large parts of that country, a stone's throw from the Panama Canal.

A Republican president will advance an agenda to restore the public's safety:

- No-frills prisons, with productive work requirements, that make the threat of jail a powerful deterrent to crime.
- Increased penalties and resources to combat the dramatic rise in production and use of

methamphetamine and new drugs such as ecstasy.
- An effective program of rehabilitation, where appropriate.
- Support of community-based diversion programs for first time, non-violent offenders.
- Reforming the Supreme Court's invented Exclusionary Rule, which has allowed countless criminals to get off on technicalities.
- A constitutional amendment to protect victims' rights at every stage of the criminal justice system.
- Reservation of two seats on the U.S. Sentencing Commission for victims of violent crimes.

We will reopen Pennsylvania Avenue in front of the White House as a symbolic expression of our confidence in the restoration of the rule of law.

Crimes against women and children demand an emphatic response. That is why the Republican Congress enacted Megan's Law, requiring local notification when sex offenders are released, and why we advocate special penalties against thugs who, in assaults against pregnant women, harm them or their unborn children. Federal obscenity and child pornography laws, especially crimes involving the Internet, must be vigorously enforced—in contrast to the current administration's failure in this area. We urge States to follow the lead of congressional Republicans by making admissible in court the prior similar criminal acts of defendants in sexual assault cases.

Millions of Americans suffer from problem or pathological gambling that can destroy families. We support legislation prohibiting gambling over the Internet or in student athletics by student athletes who are participating in competitive sports.

On both the federal and state levels, juvenile crime demands special attention, as the age of young offenders has fallen and their brutality has increased. We renew our call for a complete overhaul of the juvenile system that will punish juvenile offenders, open criminal proceedings to victims and the public, make conviction records more available, and enforce accountability for offenders, parents, and judges.

With regard to school safety, we encourage local school systems to develop a single system of discipline for all students who commit offenses involving drugs or violence in school, not the federally imposed dual system which leaves today's teachers and students at risk from the behavior of others. Any juvenile who commits any crime while carrying a gun should automatically be detained, not released to someone's custody. We urge localities to consider zero tolerance for juvenile drinking and driving and early intervention to keep delinquency from escalating to crime. While recognizing the important role of both parents to the well-being of their children, we must acknowledge the critical need for positive role models to put a generation of fatherless boys on the right road to manhood. We affirm the right of public schools, courthouses, and other public buildings to post copies of the Ten Commandments.

Finally, continued assistance to state and local law enforcement is critical. Through research, grants, and joint task forces, the federal government should encourage smarter, more effective anti-crime efforts. In particular, we advocate assistance to police for their personal protection, continuing education and training, and family care.

What Is at Stake

The rule of law, the very foundation for a free society, has been under assault, not only by criminals from the ground up, but also from the top down. An administration that lives by evasion, coverup, stonewalling, and duplicity has given us a totally discredited Department of Justice. The credibility of those who now manage the nation's top law enforcement agency is tragically eroded. We are fortunate to have its dedicated career workforce, especially its criminal prosecutors, who have faced the unprecedented politicization of decisions regarding both personnel and investigations.

In the federal courts, scores of judges with activist backgrounds in the hard-left now have lifetime tenure. Our agenda for judicial reform is laid out elsewhere in this platform, but this is the heart of the matter: Whom do the American people trust to restore the rule of law, not just in our streets and playgrounds, not just in boardrooms

and on Wall Street, but in our courts and in the Justice Department itself? The answer is clear. Governor Bush is determined to name only judges who have demonstrated respect for the Constitution and the process of our republic.

RETIREMENT SECURITY AND QUALITY HEALTH CARE: OUR PLEDGE TO AMERICA

There are those who say Americans must choose between security and freedom. They are wrong. Security and liberty are not enemies. When properly balanced, they are kindred means for advancing individual achievement. In the century past, that balance was not always maintained. There were times when the exercise of independence left too many Americans insecure, especially in their old age. And there were more times when the governmental imposition of security smothered the freedoms that should be at the center of American life.

The Republican vision for a good society restores the balance most Americans seek, by maintaining the structures that guard against unforeseen misfortune and, at the same time, encouraging individual decision-making and personal control.

Saving Social Security: Helping Individuals Build Wealth

Social Security is a defining American promise, and we will not turn back. This issue is a test of government's capacity to give its word and to keep it, to act in good faith and to pursue the common good.

—George W. Bush

"A defining American promise"—a strong phrase from a strong leader, with which we strongly agree. The Social Security program is the touchstone by which the American people now gauge the reliability, competence, and integrity of government. Unfortunately, the gauge is registering real problems. This is not breaking news to most Americans. They have known for years of the deterioration of Social Security's fiscal health but fully expected their leaders to address it. But with each passing year leading to an ever grimmer prognosis, the gauge has dropped, notch by notch, into the red zone. Since 1992, Social Security's unfunded liability has increased from $7.4 trillion to $8.8 trillion. Its trustees project that, by the year 2015, there will not be enough cash coming in from payroll taxes to pay currently promised Social Security benefits.

The current administration has treated Social Security as a slogan rather than a priority, demanding billions for new government programs instead of attending to the stability of our most important domestic program. Even worse, their proposal to let the government buy stocks on behalf of the Social Security trust fund was an unprecedented power grab over the entire American economy. Doing nothing is no longer an option, for it leads to three bitter choices in the near future: crippling levels of payroll taxation, significantly reduced benefits for Social Security recipients, or a crushing burden of public debt for generations to come.

We reject each of those outcomes and accept the mandate which others have abandoned: to keep faith with both the past and the future by saving Social Security. For starters, congressional Republicans stopped the annual raids on the Social Security trust funds by balancing the federal budget without that program's surplus. In addition, government agencies have and should continue efforts to improve the accuracy of economic indicators. Now a Republican president will forge a national consensus on these principles to protect this national priority:

- Anyone currently receiving Social Security, or close to being eligible for it, will not be impacted by any changes.
- Key changes should merit bipartisan agreement so any reforms will be a win for the American people rather than a political victory for any one party.
- Real reform does not require, and will not include, tax increases.
- Personal savings accounts must be the cornerstone of restructuring. Each of today's workers should be free to direct a portion of their payroll taxes to personal investments for their retirement future. It is crucial that individuals be offered a variety of investment alternatives and that detailed information be provided to each participant to help them judge the risks and benefits of each plan. Today's financial markets offer a variety of investment options, including some that guarantee a rate of return higher than the current Social Security system with no risk to the investor.
- Choice is the key. Any new options for retirement security should be voluntary, so workers can choose to remain in the current system or opt for something different.

This is a challenge that demands the kind of presidential leadership the country has not seen in almost a decade. Governor Bush has shown his commitment by proposing a bold alternative to the collapse of Social Security. Along with Americans everywhere, we pledge to join him in this endeavor of a lifetime.

Security for Older Americans

For most of us, retirement holds both promise and problems. Today's elderly have far more economic security than earlier generations; and opportunities for learning, teaching, and leading are greater than ever. Public policy must encourage, not inhibit, this. To that end, for half a century, the Republican Party fought to repeal the Democrats' earnings limitation on Social Security recipients, which took away a dollar for every three they earned. That fight has finally been won, and we salute congressional Republicans for leading it. We likewise note with pride the Republican legislation that has simplified pension law and made it easier for more businesses, especially small ones, to offer pension plans.

We call for full repeal of the death tax, as proposed in Governor Bush's program, Prosperity with a Purpose, and as recently passed by congressional Republicans. Hard-working Americans should not live with the fear that the fruits of their lifetime of labor will fall into the hands of government instead of their children.

The growing need for long-term care calls for long-term planning both by individuals and by government. We encourage, at all levels of government, regulatory flexibility and sensitivity to human needs in nursing homes and related facilities. In this area, as in so many other unheralded corners of American lives, heroic sacrifices are being made by millions of families to care for their mothers and fathers as their parents cared for them. We support Governor Bush's call for a 100 percent above-the-line tax deduction for premiums for long-term care insurance, recognizing and rewarding individual responsibility, and we welcome his proposal to allow an additional exemption for each elderly spouse, parent, or relative a family tends to in their own residence.

Preserving and Improving Medicare

Our nation must reform Medicare—and in doing so, ensure that prescription drugs are affordable and available for every senior who needs them. Seniors deserve a wider scope of coverage, and they deserve to have more choices among health plans. Over the last few years, both Republicans and Democrats have embraced these goals, yet the Clinton-Gore administration has blocked bipartisan Medicare reform. When I am president, I will lead Republicans and Democrats to reform and strengthen Medicare and set it on firm financial ground.

—George W. Bush

Medicare, at age 35, needs a new lease on life. It's time to bring this program, so critical for 39 million seniors and individuals with disabilities, into the twenty-first century. It's time to modernize the benefit package to match current medical science, improve the program's financial stability, and cut back the bureaucratic jungle that is smothering it. It's time to give older Americans access to the same health insurance plan the Congress has created for itself, so that seniors will have the same choices and security as members of Congress, including elimination of all current limitations and restrictions that prevent the establishment of medical savings accounts. To do that, we need to build on the strengths of the free market system, offer seniors real choices in coverage, give participants flexibility, and make sure there are incentives for the private sector to develop new and inexpensive drugs.

No one in their right mind would choose a physician who limited her practice to the treatments and procedures of the 1960s. By the same token, no one should be content with a Medicare program based on benefit packages and delivery models of that same era. For example, it denies coverage for necessary preventive services, like cholesterol screenings, and limits access to new life-saving technologies. This must change. Every Medicare beneficiary should have a choice of health care options. We want them to have access to the health plan that best fits their medical needs. In short: no more governmental one-size-fits-all.

Medicare also needs new measures of solvency that look at total program expenses and provide an honest reading of how we can guarantee benefits for decades to come. At the same time, we must dramatically reduce the program's administrative complexities symbolized both by its 130,000 pages of regulations and by its $13.5 billion in improper payments in 1999 alone. Some of that is due to fraud, waste, and abuse, but most of it comes from the sad fact that Medicare is a creaking, bureaucratic, and oppressive dinosaur in the age of MRIs. This frustrates health care providers, hospitals, and patients alike. Let us be clear: We support vigorous enforcement of anti-fraud laws in cases where there is intent to commit fraud, but it is unfair to blame honest health care providers who must seek reimbursement within a minefield of confusing Medicare regulations.

For Medicare to survive—and more important, to succeed—it must become a common enterprise of government, health professionals, and hospitals alike. Rather than continue the practice of recurrent and unpredictable cuts in provider payments, a reformed Medicare program will allow health care providers, particularly those helping rural and underserved populations, to adapt to changing conditions in health care by providing reimbursement at levels that will permit health care providers to continue to care for these patients. Republican leadership will reopen and broaden the door to health care by fulfilling the promise of medical research and innovation, by offering choice and protecting consumer rights, and by modernizing antiquated systems to deliver affordable care for all its beneficiaries.

Quality Health Care: A Commitment to All Americans

Americans enjoy the best health care in the world. Their system, the envy of all mankind, is the center of debate and controversy. This contradiction arises from the dynamism that is changing every aspect of American medicine. Change is seldom easy, and when it relates to the health of those we love, it can be downright scary. Still, the outcome of all this change is a world of unimagined promise in health. We must embrace that change, and master it as well.

The mapping of the human genome, identifying every gene in the human body, may, over time, translate into new treatments and cures for scourges like cancer, Alzheimer's, heart disease, and HIV/AIDS, as well as diseases that affect the very young, such as muscular dystrophy and juvenile diabetes. A century ago, the average American life span was 55. Today, it is 78, and children born in this decade have the realistic prospect of living into the twenty-second century. A simple blood test can now screen for prostate cancer at its earliest appearance. Biochemistry is revolutionizing the field of mental health. Millions of operations have been replaced with CAT scans. We want that progress to continue. But translating the promise of medical research into readily available treatments requires more than just money; it needs a whole new prescription for health care. That prescription is what the Republican Party offers in the elections of 2000.

Let's start with the diagnosis. After eight years of pressure from the current administration, the foundations of our health care system are cracking. We can spot the fissures everywhere.

- There are currently 44 million uninsured Americans, an increase of 1 million for each of the past eight years.
- The institutions and the people who provide health care are at risk. Hospitals in our poorest urban and rural areas are being callously closed, by the same administration that budgets far less than was originally projected, while calling for greater coverage.
- The quality of health care is in jeopardy. Recent reports estimate that almost 100,000 patients die each year from medical errors. This is more than from auto accidents, murders, or AIDS.
- Medicare, the bedrock of care for our elderly, is suffocating under more than 130,000 pages of federal rules, three times the size of the entire IRS code. It pays for only 53 percent of seniors' care, provides no outpatient prescription drugs, does not cover real long-term care, and is still headed for bankruptcy in the near future.
- The doctor-patient relationship has been eroded, and in some instances replaced, by external decision-making and managed care bureaucracy.

We intend to save this beleaguered system with a vision of health care adapted to the changing demands of a new century. It is as simple, and yet as profound, as this: All Americans should have access to high-quality and affordable health care. They should have a range of options and be able to select what is the best care for their individual and family needs. The integration of access, affordability, quality, and choice into the nation's health care system is the goal that brings together all of the following proposals. In achieving that goal, we will promote a health care system that supports, not supplants, the private sector; that promotes personal responsibility in health care decision-making; and that ensures the least intrusive role for the federal government.

Affordable, Quality Health Insurance

We will not nationalize our health care system. We will promote individual choice. We will rely on private insurance. But make no mistake: In my administration, low-income Americans will have access to high-quality health care.

—George W. Bush

Let's give credit where due: More than 100 million American workers and their families have sound health insurance through their places of employment. The job-creating dynamism of our free economy has thus done more to advance health care than any government program possibly could. The tie between good jobs and good insurance coverage is the single most important factor in advancing health care for those who need it.

That's why the Republican Party remains determined to change federal law to give small employers the liberty to band together to purchase group insurance for their employees at reduced rates, thus providing them that important security. The tragedy is that this urgent expansion of coverage has thus far been blocked by veto threats. With a Republican president, that will change.

Uninsured Americans do not have a single face. Their situations vary tremendously, with changes in family status, age, and income. It makes sense to let them decide what kind of coverage best suits their needs. To give them that power of choice, we propose an unprecedented tax credit that will enable 27 million individuals and families to purchase the private health insurance that's right for them. We also support full deductibility of health insurance premiums for the self-employed.

Truly positive market forces occur when individuals have the ability to make individual marketplace decisions. We therefore strongly encourage support for the emerging concepts of defined contribution plans and medical savings accounts. Individuals should be free to manage their own health care needs through Flexible Savings Accounts (FSAs) and Medical Savings Accounts (MSAs). These initiatives make a government takeover of health care as anachronistic as surgery without anesthesia. We will make these accounts the vanguard of a new consumer rights movement in health care. Individuals should be able to roll over excess FSA dollars from one year to the next, instead of losing their unspent money at the end of each year. MSAs should be a permanent part of tax law, offered to all workers without restriction, with both employers and employees allowed to contribute.

Still, more needs to be done. A major reason why health insurance is so expensive is that many state legislatures now require all insurance policies to provide benefits and treatments which many families do not want and do not need. It is as if automakers were required by law to sell only fully equipped cars, even to buyers who

didn't want or need all the extras. These mandates, extending far beyond minimum standards, increase costs for everyone, price low-income families out of the insurance market, and advance the interests of specific providers. They have no place in a health care system based on consumer rights and patient choice.

One area of health care that is sadly ignored is the role of primary and preventive care. This is particularly important in our inner cities and rural communities, where the emergency room may be the only avenue for assistance. People in rural and underserved areas need access to critical primary care. We will boost funding for community health centers and establish stronger public-private partnerships for safety net providers and hospitals in rural and underserved communities.

When congressional Republicans established the State Children's Health Insurance Program (S-CHIP) in 1997, they enabled us to secure health insurance coverage for approximately 8 million youngsters. Republicans want to ensure that children have access to quality health care, and that states have the flexibility to innovate, expand family coverage without interference from the Health Care Financing Administration, and reach out to eligible households that are currently not enrolled in a health insurance program or in Medicaid. In a Republican administration, the first order of business at the Department of Health and Human Services will be to eliminate regulations that are stymieing the effectiveness of S-CHIP and to stop imposing unwarranted mandates, so states can make sure children who need health care can get it. A streamlined enrollment process and energetic outreach efforts will finally fulfill the promise of S-CHIP. All it takes is caring.

Improving the Quality of Health Care

Protecting Patients' Rights. The tremendous growth of managed health care was driven by a market response to the fractured system of health care delivery that preceded it. One result of that growth has been a welcomed slowing of the rapid increases in health costs that were a regular occurrence of the 1970s and 1980s. However, this has come at the cost of patient dissatisfaction with the at-times-impersonal or -insufficient health care delivery mechanism. Simply put, patients deserve more protection if we are to achieve a patient-centered system that offers high-quality, affordable care. The parents of a sick child should have access to the nearest emergency care. A patient in need of a heart specialist's expertise should be allowed to seek that opinion. A woman with breast cancer should be able to participate in a potentially life-saving clinical trial, and patients should have prompt access to independent physicians, or when appropriate, other health care professionals, to override any wrongful denial of treatment.

The traditional patient-doctor relationship must be preserved. Medical decision-making should be in the hands of physicians and their patients. In cases when a health plan denies treatment, a rapid appeals process geared toward ensuring that patients receive the right treatment without delays that might threaten a patient's health—as opposed to a lengthy trial—must be readily accessible to everyone in all health plans. We believe a quick and fair resolution to treatment disputes without going to court is the best result. However, as a last resort, we also support a patient's right to adjudicate claims in court to receive necessary medical care. In the interest of fairness to the thousands of businesses that purchase health benefits for their employees and for physicians who care for patients, employers and physicians should not be liable for the actions of the health plan and should be shielded from frivolous and unnecessary lawsuits.

Our overall philosophy is to trust state and local government to know what best suits the needs of their people. We believe the federal government should respect the states' traditional authority to regulate health insurance, health care professionals, and health practice guidelines through their medical boards.

Medical Errors and Malpractice Reform. Our goal is to reduce the rate of medical errors, especially those that result in a patient's death. We will support scientific research to provide the public and health care providers with information about why these errors occur and what can be done to prevent them. We should not displace the current, very effective hospital peer review system.

Another key step will be reform of malpractice law. In its current form, it encourages health care providers to conceal even innocent mistakes, lest they be subject to vilifying publicity through the trial lawyers' system of jackpot justice. That is why a cloak of secrecy envelops operating rooms. We must open up the free flow of information concerning medical errors, both to protect patients and to reduce the cost of modern medicine. Patients who are genuinely injured should be rightly compensated, but the punitive and random aspects of today's litigation lottery cry out for reform. Just as we hold all health care personnel to the highest standards, so too must public policy respect their ethical conscience. No individual or institution should be compelled to assist in providing any medical service that violates their moral or religious convictions.

Women's Health. As Republicans, we hold dear the health and vitality of our families. Our efforts to build healthier families must begin with women—our mothers, daughters, grandmothers, and granddaughters. This nation needs far greater focus on the needs of women who have historically been underrepresented in medical research and access to the proper level of medical attention. We are reversing this historic trend.

Across this country, and at all levels of government, Republicans are at the forefront in aggressively developing health care initiatives targeted specifically at the needs of women. The enormous increases in the NIH budget brought about by the Republican Congress will make possible aggressive new research and clinical trials into diseases and health issues that disproportionately affect women as well as into conditions that affect the elderly, the majority of whom are women. And we are leading efforts to reach out to underserved and minority female populations, where disparities persist in life expectancy, infant mortality, and death rates from cancer, heart disease, and diabetes.

Republicans are dedicated to pursuing comprehensive women's health care initiatives that include access to state-of-the-art medical advances and technology; equality for women in the delivery of health care services; medical research that focuses specifically on women; appropriate representation of women in clinical trials; and direct access to women's health providers.

The increasing focus upon health problems of the very elderly, the great majority of whom are women, holds the promise of advances concerning osteoporosis and other ailments which should no longer be considered the inevitable price of old age. Because nutrition is intimately related to health, we advocate state flexibility in managing the various federal nutrition programs for low-income families, especially those receiving TANF assistance, most of whom are female-headed households. Their transition to jobs and independence should include nutritional improvement both for mothers and for their children.

The united efforts of Republican leaders at all levels of government and within our communities will make sure that women gain greater access to relevant care, research, and education on health care issues important to them.

Children's Health. The huge strides we have already made in improving children's health must be balanced against sobering statistics. Asthma affects nearly five million children, and the incidence is dramatically increasing. Childhood obesity has jumped 100 percent in the last 15 years and can be a forerunner of the most serious illnesses later in life. Diabetes is now the second most common chronic disease in children. Youth drug abuse has more than doubled in the past eight years. Smoking rates for youth have risen alarmingly. Every year, 2,500 babies are born with fetal alcohol syndrome. So much of the suffering caused by childhood diseases can be prevented—by increasing immunization rates; by increasing resources for biomedical research, not by crippling pharmaceutical progress; by sensible strategies against teen smoking rather than the folly of prohibition; by a real war on drugs in place of the white-flag policies of recent years. Our commitment is to address the emotional, behavioral, and mental illnesses affecting children.

With parental involvement as the critical component, we can help our youth make the healthy and the right choice in avoiding risk behaviors involving alcohol, drugs, premarital sex, tobacco, and violence.

Biomedical Research. Recognizing the critical importance of research, the Republican Congress, rejecting the administration's lower figures, has already begun to fulfill its pledge to double funding for the National Institutes of Health (NIH). This is one of the few areas in which government investment yields tangible results; and those benefits can be greatest for currently underserved and minority populations, in which disparities persist in life expectancy, infant mortality, as well as death rates from heart disease, diabetes, and cancer. With one out of four Americans contracting cancer, we need to increase not only research but also early detection and prevention efforts. Since Republicans took control of Congress in January 1995, our party has led in setting sound HIV/AIDS policy, including increased research funding and access to health services. We remain committed to, and place a high priority on, finding a cure for HIV/AIDS. With the enormous increase in resources for biomedical research comes accountability for its use, as well as responsibility to maintain the highest ethical standards. We applaud congressional Republicans for the steps they have taken for protection of human embryos and against human cloning, the trafficking in fetal tissue organs, and related abuses.

Academic Medical Centers. Adequate government reimbursement for medical services is critical to our nation's comprehensive academic medical centers, which serve as the primary health care resource for our poorest citizens, provide cutting-edge medical discovery, and teach and train our next generation of physicians.

Medical Privacy. The revolution in information and medical technology has created concerns about who has access to personal data—and how it might be used. Patients and their families should feel free to share all medical information with their doctor, but they will feel safe in doing so only if that information is protected. A related concern is genetic discrimination, now that genetic testing will become a routine part of the medical health care. Well-conceived, thoughtful action is clearly needed, action that will protect and not harm patients. In both Congress and the Executive Branch, Republicans will work with patients, health care providers, researchers, and insurers to establish new rules for dealing with these new challenges.

Safe Clinical Trials. Ensuring the safety of patients who participate in investigational clinical trials is fundamental to the future of medical innovation. The lack of oversight by the current administration in gene therapy trials put patients at risk and undermined critical research. A Republican administration will require the Food and Drug Administration and NIH to make patient protection a priority in clinical trial research.

Emerging Threats and Bioterrorism. The current administration has left our public health system inadequate to respond to the threats of emerging infectious diseases and the possibility of bioterrorism. We pledge to ensure the ability of the public health service to detect, track, and prevent infectious outbreaks, whether natural or provoked by those who hate America.

Wellness. We repeat our statement that America has the finest health care delivery system that is still the envy of the world. We also recognize that an individual's health is often a reflection of the everyday choices made.

While government's role is to help ensure a quality health care system, only individuals can make healthy choices.

AMERICAN PARTNERS IN CONSERVATION AND PRESERVATION: STEWARDSHIP OF OUR NATURAL RESOURCES

As an avid outdoorsman, I know all our prosperity as a nation will mean little if we leave future gen-

erations a world of polluted air, toxic waste, and vanished wilderness and forests.

—George W. Bush

Today's Republican Party stands in the proud tradition of Teddy Roosevelt, the first president to stress the importance of environmental conservation. We approach both the national and individual stewardship of natural resources in the spirit of his maxim: "The nation behaves well if it treats the natural resources as assets which it must turn over to the next generation increased, and not impaired, in value." Over the past three decades, we have made progress. Air and water are cleaner. Some endangered species have made comebacks. Wetlands are being preserved. Recycling is commonplace policy. The lessons we have learned over the last three decades, along with the steady advance of environmental technology, give us the opportunity to explore better ways to achieve even higher goals.

Our way is to trust the innate good sense and decency of the American people. We will make them partners with government, rather than adversaries of it. The way current laws have been implemented has often fostered costly litigation and discouraged personal innovation in environmental conservation. We need to get back on a common track, so that both the people and their government can jointly focus on the real problems at hand. As a basis for that cooperation, we propose these principles:

- Economic prosperity and environmental protection must advance together. Prosperity gives our society the wherewithal to advance environmental protection, and a thriving natural environment enhances the quality of life that makes prosperity worthwhile.
- Scare tactics and scapegoating of legitimate economic interests undermine support for environmental causes and, what is worse, can discredit actual threats to health and safety.
- Environmental regulations should be based upon the best science, peer-reviewed, and available for public consideration.
- We support the federal, local, state, and tribal responsibilities for environmental protection. We believe the government's main role should

be to provide market-based incentives to innovate and develop the new technologies for Americans to meet—and exceed—environmental standards.

- We condemn the current administration's policy of resorting to confrontation first. Instead we should work cooperatively to ensure that our environmental policy meets the particular needs of geographic regions and localities.
- Environmental policy should focus on achieving results—cleaner air, water, and lands—not crafting bureaucratic processes. Where environmental standards are violated, the government should take consistent enforcement.

While the very nature of environmental concerns at times requires federal intervention, the heartening progress made by many of the states and localities demonstrates their unique ability to solve problems at the local level. As the laboratories of innovation, they should be given flexibility, authority, and finality by the federal government. Many states have enacted environmental education and voluntary self-audit laws to encourage people to find and correct pollution; the Congress should remove disincentives for states to achieve these goals. Strong leadership by governors, legislators, and local officials is the key to states to achieve these goals. Strong leadership by governors, legislators, and local officials is the key to solving the emerging environmental issues of this new century. For example, the reauthorization of the Safe Drinking Water Act by the Republican Congress enabled states and communities to take stronger action to ensure reliable and safe water supplies. Another example is the way states are handling the problem of brownfields. In 35 states, voluntary programs are cleaning up thousands of brownfield sites faster and more effectively, and with less litigation, than under the federal Superfund program. A case in point is Texas, where, under Governor Bush, the number of brownfield sites restored to productive use climbed from zero to 451, not only improving the environment but restoring more than $200 million in property value to local tax rolls, most of it in poor communities. We will replicate Governor Bush's success on the national level. We will use Superfund re-

sources to actually clean up places where people live and labor, rather than waste it on costly litigation. The old approach of mandate, regulate, and litigate has sent potential developers away from brownfield neighborhoods. The result: no new businesses, no new jobs—only dirty and dangerous sites. Governor Bush has pledged to transform this failure into an environmental win for those communities, just as he did in Texas, and we heartily endorse his agenda for doing so.

Wherever it is environmentally responsible to do so, we will promote market-based programs that are voluntary, flexible, comprehensive, and cost-effective. The Endangered Species Act (ESA), for example, is sometimes counterproductive toward its truly important goal of protecting rare species, 75 percent of which are located on private land. Its punitive approach actually encourages landowners to remove habitat to avoid federal intervention. This serves as a disincentive for private landowners to do more to restore habitat and become private stewards of wildlife. The legislation needs incentive-based cooperation among federal, state, local, and tribal governments, and private citizens. The result will be a more effective ESA that better protects wildlife diversity.

As environmental issues become increasingly international, progress will increasingly depend on strong and credible presidential leadership. Complex and contentious issues like global warming call for a far more realistic approach than that of the Kyoto Conference. Its deliberations were not based on the best science; its proposed agreements would be ineffective and unfair inasmuch as they do not apply to the developing world; and the current administration is still trying to implement it, without authority of law. More research is needed to understand both the cause and the impact of global warming. That is why the Kyoto treaty was repudiated in a lopsided, bipartisan Senate vote. A Republican president will work with businesses and with other nations to reduce harmful emissions through new technologies without compromising America's sovereignty or competitiveness—and without forcing Americans to walk to work.

Protecting Property Rights

We link the security of private property to our environmental agenda for the best of reasons: Environmental stewardship has best advanced where property is privately held. After all, people who live on the land, work the land, and own the land also love the land and protect it. As Governor Bush has said, "For the American farmer, every day is Earth Day." Conversely, the world's worst cases of environmental degradation have occurred in places where most property is under government control. For reasons both constitutional and environmental, therefore, we will safeguard private property rights by enforcing the Takings Clause of the Fifth Amendment and by providing just compensation whenever private property is needed to achieve a compelling public purpose.

Public Lands for the Public Good

Collaborative conservation represents the future for the 657 million acres of America we call the "public lands." Working from the grass roots up, local groups are finding solutions for the problems of the public lands in their areas. Republicans want to encourage that approach, for it holds the greatest promise of sound environmental stewardship and productive use of the nation's natural resources. We will change the operating culture of the federal agencies that manage public lands, giving a greater role to states and to their political subdivisions in order to foster a creative partnership with the American people. As a sign of that partnership, we applaud Governor Bush's intention to make all federal facilities comply with the environmental laws by which the American people live.

If there had been any doubt that major reform is needed in the management of public lands, it was burnt away in the catastrophic wildfires of recent months. This avoidable devastation was the price innocent people and helpless communities paid for the extreme policies—and environmental arrogance—of the current administration. Greater tragedies await the people of our Western States if those policies are not changed. Republicans will employ the best tech-

niques of forestry science to implement a national management strategy for public lands that minimizes the risk to local communities while preserving our natural heritage.

Our national parks are the crown jewels of the country's environmental heritage. They belong to all Americans and should be accessible to all. Congressional Republicans have taken the lead in reversing years of neglect and abuse of these treasures, and we will continue that proactive agenda to keep the park system healthy and accessible to all. We should make it a priority to alleviate the maintenance and operations backlog at our national parks. Rather than adding to this magnificent legacy by unilateral executive branch action, such as the administration's recent National Monument designations, we will seek to actively involve Congress, as well as affected states and local communities, in land acquisition decisions.

We support multiple use of public lands conducted in an environmentally and economically sustainable manner. We are committed to preserving high-priority wilderness and wetlands. The Everglades are a crucial example of a special federal responsibility. We call for a review of lands owned by the national government—half the total territory of our Western States—to develop a comprehensive plan to better manage existing holdings. In some cases, that may mean transferring or sharing responsibility for managing those lands with state or local governments, while all levels of government should recognize existing rights to water, minerals, and grazing. We reaffirm the traditional state primacy over water allocations and will continue the availability of renewable rangeland under conditions that ensure both expanded production of livestock and protection of the range environment. We also reaffirm our commitment to preserve access to public lands for multiple use.

We recognize the vital role the timber industry plays in our economy, particularly in homebuilding, and we support its efforts to improve the health of the country's forests. Because so many people in rural America rely on public forests for their livelihood, a Republican administration will promote sustainable forest management, using the best science in place of the no-growth policies that have devastated communities in the Pacific Northwest and Alaska.

American Agriculture and Rural America in the Global Economy

Agriculture is at the heart of the U.S. economy. The food and fiber sector accounts for 13 percent of the nation's economic output and employs, directly or indirectly, more than 22 million people. When agriculture is hurting, the entire country aches. In all our policies and programs, the Republican Party is guided by two principles. First, to farmers and ranchers, nothing beats production and sales at a good price. As long as they have truly fair and open domestic and foreign markets, they can do for themselves far better than anything government can do for them. Second, they want to produce what makes sense on their own private property, not what official Washington thinks should be grown there. Under Republican leadership, government will never again run our family farms.

While these are not the best of times for farmers and ranchers, the hopeful promise of our Freedom to Farm Act, which finally replaced decades of controls by a federal bureaucracy, has been limited by events at home and abroad. Farmers were promised that, along with the end of governmental protection for commodities markets, there would be reforms in tax, trade, and regulatory policy. Opposition from the current administration minimized progress in all three areas. As a result, American farmers were hard pressed to deal with the challenge of increased global production and slack demand in Asia. The ineptitude of current U.S. trade policy only made it worse.

For American agriculture, prosperity depends in large measure on expansion of global markets. Our farmers already export some $54 billion in products and commodities every year. For them, for the aspirations of their families and the dreams of their children, the opening of foreign markets is essential. Governor Bush understands that. That's why he has asked for restoration of presidential fast-track negotiating authority, the key to forceful trade negotiations abroad. And it's why he's determined to open the China mar-

ket for America's farmers and ranchers. It's why he's called for the U.S. to demand, in the next round of global trade talks, the complete elimination of agricultural export subsidies and tariffs. It's why he will fight the European Community's outrageous restrictions against imports of U.S. crops and livestock. And it's why he has pledged to exempt food exports from any new trade sanctions.

Results will take time, and so, looking toward the Farm Bill of the year 2002, we call for immediate action on a safety net that will give farmers the means to manage cyclical downturns. This year's reform of the Federal Crop Insurance Act by the Republican Congress was a good start. In its wake, we propose:

- Emergency assistance to facilitate the transition to a market-driven regime.
- A farm income savings plan: tax-deferred accounts to soften fluctuations in farm earnings.
- Total repeal of the death tax.
- Immediate 100 percent deductibility for health insurance costs.
- A one-time exemption from capital gains tax on the sale of farms.
- Regulatory relief.

We reaffirm our strong support for agricultural research, including biotech and biomass research, and for a permanent research and development tax credit. We likewise support the ethanol tax credit, which is good for both the environment and for farmers. Our program of regulatory reform has special relevance to farming, which bears an annual regulatory burden of $20 billion. Every farm family has better uses for that money. Apart from costs, there are grave questions about the impact of the 1996 Food Quality Protection Act. Its implementation must not disrupt farmers' access to safe crop protection products. We reaffirm our support for cooperative partnerships between federal, state, and local governments and private landowners for the conservation of our soil, water, and biological resources on private land. The federal government should work with the states to adopt water quality standards that rely on the best science and implementation of best management practices, including addressing hypoxia and runoff issues.

We call for the elimination of outdated laws that hamper the adaptation of agriculture to the demands and opportunities of a new century. Futures trading should be deregulated. Regional restrictions on dairy products that drive up consumer prices and penalize productive farmers should be ended. We commend the livestock industry for its efforts to ensure accurate and open price reporting to ensure a competitive market.

There is much more to rural America than agriculture, ranching, and forestry. The kind of economic development that generates family-sustaining jobs is critical to small town and rural communities. We recognize the special challenges they face in working for good schools, accessible health care, decent housing, safe drinking water and waste disposal, and serviceable transportation. The federal government should be an active partner with state and local entities in that process, especially in advancing the availability of the Internet and modern telecommunications technology in rural America.

Energy

What happened? Eight years ago, the nation was energy confident. Our standing in the Middle East was at its zenith. The oil cartel was in retreat; gasoline was affordable, even as automotive progress reduced emissions from cars. Today, gas prices have skyrocketed, and oil imports are at all-time highs. Foreign oil now accounts for one-third of our total trade deficit. Meanwhile, domestic oil production has fallen 17 percent over the last eight years, as vast areas of the continental U.S. have been put off-limits to energy leasing—though we depend on oil and natural gas for 65 percent of our energy supply. Additional oil reserves and deposits of low-sulfur coal may be out of reach because of unilateral designation of new national monuments.

By any reasonable standard, the Department of Energy has utterly failed in its mission to safeguard America's energy security. The Federal Energy Regulatory Commission has been no better, and the Environmental Protection Agency (EPA) has been shutting off America's energy pipeline with a regulatory blitz which has only just begun. In fact, 36 oil refineries have closed in just the last eight years, while not a single new refinery has been built in this country in the last quarter-century. The EPA's patchwork of regulations has driven fuel prices higher in some areas than in others and has made energy supplies no longer fungible. What meets the EPA's standards in one city may not be legally sold in another. The result has been localized shortages and sharp price spikes, as suppliers scramble to get acceptable fuels to the markets where they are needed.

Environmental concerns are not at the heart of the matter. In fact, the current administration has turned its back on the two sources that produce virtually all of the nation's emission-free power: nuclear and hydro, the sources for 30 percent of the country's electricity. Because of cumbersome federal relicensing of hydro and nuclear operations, we face the prospect of increasing emissions and dirtier air. Meanwhile, nuclear plants are choking on waste because the current administration breached its contract to remove it—and then vetoed bipartisan legislation to store it at a safe, permanent repository for which the taxpayers have already paid $7 billion. At the same time, power-producing dams are being torn down, by federal edict, in energy-short areas, and the Pacific Northwest is their next target. Breaching dams would not only raise electric rates but would deny Western farmers irreplaceable water for irrigation and a cost-effective means of moving their crops to West Coast ports. We should develop and use technologies that will help entrance salmon runs while keeping the dams in place.

It's a man-made nightmare, but at last the public is waking up and demanding change. What is at stake, after all, is not just the price we pay to heat and cool our homes. What is at stake is the nation's New Economy, which relies heavily on electricity for its infrastructure and on petroleum for its trade. Affordable energy, the result of Republican policies in the 1980s, helped create the New Economy. If we do not carefully plan for our energy needs, the entire economy could be significantly weakened. The Republican

Congress has moved to deregulate the electricity industry and empower consumers through a competitive market—but congressional Democrats are holding up the process, and the administration has provided no leadership. America needs a national energy strategy—and a Republican president will work with congressional Republicans to enact their National Energy Security Act. The strategy will:

- Increase domestic supplies of coal, oil, and natural gas. Our country does have ample energy resources waiting to be developed, and there is simply no substitute for an increase in their domestic production.
- Improve federal oil and gas lease permit processing and management, including coalbed methane.
- Provide tax incentives for production.
- Promote environmentally responsible exploration and development of oil and gas reserves on federally owned land, including the coastal plain of Alaska's Arctic National Wildlife Refuge.
- Offer a degree of price certainty to keep small domestic stripper producers in operation.
- Advance clean coal technology.
- Expand the tax credit for renewable energy sources to include wind and open-loop biomass facilities, and electricity produced from steel cogeneration.
- Maintain the ethanol tax credit.
- Provide a tax incentive for residential use of solar power.

This agenda will reduce America's dependence on foreign oil, help consumers by lowering energy prices, and result in lower carbon emissions than would result from the current administration's policies. To protect consumers against seasonal price spikes, that legislation also authorizes a home heating oil reserve for the Northeastern States and allows expensing of costs for its storage. It will also make low-income housing more energy-efficient. All in all, it is a dramatic reversal of the nation's present course, and that's just what America needs: a balanced portfolio of energy options that is stable, secure, and affordable, with minimal impact on the environment.

A Nation on the Move

Commerce is the lifeblood of our economy, and the transportation infrastructure is its circulatory system. Without safe and efficient transport, the economy withers away. Maintaining that vital infrastructure has always been, in part, a federal responsibility, and Republicans have historically been the party of builders. From the era of the transcontinental railroad and the Panama Canal to President Eisenhower's establishment of the Interstate Highway System, we have championed investment in transportation assets as a cornerstone of the economy and, indeed, our national way of life.

More recently, the Republican-led Congress has enacted two historic pieces of legislation: the 1998 Transportation Equity Act for the twenty-first century and this year's Aviation Investment and Reform Act. These landmark laws represent an unprecedented federal investment in roads, bridges, transit systems, airports, and air traffic control systems—without additional taxes. They simply unlock the transportation trust funds to invest the dollars motorists and the traveling public have already paid. Those funds had been subject to years of abuse under Democrat-controlled Congresses but are now statutorily dedicated to building and maintaining the transportation system for which our citizens pay. The same budgetary protections should be extended to other transportation trust funds.

Our national railroad network is a crucial component of our public transportation system. Railroads helped build our country, and our national passenger railroad network remains a precious resource that can play a key role in transportation and economic growth. Republicans support a healthy intercity passenger rail system, and where economically viable, the development of a national high-speed passenger railroad system as an instrument of economic development and enhanced mobility. We also support a multi-modal approach to our transportation needs.

By reducing mandates, cutting red tape, and promoting regulatory common sense, congressional Republicans have given state and local officials unprecedented flexibility to set their own transportation priorities, from highways to bike trails. That will improve communities throughout the nation, and will also strengthen travel and tourism, a vital force for job creation with a positive annual trade balance to boot. But transportation policy remains inseparable from energy policy. The trucking industry, for example, is hard hit by current gas prices and would be crippled by the administration's new "hours of service" regulation. Consumers everywhere are literally paying the price both for what the administration has done and for what it has failed to do.

Republicans are going to get transportation policy back on track, both here at home through a sound, long-term energy policy, and internationally as well, by pursuing the "Open Skies" agreements, first proposed by President George Bush, to open foreign markets for American aviation services. In short, we will keep Americans moving safely and keep our country, in the words of the song, "a thoroughfare for freedom."

GOVERNMENT FOR THE PEOPLE

Trust, pride, and respect: We pledge to restore these qualities to the way Americans view their government. It is the most important of tasks and reflects the overwhelming desire of our citizens for fundamental change in official Washington.

The templates to make this happen are readily available in the 30 states led by Republican governors. These visionary leaders have opened a new era of creative federalism, making government citizen-centered, results-oriented, and, where possible, market-based. Their sound management of public dollars has led to unprecedented surpluses. Services have improved. Waste has been reduced. Taxes have been cut.

State and local governments are also far ahead of official Washington in the creation of e-government: providing information and services to the public via the Internet. Citizens can conduct business with government by going online instead of wasting hours in line. We will e-power citizens at all levels of government. And we will require federal agencies to use savvy, on-

line practices to buy smart—and save enormous amounts of money in procurement.

The leadership our governors have shown in these matters only strengthens our commitment to restore the force of the Tenth Amendment, the best protection the American people have against federal intrusion and bullying. We have limited the ability of Congress to impose unfunded mandates of the past in areas like education and social services. The dramatic success of welfare reform—once the States were allowed to manage their programs—is a stellar example of what happens when we give power back to the people.

Therefore, in our effort to shift power from Washington back to the states, we must acknowledge as a general matter of course that the federal government's role should be to set high standards and expectations in policies, then get out of the way and let the states implement and operate those policies as they best know how. Washington must respect that one size does not fit all states and must not overburden states with unnecessary strings and red tape attached to its policies.

In the Congress, a Republican majority has modernized our national legislature. They have set term limits for committee chairs and leadership positions, and they have, by law, required Congress to live by the same rules it imposes on others. And, at a time when the nation felt betrayed by misconduct in high office, the Republican Congress responded with gravity and high purpose. We applaud those members who did their duty to conscience and the Constitution.

There is much to be done, but it can be done only when a Republican president works in tandem with a Republican Congress. We will work to pass legislation to make it clear that public officials who commit crimes will subsequently forfeit their pension rights. We will ensure that IRS audits are never used as a political weapon, so innocent Americans will never again fear the snooping, harassment, and intimidation of recent years. And because an accurate census is essential for representative government, we will respect the Supreme Court's judgment that an actual headcount of persons is the proper way to determine the apportionment of congressional districts.

A Republican president will take the lead in proposing, and fighting for, the structural changes that are long overdue in the federal government. For starters, the twenty-five-year-old congressional budget process, though it has helped to make possible today's budget surpluses, has become almost unintelligible to legislators, let alone the average citizen. It has been inadequate to enforce legislated spending caps and cannot stop the phony "emergency" bills that cause the spending caps to be exceeded. It cannot control runaway spending on entitlements and "mandatory" spending; it does not even prevent our government spending $120 billion on programs whose statutory authority has expired.

Our goal is to replace the status quo with clarity, simplicity, and accountability to the budget process. We will have a biennial budget that has the force of law. To end pork-barrel abuses on Capitol Hill, we will:

- Eliminate the "baseline budgeting" that artificially boosts spending.
- Create a constitutionally sound line-item veto for the president, and direct the savings from items vetoed to paying down the national debt.
- Prevent government shutdowns by enacting a "Permanent Continuing Resolution" so the spending lobbies can never again extort billions from the taxpayers by blocking the regular order of appropriation bills.
- Define legislatively the conditions for "emergency" spending.

Like Congress, the Executive Branch must adapt to the challenges of the new century. There are too many departments and agencies with competing programs that waste resources and fail to deliver the goods: 342 economic development programs, 788 education programs in 40 different agencies at a cost of over $100 billion a year, 163 job training programs in 15 different agencies. Twelve agencies administer over 35 food safety laws. One agency regulates pizzas with meat; another regulates vegetarian pizzas.

(Still another regulates the people who deliver them. Enough said.)

We intend to downsize this mess and make government actually do what it is supposed to, simply by ensuring that all agencies adhere to the Government Performance and Results Act, which has been neglected or ignored by the current administration. By applying its procedures to all federal programs, we can stop the loss of millions of Medicare dollars for services rendered after patients have died. We can put the brakes on an Education Department that pays out $3.3 billion on defaulted student loans, and an Energy Department that spends $10 billion on projects that are never completed. Because of its history of needless partisan litigation, we call for the Legal Services Corporation to return to its original purpose of providing legal aid to the indigent, rather than pursuing political causes and agendas. We will, as an urgent priority, restore the integrity of the nation's space program by imposing sound management and strong oversight on NASA.

A Republican president will run the federal government much as the Republican governors run state agencies. Bureaucracy will be reduced and trimmed in size at its upper echelons. If public services can be delivered more efficiently and less expensively through the private sector, they will be privatized. A Republican president will establish accountability, reward performance, put civility back into the civil service, and restore dignity and ethics to the White House.

Political Reform

The First Amendment enshrines in our Constitution and guarantees indispensable democratic freedoms of speech, press, and association, and the right to petition our government. The Republican party affirms that any regulation of the political process must not infringe upon the rights of the people to full participation in the political process. The principal cure for the ills of democracy is greater participation in the political process by more citizens. To that end, we have one guiding principle in the development of laws to regulate campaigns: Will any particular proposal encourage or restrict the energetic engagement of Americans in elections? Governor Bush's agenda for more honest and more open politics meets that standard. It will:

- Stop the abuses of corporate and labor "soft" money contributions to political parties.
- Enact "Paycheck Protection," ensuring that no union member is forced to contribute to anybody's campaign—and stopping an annual rip-off of $300 million from union families by Washington-based politicos.
- Preserve the right of every individual and all groups—whether for us or against us—to express their opinions and advocate their issues. We will not allow any arm of government to restrict this constitutionally guaranteed right.
- Level the playing field by forbidding incumbents to roll over their leftover campaign funds into a campaign for a different office.
- Require full and timely disclosure on the Internet of all campaign contributions—so the media and the public can immediately know who is giving how much to whom.
- Encourage all citizens to donate their time and resources to the campaigns of their choice by updating for inflation the quarter-century-old limits on individual contributions.
- Preserve access to the Internet for political speech and debate.

Gerrymandered congressional districts are an affront to democracy and an insult to the voters. We oppose that and any other attempt to rig the electoral process.

Common Sense in Regulation

Effective government requires regulation for health, safety, and other concerns. By the same token, regulation requires review—for efficiency, economy, and plain common sense. That Republican model of regulatory reform is a good fit for an Information Age economy. It will replace a bureaucratic mentality clicking along at a Morse-code pace. We will use the advance of science and information technology to:

- Target the most serious risks to health, safety, and the environment, then put regulatory re-

sources where they best serve the public, not politics.
- Make sound science, not ideological whim, the basis for regulation, with peer-reviewed risk assessments and full disclosure.
- Require periodic review of existing regulations, to strengthen where necessary and change where obsolete.
- Require agencies to disclose the cost to consumers and small businesses of any proposed regulations.
- Let the American people know the full price they pay for government regulations, through a new regulatory budget that explains the likely cost for meeting regulatory requirements.
- Use cost-benefit analyses of regulations to develop alternatives to the outdated command-and-control attitude of recent years.
- Retrain civil servants to work with those affected by regulation rather than dictating to them.

The current administration has repeatedly evaded the normal regulatory process through executive orders, some of dubious legality. Withdrawing these orders should be a priority of a new administration dedicated to the rule of law.

We oppose and will work to end taxpayer-supported grants for projects and programs that promote religious bigotry in America.

Judicial Reform: Courts that Work, Laws that Make Sense

Americans have the right to a judicial system they can trust. There is no question that the need for reform extends to the judicial branch of government. Many judges disregard the safety, values, and freedom of law-abiding citizens. At the expense of our children and families, they make up laws, invent new rights, free vicious criminals, and pamper felons in prison. They have arbitrarily overturned state laws enacted by citizen referenda, utterly disregarding the right of the people and the democratic process.

The sound principle of judicial review has turned into an intolerable presumption of judicial supremacy. A Republican Congress, working with a Republican president, will restore the separation of powers and reestablish a government of law. There are different ways to achieve that goal—setting terms for federal judges, for example, or using Article III of the Constitution to limit their appellate jurisdiction—but the most important factor is the appointing power of the presidency. We applaud Governor Bush's pledge to name only judges who have demonstrated that they share his conservative beliefs and respect the Constitution.

Reform of the legal profession is an essential part of court reform. Today's litigation practices make a mockery of justice, hinder our country's competitiveness in the world market and, far worse, erode the public's trust in the entire judicial process.

Avarice among many plaintiffs' lawyers has clogged our civil courts, drastically changed the practice of medicine, and costs American companies and consumers more than $150 billion a year. Who profits? On average, more than fifty cents of every dollar paid out in tort cases goes to lawyers' fees, not to an injured party. This amounts to a tax on consumers to fatten the wallets of trial lawyers.

Let's be blunt about the effects of all that cash: Our civil justice reforms have been blocked in the Capitol and vetoed in the Oval Office. It's why federal agencies have colluded with the trial lawyer lobby in sweetheart litigation, to advance through the courts what they could not accomplish through the political process. We fully support the role of the courts in vindicating the rights of individuals and organizations, but we want to require higher standards for trial lawyers within federal jurisdiction, much as Governor Bush has already done in Texas—and as we encourage other States to do within their own legal codes. To achieve that goal, we will strengthen the federal rules of civil procedure to increase penalties for frivolous suits and impose a "Three Strikes, You're Out" rule on attorneys who repeatedly file such suits. We will limit "fishing expeditions" by amending federal discovery rules, curb the use of junk science in testimony, and end the abusive use of the RICO statute. We encourage all states to consider placing caps on non-economic and punitive damages in civil

cases. We also support such caps in federal causes of action. We also encourage states to examine the effects on the democratic process of advancing policies through litigation that could not be accomplished through the political process.

We will enact a Teacher Protection Act to protect educators from meritless federal lawsuits against their efforts to maintain discipline in the classroom. We will extend similar protections to non-profit organizations—churches, civic and community groups, and the volunteers who sustain them.

To reduce health care costs and keep doctors practicing in critical areas like obstetrics, we will reform medical malpractice law on the federal level and urge decisive action on the state level as well.

To encourage settlements and to discourage prolonged litigation, a Fair Settlements Rule should be enacted requiring either party in federal court who rejects a timely, reasonable, and good faith pre-trial settlement offer, and who ultimately loses their case, to pay the other party's costs, including legal fees. We also encourage states to consider enacting such rules. To improve access to justice, we will make it easier for cases of national import to be heard in federal courts.

To protect clients against unscrupulous lawyers, we will enact a Clients' Bill of Rights for all federal courts, requiring attorneys to disclose both the range of their fees and their ethical obligation to charge reasonable fees and allowing those fees to be challenged in federal courts. Because private lawyers should not unreasonably profit at public expense, we will prohibit federal agencies from paying contingency fees and encourage states to do so as well. Even more important, we will require attorneys to return to the people any excessive fees they gain under contract to States or municipalities.

An integral part of legal reform is a federal product liability law. Without it, consumers face higher costs, needed products don't make it to the market, and American jobs are lost to foreign competitors. That, too, will change when the American people break the grip of the trial lawyers on our legal system.

Native Americans

The federal government has a special responsibility, ethical and legal, to make the American Dream accessible to Native Americans. Unfortunately, the resources that the United States holds in trust for them, financial and otherwise, have been misused and abused. While many tribes have become energetic participants in the mainstream of American life, the serious social ills afflicting some reservations have been worsened by decades of mismanagement from Washington. In its place, we offer these guiding principles:

- Tribal governments are best situated to gauge the needs of their communities and members.
- Political self-determination and economic self-sufficiency are twin pillars of an effective Indian policy.
- Private-sector initiatives, rather than public assistance, can best improve material conditions in Indian communities.
- High taxes and unreasonable regulations stifle new and expanded businesses and thwart the creation of job opportunities and prosperity.

We will strengthen Native American self-determination by respecting tribal sovereignty, encouraging economic development on reservations, and working with them to reorganize the Bureau of Indian Affairs and the Indian Health Service. We uphold the unique government-to-government relationship between the tribes and the United States and honor our nation's trust obligations to them.

We support efforts to ensure equitable participation in federal programs by Native Americans, Native Alaskans, and Native Hawaiians and to preserve their cultures and languages.

The Nation's Capital

The District of Columbia is a special responsibility of the federal government and should be a model for urban areas throughout the country. Its downhill slide has at least been arrested, both through its internal efforts and the active intervention of congressional Republicans, who have taken unprecedented steps to help the city re-cover. Their D.C. homebuyers' tax credit is helping to revitalize marginal neighborhoods; their landmark tuition assistance act has opened the doors of the nation's colleges to D.C. students.

Now, to enhance the city's economic security, reverse the movement out of the city, and ensure a safe and healthy environment for families, we advocate deep reductions in the District's taxes, currently among the highest in the nation, and encourage user-friendly development policies.

We call once again for structural reform of the city's schools so that none of its children will be left behind. We strongly support both charter schools and the opportunity scholarships for poor kids that have been repeatedly blocked by the administration.

We respect the design of the framers of the Constitution that our nation's capital has a unique status and should remain independent of any individual state.

Americans in the Territories

We welcome greater participation in all aspects of the political process by Americans residing in Guam, the Virgin Islands, American Samoa, the Northern Marianas, and Puerto Rico. Since no single approach can meet the needs of those diverse communities, we emphasize respect for their wishes regarding their relationship to the rest of the Union. We affirm their right to seek the full extension of the Constitution, with all the rights and responsibilities it entails.

We support the Native American Samoans' efforts to preserve their culture and land-tenure system, which fosters self-reliance and strong extended-family values.

We support increased local self-government for the United States citizens of the Virgin Islands, and closer cooperation between the local and federal governments to promote private-sector-led development and self-sufficiency.

We recognize that Guam is a strategically vital U.S. territory in the far western Pacific, an American fortress in the Asian region. We affirm our support for the patriotic U.S. citizens of Guam to achieve greater local self-government, an improved federal-territorial relationship, new economic development strategies, and continued self-determination as desired with respect to political status.

We support the right of the United States citizens of Puerto Rico to be admitted to the Union as a fully sovereign state after they freely so determine. We recognize that Congress has the final authority to define the constitutionally valid options for Puerto Rico to achieve a permanent status with government by consent and full enfranchisement. As long as Puerto Rico is not a State, however, the will of its people regarding their political status should be ascertained by means of a general right of referendum or specific referenda sponsored by the United States government.

PRINCIPLED AMERICAN LEADERSHIP

The duties of our day are different. But the values of our nation do not change. Let us reject the blinders of isolationism, just as we refuse the crown of empire. Let us not dominate others with our power—or betray them with our indifference. And let us have an American foreign policy that reflects American character. The modesty of true strength. The humility of real greatness. This is the strong heart of America. And this will be the spirit of my administration.

—Governor George W. Bush

The Emerging Fellowship of Freedom

The twenty-first century opens with unique promise for the United States. Democratic values are celebrated on every continent. The productivity and ingenuity of American business are the envy of the world. American innovation is leading the way in the Information Age. New technology speeds an exchange of ideas that often bear the mark of American inspiration. No other great power challenges American international preeminence. There is every reason for Americans to be extraordinarily optimistic about their future.

Few nations in history have been granted such a singular opportunity to shape the future. Even after World War II the United States had to reckon with a divided world and terrible dangers. Now America can help mold international ideals and institutions for decades to come. Handed the torch by generations that won great battles, our generation of Americans with its allies and friends can build a different and better world, promoting U.S. interests and principles, avoiding the economic convulsions and perilous conflicts that so scarred the century just past. Through a distinctly American internationalism, a new Republican president will build public support for a new strategy that can lead the United States of America toward a more peaceful and prosperous world for us, our children, and future generations.

Almost all Americans know they cannot prosper alone in the world. They know that America is safest when more and more countries share a profound belief in political and economic liberty, human dignity, and the rule of law, when more and more nations join the United States in an emerging fellowship of freedom.

That is what happened during the twelve years of Republican presidential leadership from 1981 to 1992. The Cold War ended with the triumph of freedom. The Soviet empire collapsed, and the USSR followed it into history. The proud Atlantic community welcomed a united Germany and new friends in Central and Eastern Europe. Iraq tried the law of the jungle and was routed, its aggressive power broken. The Arab-Israeli peace process was revived. Alliances and friendships in Asia were robust and successful. Mexico joined with the United States in an unprecedented new economic partnership as peace and democracy spread through Latin America. Around the globe, the word, the ideals, and the power of the United States commanded respect. The American presidency showed bright and purposeful.

In the last eight years the administration has squandered the opportunity granted to the United States by the courage and sacrifice of previous generations:

- The administration has run America's defenses down over the decade through inadequate resources, promiscuous commitments, and the absence of a forward-looking military strategy.
- The ballistic missile threat to the United States

has been persistently dismissed, delaying for years the day when America will have the capability to defend itself against this growing danger.

- The arrogance, inconsistency, and unreliability of the administration's diplomacy have undermined American alliances, alienated friends, and emboldened our adversaries.
- World trade talks in Seattle that the current administration had sponsored collapsed in spectacular failure. Authority to negotiate new fast-track trade agreements was slapped down by the administration's own party in the Congress. An initiative to establish free trade throughout the Americas has stalled because of this lack of presidential leadership.
- The problems of Mexico have been ignored, as our indispensable neighbor to the south struggled with too little American help to deal with its formidable challenges.
- The tide of democracy in Latin America has begun to ebb with a sharp rise in corruption and narco-trafficking.
- A misguided policy toward China was exemplified by President Clinton's trip to Beijing that produced an embarrassing presidential kowtow and a public insult to our longstanding ally, Japan.
- With weak and wavering policies toward Russia, the administration has diverted its gaze from corruption at the top of the Russian government, the slaughter of thousands of innocent civilians in Chechnya, and the export of dangerous Russian technologies to Iran and elsewhere.
- A chorus of empty threats destroyed America's credibility in the Balkans, so that promised safe havens became killing fields.
- The administration prolonged the war in Kosovo by publicly limiting America's military options—something no Commander-in-Chief should ever do.
- A generation of American efforts to slow proliferation of weapons of mass destruction has unraveled as first India and Pakistan set off their nuclear bombs, then Iraq defied the international community. Token air strikes against Iraq could not long mask the collapse of an inspection regime that had—until then—

at least kept an ambitious, murderous tyrant from acquiring additional nuclear, biological, and chemical weapons.

- A humanitarian intervention in Somalia was escalated thoughtlessly into nation-building at the cost of the lives of courageous Americans.
- A military intervention in Haiti displayed administration indecision and incoherence and, after billions of dollars had been spent, accomplished nothing of lasting value.

Reacting belatedly to inevitable crisis, the administration constantly enlarges the reach of its rhetoric—most recently in Vice President Gore's "new security agenda" that adds disease, climate, and all the world's ethnic or religious conflicts to an undiminished set of existing American responsibilities. If there is some limit to candidate Gore's new agenda for America as global social worker, he has had to define it.

It is time for America to regain its focus. Winston Churchill, after he had lived through other years that the "locust hath eaten," declared: "The era of procrastination, of half-measures, of soothing and baffling expedients, of delays, is coming to a close. In its place we are entering a period of consequences." As idle indulgence gives way to a new Republican president in the coming new "period of consequences," the United States can again regain the hope it lost eight years ago. We can restore our country's sense of international purpose and national honor.

A Republican president will identify and pursue vital American national interests. He will set priorities, and he will stick to them. Under his leadership, the United States will build and secure the peace. Republicans know what it takes to accomplish this: robust military forces, strong alliances, expanding trade, and resolute diplomacy.

Yet this new realism must be inspired by what we stand for as a nation. Republicans know that the American commitment to freedom is the true source of our nation's strength. That is why, for one example, congressional Republicans have made political and religious liberty a cornerstone of their approach to international affairs. That commitment is the glue that binds our great alliances. It is strong precisely because it is not just an American ideal. We propose our principles; we must not impose our culture. Yet the basic values of human freedom and dignity are universal.

A Military for the Twenty-First Century

Republicans are the party of peace through strength. A strong and well-trained American military is the world's best guarantee of peace. It is the shield of this republic's liberty, security, and prosperity. Only a president, as Commander-in-Chief of the Armed Forces, can ensure that our military stands ready to defend America and triumph against new challenges.

A Republican president and a Republican Congress will transform America's defense capabilities for the Information Age, ensuring that U.S. armed forces remain paramount against emerging dangers. They will restore the health of a defense industry weakened by a combination of neglect and misguided policies. To do all this, the United States must align its military power with the strengths of American society: our skilled people, our advanced technology, and our proficiency at integrating fast-paced systems into potent networks. While we are on the crest of a new age in military technology, we will not forget that the strength of our military lies with the combat soldier, sailor, airman, and Marine.

Americans are justly proud of their armed forces. But today, only nine years after the tremendous victory in the Persian Gulf War, the U.S. military faces growing problems in readiness, morale, and its ability to prepare for the threats of the future. The administration has cut defense spending to its lowest percentage of gross domestic product since before Pearl Harbor. At the same time, the current administration has casually sent American armed forces on dozens of missions without clear goals, realizable objectives, favorable rules of engagement, or defined exit strategies.

Over the past seven years, a shrunken American military has been run ragged by a deployment tempo that has eroded its military readiness. Many units have seen their operational requirements increased fourfold, wearing out both people and equipment. Only last fall the

Army certified two of its premier combat divisions as unready for war because of underfunding, mismanagement, and over-commitment to peacekeeping missions around the globe. More Army units and the other armed services report similar problems. It is a national scandal that almost one-quarter of our Army's active combat strength is unfit for wartime duty.

When presidents fail to make hard choices, those who serve must make them instead. Soldiers must choose whether to stay with their families or to stay in the armed forces at all. Sending our military on vague, aimless, and endless missions rapidly saps morale. Even the highest morale is eventually undermined by back-to-back deployments, poor pay, shortages of spare parts and equipment, inadequate training, and rapidly declining readiness. When it comes to military health, the administration is not providing an adequate military health care system for active-duty service members and their families and for retired service members and their dependents. The nation is failing to fulfill its ethical and legal health care obligations to those that are serving or have honorably served in the Armed Forces of the United States.

It is no surprise that the all-volunteer force—the pride of America—is struggling to recruit and retain soldiers, sailors, airmen, and Marines. As recruiting lags, well-trained personnel are leaving in record numbers. Those dedicated military personnel that stay in the force face a pay gap of some 13 percent relative to their civilian counterparts. Thousands of military families are forced to rely on food stamps. The chairman of the Joint Chiefs of Staff has said that two-thirds of the nation's military housing is substandard. The calculated indifference of the administration to national defense has forced thousands of our most experienced and patriotic warriors to leave the military. We will once again make wearing the uniform the object of national pride.

The new Republican government will renew the bond of trust between the Commander-in-Chief, the American military, and the American people. The military is not a civilian police force or a political referee. We believe the military must no longer be the object of social experiments. We affirm traditional military culture. We affirm that homosexuality is incompatible with military service.

The U.S. military under the leadership of a Republican president and a Republican Congress will focus on its most demanding task—fighting and winning in combat. Readiness prevents wars. Also, by being prepared for this most exacting mission with an uncommon sense of urgency, our military will know, unlike today, that its loyalty and self-sacrifice have meaning and purpose.

In a time of fluid change and uncertainty, intelligence is truly America's first line of defense. The current administration has weakened that defense by allowing a series of shocking security breaches, from blatant espionage and its virtual abandonment of national security-related export controls, to sheer sloppiness at the highest levels of government. This must stop, immediately. Nor should the intelligence community be made the scapegoat for political misjudgments. A Republican administration working with the Congress will respect the needs and quiet sacrifices of these public servants as it strengthens America's intelligence and counter-intelligence capabilities and reorients them toward the dangers of the future.

A Republican president will challenge America's military leaders to envision a new architecture of American defense for decades to come. Our next president will balance the need to prepare for Information Age battles while keeping our conventional fighting skills second to none. To pay for profligate deployments, the administration's defense budgets have been eating their seed corn—slashing spending on modernization to levels not seen since before the Korean War, undermining the health of our defense industry, and producing what one administration official admitted was a "death spiral" for the U.S. defense capability of the future. Even our elite combat units are scraping the bottom of the barrel to find funds for basic training.

A Republican president, working in partnership with a Republican Congress, will push beyond marginal improvements and incorporate new technologies and new strategies—spending more and investing wisely to transform our military into a true twenty-first century force. A Re-

publican government will use this time of relative American strength in the world to prepare for a different kind of future. In the twenty-first century U.S. forces must be agile, lethal, readily deployable, and require a minimum of logistical support. They must also be fully prepared for possible enemy use of weapons of mass destruction.

To build such U.S. military forces will require foresight and steadfast commitment. We must be willing to act now to give the next generation of Americans what they will need to protect our country. This will also require a new spirit of innovation. Republicans believe that our military leaders will welcome and meet these challenges. Moments of national opportunity are either seized or lost. America's opportunity beckons: to demonstrate that a new approach to U.S. defense can shape the future with new concepts, new strategies, and new resolve.

The men and women of the National Guard and Reserve are an important part of the nation's military readiness, and we will maintain their strength in the States. Their role as citizen soldiers must continue to be a proud tradition that links every community in the country with the cause of national security. The Republican Party created the all-volunteer force and opposes reinstitution of the draft, whether directly or through compulsory national service. We support the advancement of women in the military, support their exemption from ground combat units, and call for implementation of the recommendations of the Kassebaum Commission, which unanimously recommended that co-ed basic training be ended. We support restoration of sound priorities in the making of personnel policies, and candid analysis of the consequences of unprecedented social changes in the military. We will put renewed emphasis on encouraging the best and brightest of our young people to join our armed forces.

As the traditional advocate of America's veterans, the Republican Party remains committed to fulfilling America's obligations to them. That is why we defeated the administration's attempt to replace veteran's health care with a national system for everybody. It is why Congressional Republicans enacted the Veterans Employment

Opportunities Act of 1998, to thwart attempts to water down veterans' preference in federal civil service hiring and retention, and why they created the National Veterans Business Development Corporation to assist vets in becoming entrepreneurs. The same holds true for their Veterans Millennium Health Care and Benefits Act, a first step toward correcting the deficiencies in medical care for vets and ensuring a medical infrastructure that will better honor the nation's commitment to those who served. In a Republican administration, a true advocate for veterans will become Secretary of Veteran Affairs.

The maintenance and expansion of our national cemeteries is a solemn duty; a Republican administration will attend to it. Many of the programs designed to assist veterans cry out for modernization and reform. The American people cannot be content with the current unemployment rate of recently separated veterans, or with the significant number of veterans among the homeless. With a backlog of almost a half million cases, the Veterans Benefit Administration needs to be brought into the Information Age. The work of the Veterans Employment and Training Service needs a stronger focus on vocational education, and the nation as a whole must reconsider the ways restrictive licensing and certification rules prevent fully qualified vets from moving up the opportunity ladder.

Protecting the Fellowship of Freedom from Weapons of Mass Destruction

The new century will bring new threats, but America—properly led—can master them. Just as the generations of World War II and the Cold War were quick to seize the high frontier of science and craft the national defense America needed, so our country can build on its strengths and defend against unprecedented perils once again.

Ballistic missiles and weapons of mass destruction threaten the world's future. America is currently without defense against these threats. The administration's failure to guard America's nuclear secrets is allowing China to modernize its ballistic missile force, thereby increasing the threat to our country and to our allies. The theft

of vital nuclear secrets by China represents one of the greatest security defeats in the history of the United States. The next Republican president will protect our nuclear secrets and aggressively implement a sweeping reorganization of our nuclear weapons program.

Over two dozen countries have ballistic missiles today. A number of them, including North Korea, will be capable of striking the United States within a few years, and with little warning. America is now unable to counter the rampant proliferation of nuclear, biological, and chemical weapons and their missile delivery systems around the world.

The response of the current administration has been anachronistic and politicized. Stuck in the mindset and agreements of the Cold War and immune to fresh ideas, the administration has not developed a sensible strategy that responds to the emerging missile threat. They have no adequate plan for how they will defend America and its allies. Visionary leadership, not the present delay and prevarication, is urgently needed for America to be ready for the future. The new Republican president will deploy a national missile defense for reasons of national security; but he will also do so because there is a moral imperative involved: The American people deserve to be protected. It is the president's constitutional obligation.

America must deploy effective missile defenses, based on an evaluation of the best available options, including sea-based, at the earliest possible date. These defenses must be designed to protect all 50 states, America's deployed forces overseas, and our friends and allies in the fellowship of freedom against missile attacks by outlaw states or accidental launches.

The current administration at first denied the need for a national missile defense system. Then it endlessly delayed, despite constant concern expressed by the Republican Congress. Now the administration has become hopelessly entangled in its commitment by its failure to explore vigorously the technological possibilities. In order to avoid the need for any significant revisions to the ABM Treaty, the administration supports an inadequate national missile defense design based on a single site, instead of a system based on the most effective means available. Their approach does not defend America's allies, who must be consulted as U.S. plans are developed. Their concept is a symbolic political solution designed on a cynical political timetable. It will not protect America.

We will seek a negotiated change in the Anti-Ballistic Missile (ABM) Treaty that will allow the United States to use all technologies and experiments required to deploy robust missile defenses. Republicans believe that the administration should not negotiate inadequate modifications to the ABM Treaty that would leave us with a flawed agreement that ties the hands of the next president and prevents America from defending itself. The United States must be able to select the systems that will work best, not those that answer political expediency, and we must aggressively reinvigorate the ballistic missile defense technology base necessary to ensure that these systems succeed. There are today more positive, practical ways to reassure Russia that missile defenses are a search for common security, not for unilateral advantage. If Russia refuses to make the necessary changes, a Republican president will give prompt notice that the United States will exercise the right guaranteed to us in the treaty to withdraw after six months. The president has a solemn obligation to protect the American people and our allies, not to protect arms control agreements signed almost 30 years ago.

Clear thinking about defensive systems must be accompanied by a fresh strategy for offensive ones too. The Cold War logic that led to the creation of massive stockpiles of nuclear weapons on both sides is now outdated and actually enhances the danger of weapons or nuclear material falling into the hands of America's adversaries. Russia is not the great enemy. The age of vast hostile armies in the heart of Europe deterred by the threat of U.S. nuclear response is also past. American security need no longer depend on the old nuclear balance of terror. It is time to defend against the threats of today and tomorrow, not yesterday.

It is past time that the United States should reexamine the requirements of nuclear deterrence. Working with U.S. military leaders and with the Congress, a Republican president will reevaluate America's nuclear force posture and pursue the lowest possible number consistent with our national security. We can safely eliminate thousands more of these horrific weapons. We should do so. In the Cold War the United States rightfully worried about the danger of a conventional war in Europe and needed the nuclear counterweight. That made sense then. It does not make sense now. The premises of Cold War targeting should no longer dictate the size of the U.S. nuclear arsenal. The current administration seems not to realize that this notion, too, is old-think of the worst order. In addition, the United States should work with other nuclear nations to remove as many weapons as possible from high-alert, hair-trigger status—another unnecessary vestige of Cold War confrontation—to reduce the risks of accidental or unauthorized launch.

In 1991, the United States invited the Soviet Union to join it in removing tactical nuclear weapons from their arsenals. Huge reductions were achieved in a matter of months, quickly making the world much safer. Under a Republican president, Russia will again be invited to do the same with respect to strategic nuclear weapons. America should be prepared to lead by example, because it is in our best interest and the best interest of the world. These measures can begin a new global era of nuclear security and safety.

Republicans recognize new threats but also new opportunities. With Republican leadership, the United States has an opportunity to create a safer world, both to defend against nuclear threats and to reduce nuclear arsenals and tensions. America can build a robust missile defense, make dramatic reductions in its nuclear weapons, and defuse confrontation with Russia. A Republican president will do all these things.

A comprehensive strategy for combating the new dangers posed by weapons of mass destruction must include a variety of other measures to contain and prevent the spread of such weapons. We need the cooperation of friends and allies—and should seek the cooperation of Russia and China—in developing realistic strategies using political, economic, and military instruments to deter and defeat the proliferation efforts of others. We need to address threats from both rogue states and terrorist groups—whether delivered by missile, aircraft, shipping container, or suitcase.

In this context, the Comprehensive Test Ban Treaty is another anachronism of obsolete strategic thinking. This treaty is not verifiable, not enforceable, and would not enable the United States to ensure the reliability of the U.S. nuclear deterrent. It also does not deal with the real dangers of nuclear proliferation, which are rogue regimes—such as Iran, Iraq, and North Korea—that seek to hide their dangerous weapons programs behind weak international treaties. We can fight the spread of nuclear weapons, but we cannot wish them away with unwise agreements. Republicans in the Senate reacted accordingly and responsibly in rejecting the Comprehensive Test Ban Treaty.

A new Republican president will renew America's faltering fight against the contagious spread of nuclear, biological, and chemical weapons, as well as their means of delivery. The weak leadership and neglect of the administration have allowed America's intelligence capabilities, including space-based systems, to atrophy, resulting in repeated proliferation surprises such as Iraq's renewed chemical and biological weapons programs, India's nuclear weapon test, and North Korea's test of a three-stage ballistic missile. Again in a partnership with the Congress, a new Republican administration will give the intelligence community the leadership, resources, and operational latitude it requires.

Seeking Enduring Prosperity

Under Republican leadership, the United States will foster an environment of economic openness to capitalize on our country's greatest asset in the Information Age: a vital, innovative society that welcomes creative ideas and adapts to them. American companies are once more showing the world breathtaking ways to improve productivity and redraw traditional business models. This is an extraordinary foundation on which to rebuild an effective American trade policy.

Under the policies of the present administration, many markets remain closed and U.S. trade deficits keep rising. New economic structures are needed to combine regional agreements with the development of global rules for opening the world economy. Collaborating with the Congress, a Republican administration will engage the Latin American and the Asia-Pacific nations, including a new dialogue with India, about political economy and free trade. As impoverished countries in Eurasia, the Middle East, and Africa accept freer economies, they will need the incentives of more open world markets. In addition, the United States can encourage the European Union and our Asian friends and allies to open more sectors to cross-investment and competition with the aim of freer trans-oceanic trade.

Republicans are confident that the worldwide trade agenda is full of promise. From the traditional goods of agriculture to the virtual links of e-commerce, gates can swing open. Tariffs should be cut further. The United States can back private-sector efforts to streamline common standards and deregulate services, from finance to filmmaking. As the one economy with truly global reach, America can set the standards and be at the center of a worldwide web of trade, finance, and openness. If some nations choose to opt out, they will see how other countries accepting economic freedom will advance on their own, working together.

This is the Republican approach, and a critical dimension of a distinctly American internationalism. It goes beyond the old choice of private-sector laissez-faire versus government regulation. Instead it is a vision of private initiative encouraged, not stifled, by governments. Private parties are already fashioning new ways to exchange goods and settle disputes, but national governments still struggle to define many of the underlying rules. Republicans will also go beyond the old arguments that pitted bilateral deals against global trade rules. Instead they envision a comprehensive approach to the more interdependent global economy, one that uses bilateral, regional, and global arrangements to spur reluctant states to become more open or to be left behind. At the same time, innovative and flexible global rules and structures can facilitate regional progress.

Rooted in America's political and economic

ideals, this Republican blueprint promotes open markets and open societies, free trade and the free flow of information, and the development of new ideas and private sectors. These nurture the human spirit, the middle class, law, and liberty.

As the Cold War ended, Republican presidents fought off protectionist pressure, eased the debt crisis then facing developing countries, signed the North American Free Trade Agreement (NAFTA), and started to enlarge free trade arrangements throughout the Western Hemisphere. They promoted the Asia-Pacific Economic Cooperation (APEC) group that could bind economic interests across the Pacific. They then used these regional initiatives to bring the global trade talks of the Uruguay Round to the edge of conclusion. Thus America began to build on victory in the Cold War to build new structures for economic liberty as well.

For nearly eight years this promising construction project has languished half-built, the old blueprint shelved and no new ones drawn.

- The administration returned to the old rhetoric of managed trade—demanding government intervention from a Japanese government that needed less regulation in its sputtering economy, not more. On the verge of a foolish trade war, the administration backed down and dropped its quota demands.
- After failing for years to make the case for free trade, the administration finally got around to seeking fast-track trade negotiating authority, but could persuade only one-fifth of Democratic members of Congress to follow its lead.
- With China, the administration sought to link normal trade relations to human rights performance. Then it flip-flopped and dropped the linkage. They tried to bring China into the World Trade Organization as the prime minister of China visited the United States in 1999, but the political waters got choppy. So the administration reversed course again. Finally the administration turned to Republican leadership in the Congress to enact permanent normal trade relations with China.
- The administration refused to fight for passage of the Caribbean Basin Initiative that was designed to extend the benefits of free trade to some of America's poorest neighbors. Congressional Republicans did the job on their own. They also enacted the Africa Growth and Opportunity Act as a companion to CBI.
- The failed leadership of the administration in international economics is exemplified by the humiliating debacle of the WTO meeting in Seattle—a conference the current administration first sponsored and then wrecked through its own indecision and inconsistency.

Republicans know that prosperous democracies depend upon the promise of shared economic opportunity across national borders. If the new globalized information economy provokes a fearful drift into national or regional isolation, hopes for a better world will vanish. Institutions founded in the Second World War and its aftermath built the basis for America's position today, but those institutions, like the Bretton Woods monetary system and the General Agreement on Tariffs and Trade, were partly sustained by the Cold War. In this new century, the United States should devise new mechanisms to enable the private sector to unleash productivity, innovation, and a free flow of ideas.

Communities of private groups can achieve results far beyond the reach of governments and international bureaucracies. Given America's strong and diverse private sector, the United States, with close cooperation between a Republican president and a Republican Congress, can gain from the widening global influence of American citizens, businesses, associations, and norms. A Republican administration will have the opportunity to fashion, with like-minded nations, the international structures of sustainable prosperity for the next several decades.

The older international financial institutions should be overhauled but not scrapped. The International Monetary Fund and the World Bank should no longer stand for unelected elites imposing their often-flawed solutions to tough problems by offering bailouts of corrupt officials and risk-taking investors. The IMF should concentrate on its original mission of promoting sound fiscal and monetary policies, advancing sound central banking practices, and easing global exchange rate adjustments. It should improve transparency and accountability, tackling corruption rather than contributing to it. The World Bank should continue to move away from counterproductive development schemes of the past to an agenda that promotes the provision of basic needs. This agenda will include support for structural reforms that will encourage self-help through efficient markets.

The United States should aggressively pursue its national interest. Unlike the current administration, Republicans do not believe multilateral agreements and international institutions are ends in themselves. The Kyoto treaty to address momentous energy and environmental issues was a case in point. Whatever the theories on global warming, a treaty that does not include China and exempts "developing" countries from necessary standards while penalizing American industry is not in the national interest. We reject the extremist call for the United Nations to create a "Stewardship Council," modeled on the Security Council, to oversee the global environment. Republicans understand that workable agreements will build on the free democratic processes of national governments, not try to bypass them with international bureaucrats.

Unlike the Democratic minority in Congress, Republicans do not believe that economic growth is always the enemy of protecting the world's common environmental heritage. Rather, the Republican vision seeks more creative international solutions. These solutions should use market mechanisms to allocate the costs of adjustment, help governments competently manage the resources they do control, and encourage application of the new technologies that offer the greatest promise to protect the global environment.

Neighborhood of the Americas

Latin America and Canada have helped shape the United States and its people. The countries of the Western Hemisphere are our neighbors. For tens of millions of Americans these neighbors are also our relatives. Latin America buys more than one-fifth of U.S. exports, while Canada is America's largest trading partner. These purchases by our Latin American neighbors are

rising at a rate almost twice as fast as the rate for the rest of the world. In the next decade, U.S. trade and investment in the Western Hemisphere are projected to exceed our trade and investment with either Europe or Japan. Future prospects for America's neighborhood are extraordinarily bright.

Secure in its strength and its principles, the United States wants strong, healthy neighbors. The next American century should include all of the Americas. Democracy and free markets are again under siege from narcotics traffickers, guerrillas, economic uncertainty, and demographic upheaval. Poverty, inadequate education, rampant crime, and corruption all tear at the fabric of several of these societies. In Peru, Ecuador, Colombia, Venezuela, and other countries, democracy is faltering or under serious attack.

The next Republican president will pay serious and sustained attention to the American neighborhood. In concert with the Congress, he will work with key democracies like Argentina, Brazil, Chile, and—above all—Mexico. His administration will be guided by the principles of respect for sovereignty, private initiative, multilateral action, free politics and markets, the rule of law, and regard for the variety of peoples and cultures that make up the Western Hemisphere.

With Mexico, whose historic recent election we salute, the United States should continue to reduce barriers to trade and investment, including the implementation of existing commitments where the current administration has backtracked. Yet a true North American community should have a wider agenda that also includes the development of civil society. Our two countries can share ideas for improving education and public services on both sides of the border and using the federal system in both countries to promote governmental cooperation between honest officials who are close to their people.

A new Republican government committed to NAFTA can enlarge it into a vision for hemispheric free trade, drawing nations closer in business, common commercial standards, dispute resolution, and education. Republicans do not want to create new trading blocs to battle rivals. They mean to encourage general political and economic reform, starting with the American neighborhood.

In Cuba, Fidel Castro continues to impose communist economic controls and absolute political repression of 11 million Cubans. His regime harasses and jails dissidents, restricts economic activity, and forces Cubans into the sea in a desperate bid for freedom. He gives refuge to fugitives from American justice, hosts a sophisticated Russian espionage facility that intercepts U.S. government and private communications, and has ordered his air force to shoot down two unarmed U.S. civilian airplanes thereby killing American citizens.

U.S. policy toward Cuba should be based upon sound, clear principles. Our economic and political relations will change when the Cuban regime frees all prisoners of conscience, legalizes peaceful protest, allows opposition political activity, permits free expression, and commits to democratic elections. This policy will be strengthened by active American support for Cuban dissidents. Under no circumstances should Republicans support any subsidy of Castro's Cuba or any other terrorist state.

Republicans also support a continued effort to promote freedom and democracy by communicating objective and uncensored news and information to the Cuban people via U.S. broadcasts to the captive island. Finally, Republicans believe that the United States should adhere to the principles established by the 1966 Cuban Adjustment Act, which recognizes the rights of Cuban refugees fleeing communist tyranny.

Across the Pacific

As in every region of the world, America's foreign policy in Asia starts with its allies: Japan, the Republic of Korea, Australia, Thailand, and the Philippines. Our allies are critical in building and expanding peace, security, democracy, and prosperity in East Asia joined by longstanding American friends like Singapore, Indonesia, Taiwan, and New Zealand.

Republican priorities in the next administration will be clear. We will strengthen our alliance with Japan. We will help to deter aggression on the Korean peninsula. We will counter the regional proliferation of weapons of mass destruction and their delivery systems and deploy, in cooperation with our allies, effective theater missile defenses. We will promote peace in the Taiwan Strait. We will reconstitute our relations with the nations of Southeast Asia. We will obtain the fullest possible accounting for our POW/MIAs from the Pacific wars. And we will promote democracy, open markets, and human rights for the betterment of the people of Asia and the United States.

Japan is a key partner of the United States, and the U.S.–Japan alliance is an important foundation of peace, stability, security, and prosperity in Asia. America supports an economically vibrant and open Japan that can serve as engine of expanding prosperity and trade in the Asia-Pacific region.

The Republic of Korea is a valued democratic ally of the United States. North Korea, on the other hand, lies outside of the international system. Americans have shed their blood to stop North Korean aggression before. Fifty years after the outbreak of the Korean War, Republicans remember this "forgotten war." Americans should honor the sacrifices of the past and remain prepared to resist aggression today. Policies to protect the peace on the Korean peninsula will be developed in concert with America's allies, starting with South Korea and Japan. What must be clear is an American policy of decisive resolve. The United States will stand by its commitments and will take all necessary measures to thwart, deter, and defend itself and its allies against attack, including enemy use of weapons of mass destruction.

After fighting together in both world wars, the United States forged a formal alliance with Australia that has stood the test of fire in the Korean, Vietnam, and Persian Gulf conflicts. American partnership with Australia is just as relevant to the challenges of Asia's future, as exemplified by Australia's leadership in the East Timor crisis.

American ties to the Philippines have been close for more than 100 years. We Republicans have supported the victory of Filipino democracy and cherish our continuing friendship with this great nation and its people who have been by our side in war as in peace.

America's key challenge in Asia is the People's Republic of China. China is not a free society. The Chinese government represses political expression at home and unsettles neighbors abroad. It stifles freedom of religion and proliferates weapons of mass destruction.

Yet China is a country in transition, all the more reason for the policies of the United States to be firm and steady. America will welcome the advent of a free and prosperous China. Conflict is not inevitable, and the United States offers no threat to China. Republicans support China's accession into the World Trade Organization, but this will not be a substitute for, or lessen the resolve of, our pursuit of improved human rights and an end to proliferation of dangerous technologies by China.

China is a strategic competitor of the United States, not a strategic partner. We will deal with China without ill will—but also without illusions. A new Republican government will understand the importance of China but not place China at the center of its Asia policy.

A Republican president will honor our promises to the people of Taiwan, a longstanding friend of the United States and a genuine democracy. Only months ago the people of Taiwan chose a new president in free and fair elections. Taiwan deserves America's strong support, including the timely sale of defensive arms to enhance Taiwan's security.

In recognition of its growing importance in the global economy, we support Taiwan's accession to the World Trade Organization, as well as its participation in the World Health Organization and other multilateral institutions.

America has acknowledged the view that there is one China. Our policy is based on the principle that there must be no use of force by China against Taiwan. We deny the right of Beijing to impose its rule on the free Taiwanese people. All issues regarding Taiwan's future must be resolved peacefully and must be agreeable to the people of Taiwan. If China violates these principles and attacks Taiwan, then the United States will respond appropriately in accordance with the Taiwan Relations Act. America will help Taiwan defend itself.

This country's relations with Vietnam are still overshadowed by two grave concerns. The first is uncertainty concerning the Americans who became prisoners of war or were missing in action. A Republican president will accelerate efforts in every honorable way to obtain the fullest possible accounting for those still missing and for the repatriation of the remains of those who died in the cause of freedom. The second is continued retribution by the government of Vietnam against its ethnic minorities and others who fought alongside our forces there. The United States owes those individuals a debt of honor and will not be blind to their suffering.

Attention to the fate of East Asia should not obscure American attention to the future of South Asia. India is emerging as one of the great democracies of the twenty-first century. Soon it will be the world's most populous state. India is now redefining its identity and future strategy. The United States should engage India, respecting its great multicultural achievements and encouraging Indian choices for a more open world. Mindful of its longstanding relationship with Pakistan, the United States will place a priority on the secure, stable development of this volatile region where adversaries now face each other with nuclear arsenals.

The Republican Party is committed to democracy in Burma, and to Nobel Laureate Aung San Suu Kyi and other democratic leaders whose election in 1990 was brutally suppressed and who have been arrested and imprisoned for their belief in freedom and democracy. We share with her the view that the basic principles of human freedom and dignity are universal. We are committed to working with our allies in Europe and Asia to maintain a firm and resolute opposition to the military junta in Rangoon.

Because of the strategic location and historical ties of the Pacific island nations to the United States, the next Republican administration will work closely with the countries of this region on a wide variety of issues of common concern.

Europe

As a result of the courageous and resolute leadership of Presidents Reagan and Bush, the Cold War has been won, Germany unified and, with the leadership of a Republican Senate, Poland, the Czech Republic, and Hungary returned to the Euro-Atlantic community. The security of the United States is inseparable from the security of Europe. Now in its second half-century, a strong NATO is the foundation of peace. Sustained American commitment to the security of Europe has paid off. Our allies across the Atlantic face no conventional external threats. American military deployments are a fraction of their Cold War size. But alliances are not just for crises. They are sustained by the kind of joint planning, political and economic as well as military, that defines and reinforces common interests and mutual trust.

Standing alongside our allies, we seek a NATO that is strong, cohesive, and active. The next Republican president will give consistent direction on the alliance's purpose, on Europe's need to invest more in defense capabilities, and, when necessary, on acting jointly with the United States in military conflict. The United States needs its European allies to help with key regional security problems as they arise, since America also has global responsibilities. Our goal for NATO is a strong political and security fellowship of independent nations in which consultations are mutually respected and defense burdens mutually shared.

For our allies, sharing the enormous opportunities of Eurasia also means sharing the burdens and risks of sustaining the peace. We seek greater cooperation within NATO to deal with the geopolitical problems of the Middle East and Eurasia. We will work with our European partners as we develop our plans to build effective missile defenses that can protect all of America's allies.

Republicans believe that the political objectives of Europe and America are mutually reinforcing and complementary. The next Republican president will ensure that the relationship between NATO and the European Union, particularly in the division of military responsibilities, is clear and constructive. The leaders of the European Union must resist the temptation of protectionism as we work together to build a Europe whole and free.

We are proud that America's longstanding commitment to the forward defense of democracy is being rewarded as Europe becomes whole and free. In the new era that resulted, some of America's strongest allies and friends have been the democracies of Central and Eastern Europe. In their recent histories, these nations have shown their commitment to the values shared by members of the Trans-Atlantic community. Poles, Czechs, and Hungarians inspired the world, assaulting the Iron Curtain again and again until finally it crashed down forever.

As the new democracies of Central Europe chose freedom, America was ready to respond. Republicans made the enlargement of NATO part of our Contract with America. Their firm stand before the American people and in the Congress finally succeeded in bringing Poland, the Czech Republic, and Hungary into the North Atlantic Alliance. Republicans recognize and applaud the tremendous achievements of the people of Albania, Bulgaria, Estonia, Lithuania, Latvia, Macedonia, Romania, Slovakia, and Slovenia in reclaiming their freedom and rejoining the Trans-Atlantic community of democracies.

It is in America's interest that the new European democracies become fully integrated into the economic, political, and security institutions of the Trans-Atlantic community. These countries are today making great progress toward developing the market economies and democratic political systems that are the best way to ensure both their long-term stability and their security. The enlargement of NATO to include other nations with democratic values, pluralist political systems, and free market economies should continue. Neither geographical nor historical circumstances shall dictate the future of a Europe whole and free. Russia must never be given a veto over enlargement.

The Republican Party has long been the advocate of independence for the people of Lithuania, Latvia, and Estonia, even when others despaired of their emergence from foreign rule. We reaffirm our traditional ties with and strong support for the courageous Ukrainian and Armenian people, who like the people of the Baltic States, have endured both persecution and tyranny to reassert their ancient nationhood. The United States should promote reconciliation and friendship not only between the United States and Russia, but also between Russia and its neighbors.

The current administration has damaged the NATO alliance with years of insensitivity and episodic attention. In the Yugoslav war the administration bungled the diplomacy, misjudged the adversary, and ignored the advice of our military commanders. Even after NATO's operations in Bosnia and Kosovo laid bare Europe's lagging military capabilities, the administration failed to persuade the allies to enhance these capabilities. The next Republican administration will work to repair this damage.

After the many trials and errors of the current administration, the United States is contributing to NATO's peacekeeping efforts in Bosnia-Herzegovina and Kosovo. Those troops cannot stay indefinitely without jeopardizing the American ability to defend other important U.S. and allied interests. Over time European troops should take the place of American forces under the NATO umbrella as the United States and its allies work together to bring peace and democracy to the Balkans. The next Republican president will not negotiate with indicted war criminals such as Slobodan Milosevic but will seek their arrest, trial, and imprisonment.

Russia stands as another reminder that a world increasingly at peace is also a world in transition. If Russia can realize the enormous potential of its people and abundant resources, it can achieve the greatness that is currently defined solely by the reach of its weapons. Russia has the potential to be a great power and should be treated as such. With Russia, the United States needs patience, consistency, and a principled reliance on democratic forces.

America's own national security is the first order of business with Russia. The United States and Russia share critical common interests. Both Russia and the United States confront the legacy of a dead ideological rivalry—thousands of nuclear weapons, which, in the case of Russia, may not be entirely secure. And together we also face an emerging threat—from rogue nations, nuclear theft, and accidental launch. For its own sake and ours, Russia must stop encouraging the proliferation of weapons of mass destruction.

The development of a democratic and stable Russia is in the interest of the United States and all of Europe. But the battle for democracy is a fight that must be won by Russians. We must avoid misguided attempts to remake Russia from the outside. The current administration's quixotic efforts have only propped up corrupt elites, identified America with discredited factions and failed policies, and encouraged anti-Americanism.

The United States should show its concern about Russia's future by focusing on the structures, spirit, and reality of democracy in Russia, embodied by the rule of law. We will do this by directing our aid and attention to help the Russian people, not enriching the bank accounts of corrupt officials.

The rule of law is not consistent with state-sponsored brutality. When the Russian government attacks civilians in Chechnya—killing innocents without discrimination or accountability, neglecting orphans and refugees—it can no longer expect aid from international lending institutions. Moscow needs to operate with civilized self-restraint.

Russia should also display such self-restraint in its shipments of sensitive nuclear and military technology to Iran. As long as Iran remains an international outlaw, preventing such transfers must be a priority for U.S. policy. Americans stand ready to cooperate with Russia in sharing technology for missile defense that can promote a more stable world, but Russia must also choose lasting stability over transitory profit and support the effort against proliferation.

Republicans welcome the historic reconciliation in Northern Ireland that is slowly bringing peace and a representative local assembly to this beautiful land that means so much to Americans. We congratulate the people of Northern Ireland for their approval of the Good Friday Agreement, and we call for the full and fastest possible implementation of its terms. In the spirit of that healing document, we call for a review of issues of deportation and extradition arising prior to the accord. We applaud the work of the Pattern Commission to reform the police authorities in Northern Ireland and urge complete implementation of the Commission's recommendations.

The sufferings of the people on the island of Ireland have been our sorrow too, and the new hope for peace and reconciliation is the answer to America's prayers. We continue to support this progress toward peace with justice and, accordingly, we encourage private U.S. investment in the North, with care to ensure fair employment and better opportunities for all. Though the burdens of history weigh heavily upon this land, we cheer its people for taking the lead in building for themselves and for their children a future of peace and understanding. The next president will use the prestige and influence of the United States to help the parties achieve a lasting peace. If necessary, he will appoint a special envoy to help facilitate the search for lasting peace, justice, and reconciliation.

We likewise encourage a peaceful settlement for Cyprus and respect by all parties for the wishes of the Cypriot people. A fair and lasting Cyprus settlement will benefit the people of Cyprus, as well as serve the interests of America and our allies, Greece and Turkey.

The Middle East and Persian Gulf

In the Middle East, the advancement of U.S. national interests requires clear and consistent priorities as well as close cooperation with America's friends and allies. We have four priorities for the Middle East. First, we seek to promote and maintain peace throughout the region. Second, we must ensure that Israel remains safe and secure. Third, we must protect our economic interests and ensure the reliable flow of oil from the Persian Gulf. And fourth, we must reduce the threat of weapons of mass destruction in the region. Because America cannot achieve these objectives by acting alone, U.S. policy must rest on leadership that can build strong coalitions of like-minded states and hold them together to achieve common aims.

As American influence declined during the current administration, the OPEC cartel drove up the price of oil. Anti-Americanism among the Arab people redoubled. Iran continued to sponsor international terrorism, oppose the Arab-Israeli peace process, and pursue nuclear, biological, chemical, and missile capabilities with extensive foreign assistance. America's closest allies expanded their political and economic relations with Iran. A Republican president will work to reverse these damaging trends.

It is important for the United States to support and honor Israel, the only true democracy in the Middle East. We will ensure that Israel maintains a qualitative edge in defensive technology over any potential adversaries. We will not pick sides in Israeli elections. The United States has a moral and legal obligation to maintain its embassy and ambassador in Jerusalem. Immediately upon taking office, the next Republican president will begin the process of moving the U.S. Embassy from Tel Aviv to Israel's capital, Jerusalem.

The United States seeks a comprehensive and lasting peace in the Middle East. America can use its prestige to encourage discussions and negotiations. But peace must be negotiated between the parties themselves. We will not impose our view or an artificial timetable. At the heart of the peace process is the commitment to resolve all issues through negotiation. A unilateral declaration of independence by the Palestinians would be a violation of that commitment. A new Republican administration would oppose any such declaration. It will also do everything possible to promote the conclusion of a genuine peace in the Middle East. While we have hopes for the peace process, our commitment to the security of Israel is an overriding moral and strategic concern.

Perhaps nowhere has the inheritance of Republican governance been squandered so fatefully as with respect to Iraq. The anti-Iraq coalition assembled to oppose Saddam Hussein has disintegrated. The administration has pretended to support the removal of Saddam Hussein from power, but did nothing when Saddam Hussein's army smashed the democratic opposition in northern Iraq in August 1996. The administration also surrendered the diplomatic initiative to Iraq and Iraq's friends, and failed to champion the international inspectors charged with erasing Iraq's nuclear, biological, chemical, and ballistic missile programs. When, in late 1998, the administration decided to take military action, it did too little too late. Because of the administration's failures there is no coalition, no peace, and no effective inspection regime to prevent Saddam's development of weapons of mass destruction.

A new Republican administration will patiently rebuild an international coalition opposed to Saddam Hussein and committed to joint action. We will insist that Iraq comply fully with its disarmament commitments. We will maintain the sanctions on the Iraqi regime while seeking to alleviate the suffering of innocent Iraqi people. We will react forcefully and unequivocally to any evidence of reconstituted Iraqi capabilities for producing weapons of mass destruction. In 1998, Congress passed and the president signed the Iraq Liberation Act, the clear purpose of which is to assist the opposition to Saddam Hussein. The administration has used an arsenal of dilatory tactics to block any serious support to the Iraqi National Congress, an umbrella organization reflecting a broad and representative group of Iraqis who wish to free their country from the scourge of Saddam Hussein's regime. We support the full implementation of the Iraq Liberation Act, which should be regarded as a starting point in a comprehensive plan for the removal of Saddam Hussein and the restoration of international inspections in collaboration with his successor. Republicans recognize that peace and stability in the Persian Gulf is impossible as long as Saddam Hussein rules Iraq.

All Americans hope that a new generation of Iranian leaders will rise to power seeking friendlier relations with the United States and a less threatening posture in the region. But Iran's record of supporting terrorism, opposing the Middle East process, developing weapons of mass destruction and long-range missiles, and its denial of human rights, most recently demonstrated in the trial and conviction of Iranian Jews on unfounded espionage charges, demonstrates that Teheran remains a dangerous threat to the United States and our interests in the region. The next Republican administration will form its policy toward Iran based on Iranian actions, not words. It will stop making unilateral gestures toward the Iranian government which, to date, have failed to result in a change in Iranian behavior. We will work to convince our friends and allies, most importantly the Europeans, to join us in a firm, common approach toward Iran.

Republicans endorse continued assistance and support for countries that have made peace with Israel—led by Egypt and Jordan. We appreciate the significant contributions by Jordan to our common struggle against terrorism, and will take steps to bolster relations with Amman, including negotiating a U.S.–Jordan Free Trade Agreement.

The United States and its allies depend on oil from the Middle East. Republicans prefer an America that is far less dependent on foreign crude oil. A Republican president will not be so tolerant if OPEC colludes to drive up the world price of oil, as it has done this past year. Yet influence also comes from friendship. The United States should restore its underlying good and cooperative relations with the oil-exporting nations, most importantly Saudi Arabia, as well as with other moderate Arab governments.

Africa

The nations of Africa have endured tremendous burdens of war, poverty, disease, and bad government. But freedom is gaining ground in South Africa, Nigeria, Niger, Mozambique, and Mauritius. Democracy can help ensure that the interests of the people are elevated above the preoccupations and self-enrichment of corrupt elites.

Some of Africa's developing countries are turning to private markets, building middle classes, and evolving toward more representative forms of government that respect individual liberties. But such transformation is not simple. A Republican president and Congress will work to encourage these efforts through closer economic integration, security assistance, and support for freedom. Republicans will replace process with outcome and rhetoric with substance.

Americans are troubled by the humanitarian catastrophes that have plagued the people of Africa including conflicts in Sierra Leone, the Great Lakes region, the Horn of Africa, and elsewhere. The risk of famine is never far away. Millions live in poverty and suffer from disease, especially AIDS and the vaccine-preventable diseases that prey on innocent children. The situation in the Sudan demands special attention, due to its employment of the slave trade and its persecution of Sudanese Christians, and we deplore the government of Zimbabwe's refusal to adhere to the rule of law. The conflict in Angola should be resolved through dialogue leading to the release of political prisoners and democratic government.

The people of Africa need economic opportunity, foreign investment, and access to markets, food, and medicine. The United States will support international organizations and non-governmental organizations that can improve the daily lives of Africans. The United States must also work to promote democracy and sound governance in Africa, and the prevention and resolution of conflict. We will help the continent achieve its economic potential by implementing measures to reduce trade barriers. Republicans will not ignore the challenges of Africa.

International Assistance

The promotion of freedom and democracy is a critical national interest. President Reagan was a champion of this idea, establishing the National Endowment for Democracy in 1983 as an instrument of U.S. public diplomacy. The National Endowment for Democracy, and other American public diplomacy institutions, continues today to advance and protect American ideals and interests abroad.

The United States must commit itself to doing more to assist refugees and displaced persons. A Republican administration will improve America's longstanding practice of aiding the innocent victims of political repression, conflict, famine, and natural disasters, and we will lead other countries in responding similarly.

Republicans fully recognize that the spread of AIDS is a terrible humanitarian disaster and will continue to emphasize action over rhetoric. In particular, we commend the Republican Congress for recently approving legislation to assist the victims of this disease in Africa.

The United Nations

International organizations can serve the cause of peace, but they can never serve as a substitute for, or exercise a veto over, principled American leadership. The United Nations was not de-signed to summon or lead armies in the field and, as a matter of U.S. sovereignty, American troops must never serve under United Nations command. Nor will they be subject to the jurisdiction of an International Criminal Court. The United Nations can provide a valuable forum for nations to peacefully resolve their differences, and it can help monitor international agreements and organize international humanitarian assistance. The United States will pay a fair, not disproportionate, share of dues to the United Nations once it has reformed its management and taken steps to eliminate waste, fraud, and abuse. All funds that the U.S. contributes for operations, conferences, and peacekeeping should count against these dues.

The next Republican administration will use its diplomatic influence to put an end to a pattern of discrimination that persists at the United Nations in denying committee assignments to Israel. It will do the likewise at the International Red Cross, which refuses to accredit the symbol of Magen David Adom, Israel's equivalent of the Red Cross. Moreover, Republicans oppose the ideological campaign against participation by the Vatican in U.N. conferences and other activities. The United Nations was created to benefit all peoples and nations, not to promote a radical agenda of social engineering. Any effort to address global social problems must be firmly placed into a context of respect for the fundamental social institutions of marriage and family. We reject any treaty or convention that would contradict these values. For that reason, we will protect the rights of families in international programs and will not fund organizations involved in abortion. This approach to foreign assistance will unify people, respect their diverse beliefs, and uphold basic human rights. It will enable us, in cooperation with other free societies around the world, to more effectively oppose religious persecution and the sex trafficking that ruins the lives of women and children.

Terrorism, International Crime, and Cyber Threats

America faces a new and rapidly evolving threat from terrorism and international crime. Meeting this threat requires not just new measures, but also consistent policies and determination from America's leaders.

Many established terrorist groups faded away in the 1990s after the Cold War ended. But the decade also witnessed a series of enormously destructive attacks against America. Increasingly, terrorists seem to be motivated by amorphous religious causes or simple hatred of America rather than by specific political aims. Terrorism crosses borders easily and frequently, including U.S. borders, and cannot easily be categorized as either domestic or international.

Republicans support a response to terrorism that is resolute but not impulsive. The most likely highly destructive terrorist attack remains a large bomb hidden in a car or truck. Yet, as with the rest of our defense posture, we must prepare for the most dangerous threats as well as the most likely ones. Therefore the United States must be extremely vigilant about the possibility that future terrorists might use weapons of mass destruction, which are increasingly available and present an unprecedented threat to America. In many instances the military will have to rethink its traditional doctrine and begin to focus on counterterrorism, human intelligence gathering, and unconventional warfare.

Republicans endorse the four principles of U.S. counterterrorism policy that were laid down originally by Vice President George Bush's Commission on Combating Terrorism in 1985. First, we will make no concessions to terrorists. Giving in simply encourages future terrorist actions and debases America's power and moral authority. Second, we will isolate, pressure, and punish the state sponsors of terrorism. Third, we will bring individual terrorists to justice. Past and potential terrorists will know that America will never stop hunting them. Fourth, we will provide assistance to other governments combating terrorism. Fighting international terrorism requires international collaboration. Once again, allies matter.

Republicans in Congress have led the way in building the domestic preparedness programs to train and equip local, state, and federal response personnel to deal with terrorist dangers in America. The administration has not offered clear leadership over these programs. They remain scattered across many agencies, uncoordinated, and poorly managed. We will streamline and improve the federal coordination of the domestic emergency preparedness programs.

We will ensure that federal law enforcement agencies have every lawful resource and authority they require to combat international organized crime. A Republican administration will work to improve international cooperation against all forms of cross-border criminality, especially the burgeoning threat of cyber-crime that threatens the vitality of American industries as diverse as aerospace and entertainment.

Nowhere has the administration been more timid in protecting America's national interests than in cyberspace. Americans have recently glimpsed the full vulnerability of their information systems to penetration and massive disruption by amateurs. A sophisticated terrorist or adversary government could potentially cripple a critical U.S. infrastructure, such as the electrical grid or a military logistics system, in time of crisis. A new Republican government will work closely with our international partners and the private sector to conceive and implement a viable strategy for reducing America's vulnerability to the spectrum of cyber threats, from the adolescent hacker launching a contagious computer virus to the most advanced threat of strategic information warfare.

Principled American Leadership

Americans have good reason to be optimistic about our role in the world. Few nations in history have been afforded the range of possibilities to shape the future that has been presented to this generation of Americans. After the wavering and ambivalence of the current administration, Americans have a fresh chance to build on the enormous opportunities of this new era and new century. Earlier generations defended America through great trials. This generation can adapt America to thrive amid great change—change in economies, societies, technologies, and weapons.

Republicans have a strategy. It is a strategy that recalls traditional truths about power and ideals and applies them to networked marketplaces, modern diplomacy, and the high-tech battlefield. A Republican administration will use power wisely, set priorities, craft needed institutions of openness and freedom, and invest in the future. A Republican president and a Republican Congress can achieve the unity of national governance that has so long been absent. We see a confident America united in the fellowship of freedom with friends and allies throughout the world. We envision the restoration of a respected American leadership firmly grounded in a distinctly American internationalism.

PART X

IMPEACHMENT OF PRESIDENT CLINTON

IMPEACHMENT OF PRESIDENT CLINTON

In 1994, a year into Bill Clinton's presidency (1993–2001), questions surrounding Bill and Hillary Clinton's involvement in Whitewater, a failed Arkansas real estate venture in which the Clintons had invested, intensified. As a result, President Clinton asked Attorney General Janet Reno to designate a special counsel to investigate the matter. Reno appointed Robert Fiske, a moderate Republican. A federal court later determined that Fiske, having been appointed by Clinton's attorney general, was not entirely independent. Thus, federal judges replaced Fiske with Kenneth Starr, a former federal judge and Republican solicitor general. The independent counsel's original mission was to determine if the Clintons had acted illegally in the Whitewater deal. However, the investigation quickly grew to include many other issues involving the Clintons, including the president's alleged sexual involvement with Monica Lewinsky, a young intern at the White House in 1995.

Allegations surrounding Clinton's affair with Lewinsky surfaced as a result of a separate sexual harassment lawsuit filed by Paula Jones. Jones, a former Arkansas state employee, claimed that Clinton had made an unwanted sexual advance to her in a Little Rock hotel room in 1991 when he was governor of Arkansas. Although the lawsuit would eventually be settled for $850,000, in 1997 Clinton was ordered to give a deposition in the Jones case. Before the deposition, meanwhile, Jones's lawyers obtained information from Linda Tripp, a former White House employee, that Clinton was having an affair with Lewinsky. Tripp, who befriended Lewinsky when the two worked together at the Pentagon in 1996, secretly taped hours of telephone conversations in which Lewinsky divulged to Tripp the details of her relationship with the president. In December 1997, Paula Jones's lawyers subpoenaed Lewinsky, and in January 1998, Lewinsky filed an affidavit in which she denied having a sexual relationship with the president.

Soon after, however, Linda Tripp contacted Independent Counsel Kenneth Starr's office to turn over her taped conversations with Lewinsky. In the recorded conversations, Lewinsky indicated that Clinton and his close friend and adviser Vernon Jordan encouraged Lewinsky to be evasive about her relationship with the president when responding to questions in the Jones case. After receiving the tapes from Tripp, Starr sought approval from the attorney general to widen his inquiry, asserting that if Monica Lewinsky's claims were true, Clinton's actions constituted obstruction of justice. A panel of federal judges agreed to allow Starr formally to investigate Clinton.

Meanwhile, on January 17, 1998, President Clinton gave his deposition in the Jones lawsuit and denied ever having had a sexual relationship with Lewinsky. Starr's grand jury investigation focused on whether Clinton perjured himself in the Jones deposition when he denied the affair with Lewinsky, whether he attempted to obstruct justice by telling Lewinsky and others to lie about their relationship, and whether he attempted to hide evidence of his relationship with Lewinsky. As the grand jury issued subpoenas for many White House aides and the scandal erupted in the media, Clinton, with support from Vernon Jordan and others, vehemently denied ever having "sexual relations with that woman, Miss Lewinsky." In the summer of 1998, however, Clinton testified before the grand jury, and later that evening, he held a televised address to the nation in which he admitted to having an "inappropriate" relationship with Monica Lewinsky.

After the grand jury testimonies had been completed, in early September 1998, Kenneth Starr submitted his report of the investigation to the House of Representatives. In the report to Congress, which included explicit sexual details of President Clinton's relationship with Lewinsky, Starr outlined a case for impeaching Clinton on eleven grounds, including perjury, obstruction of justice, witness tampering, and abuse of power. In early October, the House Judiciary Committee voted twenty-one to sixteen to recommend a full impeachment inquiry of the president. Democratic congressional leaders opposed conducting any impeachment inquiry and asked for House members to issue a bipartisan resolution to reprimand or censure the president. Democrats also proposed that limits be placed on the time and scope of a House impeachment investigation. However, Republican leaders supported the wide-ranging investigation, asserting that the Starr report had produced enough evidence to justify an impeachment inquiry.

Partisan arguments between congressional leaders over what constituted an impeachable offense ensued. While many Democrats suggested that the president's actions were reprehensible, they did not believe the Lewinsky scandal warranted further probing. Further, the Democrats argued, Clinton's conduct was a private matter that did not undercut the government and thus was not an impeachable offense. Republicans disagreed and condemned Clinton's behavior. Stating that a president held a special responsibility to maintain the law, Republicans consistently contended that Clinton was guilty of lying under oath and must be held accountable for undermining the presidency. House Judiciary Committee chair Henry Hyde (R-IL) declared the investigation was a necessary attempt to uphold the Constitution, which states that a president can be removed from office if he commits "treason, bribery, or other high crimes and misdemeanors." On October 8, 1998, the full House of Representatives voted 258 to 176 to conduct an unlimited impeachment inquiry into the perjury and obstruction of justice allegations against President Clinton.

On December 11, 1998, the House Judiciary Committee approved three articles of impeachment. Article I accused President Clinton of having "willfully provided perjurious, false and misleading testimony" before the Starr grand jury about his relationship with Lewinsky. Article II charged Clinton with having provided "perjurious, false and misleading testimony" in the Jones case. Article III accused him of obstruction of justice related to the Jones case. The votes on Articles I and III were strictly partisan, with all twenty-one Republicans on the committee voting to impeach and sixteen Democrats voting against impeachment. In the vote on Article II, however, one Republican, Lindsey Graham of South Carolina, voted against impeachment, stating that Clinton deserved the benefit of the doubt

when it came to perjury in the Jones case. The president had contended he was given a vague and confusing definition of "sexual relations," and thus, according to those definitions, Graham said, his answers as to whether he had sexual relations with Lewinsky were not false. On December 12, the House Judiciary Committee approved one more article of impeachment. Article IV accused Clinton of abusing his power in an effort to hide his relationship with Lewinsky and making false statements in his answers to eighty-one questions posed to him by the House Judiciary Committee in its investigation. As with the votes on Articles I and III, all twenty-one Republicans voted to impeach and sixteen Democrats voted against.

On December 19, 1998, the House of Representatives impeached President Clinton on Article I—obstructing justice in the Lewinsky affair—and Article III—obstruction of justice in the Jones case. Both votes fell largely along party lines. The first article passed 228–206, and the third article passed 221–212. Articles II and IV were defeated, 229–205 and 285–148, respectively. Articles I and III moved to the Senate on January 7, 1999, and Clinton became only the second U.S. president to go on trial before the Senate. At issue as the trial began was the debate over whether to call witnesses to testify. Arguing for a speedy trial, the Democrats strongly opposed having witnesses. Republicans pushed for witnesses, believing that a complete case could not be mounted without witness testimony to support the evidence. After a motion to dismiss the two articles of impeachment was defeated in a 56–44 vote, the Senate voted 56–44 to approve Republican prosecutors' request to allow witnesses to be subpoenaed in the trial. Three witnesses, Monica Lewinsky, Vernon Jordan, and Sidney Blumenthal, a White House aide, gave videotaped depositions behind closed doors.

In the final Senate vote on February 12, 1999, President Clinton was acquitted. A two-thirds majority would have been required for either of the articles to pass and to convict Clinton and remove him from office. Article I failed on a 55–45 vote, and Article III failed on a 50–50 vote. No Democratic senator voted to convict the president on either article. Ten Republicans

Article I of Impeachment

December 11, 1998: Approved by the Judiciary Committee of the House of Representatives, 21–16.
December 19, 1998: Approved by the House of Representatives, 228–206.
February 12, 1999: Rejected by the Senate, 55–45.

HOUSE VOTE

In Favor of Article I: 5 D, 223 R   Against Article I: 201 D, 5 R

Republicans Against: 5

Amo Houghton (NY)   Christopher Shays (CT)
Peter T. King (NY)   Mark Souder (IN)
Constance A. Morella (MD)

Democrats in Favor: 5

Virgil H. Goode (VA)   Charles W. Stenholm (TX)
Ralph M. Hall (TX)   Gene Taylor (MS)
Paul McHale (PA)

SENATE VOTE

Not Guilty: 45 D, 10 R*   Guilty: 0 D, 45 R

Republicans Voting Not Guilty

John H. Chafee (RI)   Olympia Snowe (ME)
Susan Collins (ME)   Arlen Specter (PA)*
Slade Gorton (WA)   Ted Stevens (AK)
James M. Jeffords (VT)   Fred D. Thompson (TN)
Richard C. Shelby (AL)   John W. Warner (VA)

*Arlen Specter voted "Not Proven," but is included here as having voted "Not Guilty."

voted against the perjury article, and five Republicans voted to reject the obstruction of justice article.

From a Republican Party perspective, impeachment by the House and conviction by the Senate was the only sensible treatment for a president who members deemed reckless, lawless, and immoral. To Republicans, the chief law enforcement officer of the United States had committed serious crimes—lying under oath, obstructing justice, and influencing witnesses—all in an effort to cover up a shameful extramarital affair. Just as important, those crimes were compounded by a campaign of lying to the public and slandering opponents for his own good.

The framers of the Constitution designed impeachment to remedy political offenses against the state and to uphold the political process. Here, at least according to the Republican Party, the president's conduct brought more than disgrace to himself and to the institution of the presidency: The president's conduct constituted a crisis of public order—a crisis that could be remedied only through the constitutionally and historically justified impeachment and conviction of the perpetrator, the president.

Lisa Hacken

ARTICLE I OF IMPEACHMENT

In his conduct while President of the United States, William Jefferson Clinton, in violation of his constitutional oath faithfully to execute the

Article II of Impeachment

December 11, 1998: Approved by the Judiciary Committee of the House of Representatives, 20–17.
December 19, 1998: Rejected by the House of Representatives, 229–205.

HOUSE VOTE

In Favor of Article II: 5 D, 200 R Against Article II: 201 D, 28 R

Republicans Against: 28

Richard Burr (NC)	Jim Greenwood (PA)	Bob Ney (OH)
Tom Campbell (CA)	David Hobson (OH)	Deborah Pryce (OH)
Michael N. Castle (DE)	Amo Houghton (NY)	Jim Ramstad (MN)
Jay W. Dickey (AR)	Sue W. Kelly (NY)	Mark Sanford (SC)
Phil English (PA)	Jay C. Kim (CA)	Joe Scarborough (FL)
John Ensign (NV)	Peter T. King (NY)	E. Clay Shaw Jr. (FL)
Mark Foley (FL)	Scott L. Klug (WI)	Christopher Shays (CT)
Jim Gibbons (NV)	Rick A. Lazio (NY)	Bud Shuster (PA)
Benjamin A. Gilman (NY)	Constance A. Morella (MD)	Mark Souder (IN)
Lindsey Graham (SC)		

Democrats in Favor: 5

Virgil H. Goode (VA)	Paul McHale (PA)	Gene Taylor (MS)
Ralph M. Hall (TX)	Charles W. Stenholm (TX)	

office of President of the United States and, to the best of his ability, preserve, protect, and defend the Constitution of the United States, and in violation of his constitutional duty to take care that the laws be faithfully executed, has willfully corrupted and manipulated the judicial process of the United States for his personal gain and exoneration, impeding the administration of justice, in that:

On August 17, 1998, William Jefferson Clinton swore to tell the truth, the whole truth, and nothing but the truth before a Federal grand jury of the United States. Contrary to that oath, William Jefferson Clinton willfully provided perjurious, false and misleading testimony to the grand jury concerning one or more of the following:

1. the nature and details of his relationship with a subordinate Government employee;
2. prior perjurious, false and misleading testimony he gave in a Federal civil rights action brought against him;
3. prior false and misleading statements he allowed his attorney to make to a Federal judge in that civil rights action; and

4. his corrupt efforts to influence the testimony of witnesses and to impede the discovery of evidence in that civil rights action.

In doing this, William Jefferson Clinton has undermined the integrity of his office, has brought disrepute on the Presidency, has betrayed his trust as President, and has acted in a manner subversive of the rule of law and justice, to the manifest injury of the people of the United States.

Wherefore, William Jefferson Clinton, by such conduct, warrants impeachment and trial, and removal from office and disqualification to hold and enjoy any office of honor, trust or profit under the United States.

ARTICLE II OF IMPEACHMENT

In his conduct while President of the United States, William Jefferson Clinton, in violation of his constitutional oath faithfully to execute the office of President of the United States and, to the best of his ability, preserve, protect, and defend the Constitution of the United States, and in violation of his constitutional duty to take care that the laws be faithfully executed, has willfully corrupted and manipulated the judicial process of the United States for his personal gain and exoneration, impeding the administration of justice, in that:

1. On December 23, 1997, William Jefferson Clinton, in sworn answers to written questions asked as part of a Federal civil rights action brought against him, willfully provided perjurious, false and misleading testimony in response to questions deemed relevant by a Federal judge concerning conduct and proposed conduct with subordinate employees.
2. On January 17, 1998, William Jefferson Clinton swore under oath to tell the truth, the whole truth, and nothing but the truth in a deposition given as part of a Federal civil rights action brought against him. Contrary to that oath, William Jefferson Clinton willfully provided perjurious, false and misleading testimony in response to questions deemed relevant by a Federal judge concerning the nature and details of his relationship with a subordinate Government employee, his knowledge of that employee's involvement and participation in the civil rights action brought against him, and his corrupt efforts to influence the testimony of that employee.

In all of this, William Jefferson Clinton has undermined the integrity of his office, has brought disrepute on the Presidency, has betrayed his trust as President, and has acted in a manner subversive of the rule of law and justice, to the manifest injury of the people of the United States.

Wherefore, William Jefferson Clinton, by such conduct, warrants impeachment and trial, and removal from office and disqualification to hold and enjoy any office of honor, trust or profit under the United States.

ARTICLE III OF IMPEACHMENT

In his conduct while President of the United States, William Jefferson Clinton, in violation of his constitutional oath faithfully to execute the office of President of the United States and, to the best of his ability, preserve, protect, and defend the Constitution of the United States, and in violation of his constitutional duty to take care that the laws be faithfully executed, has prevented, obstructed, and impeded the administration of justice, and has to that end engaged personally, and through his subordinates and agents, in a course of conduct or scheme designed to delay, impede, cover up, and conceal the existence of evidence and testimony related to a Federal civil rights action brought against him in a duly instituted judicial proceeding.

The means used to implement this course of conduct or scheme included one or more of the following acts:

1. On or about December 17, 1997, William Jefferson Clinton corruptly encouraged a witness in a Federal civil rights action brought against him to execute a sworn affidavit in that proceeding that he knew to be perjurious, false and misleading.
2. On or about December 17, 1997, William Jefferson Clinton corruptly encouraged a witness in a Federal civil rights action brought against him to give perjurious, false and misleading testimony if and when called to testify personally in that proceeding.
3. On or about December 28, 1997, William Jefferson Clinton corruptly engaged in, encouraged, or supported a scheme to conceal evidence that had been subpoenaed in a Federal civil rights action brought against him.
4. Beginning on or about December 7, 1997, and continuing through and including January 14, 1998, William Jefferson Clinton intensified and succeeded in an effort to secure job assistance to a witness in a Federal civil rights action brought against him in order to corruptly prevent the truthful testimony of that witness in that proceeding at a time when the truthful testimony of that witness would have been harmful to him.
5. On January 17, 1998, at his deposition in a Federal civil rights action brought against him, William Jefferson Clinton corruptly allowed his attorney to make false and misleading statements to a Federal judge

Article III of Impeachment

December 11, 1998: Approved by the Judiciary Committee of the House of Representatives, 21–16.
December 19, 1998: Approved by the House of Representatives, 221–212.
February 12, 1999: Rejected by the Senate, 50–50.

HOUSE VOTE

In Favor of Article III: 5 D, 216 R   Against Article III: 200 D, 12 R

Republicans Against: 12

Sherwood L. Boehlert (NY)	Peter T. King (NY)
Michael N. Castle (DE)	Jim Leach (IA)
Phil English (PA)	John M. McHugh (NY)
Amo Houghton (NY)	Constance A. Morella (MD)
Nancy L. Johnson (CT)	Ralph Regula (OH)
Jay C. Kim (CA)	Christopher Shays (CT)

Democrats in Favor: 5

Virgil H. Goode (VA)	Charles W. Stenholm (TX)
Ralph M. Hall (TX)	Gene Taylor (MS)
Paul McHale (PA)	

SENATE VOTE

Not Guilty: 45 D, 5 R*   Guilty: 0 D, 50 R

Republicans Voting Not Guilty

John H. Chafee (RI)	Olympia Snowe (ME)
Susan Collins (ME)	Arlen Specter (PA)*
James M. Jeffords (VT)	

*Arlen Specter voted "Not Proven," but is included here as having voted "Not Guilty."

characterizing an affidavit, in order to prevent questioning deemed relevant by the judge. Such false and misleading statements were subsequently acknowledged by his attorney in a communication to that judge.

6. On or about January 18 and January 20–21, 1998, William Jefferson Clinton related a false and misleading account of events relevant to a Federal civil rights action brought against him to a potential witness in that proceeding, in order to corruptly influence the testimony of that witness.

7. On or about January 21, 23, and 26, 1998, William Jefferson Clinton made false and misleading statements to potential witnesses in a Federal grand jury proceeding in order to corruptly influence the testimony of those witnesses. The false and misleading statements made by William Jefferson Clinton were repeated by the witnesses to the grand jury, causing the grand jury to receive false and misleading information.

In all of this, William Jefferson Clinton has undermined the integrity of his office, has brought disrepute on the Presidency, has betrayed his trust as President, and has acted in a manner subversive of the rule of law and justice, to the manifest injury of the people of the United States.

Wherefore, William Jefferson Clinton, by such conduct, warrants impeachment and trial, and removal from office and disqualification to hold and enjoy any office of honor, trust or profit under the United States.

Article IV of Impeachment

December 12, 1998: Approved by the Judiciary Committee of the House of Representatives, 21–16.
December 19, 1998: Rejected by the House of Representatives, 285–148.

HOUSE VOTE

In Favor of Article IV: 1 D, 147 R   Against Article IV: 206 D, 79 R

Republicans Against: 79

Charles Bass (NH)	David Hobson (OH)	Mike Parker (MS)
Douglas K. Bereuter (NE)	Amo Houghton (NY)	John Edward Porter (IL)
Brian P. Bilbray (CA)	Kenny Hulshof (MO)	Rob Portman (OH)
Sherwood L. Boehlert (NY)	Bill Jenkins (TN)	Deborah Pryce (OH)
Henry Bonilla (TX)	Nancy L. Johnson (CT)	Jack Quinn (NY)
Richard Burr (NC)	John R. Kasich (OH)	Jim Ramstad (MN)
Tom Campbell (CA)	Sue W. Kelly (NY)	Ralph Regula (OH)
Michael N. Castle (DE)	Jay C. Kim (CA)	Frank Riggs (CA)
Tom Davis (VA)	Peter T. King (NY)	Harold Rogers (KY)
Jay W. Dickey (AR)	Scott L. Klug (WI)	Jim Saxton (NJ)
Robert L. Ehrlich (MD)	Jim Kolbe (AR)	Joe Scarborough (FL)
Jo Ann Emerson (MO)	Steve Largent (OK)	John Shadegg (AZ)
Phil English (PA)	Tom Latham (IA)	E. Clay Shaw Jr. (FL)
John Ensign (NV)	Steven C. LaTourette (OH)	Christopher Shays (CT)
Harris W. Fawell (IL)	Rick A. Lazio (NY)	John M. Shimkus (IL)
Mark Foley (FL)	Jim Leach (IA)	Bud Shuster (PA)
Vito Fossella (NY)	Frank A. LoBiondo (NJ)	Mark Sounder (IN)
Bob Franks (NJ)	Jim McCrery (LA)	W.J. (Billy) Tauzin (LA)
Rodney Frelinghuysen (NJ)	John M. McHugh (NY)	Mac Thornberry (TX)
Greg Ganske (IA)	Scott McInnis (CO)	John Thune (SD)
Wayne T. Gilchrest (MD)	David McIntosh (IN)	Fred Upton (MI)
Paul E. Gillmor (OH)	Jerry Moran (KS)	James T. Walsh (NY)
Benjamin A. Gilman (NY)	Constance A. Morella (MD)	Curt Weldon (PA)
Porter J. Goss (FL)	George Nethercutt (WA)	Gerald C. (Jerry) Weller (IL)
Kay Granger (TX)	Bob Ney (OH)	Rick White (WA)
Jim Greenwood (PA)	Anne Northup (KY)	Edward Whitfield (KY)
Joel Hefley (CO)		

Democrats in Favor: 1

Gene Taylor (MS)

ARTICLE IV OF IMPEACHMENT

Using the powers and influence of the office of President of the United States, William Jefferson Clinton, in violation of his constitutional oath faithfully to execute the office of President of the United States and, to the best of his ability, preserve, protect, and defend the Constitution of the United States, and in disregard of his constitutional duty to take care that the laws be faithfully executed, has engaged in conduct that resulted in misuse and abuse of his high office, impaired the due and proper administration of justice and the conduct of lawful inquiries, and contravened the authority of the legislative branch and the truth-seeking purpose of a coordinate investigative proceeding in that, as President, William Jefferson Clinton, refused and failed to respond to certain written requests for admission and willfully made perjurious, false and misleading sworn statements in response to certain written requests for admission propounded to him as part of the impeachment inquiry authorized by the House of Representatives of the Congress of the United States.

William Jefferson Clinton, in refusing and failing to respond, and in making perjurious, false and misleading statements, assumed to himself functions and judgments necessary to the exercise of the sole power of impeachment vested by the Constitution in the House of Representatives and exhibited contempt for the inquiry.

In doing this, William Jefferson Clinton has undermined the integrity of his office, has brought disrepute on the Presidency, has betrayed his trust as President, and has acted in a manner subversive of the rule of law and justice, to the manifest injury of the people of the United States.

Wherefore, William Jefferson Clinton, by such conduct, warrants impeachment and trial, and removal from office and disqualification to hold and enjoy any office of honor, trust or profit under the United States.

SEE ALSO: Congressional Elections; Voting Behavior; Henry Hyde.

BIBLIOGRAPHY

Baker, Peter. *The Breach: Inside the Impeachment and Trial of William Jefferson Clinton*. New York: Scribner, 2000.

Coulter, Ann H. *High Crimes and Misdemeanors: The Case Against Bill Clinton*. Washington, DC: Regnery, 1998.

Gerhardt, Michael J. *The Federal Impeachment Process: A Constitutional and Historical Analysis*. Princeton, NJ: Princeton University Press, 1996.

Posner, Richard A. *An Affair of State: The Investigation, Impeachment, and Trial of President Clinton*. Cambridge: Harvard University Press, 1999.

Schmidt, Susan, and Michael Weisskopf. *Truth at Any Cost: Ken Starr and the Unmaking of Bill Clinton*. New York: HarperCollins, 2000.

"Text of Articles of Impeachment." CNN. www.cnn.com/ALLPOLITICS/resources/1998/lewinsky/articles.of.impeachment/

GENERAL INDEX

A

Abdnor, James, 276
Abortion, 18, 19, 23
    1996 party platform, 469, 496–497
    2000 party platform, 515
Abraham, Spencer, 163
Adams, John Quincy, 29, 30
Adams, Lloyd, 236
Aderholt, Robert B., 89
Adoption and Safe Families Act, 515
Affirmative access, 35–36
Affirmative action, 35–36, 40, 41
Africa, 490–491, 551–552
Agriculture, 529–530
Air Carriers Access Act, 469
Akin, W. Todd, 89
Alabama
    electoral votes, 295
    Governors, 219
        election results, 295
        James, Fob, Jr., 203, 219
    history and politics, 219–220
    population, registration, and turnout,
        296
    presidential election results, 295, 398,
        400
    Representatives
        election results, 402, 418
        party victories, 437
    Representatives (names)
        Aderholt, Robert B., 89
        Bachus, Spencer, 90–91
        Callahan, Sonny, 98
        Everett, Terry, 110
        Riley, Robert, 145
    Senators
        election results, 295, 417
        Sessions, Jefferson Beauregard, III,
          183–184
        Shelby, Richard C., 184, 219
Alaska
    drilling for oil, 22
    electoral votes, 297
    Governors, 220, 221
        election results, 297
    history and politics, 220–221
    population, registration, and turnout,
        298
    presidential election results, 297, 398,
        400

Alaska (continued)
    Representatives
        election results, 402, 418
        party victories, 437
        Young, Donald E., 162–163
    Senators
        election results, 297, 417
        Murkowski, Frank H., 181
        Stevens, Ted, 186
Albright, Madeleine, 50
Alexander, Lamar, 6
Allard, Wayne, 163
Allen, George, 63, 163–164, 193, 284
Almond, Lincoln, 193
American Dream Down Payment, 36
American Samoa, 467, 536
Americanization, 56
Americans with Disabilities Act, 41,
    468–469
Annan, Kofi, 51
Anti-Ballistic Missile (ABM) Treaty, 24, 51,
    52, 58, 488, 541–542
Archer, Bill, 89–90
Arctic National Wildlife Refuge, 22
Arizona
    107th Congress, 27
    electoral votes, 299
    Governors, 222
        election results, 299
        Hull, Jane Dee, 202–203
        Symington, John Fife, III, 212
    history and politics, 221–222
    population, registration, and turnout,
        300
    presidential election results, 299, 398,
        400
    Representatives
        election results, 402, 418
        party victories, 437
    Representatives (names)
        Flake, Jeff, 111
        Hayworth, John D., 119
        Kolbe, Jim, 128
        Salmon, Matt, 147
        Shadegg, John B., 150
        Stump, Bob, 155
    Senators
        election results, 299, 417
        Kyl, Jon, 179
        McCain, John. See
          McCain, John

Arkansas
    electoral votes, 301
    Governors, 224
        election results, 301
        Huckabee, Mike, 202, 223
    history and politics, 222–224
    population, registration, and turnout,
        302
    presidential election results, 301, 398,
        400
    Representatives
        election results, 402, 418
        party victories, 437
    Representatives (names)
        Dickey, Jay W., Jr., 107
        Hutchinson, Asa, 122
    Senators
        election results, 301, 417, 433
        Hutchinson, Tim, 177–178, 223
Arkansas Project, 18
Armey, Dick, 45, 60, 90
Arms. See Military
Ashcroft, John, 18, 36, 41, 46, 254
    biography, 164
Asia, 491, 546–547
Atiyeh, Victor, 271
Aung San Suu Kyi, 547
Australia, 546
Aviation Security Act, 490

B

Bachus, Spencer, 90–91
Baker, Richard H., 91
Balanced Budget Act, 456
Ballenger, Cass, 91
Ballots, Florida. See Florida, recount
Barr, Bob, 91
Barrett, William E., 39, 91–92
Bartlett, Dewey, 269
Bartlett, Roscoe G., 92
Barton, Joe L., 92
Bass, Charles, 92–93
Bateman, Herbert H., 93
Batt, Philip E., 193–194
Bauer, Gary, 6, 7, 8
Baugh, Scott, 225
Bayh-Dole Act, 460
Beasley, David, 194
Bellmon, Henry, 269
Bennett, Robert, 268

Bennett, Robert F., 164
Bennett, William J., 69–70
Bentsen, Lloyd, 31
Bereuter, Doug, 93
Biggert, Judy, 93–94
Bilbray, Brian, 94
Bilirakis, Michael, 94
Biomedical research, 525
Bioterrorism. See Terrorism
Bliley, Tom J., 94–95
Bliss, Ray, 279
Blunt, Roy D., 95
Boehlert, Sherwood L., 95
Boehner, John A., 45, 95
Bond, Christopher S., 45, 164, 253–254
Bonilla, Henry, 96
Bono, Mary, 96
Border Patrol, 47, 58, 470
Bosnia, 50, 486–487, 549
Boutros-Ghali, Boutros, 51
Boyd, Ralph, 41–42
Bradley, Bill, 39
Brady, Kevin, 96
Brady Bill, 53
Branstad, Terry Edward, 194, 240
Breaux, John, 55
Brock, Bill, 279
Brown, Henry E., Jr., 96–97
Brownback, Samuel Dale, 65, 164–165
Brulte, Jim, 225
Bryant, Edward, 97
Buchanan, Pat, 6, 13, 15, 51
Buckley v. Valeo, 40
Budget and fiscal policy, 21, 36–38, 458,
    461, 464–465
Bunnings, Jim, 165
Burns, Conrad R., 166
Burr, Aaron, 29–30
Burr, Richard, 97
Burton, Dan, 97–98
Bush, George W.
    approval rating, 25
    biography, 3–5, 70–72, 194–195
    election results, 15
    first hundred days, 16–25
    Florida recount, 13–15, 30
    popular and electoral votes, 30
    religious initiatives, 22–23
    style of, 19–20
    Texas governor, 279, 450
    vs. Gore, Albert, 9–12
    vs. McCain, 8–9
    See also Republican Party platform,
        2000
Bush, Jeb, 14, 64, 450
    biography, 195
Buyer, Steve, 98
Byrd, Harry Flood, 284
Byrd, Harry Flood, Jr., 284

C

Cabinet selection, 17–19
California
    blackouts, 22

California *(continued)*
    electoral votes, 303
    Governors, 225, 226
        election results, 303
        Wilson, Peter Barton, 56, 63, 215,
            225
    history and politics, 224–226
    number of electors, 31
    population, registration, and turnout,
        304
    presidential election results, 303, 398,
        400
    Proposition 187, 56
    Proposition 209, 468
    Representatives
        election results, 402–404, 418–420
        party victories, 437
    Representatives (names)
        Bilbray, Brian, 94
        Bono, Mary, 96
        Calvert, Ken, 98
        Campbell, Tom, 99
        Cox, Christopher, 45, 60, 103–104
        Cunningham, Randy (Duke), 105
        Doolittle, John T., 39, 107
        Dreier, David, 107
        Gallegly, Elton, 113–114
        Herger, Wally, 120
        Horn, Stephen, 121
        Hunter, Duncan, 122
        Issa, Darrell E., 123
        Kim, Jay, 126
        Kuykendall, Steven T., 128
        Lewis, Jerry, 130
        McKeon, Howard P., 134
        Miller, Gary G., 135
        Ose, Douglas A., 137–138
        Packard, Ron, 138–139
        Pombo, Richard W., 141
        Radanovich, George, 143
        Riggs, Frank Duncan, 144–145
        Rogan, James E., 145
        Rohrabacher, Dana, 146
        Royce, Edward, 147
        Thomas, Bill, 39, 157
    Senators
        election results, 303, 417, 433
Callahan, Sonny, 98
Calvert, Ken, 98
Cameron, Simon, 272
Camp, Dave, 98–99
Campaign 2000
    Bush, George. *See* Bush, George W.
    Bush *vs.* McCain, 8–9
    candidates, 5–7
    caucuses, 7–8
    election night, 12–13, 64
    Florida recount, 13–15, 30
    Gore, Al. *See* Gore, Albert
    presidential debates, 11–12
    press issues, 8
    See also Presidential elections;
        Republican Party platform, 2000
Campaign finance reform, 5, 38–40, 534
Campbell, Ben Nighthorse, 166–167

Campbell, Tom, 99
Campbell, William, 288
Canada, 545
Canady, Charles T., 99
Cannon, Christopher B., 99–100
Cantor, Eric, 100
Capito, Shelley Moore, 100
Carlson, Arne, 195–196
Carmichael, Gil, 252
Castle, Michael, 100–101, 230
Cellucci, Argeo Paul, 64, 196
Census 2000, 26–27
Census Bureau. *See* United States Census
    Bureau
Cermak, Anton, 237
Chabot, Steve, 101
Chafee, John H., 167, 274
Chafee, Lincoln, 167
Chambliss, Saxby, 101
Charity Tax Credit, 479–480
Charter schools, 48
Chemical Weapons Convention, 50
Cheney, Dick, 9, 12, 17
    anti-drug legislation, 47
    biography, 72–73
Chenoweth-Hage, Helen P., 101
Children
    anti-drug programs, 46–47
    gun interdiction program, 53
    healthcare, 523, 525
    at risk, 513–514
    schools and education. *See* Education
    tax credits, 514
    youth crime, 471–472
Children's Health Insurance Program, 523
ChildSafe, 53
Chiles, Lawton Mainor, Jr., 196–197
China, 24, 50, 52, 59, 491, 547
Christensen, Jon, 101–102
Christian Coalition, 273, 285
Christian Right, 220, 240, 241, 281, 285,
    288
Citizens' congress, 463
Citizens' rights, 467–470, 515–517
Civil rights, 40–42, 468
Clark, Joseph S., 272
Clements, Bill, 279
Cleveland, Grover, 30
Clinical trials, 526
Clinton, William Jefferson, 20, 223
    election (1996), 449–450
    foreign policy, 50
    impeachment, 45, 557–564
    popular and electoral votes, 30
    Social Security, 62
Coats, Dan, 168
Coats-Kasich Educational Choice and
    Equity Act, 476
Coble, Howard, 102
Coburn, Thomas A., 102
Cochran, Thad, 168–169, 252
Cohen, William S., 50
Cole, Tom, 269
Collins, Mac, 102–103
Collins, Susan, 169

Colorado
    electoral votes, 305
    Governors, 228
        election results, 305
        Owens, Bill, 207–208, 228
    history and politics, 227–229
    population, registration, and turnout, 306
    presidential election results, 305, 398, 400
    Representatives
        election results, 404, 420
        party victories, 437
    Representatives (names)
        Hefley, Joel, 120
        McInnis, Scott, 133
        Schaefer, Dan, 148
        Schaffer, Bob, 148–149
        Tancredo, Thomas G., 156
    Senators
        Allard, Wayne, 163
        Campbell, Ben Nighthorse, 166–167
        election results, 305, 417
Colson, Charles, 64
Columbia, 47
Combest, Larry, 103
Community initiatives, 22–23, 513
Community Renewal Act, 476
Comprehensive Test Ban Treaty, 51, 488, 543
Congress
    elections, 42–44, 450–451
    party composition, 434–436
    party leadership, 44–46
    party organization, 59–61
    Republican control, 24–25, 503
    seats that changed party, 439–440
    See also House of Representatives; Senate
Connally, John, 279
Connecticut
    electoral votes, 307
    Governors, 229–230
        election results, 307
        Rowland, John G., 210, 229
    history and politics, 229–230
    population, registration, and turnout, 308
    presidential election results, 307, 398, 400
    Representatives
        election results, 404, 420
        party victories, 437
    Representatives (names)
        Johnson, Nancy L., 124
        Shays, Christopher, 39, 150–151
        Simmons, Robert, 151–152
    Senators
        election results, 307, 417, 433
Contract with America, 74
Cook, Merrill, 103
Cooksey, John, 103
Coverdell, Paul D., 63, 169, 502
Cox, Christopher, 45, 60, 103–104
Craig, Larry, 45

Craig, Larry E., 61, 169–170
Crane, Philip M., 104
Crapo, Mike, 170
Crenshaw, Ander, 104
Crime and criminals, 471–473, 517–519
    hate crimes, 41
    international, 552–553
    punishment, 47
    voting rights, 64
    youth, 471–472
    See also Drugs, illegal
Cuba, 492, 546
Cubin, Barbara, 104–105
Culberson, John Abney, 105
Cunningham, Randy (Duke), 105
Cyber threats, 552–553
Cyprus, 487–488, 550
Czech Republic, 50, 486, 548

D

Daley, Richard J., 237
D'Amato, Alfonse, 263, 450
Danforth, John, 253, 254
Davis, Gray, 225, 450
Davis, Jo Ann, 105–106
Davis, Thomas, 45, 60, 106
Davis-Bacon Act, 459
Deal, Nathan, 106
Debates, presidential, 11–12
Declaration of Independence. See United States Declaration of Independence
Defend America Act, 488
Defense. See Military
Defense of Marriage Act, 468, 475, 514
Delaware
    electoral votes, 309
    Governors, 231
        election results, 309
    history and politics, 230–232
    population, registration, and turnout, 310
    presidential election results, 309, 398, 400
    Representatives
        Castle, Michael, 100–101, 230
        election results, 404, 420
        party victories, 437
    Senators
        election results, 309, 433
        Roth, William V., Jr., 183
DeLay, Tom, 45, 60
    biography, 73–74, 106
DeMint, Jim, 106
Denton, Jeremiah, 219
Department of Commerce v. United States House of Representatives, 26
Deukmejian, George, 225
DeWine, Mike, 170
Diaz-Balart, Lincoln, 106–107
Dickey, Jay W., Jr., 107
DiFrancesco, Donald T., 197
DiIulio, John J., Jr., 22
Dilworth, Richardson, 272
Disabilities, 40–41, 468–469, 510

District of Columbia, 467, 537
    electoral votes, 311
    population, registration, and turnout, 311
    presidential election results, 311, 398, 400
    Representatives
        election results, 404, 420
Dole, Bob, 30, 45, 60, 449–450, 498–500
    See also Republican Party platform, 1996
Dole, Elizabeth, 6, 74–75, 449
Dole-Canady Equal Opportunity Act, 468
Domenici, Pete V., 170–171
Domestic policy, 21–22
"Don't ask, don't tell," 41
Doolittle, John T., 39, 107
Dreier, David, 107
Drugs
    illegal, 46–47, 473–474
    prescription, 38, 55
Dukakis, Michael, 31
Duncan, John J., Jr., 107–108
Dunn, Jennifer, 60, 108

E

Earle, George H., 272
Economy, 502–508
Edgar, James, 197
Education, 21, 35, 41, 47–49
    1996 party platform plan, 475–477
    2000 party platform plan, 508–514
    bilingual, 40, 41
    budget, 38
Education Consumer's Warranty, 476
Edwards, John, 450
Egypt, 551
Ehlers, Vernon J., 108–109
Ehrlich, Robert L., Jr., 109
Eisenhower, Dwight, 219
Elderly. See Older Americans
Election Day, 64
Election reform, 64–65
    See also Campaign finance reform
Elections
    campaign 2000. See Campaign 2000
    congressional. See Congress, elections
    presidential. See Presidential elections
Electoral College
    controversies, 29–30
    criticisms, 30–32
    future, 32
    how it works, 27–28
    why it came to exist, 28–29
    See also Voting behavior
Emerson, Jo Ann, 109
Employment, 459
    worker programs and rights, 22
    workplace, 505
Endangered Species Act, 527
Energy policies, 22, 530–531
Engler, John, 63, 197–198, 249
English, Phil S., 109
English language, 470–471, 517

English-plus, 41, 58
Ensign, John, 109–110, 171
Environmental policies, 21, 22, 52,
    480–486, 497, 526–532
Environmental Protection Agency (EPA),
    18, 21
Enzi, Michael B., 171–172
Equal rights, 468, 515–517
Europe, 547–550
Everett, Terry, 110
Ewing, Thomas W., 110
Export Enhancement Program, 462

F

Faircloth, Launch, 450
Faith-based and community initiatives,
    22–23, 513
Falwell, Jerry, 23
Families, valuing, 474–475, 497, 514–515
Farm Bureau, 240
Farmer-Labor Party, 250
Farmers, 529–530
Fawell, Harris W., 110–111
Feingold, Russell, 39
Ferguson, Michael, 111
Fiscal policy. See Budget and fiscal policy
Fiske, Robert, 557
Fitzgerald, Peter G., 172
Flake, Jeff, 111
Fleischer, Ari, 20
Fletcher, Ernest Lee, 111
Florida
    electoral votes, 312
    Governors, 233
        Bush, Jeb, 14, 64, 195, 450
        Chiles, Lawton Mainor, Jr.,
            196–197
        election results, 312
    history and politics, 232–233
    population, registration, and turnout,
        313
    presidential election results, 312, 398,
        400
    recount, 13–15, 30
    Representatives
        election results, 404–405, 420–421
        party victories, 437
    Representatives (names)
        Bilirakis, Michael, 94
        Canady, Charles T., 99
        Crenshaw, Ander, 104
        Diaz-Balart, Lincoln, 106–107
        Foley, Mark A., 111
        Fowler, Thomas K., 112
        Goss, Porter J., 116
        Keller, Richard, 125–126
        McCollum, Bill, 132
        Mica, John L., 134
        Miller, Dan, 134–135
        Putnam, Adam H., 142–143
        Ros-Lehtinen, Ileana, 146
        Scarborough, Joe, 148
        Shaw, E. Clay, Jr., 150
        Stearns, Cliff B., 154–155

Florida
    Representatives (names) (continued)
        Weldon, Dave, 160–161
        Young, C.W., 162
    Senators
        election results, 312, 417, 433
        Mack, Connie, 45, 180
Florida State Supreme Court, 14–15
Foley, Mark A., 111
Forbes, Michael A., 111–112
Forbes, Steve, 6, 7, 8, 231
Fordice, Kirk, 198, 252
Foreign policy, 50–52
    1996 party platform, 486–495
    2000 party platform, 537–554
Fossella, Vito, 112
Foster, M.J., 198
Fowler, Thomas K., 112
Fox, Jon D., 112–113
Franks, Bob, 113
Free trade. See Trade
Free Trade Area of the Americas, 52
Freedom, 495, 537–539
    See also Military; Security; Trade
Freeman, Orville, 250
Frelinghuysen, Rodney P., 113
Frist, William H., 45, 55, 61
    biography, 172–173

G

Gallegly, Elton, 113–114
Ganske, Greg, 114
Gays
    in military, 494
    rights, 41
    same-sex unions, 468, 475, 514
Gekas, George W., 114
Georgia
    electoral votes, 314
    Governors, 234
        election results, 314
    history and politics, 233–235
    population, registration, and turnout,
        315
    presidential election results, 314, 398,
        400
    Representatives
        election results, 405, 421
        party victories, 437
    Representatives (names)
        Barr, Bob, 91
        Chambliss, Saxby, 101
        Collins, Mac, 102–103
        Deal, Nathan, 106
        Isakson, Johnny, 123
        Kingston, Jack, 127
        Linder, John, 45, 63, 131
        Norwood, Charles W., Jr., 137
    Senators
        Coverdell, Paul D., 63, 169, 502
        election results, 314, 417, 433
Geringer, Jim, 198–199
Gibbons, James A., 114
Gilchrest, Wayne T., 114–115

Gillmor, Paul E., 115
Gilman, Benjamin A., 115
Gilmore, James, III, 199–200, 284
Gingrich, Newt, 42, 43, 44, 48, 234
    biography, 75–76
    Speaker of the House, 59–60
Giuliani, Rudolph, 263
Goals 2000 program, 475
Goldwater, Barry, 221, 236, 251, 275
Goodlatte, Robert W., 115–116
Goodling, William E., 116
Gore, Albert
    Bush vs., 9–12
    concession, 12–13
    Florida recount, 13–15, 30
    popular vote, 30, 31
Gorton, Slade, 173
Goss, Porter J., 116
Government, 462–464, 532–537
Graham, Lindsey O., 116–117, 558
Gramm, Phil, 173
Grams, Rod, 174
Granger, Kay, 117
Grant, Ulysses S., 251
Grassley, Charles, 174
Graves, Bill, 200–201, 241
Graves, Samuel, 117
Green, Mark, 117
Green Party, 10–11
Greenwood, James C., 117–118
Gregg, Judd, 174–175
Grucci, Felix J., Jr., 118
Guam, 467, 536
Guffey, Joseph F., 272
Guinn, Kenny C., 201
Gun control, 53, 469, 516
Gutknecht, Gil, 118

H

Hagel, Charles, 22, 39, 45, 175–176
Haiti, 493
Hansen, James V., 118
Hanssen, Robert, 24
Harris, Katherine, 14
Harrison, Benjamin, 30
Hart, Melissa A., 118–119
Hastert, J. Dennis, 39, 45
    biography, 76–77, 119
    Speaker of the House, 60
Hastings, Doc, 119
Hatch, Orrin G., 6, 176
Hate crimes, 41
Hatfield, Mark, 271
Hawaii
    electoral votes, 316
    Governors, 316
    history and politics, 235
    population, registration, and turnout,
        317
    presidential election results, 316, 398, 400
    Representatives
        election results, 405, 421
        party victories, 437
    Senators, 316, 417, 433

Hayes, Robert (Robin) C., 119
Hayes, Rutherford B., 30
Hayworth, John D., 119
Health insurance, 54, 505, 522–523
Health maintenance organizations
    (HMOs), 55
Healthcare, 38, 54–56, 477–478, 521–526
Hefley, Joel, 120
Helms, Jesse, 51, 176–177, 264
Herger, Wally, 120
Hickel, Walter J., 220
Higher education, 510–511
Hill, Rick, 120
Hilleary, Van, 120
Hobbs Act, 469
Hobson, David L., 121
Hoekstra, Peter, 121
Hoeven, John, 201–202
Holbrooke, Richard, 51
Holshouser, James, 264
Holton, Linwood, 284
Home ownership, 36, 460–461,
    504–505
Homosexuals. See Gays
Horn, Stephen, 121
Hostettler, John Nathan, 121
Houghton, Amo, 122
House, George, 226
House of Representatives
    2000 census, 26
    elections
        1998, 402–416
        2000, 418–432
    leadership and party organization,
        59–60
    members, 89–163
    party composition, 434–436
    party victories, 437–438
    seats that changed party, 439
    vote on Clinton's impeachment, 559,
        560, 562, 563
    See also Congress; specific state
House Republican Conference, 60
Huckabee, Mike, 202, 223
HUD, 461
Hughes, Harold, 240
Hull, Jane Dee, 202–203
Hulshof, Kenny, 122
Human Rights Commission, 52
Humphrey, Hubert, 250
Hungary, 50, 486, 548
Hunt, Guy, 219
Hunter, Duncan, 122
Hussein, Saddam, 50, 51, 550–551
Hutchinson, Asa, 39, 122
Hutchinson, Tim, 177–178, 223
Hutchison, Kay Bailey, 178
Hyde, Henry J., 78–79, 122–123, 558

I

Idaho
    electoral votes, 318
    Governors, 236
        Batt, Philip E., 193–194

Idaho
    Governors (continued)
        election results, 318
        Kempthorne, Dirk, 206
    history and politics, 236–237
    population, registration, and turnout,
        319
    presidential election results, 318, 398,
        400
    Representatives
        election results, 405, 421
        party victories, 437
    Representatives (names)
        Chenoweth-Hage, Helen P.,
            101
        Otter, C.L. "Butch," 138
        Simpson, Michael K., 152
    Senators
        Craig, Larry E., 61, 169–170
        Crapo, Mike, 170
        election results, 318, 417
        Kempthorne, Dirk, 179
Illegal drugs. See Drugs, illegal
Illegal immigration. See Immigration
Illinois
    electoral votes, 320
    Governors, 238
        Edgar, James, 197
        election results, 320
        Ryan, George H., 210–211
    history and politics, 237–238
    population, registration, and turnout,
        321
    presidential election results, 320, 398,
        400
    Representatives
        election results, 406, 422
        party victories, 437
    Representatives (names)
        Biggert, Judy, 93–94
        Crane, Philip M., 104
        Ewing, Thomas W., 110
        Fawell, Harris W., 110–111
        Hastert, J. Dennis, 39, 45, 60, 76–77,
            119
        Hyde, Henry J., 78–79, 122–123,
            558
        Johnson, Timothy V., 124–125
        Kirk, Mark Steven, 127
        LaHood, Ray, 128–129
        Manzullo, Donald, 63, 131–132
        Porter, John Edward, 141–142
        Shimkus, John M., 151
        Weller, Jerry, 161
    Senators
        election results, 320, 417
        Fitzgerald, Peter G., 172
"Immediate Helping Hand," 55
Immigration, 56–58, 470, 517
Immigration and Naturalization Service
    (INS), 57
Impeachment, Clinton, 45, 557–564
India, 547
Indiana
    electoral votes, 322

Indiana (continued)
    Governors, 239
        election results, 322
    history and politics, 238–239
    population, registration, and turnout,
        323
    presidential election results, 322, 398,
        400
    Representatives
        election results, 406, 422
        party victories, 437
    Representatives (names)
        Burton, Dan, 97–98
        Buyer, Steve, 98
        Hostettler, John Nathan, 121
        Kerns, Brian D., 126
        McIntosh, David M., 133–134
        Pease, Edward A., 139–140
        Pence, Mike, 140
        Souder, Mark E., 154
    Senators
        Coats, Dan, 168
        election results, 322, 417, 433
        Lugar, Richard G., 180
Individuals with Disabilities Education
    Act, 469, 510
Inglis, Bob, 123
Inhofe, James M., 178–179
Intellectual property, 507
Intelligence, 494
International aid, 552
Internet
    and children, 514–515
    cyber threats, 552–553
    voting, 64
Internet Tax Freedom Act, 507
Iowa
    caucuses, 7
    electoral votes, 324
    Governors, 241
        Branstad, Terry Edward, 194, 240
        election results, 324
    history and politics, 240–241
    population, registration, and turnout,
        325
    presidential election results, 324, 398,
        400
    Representatives
        election results, 407, 423
        party victories, 437
    Representatives (names)
        Ganske, Greg, 114
        Latham, Tom, 129
        Leach, James A., 130
        Nussle, Jim, 137
    Senators
        election results, 324, 417
        Grassley, Charles, 174
Iran, 59, 550, 551
Iraq, 50, 51, 59, 550–551
Ireland, 487, 549–550
Isakson, Johnny, 123
Israel, 51, 491–492, 550
Issa, Darrell E., 123
Istook, Ernest J., Jr., 123–124

J

Jackson, Andrew, 30
James, Fob, Jr., 203, 219
Janklow, William J., 203–204
Japan, 546
Jefferson, Thomas, 29–30
Jeffords, James, 25, 39, 43, 59, 282
    biography, 179
Jenkins, William Lewis, 124
Jenna's Law, 82
Jobs. *See* Employment
Johanns, Mike, 204
Johnson, Gary E., 204–205
Johnson, Hiram, 224
Johnson, Nancy L., 124
Johnson, Sam, 124
Johnson, Timothy V., 124–125
Jones, Paula, 557
Jones, Walter B., 125
Jordan, 551
Judicial reform, 534–535

K

Kansas
    electoral votes, 326
    Governors, 241
        election results, 326
        Graves, Bill, 200–201, 241
    history and politics, 241–242
    population, registration, and turnout,
        327
    presidential election results, 326, 398,
        400
    Representatives
        election results, 407, 423
        party victories, 437
    Representatives (names)
        Moran, Jerry, 135
        Ryan, Jim, 147
        Snowbarger, Vincent K., 153
        Tiahrt, Todd, 158
    Senators
        Brownback, Samuel Dale, 65,
          164–165
        election results, 326, 417
        Roberts, Pat, 182
Kasich, John R., 5–6, 125
Keating, Frank, 205–206, 269
Keller, Richard, 125–126
Kelly, Sue W., 126
Kemp, Jack, 449
Kempthorne, Dirk, 179, 206
Kennedy, John F., 32
Kennedy, Mark R., 126
Kentucky
    electoral votes, 328
    Governors, 243
        election results, 328
    history and politics, 242–243
    population, registration, and turnout,
        329
    presidential election results, 328, 398,
        400

Kentucky (*continued*)
    Representatives
        election results, 407, 423
        party victories, 437
    Representatives (names)
        Fletcher, Ernest Lee, 111
        Lewis, Ron, 130–131
        Northup, Anne M., 136–137
        Rogers, Harold, 145–146
        Whitfield, Edward, 161
    Senators
        Bunnings, Jim, 165
        election results, 328, 417
        McConnell, Mitch. *See* McConnell,
          Mitch
Kerns, Brian D., 126
Key, Clinton, 269
Keyes, Alan, 6, 7, 8
Kim, Jay, 126
King, Peter T., 126–127
Kingston, Jack, 127
Kirk, Mark Steven, 127
Klug, Scott, 127
Knollenberg, Joe, 128
Knowland, William, 225
Knowles, Tony, 220
Kolbe, Jim, 128
Kosovo, 50
Kuykendall, Steven T., 128
Kyl, Jon, 179
Kyoto Protocol, 22, 23, 527

L

La Follette, Robert M., 288
LaHood, Ray, 128–129
Lake, Anthony, 50
Lamm, Richard, 228
Largent, Steve, 60, 129
Latham, Tom, 129
Latin America, 492, 545
LaTourette, Steven C., 129–130
Lazio, Rick A., 130
Leach, James A., 130
Leach, Margarette, 31
Leader, George, 272
Leavitt, Michael O., 206–207
Lesbians. *See* Gays
"Let America Know" legislation,
    464
Lewinsky, Monica, 557–558
Lewis, Jerry, 130
Lewis, Ron, 130–131
Lincoln, Abraham, 30
Linder, John, 45, 63, 131
Livingston, Robert, 44–45, 60, 63
LoBiondo, Frank A., 131
Lott, Trent, 45, 46, 60, 252
    biography, 79–80, 179–180
Louisiana
    electoral votes, 330
    Governors, 244
        election results, 330
        Foster, M.J., 198
    history and politics, 243–244

Louisiana (*continued*)
    population, registration, and turnout,
        331
    presidential election results, 330, 398,
        400
    Representatives
        election results, 407, 423
        party victories, 437
    Representatives (names)
        Baker, Richard H., 91
        Cooksey, John, 103
        McCrery, Jim, 132
        Roemer, Charles E., 145
        Tauzon, W.J., 156
        Vitter, David, 158–159
    Senators
        election results, 330, 417
Lucas, Frank D., 131
Lugar, Richard G., 180

M

Mack, Connie, 45, 180
Mahone, William, 283
Mail voting, 64
Maine
    electoral votes, 332
    Governors, 245
        election results, 332
    history and politics, 245–246
    population, registration, and turnout,
        333
    presidential election results, 332, 398,
        400
    Representatives
        election results, 407, 423
        party victories, 437
    Senators
        Collins, Susan, 169
        election results, 332, 433
        Snowe, Olympia J., 39, 185
Majority leader, 60
Majority whip, 60
Manzullo, Donald, 63, 131–132
Martz, Judy, 207
Maryland
    electoral votes, 334
    Governors, 246
        election results, 334
    history and politics, 246–247
    population, registration, and turnout,
        335
    presidential election results, 334, 398,
        400
    Representatives
        election results, 407–408,
          423–424
        party victories, 437
    Representatives (names)
        Bartlett, Roscoe G., 92
        Ehrlich, Robert L., Jr., 109
        Gilchrest, Wayne T., 114–115
        Morella, Constance A., 135
    Senators
        election results, 334, 417, 433

Massachusetts
    electoral votes, 336
    Governors, 248
        Cellucci, Argeo Paul, 64, 196
        election results, 336
        Swift, Jane, 212
    history and politics, 247–248
    population, registration, and turnout, 337
    presidential election results, 336, 398, 400
    Representatives
        election results, 408, 424
        party victories, 437
    Senators
        election results, 336, 433
Mattingly, Mack, 234
McCain, John, 5, 7–8, 39, 65
    biography, 80–81, 181
    Bush vs., 8–9
McCain–Feingold Bill, 39, 40, 81
McCallum, James Scott, 207, 289
McCarthy, Eugene, 250
McClintock, Tom, 226
McCollum, Bill, 132
McConnell, Mitch, 39, 45, 63, 65, 242
    biography, 81–82, 181
McCrery, Jim, 132
McDade, Joseph M., 132
McHugh, John M., 133
McInnis, Scott, 133
McIntosh, David M., 133–134
McKeon, Howard P., 134
McPhail, Evelyn, 252
Meadow, William H., 22
Mecham, Evan, 221–222
Medicaid, 477, 478
Medical savings accounts, 55–56, 477
Medicare, 54, 55, 477–478, 521
Meehan, Martin T., 39
Megan's Law, 472
Metcalf, Jack, 39, 134
Mexico, 492
Mica, John L., 134
Michel, Robert, 44
Michigan
    electoral votes, 338
    Governors, 249
        election results, 338
        Engler, John, 63, 197–198, 249
    history and politics, 248–249
    population, registration, and turnout, 339
    presidential election results, 338, 398, 400
    Representatives
        election results, 408, 424–425
        party victories, 437
    Representatives (names)
        Camp, Dave, 98–99
        Ehlers, Vernon J., 108–109
        Hoekstra, Peter, 121
        Knollenberg, Joe, 128
        Rogers, Mike, 146

Michigan
    Representatives (names) (continued)
        Smith, Nick, 153
        Upton, Fred, 158
    Senators
        Abraham, Spencer, 163
        Ashcroft, John, 164
        election results, 338, 433
Middle East, 491–492, 550–551
    peace process, 51–52
Military, 21, 24, 52, 58–59
    budget, 38, 51
    defense, 488–489, 541–543
    gays in, 41
    personnel, 493–494
    strengthening, 539–541
    See also Freedom
Miller, Dan, 134–135
Miller, David, 241
Miller, Gary G., 135
Milliken, Roger, 275
Minnesota
    electoral votes, 340
    Governors, 250
        Carlson, Arne, 195–196
        election results, 340
    history and politics, 249–251
    population, registration, and turnout, 341
    presidential election results, 340, 398, 400
    Representatives
        election results, 409, 425
        party victories, 437
    Representatives (names)
        Gutknecht, Gil, 118
        Kennedy, Mark R., 126
        Ramstad, Jim, 143
    Senators
        election results, 340, 433
        Grams, Rod, 174
Minority business owners, 35
Minority leader, 60
Minority whip, 61
Missile defense system. See National missile defense (NMD)
Mississippi
    electoral votes, 342
    Governors, 252
        election results, 342
        Fordice, Kirk, 198, 252
    history and politics, 251–253
    population, registration, and turnout, 343
    presidential election results, 342, 398, 400
    Representatives
        election results, 409, 425
        party victories, 437
    Representatives (names)
        Parker, Mike, 139
        Pickering, Charlie W., Jr., 140–141
        Wicker, Roger F., 161–162
    Senators
        Cochran, Thad, 168–169, 252

Mississippi
    Senators (continued)
        election results, 342, 433
        Lott, Trent. See Lott, Trent
Missouri
    electoral votes, 346
    Governors, 255
        election results, 346
    history and politics, 253–255
    population, registration, and turnout, 347
    presidential election results, 346, 398, 400
    Representatives
        election results, 409, 425
        party victories, 437
    Representatives (names)
        Akin, W. Todd, 89
        Blunt, Roy D., 95
        Emerson, Jo Ann, 109
        Graves, Samuel, 117
        Hulshof, Kenny, 122
        Talent, James M., 155–156
    Senators
        Bond, Christopher S., 45, 164, 253–254
        election results, 346, 417, 433
Molinari, Susan, 135
Mondale, Walter, 250
Monica Lewinsky scandal. See Lewinsky, Monica
Montana
    electoral votes, 344
    Governors, 256–257
        election results, 344
        Martz, Judy, 207
        Racicot, Marc, 209
    history and politics, 256–257
    population, registration, and turnout, 345
    presidential election results, 344, 398, 400
    Representatives
        election results, 409, 425
        party victories, 437
    Representatives (names)
        Hill, Rick, 120
        Rehberg, Dennis R., 144
    Senators
        Burns, Conrad R., 166
        election results, 344, 433
Moore, Arch, 287
Moran, Jerry, 135
Morella, Constance A., 135
Motor-Voter Law, 63–64, 462
Muldihill, M.J., 251
Murkowski, Frank H., 181
Muskie, Edmund, 245
Myrick, Sue, 135–136

N

Nader, Ralph, 10–11, 15
NAFTA. See North American Free Trade Agreement

National missile defense (NMD), 24, 52, 488, 541–542
National Republican Congressional Committee, 60
National Republican Senatorial Committee, 61
National Rifle Association, 53
National Voter Registration Act, 63
Native Americans, 471, 536
NATO, 50, 486, 548–549
Nebraska
    electoral votes, 348
    Governors, 257–258
        election results, 348
        Johanns, Mike, 204
    history and politics, 257–258
    population, registration, and turnout, 349
    presidential election results, 348, 398, 400
    Representatives
        election results, 409, 425
        party victories, 437
    Representatives (names)
        Barrett, William E., 39, 91–92
        Bereuter, Doug, 93
        Christensen, Jon, 101–102
        Osborne, Thomas, 137
        Terry, Lee, 156–157
    Senators
        election results, 348, 433
        Hagel, Charles, 22, 39, 45, 175–176
Nethercutt, George R., Jr., 136
Neuberger, Richard, 271
Neumann, Mark W., 136
Nevada
    electoral votes, 350
    Governors, 259
        election results, 350
        Guinn, Kenny C., 201
    history and politics, 258–259
    population, registration, and turnout, 351
    presidential election results, 350, 398, 400
    Representatives
        election results, 409, 426
        party victories, 437
    Representatives (names)
        Ensign, John, 109–110
        Gibbons, James A., 114
    Senators
        election results, 350, 417, 433
        Ensign, John, 171
New Hampshire
    caucuses, 7–8
    electoral votes, 352
    Governors, 260
        election results, 352
    history and politics, 259–260
    population, registration, and turnout, 353
    presidential election results, 352, 398, 400

New Hampshire (continued)
    Representatives
        election results, 410, 426
        party victories, 437
    Representatives (names)
        Bass, Charles, 92–93
        Sununu, John E., 155
    Senators
        election results, 352, 417
        Gregg, Judd, 174–175
        Smith, Robert C., 5–6, 185
New Jersey
    electoral votes, 354
    Governors, 261
        DiFrancesco, Donald T., 197
        election results, 354
        Whitman, Christine T., 18, 41, 214–215
    history and politics, 261–262
    population, registration, and turnout, 355
    presidential election results, 354, 398, 400
    Representatives
        election results, 410, 426
        party victories, 437
    Representatives (names)
        Ferguson, Michael, 111
        Franks, Bob, 113
        LoBiondo, Frank A., 131
        Pappas, Michael, 139
        Roukema, Marge, 39, 146–147
        Saxton, Jim, 148
        Smith, Christopher H., 152
    Senators
        election results, 354, 433
New Mexico
    electoral votes, 356
    Governors, 262–263
        election results, 356
        Johnson, Gary E., 204–205
    history and politics, 262–263
    population, registration, and turnout, 357
    presidential election results, 356, 398, 400
    Representatives
        election results, 410, 426
        party victories, 437
    Representatives (names)
        Redmond, Bill, 143–144
        Richardson, Bill, 144
        Schiff, Steven, 149
        Skeen, Joe R., 152
        Wilson, Heather Ann, 162
    Senators
        Domenici, Pete V., 170–171
        election results, 356, 433
New York
    electoral votes, 31, 358
    Governors, 263–264
        election results, 358
        Pataki, George E., 82–83, 208, 263
    history and politics, 263–264

New York (continued)
    population, registration, and turnout, 359
    presidential election results, 358, 398, 400
    Representatives
        election results, 410–411, 426–427
        party victories, 437
    Representatives (names)
        Boehlert, Sherwood L., 95
        Forbes, Michael A., 111–112
        Fossella, Vito, 112
        Frelinghuysen, Rodney P., 113
        Gilman, Benjamin A., 115
        Grucci, Felix J., Jr., 118
        Houghton, Amo, 122
        Kelly, Sue W., 126
        King, Peter T., 126–127
        Lazio, Rick A., 130
        McHugh, John M., 133
        Molinari, Susan, 135
        Quinn, Jack, 143
        Reynolds, Thomas M., 144
        Solomon, Gerald B.H., 153–154
        Sweeney, John E., 155
        Walsh, James T., 159
    Senators
        election results, 358, 417, 433
Ney, Robert, 136
Nickles, Don, 45, 60–61, 182
Nixon, Richard M., 32, 225
North, Oliver, 285
North American Free Trade Agreement (NAFTA), 50, 57, 461
North Atlantic Treaty Organization (NATO), 50, 486, 548–549
North Carolina
    electoral votes, 360
    Governors, 266
        election results, 360
    history and politics, 264–267
    population, registration, and turnout, 361
    presidential election results, 360, 398, 400
    Representatives
        election results, 411, 427–428
        party victories, 437
    Representatives (names)
        Ballenger, Cass, 91
        Burr, Richard, 97
        Coble, Howard, 102
        Hayes, Robert (Robin) C., 119
        Jones, Walter B., 125
        Myrick, Sue, 135–136
        Spence, Floyd, 154
        Taylor, Charles H., 156
    Senators
        election results, 360, 417
        Helms, Jesse, 51, 176–177, 264
North Dakota
    electoral votes, 362
    Governors, 267
        election results, 362

North Dakota
  Governors (continued)
    Hoeven, John, 201–202
    Schafer, Edward T., 211
  history and politics, 267
  population, registration, and turnout, 363
  presidential election results, 362, 398, 400
  Representatives
    election results, 412, 428
    party victories, 437
  Senators
    election results, 362, 417, 433
North Korea, 52, 59, 546
Northern Ireland, 487, 549–550
Northern Marianas, 467, 536
Northup, Anne M., 136–137
Norton, Gale, 18, 22
Norwood, Charles W., Jr., 137
Nussle, Jim, 137

O

Ohio
  electoral votes, 364
  Governors, 268
    election results, 364
    Taft, Bob, 212–213
    Voinovich, George, 214
  history and politics, 268–269
  population, registration, and turnout, 365
  presidential election results, 364, 398, 400
  Representatives
    election results, 412, 428
    party victories, 437
  Representatives (names)
    Boehner, John A., 45, 95
    Chabot, Steve, 101
    Gillmor, Paul E., 115
    Hobson, David L., 121
    Kasich, John R., 5–6, 125
    LaTourette, Steven C., 129–130
    Ney, Robert, 136
    Oxley, Michael G., 138
    Portman, Rob, 142
    Pryce, Deborah, 142
    Regula, Ralph, 144
    Tiberi, Patrick J., 158
  Senators
    DeWine, Mike, 170
    election results, 364, 417, 433
    Voinovich, George, 189
Oklahoma
  electoral votes, 366
  Governors, 269, 270
    election results, 366
    Keating, Frank, 205–206, 269
  history and politics, 269–270
  population, registration, and turnout, 367
  presidential election results, 366, 398, 400

Oklahoma (continued)
  Representatives
    election results, 412, 428
    party victories, 437
  Representatives (names)
    Coburn, Thomas A., 102
    Istook, Ernest J., Jr., 123–124
    Largent, Steve, 60, 129
    Lucas, Frank D., 131
    Watkins, Wes, 159–160
    Watts, Julius C., Jr., 45, 84–85, 160
  Senators
    election results, 366, 417
    Inhofe, James M., 178–179
    Nickles, Don, 45, 60–61, 182
Older Americans, 480, 520–521
Olson, Theodore B., 18
Oregon
  electoral votes, 368
  Governors, 271
    election results, 368
  history and politics, 271–272
  population, registration, and turnout, 369
  presidential election results, 368, 398, 400
  Representatives
    election results, 412–413, 429
    party victories, 437
  Representatives (names)
    Smith, Robert F., 152
    Walden, Gregory Paul, 159
  Senators
    election results, 368, 417
    Smith, Gordon Harold, 184–185
Ornstein, Norman, 64
Osborne, Thomas, 137
Ose, Douglas A., 137–138
Otter, C.L. "Butch," 138
Owens, Bill, 207–208, 228
Oxley, Michael G., 138

P

Packard, Ron, 138–139
Packwood, Robert, 271
Pakistan, 547
Palestinians, 51
Pappas, Michael, 139
Parent Drug Corps, 47
Parker, Mike, 139
Party organization, 59–61
Party platform. See Republican Party platform
Pataki, George E., 82–83, 208, 263
Patients' rights, 55, 522–524
Paul, Ron E., 139
Pease, Edward A., 139–140
Pence, Mike, 140
Pennsylvania
  electoral votes, 370
  Governors, 273
    election results, 370
    Ridge, Tom, 209–210
  history and politics, 272–273

Pennsylvania (continued)
  population, registration, and turnout, 371
  presidential election results, 370, 398, 400
  Representatives
    election results, 413, 429
    party victories, 437
  Representatives (names)
    English, Phil S., 109
    Fox, Jon D., 112–113
    Gekas, George W., 114
    Goodling, William E., 116
    Greenwood, James C., 117–118
    Hart, Melissa A., 118–119
    McDade, Joseph M., 132
    Peterson, John E., 140
    Pitts, Joseph, 141
    Platts, Todd Russell, 141
    Sherwood, Don, 151
    Shuster, Bud, 151
    Toomey, Patrick J., 158
    Weldon, Curt, 160
  Senators
    election results, 370, 417, 433
    Santorum, Richard John, 45, 183
    Specter, Arlen, 185–186
Penrose, Boise, 272
Perot, Ross, 450
Perry, James Richard, 208–209
Persian Gulf, 550–551
Peterson, John E., 140
Petri, Thomas E., 140
Philippines, 491, 546
Phillips, Rubel, 252
Pickering, Charlie W., Jr., 140–141
Pitts, Joseph, 141
Platts, Todd Russell, 141
Poison pills, 38
Poland, 50
Policy Committee, 60, 61
Political reform, 533–534
Pombo, Richard W., 141
Popular votes, 30, 31
Porter, John Edward, 141–142
Portman, Rob, 142
Powell, Colin, 18, 35, 51, 449
  biography, 83–84
Prayer, school, 476
Prescription drug plan, 38, 55
Presidential debates, 11–12
Presidential elections, 42–43
  1996, 398–399, 449–450
  2000, 400–401
  See also Campaign 2000; Republican Party platform; specific state
Presidential victories, 441–442
Pressner, Larry, 276
Prevo Conservatives, 220
Privacy, medical, 525–526
Project Exile, 53
Project Safe Neighborhoods, 53
Property rights, 528
Proportional representation, 64
Proposition 187, 56

Proposition 209, 468
Pryce, Deborah, 142
Public education. *See* Education
Public land, 528–529
Puerto Rico, 467, 536, 537
Putnam, Adam H., 142–143

Q

Quackenbush, Chuck, 225
Quay, Matthew S., 272
Quayle, Dan, 6
Quinn, Jack, 143
Quinn, William, 235

R

Racial profiling, 40, 41
Racketeer Influenced and Corrupt
    Organizations law (RICO), 466
Radanovich, George, 143
Rainey, Richard, 226
Ramstad, Jim, 143
Reaganomics, 38
Recounts
    Florida, 13–15, 30
    national, 31
Redmond, Bill, 143–144
Reed, Clarke, 252
Reform Party, 6
Regula, Ralph, 144
Regulatory reform, 465, 534
Rehberg, Dennis R., 144
Religion, 22–23, 468, 515
    school prayer, 476
Representatives. *See* House of
    Representatives
Republican National Convention, 2000,
    10
Republican Party platform
    1996
        budget and spending, 458, 464–465
        Dole speech, 498–500
        environment, 480–486, 497
        families and society, 474–480, 497
        foreign policy, 486–495
        government reform, 462–464,
            465–467
        homeownership, 460–461
        individual rights and safety,
            467–474, 496–497
        jobs, 459
        preamble, 453–454
        principles, 454–455
        science and technology, 459–460
        trade, 461–462
    2000
        education, 508–514
        environment and energy, 526–532
        families and community, 514–515
        foreign policy, 537–554
        government, 532–537
        homeownership, 504–505
        individual rights and safety,
            515–519

Republican Party platform
    2000 *(continued)*
        preamble, 501–502
        prosperity, 502–508
        retirement and healthcare, 519–526
        technology, 506–508
Reuf, Abraham, 224
Reynolds, Thomas M., 144
Rhode Island
    electoral votes, 372
    Governors, 274–275
        Almond, Lincoln, 193
        election results, 372
    history and politics, 274–275
    population, registration, and turnout,
        373
    presidential election results, 372, 398,
        400
    Representatives
        election results, 413, 429
        party victories, 437
    Senators
        Chafee, John H., 167, 274
        Chafee, Lincoln, 167
        election results, 372, 433
Rhodes, James, 268
Rice, Condoleezza, 19, 23, 51
Richardson, Bill, 144
Ridge, Tom, 209–210
Riggs, Frank Duncan, 144–145
Right-to-Work laws, 516
Rights. *See* Citizens' rights
Riley, Robert, 145
Robb, Charles, 285
Roberts, Pat, 182
Rockefeller, Winthrop, 223
Roe v. Wade, 226
Roemer, Charles E., 145
Rogan, James E., 145
Rogers, Harold, 145–146
Rogers, Joseph, 275
Rogers, Mike, 146
Rohrabacher, Dana, 146
Romer, Roy, 228
Romney, George, 248
Roosevelt, Franklin D., 249–250
Ros-Lehtinen, Ileana, 146
Roth, William V., Jr., 183
Roukema, Marge, 39, 146–147
Rowland, John G., 210, 229
Royce, Edward, 147
Rumsfeld, Donald H., 51
Russia, 24, 58, 487, 549
Ryan, George H., 210–211
Ryan, Paul, 147
Ryun, Jim, 147

S

Safe and Drug-Free Schools and
    Communities Act, 46
Salmon, Matt, 147
Sampling, 26
Sanford, Mark, 39
Sanford, Marshall Clement, Jr., 147–148

Santorum, Richard John, 45, 183
Saudi Arabia, 551
Saxton, Jim, 148
Scarborough, Joe, 148
Schaefer, Dan, 148
Schafer, Edward T., 211
Schaffer, Bob, 148–149
Schiff, Steven, 149
School prayer, 476
School-to-Work Act, 475
Schools. *See* Education
Schrock, Edward L., 149
Schumer, Charles, 450
Science and technology. *See* Technology
Securities Litigation Reform Act, 466–467,
    507
Security
    national, 493, 494–495
    See also Military
Senate
    elections
        1998, 417
        2000, 433
    leadership and party organization,
        60–61
    members, 163–190
    party composition, 434–436
    seats that changed party, 439–440
    vote on Clinton's impeachment, 559,
        560, 562
    See also Congress; specific state
Sensenbrenner, F. James, Jr., 149
Service Contract Act, 459
Sessions, Jefferson Beauregard, III,
    183–184
Sessions, Pete, 149–150
Shadegg, John B., 150
Shaw, E. Clay, Jr., 150
Shays, Christopher, 39, 150–151
Shays-Meehan Bill, 39
Shelby, Richard C., 184, 219
Sherwood, Don, 151
Shimkus, John M., 151
Shuster, Bud, 151
Simmons, Robert, 151–152
Simpson, Alan, 290
Simpson, Michael K., 152
Skeen, Joe R., 152
Small business, 505
Smith, Al, 219, 274
Smith, Christopher H., 152
Smith, Gordon Harold, 184–185
Smith, Lamar S., 152–153
Smith, Linda A., 39, 153
Smith, Nick, 153
Smith, Robert C., 5–6, 185
Smith, Robert F., 152
Smylie, Robert, 236
Snowbarger, Vincent K., 153
Snowe, Olympia J., 39, 185
Social Security, 21, 37–38, 61–63, 480,
    519–520
Soft money. *See* Campaign finance reform
Soldiers' and Sailors' Civil Relief Act, 494
Solomon, Gerald B.H., 153–154

Souder, Mark E., 154
South Carolina
    electoral votes, 374
    Governors, 276
        Beasley, David, 194
        election results, 374
    history and politics, 275–276
    population, registration, and turnout,
        375
    presidential election results, 374, 398,
        400
    Representatives
        election results, 413, 429–430
        party victories, 437
    Representatives (names)
        Brown, Henry E., Jr., 96–97
        DeMint, Jim, 106
        Graham, Lindsey O., 116–117, 558
        Inglis, Bob, 123
        Sanford, Marshall Clement, Jr., 147–
            148
    Senators
        election results, 374, 417
        Thurmond, Strom, 45, 46, 187–189,
            275
South Dakota
    electoral votes, 376
    Governors, 277
        election results, 376
        Janklow, William J., 203–204
    history and politics, 276–277
    population, registration, and turnout,
        377
    presidential election results, 376, 398,
        400
    Representatives
        election results, 414, 430
        party victories, 437
    Representatives (names)
        Thune, John R., 157–158
    Senators
        election results, 376, 417
South Korea, 52, 546
Soviet Union, former, 24, 58–59
Space programs, 494–495
Speaker of the House, 59–60
Specter, Arlen, 185–186
Spence, Floyd, 154
Spivey, Ebbie, 252
Standard of living, 456
Starr, Kenneth, 557
START. See Strategic Arms Reduction
    Talks (START) Treaty
States' Rights Party, 275
Stearns, Cliff B., 154–155
Steering Committee, 60
Stevens, Ted, 186
Strategic Arms Reduction Talks (START)
    Treaty, 50
Strategic Defense Initiative, 488
Stump, Bob, 63, 155
Sundquist, Don, 211–212
Sununu, John E., 155
Supreme Court. See United States
    Supreme Court

Sweeney, John E., 155
Swift, Jane, 212
Symington, John Fife, III, 212

T

Taft, Bob, 212–213
Taiwan, 24, 50, 52, 59, 491, 547
Talent, James M., 155–156
Tancredo, Thomas G., 156
Tauzon, W.J., 156
Tax credits
    Charity Tax Credit, 479–480
    child, 514
    healthcare, 54, 55–56
Tax cuts, 20–21, 37, 503–504
Tax relief, 456–459
Taylor, Charles H., 156
TEAM Act, 459
Technology, 459–460, 506–508
    cyber threats, 552–553
Tenet, George, 50
Tennessee
    electoral votes, 378
    Governors, 278
        Alexander, Lamar, 6
        election results, 378
        Sundquist, Don, 211–212
    history and politics, 277–279
    population, registration, and turnout,
        379
    presidential election results, 378, 398,
        400
    Representatives
        election results, 414, 430
        party victories, 437
    Representatives (names)
        Bryant, Edward, 97
        Duncan, John J., Jr., 107–108
        Hilleary, Van, 120
        Jenkins, William Lewis, 124
        Wamp, Zachary P., 39, 159
    Senators
        election results, 378, 433
        Frist, William H., 45, 55, 61,
            172–173
        Thompson, Fred, 39, 187
Terrorism, 490, 550, 552–553
    bioterrorism, 526
Terry, Lee, 156–157
Texas
    electoral votes, 380
    Governors, 280
        Bush, George W. See Bush,
            George W.
        election results, 380
        Perry, James Richard, 208–209
    history and politics, 279–280
    population, registration, and turnout,
        381
    presidential election results, 380, 398,
        400
    Representatives
        election results, 414–415, 430–431
        party victories, 437

Texas (continued)
    Representatives (names)
        Archer, Bill, 89–90
        Armey, Dick, 90
        Barton, Joe L., 92
        Bonilla, Henry, 96
        Brady, Kevin, 96
        Combest, Larry, 103
        Culberson, John Abney, 105
        DeLay, Tom, 45, 60, 73–74, 106
        Granger, Kay, 117
        Johnson, Sam, 124
        Paul, Ron E., 139
        Sessions, Pete, 149–150
        Smith, Lamar S., 152–153
        Thornberry, William M., 157
    Senators
        election results, 380, 433
        Gramm, Phil, 173
        Hutchison, Kay Bailey, 178
Texas 10 Percent Plan, 35
Theater High Altitude Area Defense, 488
Thomas, Bill, 39, 157
Thomas, Craig, 186
Thompson, Fred, 39, 187
Thompson, Tommy G., 18, 46, 213, 288,
    289
Thompson, William Hale, 237
Thornberry, William M., 157
Three-fifths compromise, 29
Three-strikes law, 225
Thune, John R., 157–158
Thurmond, Strom, 45, 46, 275
    biography, 187–189
Tiahrt, Todd, 158
Tiberi, Patrick J., 158
Tilden, Samuel, 30
Tilling, James, 268
Toomey, Patrick J., 158
Tower, John, 279
Trade, 50, 52
    1996 party platform, 461–462,
        505–506
    2000 party platform, 543–545
    Free Trade Area of the Americas, 52
    North American Free Trade Agreement
        (NAFTA), 50, 57, 461
Transportation, 531–532
Treen, David, 244
Tripp, Linda, 557
Tucker, Jim Guy, 223

U

Underwood, Cecil H., 213–214, 287
United Nations, 51, 552
    Human Rights Commission, 52
    weapons inspection, 50
United States Census Bureau, 26
United States Constitution
    Electoral College, 28–29
    Tenth Amendment, 462
    Twelfth Amendment, 30
United States Declaration of
    Independence, 495–496

United States Department of Education, 21, 48, 475
United States Department of Energy, 22
United States Department of Housing and Urban Development (HUD), 461
United States Department of the Interior, 21
United States House of Representatives, Department of Commerce v., 26
United States Supreme Court, 466
    Florida recount, 15, 30
Upton, Fred, 158
Utah
    electoral votes, 382
    Governors, 281
        election results, 382
        Leavitt, Michael O., 206–207
    history and politics, 280–281
    lawsuit against Census Bureau, 26–27
    population, registration, and turnout, 383
    presidential election results, 382, 398, 400
    Representatives
        election results, 415, 431
        party victories, 438
    Representatives (names)
        Cannon, Christopher B., 99–100
        Cook, Merrill, 103
        Hansen, James V., 118
    Senators
        Bennett, Robert F., 164
        election results, 382, 417, 433
        Hatch, Orrin G., 6, 176

V

Valeo, Buckley v., 40
Ventura, Jesse, 6, 250
Vermont
    electoral votes, 384
    Governors, 282–283
        election results, 384
    history and politics, 282–283
    number of electors, 31
    population, registration, and turnout, 385
    presidential election results, 384, 399, 401
    Representatives
        election results, 415, 431
        party victories, 438
    Senators
        election results, 384, 417, 433
        Jeffords, James, 25, 39, 43, 59, 179, 282
Veterans, 494, 540–541
Victim's Rights Amendment, 472
Vietnam, 547
Virgin Islands, 467, 536
Virginia
    electoral votes, 386
    Governors, 285
        Allen, George, 193
        election results, 386

Virginia
    Governors (*continued*)
        Gilmore, James, III, 199–200
    history and politics, 283–285
    population, registration, and turnout, 387
    presidential election results, 386, 399, 401
    Representatives
        election results, 415, 431
        party victories, 438
    Representatives (names)
        Bateman, Herbert H., 93
        Bliley, Tom J., 94–95
        Cantor, Eric, 100
        Davis, Jo Ann, 105–106
        Davis, Thomas, 45, 60, 106
        Goodlatte, Robert W., 115–116
        Schrock, Edward L., 149
        Wolf, Frank R., 162
    Senators
        Allen, George, 163–164
        election results, 386
Vitter, David, 158–159
Voinovich, George, 189, 214
Voter registration and partisan enrollment
    1998, 443–444
    2000, 445–446
Voting behavior, 63–65
    See also Electoral College
Vouchers, 41, 48–49

W

Walden, Gregory Paul, 159
Wallace, George, 219
Walsh, James T., 159
Walters, John P., 46
Wamp, Zachary P., 39, 159
Warner, John W., 189
Warren, Earl, 224–225
Warren, Francis E., 290
Washington
    electoral votes, 388
    Governors, 286
        election results, 388
    history and politics, 286–287
    population, registration, and turnout, 389
    presidential election results, 388, 399, 401
    Representatives
        election results, 415–416, 431–432
        party victories, 438
    Representatives (names)
        Dunn, Jennifer, 60, 108
        Hastings, Doc, 119
        Metcalf, Jack, 39, 134
        Nethercutt, George R., Jr., 136
        Smith, Linda A., 39, 153
        White, Richard, 161
    Senators
        election results, 388, 417, 433
        Gorton, Slade, 173
Washington, D.C. *See* District of Columbia

Watkins, Wes, 159–160
Watts, Julius C., Jr., 45, 84–85, 160
Watts-Talent Low-Income Educational Opportunity Act, 476
Weapons inspection, United Nations, 50
Weapons of mass destruction, 541–543
Webster, William, 254
Weicker, Lowell, 229
Weldon, Curt, 160
Weldon, Dave, 160–161
Welfare reform, 479–480
Weller, Jerry, 161
Wellness, 526
West Virginia
    electoral votes, 390
    Governors, 288
        election results, 390
        Underwood, Cecil H., 213–214, 287
    history and politics, 287–288
    population, registration, and turnout, 391
    presidential election results, 390, 399, 401
    Representatives
        election results, 416, 432
        party victories, 438
    Representatives (names)
        Capito, Shelley Moore, 100
    Senators
        election results, 390, 433
        Warner, John W., 189
Western Hemisphere, 492–493
White, Frank, 223
White, Richard, 161
White, Ronnie, 36
White House Office of Faith-Based and Community Initiatives, 22–23
White supremacy, 219
Whitfield, Edward, 161
Whitman, Christine Todd, 18, 41, 214–215
Wicker, Roger F., 161–162
Wilson, Heather Ann, 162
Wilson, Peter Barton, 56, 63, 215, 225
Wisconsin
    electoral votes, 392
    Governors, 289
        election results, 392
        McCallum, James Scott, 207, 289
        Thompson, Tommy G., 18, 46, 213, 288, 289
    history and politics, 288–289
    population, registration, and turnout, 393
    presidential election results, 392, 399, 401
    Representatives
        election results, 416, 432
        party victories, 438
    Representatives (names)
        Green, Mark, 117
        Klug, Scott, 127
        Neumann, Mark W., 136

Wisconsin
  Representatives (names) *(continued)*
    Petri, Thomas E., 140
    Ryan, Paul, 147
    Sensenbrenner, F. James, Jr., 149
  Senators
    election results, 392, 417, 433
Wolf, Frank R., 162
Women
  equal pay, 40
  equal rights, 468
  healthcare, 524–525
Work and workers. *See* Employment
World Intellectual Property Organization,
  507

World Trade Organization, 462,
  547
Wyoming
  electoral votes, 394
  Governors, 290
    election results, 394
    Geringer, Jim, 198–199
  history and politics, 290–291
  population, registration, and
    turnout, 395
  presidential election results, 394,
    399, 401
  Representatives
    election results, 416, 432
    party victories, 438

Wyoming *(continued)*
  Representatives (names)
    Cubin, Barbara, 104–105
  Senators
    election results, 394, 433
    Enzi, Michael B., 171–172
    Thomas, Craig, 186

Y

Yeltsin, Boris, 50
Yerger, Wirt, Jr., 251
Young, C.W., 162
Young, Donald E., 162–163
Youth. *See* Children

BIOGRAPHICAL INDEX

A

Abdnor, James, 276
Abraham, Spencer, 163
Adams, John Quincy, 29, 30
Adams, Lloyd, 236
Aderholt, Robert B., 89
Akin, W. Todd, 89
Albright, Madeleine, 50
Alexander, Lamar, 6
Allard, Wayne, 163
Allen, George, 63, 163–164, 193, 284
Almond, Lincoln, 193
Annan, Kofi, 51
Archer, Bill, 89–90
Armey, Dick, 45, 60, 90
Ashcroft, John, 18, 36, 41, 46, 254
    biography, 164
Atiyeh, Victor, 271
Aung San Suu Kyi, 547

B

Bachus, Spencer, 90–91
Baker, Richard H., 91
Ballenger, Cass, 91
Barr, Bob, 91
Barrett, William E., 39, 91–92
Bartlett, Dewey, 269
Bartlett, Roscoe G., 92
Barton, Joe L., 92
Bass, Charles, 92–93
Bateman, Herbert H., 93
Batt, Philip E., 193–194
Bauer, Gary, 6, 7, 8
Baugh, Scott, 225
Beasley, David, 194
Bellmon, Henry, 269
Bennett, Robert, 268
Bennett, Robert F., 164
Bennett, William J., 69–70
Bentsen, Lloyd, 31
Bereuter, Doug, 93
Biggert, Judy, 93–94
Bilbray, Brian, 94
Bilirakis, Michael, 94
Bliley, Tom J., 94–95
Bliss, Ray, 279
Blunt, Roy D., 95
Boehlert, Sherwood L., 95
Boehner, John A., 45, 95
Bond, Christopher S., 45, 164, 253–254

Bonilla, Henry, 96
Bono, Mary, 96
Boutros-Ghali, Boutros, 51
Boyd, Ralph, 41–42
Bradley, Bill, 39
Brady, Kevin, 96
Branstad, Terry Edward, 194, 240
Breaux, John, 55
Brock, Bill, 279
Brown, Henry E., Jr., 96–97
Brownback, Samuel Dale, 65, 164–165
Brulte, Jim, 225
Bryant, Edward, 97
Bunnings, Jim, 165
Burns, Conrad R., 166
Burr, Aaron, 29–30
Burr, Richard, 97
Burton, Dan, 97–98
Bush, George W.
    approval rating, 25
    biography, 3–5, 70–72, 194–195
    election results, 15
    first hundred days, 16–25
    Florida recount, 13–15, 30
    popular and electoral votes, 30
    religious initiatives, 22–23
    style of, 19–20
    Texas governor, 279, 450
    vs. Gore, Albert, 9–12
    vs. McCain, 8–9
Bush, Jeb, 14, 64, 450
    biography, 195
Buyer, Steve, 98
Byrd, Harry Flood, 284
Byrd, Harry Flood, Jr., 284

C

Callahan, Sonny, 98
Calvert, Ken, 98
Cameron, Simon, 272
Camp, Dave, 98–99
Campbell, Ben Nighthorse, 166–167
Campbell, Tom, 99
Campbell, William, 288
Canady, Charles T., 99
Cannon, Christopher B., 99–100
Cantor, Eric, 100
Capito, Shelley Moore, 100
Carlson, Arne, 195–196
Carmichael, Gil, 252

Castle, Michael, 100–101, 230
Cellucci, Argeo Paul, 64, 196
Cermak, Anton, 237
Chabot, Steve, 101
Chafee, John H., 167, 274
Chafee, Lincoln, 167
Chambliss, Saxby, 101
Cheney, Dick, 9, 12, 17
    anti-drug legislation, 47
    biography, 72–73
Chenoweth-Hage, Helen P., 101
Chiles, Lawton Mainor, Jr., 196–197
Christensen, Jon, 101–102
Clark, Joseph S., 272
Clements, Bill, 279
Cleveland, Grover, 30
Clinton, William Jefferson, 20, 223
    election (1996), 449–450
    foreign policy, 50
    impeachment, 45, 557–564
    popular and electoral votes, 30
    Social Security, 62
Coats, Dan, 168
Coble, Howard, 102
Coburn, Thomas A., 102
Cochran, Thad, 168–169, 252
Cohen, William S., 50
Cole, Tom, 269
Collins, Mac, 102–103
Collins, Susan, 169
Colson, Charles, 64
Combest, Larry, 103
Connally, John, 279
Cook, Merrill, 103
Cooksey, John, 103
Coverdell, Paul D., 63, 169, 502
Cox, Christopher, 45, 60, 103–104
Craig, Larry, 45
Craig, Larry E., 61, 169–170
Crane, Philip M., 104
Crapo, Mike, 170
Crenshaw, Ander, 104
Cubin, Barbara, 104–105
Culberson, John Abney, 105
Cunningham, Randy (Duke), 105

D

D'Amato, Alfonse, 263, 450
Daley, Richard J., 237
Danforth, John, 253, 254
Davis, Gray, 225, 450

Davis, Jo Ann, 105–106
Davis, Thomas, 45, 60, 106
Deal, Nathan, 106
DeLay, Tom, 45, 60, 73–74, 106
DeMint, Jim, 106
Denton, Jeremiah, 219
Deukmejian, George, 225
DeWine, Mike, 170
Diaz-Balart, Lincoln, 106–107
Dickey, Jay W., Jr., 107
DiFrancesco, Donald T., 197
DiIulio, John J., Jr., 22
Dilworth, Richardson, 272
Dole, Bob, 30, 45, 60, 449–450, 498–500
Dole, Elizabeth, 6, 74–75, 449
Domenici, Pete V., 170–171
Doolittle, John T., 39, 107
Dreier, David, 107
Dukakis, Michael, 31
Duncan, John J., Jr., 107–108
Dunn, Jennifer, 60, 108

E

Earle, George H., 272
Edgar, James, 197
Edwards, John, 450
Ehlers, Vernon J., 108–109
Ehrlich, Robert L., Jr., 109
Eisenhower, Dwight, 219
Emerson, Jo Ann, 109
Engler, John, 63, 197–198, 249
English, Phil S., 109
Ensign, John, 109–110, 171
Enzi, Michael B., 171–172
Everett, Terry, 110
Ewing, Thomas W., 110

F

Faircloth, Launch, 450
Falwell, Jerry, 23
Fawell, Harris W., 110–111
Feingold, Russell, 39
Ferguson, Michael, 111
Fiske, Robert, 557
Fitzgerald, Peter G., 172
Flake, Jeff, 111
Fleischer, Ari, 20
Fletcher, Ernest Lee, 111
Foley, Mark A., 111
Forbes, Michael A., 111–112
Forbes, Steve, 6, 7, 8, 231
Fordice, Kirk, 198, 252
Fossella, Vito, 112
Foster, M.J., 198
Fowler, Thomas K., 112
Fox, Jon D., 112–113
Franks, Bob, 113
Freeman, Orville, 250
Frelinghuysen, Rodney P., 113
Frist, William H., 45, 55, 61, 172–173

G

Gallegly, Elton, 113–114
Ganske, Greg, 114
Gekas, George W., 114
Geringer, Jim, 198–199
Gibbons, James A., 114
Gilchrest, Wayne T., 114–115
Gillmor, Paul E., 115
Gilman, Benjamin A., 115
Gilmore, James, III, 199–200, 284
Gingrich, Newt, 42, 43, 44, 48, 234
    biography, 75–76
    Speaker of the House, 59–60
Giuliani, Rudolph, 263
Goldwater, Barry, 221, 236, 251, 275
Goodlatte, Robert W., 115–116
Goodling, William E., 116
Gore, Albert
    Bush vs., 9–12
    concession, 12–13
    Florida recount, 13–15, 30
    popular vote, 30, 31
Gorton, Slade, 173
Goss, Porter J., 116
Graham, Lindsey O., 116–117, 558
Gramm, Phil, 173
Grams, Rod, 174
Granger, Kay, 117
Grant, Ulysses S., 251
Grassley, Charles, 174
Graves, Bill, 200–201, 241
Graves, Samuel, 117
Green, Mark, 117
Greenwood, James C., 117–118
Gregg, Judd, 174–175
Grucci, Felix J., Jr., 118
Guffey, Joseph F., 272
Guinn, Kenny C., 201
Gutknecht, Gil, 118

H

Hagel, Charles, 22, 39, 45, 175–176
Hansen, James V., 118
Hanssen, Robert, 24
Harris, Katherine, 14
Harrison, Benjamin, 30
Hart, Melissa A., 118–119
Hastert, J. Dennis, 39, 45
    biography, 76–77, 119
    Speaker of the House, 60
Hastings, Doc, 119
Hatch, Orrin G., 6, 176
Hatfield, Mark, 271
Hayes, Robert (Robin) C., 119
Hayes, Rutherford B., 30
Hayworth, John D., 119
Hefley, Joel, 120
Helms, Jesse, 51, 176–177, 264
Herger, Wally, 120
Hickel, Walter J., 220
Hill, Rick, 120
Hilleary, Van, 120

Hobson, David L., 121
Hoekstra, Peter, 121
Hoeven, John, 201–202
Holbrooke, Richard, 51
Holshouser, James, 264
Holton, Linwood, 284
Horn, Stephen, 121
Hostettler, John Nathan, 121
Houghton, Amo, 122
House, George, 226
Huckabee, Mike, 202, 223
Hughes, Harold, 240
Hull, Jane Dee, 202–203
Hulshof, Kenny, 122
Humphrey, Hubert, 250
Hunt, Guy, 219
Hunter, Duncan, 122
Hussein, Saddam, 50, 51, 550–551
Hutchinson, Asa, 39, 122
Hutchinson, Tim, 177–178, 223
Hutchison, Kay Bailey, 178
Hyde, Henry J., 78–79, 122–123, 558

I

Inglis, Bob, 123
Inhofe, James M., 178–179
Isakson, Johnny, 123
Issa, Darrell E., 123
Istook, Ernest J., Jr., 123–124

J

Jackson, Andrew, 30
James, Fob, Jr., 203, 219
Janklow, William J., 203–204
Jefferson, Thomas, 29–30
Jeffords, James, 25, 39, 43, 59, 282
    biography, 179
Jenkins, William Lewis, 124
Johanns, Mike, 204
Johnson, Gary E., 204–205
Johnson, Hiram, 224
Johnson, Nancy L., 124
Johnson, Sam, 124
Johnson, Timothy V., 124–125
Jones, Paula, 557
Jones, Walter B., 125

K

Kasich, John R., 5–6, 125
Keating, Frank, 205–206, 269
Keller, Richard, 125–126
Kelly, Sue W., 126
Kemp, Jack, 449
Kempthorne, Dirk, 179, 206
Kennedy, John F., 32
Kennedy, Mark R., 126
Kerns, Brian D., 126
Key, Clinton, 269
Keyes, Alan, 6, 7, 8
Kim, Jay, 126
King, Peter T., 126–127

Kingston, Jack, 127
Kirk, Mark Steven, 127
Klug, Scott, 127
Knollenberg, Joe, 128
Knowland, William, 225
Knowles, Tony, 220
Kolbe, Jim, 128
Kuykendall, Steven T., 128
Kyl, Jon, 179

L

La Follette, Robert M., 288
LaHood, Ray, 128–129
Lake, Anthony, 50
Lamm, Richard, 228
Largent, Steve, 60, 129
Latham, Tom, 129
LaTourette, Steven C., 129–130
Lazio, Rick A., 130
Leach, James A., 130
Leach, Margarette, 31
Leader, George, 272
Leavitt, Michael O., 206–207
Lewinsky, Monica, 557–558
Lewis, Jerry, 130
Lewis, Ron, 130–131
Lincoln, Abraham, 30
Linder, John, 45, 63, 131
Livingston, Robert, 44–45, 60, 63
LoBiondo, Frank A., 131
Lott, Trent, 45, 46, 60, 252
    biography, 79–80, 179–180
Lucas, Frank D., 131
Lugar, Richard G., 180

M

Mack, Connie, 45, 180
Mahone, William, 283
Manzullo, Donald, 63, 131–132
Martz, Judy, 207
Mattingly, Mack, 234
McCain, John, 5, 7–8, 39, 65
    biography, 80–81, 181
    Bush vs., 8–9
McCallum, James Scott, 207, 289
McCarthy, Eugene, 250
McClintock, Tom, 226
McCollum, Bill, 132
McConnell, Mitch, 39, 45, 63, 65, 242
    biography, 81–82, 181
McCrery, Jim, 132
McDade, Joseph M., 132
McHugh, John M., 133
McInnis, Scott, 133
McIntosh, David M., 133–134
McKeon, Howard P., 134
McPhail, Evelyn, 252
Meadow, William H., 22
Mecham, Evan, 221–222
Meehan, Martin T., 39
Metcalf, Jack, 39, 134
Mica, John L., 134

Michel, Robert, 44
Miller, Dan, 134–135
Miller, David, 241
Miller, Gary G., 135
Milliken, Roger, 275
Molinari, Susan, 135
Mondale, Walter, 250
Moore, Arch, 287
Moran, Jerry, 135
Morella, Constance A., 135
Muldihill, M.J., 251
Murkowski, Frank H., 181
Muskie, Edmund, 245
Myrick, Sue, 135–136

N

Nader, Ralph, 10–11, 15
Nethercutt, George R., Jr., 136
Neuberger, Richard, 271
Neumann, Mark W., 136
Ney, Robert, 136
Nickles, Don, 45, 60–61, 182
Nixon, Richard M., 32, 225
North, Oliver, 285
Northup, Anne M., 136–137
Norton, Gale, 18, 22
Norwood, Charles W., Jr., 137
Nussle, Jim, 137

O

Olson, Theodore B., 18
Ornstein, Norman, 64
Osborne, Thomas, 137
Ose, Douglas A., 137–138
Otter, C.L. "Butch," 138
Owens, Bill, 207–208, 228
Oxley, Michael G., 138

P

Packard, Ron, 138–139
Packwood, Robert, 271
Pappas, Michael, 139
Parker, Mike, 139
Pataki, George E., 82–83, 208, 263
Paul, Ron E., 139
Pease, Edward A., 139–140
Pence, Mike, 140
Penrose, Boise, 272
Perot, Ross, 450
Perry, James Richard, 208–209
Peterson, John E., 140
Petri, Thomas E., 140
Phillips, Rubel, 252
Pickering, Charlie W., Jr., 140–141
Pitts, Joseph, 141
Platts, Todd Russell, 141
Pombo, Richard W., 141
Porter, John Edward, 141–142
Portman, Rob, 142
Powell, Colin, 18, 35, 51, 449
    biography, 83–84

Pressner, Larry, 276
Prevo Conservatives, 220
Pryce, Deborah, 142
Putnam, Adam H., 142–143

Q

Quackenbush, Chuck, 225
Quay, Matthew S., 272
Quayle, Dan, 6
Quinn, Jack, 143
Quinn, William, 235

R

Radanovich, George, 143
Rainey, Richard, 226
Ramstad, Jim, 143
Redmond, Bill, 143–144
Reed, Clarke, 252
Regula, Ralph, 144
Rehberg, Dennis R., 144
Reuf, Abraham, 224
Reynolds, Thomas M., 144
Rhodes, James, 268
Rice, Condoleezza, 19, 23, 51
Richardson, Bill, 144
Ridge, Tom, 209–210
Riggs, Frank Duncan, 144–145
Riley, Robert, 145
Robb, Charles, 285
Roberts, Pat, 182
Rockefeller, Winthrop, 223
Roemer, Charles E., 145
Rogan, James E., 145
Rogers, Harold, 145–146
Rogers, Joseph, 275
Rogers, Mike, 146
Rohrabacher, Dana, 146
Romer, Roy, 228
Romney, George, 248
Roosevelt, Franklin D., 249–250
Ros-Lehtinen, Ileana, 146
Roth, William V., Jr., 183
Roukema, Marge, 39, 146–147
Rowland, John G., 210, 229
Royce, Edward, 147
Rumsfeld, Donald H., 51
Ryan, George H., 210–211
Ryan, Paul, 147
Ryun, Jim, 147

S

Salmon, Matt, 147
Sanford, Mark, 39
Sanford, Marshall Clement, Jr., 147–148
Santorum, Richard John, 45, 183
Saxton, Jim, 148
Scarborough, Joe, 148
Schaefer, Dan, 148
Schafer, Edward T., 211
Schaffer, Bob, 148–149
Schiff, Steven, 149

Schrock, Edward L., 149
Schumer, Charles, 450
Sensenbrenner, F. James, Jr., 149
Sessions, Jefferson Beauregard, III,
    183–184
Sessions, Pete, 149–150
Shadegg, John B., 150
Shaw, E. Clay, Jr., 150
Shays, Christopher, 39, 150–151
Shelby, Richard C., 184, 219
Sherwood, Don, 151
Shimkus, John M., 151
Shuster, Bud, 151
Simmons, Robert, 151–152
Simpson, Alan, 290
Simpson, Michael K., 152
Skeen, Joe R., 152
Smith, Al, 219, 274
Smith, Christopher H., 152
Smith, Gordon Harold,
    184–185
Smith, Lamar S., 152–153
Smith, Linda A., 39, 153
Smith, Nick, 153
Smith, Robert C., 5–6, 185
Smith, Robert F., 152
Smylie, Robert, 236
Snowbarger, Vincent K., 153
Snowe, Olympia J., 39, 185
Solomon, Gerald B.H., 153–154
Souder, Mark E., 154
Specter, Arlen, 185–186
Spence, Floyd, 154
Spivey, Ebbie, 252
Starr, Kenneth, 557
Stearns, Cliff B., 154–155
Stevens, Ted, 186
Stump, Bob, 63, 155
Sundquist, Don, 211–212

Sununu, John E., 155
Sweeney, John E., 155
Swift, Jane, 212
Symington, John Fife, III, 212

T

Taft, Bob, 212–213
Talent, James M., 155–156
Tancredo, Thomas G., 156
Tauzon, W.J., 156
Taylor, Charles H., 156
Tenet, George, 50
Terry, Lee, 156–157
Thomas, Bill, 39, 157
Thomas, Craig, 186
Thompson, Fred, 39, 187
Thompson, Tommy G., 18, 46,
    213, 288, 289
Thompson, William Hale, 237
Thornberry, William M., 157
Thune, John R., 157–158
Thurmond, Strom, 45, 46, 275
    biography, 187–189
Tiahrt, Todd, 158
Tiberi, Patrick J., 158
Tilden, Samuel, 30
Tilling, James, 268
Toomey, Patrick J., 158
Tower, John, 279
Treen, David, 244
Tripp, Linda, 557
Tucker, Jim Guy, 223

U

Underwood, Cecil H., 213–214,
    287
Upton, Fred, 158

V

Ventura, Jesse, 6, 250
Vitter, David, 158–159
Voinovich, George, 189, 214

W

Walden, Gregory Paul, 159
Wallace, George, 219
Walsh, James T., 159
Walters, John P., 46
Wamp, Zachary P., 39, 159
Warner, John W., 189
Warren, Earl, 224–225
Warren, Francis E., 290
Watkins, Wes, 159–160
Watts, Julius C., Jr., 45, 84–85, 160
Webster, William, 254
Weicker, Lowell, 229
Weldon, Curt, 160
Weldon, Dave, 160–161
Weller, Jerry, 161
White, Frank, 223
White, Richard, 161
White, Ronnie, 36
Whitfield, Edward, 161
Whitman, Christine Todd, 18, 41,
    214–215
Wicker, Roger F., 161–162
Wilson, Heather Ann, 162
Wilson, Peter Barton, 56, 63, 215, 225
Wolf, Frank R., 162

Y

Yeltsin, Boris, 50
Yerger, Wirt, Jr., 251
Young, C.W., 162
Young, Donald E., 162–163

GEOGRAPHICAL INDEX

A

Africa, 490–491, 551–552
Alabama
  electoral votes, 295
  Governors, 219
    election results, 295
  history and politics, 219–220
  population, registration, and turnout, 296
  presidential election results, 295, 398, 400
  Representatives
    election results, 402, 418
    party victories, 437
  Senators
    election results, 295, 417
Alaska
  drilling for oil, 22
  electoral votes, 297
  Governors, 220, 221
    election results, 297
  history and politics, 220–221
  population, registration, and turnout, 298
  presidential election results, 297, 398, 400
  Representatives
    election results, 402, 418
    party victories, 437
  Senators
    election results, 297, 417
American Samoa, 467, 536
Arctic National Wildlife Refuge, 22
Arizona
  107th Congress, 27
  electoral votes, 299
  Governors, 222
    election results, 299
  history and politics, 221–222
  population, registration, and turnout, 300
  presidential election results, 299, 398, 400
  Representatives
    election results, 402, 418
    party victories, 437
  Senators
    election results, 299, 417
Arkansas
  electoral votes, 301

Arkansas (continued)
  Governors, 224
    election results, 301
  history and politics, 222–224
  population, registration, and turnout, 302
  presidential election results, 301, 398, 400
  Representatives
    election results, 402, 418
    party victories, 437
  Senators
    election results, 301, 417, 433
Asia, 491, 546–547
Australia, 546

B

Bosnia, 50, 486–487, 549

C

California
  blackouts, 22
  electoral votes, 303
  Governors, 225, 226
    election results, 303
  history and politics, 224–226
  number of electors, 31
  population, registration, and turnout, 304
  presidential election results, 303, 398, 400
  Proposition 187, 56
  Proposition 209, 468
  Representatives
    election results, 402–404, 418–420
    party victories, 437
  Senators
    election results, 303, 417, 433
Canada, 545
China, 24, 50, 52, 59, 491, 547
Colorado
  electoral votes, 305
  Governors, 228
    election results, 305
  history and politics, 227–229
  population, registration, and turnout, 306

Colorado (continued)
  presidential election results, 305, 398, 400
  Representatives
    election results, 404, 420
    party victories, 437
  Senators
    election results, 305, 417
Columbia, 47
Connecticut
  electoral votes, 307
  Governors, 229–230
    election results, 307
  history and politics, 229–230
  population, registration, and turnout, 308
  presidential election results, 307, 398, 400
  Representatives
    election results, 404, 420
    party victories, 437
  Senators
    election results, 307, 417, 433
Cuba, 492, 546
Cyprus, 487–488, 550
Czech Republic, 50, 486, 548

D

Delaware
  electoral votes, 309
  Governors, 231
    election results, 309
  history and politics, 230–232
  population, registration, and turnout, 310
  presidential election results, 309, 398, 400
  Representatives
    election results, 404, 420
    party victories, 437
  Senators
    election results, 309, 433
District of Columbia, 467, 537
  electoral votes, 311
  population, registration, and turnout, 311
  presidential election results, 311, 398, 400
  Representatives
    election results, 404, 420

E

Egypt, 551
Europe, 547–550

F

Florida
    electoral votes, 312
    Governors, 233
        election results, 312
    history and politics, 232–233
    population, registration, and turnout,
        313
    presidential election results, 312, 398,
        400
    recount, 13–15, 30
    Representatives
        election results, 404–405, 420–421
        party victories, 437
    Senators
        election results, 312, 417, 433
    State Supreme Court, 14–15

G

Georgia
    electoral votes, 314
    Governors, 234
        election results, 314
    history and politics, 233–235
    population, registration, and turnout,
        315
    presidential election results, 314, 398,
        400
    Representatives
        election results, 405, 421
        party victories, 437
    Senators
        election results, 314, 417, 433
Guam, 467, 536

H

Haiti, 493
Hawaii
    electoral votes, 316
    Governors, 316
    history and politics, 235
    population, registration, and turnout,
        317
    presidential election results, 316, 398,
        400
    Representatives
        election results, 405, 421
        party victories, 437
    Senators, 316, 417, 433

I

Idaho
    electoral votes, 318
    Governors, 236
        election results, 318
    history and politics, 236–237

Idaho (continued)
    population, registration, and turnout,
        319
    presidential election results, 318, 398,
        400
    Representatives
        election results, 405, 421
        party victories, 437
    Senators
        election results, 318, 417
Illinois
    electoral votes, 320
    Governors, 238
        election results, 320
    history and politics, 237–238
    population, registration, and turnout,
        321
    presidential election results, 320, 398,
        400
    Representatives
        election results, 406, 422
        party victories, 437
    Senators
        election results, 320, 417
India, 547
Indiana
    electoral votes, 322
    Governors, 239
        election results, 322
    history and politics, 238–239
    population, registration, and turnout,
        323
    presidential election results, 322, 398,
        400
    Representatives
        election results, 406, 422
        party victories, 437
    Senators
        election results, 322, 417, 433
Iowa
    caucuses, 7
    electoral votes, 324
    Governors, 241
        election results, 324
    history and politics, 240–241
    population, registration, and turnout,
        325
    presidential election results, 324, 398,
        400
    Representatives
        election results, 407, 423
        party victories, 437
    Senators
        election results, 324, 417
Israel, 51, 491–492, 550

J

Japan, 546
Jordan, 551

K

Kansas
    electoral votes, 326

Kansas (continued)
    Governors, 241
        election results, 326
    history and politics, 241–242
    population, registration, and turnout,
        327
    presidential election results, 326, 398,
        400
    Representatives
        election results, 407, 423
        party victories, 437
    Senators
        election results, 326, 417
Kentucky
    electoral votes, 328
    Governors, 243
        election results, 328
    history and politics, 242–243
    population, registration, and turnout,
        329
    presidential election results, 328, 398,
        400
    Representatives
        election results, 407, 423
        party victories, 437
    Senators
        election results, 328, 417

L

Louisiana
    electoral votes, 330
    Governors, 244
        election results, 330
    history and politics, 243–244
    population, registration, and turnout,
        331
    presidential election results, 330, 398,
        400
    Representatives
        election results, 407, 423
        party victories, 437
    Senators
        election results, 330, 417

M

Maine
    electoral votes, 332
    Governors, 245
        election results, 332
    history and politics, 245–246
    population, registration, and turnout,
        333
    presidential election results, 332, 398,
        400
    Representatives
        election results, 407, 423
        party victories, 437
    Senators
        election results, 332, 433
Maryland
    electoral votes, 334
    Governors, 246
        election results, 334

Maryland (continued)
    history and politics, 246–247
    population, registration, and turnout,
        335
    presidential election results, 334, 398,
        400
    Representatives
        election results, 407–408, 423–424
        party victories, 437
    Senators
        election results, 334, 417, 433
Massachusetts
    electoral votes, 336
    Governors, 248
        election results, 336
    history and politics, 247–248
    population, registration, and turnout,
        337
    presidential election results, 336, 398,
        400
    Representatives
        election results, 408, 424
        party victories, 437
    Senators
        election results, 336, 433
Mexico, 492
Michigan
    electoral votes, 338
    Governors, 249
        election results, 338
    history and politics, 248–249
    population, registration, and turnout,
        339
    presidential election results, 338, 398,
        400
    Representatives
        election results, 408, 424–425
        party victories, 437
    Senators
        election results, 338, 433
Middle East, 491–492, 550–551
    peace process, 51–52
Minnesota
    electoral votes, 340
    Governors, 250
        election results, 340
    history and politics, 249–251
    population, registration, and turnout,
        341
    presidential election results, 340, 398,
        400
    Representatives
        election results, 409, 425
        party victories, 437
    Senators
        election results, 340, 433
Mississippi
    electoral votes, 342
    Governors, 252
        election results, 342
    history and politics, 251–253
    population, registration, and turnout,
        343
    presidential election results, 342, 398,
        400

Mississippi (continued)
    Representatives
        election results, 409, 425
        party victories, 437
    Senators
        election results, 342, 433
Missouri
    electoral votes, 346
    Governors, 255
        election results, 346
    history and politics, 253–255
    population, registration, and turnout,
        347
    presidential election results, 346, 398,
        400
    Representatives
        election results, 409, 425
        party victories, 437
    Senators
        election results, 346, 417, 433
Montana
    electoral votes, 344
    Governors, 256–257
        election results, 344
    history and politics, 256–257
    population, registration, and turnout,
        345
    presidential election results, 344, 398,
        400
    Representatives
        election results, 409, 425
        party victories, 437
    Senators
        election results, 344, 433

N

Nebraska
    electoral votes, 348
    Governors, 257–258
        election results, 348
    history and politics, 257–258
    population, registration, and turnout,
        349
    presidential election results, 348, 398,
        400
    Representatives
        election results, 409, 425
        party victories, 437
    Senators
        election results, 348, 433
Nevada
    electoral votes, 350
    Governors, 259
        election results, 350
    history and politics, 258–259
    population, registration, and turnout,
        351
    presidential election results, 350, 398,
        400
    Representatives
        election results, 409, 426
        party victories, 437
    Senators
        election results, 350, 417, 433

New Hampshire
    caucuses, 7–8
    electoral votes, 352
    Governors, 260
        election results, 352
    history and politics, 259–260
    population, registration, and turnout,
        353
    presidential election results, 352, 398,
        400
    Representatives
        election results, 410, 426
        party victories, 437
    Senators
        election results, 352, 417
New Jersey
    electoral votes, 354
    Governors, 261
        election results, 354
    history and politics, 261–262
    population, registration, and turnout,
        355
    presidential election results, 354, 398,
        400
    Representatives
        election results, 410, 426
        party victories, 437
    Senators
        election results, 354, 433
New Mexico
    electoral votes, 356
    Governors, 262–263
        election results, 356
    history and politics, 262–263
    population, registration, and turnout,
        357
    presidential election results, 356, 398,
        400
    Representatives
        election results, 410, 426
        party victories, 437
    Senators
        election results, 356, 433
New York
    electoral votes, 31, 358
    Governors, 263–264
        election results, 358
    history and politics, 263–264
    population, registration, and turnout,
        359
    presidential election results, 358, 398,
        400
    Representatives
        election results, 410–411,
            426–427
        party victories, 437
    Senators
        election results, 358, 417, 433
North Carolina
    electoral votes, 360
    Governors, 266
        election results, 360
    history and politics, 264–267
    population, registration, and turnout,
        361

North Carolina (continued)
    presidential election results, 360, 398,
        400
    Representatives
        election results, 411, 427–428
        party victories, 437
    Senators
        election results, 360, 417
North Dakota
    electoral votes, 362
    Governors, 267
        election results, 362
    history and politics, 267
    population, registration, and turnout,
        363
    presidential election results, 362, 398,
        400
    Representatives
        election results, 412, 428
        party victories, 437
    Senators
        election results, 362, 417, 433
North Korea, 52, 59, 546
Northern Ireland, 487, 549–550
Northern Marianas, 467, 536

O

Ohio
    electoral votes, 364
    Governors, 268
        election results, 364
    history and politics, 268–269
    population, registration, and turnout,
        365
    presidential election results, 364, 398,
        400
    Representatives
        election results, 412, 428
        party victories, 437
    Senators
        election results, 364, 417, 433
Oklahoma
    electoral votes, 366
    Governors, 269, 270
        election results, 366
    history and politics, 269–270
    population, registration, and turnout,
        367
    presidential election results, 366, 398,
        400
    Representatives
        election results, 412, 428
        party victories, 437
    Senators
        election results, 366, 417
Oregon
    electoral votes, 368
    Governors, 271
        election results, 368
    history and politics, 271–272
    population, registration, and turnout,
        369
    presidential election results, 368, 398,
        400

Oregon (continued)
    Representatives
        election results, 412–413, 429
        party victories, 437
    Senators
        election results, 368, 417

P

Pakistan, 547
Pennsylvania
    electoral votes, 370
    Governors, 273
        election results, 370
    history and politics, 272–273
    population, registration, and turnout,
        371
    presidential election results, 370, 398,
        400
    Representatives
        election results, 413, 429
        party victories, 437
    Senators
        election results, 370, 417, 433
Persian Gulf, 550–551
Philippines, 491, 546
Poland, 50
Puerto Rico, 467, 536, 537

R

Rhode Island
    electoral votes, 372
    Governors, 274–275
        election results, 372
    history and politics, 274–275
    population, registration, and turnout,
        373
    presidential election results, 372, 398,
        400
    Representatives
        election results, 413, 429
        party victories, 437
    Senators
        election results, 372, 433
Russia, 24, 58, 487, 549

S

Saudi Arabia, 551
South Carolina
    electoral votes, 374
    Governors, 276
        election results, 374
    history and politics, 275–276
    population, registration, and turnout,
        375
    presidential election results, 374, 398,
        400
    Representatives
        election results, 413, 429–430
        party victories, 437
    Senators
        election results, 374, 417

South Dakota
    electoral votes, 376
    Governors, 277
        election results, 376
    history and politics, 276–277
    population, registration, and turnout,
        377
    presidential election results, 376, 398,
        400
    Representatives
        election results, 414, 430
        party victories, 437
    Senators
        election results, 376, 417
South Korea, 52, 546
Soviet Union, former, 24, 58–59

T

Taiwan, 24, 50, 52, 59, 491, 547
Tennessee
    electoral votes, 378
    Governors, 278
        election results, 378
    history and politics, 277–279
    population, registration, and turnout,
        379
    presidential election results, 378, 398,
        400
    Representatives
        election results, 414, 430
        party victories, 437
    Senators
        election results, 378, 433
Texas
    electoral votes, 380
    Governors, 280
        election results, 380
    history and politics, 279–280
    population, registration, and turnout,
        381
    presidential election results, 380, 398,
        400
    Representatives
        election results, 414–415, 430–431
        party victories, 437
    Senators
        election results, 380, 433

U

Utah
    electoral votes, 382
    Governors, 281
        election results, 382
    history and politics, 280–281
    lawsuit against Census Bureau,
        26–27
    population, registration, and turnout,
        383
    presidential election results, 382, 398,
        400
    Representatives
        election results, 415, 431
        party victories, 438

Utah *(continued)*
    Senators
        election results, 382, 417, 433

V

Vermont
    electoral votes, 384
    Governors, 282–283
        election results, 384
    history and politics, 282–283
    number of electors, 31
    population, registration, and turnout,
        385
    presidential election results, 384, 399,
        401
    Representatives
        election results, 415, 431
        party victories, 438
    Senators
        election results, 384, 417, 433
Virgin Islands, 467, 536
Virginia
    electoral votes, 386
    Governors, 285
        election results, 386
    history and politics, 283–285
    population, registration, and turnout,
        387
    presidential election results, 386, 399,
        401
    Representatives
        election results, 415, 431
        party victories, 438

Vermont *(continued)*
    Senators
        election results, 386

W

Washington
    electoral votes, 388
    Governors, 286
        election results, 388
    history and politics, 286–287
    population, registration, and turnout,
        389
    presidential election results, 388, 399,
        401
    Representatives
        election results, 415–416,
            431–432
        party victories, 438
    Senators
        election results, 388, 417, 433
Washington, D.C. *See* District
of Columbia
West Virginia
    electoral votes, 390
    Governors, 288
        election results, 390
    history and politics, 287–288
    population, registration, and turnout,
        391
    presidential election results, 390, 399,
        401
    Representatives
        election results, 416, 432

West Virginia
    Representatives *(continued)*
        party victories, 438
    Senators
        election results, 390, 433
Western Hemisphere, 492–493
Wisconsin
    electoral votes, 392
    Governors, 289
        election results, 392
    history and politics, 288–289
    population, registration, and
        turnout, 393
    presidential election results, 392,
        399, 401
    Representatives
        election results, 416, 432
        party victories, 438
    Senators
        election results, 392, 417, 433
Wyoming
    electoral votes, 394
    Governors, 290
        election results, 394
    history and politics, 290–291
    population, registration, and
        turnout, 395
    presidential election results, 394,
        399, 401
    Representatives
        election results, 416, 432
        party victories, 438
    Senators
        election results, 394, 433